WHAT IT TAKES

Richard Ben Cramer

WHAT IT TAKES

The Way to the White House

RANDOM HOUSE
NEW YORK

All rights reserved under International and Pan-American Copyright Conventions. Published in the United States by Random House, Inc., New York, and simultaneously in Canada by Random House of Canada Limited, Toronto.

Portions of this work were originally published in *Esquire* magazine.

Grateful acknowledgment is made to Williamson Music for permission to reprint six lines from "You'll Never Walk Alone" by Richard Rodgers and Oscar Hammerstein II, on page 134. Copyright 1945 by Williamson Music. Copyright renewed. International Copyright Secured. All rights reserved. Reprinted by permission of Williamson Music.

Library of Congress Cataloging-in-Publication Data

Cramer, Richard Ben.
What it takes : the way to the white house / Richard Ben Cramer.
p.   cm.
ISBN 0-394-56260-7
1. Presidents—United States—Election—1988. 2. Presidential candidates—United States—Biography.   I. Title.
E880.C73   1992
324.9730927—dc20   91-52676

Manufactured in the United States of America

24689753

FIRST EDITION

Book design by Carole Lowenstein

For you,
Carolyn White

Author's Note

None of my friends ever thought he should be President—much less that he could be. Of course, we were all taught that it was possible (in America, God bless her). But our lives separated us from that notion by the time we left our teens. A President—*the* President—was someone altogether larger, and more extraordinary, than we. Though we might like or revile him, though we could judge him (and even send him packing) by and by . . . though a million words were written each day on his policies and politics, though millions of people might listen to his speeches, or watch a TV tour of his house . . . though his face and his voice, his wife, kids, and dog would be known to every sentient adult, though his name (or initials) would conjure up a time of our lives—for the rest of our lives . . . still, I came of age knowing, somehow, the life of this figure must be something so foreign to mine as to render it, finally, unknowable.

Later, as a citizen and newspaperman, I learned what I could about the candidates and campaigns, and the Presidents they produced. I read a mountain of newspapers along the way, probably did irremediable damage to my eyes and brain, staring at TVs. When the campaigns were over I read books about them. I learned about the polls and ad campaigns, people-meters, direct-mail fund-raising, computer-targeted media buys, and all kinds of arcane wizardry that left unanswered the only questions that I (and, I think, most voters) ever wanted to ask:

Who are these guys?

What are they like?

I still did not know what kind of life would lead a man (in my lifetime, all have been men) to think he *ought* to be President. I could only guess at the habit of triumph that would make him conclude he *could* be President.

What in their backgrounds could give them that huge ambition, that kind of motor, that will and discipline, that faith in themselves? What kind of faith would cause, say, a dozen of these habitual winners to bend their lives and the lives of those dear to them to one hugely public roll of the dice in which all but one would fail?

What I wanted, what I could not find, was an account I could understand of how people like us—with dreams and doubts, great talents and ordinary frailties—get to be people like them. I wanted to know not about the campaign, but about the campaigners. Lastly—most important—I wanted to know enough about these people to *see* . . . once they decided to run, and marched (or slid, or flung themselves headlong) into this semi-rational, all-consuming quest . . . what happened to those lives, to their wives, to their families, to the lives they shared? What happened to their idea of themselves? What did *we do to them,* on the way to the White House?

So, in 1986, I set out to write it.

— ★ —

I meant to find a half-dozen candidates in whose lives I would see my answers. I thought to pick half Republicans and half Democrats, but as a reporter (not a political expert, nor certainly a political scientist), I had to let the story pick my subjects. So the finding was a matter of much trial and error. In the end, I chose two Republicans, Vice President George Bush and the Senate's Republican Leader, Bob Dole; and four Democrats, former Senator Gary Hart of Colorado, Congressman Dick Gephardt of Missouri, Senator Joe Biden of Delaware, and Massachusetts Governor Michael Dukakis.

The final criterion for this choice developed in the course of reporting: I wanted the candidates who made that final turn in the road, who got to the point where they could say, "Not only should I be President . . . *I am going to be President.*" At that point, their idea of their own lives would change—had to change. They had to see in themselves a figure of size to bestride a chunk of history. And by the nature of the process, alas, five of the six would then have to come off of that; they would be thrown back on themselves, as they probably never were before, to examine how it was they saw so wrongly. The sixth, God help him, would be thrown back on himself in an even more fundamental way—he would have then to become the President he saw in himself. This is the drama I proposed to follow.

By its nature, then, the project had to exclude some credible and charming candidates, whose lives I dipped into but, ultimately, could not follow. The omission I most regret is Jesse Jackson, whose story is surely as fascinating as that of any man who has campaigned for the White House. Alas, I came to Reverend Jackson late, and I was never able to slow him down long enough to make him understand that help was required. We never got to the level of candor that was essential, and so, in the end, it seemed better not to write about someone I did not know well.

With the others, I have tried to tell their stories in two ways—as fairly as I could from the outside, and as empathetically as I could from behind their eyes. In doing so, I have tried not only to show *them,* but to show what our politics is like—what it *feels* like to run for President; what it requires from them; what it builds in them; what it strips, or rips, from them. The book begins with the lives of the two older men, the Republicans, Bush and Dole, and expands in Book II to include the four Democrats. By Book III, the stage is set, the race begins in earnest. The lives come together in one flooding tumble. The Epilogue tries to sketch the lives as they emerged from those rapids, to see what changes were wrought.

I would like to make note here of my reporting techniques. The narratives are based on interviews with more than a thousand people. Every scene in the book has come from firsthand sources, or from published sources that were verified by participants before my writing began. The narratives were re-checked for accuracy after the final words were written. Where dialogue is quoted, the quotes have come from a person involved in the conversation, usually the person making the statement. In most cases, the quotes have been read back word for word to the sources involved, to check them once again for accuracy and fairness. In every case, thoughts attributed to the characters in this book have been checked with them, or with the people to whom they confided those thoughts. Every section of this book has been read back to the candidate, to a family member, or to closest aides—whoever seemed likeliest to know about the events described, and who would give the time. Some family members and aides to these candidates have helped me, literally, fifty or sixty times. They know almost as much about this book as I do, and I will always be indebted to them for the time they gave, for the trust they reposed in me, for their patience with my urgencies, and the kindness with which they treated me.

A project of this size must progress with many hands on its back, and there are some who deserve more thanks than I can ever give. No author can have had better support from a publisher than I have had from Random House, especially from my editor, David Rosenthal, whose strength and intelligence helped propel this project from the first; and I have benefited from the counsel of his colleagues, Peter Osnos, Jason Epstein, Joe Fox, and boss of all, Harry Evans. So outrageously long has this project run, that I have also these chiefs to thank for support that was crucial in each case: Joni Evans assisted in shaping the labor to a book, and Howard Kaminsky gave the project its start. I also want to thank Julie Grau, Jennifer Ash, and Rebecca Beuchler for their help and good cheer; Ed Cohen and Amy Edelman for their careful treatment of the manuscript; Martha Levin, Dona Chernoff, Wanda Chappell, Mitchell Ivers, and Eve Adams for their counsel and their efforts to turn the great wheel of the mill.

In three years of reporting, there were dozens of institutions, more than a thousand individuals, who helped with information, advice, access, and inter-views, and though I do not name them here (probably to their vast relief) I remember their help with gratitude and fondness. I do want to thank by name the members of one special subset of friends and family who lent their effort or advice, time, money, food, phones, guest bedrooms or living room couches in an effort to help the author keep body and soul together. My thanks, then, to Joe Bargmann, A. Robert and Blossom Cramer, Lina Cramer, Sara Crichton, Marguerite Del Giudice, Reid Detchon, Richard Durning, Bill Eddins, Judy and Earl Fendelman, Neil Fitelson, Steve Friedman, Ken Fuson, Gerri Hirshey, Professor Christopher Janney, Elizabeth Kaplan, Sophie Lackritz, Terrell Lamb, Jeff Leen, Sarah Leen, Simon Li, Nancy McKeon, Patricia McLaughlin, Gloria Mansfield, David Maraniss, Bill Marr, Guy Martin, Joanie Miller, Jim Naughton, Michael Pakenham, Bob Peck, Chuck Powers, Gene Roberts, Mike and Jennie Roman, John Ryan, Stu Seidel, Steve and Sheila Seplow, Steven Tarshis, and Doran Twer.

Al Silverman, Robert Riger, and especially Brigitte Weeks supported this book in its formative stage, and I thank them for their interest and their faith.

Esquire did me aid and honor by purchasing three excerpts of this book to run in the magazine. I am grateful for years of support from my friend and editor there, David Hirshey; from the departed boss of bosses, Lee Eisenberg; and especially from the editor in chief, Terry McDonell.

Philippa Brophy, my agent, has been a friend to this book and to me in more ways, more ably, more constantly, and more avidly than I could ever have hoped. I have relied on, and I thank her for, her faith, good humor, and wisdom.

Mark Zwonitzer, my researcher, who stuck with this project for more than five years, was the best help and the best companion I could have had. Without him, this book would have been a poor porridge. Without him, a thousand times, its author would have been in the soup. This project had many hands on its back, but Mark's were the strong ones bearing the weight from below.

Finally, I thank the woman who bore with me, through all. Carolyn White was my partner in this book's first dreaming, my guide and my spur through all its doing. For her every line was written. And to her this book is dedicated.

—RICHARD BEN CRAMER
Cambridge, Maryland
March 5, 1992

Contents

BOOK III

BOOK I

1

The
Price of
Being Poppy

THIS IS about as good as it gets, as close as American politics offers to a mortal lock. On this night, October 8, 1986, the Vice President is coming to the Astrodome, to Game One of the National League Championship Series, and the nation will be watching from its La-Z-Boys as George Bush stands front and center, glistening with America's holy water: play-off juice. Oh, and here's the beauty part: he doesn't have to say a thing! He's just got to throw out the first ball. He'll be hosted by the Astros' owner, Dr. John McMullen; he'll be honored by the National League and the Great Old Game; he'll be cheered by 44,131 fans—and it's not even a risky crowd, the kind that might get testy because oil isn't worth a damn, Houston's economy is down the crapper, and no one's buying aluminum siding (they'd move, if they could sell their houses). No, those guys can't get tickets tonight. This is a play-off crowd, a corporate-perks crowd, the kind of fellows who were transferred in a few years ago from Stamford-Conn., you know, for that new marketing thing (and were, frankly, *delighted* by the price of housing), a solid GOP crowd, tax-conscious, white and polite—they're wearing sport coats, and golf shirts with emblems—vice presidents all, but anyway, they're just backdrop.

Tonight, George Bush will shine for the nation as a whole—ABC, coast to coast, and it's perfect: the Astros against the Mets, Scott v. Gooden, the K kings, the best against the best, the showdown America's been waiting for, and to cut the ribbon, to Let the Games Begin . . . *George Bush.* Spectacular! Reagan's guys couldn't have done better. It's Houston, Bush's hometown.

They love him. Guaranteed standing O. Meanwhile, ABC will have to mention
he was captain of the Yale team, the College World Series—maybe show the
picture of him meeting Babe Ruth. You couldn't *buy* better airtime. Just wave
to the crowd, throw the ball. A no-brainer. There he'll be, his trim form
bisecting every TV screen in the blessed Western Hemisphere, for a few telegenic moments, the brightest star in this grand tableau: the red carpet on the
Astroturf; the electronic light-board shooting patterns of stars and smoke from
a bull's nose, like it does when an Astro hits a home run; the Diamond Vision
in riveting close-up, his image to the tenth power for the fans in the cheap seats;
and then the languorous walk to the mound, the wave to the grandstand, the
cheers of the throng, the windup . . . that gorgeous one-minute nexus with the
national anthem, the national pastime, the national past, and better still
. . . with the honest manly combat of the diamond, a thousand freeze-frames,
a million wordsworth, of George Bush at play in the world of spikes and dirt,
all scalded into the beery brainpans of fifty million prime-time fans . . . mostly
men. God knows, he needs help with men.

So George Bush is coming to the Astrodome.

Disaster in the making.

— ★ —

The thing is, it couldn't just happen. George Bush couldn't just fly in, catch
a cab to the ballpark, get his ticket torn, and grab a beer on the way to his
seat. No, he'd come too far for that.

Weeks before the trip, the Director of Advance in the Office of the Vice
President (OVP) had to tell the White House Military Office (WHMO) to lay
on a plane, *Air Force Two*, and the backup *Air Force Two*. That meant
coordination with the squadron at Andrews Air Force Base, for a Special Air
Mission (SAM). Luckily, the trip was to Houston, where Bush went all the
time, so the Air Force didn't have to fly in his cars. The Secret Service kept
a Vice Presidential limousine, a black, armored, stretch Cadillac, with a discreet seal on the door, parked and secured twenty-four hours a day in the
basement of the Houston Civic Center. They wouldn't even fly in a backup
limo, they'd just use a regular sedan.

Of course, the Vice President would stay where he always did, the Houstonian Hotel (which he listed as his voting residence), and that would save
effort, too. The White House Communications Agency (WHCA, pronounced
"Wocka" by the cognoscenti) already had the Houstonian wired for secure
phones, direct to the White House on land lines, so satellites couldn't listen
in. Still, the Astrodome would have to be wired, so that meant an Air Force
transport plane to fly in the new communications gear and extra Secret Service
matériel. That, in turn, required an alert for the CVAM at the Pentagon, the
Air Force Vice Chief of Staff in charge of Special Air Missions, who would
task the Military Airlift Command (MAC) with this Vice Presidential support
mission, or in Pentagon parlance, a Volant Silver. (Presidential missions are
Volant Banner.)

Meanwhile, in Houston, the local office of the Secret Service started looking over the Astrodome, picking out the holding rooms, secure hallways, choke points, command posts, and pathways for the Vice President. This information was bumped up the ladder to the Secret Service VPPD, the Vice Presidential Protective Detail in Washington, which in ten days would have its own Advance team on scene. When that team arrived, the Lead Advance man would convene his own staff of three Site Advance and a Press Advance, along with the four Secret Service Advance, the chief of the local office of the Secret Service, two Wocka Advance men and the captain of the Houston Police Department's Dignitary Protection Division, to sit down for a meeting with the host of the affair, the Astros' owner, Dr. John McMullen. The critical question: What *kind of event* did McMullen want the Vice President for? Sure, it's the first-ball thing, but where would he make the throw?

McMullen said· Well, there's a pitcher's mound . . .

The *mound*? The Service didn't want him exposed on the field like a baited goose. Did McMullen want his 44,000 fans held at the gates and frisked for metal?

Absolutely not.

Still, the Lead Advance said, the political people might *want* him on the mound. You know, taller . . . heh heh.

Well, said the Service, you got your choice: you want him on the mound, we put him in a vest. You might ask if he can throw in a flak vest. Heh heh.

The Lead Advance said this was a matter for Washington. He bumped it up the ladder to the Office of the Vice President—Washington HQ. Meanwhile, the Secret Service Advance bumped it up to *his* Washington HQ.

"Now, what about the cocktail party?"

These things had to be decided! If the Lead Advance changed the pregame cocktail reception from a simple Mix and Mingle to a ten-minute Brief Remarks, well then, this would have operational consequence.

"Do you want him to talk?"

"*Should* he talk?"

"He talks, there's press . . ."

"No press."

"Well, he doesn't have to talk . . ."

"Okay, Mix and Mingle. . . . Who's got the motorcade?"

In the course of the next two days, this dozen men would walk over every foot of ground that the Vice President would tread, scouting this bit of his future life. They were seeing it as his eyes might, then improving the view, imagining and removing every let or hindrance. They were determined that nothing would be unforeseen. And, of course, they were timing every movement. Then, for all the following days, and most of the nights, they would fan out to their respective turfs: the Site Advance to each location the Vice President would visit; the Press Advance to local papers, TV and radio stations, then to the sites to inspect for sound cables, platforms, camera angles, and backdrops; the Service to all the sites, for inch-by-inch security checks; the

Houston PD to its command post; the WHCA to its phones, cables, switch-boxes, walkie-talkies, cellulars, and other wondrous gizmos the Vice President might require; the head of the VP's Houston operation and the Lead Advance to the three-room office created for the occasion, fully equipped and volunteer-staffed, in a wing of the Houstonian.

From this office, day by day, the Lead Advance faxed to the Director of Advance and the Schedulers in Washington the minute-by-minute breakdown of the visit. With every transmission this was refined, by two minutes here, ten minutes there; a holding room added, an extra car in the motorcade . . . And each day, by return fax, the Washington OVP sent out a new version, with its additions and refinements: Lee Atwater would be a guest aboard *Air Force Two* (need a guest car in the motorcade); approval on the interview with ABC in the broadcast booth (third inning) . . . Then, each night in Houston, the Advance team reconvened for another Countdown Meeting, preliving the trip anew.

The ultimate product of this process was a sheaf of papers detailing not only the schedule, but a description (with diagram) of each event, the staffing (on the plane, on the ground), assignments for every car in every motorcade, and phone numbers (hardwire and cellular) for every division of the traveling party at every site. In Washington, the night before the trip, all this data would be printed in a booklet, four and a quarter inches wide by five and a half high, just the size of a suit pocket, with baby-blue stiff paper covers, the front one printed with a handsome black Vice Presidential seal. This booklet was called "the bible," and in a sense, the making of the bible was the making of the trip: little that was not on its pages was going to happen in the life of the man. And with the bible's completion, a certain psychic line was crossed: the trip to the ball game was no longer a plan. It was an Event of the Vice Presidency. It was at this point, with the final retype, that the first letters of words began to jump up and salute: in the bible, that is, in the life of George Bush, every noun he touched became a proper noun. So the pregame reception had to become the Reception; or that cheap molded plastic across a steel frame would become, with the brush of his backside, the Box Seat; even as his person, the locus of Veephood, the Big Gulp of this institutional juice, became, had to become, in the bible, a black-type-all-caps monolith that began every schedule item:

6:10 P.M.   THE VICE PRESIDENT and Mrs. Bush arrive As-
                 trodome and proceed to Astrohall to attend Recep-
                 tion.

                 Met by: Dr. and Mrs. John McMullen (Jacqueline)

Now, in the Countdown Meeting, the Lead Advance was reading from the latest bible-fax from Washington. "Okay, we move him straight to the cocktail thing. Any other greeters?" There were negative shakes of heads at the table. "Okay, event . . ."

EVENT: HOUSTON SPORTS ASSOCIATION OWNERS RECEPTION

CLOSED PRESS

NO REMARKS

MIX AND MINGLE

6:15 P.M.   THE VICE PRESIDENT and Mrs. Bush arrive Reception.

6:50 P.M.   THE VICE PRESIDENT and Mrs. Bush conclude Reception and depart Astrohall en route Astrodome.

Again, the Secret Service wanted to know: "Is he gonna throw from the seats or the mound? We gotta know. It's a different route. If it's from the mound, we got a bathroom to put on the vest. . . . It's a different route! If . . ."

The Lead Advance cut him off with a glare: "No word yet from Washington. . . . Now, how's he getting to the Dome?"

"We can walk him."

"From the hall? How long?"

"Five minutes."

"Give him ten. There'll be people."

"We can close the sidewalk."

"What if it rains?"

"Umbrellas?"

"Umbrellas!"

The Site Advance for the Astrodome bent to his legal pad and wrote: *Walk to Dome: Umbrellas.*

Of course, no storm could moisten or muss the Vice Presidential person in the Dome, where giant air conditioners maintained a dry and steady seventy-two degrees. It was the Secret Service Advance—specifically, the man from TSD, the Technical Security Division—who first divined that the Vice President might have to pass three of those air conditioners in his progress through stadium halls. Of course it was the later TSD team, the fellows who swept the whole Dome with dogs, just before arrival, who actually disassembled the machines' steel covers, checked the works inside for untoward signs, and posted a man to guard each unit.

The air-conditioner guards were part of the Astrodome security force, as were the men in vigil at every janitor's closet and bathroom he would pass, as were the men who closed off the hallways he would tread. For the evening, the steady complement of thirty full-time security personnel was swelled by ninety temporary hires, mostly off-duty cops from the Houston and Harris County forces. Each was paid eighty dollars for the evening, the cost defrayed by the Astrodome—a small price to pay for the honor.

Anyway, a drop in the bucket, compared to the public cost for the FBI and the Houston Police Department's Special Ops. As there were no new threats, the FBI team had to locate only the kooks who'd made threats before, and all suspicious characters in the Houston area. Nothing intrusive or heavy-handed, just a check on their whereabouts. The Houston PD Motorcycle Squad had to cover the motorcade, but that was only thirty miles, easily handled by the normal team of twenty-two men and two sergeants. Of course, the department also had men on every bridge over the route, and officers at most intersections. Still, the bulk of the load fell to the Dignitary Protection Division, fifty men who guarded the Vice President inside and outside the Dome. The bible called for the Vice President to come off the field to the owner's box, field level, on the first-base side. He'd only stay for a while, until they moved him up to a skybox. Fortunately, the command post was set up on the third-base side, up in the catwalks, where the HPD Special Ops, the Astrodome men, and the Secret Service could keep a minute-by-minute binocular vigil.

At least they could be sure the VP would stay where they put him. Some VIPs don't, and then it's white-knuckle city. Once, on a visit to Houston, Eisenhower snuck clean away; it turned out he went to play golf. Years later, the Houston force lost Dick Nixon for a panicky hour in the old Lamar Hotel; finally found him in the coffee shop, chatting up a waitress. John F. Kennedy was the worst: he'd throw himself right into a crowd; worst thing you can do to the cops, tears them up; someone could get him with a pocket knife, an ice pick . . . *anything* . . . no way they could see it. Thank God, George Bush wouldn't do that.

He was good about being on time, too, which the motorcade fellows really liked. As it was, they spent half their lives waiting; it was dreariest when the schedule got busted and H-hour came and went and nobody even knew anymore what was *supposed* to happen. But with George Bush, they could fire up their gleaming Harleys at H-hour minus five, and he'd be there, with his crew in the cars, right on the hour. Then came the part that was their specialty, as they roared away from Ellington Field, southeast of town, and onto the wide open concrete of I-45, where seven or eight of their buddies had already closed the first few ramps and held back traffic on the northbound side. Not a car, not one truck in the way! And another half-dozen men in jodhpurs would peel away from the motorcade, and throw their hogs wide open—sixty, seventy, eighty miles an hour!—roaring up to the next ramps to close them until the motorcade sailed by. And after the trailing Harleys passed, they'd open those ramps again and thunder on past the motorcade, with the wind keening off their farings and flattening their smiles inside their helmets—ninety, a hundred, if they could—past the motorcade again to block off the ramps and road ahead. Forty minutes! From the stairs of his airplane at Ellington to the door of the Houstonian. You couldn't do it any faster at midnight Sunday—not legally, anyway. That limo was *never* gonna need a brake job. Never had to stop—not while these boys were around. And they knew the Vice President appreciated their work, the way he liked to see them lined up on the tarmac at Ellington, at the end of every trip. Always wanted them lined up there, even in the rain, when he'd get wet if he stopped to wave.

But that's the way he was. Everybody who was in on the trip talked about it—the way he was. Like when they'd get the Army to chopper him from Ellington right to the Houstonian: he wouldn't land on the hotel grounds—didn't want to disturb the guests. They'd land him instead nearby, at the Polo Club. Of course, that meant another motorcade to move him a quarter-mile, across the road to the hotel door. But that wasn't his fault. In Washington, when he went to the office, he wouldn't let them block the streets, he made them stop at the lights! A whole motorcade pulled up, *waiting for a stoplight*! He didn't want to disturb the other drivers. He'd tried that in Houston, too. But not tonight—forget it! He came in only three hours before the game, and that meant rush hour. They weren't going to have him tied up in that—no way—not in Houston traffic. And if some drivers got hot and started honking, or jumped out of their cars to see what the hell was blocking the way—well, they could always stop traffic at the *top* of the ramps, so the Vice President wouldn't be bothered.

No, from within the motorcade, you couldn't see anything like that. There was just the calm, empty highway, and the soft hum of the tires on the asphalt of the center lane. With a little motorcade like this, there wasn't even a press bus, diesel-rumbling behind. No, this one was short and sweet: only a couple of patrol cars, with the Lead Advance and the Lead Agent riding in the first one; and a lead Secret Service car, discreet, just a blue light flashing on the dash; and then the backup, which was only a sedan, carrying Dr. Gasser, the personal physician; and then the real limo, with the Vice President, and Mrs. Bush, and their old friend Jack Steel, the head of the Houston Office of the Vice President; and then the Secret Service wagon, the hulking black Chevy Suburban with the shaded windows and four agents, two facing front and two facing rear, armed with submachine guns and heavier weapons, as they were the CAT squad, the Counter Assault Team, which might have to stay and fight off attackers while the rest of the agents got the hell out with the Vice President; and then the Control Car, which carried the Chief of Staff, and the Director of Advance, and the Military Aide; and then the Support Car, with the Lead Wocka man, and the Press Secretary, and the Personal Aide, and the Vice Presidential Photographer; then, the first Staff Car, which carried the Staff Secretary and the Secretary to the Staff Secretary; then the first Guest Car, for Lee Atwater, the head of the Vice President's political action committee, which was called the Fund for America's Future, but was really his Presidential campaign in mufti; then, just one Staff Van, for the rest of the staff, typists and low-level Wocka geeks; and just one Press Van, for a few reporters who had to tag along; and then, of course, the ambulance, with its strobes flashing, red bubble-lights whirring; and another patrol car, or two at times, with their blue lights and strobes flashing, and a few of the men on Harleys, who were there in case any cars broke through the rear motorcycle cordon, a half-mile or more behind, and got too close to the Vice President . . . and that was about all.

With the volunteer drivers for the Staff and Press vans, there were occasional gaps in the train, but mostly they stayed tight and smooth. Certainly, they did at the front of the column, with the Secret Service drivers, men who could handle a motorcade without any fits or starts. In Washington or anywhere near, the Vice President always had his own Secret Service men driving, or occasionally his Capitol office driver, the soldierly Korean, Mr. Kim. But even in another city, the Vice President was almost always driven by a member of his own detail. The thinking was, he'd prefer a man from his own world, a face he knew, and a name to go with it. He'd be more secure that way, more comfortable.

Those were the twin imperatives in the Vice Presidential motorcade, and in all the effort around the Vice President: security, and comfort. They were the givens of his life, along with the thousands of hours of intense unseen labor by others. In this case, some four hundred people, a couple of hundred thousand dollars, and a couple of hundred million dollars in government equipment got the Vice President to the ball game in perfect security, and comfort. They also made it possible for him to spend the better part of a day, leave his office, board an airplane, travel halfway across the nation, land in another city and travel overland thirty miles to a ballpark, and never see one person who was not a friend or someone whose sole purpose it was to serve or protect him.

This is living in the bubble, and George Bush had long since perfected the art. By this time, midway through his second term, he had almost ceased to note the special circumstances of his being. After almost six years as Vice President, the bubble was his milieu. He had learned to accept its cost, as he had its perquisites, as his destiny, even his due, owed not to him, as he'd sometimes point out, but to the high office he held. Actually, he was seldom asked about it anymore. The public and the press expected it. They seemed to like it, really, for the glamor they imagined therein. The few who asked were old friends who came to visit and saw what had become of his life. They'd inquire, in uneasy near whispers: "Doesn't it . . . drive you nuts?" And he'd shrug it off with a quick joke, which they'd retell, as evidence of his grace, his discipline under pressure, his will to serve. But, really, they didn't see the half of it. No one who hadn't lived in the bubble could know what it was like: a trip of a thousand miles, two thousand, or more, across a *continent,* around the *globe,* without one word exchanged with a stranger; a year, two years, four years, without driving a car, without being *allowed* to drive a car; instead, the hush of the limousine and the silent smile from the Service man at the wheel; the stewards in the plane, hovering to know his pleasure; the jacket with his name embroidered as memento of his visit to the ship or the plant, the campus or the launchpad; the visor, the ball cap, the golf shirt, the golf bag, tennis racket, squash bag, T-shirts, cufflinks, tie tacks, tie clips, memo paper, matchbooks, lighters, ashtrays, swizzle sticks, the coasters, glasses, mugs, china teacups, plastic drink cups, plastic bags, all with his name and seal upon them; the minute-by-minute schedule, instructing him where to stand, whom to greet; the men in suits and earplugs, always around, talking into their wrist microphones; the men in slightly better suits, handing him typed pages, telling

him where he'd be going and whom he would see, who his friends were among
the crowd and what he was supposed to tell those friends, what the press would
be asking and what he ought to say in response; the simple, awesome fact that
from the moment he opened his door in the morning until he retired for the
night, no matter what he chose to do, or where he went, or what he wanted,
he would *never* be alone.

By this time, by October 1986, he took it for granted; wouldn't have said a
word about it, even if he didn't. The few hints to his attitude, the bright sparks
of reaction, flashed only briefly, more than five years before, when the fact of
his Vice Presidency began to sink in on him.

There was the first trip, to Massachusetts, 1980, even before inauguration,
to represent the White House–to-be at the funeral of the venerable Speaker,
John McCormack. It was as George Bush left the church, and all the other
mourners were held at the door, as he was guided through a gauntlet of men
to the limousine waiting in a ten-car train, as the agents closed him in behind
bulletproof steel and glass, and stood round the car, scanning the sidewalks
and the empty street ahead, as the motorcycles roared to life and George Bush
could no longer hear the men and women with whom he had prayed only
minutes before, and he could see only the backs of the agents and the streak
of two-wheelers past his shaded window, as even the church was rendered
invisible by the men and machines walling him away, then George Bush drew
one deep breath, as he turned from the window, and he said to friends in the
car:

"God! . . . Isn't it *great*? D'ya ever see so many cops?"

— ★ —

It takes a special man to enjoy the Vice Presidency, but George Bush was the
man for the job. Didn't matter that the writers and the pundits couldn't see
it—he had talent, and he knew it. It wasn't brains, although he wasn't stupid:
Phi Beta Kappa at Yale, if anybody cared to look. Anyway, the job didn't call
for deep thinking: if you thought too much, brought your insight and intellect
to bear on the problems of the nation, you'd get out front of the President, or
worse still, off to the side. That's the surest way down the trash chute in the
White House. There's only one question that the Vice President needs to ask:
"What's the President saying on this?" Anything else is begging for trouble,
and George Bush had brains enough to figure that out.

"A bucket of warm spit," was how Vice President Garner described the job.
At least that's how they wrote the quote from Cactus Jack, the first Texan to
hold the position, as FDR's Number Two (till Roosevelt dumped him in the
1940 campaign). Problem was, no Vice President was really Number Two, or
even Three or Four: a Chief of Staff, Secretary of State—*any* Cabinet officer—a
Senator, even a Congressman . . . *hundreds* of people had more legal and
practical power over how things went in the country, even how things went
in the White House. In fact, Walter Mondale, the last man but Bush to sit this
pointy flagpole, was the first Vice President to have an office in the White

House. (Before that, VPs were warehoused safely out of West Wing earshot, in lofty and ornate offices across the street in a gray granite pile called the Old Executive Office Building, or in a suite even more remote, equally grand and futile, in the U.S. Capitol, the locus of their only Constitutional duty, presiding over the U.S. Senate, and voting in case of a tie.)

It also fell to Mondale to pioneer in the stately Victorian house on Massachusetts Avenue, NW, the Official Residence, provided for the Vice President's use in 1974. Joan Mondale used to give over the whole ground floor to art exhibits and tour groups. It wasn't enough poor Mondale's job was to sit around in mothballs; now he was living in a damn museum! But that wouldn't happen to George Bush—not with Bar in charge. When she took over, the tours stopped and the old wooden house got homey, with tablesful of framed family photos (kids at play on the rocks in Maine), funny hats for George and his friends in the front hall closet, and grandchildren pounding through the halls to the kitchen, to see if the stewards had cookies. (They did.)

Nelson Rockefeller wouldn't even live in the house, or the bubble, they tried to make for him. He moved out after one day, said he had better security—and fewer fellas in the way—at his own home in Washington. But when George Bush began to live every minute surrounded by a half-dozen trim young fellows, he had . . . six new friends! Every day! If only he could throw a horseshoe like Jimmy here, then his happiness would be complete. (But! Wait till the next match. There *might* . . . be a *surprise* from the Veep . . . an *upset* . . . hah!)

Lyndon Johnson, the last Texan in the job, was never the same after three years as second banana to a glamor boy who disdained him. They *mocked* him, all those Kennedy guys. It ate at him like a worm inside, and it left him embittered. But when George Bush took the job, he decided Ronald Reagan was going to be his friend. George and Bar decided without even talking: they were going to *like* the Reagans. And they did, right away. They *loved* the Reagans. The only surprise, Bush told his old friends, was how easy it was. Reagan turned out to be a great guy! The way he told those funny stories! You *had* to like the guy.

But it wouldn't have mattered if there had been no charming jokes, if Reagan had been a vicious drooler; just as it did not matter that Reagan had no talent for friendship, no personal connections apart from Nancy. In fact, Reagan couldn't remember his grandchildren's names, and he had no friends, only the husbands of Nancy's friends. It didn't matter! Bush had the talent, a genius for friendship. And like every genius, he worked at it: if Ronald Reagan connected with others solely by means of funny stories, George Bush would bring him funny stories. In fact, the Vice President's staff knew he didn't want briefing memos for the weekly lunch with Reagan: the way to earn a stripe in the OVP was to give him *a joke for the President.* This was no laughing matter to Bush. It was the core of his life's method. Back in 1978, when George Bush was an obscure ex–CIA chief, just starting to run for President, someone asked him: What made Bush think he could be President? "Well," Bush said, without pause, "I've got a big family, and *lots* of friends." Later in that campaign, he learned the "proper" answer, some mumbo-jumbo about experience, entrepreneurship, philosophy of government. . . . But the first answer was true. George Bush was trying to become President by making friends, one by one if need be, and Ronald Reagan was a Big One.

It certainly didn't matter that they disagreed—that Voodoo Economics thing, and a few other differences, on civil rights, the environment, education, energy, and U.S. policy on Asia, Africa, Latin America, and Soviet relations. Of course they disagreed, because George Bush knew five times more about the governments of the world—his own included—than Ronald Reagan ever would. But it didn't matter! The fact is, they didn't disagree anymore, because George Bush would not disagree with the President. This was another of George Bush's talents: accommodation. He had the capacity to act on the judgments of others, to live within the bounds of received wisdom. It was a talent that had smoothed his path from his parents' home, through prep school and the U.S. Navy, where the lessons of life were delivered explicitly, and later through Yale, business, and politics, where things grew murkier, and the judgments one lived by had to be doped out. But he did divine them: he was always sensitive to the ethic around him. And to the extent he could accommodate himself, he flourished, and made friends every step of the way. In 1964, he first ran for Senate as a Goldwater man, and though Bush lost, Goldwater was still a friend twenty-two years later. In 1966, for a House seat from Houston, he ran as a Main Street Republican, then served and voted with the moderate mainstream, as a backer of Richard Nixon. And in 1970, when he ran and lost for Senate again (this time, slightly to the left of his rival), he asked his Big Friend, President Nixon, for a job at the UN, which he'd roundly reviled as a Goldwater man. By 1980, the accommodation to Ronald Reagan was just a walk in the park.

And it did not matter if the Reaganauts couldn't see him as one of their own. They screwed most of his friends out of jobs, stopped talking when he came into the room, made jokes about him when he was absent. He knew it, just as surely as Johnson had known. Hell, it didn't take a rocket scientist to figure it out, the way reporters would ask his staff: "People, uh, in the Cabinet meetings tell me Bush never says anything. . . . Is that true?" Or they'd just print it: "*Administration sources* said the Vice President had nothing to contribute. . . ." Of course he knew who the sources were. Some were the same hypocrites who came to his office *before* the meeting, asking him to back their schemes, talk to the President for them. . . . Then, when he wouldn't, they'd have some columnist in for breakfast and, just in passing, smiling, with a wedge of grapefruit on their spoons, they'd saw Bush off at the knees. Oh, he knew the game! Still, he never got into that White House cockfight: an eye for an eye, a leak for a leak. Could have had a pro, Jimmy Baker, do it for him. But he wouldn't: it was a matter of loyalty to the team, loyalty to the President; most of all, a matter of discipline.

This was another of Bush's great talents: personal discipline. There were no leaks from the OVP: there was *not one story* saying George Bush was unhappy with this or that decision, or the President overrode objections from George Bush. In fact, there were no stories suggesting Bush had opinions at all, even before a decision came down, even when it would have gotten him off the hook. It would have been so easy: when Ed Meese was filling Reagan's ear with some Neanderthal antiblack screed, sticking the administration's nose into a civil rights fight, putting them all in the soup . . . on the *wrong side* of the issue! And here's a reporter in Bush's armchair, gently inviting: "Mr. Vice President, it seems that you might be less comfortable with something like this. . . ." But Bush wouldn't bite. Never. Christ, the reporters were easy. One of his own aunts came at him, drove him right out of his chair, trying to have a *serious discussion*—why Ronald Reagan refused to have arms talks with the Russians. Years later, she was still half-convinced Bush was willfully stupid, or had the attention span of an eight-year-old. Didn't matter! They could all think so, and he wouldn't lift a finger to prove them wrong. He wouldn't even let his staff help. His first Chief of Staff, Admiral Murphy, used to haul every staffer in for a talk, to let them know they had only one job: to help George Bush do *his* job, and *his* job was to help the President. There would be *no* disagreement between members of the Vice President's staff and the President's staff. They *could not argue with anyone in the White House.* Admiral Dan had them all in, down to the girls who'd answer the phones. And with the same flair he'd once shown as Commander of the Sixth Fleet, he'd warn:

"Honey, tonight, you're gonna go out with your boyfriend. And you're gonna go to a bar, and you're gonna have a drink. And you're gonna want to tell him what a *wonderful* guy you're working for, and what a *great thing* he did today . . . and how he saved the President from the *most awful thing* that somebody else was trying to do. . . . Sweetheart, you don't know who's in the next booth, do you? So . . . DON'T SAY A GODDAM THING!"

It got so the whole OVP was a whisper zone in that gray granite building across the street from the White House. People and paper moved back and forth down the dark, lofty halls of the Old EOB—earnest young people, of good families, sons and daughters of George Bush's friends, would *run* between the offices, flushed with the press of business for the Vice President. And nothing came out! George Bush would go out to speak, all over the country, twenty, twenty-five days a month (he wouldn't duck a chance to help the Party, the President) . . . and nothing would be heard of him! True, the speeches weren't about George Bush, or what he was doing, or what he thought. They weren't about anything, really, except what a great country, and a great President, we had. That was fine with Bush. All the positions, all the speeches, were just politics to him. The rest, the friendships, or loyalty to the President, those were personal matters—matters of the personal code. That was where Bush's talents lay, and the only thread of steel running through his life to his seventh decade. He wasn't going to let politics change the *way he was.* God forbid! It was all personal with George Bush. He couldn't see things any other way.

Of course, he would accommodate. After he came off like such a stiff in the '84 reelection, and his personal polls took a dive, and reporters on his plane got so nasty, then his friends ganged up and made him change the staff: they told him he had to, if he ever wanted to be President; they called it a more "political" support team. That's when he signed on Lee Atwater—neither son nor friend to any old Bush-friend—to run the PAC and the campaign to come. That's when he had to let Dan Murphy go, and hire Craig Fuller as the new Chief of Staff. Fuller was a young White House pro: neat, calm, organized, and people said he knew how to stick the knife, if he had to. But he was another stranger. Jeez, Bush would call the office now, and half the people who answered were strangers! He'd live with it, if that's what it took. But it just wasn't . . . friendly. And it wasn't really fair to Dan. Those rules weren't Dan's rules, they were Bush's. Bush told him just how he meant to do the job, even before he got elected. It was the fall of '80, at the same lunch where he offered Dan the job. Murphy had been his deputy at the CIA. They could talk frankly. And Bush told him point-blank, wanted him to know how it was going to be, had to be . . .

"I've thought a lot about it," Bush said. "I know I'm not gonna have much input on policy, nothing substantive to do at all . . .

"And I've decided, I can be happy with that."

And he had been happy. That's what no one could get through their heads, except Bar, of course. That's one of the reasons he loved her: she understood things without talking. She was better at it than he was!

What was the Vice Presidency?

A *wonderful adventure.*

He had decided—*they* had decided—that it would be, just as he had decided how he was going to do the job. This was the ultimate triumph of discipline, and George Bush's greatest talent: the power of mindset. He could decide—they could decide—how it was going to be, and then it *was that way* . . . because no one, *no one,* would ever see them treating it any other way.

They loved the Reagans.

Why?

Because they *loved the Reagans.* They had decided.

And it didn't start in 1980. Talent like that comes from a lifetime. There was the time George Bush's career picked them up and moved them to Houston, and the wife of a business friend gave a tea for Barbara, to show her off to the ladies.

So they came to meet her, and one after the other, they asked: "And where do *you* come from?"

Bar said sweetly: "I live in Houston now."

"Oh. Yes, but . . . where do you *come* from?"

And Bar, with her smile still placid, beatific, replied: "Houston is my home now."

They weren't going to put her in that box, thank you. And they weren't going to hand her husband a carpetbag, either. She had decided.

But the brilliance of it was, it wasn't one party, one lunch with Admiral Dan, or one talk to the staff. It was there every day, unwavering.

What is the Vice Presidency?

A wonderful adventure. Every day.

So, every day, he did a little more, made another friend, signed more photos, wrote more notes to people he'd met . . . every day. If no one could see that . . . it didn't matter! He had it in the bank. And every day, he did a little more.

Fly across the country and back for a ball game?

A wonderful adventure! He'd get his son Jeb to fly in from Florida, and bring *his* son, George P. . . . And he'd call his eldest son, George, too. George and Laura were in Midland, just across the state, they could fly in, with friends. . . . He'd make it a friends-and-family thing. Bar'll come. Sure, she'll come. It'll be fun!

So the kids flew in to Houston, and they all met at the Astrohall, at the cocktail thing, before the game, and it was fun, sort of . . .

But then they walked to the Dome, and the Service whisked the VP away to some bathroom downstairs, or some damn place, and the others were led to their seats in the park, the Vice President's party to the owner's box on the first-base line, and the others to seats somewhat removed. And that was the first bit of trouble: George W. Bush, George Bush the Younger, who'd gotten his wife and a couple of friends, and the friends' private plane, and had flown across the state from Midland, Texas, to be with his father and mother at the ball game . . . Georgie Bush, the firstborn, first son, the biggest and most jagged chip off the old block, *Junior,* as some friends now called him, *George W. Bush* . . . along with his wife and friends, whom he'd roped into flying across the state, five hundred statute miles, and back, in the same night, for this game, to be with George *H.W.,* and Barbara Bush . . . was sitting off behind home plate.

"These our seats?"

Junior's voice was mild, but the Advance man hastily checked the envelope to make sure. There was edge on that word, "our" . . . there was a hint of ominous meaning in the glance Junior cast to his right, toward the field, toward the biblical Box Seat. Suddenly, there was more than a whiff of trouble in the air. This almost subsensory impression was reinforced a moment later, as Junior added quietly:

"Bullll-*sheeit.* "

The Advance man decided he'd better run off and check.

What the fuck is GOING ON here? They were screwing around with the wrong guy. Junior was now standing, staring at the Box Seat, watching who sat down behind Barbara Bush and the seat reserved for his father. There was Jeb, and his boy, P. *They* got seats with the old man. . . . And a lot of them were Service. Most of them would leave. Anyway, they had to be there. Wait a minute! There was Fuller, the new Chief of Staff, and one of his paper-pushers. *Are they sitting DOWN? . . . Well, wait just a damn minute!*

Fuller! There he was, with every damn oily hair in place, and his Washington suit stretched across his back like aluminum siding. It wasn't enough that he wouldn't return a damn phone call. He's going to sit right behind them, right in the front-row box! *We're being moved out!* Maybe he doesn't know Junior's here—the hell he doesn't, he *oughta*—or that he might want to sit with his parents, have a few laughs with the family . . . or that he likes to be *seen* in Texas, might want to *run* in Texas someday. What would that asshole know about running? Never ran for Sheriff! Tell you one thing: that sonofabitch doesn't know the old man, if he thinks he can move the family out. The old friends were right: This guy's an asshole! . . . *I've been replaced by STAFFERS!*

"I'm goin' down there."

Laura's voice was urgent: "George!"

But Junior was gone.

They were screwing around with the wrong guy. Junior was the Roman candle of the family, bright, hot, a sparkler—and likeliest to burn the fingers. He had all the old man's high spirits, but none of his taste for accommodation. In fact, he was more like Bar, the way he called a spade a spade. But it wasn't so easy for him to do it in the background, the way she'd done it all these years. No, he didn't mind being up front. But he'd learned some control as he'd neared the age of forty. In fact, these days, control, discipline—some of that old Bush medicine—was what he was always teaching himself. He'd just have a talk with Fuller, let him know . . . calmly, but clearly. Before the Veep even got to the seat. He wasn't going to make a stink about it. He'd be doing the guy a favor. The campaign was just beginning—they weren't even through the '86 cycle yet, and Fuller was going to buy himself trouble like this. In fact, it would do Fuller good to get a taste of *him:* Junior was thinking of moving to Washington, too, take a job in the campaign. What the hell! Oil business was no business these days. And Junior could watch out for the Vice like others couldn't: he *knew* him. . . . Atwater saw it. Atwater didn't know the family either, but he saw he could make Junior an ally. *Had* to be an ally. That's what he'd explain to Fuller. In fact, it was *just this kind of thing . . . what the family meant* to the old man. He'd explain. . . . What was the guy's first name?

Uh, Craig? C'mere for a minute? . . . He'd take him off to the side. Calm . . . control . . . guy oughta get a taste of him. . . . *Uh, listen, asshole. What's the story here?*

But he couldn't do it. He got to the Box Seat and thought how his father would hear of a showdown. It was the damnedest thing: forty years old and still shy of his father. But he knew, if he picked a fight, the Vice would be disappointed. So, instead, he said hello to Atwater.

"Hey, whuss happ'nin?" Atwater growled. Lee always talked like a rock 'n' roller exhausted from his recent world tour.

"HOW THE HELL WOULD I KNOW?" Junior said, much too loud. He knew Fuller was right behind him. "SEATS AIN'T WORTH A SHIT. I GUESS THE BOX GOT A LITTLE *CROWDED* . . .

"PEOPLE WHO THINK THEY GOTTA BE HERE . . ."

Everybody heard him. Fuller got every word. His face didn't change, but his calm brown eyes grew a millimeter wider. He could have tried to explain: he knew McMullen, who insisted he sit in the owner's box. He wasn't trying to take anybody's seat. It wasn't his idea. He didn't mean . . .

But then Junior was already talking to someone else. And anyway, Fuller wasn't going to deal with anyone who didn't talk to him face-to-face. He had enough on his plate without that. What he couldn't understand was why George was so *mad*. After the game began, while they all walked up to the skybox, he asked Junior's friend from Midland, Bobby Holt: What got *into* George?

But Bobby just gave him a big oilman grin, and mumbled some chili-mouth West Texas at him: "Y'pissed'im ohff. . . . Y'dohn' screw with th'family. . . ."

Well, apparently. But you don't screw with the Chief of Staff, either. Fuller said: "Well, he better not act that way around me."

Later, Fuller thought it through some more. Maybe he'd made a mistake. He still didn't understand what got into Junior. But he could just imagine the account the Veep might get. The Veep might be disappointed. So he mentioned the whole thing to *Mrs.* Bush.

And that was definitely a mistake.

— ★ —

George Bush didn't know about any of that yet. What he knew was they had him in a hole under the stands, behind home plate, strapped into this damn Kevlar vest, or whatever the stuff was—bulletproof . . . and it bulged in his shirt, thickened him with unaccustomed bulk, constraint, and if he arched his spine, it dug in, right *there* . . . couldn't *move* a certain way, like *that* . . . and the field looked huge from here. It looked like a mile to the scoreboard, the way the bright green carpet stretched away at eye level. The Catfish Hole, they called this place—why, he had no idea. But that was the program: he had to wait in the Catfish Hole while they did the anthem and introductions. The P.A. announcer was laying it on for every player—stats, records, hometowns and nicknames—while they ran through the lineups . . . well, walked through the lineups. They had him down in the hole for . . . seemed like hours, waiting to go to the mound.

Of course he was going to the mound. What's the point of throwing out the first ball if you don't get out there and *throw* it? He wasn't gonna stay in a seat and *lollipop* the ball over the rail, five feet to the catcher, like Eleanor Roosevelt. Jeez, what fun was that? It was his own call in the end, the only call he had to make on this trip: he knew they'd make him wear the vest. But it wasn't even an issue, really. It was a personal thing, with George Bush.

See, he'd done it before—done fine. That's what the new fellows didn't understand. He did his first First Ball in '81, the All-Star Game in Cleveland. They'd asked him for opening day, Cincinnati, when the President was still in the hospital, just a week after he was shot . . . but it wouldn't have been right, trying to step into the President's shoes. So he did the All-Star thing, four months later, and had a great time. He was on his game that night. Hell, he'd been around a ball field longer than most of these guys had been alive. He popped into both dugouts, fooling around, wrestling with his friend Nolan Ryan. (That woke up the Service, sure enough.) Then, from behind Bush, Tom Seaver growled: "What's an *Eli* doing in here?" and he threw an arm around

Bush in a Vice Presidential body lock. Bush loved that locker-room stuff. Ryan and Seaver were friends since their days with the Mets, when Bush's uncle owned a piece of the team. So the young UN Ambassador used to call up and get the best seats in the house, stop by the locker room before the game. He was always dragging along some bewildered Ambassador from Senegal or Tanzania, making friends with baseball.

Anyway, that All-Star night, they picked out a kid from the bleachers for his catcher. When they told him the plan, Bush's face fell. ("You mean I'm gonna have to take something off?") But walking onto the field with the kid was a stroke of genius. A crowd might boo a politician muscling in on the All-Star Game, but who's going to boo a thirteen-year-old kid? So they got a little round of applause, and meanwhile, Bush kept after the child: "Suppose I go with the slider? Can you handle it?" The kid was solemn, nodding, in his Police Athletic League T-shirt, with a big glove borrowed from Kansas City's Frank White, scared to death. But Bush kept talking him through it. "Well, what are our signals? How about a 'one' for a fastball and 'two' for a curve? If you get nervous about the curveball, just give me a 'one.' " Finally, the kid cracked a smile. Bush had a new friend. (Sent him a picture and a note, too.) In the end, Bush threw him two first pitches: the first was a lob, just a straight lollipop; but then he did try to break off a slider, wild as hell—almost hit a photographer in the foot—and the kid made a nice lunging grab. Saved Bush's bacon. The crowd gave a cheer, Bush gave the kid a big "Well done!" and the VP climbed back into the Plexiglas cage they'd put around his Box Seat.

After that, he'd materialize at ballparks all the time. The Service preferred it unannounced: don't give the nutballs a chance to plan. He'd just pop up in the dugout in the middle of a game; him and all the earplugs, who'd stand, glaring out at the field and the grandstands, while the VP watched the game from the bench. "Oh, great fun," he'd report afterward. And he made *lots* of new friends.

One time, back in '84, the VP actually got into a game, an Old-Timer's Day he ran into in Denver. A few of the aged stars had come to his event that morning, asked to meet him, and he said, "Of course! We *love* this kind of stuff!" Jeez, Warren Spahn, and Billy Martin, a bunch of them came. Then they told him he could come and *suit up* that evening, at Mile High Stadium. "Oh, come *on!*" he said, and then quickly, "No, I can't do that. We've got Secret Service . . . constraints." But the Service just had to work it out for him. So they snuck him in, in an unmarked car, just a normal sedan, with ten normal young men in suits trotting alongside, and he showed up in the dugout with a Denver Bears uniform on, and the P.A. announcer suddenly boomed: "*Now batting for the American League, the Vice President of the United States!*" The great thing was, they didn't even boo. People cheered him! And Spahn was on the mound, and he grooved him a fastball, but the Veep popped it up. Of course, they don't play by the rules in these things, so they sent him up again, next inning. This time, it was Milt Pappas pitching, and he served up a fat cantaloupe down the middle, and George Bush swung and rapped it cleanly over second base—solid single! How about that? He made a turn at first and got a cheer from the crowd. He was in heaven! Back in the dugout, he said he'd stay and watch another inning. They told him: Watch? Hell! He had to go out and play! So they gave him a new first baseman's mitt, lefty for him, of course, and sent him out. Just like old times—Poppy Bush at first!

Sure enough, third batter that inning: Tony Oliva . . . hits a *smash* down the first-base line. But Poppy is *there*. He lunges to his left . . . knocks it down. Stays *with* it. . . . Pappas is coming across from the mound. . . . Poppy bare-hands and hits him with the throw at the bag . . . *runner is OUT!*

And the crowd was roaring.

Bush knew his cue. He left the game. And whenever he told the story later (not often—only to friends), he was sure to add: "Should have had it clean."

Poppy Bush always had a big-league glove, if he did, every once in a while, say so himself. There was even a time—not very long—when he thought of trying to make a living with it. In the spring of '42, when Captain Bush led the Andover ball team on a spring-training trip to Florida, Clark Griffith, owner of the Washington franchise, said he'd like to have the young man play that summer for the Senators. But that was after Pearl Harbor—Griffith was desperate for talent—and all the boys on the Andover nine knew where they were going: it was their last season of ball for a while. By the time Poppy played for Yale, he had a wife and a baby son, and the war had taught him, as it had most of his classmates, that life was a serious and finite business. There wasn't much margin spending years of it as a banjo-hitting first baseman, trying to make the major leagues.

But his teammates wouldn't have bet against him. He had that kind of presence on a ball field: serious, capable, a student of the game and a hundred-percent competitor. He had to be, coming from his family, where competition, games of all sort, were practiced with a gravity and fervor that some families reserved to religion.

Pres Bush, his dad, had been a Yale first baseman, at six-foot-four, a towering slugger who'd hit the ball a mile—would have had twice as many homers if he could have run faster. Not only was Pres elected captain of the ball team, he'd occasionally succumb to entreaty from the golf team. (*Pres, we've got to have you, we've got Penn today!*) So he'd play against another school's best golfer in the morning, then suit up in Yale flannels for a one-thirty ball game. It was from big Pres that Poppy, and all the Bush kids, took their attitude toward the game itself: the seriousness of playing well, the appreciation of form. Prescott Bush demanded much of himself, and he did not play a game to hack around. He was still a scratch golfer into his fifties, and never would accept the demands of a Wall Street partnership, or later, his duties as a U.S. Senator, as excuse for shoddy play. There was one way to insure that you'd never be invited to play golf with Pres again, and that was to talk while he was putting.

Still, Pres mostly played against the golf course and his own human tendency to error. The competitive fire, the will to win, Poppy got from his mother's family, the Walkers. It was always sink or swim with the Walkers. The old man, the grandfather, G.H. Walker, was as hard a handful of business iron as the Midwest ever produced. It was he who transplanted the family from St. Louis to a mansion in New York, so he could play in capitalism's big leagues with the Vanderbilts and Harrimans. That was the same league he played as a sportsman. For a while, he kept a stable of racing horses in partnership with Averell Harriman. When his friend (and rival) in St. Louis, Dwight Davis, created the Davis Cup championship for tennis amateurs in Britain and the U.S., Gampy Walker created the Walker Cup for the amateurs of golf. In his later years, he headed the New York State Racing Commission and served as president of the United States Golf Association.

But those were the public connections to sport. It was in private that he practiced and passed on the religion of games, chiefly in Kennebunkport, Maine, where, at the turn of the century, he bought seventeen acres of rocky coastline as the Walker clan's summer preserve. For the Walkers, the long days in Maine were a whirlwind of contests. There were boat races from the harbor to Walker's Point. (And not in the genteel, silent canoes or sailboats that other families kept; Pops Walker favored powerboats, big ones.) There were pickup ball games, in the family, at the Point itself, or bigger games on the town field for the summer league that Gampy Walker created, staffed with town boys and college players brought to Maine for the summer, so his own sons could have summer baseball experience. There were daily and twice-daily golf matches, and tennis matches, pitting parents and children, cousins and uncles, Walkers and friends, against one another in an ever-shifting, always ranked, round-robin to determine *the best.* In some ways, golf was the fiercest: it was his game. By the time his sons came of age and honed their skills enough to beat him, they'd also learned a dozen little ruses ("Oh, sorry, Father . . . Bill's counting on me for a foursome") to dodge the dread despair and *rage,* somewhere on the back nine, when the old man found himself four down, with only three to play. Even when younger, tennis-playing Walkers would hit the River Club, Court One (pretty much the only court they'd play on), everyone knew it: no other members were so energetic, noisy, clannish, and competitive. No other matches had the same air of seriousness, of importance, *do-or-die.* And when there was a championship, or like cataclysm, there would be G.H. Walker himself, attending in his very clean white-and-brown saddle shoes, tweed jacket and necktie, stiff white collar, white flannel trousers, and straw boater.

One summer, when son Louis and daughter Dorothy were a mixed-doubles team playing for the River Club's junior cup, G.H. Walker appeared at Court One, but Lou was nowhere to be seen. He claimed later he didn't know the match was on. It turned out he was at the bathing beach, fooling around and drinking with friends. So the old man had Lou summoned. And he showed up loaded, *snockered,* in front of the whole club! He tossed a ball for a serve and *whiffed.* He was *staggering* on the court. The old man departed, leaving word: he would see Louis, after the match . . . in his room. When Lou got back to the Point, much sobered (by match end, he hadn't played so badly), the old man didn't wait for explanation. He announced to Lou: "You're not going to college. You're too *stupid* to go to college. You're going to work." That same evening, Lou was packed, and on his way to a year in the coal mines in Bradford, Pennsylvania.

In time, all the Walker kids got the religion. They certainly had the talent. Herbie—George Herbert, Jr.—got it all, right down to the attitude. He was as hard in business and sport as his father, he loved a *winner,* and he became the second patriarch of the Point. But Johnny Walker was certainly the best ball player: one year at Yale, he hit a glorious .600! And no one played a better golf game than Jimmy: it was he who was in line to fill the shoes once worn by the old man as president of the USGA. Even Lou might have had some sporting glory if he hadn't screwed around so much. When he was a senior, a pitcher at Yale, he got a spring-training tryout with the New York Giants. But when the great Mel Ott came to the plate, Lou's first pitch plunked the slugger in the neck. Ott said: "Get that college jerk outta here!" And that was the end of Lou's tryout.

But pound for pound, perhaps the best was Dottie, the younger of two daughters, the pearl in this pan of gravel. Not only was she bright and beautiful (they were all *so* attractive), but she seemed to have in her small form the distillate of the Walker ethic: she played to win. When Betty Trotter, a girl-friend at Kennebunkport, challenged Dottie to a swim from the River Club pier, all the Walker boys knew that Dottie wouldn't stop until Betty did. But when Betty quit, after twelve hundred yards in choppy open sea, Dottie just kept swimming, more than a mile, straight to Walker's Point. No one had to make allowances for Dottie in competition. When she married Prescott Bush, and had her own kids to raise, she served as the one-woman ranking commit-tee: it was she who made the matches, pitting Bushes against Bushes, Bushes against Walkers, and Bushes against friends, in the constant contest to be the best.

And it wasn't just summers, not just in Maine: in their year-round home in Greenwich, Connecticut, the Bush kids played games constantly. If there wasn't a ball game at the Greenwich Country Day School, or a tennis match at the Field Club, they'd gather their friends for football at the Bush house, where there was room, and a ready welcome from Dottie. The house on Grove Lane was a magnet for kids: if it rained, all the friends might still show up, to play indoor football in the long upstairs hall, or Ping-Pong on the table in the front hall (Dottie finally tired of taking it down—that table was the first thing visitors saw), or some game that Poppy made up, on the spot. Poppy never liked to be alone. And he was so good about sharing, making sure everyone was included. For a while, Dottie and the housekeeper, Antonina, called him Have-half, because once, when he got a new wagon, he turned to a friend and offered: "Have half? . . ." Of course, he had the most little friends. When Pres would come home on the train from New York and find a house taken over by children at play, he'd sigh and inquire of his wife: "Dottie, do they all have to be here?" But even when Pres was home, and didn't want a bunch of wild Indians in the halls, Dottie would sneak the boys' friends up the back stairs so they could play. After supper, when Pres was closeted with important telephone calls, Dottie, daughter Nan, and all the boys, were likely in the living room, locked in a vicious tiddlywinks match: so serious, involving, so *do-or-die,* that it wasn't uncommon for a child to leave the room in tears, after being "shot out."

Withal, Dottie brought something new to the religion: a certain refinement, a polish, the product of one more generation under the buffer of good society. In Dottie's house there was all the Walker competition, but none of the loudness about it. She did not abide bragging. Her boys were not to come crashing into the dining room, to announce: "I mopped up the court with Gerry." God forbid! They could not even announce: "I won." In the Bush household, young people were expected not only to win, but to be good winners. The proper way was to wait, to be asked:

"Didn't you have a match today?"

"Uh huh, with Gerry."

"Oh, lovely! How'd you do?"

And then, the proper answer was to offer some excuse for Gerry, avoiding the first-person pronoun altogether, or at most, to say, quietly: "I was lucky."

It was all right if a brother or sister did a bit of bragging for you: "Oh, Poppy was great! He had three hits . . ."

But if one of the Bush boys was asked about his game, and he blurted: "I had a home run!" Dottie's voice would take on a hint of edge: "That's lovely, dear. How'd the *team* do?" Sometimes, that edge could cut to the bone. When Poppy, age twelve, was asked about his tennis match and alibied, "I was off my game," his mother snapped: "You don't have a game! Get out and work harder and maybe, someday, you will."

Of course, he worked harder. He was always sensitive to the ethic around him. And he so much wanted her cooing praise. There was something special between the two of them, the way he'd make her giggle, even in church. Pres would turn and stare down the pew severely, but Dottie couldn't stop. Poppy was too much fun! And he adored her, admired her. He wrote, in 1985, in a Mother's Day tribute in *The Greenwich Times:*

"Physically she is a small woman, but she is made of mighty stuff. Nine months into her first pregnancy, she played baseball. Her last time up, she hit a home run, and without missing a base, continued right off the field to the hospital, to deliver Pres."

Yes, Pressie was the first—Prescott, Jr.—but he was different, a big boy, jovial and generous, not quite in the Walker mold. Pressie was a bruiser, a good football player, a lineman who loved to hit. But from birth, he had a problem with one eye that lent him, unjustly, the appearance of slowness. Then, playing football, he blew out a knee, and he was not so good at games anymore. It was her second boy, the one she named with her own father's names, George Herbert Walker, who had her gifts—the slender, supple form, the quickness, the charm. And she showed him in a thousand ways: he was The One. He was meant to win.

If she saved for him the bulk of that old Walker religion, he took it all, he grabbed for it. On Court One, again age twelve, with the family in attendance upon him, he played for the children's championship of the River Club. Early in the match, he turned to glower at the grandstand, and ordered his Aunt Mary, Uncle Herbie's wife, out of the stands. She was talking while he tried to play! That's how he got the nickname, in confirmation of the hope that had given him his name: *George Herbert Walker* Bush—Poppy—just like Pops.

By the time he played first base for Andover, no one else was in the running for captain. Poppy Bush was The One. Not that he was squawking for it: he was never loud, not the rah-rah sort. When you thought about it, he never seemed to mention himself. Maybe there were better ball players: better hitters probably, and Ed Machaj was a heck of a pitcher. But Ed came out of nowhere; everybody knew Poppy, he was a friend, always looking out for the other guy. One year, there was a Jewish kid named Ovie who left school when he didn't get tapped for the Greek societies. When they talked him into coming back, Poppy took him under his wing: brought him out for the ball team. One day a fly ball bounced off Ovie's head, into the left fielder's glove, and Poppy ran all the way out from first, to congratulate Ovie on the assist.

But it was more than kindness, more than friends. Elly Vose, another starting pitcher, had almost as many friends, he was good-looking like Poppy, won as many class elections. But there was something about Bush: no one could really explain it. Part of it had to be the way he dealt with the coach, Follansbee, a strange little guy, and severe, sort of a stick: never spoke like a coach at all, but like a biology teacher, which he was. They said he'd been a pretty good catcher for Princeton, in his day, but something happened to his legs: they were horribly twisted and bowed, with some kind of paralytic disease that never got talked about in those days. They called him Flop Follansbee behind his back, and some of the players never could get on with him. But Poppy was perfect, like he was with all the teachers. He wouldn't brownnose, or as they called it then, "suck," like some guys who had "drag" with the faculty. Poppy just fit in with them, like he belonged.

Still, there was something more, and this was about the way he played: it wasn't thought, or forethought—nothing studied. Just the reverse: it was release, almost the absence of self, in the focus on the game. He wanted *so hard* to be the best. They could see it before every game.

Infield practice was the last bit of business before a game, and old Flop Follansbee, he could run infield. Some coaches, who couldn't handle a bat, would just squib off grounders anywhere, weak rollers, or high-bouncing, too-easy chops off the hard dirt in front of the plate. But Flop, with his professorial scowl and his poor twisted legs, was a fine hand with a bat and ball. He could hit with different hops and different speeds, make an infielder go to his left or right, just to the edge of his range: Flop could bring out the best in an infield. And he loved to get the best from Poppy Bush. Poppy had fine, soft hands, quick moves, and Flop loved trying to hit one by him. So the last bit of infield went like this: Flop would rap a grounder down to third, and the third baseman would throw home to the catcher. The catcher would fire back to third, where the third sacker went back to cover. Then the third baseman fired the ball home again, and ran for the bench. Then, onto the shortstop, who threw home . . . and the second baseman . . . if they had a sub, they'd always give him a chance, too. But finally, there was Poppy alone, crouched on the balls of his feet at first base. And all the fellows, whatever they were doing: fiddling with a mitt, tying spikes . . . everybody stopped, to watch this *thing* between Poppy and Flop. It was so . . . *intimate;* just between them, really. But it was also a touchstone for the game to come—a check of the hands that day. Flop would hit a grounder down to first, and Poppy would throw home. The catcher would throw back to first, and Poppy would fire back to the plate. But he wouldn't run to the bench. He'd charge the plate, right down the baseline, *streaking* in. And Flop would try to rap one by him. Never too hard, he made it fair. But you could see in the jawline of that crippled old coach: he was trying to beat the kid's beautiful hands. And what they remembered most was the way Poppy came at him—flying down the line with the air and the strain pulling his face taut—*laughing* with the pure joy of contest.

That's why he was The One for captain. It was the glint of Walker steel they saw. They wanted their team to be like that.

That was the privilege of being Poppy—just playing the game, being a friend, *being like he was,* and having it come out right, without thinking too much. Having other people do the talking about him, friends who'd take up for him, praise him, so he never had to be out for himself. They always wrote about his "life of privilege . . ." like it was some snotty thing, where the family was better—thought they were better—than someone else. Wasn't like that. Never . . . wouldn't do that. That was a matter of the personal code. It was just . . . well, he just did, and people saw something in him.

That's what he couldn't understand now, why they couldn't see it anymore. Why, forty-five years later, all the guys he hired wanted him to go out and beat his own chest, to thump the tub for himself like he'd never *done* anything. Trying to tell him how to *act.* Like he had to act. . . . Goddammit, he'd played the game! And won. He wasn't gonna change the way he was now.

Sometimes it almost made him laugh, sometimes he and Bar would laugh, the way they worried about him, like he wouldn't be able to do anything—all these guys . . . straphangers, he called them, guys hangin' on for the ride. That wasn't really fair. They were all friends. But all these kids, down in the hole with him now, what were they doing? Keeping quiet because he wasn't talking. Worrying. He could feel their tension, like he'd never thrown a ball.

They were all just trying to do a job for him. He knew that. Hell, they were right about the vest. That's why he had them call from the plane this afternoon, patched it through the White House switchboard, called ahead to meet him at the hotel, with a ball and a mitt, so he could throw a few. Wasn't easy, with this damn thing on. But he had to go along. The Service . . . they were trying to do a job, too . . .

"*We've known him for years here in Houston . . .*"

The Lead Advance brushed by the VP to climb out to the field, give the high sign to the dugout, to Alan Ashby, the Astros' catcher.

In the Catfish Hole, George Bush snapped to focus on the field, the photographers . . . that's Fred! He's a friend! He raised a hand . . . his blazer caught on the vest where it bulged . . . he straightened himself.

"And he's flown in tonight to be with us . . ."

The Lead Advance was looking back toward the Hole, where the Vice President was straightening his blazer. The blazer! Why the hell was Bush wearing the jacket? On top of the vest! Christ! Why'd he have to wear the stupid vest? He couldn't move like that. At the hotel, he put on the vest—half his throws never got there!

Why didn't he just tell the Service to *stick it*?

"Ladies and gentlemen, a real friend . . ."

But George Bush couldn't tell the Service to stick it. Wouldn't be like that. . . . Alas, that was the price of being Poppy.

— ★ —

And now, to throw out the first pitch, to get the 1986 National League Championship Series under way, the Vice President of the United States . . .

In the broadcast booth, Keith Jackson segued smoothly out of a commercial for the ABC viewers.

George Bush! . . . Calls Houston home! And you know what? He knows what he's doin'. He was the captain of the 1948 Yale team . . .

He's out of the hole, and they're cheering! The noise from the crowd is washing down on him from the walls of the Dome—it's like a canyon, six decks! It's huge. This is not even noise. It's another sensation, more like touch, a feeling around the whole head, like hot air pushing in. You can feel it in your hair.

They're on their feet! Standing O . . .

Another man might have turned to wave, or raised a hand . . . another politician, surely. But George Bush lowered his head, like he was embarrassed, or he had to watch his black lace-up shoes on the turf, the dirt around the plate. The cheers rained down on the back of his neck. Oh, he heard them, or felt them, really. By the time he passed the umpires meeting at the plate, his game face had changed to a broad grin of pleasure.

You could see he loved it. Up close, you could feel the fun in him, and the force—he did look terrific. Hell, sixty-two, six-foot-two, and not a spare inch on him. Still quick on a tennis court. Only doubles now, but not too shabby. That's about the only game he had time for. Golf was too slow. Anyway, his putting was shot to hell. But tennis he kept after. Two sets last weekend. Got some sun. Did his running. Up close, you could see he was an athlete. Just a gleam of silver in his hair. Good bones, good tone in his face. Of course, if you saw that grin, you knew he was pumped up. . . . This was great! Part of it was just gettin' *moving*. Never liked hangin' around waiting, just alone, to think . . . always happier doing. And walking onto the field: "We *love* this kind of stuff. . . ." Jeez, it was great! . . . But, of course, the crowd in the Dome couldn't see that.

What did they see?

First, they didn't see him at all, couldn't tell which one was him, the way all the suits came out of the Hole together. And by the time the guys from the Service had peeled away, to stand in front of the photographers, massed on the first- and third-base lines, Bush had his head down, marching to the mound like a man to his doom. In fact, he looked small, all at once alone on the green expanse, overmatched by the huge arc of the Dome, the vast hall it enclosed, the noise from the high canyon. There was a cameraman from the Astrodome, with a Minicam balanced on a shoulder, walking behind him, relaying an image straight to the Diamond Vision screen in center field, but all he got, all the fans in the Dome got, was a fifty-foot shot of the bent back of the Vice Presidential neck. Of course, George Bush never looked up to see that.

That was the price. . . . There was no other politician, certainly no other Presidential contender, who would not give one thought, one quick glance, to a Diamond Vision screen, with a picture of *him,* looming fifty feet high, right in front of his face. Not Bush: he couldn't think about it that way, couldn't see himself as he must look to others, couldn't do "that image thing" . . . "all that me, me, me stuff."

You'd think he would have learned from Reagan, watching him for six years. You watch Reagan do something public, anything, like walk across the lawn to his chopper: every movement is perfect. There he goes . . . with his big western walk, shoulders back, hands swinging easy at his sides, the grin raised to perfect angle, then one hand aloft in a long wave . . . and every instant is a perfect picture. It doesn't even matter if they're screaming questions at him. At any one millisecond, as the shutter clicks, the President is perfect: relaxed, balanced, smiling, smooth.

Now watch Bush make for his chopper: hey, he knows that agent!—not part of his detail, but he met him on the last trip to Houston, got a kid who wants to go to West Point, wrote a letter for him. So Bush twists around and waves to the agent—lets him know he's seen him, bends his head back to Bar to tell her, that's Keith, the *agent,* remember? "MR. VICE PRESIDENT! MR. VICE PRESIDENT!" a photographer is yelling, and it's Fred, the *Life* guy, who was on the trip to Cleveland last week, so while he's talking to Bar, and pointing at the agent, he makes a face to Fred, to let him know he doesn't have to shout. He *knows* him, see. Fred's a friend! And there's Steely waiting at the chopper stairs, Jack Steel! Known him for—God! Twenty-five years? And so he's got to goose Steely, let him know he's glad to see him, and he's making a face at Bar about the way the photographers are shouting, and he twists around to see if the agent's seen him, oughta ask him, but the engine's so loud, and the wind's whipping his hair in his face, which he's screwing up to yell, as he pauses—gotta ask him—trying to balance, crouching in the engine wind, one foot up on the stairs: "Hey! How's your *son?* . . . YOUR SON? . . ."

And at any one moment, as the shutter clicks, Bush looks like a dork.

So now, he gets to the mound and turns, and stands center stage in the great canyon, stands full frame on the nation's TV screens, stands alone before the forty-four thousand, and the fifty million. And yet there is not one instant when Bush is at rest, smooth, balanced, his hands easy at his sides. Hell, he can't drop his hands to his sides: they've got him bundled up like a kid in a snowsuit!

He's got his blue blazer, and a silver tie, and the blue shirt stuffed with him and the vest, and gray flannel slacks, and a brown belt that doesn't match the lace-up shoes, which he's now inching backward at the crest of the mound, feeling tentatively for the rubber, as he balances with baby steps on the slippery dirt. And at last, he looks up . . . and there's the grin!

But, alas, no one gets to see the grin. Because as Bush looks up, what *he* sees is a *person,* Alan Ashby, the catcher, right there in front of his face, albeit sixty-and-a-half feet away. So Poppy's got to have a *thing* with him—gonna be a friend, see. So he lifts up his right hand in front of his face, palm up, and with his wrist limp, flaps his fingers up together, as if he wants Ashby to come closer. A joke, see, just between Al and Poppy. But Ashby doesn't know him, and he thinks it's serious, so then Bush has to raise both hands, *quick,* palms out, with the ball flashing white in his left hand, to keep Ashby where he is, at the plate. By this time, there's fifty million people who don't know what's going on with Bush, why he's flapping his hands in front of his face.

By this time, ABC has cut to the center-field camera, and the nation has a view of the Vice Presidential back and backside. In this cruel shot, there is none of the athlete a fan might have seen up close, on the field. There is just the squarish silhouette of an aging white man, thick through the middle like any guy at sixty-something, looking every bit the interloper, like any guy in a jacket and tie who walks onto a ball field. Just a pol muscling in on a game that isn't his—Hey, watch this . . . think he can throw?

This is it: the moment, the glorious nexus. Poppy is winding up—well, sort of. He can't really get his arms above his head, so they end up together in front of his face, and he sort of swivels to his left, and his left arm flies back—but it won't *go* back, so he gets it back even with his shoulder, and starts forward, while his right lace-up feels for the dirt on the downslope, and he can tell it's short while the throw is still in his hand, and he's trying to get that little *extra* with his hand, which ends up, fingers splayed, almost waving, as he lands on his right foot, and lists to his left, toward the first-base line, with the vent of his blazer aflap to show his gray flannel backside, with his eyes still following the feckless parabola of his toss, which is not gonna . . . oh, God! . . . not gonna even *make the dirt* in front of the plate, but bounce off the *turf,* one dying hop to the . . . oh, God!

And as he skitters off the mound toward the first-base line, and the ball on the downcurve of its bounce settles, soundless, into Ashby's glove, then George Bush does what any old player might do in his shame . . . what any man might do who knows he can throw, and knows he's just thrown like a girl in her first softball game . . . what any man might do—but no other politician, no politician who is falling off the mound toward the massed news cameras of the nation, what no politician would do *in his nightmares,* in front of fifty million coast-to-coast, prime-time votes:

George Bush twists his face into a mush of chagrin, hunches his shoulders like a boy who just dropped the cookie jar, and for one generous freeze-frame moment, buries his head in both hands.

2

The
Other Thing

BOB DOLE didn't see the ball game. He was working. Probably hadn't seen a whole game since high school. He knew what he had to know about it. Liked it, sure, as far as that went. Not too far. Might see a few pitches, in passing, on the console thing in his living room. TV, VCR, radio, all in one sort of console, right in front of the easy chair. Everything he needed, if he was home. Wasn't home much. What would he do there?

Home was kind of small, an apartment in the Watergate, his bachelor apartment, matter of fact. Elizabeth moved in when they got married ten years ago. No, eleven now. That made about ten years she was after him to get a bigger place. She was after him about a lot of things. She didn't push it, though.

Anyway, the living room was the only real room in the place. Took up about the whole downstairs. On one side, sliding doors led off to a little concrete terrace, where Bob would position a chair on the Astroturf and sit in the sun, if he had a daylight hour to rest. But it was a ground-floor place, so there wasn't any view to speak of, unless you considered other people's walls and windows a view. Inside, there was his easy chair, a couch, a breakfront that nobody used much. A foyer led into the living room from one end, and a sliver of a stand-up kitchen led off near the other end. There wasn't any dining room, or any real table. If the Doles did find themselves home for a meal, it was microwave whiz-bang and TV tables. Upstairs there was a box of a bedroom and a half-room of a study, packed tight with files and papers, the floor space in the middle taken up by Bob's Exercycle. That was it, as far as home went.

Of course, no one ever saw the place, so they probably had the wrong idea about it. You mentioned the Watergate, people thought of big, luxury places. That . . . and maybe one other thing. Actually, he wasn't living there when the break-in happened. Back in '72, he still had the house in suburban Virginia, with his first wife, Phyllis. Big house, sunken living room, a real dining room where they could have entertained; three bedrooms, a walk-in garage, yard, everything. Phyllis loved the place. Bob wasn't home much. He was working. When he was around, he stayed in a spare, monkish room he set up in the basement. Never used the rest of the house. That was when the marriage with Phyllis was coming apart. Maybe that's why he didn't want a real house now. Hard to tell. No one had the guts to ask. There was a lot no one dared say to Bob Dole.

He wasn't the kind to chat about his life—or anything else, either. Not that he was silent, Coolidge in the Cloakroom. No, he was always ready with a joke, always had a greeting for you, most often: "Howy' *doin'*?" or sometimes "How'sa *goin'*?"

Dole's voice was made for the empty distance and mean wind of the prairie. His few words were audible no matter what was going on around, especially the vowels, which would linger and fall with the kind of descending Doppler effect you hear when a race car passes.

"Howy*DOOOOnn*? . . ."

Meanwhile, Bob Dole was already on to the next greeting, or out of the room altogether. See, he didn't really want an answer. He was working.

For someone he knew, especially someone who wanted something, he'd always make up a special greeting. At a fund-raiser, he'd spot the guy—say, the lobbyist for the rice growers—who was heading for him, coming at him for something . . .

"There he *ihhhhhzz,*" Dole would exclaim, and then with his good arm raised, his left hand in a fist, his thumb jutting up, pumping the air, he'd rasp out:

"*Rice! Rice! Rice! Rice!* . . ." Like he was cheering for the guy and his rice bill. But he wasn't cheering. He was getting by before the guy could pin him for something.

Dole always spotted them first. In a crowded room, his gaze was constantly darting. He had the nervous eyes of a basketball guard, the playmaker who brings the ball up: he had to watch the whole court, he had to know first how the play would develop. Meanwhile, he had to keep dribbling.

"Agh, kinda *hot* . . . need some *rayyne* . . ."

"Howy*dooon* . . ."

"Hey, Bob *Dohhhll*! . . . Gooda meetcha . . ."

In fact, that was his job in the Senate, as the Leader, *Majority* Leader: to push the play, make something happen, meanwhile keeping track of his votes, what the White House wanted, Cabinet departments, polls, his constituents, the calendar, members' schedules, their bottom lines when votes were tight, their points of particular pride and fear. Of course, Dole had been Leader only for the last two years, but this was a case of the job finding the man: he'd kept a hundred balls in the air for a couple of decades now.

That's how it was in the Senate that day, October 8, 1986, when the budget was still hanging fire, and the House couldn't seem to send over a continuing resolution, just a simple CR to keep the government working for another few days, much less a spending plan for a year, and the bill to go along with it, to raise the debt limit, so the government could borrow; meanwhile, the President was vowing he'd veto any CR that delayed a budget past Friday, two days from now, and the Speaker of the House was threatening a lame-duck session, to reconvene and take up the budget after the midterm election; meanwhile, Goldwater couldn't get any defense appropriation worked out in conference, and Hatfield, Chairman of Appropriations, was tied up with the CR, so Dole had to schedule Hatfield's river-gorge bill when he could attend; meanwhile, the Senate was supposed to have a trial, its first impeachment trial in fifty years, of a judge who, in turn, was suing the Senate (and Bob Dole), so they had to pass a resolution to authorize legal counsel and schedule executive session for the trial and, somehow, drag the matter to a vote; meanwhile, thirty members were up for reelection and some were gnashing their teeth to get home, and Metzenbaum let Dole know that Monday next, Yom Kippur, was the holiest day of the year for the Jews, and DeConcini and D'Amato reminded him it was also Columbus Day and they had political commitments at home; and the President was getting ready to go to Reykjavík to meet Gorbachev, and he asked for a one-day ratification of the new defense treaty with Iceland, so he could take that along; and meanwhile, the White House was getting heat on this Iceland summit—the nonsummit summit, no agenda, no plan, no preparation—so Dole was drafting a resolution supporting Ronald Reagan as he went to Iceland, signing on the Senate, so it looked like the government had a plan and spoke with one voice to the Soviets; meanwhile, the House finally sent a CR, a two-day extension so the government could write checks, but someone over there tacked on a requirement to hire back the striking air-traffic controllers, so Dole checked with the White House and found out Reagan would surely veto that, and he sent it back to the House, to get the air controllers re-amended out; meanwhile, he worked out ten consent calendars with Bob Byrd, maybe thirty or forty bills they could agree upon en bloc, and got those taken up, along with Hatfield's river gorge, and Exon's used-car Truth-in-Mileage Act, Danforth's amendment to the Telecommunications Act, and Stevens's amendment to the Second-Class Postage Law, Simon's and Sarbanes's Human Rights Resolution, the conference report on the bill to keep VISTA alive, the authorization bill for the Federal Maritime Commission, and maybe a dozen other bills, along with forty-two minor nominations, and he got them all out by 8:15, after eleven hours on the floor, whereupon Dole hustled back down the grand hall, back toward his office: he had work to do.

The strange thing was, he looked just the same as he had that morning—just as good: there was no sign he'd been on the job thirteen hours; not a wrinkle in the soft, dark wool of his Brooks Brothers suit; his striped silk tie was knotted tight against the smooth collar of his white shirt; his face showed not a hint of sag, it was tight and handsome with perpetual tan. With an hour in the sun once a week, or every two weeks, Dole could keep a tan forever. And with a couple hours' sleep, and maybe a nap in an airplane seat, Dole could go forever. He was never more cheerful, more at peace, than he was in the wee hours, when a deal was going down and he was waiting for someone to crack, while he drank a milkshake and told old stories in the Senate dining room.

Now, on his way off the Senate floor, he was picking up speed. He had his right arm bent in front of his midriff, as he always carried it before him in the world. A lot of people knew that arm was useless, almost paralyzed, but even those who'd watched him for twenty-five years thought all the operations must have cocked the arm in front of him, fused the bones so the arm bent from the elbow to look almost like a working arm. In fact, it was Bob Dole who made it look like a working arm. If Dole ever let himself rest, that arm would hang straight down, like the arm of a quadriplegic. It would fall, visibly shorter than his left arm, with the palm of his bent right hand twisted toward the back. But Dole never let anyone see that—his problem. No matter how many hours he'd been up, or how long he stayed out, no matter how it ached, for hours, or a whole day, without rest, he kept that arm hiked up in front of him. He kept a rolled-up memo, or a plastic pen, in the crooked right fist to round its shape. If he ever let that memo go, or the pen, the hand would splay, with the forefinger pointing and the others cramped in toward the palm, the back of the hand painfully hollow where doctors had failed to graft in tendons. But Dole never let anybody see that. Now, as he barreled down the Capitol hallway (trailed by an aide who had to run a few steps to catch up, then tried to walk, then had to run again), Dole was canted forward, his perfect head of hair slightly atilt, his jaw set, lips pursed, his sharp black eyes in a pensive squint, like he was concentrating on something else, while his left hand, the better one, unobtrusively swung up to cup his spasming fist with its memo, and he squeezed the right fist to stop the cramping, to get some feeling back in the bad hand after so many hours of holding, holding against its rigid ache . . . but, of course, nobody saw that. What they saw was a man who moved through the idling crowd like a fullback through the line, who seemed to grow larger as he blew by, pushing forward on the balls of his feet, brushing past a question from a young man (maybe staff, press, or a junior lobbyist) with a curt, snarling "M'in a *hurry!*" that lingered in the air, as the noise of a chainsaw does when it stops, echoing off the statues and the tile floor of the grand arched hallway, as Dole disappeared into his suite.

He didn't mean to stop there for more than a minute. "Gotta gooo!" he announced to the office in general—to the press staff, which was always staying late, on the alert with Dole; to the ladies-of-all-work, who took his calls and typed his words, waited on him and lived their lives in his great whirling orbit, as stead for their own narrower tracks. He didn't have to speak to anyone in particular: they all waited for him, watched his every move, listening for the bursts of speech that leaked from him, reading in the signs of his mood their success, or lack, for the day.

But there were no bad signs that night. Only thirteen hours on the job so far, and already it was a good day. See, somewhere near the midpoint, between the closed session on impeachment and the arrival of the first CR from the House, Dole had tucked in a lunch with Howard Baker, the retired Senator from Tennessee, the former Republican Leader who stepped out of the job to run for President.

Baker and Dole stayed in touch, former colleagues who tried to keep each other apprised of their plans. That's why Baker came by today: to say he might not run, after all. He thought Dole would want to know.

Augghh! You bet Dole wanted to know! Both he and Baker had been running for the White House for the last eight years, since they started the cycle for 1980, the year both men finished as also-rans. No, for Dole it was ten years, if you started, as he did, from the day he lost the Vice Presidency, in 1976. It was ten long years . . . for the Presidency. That was "the other thing." That's what he'd call it when he told the Schedulers to put on an extra flight somewhere, a thousand miles into the country, to speak for some candidate for Congress, or Lieutenant Governor, or State Treasurer who didn't have a chance of ever getting to the Senate.

"Might be good, get his help . . . for the other thing."

It wasn't so much that he feared Howard Baker: poor Howard didn't have much taste for a fight. But it straightened his own path—after all, how many Senate Leaders could a voter keep track of? How many Senators? In the Dole cosmology, Senators occupied a special sphere. Now, in the GOP, apart from Dole, only Paul Laxalt was running. And he, too, was leaving the Senate, running not really as a Senator, but as Ronald Reagan's friend. Anyway, Laxalt had problems in his home state, Nevada: political troubles, and an investigation that threatened to drag his name down. That was all summed up in the few words, as spare and evocative as a Japanese poem, a political haiku on Laxalt, that issued in Dole's flattest prairie voice:

"Agh, got a friend . . . Nevada . . . might need a friend."

The way was now clear for Dole . . . for the other thing. He knew what he had to do. He had to get past one man: George Bush. But that meant fighting off the whole White House, all the machinery and all the goodies that incumbency could command. It meant Dole would have to work harder, hit and move with guerrilla speed, travel light.

Now he blew into his inner salon, an elegant room with painted ceilings thirty feet high, graced by two-hundred-year-old chandeliers and the fireplace the British used to start the blaze that wrecked the Capitol in the War of 1812. He strode past Dean Burridge, the former Capitol policeman who traveled with him in Washington, who now sat with his leather folder at a graceful table-desk, the kind of gleaming curvy-leg affair used by assistant managers in a fancy hotel lobby. Dole said to the air: "Car ready?"

Of course the car was ready. Dean and the driver, Wilbert Jones, had been ready for hours. Three times Dean had called ahead with updates on Dole's arrival. He'd checked the route with Wilbert. He'd checked to make sure the crowd was still there, he'd checked a half-dozen times to make sure he had any paper or files that Dole might conceivably ask for. He was ready if Dole was hungry, wanted to stop for a milkshake. . . . But he didn't say any of that. What he said was, "Yes, sir."

By that time, Dole was in his office, taking off his jacket, draping it carefully over the back of a chair. His voice cut through the stillness of his sanctum, through the doorway—maybe trying to cheer up Dean. He was not unaware of the hour, or the waiting. "Agh, Betty still at her *post*?" This was an office joke. Betty Meyer was one of the ladies who devoted her life to Dole. She'd been with the Senator nearly twenty years, almost never leaving the place, which she monitored with breathless anxiety and henlike devotion day and night. And although no one could see him, as he sat down at his desk, Dole lifted his left hand to his ear as if he were on the telephone, and with his eyebrows raised to lend his face a look of terror, he forced his prairie voice up into Betty-like squeaks: "Yip yip-yeep yeep-yeep-yeep-yeep."

Dole used his left hand to lift his right fist onto his desk and to remove the rolled-up memo from it. Then his left hand lifted his right hand again and set it on a crumpled corner of the memo like a paperweight, so he could smooth it out with the left hand. He pushed the flattened pages toward the three neat piles of paper on the desk, and picked up the phone to call Betty.

"What's *cookin'*?" he asked without greeting. And he rolled his eyes to the ceiling as he listened to the yips on the other end.

"Agh, gotta *gooo!*" he said after a minute. He bent forward to look over the piles of paper on the desk. All the memos, drafts, and requests had been stacked, each a little lower than the next, so the top of each was visible. There were three piles. The right-hand stack was for things he was saving: the new proposed tax tables, a detailed poll from California, a few memos he wanted to look over again, and two thank-you letters from Senators (he always kept those for a while). Most of these sheets already bore a few felt-tip scratchings in his painstaking lefty script. It was forty years since he started to write with his left hand, but he'd never gotten good at it. Partly, that was because the left hand worked, but he didn't have much feeling in it. So Dole had to guide his black felt tip by watching his left hand form the letters. It could take a whole minute to write a few words. But he still tried to write some response or instruction on each of the hundreds of memos he got. At times, the comments were hard to read, intelligible only to staffers who knew how he talked. For example, these thick black squiggles next to an interview request:

Writing a book?

That meant Dole had talked to the guy once last month, and never saw a story. Why should he talk to the guy again? Find out what the hell he was doing!

The middle pile was for papers he was still working on. Maybe he hadn't decided whether to give them to Sheila Burke or Mike Pettit. Maybe they awaited five minutes when he could make a phone call. Or a night when he could sit alone in the quiet of an empty Capitol, when everybody else had long since gone. Sometimes it was an angry letter from someone he knew, someone he'd worked with, taking him to task on a vote, a bill, a speech he'd made that got into the papers. Dole liked to handle those himself:

"Warren? Bob *Dohhll*! . . . Listen, some damn fool sent a letter in here and signed *your name* on it. I thought you'd wanta *know* . . ."

But there was no time for that now, so Dole carefully licked his left thumb and forefinger, and used them to slide a couple of pages out of the middle stack. It was a movement surprising in its delicacy. After he set the papers aside for Dean (they'd ride in Dean's folder tonight), the desk looked like he'd never been there. It was still in perfect order, with its three stacks and one book, a biography of Thomas E. Dewey, written by a former Dole staffer, Rick Smith. No one knew if Dole ever read the book, but it had been on the desk for months.

For ten seconds, Dole glanced at the left-hand pile, the new business, things people wanted him to see. His staff was encouraged, almost required, to put their memos, ideas, drafts, directly into Dole's hands. There was no chain of command in the office. Everybody in his orbit worked directly for Dole. So senior staff people could drop a paper onto Dole's desk, along with the rest of Dole's matters pending. Of course, that meant they could see everything on the desk. Sensitive matters, too. That didn't seem to bother Dole. Anyway, the important facts were in his head. It also meant that Dole got a lot of paper he didn't care about. Sometimes a long memo (especially a long one) would come back to its author without a word of comment. Then the poor staff guy would have to ask Dole about it. And Dole would drop one eyebrow and fix the guy with a forehead-furrowing squint:

"Don't have *time* t'discuss your political ph'*los*ophy."

That generally kept the next memo shorter.

Now Dole stood and cranked his left arm around his back, stretching to his right-rear pants pocket, and pulled out his barber's comb. He always had the long black comb. He'd never be able to get a short one out of his pocket. Anyway, the barber's comb did a better job, and Dole's hair, like his suit, his shirt, like his bills, his press releases, his letters, like everything that came from his office or reflected upon him, had to be perfect. Four strokes with the comb through the thick black hair—a bit long in the back, have to get that cut—and it lay down, like a barber had worked it over. He twisted to replace the comb, and as his left arm came around front again, he bent from the waist, almost doubled over, and the arm shot out ahead of him in a strange, twisting, lunge. It was a strain, full of effort, almost scary to people who never saw it before. (One new staff guy jumped out of his chair and leapt for Dole, when he first saw it. He thought the Senator was going to keel over!) But Dole did it just to straighten the arm. At the full extension of his reach, he bent the elbow and brought his hand back for one final smoothing pat of his hair. Then, with the left hand, he hiked up his right arm again, into its carrying position. He reached for his jacket on the chair, draped it over the bent right arm, and his prairie voice scraped through the doorway to the salon.

"Agh, Wilbert know where we're goin'?"

"Yes, sir," Dean said, as he came into the room. It was Dole's way of telling him to come get the papers. Meanwhile, Dole poked his head out the other door of the office, the one that led to the warren where the press staff worked on three crowded desks, clustered around a wire-service ticker and a console TV. With the Senate out for the evening, the staff had changed the channel, turned off C-Span, and switched back to commercial TV.

. . . so the crowd is now filling the Astrodome . . .

It was Keith Jackson's syrupy voice from the booth in Houston.

. . . and we'll be back with Game One of the National League Championship Series, after this word . . .

Bob Dole couldn't wait around for the first pitch. He had work to do . . . on the other thing. He was off to another hotel meeting room, this one rented for the benefit of Ben Blaz, the delegate to Congress from the territory of Guam. He paused to listen to the top story of the Ted Koppel news-brief: something about an American pilot—Hasenfus was the name—shot down over Nicaragua, said he was working for the CIA. . . . Dole rolled his eyes to the ceiling: the whole thing was screwy.

"Okayyy! . . . Keep it *up*!" he barked at the air, a rasping command that passed with him for enthusiastic good humor. He checked the wall clock: not even eight-thirty. Eight minutes, total, in the office. And he hustled back the way he came, down the grand hall, to the Senators' elevator that awaited him, to take him to the first-floor door, to the tunnel beneath the Capitol steps, where his Lincoln Town Car was idling in the darkness.

— ★ —

Come to think of it, even back in Russell, Bob Dole probably never saw a whole ball game. He had work to do. He had school, too, and jobs at home. With Bina Dole driving the train in that house, there were plenty of jobs for the kids. Sometimes, even before school, in the first gray light of day, Bob would run a couple of blocks to Dean Krug's place, on the west edge of town, where the houses stopped and the endless flat fields began. Dean's dad was a carpenter, but he kept cows on the side. At dawn the boys would do the milking, and Mr. Stoppel, at the grocery, would sell the milk at a nickel a quart. If they got five quarts, and Mr. Stoppel sold them all, the money from the fifth went to the boys. If they split the work, they each got two and a half cents.

In the summer, they could get another nickel digging dandelions. Bob and his brother, Kenny, one year younger—and sometimes Dean—would dig weeds from a lawn: five cents a bushel. But they had to pack the basket. If they dug for Bina Dole, she wanted to see the roots.

Then, too, Bob and Kenny sold a patent remedy, the good-for-what-ails-you Cloverine Salve, twenty-five cents a tin. The boys would pay for ten to a shipment, and the goo arrived twelve tins to a pack, so if they sold a whole sleeve—might take weeks—they made fifty cents. Their relatives had enough Cloverine to grease a herd of cows.

Weekends, if there was time, they'd deliver grocery handbills. Bob got the job from Mr. Holzer. That was the way it went: Bob got the job; Kenny and Dean would help. They'd get two dollars for the whole town, about eight hundred houses. They'd start on a Friday after school and finish Saturday morning. They couldn't put the flier in the mailbox because there was no stamp, and that was against postal law. But they couldn't throw it on the lawn, either: old man Holzer would have a fit. So they knocked on every door. And if people weren't home, they could put it in the screen door. It could take an hour to do a square block, but heck, there were whole *families* didn't have two dollars, cash.

Cash was always short in Russell: cash and water—they went hand in hand. Just a few years before the town was founded, as a way station for the Kansas Pacific, most atlases called these plains the Great American Desert. By 1870, the railroad made it through, all the way to Denver, and tried to lure settlers along the way. But Wall Street was convinced there wasn't enough rain on the empty grassland to support agriculture, or a loan for it. Still, railroad agents patrolled the eastern ports, looking for immigrants to break the prairie sod. In the 1870s, the Union Pacific sent scouts to Europe, offering a package deal: steerage across the Atlantic and a boxcar ride to Kansas, for eighty dollars a head.

That's how the land around Russell was settled, with the arrival of the Volga Germans. They were farmers whom Catherine the Great had lured to Russia a hundred years before with a grant of black Volga steppe, and exemption from service in the Russian army for ninety-nine years. Now, in the 1870s, the grant and exemption were running out, and the Volga Germans dispatched scouts to America to find a new land for an old people. They were wheat growers, a hard-headed, tight-fisted bunch. They'd have to be. The railroad never told them about the summers when it never got around to raining; about the plagues of grasshoppers; about the winter storms that screamed in across the plain, swirling snow that could bury a house in its drifts. But the Germans stuck it out, and stuck to their ways. (Sixty years later, in his cream and egg station, Doran Dole, Bob's dad, would use a few words of *Deutsch* to settle accounts on the big cans of milk brought into town by the Volga Germans.)

The Doles had lived through another generation or two in America, on farms in New York and Ohio, before they joined the tide of settlers seeking a fresh start on fresh land, after the Civil War. But Doran's family was one of many in Kansas that came up short in the struggle with the banks, and ended up tenants instead of landowners. They paid a third of their crop to the landlord, and lived on the rest; there wasn't much left. Doran came into Russell for high school, but America was shouldering her burden in the Great War, and Doran dropped out of school to enlist. He wasn't loud about it— Doran wasn't one for speeches about anything—but a call to the flag was, for him, just as basic as the other ineluctables of life: weather, work, and the shortage of cash. When he came back to Russell, he used his Army pay to rent a storefront on Main Street, which he opened as a café, the White Front, in 1920. When he married Bina Talbott, the following year, their honeymoon was a supper, cooked by a couple of friends, and served at one of the two white tables that occupied one side of the White Front Café. That was about all Doran and Bina ever got out of that restaurant. There just weren't enough folks around Russell, Kansas, who had cash to buy a meal on Main Street. By the time their first son, Bob, was born, in 1923, the White Front was a memory, a picture in their album: Doran Dole, scrubbed and proud, his sturdy form wrapped in a long white apron, standing in front of those two white tables and a sign, WE WELCOME YOU, which hung under four small American flags.

After the café closed, Doran opened up the cream and egg station. He bought from the farmers, who'd drop off their milk on their way into town, and he sold to the dairy or the grocery stores. He made about fifteen dollars a week and maybe a dozen eggs, or a quart of cream he'd take home to make butter. Doran was up by 6:00, and in the station by 6:30, getting ready. It had to be just so. He stayed late on Saturday, the farmers' big day in town, and he'd be there after midnight, scrubbing the concrete floor till it shone. If he couldn't bear to work so late, he'd go back Sunday morning, to make sure the place got cleaned just right. He was a strong man, though you wouldn't have noticed, the way he carried himself, so quiet. But a full milk can was near a hundred pounds, and Doran took them to the dock two at a time. He missed one day of work in forty years: spoiled his record, he used to say. But he gladly closed the station every Armistice Day, when the Legion marched up the brick Main Street. And, every year, when they read out the Gettysburg Address, Doran was there in his uniform, sometimes in the color guard. Then, there'd be potluck at Bina's house. That was a big day, Armistice Day.

Fourth of July was special, too, with a feast of Bina's fried chicken and potato salad. There'd be soda pop and watermelon for the kids, before the fireworks. And then the homemade chocolate ice cream. Doran would go to the icehouse and bring back a big block on the morning of the Fourth. Then he'd crush the ice in a gunny sack, and do all the cranking, for hours, by himself. That was before they got the electric icebox. That was a day of miracle! Doran built an extra ledge on the back porch, to hold the thing, and all the Dole kids sat outside, staring . . . waiting. . . . Ice, anytime! Square cubes!

By that time, Doran was managing the elevator for Norris Grain. The money wasn't much more, maybe steadier. The hours were as long, maybe longer. He opened up at 7:00 A.M., with his forty-cup coffee urn already perked. Doran made the strongest coffee in the county—used to fill up the inner basket with grounds level to the rim. He liked it so you could float a spoon, and he liked it hot—a nice, full cup, too. He'd have his gone before yours'd be cool enough to sip. When he'd go to his sisters' houses, they'd worry about making the coffee. If they made him a cup of their regular brew, he'd drink it and say, "Now, how 'bout some coffee?" In the grain elevator, he'd drink it all day, and pass it out to the farmers. He kept chairs and some four-legged stools around, just to make them feel welcome, and they'd all come in on their way out of town. They'd sit in the back, where the earthy grain smell was spiced with the steam from Doran's urn, maybe four or five old German dirt farmers and Doran, all in bib overalls, complaining about the weather, or rust got into the wheat, or something. Every once in a while, Doran would stick in a quiet comment, sometimes advice, more often a joke. He'd tell a newcomer to pull up a stool: "Sure, sit down. Doesn't matter if you work. The gov'ment'll keep you." He'd tell 'em they'd better get back home to collect their "Fare Well" checks. That's what he always called welfare. He had a way of delivering his lines so you couldn't tell if he was joking. He'd be staring off, at the floor or his single shelf of pesticides, still deadpan, while everybody else in the place cracked up. The farmers called him Doley. He called all the men and boys by name. The girls he called Sis. Mostly, he was just always there, rain or shine, any season, every day. Doran stayed open Thanksgiving if the fall was wet and the milo was late. If the farmers were cutting, he was there. During harvest, when the trucks lined up on Main Street all the way to the highway, he'd work till two in the morning, helping the farmers unload. Then he'd drag himself home for a few hours' sleep, and go at it again the next day. Bina hated that time of year. During harvests, the Dole boys used to run home from school and gulp their lunch, so they could run to the elevator and work for a half-hour while Doran marched home and ate.

During harvests, Bob Dole used to fill a tray with Cokes from the Dawson fountain and pass them out to the farmers sweating in their trucks on Main Street, "Compliments of Dawson Drug . . ." He got the job at the drugstore when he was barely in high school, not yet full-grown. There wasn't any question in the Dawson brothers' minds that he'd do the work, do it seriously. Bobby Dole had always been working, always been serious. The neighbors used to see Bob leave for school in the mornings, as they left for work, walking up Maple Street. He'd run out the door with a whoop—"Bye!"—and off he'd go. Kenny'd come trudging behind. Bob didn't visit with anyone along the way. He seemed to be concentrating. He didn't talk to Kenny, even if Kenny managed to keep up that day. "That Bob! . . . Such a little man!" the neighbor ladies used to tell Bina, who took it as the compliment they probably intended.

There were years at a time when Kenny couldn't keep up, after he got the infection in his leg. In those days, there were no antibiotics. In Russell, there wasn't even a hospital. The local doctors tried what they knew: they dipped bread in hot milk and stuck a bag of it onto Kenny's leg as a poultice, trying to draw out the disease. They tried to lance the swelling, as they would a boil, but the wounds never healed. There was a doctor named Mead who cut the leg open, swabbed it and drained it, and this time it healed. But Dr. Mead hadn't got it all, and the leg swelled and broke open again. Kenny was on crutches for most of four years, from the time he was seven or eight, and Bob was nine. For weeks at a time, the doctors of Russell had Kenny tied down on the bed the boys shared while they sowed his leg with maggots, to eat away the disease. There were hundreds of them in his leg, gnawing, eating at him all the time. You could hear them! (Like hogs eating corn, Kenny said.) The smell of sickness filled the house. Finally, Kenny was in the hospital at Hays. Bina traveled the thirty miles every day. Doran would come home after work, bathe and eat, then he'd drive his old green Whippet to Hays to join her. If Doran had a dollar saved before Kenny went to Hays, that was the last he saw of it. The other kids would listen at the table while Bina and Doran plotted payments to the doctors, in currency of chickens, or eggs. Bob didn't understand all the finance, but he knew one thing before he was ten: he was never going to be sick like that, never going to cost the family that way. Bobby Joe was going to be the strong one. He was going to be a man.

After he took the job at Dawson's—every day after school and Saturdays— he was, in fact, a little man of the town. Dawson's was the place to go in Russell, for medicine, of course, but also for ice cream, coffee, or just conversation. During the day, Dawson's drew at least one visit from everyone who worked in town. At night, they got everybody from the Mecca Theater, and the Dream, all the kids from the roller rink, the men from the pool hall across the street, shoppers and storeowners who came by after they closed. "Meet you at the drugstore," they'd call to one another across Main Street. When Bob started out, old Dutch Dawson was still in charge, but most days he sat in his back booth and the tone of the place really came from his sons. Ernie Dawson, the oldest, was the quietest: he was the pharmacist, he worked in the back. Chet and Bub Dawson were the ringleaders, working out front, with the sundries, at the fountain, dealing with the folks, giving them "the treatment." If Bub saw a lady crossing Main Street, gingerly pulling the scarf off her new perm, on her way into Dawson's for that new-style curler they'd just recommended while they worked her over at the beauty salon, he'd say, when she walked in patting her coif: "Thought you were goin' to the beauty parlor. . . . They too busy? Couldn't take ya today?" If a man walked in with paint on his pants, Chet might loudly start a collection, dunning all the codgers who did crosswords under the ceiling fans at the wooden-top tables for "a nickel apiece t'get ol' Ben some clean pants." That was if the fellow didn't really need the nickels. It got so people stuck their heads in just to get their insult for the day. Most came in and stayed for a while, listening to Chet's constant plaint about his wife, "ornery, damn fool woman . . ."

It didn't take Bob long to catch on. He had Doran's gift of deadpan humor and, soon, he had his own patter for the public. For his schoolmates, he learned to flip the ice cream or the cherry into the air, before it landed in the mixing cup, or the glass, where he'd pour the soda on top. "Nickel green river, comin' up," he'd announce, then ask: "You want the flip in it?" He talked to the adults who took their coffee breaks on the fountain stools, and he could retail all the news in town. People thought nothing of asking young Bob what happened with that wreck on the highway last night. And Chet or Bub'd call across the store: "Why you askin' Bob? He's just the soda jerk." And Bob'd snap back: "Well, somebody had to have the intelligence to mix a milkshake 'round here."

Such a little man of the town!

Such a man at school! Most of the kids who left Russell High at three o'clock each afternoon wouldn't see a thing until they came back the next day: it was home, supper, homework, maybe Jack Benny or the Lone Ranger on the family radio. But Bob was in town every night. He knew who ducked into the back room at Dawson's where they might put something extra in their Cokes. He saw the men stopping by the newsstand next to the theater where they had two slot machines, and the woman who ran it was a whore! Heck, he'd been in the pool hall! Donny Sellens's pool hall was a place kids didn't go. But Donny had a lunch counter in there, and when Bob worked a full day, Saturdays or summers, he was allowed to walk right in. He only got fifteen minutes for lunch, and Sellens's was just across the street. He'd climb onto a stool and they wouldn't have to ask: Bob got the quarter special, a hot dog, bowl of chili, and a Coke. They'd shove a box of crackers and a bottle of ketchup down the counter, and he'd eat all the crackers, and pour all the ketchup into his chili. Meanwhile, he'd watch the tables. That was as close as he ever got: pretty innocent, when you got down to it. But when Bob went back to school, all he had to say to draw an openmouthed stare was, "Guess who I saw in the pool hall . . ."

There were plenty of places kids didn't go when Bob was growing up. After oil was discovered (in '23, the year Bob was born) under a knoll on the prairie west of town, the highways into Russell were studded with neon—at least for the boom years of the twenties. By the Sheriff's count, there were twenty-seven nightclubs and honky-tonks: the Pineboard, Lindy's, Jack's Shack, and Geibel's Gables, out about fifteen miles north of town at Highway K-18; the Cotton Club, out by the stockyards, the Lakeside, the Big Apple, the Sunflower, the Red Star, out on Highway 40 East. . . . The bar rum was bootleg, there were slots, dice tables, blackjack, poker rooms. Women were expensive, in short supply. Drew Pearson passed through town in the 1930s, and wrote it up as "Little Chicago."

Well, anyway, it was little. In the twenties, Russell couldn't grow fast enough. The first handful of roughnecks who came in from Wichita, Tulsa, Oklahoma City, filled up the hotel and a couple of boardinghouses. The later ones ended up sleeping in garages, attics, and chicken coops. They were rough boys, too. The shopkeepers on Main Street called them Oklahoma Rounders— when you'd ask where they came from, they'd answer, "Aw, 'round Oklahoma." If they got work, they'd spend their weeks in cabin camps out on the prairie, slinging mud, hefting pipe. Then they'd get paid and you'd see them in their new clothes, strutting to the pool hall on Saturday night. When there wasn't work, some of them hung around Main Street, scorned as "oil trash" by the good women of Russell. If they got flat broke, they worked half-days, unloading cement at the railroad siding: that was hard labor, twenty cents an hour. But that was money in Russell, especially in the thirties, when the boom went bust.

People in Russell used to say, with an odd sort of pride, that there wasn't any family in town that hadn't been broke, one time or another. There just wasn't any money around. When the roughnecks showed up at Dawson's, got some ice cream, and slapped down a ten-dollar bill, Bob had to run to the bank to get change. When the oilmen's kids showed up at the grade school with shiny new bikes—brand-new twenty-five-dollar bikes!—local kids couldn't believe it. In Russell, you'd trade a bike for $2.50, and you might save for a year to get that. There was a lot of resentment on Main Street. And it could have got bitter on Maple, too, when Bina announced to the children that they could put their things down in the basement. Everything: clothes, schoolbooks, family pictures! The whole family was moving to the basement. *Get your things downstairs! Right now!* . . . Doran would rig a bathtub for washing and a hot plate for Bina to cook on. He'd rented the house to some oilmen: hundred dollars a month, cash in advance, for a year! That was twelve hundred dollars, cash money! . . . That night, Doran stayed out on the porch so late, the kids thought he was waiting for the bank to open.

Bob stayed awake that night, too. But he never said a word about it. Never called anybody "oil trash." Never had a bad word for anybody. Wouldn't spend the time on it, for one thing. No, he had plans of his own. For a start, he was saving for a new bike. It'd cost twenty-six dollars, but he figured all four Dole kids could use it. They could get a paper route, and that would make the money back, maybe help out at home.

Bob always had a plan. It was funny how that kind of will sprang up in a place where plans were so fragile. Back when the railroad first arrived, the town fathers had it in mind that Russell would rival Kansas City as the hub of commerce for the plains. Doran's dad was going to buy more land, before the bad years hit, one after the other, and he lost his own quarter-section. And did Doran have dreams for the White Front Café? If he did, he didn't bring them up anymore. In Russell, it was best not to talk about your hopes, past or present. Better just to make a joke, and move on. Put your head down, work for a living. That was hard enough, in the thirties—especially when the dust came.

When the dust storms hit, the sky would grow black in the southwest and the light would disappear as if a curtain were drawn across the prairie. They'd run to get the kids out of school. Kids were dying from the dust pneumonia. They had to wrap the babies in wet sheets, so they wouldn't suffocate from the dirt in the air.

Bob'd run home, and Kenny would come stumping behind, to fill the bathtub and soak the towels and pack them around the windows and doors, trying to keep the dust out. But there wasn't any way to stop it. You had to wash everything in the house so you could eat. If you left a bowl of water overnight, it'd be muddy by morning. You couldn't see the pattern on the kitchen linoleum. On the west side of town, where the Doles lived, they scooped dirt out of houses with wheat shovels.

After '33, when it pretty much quit raining for the next few years, the dust was the overwhelming fact of life. In town, they'd turn on the streetlights, and people would feel their way home, walking next to the curbs. In Hays, they

had a basketball game, and they had to stop to sweep the floor every ten
minutes. They couldn't see the lines on the court. Anyway, the Hays coliseum
was lit with skylights, and after a while, they couldn't see to play, but they
wouldn't let anybody leave, either. They'd be lost out there in the dust.

Out on the land, the dust would cover the fence posts, drift up to the top
of a barn. You'd see a pipe sticking up from the dirt, and you knew a tractor
got caught in the dust.

The trees died. The grass died. Land was selling for five dollars an acre, if
you could find a buyer. One farmer, up in Gorham, went to the bank and they
turned him down, so he herded his cattle to a corner of the fence and he shot
them, one by one . . . and then he shot himself. In Russell, one of the Krug
boys lost his hope somehow, and hung himself in his bedroom. Doc White
went over, but all he could do was hold him while his daughters cut him down.

Jack Phipps, who had a place on Kansas Street, got the dust pneumonia.
The men of the Russell Volunteer Fire Department stood in front of Jack's
house for days, doing shifts with a hose, in darkness and light, couple hours
at a stretch, spraying water over Jack's house, trying to keep the dust off.
Doran was there, of course. He was a volunteer fireman for fifty-one years. He
took his turn with the hose at Jack's house. Seemed like every man in town
did. But there wasn't any way to keep the dust out. Jack Phipps died, right
there in that house.

Bob Dole knew all that. Lord, in Russell, there wasn't any way not to know.
But that wasn't him. His life was going to be different. And it wasn't any
dream, either. It was a plan. He worked on it every day, how he was going
to make it happen.

—★—

In the Lincoln Town Car, you could feel Dole ease, you could almost see the
comfort settle on him. It wasn't just the car, although that was comfortable
enough, all pleated upholstery that creaked quiet welcome as his back settled
into the shotgun seat. The Lincoln was one of the benefits of the Leader's job.
It came to Dole along with Wilbert Jones, a solid, middle-aged Carolinian, who
knew the ins and outs of Washington traffic. Dole never had to tell him which
lane, which turn, or which hotel had a side entrance. And Wilbert knew
enough not to small-talk. Dole always sat in front with Wilbert. He respected
Wilbert as he did all working men. He always had a greeting for him, something about the weather, the hour, or how was Wilbert doing. Wilbert was
always fine.

That was the best thing about the car. Wilbert was always fine. Dean would
sit in the back, quiet, unless Dole asked for something. And after Dole
stretched his left hand across his body to pull the door shut (he never liked
people jumping out to open or close doors for him), after Wilbert hit the button
and the power windows rolled up, there was no noise, nothing pending, and
for the next ten minutes, or however long, there was no one who could get at
Bob Dole.

There was a car phone, if Dole wanted to use the time, or he might fiddle with the radio, tuning in some news. Or he might, without warning, tune in the march he had running through his head: no one knew what song it was, or whether it was a song at all. But sometimes, when this ease settled on him, Dole would lean back, get a lungful of air, and let it out in a flat rhythmic chant:

"Bup-bup-bup-bup-bup . . . bip-bip-bip-bip . . ."

Or sometimes:

"Yuuoooh, yut-dut-dut-dut-dah . . . yut-dut-dah . . ."

Sometimes it came out a whistle, more rhythm than tune, just a syncopated bit of prairie breeze. No matter. It was a way of sharing, almost like he was chatting. But he didn't need anyone to chat back.

Tonight, he got into the car and said to the windshield: "Well, 'nother day at the office . . ." That was for Wilbert, a form of Dole-code to show him Dole knew he'd been waiting. Dean, silent in the backseat, leaned forward and passed a briefing memo to Dole, who idly scanned it. Dole's political action committee, Campaign America, sent a briefing memo for every event. But Dole didn't need briefings. He did these Washington receptions every night, even if the Senate was working late. He'd schedule an hour or ninety minutes of debate, then he'd duck out and hit a couple of funders, sometimes three or four, twenty minutes apiece. He'd been at this twenty-five years now. He dropped the paper on the seat next to Wilbert.

As the car rolled through the Capitol lot, Dole spotted Senator Grassley, walking on the asphalt, back to his office.

"There's Chuckie . . ." Dole said. "Aghh, kep' him up a little *late* tonight . . ."

And while Wilbert and Dean quietly giggled, Dole rapped on the window and splayed his left hand up in a stiff wave as he rolled by, his face a mask of delight, as he said to the plate glass:

"Chuckeeeeeee!"

Then, he settled back again.

"La-di-da . . . la-di-da . . . bup-bup-bup-Bahhh! . . ."

He was always happy when he was headed out to do his thing. There was nothing that got Dole going like a crowd. Sometimes, when he'd leave an event, he was so pumped up, he was like a kid. They loved him! They were cheering! Guy came up to him and told him he was gonna win! Guy said he was gonna help! Get his name! Sign him up!

Sometimes, when he'd finish a speech and a band would strike up some brassy tune, Dole wouldn't leave the stage, wouldn't even turn around to shake people's hands. He'd stand there, watching them cheer, with the band pumping in his ears, and he'd swing his good arm in time to the music, and bounce on his feet, up and down, up and down, pumping that arm and hearing the cheers. . . . He looked like a youngster, like a hep-cat from the forties, bouncing to the big band . . . like one of those bandleaders who played the big dances, the guys who didn't play an instrument or sing, but stood up front, swinging time to the music, bringing you the *action,* Bob Crosby & His Bobcats! Bob Dole! The Bobster!

And he was action! They'd meet him at the door, he'd hit the room, and they'd all come at him. Every head in the place would turn. Here's Bob Dole! Here is juice! Here is power! Then, he'd do the place like a tornado, grabbing hands with his left hand:

"Bob Dohhll! . . . Gooda meetcha."

"There he ihhhzzz! . . ."

If it was a dinner, he'd do every table:

"Aghh, must be the *head tayy*-ble! . . ." Then he'd shake every hand, get their names.

If it was cocktails, he'd zigzag through, hitting every hand by some kind of radar. In Washington, Dean was always at his elbow, to hold things that people gave to Dole, or to hold out his leather folder, like a table, if someone asked Dole for an autograph. Usually, people asked for pictures: Would the Senator stop a second, to pose with Denise, here?

"Surrrre."

Then Dole would laugh while the picture was taken, a prairie cackle that held no humor. It was his way of making his face right:

"Agh, hagh, hagh, hagh . . ."

He never took a bad picture. Always had a great smile, unless the people couldn't work their own camera. That happened, too. They were so in a *flutter!* Here was Bob Dole!

"Agh-hagh-hagh-hagh . . .

"Agh-hagh-hagh-hagh . . .

"C'*mon!* . . ." It would come out teasing, in the middle of the laugh, but he meant it. He had other people to see.

"Agh-hagh-hagh-c'*mon*-c'*mon*-c'*mon*-hagh-hagh . . ."

Later, in the Lincoln, Dole would remember the guy:

"*Gahhhd,*" he'd say, rolling his eyes. "Hundred fifty people *standin'* there, guy can't work his *camm*'ra."

No one took liberties with Bob Dole's time. If he was going to speak, it didn't matter what the program said. They'd change the order of speakers to put him right on, whenever he got there. He never stayed to eat, never sat down at the head table for more than a minute, while they introduced him. If he had to wait to speak, while someone else finished, he worked the crowd, grabbing hands.

Then he'd get up there, and he'd lay 'em in the aisles, with the timing of a stand-up comic:

"I told the President, the other day, we *wanted* to work with him on the budget . . .

"Can't do it without Ronald Reagan . . .

"Maybe we could do it without Don Regan . . .

"But, seriously, the deficit . . ."

It wasn't a speech so much as a bracing stroll through the mind of Bob Dole.

So much going on! And now, these folks at the dinner that night, these fortunate few, these important givers, were all included, all in the swim. The laughter that rippled through the hall was always a low, appreciative, knowing male chuckle.

Of course, the guys at Campaign America were still trying to get Dole to make The Speech. Something with a theme, a *vision* for America. America at the Crossroads! . . . Don Devine, the professor-pol who was head of the campaign committee, used to fly around with Dole, giving him copies of that speech outline, over and over. Devine must have carried fifty copies of the thing. But Dole always tucked the speech into his jacket, or rolled it up to help shape his right fist, and talked about whatever was going on that week. Vision was well and good, people liked it. But Dole had a real job, solving real problems. People ought to know that, too.

That's why he did these Washington events. Bob Dole had to be in Washington. He had work to do. Couldn't spend all week flying around in Air Force planes, like George Bush. These Capital fund-raisers for every race in the country were Bob Dole's way of checking in, spreading himself around. At least, that's how his staff explained it. At Campaign America, the answer to invitations was yes to every event he could possibly get to. Then, they'd draw up a briefing paper, maybe talking points that Dole would ignore, and a contribution check for him to take along (Dole never showed up empty-handed). "What the hell," Don Devine would say with a shrug. "He's got to be in Washington anyway. So, if it's not gonna tire him out . . ." But they couldn't tire Bob Dole out. They couldn't overschedule him, or feed him too much information.

He was running the United States Senate, dealing with the White House, trying to hammer out a budget, trying to wind up a session, get his members home; he was flying all over the country to help his GOP members, trying to save his majority, working on their campaigns as if they were his own reelection. (In fact, Dole was running for reelection, but he'd scared all the big Kansas Democrats out of the race. His only opponent was a former carpet salesman from Wichita, a nice fellow named Guy MacDonald, who promised not to raise any money, or say anything nasty about Bob Dole. . . . "O*kayyy*! Guy MacDonald! Great American! . . .") And meanwhile, he was working every day on the Other Thing.

As Wilbert made the last turn, Dole picked up the briefing memo. "O*kayy*, Guam!" he said to the dashboard. "Where America's day begins! . . ." That's what they used to say at Republican conventions, when the proud Guam chairman would cast the island's handful of votes. Dole never forgot anything. This Ben Blaz, the Rep to Congress, won a tough race a couple of years ago, knocked off an incumbent Democrat, beat him by about three hundred votes. Dole knew Ben Blaz was a comer. Dole was cohost of the reception tonight.

But Dole also knew that Bush would have the Governor of Guam all wrapped up. And the Governor would control the delegates. There wasn't any way Bob Dole would get Guam, or its four convention delegates. In fact, there wasn't any plan to this night—except more, more of the same.

He rolled the briefing memo into a cylinder and used it to round out his right fist. "Ready?" he said to the air in the car.

"Yes, sir."

"'Bout a half-hour," Dole said.

"Fine."

Dole reached across his midriff and got the door handle as Wilbert hit the brakes in front of the hotel. And the Bobster was out of the car:

"Hey, Bob *Dohhhll* . . ."

—★—

The point was, he wasn't going to cut back on anything. He'd already given up enough in his life. He sure wasn't going to give up the Senate. He'd only had the Leader's job for two years—two short years—and reporters were already asking if he'd give it up for the '88 campaign. Well, maybe he would. When he was good and ready.

The problem was, he could lose it in a hurry, lose his majority this year, '86, if the GOP lost more than three seats. He knew which members were in trouble, especially the GOP class of 1980, the fellows who swept in with the first Reagan landslide. They were up for reelection this year, and Bob Dole's leadership would rise or fall with them. He knew what it would mean if his Party lost the edge in the Senate: both houses of Congress run by the Democrats, no way for him or any Republican—not even Ronald Reagan—to control the agenda. No way for Bob Dole to do what he did best—carry the ball.

So no one was going to outwork Dole in a midterm election. No one had as many invitations, no one had a feel for as many races, no one showed up in as many recondite corners of the political map as Bob Dole did.

God knows, Bush and Reagan hadn't lifted a finger for the Party last time, in '84. Everything was for Reagan and Bush. The President spent the last day in Minnesota, trying to win Mondale's own state, for a clean sweep. The Gipper wanted a landslide—well, he got it. But meanwhile they *lost* two seats in the Senate: down to fifty-three Republicans, and some of those you couldn't count on. This time, it could turn out worse! Paula Hawkins in Florida, Jim Abdnor in South Dakota, Mark Andrews from North Dakota, Mack Mattingly in Georgia, Jerry Denton in Alabama, Slade Gorton from Washington . . . might lose any one of those seats! It was so tough out there, they finally had to wake Reagan up from his nap. Now the President was going to come out in the last couple of weeks, to campaign for the Senators—but the White House didn't know how tight things were.

Bob Dole knew. Day by day, Dole got the tracking polls from across the country, every state. He knew the issues in those states, the voting districts, their histories, knew some of the County Chairmen. He wasn't shy about calling them, either.

"Heyy! Bob *Dohhhll*! Anything goin' *on* out there?"

Then he'd listen for a minute or two, while the chairman gave him a fill: whether his man was gaining or losing, what was behind the change in the polls . . .

"*Okayyy,* " Dole would say, as the chairman wound down. "Gotta gooo!"

If he got twenty minutes to spend on the phone, it meant days of hell for the Scheduler. That was always his last call: to Molly Walsh, the Scheduler, or Jo-Anne Coe, his all-purpose Office Drill Sergeant. One of them would pick up a phone, and Dole's voice would rasp in the earpiece:

"Gotta go to South Dakota."

"When?"

"Pretty sooonn."

That meant now, tomorrow, this weekend—whenever they could work it out.

He was on the road every weekend, all weekend, usually from Friday afternoon, or Thursday night if the Senate load was light, flying west in a borrowed corporate jet, picking up a time zone or two, flying against the clock to get to a Plains state, the Rockies, or the West Coast, in time for an airport press conference, a dinner, fund-raiser, or a rally for some Republican faithful, who'd light up when Dole hit the room: Bob Dole! Here is juice!

This weekend would be light: the Senate was winding up its term for the fall, and Dole wouldn't get away till Saturday morning—just time for a flight to Akron, a press conference and a fund-raising breakfast for two Congressional candidates, then a speech to a rally in the airport; then a quick flight to Sandusky, O., for a press conference and another speech at a luncheon rally; then a flight to Cleveland for a rally speech and a joint press conference on behalf of four GOP hopefuls; then a flight to Findlay, O., for another press conference and a mix-and-mingle for Congressman Oxley; then a flight to Cincinnati for a press conference with gubernatorial candidate James Rhodes and his running mate, Bob Taft, and a few remarks at their big-money funder at the home of former Senator Taft; then an hour-and-a-half flight east to Monmouth, New Jersey, followed by a twenty-minute drive to a Hilton, where Dole was scheduled to get in about midnight for his Saturday night's sleep. Sunday, he'd start with a twenty-five-minute ride to a country club in Manalatan Township to do a press conference and speech at a buffet breakfast; then another drive, another flight, this time to Jamestown, New York, near Buffalo, for a joint news conference with a House candidate; and a drive to another country club for the candidate's funder-brunch, where Dole would make a few more brief remarks; then another drive to another speech, this to a Chautauqua County veterans' group, a photo op with members of the County Veterans Council and the dedication of a bridge in honor of the nation's veterans; then another flight to State College, Pennsylvania, for a speech to five hundred Penn State students, and another press conference with a Congressman, Bill Clinger, and another drive to another hotel for another speech at a fund-raiser, and then another drive and a wheels-up for Washington, National Airport, where the

Lincoln Town Car would be waiting in the dark to take him back to the Watergate—unless he decided to stop at the office to get ready for the Senate, Monday.

He never missed a vote in the Senate. There was a certain dogged Kansas dogma to this record: a day's work for a day's pay, and the citizens of Kansas paid him to vote. So he never missed a roll call that anyone could remember, not even on wacko amendments, or a 95–0 resolution on National Teacher Week. Of course, that was easier now that he was Majority Leader: now, he was the man to schedule the roll calls; he was the potentate to cross the aisle, to work it out with Democrat Bob Byrd; he held the floor to suggest to the chair the absence of a quorum; now it was up to him when the tyrannical bells went off.

So that meant he could tuck in some time each night, for the Other Thing. He wasn't going to drop that, either. He wasn't going to do it like he did in '80, running around the country with no campaign, not enough money, no organization.

Six hundred votes! That's all he got in New Hampshire last time. It was a national humiliation! He almost gave it up, after that, after the '80 campaign. Thought about leaving the Senate, joining some fancy megamillions law firm. . . . Thought about it maybe a week.

Dole called that '80 race his "noncampaign." He always brought it up himself to audiences:

"You may not know this . . .

". . . but I *ran* for President . . ."

Here, the low chuckles would start to ripple through the crowd, laughter that would swell as Dole piled on line after line about his failure.

". . . Well, losing's tough, but you get over it . . .

". . . Night after New Hampshire, I went home and slept like a baby . . .

". . . Every two hours, I woke up and cried . . ."

But Dole was going to make this time different: he wouldn't have to make a joke out of this attempt. Anyway, if he lost the majority in the Senate, '88 might be his last chance, his only chance to hold on to power. He wasn't going to play out the rest of his years in the powerless minority—that was for sure. Bob Dole had known powerlessness.

He knew what it was to live in the minority, to scrape along in the opposition, scrambling to get into the papers, struggling to make a difference, on the edge of the fights, scrapping over the language of the farm bill, nickel-and-diming every issue for some kind of wedge, to get in on the action . . . knew it too well: he spent a political lifetime in that sour, still pond, after he came to Congress in 1961.

It was twenty years before he made it to the center of the action. He got his first heady taste of power after Reagan's first election, 1980: the GOP at last took over the Senate, and Bob Dole became the Finance Committee Chairman. Finally, he had the votes on his side of the aisle. Finally, he got a chance to show what he could do. Reagan swept into office with a mandate for tax cuts, and cuts in the budget. That was the business of the Finance Committee. But Washington's wise men were convinced it couldn't be done: once the House and Senate restored the funds to everybody's pet bill, maybe there'd be a few million cut—maybe a few hundred million. That's the way it always went. . . . Then, one day, in 1981, while he was in the Ag Committee, rewriting the farm bill, Dole stood up and excused himself: "Agh, hav'ta run over to Finance . . . got a little package of cuts to consider." The budget cuts actually ran to twenty-four legal-sized pages, single-spaced: they covered Medicare, Medicaid, unemployment, and the biggest welfare programs. In total, they would chop out $10 billion in fiscal '82, and another $12 billion the following year. In total, that was a billion dollars more than Reagan's own people suggested. In the committee room, Moynihan and Bradley started to howl: they'd had no time to *consider . . . draconian* reductions! *. . . millions of people!* . . . But then, the former chairman, the Louisiana Democrat, Russell Long, endorsed the whole package with a simple "Aye . . ." and everyone knew what had happened. Dole had greased the skids. The deal was done. So Dole let everyone talk for a few hours, then he rammed the vote home, eighteen to two. In all, he cut $22 billion in one afternoon.

By 1984, when Howard Baker retired, there was some talk that Dole wouldn't go for the Leader's job. He had power, with the Finance Committee. He might want to run for President again, might not want to be chained to the Senate's agenda day and night. But the talkers didn't know Bob Dole. If there was something to run for, Dole was running.

Still, there were more than a few doubters, and a dogfight for the job in the caucus. Wasn't Dole a slasher? Would he give every Senator a decent shake, a chance to get his bill considered, a chance to get on TV? What if the Democrats started a fight, and Dole's switch went off: What would he say? Was there anything he wouldn't say? There were four secret ballots in the caucus before Dole emerged with the job in his teeth.

There was never any doubt in Dole's mind: he'd been waiting for this chance his whole life. Now it didn't matter what the issue was—*whatever*—they'd all have to reckon with Bob Dole. The '85 farm bill, that was Dole's farm bill: he put it together brick by brick while the Ag Committee Chairman, Jesse Helms, sat on his hands; judicial appointments, Dole would get them through; Gramm-Rudman, the budget, the contras, the tax code, small business, Social Security, Star Wars. . . . There was no limit to his reach.

And now, almost two years into his term, they all came to deal with him, came to him in the morning, while he held court in his armchair in the cloakroom. "Bob, I'd really like to move this, if you could. It's been checked off, both sides of the committee—if you don't see any problem . . ."

On the floor, they called him "the Leader," or "the Distinguished Majority Leader."

"Would the Distinguished Leader yield for a moment?"

"I'd be happy to yield to my friend from Massachusetts."

And they were friends, or as close as he had. If knowing about them was a mark of friendship, then Dole was a friend. Bob Dole probably never swung a golf club in his life, even back when he had two hands to do it. In Doran Dole's house, in Russell, Kansas, golf was a sport for rich loafers. But if Quayle from Indiana slipped away for an afternoon at Burning Tree, it was Dole who'd know who made up the foursome. "Agh, s'pretty good, I guess," Dole mentioned once, to a stunned staff guy. "Handicap's 'bout seven." How the hell did he know that? How'd he know what a handicap was?

There didn't seem to be any limit to the facts he stored for instant access, the elaborate filigree of his neural connections.

Tuck the scenic river bill on the calendar for Friday?

"Agh, better not."

Dole might offer no explanation, but there were things he knew. . . . There's a Senator, border state, got a tough reelection—Dole was out there for him twice already—and his Democrat opponent's hammering him on environment: he backed a wood pulp mill, three or four years ago. Saved some jobs. But caught heat from the state's biggest paper. So he might want to be on the bill, that bit that sets aside six miles of the Wammahoochie as a wild scenic preserve. Might want to get on TV. Maybe announce it. Anyway, he's got a daughter getting married Saturday. Wife's sort of the nervous kind . . .

"Better make it next Tuesday."

Dole never had just a single source of information. That's one reason he was scary to work for. Dole would set a staffer onto an issue, something massive, like telephone deregulation, and the guy would work for weeks, bust his tail on the memo. Then one nervous, hopeful night, he'd give it to Dole, or set it on Dole's desk. The next thing the poor guy would see was Dole, wanting to know: What about the access charge? The pass-along from the local companies? What about proprietary networks?

"Gaghhh! . . . Is this the best you could do?"

See, Dole was working on it in the cloakroom. He knew who the smart guys were on every issue, whose staff was rolling on the bill, what the local companies in Kansas worried about, what GTE's guy was pushing. Then maybe he'd set another staffer in the other office, the Kansas Senate office, to finding out how much AT&T was going to drop its rates. If he didn't get the answer, he'd tell another staffer (whoever his favorite was that week, or whoever happened to be in the room) to get the chairman of AT&T on the phone—ask him to come in. . . . Of course, the guy comes. Dole is the Leader, *Majority* Leader.

The point was that everything, all fruit of this furious gathering, wound up in Dole's head. And furthermore, the complete set of facts was *nowhere else.* That's why the desk was clean, why Dole had no briefcase, and Dean carried only a slim leather folder. Sure, there was a blizzard of paper around Dole, but somehow, the written version always caught up with him after the fact. The schedule: they'd still be typing it Saturday morning, an hour before the car went for Dole at the Watergate; he kept adjusting it, fine-tuning, up to Friday night. And he'd keep changing it on the plane, if he wanted. There was no bible, except in Dole's head. Most of the speeches were still being typed as

Dole made his way to the head table. Then there was the furious dash to the Xerox, for press copies; anyway, it didn't matter: Dole would keep his own copy in his pocket and say what he wanted, any way he chose. There wasn't any speech, except in Bob Dole's head. This was an article of pride with Dole. He didn't have to read from a card in his pocket to have a talk about politics, the budget, or the tax law, dairy prices, the Russians, or anything else. It was in his head.

And that suited Dole fine. It didn't matter how many Washington smart guys told him he'd have to learn to delegate. It didn't matter how many Respected Analysts wrote columns, saying the key to his success would be to let himself be managed. If someone wanted to manage Bob Dole, they'd have to know more than Dole did. And he made sure that wasn't going to happen. There wasn't any one person who was going to know everything in his head. Sometimes, for the profile writers, a staff guy would whisper The Official Secret Explanation:

It went back to the war wound . . . when he got shot up and his arm wouldn't work. Dole had to go through law school, and he couldn't write . . . couldn't take notes . . .

He had to keep it in his head!

And that was true, in a way. But Dole had able notetakers now. The fact was, knowledge was power. If Dole had three people working on an issue, and each talked directly to Dole, then he knew more than any of them, more than anyone else. Better yet, four people digging, or six, and a colleague in the cloakroom, and some smart guys on the phone. The only place they met was in Dole's head. And there wasn't a single one of them he had to depend on.

"Agh, s'pretty good. Said he wanted to help," Dole was saying, as he got back to the Lincoln, after the Guam event. "Lotta moneyyy! . . ." He had a business card from a Washington smart guy, a lobbyist. But he didn't give it to Dean for follow-up. This was important. Dole stuck the card into his own shirt pocket.

The pocket was the ultimate action file—just the most important matters. Sometimes, the only thing Dole had in there was his prayer. He always carried the prayer, on a laminated card. It meant a lot to Dole. So, no one knew about the prayer.

Now the door of the Town Car was closed, the windows were up. It was after nine-thirty. The streets were getting quiet. In the car, silence: Wilbert and Dean waited for Dole to call it a day. In the dark, Dole's eyes shifted to the glowing green of the quartz clock. Not even 10:00 P.M.

Dole said to the windshield: "Agh, better stop at the office."

— ★ —

At 10:00 P.M., old Dutch Dawson would look up at the clock from the back booth of the drugstore, where he was doing his crossword, with his glasses on top of his head. He'd lift his squat frame out of the booth and walk to the front door. He'd look up Main Street, then down the other way. "Wait a minute.

Don't turn the lights out," he'd say. "There's a guy comin' out of the theater.
. . . Okay, turn 'em out. He went the other way." Then, he'd check the two
registers at the front, the sundries and the fountain, turn the key, and check
the ring-up. Then, he'd get into his car, and head home.

The boys and Bob Dole stayed behind, cleaning up. Bob had to make syrup
for the next day, empty the ice-cream bins, wash out the soda spigots . . . those
things had to be clean. It was always closer to eleven when he ran back to
Maple Street. Bina would have his supper waiting. And not just a plate of
something on the stove, but his place set at the dining room table, homemade
bread, soup, a full dinner. There was fresh cake or pie for dessert. Bina's girls,
Bob's two sisters, had to bake a fresh dessert when they got home from school.
There was no halfway, or good-enough, with Bina Dole.

People used to say there was nothing Bina couldn't get done. But it had to
be done just so. It didn't matter how much effort it took, or how many hours.
When Bob's older sister, Gloria, started to iron, and a shirt wasn't just so,
Bina'd throw that shirt right back on the pile. "Sista! . . ." (That was Gloria's
nickname.) "You have to learn to do things right!" She'd have Gloria, or her
youngest child, Norma Jean, standing for hours on a dining room chair, while
she got the hem of a skirt just right. "Stand *still*! . . ." When Bina set to cleaning
floors, all four kids had to get up on those chairs, and woe to the child who
jumped the gun and put a foot down on the damp floor. "You can go out back
and cut your switch, right now!" (Bina's voice could take paint off a wall: even
her name rasped with hard prairie vowels; it rhymed with Carolina, or, as she'd
likely say, Salina.)

Around Eleventh and Maple, the neighbors would hear her make those kids
hop: "Bob, you sweep off that porch! Kenny! You get that trash together!" Or
she'd call down to the grain elevator, light into Doran so hard that the farmers
having coffee could hear her on Doley's end of the line. *This was wrong and
that was wrong, and if Doran didn't care, well, that was just too bad!* Then she'd
slam down the phone without saying goodbye. Doran would just put down the
phone and go about his business; he was used to Bina; he toed the mark, best
he could. One time, they had a family reunion, and what with all the Talbotts
(Bina came from a family of twelve kids), they had to use the second floor of
the community hall. Well, it was Doran's job to set up the tables, and Doran
being the way he was, he went the extra mile, got some paper tablecloths, and
set all the places—plates and silverware, too. So Bina walked in, and she hit
the roof! "Well, my GOD, Doran! Get those papers off the tables! I've got
tablecloths and we're SURE not gonna eat on those papers!" Doran just went
back and took it all apart. "Well," he said, quietly, shaking his head, stripping
tables, "I knew there'd be somethin' wrong. I was just wonderin' what it would
be."

She didn't demand anything from them that she wouldn't do herself. She
was surely the only woman in Russell who'd scrub down her wooden front
porch, and then wax it. She'd wax and shine the garbage cans! She had the five
rooms on Maple Street done up like a dollhouse, with organdy curtains she

made herself. The girls had party dresses she made, with ruffles, all perfectly turned and ironed. And snappy pleated jumpers for their Legion Auxiliary uniforms: Bina made them, too. She'd cut down her old coats to make their coats. Each of the boys had only one set of school clothes, but they were immaculate every day, trousers creased, shirts pressed. Every day, there was a clean white shirt and white cotton pants, ironed just so, for work at the drugstore. Doran got a fresh white shirt every day, and fresh overalls, ironed smooth. Everything, even sheets and dish towels, had to be ironed, and just so. On wash day, Monday, there were four or five lines in the yard.

That's the way Bina learned when she was a girl on the Talbott farm. Joseph and Elva Talbott were reckoned the handsomest couple in the county, and at their place, a dozen miles south of Russell, everything had to be just so. Joseph used to mow the verge of the road, county land, so the weeds wouldn't spoil the look of his farm. He was so particular about his horses, he'd wash their hooves. There were eight daughters and four sons, and as Joseph was a member of the district school board, they generally had the schoolmistress boarding with them, too. The Talbotts did their own milking, they raised their own chickens, cleaned 'em and picked 'em for Sunday dinner. There were seven ponies for the kids to ride, Sunday afternoons. Monday was for washing, Tuesday for ironing, Wednesday was mending and altering, Thursday was housecleaning, Friday and Saturday they baked. When they'd get up, two boys and three girls would milk four cows apiece. After school, some of the kids would gather eggs. Some of the girls had to wash the dishes. There was a pump in the kitchen and they'd fill the kettle, boil the water for scalding. The stove had a reservoir: hot water for cleaning. They all had to pick up their rooms and make their beds before they could come down to breakfast. The evening meal was the big event. Tablecloth and silver every night. Elva's kids didn't have to be told to be cleaned up and ready in their chairs.

When Bina married Doran and got her own house, that was the way she ran it, too. In the years before Bobby Joe went to work at the drugstore (and Kenny after him, a couple of years later), everybody had to be home and cleaned up for dinner. Before suppertime, the boys would go downstairs to light the water heater. ("Your dad's comin' home. He'll want to clean up.") Then, to the dining room: tablecloth, every night. The Dole kids would climb into their seats, hands washed, faces washed, hair combed. Doran would fix the children's plates. And every night, he'd say: "Dessert's under your plate." That meant no pie till they ate all he gave them. After dinner and the dishes, all the kids did their homework at the dining room table. *The Salina Journal* came by train every evening, and Doran read it at night, in his chair in the front room, next to the round-top Philco. Saturdays, Doran had his radio shows: Fibber McGee and Mollie, Amos 'n' Andy. The kids could go out after supper Saturdays, but they got themselves home on time. Last thing they wanted was to make Dad leave the Philco, go out hunting kids, in the middle of Amos 'n' Andy. Sunday nights, after the dishes, they'd make a plate of fudge. One of the girls got to make it, the other kids would sit and watch, so nobody got to lick more. They had their fudge, and their baths. Bina would hand out the soap. "No one's so poor they can't buy soap . . ." Then it was all kids to bed, all in the back bedroom. There was a bed for the boys and one for the girls. (Later, when the kids were teenagers, Doran fixed up a boys' room in the concrete basement.) Bina or Doran would turn out the light, and that was that: time to sleep.

Even when Bob was coming home late, Bina would still be working: ironing in the kitchen, or sewing in the dining room, at her place near the south window. Sometimes, she'd sew till four in the morning, finishing something for the girls, or something special for a customer. Bina was a working mother, a rare breed in those days: she sold Singer sewing machines in the Russell district. She'd drive the country roads, sometimes fifty miles out of town, hauling her big machine in the back of her old Chevy, where Doran took out the rumble seat. Then with two trips back and forth from the car, she'd lug the machine into a farmhouse (first the heavy steel head, then the base and the treadle), and set it up to demonstrate. She'd grab whatever fabric they had—anything, a feed sack—and turn out a dress right there. Or she'd show the machine, and then, at home, stay up into the night, making a dress, or pleated curtains, for the lady of that house, where she'd show up again, next day:

"You know, I was thinking about you last night, and I decided to make . . ." And she'd give her work to the woman and assure her it was nothing, no trouble at all. It was easy, with a Singer machine. . . .

Sometimes, the kids would get home after school to find Bina out at work. The house would be studded with notes:

Do the dishes.

Put the potatoes in at 4:00.

Then, just before Doran got home, Bina's Chevy would roar up Eleventh Street (she always drove foot-to-the-floorboard, till she got where she was going), and Bina would lug the machine back into the house, along with a fistful of chickens, a couple of pounds of aluminum, or a pound of copper. . . . She'd take anything that she could convert to $1.75, the down payment on a Singer. That night, she'd be up late again, catching up on her mending, or baking, or working on her next sewing project.

There was never enough time in the day, never any time for dreaming. "If you shirk work," Bina told her kids, "work shirks you." That's what her grandmother used to say. There wasn't any point telling Bina, "I can't . . ." That was one thing she wouldn't abide. There wasn't anything Bina couldn't get done, and there wasn't anything they couldn't do, if they were willing to work at it. "Can't never could do nothin'!" she'd say. "Now, get busy!"

The only time she wasn't doing four things at once was when the headaches came upon her. It was only every so often—sometimes a year would go by without—but when they came, even a footstep on the floor hurt. Bina would shut herself into the front bedroom, sometimes for days. Doran would get up earlier to fix breakfast for the kids, and he'd be home at midday, too, to get lunch ready, and send them back to school. But there was nothing anyone could really do for Bina. God knows, Doran would have leapt to do anything. It was such a helpless feeling in the house. One time, in the middle of the night, Bina must have said something about milk. Doran jumped up from his sleep and woke Bob: Your mother wants some milk! Bob went straight to the grocery, and only then did Doran look at a clock. It was three in the morning. There was nothing open in Russell. When Bob didn't come back, after an hour, Doran went to hunt him. He found him half-asleep, eyes puffed and drooping closed, sitting on the curb in front of Holzer's grocery, waiting for the shop to open.

Bob took it to heart when Bina was sick with her headaches. There was an understanding, a shared set of standards between those two. Sometimes she used to tell her sisters, Bobby Joe was more particular than she was. One time she found him with a sweater on in the middle of summer.

"Bob, aren't you hot? Bob! Take that sweater off!"

No, he said, it was all right.

When she asked him again, she found out: his shirt was wrinkled. He didn't want that to show.

When he got older, sometimes he'd pay his sisters a nickel to iron his shirt. But it had to be ironed just so. He was worse than Bina. That was the way he held himself, in every thing he did. In a gaggle of kids outside the high school, you would always notice Bob, always with a crowd around him. Bob was the tallest, and he held himself perfectly straight. Of course, he was scrubbed and combed, with his thick dark hair in perfect trim. Lord knows, the girls noticed: in his senior year, the members of the Girls Reserve voted Bob Dole their Ideal Boy. But that wasn't why Bob did all that. He didn't have time for girls. He was just working on himself.

Bob had the first set of weights in Russell, an iron bar with blocks of cement on either end. He used to lift that thing every chance he got, until he was thick with muscle. By the end of high school, he was six-foot-one, 192 pounds, with legs that could pull like a tractor. Building his body was part of the program.

He never walked anywhere, but ran. God hadn't really blessed him with speed, but he worked at it, and he made himself a runner, held a local record in the half-mile, and beat some college boys from Hays while he was still in high school.

That was only one of his sports. He won three letters at Russell High. In the fall, he played on the football team, as an end, a pass receiver, although under Coach Baxter's single wing, there weren't too many passes to catch. George Baxter preached a brand of drive-'em-back, knock-'em-down football that relied more on stamina and will than grace. In fact, Coach did more than preach. If a boy didn't hit the way Coach wanted, then Coach would drop to a three-point stance and knock the kid on his ass. (No pads in those days, either.) He never had to do that with Bobby Dole. Bob and Bud Smith, best friends, were leaders on the team. Bud was one of the oil kids, came to Russell in '37. Bob and Bud were the best athletes. In any game, they were Russell High's one-two punch.

But in basketball, Bob Dole was the leader, the big guy on the court. In team huddles, he was the one to go around, clap every man on the backside, tell him they could win, *had* to win. "Don't give up, guys. We're gonna get 'em," he'd say. "We still got a chance. They can go sour." If things went badly, you could see his eyes tearing up and he'd turn away, go off by himself. He never told anyone, but he used to dream about basketball, how he'd make the baskets, how Russell would win. And the basketball Broncos were winners. Got to the state tournament one year. You had to be good to make that team. Bobby Dole was good. He could handle the ball, shoot that newfangled one-hand push shot, and he was big and tough under the boards.

It wasn't just his size, it was his attitude, conditioning . . . and the game itself was changing. Up until 1937, there was a jump ball after every basket. The game would stop, as the boys arrayed themselves anew at center court. But that year, just as Bob made the Russell High team, the rules changed. When one team made a basket, the other team got the ball. Suddenly, there were no breaks. For a boy like Bob, who could run all day, who *did* run all day, it was the best change possible. He was always in the middle of the action. He brought the ball up, saw the whole court. He set up the play, made it happen. When it came time to pick the Union Pacific All-Stars, the best from the towns along the railroad trunk line, Bob Dole was the only Russell boy picked by the coaches of the conference.

Basketball was the game Russell watched. Kansas was basketball country, and had been for years, ever since the University of Kansas brought in the game's inventor, James Naismith, as the chief of athletics. Naismith trained the coaches who fanned out to towns around the state—and to colleges around the country. One legend of the modern game, Adolph Rupp, the revered coach of Kentucky, played his ball at KU for Naismith. So did the next legend of Kansas basketball, Forrest C. "Phog" Allen, so nicknamed for his stentorian voice, who was the KU coach while Bob grew up, and a godly figure all over the state.

In Russell, KU had the air of the East, of money and sophistication. Snob Hill, they called it. If Phog had ever walked down Main Street, there wasn't anyone in Russell who wouldn't have stopped work, and run to the window to look. As it was, you couldn't get your hair cut or your car fixed on the afternoon of a local high school game. The gym was the newest, biggest building in town, and everybody was there. You had to go early and sit through the "B" game (for kids who couldn't quite make the grade) to have your place at seven o'clock, for the "A" game. By four or four-thirty, the men and boys would get their afternoon papers and a sack of sandwiches and head over to the gym. The women showed up later with their knitting. By midnight, there wasn't anyone in Russell who didn't know how the Broncos did, and half the town probably stopped at Dawson Drug to discuss it.

That's one of the reasons Bob got the job at Dawson's. The Dawson boys wanted a kid for that fountain job who was a leader, who'd bring in the other kids. Bob Dole, basketball star, was that boy. Anyway, there were no bigger fans in town than Chet and Bub Dawson. (Chet was a diehard K-State fan. He'd claim: "If KU was playin' Russia, I'd root for Russia.")

That was the same reason Bob got the Kaw Pipeline job. Every summer, the pipeline company gave one job to a high school kid, and that was the best job in town, the biggest money a kid could make. Usually, the job went to the best athlete. The oil companies sponsored semipro teams, and there were more than a few oil workers whose main job was playing in the weekly games. In fact, the year Bob got the job, one of those workers was Phog Allen's kid, Milton (they called him Mitt), who had better moves on the gym floor than he did around an oil rig. That's when Bob Dole's plan came together, when the pieces clicked into place.

Bob wanted to go to college. He'd kept his eyes open at Dawson's and he'd seen who it was who never seemed to want, the men everybody listened to, men of substance, respect. They were the doctors, whose word was law in any drugstore. So Bob was going to be a doctor: he was going to get to college, and then to med school. And when that was done, he'd have made it, past the dreams of any kid from Russell, past any insecurity, reach of fortune, weather, dust, or want.

But how? No one named Dole had the money for a year of college, much less seven. Then Phog Allen came to visit his son. And Mitt Allen told his dad that he ought to meet this boy named Dole, who was a heck of a nice guy, and a heck of a ballplayer, too. Phog Allen himself came into the drugstore! And shook Bob's hand! And later that year, Bob got a note from the East, from Lawrence, from KU, Snob Hill! *Bob Dole got a letter from Phog Allen himself!*

See, it wasn't a dream, after all! Bob Dole was going to KU. He was going to play for Phog Allen. They gave scholarships to the team, didn't they? It could be done!

Harold Dumler, from Russell, he was a few years older, he made it to KU. Heck, he was already rushing Bob Dole for Kappa Sigma! *Bob Dole had a letter from Phog Allen!*

When the boys from Kappa Sig made their rush tour in the summer, it was Bob Dole put on the party for them in Russell. It was real! Harold said Bob could wait tables at the Kappa Sig house. He could pay his board that way.

Bob talked to Bina. He said he wouldn't go if it would be too hard on her and Dad. He knew things were tight. He knew how hard they worked. But Bina said he'd better go. Can't never could do nothin', she said. They'd find money, if it came to that.

And there was nothing Bina couldn't get done. When Bob got the train east in September, she sent him with sixty-five dollars, cash.

3

Flyin' Around

I T WAS California that charged up the Bobster, convinced him he might keep the Senate after all. California felt so good: the crowds were huge and happy; Ed Zschau, the Republican, was closing on Cranston in the polls, the TV news in every market had Zschau and Dole, Dole and Zschau. Dole, Dole, Dole . . . like *he* was the guy running. "I can feel it!" Dole would rasp into a mike.

"I smell VICTORYYY! . . ."

That was the last week before the voting, the last days of October '86. Dole had been on the road for weeks, twenty-one states in the last fourteen days, thumping the tub for his Senators. Some campaigns were still too close to figure: one day, the tracking would show one of Dole's guys up five points— "O*kayy,* pretty *good!*"—and the next day the same guy would be down seven points, sinking like a stone. "Aghhh, numbers gotta be off . . ." The polls came from Dick Wirthlin, who had a private contract with the National Republican Senatorial Committee. ("Lotta moneyyy!") Dole would look at the breakdown in the mornings and claim the numbers were useless. Next day, he couldn't wait to see the new set.

Mostly, he went by his own sense of smell. He'd been there, had a feel for every race. Paula Hawkins in Florida, "Gaghhd! . . ." You could see she was a goner. In the farm belt, every Republican was running against five years of rural recession. And the farmers didn't want any morning-in-America crap. In the Midwest, there was no Reagan recovery. Dole was taking heat in Washington for the $30 billion price tag on the farm bill he wrote the year before. But no one in the grain belt had seen any money. Dole tried to assure them, over and over: "It's a good bill. Farmers will see the effect." But on the plains, he was talking to a wall.

It got so nasty in the farm states, Dole violated his new "Be Nice" rule. For years now, Elizabeth and his Washington smart guys had been working on Dole to be more *statesmanlike . . . Presidential . . .* or, in Elizabeth's homelier Carolina argot, "nahce." When a clever, vicious line occurred to him now, he'd swallow it, or maybe say it in the car, where it couldn't come back to haunt him. But no one was going to convince Bob Dole he should turn the other cheek, when they were *kicking him in the face. . . .* That's what nobody understood when they wrote that Dole was a snarler, a "hatchet man." From behind Dole's eyes, it was obvious: they were coming at him with knives, backing him into a corner. Well, if that's how they wanted to play. . . . They weren't gonna make Bob Dole, the Republican Senate, take the blame for the farm crisis! So Dole snarled back: "Wasn't *us* called the grain embargo in 1980. *We* didn't cause the recession . . ."

What did they want him to do? Just take it? Give up? If Bob Dole was the kind to give up, he could have lived his life in a hospital bed, or a wheelchair, with someone taking care of him twenty-four hours a day. But nobody had to take care of Dole. He made sure of that. Dole never quit. *"Don't give up, guys. . . . They can still go sour. . . ."*

So he flew into Fargo, North Dakota, where the prairie wind blew brutal cold—cold to make Dole's bones ache—and where Mark Andrews had fallen to a dead heat with his young Democratic challenger. Dole claimed that a Democratic victory would shift attention to the cities, away from the wide-open places like the North Dakota plains. (Wide open! Some of these North Dakota towns made Russell, Kansas, look urban.) Without Mark Andrews, how was Ronald Reagan going to lead the country? Without Mark Andrews, North Dakota would have two Democratic Senators—no political balance, at all! Without Mark Andrews, how was North Dakota going to get its share from a Republican administration? "He not only brings home the bacon," Dole said, "he brings home the whole hog!"

Later that day, it was gray and even colder in Pocatello, then Boise, where Dole warned that if Steve Symms lost, Republicans from the western states would lose their key chairmanships. The West would be stripped of influence! The country had come a long way since 1980, when Idaho sent Steve Symms to the Senate, but all that progress could be lost. If Steve Symms lost, it would turn the country over to *liberals,* to TEDDY KENNEDY! Without Steve Symms, how was Ronald Reagan going to lead the country? That night they finished at a shopping mall, the no-frills sort of place with discount stores that sprawl over acres in the western states. Dole's voice was going bad as he shouted out a speech for Symms in the tacky atrium. It was a bad sound system and bad fluorescent light that showed the cracks in the quick-pour concrete. He'd already done the state with Symms, done press conferences, done the satellite feeds. But Dole wouldn't give the mall short shrift. There were a couple of hundred people there, and God knows how far they'd driven in the dark. They were holding up hand-lettered signs for their favorites: Doris Jones for Deputy Clerk! . . . So Dole said he wanted *everyone* to vote for a leader, Doris Jones! . . . And for the County Sheriff! . . . And the County Treasurer! There wasn't a Republican within a hundred miles whom Dole didn't tout that night. In that grungy mall, with a few hundred votes, Dole put on a show. Said he *knew* Steve Symms would win, along with Andrews in North Dakota, and Abdnor in South Dakota, and victories in the West would more than offset any GOP loss in other parts of the country.

Next day, Dole's plane set down in Seattle in a steady rain. The only event was an airport press conference, and just a handful of press, at that. The airport room was damp and cold. Slade Gorton's campaign had the smell of death. But Dole knew he could win! The point was, he had a chance! The point was, the nation needed Gorton and GOP winners in the West, to keep the Senate in safe hands, to keep the country on a steady track. "It looks real good," Dole insisted, "for maintaining Republican control of the Senate . . ."

But it was only that night, when he got to California, that Dole started to feel it. It was the kick he always got, the rush, when it started to come together. Ed Zschau, the Republican, was gaining: the latest Field Poll had him for the first time within one point of Alan Cranston. There it was on the TV news, as Dole walked into the San Jose airport: one point! In any poll, that meant a flat-out tie. Dole knew he could win, he could feel it. Zschau's people were all over the airport, running on the adrenaline high that fuels the last days of winning campaigns. If Zschau beat Cranston, that meant the Democrats would need not four, but *five* new seats to take the Senate from Bob Dole. If Symms could win, or Gorton, or Andrews—surely, Andrews ought to win . . .

Everything looked better from here, with the next day's California sunshine streaming in the windows of his borrowed jet, with the lush wine country rolling below, with Ed Zschau and his wife, Jo, chatting in the plane, bubbling with hope. Zschau told Dole he had a new ad going on the air for the final weekend, and it was a beauty! Ronald Reagan, campaigning for Zschau, urging his fellow Californians, from the heart, to win *just one more for the Gipper.* That had to be worth a couple of points! . . . In L.A., they drove to the Sheraton Grand for a luncheon, and it was great! Huge! It looked like a convention, with a thousand people milling on the darkened ballroom floor, a horde of press and cameras all pointed at the tall dais, a spotlight stabbing through the dark in that room, size of a stadium, packed with cheers for Zschau and Dole, Dole and Zschau . . .

"I smell VICTORYYY! . . ."

And then Dole dropped his strained voice into a husky, confidential tone, as he told these Southern Californians what their work in these last few days could mean, to Ed Zschau, to the Senate, to the country—and to the man who turned this country around, Ronald Reagan. . . . God, they loved it! They stood and cheered him for a minute and a half. Then Zschau stood and made his speech, which he finished with a song, a song he wrote. He stood up there and sang to the crowd!

> Z-S-C-H-A-U!
> I can spell it, you can too . . .

Dole couldn't believe it! He'd never heard it before. Had no idea! But it wasn't bad!

> He's our hero
> Cutting deficits to zero . . .
> There'll be dancin' . . .
> When he's beaten Cranston . . .

There was a band, an eight-piece combo, and they were banging out the tune, and Zschau was singing, and the Bobster stood up and got with it! Started swinging his arm, keeping time to the music, bouncing on his feet, up and down . . . it was fantastic! They were going to win!

It was that day, the Friday before the election, on the afternoon flight to Colorado, Dole said:

"Aghh, better get a release together."

Things were going to turn out all right. And if there was credit to be shared, well . . . better put out the word on what he'd done: must be a hundred cities—God knows how many candidates, speeches, dollars . . .

"You know, all of it, miles, cities, the money . . ."

His press guy, Walt Riker, started drafting the release in his head. Problem was, how to get the totals. He picked up the air-to-ground phone and called the office.

Sure, fat chance.

Friday afternoon, on Capitol Hill, with the Senate out, Senator away? And where were the schedules? You gonna ask Betty? Yip yip yip?

The PAC must have them. Campaign America had to have them.

Sure, maybe Monday.

How about the miles?

Who's got an atlas?

Dole still had a few thousand miles to put on those totals. He had three stops in Colorado, where Gary Hart's retirement meant the GOP might pick up a seat the Democrats had held for the last twelve years. That would eat up the day, Saturday. And Dole had to be in Kansas City Sunday morning, to do a remote for *Face the Nation,* and spend at least a day in his home state, so it didn't seem he was kissing it off while he sought his own reelection. But that left him Saturday night, so he decided to fly halfway across the country and back, to pick up Elizabeth in North Carolina, do a couple of events there for Senator Broyhill. He could still get back to Kansas, maybe midnight, maybe 1:00 A.M. Sunday, to get a few hours' sleep before the TV show.

Dole looked left, across the aisle of the small jet, to the staff seats in front, facing backward. No one ever sat in the front seats on Dole's side, staring right into his face. "Agh, got the release?"

Riker was still on the air phone. "Tryin' to get the figures," he said.

Dole reached across his chest with his left hand and pulled down his window shade. He was a master airplane napper. The plane was even better than the car: no one could get at him. He didn't have to pack a 707 with staff and machinery, like Bush or Reagan, and carry around some press in the back, to badger him every time he landed. Must be nice, though, that big plane . . .

He knew Reagan's guys would be back in the press seats of *Air Force One*, claiming credit for every Senate race they won. That was the White House plan for '86: they sent Bush out to do the scut work, the Governors and House seats. The big deal, keeping the Senate, and all the credit for it, was reserved to the Big Guy. So Reagan had been out on the grand tour, brought out of the barn for one last race, with a big White House send-off, and everybody wrote about the Gip going out to win one more. Of course, it made all the papers, too, when the President flew into Oklahoma, made a speech there for Senator Don Nickles, and called him throughout: "my friend . . . Don Rickles." But no one wrote what else Reagan said. Problem was, Reagan didn't have anything to say, except the same general stuff: *America standing tall* . . . you know, the vision business. Dole tried to talk to Don Regan about getting the President onto some issues that made a difference out there, but Regan insisted he knew what he was doing. "We're going to tailor the speeches for the states involved, that kind of thing." Too bad—Don Regan didn't know anything about the states involved. If you asked Bob Dole, Don Regan didn't know politics at all.

Truth be told, Bob Dole wasn't calling Regan anymore, asking the Chief of Staff what had to get done . . . like he used to call Jim Baker: on the phone with the White House, every day or two. There wasn't any point with Regan. If you wanted to call the tune for Dole, you had to know more than he did. In fact, Dole wasn't carrying water for the White House at all—not after '85. That was the time Bob Dole, the new Majority Leader, put it on the line for the White House. Reagan kept saying the deficit was Public Enemy Number One. But then he sent up a budget that would have pumped red ink up over the window sills. It was a laughingstock! So Dole picked up the ball and ran. He'd cut the budget, like he'd done in '81. Better than '81: he bit the bullet hard, made a $56 billion package—and it was everything, not just the easy stuff. He proposed to freeze the defense budget, to freeze the cost-of-living hikes for all federal pensions—even Social Security. It meant $300 billion in savings over the next three years. It was pure Dole, brass balls . . . and he made it stick. He made Reagan swallow the freeze on the Pentagon. And he took the heat no one wanted for fooling with Social Security. It was more than just Social Security: veterans' benefits, military pensions, civil service, black-lung payments . . . every federal entitlement, the kind of middle-class welfare no one else had the guts to touch. It amounted to the toughest vote anyone had tried in years. But it was the only fair way, Dole insisted: everyone had to take a hit. For Republicans in the Senate, he made a compelling political case: unless they did something strong on the deficit, the Party was down the drain in '86—or the minute the economy went south, as it would, inevitably, someday. For farm-state Senators, he made sure their growers wouldn't suffer unduly: his farm bill would take care of them. He got Jim Abdnor with $200 million to save the Rural Electric program. For the few GOP liberals, he was offering a major prize: a Pentagon freeze. And he sweetened the pot with money for Amtrak, a bridge, a naval contract. . . . In the last couple of days, he was locked in his office in nonstop session—in his offices, really: he'd have Weicker in one room, holding out for a deal to fund some mass transit, and Zorinsky (a Democrat!) in the next room, bargaining for the wheat growers, and David Stockman in the back room, wheeling and dealing on small business—as Dole shuttled back and forth among the members, probing and nudging for their bottom lines. He was holding the package together by force of his own will and savvy, bargaining down the straddlers, vote by vote. And when it came down to an all-night floor fight, Dole finally choked off the desperate opposition by packing all amendments into a single roll of the dice, one vote, for which the White House turned George Bush and *Air Force Two* back in midflight, en route to Phoenix, and sent Bush to the Senate to break a tie. Dole was calling hospitals, trying to get John East and Pete Wilson to come back from sickbeds for the vote. East, it turned out, was too weak, and his wife wouldn't let him go. But sometime after 1:00 A.M., some forty hours after his emergency appendectomy, Pete Wilson rolled up to the Capitol in an ambulance, and medics wheeled him in, wearing his brown bathrobe, with an IV tube still in his arm, and to a standing ovation from his colleagues, he cast his "Aye," and Bush broke the tie, and by 3:08 A.M., that same night, Dole had slain the deficit vampire.

But it was Dole who got the stake through the heart. When the bill got to the House, Jack Kemp, that blow-dried windbag, started conniving with Regan, peddling his standard supply-side snake oil:

No one wants more doom and gloom on the deficit . . .

Why should Republicans take the heat? . . .

We can grow out of the deficit!

And Regan put him right in front of the President, who buckled. Reagan flapped like an old faded flag. Pretty soon, he backed off the freeze on the pensions. That was half the cuts, right there. Then it wasn't everybody taking a hit anymore. The package just came apart. The White House tried to peddle the retreat as Ronald Reagan hanging tough against the Congress. Problem was, he wasn't really tough enough. In the end, the deficit kept growing: they just swept it under the rug. But not before they'd jerked that rug out from under every Republican in the Senate. They left Dole's guys with nothing to stand on, with "a vote against Social Security" to explain, out there with nowhere to hide, while the Democrats and the AARP leisurely took aim and shot them down.

God knows, half these races wouldn't be so tough, if Reagan hadn't flip-flopped, if Jack Kemp had, for once in his life, shut up and made the tough vote. . . . Dole applied the "Be Nice" rule to Kemp only with struggle, and with imperfect success. No one was going to convince a boy from Russell-in-the-thirties that debts were going to grow away. That was the subtext of Dole's good-news, bad-news joke, during the tax fight of 1982:

"Good news is, a bus full of supply-siders went over a cliff last night . . .

"Bad news is, there were three empty seats."

When Kemp and his right-wing friends returned fire, branding Dole "the tax collector for the welfare state," Dole's jokes got more personal. During the wrangle over tax reform, Dole said Kemp must be holding out for a deduction on hair spray.

But Dole was more careful with truths about Reagan. Ronald Reagan was still huge out there, in the Party, with the people who'd vote in the primaries, especially in the South and West. At Campaign America, Don Devine made up a flip-chart, a breakdown of the voters Dole was after. It was a poll of how Americans saw themselves. More than half the voters these days called themselves conservatives. They were Reagan's voters, and now Dole had to reel in his share. At least, he had to keep Kemp from getting them, claiming he was Reagan's heir. Or keep Bush from getting them, though Dole couldn't see how Bush could get a vote from any working man. ("Gaghh! . . . I mean, guy never had to do a day's work in his life!")

Anyway, Dole had nothing but praise for Reagan, and deference, at least in public. Whenever Dole spoke in a state where Reagan's grand tour would later touch down, Dole always reminded the crowd that the Big Guy was on his way. "Aghh, I'm just doin' little *advance,* f'the *Pres*ident . . ." Whenever Dole talked about the need to cut spending, he said it was Reagan who showed the need to cut spending. It was Reagan who'd changed the tone: "Y'don't see anybody these days proposing big new spending programs . . ." And no one ever heard from Dole that Reagan had already dropped the ball; that Dole did forty-three states, this year, for Dole. No one ever heard from Dole that if it weren't for Reagan waffling, maybe they'd have some money to spend. If it weren't for Reagan's mania of self, they might have a bigger bulge in the Senate. Dole might not *have* to spend Saturday night flying an extra three thousand miles to get on the front page with Broyhill . . . wouldn't have so many tight races, wouldn't have to go to North Carolina, could have sent another plane for Elizabeth, maybe wouldn't have lost his voice, wouldn't have to listen to Riker losing *his,* yelling into a bad connection on the air phone . . .

"NO! REPUBLICAN CAN-DI-DAYTZZZ . . . YEAH, PLURAL!"

Riker was dictating the press release to the Capitol office. He'd written it on a legal pad, with blank spaces for the numbers and totals. Dole looked it over and changed the lead, made it more than an announcement of the final campaign swing. Now the top paragraph predicted a win: ". . . the U.S. Senate will remain Republican." Dole knew how to get ink: you had to make news. He also knew when to make news, and Saturday afternoon was too late. They'd already missed the first Sunday papers. And they still didn't have the totals.

"NO, *YOU* STICK IN THE NUMBER. . . . WELL, GET THE REST OF 'EM AND GET IT OUT! . . . JEEEZUS!"

The jet was flying back into weather, bouncing around in the sky. Just what they needed on that final push. At least Dole could smell the finish line. None too soon. His throat was raw, and dark circles shaded the tan under his eyes. Well, Elizabeth'd be there. She'd have everything arranged.

But there was no arranging the Broyhill campaign—not at that point. Elizabeth had no more idea than Dole what they were getting into. Dole landed late, in a rainstorm, at Hickory, North Carolina, and sat in a van while they drove him through the dark on slick mountain roads . . . for forty-five minutes! It was like a hostage scene. No one he knew had any idea where they were going. Dole Advance never scheduled *any* car ride more than thirty minutes. But this wasn't Dole Advance.

They got to a high school, some kind of fish fry: bad vibes; no media; crowd was down; Dole was late; raining like hell. Everyone wanted this to be over— especially Dole. But this was Elizabeth's home state. Of course, she was being "nahce," meeting the locals. . . . "Whah, thank you *so much,*" she'd say, in response to their effusions. Dole was halfhearted, working the crowd, as he listened for her silvery chuckles of delight behind him. He meant to keep this short and sweet. He'd say a few words—more than he should with his voice gone—then: "Gottagooo . . ."

But there was no escape. After the fish fry, they packed into the van for another forty-five-minute trek. This time, they got lost in the rain, trying to find a recreation center in the town of Lenoir.

Close to eleven o'clock, and the chucklehead with the van didn't know where he was going!

Be nice . . .

So they got to Lenoir and there's a crowd, maybe hundred and fifty, that'd been "warmed up" for about four hours . . . they looked like the people who kill time in those pay-TV chairs in airports: they're watching, but they don't want to be there. The Doles walked in and everybody sat up, waiting, but Broyhill hadn't shown yet. Elizabeth got up and delivered her remarks, and then Dole scratched out a few lines. But Broyhill didn't get there. Broyhill was lost, somewhere in the rain. So what could they do? The Doles stayed and "warmed up" the crowd for another half-hour.

It was after midnight when they got back to the plane. Dole just wanted to know the flight time. Then he sat, quiet, awfully quiet. Elizabeth was worried because Bob was so tired. Really, she had no *idea* it was *so far* . . . and on a night like this, whah, she *never.* . . . But no one else felt like chatting. Some North Carolina folks had sent along some barbecued pork for the flight, so once they were up, they set to their sandwiches, and after a while, in the darkened cabin, there was just the smell of the smoky pork, the hum from the engines, the hiss of the air vents. Elizabeth was still nervous, but she could always eat barbecue.

It'd be near 2:00 A.M. when they got to Kansas City, maybe a half-hour later when they got into the hotel. Dole would be up in a few hours to do *Face the Nation.* He'd be nice, Presidential. . . . He'd make a few jokes in the studio. On the air, he'd suavely predict victory.

But really, he wasn't so sure anymore. Somehow, it didn't feel the same. Maybe he was just tired . . . hard to tell. No one would see it on TV. He'd look fine. He always did. But somehow, when it got like this, everything seemed harder. He'd try to shrug it off, like he always did, if it came to that. If the news was bad, he wasn't going to whine.

Still, it didn't help, later that day, when Riker found out the papers were going with a story from George Bush, about all the miles he'd flown, the candidates he'd helped, the money he raised. Riker said the totals weren't as big as Dole's, but no one was going to do a second-day story on the same thing from Dole. Bush's press release had gotten to the papers in plenty of time.

Dole just made a face, and issued a mournful haiku, a meditation on the struggle against an incumbent VP:

"Agh, *Air Force Two* . . . lotta people, typin' . . . flyin' around."

— ★ —

The thing that was neat about *Air Force Two* was the way it helped him make friends. He'd be doing a state, so he'd get the Congressmen, State Party Chairman, or State Treasurer, even a County Chairman or two, and ferry them along to the next event. They loved it. They'd talk about it for the next year. That was one beautiful plane!

Actually, it wasn't just one: any plane he rode was called *Air Force Two.* In the bad old seventies, when Mondale was Veep, and the government still worried about things like fuel and noise, the Vice President flew on small, efficient DC-9s. But now, in the age of Reagan, Bush mostly flew a big old 707, the Stratoliner, a Cadillac-with-tailfins kind of plane, so heavy, noisy, and greedy for fuel that no commercial airline would be permitted to land one at an American airport. The Air Force had enough of the behemoths to keep two on call for Reagan, maybe send another overseas with a Cabinet Secretary, and still give one (or one and a backup) to Bush, to ease his travels. On most trips, he got Number 86-6970, which was the first jet a President ever flew. It was delivered for Ike, at the end of his term, and it was JFK's number-one plane. Sometimes Bush got Number 26000, the plane that flew LBJ back to Washington after Kennedy's assassination, on which he took the oath of office in the nation's darkest hour. Of course, by the time a guest learned any of that, he felt like he was riding a shrine.

And the way George Bush was, he'd never leave guests stuck in the back, even in the fine first-class seats that lined the rear cabin. No, someone from the staff would lead them up through the staff seating section, and through the office cabin, with its tables, word processors, Xerox, fax . . . and forward still, to the Power Cabin, where the Vice President would receive them in his big swivel chair. That was the grandest part of all.

Lyndon Johnson had the chair built in, along with the table and an L-shaped bench along the wall, so guests or staff could sit at the table, while Johnson held court in his swivel-throne. Johnson had them build in a button he could press to raise and lower the table. There was a TV, of course, and the highest level of Bush-friend-perk was to sit with the Veep in the Power Cabin, transcontinentally munching the public popcorn, while the latest (though, alas, not always the best) movie transpired on the VCR.

Bush used the plane as a five-hundred-thirty-mile-an-hour living room, and he dressed accordingly. Whenever he'd get on, even for a twenty-minute hop, he'd slip off his suit coat and don his AFII jacket, a short blue windbreaker made by London Fog, with "Air Force II" embroidered across the back, a Vice Presidential seal on his left breast, and on the right, in embroidered script: "The Vice President." Bar had a jacket, too, with the same decoration, and on the right breast, an embroidered "Mrs. Bush." Whenever they got on the plane, stewards had the jackets ready, his draped over the back of the swivel-throne, and hers on the table, or laid out in the very foremost cabin, the private Vice Presidential stateroom. For longer trips, the VP would strip off his work clothes and get into slippers, baggy sweatpants, a golf shirt, and, of course, the jacket.

If he was leaving an event, the first thing he'd grab was the thank-you list, which the Lead Advance handed aboard as he said goodbye to the Veep on the tarmac. These were the names, addresses, and salutations (Mr., Mrs., Miss, Ms., Dr., etc.) written out in a grid, along with the nature of each person's gift or work in aid of the event. Bush always did the thank-you notes first. Oftentimes, he'd have a dozen done before the plane got off the ground. Then he'd call his briefers in, usually the Chief of Advance, followed by the staff who arranged the next event, or the State Department briefers if he were headed overseas. Sometimes, on a long trip, he'd keep the briefers up there for hours, peppering them with questions, until he found one they really couldn't answer. Then, for some reason, he seemed satisfied. That was a note he could quit on.

But after the briefing, invariably, it was time for friends. That's when the staff would lead the pols up front for popcorn and shoot-the-shit, and maybe, if the hour was right, a martini that would fell a horse, prepared by the practiced stewards to Vice Presidential specs, in a water glass, size of a tumbler. See, the Veep allowed himself only one. (Of course, a guest could have as many as he liked: once, upon deplaning, the aged and befuddled Richard Lyng, Secretary of Agriculture, took a dramatic stuntman tumble down the back steps of the plane to cement; but he lived to buy further surplus.) Whatever the hour or the circumstance, this was the part the Veep liked best. He'd bring them up, order them drinks, and talk politics: he loved to talk politics, as some men love to talk sports. Or if he knew them better, it might be anything, as long as it was common ground: fishing, boats, children, tennis. . . . (You *play*? Y'gotta come to the house, got a court there. Why'n'cha come next weekend? C'mon! Your son play? Doubles! It'll be *fun*! . . .)

What a Great and Good God it was who gave George Bush work he so enjoyed! And work that contributed so surely to his progress on this earth below!

So, when Bush went to speak for George Wortley, Congressman from Syracuse, and then to a dinner in Manhattan, he picked up a couple of County Chairmen from the New York Conservative Party.

"Hey! Wanna ride down on *Air Force Two*?"

"*Yeah . . . uh, yes, sir!*"

So they got on the plane, and within ten minutes they were up in the Power Cabin, posing for a photo with The Man himself. Of course, next month, the pic showed up on the front of the party newsletter. And Bush used the photo a thousand times. (*Who says conservatives don't like Bush?*)

Of course, all the Governors flew with Bush, too. That's what he was working on in '86: Governors, all over the country. See, that was the White House plan: the Reagan guys, the A-Team, palmed off the grunt work on George Bush—what the hell, he'd do it. . . .

But what a Great and Good Godly stroke! Governors were just what he'd need for next time, for '88, when at last he'd turn from toil for others and, finally, do something for himself. Governors were the ones who had the contacts all over their states—and not just people who'd help in campaigns. Those were the people a Senator knew: a Senator came back just to run every six years. But Governors had to work every day with people in the towns and counties, handing out contracts, putting folks in jobs. A Governor met the local press, knew all the small papers, and the local reporters—not just the one overworked schlub who covered Capitol Hill in the Washington bureau. A Governor could make all the difference in a state:

KEAN: BUSH VISIT MEANS N.J.
HAS A FRIEND IN WHITE HOUSE

That would be the headline from Trenton, if the Governor, like Tom Kean, was a friend who'd billboard Bush's day in the Garden State—his visit to that toxic-waste cleanup site, all the help he'd offered on that Superfund. . . .

Of course, if the Governor wasn't a friend, then his appointed State Police Chief might find time to take a couple of press calls. . . .

That would be a different headline:

BUSH VISIT WILL COST
$200,000 IN OVERTIME

So Bush was focused on Governors, and not just on their campaigns: he was working on them, one by one, making friends, finding common ground. Tom Kean wasn't even running in '86, but Bush made a point of seeking him out, asking his views on two issues that interested Kean the most: education and welfare reform. Of course, Kean was a friend from way back. Same with Dick Thornburgh in Pennsylvania. But big Jim Thompson, in Illinois, he was looking for a horse to ride: had to be a good horse, to carry him all the way to a Cabinet job in Washington. So Bush had long talks with Thompson—revenue generation, what it's like to run a big state, that kind of thing. Bush let Thompson do the talking—and signed him up to be a cochair of the PAC, the Fund for America's Future. Of course, that also froze Big Jim for the whole '88 cycle, put an end to any budding plan to run as Illinois's favorite son. But it wasn't just the fellows in the biggest states. Kay Orr in Nebraska—got to know her when she was State Treasurer; Bob Martinez in Florida—friend of Jeb, Bush's son who lived down there; Henry Bellmon in Oklahoma—he was with Bush back in '80; even Mike Castle, in Delaware, who had to be with Pete du Pont, and Mike Hayden in Kansas, who'd have to be with Dole: Bush wanted to know them. He wanted to be friends.

If there was something they wanted to know about Bush, well, that was fine, too. John Sununu in New Hampshire: Bush got onto him the minute Sununu won in '82. Talked with him during the '84 reelection, and went back, over and over, during the midterms in '86. Had a real meeting of the minds there, on domestic issues, the limits on government. And Bush convinced him, worked at convincing him, that he really had flipped over on abortion: solidly against it now—except the life of the mother, or rape, incest, that kind of thing. . . . John Ashcroft in Missouri, got elected in '84, completely different background: evangelical, a gospel singer, father was a minister. He had to be convinced, too, that Bush was "right" on abortion now. So Bush convinced him, or rather Ashcroft became convinced that Bush and he had common ground.

Fact was, there was common ground with everyone, when George Bush wanted to be friends. It wasn't so much the public stuff, the speech, though that was charming, in its way. "Don't worry," he'd say on stage, in front of the flags, at the funder. He'd toss both hands up over his shoulders, palms out, a quick gesture of accommodation, half reassurance, half surrender. "Not gonna give you the full load . . ." Like they didn't really want to hear from *him*. He wasn't gonna take up their time, just talking. "Just happy," Bush would say, ". . . here with my friend, *and I mean friend* . . ." Then he'd name the guy he was with: Tommy Thompson in Wisconsin, Carroll Campbell in South Carolina, Garrey Carruthers in New Mexico, ". . . be a GREAT Governor . . ."

And he meant it, at least the friend part: even if he didn't know them well, even if they knew he'd want their help next year, they could feel how much it mattered to him. It was an animal thing, like a tail wagging, wagging his whole ass back and forth. He wanted to be their friend. And by the time they banked the gate from that fund-raiser, and they got the handwritten note he did on the plane going home, when they got another check from his Fund for America's Future, when they got the signed photo from his office, and the follow-up invitation to come to breakfast at the White House, or stay at the Residence, or burgers and bloodies in the backyard on Sunday, or troll for bluefish on the boat in Maine, when they heard from a fellow Governor, or someone they knew at the White House, that Bush was mentioning how much he *liked* them . . . well then, damn right he's a friend!

Meanwhile, he'd get them up in *Air Force Two,* or have them into the hotel suite after the big fund-raiser, and he was just terrific! Able, funny, confidential . . . and smart: he knew a few things about their states. Or, more likely, he knew people. One of the Governors would mention he was up in a certain county last week, and heard nice things about Bush there. "Oh, d'ya see Will Simmons?" Bush would ask. "He was County Chairman in '73 . . ." Bush had the name at instant command from thirteen years before, when he headed the Republican National Committee. (As a matter of fact, it wasn't Will, it was Will, Jr., whom Bush had phoned, just to say hello, when he flew in to his college town to give a speech in 1979.) And Bush knew what the issues were, what the Governor had been doing: that fight about the nuclear plant, the problem with the State Court of Appeals. . . . As a matter of fact, he'd heard about them *yesterday,* from Andy Card, who was the Bush State Chairman in Massachusetts in 1980. And what was Andy Card doing now? Well, he went to work in the White House—Deputy-Under-Something for Intergovernmental Relations—and when the A-Team started to focus on the Senate, Andy suggested that he could help out . . . take the Governors off their hands. In fact, knowing everything about the Governors (and the State Comptrollers, Attorneys General, the Speakers of the House, and other Governors-to-be) became Andy's specialty, and his work for the taxpayers of this nation. What a Great and Good stroke of fortune for Bush! . . . What a Blessed Confluence of happenstance!

It seemed always to happen for Bush—the Blessed Confluence. He just tried to be a friend, and it worked out. Even he couldn't understand why. But that's the way it worked in the five-minute devotions, homilies on how the good life is lived, which Dottie Bush read to her children, every day at breakfast.

Good things happen to good people. It was one of those truths he'd just always known.

Much later, when he was grown up, a millionaire man of the world, Bush heard the same lesson from his own minister. The Reverend James T. (Tom) Bagby, Rector of St. Martin's Episcopal, in Houston, had a homily he'd tell in church, a lesson from his own life. . . . When Tom was going to seminary, the Bishop awarded him one-third of a scholarship, the gift of a wealthy and gracious lady. That year, Tom wrote her a letter every month. The next year, the lady instructed the Bishop that Tom was to get the whole scholarship. Why, the Bishop asked her, did she want to give the full amount to a student so undistinguished? Reverend Tom always concluded:

"Perhaps it's because I did what my mother taught me. Expressing my gratitude was the very least I could have done. . . . Large rewards come from planting small seeds of gratitude."

Lord knows, George Bush had strewn the ground with seeds.

He'd see Tom this Sunday at church. He had a day off scheduled for Sunday, in Houston. Just heaven! A day with no speeches, no press. Just church in the morning and a golf game with his old friend Fred Chambers in the afternoon. Then, maybe a rubdown in the Houstonian's private health club. Then, more friends for dinner—Molina's, his favorite Tex-Mex place. It'd be a great day, a great weekend in Houston. Friday, he'd do one event for Tommy Thompson, in Wisconsin, and then he'd get into Houston about three-thirty in the afternoon. (There'd be no midnight, down-to-the-wire flights for George Bush.) Then he'd spend four nights in a row there, until Tuesday morning, when he and Bar would jump in the limo and ride five minutes to vote at their precinct, just down the road from the hotel.

It was perfect, the way it worked out. There was a tough race for Governor in Texas, too. So Bush could spend his last day, Monday, hopping his home state with his friend Bill Clements: Mesquite, El Paso, College Station . . . lots of friends in those places. Then back to Houston for one last event, the big one, at the Galleria. That would be the best of all.

In the Power Cabin, Bush had his bible out and was looking over the schedule. He could see the finish line coming. He ripped out the Wisconsin pages, wadded them up. "That's done," he said. It wasn't a gesture of annoyance, or even impatience. There was an air of satisfaction in the front of *Air Force Two*. Bush was up—everybody noticed.

The plane was packed with staff—thirty rooms reserved at the Houstonian, and that wasn't even counting the Service—and everyone telling him things were going well. Not that he had to ask. He knew he was getting a good reception. He could read a poll, too. And he knew he'd done a job: covered a lot of miles, lot of races, made a lot of friends. Anyone who stuck with him for a day saw it wasn't like '84, with the press always on him, comparing him to their darling, Ferraro, picking him over like some mysterious creature that crawled out from under a rock:

Wouldn't you call that a preppy watchband?

When did you stop wearing button-down shirts?

Why do you wear those short socks?

That was the worst, '84, when it got so nasty and personal. It got to him, he had to admit. It was "rasping." That was his word for it. Running around like he did that year—like they all did in '84—he didn't even feel like he was helping the government. No one got anything done. As for him, he was cutting ribbons. Made him wonder what the hell it was all for.

But now, that futile feeling was gone. Now, he was turning the corner. Soon, there wouldn't be any more joint events, other people's crowds to please, other people's hosts to thank. Soon, it would be George Bush for President . . . he'd waited six years to say that simple phrase again. Just a couple of days now, and it was his turn again. And he'd made it through this last go-round without any major mistakes. He was coming in strong, far better than when he started the last time—just him and young David Bates, flying commercial, flying coach! "Steerage," he used to call it.

He grabbed a fistful of popcorn and leaned back in his big chair. Yeah, different now. . . . Fuller was in the corner, quiet, as always. Atwater was on the bench, talking about Tommy Thompson. Looked good for Thompson in Wisconsin. Looked good, in a lot of the races they'd hit, Lee said.

Bush grunted assent. He had a mouthful of popcorn. He knew good news that none of them knew yet. Still delicate. Wouldn't say anything with them in the cabin. . . . Hard to know if it'd really happen, anyway. In fact, it wasn't until the next day, Saturday, at the Houstonian, he'd confide to Fuller: "Looks like we might have some good news on the hostages."

It took Fuller by surprise. The way he had the office set up, Fuller sat astride the channel for classified security stuff. And he hadn't heard anything about a hostage.

"Really?"

"Yeah, one for sure. One more, maybe two . . . maybe tomorrow."

And sure enough, on that blessed church-and-golf Sunday, an American hospital administrator named David Jacobsen was freed on a street in West Beirut, after seventeen months as a hostage of the Islamic Jihad.

That was the frosting on Bush's cake. And he was pretty sure there would be more. Timing up in the air . . . but they had a lever now. At least they were on the right track. At last, they were talking to the right people!

Bush swung into his last day, his Texas tour, with such a happy air, he was like a kid. In Mesquite, that morning, he told the crowd: "Go out and vote tomorrow, as often as you can!"

In El Paso, he appeared with the GOP's Attorney General candidate, Roy Barrera, a *Hispanic*—whose cause so thoroughly enchanted Bush that he attempted Barrera's slogan—*in Spanish! . . . "¡Voy con Roy!"* (It was the moral equivalent of "I Like Ike.") . . . By the time they hit College Station, Bush was so enthralled with his new friend that he yelled:

"*Voy con Roy!* It's not just a slogan! It's a way of life!"

By the time he'd worked through the day, back to Houston, he was ready to let it all out for the last big Monday crowd. They called the event at the Galleria mall the "Texas Victory '86 Rally." But it really had more to do with Bush, in '88. The Clements campaign didn't want a big deal: they suggested a simple press conference—just enough to get their man on the local news at six-thirty. It was the Bushies who got the bit in their teeth—insisted on a mega-event, a crowd to fill the Galleria skating rink. It was the Bush people who found the money to put down a floor over the ice, to bus in a half-dozen high school bands, to provide two hours of entertainment to pack the place. The Advance was incredible. The Clements people had never seen anything like it. The Bushies signed on the Houston Astros' announcer, Milo Hamilton, as emcee. They brought in a few Astros to build the crowd. They hired on country bands, jazz bands, rock 'n' roll bands . . . signs, balloons, giant flags. The scale of the thing was, well . . . Presidential. The Bush team didn't even observe the pretense that this was for Clements. This was for Bush, the kickoff. The Bushies wore special T-shirts while they gussied up the mall. The shirts read: "In the Rink . . . On the Brink."

And when Bush walked in, the place went sky-high. There were more than

a thousand people packed into the rink below, hanging off the balconies
. . . all the way to the roof! The bands were blaring. The noise was amazing.
Everybody agreed he got as good a reception as Clements—maybe better. It
even knocked *him* out. He stood on stage with Bar, just looking around the
balconies, his mouth hanging open in a grin. Yeah, it was going to be different,
this time. . . . It was going to be fun! Jeez, all the friends he could see in the
crowd. He was pointing, making faces at them. Bar would spot some more,
and point them out to him. Then Alan Ashby showed up, the catcher from
the Astros. They made Poppy throw the ball again. So he wound up and flung
it, good and hard this time, straight across the rink. And Ashby caught it, and
the crowd gave a terrific whoop. . . . And Bush was happy, home, among
friends, and on his own. He'd made the turn, *his* turn now, and it was coming
together, it was going to be okay, it would be . . .

How could he tell them? He'd never been too good at saying . . . people just
had to feel it with him. They were on the right track. He knew it. The people would vote tomorrow, they'd ratify . . . it was important. How could he
say? . . .

So he started with the names, the persons: Bill Clements for Governor, my
friend . . . and Roy Barrera for Attorney General, my new friend, *Voy con Roy!*
. . . the Congressional candidates . . . all the Republicans, all friends of his
. . . and he was talking without text for once, not a speech, and a lock of his
hair had fallen on his forehead, like it always did, when he really got going
. . . the most important day, tomorrow, the big day . . . we'll be voting, we'll
be sending the word, showing our colors . . .

He was standing in front of a Texas flag, twenty feet tall. And now, from
the floor, a huge Stars and Stripes began to rise in front of the Lone Star,
climbing to the rafters behind him as he spoke.

"We'll be doing the Lord's work," Bush said, "for our great city of Houston
and the state of Texas . . ."

It would be blessed.

So, the next day, he jumped into the limo, and he and Bar voted and made
for the plane. On the way back to D.C., the staff gathered with him, packed
in the Power Cabin, and gave their assessment of where he stood. Looked
good, they agreed: he'd made the turn; no mistakes.

And that night, he and Bar had a few friends at the Residence—maybe
twenty people—to watch the returns. It was a shock, the Senate thing. . . . Of
course, the networks spent the whole night on that. . . .

But the bright spots (the only bright spot for Republicans, Brokaw said)
were the Governors. The GOP just about swept those clean—picked up eight
statehouses that night. There were twenty-four Republican Governors now,
and George Bush had spent time with them all. Even he was surprised how
well that went. He spent half the night on the phone in his study, while the
White House switchboard tracked down the winners. And just when he had
one on the line, Lee Atwater would run in with more news: Carroll Campbell
in South Carolina! CBS called it for Thompson! Clements pulling away in

Texas! Wasn't it amazing the way it worked out? The only people who won were the people he helped. His friends! What a Great and Good stroke of fortune!

It was such a good night in the VP house, none of the guests could remember later whether they even heard the other news: that day, the Parliament Speaker in Iran announced that a group of U.S. officials had snuck into his country on phony passports, come to Tehran with a shipment of weapons, bearing for the Ayatollah Khomeini a cake and a Bible from Ronald Reagan.

— ★ —

Dole spent election night in his office. He'd voted in Russell, but then flew East. His home-state Republicans gathered to celebrate in Topeka, as always, in that ratty Ramada overlooking the highway, but this year they'd have to make do with a satellite feed from their victorious Senator. Dole was piling up a handsome majority in Kansas, but he couldn't stick around to commune with the faithful. He had work to do.

In Washington, the staff had the Capitol suite arranged for the business of the evening: in his inner office, a graceful antique chair and loveseat were arrayed, in state, before four console TVs. That's where the Senator and Secretary Dole would watch the returns. The outer salon was given over to camera crews from the networks: they'd be in there all night, hooked by a twisting mile of cable to satellite trucks in the parking lot, ready to feed live to their bureaus, so their anchormen could chat for five minutes with Dole. Down the hall, in the grand chandeliered Office of the Secretary of the Senate, Jo-Anne Coe's reception room was stocked as a buffet: shrimp, roast beef, cheese, crudités . . . so her staff, the Leader's staff, the Sergeant at Arms, committee staff, could gather in tribal solidarity to witness the coming of the next Congress. This was not, for them, a matter of idle, or even purely political, interest: if the news was bad, if the Democrats won, there would be no more power for them; if the news was bad, Bob Byrd, the Democratic Leader, would be coming, tomorrow, for this graceful office with the floor-to-ceiling windows that looked out on the Mall; if the news was bad, if the Democrats won, everyone from senior Finance Committee tax specialists (who'd wielded power for six years to make or break whole industries) to the twenty-year-old elevator operators (who smiled and punched buttons on the self-service consoles to make spending money for college), the Sergeant at Arms, doorkeepers, Capitol police, clerical staff, maybe two thousand souls . . . could be demoted, or fired, the next day.

And the news didn't look good: at 7:01 on the evening newscast, the nets called Florida for the Democrats. Wirthlin's last poll had Paula Hawkins only five or six points behind. But it wasn't even close. She got killed. One seat, already, gone from Dole's grasp. One minute into the news! Then, through the night, the tide rolled west, through the time zones, state after state:

Broyhill lost in North Carolina. Mack Mattingly lost in Georgia . . . Mattingly should have gone home, shouldn't have stayed for the end of the session.

NBC called a win for Jerry Denton: Alabama! At last, a state they held! Denton was a war hero, POW . . . still went a long way in Alabama.

Wasn't till late, they reversed the call—said Denton lost. Took away another seat. Took it away from Dole.

Thing was, he'd done the job. He knew he'd kept things moving, tried to make a difference, stuck his neck out to do *something* on issues that another man might have ducked. What'd it get him? What'd it get any of them? Dole saw the faces around him, the anxious strain. People thought he didn't notice. But what could he do? From the salon, amid the cables and floodlights, he heard snatches of conversation. Two of the politics guys were arriving for the tribal rite. They'd driven in to the Capitol from the Campaign America office in Virginia. One of them said, plaintively: "How can they throw us out when gas is seventy-nine cents a gallon?"

Good question. Dole couldn't sit in the throne, kept hopping up to check the ticker in the pressroom. Walt Riker had friends in the networks, so he was getting numbers that weren't on the air yet. The networks wouldn't broadcast until the polls closed in each state. Elizabeth stuck it out on the loveseat, watching as the maps and the faces flashed up on the screen . . .

Good evening, I'm Peter Jennings in New York. . . . And we have a couple of projections to make. . . . In North Dakota, that is still too close to call. The incumbent, Republican Mark Andrews . . .

Andrews ought to be pulling away. Andrews didn't make enough friends. Kind of guy who was always there when he wanted something. But when you needed him . . . He was the one who beat up Elizabeth when she testified before his committee. He was mean to her! Still asked Dole for help. Guy just had to sneeze and Dole was out there with a hanky.

The TV screens showed maps of the country, but the map in Dole's mind was the Senate floor. If they held the losses to three seats, Bush could break the tie. Do him good to stick around Washington for a vote once in a while. Even if they lost four . . . well, Dole could have another talk with Zorinsky. He was a Nebraska Democrat who used to be a Republican. Might want to switch back, if the price was right—say, the chairmanship of the Ag Committee. Dole had already sounded out Zorinsky.

The Senate in South Dakota. We now project that Tom Daschle is going to win the Senate race in South Dakota, defeating the incumbent, James Abdnor, Senator James Abdnor. . . . The issue there was the farm economy, from beginning to end.

Abdnor was the one that hit Dole the hardest. A guy Dole could count on. . . . Had a lisp, or some kind of speech problem, and the Washington press never gave him credit: Abdnor didn't go to receptions, didn't even own a pinstripe suit. But the guy was solid, knew his farmers, worked like hell . . . and what did it get him? Dole tried to put him on TV, took him to meetings at the White House. When the press staked out the West Wing doors, waiting for a statement from Dole, he'd shove Abdnor out instead. Then Dole put him up in the chair to preside on a big roll call—guaranteed TV time. Worked like a charm . . . what'd it get him?

Dole was staring down at the carpet between his chair and the TV consoles. The carpet was an intricate masterpiece, dark reds and blues, pale purples, and ivory wool knotted into tiny figures of the ancient Chinese past. Deng Xiaoping made a gift of the carpet to the distinguished Majority Leader on the occasion of his visit in 1985. *Zschau in California . . . Gorton could still win in Washington . . . maybe Andrews . . .* The carpet was priceless. Should never have been on the floor. *Four seats . . .* Dole bounced his heels on the rug.

"Senator? . . ."

They moved him into the salon, where Jennings and Brinkley wanted him live. They had Bob Byrd on another feed down the hall.

Be nice.

Dole congratulated Byrd on the air. Said he knew they could work together. They'd work out a trade bill that wasn't protectionist . . .

We can now project, James Santini, the Republican, defeated for the Senate in Nevada, a severe blow for the Republicans and for Paul Laxalt, the retiring . . .

Then it was Brokaw, Brokaw and Byrd. Dole congratulated Byrd and the Democrats, said he wasn't entirely surprised. It was a tough year, an off year, but they could work together on the deficit . . . tried to smile. He's supposed to look happy?

But the mood that you saw reflected in Senator Dole's interview is very much the mood of Republican aides here on Capitol Hill. There are lots of them around, and they are very gloomy . . .

Brit Hume was on the screen for ABC, from the Capitol.

But looking at North Dakota . . . Kent Conrad, the State Tax Commissioner, who was at one time not expected to do really well against incumbent Mark Andrews, another member of the Republican and Reagan class of 1980, is ahead out there and stands a chance. . . . And in that kind of situation, a Democratic takeover of the Senate becomes almost inevitable. Gentlemen? . . .

In the salon, Dole moved from chair to chair, wearing his own earplug, so they wouldn't have to fiddle with his ear and his neck every time he moved to a new interview. He did CBS, went out in the hall for CNN, and C-Span. Then, he did the locals. He was on TV the rest of the night. Had to be. Couldn't buy exposure like that. . . . Had to speak for the Party . . . but this was for Dole.

Over and over, he said to the camera: "We're going to work with the Democrats . . . congratulate my friend Bob Byrd . . . but keep in mind: Ronald Reagan is still President. He is a very powerful President . . ."

But this was for Dole. Reagan's power was gone. Finished. The old magic hadn't worked a lick. Reagan went into Nevada, twice. . . . Laxalt's guy still lost that race. People didn't believe in it anymore. They saw the deficit. Democrats were going to make the agenda. Finished. Bob Dole back in the minority. . . . What would he have, forty-six votes? Forty-five?

He tried to do the satellite for Kansas. The damn thing wouldn't work. "How y'*dooonnn* there? . . . We on? . . . Yeah . . . How y'*dooonnn*? . . . okay . . ."

Soon he gave up and went back to the networks for the West Coast wrap-ups. Wasn't gonna run in Kansas for a long time. . . .

It was over in the Senate. Might be years until Dole got any power again. There was only one way he was going to get it now . . .

"Well, sure, I have an interest in '88 . . . Have to see whether people have an interest in Bob Dole . . ."

He wouldn't go into Jo-Anne's office. Just had Dean bring him a sandwich, between interviews. . . . Didn't want to see the faces in there, those kids . . . some of them weren't kids. Some had spent a lot of years here, waiting for their chance . . . chance was over now. Bob Dole was sixty-three this year. . . .

We can now project that Alan Cranston has retained his seat against a strong challenge from Ed Zschau . . .

"Well, Dan, maybe it'll give me a little more time. Won't have to be here every night, turn out the lights. . . . Yeah, hegh hegh, Bob Byrd's gonna have to turn out the lights now. Hegh hegh . . ."

He was getting his face right . . . Presidential. "Congratulate my friend Bob Byrd. Lotta able people on both sides of the aisle . . ."

And standing by live, now, we have Bob Dole . . .

It was after midnight when he finished with the networks. After one o'clock when he finished with the big-foot print guys. . . . Then he went back to the cameras, started taping for the overnights.

"Of course I have an interest in '88 . . . bipartisan spirit . . . people want to see that we're taking care of some serious problems we have . . ." Exposure you couldn't buy.

It wasn't till three in the morning that he finished the last interview. Elizabeth had gone home long ago. Now Dole got into the waiting car to go back to the Watergate, too. Dole told Riker before he left: yes to Brinkley and McLaughlin for this weekend . . . yes to them all now.

He'd be back after two hours' sleep to do three morning shows. Smile. . . . "Sure we can work with my friend Bob Byrd . . ."

It wasn't till the end of the week he found out his friend Bob Byrd wanted his office: not just Jo-Anne's with the chandeliers, but the whole thing. Wanted to throw him out of his office!

Be nice.

"Hegh hegh hegh, have to see if the people have an interest in Bob Dole. . . . Walked into the cloakroom the other day, and yelled, 'Mr. President!' Twenty guys turned around! Hegh hegh hegh hegh . . . But we've got serious problems in this country."

It was the only way. . . . The Other Thing had become the only thing.

4

1944

THEY WERE all kids on the *San Jacinto*. Just past his twentieth birthday, Lieutenant George Bush looked so young he didn't seem ready to operate a car, much less the biggest bomber aircraft in the Pacific fleet. He was only a year past winning his wings as the youngest flier in the Navy. He was tall and skinny, with a high forehead and wide-set eyes that looked out at the world with a precocious gravity from under soft and delicately curved brows. The rest of his face—the narrow cheeks and the line of his long, slender jaw—was hairless and smooth, saved from prettiness only by a generous, slightly cleft chin and the quick, lopsided, aw-heck grin that dismissed his own good looks and made him, so readily, one of the guys. Still, as he sat up from a slouch in his steel chair in the ready room, and peered at the coordinates on the board, then bent to his own course calculations, he had the same buckle-down, teen-in-a-hurry look his Andover masters saw two years before, when Captain Poppy had to hustle through a history quiz, to get out to practice for the Exeter game.

But today it was a job: one more crack at Chichi Jima. They'd gone at it yesterday but couldn't wipe out the target: a radio tower and four outbuildings. They ran into a hail of flak and lost a plane. Today was their last shot: the task force would be steaming south, right after the raid, out of the sector altogether, to link up with Admiral Halsey for the landings on the Palau Islands. The radio tower on Chichi was the Japanese link to the Palaus.

Bush grabbed his gear and started for the deck. He liked to get up there early to check over his plane . . . but Ted White stopped him on his way out: he'd been after Bush for weeks to take him along on a mission. Ted was a ship's gunnery officer, not a flier. Leo Nadeau was Bush's turret gunner. It was always Bush and Nadeau, and the radio man, Jack Delaney. They'd been a crew since they were stateside. But Ted was older than Bush, a family friend, a buddy of Poppy's Walker uncles, a Yale man like them, a good, quiet fellow. Bush would be glad to take him up . . . but why'd he have to pick today? Ted had to know, it was gonna be rough. . . . Still, Bush didn't like to say no to a friend. He told White to check it out with Skipper Melvin. But he'd better step on it!

That was one more mark of the mission's import: Don Melvin would fly lead today. Melvin was the squadron skipper, the man who taught them to do things with their bulky TBM Avengers that they never learned in flight school. The guys used to say they ought to win the Bent Nail—instead of the Iron Cross—for serving in his squadron, VT-51. D.J. Melvin liked catapult takeoffs and tight formations: he liked his pilots cool, clear-eyed, more levelheaded and determined than kids should have to be.

On deck now, Leo Nadeau got the word to stand down. An officer was going up in his place, "to check out the turrets." Leo knew that was bullshit. You check that stuff on deck. But he was just an enlisted man, so he stood down, as Ted White strapped into the turret on top, behind Bush, and Delaney climbed into his regular spot in the belly of the TBM.

Anyway, there wasn't time to argue: Bush had the plane in the catapult and they were off, pressed back against their seats by the rush, as the TBM climbed into formation—tight formation, the way Melvin liked it. They had an hour's run to the island and a linkup with planes from other ships. The sky was clear, hazy blue, just a few broken clouds—too few: there'd be no cover over Chichi.

They came in at fourteen thousand, then pushed over in a shallow dive to pick up speed before they got to attack altitude, eight thousand feet. They pushed into bombing dives, an angle of thirty-five degrees. They were falling against their shoulder belts. Leo Nadeau used to say the Avenger could fall faster than it could fly. The ground was rushing toward Bush, but the flak . . . black bursts of smoke all over the sky . . . the worst flak he'd ever seen. He was third man in. He aimed his plane's nose on the tail of the man ahead—Doug West—and pushed over. There was the tower, and Melvin's plane dropping straight for it, West and Bush after him. The buildings around the tower, communication buildings, had to be hit, if the skipper got the tower. . . . Bush was hung against his harness, his plane gaining speed as it fell, a ton of bombs racked below, his eyes locked on the gathering ground, eight thousand, seven, six . . . flak on all sides and above . . . he could see the walls of the buildings . . . just a minute now, and . . .

He felt a jarring lurch, a crunch, and his plane leapt forward, like a giant had struck it from below with a fist. Smoke started to fill the cockpit. He saw a tongue of flame streaming down the right wing toward the crease. Christ! The fuel tanks!

He called to Delaney and White—*We been hit!* He was diving. Melvin hit the tower dead on—four five-hundred-pounders. West was on the same beam. Bush could have pulled out. *Have to get rid of these bombs. Keep the dive . . . a few seconds . . .*

He dropped on the target and let 'em fly. The bombs spun down, the plane shrugged with release, and Bush banked away hard to the east. No way he'd get to the rendezvous point with Melvin. The smoke was so bad he couldn't see his gauges. Was he climbing? *Have to get to the water.* They were dead if they bailed out over land. The Japs killed pilots. *Gonna have to get out,* Bush radioed the skipper, called to his crew. No answer. *Does White know how to get to his chute?* Bush looked back for an instant. *God, was White hit?* He was yelling the order to bail out, turning right rudder to take the slipstream off their hatch . . . had to get himself out. He leveled off over water, only a few miles from the island . . . *more, ought to get out farther . . . that's it, got to be now.* . . . He flicked the red toggle switch on the dash—the IFF, Identification Friend or Foe—supposed to alert any U.S. ship, send a special frequency back to his own carrier . . . no other way to communicate, had to get out *now,* had to be . . . *NOW.*

Wind of a hundred twenty miles an hour tore away his canopy, tore at him like the claws of a beast, ripped him back at the tail of his plane, which he HIT . . . and then it was quiet. . . . *Hope to God Sayer packed the damn chute right.*

By rote, he found the ripcord, and the chute opened, but it was torn. He was falling fast. He'd hit his head and chute on the tail stabilizer. He was bleeding. He had to get out of the chute . . . if he got tangled up in the water, he'd drown before he could get to his raft. *Where's the raft? Where's Delaney? And White? God, was White hit?* There were no chutes on the water in front, but he couldn't yank around to see the other side. His head hurt like hell. His hands scrabbled at the chute release, a question mark of steel he had to open. Where were Delaney and White? The water rushed up to grab him.

The water, green water, was over his head. He was out of the chute and it drifted away as he kicked up for air, air—green water—air. It was all he could see, no raft, just water and sky. . . . *Have to swim, swim where?* He was gulping water, coughing and gulping. He heard noise over him, a plane, an Avenger, Melvin! *Skipper!* He was diving for Bush. No, not for Bush . . . over there, diving and climbing and diving again to the same spot. The raft. *The raft!* Bush kicked and scrambled through the water. There it was. *Oh, God, let it inflate.* . . . He draped his arms on the side of the raft and hauled himself out of the green. Now there were other planes overhead, another Avenger, and fighters, Hellcats. The Avenger was diving—Doug West. He'd seen the blood on Bush's face, dropped a medical kit. Bush hand-paddled for it.

There was no paddle. There was no fresh water: the container on the raft had broken in the fall. Bush was paddling with both hands, puking from fear and sea water, bleeding from the head. He got the med-kit, and with a shaky left hand, swabbed at himself with iodine. He got out his .38 revolver and checked it. Fat lot of good it would do him. The wind was blowing him back to the beach. He had to keep splashing, beating the sea with his hands. If the Japanese got him, they'd kill him, for sure.

He scanned the rolling green horizon on all sides, the boundary of his fearful new world. No yellow rafts. Just air, green water. The planes were gone. They had to get back to the squadron, the carrier, the task force. They'd radio back his position. Probably had the news on the bridge already, and at his CIC, Combat Information Center. Someone would come back. There were three men out here somewhere. If he could just hold on, keep beating the water, stay away from the island, find White and Delaney, they'd have to come back. Then he remembered—the briefing: *this was the last chance . . . the task force was turning south this morning, down to the Palaus, out of the sector. . . .* They were not coming back. They knew he was down. But they were not coming back!

On the deck of the *San Jacinto,* word spread that someone was down. News leaked from the bridge, like it always did, but they never really knew until the planes came back. And here they were, circling into a string for the landing: the fighters looked all right, but only three Avengers . . . and they landed, one after the other: Skipper . . . West . . . Moore. Then they knew. And the pilots on deck took this news like they always did. What was there to say? Someone muttered: "Jesus . . . George Herbert Walker Bush."

— ★ —

That was his nickname aboard the *San Jacinto:* George Herbert Walker Bush.

Everybody had a nickname. Stan Butchart was, naturally, Butch; Milt Moore, their first replacement pilot, was renamed Gracie, after the famous comedienne of the day; the hairless wardroom officer, D.E. Garrett, was called Skin; even the revered Skipper Melvin got a handle, in consequence of his bad overbite: behind his back he was Mortimer. That was the way it had to be on a ship like that: the *San Jacinto* was tiny for a carrier, just a flattop on a light cruiser hull, only thirty-three planes aboard. With just thirteen bomber pilots in the squadron, with so many hours together on missions and patrol, with their shared loss when one of their guys didn't come back, with so much endless waiting together, so many games of acey-deucy, volleyball in the hangar wells, sunning on the forecastle, movies on the hangar deck, so many mornings in the ready room, three meals a day in the wardroom, together, for week, after week, after week, every bit of that narrow life layered with familiarity, an accretion of common memory and private slang. So flying as fourth man in formation, directly below and behind the lead plane, was called "flying snifter," a term Bush invented. So the spot where they sunned, behind windbreaks on the forecastle, became the "front porch." And a certain kind of ice-cream sundae, available belowdecks, became a "gee-dunk." (No one could remember why.)

It wasn't a bad way to spend a war. No officer on the *San Jacinto* ever handled a shovel, spent a night in a foxhole, or had to be deloused. There was a daily ship's paper with wire reports on the news of the world, and a phonograph in the wardroom with Glenn Miller records. Coffee and toast, with real butter, or peanut butter, was available in the wardroom twenty-four hours a day. Officers ate three meals on white tablecloths, served by stewards in white coats, who'd offer each dish on silver trays, from which the gentlemen could take what they wanted. They had foods unavailable at home: roast beef and steak for supper, bacon and eggs in the morning, fruit juice, cream for their coffee. The ship made its own ice cream. The ship's baker made bread daily. They had a pastry chef from the Hilton in New York, for pies, cakes, sweet rolls, crullers.

Withal, there was a brilliant clarity to the life, a sense of purpose and progress that was the greatest comfort to twenty-year-olds: they were out to beat the Japs; the Japs were evil, killers, yellow lesser-lives who started it all with a sneak attack. Hadn't the boys sailed into Pearl? They'd seen the evidence themselves! There were no shades of gray in the picture. They were a team, with a mission. They had a job, beyond survival. That was the only thing that made sense when a plane didn't come back . . . one of their thirteen, just gone. . . . What was there to say? The guy was gone. There was his chair. They didn't replace him right away. The chair would be there, empty, for weeks. Meanwhile, there was still the war. There was always, thank God, a job to do. Once, coming back from a mission over Guam, the bombers circled and settled on the deck, one after the other, all accounted for. But as Bush watched the fighters land, one of the pilots missed the trip wire. His plane spun over the slick steel, into a gun turret manned by four seamen. The gun crew was wiped out in a fiery instant, and there, just a few yards from Bush on deck, was the severed leg of a sailor. . . . George Bush, nineteen years old, just stared at the thing. . . . *The shoe is still on it.* . . . Then, the chief petty officer bellowed: "Awright, you bastards. We still got planes up there, and they can't land in this goddam mess." There was still, there was always, a job.

Problem was, on the bombing runs, they were never on their own, or even in the lead. They were such a small air group, they were always the tagalongs, joining a larger force from other ships. There were four carriers in their group and four groups in the task force. That meant hundreds of planes, and missions divvied up among the ships, according to a plan that no one seemed to know—no one on their ship, anyway. It was sobering: how huge was the war, and how small were they, their ship, their squadron, their own plane. Sometimes, it was hard to feel that what you did—you, your own mother's son— meant a good goddam in the whole million-mauling maw of the war.

But not for Bush. Hell, he didn't have any doubts, you could see that. He said it, too: he liked being part of a team. Liked the *cahm-rah-deree* of his three-man plane. On shipboard, he seemed to know more of the enlisted men than other pilots did. The Navy tried to discourage that: too much fraternization could lead to a breakdown of discipline . . . chain of command, see. In the air, that pilot was the captain of his vessel: the Navy wanted a minimum of chat, and instant obedience from the crew. But Bush would chat about anything—airplanes, baseball, the food back home . . . his girlfriend back home. . . . Despite regulations, her name was painted on the side of the plane—*Barbara.*

It wasn't that he bucked the rules; he always accommodated the rules. But his captaincy sat easy on him, and he didn't mind having fun. Sometimes, coming back from patrol, when the plane to relieve him was already in the air, Bush would get on the intercom and tell Delaney to drop a flare. So Delaney would cram a smoke flare down the tube, and when it hit the water, Bush would wheel the TBM around and throw it into a dive for the water, so his men could have a good time with their guns. In the ready room, after general quarters, if he wasn't on the first mission and running to his plane, he'd stand up from his seat in the second row and turn, always with a grin and a wave, and wander back to the enlisted men, with a "Hey, Tony . . . Jake . . ."

That was the thing they all saw about Bush: he was a good Joe, no stickler for rank. He was *not like that*. That was the point about the nickname: it was like calling a bald guy Curly. . . . His four names, his boys' school slang, his Big-Family-Back-East roots . . . he was trying so hard to be *not that way*. He was so eager to be a *friend to all* . . . that they just had to stick him with it: George Herbert Walker Bush. . . .

— ★ —

What they never knew, what they couldn't have known, was how thoroughly Bush was trained to be Not Like That. It was the central tenet of Poppy's world in Greenwich. The Bushes were always Not That Way.

You see, they so easily could have been. After all, Grandfather Walker moved the family from St. Louis to play with the Harrimans and Vanderbilts and Astors. Pops Walker had gone off to school at Stonyhurst, in England, with his valet (rhymed with "mallet"), and ever after had a taste for the life of the polo-and-ponies crowd. By the time Poppy came along, Gampy Walker not only had the Point, up in Maine, he also had the big shooting place, an old plantation in South Carolina, where the family used to gather for Christmas, and that palace out on Long Island, with the marble floors, the swimming pool, two butlers . . . you didn't often see two butlers, even in the thirties. Or, for that matter, two Rolls-Royces: Pops had one, and one for Grandmother. Ganny Walker never drove in her life. Not that she was happy about it. Her chauffeur, John, was the kind who was always talking. "Y'know, I don't think I'd like bein' President," John was saying one day in the Rolls. "I don't think I'd take th'job if they gave itta me, I wouldn't . . ." Ganny Walker just cranked up the glass that walled off the driver's seat. "As if he ever could think," she said.

Still, there was a hint of Midwest breeze that lingered in the family air, in the vigor of their play, in their open, hard-knuckled talk about business. That was the difference between the Walkers and New York's forever-monied, the ownership class of America: Astor, Rockefeller, Ogden Phipps. (Ganny used to say, a bit breathlessly: "They own the very sidewalks that we walk on!") The Walkers were only a few years removed from operation of the biggest dry-goods business west of the Mississippi. It was only in the span of G.H. Walker's career that the family made the move from St. Louis, from the class of "good families" in the heartland who owned factories or stores, who actually made or sold merchandise, to the class of pure owners, who invested in such business. So the Walkers still had links with the few families in each town—Pittsburgh, Cleveland, Akron, Detroit—who somehow knew one another, from business or from school (back East), or from some cotillion long ago. . . . And so it was, when Pops Walker's children grew up, they married children from the good Midwest: Herbie Walker married Mary Carter, of St. Louis; Johnny married Louise Mead, Dayton; Jimmy wed Sarah Mitchell, Detroit; Lou married Grace White, from St. Louis; and, of course, Dottie married Prescott Bush, the son of an officer in the Buckeye Steel Castings Co., of Columbus, O.

In Pres she found the apotheosis of midwestern virtue. Prescott Bush spent the bulk of his adult life in the monied sanctum of the Harrimans themselves: he was a managing partner of Brown Brothers Harriman, private bankers to the owning class. He belonged to the clubs of New York's forever-monied. He lived among them in Greenwich (his daily commuting pal was a Rockefeller). But Pres was forever Not Like That. Couldn't care less for anything ritzy. One time he got roped into a cruise with Averell Harriman and Pops Walker on their new boat, *The Pawnee,* a hundred-fifty-foot miracle of shining brass and mahogany, fireplace in the salon, crew of a score or so . . . the best of everything afloat. Pres was bored to death, couldn't wait to get off. He never could stand a lot of fussy feeding and primping. What was the fun in that?

Of course, once Pres brought Dottie back from the Midwest, where he started his career, and took up his post in New York with the Harrimans and his father-in-law, there was help in the Bush house, too: a woman who cooked, and her husband, who drove the kids to Greenwich Country Day School, and then, too, an Irish maid. But the Bushes didn't talk about their "chauffeur," their "housekeeper." It was Alex and Antonina, or, to strangers, "lovely people . . . the couple who live with us . . ." The point was, it was Not Like That. They were . . . like family! Lizzie Larkin, the maid, just adored Pres, jumped up aflutter in the mornings, delighted to help him on with his coat. Late afternoons, just before train time, she'd burst into the library, to plump up the pillows and make right for Mr. Bush, shooing the kids away in her brogue: "Y'chidren slouchin' around here, and yer fath'r workin' all day hard. Ah! None of you'll be the gentleman yer fath'r is. Now, get out, and let me tidy here! He'll be home in a minute now!" The message was constant, day by day: their father was a man of important work. Someday, perhaps, they'd earn their own crowns. Meanwhile, the Bush house held no princes of the realm.

Sure enough, when Alex brought Mr. Bush home from the station, Pres would go straight to the library, where he'd listen to the radio news, and then to his favorite bandleader, Fred Waring. Then, it was supper, and off to another important meeting, number three-hundred-something for the year. Or back to the telephone closet for important calls: father was not to be disturbed. Seldom would Dottie and Pres spend two nights in a row out at dinners. Though their friends, the Harrimans, the Lovetts, Ellery James, invited them always, they eschewed the constant round of parties, the evening-dress-Park-Avenue scene. Occasionally, Pres and Dottie hosted a dinner of their own, and the children were sent to the upper floor, while the flowers were arranged and the drinks table set up. But the family recalled these as stiff affairs. The real parties were Sunday afternoons, when Pres's pals from the Midwest would show: Neil Mallon from Cleveland, the Hurds from Chicago, Henry Isham from Chicago . . . or sometimes, the Howard brothers, Yale men, who could play four hands on one piano, and after spaghetti, there'd be singing on the porch. Pres loved to sing.

Practice with his quartet, or with the choir—now there was an evening of fun! He brought to the practice of singing the same talent and serious craft he required of himself on a golf course: he was not in it just to hack around. He'd sit on the morning train to New York, singing to himself, then writing down the notes, scoring a new harmony for his quartet to try later that week. When he and Dottie got their house in Florida, on the private Jupiter Island preserve, Pres abandoned the island's proper Episcopal church, and sang with the Presbyterian choir in Hobe Sound, on the mainland, with the tradesmen and their wives, who really loved to sing. But it wasn't just the singing: there was a statement in it, too. To be a Bush was to be unimpressed by money and its splendors; it was to be *not* a Mellon, or a Reed, and certainly not their acolyte; it was to be, pointedly, Not Like That.

The Ping-Pong table in the front hall in Greenwich was more than a statement about games: it was an explicit rejection of the lives ("Do lower your voice, dear. The servants will hear!") around them. Pres used to joke about the "economic royalists," and at the table, the children would hear his arch report to Dottie:

"The So-and-So's have a terrible problem. They've lost their *caretaker* in Bar Harbor! What's *worse* is the caretaker on Long Island won't go *up* to Bar Harbor! . . . What *ever* are they to do?"

Even the economic royalists at Walker's Point got to Pres, with their exclusive Sunday lobster suppers, and the pews at St. Ann's Church, up front, on the right, where no one but Walkers would presume to sit. For a few years, he summered instead at Fishers Island, in Long Island Sound, where things were Not That Way.

When Pres spoke well of a man, his admiration likely had to do with service rendered to society or its institutions. He didn't have much good to say about those for whom money was the goal. Of course, one wanted to have enough, as did he, to provide for the family. But after that, what was the point? His own father was a man of important service: founder of the Community Chest in Columbus, O. To be a Bush was to be of benefit: that was the legacy.

Pres came of age with the notion that he might become a lawyer, and somehow go into politics. But the Great War intervened, and when he came back from his captaincy in France (which was "quite exciting and, of course, a wonderful experience"), he hadn't time or temperament for three more years of law school. Anyway, he was to be a family man, so he started his career in business. But even as he worked his way to partner in the banking firm run by his father-in-law and Averell Harriman, he had the idea that service was the measure of a man. Even in the worst of the stock market slump, after all, when business was toughest, and the Harriman interests were being merged with the older firm of Brown Brothers & Co., Averell Harriman lent most of his time and talent to Franklin Roosevelt in the White House, and to the New Deal's boards and commissions. Pres was not yet asked to serve at that Harrimanesque altitude. But as soon as Brown Brothers, Harriman and Co. dug out from the crash (and the partners got their accounts out of the red), Pres got elected to the Greenwich Town Meeting, where he served as Moderator for most of the next two decades.

He cut a fine figure there, too. He knew enough of Robert's Rules to keep order, but he wasn't a stickler for parliamentary niceties. He was never afraid to take the meeting in hand and guide it simply by his own sense of where it ought to go. "A good, firm show" was what he liked to run, and after all, who'd brook him? He was six-foot-four, with a full head of hair, deep-set blue-gray eyes, a man of great stature and athletic grace, with his beautiful Whiffenpoof bass voice, and a Cesar Romero thousand-candlepower smile that was devastating to women. He was imposing enough to keep the meeting on track without ever raising his voice; he never cut anyone short, always took a lively interest and large view of the town's affairs. The great thing about Mr. Bush, other members of the meeting used to say, was that *a man like that* would listen to everybody's point of view. Most of the town services he could well afford to do without. But that wasn't the point: he was giving something back, serving, as a man ought. So night after night, he was there at the meetings; Pres knew as much as anyone about the sewers and the sidewalks, and the public schools that his children would never attend.

— ★ —

Where were White and Delaney? Did they bail out over the island? Why didn't they wait? Did they think he wasn't gonna make the water? Delaney had to know. They *did* a water landing, *did it before*. . . . The TBM was spewing oil when they took off. Bush set it down on the water, gentle as a mother's kiss. They paddled away, all three in a raft, paddling for their lives as the plane went down and the bombs went off under the sea, and they all three—twenty years old and alive, Dear God, Alive!—whaled away at the water while they started to sing, Nadeau started to sing . . . *Sailing, sailing, over the bounding main* . . . till a destroyer fished them out, singing, alive. . . . Hah! . . . Nadeau'll remember. Nadeau'll tell them, Bush was good.

What did it matter? They weren't coming back. They had orders, heading south. They were leaving, they were gone. Half the pilots in the squadron were gone—forever. Now he knew what happened to them. They were good, too. But it *didn't matter*. It wasn't about *him*. That was the point . . . what was the point now? What did it matter?

There was his service. He was good. No water. So he died.
Dear God . . .

— ★ —

Pres Bush chose Andover for Pressie and George because he thought it the most democratic school. Pres himself had put in a few years at a public school in Columbus, with German children, Italians, Irish, Negroes. He always thought that a benefit, especially in politics. But his boys had known only the privileged preserve of Greenwich Country Day. Pres chose a school that would be "broadening." In those days, Andover made a nice point of taking some scholarship boys who were "different." Andover styled itself not a standard boys prep, in the Eton-English mold, like Groton, or St. Paul's, safe green islands for the forever-rich to come of age in proper company and style. It was not like Choate, where they took you in for your name, and thereafter, by whatever means, helped you get through. No, on its own terms, Phillips Academy, Andover, Mass., old P.A., proudly, was Not That Way.

P.A. declared that its business was making the leaders of tomorrow. The place reeked of promise: great doings to come. The motto of the academy was *Finis origine pendet,* The End Depends upon the Beginning. Even thirteen-year-olds like Poppy Bush were encouraged to keep their sights on that end, that life of virtue and purpose.

The striving wasn't about scholarship: most of the study was rote. (In fact, classes were called "recitations.") And although the tweedy, absentminded headmaster, Dr. Claude M. Feuss, urged them over and over to read, to ponder "the great books, the deeper classics," the fact was, with sports and clubs, meals, chapel, recitations . . . there just wasn't time. Andover men (they were always *men*) were joiners, doers, men of action. Philosophic or political talk was all very well for "dicking" (bull sessions) at night in some fellow's room. But all the best fellows were "sound" in their beliefs—in other words, they thought pretty much what everybody ought to.

In fact, their politics weren't much different from those of their fathers in their mansions and boardrooms. The student newspaper, the *Phillipian,* hammered at Roosevelt's New Deal as "anti-democratic centralized government . . . anti-business . . . fuzzy headed theoretical nonsense." The problem with the New Dealers, of course, was they just weren't *sound.* As the paper opined, endorsing Landon over Roosevelt, the year before Poppy arrived, Roosevelt offered a government ". . . bent on browbeating free enterprise and regimenting personal initiative. . . . Many youths have been kept on the dole, because the government persisted in shackling business and free enterprise. . . . In some respects, we think the New Dealers do not know their own minds. While they mean good, they do harm. . . ."

What was the point of fiddling with the great institutions and traditions of a system that had floated their forebears (and now, them) so surely, buoyantly, to the shores of well-being? No, the Andover man was preparing to serve those institutions, to stand at the helm for another generation, lest the great ship lose its way! In fact, the icon of Andover Hill was not the bald and befuddled academic, Dr. Feuss . . . but instead, the chairman of the academy's board, Henry L. Stimson. Now *there* was a life for the Andover man: Secretary of War under President Taft, Battalion Commander of Artillery during the Great War, Wall Street lawyer in the twenties, Governor General in the Philippines under Coolidge, Secretary of State to Hoover, and then, despite lifelong loyalty to the Republican Party, Secretary of War again in the Cabinet of FDR. . . . Stimson was, said the student who introduced him for a speech to Poppy and his classmates, "a living and vital representative of our ways and of our type of existence, who is out setting an example to the whole nation, . . . living proof that the Andover Way is the way of men who guide the fortunes of nations."

What a bracing prospect was the rest of life, surveyed from the crest of Andover Hill! It was a glad and glorious path that led away from Phillips Hall, first to Yale (where P.A.'s best and brightest went to college), and thence to the boardrooms, the corridors of power, the Cabinet table.

Of course, their place at the helm was *not a birthright*—Andover was Not Like That. It was by merit that the Andover Man belonged. But what a Great and Good stroke of fortune for Poppy Bush: the Andover Way required of a man precisely the qualities he brought from home!

"The basic Andover code," said the student *Phillipian,* "assumes every student is first and foremost a gentleman." Honesty, loyalty, generosity, sportsmanship, and throughout, a becoming modesty (a bulwark for the years of triumph to come) . . . these were the qualities one needed, to belong.

He was only thirteen when he arrived, and had to struggle at first to fit in with his classmates, who were all at least a year older. (When Pressie had gone off to school at age five, little Poppy couldn't stand being alone in the house, so he'd started Greenwich Country Day a year early.) He was still awfully small, in the fall of '37, and hardly seemed marked for stardom—not at all.

But then, strangely, a great stroke of fortune: in his third year at P.A., Poppy got sick, an infection in his shoulder that threatened to spread. There were no antibiotics at the time. Pres and Dottie were worried half to death. It took a month, with the best of care at Massachusetts General, the finest hospital in the country, and then, some specialists in New York, before all the doctors were sure that the boy would recover without ill effect.

The upshot was that Poppy repeated his third year at Andover, in the fall of '40. And when he came back, of course, he'd done all the schoolwork before, and that gave him more time for sports, where he showed what a year of growth and health could do for a young man, and where he was just as big as any boy, and felt himself, in fact, older and more mature than they, having been, in a sense, through all this before, and so, better able to help them out, to lead, as captain of the junior teams, on which he starred and swelled anew in the increasing approbation of his classmates and the older fellows, who noticed for the first time: here was a fellow who could play the game, and play it well! . . . And, of course, that meant he was tapped for the best club, and then as president of the Greeks, and then elected to the student council, and secretary of the student council, and treasurer of the student council, and then a student deacon, Society of Inquiry president, editorial board of the *Phillipian,* business board of the yearbook, Tea Dance committee, Senior Prom committee, president of the senior class . . . and captain of the soccer team, captain of the baseball team, and manager of the basketball team (until the coach saw him shoot one day and made him suit up as a player). . . . He became, in the Andover man's argot, an all-rounder. Wasn't it great how it worked out?

But the best thing was, he always watched out for the other guy, the younger men, the weaker ones. The great thing about Poppy, other fellows at school used to say, was that *a fellow like him* would still talk to everybody, just as friendly to the juniors and lower-middles as he was to the grandest senior. In fact, he could drive you nuts: when the basketball coach told him he ought to suit up and play, Poppy said, "Oh, I couldn't do that! The other fellows worked hard to make the team! . . ." Finally, the coach, Frank DiClemente, had to tell him to shut up and put on his gym clothes. It was that, or wring his noble little neck. . . . But the point was, Poppy never sought his honors: he never had to, he had so many friends. And that *was* the Andover Way. One time, the *Phillipian* polled the students: "Do you think studies, friendships, or athletics are the most important in the long run?" Seventy-eight percent chose friendships. "The average student," the newspaper concluded, "came to Andover with making contacts uppermost in his mind."

It was the surest mark of his stardom that he never had to be out for himself. It was bad form to be out for oneself. Andover men not only wore the Blue like the fellows at Yale, there was an ethic they had in common, too: they were for God, Country, and Old Blue. An Andover man had to put something larger ahead of himself. Of course, Poppy was sound on that.

That was at the root of the excitement, as the war in Europe filled the papers, during their last two years, and it began to look like the men of '42 would have their chance to act in the world's highest drama: a war to rival their dads' Great War, a world for them to remake thereafter; this time, perhaps, more in their image. Clearly, Stimson heard the call to duty in 1940, when he took the post as War Secretary. (The word on campus was that Stimson was for U.S. entry, but FDR, as usual, dithered in politics.) If the U.S. did get in "over there," no one on Andover Hill doubted these young men would be called, to lead. What a chance! To serve, to prove their mettle, to lead as they'd been raised to do, to command! Stimson came to speak to the seniors that year, 1940, while the Battle of Britain crackled from the radio every night. Certainly the world faced dark days, the great man said.

"But as I look into your faces and realize your responsibilities, I am filled, not with pity for you in what you are facing, but with a desire to congratulate you on your great opportunity.

"I envy you that opportunity.

"I would to God that I were young enough to face it with you."

All at once, the alumni news was filled with pictures of dashing young men in helmets, goggles, leather jackets: flying was just the thing, the only single combat in mechanized war, the knighthood of the modern service. The Andover men were leaving Yale, crossing the border, to sign up in Canada with the Royal Air Force. How could an Andover man stand idly by?

And, then, just on that glorious autumn day when Andover beat Exeter (by one point!) to finish an undefeated football season, the Japanese fleet sailed for Pearl Harbor. And two weeks later, just as Poppy was thrashing George "Red Dog" Warren in a long, do-or-die Ping-Pong match at AUV (the top club at school), the Japanese struck Pearl, the news spread in minutes, and Poppy and Red Dog put down their paddles and hurried back to the dorm. It was the same path they trod every day, from AUV, past the Cochran Chapel . . . but now, everything was different. The air was electric. They were at war! . . .

"We stand," trumpeted the *Phillipian,* "as a unit against the common foe . . . the yellow peril of Nippon."

But all at once, their elders got cold feet! The young men of Andover Hill were told right away: they must stay in school! Dr. Feuss tried to keep P.A. calm, and bent to its business. At a special assembly, the following day, he told the men they must not run off to war, but let the draft fill the ranks, according to need and scientific methods. Pres Bush wrote to Poppy the same day: he ought to stay in school, go on to Yale. There'd be time after that to serve the flag.

But they were at war! This was his chance! Sure, Poppy would ask his coaches and teachers what they thought, but this was a personal thing, a matter of the code. The point was to know your own mind! If anyone doubted what Poppy would do, they had only to watch him on stage at that assembly, December 8, the morning after . . .

At ten o'clock, the whole school gathered in George Washington Hall, and Poppy was up front as senior class president. And when "The Star-Spangled Banner" started, the men were still slouching in front of their seats, as they always did in assembly. "Your country's at war!" said Dr. Feuss. "I expect when 'The Star-Spangled Banner' is played, I expect everyone here to be at attention!" But still there were a few wise guys who didn't know their world had changed. They were dicking around in the back! Poking each other and laughing, like they always had! And up on stage, Poppy Bush was burning! They were mocking the flag! They were mocking Dr. Feuss! The bald doctor was standing there, helpless and frail, while they ignored him! *While we're at war!* Poppy Bush took a small step forward, and stared them down. He glared at them so hard, so visibly, that soon he had their gaze on him. And from the stage, in front of the men, likely for the first time in his life, Poppy Bush curled his upper lip in an ugly sneer of contempt.

By the time Christmas break rolled around, and he went to a dance, back home in Greenwich, where he met an auburn-haired beauty, Barbara Pierce, sixteen years old (and so eager to know him!), he didn't even mention staying in school. They sat out a waltz (Poppy never could waltz), and then sat out the next dance, and the next. But in all that talk, there was no confusion about what he was going to do. He was going to war. All the best fellows were. He would turn eighteen on Commencement Day, just a week after The Game (baseball with Exeter!) . . . and that was the big day. Poppy was going to sign up to fly. The Navy had a program that would get him his wings in less than a year. Gold Navy Wings! The knighthood!

On that day, Stimson arrived once again, in his bulletproof car, to address the school: the war would be long, the Secretary said. In good time, they would be called upon to lead, to rescue the right, to remake the world. But they would serve their country better by going on to college and getting as much education as they could, before they donned the uniform.

Wait, Stimson said, and let the draft do its work.

After the speech, Pres Bush met Poppy in the hallway outside the auditorium. Pres didn't have to bend down now to look straight into his son's eyes. "Well, George," he said in his big bass voice, "did the Secretary say anything to change your mind?"

"No, sir," Poppy said. "I'm going in."

Pres nodded, then shook his son's hand.

—★—

This was where it ended? The promise, the service, great doings to come, ended here in a world of green water, blue mist, alone, small . . . *this is it?* What was all that for, all the doing, trying, dear God, the blessed . . . *life,* what was that for? . . . But he kept searching the edge of his world, the hazy divide between air . . . green water . . . for the grand, bulking, blooming island of steel with the Stars and Stripes—all the guys! They had to come back! God, where were they . . . where were they where were they where were they . . .

Have to keep going, keep away, paddle, slap, pull, paddle, nothing out here, nothing but water, no water, no water, haze and water, blue and green, a speck over there, spots, bright bursting spots, and a speck, maybe it's a ship! No, not a ship, too small, not growing, yes growing, too small, not a ship, not the guys, slap to where, my hand! What's that thing it's taller, yes it's taller! It's taller, dear God, it's there yes what? Not a ship! Can't be a ship, just a speck, black dot, is this how it ends, seeing spots? God, God it's growing. A SUB! A SUB! A PERISCOPE DID THEY SEE ME GOD DID THEY SEE ME OVER HERE! OVER HERE HEY HERE HEY HERE I AM HERE ME HERE HEYYYY!

The conning tower rose from the water, and Bush, dazed, bobbing, saw the hatch open and there was a man. *Jesus, what if it's Japs?* . . . There was something on his face. He had something up to his face. Something black. A beard! He had a beard! *NO JAPS WITH BEARDS!* A bearded seaman was holding something up, as Bush slapped and tore at the water toward the sub. A U.S. submarine, in three thousand miles of ocean, here was a U.S. submarine, come to get him! Dear God, come for HIM!

They got him, sailors on the deck now, the shape of the sub on the water, they pulled his raft, grabbed for him, pulled him up on shaky legs onto the steel deck, sweet Jesus, steel! And the seaman he saw was standing there, watching with this thing up to his face, a camera, a movie camera. They were filming. Three thousand godforsaken miles of ocean. They came to get him. They pulled him out. And they filmed it.

He'd been on the raft two hours.

"Welcome aboard, sir . . ."

The steel stairs poked up crazily at his legs as they half hauled him, half lowered him into a world of dark red light and overused air, clanking steel and the smell of men. The hatch closed. They were getting out, getting the hell out of there.

"Welcome aboard, sir . . ."

They stretched him out flat, swabbed his head. He'd be all right, he heard them say. The guys on the *Finback* always liked this, this pilot rescue duty, when they fished them out and watched them wake up to a new world below the sea. . . . What would the guy say?

"Welcome aboard the *Finback,* sir . . ."

But as the guys on the *Finback* remembered it, Bush was distraught, kept asking for his crew, half-delirious. . . . Then, no words, just tears.

— ★ —

He was on the sub for a month, while it hunted the Pacific for Japanese ships, and when the *Finback* dropped him off at Midway, he likely could have fiddled a ticket home. The Navy didn't want shaky pilots, men with second thoughts. But Bush hitched a ride west across the ocean, and then another to his ship, back to the guys. Of course, they greeted him like a lost brother:

"George Herbert Walker Bush!"

No one asked much about the day he was shot down. They knew how it was: he'd lost two friends.

There were a half-dozen more missions in the Philippines, but VT-51's number was up. By December, they were steaming home. Bush got to Greenwich on Christmas Eve. Poppy made it back! After that horrible telegram, saying he was shot down! He was *here*! Christmas Eve! Everyone was crying, laughing, hugging. He looked great! He was home! It was like a movie!

And then, after New Year's, in his snappy dress blues, he married his dark-haired sweetheart, Barbara Pierce. What was the point of dawdling? It could all end in a puff of smoke—just like *that.* There was a honeymoon, just a few days, on Sea Island, off the Georgia coast, and then a new posting to Virginia Beach. Of course, he'd have to go back to the war. They were only halfway to Tokyo. He'd get another squadron, and Bar would go back to college, to Smith. . . . But then, Truman dropped the bomb, and they got the news: the Nips had folded! No invasion! No more war! It was over! The Blessed Confluence!

Poppy was out of the Navy in a month, off to Yale the same September. What was the point of dawdling? Three years of his life were gone. There was a child on the way. There sure wasn't time to moon about the war, to talk about the day the plane went down, Delaney and White (never did know what happened to them), or the way they came to get him, Lieutenant George Herbert Walker Bush, out of thousands of miles of ocean. He had the Air Medal and two Gold Stars, and then the Distinguished Flying Cross: he was a hero, but he wasn't going to bring that up. He'd done his part. That was all he'd say.

He didn't even pick up any cheap points with Bar, saying he'd thought of her when he thought he was a goner, in the ocean. And she, being Bar, didn't ask if he did.

No one in his family could remember talking about it. Must have been dreadful, they agreed. And, being Walkers, and Bushes, they didn't bring it up.

It was only years later, when he got into politics and had to learn to retail bits of his life, that he ever tried to put words around the war.

His first attempts, in the sixties, were mostly about the *cahm-rah-deree* and the spirit of the American Fighting Man. The Vietnam War was an issue then, and Bush was for it. (Most people in Texas were.) He said he learned "a lot about life" from his years in the Navy—but he never said what the lessons were.

Later, when peace was in vogue, Bush said the war had "sobered" him with a grave understanding of the cost of conflict—he'd seen his buddies die. The voters could count on him not to send their sons to war, because he knew what it was.

Still later, when he turned Presidential prospect, and every bit of his life had to be melted down to the coin of the realm—character—Bush had to essay more thoughts about the war, what it meant to him, how it shaped his soul. But he made an awful hash of it, trying to be jaunty. He told the story of being shot down. Then he added: "Lemme tell ya, that'll make you start to think about the separation of church and state . . . ."

Finally, in a much-edited transcript of an interview with a minister whom he hired as liaison to the born-again crowd, Bush worked out a statement on faith and the war: something sound, to cover the bases. It wasn't foxhole Christianity, and he couldn't say he saw Jesus on the water—no, it was quieter than that. . . . But there, on the *Finback,* he spent his time standing watch on deck in the wee hours, silent, reflective, under the bright stars . . .

"It was wonderful and energizing, a time to talk to God.

"One of the things I realized out there all alone was how much family meant to me. Having faced death and been given another chance to live, I could see just how important those values and principles were that my parents had instilled in me, and of course how much I loved Barbara, the girl I knew I would marry. . . ."

That was not quite how he was recalled by the men of the *Finback.* Oh, they liked him: a real funny guy. And they gave him another nickname, Ellie. That was short for Elephant. What they recollected was Bush in the wardroom, tossing his head and emitting on command the roaring trumpeted squeal of the enraged pachyderm; it was the most uncanny imitation of an elephant.

Nor were "sobered" or "reflective" words that leapt to Bar's mind when she remembered George at that time. The image she recalled was from their honeymoon, when she and George strolled the promenades, amid the elderly retirees who wintered at that Sea Island resort. All at once, George would scream "AIR RAID! AIR RAID!" and dive into the shrubs, while Bar stood alone and blushing on the path, prey to the pitying glances of the geezers who clucked about "that poor shell-shocked young man."

But there was, once, a time when he talked about the war, at night, at home, to one friend, between campaigns, when he didn't have to cover any bases at all.

"You know," he said, "it was the first time in my life I was ever scared.

"And then, when they came and pulled me out . . ." (Him, Dottie Bush's son, out of a million miles of empty ocean!)

"Well . . ." Bush trailed off, pleasantly, just shaking his head.

1945

BOB DOLE didn't want to go to war. He was doing what he wanted, at KU, in the Kappa Sig house, doing what he never had time to do before: fooling around.

He was just ornery enough to be a good pledge. There was a pledge brother with a motorcycle, a big old Harley, weighed about a *ton*. Bob and some of the others hauled that bike up to a third-floor bedroom, then wouldn't help the fellow bring it down. That sealed Bob's fame. He even sailed through the hazing. Hell Week, the "actives" made freshmen wear burlap underwear to class. Bob laughed that off. The older guys got staves from a barrel factory, to whack the pledges into line. Bob said, "I've heard so much about those boards, I better find out how bad it's gonna be." So he made one of the actives haul off and whack him—hard as he could. Pretty near drove him through the wall. Bob said, "Well, that wasn't so bad." That was the last time anybody hit him.

He was going out for football, basketball, and track, so he kept up his training. He asked a friend coming from Russell to bring his concrete weights in her car. And he kept up his running, every day, before the others were awake. He was waiting tables in the house to pay his dues, and he had a milk route, dawn Saturdays, that earned him pocket money. A Big Man on Campus, like Bob Dole intended to be, had to have money to spend. . . . Grace McCandless was the most beautiful girl on campus, and Bob Dole, freshman, invited her home for Christmas. (Bina was so excited, she baked twice as many cookies.) Before he left in December, Bob was elected vice president of Kappa

Sigma. In his first term! But with all the new things he was trying that year, something had to slip: his grade point slid below the gentleman's C, and he couldn't make initiation. He was still a pledge in December, when the Japanese bombed Pearl Harbor, and Bob Dole's bright new world started to change.

He hung on at KU as long as he could. Heck, people said the war might be over before they got to him. He ran track that spring, finished the school year and started another. He played another season of football, then basketball, and more than a year after Pearl Harbor, Bob was still at school. But it got to be obvious that every man was going. Pretty soon his draft board would turn up his number—they were already coming for Kenny, back in Russell—so Bob looked to his chances, and signed up for the Army Enlisted Reserve Corps. That way, at least he'd get to finish the term.

What did he know about the war in Europe? KU, in Lawrence, was the farthest east he'd ever been. When the Army called him in '43, and sent him off to basic training, they gave him his first plane ride. Heck, his first bus ride! Turned out, Bob and Kenny ended up in basic at the same time, the summer of '43, at Camp Barkley, near Abilene, Texas. So Bina bought herself a train ticket, and showed up at the base, blew past the sentry: What was he going to do, shoot her? Bina marched down the dusty main street of camp, looking for her boys. The MPs tried to talk her into leaving, but she'd have none of it. "I've got two boys here and I've come to visit." They had to call the camp commandant to deal with her. "Ma'am, you cannot go walking around here. If you'll just wait, we'll get your boys for you."

But soon, they were far out of her reach. Kenny was shipped to the Pacific. Bob signed up for Army Engineering School, in the strange new world of Brooklyn, New York. After that, he was transferred to Camp Polk, Louisiana, then to Camp Breckenridge, in Kentucky, for antitank gunnery. By the spring of 1944, he'd made corporal and applied for officer training. The news from Europe was better and better: the U.S. was marching up the boot of Italy, Mussolini was out of power. As Bob Dole reported to Fort Benning, Georgia, for his three-month Officer Candidate School, the Allies were fighting their way off the beaches in Normandy. By the time he got his lieutenancy, Paris was free, the Germans were pulling back. . . . Who could tell if he'd get there in time to fire a shot?

There was time. The invasions of Europe had taken a fearful toll among the junior officers who led platoons. By December 1944, just as George Bush was steaming home across the Pacific, Bob Dole was headed east, across the Atlantic. It was just before Christmas when he pitched up outside Rome, where the Army maintained a replacement camp, from which to deal out officers to plug the gaps in its ranks.

— ★ —

The first thing everyone noticed about Bob Dole was his strength. He was six-foot-two, a hundred ninety-four pounds. Then, too, he always wore a tank jacket that gave his upper body more bulk. The guy was big as a house. In fact, his body almost kept him out of the fighting. In Rome, he ran into Dean

Nesmith, the trainer for Phog Allen's KU teams. Nesmith was a taskmaster, an ex–football hero with a prognathous jaw, and no tolerance for whiners or weaklings. Now he was in the Army's Special Services unit: sports and games for the guys behind the lines. He knew Dole, liked him: Bob was a kid who'd never quit. So he tried to get Dole into his outfit, as one of the trainers, a coach for the troops.

But too late: the Army had milled out orders for Dole to fill a slot with the Eighty-fifth Mountain Regiment, Third Battalion. The mountain troops were fighting their way up the spine of Italy, in a drive to the broad Po Valley, and beyond, to the Alps, to cut off the Germans before they could fall back to reinforce the Reich. At least, that was the plan: like most things in Italy, nothing went according to plan. The whole Italian invasion was a sop to Stalin, who demanded a second front in 1943. The U.S. went along, but insisted that no men or matériel be diverted from the next year's grand D-Day plunge. Meanwhile, Hitler annexed Italy and ordered his generals there to fight to the last drop of blood. The result was the war's most vicious sideshow: a meat grinder of a year and a half, where America lost tens of thousands of men, chewing north at less than a mile a day, in a campaign that history would little remark. Among the original 200 men of the company to which Dole was assigned, there were 183 casualties in four months after they debarked in Naples. When Dole got his orders, in February '45, the battalion had just fought its first major engagement: a night assault on Mt. Belvedere; in less than twenty-four hours, a company commander and half the lieutenants were gone.

Of course, Dole didn't know all that. In Uncle Sam's infantry, you were lucky to know what was going on a hundred yards to your right or left. But he knew, somehow, it was bad business up there: he told Dean Nesmith he didn't want to go. He sensed there was a bullet waiting for him in those hills. Nesmith told him to pack his kit. There was nothing more to be said.

— ★ —

That was the other thing they noticed about Dole, when he got to the mountains and took over Second Platoon: the way he held himself so quiet, like he'd stepped into someone else's war, and didn't want to intrude. He wasn't like some of those ninety-day wonders, graduates of the Benning School for Boys, who thought they owned the world because they got a strip of brass on their collars. Dole knew what it meant to be a lieutenant of infantry: he was fodder, the guy out front, the guy with the binoculars and map case, whom the Jerries tried to shoot first because it would disrupt the chain of command. German snipers went for the officers and radio men: if they got them, the unit was cut off, disorganized, without eyes and ears. . . . Of course, every man in the unit knew that: Dole could see the way they looked him over—coolly, like they didn't want to invest too much, he might not be around for long. "I'm Lieutenant Dole," he'd say, introducing himself. "I'm going to be leading the platoon. . . ." If they didn't say anything, he'd add: "Dole. Like the pineapple juice."

A sergeant, Frank Carafa, was in charge of the platoon when Dole arrived.

(Their lieutenant had moved up when the company commander was killed on Mt. Belvedere.) Carafa was small, quick, dark-eyed, a veteran; he'd been in the Army before the war, fought in the Pacific before he joined the mountain troops. Dole asked him how long he'd been running the platoon. Carafa looked him over: the wide boyish eyes under his helmet (guy was so green, he still wore his helmet!), the big tank jacket with pockets everywhere, the pants wrapped tight around his legs and tucked neatly into the top of his boots, the clean kit on the ground beside him . . . straight off the boat.

"Since Belvedere," he said.

"All right, soldier. There won't be any changes," Dole said. "We'll run it like you've been running it, until we get the knack of it."

Carafa nodded, and his eyes met Dole's for a moment.

— ★ —

He was scared twenty-four hours a day. Hell, everybody was. The Germans were giving ground, hill by hill, and when the Americans fought their way onto the next peak, the Jerries knew every inch of that position. They knew where the cover was: they could zero in their artillery, the .88s—and they were good. Carafa used to say they could hit a fly in the tail, while it flew. "Mail'll be in about five," the men would remind each other grimly. That meant artillery rounds, day after day, dawn and dusk, sometimes all night in the dark. So they dug in—foxholes, twenty-four hours a day, two men on their stomachs in the cold stony ground, one staring off at the facing hillside, watching the Germans through a twenty-power scope (sometimes, they were so close, you could spot their snipers from a puff of rifle smoke), the other trying to get his two hours' sleep, until it was his turn to wake and watch. Food came from cans in their kits: spaghetti and meatballs, or beef stew; you didn't dare make a fire to heat it.

There were daily rumors of a breakout, the big push that would carry them over the ridges and into the Po Valley. It was coming, and soon. Everybody knew it. In fact, the brass had the plans drawn up, the race for the bridges over the Po, and then for the Alps, to cut off the Germans. The generals called it Operation Craftsman; but no one on the line knew the code name. Bellied to the stones in a shell hole, they worried about the guys in the next hole, six feet away. Were they still there? . . . Were there Jerries out front? . . . The goddam fog was the worst. You didn't know who was around you.

It was scariest for the replacements, guys who never bargained for infantry. Most were "Triple-A," antiaircraft artillerymen who'd been sitting in Rome. But the Luftwaffe was finished now, so they handed these poor bastards a rifle and a shovel, and stuck 'em in foxholes. One guy they stuck in Dole's platoon was mental with the fear. Dev Jennings, one of the sergeants, went to the company command post to tell 'em they better have a look at the guy. "He's just not gonna be with us." But just as Jennings brought the exec to the guy's foxhole, they heard a shot—M-1, an American—and they found the kid standing in a corner, where he'd braced against the sides of the hole to keep still, while he fired a bullet from his rifle through his left foot. He was still holding his M-1 in position, with a blank stare on his face. They shipped him off to the aid station, wrote it up: gunshot, self-inflicted. What else could they do?

— ★ —

They were supposed to start the breakout April 12, with Dole's company on the left flank, to take a rocky, brown, flattop hill, Number 913 on the maps, to clear the way for the drive to the Po. Dole got his orders as he always did, face-to-face, a visit from the company commander. There were no ready rooms for the grunts, no meetings called on that front. Why get a half-dozen officers together, where one mortar shell could take them out?

Dole's platoon, about forty men, was supposed to stay on the left, moving down their slope and then across a thousand yards of shallow valley, over a short stone fence, and up the slope of Hill 913. Everybody knew the Jerries were dug in all over that hill: pillboxes with tunnels between them. The Jerries knew the ground like they'd farmed it for forty years. They knew where a squad leader in the field would eye a spot of welcome cover: that's where they'd strew their mines and booby traps, or zero in their .81 mortars, ahead of time. It was Dole's job to keep his guys out of those spots, to belly through that field, dodging everything the Krauts could throw, to bring his guys to the top of that hill, or as many guys as he had left: that was the awful calculus behind the brave word "breakout." How much ground did he have to take? How many of his guys would get the mattress-cover on the way?

They were Dole's guys now. A month is a long time in foxholes under fire. His tank jacket didn't look so new. Now he kept extra clips of ammo taped together, like the vets, to give him forty-five quick rounds. He knew enough to keep a few grenades on his belt, no matter what the book said about leaving that to the men. The first grenade he threw bounced off a tree in the dark and blew up just a few yards away. He could still feel where a piece of hot metal flew into his leg. When was that—last month? Ancient history. Now, in the dark before the attack, Dole went down the line to his guys, a word for each, to see they were ready, a pat on the back . . .

Funny thing about that. You go down a line of grunts before dawn of a big day, give 'em a pat, and just about every one—to a man—he'll fart. They've got their rifles clean, they've counted their grenades, their bullets, checked all their lucky little things, and then there's nothing to do, except get tight inside. Then you come and pat 'em on the ass. . . . In the Army, they call it the pucker factor. It was high that day.

But the goddam fog stopped the plan. The bombers were coming, to soften up the Krauts, but they couldn't take off from their fields near Pisa. So all the guys could do was lie back and wait. Then, that day, FDR died. The news came, foxhole to foxhole. Some men took it hard. Not that it changed what they had to do. It was just another reminder: the war was almost over, everybody knew . . . but the old man didn't make it. Would they? . . . They waited another day.

On the morning of the fourteenth, the weather cleared, the bombers came. It was bombing like the guys in Italy had never seen: wave after wave of planes, hitting the hillsides with five-hundred-pounders . . . then the heavy artillery zeroed in on the same hills for another hour. The noise was incredible, and the guys were grinning. "God, boy, they sure ain't alive in there now."

"No fuckin' way!"

By the time the bombardment stopped, near 10:00 A.M., no one could see Hill 913. The air was opaque with smoke and dust, the world was dark with brown grit, as the word went down the line and the boys scrambled out of their holes and Bob Dole went ahead, into the valley, into the dust.

— ★ —

But the Germans were alive, hundreds of them. April 14 was a daytime nightmare of cannon, mortar, machine-gun fire—flesh in uneven contest with the "instrumentalities of war." A second lieutenant named Kvam tried to take cover from artillery, dived into a shallow ditch, and tripped a Kraut booby trap. It was a steel pipe, cut on a diagonal and filled with explosives, so when it blew, it would spray burning steel in a wide, deadly swath. But Kvam took the whole load. When his men got to the hole, it looked like someone had dabbed the lieutenant a hundred times on his face and body with a tiny black paint brush. He was perforated.

Dole got his men down to the low stone wall, and started to advance in British formation. The lead squad, maybe fourteen men, followed two scouts at the point of advance. Two smaller squads were behind on the flanks. Farther behind, at the rear point of the diamond, came the weapons squad, with machine guns and light mortars. The top sergeant would move in the middle, as a belly-crawling, rolling headquarters. Dole could have stayed in the middle, too. But he knew his job, and he did it. He was out front, with the lead squad.

They were pinned down quick. The whole company didn't make a quarter mile that morning. Third Platoon got over the wall, but the sergeant told the men to advance across the field before they'd got engineers to check for mines. So the men of the Third made about forty yards and started stepping on mines. Some were killed right there, many wounded. The rest were pinned down in the field, when a farmhouse on the left opened fire: a Jerry machine-gun nest, sure as shit; the men in the field were hamburger.

Dole had to get that machine gun. The lead squad was going to have to flank that house and get that nest of Krauts. Sergeant Carafa assumed he'd be going out with the squad, but Dole said, "Sergeant, I'll take 'em." Carafa stayed behind to cover. He got the rest of the guys in position to fire at the farmhouse, then called for mortars, while they opened up with BARs—Browning automatics, the light machine guns.

Dole went ahead on the steep, rocky field. With the morning's bombardment, the mortars, and machine-gun fire, the ground was littered with bits of metal. There were still shells flying in from the slope behind the farmhouse, and German mortars dug in on the backside of the hill. Dole made fifty or sixty feet before they spotted him from the farmhouse, opened up on him and his squad. He yanked the pin from a grenade and lobbed it, but it fell short. Romberg, the first scout, was closer. He half stood to let loose a grenade, but they got him. He fell face forward and his helmet rolled off in front of him. Dole couldn't see the second scout. Jerries might have got him, too. Dole dived for a shell hole, made it, but his runner, Sims, did not, he was down. Dole scrambled from the hole on his belly, slithered out on the pocked dirt, while shells tore the air over him, and he grabbed little Sims by a handful of shirt, dragged him back, but he was deadweight, it was too late . . . and now the Jerry gunners sighted Dole, who was scrambling from his hole . . . had to get out, his guys were getting chewed up there . . . and Dole was on all fours, moving, tearing up his hands on the ground, and then . . . he felt a sharp shock of sting in his back, behind the right shoulder, he twisted in the air and went down on his face in the dirt, he couldn't feel his arms, *they shot off my arms,* he couldn't feel . . . couldn't see, face on the dirt, *can't get up to see, can't lift . . . have to get out of here!*

The others could hear him moaning. Carafa thought he heard Dole calling to *him,* heard it plain between the roar of the guns . . . *Sergeant Caraaafa.* . . . Dole only knew they were dragging him, dragging him back into a gully, a shallow depression, rolling him over . . . the tank jacket was shredded open near the neck and shoulder. You could see into Dole through the jacket, through the shoulder, like a gouged fruit, see down to the core, and they folded the lieutenant's arms on his chest, they had to get out. . . . The sergeants said they were going to push to the right, to the east, where the engineers were tripping mines. There was another company to the east, breaking through the German line. They'd get by the hill and the Krauts to the east. They had to get moving. Dole was just lying there, staring up at them, the look in his eyes a silent plea. He knew they had to get out . . . but how could they leave him?

They called in medics, but two got killed trying to get to Dole. There weren't many medics going to make it that day. That's why Sergeant Kuschik carried morphine. Stan Kuschik was a great, hairy bear of a man, son of a Jewish baker from New York. He did the best he could for Dole, more than orders allowed: he pulled up a kid named Arthur McBryar, a Tennessee boy who'd been in Dole's platoon. Kuschik told McBryar to stay with Dole, even though orders said to leave no able-bodied man behind. Dole was gray, like they get before they die. Kuschik couldn't leave him to die there, alone. Before he got out, Kuschik dug through his kit, gave Dole a shot of morphine. Then he dipped his finger into Dole's shredded jacket, and with Dole's blood traced an "M" on his forehead. That'd let the medics know he'd had a shot—another would kill him, overdose . . . if a medic ever got there . . . if McBryar could spot one . . .

McBryar was scared to death. The medics were never gonna find them, down there, in the ravine. There was cover, but no one'd come. Dole was still right where they left him, on his back with his arms crossed over his chest, still conscious, moaning, trying to talk . . . but he couldn't unclench his teeth.

He wasn't cryin' or anything. But McBryar was listening to the guns, couldn't catch what Dole was trying to say. It seemed like forever till that Kraut machine gun quit. Artillery was still comin' in. He tried to keep Dole talking, keep him going, afraid he was gonna give out.

Dole went home. He didn't know where the others were, so he went home, had to get home, wasn't cold anymore, but he could feel the air, fresh, cool on his chest, he better get home, get something on, his sweater. He was running up Maple, bright sunshine, it was so bright cold, and Spitzy was running with him, his little white dog, Spitzy, was back, running with him, going home, and there was the hoop, the basketball rim in the open lot next door, and Dole was driving for the rim, to the hoop, he could feel them trying to keep him away, trying to block him, but he could get to the hoop, he could always get in, get the ball over, get the ball up, over, could always get in, dribble once, turn and go, even if he had to bang in, bang his body, arm on his shoulder up in the air, and he was falling falling never hit the ground, falling into dark darker cold he could still feel the arm air cold on him shoving him down, down, and the bright was going, pulling away, and he was falling, couldn't stop and hands were on him shoving him down down down they were going couldn't see home or Spitzy, *SPITZY!* . . .

McBryar had a bandage pressed onto Dole's wound, had to try to slow the bleeding. Blood was soaking his jacket and uniform, turning the dry ground dark underneath. "How bad is it?" Dole said through his teeth. McBryar pulled the bandage away. Whatever hit Dole had ripped into everything. McBryar could look into him, see right down to Dole's back. His arm was connected by a couple or three white stringy . . . *Jesus, they blowed his arm off.*

McBryar pressed the bandage down again. "You gonna be fine, Lieutenant."

McBryar cradled Dole's head, gave him the soldier's mix of sulfa and water, trying to hold off infection. He rubbed water on Dole's forehead, talking to him, trying to keep him there. . . .

Dole could feel the rain on his head, legs wouldn't move in this mud, had to get by them all, get the pass, Bud can throw the ball long, Bud Smith can throw, had to get his arms up, Bud would see him, get behind, to the end zone, couldn't move in the mud, couldn't move his legs, couldn't make them go, like running through water, mud all over him, Mom'll have a fit, soaked all over, got to get home, she'll be there, get the mud off, dinner, be clean before dinner at the table, everybody's probably sitting already, at the table, Mom in the kitchen where were the others, where were they? Where were they?

After someone finally got the Kraut machine-gun bastards, McBryar left Dole in the ravine, climbed the knoll behind, trying to flag a medic. There was no one coming for them. *Jesus, we're gonna die out here.* Artillery was still coming in. Couldn't tell anymore whose it was. McBryar got hit. Hit, or knocked down. He got a concussion, they said. He was still woozy hours later, had just enough sense left to show 'em where Dole lay, in blurry dusk, when the medics found them, and packed them both off to the field hospital.

—★—

At the hospital, nine hours after he was hit, they figured he was going to die. Whatever hit him exploded inside, broke his collarbone and the shoulder behind it, not to mention his arm. Worst thing was, it smashed into his vertebrae, crushed a piece of his spine, it was broken, the spinal cord was knocked out. He couldn't move. He couldn't feel anything below his neck.

So they cleaned him up, splinted what they could reach, sent him down to the hospital in Pistoia, near Florence. But the only thing they could do there was cut him open wide, see if they could spot anything pressed against the spinal cord. Captain Woolsey was the surgeon, thought he might find out what the problem was. But when he opened Dole up, there wasn't much to go by: nothing was in the right place, and half of it wasn't there. They just sewed him up. Nothing more to do. If he lived, sure as hell, he was never going to walk. Of course, they didn't tell him that. Woolsey and the hospital chief, Colonel Prosser, told him he was going to be fine. He'd just have to give it time . . .

Dole's eyes searched their faces. His eyes were about all he could move. They had his right arm up in traction, and a sling under his chin, attached to weights over the back of his bed, to keep his head from moving. He stayed like that for weeks, with no feeling in his arms or legs, like the body on the bed belonged to someone else. There were a couple of guys from his company in the hospital, Oanes and Johnson, country boys, like him—Johnson was from Kansas. Both of them could walk, and they'd come to his bedside, try to adjust his pillows, try to tell him he'd be all right. At night, after the nurses came with his hypo, a syringe full of sedative to kill the pain, to make him sleep, Oanes and Johnson would take Bob's Army comb and comb his thick black hair to ease him, to help him go to sleep.

After a while, the doctors put him in a cast, from his chin down to his legs. They crated him for shipment like a piece of china, all but his left arm. They were going to send him out on a hospital ship. Told him they could probably do more for him outside the war zone. But he was still in Pistoia on May 2, when the Germans surrendered in Italy. The U.S. grunts had broken through, got by the hills and crossed the Po. Then the Eighty-fifth beat the Jerries back to the Brenner Pass, sealed it off, and the Germans folded. Moreover, the breakout in Italy had killed the Führer's last hope of reinforcing the Reich. In five days, Hitler would be dead in his Berlin bunker. The war in Europe was over . . . but too late for Dole. That night, they took the blackout paper off the hospital windows. He saw daylight the next day. But that was the only difference.

They were celebrating the news in Russell, how the shooting was over where Bobby Joe was, when the telegram came in to Western Union. It was funny, how the news came. The Western Union man, James Weilman, was Doran's neighbor. He used to bring the War Department wires for Doran to deliver. Doran was good at that kind of thing, a comfort, in that kind of time. Even the church used to call Doran, to go sit with someone. So this was the only wire of the war that Weilman had to deliver. He brought it over, and had to tell Doran, this one was for him.

The wire said "seriously wounded," but that wasn't what the doctors thought. The guy was finished—as far as movement was concerned, anyway. And sooner or later, that meant infection, or pneumonia, or a half-dozen other diseases that preyed on a bedridden man. The best they could do was ship him to the big hospital for the Med, the Seventieth General, in Casablanca. Maybe they could do something for him there. Maybe, if the bones healed, he'd get some feeling back in his limbs. Maybe. It was a surprise already, the way this guy hung on.

A few nights before they shipped him out, Captain Woolsey was in the ward for his rounds, and he called Colonel Prosser over.

Woolsey said to Dole: "Lieutenant, show the Colonel what you can do."

For half a minute nothing happened.

"Go ahead, Lieutenant, show him."

And then, with great effort, with the muscles in his jaw twitching from the effort, Dole raised his left arm four inches off the sheet on his chest.

— ★ —

Hello, Mr. and Mrs. Dole:

I'm sure you know that Robert is unable to write so I tried to write him a note. He told me what to write. I know you are worrying about Robert but I wouldn't worry too much because there isn't any doubt in my mind at all but what he will be just as good a man when he gets well as he was before he was hurt.

Just thank God it wasn't any worse than it was. That's the way I feel about it. In case you want to know who I am, my name is John Booth of Bethany, Mo. Robert was my Platoon Leader. He is a fine fellow. I'll write again for him. (A sniper shot me in the foot. I can't walk very well but it won't be long until I can.)

As always,
John

— ★ —

They were going to ship him back to Kansas, to the Winter General Army Hospital, some Quonset huts in a camp near Topeka. There wasn't anything they could do there, but it was policy: if they were going to die, they should die near home . . . saved the shipping cost.

Bina was there when he got to Winter General on June 12, 1945. Bob had the nurses take his arm out and lay it on his cast, so his mother could see it. She'd steeled herself, but the minute she came into the room, Bina broke down in tears. When she saw the way he looked at her, she told herself that was the last time she'd cry in front of Bob. And she sat down next to him and touched his face.

She had to pick eight cigarette butts out of his plaster cast. She told her sisters: they'd used her boy for an ashtray on the train.

— ★ —

Bina moved into an apartment across the street from the hospital. She was there every day, to take care of Bob. When she was with him now, she was brave, but she'd sob on the phone to Doran: he was like a baby again . . . she had to feed him with a spoon, wipe the drip from his chin. . . . Bina washed every bit of him that was out of the cast. Bob was always so particular . . . but the smell that came up from that cast! It was enough to make you retch! The nurses who'd fed him for the last two months had spilled bits of food down into the cast. It smelled like something died in there. Maybe something did. Sometimes she'd look at him and she had to run out of the room, to weep in a corner of the hallway.

"Don't cry, Mom," Bob used to tell her. He tried to be brave for her, too. "I'm gonna be back, good as before." That wasn't exactly what the doctors said, but if it was a matter of will, he'd make it. He knew what he had to do: get back on his feet, get his strength back. Then, he was going back to school, to play for Phog Allen. Maybe not this September, no, but he was going to play again.

As for the doctors, they talked about a long haul, chipping away bit by bit at the body cast, as feeling and movement came back to his legs, his left arm. As for the right arm, well, they didn't say much. Even at best, it was going to be months before he could start to relearn the basics: to control his bladder and bowels, to sit up, maybe turn himself over. And longer still for bigger things, like walking to a bathroom, or bringing food from a plate to his mouth. That's what preyed on him: he couldn't do anything. He lay there, day after day, one day like the last, marked, if he was lucky, by some medical event, another few inches off the cast, or a moment's success moving one leg, then the other, under his sheet.

In those moments of triumph, he was sure: he'd make it back; he was going to play again. Then there'd be days of failure, no progress, or worse, constant pain, a seizure, violent shaking when he tried to move. He itched. He felt dirty in his cast. He stunk. Then the bleakness would descend upon him, or the rage. Why him? *What the hell did I do so wrong?* What Bina saw, what broke her heart was, he was so ashamed. He was a boy who'd defined himself by the strength of his body, how he could run, how hard he could work, how much he could lift. When her sister, Mildred, came to visit, what struck her was the way Bob talked about himself, like a piece of garbage, a cake dropped on the floor. Mildred came in and saw him in the bed, on his back. The face looked like Bob, but the rest was plaster. She bent down and patted his chest, tried to kiss him. He cringed. She said, "I brought you a banana pie."

"Good," he said, but then he was silent.

She tried to smile. "Well, you listen to us jabber," she said, and she turned to Bina. Then, she heard his voice:

"Don't have anything to say, anyway."

After that, he asked his mother to keep everybody else away. Doran and Bob's sister, Norma Jean, drove the hundred and eighty miles east, every weekend. But Bina was there day after day. She'd always hated tobacco, but she sat by his head and held cigarettes to his mouth. A smoke was the only pleasure left to him. Sometimes she read to him, but she kept the papers away, in case there was news about Bud Smith. Bud was lost in the Pacific, listed officially "missing in action," but no one from Russell, Kansas, would be fooled by that. They knew they'd get the bad news on Bud.

Bob's KU housemate, Dick Finney, from Topeka, had also been shot down in the Pacific, and his mother used to stay with Bina at the hospital. Helping Bina with Bob took her mind off her own son. It was near the end of June when Mrs. Finney was called away to the hospital phone. Her husband was on the line: "We got a message from the War Department." Bina couldn't be much comfort to her friend. Bob had caught a fever, it wouldn't leave him . . . and the doctors had no idea what to do.

Bina sat helpless in the smell of the ward at Winter General, while the fever grew and took Bob away. All the progress, the tiny triumphs of movement, were lost. Finally, Bina called Doran in Russell: "You got to come down. I'm afraid he won't make it through the night." Doran and Norma Jean started racing east on Route 40. Police cars with sirens gave them an escort into Topeka. The Russell police had called ahead. When they got to the hospital, Bina was still in the room, but it didn't matter. Bob didn't know who was there anymore. The nurses kept a tongue catcher on Bob's tray in case he went into seizure. A chaplain was hanging around in the hall, to be there, "in case . . ."

Finally, the doctors decided it had to be his kidneys: he couldn't make water, even with a catheter. His right kidney was full of stones, infected. They could take out the kidney, but not with this fever. It was measured at 108.7 degrees. They'd have to wait, try to force it down with the miracle drug of the age, penicillin. It could cut the infection and fever in a few days—if he could hold on a few days . . .

— ★ —

Bob held on, and made it through the operation. The fever disappeared and the other kidney worked, and by fall, they'd chipped away the whole cast. Now they were trying to get him out of bed. They hung his legs over the edge of the mattress, but it made him weak with fatigue. It took days to get him on his legs, and then he shook so, with the pain and the strangeness, they had to set him back in bed.

When Bob would start to shake, Bina had to leave the room. But soon she'd be back smiling bravely again. Now only the right arm was in traction. Every day, they'd get him out of bed, and he could take a few steps before he got tired. He could still barely move, but the doctors said he could go home. There wasn't anything more they could do. So Doran drove east and took Bob back to Russell. The neighbors watched from their windows, while the Doles got their boy into the house on a stretcher. The biggest, strongest kid from Russell High now weighed 122 pounds.

Bina and Doran put Bob in their bedroom, the front room with the French doors that led to the living room. They slept in the back, the children's bedroom. They rented a hospital bed and a rolling tray. Bob liked to have those French doors open, while Bina rushed around, cooking and doing for him. Kenny was just back from the war, but more than ever, Bob came first. Bina would feed him, bathe him, dress him, comb his hair, hold his cigarette to his mouth, carry the bedpan back and forth, go to the bathroom with him. There weren't enough hours in the day for all she wanted to do for him. She'd wake up at dawn thinking about what he could wear that would be comfortable to lounge in, and what she could cook, what he'd like, what would make the day special. She worked herself to the frayed edge of exhaustion, though she would never let Bob see that. And when Bob got down, Bina would crumble. Sometimes, with her sisters or her daughters, safe in the kitchen, where Bob couldn't hear, Bina would cry like a baby. She'd stand at the kitchen sink sobbing. "I'm afraid we brought him home to die."

At night, Doran would sit with Bob, read to him from *The Salina Journal.* Or he'd have Chet Dawson and his wife, Ruth, over to play bridge late at night, after the drugstore closed, so Bob could listen through the open French doors to news of the town and the farmers. Chet would call in the afternoon, say: "Bina? What're you cookin'? . . . Well, save some for me. I'll be by sometime." Bob didn't mind the Dawsons, but he didn't want anyone else to see him. He was so ashamed of the way he looked. There'd be time enough for them to see, when he was whole again, when he could play. That was the dream that kept him going. He was going to play ball for Coach Allen. It was more than a dream. It was a plan. He'd count off months in his head, what he'd be able to do with his arms and legs two months from now, four months, six . . . how he'd start to run, build his endurance. . . . But then, when someone came, even a good friend, he'd see in their eyes: "Poor Bob!" Their eyes made him see himself as they did . . . "Poor Bobby Joe!" . . . And then the plan was only a dream, a pipe dream.

Bina let him talk on about how he'd play ball . . . whatever he wanted. What was the point of telling him anything else? For her part, talk of the future was bright, and immediate.

How about his favorite, liver and onions, tomorrow?

Bob, will you wear your new sweater this Sunday?

Or Christmas! . . . Christmas was always a big deal in that house, and this year, it would have to be double-special. Doran always got the biggest tree. If it didn't touch the ceiling, it was no good. And by the time he finished, that tree was a work of art. He'd trim off the uneven branches, and wherever the tree was thin, he'd drill into the trunk and insert the branches that he'd trimmed off before. Then, when he'd hang the icicles, he wouldn't throw them on any which way. He'd start on the inside and work his way out in circles, every icicle just right or he wouldn't be satisfied. Of course, that's how Bina wanted it, too.

She'd wreath every doorway in the house with evergreens. And every table had to be covered with Christmas cookies. Not just the tables. The counters, the floor . . . cookies everywhere, and all made with butter and cream, and frosted by Bina herself. Bina did everything for Christmas herself . . . her own popcorn balls, with caramel coating, or red ones, or chocolate-covered. She'd make her own taffy, so the family could come for taffy pulls. And shopping! That year, when Bob came home, she was already shopping for Christmas in the summer. And she was going to Kansas City for special things. She had her list for Bob all ready in a drawer.

But by Thanksgiving, Bob was gone again. He went to a special Army hospital in Michigan, where they did modern miracles in orthopedics. It was Uncle Sam's special center for paraplegics and amputees. Why should he wait around for Christmas?

More movement, more feeling in his left arm! The strength to walk on his own legs for ten minutes, twenty, an hour! To run! And a miracle for his right arm, to let him play ball. To be whole again. That's what he wanted for Christmas.

But there was no miracle for Bob. On the fourth day before Christmas, he woke with a savage pain in his chest. It was a blood clot in his lung, the price of lying immobile so long. The doctors in Michigan started treating him with dicumarol, a vicious drug to thin the blood. It turned him, temporarily, into a hemophiliac.

But there was no choice. If the blood clot loosened from the wall of his lung and went to his heart, he was a dead man. He was strictly confined to bed again. This time he demanded that doctors tell him the outlook, straight. And they told him, it was fifty-fifty he'd live.

So he stayed in bed for weeks, then months, while all his strength ebbed away. As the new year stretched into its second month, he was weaker and weaker, and now the fever was back. The doctors tried cutting off the dicumarol. But the pain returned, and chills . . . the fever was eating him away. So they started the drug again, with penicillin, but the antibiotic couldn't stop this infection. He was coughing and rattling in his bed. Pneumonia was filling his lungs.

Bina and Doran drove back and forth from Kansas to Michigan, but they could see that the doctors had no plan. They couldn't stop the fever, so they packed him in ice. They had Bobby Joe packed like a fish in the market! By the end of February, Bob grew worse and the hospital called again, but Bina couldn't bear to go back . . . when Bob didn't know her, when the fever had him. So Kenny went to Michigan. He figured he was going just to pick up the body. It wasn't even Bob in that bed. It was just a shell of him.

"Is there any hope?" Kenny asked. They told him about an experimental drug. The Army had the only supply, a thirty-day dose for three patients. Bob would be the third. Would Kenny authorize the treatment?

"Well, what happened to the others?"

One died and one went blind, but he lived.

"What are his chances without it?"

Without it, nothing.

So Kenny called home, and Bina and Doran came back to Battle Creek, to sign the form, to watch the treatment. They had Bob tied down in bed, so he'd be still while the new drug took hold. Doctors told them not to expect much. Even if it worked, there was no guarantee he'd know them, be able to move, get the strength back he had before. No one really knew what this drug would do. It was called streptomycin.

So, beginning of March, they put him on it. Four days later, he sat up in bed, asked Kenny to go downtown and get him a milkshake.

6

To Know

LANGUAGE, the first and most basic tool of culture, is also its truest mirror. Any culture worthy of consideration will have created language to reflect its special preoccupations. Eskimos, it's said, have a hundred words for snow.

In fact, the power and precision of language is the surest pointer to a culture's attainments, just as export of its vocabulary is the surest mark of its sway in the world. Gallic pride is engorged, with reason, when speakers of forty languages turn to French for verbs in the kitchen and nouns in the boudoir. And it is a distinction of undying greatness that half a world may call to God with names invented by a couple of small Levantine tribes.

Alas, it is the surest sign that official Washington remains a precultural swamp that it has not offered mankind any refinement of language to illumine its own constant preoccupation, the basic activity of its single industry, the work of its days and the spice of its nights, which is *knowing.* There are, in the capital, a hundred different ways to know and to be known; there are fine gradations of knowing, wherein the subtlest distinctions are enforced. But to discuss this art and passion, we have only the same bland flapjack of a verb that flops each day onto our plates, along with the morning paper: To Know.

About this preoccupation there can be no dispute: knowledge is power, and the capital is a city built on power, which means knowing and being known. But this is more than a business in Washington. It is life. Only in the bars of Capitol Hill will you hear a normal, healthy young woman responding to the blandishments of her handsome swain with the delighted, breathy question,

"You *know* Kerrey?" Only in a half-dozen Washington restaurants can a man's reputation be so quickly enhanced (and the object of his knowing so quickly diminished) by the half-bored, half-dismissive assertion: "Oh, I know Jack . . . forget it."

This is knowing in the sense of acquaintance, of *connaissance,* but this is only the most basic way To Know. Large and lucrative careers, great firms filling many marbled floors of fine buildings are built on a combination of *connaissance* and a judicious smatter of knowing in the sense of knowledge, *scientia,* as in facts or familiarity with a branch of government endeavor. "Well, you can go ahead and file the appeal," the consultant-lobbyist says to his speakerphone, "but I know the Assistant Secretary is no friend to Section 289, so we might want to pursue that avenue at the same time . . ." (Men and women with *scientia* but without *connaissance* tend to pursue less lucrative careers as policy wonks in the agencies, do-good lobbies, or think tanks.)

Then there is the matter of being known, which can be more important than knowing. If a Washington man is well known as a man in the know, then his knowing is seldom tested. In fact, it is fed daily by people who come to him to see what he thinks about what they know. This new knowledge is greeted by him with nods (I know, I know . . .) that begin before the other person has finished talking. As a result of this, he ends up knowing pretty much what everybody else knows, which is usually enough. There are companies or interest groups, officeholders or office-seekers, who will hire him to be their man in the know. He is, after all, well known.

In fact, being well known is a quality as close to a bankable asset as a Washington man can have. It's what talent is in other towns. A politician who is well known as a foe of oil and gas regulation is not going to have trouble raising money for his next campaign. In fact, a man well known for his *connaissance* of the oil and gas interests may have no opponent in his next campaign. (Why run against a guy who'll have two million in the bank?) A man who knows the President may get invited to a couple of state dinners. A man who is well known to know the President is himself a new president—of a successful consulting firm.

Then there is another shade of the verb, To Know, in the sense of *awareness.* It is about what's going on *right now,* and as such, it is Washington's highest branch of knowledge. Encyclopedic *scientia* on the theory, history, and practice of progressive taxation in America is nothing, *less than nothing,* compared to knowing (a week before the vote) Chairman Rostenkowski's bottom line on depreciation of timber assets. One brand of knowing (*scientia*) earns a ratty office and a shared secretary at the Heritage Foundation. The other (*awareness*) brings power, money, fame. . . .

But as the highest form of capital-knowing, the quest for awareness is also the most dangerous. Clearly, the lack of this knowing can undermine reputation or power, especially if one's position, or one's *connaissance,* indicates that one *ought to know.* To be unaware, to be Out of the Loop, is allied in the tribal consciousness with impotence, inability, imbecility . . . and ultimately with the fatal affliction of ridiculousness. But there is also, in success, in wide awareness, a danger just as mortal. For this is the brand of knowing that is closest to Eating from the Tree of Knowledge, and can result in expulsion from Eden. When things foul up in a massive way; when *The Washington Post,* like God, is angry; when Committee Chairmen vie for jurisdiction of the hearings that will make them well known as the scourge of evildoing, then this is the knowing implied in the most portentous of capital questions:

What did he know, and when did he know it?

And so, there has developed, in Washington, a kind of knowing *without being known to know,* for which there is no word at all. It is a nonoperational, untraceable knowing, which can seldom be proven or disproven. Indeed, its vaguely oriental essence can barely be expressed. It is yin-and-yang, knowing-not-knowing. It is knowing all about the thing without being culpable of knowing the thing itself. All of which brings us to that veteran capital personage, that longtime practitioner of the Washington arts, that most knowing of men, Vice President Bush.

Here was a man whose very job, whose only job, was To Know, as the capital understands the verb. He started early each morning, in his office in the Old EOB, getting to know someone or something over breakfast, which might last for only fifteen or twenty minutes, and always ended in time for the Veep to receive the little man with the briefcase, the gnome from the CIA who appeared each day at 8:00 A.M., to offer the Agency's knowledge, its awareness, not as a Vice Presidential perk, but as a courtesy, a tip of the old school cap, to the former Director, Mr. George Bush, who liked to know what his old shop had been doing for the last twenty-four hours; and when that was finished, he was off across the driveway to the West Wing, to the Oval Office, there to sit in on the President's Chief of Staff briefing and his National Security briefing, to sit in not because the President wanted or would seek his opinion, not because the briefings would offer material on which he'd work, that day or ever, but simply To Know, which, after all, was the point; and when those briefings were over, Bush began his formal work for the day, getting to know and to know about some federal or local officials who'd convened en bloc in the capital, or sitting in with the President to refine and reinforce his acquaintance with the President of Zaire or the Foreign Minister of Malaysia, or jetting off to meet and to know the officers and enterprise of the nation's first tall-stack-clean-coal power plant, or returning to his office for an informational briefing on the federal narcotics interdiction effort, or sitting down at his desk to work through the report on . . . no matter. . . . Every meeting, every act, each step in his daily Vice Presidential march, down to the last skip-and-jump through the briefcase full of papers which he'd tackle in his study at home, at night, had simply to do with knowing, and knowing in the Washington Way. Here was a man, after all, who owed his job to his *connaissance,* and maintained his standing in it almost solely by one pinpoint of that *connaissance:* his knowing relationship with Ronald Reagan. At the same time, his Constitutional duty required him to master the *scientia,* to know at least enough of the arms-control-throw-weight-multiple-reentry-warhead *scientia* to be President, today, should disaster strike. At the same time, his political standing, his sole shield against the dread and fatal ridiculousness of the job, depended on his ability to enhance the precious *awareness* . . . and yet . . . *and yet!* . . . He could not know, *could not afford to know,* in the full operational sense of the word, anything beyond what the administration was known to know, or anything different from what the administration Officially Knew, or anything that put the lie to any of the fond and rosy myths that swaddled, like a blessed baby, the mind of the most know-nothing President in the capital's known history.

Here was, in short, the most creative and subtle knower of knowledge in the capital.

Which brings up, again, that lamentable word: for when Iran-contra transpired, and God, like *The Washington Post,* was angry, and millions of Americans eagerly awaited a single, supposedly simple fact—yes or no?—and an answer was sought a thousand times, by a thousand of the nation's best journalists . . . it was sought only with the blunt tool at hand, the edge of that mealy flapjack, always with a question that came out this way:

Did George Bush know?

Now what could they possibly mean by that?

— ★ —

On the eighteenth of November, 1986, George Bush was to host a night at the movies: *Top Gun* was on the bill, just the kind of action flick the VP liked. In fact, it should have been a perfect night: friends, mostly Governors, in town for the Republican Governors' do, all convened in comfort and security in the armchairs of Jack Valenti's private theater on Sixteenth Street in the capital, a plushy screening room maintained for VIP entertainment by the Motion Picture Association of America. It was just the sort of soirée—twenty or thirty people he knew, gathered for activity and no heavy talk—the VP always enjoyed. He'd have them out to the house for drinks before the film. Perfect! Then he could pick off two or three, take them off to his study for a moment— no arm-twisting, nothing like that—just a friendly word or two . . .

"Well, I feel we're doing all right . . .

"And I hope you could feel, you know, I'm qualified . . .

"If you could help . . ."

It always worked like a charm. After all he'd done for them, now he was asking, so intimately, gently . . . it was so respectful and decent. If it came to arm-twisting later, well . . . Atwater did the heavy lifting with the Southerners. Andy Card was working on Governor Sununu from New Hampshire. Bush's friend, Nick Brady, went back a long way with Governor Tom Kean in New Jersey. In fact, Kean appointed Brady to the Senate, to fill out an unexpired term. So, if it came time to announce: *Hey! Bus is leaving! Get on board or be left behind* . . . there was always someone else to do it. That left Bush as the genial host . . . such a decent guy! That's the part he liked, anyway. He'd have Kean over that night, after the movie. He could stay the night! There was plenty of room! Bar would get everything set up upstairs. . . . It'd be fun!

But that was all arranged before the deal with Iran started to come out on

Election Day. Since then, there was nothing else in the news: ten minutes or more at the top of each newscast, guaranteed—they loved this crap! Ted Koppel, every night after the late news, making mincemeat out of anyone who dared say a kind word for Reagan. Turn the channel, there were Johnny Carson jokes: a cake and a Bible for the Ayatollah! That was before the *Post* started doing a special section each day, turning over every rock in town on that question: What did they know, and when did they know it? By the time the Governors came to town and Bush was to host his night at the movies, nothing seemed much fun.

Kean could tell right away when he got to the Residence: Bush wasn't happy. He was alternately pensive and snappish. He couldn't concentrate on what anybody said. Of course, Kean knew Bush from politics, and had for almost fifteen years, ever since Richard Nixon made Bush the National GOP Chairman. But Kean and Bush had also known one another in the ways that children of good families know one another. Kean's sister had met young Poppy in Connecticut. Kean's father had served with Prescott Bush in Congress. In the early years of the century, their grandfathers were classmates at a private college in New Jersey. So Kean had more than politics in mind when he took Bush aside to ask: "What's wrong? You just don't seem yourself."

"Aw, this thing with Iran," Bush said, when they got a chance to talk alone. Bar had gone to bed. The old, rambling house was silent, save for the quiet voices in the study.

"I don't know what the hell happened," Bush said, "and neither does the President. But they're gonna put him out there tomorrow for a *news conference*. . . . They'll *kill* him out there!"

Just the thought of it . . . Bush couldn't sit still in his chair. He felt so helpless. And it was his ass out there on the line! Reagan wasn't running again. If the whole second term sank into this Iran swamp, Reagan was still going back to his ranch and horses. It was Bush whose future was ruined. Of course, that's not how he said it, wouldn't even think that way. No, it was the price of being Poppy that his first thought, in fact, all his concern, had to bend to the rescue of "this good man, who has become my friend," Ronald Reagan. The code left no options. When the deal came unglued and the papers started digging up the whole sad tale, Bush didn't call any meetings, didn't take polls, didn't even talk to his political guys. There was only one thing he could do: stand by his friend in the shit-storm. Anything else . . . well, it'd be like ratting on a school chum.

But he could help, if they'd give him a chance. He knew something about this, sure as hell knew more than the President. Reagan didn't see what all the fuss was, thought he'd just go out there and say what he'd done. He didn't understand! That's why Bush went into the Oval Office that day—did what he'd almost never done in six long years. He went to the mat on this: went to the President to tell him to back off—just for a few days! Just until they knew what the facts were, what they were supposed to be. This was a covert operation! Shouldn't be coming out like this! George Bush had joined his first secret society at age fourteen. He'd been keeping secrets ever since, been Director of the CIA! He knew this stuff in his bones! Just back off, till everybody knew what they were supposed to know, what it was they could admit they knew.

But they brushed him off like a fly . . . Reagan, Meese, Don Regan. Bush talked into the President's face in a way he never had . . . but Reagan simply couldn't understand. Meese thought the Gipper could just deny it—make it all go away in front of the cameras. Regan was only interested in his own reputation—wanted the world to know it wasn't him, dropped the ball. Bush had gone at all of them, spent the capital of loyalty he'd been hoarding for six years, and got nowhere. It was incredible.

"Afterwards, I went at Regan again," Bush said that night. "Believe me, I went in there . . . as hard as I *could.*"

— ★ —

He knew Reagan was going to dig them a deeper hole. Bush knew what the President was going to say out there. (Fuller's wife, Karen, helped Pat Buchanan get the statement together.) And Bush knew some of it was plain wrong, dangerously wrong. That business about the arms fitting into one cargo plane—dead wrong. Bush had taken a private meeting (at Ollie North's request) with the Israeli middleman who started the whole deal rolling. He knew they were talking about more than one planeload, as he knew they were dealing with the genuine fanatics at the right hand of Khomeini. He never bought that "moderates" fantasy.

In fact, there were many things that George Bush knew that later emerged in the confluence of revelation that came to be known as Iran-contra. He knew, for starters, the administration shipped arms to Iran. In fact, he was for it, in a quiet, barely traceable way, not because he thought it would work, but it might . . . *and the President was for it.* He knew that if the deal went down as hoped ("planned" was too grand a word), the U.S. hostages would all come home. He knew Bud McFarlane, Ollie North, and John Poindexter were running the show. He knew the Israelis had started the whole deal, were in it up to their eyeballs, in it for their own reasons, not necessarily those of the U.S. And he knew the President didn't quite grasp the details of the operation.

On the contra side of the ledger, he had also come to awareness of most of the pertinent facts. He knew Ollie North was a cowboy. He knew Ollie was shaking every tree in the forest for money for the contras. (In fact, he was going to speak at one of North's fund-raisers, and backed off only when his staff counsel warned him he might get into trouble.) He knew—in fact, his was the first office in the White House to learn—a former CIA op named Eugene Hasenfus was shot down while flying aid to the contras. He knew Hasenfus was not the only demi-spook running around on this secret, airborne, aid-the-contras operation.

In short, George Bush had come in contact, by various means, at various times, with nearly every salient fact that later emerged in the *Post*'s special sections that bore the headline: THE SCANDAL. But that did not mean he ever put them together. Why would he, when all he had to know, the only thing he could afford to know, was that the President was for them? Why should he commit the act of overtly informing himself, when none of these matters was *on his plate*? And so, by a capital feat of knowing-not-knowing, of yin-and-yang Washington art, he was not informed, could not be shown to have been informed, of the scandal itself. As he later pointed out, he was *out of the loop!* He was not culpable of knowing anything.

What he was culpable of, on the great historical scoreboard, at least, was of practicing his art of Washington knowing to the end, to the exclusion of all else. George Bush was aware that the U.S. was shipping arms to Iran, and he did not say a word to derail the deal. George Bush was aware they were secretly shipping aid to the contras, and he did not say a word. The only time he went to the mat, spent his capital to affect the flow of events, was after the fact, when the only issue was what should come out and when, what they were allowed to admit awareness of, what they were going to be culpable of knowing. That's when he went in *as hard as he could.* . . . But, of course, no one outside the White House knew that. They were only asking a question that meant nothing: Did Bush know?

— ★ —

He was right, of course, about the President digging them in deeper with the press conference, the following day. Don Regan marched the old man out, and he screwed things up to a fare-thee-well. First, Reagan denied the deal was arms for hostages—when no one in the country believed that anymore. Then he denied the U.S. had anything to do with Israel's shipments—when Regan (as reporters pointed out) had already admitted that the U.S. condoned an Israeli shipment in September of '85. Then Reagan said there were no mistakes in the deal with Iran—they'd got three hostages back and he'd continue on the same path.

It was chaos! The spokesman, Larry Speakes, had to put out a "statement from the President" within twenty minutes to correct the stuff about Israel. Don Regan was back in the Blue Room, pounding the table and swearing he wasn't gonna be hung out in the wind as the leaker on this. Goddammit, he was gonna hold his own press conference! Poindexter wrote the correction and put in the same lies about everything fitting into one cargo plane. After that performance, seven out of ten Americans said they didn't believe Ronald Reagan anymore.

Sure enough, Bush saw the ship sinking around his ears, and there wasn't a damn thing he could do to patch the hull. He had his own small staff in an uproar, trying to do what the whole West Wing couldn't or wouldn't do: "Just get the goddam facts," Bush said. He took Craig Fuller off other business— what other business was there now?—to get to Ollie North and find out what the hell happened. He pulled Boyden Gray, his counsel, off the next big speech, the address to the American Enterprise Institute, to find out whether any laws were broken. He told his National Security man, Don Gregg, to find out what happened in Iran. Facts, he wanted. And he wanted them now. So, for days they ran around like fevered gerbils, gathering shreds of fact where they could, which they called in the same day, or they sent in memos, mostly to Fuller. . . . No one wanted to get in Bush's face when he got like this. Atwater and the politics guys stayed away altogether. Bush was in a state. If he did happen to pick up a phone while they called in, they each, to a man, felt they'd better talk fast. "Yeah. Yeah. What else?" Bush would snap on the other end. They could almost hear his fingers drumming the desk.

And every day or two, reporters would call his press office with another story they were about to unleash. And his press guy, Marlin Fitzwater, would have to walk into Bush's big office and coax a statement out of him. Usually, Bush was at his desk, working through papers, and he'd push back from the desk with a deliberate shove of both hands, and slouch back in his leather chair, with his head down, fiddling with his pen. His eyes would stay on the pen, which he rotated in his fingers, while Fitzwater told him what *The Wall Street Journal,* or the *Post,* wanted to know today. And Bush would listen with his head down, quiet, with the air of a man beleaguered, a man who had to stay composed. Then, he'd say to his pen:

"This is so unfair! Don Gregg had *nothing* to do with this."

Or, simply: "Look. The President has asked Ed Meese to find out what the facts are. When we know the facts, we'll make them public."

And then Fitzwater would have to go at it again, until he got a statement he could use.

"So I can say, 'Vice President Bush *was categorically not involved in'* . . ." Fitzwater would look up from his notepad, hoping the Veep would finish the sentence. But he'd always have to do it himself. ". . . *'directing or overseeing the contra resupply'*? . . ."

And Bush would say quietly, head down, to his pen, or off to the side, to one of his desk drawers: "Absolutely."

— ★ —

It was the weekend after the press conference that Bush got the word: Meese wanted to see him. He waited at the Residence for two days. He couldn't even sit still to read the papers. But Meese never showed up. It turned out Meese was closeted with Ollie North, to clean up "the chronology." (That was the weekend Ollie and Fawn were so busy with the shredder.)

It wasn't till Monday afternoon that Meese finally came by to see Bush, and then only for about ten minutes, just to drop this bombshell: the money from the Iran deal went to the contras. Swiss bank account. Ollie had the number. Poindexter had to know, too. They'd both have to go. There might be others. Meese was going to tell the President that same afternoon.

Bush didn't sleep that night. He came in Tuesday, looking like a man who'd got bad news on his cancer test. His mouth was a grim, lipless line. There was no expression in his eyes, no light of recognition when the staff said good morning, like Bush was looking at his own private blank wall. He had pulled completely within himself. No one had to tell Bush what this meant: a secret trail of money, had to be laws broken somehow, investigations, a Special Prosecutor, hearings in Congress . . . all they'd done for six years could go down the chute, along with his campaign. It was his ass out there now. They had to do something to curtail the damage. They had to move, and move fast, before this steamroller crushed them. . . .

But at the 9:00 A.M. Oval Office briefing, it was clear the President didn't know what to do. Meese laid out what he knew of the diversion. He said it was all in memos. (Ollie put the damn thing on paper!) Poindexter said he'd known that Ollie was up to something, but no one else did. Regan had already told Poindexter he'd have to go. Regan wanted a commission, some kind of blue-ribbon thing . . . appointed today, announced at a press conference. They had to get out in front of this. But Ronald Reagan wasn't sure. . . .

At 9:30, instead of the National Security Council briefing, Poindexter walked in, with his undertaker's face, and told the President he was sorry, he was resigning. Reagan didn't even ask what happened. He just said, "I understand . . ." Then he brightened, and with the brave smile you see at the end of war movies, he added: "But it's in the best tradition of the Navy . . . the captain accepting responsibility . . ." There was a full NSC meeting scheduled after that, so they all went in, except Poindexter. Alton Keel, his deputy, ran the meeting in his stead, and *no one said anything about it.* That's what was driving Bush crazy: they were acting so normal. At the end of the meeting, he ducked back into his West Wing office for a minute, stood at the fireplace mantel, leaned on it like it was holding him up. What the hell was going on? Was he crazy? The ship was going down and they kept on dancing!

Bush said to Fuller: "This is disaster. . . . We don't even know who handled the money . . ."

Fuller started to tell him what he'd picked up from his friend Al Keel that morning. Total weirdness! Poindexter had some early meeting, so Al ran the normal 7:30 NSC staff meeting. About 8:30, Keel walks into Poindexter's office to brief him on the staff meeting. And Poindexter's sitting there, eating a yogurt at his desk. Keel's reporting, and Poindexter just says, "Uh huh, yeah, uh huh," eating yogurt. Then he says: "By the way, Al, I'm resigning today."

Bush, still with his eyes down, withdrawn into the gloom in his own head, seemed hardly to hear the story.

"I've got to go back," Bush said. "Got the leadership meeting. Jesus. This is the worst."

So he went back to the Cabinet Room for the meeting with the Leaders of Congress, and then back again, after the President's noon press conference, for a lunch with Reagan and the Supreme Court, and then to the afternoon National Security Planning Group. . . . He walked through the day like the rest of them: reading off the cards in their pockets, going through the schedule, through the motions, acting like the ship was still afloat. . . . But he couldn't stop the baneful monologue in his head:

Disaster . . . everything they'd done, the second term, the campaign, George

*Bush out there to take the heat, they'll clobber Reagan, he doesn't understand,
thinks it's a movie . . . they'll kill him! . . .*

By the end of the day, it was screaming in his head. It was surreal, the way
no one said anything—like it would all go away if they went to their meetings!
Like The Blob That Ate Cleveland didn't exist! By the end of the day, Bush
was back in his office, at his desk, his eyes on the blotter, head in his left hand,
staring down, not seeing . . .

"It's like they don't realize . . . what's going on," Bush said to the desk.

Fuller said, across the room: "Or that it *is* going on."

And Bush looked up with his lips white, all the pain apparent now in the
long lines of his face.

"Don't they realize what this *means*?"

— ★ —

Watergate . . . was the first thing that flashed through Bob Dole's mind, in
the Cabinet Room, at the leadership briefing, when Meese dropped the bomb
about the diversion. Dole stopped in at the White House to catch the briefing
on his way to the airport. He had to get to Boston, then to Iowa, for the Other
Thing . . . plane was waiting.

Meese ran through the tale, said Ollie North did the deal on his own. That
fell onto the long, gleaming table with a thud you could almost hear. The
Leaders, the Speaker, looked at one another in silence. Lieutenant colonels
didn't *do* deals on their own. The only thing Reagan added was that Poindexter knew about it . . . and so, in the best tradition of the Navy . . . you know,
the captain taking responsibility . . .

Reagan didn't understand. There's only one captain in the White House.
Only one man could take responsibility. . . . *Watergate* . . . Dole remembered
his friend, Bryce Harlow, in an office just down the hall from this Cabinet
Room. Harlow was a Washington sage, an insider, adviser to Nixon, a man
Dole looked up to. "That break-in story doesn't have any legs," Harlow said,
back in '72. Dole was head of the Party, and he wanted to say something, to
let people know the Republican Party had nothing to do with Watergate. But
Harlow advised him: "It'll fade in two or three days . . ." So Dole didn't make
any statements, tried to pass it off with a joke.

Dole sat up at the table now, his eyes shifting from face to face. He was
trying to see the whole court. Jim Wright, Leader of the House Democrats,
was already on that portentous question:

Was this done with knowledge or approval of others?

Who else in the White House knew?

Did the CIA know?

Meese was trying to convince him that Ollie was the only one who really
knew. Poindexter only knew Ollie was up to something. Israel handled the
deal, Meese said. The Israelis thought it up, did the deed without any help . . .

Dole could see Wright didn't believe it. Who *would* believe it? He looked
down the line to Bob Byrd, his colleague, Leader of the Senate Democrats.

Byrd would have a field day, his legalistic way . . . hearings, three or four committees . . . he'd *never* let it go, the whole next Congress, it'd eat up the session, the whole campaign, the Other Thing, '88. . . . Maybe Reagan thought they'd help him, put it behind, move on. But Reagan didn't understand. Byrd always spoke with the air of the statesman, but don't get in a dark alley with him. . . . Hell, he was trying to take Dole's office. Trying to throw his whole staff out! One of Byrd's guys took Dole on a tour, to show him the "new rooms" his staff might use. They were coal bins! Walked Dole down into the basement, took him through rooms he wouldn't take his dog in . . . unless it was raining, or cold, dog wouldn't go out. . . . If they thought Byrd was going to cut them a break, well . . .

"Musta been my night off," Dole used to say about Watergate, back in '72. He never did deal with the issue, head-on. Nobody did. And they paid. It drove a President from office. Almost beat Dole, two years later, back in Kansas. The whole Party paid in blood, for eight years. A stain they never could wash off . . . still hadn't recovered, not all the way.

Well, nobody was going to tar Bob Dole with that brush now—no way. Sure, he'd support the President, as much as he could. That was his job, and he'd do it. But Reagan had to get the facts out. And if heads rolled, well, so be it. . . . Dole wasn't going to let them shove the Party down the toilet for another eight years. Not this time. This was his time.

Dole was back in the Town Car within ten minutes. "Get the office," he snapped. And then, over the car phone, on the way to the airport and the Other Thing, he asked not for his Chief of Staff, not for his National Security man, but for the Press Secretary:

"Agghh, gotta get out a statement," he said. "They took the money from Iran, for the missiles, gave it to the contras. Gaghhh, you b'lieve it? President's gonna announce it in an hour. Yeah, it's kinda bizarre . . . I wanta call it 'a bizarre twist.' Say the President's doin' the right thing, get all the facts out . . . support the President . . . yeah, point is, it's all gotta come out."

— ★ —

"I'm just not gonna say anything now," Bush snapped. He'd been through this, explained it a million times. Why couldn't they understand? His own staff, guys who ought to know him . . . they were coming at him again on this AEI speech, the American Enterprise Institute, the perfect chance to distance himself from the whole Iranamok mess. In his office in the West Wing, Bush spoke to the speech draft that was fanned out on the desk in front of him. "Look, I've spent *six years* being loyal to this President . . ." Bush's voice was high, petulant with his sense of injustice.

"This doesn't abandon the President," Fred Khedouri said. Khedouri was writing the speech—or trying, at least. He'd been back and forth with it a half-dozen times. He'd write in a line about the Iran thing—something *innocuous,* just an acknowledgment that something *went wrong*—and Bush would balk, like a horse that saw a snake. To Khedouri, it was so obvious: if the VP stuck his head in the sand, it sent a message that he was complicitous . . . or lost in the same fog of know-nothing denial that hung over the rest of the White House. It just wouldn't play! He tried to keep his voice even: "There ought to be some recognition . . ."

The Veep heard the edge under Khedouri's voice—like Bush was some thickheaded child who had to have it explained. Goddammit, he understood English! He didn't need a pointy-head like Khedouri to lead him through it. Khedouri was another stranger, one of Fuller's hires, out of Stockman's shop. A real brain—drove Bush nuts—all head, like a lot of guys who were too damn smart to have any sense. Annoyance drove Bush into his second language, Texan, the one he'd picked up along with his distaste for the Harvard Yard crowd:

"Look, I'm not gonna paint my tail white and run with the antelopes now."

Fuller let Khedouri carry the ball on this: it didn't do any good to back the Veep into a corner. It wasn't that Fuller thought George Bush could get by without some firm statement on the scandal, but he'd come at the Veep in his own way, easygoing: *Oh, on that speech thing, sir* . . . Problem was, they were running out of time. When Bush got back from his Thanksgiving trip to Kennebunkport, there were only three days till the speech. And Bush came back more convinced than ever that none of this should have come out: *Why are they releasing a chronology? . . . This is a covert operation!* . . . Worse still, Bush had turned the whole episode into an issue of loyalty, a matter of the personal code. Ronald Reagan just couldn't see that he or his boys did anything wrong, and George Bush was not going to be the one to rub Reagan's face in it.

So he said nothing. He disappeared. If the OVP was a whisper zone before, now it was a crypt. Everybody in the capital had *something* to say—except George Bush, who went to ground like the undead at sunrise. At the PAC, the political guys were catching it on the phones. Republicans were getting nervous. *Doonesbury* was running Bush every day as the invisible man. The well-fed, well-pleased men with pink jowls and red ties were chuckling about him over lunch with their clients at Joe and Mo's, Duke Zeibert's. . . . "Oh, I know George—nice guy, but Dole could eat him for breakfast . . . problem is, heh heh, you're hungry a half-hour later. . . ." He had caught the dread and fatal affliction: he was ridiculous.

He had to say something! In the office, they all told him—or, to be precise, they mostly clucked to one another about his stubborn incomprehension.

"How about, 'Sure, we made mistakes, but *they were mistakes of compassion . . . pursuit of the long-term interests of*' . . ."

"No, he won't do it. Teeter tried that."

"How 'bout: '*Everybody* makes mistakes . . . but the long record will show' . . ."

"No way. He's not gonna say the President did anything wrong."

"Yeah, but where was *he*? He's got to say something."

But Bush wouldn't budge. He didn't mind taking his share of the hit, if they'd give him a share of the credit for the good stuff. . . . But he wasn't going to cut and run now, no matter how many brainy-boy staff got into his knickers. They hadn't been around the track like he had. Reagan would be back, in the polls, they'd come around. Something would happen—always did. Good things happened to good people. Now was the time to have some faith. . . . For Christ's sake, how about some faith in *him*? That was the hardest part, when he looked up at the latest guy in front of his desk, lecturing him on the speech. His own guys! He saw the doubt in their eyes: they looked at him like he couldn't understand, or like he must be protecting himself, like he was part of the problem. They didn't understand loyalty, either. Well, they'd better start. . . . No, that wasn't fair. It was hard for them, too. They'd hitched their wagons to his, to his future, his campaign, and now it looked like the wheels had fallen off before they'd even started. Jeez, next month they were supposed to change the PAC to a real campaign committee. . . .

Bush had a dinner scheduled, the night before the big speech, with Sadruddin Khan, the Aga Khan's brother, a friend of his, just a lovely guy, played some tennis, spoke like an Englishman . . . hell, he almost was an Englishman, a Prince of the Earth in general, smooth, shiny like a brushed otter. What a credit to the Third World! . . . But Sadruddin had to cancel, and the VP already had the big table at the Alibi Club, one of the old family haunts. So Bush decided to keep the table: he'd invite the senior staff—bring the wives, make it a family thing—he'd get them together in a difficult time, get the team together . . .

And there, in the old townhouse on I Street, behind the unmarked door you wouldn't even notice unless you knew, unless you'd always known; there, in the old club with its brown, musty air and its walls festooned with tatty memento; there, where the caricature of Prescott Bush held pride of place, the drawing of Pres, singing, with the dome of the Capitol behind him and the notes of "The Whiffenpoof Song" floating around his head, there George Bush tried to tell them why he took that stuff out of the speech. It wasn't that direct, really, not a planned set of remarks: he just started to talk. And for twenty minutes, without a text, without raising his voice, or chopping the air, or lapsing into any of those gestures he employed to give force to his words when he talked to strangers, Bush made the most eloquent speech:

Loyalty, he said, was something he grew up with. It wasn't a sin. And he didn't claim it was always an asset. It was just part of him. Sometimes, it didn't work to one's benefit. There was a time in his life, when he was Republican Chairman under Nixon, when he stayed loyal to the end. Nixon had assured him—personally—that he was not involved in Watergate. And Bush got burned. But he knew that was not going to happen now. Ronald Reagan was a good man. He wasn't going to go through the case with them. But they could take it from him, as they went through this tough time, and turned to the new campaign: he knew they were going to come out all right. And he'd do the best he could—for all of them—loyally. He couldn't really be any other way.

Afterward, the room at the club was quiet. What more was there to say?

People started to drift away. They'd all have early meetings the next day
. . . Bush was about to go, too, when Khedouri made a last quiet stab, with
Bar. It was risky. She might have taken his head off—she could do it, too—for
trying to get to George Bush through her. She hated that. But she listened that
night, as Khedouri told her: Bush had to say *something* in the speech; it wasn't
against the President; no one wanted to hurt the President; this was a way to
help Ronald Reagan, to find a way out, to acknowledge that things . . . well,
to put it behind them. . . .

Bar didn't say anything. She'd never share her opinions. And no one would
ever know what she said, or did not say, that night in the Residence. All they
knew was that George Bush had Ed Meese in the office, early the next day,
and then the two of them went to the President, and when they came back,
Bush had the words: *Mistakes were made* . . . that's what he'd say. No human
beings mentioned in the sentence—nothing more. He'd talked to the President.
Mistakes were made. He wrote it into the speech himself. The press copies were
already Xeroxed without mention of mistakes—no matter. That would only
make it better. People would notice: *he would diverge from text.* It was great!
Fitzwater got on the phone to the big-foot reporters, to the networks, the
columnists. They might want to make sure they were there today: Bush had
something to say!

And they were all there, in the gallery upstairs, and CNN showed it *live*
. . . while Fitzwater spun the story like a mad hula-hoopster: George Bush
addressed the nation on the issue that mattered. George Bush said the words
everyone had been waiting to hear. George Bush stepped out front and told
it like it was!

That night, at a State Department banquet, Bush tried to shrug off congratulations. "Great speech today . . . absolutely great." They were literally patting
him on his shoulders, his back.

"He's had wonn-derful reviews, calls from all over the country," Bar confided in the receiving line. Bush's face twisted into his aw-shucks grin: "At least
I didn't get thrown out," he said.

The world was off his shoulders. He looked terrific. Everybody said so. How
did Bar keep him looking so good?

Bar said sweetly: "I beat him . . ."

Hoo hooo! Isn't that Bar a *stitch*?

And the next day, and the next, more wonn-derful reviews. And Larry
Speakes said the President *agreed* with every word. And Lee Atwater told the
networks that Republicans across the country were cheering. "The Vahz
Pres'ent," Lee growled, "hit uh gusher!"

The Era of Good Feeling lasted ten days, until Don Gregg, the Veep's
National Security man, gave his first interview to *The New York Times.* Yes,
he'd found out about the contra resupply back in August, Gregg acknowledged. His friend and fellow spook, Felix Rodriguez, had come to Washington
specially to tell him how screwed up it was. Then the next day, UPI came out
with unnamed White House sources, alleging that Bush's office knew the

contra gambit every step of the way. Ollie North kept them posted religiously.

What did George Bush know?

By mid-December, that was the only question anybody wanted to ask him. Now Bush had to issue his *own* chronology, make public a series of contacts between his staff, Ollie North, and the contras.

"Let the chips fall where they may," he'd said in his big AEI speech. Who could have known they'd fall on him?

And now, every day, Fitzwater had to march into the big office, and screw some statement out of Bush. Bush would say to his desk or his pen:

"I've answered that a million times."

Or, "That's just not true . . . I had nothing to do with that."

Or, "Salvador . . . Felix Rodriguez is a *hero* down there, to the people of Salvador."

And Fitzwater would persist, gingerly: "So I can say, 'Vice President Bush *never met with Felix Rodriguez*' . . ." And Bush would stare at his twisting pen, silent, while Marlin had to finish the quote. ". . . '*except, uh, to discuss El Salvador*'? . . ."

And when, at last, Bush would glance up with that blank-wall look, even Fitzwater had to wonder what the hell was behind that stare. Was there something he was unable to say? Was he culpable of knowing? Or just heart-sick?

At the moment, Bush was only waiting to see if Marlin was done. Was it over? When would this be over? . . . He'd said more than he wanted already. More than he ever should have. And what did it get him? . . . When Fitzwater didn't say any more, Bush replied, tersely:

"Okay. Say that."

—★—

Dole was never *off* TV. The election recaps rolled right into Iran-contra, and every time you flicked on the tube, or glanced at a paper, there was Dole. Dole by satellite, Dole on Koppel, Dole on *Face the Nation* . . . Top story: "Dole says . . ." "Good evening, on Capitol Hill today, the Senate Majority Leader . . ." Dole, Dole, Dole. No guest was supposed to be on Brinkley's Sunday chat-fest more than twice a year—they changed that policy for Dole. What else could they do? The guy made news.

Dole knew what those Sunday shows needed as well as the panelists, the host, the producers. He knew he didn't have to show up at ten, like the bookers insisted. He'd roll in at quarter-after, twenty-after, and head straight for the makeup room. He knew the girls by name, always had a greeting to settle them down, make 'em forget he was late. "Agghhh, kinda *hot* . . . Sam must be askin' all the questions. Hegh hegh hegh." Someone would bring him a half-cup of coffee from the table set with brunch. Dole never hung around to eat. On the set, no matter what went out on the air, it was always jokes and gossip during commercials: just a few Washington white men, sitting around like it was lunch at Joe and Mo's . . . what the hell, they were all well known, in the know.

Brinkley and Dole were neighbors in Florida, where Elizabeth owned a condo. Brinkley was a friend, or close enough. . . . And Dole always brought a nugget of news he could drop into the chat, somewhere, enough to make the Monday *Post* print the sentence: "Dole made his proposal (charge, comment, remark) in an interview on the ABC television program *This Week with David Brinkley.* . . ." That, and maybe one catchy sound-bite to run on CNN all day, then on the Monday *Today* show.

So, on the Sunday after the diversion was announced, Dole rolled into the studio for the Brinkley show, with just time enough. "Howy'*dooonn*? . . ." He looked terrific, tanned and healthy from his big vacation, two days for Thanksgiving at the condo in Florida. Makeup had him in and out in a minute—just powder. He looked fine. "Aghh, shoppin' *done*?" The Bobster was all holiday cheer. The music was playing in his head, the overture of the Other Thing . . . and, *heyyy*! . . . here's an issue plopped onto the ground before him like a Mexican sombrero, an invitation to the dance! A big beautiful Washington Hat Dance! No one could do it like Bob Dole. He had news to make this morning and a network to air it. . . . The White House in trouble! Bush under a cloud! What did they know and . . . da *dum*! . . . He was ready to dance . . . the Washington Dance of Death!

He'd worked to get this nugget: while he was in Florida, he'd had a chat with Bob Strauss, Mr. Democrat, a real insider, another condo neighbor. Bobster told Strauss he was thinking of a Special Select Committee on Iran— like Sam Ervin's Watergate committee. Of course, he knew the idea wouldn't stop with Strauss, and sure enough, when he got back, here was Bob Byrd on the telephone: maybe they could, uh, *coordinate* . . . So they agreed, they'd both propose it, Byrd on *Face the Nation,* Bobster on the Brinkley-fest. That would surely be news enough, but it might give Byrd equal billing. So that morning, the Bobster pulled the ace from his sleeve: he wanted a special committee to consolidate the hearings, the information . . . but he wanted it now, *this week*! A special session of Congress! Convened by Ronald Reagan to get the facts out! The first special session since Harry Truman called Congress back from the hinterlands, thirty-eight years ago!

It was gorgeous, a master stroke, raised the issue to a full-scale crisis . . . *not since 1948.* . . . Let the boys in the White House gnash their teeth. Bob Dole was *protecting* the President, making sure there weren't ten committees holding hearings, calling for documents, witnesses, all at once. And proposing that the President start it *now,* while Republicans (i.e., Bob Dole) could still control the Senate, keep a hand on the committee. What was the matter with those guys in the White House—couldn't they see? If they went along with Dole, then the action shifted to Congress, to the wrangle over the committee. It would take the heat off the President!

And, of course, it left Bob Byrd in the dust. But how could the Democrats squawk? Dole wasn't trying to outmaneuver anyone. "Agghh, been around too long for that." No, he'd be glad to let the committee reflect the lineup in the new Senate, to convene next year, the Democratic majority. . . . How could *they* oppose this? Were they trying to drag out the issue? Didn't they say they wanted all the facts out? . . . Well, let's get going!

The white men on the Brinkley set were trying not to grin, like cheap lawyers at a ten-car pileup: Uh, did that mean Senator Dole didn't think all the facts were out? Didn't he believe the White House, that North and Poindexter were the only ones who knew?

The Bobster dropped an eyebrow and rasped: "Aghh, don't think Ripley'd believe that."

Eureka! The sound-bite!

The next day, the *Post* had the story of President Reagan's first defiant reaction to the scandal of the diversion. But that didn't lead the paper. The lead story was Dole's call for a special session, along with a nice picture of the Senator, a big one, above the fold.

And that was only the beginning. That day, as Dole emerged from the White House, a meeting with Don Regan, he called for appointment of a Special Prosecutor. No, it was nothing against Ed Meese. But he *was* awfully close to the President. Republicans, Dole said, were already "suffering damage" from the scandal. That's what he told Don Regan. We've got to cut our losses! It'll be good for the President! "He didn't make mistakes. The people around him made mistakes." Remember, Bob Dole was *defending* the President!

Sometimes, in the dust from the Bobster's dancing shoes, it was hard to keep track of whom he was defending.

Nothing wrong with Meese . . . but when are we getting a Special Prosecutor?

George Shultz, a fine Secretary of State . . . "But, I must say, when people say, 'Why aren't you out there supporting the President?' . . . it's rather difficult when the Secretary of State is not doing anything."

Bob Dole would certainly not be the one to tell the President to fire his Chief of Staff . . . "But I think right now they ought to circle the wagons—either that, or let a couple of wagons go over the cliff."

Meanwhile, lest the White House make good its intention to move on to other business, Dole was on the front page again, this time calling for a summit with European leaders, to reassure the allies about U.S. foreign policy.

Meanwhile, lest anyone else miss the point, Dole made a speech in New Hampshire, and pronounced the whole Iran-contra gambit "just plain stupid."

He left Byrd and the Democrats gasping for air. The Bobster carried the ball for both sides. As for rival candidates for the Other Thing, they could only stand by, biting their tongues. Jack Kemp's Press Secretary made the papers one day with a warning that Dole was "too eager to make news over the corpse of a popular President." But that weekend, when Kemp hoped to appear on *Face the Nation,* Lesley Stahl wanted Bob Dole instead.

After that, *The New York Times* ran a page one R.W. Apple analysis that began: "Bob Dole of Kansas, the Senate majority leader who will become minority leader next year, has seen his prospects of winning the 1988 Republican Presidential nomination enhanced. . . ." That signaled the rest of the nation's press to pile on. "Mr. Dole may be the man with the most to gain," *The Wall Street Journal* reported the next week. And the week after that, came the *Post:* "Polls and political strategists indicate that, partly because of his recent high-profile performance, he has moved within striking distance of Bush. . . ."

Striking distance! It was soft-shoe on the coffin lid! Up in New Hampshire, which is where it counted, the organ of the mad-dog right, the Manchester *Union Leader,* was getting tired of Republicans who failed in their duty to defend the President. So the *Union Leader,* as it was wont, launched a foam-flecked attack on . . . George Bush! The headline: MORE MUSH FROM THE WIMP.

Of course, Bob Dole couldn't focus on the primaries now, not with the White House under assault, the credibility of the U.S. at stake. He had to appoint the members of the Special Select Committee, Senators of energy and intrepid judgment who would get to the bottom of this sorry affair and restore government to its proper business. Not that there was any shortage of candidates. These hearings could make a man Well Known! So, the Leader weighed probity, experience, intellect, savvy . . . and from among all the eager volunteers, he selected as the ranking Republican member . . . Warren Rudman, of New Hampshire.

No politics about it! It was well known that Rudman was lined up for '88 with his friend, the former Senator from Tennessee, Howard Baker. (Everybody knew Baker was running.) And Rudman did bring to the job a fine set of qualifications: he was well informed about foreign policy, national security. And he had experience as a prosecutor, as a former Attorney General of his great state. In fact, three of the five Senators selected by Bob Dole had been prosecutors. Dole meant to make sure *all* the facts came out—*he* wouldn't have to say a thing.

That's why, in all the reams of his public comment, in November and December, about the Iran affair, there was not one mention, not one word attachable to Bob Dole's name that pointed in any way to the Vice President, George Bush. It was the highest triumph of the Be Nice rule. He knew the wise guys were waiting for him to say something nasty—just one misstep in the Dance of Death . . . and it was over.

But why would he? Bob Dole never had just one source on something he wanted to know. The White House briefings and meetings with Regan were not his only avenue of inquiry on Iran-contra. And Dole was convinced: Bush was in the soup. All the connections were clear in Dole's head. The whole push on the hostages, the whole deal with Iran, had to do with the kidnapped Beirut CIA station chief, William Buckley. There was word, breathed into Dole's ear . . . the White House had a videotape: Buckley under torture . . . that's when the deal was cooked up. Buckley had worked for Bush, the kind of guy Bush loved, a secret op with an air of action about him, came from a good family . . . made his name in Vietnam, where one of his guys, his top men, was Felix Rodriguez. He was the link. . . . And when that CIA plane went down in

Nicaragua, who got called? Felix Rodriguez! And where did he report? To George Bush's office, to that other spook who worked for him, Gregg!

It was so obvious! And it had to come out. Maybe not now, or even soon. But it would come out, and the committee would prove: George Bush knew all about it!

But even Dole failed to calculate the capacity for knowing-not-knowing. Even he, the most able inside player in the U.S. Congress, underestimated George Bush's Washington art. Even while Dole danced his spectacular tarantella on the White House, the Congress, his fellow candidates . . . he made one fatal error of judgment: he thought George Bush must be something like him. If Bob Dole had sat in the VP's chair every day as the little man with the briefcase retailed the covert news of the world, or as the NSC staff in the Oval Office outlined the "initiative to Iran" . . . there was *no way* Bob Dole would not commit an overt act of knowing. There would be *not one day* when Dole could maintain he was Out of the Loop. As he said, in mid-dance, to one group of admiring reporters: "Agh, m'not one to sit on the sidelines."

So, he said nothing about George Bush. Why should he? Reporters were telling him privately that Bush was dead. All Dole had to do now was beat Jack Kemp. Hah! And not just reporters. Big guys, insiders, the kind Dole listened to, were coming on to him. Looked like John Sears, the guy who started Reagan in 1980, was going to run Dole's campaign! By mid-December, the Iowa poll from *The Des Moines Register* had Dole, for the first time, in the lead over Bush! So Dole kept dancing.

There he was with all the cameras again, on December 16, announcing Rudman's name, and the other members of the new committee. "A Watergate-style committee" is what the papers called it. And there, in the press conference, one of the young anchormen-to-be had a question for Dole, the big question now . . .

Hasn't this endless trauma destroyed the Republicans' chances in 1988? Doesn't it make the nomination . . . worthless?

Dole imperceptibly shrugged one shoulder and a little smile softened his face. He said:

"I'll take it."

7

1947

HE WAS knocked back to childhood, learning to walk, eat, dress himself, write . . . but without even a baby's physical attainments: control of limbs, the strength to reach, push, grab. And without a child's sense of wonder, without the fresh triumph of discovery. Instead, there was the knowledge of what was lost, how he used to run, pull, lift: the sense that Bob Dole was not whole anymore.

Percy Jones Army Medical Center was Uncle Sam's place for miracles, where amputees got new arms and legs, and new lives to go with them, a place where spinal paraplegics started moving, got up and walked again. It was opened after Pearl Harbor in a single massive building in Battle Creek, Michigan, an old-fashioned sanatorium endowed by the Kellogg cereal fortune, with a sweeping lawn and a grand central staircase in the echoing entry hall. By the time Dole checked in, Percy Jones was a small city in itself—with a population bigger than Russell, Kansas.

But with all the Army's assembled wizardry, there was no orthopedic short-cut for Dole. His was a solitary battle, maddeningly slow. The nurses could lift him out of traction, help him off his bed, but after that, it was up to Bob how many baby steps he could take. One day, by act of will, he might walk to the end of the hall, and his hope for a miracle would swell again. He was going to make it back, whole, good as new—back at school, he'd play for Phog Allen. . . . But then, the next morning, in the whirlpool, a therapist might work for two hours, unsuccessfully, trying gently to pry two fingers apart on the claw of his right hand. Or Dole might lie in traction all day, trying, until sweat rolled down his face, to move two fingers together, on his left hand. And if he could not, the world went black, and there was Dole alone again, just his will—that was all he recognized of himself—trapped in a hospital bed with his nemesis, this body.

The doctors could ease the struggle sometimes: if he had pain, there was Demerol. But the narcotics knocked out his will, too, and that he could not let them take. That was all he had, and he learned to hide it, deep inside, where nothing could touch it; not the false cheer of doctors, nor even his own family's brave smiles; not the pain from his body, nor even the evidence of his reason, his own racing brain that told him, screamed in his head, the ugly fact that he would not hear, that he could not accept: he would *never* be what he was.

How could he ever let that worm bore to his center: What the hell would he do then? Play bridge all day, like the guys in the ward, with his cards held in a special rack, while someone else shuffled his turn? And after that, what would he do? Sell pencils on Main Street? Sometimes, he could actually *see* himself on Main Street, Russell, in a wheelchair, with a cup. That was his private vision of hell, the spur to get him up, trying again. He didn't tell anybody about it, wouldn't let them near that part of him that still burned bright. And he didn't want it dulled with the dirty facts of the here and now, the needles, the hot-wax treatments that never loosened his hand, the bedpan-bedsore-nuts-and-bolts of hospital life. So, whenever they came to talk, no matter who they were, or how well intentioned, there was always a joke to hold them off, something about the weather, or a nurse, or another guy on the ward. The doctors and nurses marveled at him: that Lieutenant Dole was just *wonderful,* so full of good humor. They started to wheel him around to other wards. He'd cheer up the rest of the fellows.

But what about him? Where was his cheer? It got to be frighteningly clear to Dole, the Army had no miracle for him—not at Percy Jones. After months there, he could barely walk, there was still no movement in his right arm, almost no feeling in his left hand. And there was no plan to do much about it—not that he could divine. So he got leave to go home to Russell. If he had to make his miracle himself, he'd do it. If the doctors in Michigan couldn't straighten out his arm, he'd do it alone. So Kenny came back to Michigan and brought Bob home on the train. Bina and Doran moved once again to the children's bedroom, in the back of the house. Once again, they rented a hospital bed and a rolling tray for the front room. Doran, Kenny, and some neighborhood fellows hooked up ropes and pulley-weights from old sash windows on the wall of the garage, behind the house, so Bob could work on his strength, every day.

And Bob worked, alone, day and night, on his problem. That's what he called it, his problem: there were no good words for this enemy, his body. What words could anybody use that would not burrow into him and eat at the will that was keeping him alive? It wasn't that he chose to wall himself away, but what else could he do, when he heard those words that would never leave him? One day, when he was with Doran at the grain elevator, a farmer came in and, by way of chat, asked: "This your crippled son?" There wasn't a thing for Bob to say, but for days after, he was clouded over with gloom and rage. One afternoon, when he'd been home awhile, he screwed up his courage and walked to Dawson Drug. Main Street seemed a hundred miles long. He was sure everybody was looking at him—120 pounds: he was a spectacle!—the way his feet shuffled, his right arm cocked up in a lead brace that a high school pal, Adolph Reisig, made for him at his auto body shop. Bob got into the drugstore and hauled himself, without help, onto a seat at the counter. But even then his bones wouldn't sit right on the stool. Bub and Chet had to adjust him for balance, like a rickety piece of furniture. One of the geezers at the wooden-top tables said: "Gee, that's too bad. . . . You prob'ly wished they woulda finished you off . . ." Bob turned and glared, felt his face flush hot. "If I thought like that, I'da been dead a long time ago." But for months, he didn't go back to Dawson's.

He worked alone. He pulled down the dark curtain of reserve that he could not lift again, even when he chose. He'd spend all day behind the house, working himself to exhaustion with the ropes on the garage wall. Bina would stand at the back door and call: "Bob, don't you want to rest? Bob! Come in and rest awhile . . ." He'd just say: "No." He'd growl it. Or he wouldn't answer. He'd pull harder. He was trying to pull with the bad right arm. If he could straighten that out, he'd play again. Even when he was in the house, he'd be squeezing a rubber ball, or a nutcracker, with the left hand. Even when he sat in a chair, his legs were moving. Time was weighing on him: months were flying by, and he felt he was standing still. He could walk around the block, but that wasn't good enough. He pushed it, faster, harder, until he was dragging his bony form along in a shuffling run. He brought the lead arm brace back to Adolph in the body shop: he wanted more lead in it, more, and more, a constant weight, so it ached, so he knew he was working it every minute.

There was no schedule in the house anymore, except for Bob's racing internal clock. Chet and Ruth Dawson would show up to play bridge at midnight, and Bina'd do a load of wash while the card game went on around her. Food was whatever he wanted, when he wanted, and where: if Bob said he'd like to be outside, Bina would move the whole show outdoors: tablecloth, silver, the dishes with the pattern of pink blossoms and green leaves. . . . Or Bina'd ask Bob in the middle of the morning: "You want a Coke?" And everyone would pile into the car, and ride out to the highway. Norma Jean would come in the afternoons, and Bob would ask: "You doin' anything tonight? . . . No?" And then she'd stay with him in the front room and rub that arm for hours. Gloria was married by then, living out of town, but she'd come back to visit, too, mostly to talk to Bob. She'd ask about the war sometimes, in case he wanted to get it off his chest. But Bob would only say, "Agh, the heroes are still over there." He meant the dead ones. That put an end to the questions. Now Kenny was married, too, living with his beautiful Dottie in a little brick house, right next door. Of course, Kenny was still on call. If Bob had to go anywhere, Kenny took him. (He was driving Bob back to Michigan on Dottie's twenty-first birthday.) But mostly, it was Bina who did for Bob. Kenny would do for Bina. And she wasn't shy about asking. More and more, as Bob's problem wore her down, she didn't have patience for anyone else. When Dottie was in labor with Kenny's first child, Bina visited her in the delivery room and rasped: "Are you all right?"

Dottie said: "Feel like I'm gonna die."

"Aw, you'll live," Bina snapped, and went back home to Bob.

On his darker days, Kenny's marriage and his new baby girl were hard for Bob, too. It wasn't that he grudged it to his younger brother—not at all. But Bob was the elder . . . always a mile out in front of that kid. And now Kenny was a husband, a father . . . and Bob? Treading water, trying to get back to where he was. Who would *he* live his life with? Who'd take him now . . . like this? Did he even have the right to impose his . . . problem? No, he'd probably be alone. Hell, he was alone. No matter how everybody did for him, how long they sat and talked with him, how late they stayed up to see if they could get him to sleep . . . when it got down to it, it was Bob, alone. Sometimes, Dottie would wake, next door, to give the baby a bottle or quiet her in her crib. And through the darkness outside, she'd hear the music from Bina's house. It was Bob, with the record player he got when he went off to KU. And he'd play that song, over and over, Jane Froman's song from *Carousel* . . .

> *When you walk through a storm,*
> *hold your head up high*

Sometimes, after he played that song, you could see he felt better, and he'd say, "How 'bout s'more music?" And he'd play it again, and whistle along.

> *Walk on, walk on*
> *with hope in your heart,*
> *And you'll never walk alone,*
> *You'll never walk alone!*

And then, everyone was lighter. Even Bina was happy. But just as suddenly, the dark curtain could descend. One day, back by the garage, Bob fell and couldn't get up. "Never gonna work . . ." he was muttering afterward. "Terrible . . . crawling around like an *animal.*" Then there was *nothing* they could do for him. That was the awful fact at the bottom of their every day. It didn't matter what they did for him. It didn't *count* unless he could do it himself. He *had* to do it alone. Now he wouldn't let anyone light a cigarette for him. Sometimes, with a match, he'd char his numb left hand black . . . but don't try to get in his way. Or, he'd be sitting at the table, getting along okay with a fork in that balky left hand. But then a piece of food would tumble to his lap. And his face would go dark with helpless rage. And he wouldn't say a word. He'd just get up and walk out. No one dared follow him, or say anything.

One afternoon, the family came home, and there was no Bob—not in the bedroom, the living room, he wasn't out back, pulling on the ropes. Bina called Dawson's, then Doran: no Bob, not a sign of him. Finally, they looked inside the garage, and there he was, hanging from the rafters by the bad right arm. Hanging with his feet swinging off the floor. Soaked and trembling with sweat and pain. Bina burst into tears right there. Thought he was dead. But his will was alive: Bob wouldn't come down. If he could straighten out that arm, he was going to play ball again.

— ★ —

He was still hunting the miracle, when an uncle who'd served in the Medical Corps told him about Dr. K. This was Hampar Kelikian, who'd escaped to America as a boy, with twenty dollars and a carpet from his family home in Armenia, and had worked his way to eminence as a neurosurgeon in Chicago. Dr. K. knew about wars: his three sisters were killed in the massacres that posed as war in his native land; his brother, a soldier in World War II, was killed in the Italian campaign. Dr. K. also enlisted, in the Army Medical Corps: he became a pioneer in the restoration of damaged limbs. President Truman awarded him a medal for special contributions to military medicine. In 1947, Dole made his pilgrimage to Chicago.

Kelikian was a small man, with curly hair, prematurely gray. He was friendly, brisk, optimistic. He spoke with an accent, but no hesitation. He knew what could be done for Dole, and he knew he could do it. But he wanted Dole to know something, too: there wasn't going to be a miracle. He could give Dole partial use of the arm, maybe forty percent: the rest was up to Bob. He could jerry-rig a shoulder of sorts, but there was no way it would rotate: the arm would not lift; Dole would not play ball. What Dr. K could do was corporeal carpentry, not magic. . . . That was the most important work he did for Dole, and he did it with words. There was something about Kelikian, his certainty, his self-possession, the big office in Chicago, or the way he'd pulled himself up by his own will . . . or maybe Dole was just ready. But he listened. Kelikian told him: "Don't think anymore about what you've lost. You have to think about what you have . . . and what you can do with it."

Kelikian would not take a fee for his work, not from Bob, not a dime. He'd do it out of gratitude to his adopted land. To Dr. K., Bob Dole represented something fundamental about the country: "This young man . . ." the doctor said later. "He had the faith to endure."

Still, Dole would have to come back to Chicago, to check into a hospital, and this wasn't on the Army's ticket anymore. Back in Russell, Chet Dawson spread the news: Bob had to go to Chicago for an operation. And he put a cigar box on the drugstore counter: the Bob Dole Fund . . . the Dawson boys started it off with a few bills themselves. And Chet was post commander at the time, so the VFW took up the charge. Pretty soon, Bub Shaffer at the Home State Bank was taking collections, too. Then, they started across the street at the Russell State Bank, and then Banker's Mercantile and the rest of the shops pitched in. Everybody in town lent a hand, one way or another. One lady put thirty cents in the box—that was all she could afford. But there was some serious money, too, and by June, when Bina packed the car for the trip to Chicago, the people of Russell had collected one thousand eight hundred dollars to help Bob Dole get back on his feet.

It turned out there were three operations: the first to cut away the bone in the shattered shoulder, to hang the arm instead by a strip of muscle that Dr. Kelikian took from Dole's thigh. But in recuperation at Percy Jones, the arm wouldn't come down: it fused instead in front of Dole's chest, about at the level of his chin. So Kelikian went at it again, and after the second operation, the arm healed at Dole's side. It was as Dr. K. had told him: no miracle, nothing magic about it. The arm would hang shorter than his left arm, Dole would never be able to lift it much, or control it at full rotation. But the point was, Dole could do something with it. He could hold it a certain way—like this . . . and it looked like an arm again.

In a third operation, Kelikian tried to transplant muscle and tendon back to the right hand. Most of that didn't take, so Dole's fingers would always splay unnaturally on that right hand; but he learned he could roll it around a pen, a folded paper, something to give it shape. It started to look like a hand again.

The point was, he could do something with it. The biggest change was how Dole looked at it. Look what he could do! In October, Norma Jean was married, and Bob went to the wedding as best man. He wore his lieutenant's uniform—not the fussy dress stuff, but the Eisenhower jacket, with the square padded shoulders. He was thin, but his *eyes* . . . he looked so handsome. The minister put Norma Jean's ring onto one of Bob's fingers: that was the only way Bob could hold it, until the proper moment; but nobody saw that, the way Bob did it. What they saw was the way he stood up at Trinity Methodist, on Main Street, in front of all the guests, like a soldier, proud, straight as a rod.

8

1948

ADVENTURE was not a word that
would have leapt to most minds in
that apartment. Nothing wrong
with Hillhouse Avenue, of course: the president of Yale lived next door. But
37 Hillhouse was cut up into thirteen flats, divvied out to married veterans with
children. So thirteen couples lived in the house, each with a child, save for one
couple with twins: that made forty souls altogether. And they were lucky to
get the place. After the war, when almost ten million men and women suddenly
qualified for the GI Bill, the campuses took the brunt of the avalanche. The
vets lived in trailers, Quonset huts, abandoned barracks. At the University of
California, couples were living in cars.

Poppy and Bar were extra-lucky: they had their own bathroom. The two
couples with whom they shared a kitchen also had to share a bathroom. That
was apparently too much to take. So the two other couples feuded endlessly,
and there were battles about the two refrigerators that three couples (and three
children) had to share. One of the neighbors got so furious at the others that
he brought in inspectors to test their germs. He claimed there were more germs
in their fridge than in the sewers of New Haven. Mostly, the other couples
never spoke. One family ate at five and the other at seven, so they wouldn't
have to pass. Well, utopia this was not.

But adventure . . . it surely was, to Barbara Bush. New Haven was the first
place Bar had lived on her own, without her parents, or some school authority
(or the U.S. Navy, which greeted her as a bride) ruling her destiny *in loco
parentis.*

Ever since Bar could remember, her mother and older sister had imposed their wisdom on whatever Bar had to do. Her mother, Pauline Pierce, another daughter of the good Midwest (her father, James Robinson, served on Ohio's first Supreme Court), was a woman of great and refined beauty, an insatiable, somewhat spendthrift collector of beautiful things, and a woman of expert enthusiasms. Horticulture, fine needlepoint, management of the home and children, matters of dress, taste, and decorum—Pauline had firm, often idiosyncratic, ideas on *everything*, and her notions, however insupportable, were not subject to argument. She was a joiner and a ferocious doer, who had, as Barbara concluded at length, not much sense of humor in general, and none about herself or her children. Barbara's older sister, Martha, got her mother's looks, her brains, and her temperament: she had definite ideas, five years' more experience on the planet, and no discernible shyness about instructing her ungainly younger sister. What's more, Martha was thin. Barbara was not.

Barbara was what parents call a big-boned girl: at age twelve, she stood five-foot-eight and weighed, as she would forever recall, one hundred forty-eight pounds. Pauline had definite ideas on food, and the Pierces sat to a splendid table: garden vegetables shining with butter, mashed potatoes, real cream for the cereal. . . . Pauline would urge: "Eat up, Martha . . . *Not you, Barbara* . . ." It was maddening: Martha stayed thin, no matter what. Barbara might have taken the contrast more to heart were it not for her father (whose big bones, after all, she'd inherited) defending his favorite.

Marvin Pierce was a big, broad-faced man, easygoing, funny, a splendid athlete at Miami of Ohio, yet another scion of good Midwest manufacturers who'd moved the family east to New York, and thence to the stately commuter town of Rye, New York, as he climbed the ladder at McCall Publishing. By the time his third child, Barbara, was born, Marvin had long since learned to survive his wife's fierce certainties with resort to irreverent humor and the quiet pleasures of the golf course.

Barbara learned to survive, too, with her own mix of irreverence and imagination. She was a great reader, not only of the classic girls' books of the day, *Little Women, Jane Eyre,* and the dog stories by Albert Payson Terhune, but also the serial stories that appeared in her father's McCall company magazines. Then, too, there were McCall pattern books, suitable for Barbara and her friends to cut up, to dress a thousand paper dolls, for romance and daring exploit in all corners of the world. There was her dog, Sandy, to run with, her bike to ride through the neighborhood, tree-climbing, rope-skipping, swimming in Long Island Sound, tennis lessons (Barbara had her father's—ungirlish, at the time—love of sport), and a general unconcern for dainty appearance. Even after she'd slimmed down to quite a lovely young woman herself; even after she'd followed Martha's path, and Pauline's notion of proper education, to three years at a finishing school (Ashley Hall) in South Carolina; even after she'd followed Martha, again, to Smith College (where Martha had been discovered by *Vogue* and photographed for its cover as "College Girl of the Year"); even after Christmas '41, when her large bright eyes and open smile, her off-the-shoulder green-and-red dress, her flowing auburn hair and soft, pale skin had attracted the notice of Poppy Bush across the dance floor at the Round Hill Club in Greenwich, Connecticut, Barbara Pierce was a young woman notable for not putting all her stock in appearance. Identity (hers, at least) was distinct from pose. She was, fetchingly, Not That Way. In fact, as Poppy was amazed to discover, as they sat out a dance, then a second, and a third, she was better at spotting airs or airheads, better at eschewing pretense, more direct, more down-to-earth, than he! And why not? Poppy was Not That Way as an act of civility. But Bar was a natural: hers was an act of survival.

As for her, she thought he was, well . . . wonderful. Attractive, accomplished at school, funny . . . he wasn't stuck-up like some big seventeen-year-olds could be . . . he was just . . . perfect! Bar would later tell her children that she married the first man she ever kissed. (It always made them retch when she said it.) Later still, when she was campaigning, and her life was laid out for viewing on a hundred hotel coffee tables, she was always asked: *How did you know he was The One?* Well, she'd say, it was simple: "Whenever he came into a room, I had a hard time breathing."

But for the moment, for a long time, there was still the family. . . . Right after that fateful Christmas dance, Barbara came back from the Round Hill Club and mentioned she'd met a nice boy, Poppy Bush. That was at 2:00 A.M. By the time Barbara awoke the following day, Pauline had been on the phone all morning, finding out *everything* about the family. (Thank heaven, all reports were good.) Even after matters had progressed for two years, and Poppy and Bar were adult enough to plan a marriage, there was still a supply of female family wisdom:

"Now Barbara, you'll have to pick out silver, and you must get the most ornamental pattern you can find. Take it from me, dear, it's so much easier to clean . . ." So Bar scoured the stores for the plainest, flattest silver made. It was time to get out from under.

For a while, marriage only stepped up the family pressure. Greenwich and Rye were ten miles apart, and now, of course, they were in constant communication. At Christmas, and like family conclaves, Poppy and Bar would drive back and forth for breakfast at one house, lunch at another, a stop with the uncles (Poppy didn't like to disappoint), eggnog here and supper there . . . like Ping-Pong balls in a closed room! One day, when she was very pregnant with Georgie, and visiting in Greenwich with Pres and Dottie, Bar hauled herself out of a chair, and announced she had to visit in Rye, her parents . . . she was expected. . . . Pres Bush said sternly, but just as a joke: "Did we give you permission to visit those strangers?" It was no joke to Bar. She dissolved in tears.

— ★ —

She never really said to Pop: "Let's get out . . ." She didn't have to. That was one of the great things about him, about them together. There was so much they just knew . . . and from the beginning. Sometimes, people asked her: How did Poppy propose? Well, he didn't. They just started planning. Of course, she didn't propose children either. She just took care of it.

She knew Poppy was as eager as she to get out on his own. Maybe more: he'd been to war, he'd seen the world. Now he was hustling through Yale in two and a half years, but he wasn't just going to scrape through. With his straight A's in economics, letters in soccer and baseball, as the last man tapped for Skull and Bones—only fifteen chosen, the best of the best—he could have been a lock for a Rhodes scholarship, an extra year of study at a university in England. But what was the point? George Bush wasn't interested in more theory. Anyway, a family of three would never make it through a year on the stipend. Poppy would have to ask his folks for money—that's another thing he wanted to get past. He wanted to be out on his own—Bar and he even talked about farming, the most self-sufficient family life . . . but after they found out how much it would cost for land, seed, stock, equipment . . . well, Poppy wasn't going to ask Pres for that kind of dough. No way!

So, it was business. That's where the action was, anyway. With the rationing lifted and factories switching to production of cars, washers, fridges, *televisions*! . . . things were on the move . . . fortunes being made. The wave of strikes that followed the war was mostly over now, and the engine of U.S. business was never going to sink back to the sleepy sputter of the thirties. If the theories in his economics class meant anything, that was the lesson: America owned the world's markets as no other nation had before. (If the government would get its hands off the levers, there was no telling how fast, how far, the great ship of progress could sail!) American business won the war, and now it *ruled* this brave new world. And here was Poppy Bush, bred to captaincy, just itching to work his way to the helm. Wasn't it great how it turned out?

But he had to start somewhere, and fast. He was a senior already! Procter & Gamble had a trainee program; he talked to their recruiters, but . . . no soap. Lots of fellows were going into banking, or stocks, pure business, the capitalism of capital. And that would have been easy for Pop. Gampy Walker had split away from the Harrimans and formed his own investment bank, G.H. Walker & Co. His son, Herbie, was running the company now. He would have leapt to take Poppy on. For that matter, there were whispers that Brown Brothers Harriman might even bend its own strict rule on nepotism. . . . Pres Bush's son was a star!

But that wasn't the way: not for Poppy. If he'd wanted to play it safe and sound, he never would have signed up to fly on his eighteenth birthday: could have started Yale five years ago. Where was the adventure in that?

—★—

In the stiff-upper-lip world of the Walkers, no one tried to *talk* to Poppy about his choices: certainly not! . . . Unless he asked, which he wouldn't. Of course, they'd do anything for him: they were so eager, it was almost uncomfortable.

When Poppy and Bar would show up in Maine, it was like the prodigal son had returned: Kill the Fatted Calf! Uncle Herbie—the second G.H. Walker, and the second patriarch of the Point—just *adored* Poppy, idolized him. George Bush could do no wrong: George was a winner, a star at school, a hero in war, a pilot—the knighthood! Herbie's dream was to fly with Poppy. Of course, Herbie didn't know a thing about flying. He was scared to death of thunder and lightning! But he learned to fly at the close of the war, and went out to Detroit and *bought an airplane.* But then he started to fly it back East, and hit a snowstorm and couldn't go on; couldn't get back to Detroit, either. So, in the end, he landed his new plane in a cornfield and just walked away. That was the end of Herbie the Pilot.

But it didn't cool Herbie's ardor, not at all. Whenever he'd hear Pop and Bar were coming up to Maine, Herbie dropped *everything* in a frenzy of setting up golf games, tennis matches, picnics, dinner parties. He started a whole summer baseball league . . . Poppy's coming! Everyone thought it was awful for Herbie's own sons, Bert and Ray. Herbie was so obviously in love with their cousin. Poppy didn't quite know what to do about it. He always tried to be extra-nice to Bert and Ray.

It was just another thing that would be . . . easier, once Poppy and Bar got away on their own. As for going into business with Herbie, in his firm, well . . . that didn't seem like a good idea.

Pres's great friend (and fellow Bonesman) Neil Mallon, in Cleveland, had been unofficial godfather to the Bush kids. He knew Poppy was hunting a place to start on his own. So he talked to George about the Texas oil fields: that was the place for a young man to make his fortune. Mallon was the head of Dresser Industries (Pres Bush served on the board, of course), and Dresser owned Ideco, an oil-field equipment company. Why didn't George go out there as a trainee, learn the oil business from the ground up? Mallon didn't have to say the rest: he didn't have any kids of his own. . . . If Poppy liked what he saw of Ideco, and Dresser, well . . . there'd be opportunities.

Poppy liked what he heard. He'd been posted to Texas in the Navy for a couple of months. It was wide open . . . a whole new world . . . a thousand miles away. And everything about Texas oil had the air of great doings, men and fortunes larger than life. Like everyone else of his generation, Bush had seen the stories in *Life* magazine, the *Fortune* profiles of H.L. Hunt, Clint Murchison, Sid Richardson, Eamon Carter. They were Giants in a Giant Land. . . . Oil! Black Gold! . . . What an adventure!

So Poppy came back from his talk with Neil Mallon and said to Bar, he thought he'd get a job with Ideco, the International Derrick and Equipment Company. It was the oil business! . . . A trainee's job . . . *lots* of opportunity . . . starting wage just over three hundred dollars a month.

It sounded good to Bar. Reasonably stable. And she knew Pop would do well, wherever he chose to work . . . and if it didn't turn out, well, they'd find another way. Pop was Phi Beta Kappa at Yale, after all. It's not like they were going to another country . . . were they? . . . Where is this?

"Odessa, Texas," he said.

Bar paused a couple of beats and then favored Poppy with a radiant smile. "I've *always wanted,*" she said, "to live in Odessa, Texas."

— ★ —

Phyllis saw him first in March, across the mess hall at Percy Jones. He was still thin, had his arm in a splint, but what she noticed was his sharp dark eyes, his high brow and thick shining hair, the strong bones in his face. Phyllis said to her friend: "Who's *that*?"

"Oh, that poor Bob Dole. He doesn't have long to live, you know."

"Isn't that sad . . . such a nice-looking man."

Of course, her friend was behind the times: Bob Dole was going to live, and he was going to do something with that life. He was back at Percy Jones after Dr. K.'s operations, but he knew now it was just a way station.

He wasn't waiting anymore for a miracle. The hospital still gave him curare treatments for tremors, and therapy in the whirlpool every day, but he was working on himself in every way. He'd found himself sort of a job, selling Oldsmobiles modified for wounded war vets. He sold a couple at Percy Jones, and in the bargain, got himself a blue sedan with a left-hand gearshift. It wasn't long till the Army put a stop to such business. But that didn't mean Dole had to give up, to lie around in bed, or play bridge all day.

He and a couple of buddies were tearing through the books in the hospital library: there wasn't anything Bob Dole didn't want to know. At night, they'd sit up talking books, until the nurses called lights out . . . at which point, they'd sneak off the ward, and steal across the street, to a coffee shop that stayed open till two. Bob was thinking about getting out of the Army, going back to school, getting a degree. He'd talked to Kelikian about it. Maybe he could be a lawyer. "Why not?" said Dr. K.

It was March 12 when Bob showed up at the Officers' Club dance. Phyllis and her friends had done the decoration: it was Heaven and Hell—Hell, with the pictures of devils in flames, was the bar; it was in Heaven, the dance floor, under painted clouds and angels, where Bob spotted Phyllis, sitting with a group of nurses at a table. He stood straight and tall—no splint—in his uniform, as he walked up and asked her to dance.

"I'd love to," she said.

He couldn't put his right arm around her back—not by himself. But he put it on her hip, and Phyllis stepped right in. Years later, in Russell, she'd advise their women friends: "Dance close to Bob . . ." They always thought she was making a joke.

— ★ —

Phyllis Holden wasn't the kind to make jokes—not about things that mattered. She'd grown up in rural New Hampshire, a girl so tenderhearted she never could stand teasing. Sometimes, like every well-loved child, she'd do something so cute that her parents laughed with joy. But Phyllis thought they were laughing at her, and she'd start to cry. As she came of age, there was a softness about her that drew a flock of young men. But until she got to Percy Jones, she was not lucky in love.

At the University of New Hampshire, in the new program for occupational therapy, she'd got engaged to a fellow named Joseph Bennett, who was badly infected with malaria from his days on Guadalcanal. That engagement lasted almost three years, but in the end, it fell apart. After college, in her resident training, she got involved with a young man who had osteomyelitis. That never got beyond a "serious friendship," but her parents were horrified. "My God, Phyllis," her mother scolded. "Why don't you get away from these lame ducks!"

But she loved the work. It was a new field, exciting, and Phyllis felt like a pioneer. She worked in the psychiatric wards, teaching crafts, silver and leather. She was never scared of the men. She thought even a schizophrenic would maintain some respect for a woman. And the alcoholics would protect her, if need be. Meanwhile, she was helping, she was needed, she was good at her job. In '48, she decided to follow her college friend, Elsie Deming, to Michigan, to the Army Medical Center, where the big job was being done. She and Elsie would join the Army, they'd see the world: Phyllis had never been west of New York State. Anyway, there was not, at the moment, a love in her life to keep her in New Hampshire. When Elsie met her at the station in Battle Creek, Phyllis laughed and said, "Tell you one thing: the next time I get engaged, I'm going to get *married*. Just give me time to get out the invitations . . ."

She almost didn't have time. Two days after she danced with Bob Dole, he called—nine-thirty at night!—and asked her out for a coffee. If it'd been anyone but that nice Lieutenant Dole, she wouldn't have gone: he'd think she was sitting alone by the phone. But everybody knew Bob was a nice guy, always had a good word for everyone, had a job selling cars . . . he didn't try to flirt with the nurses, like some of the men. So, she said yes. And he told her about Russell, Kansas, and his father in the grain elevator, his brother and two sisters, and Dr. Kelikian in Chicago, and the operations. . . . Then it was the Easter dance at the Officers' Club, and more coffee dates, always at night. She had her work and he had his therapy, so it wasn't like they spent every minute together. And Phyllis wasn't looking for anyone special. . . . But Bob was always fun, always so gracious, always opened the door of the Oldsmobile for her, always did the driving, always wanted to know about *her,* how *she* was doing. And he was brave about himself, and handsome, and smart. It was only a few weeks before she felt she wasn't interested in a date with anyone else. Then Bob had to go to Chicago, to see Dr. K., and Phyllis went with him. Kelikian was urging Bob to go to school. He smiled at Phyllis, and said: "She can go with you and take notes."

— ★ —

In April, Bob went back to Russell for a visit, and Bina got on the phone with her sister, right away. "I think Bob's fallen madly in love with a therapist."

"*Really?* How do you know?"

"That's eighty percent of his conversation! What a difference!"

Bob was like a kid again. He'd get up in the morning, jump into his car, and drive right down Main Street. Visit with Doran and the farmers in the elevator. Stop in at Dawson's, stay two hours! On and off the stools, over to the jukebox . . . "Heyy, how 'bout some music? . . ." Then back home, next door, to Kenny and Dottie. Told Dottie about the beautiful things Phyllis made with her hands. Phyllis can do this, Phyllis can do that. She's got long dark hair, dark eyes, real pretty, real slender. . . .

He told one friend: "Boy, she's filled in all the right spaces!"

Bina was teary with joy on the phone. "Lord, what a difference!"

— ★ —

A month after the dance, Phyllis got the test results for her Army enlistment. She had allergies the Army was concerned about. "Well," Bob said, "you could prob'ly get out . . . if you got married . . ." Phyllis didn't speak. Bob said: "Aghh, think you could live in Russell, Kansas?" She said she thought she could, with Bob.

She called her mother on April 27th, her birthday, and said she was getting married. "He's been paralyzed, but he's had a wonderful return. He's still got some paralysis in his right arm, but it doesn't seem to bother him . . ." Her mother hit the roof.

"Phyllis, you *can't* have another lame duck!"

"Oh, Mother!"

"My God, Phyllis! *You* said he can't button a button, zip a zipper! How's he ever going to earn a living?"

"He's going to go to college!"

"Well," Estelle Holden insisted, "your father and I think it's just too soon."

Within days, Estelle got a letter from Bob, analyzing his time in courtship with Phyllis. The way he figured, if it had been normal dating, say once or twice a week, it would have worked out to three years!

Estelle wrote back with her real reservations: "Phyllis is a very precious child to us, and we want the best for her. And unless you are capable of becoming a husband to her, in all ways, we don't think it would be a good idea."

That was hard for Bob to take. But Phyllis wouldn't let him get down about it. "Bob, it's just because they haven't met you."

She told her mother: *Make the announcement!* And she and Bob started driving east, to New Hampshire.

Two weeks later, Bina and Doran arrived, and Bob and Phyllis were married, June 12, 1948.

— ★ —

In June, after the College World Series and Graduation Day in New Haven, Poppy packed up his new red Studebaker (a graduation gift from Pres), and started driving south. Bar and Georgie went up to Walker's Point, to wait for Pop to find them a home. It was just a few days before they got the letter with the good news: Poppy was a star! Of course, all his Yale training was wrong, but he was getting better with a broom, and the boss said he was the best warehouse sweeper that Ideco's Odessa Branch Office ever had.

And he'd found them a house—well, half a house. (He wrote that it was "kind of humble.") So Bar and Georgie got an airplane to Dallas and then to the Midland-Odessa field, a propeller-flight journey of more than twelve hours, to join George in their strange new world . . . and my, wasn't it exotic!

First, it was flat, perfectly flat, like no land they'd ever seen. No brooks, streams, rivers. No native trees—no trees. It was bright, and hot like they'd never felt heat, and gritty everywhere with dust. The blacktop into town from the airport shimmered between opposing ranks of strange, hulking drill rigs, piles of steel pipe, casing, tubing, decking, cable . . . all baked in the sun-grit, like ossified armies standing guard on the tatty tin or cinderblock sheds housing the businesses behind. And then, as George and Bar turned onto their street, East Seventh, the pavement gave way altogether, and they rolled on two ruts of dust to a stop, in front of their new home.

It was a shotgun house—tiny in the first place, but now partitioned down the middle, so two families could each have a narrow, half–living room, just inside the concrete front step, and then a counter giving on to a tiny kitchen, and one narrow bedroom in the rear. The partition ended at the back, with the bathroom, which both tenants shared. It was one of the few bathrooms on the street. Most had an outhouse in the boxy backyard, like Mr. Wagley, two doors down, whose outhouse shared his rear plot of dust with the junk he collected for a living, and his wagon, and his horse. The immediate neighbors, in the other half of the shotgun house, were a mother and her daughter (and the daughter's toddler daughter), who made their living entertaining male guests, which pretty much tied up the bathroom, from sundown on.

It was all so . . . interesting! You just didn't *see* stuff like that in Rye, or Greenwich—even New Haven. In fact, back in Rye, Pauline Pierce thought poor Barbara must be desperate: *Odessa!* It smacked of Russia and want. She kept sending cold cream, and boxes of soap flakes, convinced that privation dogged her daughter at that edge of the earth. But there was no privation, no desperation. In fact, it was only thirty-five years later, when George Bush had to convince the world that he wasn't some timid toy poodle, that it ever came to be described as a roll of the dice, a gamble. . . . At the time, it was just *a wonderful adventure!* See, it *wasn't* really their world. George and Bar always knew that—they weren't trapped. They could always go back . . . or go somewhere else. They were in it, and yet, not quite of it, immune to enjoy it like expatriates who talk with fascination about "the locals" and their strange folkways.

Such *fun:* high school football on Friday nights, with a crowd twice as big as Yale ever drew, all in their shirtsleeves, fanning themselves in the twilight heat, and girl cheerleaders! Never saw *that* back East! . . . And barbecues over a fire in an oil drum, and grits, and chili, and chicken-fried steak at Agnes' Café. *Oh, we love that stuff!* . . . And the strange and humorous things that George would report when he came home, about the squinty stares he drew at the oil field, or out painting pumps, with the good ol' bubbas in the heat and the grit . . .

Boy. Jus' whu'the hayl'r yew dooin' out 'ere ennuhways?

The short answer was: living high and free, on three hundred seventy-five dollars a month. And learning, sometimes the hard way. . . . A couple days after they moved onto Seventh Street, Bar woke them all up in the middle of the night. Gas! She smelled it . . .

Get out!

Get Georgie!

GET OUT!

DON'T LIGHT A MATCH!

Thing was, there were always a couple hundred wells flaring off within the city limits, a refinery, a few hundred tanks. . . . Odessa, as the wakened neighbors pointed out, always kinda smelled like that . . . ma'am.

—★—

It was land like Phyllis had never seen. No trees for miles, no hills or rocks like her home ground. But it was beautiful to her, at the end of that June. Phyllis was in love, and the harvest was on, the milo and beans were like rich green carpet, the ground checkered in emerald, gold, and deep brown, as Bob raced the Oldsmobile west on Highway 40, and told her about Russell. Bob said the earth there was *so flat* . . . on a good day, you could see Kansas City. Well, it wasn't quite like that. Kansas City was two hundred miles away.

But she would have believed him, if he'd insisted. She was so willing to see it as his eyes did. If this was to be her adopted home, then she'd embrace it, too. But in Russell, it wasn't quite that easy. For one thing, she came to make a home in a nest of ferocious homemakers. Actually, Phyllis knew how to cook—or thought she did: she'd even won a prize for a cake at the state fair in New Hampshire. But that wasn't cooking in Russell, heck no. She couldn't make the fried chicken like Bina (who could?), or the brownies, or the ice cream, or . . . the problem was, Bina's house was perfect, from the flowers bordering the lawn, to the shrubs and roses, the shiny scrubbed porch, and inside, the smell of flowers and wax, and the pie cooling on the dining room table, and not one dish out of place, unwashed, and the big embroidered white feedsack towels, the pink-and-green curtains on the French doors in the living room. It wasn't that Bina was mean about it, no . . . but you could see she noticed when something wasn't just so, and Bob must have noticed, too. Of course, he didn't say anything.

But Phyllis felt she had to be perfect for him—it was *expected.* She'd stand next to Bina for hours in the kitchen, watching and measuring what went into the bowl—Bina never had recipes. When Bob went to buy clothes, the tailor at Banker's was going to take in the shoulder of the suit, but Phyllis figured out how to pad it underneath, just so, and it looked perfect. . . . Then there was the matter of his neckties—she tied them. But she couldn't get the Windsor knot, with the dimple just so, and the front just a hair longer than the back, like Bob liked it. And this went on for *years,* and she asked their men friends, and the salesmen at Banker's to show her . . . but it still wasn't right. And, of course, she could see he noticed, they all did. . . . They were always watching Bob, jumping up to help him, getting something for him, or fixing something near him that wasn't quite right. . . .

That was the heart of the problem, how they treated Bob, too tenderly, like a thousand-year-old vase. It just reinforced his feeling that something wasn't right, wasn't whole, about him. One day that summer, in lawn chairs out in Bina's backyard, a glass of iced tea slipped from Bob's numb left hand and spilled at his feet. "Oh, God," Phyllis said, "can't you hold on to *anything*?" Bina and Kenny looked at Phyllis like she'd just spat on the Bible. How could she talk to Bob that way?

But, of course, that was the right way. That's one of the things Bob loved about Phyllis: she never treated him like a cripple, an invalid . . . God, how he hated that word. . . . She'd tell him flat out not to wait to be waited on: "Do it yourself . . . you can do it!" She'd get after *him* to work on his body. "You've got that leg exercise to do . . . why don't you get that out of the way?" And she was so matter-of-fact, so sure of him and what he could do. "Pick up your feet, Bob. There's no reason to shuffle like that!" In time, Bina and the rest realized it was good for Bob. In Phyllis's eyes, he saw himself whole. And why not? She never saw him any other way.

Around town, where the citizens looked at Bob like their own prize experiment (they were the ones who put him back on his feet!), there was a myth already spreading on Phyllis, that she was Bob's therapist at the big Army hospital. Or, better yet, his nurse. She was the gal who nursed him back to life . . . and fell in love. . . . And no matter how many times Bob explained, or how many times Phyllis protested that Bob was well and strong again before she ever met him . . . well, people believe what they want to believe. Even years later, when he'd risen so high, no one wanted to believe her when she said that he was always the strong one . . . but she knew.

That September, they packed up the Oldsmobile again and started south, to Arizona, where Bob would go back to college, as a junior. The doctors recommended a hot-weather climate, after all the blood thinners Bob had taken. Of course, Bob drove all the way, and Bob found their two-room house . . . and although Phyllis did take notes (and wrote test papers from his dictation), it was Bob who did the work, who studied all night, each night, by memory, pacing their living room, barking German verbs in his prairie voice, over and over, until he had them in his head, until Phyllis finally had to ask: Bob, why? . . .

"Why do you have to get an A? Isn't a C good enough?"

And Bob snapped: "*You* tell me how to study a C's worth, and *I'll do it.* All I know's how to work till I get it."

He taught her how to play cribbage, but he didn't play, he had work to do. No one was going to have to cut Bob Dole any slack. There was a couple nearby who became good friends, and they'd go swimming, but Bob wouldn't undress. He didn't want anyone to see his problem. She could cut up his food for him at home, but not at a restaurant. He'd have them cut it in the kitchen and bring it out that way. He meant to be strong, and she relied on that, too.

One night, that autumn, when they were at dinner, Bob suddenly lurched in his chair, slumped over his plate and gasped: "Omigod . . . s'get to the VA . . . on the double."

Phyllis was scared to death. She was twenty-three, had never stayed a night alone. She'd never even driven in Tucson by herself. And now Bob was in the hospital. . . . It turned out he had another blood clot, but thinners took care of it. He was fine, in a week. Yet what she remembered was her shock, the way he looked at that moment, so frail! . . . It had never occurred to her that Bob could get sick.

— ★ —

The big excitement that fall was the Jugoslav who came to visit, to study American oil operations. The head office of Dresser sent him down, with carte blanche. But that didn't mean the good ol' bubbas wanted foreigners—a commie!—snoopin' around. So the eager Jugo gentleman got kicked down the ladder and landed in the lap of . . . George Bush.

What fun! It went on for days and days. George and Bar took the guy all over West Texas. Took him for barbecue. Took him to a football game. The fellow had his notebook, with everything he wanted to learn, and anytime a fact penetrated the language haze, he'd write this, too, in his book. The big thing he wanted was . . . *skiddarig.* That was a shortcut they'd figured out in West Texas. If a hole was dry or played out, and the drilling equipment was needed elsewhere, they wouldn't have to take down the rig: they'd move it whole, *skid* it, sometimes hundreds of yards down the field, to the next location. Well, that was the cat's pyjamas at the Ministry in Belgrade, in '48. "*Skiddarig?*" the Jugoslav implored. So George Bush, whose highest attainment in the oil business, to that point, was a clerkship in an equipment warehouse, learned how to skid a rig . . . and how to explain it without benefit of words.

Words weren't Bush's strong suit, anyway. There was something extraverbal about his friendliness, his eagerness, the way his smile bent his whole body toward the guy, or the light, friendly bubba punch to the shoulder to show he was making a joke, the way Bush flung his legs out when he sank into a chair at home, told the Jugoslav that *he* could feel at home there, too. It was an animal thing . . . the same bodily aw-shucks with which Bush let Texans know they needn't mind his back-East college-boy talk.

How could they mind, when he was so happy to get to know them, to make their home his, to have them think well of him? Hell, here he was, after a few months, West Texas's own ambassador to the foreigners. Thing was, he was so . . . accepting. Here was a fellow who came from outside, but he didn't act like it . . . didn't judge them like a stranger. Wasn't that way. The way they saw it, the way they said it, Bush was just a hell of a good guy, tried to fit in, played the game.

As for him and Bar, they'd decided: they *loved* West Texas. The way people took you in! . . . You couldn't find nicer folks, no matter where you went. . . . Late that fall, they decided they weren't even going home for Christmas. Of course, they'd miss everybody back East: they sent out, must have been a *hundred* Christmas cards . . . but it was just too long a trip with a two-year-old in tow. And they had their own life to live now, even for the holidays. So they made their own preparations in their half a house, and they did their shopping and found a tree, and everything was ready by Christmas Eve. . . .

Ideco had a party that afternoon—a West Texas custom, Bush figured—and customers and friends dropped in, and George helped out, mixing drinks. And he wanted to fit in and be friendly, of course, so as they hoisted each glass he poured, he'd hoist one, too . . . and he did fine until a whole 'nother set of guests trooped in, a second shift to the office party . . . but he poured more drinks and, just to be friendly . . . It got to be dark, and well past dark, and Bar was still waiting with the dinner at home, and the tree was there, undecorated, and it got quite late, and George was being friendly, fitting right in, on his own now, and . . . Anyway, they brought him home in the bed of the company pickup, rolled him gently out onto his lawn, and that Christmas Eve he was truly on his own, though he didn't know much about it, shitfaced, on his back, under the stars, in Odessa, Texas.

9

God Rest Ye,
Merry Gentlemen

AT THE PARTY, George Bush held a tall Perrier. He hadn't been drunk for almost forty years: one martini, maybe two, for Christmas. Still, you'd have to say he had a rosy glow, mostly from his bright red blazer. He wore it to all his Christmas parties, then stuck it in the closet for another year. You wouldn't catch him wearing anything like that any other time . . . but the holidays were special, for friends, family . . . didn't matter what else was going on.

George Bush was serious about spreading cheer. He had to make sure to take care of everyone. That's why he had eleven parties that Christmas. Most were minestrone guest lists: any Bush family in the region, of course; a few friends from the White House, maybe a handful from Cabinet departments, notably Commerce, where Bush got a lot of jobs for friends; some friends or friends-to-be from the press (off the record); some fellows from Congress, friends from embassies, from the CIA, the Pentagon, politics . . . and, Hey! Bring the wife! . . . Bush worked over the lists himself, always threw in a few surprises. A couple of parties were just for staff, of course, and two for the Secret Service, their wives and kids. In fact, the Secret Service was the reason Bush stayed in D.C. for Christmas. He wanted to let the agents stay home with their families.

Anyway, you couldn't miss him at the party, leaning against the door jamb of the big entry hall of the Residence, watching as the Air Force Choir sang carols . . . smiling and saying thanks all night, while the friends came up and shook his hand, wished him merry, then posed for their pictures with him. He

posed perhaps a hundred times each party, over and over, in front of the
mantel on the first floor, or before the big Christmas tree in the dining room,
where the Filipino stewards manned the buffet of roast beef, ham, shrimp,
salads, fruits, fruitcake, Christmas cookies, eggnog. . . . Of course, there was
a gift, too. This year, it was a porcelain model of the VP Residence. Must have
given away hundreds of those. But the photo gave each friend something to
remember, something to put on the wall. And Bush always had something to
say, a funny moment to recall, a teasing needle, through his smile, as the
cameraman clicked away. The VP thus bestowed his highest gift, his company,
a personal moment with him, the currency that had paid his freight all the way
from County Chairman. The photo was remembrance of that moment in the
glow. Being with George, as his sister said one Christmas, was like feeling the
sun on your back.

"You know, if every voter could just *meet* him . . ."

"He'd be President already. I know."

The guests nodded murmurous agreement as they watched him, fondly,
across the room, enjoying his friends, spreading the glow.

"If he could just show himself . . ."

"Like he *is* . . ."

"I know."

Some went so far as to tell him, as if to make him *understand,* as if he could
somehow unlock it in a speech, or on TV someday. "You just have to let people
see you . . ."

"Just go out there and *be yourself*!"

Bush always countered with his old one-liner, the punchline to a joke he'd
heard years back: "Yeah, they told me, just be yourself . . . so I did. Maybe
that was the problem."

But now with Iranamok around his ankles, with Dole climbing past him in
Iowa, with his polls at an all-time low, some friends wouldn't be put off with
a joke. One of the oldest friends, FitzGerald Bemiss—an usher at George's
wedding, known him forever, since boyhood summers in Maine—tried to sit
Bush down for a serious talk: George *had* to define himself, to show the people
who he was!

And Bush unloaded on him, blew up! Set poor Gerry back on his heels. Bush
wasn't going to cut and run from Reagan! He wasn't going to duck out on his
friend now!

Of course, that wasn't what Bemiss meant. But Bush couldn't see the
difference between *showing himself* and *showing up a friend.* And that was just
out of the question. George Bush would never lose a friend.

That was the reason for the Christmas cards, at least at the start: a way for
George and Bar to keep beaming the glow to the folks they'd left back East,
when they moved to Texas. But the way those two were about friends, the list
just kept growing. Every year George Bush was alive on the planet, there were
more friends to take care of. And the way Bar kept her file cards, no one ever
dropped off the list. Bar moved her box of file cards from Midland to Hous-

ton, to Washington, back to Houston, to New York, back to Washington, to China, back to Washington, then back to Houston, and to Washington again. Of course, every year it grew, from family and schoolmates, to oil-business friends and new Texas neighbors, and Texas pols, to Washington friends and neighbors, fellow Congressmen, then UN Ambassadors from all over the world, and then local pols from all over the country, and more new neighbors, and Chinese officials, and CIA colleagues and foreign intelligence pooh-bahs, and more pols, now from all fifty states and a few from the U.S. territories, and campaign contributors, and volunteers, and staff, and ex-staff, and that wounded soldier he met at the VA, and that lady who told him *such a sad story* at the shopping center in Waco, and the cop who used to stop traffic every afternoon, as George Bush nosed his car out of the Houston Club garage. Some of the older entries were written over a dozen times for that friend's successive new houses, amended for that family's every new child, and when a child moved away from home, that child got a new file card. By the mid-seventies, say, while the Bushes sojourned in China, Bar had four or five thousand file cards, all updated by year-round effort, stored in a gleaming wooden four-drawer case that held pride of place, like the Roman gods of the household, in the upstairs family room of the residence of the U.S. compound in Peking. Bar used to point it out to guests, as one might mention a family heirloom. One visitor who saw it protested:

"Some of those must be just political friends."

And Bar's eyes turned icy as she snapped: "What's the difference? A friend is a friend."

It wasn't till 1979, in the first George Bush for President campaign, that staff intruded in any way upon Bar's Christmas card suzerainty. The friend list was growing geometrically as George flew around the country, and Bar was busy campaigning, too. So a group of volunteer ladies in Houston took over. Of course, Bar came by, every chance she got, to see that the cards were done right, addressed by hand with blue felt-tip pens, to give them a soft, kitchen-table look; and the cards for the closest friends pulled out of the bulk mailing and brought to the house for a scrawled P.S. and signature from George Bush.

Two years later, when the campaign was over and, in Bar's phrase, "we became Vice President," there was a VP Christmas card budget from the Republican National Committee, and a Houston Branch Office of the Vice President to do the heavy lifting. To be sure, the friend list was bigger now, embracing all U.S. Ambassadors overseas, and foreign dignitaries, and all members of Congress, and Governors, Republican Committeemen, campaign contributors, County Chairmen, and like stars in the new George Bush cosmology. By 1983, the ladies in Houston had the list cross-indexed on an IBM database. And a gentle, white-haired woman named Dot Burghard (a bit hard of hearing of late, but still possessed of *beautiful* penmanship) sat at a desk in the workroom of the Houston OVP, attending to the friend-list updates and then addressing envelopes, every day, beginning each year in May. By December, of course, it wasn't just Dot, but a whole roomful of volunteers, bent to the three S's (stuff, seal, and stamp) at the long table in the workroom, amid a murmur of old Bush-stories, and occasional shouted queries to Dot, and Betty Baker's Texas trail-boss voice, on the phone, trying to rustle up more volunteers: "Hah, Suzie! Did Santa Claus visit yet? . . . Oh, well, tellya how ta assure it. Come on down here and give us a hand. . . . Well, we're doin' all *right,* but we could always use s'more. . . . Gloria! What're we up to—the H's? . . . Fact, I'm a little worried 'bout gettin' 'em *out!*"

And even after the bulk mailings, there were response cards to fire out, to people who were not on the friend list but who sent George Bush a card that year. And then, of course, returns started boomeranging in—someone moved, or dead, or God knows what—so the ladies had to peel back the stamp to read the code to find out which substratum of the friend list it came from: the Ambassadors, or contributors, or the 1944 crew of the USS *Finback* . . . or, in the worst case, it might be a card with the "CC" code hidden under the stamp, which meant "Christmas Card," and which meant the name was from the *crème de la crème,* the Original Barbara Bush Christmas Card List. And that person had better be found. That card HAD to get out. It was often February and sometimes March before all the returns were investigated and rectified. Better late than never: people saved those cards, after all, and watched the kids (now the grandkids) grow up in the annual family pictures. This year, 1986, with new friends for the new campaign, it was bound to be March before it ended. They could almost count on that. This year—in fact, on the night of this party—there were thirty thousand George Bush Christmas cards in the mail.

> *God rest ye merry gentlemen,*
> *Let nothing ye dismay . . .*

In the foyer, the Air Force Choir was in song, but there was no rest for a man with thirty thousand friends—certainly not at Christmastime. There were the hundreds of cards sent to Washington, still waiting for his personal P.S. And then the hundreds of pictures, each to get an inscription, personal, jovial, sometimes intimate. Bush could knock them out, one after the other. And, meanwhile, the parties, night after night, and Bush telling stories, teasing, pointing, punching shoulders, introducing, pollinating his garden of friends in a buzz of happy talk and laughter. But now, for the moment, the buzz died away, the choir was silent, and a rustle of whispers swept the ground floor of the Residence.

"Isn't that? . . ."

"Where? It sure is . . ."

And Bush called out across the foyer (as he called whenever he spotted a new guest), called through the sudden silence . . . "Ollie!"

Of course, they were all stunned: Ollie North was too hot to touch now. The hottest! A pariah! Jeez, and the house held a half-dozen reporters! What was Bush *thinking*? Didn't he, uh, talk this out? Couldn't the staff head this off?

The short answer was, not many of the staff knew. Fuller heard about it, but he knew better than to say a word. The PAC, the political guys . . . why would Bush bring it up with them? This wasn't politics. A personal thing. His own guest list. Christmas! His own house. Friends! If they couldn't understand that, well . . . That stuff about Ollie lying to Congress, shredding papers— nothing proved yet! Anyway, it wasn't *about* that. Ollie was a guy he knew, he'd worked with. (And not just Ollie: Poindexter showed up that night. And Bud McFarlane made the list for another party.) The point was, that was all politics. Bush couldn't let it change the way he was. They were friends. Shouldn't be shunned.

Instantly, Bar was there at his side in the foyer, to greet Ollie. . . . How about a drink? Eggnog? . . . Of course, Bar wasn't surprised. It wasn't that George Bush discussed it with her. Didn't need to. . . . Thirty years before, back in West Texas, where deals were done on a handshake between men, there was one fellow who didn't play the game right. Soon enough, of course, everybody in town knew. And no one would touch him with a ten-foot pipe. That year, George and Bar had a party, and Bar was surprised to see this man appear. She said to George: "I thought we weren't going to have anything to do with him." And Bush said: "Just because I'm not gonna ever do business with him doesn't mean he can't be a friend."

The funny thing was, everybody heard Bush use that word, "friend," a hundred times a day, but they never could see what it meant to him.

By what extravagance of need and will did a man try to make thirty thousand friends?

By what steely discipline did he strive to keep them—with notes, cards, letters, gifts, invitations, visits, calls, and silent kindnesses, hundreds every week, every one demanding some measure of his energy and attention?

And by what catholicity (or absence) of taste could he think well of every one of them?

He could not.

But they would never know that.

The funny thing was, the friendship depended not on what Bush thought of them, but what they thought of him, or what he wanted them to think. If they thought well of him, then, they were friends.

And he would try to the point of contortion not to lose them. On the altar of what idea would he sacrifice a friendship? For a *speech*? For that show-biz? For some brainy-boy staff guy's idea of *self-definition*?

He *was* defining himself, as he had for sixty years: eleven parties, a thousand pictures, thirty thousand Christmas cards, to *friends*. It was by their fond gaze that George Bush saw himself. By them was his fortune counted. By them was his progress marked in the world. Only by their loss would he be diminished. And George Bush could not afford that loss now. It was by their number and approbation that he measured himself the size of a President.

— ★ —

The great thing about Christmas was, it gave Dole a chance to catch up on work. Interview requests that stacked up while things were hopping, while the Senate was in—Dole would take the list and mark them off: 10:00, 10:30, 10:45, 11:15 . . . bingo, a half-dozen profiles in the works. (They were all trying to write up Bob Dole now, to "explain" how he took the lead away from Bush.) Or something would happen, and the networks would phone to ask where Dole was vacationing: Could they get a call to him?

"He's right here."

"*Really?*"

"Sittin' at his desk."

They'd send a crew right over.

And there they'd find the Bobster, friendly, relaxed, charming . . . they were amazed. He sat and *talked*—asked them what they'd heard in New Hampshire, let slip a knowing aside on Regan ("Gaghh! Guy's hangin' on f'dear life!") . . . didn't even seem to mind the stupid profile questions:

"How about hobbies?"

"Well, agh, kinda don't . . . I mean, politics . . ."

"No *hobbies?*"

Lord, what did they want him to do? Play golf?

The point was, this *was* relaxation: no one around, nothing stirring on the Hill except Dole's office. It wasn't that he didn't pay attention to the holiday. Half the staff was gone the week before Christmas. Half took off the week after that. Dole meant to get away, two or three days, to the condo in Florida, but then, Elizabeth was tied up with *her* job. Still, Dole came in late most mornings, nine or nine-thirty, sat down at his desk and had his oatmeal. Sometimes, he wouldn't even wear a suit, just slip a sweater over his tie. This year, he wore his new Christmas sweater, a hand-knit beauty, white cardigan with clasps down the front and bright green and red snowflake patterns across the chest. He looked terrific: white shirt crisp under the sweater, flipping the fingers of his left hand idly on the smooth gray flannel of his pants-leg, occasionally emitting a tuneless whistle as he padded around the office in his black tassel loafers.

"Agh, anythin' new?"

Sometimes he'd pull his chair up to an empty desk, next to some staffer. "D'you see the figures for those car comp'nies? Makin' out like *bann*-dits! . . ." (That was from a story in the Bobster's clip file, waiting for him next to the oatmeal that morning.) It was almost like Dole was trying to chat! Thing was, most of them couldn't think what to say back to him. So he'd get up and whistle around some more.

He made a point of remembering the staff at Christmas. Always had a party in the office—last a couple of hours. And he gave the staff all the gifts that piled up under and around Betty's desk, from lobbyists, constituents, admirers of all kinds: cases of wine, whiskey, cigars, clocks, cameras . . . and weird stuff, Kansas figurines, sampler flags, paintings of Dole. Fruit baskets, things like that, he'd send off to hospitals. Popcorn and candy he'd open right there and grab a handful each time he padded by.

Then, too, for the women in the office, he'd send Betty out to buy scarves or bracelets, or something. For men, he'd send Dean out to buy twenty-five ties. Dole wouldn't pick them out himself, he was color-blind. (For his own ties, Tito, his Brooks Brothers salesman, sewed numbers on the back so Dole could match them. One time, at dinner in Kansas City, Dole's tie flopped over to reveal a big 4. Max Klein, the drawly old Southwestern Bell lobbyist, remarked: "Senator, you ought have 'em number it 104 or something, so people'll think you have more ties.") Then, too, Betty had to go out to buy extravagant gifts for all the family back in Kansas. And Dole would get something really expensive for his daughter, Robin, and Elizabeth. And then, at his desk, he'd make out his list of checks—for the barbers in the Senate shop, the cooks, waiters, and hostesses in the Senate Dining Room, the shoeshine guy, the parking guys, and the Watergate doormen and janitors . . . they all got generous checks from Dole.

And, somehow, the Christmas cards had to get out. Betty and Jo-Anne Coe would honcho the job, but what they'd end up doing was plopping a hundred, two hundred names and envelopes on an intern's desk . . . in fact, the desks of all interns and some of the Kansas and legislative staff—everyone would have to crash those addresses out *right away:* it was usually down to the wire. People Dole actually thought of got calls. That's what he did with most of those easy days: he fired out calls to Kansas; hundreds to Iowa and New Hampshire, South Dakota, Minnesota, and the other early primary states. Then he'd call his big guys and smart guys, political sages and men in the know, in and out of office or retirement, men like Alf Landon, and Richard Nixon, and the thousand-dollar-suit lobbyist crowd, the boys at Gray & Co., Timmons & Co. Christmas was a perfect chance to check in, wish them well, find out what they'd been hearing.

Dole paid attention to those big guys, mostly because, in one way or another, they had been, or had made, or had served a President. In the Dole map of the universe, that placed them in a special galaxy. ("Agh, guy worked in the White House, oughta know *some*thing . . .") Yet, in some corner of consciousness, Dole could not be unaware that he seldom mentioned a *current* crowd in the White House without, in the same breath, complaining that they were out of touch, wanting in tact or political awareness, mistaken on some policy, or, generally speaking, out to lunch. This Dole-forged alloy of reverent contempt was familiar, comfortable to him. It was the same combination he reserved for other attainments, including:

"Agh, guy's a Ph.*Dee* . . ."

Or, "Lotta moneyy . . ."

Or, any connection to the Ivy League. (If Dole had a staff assistant with a degree from Harvard or Yale, he could not introduce that person without mentioning the school. And just as often, he'd remark privately, almost to himself, that he knew ten times as much as that guy.)

Anyway, this Christmas, the big guys, the car-phone-in-the-Jag crowd, the former White House Special Assistants, now lobbyists for McDonnell Douglas, consultants to the Republic of South Korea, were telling him he was doing fine, but he needed to build an organization: he couldn't try to do it himself this time. He had to get someone to run the campaign, someone who knew the ropes, who could keep the operation on track (they meant: keep Dole on track), someone who commanded respect, who could speak for the campaign, who could take the heat, someone with national standing. . . . In other words, he needed . . . a real Big Guy.

Thing was, Dole knew that: he'd been hearing that for months; he was trying! Nothing wrong with Don Devine, of course. Nice guy . . . a professor, got a Ph.D.! . . . but who was listening to him anymore? Not Dole. Dole got new advisers like Christmas sweaters . . . liked 'em for a while, then got tired of them. Got tired of anyone who kept telling him the same thing, like he didn't get it the first time. Lately, he'd been talking to John Sears . . . the guy who put Reagan on the path in '76, then in '80, till Reagan fired him when he lost Iowa. Sears was a Big Guy. Big ideas: how to structure the campaign staff, set up machinery in the early states, how he'd take care of the whole campaign while Dole went out and made speeches, got a *vision*—you know, Presidential. But Dole would have to let go of the rest, the money, the ads, the schedule, everything. . . .

O-kayy! Dole knew he had to give it all up—or at least look like he did. That's what the press was writing: Dole's big problem was organization, flyin' around with the map on his knees, making up a campaign as he went along. Maybe they were right. Let someone else sit in the office, chair the meetings— near as Dole could figure, that's all they did in the campaign: everyone was always in a *meeting* . . . for what? Is that what the press wanted to see? But the Bobster was going to show them now—sign on a Big Guy, even before the *exploratory campaign*. Sign him on and *announce it*. Raise a million dollars a month, and announce that, too. That'd wake them up. Ring Bush's chimes. Show the world that Dole was going to play this one like a Big Guy.

So right around Christmas, Dole arranged a secret meeting in the Maryland hills, at his friend Bob Ellsworth's country place—not too far from Camp David, matter of fact! Ellsworth was all class, possessed of the attributes that registered with Dole. Came from Kansas, but *eastern* Kansas, Snob Hill, fine family . . . in fact, there was a county, Ellsworth, and a town, Ellsworth, Kansas . . . and Ellsworth's dad had been alumni director of KU, a position of such clout in the state that, during the thirties, he took on the Ku Klux Klan—single-handed—and won, faced them down! . . . And Ellsworth the younger went to Congress with Dole, freshmen together in 1961, and by '68 he was Nixon's Political Director, working the country with the Big Guys, for the White House . . . and then Ambassador to NATO—people still called him Ambassador, though he had his own consulting firm now—lotta moneyy! . . . Perfect host for the meeting! And Sears drove out, of course; and Don Devine refused to come at first, but then he showed up; and David Keene, a consultant to Dole and a friend to Devine. . . .

And Ellsworth, with his wife, Vivian, went up to the big new Giant Food in Frederick, and laid in a small fortune in deli stuff, and chocolate cake, and a fine new Silex coffeemaker. (They weren't much for coffee themselves, but they were hosting a political meeting!) And they set out this feast in the old farmhouse, and everybody dug in, while Sears started talking about what ought to be done three months from now, and what ought to be done six months from now . . . and Dole sat in Ellsworth's rocker, in his Christmas cardigan, listening and nodding, eyes drifting from Sears to Devine, to Keene going back for more chocolate cake, to the windows overlooking the pond and pasture, while the scenario of his White House win hummed in his ears. This was it: the Big Guys, The Plan . . . the kind of meeting Teddy White used to sit in on in Hyannisport!

But Keene was cold (Ellsworth couldn't get the goddam wood stove lit) and laying into the coffee and cake, and pretty soon he was working on the sort of sugar-caffeine frenzy that crops up occasionally as a defense in murder trials. He said to Sears:

"You can't manage a thing! When my people came back to me in Iowa, told me what you were doing for Reagan, I told 'em I ought to fire 'em if they couldn't collect intelligence better than that. I thought you *had* to be doing more than that. But you weren't. And you lost. So, don't start telling us now what *we* ought to be doing . . ."

And then Sears was off again, explaining why he was right seven years ago, in Iowa. And Keene started shouting back at him, and Devine let everybody know that if they thought he'd take the number-two job under Sears, well, forget it. It was only Dole talked him into running this campaign—never wanted it, wasn't doing it for his pleasure . . . and Ellsworth sat near the buffet counter, waiting for Dole to call a halt to this drivel . . . but Dole never said a thing. This was Dole's nightmare—trapped in a room with a vicious interpersonal quarrel to sort out. And it went on for *hours*. . . . Aagh! Meetings!

So finally, they all just drove away. And Dole didn't have his Big Guy to announce. Didn't matter. There was time. Anyway, it wasn't going to change what he did. "You know," Dole used to say, "I came to Congress, I answered every letter, answered it by hand. I was my own AA, my own Press Secretary, my own Advance man, my own office manager, my own political adviser. Funny thing: we kept winning."

He had work to do. Do it himself, if he had to. Wherever he was, that *was* the campaign. Elizabeth was ready to head down to Florida December 24. That was all right with Bob. Of course, by that time, there was no one around for him to call. Unless he had their home numbers.

His Midwest coordinator, Floyd Brown—best guy Dole had in the field— took off the day before Christmas, too, and flew to Olympia, Washington, to his parents' home. It was Christmas Eve, and not too early—must have been eight or nine at night, back East—when the phone rang in Olympia, and Floyd's dad picked it up.

"How's it *lookinnnn*? . . . What's *cookinnn*?"

Floyd's dad almost hung up. Thought it had to be a crank call.

BOOK II

10

Right
from the Start

IN THE tiny elevator, after the meeting, no one said a word. No one wanted to spoil the moment. Anyway, together with the two Kremlinoids who rode along and pressed the buttons, there was hardly room for the three of them to face one another. They grinned straight ahead.

Kind of funny, this narrow old elevator, in the grand Seat of Empire. He had seen things like that everywhere in Russia: deficiency, a want of resource, of precision . . . things that didn't match the image of Soviet superpower. Less than a day in the country this time and Hart already took it for granted: the Soviet system was decayed from within, deficient economically, industrially, in investment in the lives of its people. . . . That was the enormous fact that underlay all the new buzzwords: "glasnost," "perestroika," "the Crisis of Communism" . . . and made possible the brave new world-without-warheads that Ronald Reagan flirted with, then kicked away, at the summit in Iceland.

The Soviet Union was rotting from within.

It was the kind of defining fact-on-the-ground that made opportunity, new rules of the game. It was the kind of fact that Hart never missed, and never forgot, the kind he'd built his career on: simple, fundamental, so *apparent* . . . why didn't others see it? They never seemed to catch on. But once weighed for the ripples it would launch as it hit home, such a plain, radical truth could change . . . everything. From that kind of fact, a Gary Hart fact, he could reckon out to the ends of the earth.

That was the joy of being with Hart: the shared, secret knowledge. Once you saw one of those Hart-facts, saw it as he did, started riding the ripples, you belonged. Not that you could keep the secret to yourself: it was the ethic of his life, and of those in his orbit, to build the power of those truths by sharing them, spreading them, if need be, by forcing them upon the world.

But the awareness was the fun. It was like seeing the world (watching even yourself!) with a second set of eyes, more knowledgeable, privileged, as if removed to a hillside above the action. . . . And always, with Hart, *you knew he knew*! That was shared, even without words: by a lungful of laugh that burst from Hart, like a bark, when some absurd detail caught his eye. Or he could include you without a sound: with his lips pursed, he'd just toss you a look, and a slight, intimate shrug of his eyebrows, with the joke—*he knew you knew*—lurking in his eyes beneath . . . like the look he flashed for a half-second now to Doug Wilson, his foreign policy staffer, as the elevator lurched and sighed to a halt at the ground floor.

Everything made such delicious sense, once you knew . . . and Wilson knew. He'd worked with Hart for five years now, worked his way into the First Circle, worked for two years on this meeting: researching, scouting expert help, writing letters, nudging the Soviets toward a face-to-face, visiting the embassy with articles and opinion polls: HART URGES SHIFT IN U.S. POLICY . . . HART FRONT-RUNNER AMONG DEMOCRATS . . . No one knew better how hard Hart had worked for this, his elation now, his relief . . . what it *meant.* Wilson looked at his watch: three—no, three and a half hours! His mind flashed back through the meeting: it was amazing, in its sweep—and rich with ironic detail. For Wilson, the detail was the pastry, that blueberry pastry, so delicate, finely wrought, so unlike *anything* any normal Soviet citizen would ever see . . . the pastries, on two little plates, which rested for four hours, on the green felt of the table, in front of Mikhail Gorbachev.

God, Wilson wanted one of those pastries! Gorbachev even offered—urged Doug to leave his notes and eat! But, no, he bent to his frantic scrawl, like the Soviet notetaker, across the green baize. And Hart, of course, didn't touch them. Probably never *looked* at them, he was so intent, so on his game, so . . . excited. He was right! What he'd said about this new Soviet leader, what he'd seen, that new and enormous Hart-fact, it was . . . *so apparent:* Mikhail Gorbachev was riding the ripples, too, reckoning out to a new world order. The old Cold War rules *did not have to apply.*

Of course, you had to know Hart: you couldn't *see* his excitement. Hart was especially still in his moments of apotheosis—the '72 convention when he watched George McGovern go over the top, the night in '84 when Hart won New Hampshire. . . . It was as if the new certainty that he was right—from the start—gave him ease instead of adrenaline. There was excitement, yes, but he did not permit himself amazement.

That was left to his daughter, Andrea, who was twenty-two, and had just spent three and a half hours with the leader of the Soviet Union and her father, who had sat down across from each other and discussed the world, the *planet,* with no apparent discomfort, but with intensity, understanding, and such a calm, shared sense of future and purpose—like two guys getting together to build a boat. In many ways, Andrea was like her father: there wasn't much gee-whiz about her. In fact, her usual gaze on the world gave even less away than his. But every once in a while, she was suddenly shocked: that guy on TV, the man at the podium in front of thousands, was her father!

She always remembered the first time it happened, that dizzying hour on the platform of the Moscone Center in San Francisco. It was the night of Hart's speech to the Democratic Party, to a convention that should have been his. It was the night of the eighteenth of June, 1984. She'd asked him if it was going to be, you know . . . was she going to be in tears? And he'd said, well, yeah, perhaps. So she brought a wad of Kleenex, and she thought she was ready, as she sat down just behind the podium, a little to the right, with her mother and brother. And all the delegates were before her, thousands, and the alternates stretched off to both sides, and the guests in back, farther than she could see, as if the people of a nation were massed in the hall, and rising from their midst, two great black towers, where the networks, CNN, NBC, ABC, CBS, had their studios and signs, and light poured down on them all. And then, he passed in front of her, to the podium, and the ocean of people rose and began to roar, and the great force and heat and noise rushed up and struck her . . . and she knew somewhere in her head that their staff had passed the word to the floor to scream and shout just as long as they could, but these *people*—this had been their life for a year and a half, and it had been her life for a year and a half, and she looked at him at the podium, and it was so strange . . . all the months, the days and nights, the frustration, joy, the fear, hope, hate, came through her, welled up in a jumble-rush like the signs HART HART HART HART HART HART HART HART HART leaping red everywhere in front of her eyes, and she looked over and she *saw* him . . . Dad! . . . It was like she realized for the first time. He'd come from *Ottawa, Kansas* . . . to this . . . from parents who never finished high school . . . to *this*. . . . And she must have looked like a raccoon, with her eye makeup streaming down, as she searched her hands for Kleenex, but it was gone, and she looked down and there it was, on the floor in twisted shreds, and she bent to pick it up, she'd clean it up . . . but the people were screaming and she looked up at him, and he was saying softly, thank you, thank you . . . trying to calm them.

She guessed another man might have pinched himself, just to know it was real, when it was so . . . *amazing* like that, like it was now, this morning. . . . But it wasn't another man, it was Dad, who wasn't like that, usually. No . . . then again, this wasn't usual, was it? Hart did the next best thing to squeezing himself. Without looking down, he reached out and grasped his daughter's hand, held on to her, as they walked to their car through the Kremlin.

—★—

The surprise for Hart was how easy it was, how natural, right from the start. Of course, by the end of the meeting, he'd come to expect that from Gorbachev. But it was like every step Hart had taken: he never really knew until it happened, couldn't be *sure* how it would be. This was just as much an act of bold and blessed faith as the first step, from Ottawa out to the wide world. He couldn't be sure when he went off to college that he even belonged out there— maybe they were all geniuses . . . how could he know? . . . until he made that push and the door swung open . . . just as Yale's door did afterward, and Washington's, the McGovern campaign, the Senate. . . . There it was, every time, the opportunity, just like he'd imagined.

That's what he never could make them see—the writers, the Washington big-feet, the pols (what Gary Hart, front-runner, at the doorstep of the White House, still was pleased to call the Establishment). He never could make them understand that he was not a plotter. He didn't have any grand strategy to advance himself. He had ideas. He put them forth. And people accepted them . . . or they didn't. What had to happen, happened. But they always wrote about it like it was some kind of trick, a tactic, like he was some master schemer.

He'd try to explain: "I'm very existential."

Of course, that only made it worse.

But it wasn't like that today—not at all. (Funny, it never was overseas.) Gorbachev was so ready. From the moment that door swung open, and there he was—no fanfare, entourage, announcement, just him and Dobrynin, and a guy to take notes—it was natural, obvious, that they met to discuss important matters at the highest level of engagement. The only moment of uncertainty, the only stutter-step, was at the beginning, when Hart introduced Andrea. He said he'd brought his daughter so she could meet the General Secretary, get a chance to shake his hand. The implication was, she'd wait in an anteroom—if there were somewhere she could go, if the General Secretary could suggest . . . but Gorbachev couldn't have been nicer: she should stay . . . he insisted! Sit! Sit!

And then Hart started, by way of introduction, to tell the General Secretary something about himself. He meant to do all that in a minute (he thought he'd only have a half-hour, tops): two terms in the Senate from Colorado, the run for President in '84, a voting record that differed . . .

But Gorbachev waved him off.

"No, I know about you," Gorbachev said. "They call me the Soviet Gary Hart. They say I have New Ideas . . ."

—★—

Back at the hotel, there was a gaggle of press: cameras and correspondents in the lobby of the National; lights came bobbing at him like an attack of killer fireflies. It was an onslaught of the eighties in this perfect 1930s lobby: the heavy curvilinear chairs with their standard Stalinist upholstery that looked exactly like the carpet; the smell that hung in all Soviet lobbies, stale black tobacco smoke atop oily fumes from the heaters . . . and here were the halogen fireflies, and the Minicams, and cameramen with vests of ripstop nylon, and battery belts, and Velcro pockets, and the questions:

"How would you characterize the meeting?"

"Senator! What did you think of Gorbachev?"

Hart's eyebrows leapt again: surprise mingled with amusement. To the cameras he said only: "I'll be back . . ." and he strode past to the elevators. He had to have a minute to collect himself, throw some water on his face: What was he going to say? With the Kremlinoid driver at the wheel, he hadn't even had a chance to talk to Wilson or Andrea. Not even: "What did you think? . . ." which was always his first question, open-ended, a challenge for them to put words on it.

"Well," Wilson answered with a happy shrug. "I mean . . . what can I say?" That was the confirmation, the assurance that it was as it seemed . . . extraordinary. Andrea was surprised at Gorbachev's warmth. He'd been charmed by her greeting in Russian—Russian Language 101, from the University of Denver. He'd invited her back to the Soviet Union, *as his guest,* whenever she wanted. She was so surprised, she told him she'd have to think about it.

Hart's voice held a fond, fatherly needle as he said to her now, up in the suite: "Well, I guess that's the nicest way to kiss off one of the most powerful men in the world." And Andrea was stunned, suddenly fretful: Did it sound like that? She'd just told him what came into her head: her father's campaign was starting, and that was her priority for the next two years. . . . It wasn't that she wasn't grateful, but it was true!

Hart knew that. It wasn't that *he* wasn't grateful . . . but as a father he wanted that trip for her. He knew how she felt about the campaign. They'd always had that understanding, an identity of feeling that didn't need explaining. His daughter was, in Lee's homely phrase, the apple of his eye. Hart didn't permit himself that kind of cliché. He'd say it was just . . . easier with her.

John was the hard one, his son, now twenty. Hart worried about him. Sometimes he seemed so bitter! And Hart had asked himself a thousand times if he was being unfair, twisting John's life for the sake of his own. John didn't want much part of the campaign—not the last one, anyway. He took off to Europe, in the winter of '83, got the hell out. He didn't want to be a spectacle, to be interviewed, and watched, and filmed. Hart knew how that was. He'd talk to John—next week, home, Christmas—to tell him he understood . . . really.

Words never came easily between them. They were freighted with too much meaning. Hart had to make John see it was all right: if John didn't want a campaign, *there would be no campaign.* Hart told himself, as he had so often: No campaign. No interviews. No Secret Service. No White House. None of it. Not if John didn't want it. He'd tell John, next week . . . if they could talk. Hart didn't know. He'd talk to Wilson first.

John talked to Wilson more than his father. It was strange, but Hart had come to depend on Doug. One time, a couple of months back, on another trip, Doug and Hart had a walk through London, after dinner at the Wilton Inn. They talked for hours, through lanes and mews, in the misted lamplight. Hart was so worried about John. He'd gotten into a scrape in Washington, got mad, punched a dent in the side of his own car. Hart couldn't understand that, John's streak of violence, that temper!

"Don't worry," Doug said. "John's headstrong. He has a temper. But he'll never hurt anyone."

"How do you know?" Hart said.

"Because he's just like you. What provokes his anger is injustice . . . like you."

Hart stopped and peered, eyebrows up, at Doug's face.

Doug said: "You two are more alike than anybody I know . . . even more than Andrea." They passed another few houses, silent, Hart looking down.

"You really think so?"

He sounded relieved—but puzzled, too: he never thought of himself as angry.

—★—

That's what Lee tried to tell him—must have told him a half-dozen times over the years, when things were difficult, when they had to talk: It's *okay* to be angry.

But words were hard with them, too. Sometimes what one of them said just sailed past the other. Lee would tell him: "It's okay! You don't have to like everything about me. It's all right to be angry with parts of me . . ."

But Gary would give her that blank look, or stiffen at the edge of annoyance, and insist, like she didn't *get* it: "Babe, I'm *not . . . angry.*"

And she knew (she'd grown up in the church, too, wrapped even tighter in it than he) that he could not allow that. Frustration, yes, but anger was . . . unworthy, like swearing, or the sin of pride. And you could not push Gary—not into something he considered unworthy. She could not.

But she knew. . . . Funny, on a lot of things she was smarter than he, though you'd never know it to hear her talk. Ten times a day, she'd break off, amid something she was saying, and skitter, breathless, into explanation that, of course, she didn't learn all this herself, but *Gary* always said . . . You had to be a very good friend indeed before Lee would let an hour pass without reminding you who was the intellect in that household. When he was around, she'd do it every ten minutes, sometimes with every sentence, like a nervous tic, a dripping faucet. Of course, it drove him nuts.

But she believed it: look what he'd done! He'd been right from the start, on all the big things: when Gary said George McGovern could win the nomination; when Gary said he, Hart, could come from *nowhere* (against three people well known in the state!) to win the Senate seat from Colorado; when he said the race in '84 would come down to him and Mondale—Glenn wasn't a factor, Glenn was no choice—forget the polls, endorsements, forget the money (he mortgaged their house!) . . . the choice would be between the old way . . . and him. How could she not believe in him? She guessed (this was *not* something Gary said) that they were all smart, all the men who got to run, who got to that level. But Gary was different, she knew that.

And she was right. They were all smart, but Hart's mind was of another order. If, say, George Bush's intelligence was a silken windsock, so supple, so brightly sensitive to the currents of air around him, Hart's was something harder, unyielding—industrial-grade, a diamond-pointed tool on the landscape. It was proof not only to shifting air, but to layers of surface "fact," the lava-crust from Washington's eternal volcano, this year's, this month's everybody-knows it-goes-without-saying op-ed magma.

"I don't understand why . . ." he'd start, and the staff would brace in their seats, knowing they were in for a trip to the center of the earth . . . or at least to the nearest stratum of rock, the first available Hart-fact. Sometimes, in a rush toward some bold idea, which captivated him just by its boldness, he'd auger and slice, kick up only ash and dust. But he never stopped bearing down on that diamond bit, weighted as it was with his will. In fact, it was that process of continuous cutting, always against the grain of common wisdom (Mondale had that nomination *all locked up* . . . Reagan wins elections *'cause he's good on TV*) that kept Hart's edge so sharp.

But who would turn that vicious tool inward, into his own soft center? The answer was: *he* would not, no matter how many profile writers and armchair political shrinks wanted to see him sliced open like a mango. He kept telling them: it wasn't about him. That's not what people wanted to know. They had to know where he stood, that he stood for *something,* something that made *sense.* He had a long public record. He'd given half his life to building that record, and it was out there. He'd never tried to hide. He'd gone against the grain, tried to change the Party, the country. And he'd been right.

That must be what threatened them: if he'd been right—every step of the way—then all the big-feet, the consultants, the Party pros, the inside players, had been wrong, from the start. That's why they had to come *at him,* to make *him* the issue: Who *is* this guy? . . .

It was different with Hart and the voters. He couldn't stomach a profile interview of fifteen minutes, wouldn't sit for a picture for thirty seconds. But he'd stand for an hour in a Legion Hall, trying to explain military reform to a guy who thought Hart must be antidefense. That man wanted to know what he thought! Hart had the greatest respect for the citizenry. He thought they were like him.

— ★ —

That's what he'd tried to tell Gorbachev: the American people were not confused. They understood the need for arms control, an end to the crazy spiral. They were not distracted by the Iran scandal. There was no point in Gorbachev's waiting for an end to all that hubbub, or waiting two years for a new administration, to try to get an arms deal.

Actually, it was Gorbachev who bore down on the subject: he couldn't understand Reykjavík, why Ronald Reagan kept retreating to the same stupid formulas—wouldn't try to make the world new with a bold stroke. Reagan *wanted* to—Gorbachev knew that, he could *feel* it. He and Reagan had talked well together, they *agreed* . . . as long as they were alone. Then they'd break, go back to their own delegations, and when Reagan returned, everything had changed! Reagan couldn't deliver! Gorbachev would say something they'd agreed upon two hours before, and Reagan's old head would begin to shake, and he'd say: "Well, uh, no . . . no, we, uh, don't accept that."

Gorbachev ran through every talk in Reykjavík, for an hour and a half, glancing down from time to time to his little leather book with handwritten notes. Hart was fascinated by the man's mimicry, his recall, but he could not take up the invitation to dump on Reagan: Hart was here to advance, not undermine, American policy.

Still, Gorbachev kept asking, demanding: Why? Why could Reagan not come up to it, when the moment was so right? His hands were tied! Reagan's hands were tied! . . . Gorbachev was like a guy on a barstool, poking a finger into Hart's chest: Why? You tell me. *You're* from that country. *You* explain it. . . . And with every question, it was clearer: Gorbachev was looking for someone to ride the ripples with him. And with every question, Hart's excitement grew. There would be someone, there *is* someone. . . . But he could not say that.

All he could do was try to keep Gorbachev from retreating to *his* old formulas. At one point, Gorbachev suggested that Reagan was captive to the *military-industrial complex.* It struck Hart false, tinny, like a phrase from the old Gromyko textbook. (Hart had met, two years before, with Gromyko; that day Hart said two things: "Good morning . . ." and "Thank you very much for your time." In between, Gromyko ranted and pounded the table.) Now Hart told Gorbachev: there was no monolithic "military-industrial complex" that had to make puppets of American politicians.

The phrase was not *his,* Gorbachev objected. "That is from one of your Presidents."

True enough, Eisenhower said it. But that did not tell the whole story, Hart said. He, for example, was a Senator from Colorado, where the MX missile system was made—and yet, he voted against the MX. There were subtleties to the United States system that, perhaps, the General Secretary had yet to learn.

No, Gorbachev said, his research was good, his advisers well informed. . . . Here, he gestured with a courtly nod to his left, to Dobrynin. . . . Anatoli Fyodorovich Dobrynin was newly back in Moscow, to serve at Gorbachev's elbow, after more than twenty-four years as Ambassador in Washington. He'd observed American government under six Presidents, back to JFK. Now Hart, in turn, glanced at Dobrynin with the hint of a smile. He and the old Ambassador went back a few years, too.

Yes, it's true the Ambassador is well informed about American politics, Hart allowed. Indeed, the Ambassador is probably better informed than most American citizens. . . . Of course, that did not stop the Ambassador from maintaining at lunch three years ago that John Glenn was a *sure thing* for the Democratic nomination for President; did not stop the Ambassador, in fact, from suggesting to his friend, Senator Hart, that he *give up the race*—Glenn was just too popular!

Hart sat back and allowed himself a small chuckle (no more than Gorbachev allowed himself at that moment) and noted with satisfaction a becoming tide of pink that rose from the ancient Ambassador's neckline, toward his snowy brow.

Days later, in Vienna, the memory of that blush still drew a bark of laughter from Hart, as he retold the story. Of course, he hadn't breathed a word of the joke in Russia. In fact, to the reporters in the National Hotel, he'd held himself to general, positive comments: Gorbachev was open, and interesting . . . the meeting had been long, informative . . . the General Secretary and he had agreed on the need for arms control progress with the current U.S. administration. . . .

It was left to Tass, the Soviet wire, to let the world know the important fact. The meeting with Senator Hart, Tass said, was "friendly and relaxed." That was standard Soviet code for the essence of the matter: they'd hit it off fine.

—★—

Vienna was celebration, and a day of decompression. The staff knew Hart had to have a day somewhere to rest and think. (This trip had started with a conference in Korea and a stop in Japan—Hart had flown around the world in a week.) And there were arms talks in Vienna that Hart could check in on: Mutual and Balanced Force Reduction talks—right up Hart's alley. Warren Zimmerman, the chief U.S. negotiator, was a friend. His son, Tim, had worked on Hart's New Hampshire campaign. And Zimmerman *père* was a pro on East–West relations: knowledgeable, experienced, but without a vested interest in the wisdom of the moment. Hart could run the Gorbachev meeting past Warren; it would be useful. . . .

Anyway, there had to be a stopover somewhere, and Vienna was the perfect middle ground between East and West. It was old, cultured, suffused with the half-decomposed air of empire, Hapsburgs, Mitteleuropa, of spies and assignations, of plots whispered over café tables . . . the kind of place Hart liked to set scenes in his novels. (His second novel, *Strategies of Zeus,* had just been published in the United States. It was the story of a U.S. arms control negotiator, a quiet, raw-boned man from the Rockies whose life was caught up in a desperate struggle to save the world—a goal that came clearest to him whenever he gazed at his beloved daughter. . . . Hart, of course, insisted it was not, in any way, autobiographical.)

Withal, there was another reason for Vienna: Hart was determined to take Andrea to the opera, and when he got an idea like that, he was seldom brooked.

No matter he was not a big opera fan, no matter the tickets would cost a fortune; the *Staatsoper,* the state opera house, was one of the world's grandest, most sublime sites for music. Hart was resolved (as his parents had been on an education for *him*) that Andrea would have the advantages *he never had*

... the familiarity, the ease with the world ... and with the worldly: in Ottawa, young Gary Hartpence never even went to the *movies.*

So he had the day all planned: they'd fly in from Moscow early, check into the Imperial . . . the hotel manager had figured out *who he was* (as so many hoteliers had, since '84) and had bumped them up to a two-bedroom suite, all white-on-white, with huge bathrooms of gleaming white marble, towels as thick as a carpet, bathrobes even thicker, white linens, white upholstery, and ivory-intricate carpets: the perfect hotel antidote to Moscow's grubby National . . . like diving into an ocean of *Schlag.* Then off for a late breakfast, or at least one of those wicked Austrian treats, a ten-thousand-calorie orgy of hot chocolate and whipped cream. And then a walk around the city, Hart-style, into every old bookshop and twisty street that held mystery, promise. And then, perhaps, lunch, and a stop for a talk at Warren Zimmerman's apartment, and then to the hotel, to rest, to make a few phone calls, and dress . . . and on to the opera, and a glorious supper, and a fine night of sleep in a room constructed a hundred years before . . . built for the Duke of Württemberg. It would be exquisite.

But at the last minute, as a last mark of esteem for Hart, the Soviets decided to send on his plane (in fact, in his care) one of the refuseniks whose case Hart had brought up with Gorbachev—Rimma Brave, a Soviet Jew who needed cancer treatment in the West. Actually, she was kind of a pet case of Al D'Amato, the Senator from New York.

So Hart escorted her out of the plane in Vienna, and someone from the embassy took them both to the VIP lounge, where there were cameras waiting . . . along with *Al D'Amato,* who was looking a bit sour about Hart horning in on *his refusenik.* Unhappily for Al, the pic in *The New York Times,* the next day, showed Rimma Brave with Hart.

Unluckily for Gary, the business with Al took some time, and when he got to the Imperial, breakfast was out of the question. Hart was still up for a whipped-cream treat, but Andrea and Doug had spotted a McDonald's across the street. So they snuck over for a Big Mac, despite a look of unalloyed scorn from Hart, and when they got back, it was almost time for Gary's stand-up on *Good Morning America.* This was something arranged by his staff in the U.S., a live satellite feed back to Joan and David and the whole of the U.S.A., just then waking up to a grisly gray working Thursday. So Gary had to leave the white-on-white suite to go to a rooftop somewhere in Vienna, to stand under a dripping tarp (it was fairly grisly in Vienna that day, too), chatting brightly with the anchor-humans.

Thence he scooted right into his walk, and then to Warren's for a talk about Gorbachev—had to cut that short—and back to the hotel, where he called Billy Shore, his number-one aide, who'd just moved to Denver, along with the rest of the Hart campaign crew. Billy was full of good news and arrangements: good press in Boston and New York, "Hart, Gorbachev Exchange New Ideas" . . . That was the wire copy in other papers, too, and a new poll from *U.S. News* showed Hart well ahead of the Democratic pack; Hart at thirty-one percent,

to Cuomo at nineteen, tied with "don't know." Nobody else was even close.
. . . And another poll from *The Des Moines Register,* arbiter of the nation's
first caucus, showed Hart in a cross-party race beating Bush—sixty-five to
twenty-nine. . . . And then there was the schedule for the weekend, as a matter
of fact, day after tomorrow, when Hart, back in Washington (after another
eight hours in the air), would make the radio response for the Democrats after
Reagan's weekly chat—Hart would have to get something written, maybe
tomorrow, could they fax it? . . . And day after that, *Face the Nation,* and Billy
wanted to set up a conference call with Hart and the campaign brain trust on
that: just the standard stuff—what's our message, what's the headline, what's
the sound-bite . . . just had to be arranged.

As always, Billy was quick and precise, calm, good-natured. Billy Shore,
who'd worked with Hart since '78, was a neat man, with thin blond hair and
a round, boyish face that always seemed to look upon the world with quiet,
self-sufficient pleasure. Shore was Hart's point man, his gatekeeper and usual
traveling companion. If you wanted to tell Hart anything, you could tell Billy,
and he'd write it down in two or three neat words, on one side of his Hart-
sheet, always an accordion-folded page from a yellow legal pad, which he kept
in the same suit pocket, one sheet a day, every day. And when the time came,
he would rattle them past Hart, and write the responses, in two or three neat
words, which he'd then relay from the next stop, the next pay phone, the hotel
that night . . . Nothing got lost. Shore was impeccable. And the best part was,
he was a man of sweet juices, which he used to lubricate Hart's path through
the world, or patch things up in his wake.

Now, in the grand white suite, Hart was perched uneasily on the edge of
a white chair, closer each minute to the front edge of the cushion, and his
answers to Billy grew steadily shorter as Billy ran down another half-dozen
notes—all arrangements. Billy could hear the growing edge in Hart's voice—
he knew his man. Mostly, it seemed to Hart, his life was consumed by
schedules, arrangements, things he had to do before he could do what he meant
to do . . . like a man who lived in too small a house, who always had to move
three things to get to the thing he wanted. (In fact, at that moment, Lee *was*
moving them into a too-small house, their log cabin in the mountains outside
of Denver, whose three rooms she'd already filled with stuff, while sixty-three
cartons from Washington waited, stacked on the porch. . . . That was another
thing, he had to call Lee back: their friend Terry Tydings had called Lee from
D.C., where she had ten copies of Hart's book for him to sign. Should she
take them to the office, or the Washington town house? It had to be arranged. . . .) Mostly, it seemed to Hart, he never got a day to think—or even
not to think—just to live, be himself, read, go to a bookstore, see friends, a
movie . . . to feed the individual mind, which, after all, was what he had to
offer.

Instead, what he got was arrangements—sixteen hours a day of arrangements. Things had to be done *now,* or yesterday, by the time he got to them.
That's what the staff in Denver was supposed to take care of—this time, he'd

have a real campaign staff, not like '84. No, this time, the machinery would all be in place. The First Circle was already moving, hauling lives, homes, and families out to Denver, where offices were already assembling . . . 1600 Downing Street, a propitious address—and cheap rent. But somehow, it didn't lighten the load on Hart. It was just more people for him to teach that it *wasn't about arrangements* . . . that he wasn't going to stop, today, now—this minute!—to call the Democratic Chairman of Cumquat County, *who was so pissed off* . . . not even if Hart's own county coordinator, Mary Makeadeal, said he *had to call the Cumquat County Chairman, NOW . . . or she'd walk*! No, that's not how it was going to be . . . not this time.

"You feel good about it?"

Billy's voice in the phone—he wanted to know about Gorbachev.

Hart said: "It was . . . incredible." And he gave Billy the outline of the meeting, its length, its sweep. He did, he told Billy, what he'd come to do: he had opened a relationship . . . it was important.

"Yeah, that's great. I talked to Hal and Dixon"—two of Hart's senior campaign staff—"and everybody said it was, you know, a really good move. Politically, it played really well, people were just really proud of you, you know, dealing with another world leader. It's perfect, in terms of what it does to your stature, you know, fits perfectly with that strategy, and *Face the Nation,* Sunday . . ."

Hart cut in: "No."

Hart's voice had that clipped tone.

". . . No, Billy. This was *important. "*

He shouldn't have to tell Billy that it wasn't about talk shows, or polls, stature gaps, strategy, not even about becoming President. This was about *being* President.

That was the Hart-fact underneath: Hart was getting ready to be President. Not because he thought he had the race won—just the reverse. He knew, somehow, in that extrarational way that led him to most of his truths, that this would be a difficult campaign—vicious, more like it—that's what he feared. That's why he had to be ready, now. He had to decide, to know, where he wanted to lead the country. There would be no time to do the work, no time to think, in the campaign. Hart knew what the campaign could do to a man, the constant, restless, know-nothing drive that the system now demanded. Save for Jesse Jackson, who'd run in '84, Hart was the only Democrat who knew about the bubble. Hart remembered '84, after New Hampshire, when he touched down at a hundred airports in the space of twenty days, screaming out his New Ideas into the wind on the tarmacs until he was hoarse, weary, shrunken inside around a kernel of himself that he had to protect . . . or lose himself altogether. He knew he made mistakes in exhaustion. He knew exhaustion would come again. Hart knew the American campaign system like no one else: he'd helped to invent the long march with McGovern in the run-up to '72.

And he knew, they'd have to come *at him.* They'd try to make him the issue. Like Mondale did in '84, when Hart had him down on the mat: "Where's the beef?" Mondale said. That wasn't about issue papers. Hart had spoken on the issues for two years. What Mondale was saying was: *Who is this guy? Where'd he come from? . . .* And it worked, God knows. This time, they'd come at him harder. And the only thing Hart could do was to get his ideas out there *now,* to make his ideas the issues. They were his only protection. That's why he'd spent the last two years, since '84, building his program, like a brick wall: the book on military reform, the comprehensive trade bill, his own version of the federal budget, the Georgetown lectures on foreign policy, and, soon, the education speech. . . . Where is that speech? What are they doing with the time? . . . That speech would be another brick. That wall had to get built.

And people would see. He trusted that much. That's what he kept trying to tell the staff about the "stature strategy." It wasn't just a trick to make him stand above the others. It had to be based on a rock-solid fact: he knew what he wanted to do, when the others were just peddling sound-bites. And he knew, now . . . much better since the morning with Mikhail Gorbachev. He knew it like he knew every grand Hart-fact, knew it whole and instantly, without a train of reason. . . . It was the same feeling, the same rush of glorious certainty he'd had six months before, in the Middle East, with King Hussein, and Shimon Peres, and Hosni Mubarak. The old formulas were dead. That's what Gorbachev was saying to him in a dozen different ways: something great, and new, could occur.

And it *fit.* It made perfect sense with the first year in the White House, the agenda that Hart had, even now, running through his head. He hadn't told anyone, not even Lee. . . . But he knew: Gorbachev would be first. Hart would send an emissary to Moscow, even before he took office, to plan an early summit *with the Reykjavík agenda:* the zero option—no more missiles. They could make it *happen.* Within ten years, there would be no arms race. *He'd invite Gorbachev to his inauguration.* Hart knew it whole: Gorbachev would come . . . and that would wake the world to the change within its reach. And after that summit—as early as February '89—Hart would set the Secretary of State to detailed negotiations to make real the end of the Cold War. And when those talks were under way, then . . . he would go to the Middle East. Himself, *he* would do it, and in a room with Hussein and Peres and Mubarak, he would work out an end to those wars, that madness. He had already talked to them all, and he *knew,* there was basis for an agreement. Real peace would take years. But the framework could be set up now, *had* to be set up now. . . . And by the summer of '89, he'd be back in the U.S., where he'd set in motion a reform of the nation's basic institutions: military reform—only from the White House could America change *how it thought about defense,* and then work out what that meant for weapons, basic equipment, training, troops. And education: a total overhaul, freeing up new ways in which people could study, but all based on conservative *subjects*—languages, classics, more science, mathematics. It *had* to be done from the White House. . . . And there was more: industrial policy, trade, energy, environment—fundamental changes. He saw it whole. And he could do it.

But he could not do it without a campaign to match that boldness. He could not get there by cutting deals with the politics-as-usual pros who signed on because they liked his chances. It was not going to be that way—could not be. And he couldn't get there if the campaign was about him, even if magically he could transform himself to the perfect pitch of slogan and slow grin—it would not work. Unless he was hauled into office by his ideas, there would be no mandate, no way to govern. And there'd be no point: Why would he give his life over to this, if it were not for the notion that he could do something great? He didn't have to be President, not for him—maybe for the kids; he could see it that way, sometimes, for their future—but for him, he could live without. He could write books. He could have . . . a life of his own. That was the other truth: he could not do it by losing every shred of himself in ninety-nine Iowa counties, by shaking every hand at every steak fry, press conferences at every airport in every state. What was that for? Ideas did not come from meetings of consultants thinking up slogans, certainly not from press conferences. Ideas came from something deeper, from the life that underlay the candidacy. If there was no life, no time to think, what was the point? That's what he kept telling the Schedulers: he had to have time, somewhere—anywhere—a day to live, to graze on the world. It wasn't because he was lazy, God knows. He'd work like a beast, a wiry old donkey. But what was the point, if there was no life inside him? What use would he be then?

It was, for Hart, a matter of simple independence. If he lost that, he was lost—and they might as well fold up shop. Independence was, for him, in equation with individuality. And it was his individual thought—the power of one man's ideas—on which the whole edifice stood. Just a day, just once in a while . . . to read, have a drink, talk about ideas, or not talk at all, see a city, go to the beach . . . or the *opera!*

So, they dressed, he and Andrea, dressed for the evening in their splendid suite, and stepped down to the lobby and asked for a cab. . . . *Staatsoper!* the cabbie confirmed with a nod, and they drove through the capital of the Hapsburgs, to the glorious theater. . . . No matter their seats were not too good, stuck up in nosebleed city, third balcony—Boy! Wish we had glasses!—no matter: they were at the opera! And the glittering chandeliers dimmed and died, the orchestra began to play, the audience settled with a susurrous sigh, the curtain rose, and . . . Gary and Andrea Hart fell quickly, blissfully asleep in their seats.

—★—

In Ottawa, there was always time. Sometimes it seemed like time didn't pass at all, in the dreamy wait for sleep in the front bedroom on Mulberry. The sounds of the house were always the same, reassuring. There was hardly sound at all from his parents' room; his dad had already turned in. Carl Hartpence was still a farmer in his rhythms, early to bed, up about dawn, though he'd worked in town for years now. Nina was the night bird. Even after he put down his own book, Gary could hear her in the living room chair, where she read—probably her Bible, or church magazines—though lately, since the new thing, television, she kept that on, too, with its murmurous song or riffling laughter in the background.

Gary knew what show was on, knew the whole schedule, matter of fact. In those days, there was only one station, WDAF, Channel Four, from Kansas City, thirty miles to the northeast. Nina and Carl got one of the first TVs in Ottawa. The mystery in the family was: How'd they afford it? Everybody knew Carl never made much. He sold farm equipment, and every once in a while, a car. But it never, well . . . Nina used to say Carl was too honest to be a good salesman. Her family used to say it just wasn't in him to do any more than get by: it was Nina who had all the get-up-and-go. And that's how you'd hear it in town, as Nina came from a family of thirteen children—and ten of them lived—so there were Pritchards everywhere. On the other hand, the Hartpence side came from a farm out of town; Carl only had a couple of brothers, and one of them, George, didn't cut much of a figure . . . in Ottawa, Hartpence wasn't a name of great lustre.

Anyway, hers were always the last sounds Gary heard, just as they were, years before, when she would read to him, until she switched off the light and he sank into the smell of fresh bed linens. There was always the scent of just-cleaned in the house: Nina (her name even rhymed with Bina Dole's) was another Kansas woman for whom everything had to be just so. There wasn't much in the place—furniture, or fancy things—but Nina cleaned every day, as her Pritchard sisters used to say, "top to bottom." And sometimes, there'd be the smell of fresh cookies, or a cake with sweet promise for tomorrow. In later years, after Gary left, and Nina stopped cooking, people forgot: talked about her like she couldn't cook at all. But while he was there, it was Nina who did for the whole family. On big days—Thanksgiving, Christmas—she'd overdo: turkey, oyster dressing, candied apples . . . and a coconut cream pie that would absolutely curl your toes. Nina could bake the best chocolate cake (no recipe, either—she'd just start stirring), and she'd never get a speck of flour on the counter: she was neat, organized. That's why the other Pritchard children leaned on her so: "Well," they'd say, "it's no trouble for Nina . . ." Of course, it was: she just didn't show it. Gary knew. Sometimes, as he lay in the dark, he'd hear her still going, snapping things back into kitchen cupboards (nothing stayed out of place overnight) and sliding drawers shut, the sounds punctuating the song of crickets outside or perhaps the mile-long rumble of a freight train rolling through town in the night.

East–west train . . . had to be the Missouri Pacific. There was a time when Gary knew every train, and not just the Mo-Pac, but the Santa Fe, too, and not just the names and destinations, but the roaring steam locomotives that pulled them, and their wheel bases and their engine weights. He and his cousin, Jon, fell in love with trains—of course, they were Pritchards, and the men in that clan had all put in time on the tracks: they were section hands, gandy dancers; but Gary and Jon made a *study* of it . . . till the diesels came in, and then it wasn't the same . . . just a train in the night.

That was the way Gary was about things: a boy with a restless hunger to know. He was a reader, like Nina, and with that, too, he'd run through periods of particular infatuation. He read everything by L. Frank Baum (the fellow who invented the Wizard of Oz), and then Gary lived and dreamed the Wild West, eating his way through a score of Zane Grey books in the little stone library across from school. Lately it was Robert Heinlein, sci-fi books, which coincided with Gary's interest in rocketry. He and Art Harkins, the school's science geek, made their own black powder (enough to blow up Art's house, they figured), and now they were building a rocket.

Gary wanted to know everything. In fifth grade at the Lincoln School, his teacher, Mrs. Hannah, put up a chart with everybody's name, and each time a student read a book, she'd paste a star next to that name. After a while, Gary's name looked like the Milky Way. But he didn't read books for the stars on his chart, or even marks—though he got straight A's. It didn't even start with school. When he was six years old, he signed a family guest book: "Professor Gary."

Education was an absolute in that household. Both Nina and Carl had to leave school to work. One thing Gary always knew: he was going to study; he was going to college; he was going to be better off than his folks. He could never forget the hurt in the house when his older sister, Nancy, left school to get married. Nina was crushed. She felt such a failure. Nancy was willful, full of life and fun, but the kind of girl who just got by in school. When Nancy took up with boys, Nina saw her off to an all-girls academy in Arkansas. But Nancy soon came back. When she met Bob Brenner and things got serious, Nina just fretted herself sick. Bob was a big, easygoing man, come up from Texas to Ottawa on a construction job. Whenever he'd come over to the house, Nina would go stiff with worry and anger that she couldn't let out. It used to make Bob laugh to see Nina fidget on her couch, plainly dressed, with her hair pulled up in a severe bun, as the Nazarene Church prescribed. Nina finally made Nancy vow she wouldn't see Bob anymore. Nancy promised. But she married him anyway.

It was different with Gary: Nina never had to scold him, never even raised her voice. He always minded. He was quiet and polite, a bit formal for a boy his age, and respectful of her—of all adults. When the Pritchard ladies would come by for coffee and a good giggling visit with Nina, the talk would drive Carl out of the house. "Aw, come on, now," he'd say, as he got up, "you just sit around and gossip, and you don't know what the truth is . . ." He'd go out to the backyard, or to Lee's Downtowner, a restaurant on Main Street, to talk with his pals about hunting or cars. But Gary would stay in the room, he'd listen to *everything*. You could almost *see* him listening, with those big ears sticking off his head.

Gary had strong Pritchard bones that gave his face a serious look beyond his years, like his features had got to full size before he did. In fact, since his birthday was late November, and the cutoff for school enrollment in each grade was January 1, for many years he was small among the kids in his grade.

And you couldn't call him stylish. He never had, for instance, just the right shoes, the Nunn-Bush, or the whippiest Florsheim's, from Paine's Shoe Store on Main Street (where they had an X-ray machine so you could wiggle and watch all the bones in your feet!), and certainly, he never wore his sleeves and cuffs rolled up, like the athletes. He was, instead, always neat, with clean wash-pants and a sport shirt. (Carl's brothers used to say that kid never once got dirty!) Nina laid his clothes out for him, all the way through high school. By the time he was older, he wished she'd stop, but he never said anything.

That's one of the reasons there was always time: she organized him. Nina made sure there was time to study, time to do his assignments, and more. Nina put the fear of God into Gary's friends. They'd show up at the door, and ask if Gary could play, and she'd just say no. Nothing more . . . no. To hear them talk, she was ferocious, standing in the door, plain and pale, with her hair yanked back in that churchly bun, and her eyes just staring them down. Scared them to death! But Gary never saw her like that. In fact, everyone who really knew her noticed her softness whenever she looked at him, the tenderness, devotion: there were no words for it, except Perfect Love.

That's what they talked about at her church, Perfect Love: of course, they meant it toward God, as well as man. The central doctrine of the Nazarene Church was Entire Sanctification, which meant a second, higher level of religious experience, *after* salvation and acceptance into the church. It was, for Nazarenes, a distinctive act of God *for them,* a personal intervention by the Holy Spirit, to cleanse the deep stains of inherited sin, to imbue them with holiness, which would not wear off, which should only grow, which made possible a life of thoroughgoing grace. In the words of John Wesley, the great Methodist, whose teachings were the inspiration for the movement, this Entire Sanctification made possible Christian perfection . . . Perfect Love.

Nina wasn't so much caught up in the theology. When she found the Nazarenes, just after the war, when Gary was maybe eight or nine, she simply found a church home for herself and her family. It was mostly outsiders who made such a fuss about the rules (the Godly Walk: no alcohol or tobacco; no personal adornment; no secular entertainments, movies, card games, dances, or the like). But Nina had been raised strict Baptist—no alcohol or cards in the Pritchard house, either (though her father, Willard, did enjoy his pipe)—so the rules weren't strange, or severe. In Ottawa, there were always more churches than bars, and most people were straitlaced. In fact, in those days, Ottawa U, which was a Baptist institution, still played basketball in long pants. For Nina, the difference lay in size, and sense of purpose: the Nazarenes were a small congregation, a fellowship—the pastor was always a family friend— and the church wasn't so worldly, caught up in wealth or status. In Ottawa, the Church of the Nazarene still wore with pride the air of a movement, of a Wesleyan mission where the Lord's poor and needy were ushered to the front pew.

That was a part Gary liked, too: the church was there to help people in this life. Everybody talked about how tough the Nazarenes were, but really, they weren't so fixated, like others, on the sins of man. The point was redemption, on this earth, now. The point was people could be better . . . perfect! It was a beautiful idea. Of course, Carl joined the church, and Nancy went along, too—she was a gifted singer in the choir. But the way Gary was, he went into it to know, to understand: he was serious about things. . . . He was about ten when he went to the front of the simple church on Seventh Street, to accept the Lord Jesus Christ as his personal Savior. It wasn't more than a year later, he said he was going to be a minister.

Nina was so proud! She'd beam as she told her sisters and his cousins: Gary's going to pastor a church! It was a great work, bringing salvation. In those days, before the television came, Nina'd do housework with the company of the radio, a big stand-alone tube set, aglow with the voice of Billy Graham. And sometimes, she'd mention what a wonderful man that Mr. Graham was, all the important work he was doing. She didn't talk like that about too many people. She may even have sent him money—although, Lord knows, there wasn't a pile to spare. Carl and Nina usually rented their houses (there were lots of houses; Nina liked to move), but the one they owned on Seventh Street they sold, without profit, as a good deed, to the church for a parsonage. Nina believed in living her ideas. Of course, Gary understood. That was one of the early things he knew whole—ideas had power, they had to make a difference in life. If not, what was the point?

And it was the great joy of Nina's life that *she knew Gary understood.* She had such confidence in him. Years later, when he turned away from the ministry and went to law school, people thought Nina would be heartbroken. But they missed the point. She wanted for him what *he* wanted. She knew he would always do good works in the world. He didn't have to be a minister . . . for God had already worked His blessed way in Gary's life, and in hers.

See, Nina was told she couldn't have children. That's why she and Carl went to Kansas City and adopted Nancy. Then, a few years later, Nina thought she had a tumor. She had no idea . . .

She was twenty-eight when she delivered. She was in hard labor for three straight days. They were just about to bring in a doctor from Kansas City, to do a C-section, when Gary finally came out. Leila, her sister, was in the hospital with her, and she took the baby off to the nursery, cleaned him up, and put stickum on his head, to curl his baby hair. Nina was so thrilled that she had a curly-headed little boy! It made the delivery somehow more wondrous. Of course, the next day, when the nurse bathed the boy, his hair was straight. In fact, it looked like a brush pile!

But it didn't matter. Not to Nina. Gary was her personal gift . . . a distinctive act of God *for her*. . . . And that was the first thing Gary just knew: it didn't matter what else happened . . . he was her miracle.

—★—

You could tell it was Hart in the photo, though the winter-morning light was not the best—his hair looked like a brush pile!

Actually, there were two photos—one was of the woman. The detective's report said the woman came out to her doorstep, about 7:00 A.M. that Sunday, December 21, 1986. That was her in the first photo. She looked up and down the street, she picked up her paper. The second photo was snapped a minute later, when Hart came out. You could read the number of the house, behind him: 1006. That's how they'd retrace the trail . . . months later.

Months later, everybody-in-the-know would say: this was the wrong woman! Word around Washington was, the detective was hired by former Senator Joe Tydings—trying to catch Hart with his wife, Terry. (They were in the middle of a horrible divorce.) Just Hart's bad luck—the detective trailed him to someone else! . . . For his part, Joe Tydings told anyone who asked that he had nothing to do with that report, he never hired a detective.

Hart was convinced, he'd been followed for months. Joe Tydings was too cheap for that. ("A notorious tightwad," Hart insisted.) Anyway, *any husband* who is trying to get the goods on his wife has the wife followed—not the man. (Why would the detective follow Hart to Virginia, to a radio studio, where he made the response to Ronald Reagan?) Hart thought maybe it was organized labor, or organized crime, or organized . . . well, he loved spy plots.

But by the time those pictures and the detective's report surfaced at *The Washington Post,* no one wanted to hear any theories from Hart.

By that time, *everybody knew,* the real issue, the only issue, was . . . him.

11

Don't Tell Michael

USUALLY, it took a few days before Michael would be his old self. For at least forty-eight hours you could count on finding him quiet, reading in a corner, not eager to do much—oh, maybe he'd cook . . . he'd always do the salad. Michael was great in the kitchen. And he'd do his walks, steaming down the sidewalks with weights on his hands. He loved to walk in their neighborhood, with the bridges over the finger creeks and the water lapping at the smooth back lawns, on both sides of the street, every street an island . . . and the great tropical fruit trees, avocado and guava; they lost the tall coconut palms a few years back, to the yellow disease that spread from Jamaica—Michael knew all about that. Of course, he was the expert on everything; found out all about the trees, and then he'd *argue* about them *with Tiky, who lived there,* in Fort Lauderdale . . . but not right away: at first, he was just walking, working his vents and valves. Even without visible joy, Michael kept his machine in tune.

If they dragged him out in the car, he'd fall asleep. It shocked Vivian, the first time they went on a trip. She and Tiky borrowed a big car, so they could carry Kitty and Michael in a comfortable backseat. They were driving some-where—down to the Keys?—and she was talking . . . they were all talking, she thought. But then she turned around, and Michael was dead to the world, with his face in folds, curled like a kid in a corner of the backseat! Happened three or four times that first day. Pretty soon, Vivian had to wonder: *Is this man bored with us?* But she was new to the family then, Tiky's new bride. She learned, after that, about Michael and his naps. . . . Anyway, second or third day, Michael would appear next to Tiky's chair. "Okay, Doc. What're we gonna do this afternoon?" And Tiky'd drawl out: "Ah'm not gon' do a damn thing. Ah'm a read." Michael would snap: "No, you're not. We're going swimming. That's the trouble with you—you never get up. That's why you look like a beached whale . . ." And then they knew: Michael was back; he'd got some rest, got the steam back; it only took a couple of days. A marvelous machine, was Michael Dukakis.

You couldn't keep him down for long. You sure as hell couldn't argue him down. Not that Tiky didn't try. That was how they loved each other, those two. Tiky was on him about everything! . . . How cheap Michael was, what a know-it-all, always politicking! . . . When they really got going, it was in Greek, needling, sarcastic, interrupting one another's interruptions, correcting one another's Greek . . . in Greek.

"Mr. Expert! You don't know what you're *talking about!*"

"You don't even know how to *say* it! . . ."

"That's ancient Greek, the way you said it."

"This is my cousin," Michael would say, "who talks Greek with a southern accent."

And giggling . . . like boys. Fact was, they'd been boys together, when cousin Stratton (that was Tiky's real name, Dr. Stratton Sturghos) came up to Brookline for visits at the Dukakis home. Stratton's mother was a cousin of Michael's father. You had to be Greek to know what that meant: cousins together, in the family home, sons of cousins, grandsons of brothers, back to . . . well, back forever, to the village. It was absolute comfort that they were of the same flesh . . . and absolute license, open season:

"Look at him, big doctor! Flat on the couch . . . Chubby! You eat that whole bag of cookies?"

Michael could never understand how Tiky could *live* like he did—not a shred of discipline! Michael was the kind who'd eat one cookie. Tiky'd just eat till they were gone. Tiky and Kitty, they'd race for the couch—winner take all, sprawled flat out. Michael and Vivian were the run-around kind, always in the kitchen, fixing something, doing something. Michael fetched for Kitty. Vivian fetched for Stratton. It was perfect. Sometimes they got to laughing so hard, they were crying. Tiky and Kitty were fighting for the couch, so Michael dove for it, and they were wrestling, grunting, giggling. Once, in the Berkshires, Michael got a fish; Tiky hates fish, just can't stand it; so Michael cut off the head, and he snuck in on Tiky, who was reading in bed, and all of a sudden, a disembodied fish head jumped at Tiky from over the edge of his book. And he yelped, hit the deck, whereupon Michael chased him, all over the house, trying to zap him with the fish head, on a skewer, shouting in Greek: THE FISH! THE FISH IS COMING! . . . waving that plug-ugly severed head till it flew off the skewer and landed behind the fridge, and they had to move the fridge, but Tiky wouldn't help, and the rest couldn't budge the box, for laughing.

That's why Michael always came—to let go, like he could when it was family. You wouldn't see him waving a fish head in Boston, no—not with the animal-rights coalition, reporters, Republicans . . . not with any strangers to see. No, in the State House, even around town, no one would see Michael Dukakis without his dark suit, his dark eyes sober and composed, hooded under his bushy brows, watching, wary, thinking his way through. You could almost hear the gears in his head. Even when he was happy, supposed to be having a good time . . . you could see him thinking. Michael didn't lose control. People in the State House, it drove them nuts: Governor Robot! They didn't understand: in the Mediterranean mindset, there are only two kinds of people. There is family, and there is everyone else.

That's why it worked with Tiky; it wasn't a meeting of the minds. Michael didn't have much use for Tiky's politics, which tended to echo the standard Sunbelt war cry: get the damn gov'ment offa mah back! There were topics that Michael wouldn't even get into with Tiky: medical care . . . Michael thought it a scandal, a *disgrace,* that millions of people didn't have insurance, had no access, not even *basic care*! . . . Dr. Stratton Sturghos, on the other hand, would have no *truck* with "sosh'lahzed medicine." Once or twice, he tried to tell Michael what happened when the county took over *his* hospital, where *he used to practice* . . .

"Jus' fell apart . . . completely to hell—no better'n'a charituh ward in Miamuh! . . . Michael, you're not list'nin' . . . Ah'm try'n'a *talk* to you now!"

"Don't even start," Michael would say, with a quick, dismissive show of one palm, a grimace off to the side.

Tiky wouldn't push, not on politics. When you got down to it, Tiky had too much respect. He honored Michael. The most admirable man Tiky knew. Michael never lied, never took advantage, never played favorites, never cut a deal with one against the other. And he was exactly the same at twelve years old!

It was always special, even forty years before—Tiky's visits to Panos and Euterpe's house in Brookline. He and Michael were born nine days apart, forged of the same metal. And yet . . . Brookline was a different world. It was . . . a privilege, going up there. That's how much respect there was for Michael's family. Panos was a *doctor,* a man of learning, a helping man. How many Greek doctors were there? Not too damn many. Stratton's dad ran a restaurant in Greenwood, South Carolina. Of course, all Greek men could cook. And Euterpe, Michael's mother, was an educated woman. How many Greek girls had been to college? She might have been the first in the country, to hear the family talk. So, inside that house you watched your step, you behaved. When Panos arrived, you shook his hand. (It wasn't all hug-and-kiss, like Tiky's family in Greenwood.) And when Panos talked, you listened. Of course, that wasn't often. He worked day and night. But he'd show up for meals, in his wool suit, with his vest still buttoned, at the head of the table, and when he told you to eat everything on your plate . . . well, then, you sat straight up, and worked your fork on those carrots!

Panos was stern, but an upright man, a model in that family. *The* model, in fact: growing up, both cousins knew they were going to be doctors, like Pan. At least, that's what Tiky always thought, until one day, on a visit, during high school, Michael and he took the trolley into Boston. And they were walking through that park, the Common, the green in the middle of town, looking at the old buildings, and Michael said: "I'm gonna be there someday." And he was looking up the hill at a building with a golden dome, and Tiky didn't even know what he meant. But he learned, later: that was Beacon Hill, and that building with the dome was the State House. Michael knew even then, what he wanted, where he had to go.

And he got there. That's what Tiky had to admire. Michael picked out one job in the world, and worked, and worked, and never took his eyes off the top of that hill . . . never cut a deal, never went against his own ideals, never wavered, never changed *at all*—the guy *weighed* the same as he did in high school. And he got there. He made it work. . . . *Work?* Hell! Tiky's cousin had to decide now whether he wanted to be *President*! Tiky knew the decision Michael had to make. (With Kitty around, everybody knew.) That's why they had come down for another visit, second time in two months. Michael couldn't talk about it in Boston—every word would be retailed in the State House halls, and then right into the papers. Michael wasn't going to show uncertainty, not to strangers. With family, he could talk about what he *didn't* know . . . maybe. Tiky didn't mean to push. Michael would talk, if he wanted to. Tiky wasn't going to get into politics now. But he couldn't help *asking,* first time he had a chance:

"Michael, what're you gonna do?"

"I don't know. Kitty says I'd be good. . . ." Michael's mouth twisted into a small, ironic grin. "She thinks her husband would make a terrific President."

"Well, if you won . . ."

Michael cut in: "I'm not gonna lose!" Then he added, softly: "If I'm gonna do it . . . I'm not going into it to lose."

Tiky nodded, backed off. But Michael was talking. That was what they all noticed, that time, at the end of '86: Michael didn't have to rest, didn't need to cool out. He had that snap the minute he got there, first day. "Let's *go!*" He was, well . . . ebullient!

"Whadda *you* care, Doc?" Michael said to Tiky, with the needle in his voice. "You wish Reagan were running again?"

—★—

Why wouldn't Michael be happy—on top of the world? It was, to use one of his favorite words . . . *appropriate.* Michael Dukakis was, at the end of 1986, in control of his life, master of his fortunes, victor in his struggles, as few of us can ever hope to be, on this earth.

In the neat and narrow ellipse of his life, there were two long sides. There was work, and there was family, anchored by the two poles of his daily orbit: the State House on Beacon Street, and his home on Perry Street, in Brookline. Within this universe, he was master, and masterful: proud father to three splendid children, a son and two daughters, who were flourishing, each in his or her own way, and all lovingly proud, in turn, of their father. He was husband to a woman who was the object of all his earthly desires, his bride, Katharine, who was beautiful, bright, emotional, exciting, and—here was the miracle!—still in love, after twenty-three years, *devoted* . . . to her solid (sometimes, he suspected, stolid) husband . . . him. It was . . . well, Michael wasn't good at describing emotion, but to him . . . and when he did, it always rattled out in bursts of quick monotone with pauses not . . . at the end of thoughts, but for breath while he thought more . . . lawyer-words-and-State-House-words-and . . . that's why he seldom tried it, but . . . it was the greatest thing that could happen . . . to a guy like him, his family, they were (shrug, pained smile, hands-turned-up-in-hopeless-seeking, head-shaking-no, no, words fail him) . . . just terrific.

Sometimes he was so proud of the kids—on occasions, appropriate occasions—that he'd start to mist up and couldn't talk. Kitty—you could always see how he felt about Kitty, he was like a high school kid, nuzzling her, kissing her . . . and when he knew he pleased her, a boyish pride swelled him, puffed him up like a bantam in the henhouse yard. . . . But away from her gaze, he didn't think of himself as special. He hardly thought about himself at all. It was untoward, a breach of discipline, to dwell on the self like that. That's one of the things the family did for him: in their eyes, he found the fondest view of himself, his best self. And not just on Perry Street: he was much blessed with family. There was, God love her, his mother, still hale at eighty-three, still in perfect mastery of her own life (though she did, last year, in light of her age, finally give in to an automatic lawn sprinkler), still thoroughly attentive to Michael and his progress in the world, still taking care of the house he grew up in, on Rangely Road, in South Brookline, just a few miles from Perry Street. There was Kitty's dad, the warmest of men, a brilliant musician, first violinist with the Boston Symphony, assistant conductor for the Boston Pops, and a great admirer and booster of Michael. There was Kitty's sister, Jinny Peters, and her husband, Al, who would move the earth for Michael. And then, all the cousins, who were so proud of him, as were all the Greeks in Massachusetts—in fact, Greeks all over the country . . . but that was work, and that was different. . . .

Dukakis took quiet pride in the way he cleaved the two halves of his life. He kept a rigorous balance that was, well, Greek in its symmetry. He got to the office early each day: by 8:15 he'd be there at his desk, with his coffee in a Styrofoam cup, looking over the papers that were lined up for him, while he demanded of his secretary, Jean Hines: "Well, what've you got?" . . . But, just as surely, by 6:00 P.M. he'd be on his way home, for dinner at his own table, in the embrace of his family. True, he might have to leave again, some nights, for meetings or political events. But, just as surely, he'd save a night to get the family groceries at the Brookline Stop & Shop, marching the aisles briskly, behind a cart half-full with the weekly produce specials, and the plain-paper labels of generic foods. ("Go on, read the label! You tell me the difference!")

. . . Michael Dukakis insisted—Governor or no—he was going to have his life, a life that did not lose touch with reality. So, in the summer, he tended his own garden (not too strong on flowers, but what tomatoes! And his berries!), and he cut his own lawn with his old push-mower. While he was out, he might see his neighbors, talk about kids, crabgrass, or gutter screens . . . bits of home-owner life that another Governor might have dropped. But with Michael, nothing was dropped, nothing was wasted. Come to think of it, not much was added, either.

He had a car, an appropriate car: a Chevy Citation, made in Massachusetts . . . perfectly good car. Or, on appropriate occasions, he would let a state policeman drive him—when a driver would save time. But there were never any limousines idling on Perry Street. Most mornings, Michael preferred to walk to the trolley stop, get a paper, pay his sixty-cent fare, and ride into Boston on the T. Sometimes, when they picked up a security threat, the state police would try to station a car in front of the Governor's house. But Michael would go out and order it away. He didn't like a fuss. And he was not going to let his life be consumed. He was busy, all right—he never had time to read anything that did not have facts he might use someday; he had a lot of meetings, had to turn down invitations. But he made time, every Sunday night, to type out long and lovingly newsy letters to his daughters at college. That was family. That was important! Anyway, a twenty-two cent stamp was *much* more economical than a call to Princeton, New Jersey.

It all fit together so nicely—the wheels and gears of Michael's wonderful machine—and it was not without power: to use another fine Greek word, it had synergy. There was strength in having a Governor who knew the price of milk. Price-gouging was one problem that would never sneak up on him. Michael didn't need a meeting on maintenance of the mass transit system. He knew the T as well as any working stiff. The Governor didn't need a staff report on the highways from Boston to Jinny's (rent-free weekend retreat!) house on Cape Cod, or the routes to Harry's (Tanglewood, rent-free!) place in the Berkshires. He lived in the state like a working man lived. The problems of his voters were his problems, too. And in his second go-round, after he lost and made his comeback, after John Sasso and his roundtable of wise guys managed to create Dukakis, the persona . . . well, then, the synergy worked the other way, too. It got easier to screw a $100 million out of the legislature for job training—what the hell, the voters knew Dukakis wouldn't throw money around. Ha! Sonofabitch was too cheap! When he cracked down on tax cheats, they knew he was playing fair and square: first business his G-men padlocked was a Greek restaurant!

It was beautiful, when it worked like that, it was mastery, that second term: Michael's pistons pumping, Sasso greasing the wheels. After his first term, in '78, the voters turned Dukakis out on the street because he wouldn't listen; he wouldn't even discuss anything. When you boiled it down, all he'd ever say was, he was right. He was right about this, right about that . . . and anyone who knew *anything* would *see* he was *right.* Governor Asshole! Then, he had to raise taxes, and he was dead: the thing just blew up in his face. But it was different when he came back, in '82. For one thing, he went around the whole state and apologized. He hadn't listened. He'd been an asshole. Of course, that's not how he said it, but he showed everybody what he meant. When he got back in, he scheduled meetings just to listen. He listened to the cops, listened to the teachers, listened to the doctors. . . . When he set out to do something, he consulted: called in the legislative sachems and asked—what did they think? (Then he went ahead and did what he wanted.) Everybody ate it up. The papers started calling him Duke II, like he was another person, a total redesign, a fundamental improvement, like a solar-powered car. . . .

Of course, the papers peddled the New Nixon, too. What human being in our own lives remakes his personality after age forty-five? We wouldn't believe it of our own brother or sister, but for some reason, it sells with pols.

There wasn't any solar–Duke II. What they saw was the same old Michael Stanley Steamer . . . but with new valves, better lubrication. That was John Sasso's genius. The legislators still couldn't talk to Michael about what mattered to them: a new bridge on Route 464, or a job for a nice young man of good family. . . . Dukakis (I or II) would look at them like they'd brought dirt into his office. But with Sasso as Chief Secretary, they could come in, have a drink, a cigar, and a sympathetic chat; John would try to help, but, he'd add: "*You know how the Governor is* . . ." Then, perhaps, John would call Fred Salvucci, the Transportation Secretary, or Nick Mitropoulos, the patronage chief, and take care of the matter. Michael never had to know. On bigger things, when Michael did have to know, John could slowly lead him to the deed, showing him, every step of the way, how this move would make possible another, and another, which led to the goal they had discussed, which was *exactly the right thing for the state* . . . exactly what Michael wanted to do. Still, there were afternoons in the State House when the Senate President, Billy Bulger, would travel back and forth to John's office by means of the outside balconies—so Michael wouldn't see. The funny thing was, they weren't doing anything wrong! They weren't getting rich, or defrauding the citizens. They were doing the state's business, making the wheels turn. Don't tell Michael!

The other funny thing was, Michael was now the master mechanic, explaining at the Conference of Governors how he'd learned to make the wheels turn. To be fair: he *had* learned some new tricks. In the second term, when he had another deficit, he didn't cut programs, and he didn't raise taxes. Instead, he called in his revenue guy, Ira Jackson, and told him: You figure out a way to get me more of the taxes that people already owe. So Ira came back in a matter of days with a plan for an amnesty and a crackdown: the carrot and the stick . . . pay up now and no one gets hurt. If you wait, you'll get busted, and you'll pay more. Michael looked at the plan and said: Okay, do it.

And it worked. Even Ira never dreamed it like this: millions of dollars started coming in—hundreds of millions! And then a couple of businesses were padlocked, cars seized, boats, that kind of thing . . . and more millions rolled into the state—$900 million in three years. People started to pay up. They

knew about the new plan. It was called REAP, Revenue Enhancement and
Protection. The important thing is, it had a name that people could remember,
like all of Michael's new programs, and a rollout, with posters, or TV ads, or,
at the least, a ream of newspaper stories. Telling the story was *just as important
as being right*! Sasso and his Boston wise guys would sit around, two Thursdays
a month, and figure how to show it all in the best light, "to create the right
climate in the state." Then Sasso would synthesize, dis-aggrandize and memo-
randize, and that would be the new plan for Michael to look at, next week,
next month, next quarter of the year.

The stuff was good . . . but this wasn't subatomic physics. Most of these ideas
had been around for years. The trick was to make the wheels turn. Welfare
was the biggest budget in the state—even though unemployment was down,
and you couldn't *find* a worker to take an entry-level job. So Michael said:
Why don't these welfare people work? And the answer was, they didn't have
any education. So Michael said, well, let's send them to school, and *then* find
'em a job! . . . But they're mothers! What about their kids? Okay, we'll do day
care. . . . Well, how are they going to get to the school? Uhmmm. . . . *Give
them money for the T!* So, they tied it all up into one package, and they called
it ET ("You see, Michael, there's this movie . . .") for Education and Training.
And they rolled it out, they sold it and sold it, and . . . it worked! Thousands
of welfare women got training, and thousands got jobs (forty thousand in four
years). And the jobs paid more than welfare ever did, and the women stayed
in the jobs. And instead of getting welfare, they were paying taxes. And though
ET cost money, it saved more money. And women's lives were changed. And
their stories were stories that Michael could tell.

So he told them, all over Massachusetts, and then to the other Governors
at their conference, and he told the stories in Washington, where he testified
about ET. That was another part of Sasso's plan: the well-timed, well-planned
appearances around the country . . . along with Sasso's quiet, friendly phone
calls to the national columnists, the networks, *The New York Times*. . . . Ever
since the middle of Michael's comeback term, since '84, when Sasso took a
leave to help run Geraldine Ferraro, he was thinking bigger, constructing a
national reputation for Dukakis, the doer, the man who could make government work. What the hell, Dukakis was smarter, more able, than most of the
national Democrats . . . what about The Duke in '88? So that's what the
Thursday night sessions turned into: Sasso and his guys were plotting a platform for a national campaign. Dukakis could offer a record, a litany of achievement, all wrapped up under one grand rubric—the boys made it up one
Thursday night: the Massachusetts Miracle.

Hey, it was catchy! This could fly! The race was wide open. Hart could be
beaten—John thought people were uneasy about him. And Dukakis would
have a story to tell: the state was in the gutter—Taxachusetts—but he pulled
it out, turned it around, changed people's lives . . . with government that
worked!

God! It was *perfect* . . . don't tell Michael.

—★—

Michael didn't want to hear it. All through 1986, people tried to talk to him about President, and he'd duck his head into his shoulders and insist: "We've already *got* a campaign."

That meant his reelection. He wasn't going to get cocky and let the voters throw him out on his ear again. This time, he wanted ratification. This time, he wanted affirmation that he'd done the job, done it right. He wanted to win big.

It didn't matter how good things looked. Michael didn't want to hear that. "Nope. You know me . . . steady as she goes. . . ." That meant keep away from his face with predictions that he'd win in a landslide. He'd get that rueful little smile, and say: "You know how I feel about polls. . . ." After all, he'd been fifty points ahead, back in '78, before the roof fell in, and he lost the only job he'd ever wanted.

It didn't matter that no Democrat filed against him—first time in thirty-six years when there was no primary: Who would take on a governor who'd already cut the tax rate and still had a $500 million surplus? . . . It didn't matter that the Republican candidate had to drop out of the race: his former co-workers said he spent his time sitting naked in his office, smoking cigarettes, talking on the phone—with no one on the other end. . . . Then, the GOP put up a guy from the legislature who *hated* Dukakis. Guy was a killer! But lamentably, he lied in his campaign fliers about combat service in Vietnam. So, he dropped out, too. . . . Finally, the Republicans put a third guy in the race who'd never run for *anything*. Nothing. No one knew him. And the guy was a Greek! Kariotis. (He and Michael would go head-to-head for that *crucial* Greek vote—fine piece of planning!) . . . Didn't matter. Michael didn't want to hear about it. After all, back in '78, he thought Ed King was a schmuck—a *bufo,* to use the nicer Greek word . . . and King took the Governor's chair away.

So, people would come up to Michael and say: "I saw you got a nice mention from Mary McGrory . . ." (Or George Will, or *The Wall Street Journal,* or *The New Republic,* even James J. Kilpatrick! . . .) And Michael would hold up one dismissive palm: "I don't want to talk about it." When Michael didn't want to talk about it, well, there was no one who'd make him talk. He said no. He meant no. . . . Michael Dukakis was the King of No.

Even Kitty! Of course, she read every word. And there was no one who thought more of the idea: President Dukakis! But she wasn't going to get into Michael's face. So she'd ask Sasso: "What does he say?"

"Nothing."

"Even to you?"

"I thought he'd talk to you."

"Not yet."

"He's not there yet."

Then, her son, John Dukakis, would call from D.C., where he worked for Senator Kerry. And Kitty would tell him: "He's not there yet. . . ."

John was eager for his dad to run, too. But he knew his mother wouldn't blow it, let that out, and make Michael feel pressured. Kitty was the Queen of Don't Tell Michael.

That's how it worked for all those years. Michael thought a dress for Kitty cost—what, he never really thought about it . . . fifty dollars? Well, that was twice as much as it *ought* to be, but . . . what could he do? She looked, well . . . terrific.

Of course, Kitty couldn't buy a scarf for fifty dollars. But she worked. She made a little money of her own, and if she spent four figures on an outfit, well, there was no need to bother Michael with that. If there was some frock, an extra pair of shoes, that she couldn't risk Michael asking about, well, there was always room in her father Harry's closet. (More room than hers! Michael would never spring to build a walk-in closet on Perry Street, just as he never saw why a family of five could not get along *just fine* with one bathroom . . . for two men and three women . . . who all had to be dressed at the same time . . . God! Sometimes she could just wring his neck!)

Smoking—same deal. Kitty smoked. Michael disapproved. So, Kitty smoked all day, and just before he came home, she'd air out the kitchen and wash the ashtrays.

Did he know? Of course he knew. Just as he also saw the gleam of Sasso-grease on the wheels of government at the State House. But that wasn't the same as having his face rubbed in it.

The point was, he was right about the smoking. Terrible habit. Kitty knew he was right. But loving her entirely, he accepted in her certain . . . weaknesses, breaches of discipline that he would never tolerate in himself. That was how it always worked: strong, steady, disciplined Michael *took care of* high-strung, fiery, fragile Kitty.

One night, in the '82 campaign, he dragged her to some political dinner, some jerky fund-raiser, the kind she hated. But she did it, for him, and she sat there all night, and smiled, and talked—and, of course, she couldn't smoke. She'd never smoke in front of him, like that, with a crowd around. So, finally, they got back to the car. The campaign had sent a kid to drive them. And Michael rode shotgun, and Kitty sagged into the backseat, fished in her purse, and lit up a cigarette. Right away, he's on her: "*Katharine* . . ." In that little singsong scoldy voice he used sometimes: "*Kath*-ar-ine . . ."

Kitty said through a mouthful of smoke: "Aw, fuck off, Michael." The kid who was driving almost ran off the road.

But there wasn't anything uneasy between them. They knew how far they could push. They both knew their roles in this long-running drama. They played it to the hilt: they could play it for laughs.

Once, when she led some friends on a trip to Japan, and they were coming back—terrible flight, across half the world, and then they had to land in New York, and take a *shuttle* up to Boston—Michael met the plane at Logan, and he stood there while a score of people got off, then fifty more, and all her friends were off, a hundred people came through that gate . . . and no Kitty! She'd been sitting in the back row, smoking. He knew it! She was going to be the last one off! So he marched down the ramp and grabbed the microphone for the plane's P.A., and he announced, to the crowd at large:

"Attention Katharine Dukakis! Mrs. Katharine Dukakis! If you weren't smoking, you would be off the plane and with your husband now!"

She really could kill him sometimes. But, see, he never would have done it if he weren't so eager to see her walk off that plane. He was like a kid who stayed home from camp. He missed her so terribly when they were apart . . . like half of *him* was gone.

Everyone agreed, it was a wonderful marriage. Michael and Kitty agreed, tacitly—not everything had to be said. Not out loud. Not all the time. Certainly, not when things were so good. And they were: things were just about perfect.

Michael won big in '86, won bigger than any Massachusetts Governor in modern times. He won with sixty-nine percent, four points better than Mario Cuomo, his Governor-neighbor in New York. (And don't think those two weren't keeping score.)

That night, in front of the crowd, he reminisced about the races of the past, the victories . . . "But this, my friends, this . . . is the sweetest of them all." Then, he borrowed a line from a rock 'n' roll song: God knows who taught it to him, but he used it. "The future's so bright," said Dukakis, "I gotta wear shades."

Two days later, Sasso gave him the memo, the President memo he'd been holding in his locked briefcase for the last three weeks. Now it was . . . appropriate. But Michael's head started shaking, no, almost imperceptibly, but . . . no, he just didn't want it . . . not yet. He told John that he might not get back to him on it right away.

"Yeah, well, some decisions have to get made . . . in this kind of thing," Sasso said. His solemn brown eyes locked onto Michael's face. He was doing it like he always did, nudging Michael along with veiled warnings that he could do what he chose . . . but, of course, he might be screwing up the plan. Michael liked to stay on the plan. "This kind of thing, you have to be rolling by February or March. . . ."

Michael got the message. But his head was still shaking. His face had that little grin of rue. His heavy eyebrows were arched in silent irony, almost a plea: *We just got here, to this peak—can't we just . . . sit?* All he said was, "I just want to enjoy the holidays, the family . . ."

Sasso understood. His own face relaxed into a quiet, conspiratorial smile. It was a gift, that smile of Sasso's, a confidence he bestowed. His head inclined once, slightly, on the wrestler's neck that his suit never quite disguised. All he said was, "That's fine, Mike. Fine."

To his friends, who called in that day, Sasso said, "I don't think he'll go. I don't know. Depends on the family."

—★—

There wasn't much discussion in the house on Rangely Road: certain things were expected, and once those were clear, what was there to discuss?

True, every once in a while an adjustment in the pattern had to be made. But generally, that could be taken care of with a quiet word from Euterpe to Panos. She was the only one who could change his mind. When his practice grew so busy and he was working thirteen- and fourteen-hour days (not to mention calls in the middle of the night), it was Euterpe who changed his life. "Now, listen, dear," she told him one night. "The children are never going to see you if you keep the office hours through six, seven, eight o'clock, and you come home at nine or ten. We're not a family. You come home and eat dinner, and then you can go out again."

So he would come, every afternoon, five-thirty or six o'clock, and he'd listen to the CBS Radio news, and he would eat, and then rest. He'd sit in his chair, with his paper, put his feet up, and in five or ten minutes, he was asleep. Five or ten minutes later, he'd be up again, a new man: he'd be back in his office by seven, seven-thirty. And he was happy: he loved his family, his home, he loved the practice of medicine. And he loved the country that had opened its arms to him. A placid man was Panos.

Sometimes, he'd start working up a case about the boys' behavior: something that just didn't look right, or reflected badly on the family . . . those bicycles all over the front yard! They were ruining the grass! But Euterpe would step in, before he forbade it, and reason with him. "Now, Pan," she'd say, "didn't we get the house for the boys? So they would have a place to play? Soon they'll be gone, and we'll have a nice lawn." And that would end the matter.

It was funny: he was such a softie, she could do almost anything with him. And when she'd met him, as a high school girl, she thought he was stiff . . . so forbidding! Pan was at Bates College then, in the premedical course, and a member of the Philhellenic Club. Each year, the club put on a play, and that year, in the *Hippolytus,* Panagis Dukakis played the title role. Euterpe's older brothers, Nick and Adam Boukis, haberdashers, men of substance among the Greeks in Haverhill, Massachusetts, brought the student troupe down to perform, and although Euterpe missed the show (she had a gym exhibition that night), she ran to the train station, early the next day, to meet the actors and their professor. And there was Pan. He was so solemn, she thought—perfectly humorless. Nice-looking, yes, but he had no spark.

He was just shy, she found out later—very self-conscious was Pan, all his life. It was much later, she learned to love him. He didn't call her for almost a decade, until she herself had gone through Bates College and was off on her own, teaching school. And then, Panos called to say, he had not thought of anyone else since he saw her at the station, ten years before. But being an upright Greek man, he could not come courting until he was on his feet, with his medical practice well established. Of course, she could not have talked to him, either—not seriously, not before both were ready to give their promise— as that was the way with the Greeks. In fact, it was quite daring, ultramodern, that he called *her,* directly, to talk. It would not have been permitted in the old country. But no one was going to arrange a marriage, in the old way, for Euterpe . . . they wouldn't dare. She had come a long way since Pan first saw her, the immigrant girl with the two long braids and the eager dark eyes, at the station that morning. She was the first Greek girl to go all the way through Haverhill High. And then she went on! To a coeducational college! Alone! No, Euterpe Boukis was quite the *Amerikana*.

She was always a special girl, even in that special family. She was born in a Thessalian mountain village of stone and mud-brick, in a whitewashed house on a path of dusty rock, where she and the other children used to play a sort of hide-and-seek called the Rescue of Helen of Troy. Her mother washed clothes in the shallow, stony Piniós River, and spread them on the bank to dry. The Boukis family had no more than the rest, but her grandfather had insisted on an education for his son: Euterpe's father, Michael, had studied at Smyrna. He was only a bookkeeper, a clerk by trade, but he had the standing of a learned man, and the Philosophical Society would not meet unless Michael Boukis was present.

Her oldest brother, Nick, was almost eighteen when he determined to go to America to work: the family had no land, and alas, three daughters. (How would they get dowries? Who would marry them without?) So he wrote to a cousin in New Hampshire, who sent money for the passage, but still, Nick paused. His mother was pregnant again, and he waited for the birth. When he walked into his mother's room, on the day of delivery, she was in tears. "Oh, Nick," she wailed, "another girl!" Nick said: "Don't worry, Mama. I'll work two more years in America for her."

But soon, they were all in America. Nick wrote back of the marvels in the New World. The Americans, he wrote, had so much wood, they built houses of it, and sometimes, he wrote, they would pick up a house—and *move it*. No one could believe it! Soon, he sent money for his brother, Adam, to come and work beside him in the mills—good wages! And when Nick and Adam were both at work, they pooled their savings to open a business: a clothing store in Haverhill. There, they got their own apartment, and then bought (from an older Greek) three houses on a corner of a poor street, in the factory district, where the Greeks lived. Then the brothers sent for all the family. The father, mother, and four daughters left their village in the spring of 1913. Euterpe, the third girl, was nine years old.

And, like her brothers, she took to this new land. It was easier for her than her older sisters. They had come of age in Greece. They had trouble with the odd new language, the loose customs, the want of everything they knew. But Euterpe had her father's love of learning. She and the youngest sister, Eftie, just absorbed all the strange English words. Euterpe would stand before the mirror, watching her mouth, to make sure she pronounced each new word correctly. She so wanted to fit in. She went to school and she understood. She brought home all A's to show her father. The principal at her elementary school, Stanley Grey, was a Yankee, but a kindly, childless man who took this young Greek girl under his wing. He taught her about reading, for pleasure, just to know a new book, a new world. He'd take books out of the library for her, and send her home with them, three or four at a time. *Little Women, Little Men, Treasure Island, Jane Eyre* . . . In Euterpe's house, all the girls had chores, but if you had a book in your hands, you were not to be disturbed. So Euterpe spent all of her time reading. Her oldest sister, Lica, left grade school and was apprenticed to a dressmaker. The second daughter, Helen, only finished the eighth grade. But Euterpe not only stayed in school, she skipped the ninth grade and went right into high school. There were plenty of Greeks in Haverhill who couldn't see the point of so much schooling for a girl. (Who would marry her after all that?) But in the Greek café where he spent his years in the New World—happily arguing philosophy, reading his Bible, railing against the ignorant priests who deceived their poor flock—Michael Boukis would shake his head and laugh at the doubters. He was proud of his learned daughter.

This was the pride Euterpe had in her own sons, and the expectation: that they would apply themselves to their learning, to all their tasks; that they would excel beyond their peers; that they would make their own way in this opportune New World, farther even than their parents had gone. She and Pan named their two sons in the traditional way, the first for Pan's father, Stelian, who had died in the influenza epidemic just before the First World War. It was the second son, her last child, who would be named for her family: he would be called Michael, for her learned father . . . and she gave him a middle name, Stanley, to honor that kindly WASP principal who had seen the spark in her. It was just right, the way it worked out . . . because her first son, her Stelian, was such a Dukakis! A kindly boy, good-natured, he had Pan's broad face and sturdy frame—he loved to play sports with his friends. But the second son, Michael, was a Boukis, sure enough: he had her looks, her slender quickness, the gift of easy learning, the near-photographic memory. . . . He had her discipline: now it was little Michael who stood in front of the mirror, learning his new words. . . . And he had her will: with pride, she always told strangers that the first Greek words he ever learned were *monos mou,* "by myself."

Both the boys learned Greek when Pan's mother, Olympias (Lymbia, they called her in the family), came to live out her last years with her doctor son. That was just after Michael was born, and from that point, they spoke Greek in the home. Lymbia loved all her grandchildren, but she could not get enough of Michael. She would sing to him, in Greek, and tell stories of her old home in Adramiti (now Edremit, in Turkey), how her old stepmother kept cocoons in the house, and spun out raw silk to make the sheets, and men's shirts, for Lymbia's dowry. . . . In fact, Lymbia still had one with her: a silk shirt with no neck opening (because every girl had to have so many shirts for the man she would marry—but, of course, no girl knew how to cut the neck until she found the husband). . . . And little Michael would regard the shirt, listen to the story, in solemn fascination. Stelian would be outdoors with his friends, whooping around the neighborhood. But Michael loved to sit and listen to his *yiayia* (grandma). He was so gentle with her. Every night, he would bring

Yiayia from her room to the table. And he'd pull her chair out, hold it for her. She adored him for that.

Lymbia, in fact, was the reason they moved from their apartment to the house in Brookline. Euterpe wanted an extra bedroom on the ground floor, so Yiayia Lymbia (who could not manage stairs) could sit with them at the dinner table. Pan only had two conditions for a new house: it had to be within fifteen minutes of his office, and it had to have a two-car garage. When they found the house on Rangely Road, it seemed perfect, though there were no other Greeks in the neighborhood. In the midst of the Depression, they bought the house, new, for $12,500. Panos paid cash. That was the way Dr. Dukakis did business. No debts allowed—not to strangers. Family, that was different: it was Pan's brothers who had helped him through medical school. That was a debt he never forgot.

Panos would never take a dime for doctoring anyone in the family. This was a matter of pride: What good was a doctor in the family, if a cousin had to pay a stranger to look at him? Whenever a cousin anywhere in this country took sick, the family called Panos. Sometimes, half-asleep, three o'clock in the morning, Pan would be on the phone to New Jersey (or New York, or South Carolina), listening to the symptoms of a niece or nephew. Even in later years, when his brothers, and their wives, and wives' families, could well afford their own local care, no one's doctor was allowed to make a move without consulting Pan, by telephone in Boston. After all, he was their pride, too, the ornament at the top of their tree, *a doctor in their family.*

And what a doctor! By the time Panos made a bride of Euterpe, he had long since wed the practice of medicine. Throughout his life, it remained his first love. When Euterpe joined him, he had already worked his way through premed and medical school, practiced as an intern and resident for nearly five years, and opened his office at 454 Huntington Avenue (just across from the Greek Orthodox Cathedral). He and his bride took an apartment in the same building, across the hall from the office, so Pan could be there on a moment's notice. Even after they moved to leafy South Brookline, Pan still spent the bulk of his life in the office on Huntington Avenue, or in the car. He made house calls for more than forty years, even after he couldn't do the driving. (Euterpe had to chauffeur him, and read or knit at the wheel while he went inside.) Through five decades, he delivered three thousand babies, and in later years, he birthed the babies of his babies. They were his pride and his testament, his patients. For the first-generation Greeks who came to him, he was the first doctor who spoke to them gently, who did not lord it over them, as they expected an educated man to do. Panos was always respectful of them, sometimes even tender. There was a young priest, named Iakovos, who served for a time at the cathedral. One night, about 2:00 A.M., Panos called him to the hospital: one of his patients, a Greek man, was dying. The young priest ran to the church and then straight to the hospital. But he found Dr. Dukakis in tears, because his patient had died before the priest arrived. The priest had never seen a doctor cry. Iakovos, the future Archbishop of all the Greeks in America, concluded: "Panos was a very human man."

But at home, it was not humanity but stern expectation he showed to his boys: Stelian and Michael were ever reminded of the great blessings they'd enjoyed since birth. "Much has been given . . ." Panos would say. "And much is expected of you." They could never forget (as he could not) that he never had a fine school like theirs, a luxurious home, all the food he wanted, a car to ride around the town, green lawns for sports and games. No, when Panos came to this country, at age sixteen, without money, education, without his parents, without English . . . he had to work, he had to save, he had to sacrifice! He worked in the mills, and behind a lunch counter, he went to night school to learn English, and then to another job, cleaning out meat cases for a grocer. He came to this country in 1912, and twelve years later, he was the first Greek to graduate from Harvard Medical School. How could they ever forget that? How could they ever match it? Certainly not by fooling around: one time, *once,* Michael brought home a B-plus on a report card. Panos asked: "Why did you not get an A?" . . . And certainly not by ungrateful waste! If, God forbid, Michael left a scrap of food on his plate, Panos would command from the head of the table: "*Ekonomia,* Michael. *Ekonomia!*" . . . And certainly not by giving in to trouble, crying, being weak: when Michael had a paper route, there was a dog at the top of the hill who never let him pass, but snarled and attacked him. Michael lived in terror of that dog. In fact, he would fear dogs for the rest of his life. But he would not, as another boy might, tell his father, who could likely solve the problem with a phone call. He would *never* tell his father he was scared.

There were no failures in that household, no tales of woe or loss brought home to Rangely Road. The boys were expected to do their work and succeed: simple as that, simple as Pan. Euterpe was, if anything, tougher. Although she was a former teacher, she would never help them with an answer for their lessons. Instead, she would tell them where they could find it, then quiz them to make sure they did. Of course, both boys did well in school. It could not be otherwise. She made sure they set aside time for their studies, along with their other obligations: orchestra practice, music lessons, sporting events, club meetings. Euterpe would arrange their schedules with them at the beginning of the week, along with their obligations in the home. No Dukakis boy would stay up till dawn the night before a school exam. There was no excuse for running out of time. Stelian and Michael always knew the schedule and the expectations for the following day, even before they hung up their clothes and got into their pyjamas, even before Euterpe set four places for the next day's breakfast (cup, saucer, orange juice glass, plate, fork, knife, and spoon . . . all covered with a napkin, to ward off dust) and switched off the light in the kitchen.

She'd be up again at six or six-thirty, and she'd have her bath while Pan went downstairs and read the paper. Then she'd come down to make breakfast while Pan went up to the bath. Soon, there would be three of them, downstairs, for breakfast, while Panos shouted up the stairs: "Stelian! You're going to be late for school!" Stelian hated to get up for school. But he was late only once. He had to bring a tardiness excuse, a note from home. So, Euterpe wrote: "There is no excuse for Stelian's being tardy. He was wakened with plenty of time, and he should have been ready." Stelian had to stay five nights after school.

Michael was never late. He just got up and went about his business. That was always the way in the house. Stelian, three years older, had to do everything first, of course. He was popular with the other kids (they called him The Duke, at Brookline High), and he taught Michael all the games—even made sure he was picked when the big boys in the neighborhood were choosing teams. He took care of Michael. But then, the little guy would come along and do everything quicker, better than Stelian! Things just came easier to Michael.

By the time he got to high school, he was Mr. Everything. Not socially: he never had time for that, and anyway, he did not approve of the social clubs that excluded some students. Michael was friendly to all the students—one of the few who talked to both the poor Irish kids and the richer Jews—but not too friendly. He didn't have time to hang around. With letters in cross-country, basketball, track, and tennis, trumpet lessons, the school band, orchestra, class office, student council, the honor society . . . even Pan had to wonder after a while. He told Euterpe one night: "If this boy doesn't slow down, he'll get sick." But Michael didn't show any ill effect. And at the end of every semester, he brought home another card full of A's. Panos said to Euterpe: "How does the fellow do it? He's amazing!" Of course, neither parent said that to Michael.

But there are a thousand ways a child knows, when he is favored, some of them small—like Euterpe's little nod of satisfaction when he'd report another perfect score on a test—and some of them more dramatic.

It was Stelian who first took an interest in politics, brought the subject and his zeal for it into the household. But, then, as always, Michael came along behind him, and just absorbed it—he could discuss elections like a committeeman! When the cousins came, talk would fly around the table. Uncle Constantine was the sparkplug—he'd stake out some far-out position and hold it against all comers. The others would argue, at first, then subside. (If they asked Panos, he'd only say: "Don't look at me . . . Leave me out . . .") But Michael would hold his ground. No matter what Constantine or Stelian said, Michael would never give in. And then Euterpe would take Michael's side. Michael knew what was right.

Panos was never much for politics. He registered Republican, against FDR's New Deal. (Like most Greeks, Panos didn't believe in the dole—something for nothing—let the people work!) What Pan wanted was a son to take over the practice, to become a doctor, to inherit all he'd built. There was never any question in Pan's mind that one of his boys should have the office at 454 Huntington Avenue. That was their legacy. And that was his plan for Michael, his second son. Stelian was a good boy . . . but Michael was the heir.

Of course, no one had to tell Stelian. There was nothing said at all. In the house on Rangely Road, the expectations were just understood. After that, what was there to discuss?

— ★ —

"Look at him! Just like Euterpe!" Tiky was crowing, needling, all over Michael. "Lookit'im! For God's sake, Michael! The kid's out of school!"

Michael always liked to meet the Greek kids in Florida. He'd quiz them on their Greek language, their schools, their schoolwork: Who's the teacher? . . . Is she good? . . . What are you learning? . . . Oh? Did you learn about Samuel Adams? . . .

"Michael! F'God's sake!"

"Wait a minute," Michael protested. "I'm trying to learn something here."

"Lookit him, always lookin' for an edge! Kitty! He's politickin' again!" Tiky always got on Michael for not being able to stop. That was Tiky's trump card, when Michael started riding him about his cookies, his diet, his weight. Tiky always told the story about a visit in 1958, when he was in medical school and Michael was at Harvard Law. He went up to Boston to visit Michael, and spent the *whole damn weekend* on the back of Michael's stupid Vespa, handing out stupid fliers for some stupid town election in Brookline. "Pretty soon, I'm thinkin' . . . 'What the hell am I doin' this for?' . . ."

The short answer was: because Michael couldn't stop. Tiky learned then: that was Michael's life.

But it wasn't really politics—not the way Tiky liked to caricature it. Michael had spent his life fighting that sort of politics, the glad-hand, back-slap, blarney-*paisan,* ethnic-joke, one-hand-washes-the-other, job-for-a-friend politics he found when he started in Massachusetts. It was always young, clean Michael and his Harvard-Law-Democratic-Study-Group allies against the dirty old hacks, the hoary Irish machine, against the bosses, the rake-offs, the patronage . . . *against the politicians.* . . . That's what carried him into office, and carried him to the top. Michael always had to operate from that narrow, moral axis. In every race, Dukakis had to prove himself abler, smarter, cleaner than the other guy—*even if they agreed on policy.* He didn't get into contests of philosophy. Michael's career had more to do with another old Greek word: philotimy . . . *philotimo* . . . the love of honor. A Dukakis campaign was never about how he saw the world so much as how he (and the voters) saw Michael Dukakis.

Politics was, for Michael, a means to an end. And the end, for him, was always the same: putting good law, and good people—the able, decent few— into the slots of the system, so the mechanism of government could run cleanly, efficiently, to solve the problems of the many. Michael Dukakis, master mechanic.

And the problems? Well, there were always problems. Michael could tick them off all day: there was housing and the infrastructure of the neighborhoods; Michael had worked on that for thirty years; in fact, that campaign Tiky saw, in '58, was Michael's first, for the local urban renewal board, the Brookline Redevelopment Authority. There was transportation, which was always one of Michael's interests; not just urban transit, but interurban, too; in fact, he was the champion of high-speed rail, bullet trains for Bos–Wash. (Now, there was a dream!) There was economic development, where Michael had also made a name for himself, with the explosion of high-tech business around Boston, and the state-aided renaissance of old mill towns. And there was taxation, which Michael studied, labored to reform, long before REAP and his current success; in fact, that's where Michael met John Sasso, at a 1978 rally for a fair-tax referendum; Michael cared about the tax system, talked it like some men talk fishing. And there was education, health-care costs, welfare reform. Open space, and acid rain . . . healthy air for healthy people to live healthy, productive lives . . . the kind of lives he knew they would live, simple as that—if good government could cure the ills of ignorance, poverty, pollution, crime. . . . In Michael's neat world, the problems could be solved. And government, by the clean, the good, could spur the cure. See, he'd gone into doctoring, after all.

That's how he talked about the Presidency, at Tiky's house. He saw the problems. He dealt with them every day. And God knows, Washington could use some doctoring, Dukakis-style. That thing about Iran? Never would have happened, *never*! Free-lance foreign ops from the basement of the White House? No way—no loose wheels, rolling free—not with Dr. Michael tuning the machine. Hands on—that's what it took . . . Michael Dukakis never took his hands off!

"Michael would be great at that. Terrific! You know he would. . . ." That was Kitty, talking about how Michael could run the government. These days, she was always trying to show Michael how great he could be . . . but she wasn't pushing: she *told* Michael it was up to him . . . so now, she was telling *Tiky* how great it would be. Of course, Michael heard.

"Oh, ah'm not sayin' he couldn't do it. Ah got no problem with that. It's just . . ."

"What?" Michael said, eager, combative.

"Well, yours and *mah* relationship isn't ever gonna be the same. Ah admit it: mah reasons are selfish . . ."

"What are you talking about? We'll be the same."

"You're gonna be unda a damn microscope! You know that. You get shot, God forbid, and you got on bad shorts, they gonna write about your shorts! They'll pick ya to *death*!"

"Aw, come on," Michael said, in his most dismissive, get-serious voice. Strong, steady Michael had taken the heat before. He wasn't afraid of the press . . . if they wanted to test his marvelous machine . . . if they made Michael Dukakis the issue: that's what his campaigns were about. That's how he won!

"The spotlight . . ." Tiky said. "It's jus' gonna be a whole new ball game." He knew he wasn't getting across what he meant.

"You won't have to say anything," Michael said.

Tiky just shook his head. It wasn't himself he was worried about.

Michael's eyebrows were arched in mock-serious consideration: "Vacations at Camp David . . ." He was starting to see it like Kitty did: this could be fun . . . the big time.

Tiky could see Michael getting used to the idea. And cousin Stratton had too much respect to argue. "Well," he said, "ah don't mind sleepin' in the Lincoln bed, if that's what . . ." He trailed off, his eyes seeking Vivian's. Tiky never could get Michael to see: it was never going to be the same.

But the way Michael was, he always thought: whatever happened, he'd handle it. Strong, sturdy Michael . . . steady as she goes. How could Tiky challenge that? How could he even bring up the question? He couldn't. Instead, he said to Vivian, that night: "We're gonna lose the Michael we have."

— ★ —

Michael never talked about loss, not like Tiky meant it—lose oneself?

Loss, in a vote, he knew . . . too well. That first campaign that Tiky saw, in '58, for the urban renewal board—Michael lost it: came up fifth in a race for four seats. But the point was, he came back stronger. Two years later, he and his friends organized every precinct in Brookline, and took over the Democratic Party. In 1970, Michael lost a bid for Lieutenant Governor. Of course, that wasn't his race to run: Kevin White was at the top of that ticket. But anyway, Michael came back stronger. Four years later, he'd organized the whole state, won the nomination for the top job, and ousted Frank Sargent from the Governor's chair.

In '78—now, that taught him loss—the voters threw him out. They didn't really choose that moron, Ed King. They voted against Michael Dukakis. He had to face that. And it hurt. He was the first to admit . . . how it was. Michael said, over and over, "I blew it." Kitty called it "a public death." Actually, it was harder for her. His bride was the one he worried about. She never had his stoic calm—things got to her more, he . . . well, she counted on him . . . and he blew it. That's what made it so hard to take, sitting home, in the kitchen, every time he looked at her. That was hurt. And for a while, he sank inside himself: What went wrong? Why did the people turn on him? He got a job at the Kennedy School, teaching government, and he applied himself, as he always did, to find the answers, to learn, and he signed on John Sasso, a terrific help, and they started again. . . .

It wasn't easy. But four years later, he was back. And he was better. He and Kitty were better. She'd had to look inside, too . . . and she did. In the middle of that comeback campaign, '82, she told him about the diet pills: she'd been taking pills for twenty-five years. He couldn't believe it! How could he not have known? He should have seen somehow. He blamed himself. . . . He'd found them once, found a bottle of pills, a few years back, and she told him she would quit—but she never did. Not until that campaign, when she said she wanted to go away for treatment, a place in Minnesota. And Michael listened, he supported her. It all went together somehow: learning to listen, listening to her . . . the better Michael, the better Kitty . . . whatever she needed, he was ready to help. So, he told everybody she'd gotten hepatitis, had to get away to rest . . . and he kept on plugging. And when she came back, she was better—she'd beaten it—and he was back on track. And they won, stood together on stage, that night, while people cheered, and that was a great . . . the feeling was

. . . the way she looked that night—God, the light in her eyes that night, his bride—it was . . . well, just terrific.

The point was, he was better now. This last election proved it. Sixty-nine percent! . . . And he'd be okay, whatever happened, with this Presidential campaign. Like he told Tiky, he wasn't going in to lose. Of course, he wasn't going to rush into anything. That's not how Michael did things: he'd construct an orderly process of decision. He had questions, and, in an orderly fashion, he had them catalogued. In fact, in the fashion of Michael Dukakis, he already thought he had answers. But he'd listen. He'd learned that.

Family . . . that was first. They'd have a talk, a real family conference—next week, when they'd all be home for Christmas. But Michael had been promising that talk for a month. He knew what they wanted. It hung in the air every time he saw them. The kids all thought he should go, especially John—quite the politician now, and just as eager as his mother for this. . . . Kitty must have told him a thousand times: it was up to him, whatever he chose . . . but Michael knew how she wanted it. He always knew more than she thought he did.

Well, they'd have their talk, next week, back in Boston, after he got back to work, saw how things stood in the State House. That was the other question, the other pole of his orbit. He wasn't going to let everything he'd done slide down the tubes—his programs, his promises for the next term. . . . Could he govern, hold the reins in Boston, while he slogged around a cornfield in Iowa? . . . Sasso said it could be done. That's what John said in the memo: twelve days a month outside the state . . . at the start, at least. If he used the weekends, that's eight days right there . . .

The fact was, Michael knew he could run the state with one hand. Michael never doubted his own ability. At one point, in Florida, Tiky suggested: "Isn't there a Lieutenant Governor up there? Whyn'cha just turn it over to the Lieutenant, let 'im run it?" Michael just shook his head. That wasn't his style. Dr. Dukakis, hands on. One hand? Well, so be it.

There'd be time, certainly time enough in the year to come . . . even in '88, if he got into '88 . . . if he didn't fall on his face. That was the real question for Michael. Could he win, or at least do well? That's what he wanted to know, when he talked to people who'd been through one of these. Did he have a chance? How could he do it? How much money? What kind of theme? . . . He didn't want to get into this to be embarrassed. That would be loss. Once again, for Michael, it came down to philotimy, to Michael's (and the voters') view of himself. Him? President? That's how he thought at first. Then this Iran thing showed him what he could do. They were shredding papers in the basement! Lying to Congress! That was the stuff Michael Dukakis was born to clean up!

Anyway, Sasso said he had something to offer: it had to do with development, jobs, opportunity for all. Michael didn't have the words yet. He'd have to ask . . . figure out how to phrase it . . . he'd ask John, when he got back. No, if he asked John, he'd only see the question in John's eyes again: John said he wasn't taking sides . . . that's how the memo was written. But Michael knew how John wanted this: if he didn't go, he could say goodbye to John. Sasso would be on the phone to Cuomo. Now that would be loss. . . .

Michael didn't talk much about loss—but he knew how to avoid it. And every which way he looked at this thing, all the loss was on the side of not running:

If he did not run, his own career was crested. What victory night would ever be as sweet as this last one?

If he did not run, he would lose John Sasso . . . like losing a brother. Michael knew.

If he did not run, then that special light would leave the eyes of his bride. In that light—in the eyes of his wife and his kids—was his own brightest view of himself.

One more possible loss: if the family would be okay . . . if the state would manage to survive without him for a day here and there, maybe a week, a week or two . . . if the only question that remained came down to, "Was he able enough?" . . . and Michael Dukakis had to answer, "No," and for the first time in his life, back away . . . well, that was a loss he could not take.

There is a second meaning to that old Greek word, philotimy: it also means ambition.

Tiky asked him, quietly, just before Michael was ready to leave: "Well?"

"Looks like . . . well, I'm gonna look at it."

"You thoughta everything?"

Michael said, with a half-shrug: "Everything I can."

12

Stelian

THE DIFFERENCE between the boys was that Michael was always so serious. You had to admire him, but you got the feeling you were taking up his time. Stelian was happy to see you. He'd shake your hand, bring his left hand up on top of yours, and smile while he held you. He had Pan's smile, the same square, open face, the same fair skin, Pan's courteous manner. And always, a word of encouragement. He'd say to a cousin who was applying for a job: "Oh, I know you're going to get it . . . you'll be great." And they could feel close to him, the way they never could with Michael. The other difference was, it was harder for Stelian. He had to struggle to make his grades. He was bright enough, eager enough. In another house, he would have been an easy success. It was only in comparison that he seemed to be laboring. Not that he complained.

No, Stelian—The Duke—did well enough, and had plenty of friends at school, mostly guys: he never developed any ease with girls. He didn't have money to throw around on dates, for one thing; or a car, which could have made a difference; he didn't dance, either. Neither boy could dance a lick. It was odd: they were so determined to learn everything else; they had lessons for music, practice for sports . . . but dancing, never. Sometimes when the cousins were there, after dinner, someone would call for a dance, and cousin Olympia, the only girl, would be nominated (dragooned, more like it) to teach the boys in the living room. But after a few halting steps, they'd start to joke around, and forget it. Life was not about dancing.

In fact, Michael never did learn, even into his senior year at Brookline High.

And there was the prom coming up, and a girl . . . first girl he paid attention to, Sandy Cohen (of course, Michael called her Sandra). She was smart, pretty, blond, popular . . . and she thought Michael was *so cute*. (He said he hated that word.) She wanted to get all A's, so he would like her. And he did: he asked her to the prom, and although she'd already said yes (a year in advance!) to the most popular boy at school, Bobby Wool, she wanted to go with Michael . . . and she was going to break her date, and she even came over, after school, to teach Michael to fox-trot . . . but in the end, she couldn't do that to Bobby. So Michael went to the prom alone, worked all night in the coat-check room.

Anyway, that's when it happened, Michael's senior year, when everything was going so well, in the winter, before the prom. . . .

— ★ —

Stelian had gone to Bates College because Pan and Euterpe went there. Michael applied to Bates, too, and got in, but he turned it down. Maybe he thought he could do better. Maybe Pan and Euterpe believed Stelian would do better without Michael around. Maybe they had some hints, after all. . . .

It was the winter of Stelian's junior year, when Panos and Euterpe got the call. Stelian had better go home. He wasn't well . . .

Is he sick?

Well . . .

What?

He is very depressed.

What was it? Why? How could it be? Their son? He was fine!

Stelian had attempted suicide.

Over the next months, and years, the parents and Michael would learn scientific terms for Stelian's psychological condition. But the truth was, as Michael phrased it, through tears of incomprehension and pain: The Duke did not want to live anymore.

— ★ —

The polite phrase for it, in 1951, was "a nervous breakdown." The doctors wouldn't put words on it without an extensive mental examination, long-term evaluation in a hospital environment. Psychoanalysis was, at the time, in its prickly adolescence. It wasn't more than a decade before that doctors had labeled schizophrenia (which could not be ruled out here, no, not yet) as "neuro-syphilis." And not long before that, its cause was thought to be masturbation. Science had come a long way since, but the mystery still cast a shadow of shame. There was nothing good to be said about this. Outside the house on Rangely Road, there was to be nothing said, at all.

The family would tell no one. Not even the cousins could know. It was trouble they would bear alone, the three of them, Panos, Euterpe, and Michael. It went without saying: they would be strong.

And they were strong. Pan went to work every day, and on weekends and holidays he'd drive them to Stelian's hospital, where they'd chat in the com-

mon room for a while, or walk the grounds outside. And Euterpe kept the
house going, every day, and worked out Michael's schedule with him, including visits to the hospital; and every night, she'd set out three sets of breakfast
dishes, covered with napkins to ward off dust. And Michael went to school
every day, and played basketball, and brought home A's, and was president
of the honor society and the student council.

"Hi, Michael, how y'doing?" they'd ask in the halls of Brookline High.
"Fine."

And it was true. He was only stronger. That was the winter he decided to
run the Boston Marathon, and he went into training, miles and miles every
day, and that spring, he faked his age, entered the race, and did very well:
finished fifty-seventh in a field of almost two hundred runners. That special
girl, Sandy Cohen, stood on a corner of the course, in Brookline, near the
finish, holding an orange with the top sliced off, so he could squeeze the juice
into his mouth for a last burst of energy. She was proud of him. She kept a
photograph of him, running, in a T-shirt, with his number across his chest, his
hands in loose fists pumping at his sides, dark eyes down with intense, inward
concentration.

She was the only one who really knew what it meant to him, that race. She
was the only one he ever told about the sorrow in the house on Rangely Road.

— ★ —

Inside the house, just the three of them . . . what else was there to talk about?
Stelian's trouble was of overwhelming moment for the family, at the kitchen
table. But really, what was there to say?

He's getting the best care . . .

He seems to like the new doctor . . .

He seemed more like himself . . .

There was just no way to talk about why. What had they ever *done*? Pan
was so pained. What got into the boy? Had he ever lacked for anything? For
Michael, a pillar of existence had crumbled: the big guy, Stelian, The Duke
. . . was down. Had Michael done something wrong? Had he not done something? Could he have helped?

It was not the kind of thing they knew *how* to talk about—even before, when
things were good, the language of psychic need was one they'd never tried to
learn. So, sometimes, there was just silence at the table, ten minutes at a
stretch, while the three of them stole glances at each other, and interested
themselves in their food.

It was worst for Euterpe. She felt everyone was looking at her. And they
were. That was the state of psychiatry at the time. The doctors looked nowhere, save to the home, the dysfunctional family, the mothering . . . it was
the dogma of the day: momism. The child got sick, the cause was in his
rearing—had to be early on—bad mothering . . . a psycho-pathological
mother. There was no comprehension of biochemical dysfunction, there was
no credence for inborn instability: there was only one cause—Mom.

And when the doctors talked to Euterpe, they didn't want to hear about the bikes on the lawn, how her boys did their homework, got to school on time, and did so well—enough of that. . . . They were only after the pathology. How had she messed up her son? *They asked her.* They had the *nerve.* They looked at her as if she were a monster. She tried to tell them: there was *nothing* wrong with her sons. They were better than anyone else's sons. That's the way she raised them. They'd done very well, all their lives.

But there had to be a reason. Surely she must understand. There was Stelian, withdrawn, in pain . . . after shock treatments to his brain . . . in the dayroom of Baldpate Hospital. . . . What did she have to say to that?

She didn't have anything to say—none of them did. All they could do was keep their pain, their shame, their questions . . . in that house. They went into a Mediterranean hunch, erecting a wall of silence against the outside world. After all, there is family, and there is everyone else. And for everyone else, they were just fine.

—★—

Especially Michael, who became, in a matter of days or weeks, something akin to an only child. It wasn't that they stopped thinking of Stelian. They had trouble thinking of anything else. But all the formidable expectation of that household now descended onto Michael's narrow, rounded shoulders.

He was ready, certainly able enough, and fit for the weight by temperament, too. He bore it as he'd been taught to bear all: with stoic determination and hard work . . . steady as she goes, one foot in front of the other . . . especially on Heartbreak Hill. And he never talked about Stelian's troubles, not to his old friends in Brookline, nor to his new friends at Swarthmore College.

That was the school he decided to accept: with his grades, he could have had his pick. But Swarthmore (it was Stelian who'd first mentioned the college) was small, quiet, not too far away, outside of Philadelphia, in a well-to-do town not unlike Brookline. It was not socially elitist like Harvard, but committed to a brainy meritocracy, and serious about the business of learning, as serious as young Michael.

It was a perfect fit, and he dived into noetic training as he had into the marathon. He would not falter and he would not stop. His classmates marked him right away as a young man with much on his mind:

"He just seemed more mature . . ."

"He wasn't going to waste two minutes . . ."

"More than the rest of us, he had his priorities . . ."

It was all true, as far as it went. Michael was on his own program. It wasn't that he was a grind, a drudge. Not at all: he played his trumpet, ran cross-country, made the JV basketball squad (at five-foot-eight, the shortest player), and even wrote sports for the student *Phoenix* in the larded style of the Boston sports pages (*the crack of the ash on the old horsehide . . . Cooper flung the pigskin . . .*). That first year, he led his classmates, two nights a week, into Philadelphia, where they canvassed for a slate of clean, smart Democrats—

reformists, the able, decent few—to unseat a corrupt Republican machine that had held power in the city for almost seven decades. That fit into the program, just right . . . as did the campaign to organize students against a McCarthyish loyalty oath then under discussion in the state legislature . . . and the campaign against fraternities whose national charters barred Negroes, or Jews . . . and Michael's own makeshift dorm-hallway barber shop, which he set up when barbers in the "ville" refused a haircut to a black student from Nigeria. Michael had learned to cut hair when he worked as a counselor in a camp for underprivileged children. Now, for sixty-five cents a head, he offered a flattop and a political lecture. What he got was campus fame . . . and pocket money.

What he erected was a neat system in which everything fit—or it was dropped. Some kids hung out at the Turf Villa (pizza and beer), or at the "druggie in the ville" (sodas or coffee at the fountain). Not Michael. Around exam time, the campus was wired. (Professor Laurance Lafore used to say he'd never seen *anything* like Swarthmore in exam week—except London during the Blitz.) Everybody was up all night. Not Michael. In later years, when he had to tell something about his life, he liked to say he ran into freshman physics, and that put an end to his medical career. In fact, his D in physics fit just right—it allowed him to tell Panos, finally, that he wasn't going to be a doctor. At that point, Panos was a gingerly father: he did not insist to Michael that he could do well—in any class he chose. But that was true, and Michael knew it. One day, before psychology class, Michael and a friend were leafing through the thick text, studded with terms of mystery and menace. Leighton Whitaker, who was a sophomore, figured it would take hours to get through any one of these chapters. He asked Michael Dukakis, freshman, how much time he figured he'd need. "Twenty minutes a chapter," Michael said shortly. "I'm just going for a B in this class."

By his own sophomore year, Michael was head of Students for Stevenson, and he helped sign up a quarter of the campus for the ACLU mobilization against Joe McCarthy and the Red Scare hordes. These were serious endeavors at Swarthmore; the school's Quaker-pacifist roots fed the free-speech, free-inquiry doctrines of the present. With the nation at war in Korea (Swarthmore voted *not* to host a ROTC corps), with an Army general heading for the White House, with loyalty oaths waving as weapons in the hands of the know-nothing right, the values of liberal education seemed to hang in the balance in 1952. But at Swarthmore, there was always the faith that intellect, knowledge, the Truth, would triumph, when spread by effort of the enlightened few. True, in Michael's sophomore year, Stevenson was drubbed in the national vote by that general, Ike, the people's choice. But one day in the spring of his junior year, the cafeteria was abuzz with the news that the Supreme Court had struck down segregated schools. (And wasn't that Justice Black's daughter, Jo Jo, eating lunch with her classmates over there?) There was no doubt that advancing enlightenment would solve the problems of race relations, just as surely as advancing medicine was finding a cure for polio, just as surely as urban renewal would cure the blight of city slums. . . . And there was no doubt that these brainy, young Swarthmore savants would march in the forefront of Improvement. By the time Michael was a senior, spending a semester in Washington, D.C., he had the satisfaction, and confirmation, of *seeing* Joe McCarthy censured by the Senate. Truth and Knowledge were on the march.

Now, there was less and less doubt in Michael's mien, less hesitation in his talk. He participated in all issues of the day, large and small, but not in debate. He knew what he thought. If the question was, say, whether a communist should be allowed to speak at Swarthmore, others might resort to arguments from Jefferson or Rousseau . . . not Michael. "What is this?" he'd snap. "It's a *campus.* Of course he should speak." End of argument. If someone in the dorm liked the Indians' chances in the World Series, Michael had three reasons why the Giants were clearly superior. Cleveland would be destroyed. End of argument.

There were lots of fellows in the Wharton dorm who thought they should end up in Washington: the capital, after all, was the locus of great doings, and the federal government was the engine of progress. . . . Not Michael: he claimed it was state government that affected people's lives, the State House was where the action was. Not for him some vague plan to climb the great greasy federal pole. He knew what he wanted, and he wasn't afraid to say it:

"I want to be Governor of Massachusetts."

— ★ —

In their fourth year in that hothouse (they used to say: at Swarthmore, you major in Swarthmore), most of his friends were planning, scheming, to see the world, to go somewhere far away and new—Europe . . . or, at the very least, California. But there was no doubt where Michael was headed: he was going home. The only question, he told friends, was whether to head straight to Boston for law school, or get the Army out of the way. In the end, he decided it would disrupt his career less if he got through the Army first. So he made plans, in an orderly way, to sign on for a two-year hitch, right after college. Meanwhile, for holidays, and some weekends, he went . . . back home to Brookline.

Sometimes, he'd bring a friend along, and proudly show them his home. There they'd meet his imposing father, and Euterpe, who was the life and warmth at the table, explaining and proffering the strange Greek dishes, asking about their schoolwork. There, too, some of them met his big brother, The Duke (Michael was probably the last still to call him that), who was quiet, diffident, but obviously fond and proud of Michael.

Stelian had made it out of the hospital, and after a hiatus of more than a year, back to Bates, where he made it to graduation. But he did not emerge with Michael's confidence in his armor, or Michael's determined route-of-march toward his chosen destination. In fact, somewhere along the line, Stelian lost track of destination.

For a while, he lived and worked in a settlement house, doing social work in Boston's poor South End. He didn't want to live at home anymore. He

wanted to make it on his own. The settlement house only paid a pittance, but
it offered a room and communal meals, and there was the wonderful, WASPy
director, a kindly woman named Beatrice Williams. Beatrice became like a
mother to Stelian.

In 1958, Stelian entered the Boston Marathon . . . but he doubled over after
sixteen miles and could not finish the race. In 1960, he ran for Brookline Town
Committee, and won. But that was the year Michael and his friends took over
the whole Town Committee.

In later years, he had his own apartment, an efficiency near Coolidge Corner,
in Brookline. And he had brief jobs as an assistant in the City Manager's
offices, in a couple of small towns around Boston. For several years, he taught
government at Boston State College. The job never paid much. Stelian never
could afford a bigger place, or a car: he rode his bicycle everywhere, sometimes
thirty miles and back, to see an aunt or a cousin in Lowell, where the Dukakis
clan had started out in America. But the subject matter of his classes was
congenial: politics was still his abiding interest.

He was always active on the fringe of Democratic politics in Brookline—
always around, anyway. A few more times, he filed to run: for the Town Board
of Selectmen, or the Massachusetts House. But he wasn't well known, and
often, not a comfortable presence. He was friendly, sometimes too friendly,
somewhat odd. A few old friends tried to fix him up with dates, but he didn't
have much money for that, and he never did find a girl to share his life. He
even stopped going home to Rangely Road for Sunday dinners, or holidays. He
was, through the sixties, a solitary man, always with dreams of office, but
never with much chance. Sometimes, he'd buttonhole a cousin, or someone he
knew in the past, and urge them: "You'd be great in office. You run . . . I'll
be your campaign manager." But they never did, and nothing came of Stelian's
dreams. His final race, he ran as a Republican, for the House seat Michael
vacated when he was on his way to his first run for Governor. But Stelian
finished last in that vote. The way his old schoolmates described him, he was
a shadowy figure, at the end.

And the shadow was getting longer. A couple of times, Stelian was back in
the hospital: now, it was drug therapy, instead of shock . . . and endless talk
with psychiatrists, about his family. And one night, in the sixties, something
finally welled up in him and burst into the open. Michael's volunteers were
leafleting Brookline for Michael's reelection to the House of Delegates. They
were going door-to-door, leaving fliers in the boxes, and after they'd passed,
Stelian came, and took out Michael's literature and put in his own:

Not Michael Dukakis . . . STELIAN Dukakis . . .

No one was sure if Stelian was even running for an office. But that wasn't
the point:

DO NOT VOTE FOR MY BROTHER . . .

MICHAEL DUKAKIS IS THE LAST MAN TO VOTE FOR . . .

*I, STELIAN DUKAKIS, WILL RUN AGAINST HIM AND RID THIS
DISTRICT . . .*

Michael's friends were horrified, for him, for the family. They called each other frantically all night: go down your street and get Stelian's fliers out of every box!

And they did. They got most of them. Stelian had only poked them into the slots of the mailboxes. He hadn't stuffed them all the way in. For the most part, his leaflets of pain never saw the dawn. Their existence was only whispered.

The following day, Kitty called her friend, Sandy—that same special woman who'd been Michael's first girlfriend—but all she could say was, "Oh, God . . . you don't know what we're going through here." Michael never talked about that night. If someone, a close friend, asked about Stelian, Michael would literally hunch his shoulders, shake his head, sadly, and mutter: "We have to live with it . . ." But that was all: the wall of silence remained.

It wasn't too long after that, just a few years . . . a Saturday night . . . a car—someone—hit Stelian as he pedaled his bicycle down Winchester Street, near his apartment, in Brookline. Stelian's skull was smashed. The motorist drove away.

Stelian lay in the hospital with the membrane of his head exposed, still pulsing with life. But he never came out of the coma. Panos and Euterpe and Michael all came, and stood by the bed. Then, they sat. The parents came for months. Sometimes, one or the other would hold his hand and call to him, *Stelianos!* . . . and think they felt something in his hand. But probably they did not. Stelian died four months after the accident, July 29, 1973.

13

1951

THERE WAS no man more equable, sweet-natured, than Carl Hartpence, who had a few things to blame the world for, if he had been so disposed. There was, for one, the pressure of money: the family finances were always a strain. But that did not alter Carl's disposition, and the kids grew up without much thought that they were poorer than anyone else.

One of Nina's brothers, Neal Pritchard, was a prosperous man, owner of Ottawa's finest grocery store. The family story was, Neal stocked the basement of his store with foods just before World War II . . . and when the rationing hit, well, Neal had money. After the war, it was Carl who sold Neal a new Packard, and that helped out in Nina's household. Anyway, if Neal's son, Jon, got a new bike, Neal made sure that cousin Gary got one, too. Carl never seemed to mind that, just as he never seemed to chafe at abiding amid a gaggle of Pritchards, in general.

It was with quiet resignation, too, that he accepted his status in Ottawa, Kansas, which was pretty much nil. Ottawa had four distinct social orders, which offered the advantage that three of the four had someone to look down on. Within the top stratum, there were the bankers and professional people and the high-muckety-mucks of Ottawa University. That was the country club set. Just below that was the Main Street crowd, the merchants, contractors, land-lords, and other businessmen who formed the Chamber of Commerce. And then there was the general run of working people and farmers, into which third stratum Carl Hartpence was born, and in which he stayed. The only stratum below was peopled by blacks and Mexicans, who were talked about with disdain and mistrust by many people in town. But Carl never went in for that.

In fact, you could go years and never hear Carl utter a harsh word about anyone. He'd try to find the good in whatever came. When his own leap for the next stratum foundered . . . when he went into business with a cousin, trying to start an insurance agency . . . when the cousin then left Carl high and dry, without means to keep his dream afloat . . . Carl just went back to selling farm equipment, and all he said was: "Well, Jim had a different way a doin' things. . . . Jus' couldn't work it out."

Carl seemed oblivious to inequity. Which is what made it so remarkable, that Friday night, on Main Street, when Carl and Gary were sitting in Carl's car, his old Chrysler, which he'd nosed into a parking place, diagonal to the curb, like folks did in those days—in Ottawa, anyway—just to take the evening air and watch the people go by. Carl was talking quietly, and just what brought it on is lost in time now. Maybe it was something Gary said, something with a shot of ambition behind it. Or something about the wider world and what a man might do in it. Anyway, the remarkable part was what Carl said when he half turned away from the windshield, toward his son, and tried to explain how the world was.

He said, there are people with money in the world who can do pretty much what they want, and then there's a lot of others. And the ones with most of the money keep the money, and do not care much about the others. The ones with the money, Carl explained, mostly live in New York, and do what they choose. The rest of us work, and get by.

Of course, the way Carl was, he said it without rancor, just stating facts in his quiet way. Still, Gary never forgot it. It was the most political statement he had ever heard in his family.

— ★ —

Politics wasn't something you'd hear about in Ottawa, not the politics of social movements, certainly not at Ottawa High. It wasn't till years after the Supreme Court decided that school case forty miles up the road, in Topeka, that Ottawa kids even heard the rumblings of protest, or civil rights, or free speech, or anything like that. In fact, when a few kids at Ottawa High finally did mount a tiny echo to the great movements abroad in the nation (they parked themselves in an upstairs hall one day, between classes, and called it a "sit-down"), Mr. Hood, the principal, marched by, clapped his hands twice and shouted, "All right! That's it! Let's get back to class!" . . . and they were up and on their way before he got to the end of the hall.

While Gary Hartpence was there, things hadn't even gone that far. When he looked back much later, and tried to describe Ottawa High, he said it was like the television show *Happy Days*. Fact was, they weren't all happy. There were strata in the high school, too—cliques, more like it—and Gary wasn't in them. Everybody knew he was smart—a hell of a reader—but that and a quarter would buy an ice cream soda at the Dutch Maid.

Jocks were the heroes, and he was not a jock. He had played football before high school, when one of the older kids organized an eighth-grade team. Gary was an end (he could catch, and, yes, he did get dirty) and he loved it. The coach, a high school player named Dick Martin, called him Harts, and Gary liked that. But after that, Gary didn't have the speed, or size—by the middle of his high school years, he might have weighed one-fifty, maybe, with his clothes on. In fact, he stayed scrawny. And with those jug ears, and a complexion that wasn't just right, well, he was no social lion, either.

That was the other whippy thing to be. But in that ethic, the whippiest kids had to show a streak of wildness—nothing too awful (one farm kid did sock the principal in the jaw, but that was over the line)—maybe a sack of garbage strewn on somebody's porch, or a sack of crap at their front door, or stuff nailed up on telephone poles, like wheelbarrows, or porch furniture. Wildness was getting your father's car and driving the tires up onto the railroad tracks, around Third Street, or Fourth, and then riding the rails, with your fists frozen around the wheel and your face a bloodless grin of fear, out to Thirteenth Street, or even Fifteenth . . . before you yanked the wheel and got back onto the street. (Larry Larkin and Richard Fogel, they'd do *anything* . . . rode the track fifteen *miles,* out to Williamsburg!) Wildness was bushwhacking parkers while they petted behind their steamy car windows . . . and other drive-in movie stuff. But wildness was not Hartpence—not at all.

For one thing, he couldn't go to the drive-in, or even to the Plaza Theater on Main Street. That was a Nazarene rule: no movies. Same with dancing at the youth center, which was open Wednesday, Friday, and Saturday nights (weekends, till eleven) and was a must on the high school social circuit. Sometimes, there were pyjama parties, and the girls would go out on the street, middle of the night, in their baby-doll pyjamas . . . or they'd go skinny-dipping at the country club, while the boys hid in the bushes to watch. Not Gary. . . . Kids would hide their cigarettes out at the quarry—then they'd get rained on and ruined, so the kids would crush up leaves and smoke the stuff from straws. Not Gary. Smoking was explicitly barred in the Godly Walk of the Nazarenes.

But it wasn't the church that set Gary apart. It was Gary. He was shy, and just . . . didn't belong. After a while, maybe he didn't want to belong. He'd say he couldn't *understand why* the rest of the kids acted like they did. Things most people just took for granted . . . bothered him: Why did they have to be that way? Marvin Wilson was a heck of a nice guy, good athlete, smart, good-looking . . . but Marvin was Negro, so he and his family had to sit in the back row of the Plaza Theater. Why?

Friends would say: Gary, that's just how it is. Who cares?

"Well, why is it like that? I don't understand why."

He couldn't small-talk, the way most kids could, about dragging Main in Doug Shade's car, or who was dancing (and with whom) when the youth center closed last night. . . . He couldn't see the point of that stuff, like the endless cycle of *Hi! Howareya?* in the halls at school.

How you doin'?

Fine.

Hiya, Gary!

Eight times a day, they'd say the same thing! "Why do we *do* these things? . . ."

At one point, he worked out his own answer:

How are ya, Gary?

"Well," he'd say, "I feel much more like I do now than I did when I got up this morning."

His humor was a bit quiet for the crowd.

— ★ —

Tell the truth, he probably would have loved it if his talk had been just the right talk, or Carl's car had been just the right car, instead of the solid, family Chrysler sedan (with wheels so wide, you couldn't even *try* to ride the rails). He always half admired (more than half!) the ease some guys had: his friend, Kent Granger, a good athlete, had a way with girls that was so natural. Another friend, Dick Martin, was so ornery as a kid, his mother used to chain him to the clothesline . . . but Dick's dad was president of Ottawa U, and so, by right, he just belonged.

It wasn't that Gary didn't want to get into the swim. And it wasn't his fault that by the time he got to the edge of the pond, he had the wit, the discernment, to see it was *empty.* . . . It just happened that he wasn't a jock, or easily social, so he had to find another way to get what he needed, to see himself whole.

He was not going to make the football team, no . . . but he made the tennis team. He was not going to play varsity basketball . . . so he became the team manager. For a while, he went to games as announcer for Ottawa's first and only radio station, KOFO (*twelve-twenty on your dial* . . .). He was the only boy to apply for editor in chief of the student paper. So, Florence Robinson, the faculty adviser, asked the other teachers, and . . . Gary was the chief. And then, too, he ran for class office: not yet for president; that was still the province of jocks, heroes . . . but everybody knew Hartpence was smart, and serious, so they voted him vice president. (It wasn't till his senior year he tried for president, and almost sailed in unopposed, until his friend Willie Hoobing filed on a whim, and Willie, who always small-talked *everyone,* took that prize away.)

Meanwhile, Gary did his reading, kept out of trouble. There was a mini-scandal in chem class one year when someone stole the final exam, and Lester Hoffman, the teacher, hit the roof and made everybody take the test again . . . but Gary didn't need that kind of shortcut. (In fact, Bill Meucke offered him a peek at the test, but Gary was scared, and said, "Get that thing out of here!") Grades were never a problem for Hartpence. Like most of the smart kids, he knew he was going to college. Even had the school picked out: Bethany, a Nazarene college near Oklahoma City. Of course, that wasn't a big school, with teams that people talked about, like KU, or K-State, or even Ottawa U . . . so it wasn't something he could small-talk about.

But even with that, he found another way. He found out he could *not* talk.

It worked like a charm! In fact, it was charm . . . you could almost see it happening in him, about the time everybody got their licenses, sophomore year, '51–'52. . . . Gary and a friend, or a couple of friends, would be riding around, dragging Main, like everybody else, in the evening. Maybe they'd check in at the Dutch Maid, or Scott's (seven burgers for a dollar) on Fifth Street, near the library . . . and then, they'd go to the youth center . . . where Gary found he didn't have to dance, and he didn't have to play Ping-Pong, and he didn't even have to small-talk. He found out he could sit in the back, alone, near the fireplace, lost in his thoughts, a bit melancholy, silent . . . and, sure enough, some girl would come over to say, "Oh, Gary, don't worry . . .

"Gary, things're gonna be all right. Are you sad?"

And Gary'd say, no, he was all right, just thinking . . .

"Really?"

And sometimes, they'd get to talking about what Gary was thinking, maybe what he'd been reading . . . he was so smart! And he made them feel smart. He always wanted to know about them, what they thought . . . (Really? That's what they thought? He never *knew* that . . .) And he spoke so softly, almost purring, and they could see how he brightened, the fun in him, his eyes . . . if they were a year or two younger, it was even easier, and almost more fun, and it made them feel important.

Sometimes, they'd get back in the car, Gary and the girl, or him and a friend and a couple of girls, and they'd drive out to the south edge of town, to the airport, just a strip of concrete in the fields—no lights, no planes at night . . . and they'd pull out onto the runway, and stop the car, and open the doors. And with the radio glowing, the Mills Brothers piercing the dark, they'd dance on the runway, under the stars. . . . Gary liked to dance slow, and close, almost motionless. . . . That concrete was rough on the shoes, but what the hell—Gary hardly moved his feet.

14

The Diddybop Bostons

HERE THEY COME, off the plane, the diddybop Bostons, jangling down the ramp to get ahead of their man. There's nothing like them—not out here, anyway. First thing is their color: they're gray. In Iowa, the only people that color are sick. But the Bostons are always soot-color in the winter—like streets after snow, after the salt trucks come through and it dries during the day . . . asphalt gray. They don't notice: they feel fine, full of nervy energy and quick talk. And busy, always—maybe that's what makes them gray, those women with the skin stretched around their eyes, like they've been in traffic for the last ten years, their jaws narrow under tight haircuts. The guys seem to have more flesh, and flush to their cheeks, but when you get close, it's only broken veins . . . their capillaries all had little strokes, practicing up for the Big One. The other thing is the way they move, so busy: the first ones are hunched over fast mincy steps, like they're getting out of cabs in the rain; they've got to get off the ramp, to get the shot, and their cameras, lights, boom mikes all stick out, giving them a six-legged look, like something skittering under the stove when the light switches on in the kitchen. Then the lights *are* on, and the others come out, bouncing down the ramp, with the jingle of all the crap they carry (even the guys have little bags), with their heads bobbing time, and their gray eye sockets shifting back and forth, looking the place over, while their heads are nodding, like they'd buy it—if it weren't such a dump. A couple of the guys have a hand in a pocket, like they're holding shivs, and there's one chewing gum, and they're off the ramp, still bouncing and jingling, while they trade bursts of rat-a-tat talk down the concourse, and quick snorts of laughter, and two of them stop at a picture on the wall, the sort of color-chocked promotional photograph that airport authorities select by committee, and one of them is digging in a bag for a notebook. It's a *farm scene* . . . with *animals* . . . which is just what the diddybops came out to *see* . . . and now a third one comes up behind, and says, as if the first two were wondering, "That's a cow." And they all have a giggle about coming out here—"hog-hopping," as the *Globe* would call it the next day.

Make no mistake, though: these people were in deadly earnest. For one thing, besides the Governor and his wife, and Sasso, and a couple of staff to tend to them, there were about twenty-five reporters, and each would have to get a story, to justify the trip. All the affiliate TV stations had three or four people each, not to mention Channel Fifty-six, and public TV, and Ken Bode with his crew from NBC, and the big papers had at least two, or two and a columnist, and the smaller papers—*The Quincy Patriot Ledger, The Worcester Telegram*—had their State House guys out there, with plane tickets and hotel rooms . . . and those guys weren't even political writers, who were used to spending a fortune to learn . . . well, not much. No, these guys had to have a story, and the story was: Is he running, or not? So every few minutes, they'd poke their mikes in, like thermometers, to see if the fever was rising.

The official line on the trip was that Governor Dukakis, a prominent member of the National Governors Association, was *invited* to Iowa by the Governor, Terry Branstad, for a *hearing* on rural America . . . just part of the Governor's continuing process of self-education. But that polite fiction begged the question: as if Neil Armstrong stepped off the lunar landing module, and tried to explain, "Hey, no big deal, I'm just here to collect some rocks." No, the point for the Bostons was the trip itself, and they were in full Presidential cry. The Bostons always expect to have a piece of this President business: it's a regional industry with them—like ham is in Virginia. There was no Kennedy going this time, so . . . The Duke was the ticket. The Boston TVs had already commissioned exclusive polls to see where he stood in Iowa. The *Globe* had a guy on the streets of Des Moines two days early, showing a picture of Michael, like a runaway child, to see if anybody knew him.

They didn't. But the process already was feeding on itself. The moment the diddybops hit that ramp, Gate 3B, Des Moines Airport, it did not matter that no one in Iowa wanted Michael Dukakis to be President. The local TVs and *The Des Moines Register* showed up to cover the arrival . . . as news! . . . *He has come!* Hey, more than a year to the caucuses, and this guy already needs a Greyhound to carry his press corps—*we better get out there!* At one point, one of the Bostons asked one of the Des Moineses why the hell he was there: "If so many of you guys weren't here," said Michael Day, of KCCI, Des Moines, "we wouldn't *be* covering this today." Meanwhile, Day complained that Dukakis wasn't *saying* anything. Which, of course, filtered back to Michael. Why didn't he say something?

And from that moment, it did not matter that Michael Dukakis had nothing

to say about Iowa—in fact, knew nothing of the problems of its farmers
. . . in fact, had never been sufficiently interested in Iowa to visit in his
fifty-three years, save once, as a college student, thirty-three years before, when
he hitchhiked through, one blurry night, on his way to somewhere that did
interest him, which was Mexico. Didn't matter: the Des Moines TVs and the
Register were there, to give the people of this state their first impression. What
did he have to say? . . . And Lowell Junkins, who had run and lost for
Governor in Iowa, got into Michael's car at the airport (he had to know some
farming—didn't he?), and Junkins was talking diversification: problem was too
much corn and cattle and hogs. You know, Junkins said, forty years ago, the
second biggest crop in this state was apples, but people lost track of that.
. . . So by the time he got to his first stop in Iowa, Michael was talking
diversification. Sat down in a cattle barn and started telling ranchers about
diversification. How about lamb . . . or fruit? In Massachusetts, he said, *his*
farmers had branched out into berries, lettuce . . . Belgian endive. (You know
what Belgian endive brings at the Stop & Shop? A fortune!) And it did not
matter that these cattlemen had spent their lives raising cattle, and were
looking for a way to perpetuate that life. It did not matter that, in Iowa, a
Massachusetts-size farm is called the front lawn. Michael had come out to talk
to farmers . . . so, he talked. And he said to the cameras, after a half-day: "I've
learned a lot. We've had some . . . terrific discussions."

But it really didn't matter: the bubble is its own show. By 5:00 P.M., that
first day, Michael steamed into downtown Osceola, Iowa, supposed to march
Main Street, meeting and greeting ("Hi. Mike Dukakis. Tell me who you
are . . ."), and right away, the cameramen and sound men were running,
six-legged, out of the Greyhound, the rent-a-cars—counting cops, seventeen
cars in the motorcade now—and the lenses and mikes were poking over his
shoulders, next to his ears, driving him nuts . . . but Osceola will never forget.
There was a Boston TV lady, Janet Wu, a *Chinese,* cabled to a satellite truck
on Main Street, doing her stand-up, live, back to Boston for the six o'clock
news. There were *three satellite trucks* parked in Osceola, with their dishes
turned aloft to the stratosphere, while the halogens stabbed at the storefronts,
and strobes whirled atop the state police cars, and, of course, people came out,
stood on the street, staring, and then the diddybops grabbed them and poked
tape recorders or notebooks at them: "C'nIgetchurname? . . . Spellit . . .
Y'farmer? . . ." And people were asking: "What is it? Who is it? Who?" But
that wasn't important: three high school girls were standing on Main Street
in the middle of the trucks, and cables, and cop cars, and press-pack-rent-a-
cars parked crazy-quilt over the curbs, and by the time he came, almost
trotting, Michael Dukakis, five-foot-eight in his wing tips, almost lost in the
press pack, and not too happy about it, either . . . it simply did not matter.
The halogen fireflies came at the girls, and it was . . . *so exciting* . . . *Oh, GOD,
there he IS* . . . *EEEEEEEEEEEEEEEEE* . . . that they started to scream.

Michael only worried about the cameras. Did they have to be there? Were
they always going to be there? How could you have a discussion with people

while boom mikes were brushing their noses? Sasso shrugged: "This is what it is, Mike. Part of the process." And he watched for a sign—a frown, a grimace—that would have told him Michael could not take the bubble, that he was going sour. But Michael tried to shrug it off. He talked to Kitty—of course, she thought it was ridiculous, an *outrage,* the way the camera people trampled everywhere: they could *kill* somebody . . . and they wouldn't care! But she didn't make it an issue. She was so eager for Michael to have a good time. That night, they were going to have dinner with Governor Branstad and Governor Clinton in a private home in Osceola . . . and then each Governor would sleep in a farmhouse . . . to have another talk with a farm family. And Kitty professed herself charmed by these arrangements . . . smiling all evening, talking hogs, chewing nicotine gum . . .

Oy! A *waterbed*? . . . "Oh, how delightful! We've never tried one!"

It was during dinner that night, while the camera people were out on the lawn, shining their halogens at the windows, standing on the flower pots, tipping two over, that their hostess, Judy Barrett, brought up the subject, life in the bubble: "I don't see how you can stand it," she said. "People writing down everything you say, putting it on tape. On stage every minute of the day . . ."

But the process was already feeding on itself: Michael and Kitty were already inside, playing the roles assigned.

"Oh, we *love* it," Kitty said.

"We like politics . . ." Michael said, ". . . meeting people, talking to the people out there, today, just . . . terrific."

Meanwhile, Sasso was doing his part, out to dinner with the rest of the press, a steak joint, the only place in town. They filled up four or five tables with the Bostons, who were having a great time, knocking back a few, while Sasso worked, from table to table, like a bar mitzvah boy, dispensing quotes and the gift of his smile, his enjoyment of them. This could be fun! . . .

You bet it could: the reporters knew where their interest lay, too . . . a story that would take them all over the country, maybe to the White House. . . . They were going *national,* not to mention all those steaks on the cuff. . . . There was a TV in the restaurant, and when the local news came on, there was a bit of a hush. And then . . . there it was . . . The Duke, their guy, lead story! And from the Boston press rose a quiet, but unmistakable, cheer.

—★—

The startling thing about the Hart campaign, when he started out again, after New Year's, was how quiet it was, how sane, even here in New Hampshire, where he'd won before, where he had so many friends. You would have thought that a guy thirty points ahead in the polls (no one else was even in double figures) would be packing in huge crowds, stuffing the high school gym, with a big flag behind him and a platform for cameras. But Hart was wise to that: he did not want to climb into the bubble.

What he wanted, what he got, were living rooms, holding anywhere from a dozen to forty people, places he could talk for an hour, and listen, answer questions, have everyone feel they'd met him, feel they knew why he was running. That's how he started out, last time, '82–'83, and it worked—better than anyone dreamed . . . anyone except Hart. Of course, last time, he didn't have a choice: a year before the first votes were cast, he *couldn't* have packed a high school gym—nobody knew him. (One time in Portsmouth, Hart tried to work a bingo hall. "Hi, I'm Gary Hart. I'm running for President." One bingo player turned and snapped: "President of what?") This time, he had his choice, and he took it: he wanted it small, at the start.

It had to do with Hart's theory of campaigning. (Hart always had a theory.) He liked to build from the bottom up. That meant all organizing was local: once a person signed on to run a town, they need only turn to the state office for supplies, resources, and requests for the candidate's time. In the same way, the state campaigns never had to follow orders from the national staff. The national staff was there to serve the states. When Hart explained the theory, he talked about concentric circles. The base of the campaign, and the locus of his greatest effort, was that first circle. It wasn't too big—could not be—maybe ten or twelve souls in any one state, handpicked for their energy, credibility, and contacts, who knew Hart, knew what he stood for, had internalized the message. Those ten or twelve would then create a second, larger circle: people they knew, in their neighborhoods, or places of work. They might invite a group to their house to meet Hart, or get a member of the second circle to host a coffee, with *his* friends, which would start a third circle. The point was, the message would radiate out to the final, largest circle, the voters as a mass.

It was like Amway . . . or saving souls. More like the latter, because it rested on faith, ultimately on Hart's own faith: he was the only one who fed all the circles. In '83, Hart had to explain the theory, how it would work, over and over: forget about the polls—once he started to win, the polls would turn around overnight. Forget about endorsements: he could do more with half a dozen good twenty-two-year-old organizers than a score of State Senators who climbed on because they thought he was a winner. Before the votes went down in '84, Hart even had to tell his people to forget about money—their salaries, which he could no longer pay. When he started to win, the money would roll in. It was the same thing he said about charisma: they called him aloof, too cool, couldn't lift a crowd . . . well, when he started to win—suddenly—they'd see the charisma. Americans love a winner, he said. They were going to love him.

And they did. After he won New Hampshire in '84, he was instantly the candidate of charisma—funny, how he'd changed so much in a week. . . . That's what he thought this time around, when everybody said how much better he was. All the writers with him in January '87 came away with the same psycho-political mumble about Hart—"more at ease with himself . . . more relaxed . . . more at peace . . ." Yeah, he was more at peace: he was thirty points ahead.

But there was no doubt it was clicking, whatever "it" was. In those living rooms, Hart was self-possessed, self-assured, funny sometimes, always full of purpose. He knew what he wanted from that room, that day. He knew what he had to say, and why. His issues made sense, they hung together: it was a worldview; that's what Hart had spent the last two years on. He had connected the dots. So, when he brought up an oil-import fee—a ten-dollar-a-barrel tax on imported oil—it may not have been a popular stand in New England (where heating-oil costs are a cutting issue). But Hart did not justify the tax just on the basis of energy policy—to spur production in the Southwest. It would also help reduce America's killing trade deficit. It would raise money for his education proposals. Most of all, it was a national security issue: if America had to send troops to protect "our" oil in the Persian Gulf, the result, he insisted, would be disaster.

And always, in the question-and-answer sessions, he found his own over-drive, bringing the questions of policy back to the bedrock of Hart-facts. Yes, he was against protectionist tariffs. But not just because they were a bogeyman since the thirties, when tariffs caused a worldwide depression. It was because the goals of trade had changed. America could not, and would not, dominate world markets as it did after the Second World War. The goal of trade had to be a mutual enrichment, the size of the worldwide pie expanding as nations bought ever more from one another: if the America-first crowd ever won, if the U.S. somehow restored its domination, the result would be enmity, isola-tion, and war.

You could see it starting to sink in, in those living rooms, in the faces locked onto his. It wasn't so much they agreed . . . but this guy was the size of a President. That was the measure people were taking, a year before the voting started: Hart was of size. People asked him questions they would ask a Presi-dent. People told him they wanted to help. People signed the sheet in the back of the living room, and Hart knew the follow-up would be there: those people would be brought into the circle; the machinery was in place.

Was he more at peace? Well, yes. . . . He still had debt from the last campaign—a million and a half—but the money would be there. The debt was down from almost five million—of course, nobody wrote that. He still didn't have many endorsements. (He only had one elected official in Iowa, and *that* guy just got caught getting a blow-job from his secretary in a car, so the Hart campaign wasn't using his name.) But elected officials could read the polls. The point was, Hart was winning.

Now he'd wind up a day of campaigning with a dinner for the staff, the local drivers, all the reporters, an easy, off-the-record talk about anything. He'd even talk a bit about himself. He let a photographer take his picture, with his family . . . watching football . . . *at his cabin*! He'd never let them near the place before.

He even sat down with *Us* magazine . . . and had a good time, mugging in his mirrored shades, jumping up to turn up the Mozart on the radio. . . . "Gary Hart is relaxed today," *Us* averred in surprise. "He is funny, charismatic, witty—even a bit goofy. He is startlingly unlike the Gary Hart a good portion of the public sees as aloof, too intellectual and boring. . . . *Why aren't you like this all the time?*"

"But I *am* like this all the time!"

The *Us* lady was in New Hampshire on one of those great campaign days, along with a few of the national big-feet, Bob Healy from the *Globe*, and Jules Witcover, the columnist. It was Healy and Jules who had the idea—hey, they were all going down to Boston to get their planes the following day: why didn't Hart and Billy Shore join them for dinner in Boston tonight? They'd do Pier Four, have a couple of pops, kick back . . . have a talk.

So they did. They were a half-dozen at table, Hart and Shore, Bob and Mary Healy, Jules and the *Us* lady, and it was fun! . . . especially after a couple of pops. Hart had his white lightning special—vodka on the rocks—only a couple. He was telling wickedly funny stories: Jacob Javits's funeral, when Hart was sitting in one of the front rows, and plop, into an open seat drops . . . Richard M. Nixon!

"So the organ music is playing, and Nixon says, 'What is it? BACH? . . . *or Brahms*?' "

Hart is a splendid mimic, and with Nixon, he had it all: the furrowed brow, the shaking scowl, the deep voice from the stiff thorax . . . " 'BACH? . . . *or Brahms*?' . . .

"Then he sees Kissinger in the row ahead, but Kissinger won't turn around. *'Should I say hello to Hank? You think I should say hello? . . . BACH, or Brahms? . . . I ought to say hello to Hank'* . . ."

They were giggling at the table. It was a wonderful dinner. Of course, those guys went back a long way—at least to '71, with McGovern. And Jules was out there writing when Bobby Kennedy, Hart's hero, ran in '68. They were all big-feet now. They ought to understand each other.

"You know, Gary . . ." Jules said, as he rattle-slapped his glass down onto the table. "One thing. . . . I never did understand all that shit you said about why you changed your name . . ."

Hart stiffened in his chair, and the pleasant pink began to drain from his face. These people had known him for *fifteen years*—why were they doubting him now?

Jules didn't see. He was just talking about something that bothered him . . . like a New Yorker on the subway platform: *Why don't they clean up the spit on the floor?*

"I mean, seems to me, you gave about five different stories . . ."

Hart could not *believe* they were doing this to him. Fifteen years! They knew his record—or, by God, they *ought to*—fifteen years they never doubted his veracity . . . not *once*. What was it about him now? Who did they think they were, to pick at his life? Hart was pale, holding a single trembling finger in front of his face: "One story, Jules . . . *one.*"

"I mean, I don't give a shit . . ." Jules was rattling on, like the ice in his glass. "I mean, whatever the story is, you know . . ."

So Hart told him the story: the same story he'd told for the last three years: his family had always talked about changing their name from Hartpence, to what they thought it was, used to be . . . and when he was home from Yale, his father had taken them down to the courthouse, and . . .

"Yeah, I know, but then you said some kinda thing about your mother, and . . ."

"And we changed it to what we thought it must have been *originally* . . ." Hart was now enunciating every word. He was not going to talk about his mother. Nor were these self-appointed psycho-police going to talk about his mother. He bored on, with the tone of a man saying something for the *last* time. His lips were thinner and thinner. No, you couldn't see his lips anymore.

". . . we changed it to Hart . . . and that is all."

That was all. Within minutes, Hart rose, dropped his napkin on the table and, without another word, walked out of the restaurant.

— ★ —

This is the speech? Eight months on the education speech—and this is what he gets? Maybe they thought this was just an exercise, some kind of fun and games. It was not. He was running for President of the United States—and this is the speech he gets?

As usual, Hart started editing, then rewriting, before he got off the first page. He crossed out lines, then whole paragraphs, noting in the margin: *rhetoric.* There was no one who went after a speech like Hart. He was relentless, vicious. And this was after months of work: the labor involved was on the scale of a pharaoh's pyramid. Like Cheops, Hart wanted it to stand forever.

First, his two issues chiefs, David Dreyer and Mark Steitz, had to empty their own files, the Library of Congress, Lexis-Nexis . . . a total data-dump. Then, working on an outline from Hart ("It has to step on a lot of toes," he warned), they farmed their questions out to experts—a hundred famous and near-famous thinkers. Hart insisted on rattling the experts' cages. Of course, half of them wouldn't respond, and maybe another twenty-five would answer with a copy of their latest speech . . . canned stuff—Dreyer and Steitz could always tell. But then there would be twenty, or twenty-five, who actually tried to think up answers . . . and those were the ones Hart wanted. It wasn't just their ideas—though they had to be considered. This was another way to build from the ground up: if—when—he became President, he would have a constituency, all over the country, to carry the mail for his education program. He was getting ready to govern—not just make speeches.

So the boys got all this stuff together, working back-to-back in a single office, and rammed it into computers (they called it "feeding the beast"), then knocked out a first cut of a speech, which they sent to Hart's desk . . . whence it came back. There wasn't a mark on it—just a note from Billy Shore: *Returned by GWH.*

That meant try again. But there wasn't a whiff of evidence that Hart'd even looked at the thing . . . until six months later, when they were trying to get the latest draft approved, and Hart leaned back in his chair and said, "Yeah, but you've totally omitted Sizer's argument that the seven-period day is now obsolete."

Oh, so he'd read it. . . .

Yes, he'd read it, and complained about it, and wondered what the hell they were doing all those months . . . while he simultaneously asked them for stuff he wanted against the Gramm-Rudman bill, and for the drug bill . . . and while the speechwriter quit, and they had to find another, who didn't really work out, and then Hart left the Senate and they had to pack up their stuff, box it for shipment to Denver . . not to mention move their own households, drive their cars out to the Rockies, set up a new office . . . and Hart wanted to know . . . *where* is his education speech?

So, by New Year's, Dreyer and Steitz were back-to-back at new computers, folding in more stuff from the experts, feeding the beast . . . with Hart demanding something tougher, something more: more school days, more hours each day, competency tests for teachers. . . . "There is a price for the generosity of the Hart education plan," he said with an evil-scientist grin. "We're going to spend a little money here. But we're also going to make demands . . . teachers, parents, students . . ." Hart wanted to shake them all by the neck. Meanwhile, he'd inquire, every few days: *Where* was his speech? So, finally, Dreyer and Steitz had to crank it out themselves. They still didn't have a writer who could work with Hart for ten minutes. They gave him a draft, and he hit the roof: *This* is the speech?

Now he was working on page twelve, halfway through. The pages looked like subway art. His block-letter print filled the margins:
Why all these words to make simple points?
What's this?
Awful.
Awful.
Then spell it out.
Awful grammar. D–

They were wasting his time! It was 1987. His two years for issue preparation were gone. He was three months from announcement! He had Iowa to work on, New Hampshire, the South. Millions of dollars had to be raised, *now*. He had speeches to make for money, too, money of his own—he had to make the mortgage for the land around the cabin. (He was not going to give up the grounds of his castle!) He had his law firm in Denver, and they wanted hours from him—billable hours! He didn't have time to screw around with bad work.

So he tore up the speech and they wrote it again. And he tore it up again, and they wrote it again. And this time, he did the rest with a pen. The packets for the press had to go out. None of it would make any difference if no one heard about the speech. There was a crack Advance man dispatched to the University of Virginia—Hart would issue his call for a new American Revolution in Education at the seat of learning founded by his idol, Thomas Jefferson. It was the last week of January when everything was ready.

And then it snowed.

It snowed all day, and the next day: it broke records. And Washington shut down, and Virginia shut down, and roads were closed, and there was . . . no

way. The Hart campaign was up and running now, in Denver, and people there
did the best they could. They called around the Southeast for a campus that
would, at least, offer a hall. There was no question of delaying for a week: the
speech was ready, the packets were out . . . the brick was baked—it had to go
in the wall.

They booked him into Duke—good weather there—for the next day. Of
course, none of the big-feet came. Hart was let down. It just was not how he'd
imagined. . . . Duke was . . . well, it was just a speech. The ideas were there.
The statement was made. He'd repeat his call throughout the next week in
California, and Iowa. Meanwhile, the press packets did their work: the leader
of the pack, David Broder, wrote under the headline A NEW GARY HART:

"In the midst of the East Coast blizzard last week, former Senator Gary
Hart of Colorado went college shopping for a campus that was clear enough
to provide him a lecture hall. He wound up at Duke. And what he said there
about the education challenge facing the nation was another indication that
the early front-runner for the 1988 Democratic Presidential nomination is
ready to meet the test in the issues area. . . ."

Yes, that eased the sting. And Hart was ready with his most characteristic
compliment: "Where do we stand," he wanted to know, "on the economics
speech?"

—★—

"I agree, it's gone fine, but this is *different.* This is you. They have to feel you.
This has got to come from *you!*"

In the kitchen, Ira Jackson was prodding, insistent. Michael was going to
have to do better for this, the first big speech, the New Hampshire Democratic
Party. But Dukakis was shaking his head, between his shoulders, like he
always did when he dug in . . . what the hell were they beating on him for?
This was not the first speech he ever made.

Across the table, Ira read the head-shake, the shoulders. "Michael, it's not
just a speech. This has gotta be Presidential league. This is New Hampshire.
This is where you say what it's all about. It's Broder, Healy, every columnist
in the whole goddam *country,* watching to see if you make it over the bar. You
know what it is? This is your *bar mitzvah.* . . ."

Ira had a talent for hyperbole, and no fear of Dukakis's scorn. Ira was the
State Revenue Commissioner, the man who invented REAP: he was thirty-
eight years old, dark-haired, slender, smart as hell—one of the most visible
stars in the State House. But that wasn't how he got to Michael's kitchen table.
Ira was a Brookline boy, he used to baby-sit Michael and Kitty's kids . . .
almost family. That's why Michael picked him to write the speech. He had
confidence in Ira. That's why Michael thought he could give him one line—
"Opportunity . . . for every American"—and know Ira would surface in a
week, with a speech in his mouth.

But not this time. No goddam way! Ira wrote the whole inaugural speech
in '82—six days to write the thing, and not much guidance. Not this time.

It's only the most important speech of your whole goddam life. . . . Ira had asked him point-blank in the office last week: Why are you running for President? And Dukakis just stared him down and said: "You tell *me*. . . . Why would you think I'm running?" Like some kind of stupid riddle game! And when Ira started to mumble some crap, Dukakis got pissed off . . . *at him*! No, that's *not it,* he says. . . . "It's opportunity . . . for every American. *That* is my ideology."

Okay . . . opportunity, fine, the American dream, the immigrant story . . . Ira could do that. But not if he didn't know the story! And Michael had never told the story. Never! That's why Ira was back in the kitchen on Perry Street. That was where you had to go, to get down with Michael.

"You know what this is?" Ira insisted. "This is: '*Tonight, I am a man.*' You either do it here . . . or you forget it!"

"Mike . . . Ira, wait a minute! . . . Mike, listen . . ."

This was Sasso. He was the only one to call Michael "Mike." It was the name that went with Dukakis, the persona, which was Sasso's doing, and which he reinforced constantly. Now he broke in, an octave lower, and half as loud as Ira. "Mike, there's an intimacy about a candidacy for President. There's an intimacy with the voter, the most personal vote anyone ever makes . . . and there's got to be something shared, a personal, intimate connection, or it doesn't fly."

"Exactly!" Ira crowed across the table. "It's you, your story, *you. You!*"

"All right, guys, knock it off," Michael said, in his parent voice. This was business. "What're we doin' here? What do you want to know?"

"The immigrant story is powerful, Mike . . ." Sasso was still talking low and calm, like this was the Economic Development Council. But Ira didn't wait for Sasso to jolly Michael along.

"When did your father come?" he demanded.

"How old was he? . . .

"How much money did he have with him? . . .

"Did he know any English?"

Michael had to think about the answers. It was incredible: he'd never told the story. The fact was, Michael had never spoken of himself as a Greek American till just the last few years. He only talked about what he knew: insurance, or welfare programs, housing, or transportation . . . a disembodied brain . . . who should be Governor because he knew more than any other brain. It was only in '82, when he made his comeback, that he let his adman, Dan Payne, make a couple of spots about his "roots." And there was Michael, in front of the house in Lowell, where the Dukakis clan had settled, talking about his run in the marathon, and his days in the Army, in Korea . . . and people loved it! They never knew!

But this was different. He'd always stopped short of this, his family.

"Where did he land in this country?" Ira demanded.

"In New Hampshire, in . . ." Michael had to think. "Manchester."

"You're kidding!" Ira said. New Hampshire! There was the connection.

"How'd he learn English? . . .

"The Y taught English? . . .

"He ran there? . . .

"At night?"

The stuff was incredible! Eight years after his arrival, Michael's father entered Harvard—the Medical School. The American Dream: there it was, in Michael's life.

Ira took away his notes and wrote that night. He didn't need a week: he was back in the kitchen the next day, with a draft. It had everything: the link to New Hampshire, lines from Robert Frost . . . Ira even put stuff in about the Russians: he called for an era of "peaceful competition with the Soviets." It sounded good! And there, throughout, was the theme for a campaign: opportunity for all, the American Dream . . . the story of Panos and Euterpe Dukakis and their Greek American son . . . *who stands before you tonight . . .*

Michael took the draft, and read it through. Ira knew he'd hit something . . . but he didn't know what.

Maybe it was Michael seeing his parents' life in black and white. Or maybe it was just, he'd never told the story, and there it was now, for the whole world to hear. Or maybe, as Ira came to suspect, there were feelings in that story that Michael never shared with his father, never had a chance to say . . . maybe this was Michael's way of saying to Panos: I love you . . . a way for Panos, dead these seven years, to say, at last, to Michael: I am proud of you.

There was no way to know. Michael finished the speech, said nothing. He pushed back his chair and left the kitchen. Ira saw the tears in his eyes, but all he heard now was Michael's tread on the stairs, and his footfalls in the hall, to the study he kept up there. Then Ira waited. But after a while, there was no point. Michael had gone. He was not coming back. Without goodbye, Ira packed up his papers, and left the house on Perry Street.

15

1952

THE COUNTY ELECTION was the first chance folks had to get a good look at Bob. Of course, people knew him from Dawson Drug. But that was before. . . . And the farmers who knew Doran from the grain elevator, they'd heard about Bobby Joe. In fact, one way or the other, almost everybody had heard the story of that poor Dole boy, or if they hadn't, someone would whisper it ("carried 'im home on a stretcher, couldn't even feed himself . . .") as they watched him around town, campaigning for County Attorney.

It wasn't much of a job, when you got down to it. You had all the criminal prosecution, all the county's civil legal business, and then, if you had time, you could take on private clients. You pretty much had to take outside work; the county job only paid $242 a month. The courthouse janitor made ten dollars more. (In the old days, there was always something extra from the bootleggers, but Kansas had gone wet in 1948, so that put an end to a source of steady income.) There were only a half-dozen lawyers in Russell, and the county job usually went to the last one, the youngest, who was trying to build a practice.

That was the problem in '52: there were two good boys come back to town, after the Army, law school, and all. And people said it was a darned shame there wasn't a pair of jobs. Dean Ostrum, Bob's opponent, was a boy of excellent family, too. He was Oscar's son; Oscar Ostrum was probably the best lawyer in Russell. And Dean was always smart: a debater at Russell High, where he likely did even better than Bob Dole; everybody knew Bob as an athlete, but Dean was the brainy sort. People naturally thought of Dean in the law—in that county job, matter of fact . . . till Bob announced.

Actually, he didn't so much announce it as murmur. . . . There was a political meeting in June, at the high school in Bunker Hill, a tiny town nine miles from Russell. Ray Shaffer was the Republican boss in Russell County, and he introduced Bob to the crowd. Bob stood with his arm hanging down, crooked at the elbow, his body canted a bit to the left, so he could try to hide "his problem," and he said to the crowd, in a single sentence, that he wanted the County Attorney job. Said it so fast and low, it didn't really sink in—people just stared—until he stopped, and sat down again. That was all the announcement he made. Next day, he got a new blue suit, on credit, at Banker's Mercantile—Phyllis taught the tailor how to put in the special shoulder pads—and Bob started passing out fliers on Main Street.

That was about as sophisticated as things got in that race. Oh, Bob had his brother, Kenny, and his friend, Adolph Reisig, and maybe a couple of the Krug boys—they called themselves the "tack and hammer men"—who'd nail up posters to get Bob's name in front of people's eyes. And maybe at the end, each candidate would drop twenty-five dollars for ten spots on the radio for Election Day. But mostly, this was one-on-one campaigning: Bob and Dean Ostrum, dogging one another's steps up Main Street, Russell, and then out to Bunker Hill, Gorham, Lucas, Luray, Fairport, Dorrance, Waldo, Paradise. . . . At least, Bob Dole made all those stops. Heck, if he was driving back from some one-street prairie town, and he spotted a light off in the endless fields, he'd dirt-road up to that house in the night, and let the dogs yowl until a light came on behind the screen door, so Bob could say: name is Dole, and he just stopped by to let them know—name's Bob Dole—he hoped, he'd be grateful—Dole, like the pineapple juice—to have their support on Election Day.

In theory, Bob was already a practicing attorney in Russell. He got a used desk and a brand-new hundred-dollar leather chair, and set them up in Doc Smith's office on Main Street. But really, what he was doing, from the time he got out of law school in June, was running flat out for that county job. By happenstance (and the boom in oil, sparked by the war), that was the year Russell peaked in population—maybe seventy-five hundred people in town, another five thousand spread out around the county. Still, there couldn't have been any more than five thousand voters, and Bob probably asked for every one of those votes, personally.

In theory, he was already a veteran of public office, having been installed for a single term in the lower house of the Kansas State Legislature, while he was in Topeka, at Washburn University Law School. But that wasn't anything like this. The legislature only met for three months during his two-year term—it wasn't a job for a grown man, not full-time—and Bob (or, to be precise, his Republican backers in Russell County) had the powerful argument that Bob was already there, in Topeka, and at least the voters wouldn't pay for gasoline, back and forth. As for Bob, he held that post in his spare time—didn't even break stride in school. Barely mentioned to Phyllis that he was going into politics: she wasn't that interested; and what the heck, he'd be home every night, same as always.

In theory, Bob was already fully recovered from his injuries. That was the party line, anyway. He was still thin, of course, and he had that arm—everybody could see that, no matter what he did. But you wouldn't think of him as still healing, not by seeing him on the street, or talking to him, watching him work. Bob made sure of that. In fact, this was the recovery: showing himself, and his nemesis, his body, in every corner of the county, to any voter who'd stop and chat. That, and winning . . . that would be the ultimate recovery: to have those thousands of his home folks—everybody who knew him, really—ratify with their ballots that he was a man who could work for them. For that he'd keep going, till his was the last light you could see on Main Street. And he'd be up and at it by seven the next morning, as soon as Phyllis finished tying his tie. . . .

He wasn't afraid of work—only of no work. It wasn't so long since he'd starred in his own private nightmare, the vision of Bob Dole in his wheelchair, selling pencils on Main Street. What he feared were the silent flashes of that vision in other people's eyes—he searched their faces when he asked for a vote: Did they think he wasn't up to a "real" job? In fact, a lot of people thought this might be just the way to get Bob into a job "he could handle." But nobody said that to Bob. There was something in the way he carried himself that warned off sympathy—would have broken his heart.

Of course, there were also some codgers who just didn't care. One old farmer greeted Bob at the door and told him he knew his granddad . . .

"Agh, good," Bob said.

"Used to butcher for me . . ."

"Yeah, he was a pretty good butcher . . ."

"No he wasn't," the farmer said. "Gave me bad sausage. Never liked him."

Back in town, Bob would tell that story with relish. He'd tell it with an air of droll complaint—can you *believe* some people? It was funny, but it showed—he hoped it showed—that no one was cutting a break for Bob. No, sir. Bob was never afraid of what people would say—only of what they wouldn't say.

And he never forgot anything people said, the way they looked, their kinfolk he knew . . . kept it all in his head. If someone mentioned they'd be at their church Sunday after next for their parents' anniversary—everyone in the family's coming by for ice cream and cake . . . well, they learned after a while, they'd see Bob that Sunday, too. He wouldn't make a show of it: just stopped by to say hello . . . but the people were so surprised he showed up, they'd always make a point of introducing "their special guest." Then, of course, they'd want to feed him ice cream and cake, but he wasn't going to try to work a fork with his left hand in front of everyone, so he wouldn't be able to stay, and they'd wrap up a couple of pieces for him, which, of course, he'd remember when he saw them again, and mention how good that cake was, how he'd like to get the recipe for Phyllis. . . .

There didn't seem to be any limit to what he could keep in his head. Nobody much remarked on it: they all thought he just remembered *them*. The only one who really knew was Phyllis, but it was old hat to her. That's the way she'd seen him go after law school, night after night, in their tiny apartment (in a building named The Senate) in Topeka. In his first year back at college, Phyllis had gone with Bob to take notes, in a few of his classes, but after that, the VA gave him a machine, one of the first recording machines manufactured. It was called a Sound-Scriber, a big, clunky brown box with a black microphone-mouthpiece and a heavy needle arm that grooved a recording into green plastic disks, like little record albums. Bob would carry that machine into class and set it up on the arm of a chair, up in front, where the professor's words would be clearest. At night—sometimes all night—he'd sit at home (while Phyllis tried to keep quiet), playing those scratchy green disks, over and over, noting a couple of words in his painstaking left-hand squiggles, then putting the pen down, lifting the needle, and carefully setting it back on the disk to get the next few words. In those days, the law was practiced without dictating machines, and that box in the classroom spooked some people—even professors. Bob had to get official permission to use it, after one student complained that those disks gave Dole an advantage. But it never felt that way to Bob. He never could take many notes. Mostly, what he could do was hear that voice, on the disks, over and over, until he could say it in his head, until he knew that case, with all the citations—until he could literally dictate that learning back to Phyllis, who would write his exam.

Sometimes, he'd study with his friend Sam Crow—of course, Sam had notes. He even offered to copy them for Bob. But that wouldn't do Bob any good. He had to have it in his head. That old apartment building, The Senate, had louvered doors out to the hallways, to let the air circulate, and when the weather was warm, you could hear a whole lesson on contracts or torts, in the hall, before you even got to Bob's door. Then, inside, at a little desk, just to the right of the door, there he'd be, sallow and skinny in his T-shirt, which hung uneven on his neck, sloped down on one side, where there was no shoulder: that was the side Bob kept his pack of Camels rolled up in the sleeve. Sam and his wife, Ruth, would come over in the evenings, and the girls would take turns treating each other to the movies, while Sam and Bob went at the cases—Sam had his notes, Bob had his head. When the girls came back, they might stop for coffee, after which Sam and Ruth would head home, and Phyllis to bed. She would still hear Bob on his cases, as she dropped off to sleep.

Bob never talked to Sam or Ruth about his injury, about the war. He was still painfully shy—considered himself a ruin. But he knew he'd have to get over that. Even then he was thinking politics, as a career. So Sam and Bob enrolled in a night class at the local high school—Beginner's Speech. For Bob, it was the moral equivalent of fire-walking: a test every time he showed up. In one of the first lessons, the teacher asked: "If you saw someone you knew walking down the street, would you cross the street to avoid him?"

Bob answered, "Sure."

But in class, he couldn't avoid showing himself. He had to get up on the raised stage, stand up tall, and talk, while the eyes of the rest were upon him.

The little podium, at center stage, wouldn't hide his arm, no matter how he shifted. . . . "Bob!" the teacher would prod. "Why don't you say what you want to say, instead of shuffling around, and making us all wonder?"

After a while, speech class was like law school—sure, it was hard. But Bob had to be good. No matter what he had to do, no matter what he feared . . . nothing compared to the fear that people would pity him, expect from him any less than the rest, figure they had to cut slack for Bob Dole. It was never going to happen. Getting by was just not enough. He had to graduate from law school with distinction. He had to stand up in speech class and get his point across.

And now, he had a point to make, all over Russell County. He wanted that County Attorney job. He needed it. It didn't matter what he had to do. So anytime Bob could buttonhole a voter, better yet, a dozen, he'd stand up and say what he meant to say:

"Well, I didn't grow up with all the advantages," Bob would begin. "Had to work . . ." And he could almost see heads start to nod, as he bore into it. He never had to mention Dean Ostrum's name. People could fill in the blanks: son of a prominent attorney, had a car to drive to school, didn't play football—probably tennis was more in his line . . . the message was clear enough. Dean Ostrum didn't need that job, not like Bob. Bob Dole came from the world of work, weather, and want, like the farmers who would vote him into office. . . . Dean Ostrum would find a job, and if he didn't, he'd never go hungry. Bob wanted those farmers to know who was their kind, who would understand them, who grew up with Kansas dirt under his nails . . . like theirs. It got so tough out there for Dean, he started wearing frayed shirt collars, just to show he had some. But the people knew who Oscar Ostrum was, just as they knew Doran Dole.

Funny thing about it, Dean knew, too: from the day it came down to him and Bob, Dean figured he was going to lose. Bob Dole would just out-need him, and out-work him, run him into the ground. Dean kept at it, but after a while, it was like the steam just came out of him. Dean knew in his heart, it didn't matter what he did. . . .

"How long was my day?" Dean said, later, when it was just a wistful memory. "I don't know, but it wasn't as long as Bob Dole's. I'm sure of that."

When the votes came in, it was Dole 1,133, Ostrum 948. And Bob Dole was in politics.

— ★ —

They called it the independent oil business, and that was one of the lures for George Bush: it even sounded right. He liked the strange, fierce language of this last American frontier, the barren Texas plain: the land men, promoting a deal, to carve out an override . . . buying mineral, or royalty, at The Spot, over a bowl of red . . . grabbing off a farm-out from a major, or wildcatting a field where there was show, but they plugged and called her a duster. . . .

It was the only foreign language George Bush ever took to. But, for him, its highest incarnation was the honorable title borne by all the young go-getters: *independents* . . . now, that was something to be. That's what he was out here for, and it worked: he won his independence. It wasn't till he'd been a Texan for years, and was an oilman himself, shopping around for investors one day, that anybody thought to introduce him as "Pres Bush's boy. . . ." It sounded so strange, by that time, struck him so odd, that he went home and told Bar about it: first time in *years* he'd heard that.

But, of course, there was more than the name: there were all the truths it implied. It was a perfect business for George Bush—he had everything it took. The first fact was, the business rested entirely on personal relations. The goal of the independent was to put himself in the middle of deals. That meant finding out where deals were being done. You could find out some from the maps, where a dot marked each oil well, and you could find out more from the county land records, which showed who was buying land, or leasing mineral rights, in which tracts, and for how much. But once a deal hit the maps or the courthouse, it was done. What you wanted were deals in the making, the newest geology, the plans of the majors . . . and for that, well, you had to chat up the geologists for the majors, and their scouts, and the ranchers around the countryside, the abstractors around the county courthouse, and your fellow independents . . . you had to ply them, wine and dine them, ask about their kids, be sure to say hey in church. . . . In short, you made friends. And no one would have more friends than George Bush. Once a deal was in the works, it was all done on handshakes—there were no lawyers around a table. Hell, lots of times, there was no table! Your word and your good name were your primary business assets: you had to play by the rules, the code. And no one was more sensitive to the code than Bush. It was like school, but better: the rewards weren't grades, or honors, but cash.

In fact, it was like an eastern boys' school, in those days, in Midland, Texas. Many of the young independents came from back East, from Ivy League schools. The locals called them "the Yalies." Actually, they weren't all Elis. Toby Hilliard and his partner, John Ashmun, were from Princeton, as was Pomeroy Smith—class of '46, was Pom. There was a Princeton Club in Mid-land, with thirteen members. . . . And the Liedtke brothers, Hugh and Bill, were Oklahoma boys, from an established oil family in Tulsa, but they came out of Amherst and Dartmouth. . . . Earle Craig, like Bush, was from Yale. There was an ad hoc Yale Club in Midland, too. And, of course, a Harvard Club—there were dozens of these bright, young Yankees around. They were the best and the bravest of the Ivy League, the boys who weren't going to sit in some office, after they'd seen the world in the war. And smart—they were all smart, it went without saying—but that was another thing about this business: it was better to be lucky than smart. It didn't matter what you knew, or even whom. You could have all the geology on a formation, and production figures from working wells five hundred feet away on every side, and you'd put a hole smack in the middle . . . and nothin', not a drop, a duster. Go figure. . . . So, no matter what else he did, an independent had to roll the dice. At a certain point, you had to trust to your luck. And no one was luckier than Bush.

The third thing about the business had to do with the same hard, dusty fact: everyone bored some dry holes. So, the trick was to drill a *lot* of holes. If you were in one deal, it was make or break; but if you were in forty deals, you'd get production *somewhere*. The essence of the business was activity: new friends, new deals, a sixteenth of an interest here, an eighth there, maybe three thirty-seconds, and you'd carry the friend who got you into it for the drilling costs, down to the casing point. . . . The deals were anything the market would bear: whatever you could get a handshake on. Most of the independents didn't have the capital to act like majors: simply lease the mineral rights under a piece of land, drill the wells, and sell the oil. Instead, they had to do a lot of little deals: maybe leasing mineral rights from a rancher, then running, that very afternoon, to the office of a major to sell that lease for five percent more. Or they'd take on a drilling contractor as a partner, and keep a share of the production, if a well on that lease hit. But even for the littlest players, it was the same game: in general, the business would reward hyperkinesis. And George Bush never could sit still.

In fact, none of those boys could: it was go-go-go, every day during the boom years—and most of the nights. By seven or eight in the morning, you'd see the Yalies hustling up Wall Street (for a long time, the only paved street in town), to The Spot, which was the coffee shop in the Midland Tower, or to Agnes' Café, or the Scharbauer Hotel, with the flush of a big-deal-to-come on their cheeks, and maps under their arms, ready to unfurl on the first table they saw, after which their finger would trace the line of that trap . . . right there, see? . . . while they explained that this thing was surefire! Just barely got in there ahead of those bastards at Texaco! . . . At night, while they sipped beer and barbequed in empty oil drums, they'd talk about one thing—oil—who was buying where, who was drilling, what kind of rock they hit at three thousand feet, and what royalty was fetching now on the west edge of Ector County. They'd dream and scheme and talk about the Big One . . . the one they all meant to hit, the one that would put them on the map. It only took one. That was the beauty of the game. At one party, when all the Yalies gathered (they always were together, it seemed), Toby Hilliard leaned back in a chair and mused to the crowd at large: "You know," said Toby, "some of us in this room are going to be *very, very* rich."

The thing with Bush, it wasn't just about wealth: sure, he wanted to get rich, like anyone else . . . but not private-island rich, Monte-Carlo-in-the-winter rich. What drew him, what he had to have, was the game itself, the great doings . . . so absorbing, so *do-or-die*. This was a game where he could shine! But, alas, by 1950, when he and Bar moved back to West Texas (over two years, Dresser Industries had moved him from Odessa, Texas, to a subsidiary in Huntington Park, California, and then to Bakersfield, then Whittier, then Ventura, then Compton, and, finally, back to Texas . . .), George Bush was not in the game—not really. He was only a salesman of drill bits.

By the time George and Bar came back, the Scurry boom, a couple of counties away, to the northeast, was pumping out a fortune in oil, and the fortune was landing on Midland. Ideco, where Bush was employed, had its warehouse in Odessa. But Odessa was just a blue-collar town, home to rough-necks and equipment engineers (whose sons were perennial champs in the local high school football league). The West Texas offices of the major oil compa-nies, and the brightest of the Yankee independents, were twenty miles north-east, in Midland. That was the place for Bush. . . . Problem was, finding a place. Midland now had *three* paved streets, but almost fifteen thousand souls packed into a town built for half that number. Oil was booming during the war, and for all the years thereafter. But it wasn't till a few years after the war that anyone, or anyone's money, could beg or buy enough wood, steel, or cement to build a block of office space, not to mention a thousand houses. So when the Bushes got back, there was no house. And now they were four. Little Georgie was almost ready for school, and back in one of those godforsaken California towns, he'd been joined by a baby sister, a beautiful little blonde whom George and Bar named Pauline Robinson Bush. Still, best they could do, for the moment, was a ratty motel called, by happenstance, George's Court.

Well, it was a wonderful adventure. They checked in, and every day, Bar-bara Bush would entertain two kids in one room, while George Bush drove the twenty miles southwest on Route 80—as bleak a drive as the U.S. offered; the sandstorms would take paint off your car—to his Ideco warehouse in Odessa, then back, at night, to his wife and kids in their motel. At last, someone built a tract of houses—wrong side of town, and no great shakes: all the same floor plan, 847 square feet (including carport), and an extra slab of cement, called a patio, that was buried in sand whenever the wind kicked up—but hell, they were houses. The tract got the nickname Easter Egg Row, for the way the developer painted these boxes—yellow, green, blue, or pink— mostly so you could tell which was yours. George and Bar bought one for $7,500—a bright blue egg, on a street called Maple. Of course, there wasn't a maple within five hundred miles.

But a lot of the independents were moving into Easter Egg Row. Red and Ferris Hamilton (brothers and proprietors of the Hamilton Oil Co.) lived one street over. Ashmun and Hilliard got an Easter Egg to share, couple of blocks away. John Overbey, who was a Texan, an independent, just starting out, got a house across Maple from George and Barbara Bush. And that was how Bush made his move. Even at the start, it was all about friends. George would get home around six at night, and sometimes, Overbey would get back then, too. George would call him over for a drink, a cold martini on the patio (inside, if the dust was blowing), or maybe burgers from the backyard grill. He'd say to John, "Whad'ja do today?" And Overbey would tell his stories.

Overbey was a land man who'd scout out a likely property and try to cut a deal with the rancher who owned it, for a lease on the mineral rights. Overbey never had a pool of capital, so usually, he'd broker the lease, quick as he could, sell it to a major, or a big independent, who might be interested in drilling there. Sometimes John would take the money and run, maybe make a few hundred dollars over cost. Sometimes he'd sell the lease at cost, but carve out an override: that is, he'd keep a sixteenth or a thirty-second of any future production. The point was, he was in the game, and he always had a story to tell. . . . Maybe, that day, it was a tale of his travels to a dusty little town called Monahans, where he took the local abstractor out for a beer at the only joint in town, and found out Gulf Oil was buying, right there, on the edge of Rattlesnake Air Force Base. Or maybe he'd spent the day on his maps in his office, which was a single room in the old Scharbauer Hotel, which he shared with five fellows, one of whom, Charlie Roberts, always had a crap game going in the back. . . .

"Well, I had a hell of a day," Overbey would start out, after a few sips. "Took a trip downta Rankin . . . piece-a land looked pretty good. Looked like, on the map, like it might be open, so I went down to have a talk with this ol' rancher, Ad Neil . . ."

"Yeah?" Bush was soaking this stuff up.

"Yeah. So, I hunt him up, see if I could get a price outta him. . . . Well, he's brandin' cattle . . . he wouldn't come outta damn corral. So I sat around on his fence half a day . . . *then* the sonofagun wants me buy him a beer, before he'll even *talk* to me."

"So did you?"

"Yep."

You could just about see Bush's eyes shining with the stories, the exotica of old Texas ranchers, the snooping around on the majors, the lure of the game. . . . Poor Bush only had a few stories about the guys he worked with at Ideco, and occasionally something funny some old roughneck would say at a well site, when George Bush stopped by to see if they'd need any bits. But that wasn't the game, no. . . . Overbey, even in his tiny way, was just where Bush wanted to be.

Pretty soon, with every story, he'd be asking Overbey a raft of questions. How much money could you make from a lease like that? Well, what could you have made, if you'd kept it, instead of brokering it? How much would it cost to drill one test there? . . .

Finally, one night, Bush said: "Geez, if I could raise some money, do you think we could do that? . . . Maybe get in business?" Overbey considered the proposition for about thirty seconds, before he said, yeah, he figured they could.

In the short run, money was equal or better than know-how. And money— to be precise, OPM, Other People's Money—was the calling card of the best young Yalie independents. Earle Craig was playing with Pittsburgh money. So were Ashmun and Hilliard. (H.T. "Toby" Hilliard was actually Harry Talbot Hilliard, of the Talbots of Fox Chapel, where the Mellons and friends had their houses.) Hugh and Bill Liedtke were keyed into oil money from Tulsa. Without outside money, you could spend a long while hustling leases before you could call any oil your own. So Overbey would be happy to show Bush everything he knew . . . Bush happily flew east to talk to Uncle Herbie. And Herbie Walker was *delighted* to place a bet on his favorite, Poppy, and to tell his Wall Street friends all about the doings of Pres Bush's boy. Pres himself went in for fifty thousand, along with Herbie, and some of Herbie's London clients, who all got bonds for their investment, along with shares in the new company—Bush-Overbey, they called it. Herbie Walker had decreed the name. After all, it was his money.

It was about $300,000, when they added it all together. So Bush and Overbey rented an office on the ground floor of the Petroleum Building—got it from Fred Turner, an independent who was moving up. But Bush-Overbey only took half—one room (the other was rented to insurance agents). A cautious player was George Bush. He wanted to be in the black every quarter. One room was enough, and a desk for each, two chairs, two typewriters, file cabinets, and a map rack. That was the sum total of equipment of the Bush-Overbey Oil Development Co. They weren't going to sit in the office, anyway.

Soon enough, Overbey had Bush out in his Chevy, plowing through the gritty wind out to Pyote, Snyder, and Sterling City. . . . Overbey had a few irons in the fire, and there was a piece of land right next to a dry hole that actually had a little show—just not enough to make a commercial well. But a half-mile south, now, maybe different story . . . you never could tell. No one was perfectly smart about this . . . it's like old H.L. Brown—Windy Brown, outta Fort Worth—used to say about the Scurry County boom, he used to say: "There was a time, if my land man even drove across that county, I'da fired him." See, you never could tell where the next boom was coming.

And Bush drank this all in, the lore, the lingo, all the names. He and Overbey scurried around, spending Herbie's money, trying to get it back as quick as they could. Kept a sixteenth here, a thirty-second there. . . . And now, Bush had maps under his arm as he breezed into The Spot for lunch. ("Just a bowla red, Helen. Gotta run. . . ." Bush was the first of the Yalies to go local with his diet—bowl of chili and crackers for lunch, chicken-fried steak at night.) Bush got to be a good hand with the records, and he was great on the personal side: people who came by the office to bullshit a minute, on their way somewhere, would find him, in the mornings, typing out friendly notes to people he met the day before. Sometimes, if you didn't have something he ought to hear, you couldn't pull him away from that typewriter for two minutes! He was always on the go, assiduous about the work. He was head of a family of four, steward to his father's money, and his uncle's, and his uncle's friends' . . . a man with rent to pay, a balance sheet to fret into the black . . . a man with a deal to promote—*Hey, this thing is surefire!* . . . a man with stories to tell ("Head geologist for the whole damn *region* gets up in the middle of the meeting . . . and pisses in the sink!") . . . a man twenty-seven years old . . . an independent oilman.

—★—

Well, there never was a County Attorney like Bob Dole. People said it was probably because he had a question in his own mind—could he do it?—that he worked so hard. There never was a time when he wasn't working, seemed like. He'd get to the courthouse, his second-floor office, maybe eight, eight-thirty. Usually, he'd have court in the morning, if the judge was in Russell that day. It wasn't that crime was such a problem—crime like we know it, any-way—but there were disputes about land and water rights, sometimes a bit of cattle rustling. (One fellow asked his neighbor, nice as pie, to borrow his truck one night, then used it to go steal cattle—that's the guts of a burglar: Sheriff Harry Morgenstern caught him at the auction house, with the check still in his pocket, and Bob sent him up the river.) There was always farm thievery and the usual run of drunk and disorderly. . . . In the beginning, Bob would generally go home for lunch, then be back for the afternoon, when he'd go home again, then he'd be back in the office at night. Evenings, he'd try to do his private work: wills and license applications that the farmers brought in. Bob never charged them much—maybe five or ten dollars. He needed friends more than money: there was always another election in two years. Springtime, they'd bring him their tax returns, and Bob would fill them out ("How many those steers d'you sell last fall? . . .") for two bucks, or even free. There was one CPA in Russell, but he had his hands full with the bankers and the oilmen. And Bob didn't mind. He had the time—or he made it. At Dawson Drug, when Chet and Bub would get the fountain clean, get the floor swept and the door locked, maybe eleven at night, they could always look down Main Street and see Bob's light in the courthouse.

Phyllis didn't mind, or said she didn't. She kept busy—in two or three bridge groups. She got Bob to go with her to a Sunday night game, and he was good, but after a while, he didn't have time. They rented a house on Sixth Street, and Phyllis had that to fix up: she did it early American, with stuff all stenciled and hand-painted like they did in New England. No one in Russell had ever seen its like. Phyllis taught some crafts to the local ladies—ceramics: no one in Russell had used that word before. Of course, there were friends, too, and family—Bob's family. Sometimes Phyllis would fill in alone, at Bina's house, for Sunday dinner, or potluck; Bob was working. Bina and Phyllis got along fine. Phyllis even learned, in time, how to make fried chicken. When all that wasn't quite enough, Phyllis took a job, part-time, at a florist's. Bob wasn't happy about that. In those days, if your wife went to work, it said something about you, as a man. But he didn't say anything. It'd be different . . . if they had kids.

It seemed like they never were going to have a child. Phyllis got herself tested, and the doctors didn't see anything they could do. Bob was always ready, in those days, to fear the worst about his own body, and one time, he went all the way to Chicago for tests. (Dr. Kelikian set that up.) But none of the doctors could say what the problem was—if there was a problem. After a while, they figured it just wasn't in the cards . . . maybe they'd adopt, but for that you had to do a home visit, it was part of the routine with the agency in Topeka—and that cost money, and . . . well, it dropped through the cracks, for a while.

Anyway, it wasn't like Bob had time to sit and worry. It seemed like he was always pushing harder, just to see how much he could do. Sometimes, he and Phyllis would go to someone's house for dinner, or bridge, and, come eleven, Bob would stand up and say he had to get back to the office. After midnight— till the bars on the highway closed—Sheriff Morgenstern would drive around, nab a drunk driver or two. And generally, when he got them back to the courthouse, he'd find Bob still at his desk. They'd book the drunks and arraign 'em, right there, 2:00 A.M. . . . Bob figured it was his job to get those cases out of the way. That's how he met Huck Boyd. Huck was a small-town newspaper editor and a Republican bigwig—National Committeeman for the state of Kansas. Anyway, one night Huck was driving through, on his way home to Phillipsburg, in northwest Kansas. Must have been midnight, and Huck looked up, saw a light in the courthouse. He thought there must be a break-in . . . got out of his car and went to investigate, and he found young Bob Dole, working at his desk. County Attorney . . . at midnight! Huck told the story to friends around the state. Meanwhile, he marked that boy Dole as a comer.

That he was. Summertime, when the farmers were lined up with the harvest on Main Street, Bob'd work his way down the row of trucks, just like he used to for Dawson Drug, except this time, he was only saying hello, shaking hands. Sometimes, he wouldn't even make it home for meals—he'd stay downtown for lunch with Harry, the Sheriff, then catch dinner at a Legion affair, or the Rotary. Sometimes, Phyllis used to say, it was like they didn't have time to talk . . .

"What do you wanna talk about?" Bob would say.

She didn't ask about his work. She got that piece of advice from another lawyer's wife, Doc Smith's wife: "Sometimes, it's better not to know." So Phyllis steered clear of his work life. It was just . . . that didn't seem to leave any life for her. When she did catch him, long enough to have a conversation, it was generally whether they were going this weekend to someone's house for dinner, or when Bob was going to get home that night. To which Bob would issue his standard reply, which was: "Depends."

Depends on what?

"On a lotta things."

Thing was, everyone talked about how well Bob was doing: Bina, the Dawsons, the old crowd in general. And Phyllis, for her part, certainly wasn't going to complain: she told her mother, who came to visit, that she loved Kansas— the people in Kansas. Her mother, Estelle, couldn't stand the place—it gave her the creeps, driving through the flat emptiness, past nothing but a thousand telephone poles, and then, on one pole, you'd see a sign: CITY LIMITS. How could you live like that? One time, Estelle and Phyllis's dad drove through Russell, all the way to Denver, and when Estelle came back she announced to the Doles: "Now I understand that cowboy music . . . it's nothing but a howl of human loneliness."

Phyllis was lonely sometimes, too, but she did what she had to—she found plenty to do. One springtime, she devoted weeks to learning how to make sugar Easter eggs. They were tiny, ornate, something she'd never seen before. Finally, one night, when Bob was home for dinner, she showed him: "Look, aren't these wonderful?"

"Yeah," he said, "was it worth walkin' on sugar for two weeks?"

It would be different, she thought, if they had a family. So they filed the papers to adopt in Topeka, but it took a long time, more than a year . . . and by that time, Phyllis found out she was pregnant. Bob and Phyllis had a little girl, whom they named Robin. And Bob was very pleased. He even came home in the evenings, for a while.

16

1953

EVERYBODY showed up for touch football, except Hugh. It was the big event of the week. The fellows would gather Sunday afternoons, after church, at the high school practice field, mostly just to hack around, while the wives on the sidelines peered into one another's prams and talked about houses, schools, and kids. It was a family affair, start to finish. No one brought beer. And no one took the game seriously—save, perhaps, for Bush, who was always the quarterback, and called the plays, did the passing, and most of the running, too.

Sometimes, there was a real game—when they challenged the fellows from Lubbock, for instance. But even that was tongue-in-cheek. The Midland guys named the game the First Annual Martini Bowl. They named their team the Midland Misfits. They even printed a program, with ads from Bush-Overbey, and Liedtke & Liedtke, Attorneys at Law.

Not that Hugh was going to show up. Bill Liedtke would play football with the guys, or tennis, even golf, but brother Hugh, the fellows used to say, only thought about deals: probably worked up deals in his sleep. Hugh and Bill Liedtke, as the ad said, operated as a law firm, but the only legal business they ever did was to bail a few of the Yalies out one night after they got liquored up in someone's apartment and went after the miller-moths with croquet mallets—busted up the walls pretty good. Anyway, three or four of the boys ended up at Sheriff Darnell's jail—and Big Ed's jail was not a place to spend a night, if you could help it. So Bill Liedtke came down to spring them. Of course, Hugh wasn't going to come . . . probably busy thinking up deals.

It wasn't that Hugh was unfriendly. Just seemed like when he was friendly, he always had something in mind. No, to be fair, it was the other way around: he always had something in mind; if he was friendly, that was just bonus. Anyway, you learned pretty quick that behind the deep drawl and jowly grin was a mind that was two or three sharp steps ahead of you, maybe a step or two ahead of what he was telling you. The Liedtke boys had grown up in the business—their father was a lawyer for Gulf, in Tulsa, and well connected there—and the way Hugh thought about the game was different from the rest of the Yalies. With the money from Tulsa, Hugh put Liedtke & Liedtke right into operation of wells. Hugh was buying and selling oil when most of the boys were hustling leases that *might* get drilled, and *might* have oil. Hugh Liedtke was building equity. He didn't talk about the Big One, the quick strike and a gusher of cash. He had a long-term, corporate view of the business. Hugh didn't mind buying into someone else's production. He'd try to work out a deal where he'd pay for the purchase, down the line, with proceeds from the oil he bought. Hell, if it came to that, Hugh wouldn't mind calling a broker in New York, to buy the stock of the company that owned a share of the partnership that owned the oil. He always saw five ways to skin the same cat. One of Hugh's stops in the Ivy League was the Harvard Business School, and what he brought to the West Texas oil fields was not romance, but a genius for finance.

The Liedtke brothers had an office across the street from Bush-Overbey, and, of course, George Bush made friends. Still, it came as a surprise in Midland when Bush let out word that he and Hugh—or, to be precise, the Liedtkes and Bush-Overbey—were going into business together. "I've been talking to Hugh," is the way Bush said it, "and we're going to go the corporate route." It seemed to the other fellows in Midland that with less than two years in the business, George Bush was a bit dewy for Hugh to pick as a partner. As usual, Liedtke had a different view. What he saw was a man who worked hard, who would work with him—maybe he wouldn't bring to the firm long experience, or deep knowledge of the business, but that would come. Hugh had the long haul in mind, and what Bush would bring, right away, was access to East Coast money. That was in the nature of Hugh's proposition: the Liedtkes would raise a half-million dollars, and Bush-Overbey would do the same. What they'd have was a real oil company—a million-dollar outfit—some staff, maybe a geologist . . . in the argot of the game, which Bush so enjoyed, "a little more muscle, a little more stroke."

That they did, when they joined up in March 1953, with Hugh Liedtke as the new company president. George Bush would be vice president. . . .

"What should we call it? . . ."

President Hugh said it had to stand out in the phone book: "It oughta start with A . . . or a Z."

There was a movie playing that week in downtown Midland: *Viva Zapata!*, with Marlon Brando . . . so that's what they fixed on—Zapata, the name of a Mexican rebel *comandante*.

Hugh was right: it did stand out. And at twenty-eight, George Bush was not just in the game, he was on the map. In The Spot, or at the Ranch House, where the guys would kick back over dinner with a couple of drinks, people talked about Bush now in a different tone of voice. Zapata was a player—a clean million in equity. But Bush? . . . For the first time in his life, people talked about George Bush as a man whose résumé may have outpaced his attainments.

"Smartest thing he's done was to hook up with Hugh . . ." someone would say.

"Yep. Ol' Hugh, though: he's the one who makes the snowball . . . and he throws it."

"Yeah . . . bring s'more snow, George."

Even a year later, when the other independents learned, to their shock, to their admiration, and later still, to their envy, that Liedtke and Bush had bet it all on one roll of the dice—$850,000 on one lease—no one made much point of crediting Bush's steady faith, his assiduous work, his hyperactive friendliness . . . or even the good fortune that had followed him through three decades.

They leaned back in lawn chairs, around the barbecue in someone's backyard, and shrugged: "Well," they said, "that's Hugh . . ."

Of course, by that time, no one who'd been close to Bush would have talked about his Great and Good Godly fortune—not that year . . . not at all.

— ★ —

They called her Robin, but her full name was Pauline Robinson Bush—named for Barbara's mother, who died in 1949, in a car accident, with her husband at the wheel. Marvin and Pauline Pierce had left home together one morning. Pauline took along a cup of coffee. As he drove, Barbara's father saw the coffee start to slide on the dash. He lunged to steady the cup, but he lost control of the car, hit a stone wall. He was hospitalized with broken ribs. Pauline was killed.

Bar did not go to New York for the funeral. She was seven months pregnant, and her father insisted she stay home and take care of herself. It was five days before Christmas when Bar gave birth to Robin. She would always remember the sight: it was the only birth for which Bar was awake, to watch, as her daughter came into the world.

Robin was still an infant when the Bushes moved back to Texas, just a toddler when George Bush swung full-time into business as an independent. Bar took care of the two kids, Georgie and Robin, in the house on Easter Egg Row, and then, in 1953, another child arrived, John Ellis Bush, whose name father George initialized: J.E.B. They called him Jebbie.

Among the Yalies in Midland, everybody kept having kids. It seemed the natural way of things: at the time, Bar didn't think twice about her choices in life. It was decades later, when she looked back and labeled her state of mind in Midland as "dormant . . . just dormant." Or when, with a shrug, she dismissed all the might-have-beens and ought-to-have-beens with a smile of ironic self-mockery. "In a marriage," Bar said, "where one is so willing to take on responsibility, and the other so willing to keep the bathrooms clean . . . that's the way you get treated." (Of course, by that time, too, Bar had perfected her own power of mindset: she could have gone back to college, she said. George would have applauded. But she did not go back, and did not look back. . . . "I think," Barbara Bush said, "people who regret something they did not do are liars.")

At the time, 1953, what she knew was, she was plenty busy, getting Georgie off to school in the morning, and getting Robin, who was still home all day, set up for play, and feeding the baby, Jebbie. . . . She'd wonder later, if she hadn't been so busy, would she have noticed sooner?

She never saw the little bruises on Robin's legs, or never observed them— every child got banged up playing. What she noticed, what worried her, was when Robin would not play. "What are you going to do today?" Bar asked her little girl.

"I'm either going to lie on the bed and look at books, or I'll lie on the grass, and watch the cars . . ."

That's when Bar took Robin to the pediatrician: Why should a three-year-old want to lie around all day? The doctor, a family friend, Dorothy Wyvell, didn't tell Bar her diagnosis. "Why don't you come back this afternoon, with George?" That rattled Barbara, sure enough.

She tracked down George at the Ector County Courthouse, where he was digging into land records. That afternoon, Dr. Wyvell told them that Robin was very sick. She had leukemia.

It didn't sink in with George—not at first. He said: "Well, what do we do?" Dr. Wyvell started to cry.

"Well, what's the next *step*?" he insisted.

She told him there was no next step. Or, at least, she offered her advice, which was: do nothing. And tell no one. Just make Robin's time the best she could have. The child only had weeks to live.

George Bush, young man about business, could not believe it. He refused to believe it. He called his uncle, John Walker, a cancer specialist in New York, president of Memorial Hospital.

"I just had," Bush said, "the most ridiculous conversation . . ." and he told Johnny Walker what Dr. Wyvell said.

"Why don't you bring her up here . . . have her looked at," Dr. Walker said. He'd arrange treatment by cancer specialists at the Sloan-Kettering Foundation. But, he warned his nephew, Dr. Wyvell might be right: leukemia was a killer. In '53, doctors had no sure way . . . in fact, little hope, of reversing it.

Bush kept replaying that conversation where he heard it was helpless, hopeless . . . he *could not do anything for his daughter.* . . . It was incredible. What was he supposed to do? Just take it? Sit on his hands?

"You'll never live with yourself if you don't treat her," John Walker told him over the phone. George, Bar, and Robin were on the plane for New York the next day.

That began a roller-coaster ride that went on for months. Bar was in New York, full-time, and George was father and mother in Texas, until the weekends, when the boys would stay with neighbors while George flew to New York to join his wife and daughter. The doctors at Sloan-Kettering gave Robin an experimental drug—it was new that year . . . no one could promise . . . but she got better . . . she could eat, she sat up, she could play . . . doctors called it remission. And after a couple of months, Bar and Robin were home in Midland. . . . But then the child started to sink again, and the drug was no help, the roller-coaster screamed downhill, Robin and Bar went back to New York, and George was flying back and forth.

It was hell for all of them, but George was the one who just could not stand it. Bar made a rule that there would be no crying in front of Robin: Bar meant to make her daughter's days happy ones. And she did: Bar stayed with Robin hour after hour, playing with her, reading to her, tickling her, talking, holding her as she slept, smoothing her blond hair. Barbara Bush stayed with her daughter through it all. Like an oak in the wind, she was tossed, but she would not be moved. No one in Midland, or in New York at the hospital, ever saw Barbara Bush cry, through seven months, while her daughter slipped away. George could not sit and take it like that. He marveled at his wife's strength—it was beyond strength, it was heroic, an act of will and love that he could not match. He could not look at his daughter without fighting tears, and a helpless rage, or despond that he could not bear. He was so grateful to have work to do, places to be, people to see. He'd burst out of that house in the morning like a man trapped in smoke lunges toward fresh air. Sometimes, he'd stop at church to say a prayer. Then he'd immerse himself in the game, the cares of the living.

Of course, he could not follow Dr. Wyvell's counsel of silence, either: everyone in Midland knew . . . all their friends, and their families. Some of the friends in Midland gave blood for Robin's transfusions. When Bar and Robin were home from New York, Betty Liedtke, Hugh's wife, would come to the house almost every day. And she'd cook, hoping to tempt Robin to eat . . . and tempting Barbara, who might not have thought of food for herself. In New York, Barbara had her own family to support her. She stayed with George's grandparents, just blocks from the hospital. Her old friends, and George's, were everywhere around. From Greenwich, George's mother, Dorothy Bush, sent a nurse to Texas, to be with George and the boys. And Prescott Bush, newly elected to the United States Senate, called Bar one day, to come out with him in Connecticut. He said he wanted her help, picking out his gravesite. And gently, he led her through the cemetery, until they found a lovely spot . . . a place, Prescott said, where he would be comfortable . . . and there he planted a hedge, *a bush* . . . of course, that was just his tender way of making a place for Robin.

Uncle Johnny Walker was at the hospital every day. He was more than counsel, he was inspiration: his own career as a surgeon had been cut short, a few years before, by polio, and doctors said he'd never walk again, but John

Walker not only made a second career in business at the G.H. Walker firm, he also served medicine as president of Memorial Hospital—and with crutches he got around New York, every day, on the subway. In the end, in October, it was Dr. John Walker who tried to tell Bar: she could let Robin go. The girl was failing, the cancer drugs had eaten holes in her stomach. She was bleeding inside. She was very weak. The Sloan-Kettering doctors wanted to operate: they thought they might stop the bleeding . . . anyway, they knew so little about these cases, they wanted to try. . . . Bar was twenty-eight years old, and this, she had to decide alone. George was in the air, on his way to New York.

"You don't have to do it," Dr. Walker told Bar.

But Bar felt she had to. Those doctors were half killing themselves, trying to save Robin. And there was always hope—wasn't there? She gave the go-ahead, and the surgeons went to work.

But Robin never came out of the operation. George was there that night, when Robin died. She was two months short of her fourth birthday. George and Bar did not bury her, but left her for the doctors at Sloan-Kettering. They wanted her death to mean something for other children who would face this, in years to come.

After Robin died, the world changed for Barbara Bush. All at once, the unfairness, the pain and loss, came crashing down on her and she was without strength, without will. It was George now who took her in hand. And he did what he thought best: the day after Robin died, it was George who went to the hospital, to thank everybody who had worked on his child. And then, in Rye, he took Bar to the club, and they played golf.

Barbara was lost in her grief. It was only George who kept her going. After Robin's death, he was released, to act, to keep moving. He knew so well how to do that. And he would not let his wife sink into her mourning. They had to go on, he told her. But for a while, she did not know how. He was like a man holding on to her at the cliff edge: they had to keep moving, to live—there were the boys . . . there was him! There was their life, still, to live! . . . In later years, she always gave him credit for saving her, for saving them. Somewhere, she learned a statistic: two-thirds of the couples who lose a child, as they did, end up divorced from the strain and the grief, the guilt and blame . . . but not George and Barbara Bush. They were stronger, and she always blessed him for that. Sometimes, when she thought back, she would tell of the critical moment for her . . . it was so strange, and small, when she told it, she was sure no one would quite understand, but that was the instant she turned away from the cliff edge.

It was the day of the memorial service, and the house was filling with friends and family, and Bar was upstairs getting ready, in the bedroom . . . but she wasn't getting ready. She could not. She could not *get* herself to go down those stairs, to face all those people, and have the sad wound in her opened to them . . . she just *could not* go down there. Did he know? Hard to say. He was not urging her, or even looking at her. George was standing at the window, looking over the yard and the walk, his lanky form silhouetted in the light . . . as he watched Bar's sister, Martha, and her husband, Walter Rafferty, coming toward the front door. And he said, as if to himself, just one of his wry play-by-plays . . . with a hint of an Irish brogue: "Ah, here come the O'Raffertys. It's goin' to be a helluva wake!"

With that, somehow, it came to her, penetrated her pain: there he was, her George, and he was so . . . all right. They both were. They had so much. . . . It didn't stop the pain. Back in Texas, the pain would be a physical presence, an ache inside . . . but she would go on.

As for George, he seemed never to doubt, never to waver, from the instant Robin was lost to them. He always seemed to have the articles of faith he'd taken from his mother's breakfast readings. Life was good. Life was for the living. Good things happened to good people. It wasn't so much what he said, as how he lived. The point was, to keep moving, doing, turned ever outward: when Bar and he flew back to Midland, George Bush did not take them home, but directly from the airport to the houses of their friends—all over town, visiting friends. . . . He said it would be hard for people to come to them, in that situation, and he wanted so much to tell people, thank you.

— ★ —

And he was moving. That was the moment he and Hugh Liedtke rolled the dice. There was a big swatch of land in Coke County, about eighty miles from Midland, and Sun Oil had wells, producers, on a parcel just to the east. Zapata bet $850,000—for all practical purposes, Hugh and George bet everything—on the proposition that a huge pool of oil extended west under eight thousand acres of sand.

Two-thirds of that lease, called the Jameson field, was owned by a Wichita Falls outfit called Perkins-Prothro. But the other third was held by an oilman named Green, who worked out of San Angelo. When Green wanted to sell his interest, Hugh Liedtke wanted that lease. Problem was, a couple of independents out of Midland beat him to it. Bob Wood and Leland Thompson got in there and made a deal with Green a week ahead of Zapata. But Hugh always saw five ways to skin the same cat: he and George Bush worked out a deal to pay Wood and Thompson $50,000 and *then* carry them for a quarter interest. . . . Zapata had its deal.

How could they be so sure? They could not. You never really knew until you drilled each hole. They had some geologists working for them now, and there was a senior geologist, just retired from Gulf, whom George and Hugh kept taking to lunch . . . but still, you could never *know*. Call it instinct, or faith (good things happen . . .), but no one among the independents in Midland ever bet it all like that. No one in their crowd had done that before.

So they drilled—Perkins-Prothro was the official operator on-site—and probably sank another hundred or a hundred twenty-five thousand on that . . . and they hit.

So they drilled again . . . and they hit. And drilled again . . . and they hit. The way books were kept in the game, there were two classes of drilling expense. The first was capital expense, which was the wellhead, and the pump, the pipe and like tangibles, all of which could be depreciated over a ten-year term. The second class was called intangibles, and covered things like rental of a drilling rig, special mud to lubricate the drill bits, diesel fuel to operate the rig, labor costs . . . and all of that was written right off the top of your taxes. With a setup like that, it almost paid you to keep drilling.

So they did . . . another hole . . . and they hit. And another, and another . . . and they hit.

In the span of a year, Zapata and Perkins-Prothro drilled seventy-one holes . . . and seventy-one of them hit. By the end of that year, they were pumping out 1,250 barrels of oil each day, at that time worth about $1.3 million a year. By the time the Jameson field was fully drilled, the partnership had bored 127 holes . . . and 127 wells produced.

George and Hugh were the first of the Midland independents to be worth a million apiece. All the fellows talked about them . . . well, mostly they talked about Hugh. It was hard to talk *to* him anymore. Never around—too busy. George Bush they still saw—hadn't changed a bit. Except now, you wouldn't find him hanging around The Spot. He might take his lunch at the Petroleum Club. Sometimes he'd go with John Overbey—probably neither one was a member, but they'd go on Bush's invite. Overbey had dropped out of Zapata— didn't have much taste for the corporate business, went back to what he knew, which was land work, and leasing . . . dropped off too early, as it happened. He lost out. But George Bush never lost a friend. Bush also teamed up with Bob Wood, one of the fellows who snuck in a week ahead on that Jameson deal, and those two started the Commercial Bank and Trust Company. Bush wasn't quite thirty years old. Meanwhile, Zapata built its own office building in Midland. And hired more staff . . . a little more stroke. And George and Bar got a new house, and then another, a bigger house. And then, they were the first of their crowd to have a swimming pool. . . . And George Bush really liked that—everybody came over.

17

The
Night of
the Bronco

THE FIRST THING you've got to know about Joe is the house. Probably the first thing he'd show you, anyway. You talk with Biden about anything . . . somehow, it gets back to home. And the house is gorgeous, an old du Pont mansion, in the du Pont neighborhood called Greenville, outside Wilmington. It's the kind of place a thousand Italian guys died building—hand-carved doorways, a curving hand-carved grand staircase that Clark Gable could have carried a girl down, a library fit for a Carnegie, or Bernard Baruch, someone like that. And a ballroom—can't forget the ballroom. And a living room, about half an acre, and a bathroom upstairs the size of a gym, and all dusty rose outside, with beautiful brickwork over the windows, black shutters, white porches, a fountain, a pool . . . the place is drop-dead *stately.*

Joe found it one night, a couple of years after he became a Senator. He was driving around, like he did back then. He was snooping around Greenville, streets of his dreams, when he saw it, all overgrown, boarded up. Some developer was going to knock it down because the four and a half acres were worth more than the house. The du Ponts couldn't take care of the place! . . . But Joe had to have a look, so he pulled in, and shinnied up a pole in the darkness, onto a second-floor porch, and broke in through the plywood. And when he came out a few minutes later, he had to have it.

Joe did a $200,000 deal for the house. That was more than he had, of course. But Biden never let money stand in the way of a deal. He got in the developer's face and started talking—fast. Joe can literally talk fast. It's like the stutter left it all pent up, and when he starts talking deal, he goes at a gallop. But the

beautiful thing is the *way* he talks deal. By the time Joe's finished talking, it
wouldn't matter if he didn't have a thousand dollars cash . . . in fact, that no
one would see any cash, for *years.* When Joe Biden gets going on a deal, he'll
talk that deal until it's shimmering before your eyes in God's holy light
. . . like the Taj Mahal. . . . *Where do I sign?*

Anyway, when he moved in, he started finding out about the place. First
winter, first three months, he used three thousand gallons of fuel oil. The top
of the house was wide open. Squirrels were living on the third floor. So the
second year, he had to get storm windows for the whole place. Of course, he
didn't have the money, so he had to sell off a couple of lots. He lived in fear
that the place would need a new $30,000 slate roof. Meanwhile, the place was
chock full of asbestos. He had to hire a guy to clean that out, but the guy
wanted too much money for labor. So there were weeks when Joe was down
in the basement, in a moon suit, ripping out asbestos.

When he moved in, the old winding driveway led from Montchan Drive. But
Joe couldn't buy all the land that held the right of way, and then he pissed
off the owner of the front lot, who put boulders in the driveway . . . so Joe
had to build a new one around the front—which was great because everybody
who drove in would have to see the whole place. But he didn't have the money
to get that paved, so it turned to soup when the weather went bad . . . and
anyway, he sold the corner lot that held the start of that driveway, so he had
to build a *third* driveway—a little one in the back that he could actually use.
But he never liked that dumpy little third one, so eight years later he made
a deal with the new owner of the front lot—cost him another fortune in
landscaping—but he got the original driveway back.

He killed one riding mower a year. He'd let the grass get three feet high,
until he was going to have someone over, or a function at the house, or
something . . . then he'd attack with his riding mower, which had been out
in the rain for six months. "These damn things aren't built right," he'd complain. "I gotta find one that works."

Upstairs, the third floor was still driving him crazy. At one point, he was
going to lop off the whole thing. Brought in the architects for plans and
everything. Why not? The house, the world, were malleable to his will. Then,
he decided he'd keep the third floor, but close it off, with its own heating plant
and a separate entrance. He could rent it. Maybe offices. He'd make a mint!
He brought the architects back, and a contractor. Then he thought of the
strangers around his home. He couldn't stand that. No strangers were going
to tromp around his dream world.

Next, he envisioned a scheme where he'd take the ballroom, library, the
entry hall and the carved staircase, the dining room, the living room, and *he'd
have them disassembled.* Then he'd have those rooms reassembled, *just like
they were,* in a house that was smaller, and new, and wouldn't be so hard to
run. See? Then he'd stick in wallboard where the great rooms had been and
he'd sell the big place. So he brought back the architects and the contractor
. . . but it was too hard, so he stayed.

Meanwhile, he planted. He liked hemlock trees. He found some old Czech guy who ran a nursery up in Pennsylvania. Joe didn't want any three-foot saplings, no. This guy had big hemlocks. Rhododendron bushes, great ones. Yews—big old yews! See, Joe had to have privacy. When he started having to sell off lots, he had to plant more, so he'd have privacy. When he found this old nurseryman, Joe went bananas. . . .

Joe kept asking: "What's the biggest you've got?"

Twenty-foot hemlocks! Bushes! Huge bushes! A ton of dirt around the bottom of each.

His pal Marty was with him that day: Marty Londergan, a dentist, Joe's buddy from high school. "Joe," Marty said. "How we gonna get all this shit back?"

"Get a truck," Joe said. Like everybody's brother had a forty-foot flatbed in the garage.

"Yeah," Marty said. "Who's gonna drive it?"

"I'll drive," Joe said. "Used to drive 'em all the time."

Sure enough, Marty found somebody's brother who'd lend a truck, and Joe drove the thing, overloaded, rocking and pitching, with trees hanging off the tail, down the back roads, an hour and a half, back to Wilmington. Then he started digging—a forty-five-foot trench, three feet deep and three feet wide, through blacktop and paving stones. He was out there in gym shorts and hiking boots, sweating like a pig, with the headlights of four cars shining upon his ditch, with Jill leaning out the window to yell, "Come to bed, honey!" . . . while an old friend or two propped the trees and bushes up in the ditch, so Joe could wall away his realm.

"No, tighter!" Joe'd say.

"I don't know, Joe . . ."

"Tighter," Joe said. He had to have privacy. The rhododendrons, he planted them two feet apart. Next weekend, he's back for yews. He built a wall of yews around the swimming pool. Never mind there was no room for them to spread their roots.

"Whaddya think?" Joe asked, grinning.

Two years, of course, they're all dead.

But every time he sold a lot, he needed more trees. When people actually built on the lots, he couldn't stand it. He spent thousands of dollars on a stockade fence around the whole place, a mile of fence. His friends started calling the place Fort Apache. But Joe had to have it. The day he got it all up, the neighbors began to complain. He had to take it all down.

And each time he'd get a new scheme for more privacy, he'd have to sell another lot.

After a while, he was down to three acres. One day, his friends came over to find the swimming pool area staked off. Joe was going to sell that land as a lot, and pick up the pool and move it. "Whaddya think?" Joe said.

"I think you're fuckin' crazy."

The thing is, he never did get it sorted out. And now his older son, Beau, was getting ready for college, and Hunter, the second son, was just a year behind. And, of course, Joe hasn't got cash—whatever he gets, the house eats for breakfast. That house *loves* cash. . . .

So that's why Joe decided he had to have another house. This time it was seventeen acres, a $1.1 million estate . . . an enormous main house with a sauna in the master bath, a swell apartment over the four-car garage . . . and the outdoor pool had a separate cabana that was, itself, like a nice, suburban home . . . and then, there was the tennis house, with the *other* sauna, and the *indoor* pool, and, of course, the indoor tennis court.

He had the thing all gamed out in his head, the way he always did before he made a move, and he could *see* it, with his parents in the apartment, maybe brother Jimmy would build onto the little house, or take a couple of acres, build something new . . . Joe and Jill and the kids would take the big one, and then a guest house . . . it was a compound, it was . . . *Hyannisport!* He could see the goddam thing in *Life* magazine, he could just about lay out the photos *right now* . . . touch football on the grass, the house fuzzy in the background, him and his brothers, and the boys, sharp, in white—no, blue jeans!—with Beau-y running out for a pass, which Joe would throw—on a line, tight spiral—maybe catch the damn ball spinning in the air, if the photographer was any good. . . . The Bidens. First Family.

It was beautiful. And he could do it! He could make the deal! . . . That's what his guys were afraid of. The sonofabitch was just crazy enough to do it. That's why they came up to Wilmington that night, that January—to tell Joe he couldn't have the new house. And that's how it began: The Night of the Bronco.

— ★ —

But wait. Consider for a moment the deal and what it took. Not the money, or, rather, the paper flying back and forth—Joe could explain that, no one else could. Consider the psychic foundations of the deal, the pillars of its possibility.

There was (to be perfectly blunt, as Joe would say) a breathtaking element of balls. Joe Biden had balls. Lot of times, more balls than sense. This was from the jump—as a little kid. He *was* little, too, but you didn't want to fight him—or dare him. There was nothing he wouldn't do. Joe moved away from Scranton, Pennsylvania, in '53, when he was ten years old. But there are still guys in Scranton today who talk about the feats of Joey Biden. There was, for example, The Feat of the Culm Dump.

Culm is the stuff they pile up next to the mine after they've taken out the coal. Every mine shaft in Scranton had a mountain of culm, and in the fifties, when people weren't so picky about the air, the stuff was always on fire. There was just enough coal carbon left in the soot to cause spontaneous combustion; pile would burn for twenty, thirty years. So what you had, for instance, at the Marvin Colliery, down the hill from Green Ridge, three or four blocks from Joey's house, was a mountain on fire, lava-hot on the surface, except where it burned out underneath, and then there'd be a pocket of ash where you could fall right into the mountain, if you stepped on it . . . but, of course, no one was going to step on it . . . until Charlie Roth bet Biden five bucks that Joey couldn't climb the culm dump.

Actually, Charlie bet two guys: Joey and his friend Tommy Bell. And they both started up the black mountain, but Tommy got to the first swath of fire, and the flames were a foot away from his feet, and he thought about the voids under ash above—it was maybe two hundred feet to the top, maybe twenty-five million tons of burning soot—and Tommy thinks: *What the hell am I DOING?* . . . There is no way in *hell,* not a Chinaman's *chance* in hell, that Charlie Roth is going to part with five dollars. Charlie did have a paper route. Maybe he had a couple of singles, but . . . to this day, Joe Biden has never seen the five bucks. Of course, by the time he got to the top, the five bucks wasn't the point anymore. It was more like . . . immortality.

That was certainly the point in the horrifying incident of The Dump Truck. This was a feat of Joey Biden that is still talked about in hushed tones, with rueful shakes of the head. Regret weighs most heavily on Jimmy Kennedy, who is a parent now, and a judge, and an upstanding citizen in every regard . . . but who was four or five years older than Joe, and the one who dared him to run under the wheels of the moving dump truck. Thing was, Kennedy never, *never*—NO CHANCE—thought the kid would *do* it . . . but Joey did it. The dump truck was loaded to the gills and backing up—not too fast—and Joey was small, only eight or nine, and he ran under the truck from the side, between the front and back wheels . . . then let the front axle pass over him. If it *touched* him, he was finished—marmalade—but Joey was quick. The front wheels missed him clean.

Joey was always quick, with a grace born of cocky self-possession. He didn't—like some kids that age—doublethink himself, so his movements got jerky and he screwed up . . . no. Once Joey set his mind, it was like he didn't think at all—he just did. That's why you didn't want to fight him. Most guys who got into a fight, they'd square off, there'd be a minute or so of circling around, while they jockeyed for position. Joey didn't do that. He decided to fight . . . BANGO—he'd punch the guy in the face. Joe was kind of skinny, and he stuttered, and the kids called him Bye-Bye, for the way he sounded when he tried to say his name. But Joey would never back down, and he knew how to box, when no one else did. His father must have taught him—just the kind of thing Mr. Biden would know—manly art, and all that. So Joey got into fights, and BANG—it was over quick.

What he was, was tough from the neck up. He knew what he wanted to do and he did it. That's why he was the center of the wheel with the guys in Green Ridge, even with the stutter—might have beaten another kid down . . . not Joe. Even after he left, after Mr. Biden got the job selling cars in Wilmington and moved the family away, Charlie Roth would still (in moments of duress) tell guys that his friend Joey Biden would come back and beat them up, if they didn't watch out. (When Joe did come back, Charlie always had a list.) But it wasn't just fights: if you could run, Charlie, or Larry Orr, or someone, would say Joe Biden could run faster. If you had a dog, they'd say Joe's dog, King, could murder your dog. Joe was the guy they turned to when the question arose: What are we gonna do? Joe always had an answer.

Sometimes, Saturdays, they'd go to the Roosevelt Theater, where the matinee, a double feature with a serial adventure, cost twelve cents—but they'd try to sneak in, anyway. When the villain was creeping up in evil ambush on the rocks behind Hopalong Cassidy, Joe was the one who'd stand in the darkened theater to yell: "LOOK OUT HOPPIE! HERE HE COMES!" But the best part was coming back from the Roosie: with the route Joe led them on, it always took hours. If they'd managed to sneak in and still had their money, it could take an hour just to get to the corner: stops at the Grace Farms Dairy for milkshakes, and Mueller's Drug Store for candy, and the Big Chief Market, just to raise hell. Then they'd head off, reenacting the movie on the way home, through the alleys, over lawns; they never used the streets, never touched a sidewalk. They climbed all the fences, cut through the backyards . . . if it was a western, they were the posse . . . up on garage roofs, along the top of the wall at Marywood College . . . after war movies, they were up against the Nazis . . . climbed a tree here, to get over the fence, or used the latch on a gate, or the garbage cans, for a boost (knocked one over back there, too), down past Joey's house into the woods, and back across Maloney Field, where sometimes they played Little League ball . . . and today, staged the final shootout: the bad guy dead in the dust on Main Street . . . High Noon . . . but actually, it was almost dark when they got home.

Here is another game Joey devised: the sisters at Marywood College were building a new arts building, with a big theater, and at one end, behind the stage, where the sets and scenery would hoist up out of sight, the building would rise to a height of six stories. The builders were raising the steel beams with thick hemp ropes that held them in place until the riveters could secure the steel. Joe's game was to climb the superstructure to the top, where you could edge out on a girder eighteen inches wide, maybe fifty or sixty feet in the air, and then you'd grab the rope and swing out over the stones and cinderblock, out over where the seating would be, screaming through the air, to the end of the rope's reach, after which you'd come flying back toward the steel beams. Of course, Biden was the first to do it. He was ten. But he'd seen a Tarzan movie . . . anyway, Joey had imagination.

That was the imagination that went into the real estate deal, or this President deal—same thing. Imagination was the essence of his method, the first and most crucial step: Joe got the picture in his head, like he was already there, and he knew how it was going to be . . . and most important, *how he would be.* Joe was continually creating himself. This was how he made things happen. . . . Then, once he made that imagination into fact, once he made his move . . . BANGO—that defined the game. Others could only react. Same in fights, games, politics, real estate, love—imagination.

In '72, when he was twenty-nine, and a County Councilman, working and voting, like any Councilman, on planning and zoning, sewer bonds, paving contracts, and stop lights . . . no one in Delaware could see Joe Biden moving, by one giant leap of imagination, into the United States Senate. Hell, no! Not against Cale Boggs—an institution, a man beloved in Delaware, a man who had won seven straight elections, who had held statewide office for *twenty-five years*. There was no Democrat who even wanted to run against Boggs. But Joe could see it—had seen it already, a thousand times in his head—how Boggs would wake up one morning and find Joe Biden breathing down his neck. And most important, how Joe would be, how he'd look: young, handsome, smart, self-assured. And the way he'd act, toward Senator Boggs: respectful, friendly, fond, like a grandson . . . *who knew the old man wasn't quite up to it anymore*. . . .

Joe could see the thing whole in his head, and what's more, he could talk it. Not too often—he didn't let most people in on a vision, but family . . . Neilia, of course: he joked that his wife was the brains of the family, but it wasn't all joke. And Val, his sister, twenty-seven, who was the manager of his campaign. And Jimmy, his brother, who was twenty-four—he was the fund-raiser. Of course, in that family, no one ever doubted Joe. But then, too, every once in a while, Joe would let in people from the outside, people he needed, people who had to believe. And then Joe would get to talking fast, with conviction—something near joy in his voice—and he'd haul them along, until they could feel his belief like a hand on their backs, until they could see it as he could, until the thing was shining in the air . . . and they only hoped they were good enough to be with him, there, at the end. . . . You could feel the thing happen in the room—the "connect." People called it the Biden Rush.

The funny part was, the people who saw him—the press, the political pros—only talked about the last stop of the train: they praised his "oratory," but wondered whether there was any thought behind the waves of stirring words. Even his own guys—the experts and consultants buzzing around this honeypot—talked about him like a wild stallion who'd never felt the bridle. They said they were with Biden because he could "connect," he could "move the people." Of course, now that they'd signed on, he'd also have some direction, some savvy. . . . That only fed the common wisdom that Biden was an unguided missile. Every week or so, his experts were quoted ("Don't use my name, huh? . . ."), analyzing his appeal under headlines like: THE POLITICS OF PASSION. . . . But it didn't feel like passion to Joe. Not the way they meant it. Not when it was working. What he wanted it to feel like was the organized emotion of a football play—practiced for months, until it was clockwork—where he knew, where he *saw* in his mind, before the snap of the ball, how he'd run, exactly twenty yards down the field, where he'd feint for the goalpost and cut to the sideline . . . like it already *happened,* he saw how he'd plant his left foot . . . saw the tuft of grass that his cleats would dig into . . . the look on the cornerback's face . . . as he left (as he would leave) that sonofabitch *in the dust*!

In the end, when you took it apart, it all rested on Joe's certainty. He tried to tell his experts and gurus: he had to see the moves. He wanted to play them out in his head, with scenes, with dialogue . . . until he had worked them, refined them, rehearsed every line . . . until he was sure what would happen. Joe called that process "gaming it out"—and it went on continuously in his head. Then, once he'd seen . . . he could do anything, he could stoke the fire hot enough to get the "connect," he could swing out to the end of that rope. That was his view of his history, even the stuff that looked so ballsy: never had a doubt in his head that he could wiggle under the bumper of that truck, get to the top of that culm dump . . . that he could fly over the earth from those girders (he'd been looking at those hemp ropes for weeks) . . . that the owner of that house would take a half-million pullback (he knew what the sonofabitch paid for the place) . . . that Cale Boggs could not react in time (Biden was at three percent in the polls when he rented the best and biggest ballroom in the state for his "victory celebration").

Once he'd seen . . . then it was singing in his head, and he didn't have to think . . . he just did. He knew what was supposed to happen. Hell, it was a *done deal* . . . and then it wasn't imagination, or even balls. Not to Joe Biden. It was destiny.

—★—

That was the problem. So, Ridley and Donilon came up to Wilmington that night, one week into 1987, to tell Joe he couldn't buy the new house. Actually, they had a few things to straighten out. For instance, was Joe going to run? (They couldn't seem to get a clear answer.) If so, what was he doing for the last two weeks on vacation in Hawaii with Pat Caddell? And if he meant to run, what the hell was he trying to pull with a one-point-one-million-dollar house?

It was an odd summit on the shape of Joe's life. Tim Ridley was thirty-one years old and had worked with Biden for about three months—signed on last October as Joe's new Administrative Assistant, after a four-hour Biden Rush—and now he was supposed to manage the Presidential campaign that Joe wasn't sure he was going to make . . . and supposed to make peace among a half-dozen experts, gurus, and self-appointed Rasputins, who all wanted to run the campaign that might not happen . . . who all loved Joe, and all mistrusted each other, and Joe wasn't sure about any of them . . . and now Ridley had a U.S. Senator in rut for a real estate deal that would sink the whole ship anyway.

"Look, Senator," Ridley said, earnestly. "In the mind of a voter, there's *no way* you get from a Senator's seventy-five thousand a year . . . to a million-and-a-half-dollar *estate.*"

"One-point-one . . ." Joe said absently. "I said I could *sell* it for a million-and-a-half." He was in his big chair, listening. Ridley and Donilon were on the couch in Joe's study. Joe had offices, three or four of them, but the serious stuff happened at his home, in the study during the colder months, on the side porch during the summer.

"One-point-one, one-point-five, whatever you say . . . it *doesn't matter.*" Donilon had his face set in its grimmest lines—which were not too grim, when you looked at his baby cheeks and the friendly half-smile that always played on his mouth. Donilon knew about campaigns. He was also thirty-one, but he'd started as a Carter field man at age twenty-three. He lived with Mondale on the road for years, shared the same hotel suite, watched the guy walk around in his underpants, chomping a cigar and fuming about his campaign. Donilon was a lawyer, smart, and tough enough. But you didn't see it right away because of that baby face . . . no matter what he said. It was like getting a lecture from the Pillsbury Doughboy.

"You can't run as a Democrat, a guy who's in touch with middle-class values, when you're on TV in your *indoor tennis court.* How the hell do we explain it to Brooks Jackson?"

Brooks Jackson was *The Wall Street Journal* guy who made a specialty of candidates' finances. Joe seemed to brighten at the name. Brooks Jackson was the one guy who *would* understand. "C'mere, I'll show you how we tell him. C'mere!"

And he took the boys over to a table, where he had the plans of the place, and the numbers, and he started talking deal. This house was going to make Joe rich! . . . "See, with a four-hundred-fifty-thousand pullback, and the fifty up front—that's all up front—that means, with the interest and all, and the balloon, in '91, I'm only paying, cash, five hundred thousand. I got this place listed for seven-ninety-five! And for the rest, I sell two pieces, I already got 'em sold, see—here, and here; I sell this, that's gone—and that's three hundred fifty thousand right there, so . . ."

Ridley was looking at the plans while Joe kept moving money in his head. Ridley stared at the block marked "Tennis House," thinking, "Oh, my God, migod, migod . . ." and he thought of the headlines, like he always did when there was trouble coming: JOE BIDEN'S NET GAME . . . DOWN AND OUT WITH BIDEN . . . because in his right ear Ridley could hear the high ground creeping into Biden's voice: Hey, it's a righteous deal!

Tom started again: "Senator, I know you can buy it. The point I'm trying to make . . ." But Joe had moved beyond talk. He wanted to show them. So they could see it like he did, see it whole . . . *Life* magazine! "C'mon," he said. And he dragged them out to his car, or his truck, to be precise, a four-wheel-drive thing. It's actually a Wagoneer, but Washington guys don't know about trucks, so the night has gone down in history as The Night of the Bronco. And Joe rode them all around Wilmington—hell, they covered half of Delaware, for hours, driving to different properties, which Joe pulled into in the darkness, and raked the houses, the land, with his headlights, and showed them the features, the problems, and told them what it went for in '76, and what this sold for last year . . . and what that said about the value of *his* house, his new house, seventeen acres! . . . which he could get, with the pullback, the balloon, and everything . . . "in *Greenville,* ninth most expensive real estate in the *country* . . . and it's perfect. All brick! Perfect shape. Wait. We're right near it . . ."

Thing was, both of them had already seen the compound. Like all decisions in the Biden campaign, this thing had been hanging fire for months, while Joe sifted out his moves. The staff in Delaware had named the place "The North Forty." And Joe had shown them everything, taken everybody out there, walked them through the tennis house, to make them see . . . and it was splendid, there was the sauna, the indoor pool. Ridley had taken one quick look and was sure the campaign was over. "Oh, God," he murmured, looking up, into the vast, airy hall of the tennis court. "We're fucked. Completely. Oh, my God . . ."

But this was the night they would not quit, and they were after Joe. "You're not going to take every goddam reporter in the country out in your truck. You can't. You don't know what this is like. You can't explain to everybody. Things just come out. Everything comes out, and everything looks . . . worse than you can think. Joe, if you run, your life is going to change. It's got to change . . ."

They were back in the Bronco, and the boys were pressing: "Look, if you think you can live your life like you been living, like you want, in the middle of this, you've got it wrong. If you do this thing, you've got to want it more than you want *anything else in the world.* You're going to give up . . . *everything.*"

And then, they were back in Joe's old house, with takeout Chinese, and Ted Kaufman was there, who was Biden's old Chief of Staff, who these days was running around the country, raising money for the campaign that might not be. And Joe was trying to tell them he had to do it *his way,* there wasn't any point in running if he had to twist into some new shape. And he didn't just mean the house . . . he meant everything, his work in the Senate, the Judiciary Committee, his home, his family . . . weekends—he had to have weekends home.

Weekends!

"Look, Joe . . . it's not going to happen. That shit you been telling Jill— weekends home, campaigning together, she won't have to go out alone . . . that's bullshit . . ."

"If you guys don't think I can do it . . ."

"It's not that . . . you can do it!"

And Joe knew he could do it—not a doubt in his head, honest to God, his word as a Biden—it was destiny . . . *if he could see the moves.* He had to figure out . . .

Joe was thinking of Jill, what she said on the plane, coming home from Hawaii, just a few days before. They'd done a round of fund-raisers on the Islands (turns out that's where the Jews from L.A. spend their Christmas) . . . and they'd stayed with Pat Caddell, who had the use of a house there. Joe and Pat went back a long way, to the start, to '72, when Joe made his first Senate race and signed on a brilliant twenty-two-year-old pollster from Harvard—that was Caddell . . . before McGovern, before Carter, before the White House and all that bullshit . . . hell, Joe knew Pat before Caddell had any enemies, and that was going back some. They were like brothers. They'd helped to create one another.

Anyway, the strange thing was, this time, they almost didn't talk about the campaign. After so much talk before. After Pat tried so hard to get Joe to make the race, in '83 . . . they'd talked forever about that. But now, this time, when they both knew it was Joe's time, neither wanted to bring it up. And the conversation Joe remembered from that trip took place on the plane, coming home from Honolulu. The airline pulled one of those stunts where they get you in the plane, and then it sits on the tarmac, for hours, waiting for something . . . and Jill was staring out the window, they were quiet, until a sigh of such concentrated sadness escaped her that he turned to ask: "What? . . ."

"Nothing . . . just . . . it's never going to be the same—is it?"

Joe asked, gently: "Don't you want to run?"

"It's not that, it's just . . . everything's so perfect now."

Even Joe, who was always looking to move up, had to admit . . . the kids were doing great, Jill was going back to school . . . Joe was forty-four, had a lock on his seat, on his state, just became chairman of one of the Senate's most powerful, visible committees. And he could do that job, he could be . . . a force. It was perfect. But Joe was not a man to let perfect alone.

This could be his time . . . he had seen the way he would be, a thousand times . . . back in college, '63, '64, when he was driving back and forth to Syracuse to see Neilia, every weekend, he went over and over his statewide race—Governor, or Senator—he knew how that would be, every move . . . and after that, there was President. Like night followed day. He would make that move, that race, and in his mind's eye, his race looked like John Kennedy's . . . a young man's race, an excitement in the nation, a call to get America moving again, after a sleepy two Republican terms, against an unpopular Vice President—and Kennedy was forty-three years old, and not well known in the nation, but the time was right to move the spirit of the country . . . and it looked . . . *just like this.* Hell, Pat could see it in the numbers—Pat was a prophet with a poll—and he told Joe, must have told him a hundred times, that a new generation was ready, now, to shove the country toward its ideals. This time, '88, would be the first election when more than half the voters would come from the postwar baby boom . . . the bulge in the bell curve would inherit the earth. But Joe didn't need numbers: he could see it himself, when he spoke, when he seized a room, a campus hall, or a roomful of Democrats, and the feeling, the "connect," rushed back at him, and he could see the faces, the women in tears, when he talked about the dream they'd all shared, twenty years ago. . . . He remembered the first time it happened, Atlantic City, the convention hall, three years ago, a room full of regulars, sixty-year-olds, party pros . . . a thousand muldoons and the smell of cigar smoke, and perfumed women stiff with makeup, and still, even so . . . when he got to the end, where he spoke of the dream and the dreamers, John Kennedy, and Bobby, and Martin Luther King: *Just because our heroes were murdered, does not mean that the dream does not still live . . . buried deep . . . in our broken hearts* . . . he saw it happen, saw it that day as he would see it again in his mind, another thousand times . . . that crowd of party hacks, who'd heard a million speeches, who didn't give a *shit*... did not know what to do. There was silence. Then they stood. And then, only then, they began to cheer . . . and some of them wept. And they did not talk to one another, or pick up their coats, or look for the exit. They stood, looking up at him, and clapped and cheered, for . . . must have been five minutes. Joe knew, his time was coming.

Joe found Ridley's face talking to him in the kitchen. ". . . No way Pat can be any part of this campaign. When *The Washington Post* reports you and Pat lounging on a beach in Hawaii, it's a red flag, and they're gonna do anything to get Caddell . . . they'll *kill* you, just to nick him, make him bleed, and you're on the beach with him. Taking a condo he arranged! You know whose condo? For your information—this must be Pat's idea of, like, a neat move, right?— the condo belongs to the manager of *Alice Cooper.*"

Joe met this information with a blank stare. He didn't know any such woman. He had not a clue about rock 'n' roll stars who performed in drag, who assaulted live chickens on stage, who spat on the audience or performed strange acts on inflatable toys. Biden was still a bit hazy on the Beatles. Alice Cooper? . . .

Ridley lapsed into a painful, tuneless rendition of "School's Out for Summer" . . . while Donilon told Joe, *that's what they meant:* borrowed condos, real estate deals . . . things had to change; the bullshit had to stop; if Joe meant to run, this was serious, total.

"You give up *everything* . . . give up your life. It's gone. Home, friends, you're not there. And you're all alone. Completely alone. Your relationship with your wife, your whole family, is going to suffer. . . . You know why? Because you're going to want this worse than anything, and it's going to take over. And there'll be *weeks* when you're not even gonna *see* home, whatever house . . ."

And it dawned on Joe that these sonsabitches were still beating on him about the house . . . and he made a move, he planted and wheeled for the sideline . . . he held up a hand in the kitchen and told Donilon, and Ridley, and Ted, that he had news for them. They could shut up . . . because what they didn't know, what he hadn't said, was, he'd already *decided . . . he didn't have to buy the house.*

No, he said, with a dazzling Biden smile, into the sudden silence . . . there was *another* house. ("Believe it or not . . . this *other* thing happened . . .") And this time he got all three of them into the Bronco for the trip to the city, while Joe explained, it *was* in the city, but you'd never know, with the green around, in a cul-de-sac, but it wasn't big, the kind of house no one would even notice, if they were driving by, like this, see—see, where the headlights . . . see there? . . . "Wait, I'll show you next door—know what it went for, last year, this time last year? Guy bought it, moved in last spring—look at this!" . . . It was after midnight now, as Joe stabbed the houses with his Bronco lights . . . and he already talked to the guy, there was a deal . . . (in fact, he'd talked to the guy yesterday, when he knew Ridley and Donilon were on their way up, to talk about the big house).

. . . And he could build the wall up in front, there, see? . . . "Wait, I'll drive in, you'll see." With a gate, like a compound, but smaller, see? And the whole deal, he could have the whole thing for . . . and no way *anyone* could say a goddam *thing*.

And it *was* quieter in the Bronco as they drove back, and Joe said he knew what they meant. He'd talked about it with Pat. This time, the whole thing would come down to character. That's one of the reasons he thought he could do it. . . . The issues, the Senate, people might pick him apart . . . (God knows, they'd been talking him down, for years, since he made it clear he'd rather go home each night than be in the club . . .). But one thing he knew: they would never take him apart on character—his basic honesty—his fabric as a man.

And the boys in the Bronco said they knew that, too . . . but Joe could not imagine how the press would come after him. There were only two papers in Delaware, and everybody knew Joe, or thought they did. . . . But this was the big leagues. They'd try to kill him, and Joe would have to watch every move. "Stuff you been saying . . . won't wash . . . stuff about your history . . . it's all going to come out. Anything you did to get the house . . . women you went out with . . . stuff you said, ten years ago . . . everything comes out."

And back at the house, Joe said he understood. He wanted them to know everything. And he started then, with his recitation: the anatomy of Joe Biden—confession and apologia . . . it went on for hours. Must have been close to one A.M. when he started, but that was the Biden campaign: there was no clock.

The debts—he went through his finances whole, the mortgages, the credit cards. He was into Visa, Amex for thousands.

The women, between his marriages—a list, with commentary—and how Joe was: that was a hard, hard time for him . . .

And Jill's first marriage . . . not the greatest guy in the world. And then he brought Jill in—must have been two in the morning, or after—got her downstairs to tell the guys about *her* inventory . . .

And farther back, Joe's life with Neilia—before the accident—when he was a County Councilman, and a lawyer before that . . .

And law school, before that . . . Ridley would remember, Joe mentioned that he'd flunked a course in law school. But the others, Kaufman, Donilon, would not remember anything about the law course . . . how could they? Joe talked for hours, until the boys were slack-jawed and yearning for bed . . .

And before that, University of Delaware, where he only screwed around, trying to be Joe College—got probation for dousing the dorm director with a fire extinguisher. . . . Then there were hijinks from high school, streaking the parking lot. . . . They were getting back to childhood sins, stuff where the priest says, "Two Hail Marys" . . . but Joe was still talking.

And there were streaks of light in the sky when he finally put the guys to bed in the guest rooms, and they were all played out. It had been quite a night, Night of the Bronco, and they'd had their talk . . . more talk than they'd ever imagined. . . .

It was only the next afternoon, on the way back to D.C., that they tried to sort it out. Would he run? Never did say, that whole night . . . Joe was still looking for the moves. Could he run for the White House and run the committee? Keep the life he'd made with Jill? Time with the kids? Money for college? Hit the connect that fed his own engine? . . . It was all tied together in Joe's life, in Joe's mind . . . with the house. That was the other thing: he never did say, that night, exactly what he would do about the house.

—★—

The house on North Washington Street was a middle-class home, as Scranton defined it. In fact, Washington Street itself was an inventory of Scranton's strata, a serial history. Close to town, nearest the valleys where Scranton first grew, the houses were small and mean—built for coal miners, who packed the place during the great age of steam. Farther out, say fifteen to twenty blocks from the town's center, the houses grew bigger, almost grand—for a pocket of professional men, managers of industries and the anthracite mines that were the bedrock of all. And then, in the twenties, the trolley pushed out past that "millionaire's row," and modern smaller houses sprang up along the route, another ten blocks or so, almost out to the old city dump. That was Green Ridge, and a good neighborhood—not easy for an Irishman to buy there, not back then.

But Pop Finnegan made it. He was a college man, and a pretty tough cookie, Little All-American quarterback for Santa Clara College (or so the family always maintained), when he and the century were young. He was in San Francisco, trying to finish college, when the earthquake hit, and that drove him back to his birthplace, Scranton, where he went to work for a coal company, then the gas company, then the newspaper. He married Geraldine Blewitt, the daughter of the former City Engineer (and then State Senator), Edward F. Blewitt. And by the thirties, when Ambrose Finnegan moved his wife, Geraldine (and her unmarried sister, Gertrude), his four sons and his daughter, Jean, to Green Ridge, to North Washington Street, there was no one to deny that the Finnegans were a family of respect.

True, the home was in no way fancy—the Finnegans had no airs—but it was full of life and family; the noise of five kids pounding up and down stairs; big, crowded, clamorous Fourth of July barbecues; and long, loud arguments at table (Pop was a newspaperman, after all) on politics and affairs of the day. The Finnegans were all opinionated. A guest for dinner would get a fine feed, but at the same time, he'd better watch what he said. All his ideas were fair game: they'd take him apart. That's what they did to Joseph Biden—Joe, Sr., as he would come to be known—when he showed up as a dinner guest, just after he moved to Scranton, in 1936. See, Joseph Robinette Biden was not of their world. In fact, they'd never met anyone like him.

He was an elegant boy. Handsome, yes—movie-star looks—but that wasn't his distinction. It was a matter of style, of carriage . . . class. Joseph Biden, just a senior in high school, had already seen a bit of the world, seen the best

... and to him, this coal-cracker town of Scranton was, well ... *not* the best.

Not that he grew up with money of his own: Joseph was born in Baltimore. His dad worked there, for American Oil ... which sounded great, but actually, his father started out delivering oil to homes, in a wagon. Still, Joseph grew up with a consciousness of his lineage: the Robinettes, his mother's kin, traced their path in this country from a tract of land near Media, Pennsylvania, which was an original grant from William Penn. And even in Joseph's time, that side of the family flourished. His mother's sister married a man named Bill Sheen, a two-fisted Irish business baron, who held the patent on a substance called asphalt-gravalt, a hard mineral pitch used for sealing coffins. Bill Sheen sold tons of this stuff, and made a fortune, which he quickly converted to estates in the horse country outside Baltimore, and then a baronial manor in Connecticut ... and a boat, or two, and then an airplane ... and lots of cars, some for him, some for his son, Bill, Jr. ... . Junior was a young man who used up cars like tubes of toothpaste.

Yes, the Sheens knew how to live, and how to take care of family, too. And Bill Sheen, Jr., had a favorite cousin, who was just his age ... and that was Joseph Biden. So Joseph spent every summer with the Sheens, and he went to their parties, and played their golf course, and he used up their cars, and he rode to their hounds ... and you can believe that handsome Biden lad cut a fine figure in his riding pinks. He was a young man with all the graces ... save one: he could never pick up the check.

But what did that matter, really, when he was just like another son to the baron, Bill Sheen? And Joseph took to the life so naturally, as a child of that age will absorb a foreign language, and speak like a native, forever after. It became him, that style—everyone said so—and went with his good looks, his slender grace, his dignified walk, the seersucker suits, white bucks, and straw boaters that he favored, in the summertime. . . . He was, in sum, a lad of preternatural polish.

So, of course, he did stick out ... when his father (something of a drinker was his dad) was exiled by Amoco to the outback, to the boonies of Scranton, Pennsylvania. Scranton was a football town, a shot-and-a-beer town, and here was Joseph, come to finish high school, just for a year or so, who talked about golf, shooting skeet, jumping horses, and racing cars that no one had ever seen. He got an earful in return from his schoolmates, not least from the Finnegan boys ... but all that guff was well worthwhile, when he went to their house for dinner, and met their sister, Jean.

Jean Finnegan was the homecoming queen, the object of a hundred boys' dreams. But all those dreams were dashed the minute Joseph Biden walked through her door, in his perfect suit, with his brilliant smile, his shining fingernails, his manners—so soft! ... She was a goner. Yes, he wooed her, and brought her flowers, and took her riding, and told her about the glowing life that was his ... well, almost his.

They married young. Time was a-wasting, as Joseph was swept into the empire of the Sheens ... and now, Jean with him ... whirled along in a dizzying twister of money, pleasure, power. The Sheen family business had evolved, with the times, to supply a type of armor plate, chiefly for the merchant ships that plied the dangerous Atlantic. Old man Sheen had smelled war in the wind, and money—which descended in truckloads upon him, when Congress passed a law *requiring* his armor on every U.S. ship in the North Atlantic trade. Bill Sheen, Sr., ran the New York operation. He sent Bill, Jr., south to run Norfolk. And Joseph Biden, five years out of high school, was general manager, and maximum boss, of the Sheen Armor Company's Boston division.

God, it was a wonderful war! They drove up to Boston in Joseph's four-hole Buick convertible. (Bill Sheen always sent the chauffeur out to buy cars four at a time—three Cadillacs and four-hole Buick. Sheen, Mrs. Sheen, and Sheen, Jr., got the Cadillacs; cousin Joseph got the Buick roadster.) Joseph and Jean moved into a beautiful Dutch colonial house, outside Boston: four bedrooms, three baths, for the two of them. (They were planning on a family, after all.) As a defense contractor, Joseph Biden held a triple-A priority with the nation's airlines. That meant he could bump a general, if Jean fancied a weekend in Scranton. Joseph, too, did his share of flying, on the airlines, and in the company planes, which he piloted like a fighter-jock. (He and Bill, Jr., ditched one plane in New York harbor—that was a show!) So, weekends, if he could spare the time, he'd fly out with Junior, off to hunt pheasant, and then fly back to Boston, or New York, where they'd march, in their hunting togs, into the Barclay, and directly to the kitchen, with a brace of birds, which they'd present to the chef for preparation.

Plenty . . . and more than plenty . . . and Joseph Biden was not small with wealth. He took care of friends—plenty of them. He bought an interest in a furniture store—a whole city block—and put a friend in charge . . . (but the friend took off with the money, and Joseph lost that store). He knew how to take care of family, too, triple-A-flying sundry Finnegans up to visit in Boston, or sending lavish gifts down to Scranton. When Frank, his brother, came back from the war, shell-shocked—problems with his vision and balance—Joseph took him in as manager of the works in Boston. Frankie screwed that up to a fare-thee-well (actually, spent most of the time getting snockered on the yacht with Bill Sheen, Jr.), but Joseph swept up behind him, and never said an unkind word. Nothing was too good for a Biden. That was the same way he treated his son, Joseph R., Jr., born 1942. The Biden home movies from the forties show Joey in his perfect little sailor's suit . . . Joey on his brand new pony . . . Joey with his gorgeous toy car . . .

And why not? It was all still up and up. Sure, the war was ending, but business was business. There'd be something else, Joe, Sr., told Jean. . . . But less and less did she believe. She was a Finnegan, after all, and stubborn like that breed. She loved his great gestures, his magnificent style . . . all his Biden ways: she knew what it meant to be a Biden; she took that to heart till she was more fierce than he. But she could not really approve of the life, the high times

. . . the expense! "We're just on their train . . ." she told him. "It's Bill's money . . . Bill's plane . . . Bill's company . . ."

"Yeah," Joseph said, "but he's a *pal*." Surely she knew what that meant to a Biden. . . .

But less and less could she see it as he did. Bill, Jr., she decided, was a lush and a liar, who made promises he forgot on that yacht, with a glass in his hand. After the war, when the armor business folded, Bill, Jr., dreamed up a scheme to buy a country airport, on Long Island: they'd run it together, him and cousin Joseph. And Jean was against it. But Joe, Sr., wouldn't duck out on a pal. He'd already agreed . . . *his word as a Biden.* So they bought into the airport, and got a couple of crop-dusting planes—Sheen, Sr., helped put up the money—and they were in business.

Well, sort of . . . the crop-dusting contracts were few, and difficult. It was Biden who humped all over the Island, drumming the farmers for jobs. Bill, Jr., wasn't around much—still on the yacht, drinking the company dry. In the Biden home, things were dry, indeed. Two children now: Joey's sister, Val, was born just at the close of the war . . . and nothing but debts in the household budget. Jean Biden was in a boil: the Irish was up in her now. "Joe Biden, I'm not going to do it! I'm not going to have dinner with that lush! He did not do what he said. . . ." Jean had no tolerance for people who fudged, or did less than they vowed.

But Joseph was still swept up in his Sheen-dreams. It would turn around, he said. Bill would be back . . . and he'd bring the money, like he promised . . . he's a pal!

But Bill did not come back . . . and finally, Jean left. She went back to Scranton, in 1948. It wasn't long after, that Sheen, Sr., smelled failure . . . and pulled the plug. He yanked the line of credit. Probably good for Junior, he figured—teach him a lesson. But it was more than a lesson to cousin Joseph. It was the end of his dreams . . . and a plunge into ignominy.

Joseph Biden had no choice—he went back to Scranton, too. He drove in, and the next day, Sheen's chauffeur showed up to take back the Buick. . . . And that was the end. Joseph and Jean and their children moved in with the Finnegans, in the modest yellow house, at 2446 North Washington.

And that's where Joey did his growing up, in that packed house, with his parents, and Val, and soon, another brother, Jimmy . . . and all the Bidens in two bedrooms now—kids in the garret.

Mom and Pop Finnegan still had their room, of course, although since Pop's stroke, he mostly sat in silence, in his overstuffed chair, in the living room, day and night.

And the top floor, front, that was Aunt Gertie's room—Gertrude Blewitt, Mom Finnegan's unmarried sister—she never left the property. Gertie was usually at the kitchen window, the one near the sink, that looked out over the back, where she'd watch Joey and his friends. She doted on Joey—always cooked his favorites, spaghetti and meatballs (Gertie made meatballs the size of your fist), and apple pie, still warm, just the way he liked it. Gertie was odd—with the hairs on her chin, the way she wrote on the walls in the kitchen: phone numbers, recipes, anything else she thought of . . . but a five-year-old doesn't know what's odd: she was a fixture in Joey's life, and she always watched out for him. (Once, Joey and his pals were throwing snowballs, and when the Kelleher Coal truck happened by, that was the biggest, best target they'd seen. So, they let loose, and a snowball shot right through the window, right in the guy's kisser! The driver ground metal-on-metal to a stop, and chased the fleeing boys up the Finnegan driveway. But then, Aunt Gertie burst out of the house, with her apron on, a broom in her hand . . . and chased that coal man down past the curb, all the way back to his truck: "Get outta here, you sonofabitch!" It was the only time anyone ever saw her feet hit the pavement past the Finnegan yard.)

Then, too, still living at home, there was Uncle Edward Blewitt Finnegan, Jean Biden's unmarried brother. They called him Boo-Boo. He stuttered, hard, and that was what came out when he tried to say his name, *B-b-buh-buh-buh-Blewitt.* He had a room on the second floor, but he was a presence everywhere. For instance, the garage: Boo-Boo collected things, and he must have had eighty bicycles tossed into the garage, all twisted in one massive sculpture, all inextricable and perfectly useless. He also made his mark on the backyard, or his dogs did, Lobo and Diablo: they were a total pain in the ass.

Actually, the backyard was kind of a problem, once Lobo and Diablo did in the grass. The Finnegan-Blewitt-Biden clan liked to spend time out there—they'd barbecue—things were so tight indoors. But once the grass was gone, the back turned to swamp in the rain. So Joseph Biden determined to build a backyard patio, with red concrete tile. And he did a good job—got strings up, and levels, the whole deal. It wasn't the sort of work he was cut out for . . . but there he was, in his wing tips, him and his brother, Frank, who came to help out. That's when Boo-Boo came back to the house, and there was a huge fight. You could see Joe, Sr.'s, point in the thing—he was trying to do something good for the place . . . he was there every night, after work. Boo-Boo was a salesman—away all week peddling mattresses. But you had to see Boo-Boo's point of view, too. He was a Finnegan. He was the son. It was supposed to be *his* house . . . not some goddam fancy-pants Biden who'd been lording it over them for years, sending airline tickets and fancy shit from Boston . . . like Scranton was some starving African country! *Where's all that f-f-f-fancy shit now, Lord J-Juh-Joseph?*

God, it was terrible. Boo-Boo went nuts. Joe, Sr., just got quiet. When you got down to it, it wasn't his house. He was quiet more and more in those days, although it wasn't something a kid would notice. Joey's friends just knew Mr. Biden worked a lot. When he'd get home from his job at the Nu-Car company, he just seemed to accept whatever he found. Of course, the Biden kids knew more. Dad didn't talk much about the old days, but there were the pictures—Dad with his plane, Dad with his horse—in Mom's photo album . . . not out front, like she was making a point, but they were in there, the pictures. And then, in the back of the closet, where kids always look, there were the riding boots, and the beautiful red jacket. . . . It was something those kids knew without words: life was not now as it had been . . . their father had come from better things.

It was left to Jean to make the message explicit, which she did in her own fierce Finnegan way. She told those kids, every day, over and over, that they were Bidens. And there was *nobody* better than a Biden. *Nobody was better bred.* In fact, Jean Biden had a set of lessons for those kids—all interlocking, all important.

The most important was: tell the truth, and do what you promised. "Whatever you do," she'd say, "if you tell us, we'll do anything we can to help. But if you ever tell me *one lie,* I'll never trust you completely again." And the most solemn thing you could say was, "I give you my Biden word."

Whenever a Biden kid needed help, all Biden kids had to drop what they were doing. Jean told them, again and again: "There is nothing in life but family. . . . There is no one on earth closer than brother and sister. They're the same blood! Even closer than parent and child. It's the same blood!"

And they must take care of themselves. They didn't have to put up with guff. They were Bidens, and Bidens did not have to take *anything.* If someone in school was bothering her child, Jean would counsel: "Well . . . punch 'em in the nose!" Or sometimes, to Frankie, or Jimmy, she'd advise: "Why don't you take your brother Joe along? He'll show you how to throw a punch." . . . One time she *paid* Jimmy two bucks to give another boy on the block a bloody nose. That kid was *impossible*! . . . When a nun at school got it into her head that Jean's daughter *ought* to be named Valeria (which she pronounced Val-er-*ee*-ah), Jean told Val not to stand up if that nun could not learn her proper name. "You have to respect the habit," Jean said. "But not necessarily the person in it." And the next day, Valerie, trembling for her mortal soul, refused to stand in class. She was scared to death of what the nun would do . . . but she was more afraid of coming home and telling Mom that she'd knuckled under.

With Joey, Jean Biden never had to supply the will: he knew what he wanted to do. She would always recall, when he was two, and playing on the kitchen floor, with a spoon, whanging and banging her pots and pans—noise to wake the dead!—she asked him, please, to stop. Joey looked up at her with his blue eyes flashing anger, and he said: "Look, Mom. You do your work, I'll do mine. Okay?"

And that was fine with her. The one thing she didn't want was followers—anything but that. She wanted her kids to drive their own trains. Whatever they wanted to do—that was fine. As long as it was *theirs* . . . and their way, as *Bidens.* That's what Jean's lessons always came back to:

"You're a Biden. You can do anything. There's nobody, anywhere, better than you. Maybe just as good, in a different way . . . *but not any goddam better."*

— ★ —

"Look, I don't want Bobby Kennedy. I want my own stuff. I'll say it my own way. And I'm gonna say it better than any . . . well, okay, look, here's what

I'm gonna say . . . first, I'm gonna tell 'em they may not like it, but it's time to stop screwing around. We'll use the economy thing—'. . . forces of decline.' Then, I'm gonna go for the other problems, the education thing first . . ."

Joe had his hands on the speech now, and he was running through the moves in his head, making his guys into the audience, trying out each line, the order, the cuts. . . . These meetings could go on all day, all night, when a big speech was in the works.

"You guys may not believe this, but I'm absolutely convinced—absolutely . . . I was talking to Jill about it—that the most important thing I'm gonna do in this whole campaign is education: okay, listen to this . . ."

Sometimes, it was hard to see what the other guys were in the room for—what they *thought* they were doing. Except Caddell: Pat would break right in and start correcting Biden, arguing . . . and then those two would go at it, an hour at a time, one-on-one, while Joe chopped up Caddell's text, and Pat fought a bloody, line-by-line retreat. Caddell would stew, and start muttering into his beard: "You just don't understand this, Joe. That's the problem. This is very, *very* important, that this stay exactly here . . . said exactly like this."

"Why, Pat?" Joe's jaw was clenched, and his teeth showed in a little grin.

"Oh, well, okay, *fine.*" Caddell was steaming, too—he wouldn't look at Biden. "Do it your way. Fine. We'll do it your way."

"Pat, don't give me that crap. What's the problem?"

"Well, if you don't understand, Joe, you know, I can't explain it to you."

Then Joe blew. Exploded:

"It's my fucking campaign! I'll say this the way I want to. I don't like this. This is yours and Mark's bullshit. I know your bullshit. Remember? You think this is some kind of fucking crusade. It's not. We've got to talk to regular Americans."

When Pat knows he's lost the argument, he just laughs. So now he was forcing a chuckle. It wasn't that they wanted to make Joe into Robert Kennedy . . . it just happened that Robert Kennedy was important . . . to the *time,* to a whole generation. And *that was the message:* that a whole generation was lost, submerged, driven off from the struggle for a better world, twenty years ago, in '68, bloody '68, the Year of the Locust, and the Tet Offensive, the Chicago Convention, and Richard Nixon, and the murders of Martin Luther King and . . . Bobby KENNEDY! That was the whole fucking point! . . . That a whole generation had to come back now, that they had to wake up!

That's what Caddell and Mark Gitenstein talked about for months, that's why the California speech was hung up—why there was no speech, for months—while they tried to get it right. That was the *generational message.* And now, they got a speech . . . and it was like Joe didn't *get* it.

Joe said he got it. He also said he'd heard the same shit from them for three straight years, since Atlantic City, and this speech had to be more. This speech had to be about *him,* why *he* should be President. And now there's only days till he has to give the goddam speech, and he wanted *his* words. So Joe took out a lot of "my generation" stuff. Meanwhile, he marched around the room, running through the lines, like *he* wanted them to sound.

"Then I tell 'em: the education system—the *dual* education system—is exactly the model of what Reagan has done . . . on everything. Dividing the haves and have-nots. That's what we're really trying to get to, right? . . . Well, that's what I'm trying to get to . . ."

This is how he always did it—out loud, with his guys in attendance upon him, to listen, to react, while he worked the thing around in his head. Always been the same way, since the start, since '72, when he'd get Caddell and John Marttila down to Delaware, and they'd sit down in the kitchen to figure out the moves. And it worked, God knows: he won three terms, won bigger each time he ran. That's why Marttila was still on board, still came down from Boston to run the meetings—as much as anyone could run those things. And Caddell was heading off to California, to teach at Santa Barbara, but Pat would still do the message. Like everyone in the Biden world, Joe was just waiting for Caddell to find the message, to hit that big nerve in the public knee that would focus the whole Biden campaign. Pat was a fucking genius! That's why Biden would wait for months. . . .

But for months, Caddell was dry. Around the turn of the year, he gave Joe some kind of mega-memo that concluded this was the sixties, all over again. Twenty years since *Sergeant Pepper.* Twenty years, and we're coming full circle. And look! Here's proof! *Even the Monkees are coming back!* Well, that was nice, but what about the *speech*? . . . So, by that time, everyone in Joey's orbit was trying to come up with message—hey, without message, Biden's not going to run; he said that a hundred times, he's got to have a message! And what made it harder: it wasn't just two or three guys sitting down now— sometimes there were twenty guys in the room, each with his own idea. It was a tribute, when you thought about it: guys wouldn't be here if they didn't think Joe could do it—do it better than anyone else. That's why they kept coming at him . . . why they wanted him to run. The best in the business, coming at him for years . . .

Lots of politicians say people come to them, asking them to run for the White House, but with Biden, it was true. Caddell and Doak and Ridley all ganged up, in '83, wanted Joe to go against Mondale . . . and he almost did. Filled out the papers, almost filed for the primary in New Hampshire. Hell, you had to think about it, when guys that smart believed you could do it. Joe knew they were smart. In fact, that was one of the reasons he called them all in, wanted to have all the gurus around: just their presence, their willingness to be there, was proof . . . he's doing something right.

But the problem was Guru Madness—and it didn't have anything to do with Joe. They were after *each other.* Doak—David Doak—Joe liked him. He could be *very influential* with Joe. And Doak loved Biden, always wanted him to run . . . always. But Doak was partners with Bob Shrum, the old Teddy Kennedy speechwriter. They had a consulting firm, Doak and Shrum . . . and Shrum thought Biden was a *looneytune.* So the whole thing with Doak was on-off, on-off, while Doak tried to work it out with Shrum.

And the two of them, together, used to be with Caddell, except now they

hated each other. In fact, it was Joe who had to sit them all down, back in
'85, and work out their separation agreement. He got them all in a room for
a whole day, with these big bowls of candy on the table, and he made them
crazy with candy, until they sugar-shocked, and finally he got them to sign the
deal. But Caddell said Doak and Shrum still owed him money—a couple of
hundred thousand dollars from campaigns they did together—and he was
going to sue, he wouldn't drop it . . . when did Caddell ever drop anything?
So Doak and Caddell both loved Joe, but they weren't going to work together—and Shrum didn't want to be listed on the same sheet of paper with
Caddell.

So, instead, Caddell formed a consortium with Marttila, and those two
figured they'd buy the airtime for the commercials. That's where the money
is in campaigns—from commissions on the purchase of TV time . . . that's
worth millions. So Ridley was working on Doak and Shrum (fuck Caddell—
Ridley would lose Caddell in a minute!), and he'd almost got Shrum convinced
that Biden was for real, serious about this, and, of course, Doak would have
come along, with pleasure, even would have worked with Caddell . . . but then
Ridley and Donilon mentioned their progress with Shrum to Marttila, and
Marttila had a fit. Shrum, he said, is not *ethical.* Of course, that's what
Marttila said about anybody he didn't like. Marttila's a big guy, Nordic (the
name is from Finland), and imperious. So when he didn't want something, or
someone, he'd pull himself up to his full Viking height and say they were not
up to moral snuff. This time, he added: *"I would have to reconsider my participation in the campaign."* Of course, he really didn't know shit about Shrum.
The real problem was, Marttila didn't want to cut Doak and Shrum in on the
airtime. No fuckin' way! So, then, they were going to lose Marttila.

But it wasn't just these professional pitbulls—no, with Biden, there had to
be more. He'd also got, from Boston, Tommy Vallely, who used to serve in
the Massachusetts State Legislature, and ought, by all rights, to have been with
Dukakis—except he didn't like Dukakis, and he loved Joe Biden. So, Vallely
had to be factored in, with full guru status, on account of his personally ballsy
move. And from Chicago, Joe had Bill Daley, son of the old Mayor, and a hell
of a pol, and a Daley has to get listened to—which, in this case, probably
wouldn't do any harm. And sometimes, Daley was joined by Joe Cari, another
Chicago op, who also was there on account of a personal relationship to Joe,
and also quite savvy on politics. But the way things were going, it never got
to politics . . . Joe couldn't say if he was *running,* they couldn't get a *speech*
out the door . . . so how was anybody doing politics for him? And then there
were more Washington guys—came in like roaches. The one Joey wanted was
John Reilly, Mondale's main man for thirty years, a guy who knew a hell of
a lot, and Reilly was in there, but he wasn't dropping anything else, which
bothered Joe. What the hell did he have to do to come first with these guys?
They were still in their consultancies and their law firms, and no one was
coming in every morning, to run his campaign. Hey, what gives? . . . So, there
was endless talk about how to get Reilly signed on. And then there were a

bunch of free-lance gurus, who couldn't even decide whether they were in the campaign *business.* Hodding Carter showed up at meetings, and he was working for public TV. And William Schneider, the ubiquitous pilgarlic, who worked for anybody, wrote a column, and showed up on TV whenever anyone spent a dime to call him—he was in there, too . . . no one knew why.

And, of course, all these guys wanted to talk—that's all these guys do is talk—but with Biden in the room, what they mostly did was listen (". . . So all I'm gonna say about Japan—the whole competitiveness thing—is . . . *I don't want to compete. I want to win! . . .*").

So what they did was, they'd get out of the meetings, and *then* they'd talk . . . to their friends in the press. Hell, some of them *were* press. So everybody in the country who could read knew that Biden wanted to run, but he wasn't going to run without message . . . and he didn't *have* a message . . . nothing to say.

Great.

Of course, that meant every day, every few days, there's another columnist on the phone to the staff—they want Joe's comment on the "message problem." And that meant the staff had to come to the meetings, too. They were the ones had to answer this shit. Anyway, they had to keep an eye on Joe and the gurus, make sure the Senate stuff didn't get screwed up, and committee stuff . . . Joe must have said a hundred times, he wasn't going to run unless the Senate piece, the Judiciary Committee, could be kept on track . . . that was Number One, right? And when you got down to it, the staff people were the only ones who were *doing* anything. The gurus talked about the Senate staff like misfits and weak links—like Joe would fire them all, if he wasn't such a softie. Meanwhile, the only thing the campaign could do right was raise money—and that was Ted Kaufman, the Chief of Staff. And the only guy who actually wrote a speech that Biden liked was Mark Gitenstein, from the committee staff. Gitenstein wrote the Atlantic City speech, and that was the biggest "connect" Joe had. Gitenstein was supposed to be organizing the Judiciary staff—that was Number One, right? But he was also talking to Ridley, every night, and trying to plug pennies into Caddell's fusebox . . . they had to get a speech that connected—or Joe wouldn't go.

"And the first cut on this," Gitenstein counseled Ridley, "*has* to come from Pat. . . ." In other words: back off of Caddell. Joe wasn't going to take message from anybody else.

So for a while, Ridley stopped trying to ax Caddell, hoping maybe they'll get the goddam speech. And he made a resolve, to live with the Guru Madness—he would work with them all, get them all to work with Joe . . . whatever it took. And then, one night, he was up in Wilmington with Biden, and Joe said: "Fuck 'em. Let's get rid of 'em all."

And Ridley just stared at Biden, like he must have heard wrong, while Joe said: "You know, it's like pulling a tablecloth out from under the dishes. I always worried I was going to bust all the dishes. Now, you know, I don't even care. I just want the table clear. . . ."

Then, with barely a pause for breath, Joe said: "This is between us. Don't tell anybody."

Now, what the hell did that mean? If you're going to get rid of them, who cares if they know? Was Ridley supposed to do this secretly?

Turned out, they couldn't do it at all. Because the message had to come from Caddell. And if they fired everybody and kept Caddell, the press would immolate Biden. What a story! Pat Caddell body-snatches another candidate . . . this time, it's the Biden-pod! . . . The only reason they could keep Caddell was, the Washington wise-guy pundits thought that Doak, and Donilon, and Marttila, and Reilly were *adults*. Otherwise, everyone would just assume Pat was pouring his screed nonstop into Biden's ear . . . they didn't know, of course, Pat was stuck on the first goddam speech.

But Gitenstein was on the phone to Caddell: "Pat, I think I got it. You've got to listen to this song." So Pat went out and got the album—*Invisible Touch*, by Genesis—and listened to the track that Mark named, about saving the world, just us together, the one that had the hard sixties beat, "Land of Confusion."

That was it—exactly—what they were trying to say, what Joe should be saying: what he *had* said, a dozen different ways. It was time to bend the spirit of the country to renewal. It was not a matter of position papers, or fourteen-point programs on trade, or higher ed. It was about waking up the whole damn country!

"That's *it*," Caddell reported back. He was writing, finally. He was writing a speech. He actually *produced* a speech. It was about renewal, healing the wounds that had only scabbed over since '68 . . . fateful '68, the end of the dream. And that's what Joe Biden would be out there to do. To reawaken the dream of a better land.

> *I won't be comin' home tonight.*
> *My generation will put it right.*

That was the song. . . . In the Biden campaign, every message had a song. This *was* a new generation, the first MTV campaign; every message guru had a song to back him up, or a video, or a whole *movie* . . . they were always talking movie-talk.

"What Joe has to do," said Gitenstein, in epiphany, to Ridley, one midnight, ". . . he's got to break through The Big Chill!"

And Ridley was earnestly nodding. Movie-talk meant something to him. That's what Ridley would do to cool out, he'd rent videos. One night, that January, after another day of Guru Madness, Ridley brought home a British movie, a George Stephens, Jr., film. And Ridley was flat on his back, idly watching, and there was a speech in the film, a quote from Shakespeare, *Henry V:*

> "We few, we happy few, we band of brothers;
> For he to-day that sheds his blood with me
> Shall be my brother . . ."

And Ridley concluded, right there on his couch, that *this* would be the tenor of the Biden campaign . . . *a band of brothers* . . . that's what he would make of them . . . *no matter what* . . . united to move the world!

And then, his phone rang, and he said, "Hello?" . . . and he heard in the earpiece:

"You tell Doak . . . I am going to . . . FUCK HIM! . . ."

It was Caddell's voice, dripping bile and deadly resolve. He had a message for Ridley to pass on, about his dispute over the $200,000 . . .

"You tell Doak . . . all I have is *time* and *money.*"

Maybe Pat didn't see enough movies.

Thing was, Joe didn't see those movies, either—and rock 'n' roll, well . . . it wasn't him. Joe didn't know what The Big Chill was, much less how to break through it. Sometimes, he tried to explain to his guys, when they got into this generation thing: '68 . . . he really wasn't, you know, *in* that. . . . He was married. He had kids. Anyway, even in college, he was the guy who wore a *suit jacket* to class.

But that didn't matter—not to the gurus. There was truth to be sung: a generation, a nation, to awaken!

So, Joe ripped up the speech, chain-sawed half the stuff about the sixties. But Pat's stuff was like kudzu—kept coming back. Caddell and Gitenstein got another draft together, and took it up to Wilmington—to the house—January 31, only hours before Joe was supposed to go to California.

But Joe took a look—read the first page—and ripped into the damn thing again. He started crossing out lines and writing between the typescript . . . and then he started pulling it apart—physically ripping pages off and putting them in piles on the study floor, the couch, the desk . . .

"Okay, here's what we're gonna do. Pages 3 through 6, now that's gonna go in roman numeral III. The rest of that shit from that section, that's out. Then, we're gonna make a new roman numeral VII. That's the stuff about me and the Kennedy funeral train, and all that . . . then we're gonna make a new transition . . ."

Now Biden had a legal pad, and he was writing a transition, on the spot, that was supposed to bridge to the new section VII, and then he read what he wrote to the others, and then he said it, off the cuff, in a different way, and he wrote that down instead . . . and he was pointing at the piles of paper and the odd pages on the couch, with the chicken scratching, where he wrote on them, and he had the idea, somehow, that one of the Delaware staff guys, Bob Cunningham, was going to get all this *retyped* before he had to go . . . but Joe already ought to go . . . and Caddell was on the floor, on his knees, bent over the piles of paper—overweight, overwrought, the smell of burnt wires coming off his head—arguing: You gonna cut *this*? This shit is *important*! . . . And Gitenstein was trying to make notes on Biden's notes—because *someone* was going to have to get this shit together again, in a hurry . . . and Spike, Tommy Lewis, Joe's old high school friend, who worked in the Delaware office now, edged into the room with a little smile that said, *Joe, don't pull this shit on me* . . . and he said aloud, "Joe, I can get to the airport pretty good, but . . ." Joe was still writing, and talking at the same time, telling Pat to leave that goddam pile alone: That shit's *out*! He's not gonna say it. And Pat said, what about *11 and 12*? Eleven and 12 are *not out*! And Joe said he's *got* those pages—from the other copy, right *here*. And Tommy Lewis edged back into the study, but this time, he had his coat on, he meant it . . . and Joe glanced up with a look that said, *Awright, Spike, I KNOW.* And Joe ripped a couple of pages off his pad, and put them on the pile that he said was roman numeral II, but the pages he ripped out from the beginning were on there—they were supposed to be in roman numeral *III*, over there, near the fireplace, so Joe headed for them . . . when Jill came in and grabbed him—laid hands on him, and looked in his eyes, and said:

"Joe. Now. It's time."

So Caddell started grabbing papers, got them under his arm in a raggedy yellow-white pile, and said, "Well, I guess I'll just have to go with him . . ." Which was probably his plan all along.

And Joe said to Gitenstein, "You wanna go, too? . . . No? . . . Okay."

Joe slipped his coat on, and stretched his jaw up and out for an instant, while he pinched with a deft thumb and forefinger at the tight little knot of his tie, under his Adam's apple, and he shrugged once, almost a shiver, that magically straightened out his jacket and coat. . . . And, all at once, there he was, Senator Biden . . . svelte, handsome, calm, clear, stepping with a smile, out the door of his mansion. . . . He had a speech to make, across the country, three thousand miles away, today. And he was ready.

— ★ —

Almost ready. They did use the whole flight to work over the speech. And they had to find a typist in Sacramento. And even then, after they landed, there was an emergency call back to Gitenstein:

"Mark, you still got roman numeral VII? The old section VII? Could you telecopy it? . . ."

Somehow, those pages got lost along the way.

But, you know, some of that shit wasn't half bad, once Joe got a chance to hear it, in his head.

From Sacramento, Joe called home, to Jill. She was the one with whom he shared his satisfactions. "Listen to this, honey . . ."

And he read her two paragraphs from the speech, a critique of Reagan's Religion of the Bottom Line:

"*But this standard cannot measure the happiness of our children, the quality of their education, or the promise of their future. . . . It cannot measure the intelligence of our public debate, or the integrity of our public officials. It counts neither our wit nor our wisdom, neither our compassion nor our devotion to our country.*

"*That bottom line can tell us everything about our lives . . . except that which makes life worthwhile. And it can tell us everything about America . . . except that which makes us proud to be Americans.*"

Joe said to Jill. "I *told* you we had the best speechwriters."

And she could hear in his voice that game-day quiver. Joe was taking the speech *inside,* letting himself *feel* it. That's how the "connect" happened: on game day, Joe stopped planning his moves, and just did, by feeling, by the spring of the field beneath his feet, the sound of the crowd, and the words, singing in his head. . . . And when he felt it—he could make them feel it . . . he could make them feel *him.*

And he did. Lord, he laid it out that day. It was a big hall in Sacramento, maybe three thousand souls, and he grabbed them, and held on. He could feel the whole hall sit up and listen, when he got to that stuff about the bottom line. And when he got to the end, when he did the dream, and the dreamers . . . with conviction, and something like joy, ringing in his voice:

"Just because our heroes were murdered . . . does not mean the dream does not still live . . ."

They stood up—three thousand people, who did not know him, who'd never *seen* him until that day, that hour—stood up at the close of that line, and stopped him with applause and cheers, a standing ovation. . . . God, they were hungry, for something, someone . . . and he could be that someone: Joe Biden could make them *feel.*

And when that happened . . . then, it was not so important that he could not see himself already in the end zone. Goddammit, he was doing *something* right. He was halfway down the field. He had the "connect." And in the end, that's what he needed, what Joe Biden had to have. In the end, he was as hungry to feel it as they were.

When that happened . . . then he really believed—not a doubt in his mind, word as a Biden—he was going to be President. They'd figure out the moves, they'd hit the nerve in the knee. He had a lot of smart guys with him . . . and Pat was a genius—if you knew how to handle him, he could do miracles . . .

Yes, he could.

Pat tried another miracle that afternoon: he tried to change a speech that was already given, the speech he'd handed to Joe that day, in Sacramento. Joe was still receiving congratulations, still working the hall, pumping hands and meeting new friends, shrugging off compliments, when Pat made another emergency call, back East, to Gitenstein:

"Mark . . . have you put out a press text?"

"*Text?* . . . Pat, I don't even know what he ended up *saying.* You assholes never even called me. I'm sitting here and nobody calls me to tell me how it went."

"It went fantastic," Caddell said, but his voice was nervy, spooked. "Mark, we got a problem. This paragraph . . ."

"What paragraph?"

Caddell said it was the stuff about the "bottom line."

Gitenstein was relieved. "Oh, I love that paragraph."

"Yeah. Well, if you put out a text, it's gotta have quotes around it."

"Shit. Who's it from?"

"Well, it's from a great American."

"Who?"

"It's a great American."

"Pat, don't fuck around with me. Who is it?"

"Well . . ." Caddell's voice was small as he said it, the name he couldn't bring up with Joe . . . Caddell murmured into the phone:

"Bobby Kennedy."

18

They Expect to Be Cold

WHEN THE END CAME, it was six months after Tet, and LBJ already had shocked the world with his announcement, that he'd pack it up and walk away . . . in '68, Year of the Locust—that was a big year for Dick Gephardt, too. Actually, it happened after the convention in Miami, where they nominated Nixon, and just on the day when the Democrats gathered in Chicago, where Humphrey would beat back McCarthy's legions, and Mayor Daley's cops would beat up anyone they saw, in bloody Grant Park. . . . That was the end of the dream, after Dr. King was gunned down, and the riots scorched a score of cities, and Bobby Kennedy lay dying in a hotel kitchen . . . a year of terrible death it was. But the big one, the one that changed Dick's life, didn't happen in Memphis, L.A., or Chicago. It happened in sleepy South St. Louis: the death . . . of Phelim O'Toole.

You couldn't really call it a shock. Phelim would have been seventy-five that year, he'd been failing, arthritis had him down, and, of course, his lungs were in no shape, either, after half a century of his cigars. It was almost that long he'd been a ward leader, and maybe half that time he'd had his job downtown as Clerk of the Circuit Court. In those days, the Ward Committeemen still got jobs. And after forty years in the game, Phelim had one of the best. See, with the clerkship came some bailiff jobs, and under-sheriff jobs and office jobs and such, not to mention a certain amount of legal work to direct to your friends, or to friends of your friends. In fact, the Fourteenth Ward was *entitled,* by custom and its Democratic primary vote, to pluck from the great City Hall tree about fifty or sixty jobs. It was all part of the system that started block-by-block in the precincts and went all the way up to the Mayor, Al Cervantes. Wasn't any different, in substance, from Dick Daley's system in Chicago— that's why Daley's army of cops was out there, that August, cracking heads in Grant Park, loyal to the Mayor rather than the law . . . it was the system. And in South St. Louis, in the Fourteenth Ward, Phelim O'Toole was that system.

Not that Phelim was the kind to crack heads—he was conservative, yes (matter of fact, his son went on to write the hard-line Missouri abortion law at issue in the Supreme Court's Webster case), but that's how the whole Fourteenth was. It was a hardworking, white, Catholic neighborhood—Germans (Scrubby Dutch, they used to call them, for the way the housewives would scour the front steps, with cans of Bon Ami next to their buckets) who were hardheaded voters, who stood for no nonsense, and when they called City Hall, they by God wanted that dead dog picked up out of their alley! . . . Today! That was part of the system, too. And Phelim obliged, unfailing, for forty years, and saw that deserving officials got votes, and faithful Party workers got jobs, and did it with a smile—even in the worst of times, even when his colleague (supposed to be his partner!) Margaret Butler, the Fourteenth's Committee*woman,* was busting his chops, splitting the ward, running on her own ticket—yes, even in tough times, Phelim worked with a glad hand, a wink for the girls and a sharp eye for young men of talent and energy, young men who had the values, and the good sense, to play ball.

That's how he met Dick Gephardt: met him, in fact, not long after Dick came back to St. Louis from law school, just embarking upon his career, and he had to come into the Clerk's Office to register, to sign the scrolls as an attorney in practice in the city . . . and there was Phelim, who heard the address—Fourteenth Ward!—and he looked this young man over. Clean, respectable; you could see that right away. Suit, blond hair short—"neat" was the word Phelim used—and Phelim O'Toole called out right there in the office: "Young man, you ought to come to our meetings!"

That was 1965, when Dick started coming to the meetings: Dick and Jane, that blond and handsome young couple—she was twenty-three and he twenty-five (about the same age as Tom Hayden, or Rennie Davis, the two past presidents of Students for a Democratic Society . . . not much older than the thousands, the hundreds of thousands, who would take to the streets to tear down the system)—they walked into the smoky storefront at 4524 Morganford Avenue, took seats in the back, and that day joined the Fourteenth Ward Democratic Organization, to serve as the club's youngest precinct workers. In fact, the next youngest member was more than twice their age. And Dick came to every meeting, until Phelim and Margaret Butler made him Captain of his precinct—it didn't take long—and Dick was part of the system, too. And Phelim O'Toole, who'd seen so many men work, had to go back a long way to remember one who worked like Dick Gephardt—so eager to learn, to listen, to work his blocks, door-to-door. It got to the point where Phelim even talked to Dick about the Alderman job. The Fourteenth Ward was represented

on the St. Louis Board of Aldermen by a Republican. A disgrace! And Gephardt might be just the young man to take back that seat for the Party. . . .

But alas, Dick Gephardt was still new in the system—just learning the ropes,
Phelim said—more than two years before the next election, when Phelim went
into the hospital for his arthritis, and right there it was, he had his heart attack.
. . . And everyone who knew him was saddened—that's the kind of man Phelim
was, all those years, a lot of friends . . . and among them, that young Dick
Gephardt, who was twenty-seven now, who'd learned a lot from Mr. O'Toole.
Maybe he knew more of the ropes than Phelim figured. For instance, he knew
just what the system required now.

When he heard the sad news, Dick got right on the phone. Called the
Committeewoman, Margaret Butler, and told her he'd like to have Phelim's
job. And when he had it, he called the family, to offer his condolence.

—★—

Thing about Gephardt was, he never stopped. He got that Committeeman job,
and he was *off*, door-to-door. He'd go down some little street in the ward, and
hit every house on every block, to ask the people: Would they like to have their
street made one-way? Nobody *asked* him to make the darned street one-way.
It was just his idea of something to talk about. . . . See, that way, they could
park on both sides of the street! . . . Of course, at every house he introduced
himself. And if those people didn't want to talk about the street, he'd talk
about their alley, or the storm drain that clogged whenever it rained, or the
tavern two blocks down, where careless patrons left their beer cans on the curb
. . . or whatever else that voter wanted to discuss. Actually, they did the
talking: Gephardt listened. That was the essence of his method, right there.
That, and the fact he never stopped. If someone wasn't home, he'd come back
some evening later in the week (he was doing the next street over, anyway),
or he'd leave a note, to let them know he stopped by . . . to talk about their
street. If he'd already made the stupid street one-way, he'd come back in a
couple of months . . . to see if they liked it. Was there anything else they wanted
him to do?

See, it didn't matter what it was—that was up to them. He was for them:
that's what they had to know. His message, his program, consisted of showing
up at that door. *He was* the program: that good-looking young fellow who was
so smart, respectful, eager, honest, helpful, neat—the embodiment of the
values he meant to represent. He was there to help them do *whatever it was*
. . . same way he operated inside the system. Dick Gephardt, fast as he climbed,
seldom pissed anybody off. He seldom had to. In the end, he wanted the same
thing they wanted: to make the system work . . . for everybody. You could bet
the Fourteenth Ward didn't have a split ticket again, not with Dick Gephardt
hitched in the traces with old Margaret Butler—no, they trotted in lockstep.
A unified ward was the *first* demand of the system, the basis of all further gain
. . . so Dick got that done in a matter of months. And it worked. (See? The
system *did* work.) They got their Democratic Alderman, a terrific young

lawyer, a bright new face, first time he ever ran, but he got out there early, worked long and hard, door-to-door . . . Dick Gephardt.

And after one term on that board, after he'd run for reelection, and led the ticket, he started thinking about the next step up. There were people talking to Gephardt about Governor! And his friends on the board wanted him to run for Mayor. Dick was a heck of an Alderman. Saving the city was what he was all about, right? Dick agreed. He was going to run for Mayor. But just as he was about to go public, the Congresswoman from his district announced her retirement—after twenty-four years! So Dick filed for that seat . . . (see, the Mayor's race could have been bloody, but Congress, well, it was almost a straight shot) . . . and after the '76 election, he was off to Washington.

And with every step up, he got better. Gephardt always—in the argot of ward politics—made a nice appearance. He was blue-eyed handsome, with strong, high cheekbones and a full firm jaw, always unexceptionable in dress, ever sober in demeanor, but friendly, and patient, helpful with the voters. But after a few years in the system, he had command of more subjects. He could explain . . . well, anything. He'd get a question in a town meeting about Social Security—just some old coot who wanted to know: Was there going to be any money for him? And Congressman Dick would make a learned, lucid disquisition on the history, current status, and prospects for the trust fund, including a history of his own efforts (and those of his Democratic colleagues) to make sure . . . yes, there will be money for you, sir. . . . Housing, taxes, small-business loans, veterans' benefits, deficits, interest rates, banking, insurance, postal regulations . . . Gephardt knew about all of them. He was impressive—and so young! It did your heart good just to find a young man like that in politics. . . . See, the message—which was the method, which was him, the balm of Gephardt *in se*—never changed.

Let's say you had a problem. And you wanted to talk to Congressman Gephardt. . . . The first fact: you *could* talk to him; you'd get an appointment. He'd be late, he'd be rushed, but he'd get there. ("Great to see youuu," he'd croon.) Then, what he'd do, he'd listen. That was the second fact: Gephardt listened as hard as any man in America. With Gephardt, listening was a positive and physical act. You could *feel* him listening. It was not like, for instance, Biden, or Dukakis, where listening was the absence of other action. (They weren't leaving, they weren't saying their next thing yet, so, therefore, they were still listening.) When Gephardt started to listen, his whole person went into "receive" mode. He locked his sky-blue eyes on your face, and they didn't wiggle around between your eyes and your mouth and the guy who walked in the door behind you: they were just on you, still and absorptive, like a couple of small blotters. Then, as you talked, his head cocked a bit, maybe twenty degrees off plumb, like that dog in the old RCA ad. Matter of fact, his face bore the same expression: that keen canine commingling of concern, curiosity, interest. . . . Gephardt could keep that intelligent-dog look through a six-hour meeting. If it was just you and your problem, he'd stay on "receive" until your tanks were dry . . . until you were *weak* from being listened to.

Then, he might talk, at the end—it usually was the end, because . . . he agreed! Or he thought your idea was a good one. "Yup, very good . . . right," he'd say. "Well . . . we'll do it."

Or sometimes, he might explain that he agreed, but this *other guy* had a problem, and then he'd explain the other guy's problem. But usually he'd have a plan to get the other guy half of what he wanted, to solve his problem, and that way, you'd get what *you* wanted, or some of what you wanted . . . if Dick could pull it off . . . anyway, he was for you.

And sometimes, if it was a planned disagreement, like a caucus, or a conference on a bill where the Senate and House could not agree, or some other forum of organized bitterness, Gephardt would go onto "receive" for a whole day . . . and when everybody was exhausted, and sour, and stinking from flop-sweat, and the whole ship was on fire from the cannonades on either side, there was Gephardt, fresh and bright, not a single strawberry-blond hair out of step with its brethren, his jacket unrumpled on the chair-back behind him, his shirt crisp, dry, and dazzling white, who would suddenly take his chin off his fist, break his RCA-dog face into a smile of empathy for all, and he'd say: "Lemme see if I can make a suggestion. . . . Bob, Marty, isn't this where we can agree, for a start? . . ." And then he'd lay down some narrow gangplank of common ground, where everyone, from any deck, could get off the burning ship before it sank. And it was beautiful the way he could do it, because everybody would leave with *something* to tell the voters. He would draw for them their bottom lines—what they really needed, to get away with their skins . . . because he did understand, and the way he did that was, he listened.

Of course, it also helped that he didn't care what came out. Well, to be fair, it wasn't that he didn't *care:* if that were true, he wouldn't have sat there for the last eight hours, watching all those sperm bulls paw the ground. But he didn't care that much if the top tax bracket ended up at twenty-five percent, or twenty-eight, or thirty. He didn't walk into that room with his jaw out, and the certain, God-given truth in his breast that the cutoff for aid under Subsection 328-A had to be $14,300 a year (and not a penny less, goddammit). No. What he cared about was doing *something,* and that something he did was to make a bill, and the bill had to get out of committee, and get to the floor, where it could get a vote, and if it passed (and passed the Senate, God willing), and went to the President's desk, and he signed it, well . . . then the system had worked. That was the goal. Right?

— ★ —

Well, that was *his* goal. Gephardt thought his job was to make the system work on the problems. (Kind of radical, but there it was.) Anyone could see, there were problems, right? Biggest budget deficit in *history* . . . biggest trade deficit in *history,* and getting worse . . . factories closing, the jobs ending up in Japan or Taiwan . . . farmers drowning in debt, selling out, shutting down . . . kids dropping out of school—they couldn't even *read* . . . what kind of country was this going to be?

What did people need—a pail of water in the face? *The system was not working on the problems!*

What's worse, Gephardt could not get it done in the House, couldn't make the system work there—not really. Not that there was anybody better at the game.

In his first year, his fellow Missourian, Richard Bolling, a senior statesman of the House, wangled Gephardt a seat on the Ways and Means Committee, a hell of an assignment for a freshman—happened once in a blue moon. Gephardt did not waste the chance. By his second term he was a leader on health-care costs—he fought President Carter's proposals to a standstill, and offered instead a massive substitute that he worked out with a brainy new-right Republican named David Stockman.

By his third term, he was a leader of the young House Democrats who wanted to grab hold of the system, shake it up, make big things happen. The Democrats had lost the White House in '80, they'd lost the Senate. The House was where the action was on the Democratic agenda, and these young fellows wanted seats at the table—they wanted to shuck off the old-guard leaders . . . and *take over.* But Gephardt wouldn't coup the system. He wasn't going to pick a bloody fight with Tip O'Neill. Instead, he took jobs from Tip: he got a seat on the Budget Committee (with Ways and Means, the tandem gave him a say on every cent the government raised or spent). Tip made him Chairman of House Task Forces, a designated hitter whenever a hot issue hit the House. From that point, Gephardt was the bright young man to see on all the big stuff—money stuff. That's why Senator Bradley came to Gephardt with his big-league proposal for tax reform. That became the Bradley-Gephardt bill, the major tax bill of the session.

By his fourth term (after six years, just a stretch and a yawn in a normal House career), Gephardt was turning back talk of Gephardt for Speaker. He became a part of the leadership, Chairman of the Democratic Caucus, fourth in line in the majority. And he was doing more: Senator Tom Harkin came to him with his radical farm bill (which became the Harkin-Gephardt bill, the major point of discussion on Democratic ag policy). Gephardt introduced his own trade bill (which came to be known as the Gephardt Amendment, the lightning rod for discussion on the nation's trade deficit). Gephardt had a bill on *everything.* But it wasn't enough.

What he wanted to do was to *get everybody together* . . . get them into one room, and say:

"Okay, guys. What do you want to do about this?

"Okay . . . good. Let's get it done."

But you couldn't get it done that way in the House. There were 435 members, who didn't pay attention to *anyone.* They didn't pay attention to their Party leaders. What the hell did they need their Party for? All they needed was their half-dozen big contributors, a guy to make their TV ads, and . . . they were bulletproof. You couldn't get them together to do . . . anything. Anyway, after '81, with Reagan and that bastard Stockman running the show, the only thing a Democrat could do was damage control, try to save a program here or there . . . *something* besides the Pentagon. . . .

There was no way to set an agenda, and make the system work. Not for Gephardt . . . unless he did it from one special chair . . . and that was in the Oval Office.

—★—

So he set out to run for President. Sure, it'd be hard to make the jump from the House (hadn't been done in this century). But there had to be a system, right? He'd learn the system, and he'd get out there early, work longer and harder than *anyone.* . . . So Gephardt set out to learn what it took. He asked around, and when people told him, he listened. Here is what they said:

They told him he'd have to raise a hell of a lot of money, maybe five million to start, just to get him through Iowa and New Hampshire, just to the first primaries. Gephardt hadn't raised five million dollars in his whole career. So he said, "Yup, okay, I hear you . . . five million, good. We'll do it." And he got himself a Finance Chairman, who started giving Dick names to call. There were hundreds of names—fat cats and do-goods—none of whom knew Dick from a hole in the ground. And Gephardt made those calls—called them cold, if he had to—and then called some names he heard from other people, and called back the ones he missed, and made visits with anyone who said yes, and called back anyone who said maybe . . . until his finance guy, a St. Louis banker named Lee Kling, who was the Party Finance Chairman under Jimmy Carter, finally figured out: "You got to fight not to give Dick too *many* calls. . . . He'll make as many as you want."

They told him he'd have to jump-start a national organization. With Gephardt, it had always been just him. He was the organization. But not this time, not in this league. The wise men gave him lectures: he'd have to be *just the candidate.* He couldn't think anymore about his own schedule, his own ads, his own speeches: he'd have to sign on professionals for those. He'd have to sign on gurus, and a pollster, a Campaign Manager. He'd have to start a PAC. So Dick took some of the money he'd pried out of folks with his fingernails, and set up a PAC, a political action committee, and he got a smart guy to run it, Steve Murphy, who was a thoroughbred political hit man, and Murphy daubed Gephardt's money onto dozens of deserving Democrats, who were running deserving local races, in deserving states such as Iowa . . . and things went fine. Dick even bought a few friends. And so pleased was he with the progress that he talked to Murphy about becoming the Campaign Manager . . . or, to be precise, Murphy talked . . . and Dick agreed! And then he started looking for a polling firm, and he got a hot outfit from New York, Kennan Research, which would cost another fortune, but provided not only a young killer pollster, Ed Reilly, but offered the services of Ned Kennan himself, who talked like a Viennese shrink, except much louder, whose part in the drama it was to sit Dick down (along with his wife, Jane, and his mother, Loreen, who flew in from St. Louis for this), and to scream at him: "DEY VILL

ATTACK YOU! DEY VILL TRY TO KILL YOU! DE PEHRSONL LIFE
DE FEMMLY LIFE VILL BE *RUINNN!* YOU *VANT* DIS?" . . . which
performance Dick greeted with his eager-dog stare, and an occasional murmured: "Okay . . . yup, I can handle that. Fine. It'll be fine."

Above all, they told him, he'd have to win Iowa. That was the old Carter
'76 scenario . . . guy sneaks up out of nowhere in Iowa, by working every
chicken dinner and corn boil in the state . . . and once he wins the caucus—he's
a *star* . . . got *momentum* . . . the polls shoot up, the money rolls in . . . it's
a *lock.* So Dick thought: Hey, perfect! Door-to-door! And he went to Iowa,
to present himself, as he had on so many St. Louis stoops. He started in 1984,
and after Mondale went down the tubes, Dick started working Iowa in earnest:
made a dozen trips into the state in '85. He went to Des Moines in the center
of the state, and Sioux City in the west, and Waterloo, Cedar Rapids, Davenport in the east, until someone asked why he was spending all his time in such
big cities, and then he went to places you never heard of. For the PAC, he hired
a couple of big names who'd worked Iowa for Carter and Hart. By '86, any
Democrat who was running for Sheriff or better got more than a check in the
mail from Dick's PAC. They got Dick, who'd show up at their twenty-five-
dollar fund-raiser, happy to make a few remarks, to help out.

And there he'd tell the faithful—whoever showed up—how fortunate they
were to have this fine candidate . . . for the sake of their Party, their state, this
whole country . . . because, ladies and gentlemen, this country has problems.
And then he'd set out explaining the problems ("I see an America beginning
to decline . . .") and how the system could be brought to bear on the problems.
And he'd work through it patiently, lucidly, explaining his bills and how they
would address the nation's ills . . . until his wise guys told him that *explaining
wasn't enough.* He had to *move* the voters, inspire them, scare them . . .
something. So, Dick would show up in Iowa and *decry* the problems, with
heat, with passion (or maybe strain) constricting his throat . . . and he'd chop
the air and whack on the podium ("It's not morning, Mr. Reagan . . . It's
MIDNIGHT IN AMERICA! . . .") and *then* he'd explain the problems
. . . until his wise guys started whining that his whole speech was, you know,
a downer. So then, back in Iowa, Gephardt would decry the problems, chop
the air, and smack the podium, then explain the problems, how the system
could be brought to bear . . . and then, when the audience was totally becalmed,
he'd tack on this strange and churchly breeze: "Now wait . . . lemme tell you
how *good* it's gonna be, when we solve these problems. This country is gonna
be soooo great! . . ." And he'd go on like that for maybe two or three minutes.
The close had to be upbeat, see, so he got this long quote to use, some blather
about "I see America . . . not in the blah blah light of a setting sun but in the
blah blah blah of a rising sun . . ." It was a Carl Sandburg quote, supposed
to be inspiring . . . except, for months, Dick went around, introducing it as
a Steinbeck quote ("I think John Steinbeck said it best, when he wrote . . .")
or maybe it was the other way around. Maybe it *was* a Steinbeck quote. Didn't
matter: no one cared who said it. It was like the rest of the speech: paint-by-

numbers . . . he was doing everything they told him. It's just that he wasn't *doing* anything.

Which, of course, started to eat at the wise guys he'd hired. Gephardt was only months from his announcement, he'd been running in and out of Iowa like a drug courier for two years . . . and the polls there put him at one percent! (By late '86, Gary Hart was at *fifty* percent.) So they decided what wise guys always decide: they had a problem, and the problem was . . . the candidate. The hot pollster, Reilly, ran a series of focus groups. That was the latest wheeze in the pollster game. You got a group of voters in a room, showed them things, and then, while they talked, you taped them and watched them through a one-way mirror. It was supposed to tell you *attitudes* . . . to unlock their wallets, or their votes. So Reilly showed these Iowans tapes of Mondale, Ferraro, Reagan, Hart . . . and Gephardt. And what the people said was . . . *he looks too good.* Too smooth: this guy's just rattling off answers . . . like it's rehearsed. So the wise guys came back to Gephardt and they said: too smooth . . . too lucid. What people want to see is passion, commitment, they want a window *into your soul.* "You've got it, Dick . . . your life *is this* commitment . . . what you've got to do now is . . . just, you know, *let it out!*"

"Okay, good. Very good. I hear you. Let it out . . . okay, very helpful."

Let *what* out?

"You've got to have a message," Don Foley said. Foley was Dick's press guy—went back with him all the way to St. Louis, to the first campaign for Congress. Just about the only guy left in Dick's office who knew anything about Gephardt . . . *last* year. "And it's got to come from you," Foley said. "So, Dick, what you have to do, is take a weekend, or a *week,* and don't go to Iowa. Go off somewhere, by yourself, with Jane, and just write down what you really want to do, just write why you think you ought to be President." So Dick said he understood, but it took months before he could get away, and when he did, it was only a weekend, but still . . . he sat down and he thought to himself why he really wanted to be President. But it was obvious. There were problems . . . and the system . . . and he wrote that down, and brought it back, but it ended up like a laundry list, like the roster of bills at the start of any Congress.

Meanwhile, the chief of Gephardt's wise men, Richard Moe, another graduate of Mondale U, told Dick that his campaign wasn't *big league:* here they were, heading for announcement, and the message wasn't getting through. Gephardt for President needed a Campaign Manager with national experience . . . no, Steve Murphy was a fine, good man . . . but Moe knew that true professional killers are quiet, heady guys in suits, who leave no fingerprints. Only two fellows who could run this thing, Moe said, were that guy in Boston, John Sasso . . . or a fellow from Teddy Kennedy's staff, a murmurous South Carolinian named Bill Carrick. "Okay. Got it," said Gephardt. But Sasso was otherwise engaged, so Dick started talking to Carrick. Talked for months . . . well, Carrick talked, and he sketched out the way a campaign should go: most important, there would be discipline, focus . . . while the manager *ran things,* and the candidate would be . . . just the candidate. Dick agreed! And when Carrick finally said yes, just at the New Year, 1987—only two months to announcement, time to get *moving*—Dick dropped Murphy like a sweaty gym suit (put him in another job, director of the Democratic Caucus, after Foley reminded Dick that he had to do *something* for Murphy), and named his new manager, Bill Carrick.

And Carrick got in, looked the thing over, and discovered there was no message. . . . *Who's doing message?* . . . And Carrick said, there's only one guy to do message: guy's a genius—Bob Shrum. They'd worked together for Teddy Kennedy—Shrummy and Bill, pals, you see . . . so Carrick told Dick he *had to get Shrum.* So Dick called Shrum, and called him, and called him back, and finally invited him to dinner . . . out to the *house* to dinner. So they made a date, and Jane cooked, and everything was ready, out in the woods in Virginia, where Dick and Jane had their lovely, airy house . . . except that day, Shrum was meeting about Cuomo. Had an appointment with Mario's son, Andrew— supposed to talk for an hour or so. But Shrummy and Andrew got to talking and the time . . . well, it just went! . . . and it got to be awfully late. And there were Dick and Jane, in the woods in Virginia, and no Shrum, and the dinner was drying out in the oven by the time Shrum finished talking up Cuomo . . . and that was in *Washington,* forty-five minutes, at least, from Dick's house, and Shrum would have to find someone to drive him (Shrum's a genius and does not have to drive himself—he once took a cab in Washington . . . to Harrisburg, Pennsylvania), so Shrum had to go back to his office and get a colleague to drive him out to Dick's, and by the time they got there, even Shrum thought Dick might be, well, a little pissed off . . . but no.

"Good to see youuu . . ." Dick said at the door. Jane was in the kitchen, taking the supper off life-support. And Shrum and Dick started talking . . . about the campaign, the nation's ills, the Congress, the White House, the field for '88 . . . and it was great. Shrummy talked a lot . . . but the amazing thing was, how well they agreed! And by the time Dick jumped into his own car, to spend an hour and a half driving Shrum back to Washington (Hey, no problem—after midnight there's hardly any traffic at all!), Shrum forgot all about Cuomo. He wanted to talk about Gephardt to his partner, Doak. They'd have to be together on this, Shrum and Doak, but Doak was still sniffing around Biden. . . . So, it was hung up while Shrum tried to work it out with Doak, and it was coming up on February '87, Dick's time to announce—Dick wanted to get out there early, earlier, harder, longer, than *anyone*—when Shrum finally signed on to help . . . at least he'd write the announcement speech. And Dick kept talking to Shrum and Doak . . . must have called back a dozen times . . . and finally, he got them—Doak and Shrum—signed them on, as a firm, his *media consultants.* (That meant they'd buy the TV time.) Now Gephardt had gurus, too.

And then, all the new hired killers got busy: announcement had to be right. Had to set out themes that Gephardt could ride to the White House. Had to look right, too—big, professional. . . . And Carrick sat down with Shrum and

Doak to bring them up to speed . . . after all, Carrick had worked with Dick for *weeks* now. And he told them straight out, what he'd learned in that time . . . reviewed the campaign that Dick had created—by white-fisted will and his own febrile effort, made from thin air—and Carrick warned Doak and Shrum what the real problem was: this guy might not be hungry enough . . . too polite, too nice . . . might not go for the kill.

"You don't wanna let up on this guy," Carrick murmured. "You can't push hard *enough* on this sumbitch . . . you let up, he'll pussy out on you."

—★—

And in the middle of this, thumped and prodded from every side, Dick was . . . just fine. See, he *didn't mind.* All he wanted to do was to climb into that bubble . . . he'd find out how to be, and then just *do* it—he'd be the best darned Just The Candidate anyone ever saw.

When he'd show up on the floor of the House (less and less—he was on the road four days a week), his friends, fellow members, would ask, "How *are* ya?" And Dick would croon, "Fiiine, greeaaat . . ." Sometimes, with solemn eyes, they'd try to talk to him about how it really was: Wasn't it . . . crazy? Impossible? And Dick would agree: "Yeah . . ." and maybe laugh with them for a minute. But it wasn't his real laugh—the cackle, where his cheeks get pink and sit up like a couple of chipmunks on their hind legs, the laugh that offers a flash of the freckle-faced boy underneath Dick's system, the unbridled, shockingly loud, hacking laugh that his kids hear in tickle wars. Most of his member-friends never heard that laugh.

See, it wasn't really funny to Dick, or crazy, or impossible. . . . You do not, can not, get up at five-thirty—again—in another shitty motel room, to work another six events for the next sixteen hours . . . *again* . . . if you think the system is absurd . . . not for years at a time, like Dick did. If the system has absurdities, or discomforts, well, you just bore through them, or ignore them, or get by with a quick chuckle . . . just as Dick chuckled by the needy question in those members' solemn eyes: the system had to be absurd—right? Impossible, crazy—right? (Otherwise, why you? Why not me? *I've been here ten years longer!*)

No, Dick already knew this much about the system: it would be *greeaaat, fiiine . . . had to be:* it was just a matter of *attitude.*

This is what Gephardt had always known, took it in with mother's milk: with the right attitude, you could do anything. And Gephardt's attitude was . . . *perfect.*

"Tell you a story," Dick said late one night, while he bounced up and down and sideways in a shitty four-seater airplane—no heat in the back—over Iowa, on the way to another shitty motel room and five hours' sleep before he got up to do it again.

"The Air Force had these bases up in Alaska, way up, Arctic, *freezing* up there. And they noticed, the Eskimos, the native guys, could work out there— three hours, six hours—whatever you needed. But the guys from the lower forty-eight states, you'd put 'em out there, and after an hour, they'd be finished, *frozen stiff,* just couldn't do it . . . same clothes, same jobs, everything . . .

"So they ran these tests, physical exams, complete work-ups, everything—nothing. They couldn't find any physical differences at all. So then they ran psychological tests, the whole battery—the Pentagon, right? You know how they do things. But they had to find out: What was the difference?

"You know what they found? . . ."

Now the chipmunks leapt up on Gephardt's cheeks, and he started to cackle, loud, *hackhackhack . . . this* was funny:

"The Eskimos, the natives, *hackhackhackhack,* what they found? . . . THEY EXPECT TO BE COLD! . . ."

Hackhackhackhackheeheehee.

— ★ —

That was the issue at home: attitude. That's what it always came down to. It wasn't nasty—not often—but after decades on the same course, any steady stream will cut deep into rock. Thing was, Loreen Gephardt could see no place for pessimism, for complaint. What good did that do? But Lou, her husband, father to her two sons—a good man, a fine man, but . . . sometimes, he was so *sour.*

"Lou! No one wants to hear all that," she'd call out from the kitchen when Lou was on one of his streaks—some screed about Harry Truman and the damn Democrats ruining the country, or the way the big shots laid out the roads, so they could make the money, steal all the money, and to hell with the little people . . .

"Lou, you've made your point! . . ."

Thing was, Lou was a talker. He'd tell long stories, then follow up with long explanations, and . . . sometimes, seemed like he never stopped. That was always the way with his talk.

Amid the dour and taciturn Gephardt clan, in Washington, Missouri, Lou was a talker without peer. He was the star of the one-room schoolhouse, the kid who got to school early, to light the stove for the teacher. And he always meant to finish high school, and go to the city, to St. Louis, forty miles to the east, to enter business, to earn his bread by his gift of gab, and to see the big, bright world. Heck, Washington didn't have a single electric light till after the Second World War. While Lou was there, it was coal-oil lamps, and horse-and-buggy into town on Saturdays. The Gephardt farm wasn't bad, in the scheme of the local economy, but there wasn't much cash money for a family with six kids . . . as Lou, the oldest boy, found out when his dad died of typhoid at the age of forty-four, and Louis, then fourteen, was pulled out of high school and set to tending the farm.

He became the man of the family, a man of care, before his time. And he worked at it—no quit in him—up before dawn, aching by dark. That didn't mean he liked it, no . . . nor would he ever forget how his mother pulled him out of school—took away his chance to shine, his chance . . . no, how could he forget?

As soon as a couple of his brothers could do a man's work, and an uncle showed up to help out . . . Lou was off to St. Louis, where he enrolled in Brown's Business College—just a trade school, really, for bookkeeping and clerkly skills of the office. That was fine with Lou.

If there was one thing he knew by his early twenties—as he'd be glad to tell you, volubly, in no uncertain terms, in detail, and at length, maybe more than once—he loved the land . . . but he'd had enough of rising in the chill before dawn, and he would work at whatever he had to, henceforth, to rise in God's daylight, to use his head, to earn a living in a white shirt and tie, and . . .

That was the way Lou went at talking, doggedly plowing up furrow after furrow of talk about his point until an acre of soil lay bare. That's the way he went at everything, which was in the tradition of the Gephardts of Washington, Missouri . . . but it did not cut much mustard in St. Louis with Mrs. Stella Cassell. Stella was a woman of the city, who took a lively interest in people, which translated to an interest in lively people, and there was just something stolid about that young Mr. Gephardt that gave her pause, when he showed up at her door.

Mrs. Cassell's husband, King St. Clair Cassell, was a railroad man who worked the Pullmans out of Union Station. So, rather than languish as a railroad widow, Stella Cassell took in boarders, and cooked for them, cared for them, along with her children . . . and the big house on Vernon Avenue was always the liveliest place. It was at church that Lou Gephardt heard about Mrs. Cassell's, and so, that Sunday afternoon, he presented himself at the door, to ask for a room. And Stella Cassell told him there were no vacancies, at present.

Then, next Sunday, he showed up again. And she turned him away. And he showed up again. And she told him there would be no room . . . but he turned up again, and again, and again. So finally, just to have an end to this, she took him in, and let him sleep on the third floor, with her son. So Lou Gephardt moved into the Cassell family quarters, and there he met Loreen, the family's oldest daughter, who was just as lively and popular as her mother, and beautiful to boot, so Lou asked her out for a date . . . she refused. So he asked her again, and she turned him down. And he asked her again, and she said she didn't think it was a good idea. And he asked again, and she said no.

For *two years,* while he lived in her very household . . . Loreen kept telling this Gephardt no. For two years . . . until she finally said yes. And they went out on a date, and then another. Sometimes, they'd go to the grand Ambassador Theater, where in those days you'd see a spectacular show: Ginger Rogers and Ed Lowry, singing and dancing as the featured act, and a whole vaudeville troupe, and a sing-along with the organist, and then, finally, the movie. And on the way home, they'd stop at Garavelli's, for honey-baked ham on rye— Lou knew something about food: he was quite particular about his produce, the freshness, the varieties, all of which, of course, he'd explain . . . and it was, well, interesting. Sometimes, she'd go back with him to Washington, Missouri, where he was a drummer in the town orchestra. Lou would go up on the bandstand to play, and Loreen would dance with all the men of the town. And that was interesting, too. Very interesting: in fact, that's where she decided.

There was something the townsfolk said about the Gephardts, stuck in her mind: "Good stock . . ." That's how they put it, in that farm town . . . like she was shopping for stud. They didn't say, lovely family . . . distinction, charm, beauty, wealth—no—but, good stock.

And Loreen thought that over. Lou was steadily, persistently proposing: they were of age and prospects were good. Even through the depths of the Great Depression, he'd persevered, and now held a territory, selling insurance, for a fine company out of New York, the Metropolitan Life. Loreen thought, surely, they could make a go of it. (Loreen was generally of the opinion that with application, and trust in the Lord, one could do anything.) If she could lend to Lou just a touch of her own sunny, determined faith, well then, they'd do fine. So, she accepted his proposal, and they set out to raise a family. That was the mission for Loreen.

And they were happy. Loreen, like her mother, was a prodigious doer in the home. Lou was a proud head of household—just the role to which he'd been raised. And every morning, he dressed carefully in his white shirt, dark suit, to set out for his territory. In those days, life insurance was a door-to-door business (and sometimes up the stairs to the third- and fourth-floor apartments), and Lou's territory was hardly rich—a narrow southside neighborhood of Brewery Dutch, second-generation Germans, who'd left high school to make beer for Anheuser-Busch, to make cardboard cartons for Gaylord Box, or pound nails into leather for International Shoe. Lou's major "product" was Industrial Debit Insurance—designed for the working man, who could pay a quarter or fifty cents a week. The agent came by every week to collect, and the coverage was good for that week. A twenty-five-cent policy would yield about a thousand dollars in coverage for a newborn infant. A forty-year-old man might get five hundred dollars' coverage for his forty cents a week. It was really just burial insurance, but it was all the certainty those families could buy.

Of course, the agents were authorized, eager, to sell Regular Insurance— say, a five-thousand-dollar policy with a premium of a hundred fifty a year. But there were few takers in those days, before the war, when times were tight. Some agents tried to pump up their policies, overloading their families with coverage, but Geppy (as his fellow insurance men called him) was conservative, and steady: sometimes (to Loreen's great dismay) he'd talk a family out of extra coverage. Geppy played the game fair and square: the trick was to stay in touch with your families, to know who was expecting a new child, which wage-earner had just won a raise; a good agent would become a friend, a financial and family counselor . . . and Geppy was good. In fact, this was just the sort of steady, chatty, incremental business that Lou Gephardt was made for . . . but then, the business changed. Now the big shots in New York weren't so interested in nickels and quarters; they wanted to sell major policies—no more Industrial Debit; they consolidated offices, let go a lot of men in the neighborhoods, and just when things with Lou seemed so good, just when Loreen's prayers were answered and she was pregnant with their first son (the Lord does hear the prayers of the faithful—both of her children would be boys) . . . then Metropolitan Life pulled the rug, and Lou Gephardt was tumbled out of work.

Oh, he tried to find something congenial, something like his territory for Metropolitan Life. But the way the big shots were running things then, he knew the odds were against him. He'd put on his white shirt, his suit, and he'd go out hunting work, but there was none . . . nothing in his line, anyway. The only offer he got was a job with the Pevely Dairy . . . a horse and wagon, and up before dawn—that was the *last* damned thing he wanted. So he held out. He dug in his German farmer heels and turned down the milk-wagon job. And he put on his white shirt again, and tried all over town . . . but nothing. And he tried again—Lou always persisted—but no soap. Problem was, Lou and Loreen didn't have much cushion. It was week to week, in the best of times, and now . . . times were not the best. In their apartment, upstairs on Gaynor Avenue, Loreen was feeling desperate.

"Lou, you have to take something . . ." she'd say.

"Lou, you could just try the dairy. It doesn't have to be for long . . ."

"Lou, I don't see how you can just turn your nose up at a *job*. You have a family now . . ."

Lou had always had a family. Lou had always taken care of a family. Lou had always . . . but not this time. No way he was going to wrestle with a horse all day . . . *no way*!

Until Loreen played her trump card, and told him she was going out to look for work—herself, his pregnant wife, going out to work, if he wouldn't. . . .

So he took the milk-wagon job. Wasn't forever, she told him; but it was . . . or it seemed forever, for nine long years, every morning, up at three, out to wrestle with the horse and the harness and the ice—big blocks of ice that the drivers had to chop at the depot . . . and the clinking crates of milk, and the goddam horse—ran away from him one day, had to chase the beast all over the streets . . . nine years, and he hated every day of it.

And that's when Lou became convinced—didn't matter what she said anymore—he knew: the world was set up to screw you in the end, the big shots would beat you, if you gave 'em half a chance . . . the way people get treated . . . it could make you . . .

Well, what it made him was angry, but that couldn't come out, could it? Not in that house, with the boys, and Loreen, and they were all good Christians, and Lou was a good husband . . . and he wasn't angry at Loreen—was he?

No, it had to be the big shots, and the way of the world, which Lou would explain, at length, if you asked, or sometimes even if you didn't . . . until Loreen could not stand any more of his sour talk.

"Lou! No one wants to hear all that!"

"Lou, don't you have anything positive to say?"

Well, no, he did not. He had his farmer heels dug into the earth. And it didn't matter anymore what she said. Whatever she said bounced right off Lou Gephardt's solid milkman shoulders . . . and straight into his son's breast.

— ★ —

Jane had to run to catch him—literally. She had to get up in the mornings at five or five-thirty, and put on sneakers and run with him, up their street in Virginia, to the cul-de-sac, and back. Jane *hated* to run: a very smart woman was Jane Gephardt, and sensible—never could see the point of doing something that felt so much better when you stopped . . . but that was the only way to talk with Dick about this President business. Once he got to the office, he was a man possessed: and these days, he wasn't even going to the office—it was the airport instead. He was on the road, pecking and sniffing at this White House race for two or three years before he gingerly brought up the subject with her. So, now, gamely, she laced up her sneakers . . . anyway, they couldn't talk like this in front of the kids.

"I'm just not sure . . . this is the right time . . ." she'd say between puffs, pounding up the street in the half-light. ". . . We just . . . can't be away . . . that much . . . right now . . ."

What she would have said, with more breath, was that none of their three kids was out of the house yet. Why did it have to be now? Katie was only eight years old, Chrissie was eleven, Matt was sixteen, still in high school, a rough time for him. They needed Dick. How could he push them into a whole new league, blow up every routine they had, and then take himself off to Iowa, New Hampshire, every week? It wasn't fair—what about her? She needed Dick, too. What about what she'd have to do? She'd always helped with his campaigns— door-to-door—she liked door-to-door . . . but this was different, this was speeches, and TV, people writing about what dress she wore—could she do that? Did she want that? Did it matter what she wanted? That wasn't the way she said it, though.

". . . Suppose Matt needs you? . . .

"You're the one . . . he's close to . . ."

So often it came down to Matt: ever since he'd gotten so sick as a baby— cancer at one and a half years old, their firstborn; he was the one they worried for. And now, when he so much wanted Dick to be there. . . . Jane didn't worry so much for the girls. Chrissie would have a ball on the campaign, watching the people. Chrissie and Dick would get going on people—she noticed the tiniest details—and they'd never stop laughing. Katie would be fine, too: she'd motor right through it, organize her way through it. (Katie was only eight, yet she was the one who got her sister off to school. "Okay, here's your lunch, here's your backpack. Bye!") Matt was the tender one . . . so *angry* now. . . .

"It'll be fine," Dick said. "It might be good, meet a lot of people, it could give him something, you know, a focus, outside himself . . ."

(Dick could talk while he ran—never puffed or paused. In St. Louis, he used to run in Bermuda shorts and a golf shirt. He'd finish his run in Tower Grove

Park and walk right into a bakery for donuts, start saying hi, shaking hands. Dick was such a white guy, he'd never even sweat.)

"It could give him confidence," Dick said. He always saw the positives. That's how he worked on Jane:

"It'll be great. We'll all be in Iowa together . . .

"Sundays home, that's for sure . . . Wednesday nights, too, at *least* . . .

"Won't have to run back and forth to St. Louis . . ."

Jane knew he was working on her. And she knew herself. She could get through a campaign, if she had to, one day at a time . . . she could do anything—for a while—she'd learned that, when Matt got sick, she learned what she could do . . . but what if Dick *won*? Four *years*? *Eight years*? . . .

"If we win, we could sell this house, you know, and there's the college money, right there . . ."

Dick was so full of good hopes. That's what made it so hard for Jane. By the time they started to talk about it, he was so *into* the thing, he was on that weird white tractor beam, that focus he got, that made everything else small . . . and she knew she wouldn't stop him. How could she? Holding him back, saying no to him—that would be terrible for her. And she knew he'd haul them all into it . . . carry them into his zone of zombie will. She knew she'd fold, but . . . couldn't they talk?

So Dick would say, "Well, let's make a time when we can really sit down, you know, decide . . ." And they'd set a date: July Fourth . . . and then Labor Day, and then Thanksgiving—Thanksgiving for sure . . . but it was hard to get the time carved out, you know, with everything else. . . .

Meanwhile, Matt would lash out . . . to Jane: "I don't want him to do this. It's just wrong . . ." She was driving Matt to a tennis lesson, Old Dominion Lane, on the way to McLean.

"It's just . . . *selfish*. He isn't even *thinking* about us. Just for him. Why does *he want* to do it?"

And Jane would say softly, "Matt, don't tell me this. You have to tell your dad this . . ."

But Matt would not tell his father: he would not be weak, he would not disappoint. To Dick, he'd say, "Whatever you want, Dad." And then he'd scream at his mother, with an edge of tears near the top of his throat: "I don't wanna be looked at. I don't want to be . . . I don't want them LOOKING AT ME."

And Jane would tell Dick, who'd try to have a talk, some night, when he was home for dinner . . . and Katie, on his right, would make a face: "Aw, Daaad. Stupid conversation . . . again?" But Matt would listen, eyes down, while his father tried to emphasize the good things.

"Think of the people you could meet . . .

"This'll help you get into a really good college . . .

"Don't you think it'd give you a special, uh, identity at school?"

Matt's answers were short, conclusive—mostly said to his plate.

"People'll look at me funny . . .

"I don't wanna go with Secret Service . . .

"I'm gonna get into college on my own."

And sometimes, all the kids would start piling on:

"*Am I gonna get to go to my same school?*"

"*We'll never see you!*"

Dick would say, "No, it'll be greeaat . . . we'll be together in the White House."

"*It won't be the same . . .*"

"*We gonna go out and shoot baskets on the garage?*"

"*You'll have people around you all the time!*"

They knew he was different when there were people around. No more tickle wars on the floor. No more wrestling and cackling, no nicknames in front of the Secret Service. They knew . . . but they also knew they would not stop him—it would only hurt to try. So they tried instead to have a good attitude. They were Gephardt's kids, after all.

And one day—it was a Sunday, Dick was home—they went to a movie. It was *Rocky IV.* And coming out of the mall, Matt said to Dick:

"That's you, Dad. You're like Rocky. You have to do this. . . . Don't worry. I know that. You just go ahead."

— ★ —

Her first son, Don—sometimes Loreen thought he was Lou all over again: the same sharp features, the musical ability, the long silences she'd hear when they'd visit the farm in Missouri. Don was neat, organized, persistent. He wouldn't go to sleep with something out of place in his half of the boys' room.

And Dick was just like her—she knew it the minute she saw him born. He had her smile, her curiosity . . . before he could walk, he'd crawl across the floor to visitors in the living room: "Whuzzat? . . ." he'd say, and he'd point. He wanted to know everything. He wanted to hear what everybody had to say. And she bred this in him, praised it steadily, took such joy in him, and pride. . . .

She loved both her sons: fine boys. But so different from one another, it was . . . a miracle, the way God worked. She knew it was God's hand, His plan manifest on Earth. A strong faith was Loreen's, and this, too, she bred into the boys—with faith, they could do anything in the world. That's what they heard, too, each Sunday, at Third Baptist, a large and imposing church, all the way downtown, where during the war, when the boys were young, fifteen hundred worshipers would pack the place, four deep in the balconies . . . and while the flags of the church and the nation were marched down the center aisle, the great and stentorian pastor, Dr. C.O. Johnson, would boom out: "All those who will pray for our military men, until the lights come back on, STAND WITH ME NOW . . ." And the place would leap up with a roar.

That was a new church for the Gephardts, when Dick was born. So many things changed when Dick came along: they moved to the house on Reber

Place, a two-story brick bungalow, with a wooden front porch behind a low white railing. On the first floor, there was a living room, dining room, kitchen . . . and behind, a tiny backyard, and then the alley. Upstairs, the boys shared the front bedroom; then there was a bathroom, with Lou and Loreen's room behind. It was a modest house, by any standard, but a wonderful place for the boys. Reber Place was a dead end, with lots of kids—perfect for ball games in the street. There was the Mason School, where both boys went, only three blocks from their own back alley (and just a block past Hill's and Bill's, the corner store, with penny candy, and bubble gum). The backyard was just the right size for one red-haired kid (in his red Cardinals' ballcap) to throw a baseball against the wall, and catch it, and throw it again . . . calling the play-by-play of his game, like Harry Caray did for the Cardinals. In the basement, there was just space enough for Loreen to host the Cub Scouts and the den mothers . . . most of the basement was taken up by the furnace and the big coal bin, where Don had to shovel. Of course, just as Dick came of age for shoveling—wouldn't you know it?—the Gephardts made the switch to oil heat.

Everything changed just in time for Dick: even Lou, who didn't do much changing. . . . But when Dick got interested in the church, Lou took an interest, too. He became a deacon, and president of the Agoga Bible Class. When Dick became a Boy Scout, Lou joined the club of Scout dads, went on the cookouts, cooked for the camping trips. (Somehow, he never had the time when Don was a Scout.) And in time, with steady application, Dick made Eagle Scout. (Don just missed.) It was strange, the way it always happened for Dick, though he was never loud, never demanding . . . like he was the heavy lump of iron, and the magnetic field of the family bent around him. . . . When Lou and Loreen would start to scrap—always about attitude—it was Dick who took it to heart. Don would just go up to his room, close the door, and practice his saxophone . . . but Dick couldn't block it out like that. Sometimes, he'd have to jump on his bike and ride away. But then, as he came of age, he could do more: he could deflect trouble, he could talk his dad off a streak ("Dad, isn't that just like you used to do on the farm?"), he could josh him out of sourness, he could change the subject ("D'you see Musial was four for four?"), he could turn the tide with a joke about Ike. . . . Dick himself, in his person, at the dining room table, could be the bridge . . . to straddle the poles of the household . . . to make the family work.

He was always so good with adults, so respectful, so *interested* . . . better than he was with kids. When the relatives—uncles, aunts, cousins—came for dinner, and all the kids went outside to play, Dick would stay in the living room, listening to what the grownups said. His aunt, Lucy Cassell, used to call him Hothouse Rose, because he always stayed inside with her. He was great, too, with his uncle, Loreen's younger brother Bob, who was a commercial artist, had a studio downtown (on a boat, anchored at a river dock—very Bohemian for those days!), and he used to ask Dick to model for him. And Dick would catch a streetcar on Southwest Avenue, and ride downtown—

quite a trip for a twelve-year-old—and go to the boat to pose for Bob . . . he was terrific at that. Bob would say: "Okay, now look like you're reading . . ." or "Good. Now put the book down and just gaze off, like you're thinking about it . . ." And whatever Bob asked, Dick could just *do* it . . . no problem. It was fun! And, then, too, on that riverboat, apart from Bob, the studio was staffed entirely by women, and they *loved* Dick—he was so cute, with his freckles, that red hair!—they praised everything he did.

It was always praise with Dick. That's how Loreen ran her home: she meant to fill those boys with confidence. . . . If they told her they had an assignment for school, she'd reply: "Oh, I know you'll do wonderfully. You are *so* good at writing." When Don would play his clarinet in the school orchestra, she'd tell him how *beautiful* that music sounded. When Dick had the lead in the Mason School play, she stopped him in his costume, as he went out the door, and bent down, with him looking straight into her eyes (she insisted her boys look right *at* her, whenever she talked—that way they'd know she meant what she said), and she told him:

"You know . . . I am *so proud* of you . . ."

And she was. She knew she was doing God's work in the building she did: that self-assurance, that will . . . Loreen always knew that if you were doing God's will, He would help *you* work *your* will on this Earth. She told her boys, over and over: "Ask and ye shall receive. . . ." Except with her, they didn't have to ask—they had only to do, to shine in the world, to hear her praises flow.

And they did shine. The principal of Mason School, Miss Marie Thole, personally called Loreen to the school office, to tell her: "Mrs. Gephardt, your boys are college material. I would like to see them both go to college. And I would like to see them go *away* to college, because that is an education in itself."

So by the next week, Loreen had a job—two days a week, at a law firm downtown, to save money for college. The Lord does answer the prayers of the faithful.

And lest a son go, for an afternoon or two, without reminder of his opportunities, and his talents, she brought in a teacher from the Mason School, a lovely younger woman named Helen Baldwin, to stay with the boys on Reber Place, while Loreen was at work. And Helen, too, a woman of faith, reinforced the message.

When Dick graduated from the Mason School, at the end of eighth grade, he had a little autograph book, which he passed around for the signatures of his classmates, as memento. Most of the entries were kids' block printing, with well-worn rhymes and jokes:

> *Roses are red, violets are blue,*
> *If skunks had a college, they'd call it PU.*

But in the center double page—where the book would open naturally, if Dick ever chose to look in it again—there was a long, tightly written poem about teaching, and molding men. This was from Helen Baldwin, who followed the verse with this reminder:

"This little bit of poetry inspires me, Dick, and reminds me of you. Of all the boys I know (and that's quite a few), you have the greatest potential for doing great things."

—★—

It's ten days before announcement now, and Dick is supposed to be rolling, presenting himself to the people—today, it's New Hampshire, and the morning bids fair: sunshine on white snow, white steam whenever you talk, and Dick and Jane, campaigning together, as promised . . . this is how it ought to be, right?

But on the schedule, it's one morning speech (a poli-sci class at Daniel Webster College—twenty sleepy, vacant-eyed kids and two Minicams—with Dick pounding the lectern and decrying the problems, like it's a hall packed with five thousand union men . . .) and then mostly private meetings: lunch with the Mayor of Nashua, kiss-ass at the statehouse in Concord. . . . What happened to the famous door-to-door Dick? ("He'll do it," his press guy, Foley, insists. "That's how he *really is*. Do you know that in his first Congress campaign, '76, he hit thirty thousand doors?")

Well, the day holds promise of one such event, a visit to Jean Wallin, ice-cream parlor proprietress, a "Democratic activist," the kind of woman around whom campaigns in New Hampshire are built. She's only had the ice-cream shop for the last six months, but she's had winners for the last twenty years: McCarthy in '68, then McGovern, Carter in '76, Carter again, and then Mondale. She has a nose for nominees, and Dick is coming to ask for her support.

In the Chevrolet, Jim Demers, a local pol, is driving, and Dick is riding shotgun. Jane is hunched in the back, just behind Dick, and next to her rides the new body man, Brad Harris. Brad, a Georgian, about twenty-two, with razor-cut hair and premature jowls, with the standard Washington aluminum-siding suit and a quiet, responsible, striped rep tie, is the first bit of bubble that Dick has accreted for his new road show. The body man holds the briefcase, writes down the names of people who'll help, holds the notecards or the text of the speech, sees to the phone calls and messages, gets water to the podium and snacks to the car, lines up the plane tickets and hotel rooms . . . he is a man of all work, an indispensable man, and of this last fact, Brad is aware. "Dick, this is *people-to-people*," Brad says now, with the air of a major explaining a mission to a young lieutenant. "*Jean . . .Wallin . . .*"

In the parking lot, someone says to Jane: Hey, this is more like it! Pretty soon, Jane and Dick would be peddling brochures on doorsteps in the Manchester suburbs. "Well," Jane says brightly, "door-to-door is something we can really do! You should *see* us go door-to-door! In 1976, we hit fifty thousand doors, you know. And Dick's mother! She won't leave the porch until she gets a commitment. She won't leave!" It is the most voluble speech from Jane all day. Here is something she *knows.* Meanwhile, Dick is still in the car, fidgeting with his shirt. Turns out CBS has him miked up for this homey little people-to-people. . . . Later, it emerges that Jean, the ice-cream lady, is miked up, too. God bless America!

Dick walks into the ice-cream store and seven cameras swing around. The anchormen-to-be are yelling questions into their own microphones:

"What are you going to do about being an asterisk in the polls?"

"Congressman! Are you counting on your trade bill to raise your polls?"

Dick tries to answer, as he edges through the Minicams, toward the counter, to meet Jean and get some ice cream. Jane is in already, carrying the freight with Jean . . . "Mmmm, good! That's great! Our kids'll love this! . . ." Dick fishes in his pocket for two dollars. The TV lenses are whirring in full zoom for this picture of democracy at work. Jane asks for coffee. She got to sleep at 1:00 A.M. and they woke her again at 4:30.

Finally, one of the TVs shouts at Dick:

"How much help can Jean be?"

"Well, she can be of immense help," Dick says, forbearing. "But we've got to sit down and *ask* her if she's *willing* to help."

So they sit: Dick, Jean, Jane, and Jim Demers, hemmed in with their knees together like people in a crowded bus, all on one side of a tiny ice-cream table; they have to stay in camera frame. Dick tells Jean that he loves this kind of campaigning. "You know, we hit sixty thousand doors in '76, when I ran for Congress . . ."

"Well, that's good," Jean says. "If you're not out there meeting the voters, you can't go from Jimmy Who in 1975 to a winner. And frankly, I'm looking for a winner."

"Well, you should be," Dick says. "And I am one. I, uh, am the winner. Um. I'm going to win it . . ."

Jean stares at him, waiting. Dick adds lamely: "See, I believe in talking to people one-on-one."

"Well, uh . . ." Jean is trying to help, prompting: "What do you tell them when you sit down?"

"Well, you tell them why you're running. I tell them we can do better than a deficit of two hundred billion, and we have to get a policy that makes this country Number One again in trade. You know, there's no reason why this country . . ."

Dick is rolling now. Through trade, to retraining, education, our schools, our kids, our values. . . . He's got the baby blues locked onto her face and he's telling her, quietly, firmly, what he tries to tell people in his stump speech, while he's busy pounding the lectern. And all of a sudden, it starts to click. The private foreign policy, Iran-contra, is lawless, and lawlessness is seeping out of the Reagan White House, into the country at large. It's greed that's the message when Deaver and his ilk leave government to cash in as lobbyists. It's lawless greed that's the ethic now, and that's what Dick wants to change. And she looks into his boy face (he's got her eyes now, she couldn't turn if she tried) and she can see that he means it, that everything he is to his marrow is a good boy, clean of heart, so different from the hard-eyed men in the White House, and that's what he's saying: *Put me in and it'll be different. It has to be me because I am the policy, myself, the embodiment, the difference, look! Here in my eyes. Don't you want it to be different? Can't we be better?*

Sweet Jesus, he is terrific. There aren't ten voters in the country who'd work against him, once he's had them face-to-face. And Jean is catching it, too. She's lost that studied helpful air of the prompter for the cameras. Now she's just watching, and her mouth is parted, and her head bobs accord with his words. He's slow now, just explaining, like the words echo in his own head. "And a House member can *do* it," he says. "Mo Udall proved that a House member *can* do well in New Hampshire. And a House member is the one who can work *with* the Congress. I think that *I* could work with the Congress to get us moving, which is what we *need* . . ."

She's nodding as he finishes. He's talked for maybe ten minutes straight. She sits back and she wants to gush, but it takes her a moment to shake off his eyes. "Really," she says, "you have more ideas! I mean . . . I feel I've gotten an education in fifteen minutes, and, really, I have *never* . . . well, you're great!"

Dick is still locked on her, taking this in, unblinking, unblushing. A little smile is his only acknowledgment of her words. He's watching to see the hook set.

"And another thing," Jean is saying, her eyes taking in the room now, conscious once again of the cameras. "I've heard answers from people . . . but I feel like it's coming from a computer. With you, I feel like it's coming from a person." . . . Yes, the hook is set.

"Well, I've been studying this for a long time," Dick says, a modest merit-badge winner.

"Well, I've just never had anybody sit down and tell me, like that, exactly what they want to do . . ."

"Oh," Dick says, and it just pops out, the most honest thing he'll say all day: "Oh, I know what I want to do!"

"I think you can do it," Jean replies. "I really do."

"Can we count on your help?"

"I'd love to. I'd really love to. I really . . ." She hasn't words. She shrugs and says to Gephardt: "You're great!"

There is a small scraping sound as Dick's feet gather under his chair. He bends, suddenly, to his ice cream, gooey now, almost untouched. He says to the dish of chocolatey mung: "We're gonna have to go."

Jean is saying to a local Minicam: "I've never seen such a depth of knowledge along with a vision of what he wants to do. And in a way where he's not really criticizing the American people, but telling them what to do . . ."

The furrowed brow behind the camera asks: "And you didn't have your mind made up before?"

"No, uh, no. Absolutely."

"Isn't she a nice person?" Jane says, as she and Dick, Demers and the body-Brad get back to the Chevrolet. "So genuine!" Jane's step is light; there's no sign now of her protective hunch. Dick has brought his ice cream along. He turns on the all-news radio and opens the *Globe* as the car starts to move. He's scraping the dish. He loves ice cream. For the first time all day, the car feels right.

"Uhh, *Dick*? . . ." This from Brad, in the backseat.

Gephardt doesn't turn around. He's got his face in the *Globe,* his mouth around the spoon. "Hmm?" he murmurs. He doesn't sound eager. "Never get to eat on this job," he mumbles.

"Uh, *Dick*? One thing." Brad is insistent. He knows campaigns. He helped Hamilton Jordan lose a Senate race in Georgia. His voice is hectoring over the radio and road noise, and lands with a slap on the back of Dick's neck. "On an event like that, uh, that one. That was s'posed to be a people-to-people event. Now, uh, the thing we wanted to do there was to show you sitting there talking to that woman and, if you noticed, most of the cameras were packing up after you answered their questions . . ."

"Mmm . . ." Gephardt is trying to ignore him. Dick still won't turn around, but from the back, you can see his head sinking bit by bit between his shoulders.

"So, uh, *Dick.* On an event like that, when you come in, uh, don't answer any questions. We have to control, uh, we have to dictate the uh, media, uh, *hit.* So, when you go in, just, um, do what you're s'posed to do. All right?"

Gephardt's head is now thrust forward into his paper. The exposed back of his neck is pink. All the good feeling in the car is gone. Gephardt says into the folds of his *Globe:*

"Mmm hmm, I understand."

19

1954

HE MUD in Delaware stinks. It's clay, really, and you get used to it—it's not bad unless you dig it up wet. But when you get a whole soggy swampful dug, it smells like someone died in there . . . and that was the smell, the day they got to the new place, the day they were going to start their new lives: Joe, Sr., Jean and Val and the boys, the Bidens, of Wilmington, Delaware.

Actually, it wasn't even Wilmington, but Claymont, a steelworking suburb to the north, near the river, where in the fifties they were putting up ticky-tack houses, and garden apartments (except there were no gardens, just this malodorous mud), and when the Bidens drove in that day, to Brookview Apartments—they were among the first tenants—the place was a bulldozed moonscape, a stinking mess. Brookview would never be beautiful: strings of one-story yellow stucco boxes—efficiencies—appended to larger, two-story units at mid-horseshoe . . . so there were these horseshoes of stucco marching across the gray mud with the promise of eventual, unlovely overcrowding: an instant slum. You could see it at one glance, through the windshield, as you drove up. . . . And from the backseat, where he sat with his sister and brother, Joe Biden looked at his mother, and she was crying.

"*Mom,* what'sa matter?"

There was an instant's pause, as Jean Biden tried to make her face a smile. "I'm just so happy," she said.

"Honey," Joe, Sr., said from the driver's seat, "it's gonna be okay. It's gonna . . . it's just to start . . ."

Now, from Joey in the back: "What's *wrong*?"

Jean Biden turned quickly and said: "Nothing's wrong, honey." And then she turned back—must have taken all the will she had—turned back to Joe, Sr., and hugged him:

"It's wonderful—thanks . . ." Jean said. "I'm just so happy . . . I can't stop crying."

—★—

Joe, Sr., just couldn't hack it anymore in Scranton—not with the old man, Jean's father, silent in his armchair, and Gertie in the attic, and Boo-Boo all over the house (*his* house, the *Finnegan* house). When brother Frank Biden called from Wilmington and said he knew of a job there . . . well, it didn't matter what the job was, it would be easier than swallowing another day in Scranton.

So, Joe, Sr., started driving back and forth, each week, started cleaning out boilers—that was his work in Wilmington. And then he landed a job at Kyle Motors, in sales, and they liked the way he carried himself, the air of distinction he lent to the place, so right away they made him manager of sales . . . and that's when he moved the family, to Claymont.

It was still a far cry from the big place outside Boston, the beautiful house in Garden City, Long Island—wasn't half as nice as the place they left in Scranton. But at least they'd be on their own. And Joseph was going to get back, see: he never liked that used-car job, never—it was only a start. And the house, well . . . there'd be a better house. After a year, he moved Jean and the kids to a real house in Arden, a rental place, but better . . . and after another year, they moved to the house on Wilson Road. For nineteen years, they lived on Wilson, but to Joseph, it was always temporary. He was going to get back to a *really good* house, he was going to make it again, *every day* . . . he'd get up, and he'd say: Today, I'm going to turn that corner, get the big break, today. . . . That was the great thing about him: he would never, never quit.

And to Joey, who watched this . . . every day . . . that was the difference between balls and courage. That was better than daring . . . that was guts. And Joey meant to have guts. He would never, *never* quit.

—★—

A stutter is a cruel affliction for a kid, because no one, not even he, can see anything wrong. It's not like a club foot, or a missing finger—where there's something physically, visibly wrong, and you have simply to shrug and do the best you can. No, a stutter is more insidious: it attacks directly a child's ability to make himself known and felt in the world. But indirectly—because there's nothing wrong—it attacks his own idea of himself, his self-esteem, his confidence: Why can't he talk right?

Joe did not stutter all the time. At home, he almost never stuttered. With his friends, seldom. But when he moved to Delaware, there were no friends. There were new kids, a new school, and new nuns to make him stand up and read in class: that's when it always hit—always always always. When he stood up in front of everybody else, and he wanted, so much, to be right, to be smooth, to be smart, to be normal, j-j-ju-ju-ju-ju-jus'th-th-th-th-*then*!

Of course, they laughed. Why wouldn't they laugh? He was new, he was small, he was . . . ridiculous . . . even to *him*. There was *nothing wrong*. That's what the doctors said.

So why couldn't he talk right?

He learned to dread. He'd be coming to school, running from the bus—flushed, healthy, full of juice—and then he'd remember: *Oh, God, it's my day to read in Latin class. God!* . . . and the joy was gone from the morning.

He learned to scheme. In Catholic school, kids sit in rows. "A-a" takes the first seat, front of the row on the teacher's far left. "A-b" will have the next seat back, and so on. Biden would usually sit in the middle of that far left row, maybe four or five seats from the front. And when the nun would start the readings, it was easy for a smart kid like Joey to count the paragraphs down the page . . . three, four . . . *five*—to find his paragraph, and memorize it. Somehow, it was easier, his mouth worked better, if he didn't have to look at the page.

He learned what cruelty, unfairness, was—a dozen ways, but all from the wrong end of the stick. There was a kid in class, Jimmy Lanahan, who used to give Joe fits. Every time he stood up to read, Lanahan would start on him:

"B-b-b-b-b-b-BIDEN!"

Of course, that only turned the screws tighter, and Joey would stumble, have to look down at the page, and then it was over:

"P-p-p-p-ar-r-r-ret omn-n-n-n-iamqu-qu-qu-qu-"

In a whisper, from behind: "B-b-b-b-b-BIDEN!"

". . . qu-que v-v-v-vi-v-vinc-c-c-c-it . . ."

And from the sister at the head of the classroom: "All right, Mr. Biden. That will be enough."

Thing was, he knew they were wrong to mock him. There was a saying in Jean Biden's house: "Never kid a fat person about being fat." You could punch some kid in the nose—sure—but you did not, could not, attack his dignity.

One day, he stood to read, and from behind, Lanahan let him have it: "B-b-b-b-b-b-Biden!" And Joey turned around and got Jimmy—by the neck—and held on, shouted in his face:

"You sh-sh-shut up! I'm reading here!"

Mostly, he got mad at himself: ashamed of his own helplessness. He always felt he was imposing on *them*. The class should not have to sit there, and l-l-l-li-lih-l-listen to him, t-t-t-t-trying to get out a p-p-p-p-pa-pa-paragraph th-tha-th-that everyone else w-w-w-w-wuh-wuh-would've f-f-f-f-ffinished!

One of the nuns in Scranton had told him he'd do better if he got into a rhythm, a verbal march that would help him keep step while he read. So when Joe got to Wilmington, and schemed ahead to find his reading, he'd break each sentence into rhythmic bursts, till he could hear it, by memory, bouncing in his head. One day, that first school year in Wilmington, Joe skipped ahead to find his paragraph in the story of Sir Walter Raleigh:

"Then, the gentleman put the cloak across the puddle, so the lady could step . . ."

And he broke it up in his head to hear the footfalls of its march:

THEN the GEN-tle
MAN put the CLOAK
a-CROSS the PUDdle
So the LA-dy could
STEP . . .

And that's the way he spoke it—he was getting along great!

Then the nun broke in: "What is that word, Mr. Biden?"

"W-w-wh? . . ."

"The *third word*, Mr. Biden! Read it!"

Joey froze. He could only say it as he'd heard it in his head: "GEN-tle MAN . . ."

"Mr. Biden! Look at the page, and *read it*!"

Joey could not look at the page and read it—he knew he'd lose it. What was the word? Did he have the wrong word?

"*GEN-tle MAN . . .*"

"That will be all," the teacher snapped, "Mr. B-b-Biden."

Joe put his book down, silent in his shame, and just walked out of the class.

— ★ —

Thing was, Joe, Sr., never could get out of selling those cars: there were four kids now—the youngest, Frankie, was born in Delaware—and Catholic schools for all of them, and the mortgage for the house on Wilson . . . so, it was the sales lot, every day, and evenings till nine, and Saturdays, too. He never could trade up to a house of distinction . . . no, it was a three-bedroom tract house, like its neighbors.

And no room to spare—that was for sure. His daughter, Val, had to have her own room, so the boys, all three, slept in one small bedroom . . . and the dining table was spread with their homework, and the living room was an obstacle course of kids asprawl . . . and then Boo-Boo showed up. At first, he only came to drop off his father—Joey's granddad—to stay with Jean for a few weeks, while Boo-Boo was on the road, selling Serta mattresses. But even after Pop Finnegan died, Boo-Boo would drop by for visits. And then one weekend, he came to visit, and stayed for eighteen years. Then, it was four in the boys' room: two bunk beds, top and bottom. . . . And meanwhile, the Widow Sheen moved to Wilmington and lived with the Bidens for two years. Even after they found her a room in a private house nearby, she'd still put on her white gloves and come to lunch almost every day. . . . And then her son, Bill, Jr., moved into the Bidens' rec room for a year or so . . . and then, too, Frank Biden's wife died, and he was so lonely, he had to move in. Joseph and Jean took care of them all. That's the way it was, with the Bidens.

But the big one was Boo-Boo, a presence in the house, and an object lesson for Joey: Boo-Boo stuttered. Edward Blewitt Finnegan was a smart man, a college man—had dreamed of becoming a doctor—but he stuttered. And the way Boo-Boo styled his life, it was a t-t-t-tuh-tuh-tragedy: he *couldn't* go to med school when he talked like that! . . . It wasn't that he didn't try, was it? The stutter was his explanation, an alibi in constant evidence.

But Jean Biden would have none of it. Blewitt was her brother, and she told it like it was. He could have gone to medical school, if he'd tried—if it took *twenty years.* There was no excuse, in Jean Biden's book, for giving up. She would not let Boo-Boo *mention* his stutter and his failure in the same breath, without shaking her head, rolling her eyes . . . or calling him out, right in his face, in true Finnegan style: "Edward Blewitt Finnegan! That's a goddam lie!"

And she would not let Joey give up—not for one day, not for an hour: he would beat this . . . there was more to him than stutter. He had his Biden grace. He had talent. He had brains. She must have told him ten *thousand* times: "Joey, it's just that you are *so smart* . . . your mind outruns your ability to say your thoughts."

"Joey, you have *such* a high IQ . . ."

"Joey Biden, you're just smarter than anybody . . ."

But she needn't have worried. Joey was not short on will. And he had eyes to see what he didn't want to be. He did not want to be Boo-Boo, arguing with schoolboys about their lessons, to show how smart he was. He did not want to have to alibi. He did not want to drive every week through five states, selling mattresses—no.

He knew it just as surely as he knew the other truth of his young life: he was not going to sell cars—no way. He didn't know how his father could stand it. He would not be slave to a mortgage on a tract house; he would not end up trapped on that treadmill. No. He was a Biden and he could do . . . anything.

—★—

It wasn't quick, it took years. But he learned to game it out. He learned, always, to see himself in the situation to come, to think what he'd say, how he'd sound, what the other guy would say, and what the answer would be. . . .

He had a paper route, and a neighbor, an old chatty man, who was always around . . . and Joey knew (he could see it, like it already happened!) that if he wore his Yankee baseball cap, the old man would ask him about the Yankee game last night, and Joey would say:

"Mantle hit a home run . . ."

"Man-tle-hit-a-home-run . . ."

"Mick-ey-Man-tle-hit-a-homer . . ."

He could see where he'd be standing on the walk, in front of the porch, and he'd hand the man his paper . . .

"Yeah-Mick-ey-Man-tle-hit-a-homer . . ."

"They-beat-Cleve-land-four-to-one . . ."

He'd play the thing over and over in his mind: everything the guy could ask him . . . everything Joey would have to say. And he'd make sure to wear his Yankee cap. That was the key.

He lived so much of his life in his head, in the future, that he had more than a child's understanding of how people were likely to react. Of course, every kid thinks that way about adults, to a certain extent, if only to stay out of trouble . . . but Joey had to know more. He had to know what they'd say, what *he* could say, how he'd be, how he'd sound, how he'd look. *And then, if they said that . . . what would he say then?*

And so, he had more than a child's understanding of what he wanted to do. That's what his new friends in Wilmington saw. Joe always had an idea. . . . If their notion of a summer evening's prank was to put a bag of dogshit on old man Schutz's doorstep, Joey would say, "No, here's what we'll do. You know behind my house, where they got all those little trees? Get a shovel . . ." And they did: they went out with shovels and planted a forest of saplings on Mr. Schutz's lawn. It was so much more elaborate—all thought out, the way Joey had it figured.

The other thing was, the moms loved Joey: as long as young Biden was along, the thing was okay. . . . Part of it had to be, he was so nice to them—he seemed to know how they would feel about things. They might have seen, too, how he was about his own mom—so sentimental. (The way to get a punch in the nose was to say *anything* about Joey's mom. BANGO! Right in the face.) But what those ladies saw most clearly: here was a boy unswayed by peer pressure, who always seemed to have his own idea—such a sense of himself. . . .

Yes, and that's why it mattered so much to Joey to get into Archmere—Wilmington's smallest, most serious, preppiest Catholic high school. It was crucial to the picture he had of himself—in the future, which was so real, so present, in Joe.

— ★ —

He was so happy when he got to go—so grateful. (He knew it was a strain. He'd heard his parents talk at night about the bills . . . he knew.) But Archmere held its terrors, too. There was speech class—required for all ninth- and tenth-graders—and weekly Tuesday assemblies, where four underclassmen would each have to make a speech, in front of the whole student body, and all the teachers, and Father Diny, the head man.

What could he do but scheme ahead, and dread the day, and practice? He went into training. If memorizing helped, then he would train to memorize: he used to time himself, committing to rote stock pieces, like the Declaration of Independence. He'd grab the text and peer at it, like he wanted to bore holes through the page, and then he'd put it down and try to say it, whole. . . . How fast could he get the thing in his head?

Someone said a stutter was caused by facial muscles seizing up in nervous convulsion. So Joey stood for hours in front of a mirror, reading aloud or simply talking to his own image, while he tried to relax the muscles in his face, to attain that droopy, logy, sloooow eeeease that he thought would solve his problem.

And in class, he read about Demosthenes, who made himself the greatest orator of his day by putting pebbles in his mouth and declaiming to the sea, above the roar of the waves. So Joey Biden, of Wilson Road, would stand outside at the wall of his house, the blank wall that looked out toward the fence and Mom-Mom's roses, and with stones in his mouth, he'd try to read aloud, until he could read that page without a miss, and then he'd go to the next page, and the next . . . until it was the book in one hand and a flashlight in the other.

And he got through: ninth grade, he had to stand up at assembly and give a talk, like the rest . . . but the rest could not have known such triumph. His speech was not perfect, no . . . but it was a great day. And like a kid who beats his big brother at a footrace, and devotes himself to running ever after, Joe Biden decided he would be a speaker. He would be the best goddam speaker at Archmere.

So he trained. That summer, after his job on the school grounds crew, in the hours till dinner, after which his friends would show up, he'd practice. He'd read aloud. He'd speak aloud. . . . And that was the same summer he grew so much, came of age and of size . . . and still good-looking—a wonderful smile—and plenty smart, and less wary now when he came back to school, which wasn't a new school anymore, but a small place, really, where everybody knew him . . . or thought they did (He's changed somehow, hasn't he?) . . . and that was the same time that girls got important, and Joey was always sweet and serious with girls—they loved him—and his sister knew plenty of them . . . and that size made a difference on the football field, and Joey could run, and he could catch, and most important, he believed he could catch *anything* . . . and that was the difference, really: he believed he could master . . . anything. It seemed he could: he was in just the right circle, with the athletes, and the cool guys, and when the question came up—what're we gonna do?—well, still, it was Joe who had an answer. He was a leader—that's what his teachers said. And a player—that was from his coach. And the other guys, his classmates, they remember those things, too . . . but what they all say about Biden at Archmere:

Joey Biden, he could really talk.

20

1955

H E CAME OUT as a mother's idea of a perfect kid: Dick was an Eagle Scout, obedient and helpful at home, respectful to his elders, a quiet and steady success at school, confirmed in his belief at Third Baptist Church (he'd been dedicated in his cradle). The church financed his summers at Camp Minnewonka, a Christian leadership camp on the shore of Lake Michigan, where the four-square (physical, mental, social, and religious) life of Christian virtue was developed by dividing the camp into tribes, each identified by a different-colored headband, each competing in disciplines like swimming, archery, and Bible history. Dick was a Tribal Chief. (The head man, named Steiger, was a square-jawed, inspiring, evangelical type. He was the Big Chief. At the Great Council Fire, if you wanted to speak, you had to raise your hand and call out, "O Big Chief!")

Back in St. Louis, Dick evinced an interest in current events. Both of Loreen's boys used to pop out of bed and run downstairs by 7:00 A.M., to get the paper. They'd have it read before school. Dick tried to talk to his friends about the wider world, but none of them knew what was going on . . . so, in eighth grade, his last year at Mason School, Dick started his own paper, *The Voice of Mason*. Much of the mimeographed sheet was taken up with school events, PTA news, and honor rolls, but Dick wrote the world news column. For instance, he analyzed the Army-McCarthy hearings, and concluded with this declaration:

"Throughout the history of the United States the greatest men we have known were those who were the most criticized and discussed. A good example is that of Abraham Lincoln, who during his time as President, was probably the most hated man in the United States. Now he is recognized as a great man, in fact, one of the greatest men the world has ever known.

"Will this be McCarthy's case? Only time will tell."

See, Dick was not going to offend anybody—that was not the system, at all. With Loreen a quiet Democrat and Lou a loud Republican (and his grandma, Stella Cassell, writing letters to the *Globe-Democrat* about the menace of Godless Communism at home and abroad), Dick could discuss almost any political question as an ally of the adult involved. In fact, there was no adult he knew who did not regard Dick as a boy with exceptional judgment, sound information, precocious understanding. . . .

— ★ —

In short, he was sort of a nerd—even by standards of the mid-fifties, when he entered Southwest High—or as they said in those days, in South St. Louis, kind of "fruit." Actually, he wasn't total fruit, because he was good in drama, and that counted for something—though being in a play didn't automatically make you "neat," like being on the football team. For example, the football guys always put up the student council president—and Dick never did get to run for council president, or any other office. He was a bit small (he'd skipped half a grade), and with kids his own age, he was shy. He didn't have a girlfriend, though his neighbor, Carol Rauscher, was one of his oldest friends—the girl Dick would go to when the Scouts had an outing: "Hey, Carol, we gotta go on a hayride . . ." She wasn't a girlfriend, in the high school sense of the word.

What made matters harder was, the Mason School kids were joined at Southwest High by kids from St. Louis Hills. And St. Louis Hills was money—mansions!—a different world. That's where the cheerleaders lived, and the neatest guys, the social stars. They had cashmere sweaters, and Spalding saddle shoes, and the girls had dyed-to-match sweaters and skirts, and big bobby sox (that cost *two dollars a pair*). There was no way kids from Mason could keep up with that . . . so, they were not neat.

Anyway, Dick was too neat to be neat. He came out of the house on Reber Place, every day, looking like he'd been inspected, which he had. In school, Dick was mannerly, his locker was impeccable, with his books in order and his jacket hung up. He did not use bad words, never drank, never smoked. He had oversized hands, a nice, firm handshake, like a little man . . . but his face looked so young—red hair, blond peach fuzz (he was still years from his first shave), no pimples, freckles in the summertime . . . and always spanking clean, with his wash-pants and socks matched to his Oxford shirt, which showed the creases on the sleeves where Loreen had pressed them.

He had none of the sloppy excess requisite to teenage élan. True boppers, in those days, were moving on to sideburns, skinny ties, and blue suede shoes, as affected by his brother, Don, the saxophone man, when he formed his combo, the Aristocats, which played for teen parties and talent shows. Dick's talent entry had nothing to do with hep: he'd dress in a suit and hat, with spectacles, a white goatee and mustache, to perform Senator Claghorn, a drawling and bombastic character who strolled and preened before the crowd, making speeches and telling jokes about politics, school affairs, and the vagaries of life. Loreen helped him get the costume together. Helen Baldwin helped with the writing. But then it was up to Dick (or rather, Rich, as he'd started to call himself) to hold the stage in this seventy-year-old southern solon persona. The amazing thing was: he could do it. He seemed to have no teen self-consciousness about sticking out, looking weird, being seen. It was as if Uncle Bob had told him, one day, on the boat: *Okay, now, act like you're a self-important fifth-term Senator* . . . and Dick could just *do* it. No problem!

Here's the opener:

"I was down to th' fillin' station, this mornin' . . . you know what th' fillin' station is, don't you? . . .

"It's where they fill up th' *car* . . . and drain the *family*!" (Ka-thump)

And people loved it—thought it was great—especially his teachers. Miss Meenach, the drama teacher, thought that darling Rich Gephardt walked on water. . . . That was the year, sophomore year, '55, when he enrolled in drama class. And that's where it happened, in Miss Meenach's class, where Rich became such a star. . . .

— ★ —

Gould Meenach had her eye on everything happening in her field. Every year, ever since they were young, she and her sister traveled to New York, to see what was what on Broadway. That was something, in South St. Louis. She started the school's radio workshop, with full sound effects, and scripts from the networks. Of course, she didn't have the budget for video, so she made cardboard dummy cameras and started a television workshop. And, of course, every year, there were the junior and senior plays, and the drama workshops, and the sophomores in drama class—and Miss Meenach was not young: she must have seen a million kids perform. But seldom did she get one like Rich Gephardt. That boy was a natural! She'd tell the class: "All right, now, I want you to act like you're in an elevator . . ." And that Gephardt boy could just *do* it. Not a moment's pause, no giggling, no unease . . . he'd back right up against a wall, stick a hand in his pocket and gaze up toward the ceiling, like he was watching the lights of the floors flash by, then lower his eyes, just at the right time, just as the cab was slowing to a stop, and then he'd walk off . . . and hold the door to let an imaginary lady by! . . . He was impeccable! And the way he listened, she never had to tell him anything more than once.

Of course, some things about Gould Meenach were very much of the old school—seating, for one. None of this open-classroom-sit-anywhere-you-please for Miss Meenach, no. Students sat in alphabetical rows, which was why Gephardt was next to Hahn. . . . That made all the difference.

Carol Hahn was a big girl, stylish, athletic. She was a cheerleader, pretty, with dark hair cut short in just the right style, and she hung out with football guys, the neatest guys. She came from St. Louis Hills, had the right clothes, the right friends. She belonged. But she did not belong in drama class. See, in sports, or even cheering, where Carol excelled, she was on a squad, part of the team . . . but this, this *acting,* she was all alone, with everybody watching *her.* It was . . . so awkward. She couldn't figure out how anyone could do it . . . until she looked to her left, and there was this red-haired kid, who could do . . . everything. Miss Meenach adored him. He was a star!

She'd met Rich Gephardt as a freshman, of course, but she never paid attention. He was fruit, wasn't he? But now, in drama class, she decided he wasn't fruit. He was neat. So, she started to talk to him. And pretty soon, he wasn't so shy. And as social girls could do, she gave him to understand that if he asked, she would go out with him. So, one day, blushing to the roots of his strawberry hair, he asked . . . and she said yes.

They went to a play, which was kind of his turf, and it was fun . . . so they went out again, and again. And all at once, that freckle-nosed Rich Gephardt had a girlfriend, who was a *cheerleader . . .* who hung out with *football guys.* And who dressed right, and was rich, and popular . . . it was *so neat.* Oh, it took some adjusting: he had to tell Loreen he needed new clothes—Spalding oxfords, different sweaters. . . . But Loreen was working, and she made sure he got the clothes . . . just as she made sure Lou took the trolley to work when Rich needed the family car for a date. And she'd have gas in the car, too, and she'd iron and lay out his new clothes, and leave money for him. And he was neat.

Anyway, Carol always had a car. The Hahns' house in St. Louis Hills had *seven bathrooms.* It was another world. And Rich loved it. Carol's parents belonged to the country club, and they took Rich and Carol there for dinner. And Rich drank that in like a thirsty man. Carol couldn't stand the people at the country club—they were drips. But Rich thought they were neat. And Carol's father was a talker—talked forever, to hear Carol tell it—but Rich was great with her dad . . . he'd just sit there and listen, for *hours.* Both the Hahns thought Rich was just the *nicest* boy. . . .

And he was—even as he grew into his neatness. Sometimes, Rich would take Carol along on his private errands to an old-age home, where he'd dress in his suit and hat, with the goatee and glasses—Senator Claghorn. Rich would tell his jokes for the old folks, and they loved it. Meanwhile, Loreen introduced Carol to a life of faith, the Christian life that centered around Third Baptist. One New Year's Eve, Rich and Carol's date was a service at church . . . it was beautiful. But Carol would not tell their neat friends where they'd gone for New Year's. People would think she'd changed . . . maybe she had.

So had Rich, in some ways. He was not so shy about himself. For the talent show on their last Hello Day (an annual program of welcome for new freshmen), Rich did not do another Senator Claghorn, but instead, in his own clothes, alone on the stage, he acted out a long verse about the creation of the world.

And God stepped out on space.
And He looked around, and said,
I'm lonely . . . I'll make me a world . . .

And Rich stepped out on stage, and looked around, and said . . . "I'm lonely . . ." and then with a gesture, he rolled the light up one side of the stage, with the darkness still cloaking the other, and Rich said (as did God, in the poem), "That's good!"

. . . this Great God,
Like a mammy bending over her baby,
Kneeled down in the dust,
Toiling over a lump of clay,
Till He shaped it in His Own Image.
Then into it He blew the breath of life . . .

And there was Rich, on his knees, center stage, forming with his hands God's own image in clay . . .

And the audience was silent, and Carol was in tears. And Loreen had come to school, too, and snuck into the back, and she was crying. (Helen Baldwin was backstage, doing the props and lights.) And the whole thing was a huge success.

And in his last summer at Southwest, Rich did not go back to Camp Minnewonka; instead, Miss Meenach proposed him for a special drama workshop—just one Southwest student each year—at Northwestern University, in Evanston, north of Chicago.

And there he got to measure himself against students from everywhere in the country—and it was fun! It was just like Uncle Bob's boat, or Miss Meenach's class. And when he came back, he'd found his college—and his course of study: drama at Northwestern. See, he'd been there, he knew he could succeed: there were not too many kids who could take a role, or an improv, and just *do* it . . . who could be any way they told him to be. But Rich Gephardt could. And that could take him a long way.

Like They
Always Did

I T WAS sort of a good-news-bad-news thing. No one picked up on the Kennedy stuff in the California speech . . . because no one was listening: Joe still couldn't say if he was running. That's all anyone would ask him, for *months:* Could he do it all—be a candidate and a chairman? He was already taking heat in the press about the Judiciary Committee: Why were they off to such a slow start? And any time he'd show his face, doing politics, some sonofabitch was sure to ask: Wasn't that taking time from the Senate?

How about candidate, chairman, and family man? Jill still regarded the campaign with dread. What about her life? What about their life together? What about Ashley? Ashley was only six . . . didn't know anything about Neilia. (In '84, when Joe ran for reelection, his media gurus made a fine bio ad—cost a fortune—but Joe had to kill it, afraid that Ashley might see the part about Neilia.) And Hunter, Joe's second son, was at that shy and tender teen age where he didn't want everybody looking at him: didn't want interviews, pictures of the family—didn't want life turned inside out . . . so, he talked to Jill.

The gurus took Jill for a political infant, or a problem to be circumvented. But Jill Biden was a woman of realistic judgment: she'd been around politics for a decade now, and she had good eyes. She didn't think about songs, sleeping generations, or movie titles. She thought about how it was *going to be.* What if Hart was too strong, and Joe couldn't break out of the pack? What if Cuomo decided to run, and there were two brilliant speakers in the race? (Two *Catho-*

lic brilliant speakers, one with New York money.) What if Joe did break out
and made a run for the finish, and came in . . . just short. Then they'd run
again . . . and again. That was her nightmare: that he'd run, come close, and
then it would never stop. Why did it have to start now?

That's not how Joe talked about it. No, Joe mostly talked about time: like
he knew he could do all those things—hell, he *was* doing all those things—if
he could find the time. He talked about it that way for so long, so often, that
the staff came up with the brilliant idea that Joe must want to see a *schedule.*
They would put all the dates into the computer, see . . . the days in Iowa, days
in New Hampshire, and committee hearings, Senate sessions, fund-raisers,
trips around the country . . . and then the computer would print out a schedule.
And then they'd know, right? The problem would be solved! . . . Like
McNamara's computers were going to win the Vietnam War.

(In the end, they never did mash it through the computers. Instead, Ted
Kaufman and Ridley taped colored file cards all over the walls of Joe's study.
Red for Iowa, green for New Hampshire, blue for the South, pink for the
committee . . . something like eight colors. The room looked like one of those
op-art pieces that vibrates when you look at it. Then they spent the first hour
or so with Joe on the couch saying: "Wait a minute—tell me again—what's
pink? . . ." and then more hours moving cards around on the walls, swapping
dates, and finally, Ridley and Kaufman stepped back and announced, with
pride . . . no, with triumph: "There . . . *that's* how we get through the next
six months." Whereupon, Biden pointed out, with some justice: "Yeah, but
this thing lasts more than six months.")

In the end, no schedule could solve Joe's problem. It wasn't about time—not
really. The heart of the problem was: Joe could not see his way through. How
was he going to be a husband, father . . . the way he meant to be? He made
a rule: the kids could come along, all the kids, or any kid, or Jill and the kids
. . . whenever they wanted, whatever the cost. If that meant a change in the
schedule, a larger plane, if it meant another thousand dollars, or five, or ten
thousand . . . no matter: *any Biden . . . on any trip.* But was that father enough?
What if they wanted *him* to come with *them*? What if they had a game, or
a play, a debate? Christ! Beau's graduation! . . .

How would he be a brother . . . the way he meant to be? Val's divorce,
Jimmy's bankruptcy, Frankie—Jesus! Frankie had gone through some serious
personal problems in California. And now the kid was home again, going to
settle down, get married, and . . . boom—Joe says the word and every paper
in the country would be turning over rocks on Frankie.

And how could he be a Senator, a chairman . . . the way he meant to be?
He could not afford to give short shrift to the committee. There were already
people in the Senate who talked him down as a lightweight. If he walked away
now, they'd savage him. He had long talks with his senior staff guys, Gitenstein, Kaufman—they thought it was impossible to do everything. That's what
they all thought, last November, when the Democrats won back the Senate and
Teddy Kennedy gave up the Judiciary chair. They just assumed Joe couldn't

do both—chairman and candidate . . . Joe couldn't see it either. He tried to get Kennedy to take the committee. He just about begged the sonofabitch. But no, Kennedy wanted the Labor chair, and Biden was saddled with Judiciary, the toughest, most fractious, most . . . Jesus, if a Supreme Court justice dies, they get a nominee—well, that's it: the end of the campaign. No way in hell . . .

Thing was, Joe knew there was no way—that's why he told Jill not to worry. That's why Ridley had the statement all drafted, carried it around in his briefcase: *Why Joe Biden Is Not Going to Run.* That's why the papers were picking up hints: writing the obit for the campaign before Joe even said the word. That's why Joe himself told reporters: "Right now, quite frankly, I don't see the way. . . ." Then he went to Florida.

The venue was a conference of union chieftains, about half the AFL-CIO, at the Sheraton in Bal Harbour. Joe was on the program, with Hart and Gephardt. Hart was there to make amends, to tell the unions that just because he'd called their main man, Mondale, a "candidate of the special interests" . . . didn't mean he was *against labor . . .* no. Gary Hart was a Friend of Labor! Gephardt came with the goodies: his trade bill, which promised to save U.S. jobs by opening foreign markets . . . or else. After all, labor had been saying, all these years, that foreign competition was unfair, and Dick was there to let them know—he agreed!

But it was Biden who blew the crowd away.

"You kid yourself half the time," he told the union nabobs. "*You* don't understand what's *happening . . .*"

Joey got his chin out, stuck it in their faces, like a dock boss who wants to see things *shape up:*

"There has been an *outright war* declared on you these last eight years. This is not some minor conflict. The Chambers of Commerce of America understand what's at stake, and they are about the business of *seeing to it* that *your* say, and *your* share of the economic bounty and prosperity of America are fundamentally changed.

"If you don't understand that, then, with all due respect, you're in the wrong business. You've been coming to Florida and sitting in the sun too long. . . ."

Of course they jumped up and started to cheer. There's nothing labor likes more than a war—and nothing labor sees more often, more readily, than a business plot against the God-given right to pull down twenty-two dollars an hour.

After that, it was Biden's crowd, though he talked for another forty minutes: he wouldn't leave the podium until he *knew* he had the connect. And he got it. They loved how Joey made them feel.

Of course, he felt it, too. Joe's committee press guy, Pete Smith, was along in Bal Harbour, and he was with Biden when reporters cornered Joe at the elevators.

Sure enough, someone asked about the candidate-and-chairman thing, and BANGO—it was all over. Joe said: "I think I can do 'em both."

Then someone asked about Cuomo, and Biden snapped that he didn't worry about Cuomo. Then, he seemed to think that might sound cocky, so he explained: "I think only one of us is going to run—and it's probably going to be me."

So was he in?

Was that an announcement?

When would he announce?

"I plan on running . . ." Biden said.

"I want to be President . . ."

As to announcement: "Well, it depends . . ." Joe was making this up on the spot. "It depends how things are going . . . after June." (And he thought to himself, ". . . after Beau's graduation.")

In the Sheraton hallway, Pete Smith gave Biden a grin . . . meant to be congratulations . . . a moment of shared relief, at a return in the road, taken at speed.

"Well, I guess that's that," Pete said.

But Joe wasn't sharing any relief. He was all steel: "Well, I've done my part," Biden said. "Let's see now if the staff can do its part."

Staff? . . .

That's what Ridley said, when Joe got back to Wilmington, and Ridley came up for another talk. Joe still had a score of gurus, and demigurus, but no one was signed on, no one was coming in every day. All they really had were the same few guys: Ridley, Gitenstein, Kaufman—and they were stretched to the limit.

"Joe, it's sort of a good-news-bad-news," Ridley told him. Joe looked over from the driver's seat. They were riding around in the Bronco again. "You know, the good news is, you're running. The bad news is, your first team's already burned out."

— ★ —

Back from Bal Harbour, Sasso was in a stew. These guys were *good*. There was no way Michael could stand up and do a labor crowd like that. . . . Chrissake, the man could not utter the word "President." That February, Dukakis was on the road, two weeks out of four, but he still could not get the word out. He'd say: "And if I run for national office . . ."

That was not going to feed the bulldog. That's what Sasso found out in Florida. Hart was better than Sasso had ever seen him—funny, relaxed, like a man who knows he belongs on the national stage. Gephardt was about five times better than he was a month before . . . and that trade bill was red meat for labor. Biden was amazing—he had the speech, had it *down*. Michael was still getting ready to make his first *national* speech—the New Hampshire speech—but he wasn't ready.

That's how Michael ended up in the office of the speech coach, Frances LaShoto. Fran was a professor at Emerson College, and she'd seen them all; she was Jack Kennedy's coach. She had a studio upstairs on Newbury Street, not too far from the State House. Michael did not want to go. But he went.

It was supposed to be an easy hour, tucked into a normal day: 11:00 A.M.—Michael would be back at his desk for his brown-bag lunch. Ira Jackson dashed across Newbury Street for some croissants and French coffee, to keep everybody going. Ira was along with his speech text—and Sasso, and his deputy, John DeVillars. DeVillars would take over the First Secretary's job if Michael decided to run and Sasso moved over to the campaign. It'd be good for DeVillars to see this, a chance to see the man work . . .

But DeVillars left within minutes, after Fran started ripping into Michael. Even Sasso had to leave the room a couple of times. It was too close to the bone, too private: like watching your friend fight with his wife.

"You think you work hard at your job, don't you?" she was saying to Michael, in the middle of the speech. He'd just got to the stuff about his parents.

"I work as hard at my job," Michael said, "as any public servant in America."

"So how come you don't sweat?"

"Whaddya mean, I don't sweat?"

"I don't see any pain," Fran said. "I don't see any pain in your face. I don't see any clutching in your gut. I don't see that you're working. All you're doing is going through the motions."

Doubt and annoyance clouded Michael's face. He was just here to learn to keep his hands still, look at the audience . . . you know, get some tips! He was just trying to read the goddam speech!

"Exactly!" Fran spat. "You're not working. You're not hurting. I want to see you get to the marrow of your bones, and you're not even getting into your gut. You're just getting through it with your head, aren't you, Michael?"

So Michael went at it again, and she came at him again.

"You think you're so smart, don't you, Michael?"

"No, I . . ."

"Yes, you *do*. Smart Michael. Perfect Michael! Don't have to show anybody how you feel, *do you*?"

It seemed like it went on forever, like a war. No one ate croissants. Ira was jittery . . . and satisfied. He was the one who lined up Fran LaShoto. And she was right: this had to come from Michael's gut. That's what *he'd* been trying to say. Sasso looked like a mother with a sick child. There was no point worrying about the field if he was going to lose Michael—it could happen, too. Sasso knew Michael was the kind of guy who could walk to the brink, look over the cliff, then say, No. ("Nope . . . it's just not me." Sasso could almost hear him say it.)

But Michael didn't say it. He took the blows, he tried to do the work. He didn't know quite how . . . but he stayed. He wanted this New Hampshire speech to be something special. More than any of them knew: this was *his* test, for himself. And he was in this to listen, that's what he always said—to get his feet wet. He wasn't going to turn around at the first puddle. No, he was tougher than that.

—★—

They sent Gary Hart to a speech coach once. He didn't have any choice. It
was '83, and his contributors insisted. Hart was in no position to lift his leg
to contributors.

What happened was, these guys would send money to his campaign . . . then
he'd come to their town, and they'd watch him speak—he was *terrible*—it was
like sitting through a chemistry lecture: no attempt to lift the crowd. Of course,
that's the way Hart liked it: appeals to emotion made him feel *cheap*. But they
couldn't see it, the money guys, so they'd call Billy Shore. "You *gotta* get him
to a coach . . ." They didn't have to add "or else."

So Hart walks into this place in New York, with his jaw already working
and his mouth a grim white line. And the coach takes one look, and figures:
I got it. This guy's got to loosen up!

Good eye! That's like looking at a cocked howitzer and deciding there's
some tension in that gun. When Hart has to do something that Hart does not
want to do, he immediately decides it is unworthy. And then (if he still can't
get out of it) he goes *rigid:* like he's wearing some new du Pont polymer (five
times stronger than steel).

The coach says, "First, we're going to go out to the hallway . . ."

And Hart's mandibles open an inch, so he can enunciate: "*Why* are we going
to the hallway?"

"I want you to wad up this paper, and play catch with me."

"I am *not* going to wad up paper, and play catch . . ."

"It's just an exercise . . ."

". . . with *anybody.*"

"Well, look . . ."

"No."

"It's a way to . . ."

"No."

"Senator, if you can't do this, there's no way I can help you . . ."

"That's correct," Hart said, and with his first smile of the day, he walked
out of the office.

Turned out, people found all sorts of drama in his words, once he made his
move in Iowa and won in New Hampshire. . . . And this time, '88, he was
running with the wind: this time, he didn't have to show anybody he could
win. No one was asking anymore *if* he could win.

This time, he wasn't going to sand any sharp corners off his positions: Tax
the rich! . . . Yeah, let's show 'em what we're gonna do. *We'll put out a full
budget!* . . . It drove his Campaign Manager, Bill Dixon, crazy. But Hart loved
it. He'd stick it in their *faces*. This time, the staff would line up a speech before
some Jewish group, and Hart would talk for an hour . . . about supply
management in agriculture (addressing the concerns of all those Jewish farmers). But it worked. People left the room, saying, "This guy is *serious.*" When
you look like a winner, everything you do is a winner. When you're taking
strong positions, it gives the look of a man who is strong. Most important, it

undergirds the assumption that *something can be done.* That is the essence of optimism. All winning campaigns communicate optimism.

So this time, his staff had to show him a reason—policy or high politics, some way this would move the country toward his ideas—or they couldn't get Hart to do . . . anything.

"Look, it's one day . . ." they'd say around the big table in Denver—the schedule meeting: that's where the rubber hit the road. "He's just got to show up at the statehouse—*one day.* Just so he can say he's been there, he's *talked* to those people . . ."

"I don't know . . ." Sue Casey, the Scheduler, would say. She was the one who'd have to run it past Hart.

"Casey, those people can kill us. He's got to talk to them. He doesn't have to agree with them. He's just got to *show up.*"

So Casey would take the block schedule into Hart's law office, where he held court in Denver, and she'd try to scoot it past him:

"Absolutely not."

"They think you have to just . . ."

"No."

"What if it's just . . ."

"No."

The awful thing was the look he'd give her—it was scorn, and hurt. And Casey loved Hart . . . she did understand him. She knew he meant to create his own campaign events. And she knew why. Casey was one of the women who engineered the win in New Hampshire, in '84. She knew the concentric circles, all the theories—she *believed.* . . . And here was Hart, staring at her with that *look* on his face: *Don't tell me YOU'RE gonna be an asshole, too!*

When Hart would give that look . . . it was over. You couldn't stay in his face. You couldn't bear to be one of *them* in his mind. It was the same look he'd flash at the guys—Dixon, Hal Haddon, John Emerson—who tried to talk to him about women, about the way things *appeared,* how Hart had to watch himself. . . . These guys were supposed to be *friends.* They were supposed to know him! And he'd told them—told them *all*—that was *not* going to be a problem.

So they backed off, never brought it up anymore . . . you couldn't push Hart. And he wasn't stupid. If you could show him why something made sense . . . well, he'd do it. Might not like it. Might go stiff in the middle of it . . . but he'd do it. That was how he was about the big stuff, anyway, like the date of announcement. . . .

Hart didn't want to declare his candidacy early. He didn't see the advantage to inviting that kind of scrutiny *now.* . . . "I don't understand why . . ."

But they convinced him: Dixon, Haddon, Emerson, Paul Tully . . . hell, no one was more of a political pro than Tully. He'd been in the business twenty years—with the sole aim of electing a progressive Democrat. Tully had no ax to grind. He wasn't trying to change Gary Hart—didn't want to mess with the man, at all. And Tully was convinced: it was just good politics. It would highlight the hollowness of Cuomo's posture (still on the mountaintop, waiting for God to speak to him) and Senator Sam Nunn's calculation (could he make it? could he make it? could he make it?). Anyway, you get out there early, flatten the grass, none of the little guys can sneak up. Tully had argued the same strategy for Mondale four years before—and Mondale ended up the nominee. . . .

So they convinced him—they'd schedule announcement for April . . . and with a sigh, Hart acceded. It *was* good politics. It *would* flatten the landscape. It's just that Hart knew: the only man with his head above the grass would be . . . Gary Hart. For Tully, Haddon, Emerson, Dixon, it would straighten the road: it was the start of their campaign. But Hart knew: it was the end of life, as he chose to live it.

— ★ —

They all said, the gurus and political hit men: an early announcement, earlier than anyone . . . and Dick agreed!

Of course, before that, he had to hit the statehouses, the courthouses, the activists—give them a chance to feel they were in on the ground floor. And Dick agreed! He was hitting doors as fast as he could. Big doors, little doors . . . he didn't just hit the big union meeting at Bal Harbour, like the other candidates. Dick hit the Machinists' Midwest Regional Leadership Conference. He showed up when the chieftains of the bricklayer locals gathered in Washington. He must have made a half-dozen personal calls to Chuck Gifford, the head of the United Auto Workers in Iowa. Another half-dozen to *Mrs.* Gifford . . . you couldn't give him too many calls.

That's the way he always did it . . . since '76, every campaign for Congress: "How many doors did we hit today?" That's all Dick wanted to know. Of course, it wasn't Dick alone: Jane could work one side of a block, or Jane and Loreen . . . and there was Dick's cousin, Joe Kochanski, who'd bring a van with the helium tanks, balloons for the kids . . . and Dick's campaign coordinator, the large and hyperactive Joyce Aboussie, who'd organize the thing, run the phones and volunteers. Even Joyce, who'd made a career helping Dick, had to wonder about him sometimes—Saturday night, when she and Jane would finish, they'd wait hours for Dick to quit. He'd get that weird focus, and he wasn't going to stop for something stupid like dinner.

"Jane," Joyce said on one such night, "you married a dork."

And Jane, who'd made a life loving Dick, said, "I know. He is a dork."

This time, Joyce was still in St. Louis, and the new people couldn't figure Dick, at all. Most of them had worked campaigns before, but they'd never seen a guy who'd just *do* it. They'd get around a big table for a schedule meeting, and they'd throw together whatever invitations they had: two states a thousand miles distant, the same weekend, flying coach, night flight through Chicago, on to Des Moines, and *then* a two-hour drive in a van . . . and Dick would just *do* it.

One time, the Scheduler lady said in the meeting: "Lemme ask you guys something . . . does Dick always agree with you?"

Don Foley, the press guy, the only one who went back with Dick, smiled as if to himself, and said: "As a matter of fact . . . yes."

And they all started giggling at the table.

But announcement was different. You couldn't just toss it together—even with Dick, who could make up for a lot of sloppy work . . . no. Announcement was big, had to be right. That would be the tape clip that would run for the next year and a half. That day would define the theme, the melody of the whole campaign.

That's why the speech was so important—but a week before the announcement, they still didn't have the speech. See, Shrum was a genius . . . genius needed time.

So they worked around the speech. They had the site: Union Station, St. Louis. It was perfect: there was the echo of Harry Truman, the underdog from Missouri, who got the '48 election-night papers on that Union Station concourse, and gleefully held up the headline from Chicago: DEWEY BEATS TRUMAN. Harry had the last laugh. . . . There were echoes there of Dick's own career: Union Station was the city's most conspicuous renovation, the emblem of its downtown renewal, a renaissance begun by Dick Gephardt and his fellow Young Turks on the Board of Aldermen fifteen years before. . . . And there were echoes of Dick's own family, of King St. Clair Cassell, Loreen's dad, who worked the Pullmans from that station, so many years, so many years ago. . . .

Problem was, the Advance staff couldn't hear the echoes, didn't know Dick's history. They were pros, and proud of it. Carrick had gone out and bought the best: Barry Wyatt, from California. He'd done White House Advance, done Kennedy Advance all over the country. Wyatt and the boys— there were twenty-four deputies by the day of announcement—knew how to treat a man in the bubble. (That's what the campaign wanted, right? A *professional* operation.)

So they flew in a week before, rented a room in Union Station (The Cannonball Express Room), and sat down with the locals. But the locals didn't have much to say, once the pros started putting together a bible:

10:08 A.M.   RAG to holding room, Union Station.

Dick didn't have a truly biblical title yet, so they just used his initials. Loreen was upset: "It just makes him sound, well . . . like a *rag.*" But they didn't ask Loreen, didn't even know her. They did know about her: she was on the list . . .

"We move the family on stage with him?"

"Move 'em before. Let people see him come up alone."

"Okay, we move the candidate's wife . . . kids—what is it, four? . . . three, okay . . . candidate's mother. Is the mother with the wife?"

"Who's gonna move the candidate's wife?"

"I got the brother, brother's wife . . ."

"Who's got the candidate's wife?"

Finally, someone who knew Dick and Jane interrupted. It was just . . . *wrong,* somehow. She had to say something. JoJo Crosby, the wife of Dick's old friend John Crosby, broke in to say: "Her name is Jane."

"Who?"

"Dick's wife. Her name is *Jane.*"

They looked at JoJo like she'd landed from Mars. What the hell difference did that make?

—★—

He was in this to listen, but listen to what? Michael had scores of meetings about this campaign question . . . but it was he who asked the questions, so he got the answers he wanted. Michael was enough of a lawyer for that.

What he wanted were the mechanics, tactics, politics:

How does a Dukakis sell in the South?

Would I have a chance to finish well—well enough—in Iowa?

What is it like? Say, an average week—what would I have to do?

What he didn't ask was about the job, save in the broadest terms: Could he do it? Of course, they said he could. They were all politicians. What was their percentage in telling him anything different?

Anyway, he was sure he could do it. Michael did not have a small opinion of his mind. Governing was what the job entailed. Governing was what he knew. For the rest, the *scientia,* the programs, the federal system, the foreign arcana, the bureaucratic lingo . . . well, he'd pick that up as he went along. He was a superior student.

So they told him all kinds of wonderful stuff:

There's a New South, where Democrats get elected on a biracial base of blacks and white liberals . . .

The Iowa race was still wide open—people there wait till they get to know the candidates . . .

Michael was already a hero to New Hampshire Democrats, since he stopped the Seabrook nuclear reactor, just over the border. (Michael had refused to file the required evacuation plans.)

Michael took all this into his head, with quick nods, like little check marks: he was in his professional listening mode. Since his loss, in '78—as he said, so many times—he'd become quite the determined listener. The signature of this new style (what the press liked to call "Duke II") was always the last question: an open-ended invitation for anyone in the room to talk. "Well, any questions, any comments? . . ." That showed he was listening—didn't it?

What it usually showed was he thought he'd got it. It was up to them now to show him something he'd missed.

Thing was, his method hadn't changed. Why should it? He had an unshakable faith in his power to arrive at a rational decision. He'd get the facts, he'd make the *correct* decision—simple as that. It's the same process he went through deciding whether to go to Harvard Law straight out of college, or do the Army first, and *then* go to Harvard. He asked people who thought they knew him. He asked people who'd been to the Army. He asked people who'd been to law school. Then, on a timetable previously determined, he made a considered and rational judgment.

Of course, he hated the Army. Most useless two years he ever spent. But that did not shake his faith in the process.

So he filled up his checklist . . . anything missing? And he was so much master of this game that no one stopped to ask *him,* what was it about? Why did he want to be President? What did he mean to do with the job? What was the inarguable base of mission that would drive him on when the taste of his own words was shit in his mouth?

There was that one time, when Ira asked . . . but Ira had to write the New Hampshire speech, so that was practical. And there was one time, when Michael brought in his ad guy, Dan Payne, brought him into the State House office for a sitdown at the table, where Michael held most of these matter-of-fact meetings . . . that familiar room, with the cool blue carpet bearing the Great Seal of Massachusetts, and the portrait of Samuel Adams, and Michael's straight-back chair, behind the big desk, with his Styrofoam cup . . . the room where Michael was so much at home, where he could solicit efficiently the facts he sought, the facts required for a reasoned conclusion . . . in this case, from his adman, some notion of how his campaign would look and sound. What would the words be? . . . What look, what themes, would a Dukakis campaign present to the voters?

And, as much as Payne wanted to help, wanted at least to be perceived as a player, he just stared at Dukakis like Michael was talking Greek.

"Governor, it's not the kind of . . . you know, I don't have a kind of one-size-fits-all *thing* that I can do . . . I mean . . ."

But Michael was insistent. Payne had worked on his '82 comeback, and in '86. Michael knew he was a charter wise guy at Sasso's Thursday night sessions. "What would you do?" Michael said. "I mean, what would, what would the themes, you . . . I think you know as well as anybody what a Presidential campaign for me would be like. . . ."

But Payne didn't know—thought he could not know until Dukakis came up with something *that mattered to Dukakis.* That's what he tried to say, politely. But Dukakis kept looking at him like he was holding out: Come on! Let's think up the words!

Kitty was there, next to Michael, and looking at Payne like he was a traitor to the cause. Finally Michael said to her: "Katharine, what do you think? Any questions? Any thoughts? . . ." But Kitty had nothing to add, so that's where it ended.

And Sasso was there, of course, but John wasn't asking anything. He figured the mission would come, in time. There had to be—there would be—a process of growth. Sasso had no small opinion of his own abilities, either. He would manage this process. He would lead his horse to water. . . . Meanwhile, they had something to say: the story of the comeback, the Massachusetts Miracle. That was enough, for the moment. Meanwhile, they had money to get. They had staff to line up. They had press to massage.

Sasso still worried about the field: Biden was in now, and Biden had talent. Gephardt was announcing, and he'd *live* in Iowa. Hart was doing everything right this time. . . . And Cuomo: John worried about Cuomo, the one man who shared their natural advantages, and had some others uniquely his own—the man they could not get by. But John had talked to Cuomo just the week before (Mario loved Sasso—they talked very well), and Sasso took one comfort from that talk. Cuomo had asked him, twice: *When* is Dukakis's date of decision? (Middle of March, middle of March, Sasso said.) So John knew Cuomo would not play it cute—he would make his move, he would let Michael know before Michael had to decide.

Mostly, Sasso worried about Michael—would he go? For the moment, that was the ball game. What was the point of pushing this, or stressing that . . . if Michael walked away? Sure, there had to be a theme for the campaign— but first there had to be a campaign. Sure, Michael ought to use the time, now, to learn—but first Michael had to hear what he needed to hear.

There was one time, by happenstance, Michael collided with a chance to learn. He had an event at the Harvard Club, in Boston. It was early evening, after a day at the State House; Michael was making for his meeting room . . .

"Hey, great to see you, Mike. Glad you're here . . ."

That was Teddy Kennedy, the first guy they ran into at the club. Kennedy was hosting a confab on arms control, and the major-league multiple-reentry-first-strike-throw-weight muckamucks had flown in.

"Listen," Kennedy said. "I'm having a few of these guys up to my hotel room, after. You know, just to kick things around . . . love to have you sit in . . ."

This took Michael completely by surprise, so he murmured thanks . . . said he'd certainly try.

But after Michael's event, when it came time to go to Kennedy's soirée, Dukakis was antsy.

"This isn't gonna be all night, is it?" That's what he wanted to know from Mitropoulos.

"We'll stay as long as you want, Governor."

Michael knew he ought to go—the words "D-5 missile," after all, had never escaped his lips, and soon he'd have to talk about how many the U.S. ought to build, and why. . . . But Dukakis does not like to be the dumbest guy in the room. Michael is always the smartest guy in the room.

"I don't know . . ." Michael was frowning at his watch. "Ahhh . . . I don't wanna go in there."

Mitropoulos shrugged, and stopped. "Up to you," he said.

Michael's eyes were down at his watch again, and he muttered something about the Stop & Shop. He said: "It's my night for groceries."

— ★ —

What he wanted them to have was a sense of mission. It could not be just a campaign for office. Wouldn't work that way . . . and wouldn't matter. He wanted them to feel they were working for the people, to change the country . . . not just for Gary Hart. It was not about him.

That's the way he'd always worked: the mission, this *crusade,* was his lever to move the earth . . . ever since 1971, when he marched in his cowboy boots straight to the big time in American politics as manager of George McGovern's campaign for the White House. Of course, in those days, it was easy. They were all young, for one thing—McGovern's "army," and its general, Hart— and they didn't fit in with the pros who ran politics. Hart would show up in those boots and his skinny blue jeans, shirt open at the neck, and too-long hair, and he'd start to talk, and you could *see,* you could *feel,* how different it was with him, the freshness of his thought and his faith in the power of ideas.

He was quiet, and mannerly, with that diffident Kansas politeness that had nothing to do with *politesse,* and a preacherly belief about the campaign—like his boss, Senator McGovern, from Hart's neighbor state of South Dakota, the son of a Methodist pastor (that same crusading Wesleyan gospel), who was so *decent. . . .* "George McGovern," Hart used to tell the kids in the office, "is who we are." It was easy to see that theirs was a campaign to change American values, a campaign for the dignity of each man, the future of all men. Then, too, if matters got muddy, they had this gyroscopic certainty: they were working to unseat the evil Nixon. They were working to bring the boys home from Vietnam. To change the system . . . end the war . . . bring the country back to its senses. That's why Hart could tell those college kids: it didn't *matter* that they were sleeping on floors, fifteen to a room, with hot dogs to fuel another day, canvassing through the snow. They had a mission. . . . That's why the McGovern campaign could take a dive at the convention on the South Carolina credentials challenge: sure, purity would argue for more blacks, more women, in the South Carolina delegation. But not at the risk of losing this prize. "Now, wait a minute . . ." Hart would tell the black caucus, the women's caucus. "Remember who it is we're running against. It's *Richard Nixon.*"

It was easy then for Hart to construct a *new kind* of campaign: there was no model for that sort of insurgency, and they had no choice about being different. Hart had a list in the office: all the Party chairmen, local officials, Congressmen—the regulars. And Gary insisted that his kids make an effort to call them, try to include them, let them know when McGovern was coming to their districts. But none of the political pros took much note. They couldn't feel the ground moving under them. The press couldn't see it coming, either, kept writing that McGovern was "a one-issue candidate" . . . "from a small state" . . . "no money, no endorsement" . . . "lacks Muskie's broad support." Hart would fume at the morning papers—it was so *frustrating:* "They just can't get it, can they?"

No, they'd have to be shown. So whenever someone *within* the campaign would complain that McGovern was slighted by Party bigwigs, or McGovern was left out of some news story, Hart would quote Tolstoy's General Kutuzov: "Time and patience . . . patience and time." Hart would never authorize the purchase of a conference table, or chairs, for the meeting room. He hated meetings: theory was, if there were no chairs, people would say what they had to, and wrap it up. Yet, as often as he had to, Hart would sit for an hour, two hours, with his rangy frame folded atilt into a straight-backed seat, his cowboy boots propped on the edge of his desk, explaining: sure, they were thirty points back in the polls, but that'd *change* if they won Wisconsin . . . and here's how they could win Wisconsin. . . . He'd listen for hours on the phone to his man in Milwaukee, Gene Pokorney, bitching and moaning: How was he supposed to win Wisconsin with no money? Then he'd listen to the daily whine from his New Hampshire coordinator, Joe Grandmaison: "I'm doing everything for this campaign. I'm going to the wall for the candidate. What are you doing for me, Gary?" He'd listen forever to Jesse Jackson, hectoring about what was owed to South Chicago, punctuating his demands with his favorite phrase of the time: "You hear where I'm comin' from? . . ." Hart heard, and heard again and again, and he'd sympathize, reason with them, try to explain . . . he never blew. They shared a mission. There was no end to his patience.

And that's how he wanted it to be. A different campaign, a shared sense of mission, a battle plan for a great crusade . . . But somehow, now that it was his candidacy, now that he was thirty points *ahead* in the polls, now that there were *professionals* in Denver, plotting for him, moving him, and there were chairs in the meeting room, and a conference table, conference *calls* . . . it was harder to keep it straight. Fifteen years . . . time and patience. But time was short now. They *gave* him no time. He couldn't sit around, for hours, explaining. He'd have to cut past explaining: they'd just have to be shown. And, tell the truth, that suited him now. Somewhere, in those fifteen years, the patience had worn thin. If they just couldn't get it . . . well, that was their problem. If they wanted him in Iowa, and the best they could come up with was a *full day* of kissing ass in the state capitol, "private meetings" with "important Democrats" . . . well, then, they'd just get it back in their faces: No. It didn't matter if they sent in *twenty* call slips for Hart to phone this important local candidate from the last election. He'd already talked to the guy in person . . . *visited* the smarmy creep. So every one of those call slips would slide into the side pocket of Hart's sport coat, and that was the last they were seen. It wasn't that he disrespected his staff—for God's sake, he'd made himself slave to their schedule! Hart had the best in the business in Denver. He'd seen to it. But he wasn't going to lower the level of his game. Not for anyone. Not this time.

So the white boys would visit the law office, whenever Hart had a day in town . . . and they would talk. But for the rest—the colonels and captains in the "army"—they seldom saw Hart. They'd have to make an appointment. Even the ones who went back with him, all the way to '72—they were middle-aged now, and there weren't too many who could move their lives to Denver for this new crusade . . . but there were a handful. Even they never sat and talked with Hart anymore. Judy Harrington worked on the field desk for McGovern, fifteen years before, and now she was running Hart's tank. It was her people who monitored the states, and she was the one who had to pass on their urgencies:

"He's just got to speak at this one Jefferson-Jackson Day Dinner. It's their Party's only big event of the year. And we promised! . . ."

". . . This guy is getting pissed off. Gary saw him in Des Moines, told him he really wanted to get to know him. And now he can't get through! Gary's *got* to call him back!"

So Judy passed on the call slips, and the schedule requests, and memos . . . for months. But she never saw Gary. And all she heard was: they could forget the J-J Dinner. No. No. . . . And as to the calls, well, he had the slips. . . .

So she made an appointment. It wasn't about the calls, really, or the schedule stuff, any of that. She wanted to connect, to talk to him, to tell him how proud she was of him, how far they'd come . . . she wanted to *see* him. But, of course, that had to be arranged. So it was late February when it finally got scheduled, and she went to the law office. But it was zoo-time that day.

The night before, Mario Cuomo had announced, on a New York radio station, that he would not run. Bill Dixon and Billy Shore tracked Hart down at a downtown restaurant, where he'd taken Lee out to dinner for her birthday. Now, the next morning, Gary was rushed. Dixon was flitting in and out. They wanted Gary to go to New York, today, right now, to tie down some New York money, now that Cuomo was out. Elsie Vance, Gary's personal assistant, was poking her head in the door to tell Gary about new meetings, people waiting on the phone, she had his ticket for New York. . . . And Gary had his game face on. He was brusque. He greeted Judy: "What should I be doing better?"

This wasn't what Judy wanted, or expected. She just wanted to talk.

"Well, you really ought to be taking care of these phone slips that come over here . . ."

"Yeah. I got this one right here."

"Yeah, you left him with the impression that you wanted to extend your friendship with him. You wanted him to come to Colorado or something . . ."

"I don't want to be friends with him."

"Well, Trippi says . . ."

"Look. The guy's a creep. I don't want to be friends with him. I don't want him here."

"Well, the guy's poisoning the well in Des Moines, and it takes a thousand staff hours to make up for what you can do with one phone call."

"Well, you people think it's so easy to make phone calls. I must call three times for every time I get through. And the phone's always busy, or I don't get through. And I can't sit around here, waiting for them to call back. Or I try to call them from the road, and then it's impossible . . ."

This was getting worse and worse. "What else?" Hart demanded.

"Well, why don't you relate your candidacy in more personal terms?"
Gary's face flashed annoyance. Well, he'd asked for it.

"Like last night, today . . . why don't you say, 'I was really surprised about
Cuomo. In fact, Lee and I were out to dinner, celebrating her birthday' . . .'"
Hart cut in: "I'm not going to drag my family into this."

"You *have* to use your family. You had the perfect opportunity today, and
you didn't use it."

Hart was shaking his head. "I don't want to relate to things in those terms."

"You just have to *mention* it . . ."

Now Hart flashed at Judy that look of scorn and hurt. What business did
the press have, knowing where Hart was at dinner last night? What he said
to Lee? What he and Lee were doing? He wasn't going to talk about Lee.
Wasn't going to talk about any of that! And, for God's sake, he shouldn't have
to explain *that* . . . to *Judy*!

Across the desk, she shrugged sheepishly. "Why do I have to bring up two
things that piss you off?"

Hart just stared at her. *He* wasn't pissed off! . . . But he had no time to
explain. He had to get to New York.

22

Gary and Oletha

IN 1955, after their first year at Bethany Nazarene College, Gary Hartpence and Oletha Ludwig were named Freshmen of the Year. Oletha said she had no idea why they gave it to her—that's how she was, so offhand about herself.

Of course she knew. She was the princess of the place, by right, almost by inheritance. Her father, S.T. Ludwig, had been president of the college some dozen years before—he'd appointed many of the faculty. It was the faculty who ordained the Freshmen of the Year.

Which is not to say she was undeserving: Oletha was attractive, full of good cheer, outgoing, chaste of heart and mind, observant in the faith—a model Nazarene girl. She was smart, or, to be precise, she was good at school. She'd always done well with grades and teachers. She had an easy, daughterly way with adults, especially church officials, who were around her home ever since she could remember.

The name Ludwig, see, was a great name of the church, its history stretching back to Oletha's grandparents, Theodore and Minnie Ludwig, who were traveling evangelists when the Nazarene sect was young. Theodore was a German Methodist, preaching to the faithful in the old tongue, before he came over to the Nazarenes (at that point, a church only six years old) after his entire sanctification at a service near Sylvia, Kansas, in 1912. Minnie Ludwig was every bit the speaker and evangelist he was: in fact, she was even more of a drawing card at tent revivals and camp meetings. ("Come on in close," she'd urge the faithful, in her piercing plains twang. "I don't know whether my gospel gun will hit all of ye, s'far scattered . . .") For decades, they traveled town to town—forty-seven states, Canada, and Old Mexico, as Theo used to say—sharing the Good News, and winning souls for Jesus. By and by, their handbills also advertised a cornet player, who would complement their preachings . . . that was their son, young Sylvester Theodore, or as he would come to be known, S.T. Ludwig.

And in S.T., Oletha's dad, the Nazarenes found a compleat churchman: raised on a steady diet of revival, schooled in the Nazarene Academy in Hutchinson, Kansas, where he later served as principal, then president—at age twenty-three. That was the same year he felt the call to preach, and so, in time, he was ordained, and as a pastor and educator, he served the church in another dozen jobs. After his presidency at Bethany College, in Oklahoma (where he wiped out the school's debt in a single year), he was called to church headquarters, Kansas City—the First Church, the Nazarenes called it—to serve as general secretary, sixth in command of the church, worldwide. There, in comfortable circumstance, he raised his two daughters, Martha and Oletha. Meanwhile, he poured out a steady correspondence to Nazarene churches everywhere; he traveled widely; at home, he hosted a procession of visiting churchmen: deacons, parishioners, preachers, professors—and not just Nazarenes, but Protestants of all stripes. S.T. was surely the most outgoing and open-minded Nazarene in the top leadership. He was a neat man, a careful talker, strict in his doctrine, but considerate and friendly . . . he always had a kindly word, and he enjoyed a joke, of the broad slapstick sort. He may have been the best-loved man of the church, and wherever there were Nazarenes, his girls had only to say their names, for someone to answer: "Ohhh! You're S.T.'s daughter! . . ."

Yes, a princess of the church was Oletha Ludwig, and determined to wear that crown lightly, with grace. At that point, at Bethany, she didn't want to be singled out, even for honors. She was shy, actually—very shy with boys— and her vivacity was a shield to hide that discomfort. It was a ruse of long standing with Oletha, who'd developed a dozen tricks like that, through a childhood on display for all those years, for all those dinner guests, all those eyes looking down the table at her . . . when she'd ask a dumb question (that she *knew* was dumb—see?), which made everybody laugh and pay attention in fond and fatherly ways to a little girl who always saw herself in second place.

Of course, to understand *that,* you'd have to know Martha, who was perfect—beautiful, petite, polite, smart, a musical prodigy—and five and a half years older than Oletha, who *never* thought she could stand as the equal of her sister. Oletha was so different: louder, big-boned, with her father's social and organizational skills, but alas, little of the musical talent. Oletha felt gawky, clumsy (though she was actually quite athletic, once she'd grown into her form). She never thought she was as pretty as Martha, nor as smart. She certainly could not entertain, the way Martha could astonish and charm all those guests, at the piano in the living room, after supper.

What could Oletha do? Well, she could seek approval in a hundred other ways. She could, for instance, shine at school, which she did. It seemed she was president or secretary of everything in her high school, which was a large one: more than a thousand kids, in five grades. Girls did not often run, in those days, for student council president, but she could manage a campaign for a boy, so she did . . . and then, next term, she got up the gumption, and ran herself—though she lost out, to a football hero . . . but she served as vice president, and as a class officer, on the newspaper, and the yearbook, and the choir, and whatever else. . . . On the playground, the kids nicknamed her Bossy—she always hated that, but she *could* organize—and she could chat a blue streak, amiably, volubly, to *anyone,* which Martha, after all, could never do. . . . In short, Oletha became a very popular girl.

And when she got to Bethany College—a school no bigger than her high school, in a town much smaller, and less worldly, outside Oklahoma City— well, it was . . . no big deal. Many of the students came from farm towns (like Ottawa), and she was from Kansas City—*First Church.* . . . She knew more church bigwigs than any of the teachers, probably more than the college president. Their authority struck no awe in her. . . . And she'd had all those honors in high school, done all those clubs, all that razzmatazz: she really didn't have anything to prove. In fact, her one social fear was that people might think she was stuck up, because of her family and all. . . .

So when she was named Freshman of the Year, in 1955, Oletha Ludwig said quickly: she had no *idea* why they'd picked her. She was *so* casual, *so* offhand about the honor . . . it only increased her campus cachet: Freshman of the Year! And she just shrugged it off!

Of course, no one at Bethany had any idea what a complicated little shrug that was.

— ★ —

When Gary Hartpence was named Freshman of the Year, he wasn't sure why. He didn't feel like a Big Man on Campus. Even on a little campus like that. In fact, when he came, he had no idea whether he'd even make the grade . . . how could he know?

He felt, in fact, that he was a nobody: his father wasn't a minister, or a churchman of any kind, and he came from a town no one knew—there were no other kids from Ottawa there. And he wasn't handsome, or well dressed, or rich—didn't have a car . . . and shy was too mild a word.

But his name got around after the entrance exams: everyone knew everything about everybody in the tiny world of Bethany . . . and Hartpence aced the tests—*clobbered* the tests. Of course, the faculty knew that first, and that's why Prescott Johnson came after Gary.

Dr. Johnson was head of Bethany Nazarene's philosophy department: tell the truth, he was the department—he and a half-dozen students who were his coterie, whom he'd picked out for their raw smarts, which he meant to turn into a capacity to think. Johnson went through those entrance tests like a major-league scout, culling from each new crop the boys and girls (mostly boys, in those days) who had the talent to make his league. In his league, the

game hinged on the fundamental questions of Western thought. Prescott Johnson was a quiet and unassuming man, but a serious teacher of serious subjects,
and he meant to make serious students of his boys. He meant to make philosophy at Bethany something more than multiple-choice learning (*Which of the
following analogies is found in Plato's* Republic? . . .). He meant to make
theology more inquiry than rote.

Of course, that made him something of a subversive at Bethany Nazarene.
Oh, everybody recognized that there had to be philosophy—three credits were
required. But it shouldn't interfere with the business of the school, which was
propounding the truths of the faith. And here was Prescott, spurring his boys
to consider: In what did salvation really consist? . . . What was a personal
relationship to God? . . . What had that to do with religion? . . . What was
the soul? How might we know? . . . What certainty was that? . . . How were
those assumptions defensible? . . .

For Heaven's *sake*! He was chewing at the foundations of the church!

Prescott was always willing to challenge assumptions—even his own, especially his own. That was the essence of his method, that questioning. And
although he was a man of faith (he preached at assemblies, once or twice a
term), his practice and profession (and perhaps his profoundest belief) was
about rigor in inquiry. So his own readings, and those of his boys, ranged far
beyond the safety of the Aristotle-to-Aquinas axis, and into dark, provoking
modern realms: Heidegger, Jaspers, Sartre, Kierkegaard. . . . There were times
when Prescott's boys could be *seen* leaving his office, carrying Kierkegaard's
slender and dangerous book: *Attack upon Christendom.*

Lord, help us!

Of course, Prescott knew how he was regarded by much of the faculty, and
certainly by the administration. There was one time *he* was carrying *Attack
upon Christendom* down a school hallway, and he came upon a dean with the
Dickensian name of Ripper. And as he passed, Prescott held the book before
him with two fingers, like a dirty diaper, murmuring past Dean Ripper: "I am
unclean . . . I am unclean . . . I am unclean." (Prescott's humor didn't much
help him, politically.)

But there was no way Gary Hartpence could have known all that when he
stood in the registration line and a small man with wire-rimmed glasses and
slicked-back hair presented himself:

"I'm Professor Johnson, head of the philosophy department. I'm your adviser . . ." (In fact, Prescott had rushed right over when he saw Gary's test
scores—two national tests in the ninety-ninth percentile, a third in the ninety-
eighth percentile. Gary was supposed to have another adviser, but Prescott
meant to swipe him.)

"Just thought I'd come by," Johnson said, "see if you need any help."

"Well, uhm . . ."

"Let's see what you've got there."

So Hartpence showed him, and Johnson began shaking his head. "No, no
. . . what *you* want is some *philosophy.*"

So by the time Hartpence got to the head of the line, Johnson had him signed up for twenty-one credits in philosophy—the first year. Gary was going to be one of Prescott's elect.

But even Professor Johnson could not have known how ripe was this lad for election. What Johnson wanted were young men who would dive into things, take them apart, proposition by proposition, testing all assumptions, to the *root,* where knowledge stopped and belief must take over . . . or doubt: Johnson was not averse to honest doubt. And that was always the way young Hartpence went into things, bearing down with that diamond bit, toward the center of the earth, to the rock of inarguable fact, or a truth so self-evidently solid that he could build a mountain of belief upon it.

Even Johnson could not have known how willing Gary was to dispense with the common wisdom; how even as a boy, in Ottawa High, he always had to know *why.*

Nor could Gary have known that in this "prof" (as the students called the teachers in those days), in this adult (who must have looked in the eyes of an eighteen-year-old like a finished being, a man possessed of the truths of life), in this *adviser,* he had found a man who was working off the certainties of his own strict church upbringing, who was wrestling with his own doubt, and his growing contempt for the unexamined dogmas of the Nazarene establishment.

What Gary did know (once he got back to the dorm that night) was that no one else had a schedule like his, so the next day, he went to Prof Johnson's office, to ask:

"Uhm, do you really think I can do this?"

And Johnson, who was anxious to get out of there, to tuck in an afternoon's work on his own dissertation, snapped at this crew-cut kid who didn't even know what he had between his jug-ears: "Of course you can, with a mind like yours. So shut up . . . and get to work!"

So he did. Gary Hartpence dived into philosophy as he had into every study in his life, whole hog, to *know.* And he hung out among Prescott's boys, the most brilliant one or two from each class in the school. There was Don Conway, the sharpest wit among a thousand kids; and Dale Tuttle, the drama star, the campus's leading man; and Tom Boyd, who was such a dynamic speaker that he was already featured, at age nineteen, in revival meetings in towns nearby—Tom could draw a thousand souls to his *Sunday school* class.

And they all hung out with Prescott, who was the chief character, so deliciously, unflappably individual . . . driving through town with his wife and two kids in his '38 Olds, an old whoopee of a car, which Prescott maintained lovingly, in mint condition, by his own labor. He was not a man of wealth, after all, and he had better things to do with his small salary than to buy new cars . . . or new suits. He only had a couple of suits (an old-fashioned double-breasted navy blue was his standard), but he *dressed*—coat and tie, all the time. And then, there was his music. He was always running off to Oklahoma City for the symphony . . . his students would baby-sit. But then, too, they were welcome in his home any evening, or he'd come with them to their hangout, Ned's Pizza, and happily spend his evening helping them work through a philosophic problem. Prof Johnson always had his own ways—and his own opinions, which he shared without fear, no matter how subversive.

He didn't mind asking aloud why so many cigarette lighters were sold on campus. No cigarettes were sold, of course. No tobacco, no smoking allowed. That was one of their precious rules, which they substituted for personal faith . . . so why were they all buying lighters? "It's not for lighting candles, I don't think," he'd say to the chuckling young men at his side. "Last time I looked, we had electric lights."

He did not mind standing alone—and he was alone, a pariah to the powers—against the theology of the whole college . . . which was almost solely devoted to making sure these young men and women were *saved.* That was the shame of the college, at the time, and the Nazarenes generally: from a movement to make a difference in men's lives, to *change the world* by the power of faith, the doctrine had dried down to a barren set of rules, meant to insure *personal* salvation—as if God were the Great Hall Monitor, making sure the faithful carried their notebooks neatly, lest they plunge forever into the Fires.

The ministerial students were the worst—they were maybe one-third to one-half of each class, and this was their trade school. They came to learn the right words, all the proper formulae . . . which they wrote down and memorized from the lectures of their profs. (Woe to the student who tried to mouth those comfortable truths back to Prof Johnson: "How do you know that?" he'd demand. "What does that mean?" . . . "Can you support that?" . . . Of course, most students got through without attending a single class with Johnson.) The idea was, these students would emerge, to live out perfect, and perfectly unexamined, lives . . . until they earned their just rewards in Heaven.

Prescott Johnson could not abide the safe hypocrisy of it. It was selfish. It was obsessive. It was *sick.* For him, as for young Gary Hartpence, ideas had to have force in this world. They had to make a difference in people's lives— otherwise, what was all the talk about? What did religion mean? What was it for, save to make the world better?

And so, by the end of that first year, Gary was fairly sure in his mind that he would not be a ministerial student—a professor, more likely, an examiner of truths. . . .

And he knew, by that time, that he could hold his own in the world of ideas, even in the rigor of Prescott Johnson's Socratic circle.

And he knew (as he'd always felt in Nina's house) that ideas were of substance in the world, *had* to be of substance, had to make a *difference.* . . .

And so, when the faculty, in recognition of his obvious intellect, his seriousness, his studiousness . . . voted him Freshman of the Year, Gary Hartpence did a very logical thing, a very simple act.

He came back to Bethany for his sophomore year, and he refused to sign The Pledge.

—★—

The Pledge wasn't any big deal—or it wasn't till that point. It was a simple affirmation that the student undersigned would abide by all rules of the college. Just one simple line at the bottom of the entry form. Everybody signed it—except Gary.

See, there was a rule that you had to be in bed, with lights out, by eleven o'clock. But the way it worked, the rule only meant girls—no one checked on the boys, no one cared. In fact, in the boys' rooms, the bull sessions went on into the wee hours—Hartpence knew: he was in there, arguing philosophy, two out of three nights. But the point was, he wasn't in bed by eleven, and he wasn't *going* to *be* in bed by eleven—and he wasn't going to swear to abide by a rule by which he did not plan to abide.

Well!

The head of the college, Roy Cantrell, didn't know what to make of it. Neither did the dean of students, or the dean of instruction, or any other dean. The students had to sign, and this young man refused to sign, and they couldn't let a student change the *rules,* whenever he chose. . . . They could go to his adviser, try to reason, cajole . . . but his adviser was *Prescott.* He'd laugh in their faces! Of course, they could—they had the *right* to—refuse the lad admission, but, ah, ahem . . . there *would* have to be some explanation. Perhaps the Board of Trustees would want to know why the rule was not enforced in the first place. And then, President Cantrell was reliably informed that the young man in question . . . what was it? Hartpence? . . . was the Freshman of the Year.

There ensued a Mexican standoff.

This went on for days.

Of course, Prescott Johnson was enjoying a tremendous hoot from it all, advising his student to stick to his guns. He was absolutely right! What did they mean, forcing these students to swear false oaths as the price of admission!

But he needn't have worried about Gary's resolve. Gary knew he was right: it was *so obvious.* And he knew (as Prescott used to say in class) the deans could not *justify their assertions.* In his shy and serious way, he'd explain this to anybody who asked.

And they did ask, as word got around. (Sooner or later, everybody knew everything . . .) A lot of students thought Gary must be a troublemaker to challenge the rules . . . or stuck on himself . . . or *awfully liberal.* (Liberal, which at Bethany meant *theologically* liberal, was a term of great contumely among the ministry students. It went with drinking, tobacco, jewelry, cards, and dancing. . . . Liberality paved the road to Ruin.)

But Gary was quiet, and modest, and they could see, if they talked to him, he wasn't trying to raise a fuss (at least, he didn't *look* like he was) . . . and some people thought, well, he was just honest. And straightforward. He had integrity.

That's what Oletha Ludwig thought.

She didn't really care about The Pledge. (She'd signed, without a second thought. Of course, girls *did* follow the rules.) But she knew Gary now, from their shared honor, and the Freshman Banquet, and he mentioned the whole hullaballoo to her . . . and he *was* right.

And it was awfully funny, when they had to just *drop* it—Cantrell and the deans. They finally just let Gary in, when they figured out there was nothing they could do. And they didn't change the rules, or *say anything*. They just swept it under the rug (so much for *that* rule) . . . like Gary said they would. He was awfully smart . . . and funny. What was really funny was Cantrell's face—when he saw them together . . . Gary and Oletha.

— ★ —

Tell the truth, it was a surprise to everybody—Gary and Oletha. She was so pretty and popular, so much at ease in her standing at this place. And so much fun! She was a sparkplug—she and Talmadge—the way they got everybody to pile into cars and head off to Oklahoma City for pizza. Everybody would just *scramble* to go along . . . with her and Talmadge. Now, *they* were a pair.

Talmadge Johnson was a handsome young redhead, with a drawling bravado; an accomplished speaker and promising preacher, and quite well known. In fact, he was known to hundreds of students from Oklahoma as the son of an Oklahoma district superintendent. Talmadge was conservative—theologically strict—he believed the rules paved the path to Personal Salvation. But that didn't mean he didn't like a bit of fun. For instance, there was the time—this was when Talmadge and Oletha were dating—when the ground near the Student Union was dug up in huge mounds of dirt . . . some construction project, and the students snuck out of the dorms *at night* . . . after *lights out* . . . and put up signs with the names of profs and deans on the mounds, like they were graves, with a funny epitaph for each . . . it was a riot.

That kind of thing.

As for Hartpence, he wasn't into that kind of thing. That was partly because he lived in The Barracks, a makeshift dorm in old Quonset huts—they were off-campus, and uncool. (In fact, when Nina first delivered him to Bethany, she took one look at The Barracks and thought about taking her boy back to Kansas—that place was nothing but a slum!) But, tell the truth, it was partly how Gary was. He did have humor, when you got to know him, but it was quiet: witty asides about things going on, things people said, funny ways they acted. As far as pranks . . . forget it. If he was in attendance, he'd be off to one side, gangly like he was then, his ears sticking out under his short hair, his bony jaw set, while he stared . . . like he didn't *get* it. Well, they knew he was smart . . . but the girls in the dorm (the best dorm, Oletha's dorm) had him figured as a geek.

Imagine the suprise, then, when *Oletha Ludwig* started going out, sophomore year, not with that dreamboat, Talmadge Johnson (who adored her—at least he did last year), but with Gary Hartpence!

Talk *about* it!

And imagine . . . sophomore year, when the guys would be out on the lawn in front of the Student Union, shooting the bull, killing time until dinner, talking and talking, like they did all the time, and there'd be Oletha Ludwig, her skirt arranged on the grass over her knees (all the girls had to wear skirts), listening to every word Gary said, never breaking in while he talked (like she could, and would, with anyone else), but just watching him, with such interest—no, excitement—like she could see something that no one else could.

She knew he didn't think he would ever be a minister. Maybe a teacher . . . and that was fine. That wasn't what it was about—not at all. She was looking at the way he could be with her. The way her ease, her graces, complemented him. How he coveted that ease . . . though he was so smart. And he was of another order of smart; he showed her a whole new way of looking at things—looking for yourself, asking, and deciding . . . about things she'd always accepted . . . like she always ate her vegetables at dinner. It was just part of growing up in her home, the tenets of the faith. And now, here he was, *asking* her about them: *Why?* . . . Gary wanted to know what *she* *thought.* It was intoxicating.

And he knew . . . it was that ease of hers that drew him, the wonderful way she had of plunging in—on the hockey field, in a group of friends—she didn't think twice . . . it was beautiful to him. God knows, there was no one more acutely aware of Gary's social unease . . . than Gary Hartpence. If the Good Lord had suddenly appeared to him, and asked him what was the *one thing* . . . well, of course, the way Gary was, he'd take it *seriously,* and ask for Salvation for All Mankind, or something . . . but if the Good Lord had *snuck* *up* and asked, well, the one thing Gary would have wanted, what he coveted, was to be able to fit in, or even better, to lead, *without even thinking,* just as a matter of natural grace. That was his lack, his one mortal envy, that ease of belonging, and Oletha had it, in her every move at Bethany, that sense of acceptance, that sense of right without thinking . . . and she liked *him.* It was intoxicating.

And soon he *was* more at ease, with her friends and their dates, when they'd pile into cars and go off to the city, or to someone's house off-campus. Once they got to know him, Gary said things that were *so funny.* He was so quick, the way he'd mimic the profs: he was a wicked mimic. He had natural acting skill, which was why he got a part in that year's *Hamlet.* Gary played the Ghost, and Oletha was Ophelia (of course, Dale Tuttle had the lead), and it was a terrific production. (Better than Oklahoma U's *Hamlet* that same year, everyone said.) And, of course, everybody knew that Gary was Freshman-of-the-Year smart, and that's probably why he got elected to the student council, and anyone who was at those meetings knew he was the brightest guy in that room—though the officers sometimes thought he was, you know, off in left field, a rebel . . . you could count on Hartpence to question *everything.* . . . But the point was, he was in the swim now, and very determined about that, too. He meant to make an impact on the place. And what with the people he knew from the council, and from the play, and Oletha's friends, and people who would have liked to be her friends, and, of course, that band of brainy brothers around Prescott Johnson . . . well, Gary Hartpence got to be quite well known.

So that was the year, spring of sophomore year, when he stood for election as student council president—he'd be sworn in as a junior, if he won. But it wasn't automatic—no, not by a long shot, not the way it turned out, in a two-man race . . . Gary Hartpence against Talmadge Johnson.

See, Talmadge was a young man of ambition, too, and definite ideas: he meant to arrest the school's long slide into looseness and liberality. Why, there were students (who called themselves *leaders*!) who'd sneak into town and go to *movies* . . . and then come back and *brag* about it! The girls were wanting to wear pants . . . and the basketball team wanted to play in shorts! Things at Bethany were rumbling downhill fast. . . . Talmadge and his friends smelt hellfire from the valley below.

Of course, Talmadge was greatly admired, and *everybody* knew him, so that gave him a head start. And then, too, he campaigned on what he called his Strong Christian Character. He didn't have to draw the contrast directly with Hartpence, who after all, had lapsed from his ministerial studies . . . Hartpence, who was a linchpin of the freethinking cabal at Prescott Johnson's knee . . . Hartpence, who (as everybody knew) refused to sign The Pledge. . . . Well, the contrast couldn't have been clearer: this was a battle for Bethany's soul.

But Hartpence—well, you couldn't count him out . . . or just when you thought you could, you'd find someone else won over. He'd get to people so quietly, you'd never know they'd gone liberal. He'd just get to talking, asking them questions . . . why they thought the girls shouldn't wear pants, on outings, say . . . did God make that rule about skirts? Or did the Good Lord simply want His faithful to be modest? Weren't pants more modest than a skirt for a girl climbing hills . . . what did they think?

And pretty soon, you'd see some fellow (or more likely, some girl) start nodding with Hartpence—or they were *laughing*—and *there* was a sign. . . . He got people fired up, sure enough. And then there were the girls in Oletha's crowd. She was strong for Gary now; and, of course, everybody knew she used to date Talmadge . . . so *there* was something to think about. And what with everything rolled in like that, it was a very hot election for Bethany, in '56 . . . and neck and neck, near as anyone could figure.

And then, disaster struck . . . but not so you'd hear it, in anything other than a whisper. Gary and his crowd (a lot of Prescott's boys) were in Ned's Pizza, in Oklahoma City, and somebody *saw them* . . . passing a beer around the table. Well, of course, word got back, right away—they were passing that mug, and they *each* took a sip . . . right *out in the open*! BEER!

Well! Wasn't that *exactly* what Talmadge was *talking about*?

What did that say about people who called themselves *leaders*?

BEER!

And it did not matter that Gary insisted he was the one at the table who *did not* sip the beer. How could he prove a negative? How many people could

he tell, anyway? He just would not do it. He was not going to say who *did*
have beer—he would not dignify that kind of slur, *at all.* . . . That was not
what this campaign was about!

But, of course, it was.

Talmadge Johnson won the presidency by a handful of votes . . . and
Hartpence was crushed.

—★—

Thing was, Gary won the greater prize. Oletha was disgusted by the unfairness
of the election. That's the same way Gary felt. It wasn't the result that
bothered him so much, he told her, quietly, with sadness in his voice. It was
how it happened, and *what that said* about the place . . . about how people
were. Of course, she understood. She was coming to understand him, more and
more.

It was '56 that Gary and Oletha started dating steadily, and in those days,
that meant seriously. Their classmates were already pairing off to marry, and
to move off campus. (At Bethany, that was the only way they could sleep
together . . . and even among the faithful, that thought did occur.) Junior year,
the question occurred to Oletha and Gary: Where was their relationship going?

The difference was, Oletha got more serious. It wasn't just the pressure of
advancing age (though she was *twenty* now, and a girl had to think of *what
she would do,* if she wasn't married by the end of college). At the same time,
she was getting more serious about herself: What kind of woman did she want
to be? Gary made her think about herself: Why did she do those things, why
did she believe that, why did she say things like that? . . . It wasn't that he
pushed or demanded that she change—not at all. He was sweet to her, so
courtly. (Valentine's Day, he gave her an adorable furry kitty, a stuffed animal—she kept it for years.) It was just that she saw herself, as if for the first
time, with the help of his eyes. All those little tricks, the ruses she'd learned
as a girl . . . what were they for? She didn't *like* playing those games. She didn't
want to be that way. . . .

She wanted to be straightforward, and honest—as honest as Gary. Somehow, other boys she'd dated now seemed . . . just full of hot air. She'd never
be as smart as Gary. She used to say that. (Her girlfriends would stare at her
cockeyed. What was she talking about? Oletha always got straight A's!) But
she could think for herself. Had to think for herself. And had to make a
difference in the world. That was the other thing. She wasn't just going to stare
into herself, checking her soul, every day, every hour, for its purity, its standing
on the scale of salvation. (That's what half the stupid chapels were about, and
the big revival meetings, with President Talmadge there on stage, whipping up
the believers—it almost made her laugh.)

No, there was a great and needy world outside the gates of Bethany . . . and
outside the self. Gary felt it—that was the year he went to Oklahoma City, to
the arena, to hear Eisenhower speak. Gary always had his eye on the wider
world (he was already talking about graduate schools, the best schools, in big

cities—he would get there, too), though he'd hardly been anywhere. It was Oletha who'd traveled, with her dad, in the summers. She'd been to New York! Her father had gone to Europe! But she knew (and it wasn't just her who said this—Gary always said . . .) that their church was born as a movement, a drive to *remake the world.* What happened to that? They lost track of that. Even her dad said so. He gave a speech about the role of the church college, and he told them all, they'd lost the way . . . the orphans' homes, the street services, the missions to the jails . . . what happened to them? *We have lost our sense of social vision.* That's what her dad said, her junior year.

That was the year . . . she just knew. It wasn't just dates anymore. They were together, all the time, whenever they could be. They'd eat together in the dining hall, and sit in the student lounge, or study together, or baby-sit at Prescott's. And weekends, they'd double-date, find someone with a car, or Oletha would check out of the dorm for the weekend, and stay with a friend who had a place off-campus, and then, Gary could come, and they didn't have to worry so much about the rules. . . . And they could kiss, and hold each other, and have the time. And they could talk. Lord, how they could talk—all day, all night—about what they could do, if they were off on their own . . . together.

And she could feel Gary's sense of power growing, the unease slipping off him. He'd made the grade, with Prescott, with his friends, with her, with her friends . . . and now, he was looking onward. He would not stop. She knew that about him, without talking. So much had changed: the stars of Prescott's circle moved on in time, Dale Tuttle, Don Conway, Tom Boyd . . . and now, quietly, with unstated authority, Gary was the leader. Now he was president of the junior class, and he didn't even run—not really. His friends put him up . . . and he accepted. Now he'd moved in from The Barracks; he was a counselor in a campus dorm. There were younger men now, who'd come to his room, to listen to the talks there about the Great Questions. That was the spring Gary got a car—Carl had a Buick he let Gary take to school . . . and then, they weren't scrambling for double dates. They could go where they wanted . . . together.

And he stood again, that spring, for president of the student council. Talmadge's term was ending, and this time, there was almost no contest. Friends put Gary's name up, and he won. People knew him, see, and admired him. And she was pleased she'd had something to do with that, with his own growing ease . . . so he could *be himself.* He'd told her—this meant a lot to Oletha—with her, he could be himself.

That was the wonderful thing.

And so, in the spring, at the Junior-Senior Banquet (it was always banquets for the Nazarenes, as eating was the only licit sensual event), when Gary was emcee, as president of the junior class, he stood up at the head table and read his announcement, to Bethany and the world, that he and Oletha were engaged to be married . . . and there was no surprise in that room, just great applause and joy.

—★—

Oletha always remembered that last year as a busy time, not especially romantic. She and Gary had moved beyond the point of decision. Now they were making plans.

Big plans: Gary had applied, almost on a flier (at least that's how he talked about it) to Yale, to the finest divinity school in the country. It was eastern, urban, Ivy League, it was the big time.

He pushed on that door . . . and it swung open. Just as he'd imagined, just like they talked about. And there was quite a bit to talk about. They'd be married, that summer, after graduation. (S.T. Ludwig would give the graduation speech.) Then, a short honeymoon, and they'd drive east. Yale would offer Gary financial help . . . but it wasn't going to be easy. They wanted to get to New Haven in time for Oletha to find a job.

But first things first—there was a wedding, her wedding! A big church wedding—First Church, Kansas City—and five bridesmaids, and her sister, Martha, would be maid of honor. (Dale Tuttle, Bethany's leading actor, would serve as Gary's best man.) Meanwhile, she was a senior, and she had her solo drama recital, and there were parties, and the banquet, of course, and graduation . . . well, she was awfully busy.

—★—

As for Gary, he would remember that year as a quiet time. Perhaps it was his first and most languorous moment of attainment, of pause, looking to the next hill.

He was going to Yale, with the best of the best. Would he make the grade?

Bethany . . . well, he had that licked. He had a pretty sweet deal that last year. His position as student body president afforded him tuition. His room and board were free, as a resident counselor in a campus dorm. He even had a job as campus mailman—that earned him pocket money. He had the Buick, he had his girl . . . not just a girl, the campus queen.

He felt he'd come to some peace with that campus—or at least an understanding. The deans didn't look at him like a bomb-thrower anymore. They knew he was serious, maybe even fair-minded. And if he liked, from time to time, to poke the powers with some uneasy questions, well . . . at that point, it was mostly for fun. In his own mind, he had moved on. That was his way with attainments.

—★—

Gary and Oletha wrote their own wedding vows (which raised a few eyebrows in 1958).

Then there was a week in the Ozarks, and off to New Haven, where Oletha did find a job—at the Yale registrar's office. It gave her a window into their new school.

And it was awfully exciting, the new school, new city, the new world. She even got a new name with her new job: they just couldn't handle Oletha, so they called her Lee—and somehow that fit. Everything was new, see . . .

Lee saw her first movie, Walt Disney's *White Wilderness.* And she had her first glass of wine, and got her first pair of earrings: faux pearls surrounded by tiny paste diamonds. It was the first time she could wear jewelry . . . that is, if they had someplace to go.

Mostly, their life was constrained by the limits of her salary ($199 a month) and by Gary's work. He worked hard (though within months he was not too sure he ever wanted to teach), and thought hard, and read constantly, working through the Great Questions. So much was new, even to him—the Divinity School was peopled with all stripes of seeker: Protestants, Catholics, foreigners! . . . When they'd get together, it was pig heaven for Gary, who wanted to know . . . everything.

It was hard for Lee, those discussions—the boys arguing and one-upping each other like philosophic toreadors. (So, I said to him, "Well, if you countenance *teleology* . . . " Haw!) Like any graduate students, or med students, or other bores, their world was The World . . . they were in thrall to its tiny fascinations.

And the funny thing was, it was because of how hard she'd thought about the way she was . . . she wouldn't play her old social games—those little ruses, what were they for? Gary was always reminding her, when she'd say something stupid, like about how somebody looked, or dressed: "Now, Lee," he'd say, or, "Lee-ee . . . we don't need any of that." But it was hard to have a new way to play, just like *that.* And the way Gary's conversations flew, with those jousting boys . . . well, she really didn't feel she had the background. (She'd only taken one philosophy course, and she thought she'd only got through because Gary was grading the papers.) And anyway, she wasn't reading all day, she was working, and working hard.

So a lot of times, she wouldn't talk. It was fine, she'd say. She'd just listen. . . . But somehow, even listening was hard. It was easy to get lost, and she did not want to ask anything dumb—not then. So, mostly, she was quiet. And she'd say, if she did speak, that it wasn't just her—*Gary* always said . . .

And often, it was something Gary had said about what she did, or the funny way she acted. That was always the safest thing, some funny self-deprecation. She really did remember everything he said, and she'd think about it, too, whenever the same thing came up.

She only wished he'd say more—he got so wrapped up in thought. Like she wasn't even there! After that first year at Yale, they were driving back to the Midwest—two cars, the Hartpences and the Boyds. That was Tom Boyd, and his wife, Beverly, friends from Bethany who'd also moved on to Yale. And somewhere beyond the Appalachians, they stopped at a station, Gary hit the men's room, and Lee came up to the Boyds' car to chat . . . but not idly. Lee wanted to know:

"Let me ask you something. Do you two talk?"

They stared at her, murmured: "Well, yeah . . . sure."

"Well, what do you talk about?"

It was hard to say, exactly.

Lee said: "We haven't said a word. We just sit there. I don't know how to talk."

— ★ —

Sometimes, Gary wondered why Oletha, why Lee, did not have that ease that was her accustomed grace . . . but he didn't say anything. Not to her.

One day, at lunch in the Divinity School basement, he said to his friend Tom Boyd:

"It's so strange . . . you go to the school you're supposed to, and you date the kind of person you're supposed to marry, you get married. . . . And you wake up six months later, and you say, 'What am I *doing*?' . . ."

But Tom knew (he was an old hand at marriage—three years!—he'd gone through the same thing), it wasn't that Gary didn't love Lee, it was just . . . he was questioning *everything*.

To Gary, it was just . . . everything was different: it was Bethany that now seemed another world, a smaller world, a narrow place. Gary and Lee went a couple of times to the Nazarene Church in New Haven, but it was . . . well, it was nothing: it was no more sophisticated than the church on Seventh Street in Ottawa!

It was almost funny, for Gary to look back . . . at that church, his little college . . . it was so strange, how they shrank, as he moved outward . . . it would be funny—if it weren't tragic.

Years later, he would still be startled—shocked—when confronted again with the power of those places, the grip they had on some people's lives . . . even when they tried to wriggle free.

Don Conway, God bless him, killed himself while he was doing graduate study at Berkeley, in 1967. . . . Then, Dale Tuttle, Gary's best man, killed himself in 1971. . . . They were brilliant, both, the best of the best. Dale was likely gay. He suffered with it terribly. Don . . . well, who could know? But whatever it was, they could not turn away from the dark battle with their imperfect selves, their failures, their *humanness*. That was the Bethany disease: that morose, myopic self-investigation that never ended, never stopped cutting away inside. . . . And here was the horrible cosmic joke: it happened to the best! . . . Well, it would not happen to Gary.

He was not going to turn that diamond bit on himself. He was faced determinedly outward, to the wider world. He would not stop now—would not stop *ever*—to peer into, to pick apart the layers of his life. That was morbid. It was obsessive. It was not what *his* life was about!

And Bethany—well, he would not soon go back. (Not even when Lee did, in 1984.) And he would not look back. He would not concede it any hold on him. Not for years, anyway . . . not even to recognize the comic twist, the cosmic joke that God and Bethany played on *him:* he fell in love with Oletha Ludwig for her queenly ease, never knowing—how could he know?—that past Bethany she would so seldom find it again.

23

Family Values

I T WAS AT DINNER, two nights before announcement, that Dick made them all sign. There was a form he had to fill out for the Federal Election Commission—a notice that he was seeking the office of President. But instead of just signing, he brought it to dinner, passed it around. He wanted Jane to sign, and each of his three kids . . . Dick called it their "bond."

This bit of family hardball was mostly aimed at Matt. Already, Gephardt had worked it around to where Matt *asked him* to run. But this sealed the deal. It was like cosponsors in the House. (What do you mean, you don't know? Your name's on the bill!) Dick was so sure: Matt would learn a lot, it would take his mind off things. . . . Wasn't it exciting already?

Everyone was flying into St. Louis: from Long Island, brother Don and his wife, Nancy, and their kids, and Cassells from all over, and Gephardts—cousins no one had seen for years . . . and old friends, guys from Northwestern, and law school at Michigan . . . and from Washington, a whole planeload took off, despite a killer snowstorm. The chartered DC-9 would cost the young campaign something like thirty thousand dollars, but on the big day, Monday, February 23, there would be twenty-one Congressmen standing behind Dick. That was backing from all over the country, entrée into a score of states. And why not? Dick Gephardt was one of their own, a man of the House, a guy who would play ball, to make the system work.

Anyway, the money would be there: that was obvious now. The campaign had scheduled a fund-raiser dinner for the night of announcement at the Adam's Mark Hotel, sent out invitations . . . and money *poured* in. They

banked a quarter-million in two weeks! (There were some *years* Gephardt
hadn't raised a quarter-million.) They had a hundred takers on the predinner
cocktails-with-Dick . . . at a thousand dollars a pop! By the weekend before
announcement, there was more than a half-million committed. No one had
ever bled St. Louis like that. The campaign reserved a second banquet room
with TV monitors, so people could watch Dick's thank-you speech. And still,
Loreen was working the phones, calling the members of Third Baptist Church,
and the Cub Scout moms, to make sure they were coming—how about the
dinner? ("If there's one empty seat," Loreen explained, "that's what the cameras will show." Dick's mom was a woman of faith—not naïveté.)

And that was just part of the hubbub: there was *Meet the Press* the Sunday
before, and *Today* and *Good Morning America* on announcement day, and a
segment on *MacNeil/Lehrer,* not to mention the St. Louis shows. And Sunday
night, the bunting went up in Union Station, and the high school bands came
out for practice, and there were volunteers hanging signs in the rafters, crawling over the stage, taping wires, mult-boxes, and microphones. The volunteers
were coming out of the woodwork at Joyce Aboussie, who was the honcho of
announcement day. She'd expected twenty-five—if they got lucky—and by
that last weekend she was trying to find work for a hundred. And these were
not high school kids. She had $300-an-hour lawyers driving Ford sedans
around town, seeing to the fruit baskets in the Presidential Suite, or on call
for last-minute shopping.

They all had the feeling this was big—once in a lifetime. They could make
history. Hell, look at the Sunday papers! Nothing on the front page but
Iran-contra, the Reagan revolution falling apart. Dick could make it! And they
wanted to be a part, to be inside. They had to help Dick! This was their chance
to show the guy they were *for* him. And there were more than a few who
brought along ideas—campaign themes and issues, lists of names for Dick to
call, zingers for speeches, slogans for ads . . . hell, they had whole ad *campaigns*
. . . (just for him to look at, you know—maybe at the house, they'd stop by
his house . . . they'd give them to Dick, when they sat down to talk).

Of course, they never did talk with Dick. Never even saw Dick, except on
stage that Monday. By the time Gephardt flew in Sunday afternoon, the bubble
was in place to receive him. He couldn't stay in his St. Louis home (where
Loreen lived full-time, amid pictures of Dick and Jane). Didn't see any friends.
Talked mostly to anchormen. His professional Advance team whisked him
from the airport to the Presidential Suite of the station hotel. He had a
schedule to keep, and a run-through—the speech!

It was eighteen hours till announcement when Gephardt saw the speech for
the first time, in his hotel suite, on a TelePrompTer flown in from California.
See, Shrummy was a genius, and the speech wasn't done until Saturday. And
by the time Dick got there, and got a look—well, delivery was the thing. He
had to work on the timing: *Look out at the crowd when you talk about St. Louis
. . . slow up, there . . . don't step on that next line!*

"Okay, good . . . let's do it again," Dick said. He was better each time he read it through. Everybody said his problem was he looked wooden, like he didn't care. So Dick was working on emotion—that's when he'd hammer the podium, to show how deeply he felt, about that last applause line.

The speech had lots of applause lines. The theme was *Make America First Again* . . . and it worked great, with his trade amendment, his farm bill, and his line about wiping out illiteracy by the year 2000. There were plenty of Dick's ideas in the speech, because he and Shrum had had a breakfast—three *hours*—and Shrum, as Dick knew, was big-time, the guy who wrote for Ted Kennedy! So Dick didn't have any problem with the speech itself—for instance, what was in it.

He just had to hit the lines, one by one—loud and clear. He had to look at the crowd, look at the prompter, remember where the cameras were, where he was in the speech, and just . . . keep it together. As it turned out, that was hard enough, when he finally did get introduced, and the bands were playing and the crowd was cheering, and he got up there on the station stage and kissed his mom, and she whispered to him: "I wish your father could see you now." And he looked out over that concourse, with the skylight streaks shining down on the crowd, and *everyone* was there—friends from school . . . kids from camp . . . lawyers from his firm . . . fellow Aldermen . . . fellow Cub Scouts! . . . And the cheering wound down, and he was supposed to start, but it was like his life was there, assembled for him, in *support* of him, and for a moment, he felt he couldn't talk.

But he did. He delivered the speech word for word, didn't change a line. And everyone said it was great. He hit the gong for his trade bill, and then education, then the zingers on Iran and contra aid . . . and with each, he slowed, and stopped, and just like they'd planned, the crowd filled the air with cheers. And that was great TV, in the packed station hall, with the camera angles just right, and the cutaway shot from behind Dick to show the hometown crowd approving, urging, like the Cardinals had a rally in the ninth. . . . It was beautiful, it was professional. Not one foul-up, not a hair out of place! (How could anything fall awry? Once she got the hall set up, Joyce never let it out of her sight. Sunday night, she brought a pillow and slept on stage.)

Dick couldn't tell how it looked on TV, but he knew he was exactly where he wanted to be. He was so happy that day. There were so many friends, and his fellow House members—even they thought this was a hell of a show—and the family, all together. . . . That's what made it so special, when he got to the end of the speech, the part about his family, Lou and Loreen and the brick bungalow on Reber Place. . . .

It was all about family values, see. And Shrummy wrote that beautiful ending about how Dick and brother Don would sit with their parents, summer nights, on the front porch, listening to their lessons of hard work and high aims:

"The air was hot and muggy," Dick said, "but it was full of dreams."

And Dick read out, with evident emotion, how Lou's dreams were shattered when the Gephardt farm was lost in the Great Depression. But still, Lou worked and saved to make sure his sons would have the college training he never had.

And it didn't matter that Lou wasn't much for inspirational speeches on the front porch (the Cardinals game was the more likely soundtrack), or that Lou's farm was not lost in the Depression (in fact, Lou left that farm at a trot, but there were Gephardts, still, on that land today), or that Lou was never quite convinced about the value of college for the boys ("I made it without college!" he used to grouse to Loreen).

The point was family values, see . . . and Dick was so eager to do this thing right . . .

Anyway, who was going to argue? The two-score national press in attendance knew even less about Gephardt than Shrum did. They were here to see if he could pull off a big-time announcement, Presidential grade. And he did. There was not one glitch to write up. The crowd was big enough, loud enough. The rhetoric—well, it was just what they'd come for. . . . "God!" Peg Simpson from Hearst newspapers said to Don Foley in the press pen. "He's good! He sounds like Ted Kennedy!"

And who could miss the subtext of family values when Dick finished his speech, hugged his mom and kissed his lovely wife, Jane, and his two pretty daughters, then wrapped his son in a bear hug that lasted until Matt woke up to all those eyes upon him, and started in his father's embrace, and stepped back a couple of paces . . . and then Dick swooped up his youngest, Katie, and held her aloft with one arm while they waved to the crowd . . . and that was the picture in *The New York Times,* where E.J. Dionne reported: ". . . the family presented a striking tableau before the crowds and television cameras this morning."

Of course, the national press left town the next day, when Dick flew off to points west and south to continue his announcement barrage, and Jane was left in St. Louis, calling around to friends, trying to find a ride to get Matt to his appointment at Barnes Hospital, trying to figure a way to get herself and three kids to the airport thereafter, for the flight back to Washington . . . whither she arrived in the snow, late that day, and got the three kids off the plane, through the airport and into the car, and got them back home, sent them into the house, while she parked on the street, so she could shovel out the driveway.

—★—

Ski trip was Family Time—been on Joe's schedule for weeks: third weekend in March, northern New Hampshire, just the kids and Jill. Of course, the campaign had to coordinate, because after that weekend, Joe would do politics up there, and anyway, they'd arranged for a condo on loan from New Hampshire's Senate Democratic Leader. But they kept it simple: just the New Hampshire Scheduler (who drove the family to the condo), and Ruth Berry, who'd signed on as the traveling aide, the body woman—Trip Director, she preferred to call the job. Whatever . . . the work was the same: she had to take care of Joe, make sure he got his plane, and his rest, had a clean shirt and food in his belly, a copy of his speech, a ride to the next event, a rundown on who'd be there . . . and why. Ruthie was a pro: a young woman still, but she'd served in her twenties in the Carter White House, and before, with the venerable Senator Henry "Scoop" Jackson. Ruth had been with Biden only a few weeks, but already she knew Joe's acid test: love him, love his family—in fact, take care of the family first!

So they got to the Leader's condo—North Conway, New Hampshire—and Ruth got the family in, she was about to disappear . . . when lo, came a knock at the door and who should appear but the Leader, and Mrs. Leader, and the Neighbor, and Mrs. Neighbor . . . and they had an idea: How about *dinner*— all together, the Bidens, the Leaders, and the Neighbors? So, Ruthie asked Jill, who said absolutely not—*This is Family Time . . . please pass on regrets.* This Ruth did, and proceeded to disappear.

It was only the next morning, on the way to the ski slope, when Jill was so pissed off in the van, that anyone found out that Joe had gone to dinner. In fact, Joe and the kids had gone, and Jill stayed home, or almost home, at the condo. And that was the weekend Jill found out there wasn't going to be any Family Time, or private time, or whatever Joe called it. It didn't matter what was on the schedule . . . that's what she figured out. Because there wasn't any life outside this thing. They could go to dinner with their oldest friends—what did those folks want to know? How's the campaign? . . . They could go out together, just Joe and Jill, and she'd still have to think, look over her shoulder, before she touched his cheek, or kissed him. Every move, any move, was now a public event—she could face it, or she could stay home. If she went out, even to the Pathmark, there was the campaign. The checkout girls were for Joe— *knew* he was going to win—and Jill would have to smile and say, "Hope so . . ." Where was private time? Some sun-stunned one-street gila-monster town in New Mexico . . . you think they don't get CBS News?

CBS News was with them on the slopes—by prearrangement—taping a story about Joe, for *West 57th Street* . . . a nice producer and his crew. Jill couldn't be mad about that: they were so polite . . . and it was good for Joe, wasn't it? That was the funny thing: there was nobody to be mad at. Everybody was trying to help. It's just . . . their life was gone. The way Joe got in, the campaign just came at them: no time to think. It was pulling *them.* And Joe had to do everything at once. She couldn't even stay mad at Joe—dinner with the Leader, that was just Joe. Politics was so much a part of him that she never expected him to be another way. It was like breathing for him, part of life, like family, or home. When she married him—in fact, when she met him—he was already in the Senate. It wasn't like politics snuck up on her. She'd always helped—and not just with the public parts. She got the mail at the house. It was a point of particular pride with Jill that Joe never saw one piece of hate-mail. All the vicious anti-Catholic stuff, the threats from the sickos. She took them to the FBI, or she trashed the stuff. He never even knew. She'd always helped in the campaigns, too. But before, she'd always had the choice.

She could go along if she wanted . . . what she didn't want, she could leave alone. Now it wouldn't leave her alone.

She would not be the one to tell him no. This was his dream. He would never have said no to her dream. And she would never be the wife who kept him from his destiny. That would . . . destroy his soul. She would keep what she could of her life—at least, her life alone. She had her work—teaching disturbed kids at a hospital in Wilmington. And her graduate English course at Villanova. (She'd registered under her maiden name, but even so, people in her Faulkner class recognized her from TV.) She was not going to give up grad school. Joe said she had to do what she wanted. And they'd get through the campaign—a year, eighteen months at the max. Unless he won . . . God, what if he won?

That was the weekend Jill started asking what it would be like . . . if they won . . . the White House. Ruthie had been in the White House with the Carters. It was in the plane, flying south that Sunday—Joe was catching a nap, he had three political events to hit that night—when Jill asked Ruth Berry what would it be like. What could she do? What would she have to do?

And Ruth started to tell her about the life: she could do . . . anything she chose to do. She could help Joe in a hundred ways. Or she could work on her own issues—things that mattered to her—education, family services, better day care . . .

That's when Joe woke up, and the only part he heard was Ruth telling Jill how she could work on those issues. And he jerked into instant fury. He was not in this goddam thing to have his family bossed around. His jaw started working and his teeth clenched in that killer grin. No one was going to tell his wife what to do!

"Honey, don't listen to anyone. You just do what you're comfortable with . . ."

And to Ruth, Joe snarled through his teeth: "Goddammit! Don't you *ever* tell Jill what she's got to do."

Later, in the bathroom, Jill told Ruth: "When he gets like that, just ignore him. He just gets that way, sometimes."

— ★ —

There was Sasso, like a brother to him, smoothing every trip, every meeting. There was his son, John, prepping him, pushing him, for his first big speech. Pick up the paper, and there was Kitty, confiding (just between her and the Hadassah, understand) that the family wanted Michael to run. . . .

Only with family could Michael show doubt . . . but there was no doubt discussed in the family now. Only in their eyes could he find the fondest, largest view of himself . . . and they saw him as either a candidate, or a man who would not match their dreams.

Even at the fringes of his tight life, at the third and fourth remove, everybody had such confidence for him. He asked their help to peer down the long track ahead, and they told him: all the lights were green. What engineer, like

Dukakis—at the levers of his marvelous machine—could stay his hand on the throttle?

A thousand Democrats (along with a score of diddybop press, and local wise guys, national big-feet, Ken Bode's NBC crew, and then, too, Michael's State House brain trust, his old Greek friends, his speech coach, his family) packed a hotel ballroom in Bedford, New Hampshire, to hear his first "Presidential" address. Democrats in New Hampshire are such an oppressed breed that they have to look past their borders to see what a Democratic officeholder looks like. And Dukakis was the man they had turned to for years, to stop their Seabrook nuclear plant, to face off with their hated and hostile Gov, the Republican, John Sununu. In effect, Michael Dukakis was New Hampshire's leading Democrat. They owed him. And that night, the Party loyalists paid him back.

It wasn't the Gettysburg Address, after all, but a good speech, yes . . . a call to let the road to renewal begin, there, in New Hampshire. Michael was nervous, careful at first. His son, John (a professional actor), had plastered sticky tape on the podium to remind Michael: Keep those hands down! At first, Dukakis was thinking his way through . . . *hands still . . . slow here . . . let your voice fall* . . . but as he got untracked, more confident, his hands started slicing and dividing the air over the podium . . . and he sounded like he meant what he said. He even slowed down and looked up when he got to a zinger . . . and they stopped him with applause! He looked so startled, first time it happened—like he wondered what it was he said. But it happened again, with the next line, and the next—twenty-four times!

And when he got to the part about Pan and Euterpe, their voyages to this land, their hard work (in New Hampshire!), their dreams, their success in the New World . . . well, it was a real connection with that crowd. Then Michael introduced Euterpe Dukakis, and at eighty-three years old, queenly and calm, she rose to acknowledge the cheers. And some stood to applaud now . . . and, therewith, Michael passed his test: a standing ovation from New Hampshire Democrats, "activists" in the first primary state. And when he finished, there were a thousand people standing, as Michael, with a small, pained smile, held a hand up, as if to still them . . . but they did not stop. They were grinning and clapping, even after he sat down. And Michael's smile had grown wide. . . .

And so, two days later, a Sunday, while the press was asleep (the Boston press knew Michael *never* worked on Sunday, his family day), Michael and Sasso flew down to New York and met with Jimmy Carter. And Michael asked his questions: Could he win in the South? Could he do the job? . . . Carter said yes, and yes.

Then Michael and Sasso caught a train (Michael loved trains—and no reporter would look for anyone on a train), and traveled to Albany, where he and Mario Cuomo—these two Democrats, Governors, each at the peak of his form; Mediterraneans, sons of immigrants, products of the American dream, both acutely conscious, proud, and grateful of how far they'd come—sat down in Cuomo's grand and Sunday-silent capitol to talk about the top job in the United States.

Cuomo was in a sport shirt. Michael was in his suit, small, neat, cautious; he propped his right elbow on the arm of his chair, then brought his other hand across his chest to hold his right forearm. Then his legs crossed, left over right, so his whole body was canted into a corner of his armchair. His every move revealed more chair and less Dukakis. But his thick eyebrows were lively, raised in self-conscious enjoyment of the moment. His mouth twisted into a little smile. Michael had a sense of occasion. And this—him and Cuomo, this Sunday, this . . . was rich.

He knew Cuomo understood his doubts about governing and running at the same time.

"That's your advantage, Mike . . ." Cuomo said. "You've got what the country needs. You know what I mean. . . . You *govern*. We *govern* . . ."

And Michael nodded. He did know. All the big-foot punditry, all the op-ed magma, was hardening on the conviction that "hands-on management" was what the nation lacked, under Reagan.

Cuomo pressed on: "When people want to know what you'll do, you stack nine budgets on the table. There. That's your answer."

Nine balanced budgets, a record of success . . . Michael did understand. So, three nights thence, in Washington, when he spoke at the Children's Defense Fund banquet, he did not confine himself to an airy encomium on the American family. No, he talked about his record: thousands of welfare mothers who found jobs with ET . . . a model teenage pregnancy program in Holyoke, Massachusetts . . . a bill to force delinquent fathers to pay child support. "Idealism that works," Michael called it. And again, they saluted him with cheers.

It was that night, nearly midnight, in a hallway of the Capital Hilton, on his way to sleep before a flight, the next morning, to Louisiana and another speech, Michael said to Sasso:

"You know, we said we were going to announce this thing mid-March . . ." Michael's voice was casual. "You thought about how we'd actually do it?"

Sasso stopped in the hallway. "Yeah, I've thought. But if you're closing in, I better start thinking harder . . ."

So Sasso flew back, the next morning, Thursday, March 12, to Boston. Michael went on to Baton Rouge alone. By the time Dukakis got back to Boston, John had been closeted in his office for a full day and a half. He had the curtains closed, the outer door locked. No one inside or outside the State House could know he was there. And now he had a plan. . . .

In the half-house, on Perry Street, Saturday morning, Michael was at the front door, getting the morning paper. Kitty was behind him, down the narrow hallway that led to the kitchen. Michael did not turn to look at her, or even raise his head. He was hunched, his eyes on the headlines, as he said, "Well, I guess we're gonna do it."

And it took a moment, even for Kitty . . . and then she got it, and ran to hug him. She was so excited! So proud! God, she had to tell someone, just the girls—she'd call the girls! . . . But, no, Michael was on the phone, the wall phone in the kitchen, next to his chair at the dowdy Formica faux-wood table. "John . . ." she heard, but she knew it wasn't their son. Kitty could always tell when it was Sasso on the other end. "Can you come over to the house?"

Sasso was there in a hurry, and Michael walked him back to the kitchen table—it was always that table. When John sat down, Michael said, without preamble: "I'm gonna do it . . . I think we can do it." Michael's voice carried no heat. It was almost clinical. "It's gonna be tough . . ."

"Yeah. It's a brutal business." Sasso's face kept faith with the solemn words, but his heart was singing.

John already had the schedule in his head. In a matter of hours, on Friday, he'd got Marty Kaplan in California to write a speech . . . which he whipped out now. "I've got a draft of something here that I think is consistent . . ."

And that was the speech Michael would give Monday, a message to the people of Massachusetts, announcing his intention to announce his candidacy. He'd tell a joint session of the legislature (arranged by Sasso on three hours' notice):

"I love my family, I love this Commonwealth and its people, and I love my country.

"I have the energy to run this marathon; the strength to run this country; the experience to manage our government; and the values to lead our people."

That day, Michael did sound certain.

"With your help, and with your prayers, a son of Greek immigrants, named Mike Dukakis, can be the next President of the United States."

There could be no doubt for him now.

Save for the morning after, when Michael picked up the paper: Duke for President was just about the whole front page. But Michael was most surprised to see one picture in that paper, a photograph of him that Monday, that great day, at 7:00 A.M., taking out his garbage on Perry Street.

What the hell? . . . They must have *staked out his house*!

—★—

The white boys warned Gary: there were people, press, going to stake out his house, try to tail him, spy on him wherever he went. "NBC has a stake-out . . ." That was the most common rumor. Sometimes they said CBS, *The Washington Post, Newsweek* . . .

It didn't matter to Hart who it was. "I expect that," he'd say, and that was the end. He wouldn't discuss it. He'd get that look on his face, and go silent. He'd told them all before: that was *not* going to be a problem.

Actually, it was all the same problem, what the big-feet called the Character Issue. They said the whole election—at least Hart's bid for nomination—would boil down to one question: *Who is this guy?*

"People want to know who you are," the white boys told Gary.

"They know who I am." (And he thought to himself: they've had fifteen *years* to know who I am . . .)

"No, there's a *perception,* you know . . . they don't know, really . . . where you're coming from."

So the white boys went at this . . . *problem,* as white boys are paid to do, head-on, with breathtaking literalness:

Hey! Let's show where he comes from!

That's why they get the big bucks.

So, they told Gary he had to go to Ottawa, Kansas. They told Gary he had to give people an idea of his roots, that he wasn't just sprung, full-blown, in suit and tie, on *Meet the Press* some Sunday, while the nation rubbed sleep from its eyes and waited for football to start.

"People want to know about your values, Family Values!"

"People don't want to know any such thing. It's only the press that's asking . . . nobody else ever asks me about those things."

"Don't take it so personally. It's not you. It's just the way they are. It's just the *system.*"

"It's morbid curiosity," Hart complained. "It isn't natural."

"Look, Gary, just go for a day . . ."

"No."

"Gary, it's just . . ."

"No."

"They're voters."

"What?"

"They're voters in Ottawa, too. You don't have to talk about your family . . ." This was from Hal Haddon. Hal was brilliant, a Denver trial attorney of ferocious reputation. And he knew Hart cold—ran his first race for Senate, back in '74. "Talk to them as voters. You can tell them why you're a Democrat, and not a Republican, like all of them."

"Well . . ."

So they scheduled a speech for him at Ottawa U, where Hart could talk *political philosophy* . . . and everybody was happy. Hart was actually, quietly, excited. There were aunts—Nina's sisters—and cousins, still in town . . . and friends from school . . . people he'd love to see. He'd gone back in '84 (after his campaign—he purposely went *after* he was out of the race), just to see friends . . . went to his high school reunion. And he had a *great time.*

So Sue Casey scheduled time for a private meeting with family . . . before the speech. Just an hour, maybe less, but he'd have time to visit.

And Hart wrote into his notes some lines about the ethic of the town, his school, his friends, his parents . . . what he'd learned from them. He was actually going to talk Family Values.

Well, the white boys were in a lather, and they put out the word: this *showed* how much Hart had grown—see? He was playing by the rules. He was sharing his life! He was so . . . comfortable!

But when Gary and the press herd got to town, *The Ottawa Herald* greeted them with a front-page streamer about the *sixteen different houses* where Carl and Nina Hartpence lived, while Gary grew up . . . and there was a big map, showing the locations, and a long story of explanation:

It was his mother, see . . .

Then, there were interviews with people who lived in the houses now, the first with Ronald D. Cowdin, a schoolmate of Hart's who owned the house where Gary was born in 1936: "I knew him as Hartpence," Cowdin snarled to the *Herald*. "I don't remember him as Hart. I try to forget those deals."

And that afternoon, while Gary and Lee cut away to visit his parents' graves . . .

("No pictures.")

("Gary, one photographer . . .")

("No pictures.")

. . . the herd found his uncle, Ralph Hartpence, who entertained on his front porch with stories of Gary as a strange, persnickety kid . . . "Never once did get dirty—thought he'd catch the dickens from his mother . . ."

And Gary tried to eat a chicken-fried steak at the L&L Restaurant, where Carl used to eat, but the cameramen started crowding and shoving, and he had to finish and go. And then he got to his private session with the family, in the chapel at Ottawa U—no press, absolutely not, no—and he walked into the room and found . . . about a hundred people. Hart's face froze.

There was family . . . he could see his Aunt Louise (who married Nina's brother), and Nina's favorite niece, Letafay Weien, and a few cousins—maybe six or seven Pritchards in the group as a whole. But the rest . . . well, they said they were Hartpences. Cousins . . . somehow. One had an autograph book, and he came right at Gary, wanted him to sign. So Gary signed, and then another one came, with a loose piece of paper for Gary to sign, and then more: they were around him two and three deep, with napkins, telephone bills, whatever they could find—they wanted his autograph. Wanted him to pose for pictures. Gary only had a half hour to the speech, and this went on twenty minutes. They treated him like a movie star—and all the time, Gary's wondering: Who are these people? Why are they doing this? Why can't he have a *few minutes' peace* to see his family?

Aunt Louise got to him for a minute, just to tell him how proud his mother and dad would be now, if they could see him. And she saw his eyes grow shiny with tears, though she didn't know whether that was the thought of his folks, or frustration. . . .

And Gary got up to the podium in the chapel, and stood before the crowd, and gracefully thanked the Mayor for the welcome of the city . . . and the university . . . even *The Ottawa Herald.* And then he meant to thank his family, but he'd barely got to talk to anyone *he* remembered as family. So he said:

"I'm constantly amazed at the increasing number of relatives that I have . . ."

He meant it as a joke, but it set off an anxious, whispery rustle in the hall. Gary tried to lighten it up:

"Actually, what happened was . . . I didn't have that many relatives in 1983, during that period . . . I was only one or two percent in the polls. Then after the primary, I had a lot of relatives . . . and then after the convention, I didn't have as many relatives . . . no, I'm just kidding."

Kidding! Jeez! The press herd (absent perforce from the "family visit") was slapping this stuff right into notebooks. *Christ! The guy's mocking his own family!*

But Gary hadn't come to mock; he came to tell what Ottawa had given him, and he was making an honest effort now, in the body of the speech . . .

The Church of the Nazarene gave him the moral foundation of his life; the Santa Fe Railroad gave him a job and a chance to know how working people lived; the Main Street merchants, *The Ottawa Herald,* the radio station, KOFO—they were all teachers to him. The town itself taught its values of hard work and community, the way Ottawa pulled together when the river rose and flooded the downtown, and the north side was cut off from the south, and people drove a hundred miles to help their friends on the other side. The schools taught him to read and study, offered him friendships that he felt he still had, thirty and forty years down the road. . . . And then his parents:

"I don't think anyone's had . . ." Hart said, and he stopped. He could not continue. Ten seconds passed, then twenty, and the camera shutters began to click and whirr, as Hart fought off tears. His parents died in this town.

"I don't think there is anyone in this country who has ever had better parents than I had . . ."

And then he stopped again. What would they say, if they could see him now? With the keys to the city . . . what would Carl have given for that recognition in his town?

"My father," Hart said, "was as honorable and decent a man as I think ever walked the face of the earth . . ."

The Wall Street Journal wrote that his mother was *crazy* . . . and she could not speak now, to show them, to defend. . . . What did she have to explain? Her love?

"My mother *loved life,* she loved the people around her, and she loved good humor . . .

"You've often heard the term 'salt of the earth,' and I think that's what they were . . . and they represent about the best that this society has to offer . . . and what they gave to me, I don't think I could repay, except to try to raise my children as well as they raised me."

After the speech, when Hart shed the last reporter . . . (*Senator, were you crying? . . . Senator, why did you stop in your speech?*), he and Lee snuck over to Letafay's house. She was Nina's favorite; he hadn't even got to see her. And he'd be leaving tomorrow, after a visit to Ottawa High.

Gary sank into the armchair near the fireplace. He looked so tired. Lee did, too. But with Gary, Letafay thought, there was sadness. . . . Lee was complaining that she had to pack her own bags, make her own arrangements, get herself to the airport.

"Lee, you need somebody," Letafay said.

"I know I do, Letafay. But I don't have *anybody*."

Gary was staring at the floor, with that somber look on his face. He didn't respond to what Lee said. Letafay looked over at him, and thought with a start that he'd have to get up early—have to travel again tomorrow. Letafay felt she was keeping him, that he just came over to be nice.

Hart looked up, and said, "Letafay, why would *anybody* want to run for President of the United States?"

"Why, Gary, that was my question to you!"

Gary didn't say anything.

They visited for a few minutes about the family. Then Gary and Lee stood to leave. Letafay felt she must have been boring. He just came out of the kindness of his heart.

"You know, Gary, I'm honored you came here to visit like this."

Hart's eyes gathered slightly and a furrow appeared in the center of his brow, like he didn't know what language she was speaking.

She stumbled on. "And, you know . . . I really appreciate it."

Hart still stared at her, pain mixed with confusion on his face. "Why would you say something like that?"

Then he kissed her, and went into the night.

24

1960

Yale Divinity was a school of social conscience: all but the most academic types had to mull, on
occasion, the place of the church in society, or the duty of a Christian in
combating the miseries of this earth. There were students and teachers committed to the struggle for civil rights. One divinity student was crushed to
death under the treads of a bulldozer in Cleveland, trying to block the
"urban renewal" of a poor people's neighborhood.

But that was social service, commitment, idealism . . . something other than
politics. Politics was crass, too clearly part of Caesar's realm. Even Gary
Hartpence, on whom the Nazarene Church had lost its hold, who was not sure
anymore whether he could sit still for a lifetime of philosophic inquiry and
teaching, would never have named politics as a possible career. Hartpence was
a young man of ideas—commitment, yes, but to principle. Politics was the
province of cigar-chomping ward bosses: patronage, payoff, one hand washing
the other . . .

And then came John Fitzgerald Kennedy.

Gary heard about him in a social ethics class—where Professor Miller
asked, one day, what they thought of a practicing Catholic in the nation's
highest office. This young Senator, Bill Miller said, might *force* the question.
Gary didn't have any trouble with that issue—any opposition to Kennedy on
those grounds struck him as simple intolerance. But the more he heard about
the Senator, the less was it a matter of academic interest.

Kennedy was new, young, bold, intelligent (qualities, each and all, that struck a gong with Hartpence), and yet possessed of a polish, a sense of irony, *personal grace.* He was the embodiment of that ease that was Gary's great envy and aspiration, but he bent it (along with his talent, his time, and gobs of his father's money) to the service of those social principles that were the core of Gary's own belief. Lord, what a combination! What a man!

It seemed to Gary a Providence, surely, for the nation: after eight long years of Ike, of tired, gray businessmen speaking for the country, years of inwardness and self-satisfaction, here was Kennedy, calling, demanding . . . to get America moving! It was time for youth, experimentation, *action:* the best of a new generation, hauling the nation forward toward its ideals . . . and just as Gary Hartpence was searching out a new way to serve his ideals.

Yes, surely, a Providence . . . after all, Gary was at Yale because his idea of service could not fit in the narrow ambit of the Nazarene ministry (in the end, that had so little to do with the great and needy world outside). By instinct, by philosophy, by his stubborn insistence that faith must make a difference in *this world,* he had turned away from the Nazarenes' endless dark struggle for salvation—soul and self. He would never fall prey to that baneful self-dissection that would make suicides of his two brilliant Bethany friends. . . . But even Yale Divinity, so much larger in its view, so richly oxygenated after Bethany Nazarene . . . seemed still, somehow, at one Platonic remove from the world as Gary longed to know it. Sure, the path to professorship was wider than the dog track to personal salvation . . . still, it was not the grand boulevard of life.

In that first year at Yale, his friend and fellow Nazarene, Tom Boyd, came to Gary's apartment to study for the big test on Aquinas, only to find Hartpence with his feet propped up, his face in the new issue of *Time.* "This is my question," Hartpence announced. "*Why* do I find this magazine so much more interesting than Saint Thomas Aquinas?"

By his second year, fall of '59, Gary had almost decided that a life as professor of philosophy was not for him. Maybe literature, which after all, dealt with every sort and shard of life. And so, he began to roam the campus, sampling here and there—modern culture, history, comparative lit. . . . By the spring of '60, he'd applied for the honors program, which would give him the run of Yale's riches. (In his third and final year, still nominally a divinity student, he would spend his time in study of Faulkner, Tolstoy, Dostoyevski . . .)

But by that time, too, he had marched himself to Democratic Party headquarters, to volunteer for Jack Kennedy—offered himself not at Yale's student union, but the office in New Haven . . . the real world. He may not have been the only one in his class, but there weren't too many, that was sure. Even at "liberal" Yale Divinity, there were plenty who thought a Papist had no business in the White House . . . even more who thought this Kennedy fellow seemed too young, too sharp, too worldly—awfully hard-eyed. (Stevenson was more their style: mild, intellectual, impeccably Protestant.)

Not Gary. More and more, Kennedy's progress (or lack) came to color his days. More and more, the evening talks in the apartment drifted off philosophical swordsmanship, onto politics, primaries, the agenda for the nation. What lure had Luther . . . when Ribicoff was endorsing the young Senator? Of what moment the torment of Vronsky . . . while, in West Virginia, that old pol Lyndon Johnson was threatening to unhorse Our Hero?

Well, not everybody's hero.

Even in Gary's own social set, the three or four couples with whom he and Lee spent their time, Gary was the only Kennedy man. Of course, he knew more about the campaign than most people in the graduate building. That's how he went into things—whole hog, to know. Then, too, there was the way he held to his judgments. (Gary, as one friend put it, "could argue like a dog.") He became implacably a Kennedy man. He was so in love with his hero, so obviously, teasably in thrall, that a couple of neighbors got a picture of Jesus (the best-known one—Jesus with long hair and arms extended downward, palms out) and pasted a cutout of Kennedy's face over Christ's . . . and tacked the thing onto Gary's door.

But Gary would not be laughed off this; it didn't matter if no one else saw it as he did. In a way, that made it better. It mirrored the crusade he saw in Kennedy's quest. More and more, Gary became convinced that Kennedy was not the choice of the Party—the insider, politics-as-usual hacks would *never* gamble on a Catholic, *never* choose his bold brand of leadership, no. . . . JFK would have to take over, from below, from the outside . . . by the power of his ideas.

And so he did, week by week, state by state . . . New Hampshire, Wisconsin, West Virginia . . . as Gary watched, and leafleted New Haven, and had the satisfaction of seeing its citizens, and his classmates, come around. That summer, back to work for the railroad, Gary pressed his case on the folks back home, the Republicans of Kansas, and that was a tougher sell. His own folks were simply bemused by his zeal. They weren't much for politics, after all . . . though, like everybody in Kansas, they'd been proud to vote for Ike . . . and Nixon was Ike's Number Two. Experience had to count for something! Still, Carl and Nina Hartpence were easy, mild, compared to S.T. Ludwig, Lee's dad, in Kansas City.

For all his reputation as a "liberal" Nazarene, S.T. was a man of entrenched ideas, and some familiarity with politics. He was Republican, when pressed on matters of party . . . but this had little to do with party. S.T. was a churchman, and that Kennedy boy was *everything* that good Nazarenes mistrusted: he was eastern, worldly (i.e., corrupt), stylish, handsome (i.e., vain), Harvard-polished (a rationalist) . . . with a shine bought and paid for by his father's money—*dirty liquor money*! (The Republicans made sure Joe Kennedy's history made the rounds in the dry Midwest.) And those were just S.T.'s *stated* reasons! By the time he and Gary thrashed it out, Gary, in his maddening way, had peeled back the layers of S.T.'s argument, to reveal the hidden, glistening core: that boy was a *Catholic*! And if the Pope of Rome meant to place his minion in the White House—well, he'd have to do it without S.T.'s help.

Gary called that simple prejudice. As for S.T., he could not understand what got into his son-in-law, Hartpence—or, for that matter, a whole generation of his family! Lee's sister, Martha, was touting that Kennedy boy, and her husband, Sam, was just as wildly liberal as Gary (though, thank Heaven, he favored Stevenson). Even dutiful Oletha . . . well, Lee, as she called herself now . . . was sticking up for Kennedy, or at least sticking up for Gary.

It was a summer on the griddle for Lee, Oletha, caught between the two beloved men in her life, between her old life and her new. She wished Gary wouldn't be so hard on her dad . . . of course, she knew Gary was right. What she tried to explain to her father—though the words were not so clear that summer: it wasn't just Kennedy; it wasn't even politics—not really. But Kennedy wanted people to do something for the country. That's the call she and Gary heard: not to politics—it was Public Service! If they all did something, if they all bent their talents to the needs of the age, there was no limit. They could change the world!

And there was another reason—though she couldn't have begun to explain, at the time. This call, this Public Service, this politics that had taken over their home was something she and Gary could share. That spring, that fall, 1960, the arguments in her living room were not arcane philosophic ponderings, the fruit of lectures she hadn't heard, or books she had no time to read. Kennedy, politics, the campaign, they were hers, too—as accessible to her as the newspaper, or TV news. She'd always had good sense about people . . . that's what politics was, after all. If it came to that with Gary—Public Service, as Kennedy said—if the agenda of the nation became the agenda of the household . . . well, Lee Hartpence would be in that mix. In fact, she'd be darned good at it!

And she knew, the way Gary was when he believed, it would have effect in life. He'd been searching, she knew. It would not be small, this change of focus. It *could not* be small with him. It was after Kennedy won, that fall, and excitement was high in the country—the most brilliant people from every sort of life were heading for Washington, heeding the call—that Gary decided he'd apply to Yale Law School, and not just for law, but for Public Service. And the next summer, there would be no more work on the rails. He got his summer job in Robert F. Kennedy's Department of Justice. The country was on the move. He and Lee, together, were headed for the engine room—Washington . . . and, yes, a new life. That was the summer they got the name changed to Hart. Gary had wanted to do it for years. And now was the time. Carl and Nina went along. Gary's hair got longer, his ties narrower. But those were just the outward signs, not the big changes—they were in his head. That was the summer he began his new study—power, the means of moving a nation—a study that would occupy his next thirty years. It was a heady subject for a new life, yes . . . there were no limits! Not for the nation, nor even the world . . . not for Gary and Lee Hart, together.

— ★ —

It was actually 1958, the first time Michael saw JFK. The Senator had come back to Massachusetts, running for reelection. But that was no contest (he'd end up with seventy-eight percent of the vote). And Kennedy wasn't interested in disguising his aim. At a meeting of the Harvard Law Graduate Democratic Club, he strode to the podium and announced (in fact, this was the full text of his speech): "My name is Jack Kennedy. I'm a candidate for President of the United States. Are there any questions?"

It was, as Michael would ever remember, a commanding performance. Kennedy was home at Harvard, after all, and these young men, with their earnest eyes fixed on him, under their earnest crew cuts, they *were* the best, the brightest, they would people his New Frontier. Kennedy's message was made for them:

During the American Revolution, Thomas Paine said the cause of America was the world's cause. But now the cause of all mankind was America's cause. . . . Their nation was the hope of the planet, and *they,* the most fortunate, the enlightened, the blessed, would bring that hope to flower in the new decade. There must be no limit to their aspiration. No problem was too big, too tough . . . nothing less than a new Enlightenment was in their grasp, if they would but reach. . . .

So, you could understand if all those young men—and Michael in their van—ran to Washington in fever (or at least to Wisconsin, to set up for the primary two years thence). But fever was not Michael's style—even at twenty-four years old, in his first year at Harvard Law. Anyway, he already had a tough campaign—his own: Michael was running for one of four seats on the Brookline Redevelopment Authority, a new-but-already-obscure board that would advise the town government in its early efforts at "urban renewal."

See, Michael believed in Public Service, was raised to it, in fact—he didn't need Kennedy to wake him to that—but as for causes, new ages, America's hand reaching for the stars . . . that was a bit airy for Dukakis. Sure, he caught the excitement, and pride, as Kennedy, fair son of Massachusetts, rose in the eyes of the nation. But that didn't change the sorry facts on the ground, in their home state, or in Brookline—Michael's town—where JFK was born. The fact was that Brookline, like most towns around Boston, like Boston itself, like the whole benighted state, was locked in the arid and archaic politics of the early century: the well-bred Yankees (Republicans, alas) vied every four years, with mixed success, against the Democrats, who were Irish and Italian clubhouse pols, more numerous, of course, than the Yankees, but corrupt, old-fashioned . . . well, in Michael's view, they were ignorant hacks. In Brookline, with its tradition of clean government (as clean as the air, as clean as the lawns that drew the escapees from Boston in the first place), the Yankees held the upper hand. But still, the Democratic Party there was the province of old Irish muldoons, who made their living trading the town's small machinable vote for a few jobs and favors (and maybe a spot on the state payroll for themselves).

Therein lay Michael's crusade.

That's why he ran for a spot on the redevelopment board, to get a leg up in this system—that cried out for *reform*! That's why he and a few friends from Harvard—Fran Meaney, Carl Sapers, another Greek kid named Paul Sarbanes—were out on street corners, at trolley stops, every weekend, pressing

upon the citizenry the *importance,* the *seriousness,* of this board and its contribution to *rational planning.* This was *too important* to leave in the hands of
the same old hacks. But Michael didn't have to say that. The big thing was
to get his name around, and his qualifications: born and bred in Brookline,
Swarthmore College, service in Korea, Harvard Law . . . it was a résumé of
obvious merit, clean as the lawns on Rangley Road. And really, one look at
the guy would tell you what you had to know: he was living home, commuting
to Harvard on his Vespa motorscooter (cheap, easy to park, plenty vehicle
enough, thank you), and weekends, he'd jump on the scooter to campaign.
He'd work a corner, standing straight up, hands on his hips, his button on his
suit jacket, and an earnest look on his clean, sharp face, a look of such
concentrated purpose that it seemed to pull down the front of his dark crew
cut in mid-forehead, toward the line of black eyebrow, as he explained in a
clipped, rational tone, the important agenda of redevelopment. What he looked
like was a little Mr. Spock—without the ears—on the bridge of the *Enterprise.*

But so hopeful! Times were changing, even in Brookline, even in the sleepy
fifties. Prosperity brought a new wave of escapees from Boston—mostly Jews,
these were, drawn like moths to the light of Brookline's schools—and unlike
those who had moved in before (the German Jews, for instance, who worried
so much about fitting in), these people didn't feel they had to act like "Yen-
kehs." They were Democrats—active Democrats, who owed nothing to the
Irish machine. And they were at the core of the breakthrough—the election
of the first Democratic officeholder in Brookline, since . . . well, probably since
the Civil War. He was Sumner Kaplan, and if Michael had a political model,
it was not JFK, nor any Massachusetts Irishman: it was Sumner Z. Kaplan,
of the Massachusetts House of Representatives. It was Sumner's energetic
street-corner style (door-to-door, apartment-to-apartment, if possible) that
Michael and his friends emulated. Sumner showed they could do it—maybe
not the first time, maybe not every time . . . but Sumner had broken through
in 1954. Surely, times were changing now. Intelligence, reason, and decency
were on the march!

Alas, not in '58, not for Michael. He came in fifth, in a race for four seats.

But he'd be back. (He'd got more than four thousand votes! . . . He'd done
well. *Sumner said* he'd done well!) The next year, there was a special election
for the members of the Town Meeting, that old and venerable New England
institution that still survived in Yankee enclaves like Brookline (or Greenwich,
Connecticut). And when the special election was called, Sumner said, "Run!"
And all the boys ran. They leafleted the houses, street by street; they worked
the trolley stops and corners on Beacon Street; they rounded up their friends—
volunteers!—to make calls. Brookline had never seen such effort! (In fact, the
Yankee tradition frowned on such effort—one didn't run, one *stood* for election.) But it worked. This time, Michael won. And a few friends with him, who
took seats at the Meeting . . . duly empowered holders of office in Brookline,
Massachusetts.

Problem was—empowered to do what? Town Meeting was much more a

sounding board than a paddle to bestir government. Michael and his Young
Turks had no sway in the Meeting, the town, or even within their Party. The
Democratic Party Town Committee was the machine's committee. Those
people wouldn't even get off their duffs to mobilize the faithful for Jack
Kennedy! Michael and his friends thought it was an outrage. Here was their
Senator sweeping the country, and his home-state Party was still sunk in
back-slapping clubhouse torpor! That's not how Michael said it: he said *the
process* was being ill served. But in his mind, that was the same. Same problem:
ignorant hacks. And only one solution: Michael and his friends would take
over. In 1960, there'd be a big turnout for Kennedy in the primary—the
Presidential preference vote. But what that primary would also select were the
down-ballot Party officers, Town Committees, the machinery of the machine.
    So Michael made a slate of his young, clean, intelligent friends, and they all
filed for Town Committee: thirty-five seats at the table . . . and Michael's
friends filed for every one. Michael made the budget and the plan: they'd each
chip in five dollars for the campaign (to buy a button for each, and one
newspaper ad); they'd each come up with a list of twenty-five friends (names,
addresses, and phone numbers) who were voters in town. Then each candidate
would get all the lists, and make sure to call every name. . . . And for every
candidate, with every voter, the message was the same: Vote Group Two.
Straight ticket, one lever—Vote Group Two. Well, no one had ever campaigned for this committee . . . only hand-picked boy-os ever ran: the job didn't
even pay. And certainly no one campaigned like these kids. They were all over
town, quietly (so as not to wake Group One, the machine) talking to their
friends, and their parents' friends, and friends of their friends . . . Vote Group
Two. They even had a platform, a program! It was all about the fairness of
the process:
    Group Two pledged to have a Campaign Office in Brookline, where the
brochures of every Democratic candidate could be displayed.
    Group Two pledged to hold an annual Garden Party, a fund-raiser, where
every Democratic candidate could speak.
    Sounded fine . . . but what was the big deal? Well, to see the big deal, you
had to look at the thing like a third-year student at Harvard Law in 1960
. . . when Process was at its peak. . . . There are fashions in law, though they
aren't called fashions while they're in vogue. No, while the hot professors still
believe in a fashion, it's called brilliant scholarship . . . until those scholars are
judges, and then that fashion is called law. . . . Anyway, in the late fifties, there
was a most influential Harvard prof named Kaplan (Benjamin—no relation to
Sumner), and he taught Civil Procedure, the highlight of the first year. Kaplan
contended that a lawyer, because he understood process, could do anything.
Later, students were treated to lectures from Professor Al Sacks, who teamed
up with Professor Henry Hart for a course on Legal Process. That was the
most important course at the school, a near-universal analysis of how to make
things work better. The underlying jurisprudence was debatable (and out of
fashion in a few years—then it was called a fad!), but for Michael and his

friends, for all the young Harvard Law men whose mission, whose burden it was to be learnedly sure, to be right in every regard (a fashion never out of vogue at Harvard Law), there was only one thing worth looking at: Process.

Sure, Jack Kennedy was calling the young of America to greatness, but you had to look at this thing like Michael—that is, correctly: if you wanted the Party to put forward men like Sumner, like Stevenson, like John F. Kennedy . . . well, then, you had to put good people at the levers of the Party. You had to reform the process to control it. You had to increase your power at the Party's state convention, which meant increasing the size of your town's delegation, which meant increasing the town's vote for the Democratic candidate for Governor, which meant invigorating the Party in town, which meant taking over the Party committee. It was like a set of those wooden eggs from Russia, with one egg inside the other, forever . . . until you got back to Michael and his friends, hatching their tiny . . . Vote Group Two!

Well, sure, Kennedy won the primary that day, in the spring of 1960. But the big surprise in Brookline was . . . Group One never knew what hit them! The muldoons were history! Michael and his friends took thirty-four of thirty-five seats (one of their candidates had dropped out) . . . and the new Chairman of the Democratic Party in Brookline was twenty-six-year-old Michael S. Dukakis.

And the great thing about 1960, with the Kennedy youth thing in the air, was that Michael was not alone in triumph. His law school buddy Carl Sapers took over the committee in Boston's Fifth Ward, Beacon Hill . . . and there were reformers in Waltham . . . stirrings in Lexington. . . . So two months after their primary-day triumph, Michael and Sapers called a meeting of all the reformers, from every town, at the state convention . . . and announced the formation of the Commonwealth Organization of Democrats—COD. The mission: nothing less than a takeover of every Town Committee in Massachusetts, the promotion of good, clean, qualified candidates, for every office, in every town, in every courthouse, and in the State House . . . complete control of the process, statewide . . . reform, everywhere!

25

The
Tinsel
and the Tree

IT WAS the joy of being with Joe that you were included—not just in his politics, but in his life, and the lives of his family. You were more likely to hear from Biden what Jill said the other day about teaching . . . what his mother used to say . . . or a wonderfully embroidered story about a nun in Scranton . . . than you were about his five-point education plan. Joe Biden shared his life—or his version of it— continuously. He confided it, displayed it, spread it profligately, even expanded it to connect with *your life.* He could settle for nothing less.

This was the bane of his Schedulers' lives. Biden could run an hour late—to his second event of the day. But if a room held *one vote* still hanging on the cliff edge (Joe could always tell—he'd talk right to them, till he had their eyes) . . . Joe would not leave! This was the great cause of heartburn, too, for his staff, for his gurus. Joe would get a crowd of Democrats, his age, maybe older, and he'd work until he had almost *every one* . . . but he couldn't stop there . . . he'd reach for the others, talk right to them . . . until, BANGO! Joe was off on his life . . . how he started in the civil rights movement . . . *remember*? . . . *The marches? Remember how that felt?* . . . And they're nodding in the crowd, and he's got them, sure. . . . Trouble is, Joe didn't march. He was in high school, playing football.

(But there was one teammate, a black guy, and one day they all went to the Charcoal Pit for french fries, and the counterman was not going to serve the black kid—so Joe walked out . . . and so did the rest of the guys, they *walked out* . . . and that was the same feeling in the marches, right? And that was the feeling Joe wanted to share, see? . . . The gurus would shake their heads. "That's *not marching.* " And Joe would say, "I know. Okay." But then, a week later, another crowd . . . and Joe would do it again.)

Still, this was also the reason they were working for Biden: for the abandon with which he stretched himself (and not just by exaggeration) to touch a thousand lives in a day . . . for the talent, extravagant effort, the generosity of spirit that made every event with Biden a festival of inclusion . . . for the death-defying-Evel-Knievel-eighty-miles-an-hour-over-twenty-five-buses *leap* he would make to get the connect—if that's what it took—before he had to land, dust himself off, bow to the crowd, and leave that room. The gurus would come back from trips with him, rolling their eyes, telling stories. . . .

One time, an Iowa room, Joe was in mid-monologue, and there was a woman at a table, facing away, who would *not turn around.* Joe didn't break stride in his talk . . . ("Folks, think of it! We have the chance now to make that difference. I'm absolutely convinced . . .") or his walk—he was always moving, fixing one with his eyes, then another. And he got to this woman, came up from behind . . . ("So, folks, look me over. If you like what you see . . .") and gently, but decidedly, he put his hands on her. In Council Bluffs, Iowa! He got both hands onto her shoulders, while he talked to the crowd over her head, like it was her and him, through thick and thin. The woman looked like she'd swallowed her tongue.

And the gurus would shrug, and say, in wonder: "You can't teach that . . ." Hell, they couldn't even gauge it, it was off their charts! What was the effect in that room . . . or on that woman? Who knows? Maybe she became his voter. Maybe she was offended. But one goddam thing was no longer in doubt: she heard him, she felt him. At that moment, for good or ill, she was at that here-and-now, with Joey Biden.

—★—

They didn't want to clip him back—you don't fool with magic, and when Biden was on, well, that was the only word. (That room in Council Bluffs— seventy people, and they signed up more than fifty that morning.) And Joe sure as hell wasn't trying to hold himself in check. His effort, the labor of his days and nights, was to get himself up, stoke the heat, do the next room, the next hit. With everything clawing at him—the family, the Senate, the committee, the interminable message meetings with the gurus—it was a wonder he stayed clear enough to make any sense, much less move a crowd.

His days were a dance, which he could not slow down—if he let that energy slip from his grasp, then he couldn't get it back for the next room, or the next . . . sure, he could fly over twenty-five buses (absolutely convinced, not a doubt in his mind . . .), but *it had to be done at speed.* So many times, in the office, in meetings, in a plane or van between events, Joe was just spinning, talking a streak, going too fast to listen. If he asked a question, he wanted the answer *now.* When he snapped about arrangements, Advance or staff work, it was always about delay—they were *slowing him down*! . . . That spring, Tommy

Donilon, senior guru, was trying to explain to a friend what Joe was like in a meeting. "Did you see *Beverly Hills Cop II*?" (Of course, it had to be movie-talk.) "You remember the scene where Eddie Murphy goes deep undercover to buy the stolen goods? He walks into this bar, right? And the guy doesn't know if he should do it, so Eddie's like this . . ." (Now Donilon was snapping his fingers, fast, both hands, in front of his face.)

"Hey! I'm a bidnessman . . . I got to make MOVES! . . ."

In Washington, in the life he knew, Joe had a vent for his steam—the Senate gym . . . you could find him there for hours each day. Well, actually, you couldn't find him—that was the point. No staff, no outsiders allowed. Joe's schedule would say "staff time" at least once a day, usually twice, and what that meant was *gym time*. Somehow, he had to blow it off. . . . But on the road, there was nowhere to vent, save public events. If he got through talking and wouldn't leave, if he kept working harder till the whole room was sweaty, if he had them all . . . and then *lost them* because he couldn't stop . . . well, you had to understand that these were his workouts.

Now, at the close of his ski-trip weekend, he has to check in on a funder for Paul McEachern, the Democrat who lost to Sununu in the last New Hampshire gubernatorial election. So Joe shows up with the whole family: Jill (who's still not happy—she and the kids have to get to the airport—but Joe said they'd just stop in) and the boys, Beau and Hunter, and little Ashley . . . and a couple of staff, and the CBS crew, and three or four reporters . . . and every eye in the banquet hall is on the Bidens as they file in . . . late . . . but what a beautiful family! Joe is lithe, balding, rich with charm: light on his feet, suddenly eye-locked with the ladies, full of good-humored candor with the men. He has a woman's hand in one of his own, and he raises his other hand to greet her whole table, "Hi, how're y'all doin'?" while he keeps his gaggle together, through the crowd, with asides, jokes, confiding patter. . . . "Hi, uh, oh, we met at the door . . ." (Aside: "I always watch for my reporter friends with their notebooks to see, uh . . .") "Can we all fit here, honey?" "Hi! How are you?" (". . . see that I don't wear out my welcome.") "Hi! Good to see you!"

Of course, they bring him right on stage to say hello, and he doesn't mean to talk, so he just says what a fine man Paul McEachern is, and what a fine campaign . . . which reminds Joe of an Irish joke, an old Father Ryan joke . . . and after they all have a laugh, he really doesn't want to take their time, so he just thanks them for the invitation, urges the crowd to look him over . . . and he really has to go . . . but McEachern gets up to speak, and Joe can't say what a sterling and important guy Paul is and then leave at the start of his talk, so he sits back down with the family, but it's a hell of a place to ask the kids to sit still, especially a six-year-old, so while he whispers something to Jill, he sweeps Ashley onto his lap, where she stands on his knees, facing his face, which he tries to keep smiling toward McEachern, who's thanking supporters, a list as long as his arm . . . while Ashley strips from her wrist her colored plastic bracelets, and piles them (as the TV lights flash onto Joe—CBS *has* to have this) . . . on top of daddy's head, on the bald part, where Joe has the transplant hairs raked across the scalp . . . a yellow bracelet, then a red one, and a green one, until they cascade onto daddy's nose, and Ashley is giggling with delight.

And by the time Jill and the kids get to the airport, Joe is late for the next thing, a coffee-chat with a houseful of folks, so he's urgent once he gets them into the living room and starts to talk—he's hot tonight—but there are folks in the dining room who might not hear . . . anyway, he can't see them to make sure he's got them . . . so in mid-breath he's asking the folks in the living room to squeeze in this way, "so we can all see . . ." and then in the middle of his next riff, he sees that he's jammed CBS into a corner—and Christ! That's a million people!—so he adds, as aside, just to them: "I don't mean to back you in like that. I'll move over here . . ." which means the young woman from the local radio has to stretch her arm to get her microphone closer, so Joe says, in the middle of his thing about how this people, this generation, hasn't lost its idealism, no, not at all—"You want me to hold that, dear? Your arm'll be killing you . . ." and Joe holds her mike in front of his chest, as he singles out the hostess with his eyes, and he says, to close his message, "Bev, I *know* we can do better . . . I am absolutely convinced . . ." Yes, he's on tonight, he's got them, you can feel it in the room, and they can feel his conviction, or at least his need, and they're itching to applaud him, but he's taking questions, and the answers are twenty minutes long, because he wants them to *know* him: "Folks, when I started in public life, in the civil rights movement, we marched to change attitudes. . . . I remember what *galvanized* me. . . . Bull Connor and his dogs . . . I'm serious. In Selma." Joe's voice drops to an urgent whisper. "Absolutely . . . made . . . my . . . blood . . . run . . . *cold.* Remember? . . ."

Yes, they remember . . . but Joe is an hour and a half late to his last event, in the basement of a restaurant. It's after ten when he gets to the place, through sleet and snow, and he's tired. There are only twenty people left, but still, he's got to get up to full steam for them, about eleven o'clock, and when he starts to take questions . . . well, he's still talking an hour later, and people are almost forced to walk out on him. But the staff always lets him run, on his last event. There's no way they can stand at the back and say, "Uh, Senator? Last question. We really have to go . . ." Go where? For what—sleep? There are people here! . . . So Joe calls his own last question, and then another, and another, and it's after midnight when he says goodbye to the last hardy dozen, and he wants pizza with the staff, but Ruth says no—he has to sleep—a big speech at lunch tomorrow, another at dinner, and four events besides . . . so she gets him to the motel and gets him squared away, but how is he supposed to just *shut down*? He'll be up for *hours* . . . Ruth will know in the morning, when she calls—the moment he says two words . . . she always knows.

"I'll call back in fifteen minutes," she says. She can hear the woozy fatigue in his voice. They'll start late that morning, again. . . . But just to be sure, when she checks him out of the motel, she'll ask to see the bill: Was it a two-night, a three-night? . . .

How many of the pay-per-view movies did he have to watch before he could crash?

— ★ —

The funny part was how normal it seemed to Joe. He'd always loped with a smile on this raggedy precipice of excess. Of course, he would explain, afterward, that he knew *all along* how it would come out. He had the whole thing gamed out . . . see?

Well, mostly, it was hard to see. It felt to the others, who were with him on the edge, like they were making it up *right now* . . . that's why they were jumpy. But Joe wasn't uncomfortable at all. Tell the truth, he liked it when there was no more time to think—High Noon on Main Street, Joey and the other guy in the sun . . . when you had to just *do*, or shut up and walk. That was Joe's time—game day . . . BANGO!

Sometimes, in the Senate, Joe would push away his briefing books and walk into a hearing with just one question—something Mom-Mom asked him on the phone twenty minutes before. And there were all those times Joe would hunch at the head table, writing notes for his speech, while they were introducing him. He courted that showdown in the sun—it made his motor run.

That's why they had to charter a plane to Iowa, that day in March . . . *right now* . . . *a jet.* Joe had to get to Des Moines! The UAW was holding its state convention, three days in the ballroom of the beautiful Best Western Starlite Village. Of course, Joe knew about the convention . . . knew also that the union's head of politics, Chuck Gifford, was just about working for Gephardt (Gephardt just about moved into Gifford's house, didn't he?) . . . and some of the members were already leaning to Gephardt (Why not? That's what Dick's trade bill was *for*—for the auto workers who'd been whining about the import cars) . . . and Joe knew, too, that Gephardt was scheduled for the keynote address. . . .

But then Joe got a call—his guys in Iowa, they were frenzied! The convention was a Gephardt jamboree! Chuck Gifford and his wife were greasing the skids—the whole damn UAW was sliding into Gephardt's lap!

So Joe had to go. Had to turn it around!

But wait—was he invited?

Even better! He'd storm the place, crash the party!

So he called a couple of his UAW guys from the Delaware council, got them to come along ("No, today . . . yeah, now!") . . . no way the Iowa men could freeze out their own union brothers, right? And then, just to be sure, Joe called up Owen Bieber, the National High-Cheese-Maximum-Muckety-Muck-Auto-Worker-Wallah, *himself.* Joe wanted Bieber to tell that asshole Gifford to *back off*—what the hell was he trying to pull? Bieber said he'd look into the thing . . . and Joe rode off to the airport.

Well, by the time they came steaming into the Starlite room—Joe, the Delaware union men, and Ridley, puffing and jiggling and talking a mile a minute from adrenaline and coffee in the plane—Gifford had got a call from

Bieber, see . . . so he said: *Of course* Joe Biden can come. He can speak! I will *personally* introduce him . . . right *after* these three union men, who, of course, were *scheduled* to speak, and who would rumble on for *more than two hours* . . . while Joe steamed and fretted and bounced his knee, while he shifted on a chair and tried to look like he was listening. And just when Gifford judged there was *no one* in that room who wanted to hear another word . . . when it was obvious it was time to head for the bar . . . he stood up and, coolly, introduced Joe Biden.

But Gifford and his guys didn't know about Joey on game day . . . how could they know? The guys in that room had never seen him until he walked in—just another Senator, running for President . . . until Joe started to tell them about his life. In fact, he started with the UAW and his life—because it meant something to him—that was the first union to break away and support him in '72. He never forgot that—never. . . . And he introduced the two fellows who'd come with him from Delaware, left their families and homes, on awfully short notice, to be with him tonight—and that meant something to Joe, too . . . as it did to the union men and women in the hall.

And then he told them why *he* was there, tonight . . . about the outright war that Reagan and his pals had declared upon the working man, and the way the nation slept while its factories slumped and its jobs went overseas . . . and he asked if they wanted America to be something more than the biggest McDonald's outlet in the world. . . . Well, *he* did . . . and *now* . . . *was the time.*

And the room got quiet, though it was late and there'd been too much talk. Joe was into the speech now, where he knew just how the words should dance on the ear.

"For a *decade,* ladies and gentlemen, the *cry* of the Reagan years has been: 'Got *mine!* Go get *yours!*' . . ." Joe's voice was harsh with flat and wheedling greed, as his gaze shifted, almost accusing, to another table. " 'What's in it for *me?*' . . ." And they saw, he didn't have any notes, he didn't have to read this, or stop to think it out. He was just talking to them.

"Ladies and gentlemen . . . something is *wrong.* "

And he told them what he thought was wrong, and how they were going to fix it—not by a fifteen-point program diddled through Congress, and signed at a Rose Garden media-op by a President smiling for the cameras . . . no! It rested with them . . . in this room. It was about waking up the whole damn country!

"Folks . . ." Joe said, and he stopped. He stopped for a full two beats. "Let's not kid each other. *You* have the same problem I have. You walk into your meetings, and your folks look at you and say, '*What the hell do you know?*' . . ."

Now they're nodding, there's knowing laughter from the well of the hall.

"So you have the same problem—leadership—that faces us in government. . . . But I believe (I am absolutely convinced of this) that our citizens and our workers offer untapped resources . . . the country is not as afraid as we are.

The people are willing to take chances; they're willing to take their shots. They're not looking to be coddled. They're looking to have a chance to fight.

"And, folks, this vision is not just some pipe dream. . . . It is nothing *less* than the *legacy* of *our generation*. . . . When I was seventeen years old . . ."

And Joe was off on his life again. The amazing thing was, no one moved, made a sound . . . Joe talked for an hour and twenty minutes, and nobody left that room. And when he got to the end, the heroes and the dreamers . . . and the quote: "*He will lift you up on eagles' wings . . .*" and he finished, there was silence for a moment, two beats, three beats—ten seconds of hush—and they started to clap, and Joe could see people looking over at Gifford and the state nabobs . . . everybody knew, see, what Chuck wanted. But some stood up, they were cheering, and then there were maybe fifty men and women on their feet, and then the others, table by table—you could almost see them say to themselves, "Aw, fuck Gifford!"—they stood up, too, and the whole crowd was on its feet, cheering . . . and when it ended, there must have been seventy-five who lined up to shake Joe's hand.

Of course, Joe was pumped up, too, and his friends, the union men from Delaware, had found folks they knew, and they told him about the hospitality suites, upstairs in the beautiful Best Western, where the real talk went down. So Joe went upstairs to meet those folks, and they were stunned when he walked in—amazed he'd take the time. But he wanted so much for them to know him—they felt that—and Christ, he stayed till after eleven.

And it was after midnight, when his rented jet was in the air again, that Joe even started to wind down. And everyone in the plane said he'd done a hell of a job. Maybe he'd even turn Gifford around! Or his wife! Who knows? It was off the scale. One goddam thing was sure, though. There were Biden people in that union now.

Ridley was next to him and he asked Joe:

"How do you *do* that?"

Joe shrugged, and told Tim how he talked to one table, and then another, and when he had them, he moved on. . . .

But that was technique, and not what Ridley meant.

In fact, Joe didn't know exactly how it happened, or what the connect *was*. What always occurred to *him* . . . what he felt when it happened in a room . . . was a tingle of fear. He hoped to *God* that what they understood was what he was trying to say, because he could feel their need coming back at him, and their willingness to be led—he just had to pray they got it right! If they didn't . . . well, God only knew what someone could do with them. . . . That's what always scared Joe: *If I can do this to these folks, what happens if someone comes along who can really SING?*

But Joe didn't say that to Ridley. What he told was what he saw—when he knew he had the room. There was a couple, husband and wife, way in the back, in the dark, and Joe was working on them when he got to the end, the dream and the dreamers ("Just because our heroes were murdered . . .")—and Joe saw the guy's arm go around his wife's shoulders . . . and he knew then.

Then, too, Joe said he'd known how it would be, all along.

— ★ —

The most frightening thing was, he didn't know why it disappeared . . . the magic. He knew he felt bad—that's all he knew—and he looked scared. It was the morning after the big ski trip, and Joe had a hell of a day on his plate, even before it got so screwed up.

He had a big speech at the Nashua Country Club, where all the city's movers and shakers gathered for their monthly Rotary luncheon. Joe was going to preview his arms control speech. Then there was another address on Constitutional issues at a law school that night . . . and in between, he was supposed to announce his New Hampshire campaign committee, and Valerie, his sister, his Campaign Manager, was supposed to fly up for that . . . but it was getting on to lunchtime and where was Val? . . . Meanwhile, CBS still had him miked for *West 57th Street,* and Paul Taylor, the new big-foot for *The Washington Post,* had come to listen to the speeches, maybe talk with Joe, and Boston TV was choppering in for the country club speech at noon . . . and Marianne Baker, his personal keeper in the Senate office, tracked him down in Nashua to tell him there might be a cloture vote on contra aid—Joe might have to fly back, they'd have to charter a plane . . . so they were trying to find Larry Tribe, Harvard's reigning Constitutional scholar, to fill in for Joe at the law school speech—if it came to that, if the vote was late—but no one could find Tribe to get a commitment . . . and Joe had to go on at the Rotary, *now,* and do the press conference on the committee, after . . . and where the hell was Val? . . . Did anyone get Tribe?

And Joe was off. You could feel it the minute he got to the podium. His voice was flat, his face was drawn, and the TV lights only made him paler, thinner, less substantial . . .

"But I do congratulate you for coming out to hear me speak . . . because I *am* one of the most important men in America . . ."

No! *BZZZZT!* Wrong!

It was an old joke with Joe, but today it didn't sound self-effacing, ironic.

He tried to tell another joke, a long story wherein he's mistaken for the baseball commissioner, Ueberroth . . . but he never got through it.

"Uhnnn . . ." Joe said, and he stopped, like he couldn't think. "Something I ate . . ."

His face was flushing as he stopped to draw breath, he looked confused, out of place. He was turning an awful color in the lights—almost purple.

". . . is, uh, really giving me difficulty, and uh, I mean that sincerely . . ."

He had to get out of there. The pain in his head! Like boiling water up the back of his head. Like it would blow off the top of his skull. He was nauseated. He couldn't focus on the words of his speech.

"Could I go downstairs? . . . And come back? . . ."

There was a bathroom downstairs. He didn't say more, he just walked out.

In the press gaggle, there were a couple of jokes about Rotary food—chicken surprise, heh heh. . . . A Rotary member went to the mike and told racist jokes about his travels in India and Africa. The TV guys flicked their lights off, looked at their watches. . . . Joe's staff was trying to cook the schedule. If Joe took fifteen minutes here, he wouldn't get to the press conference till two—he'd have to cut right out to Washington: How many seats in the plane? Would Val go back? Any seats for press? . . . Paul Taylor was holding court in the country club lounge. Some editor-lady had called from New York—wanted him to do a book—inside the campaign . . . you know, with the *Post*. The *Post* is a player . . . Taylor thought it would be interesting: this was the time of *his* coming of age, along with his generation, accepting the responsibilities of the big time, just as he, Paul, was inheriting the mantle of leadership from David Broder . . .

And Joe was dying. At least he felt like he was. In the bathroom downstairs, the pain had hold of him and he couldn't think. He had to think . . . *what was this?* He couldn't remember pain like this. Nauseous pain. He should puke. He tried to puke, down on his knees, grunting and heaving. He couldn't breathe. He'd call out—for what—a doctor? Val? Where was Val? He hadn't air. He had to have air. He threw open the window—basement window, ground outside, and snow . . . and he laid his head onto the snow, tried to breathe. It was cold. The air . . . didn't help. Was there anything like this? He couldn't remember pain like this. Sweet Jesus God—he had to think—was this what it felt like when you had a heart attack? . . .

He didn't know how long he was there. He was alone . . . how much time? He had to get back up there—there were people, his speech . . . the cameras. How would he look? He smoothed his tie . . . holy shit! He had a mike on—CBS!—those noises, puking, groaning! Holy shit! He had to pull himself *together. This could not come apart!*

And he did it. He washed his face. He came out and went up the stairs at a trot. He strode back into the dining room, straight to the mike. He apologized, said it wasn't their food. He started reading his speech.

"Mr. Reagan intends to continue with his Star Wars program . . ."

It was a good speech—an interesting point: a President had twenty minutes now, to react, if missiles were fired into the air. But with Star Wars, Reagan's crowd would cut that to five minutes: man-the-scientist was going to outrun man-the-negotiator. Well, okay. . . . But it seemed, suddenly, academic. The Boston TVs wanted to know: Was this Biden the orator?

Joe couldn't even hear himself reading—that word, next word . . . what the hell was it about? He clamped both hands on the sides of the podium. He never looked up. All he knew was, his head hurt like hell.

In the dining room, all the Rotarians knew was, there wasn't any magic to this guy—none at all. Senator Joseph R. Biden, Jr.—just a tall, skinny, balding man . . . reading a speech.

—★—

His gurus used to say there were moments in campaigns—the big debate, the acceptance speech, or just some serendipitous collision of fate with publicity along the trail—moments of decision, maybe even truth, when the halogen lights and the eyes of the nation snapped to shining focus on a campaign and candidate . . . and that's when it counted. If they could just get Joe and his magic, intact, to one of those moments, then millions would see, in a flash, his brilliance, his balls . . . and they would make a President.

And Joe believed them. That's why his effort, his every day and night, was bent to straining, ever, to *make something happen.* Make the magic now— *something* . . . the feeling, the connect. Who knew? This could be the time. And so, where his instinct drove him to share some bit of his life, he'd strew the gaudiest, shiniest trim that fell to his gaze . . . right *now.* "Folks, when I was seventeen years old, I took part in demonstrations to desegregate restaurants . . ." Somehow, it was easier to show the tinsel than the tree.

Lost, alas, was the solider stuff: the way he fiercely, doggedly, held his family together through loss; the way everybody he touched that day—every day— felt more like his better self than he did before Joe showed up; the relentless way he drove himself to be *always* the one they could count on. This was the common grit at the bed of his life—family, loyalty, humor, guts—that was ever there.

See, he thought they'd *have* to get that stuff—that's character, right? . . . *One look* at his kids, Jill, his home, his *life*—they'd pick it up, right?

But it's hard to show the grit underneath the bits of glitter—hard for Joe, took time . . . and never hit with the hot splash he craved. Anyway, the big-feet, the pundits—it was not their business: they were writing about politics, not life. Not even the near end of life.

What did they know about bleeding in the skull? . . .

What did Joe know, for that matter?

So no one wrote about the moment Joe lost the magic, or the common guts it took to finish the day.

— ★ —

Oh, he did finish—and not just the speech. He did the press conference after, announced his committee, and flew down to Washington, cast his vote against the contras, and decided to fly back. He might still make the dinner in New Hampshire—late, but hell . . .

And the plane was small—no room for press—so he only took Paul Taylor, and Joe made sure they had a chance to talk. Taylor was important, see, and Joe wanted Paul to know him. And Joe talked about his life, what it felt like now, with everything in the air at once. And the great thing was, Paul talked about his life, too . . . and the most amazing thing—he was talking about . . . *their generation,* just like Joe had been saying out there!

Joe didn't know about the plan for the book, the way Paul was thinking . . . but he knew this was important, him and Paul—if Taylor could really know him, his character . . . the *real stuff*! And Joe got pumped up—he did feel better. If only he could shake this goddam headache!

He got to the dinner, and Tribe was at the podium . . . but Joe got on after him, and did his speech anyway. It was late, but he gave it what he had.

It was after midnight when his plane was in the air again, heading south to Delaware—Joe insisted on getting home. And when they climbed down onto the tarmac at the Wilmington airport, about 2:00 A.M., Joe asked Taylor to come home with him, stay with the Bidens for the night.

Taylor looked uneasy. No, he said. He could go to a motel . . .

Joe wouldn't hear of it. "Plenty of room!"

So he took Paul home, and walked him through the silent, stately house, took him to a guest room . . . but a nanny was asleep there. So he led Paul upstairs to his son's room—Beau was asleep, too—and Joe laid a hand on his son's shoulder for just an instant, to tell him: "Beau-y, this is Paul . . . he's gonna sleep in the other bed."

"Hnnuh! . . . okay, Dad . . ." And Beau was asleep again.

So Taylor slept that night with the Bidens, *en famille,* and woke the next day among the family . . . but he never did write about it for the *Post.*

Taylor did write his book, about him in the campaign and all . . . and in the book, he explained his technique:

"I'm a 'good cop' interviewer. I try to ease, tease, coax and wheedle information from sources. With body language, facial expression, tone of voice and other verbal and nonverbal cues, I hope to let them know that I see the same world they see; that I empathize with them; that, beneath my aloof reporter's exterior, I may even secretly admire them."

In fact, Taylor noted, he does admire them. But he will not write that.

"Once a reporter ventures beyond the neutral zone of objectivity into the netherworld of approbation, he makes an almost tactile investment in the subject of his praise. By morning, tons of newsprint (seventy-five tons in the case of *The Washington Post*) will convey his judgment to millions of readers. It's risky. Suppose the ingrate embezzles the orphans' fund next Tuesday. Then who looks like a fool?"

Taylor was not going to look like a fool . . . no. So there was nothing in the book, either, about that night with Biden, the speeches, the flights, the talk about life, the house in its stillness, the practiced hand with which Joe brought his son to the edge of waking, so he would not be alarmed in the morning . . . no.

Paul was asked about that night, one time, long after, when Joe's campaign was history:

"That kind of thing . . ." Paul said, and he squinched his face briefly and blinked a couple of times. "It was like a scene that he liked to show. . . . He thought it showed him to advantage."

26

The
Steaming
Bouillabaisse

HART NEVER EXPECTED reporters
to admire him, just to do their
job—was that too much to ask?
Of course, he didn't understand their job. He couldn't understand why they
wrote the *same things,* over and over . . . it wasn't anything he'd said to them.
Who were they talking to?

E.J. Dionne, in *The New York Times,* began his dispatch from Ottawa:
"Gary Hart came home and, for a moment, he did not live up to his reputation.
He nearly cried."

Time magazine crammed the visit into two paragraphs in "American
Notes," and dispensed with any facts about the trip till the latter paragraph.
The lead paragraph began: "In his quest for the Presidency, Gary Hart is
plagued by two troublesome perceptions: that he is cold and aloof, and that
he has tried to reinvent or run away from his roots."

Paul Taylor, in *The Washington Post,* led with *The Ottawa Herald*'s report
about the Hartpences' sixteen houses. Then he brought the reader up to speed
on the trip with a paragraph that began: "It was but one of many morsels of
biographical detail to emerge from a campaign visit that seemed programmed
to unearth nostalgia and emotion in a frontrunner sometimes accused of being
too icy to be elected President."

Three reporters, three big publications . . . but one common element in all
the stories: Dionne's "his reputation" . . . or *Time*'s "troubling perceptions"
. . . or Taylor's "sometimes accused." Hart could do nothing without reporters
reminding us: they thought Hart was weird.

Note that Dionne adduced no imputers, Taylor named no accusers, and *Time* had room for no troubled perceivers. This was such standard Washington poop, so well known by people well known to be in the know, that they didn't even need to trot out the garbage source-codes ("political observers," or "campaign staffers," or "Capitol Hill sources," or other lunch-buddies) that pass for attribution in the daily political smegma.

No, *everybody knew* Hart was weird.

— ★ —

Wait—who was everybody?

Well, when you talk about the pack, you first have to mention the Leader of the Pack, David Broder, who had attained that status by thirty years' work as a Washington reporter, and lately as a columnist for the *Post*. He was the biggest of the big-feet . . . balding, bespectacled, soft-spoken, kindly, a thoroughgoing gentleman, well informed, hardworking, fair-minded, and, in general, exemplary—which is exactly the point.

Because that was the year Broder wrote the book *Behind the Front Page,* and the very first story in that book was about campaigns—how mistakes in coverage are made. Specifically, the story was about 1972, when Ed Muskie cried (or didn't cry) one day in Manchester, New Hampshire, and his campaign slid straight into the shithouse after that. Part of the story was missed, Broder said, because no one knew until the next year that the whole scenario was launched by a Nixon campaign "dirty trick." But at the same time, Broder defended his coverage (and that of his friends), which concentrated on the crying, the way Muskie came apart at the seams. Why was it right? Why was Broder so sure? Because everybody (secretly) knew that Muskie was wound too tight—*the guy was weird*!

"All of us suspected that under the calm, placid, reflective face that Muskie liked to show the world, there was a volcano waiting to erupt. And so we treated Manchester as a political Mt. St. Helens explosion, and, in our perception, an event that would permanently alter the shape of Mt. Muskie." (Alter it they did—they took the sorry sonofabitch *down*!)

One of the reporters whom Broder commended, in that instance, was Jack Germond, who then worked for Gannett, but who now wrote a syndicated column with his partner, Jules Witcover—and those two were the only other snowshoe-size big-feet who actually worked on the trail. On some trips, you'd see Germond, reclined, as was his wont, in a bar chair or an airplane seat, wisecracking with those in the know, smiling, bald, round with a firm and blessed roundness—Buddha with an attitude. Or sometimes, Jules would appear behind some candidate on some Iowa Main Street, wearing an overcoat and a patiently mournful look on his long face, walking his practiced and careworn walk—the walk of a policeman who has ever walked, ever mindful these days that there are two years (still!) to retirement. Their column ran in hundreds of papers, and was read religiously by the wise-guy community. And where Broder would stray, at times, into the thin air of government, Germond and Witcover wrote pure politics—a column you could count on. And with their book, every four years, settling the record and the scores on the last race, they, too, were exemplary—the ranking diarists of Presidential politics.

The way they cranked out books, see, you didn't have to wait fifteen years to find out you'd better save string on this weirdness. It was all in their '84 book, the candidly titled *Wake Us When It's Over.* The name thing . . . the age thing . . . the *signature* thing. (Hart changed his penmanship! . . . Jeezus!)

And you didn't even have to wait for the new book, because Jules would tell you! They had this dinner with Hart, see, in Boston . . . and it was going great until they asked about the name thing . . . or the age thing . . . or some goddam thing. And Hart just stood up and walked out. The guy is . . . a weird duck.

Anyway, you didn't have to scale snowshoe Olympus to get the poop: younger big-feet, big-feet-to-be, and wannabe-big-feet were all aware of Hart's weirdness, and being younger, perhaps more eager—each with his way to make in the world, each eyeing the other, elbowing by on the path to greatness—they were going to *expose* the weirdness.

Taylor was right about one thing—it was a new generation trying on the big shoes, a generation that learned its craft (in journalism schools, or in first jobs) just as Woodward and Bernstein were taking a President down. So, among the shared attitudes of these big-feet-to-be was an abiding cynicism about the process they were sent out to cover. Oh, they'd read the books, they'd been around: they'd all smelled the elephant shit behind this big top . . . yes. Sharp-eyed they were, every man and woman aboard, long on suspicion. A serious-minded pack it was, too, and abstemious in personal habits. They'd work the hotel bars with Perriers in hand. They'd vote campaign planes smoke-free zones. They made their deadlines, and got up extra-early to run. . . .

Of course, each had his own style, his own view of himself. Just by way of example: Taylor, who was cool, handsome, and detached, was by his own lights a man who "saw nuance" and "took a fair-minded approach." . . . E.J. Dionne, from the *Times,* was short, quick, awfully busy, harried like a border collie with a bad herd. Like so many *Times*-men, he was an expert—a Ph.D. historian from Oxford, no less—and he'd learned his politics at the knee of guru-columnist William Schneider, so he could seek from the latest polls the undertow in the great sea of voters. . . . Smooth Howard Fineman from *Newsweek,* with the soft hands and bottom-line eye of an up-and-coming junk-bond salesman, just meant to hit with a thump—wherever, however. (Howard, it should be noted, was the first of his generation to earn a panelist's chair on the Hour of the Living Dead, *Washington Week in Review.*)

Yet different as they were (and as many as they were—for these were but three conspicuous flowers on a stalk that bore profusely), none got to this campaign, or got through it, by being shy of reputation. (Being well known was their bankable asset.) And although they could emerge better-known by any of a half-dozen routes—by the grace of their prose, their consistent good judgment, their steadiness through a campaign's sharp turns, perhaps by spotting early some lesser-known candidate with a spark of greatness—those were, well, mild . . . much too easily lost in the shuffle. The only sure route to celebrity, and beyond, into *history*—to their own index entry in the next Germond and Witcover epic—was to take somebody down.

Of course, best of all, a front-runner . . . hell, they didn't have to be ambitious to want to knock Hart off his horse. Not only was he weird, he was four-to-one over the next guy in the polls—and the next guy was black! It's a year to the first convention and there's no horse race! This thing—*their* thing—could be over!

Unless they could . . . somehow! . . . write the weirdness.

—★—

But they couldn't, you see—couldn't just come out and say, *this guy makes me uneasy.* There's a standard of conduct in the trade, and the standard requires some evidence, preferably public evidence, that there is *reason* for uneasiness. Even pundits—columnists, editorialists, commentators, and like pooh-bahs—who are mostly relieved of the strain of actual reporting, feel *comfier* if they can adduce some "objective" evidence of the character flaw they purport to discern.

So what they'd do, they'd take a wise guy to lunch, and quote *him* on why Hart was weird. But by April '87, with Hart at fifty-five percent in Iowa, it was hard to find a wise guy who'd let his name appear with the quote. Anyway, even if they could use the name, and the guy stuck Hart until he bled all over the page . . . even if they could do some *damage* with the quote . . . well, the wise guy would get the index entry with Germond and Witcover—not the writer.

It was very frustrating.

So what happened was, the stuff would seep into stories as code, phrases that attached to Hart, whatever he did, wherever he went—because everybody knew them. True, the code words might have meant different things to different writers (God only knows what they meant to readers), but they gave the illusion of knowledge of the man . . . and they were safe. There was more than a grain of truth to them—*everybody knew* that—and even if they explained . . . well, actually, nothing . . . no one felt out on a limb, calling Gary Hart "cool and aloof."

That was number one, the hoary "cool and aloof." The standard evidence was the way Hart would stand in a corner in a room full of people he didn't know—wouldn't act like a pol, would not press the flesh . . . no. Hart would not small-talk. Nor would he slap backs—not even *big-feet* backs—and he could not, or did not, hide his contempt for their questions. In fact, he thought they were stupid. Worse still, he made the interviewers *feel* stupid.

One time—this was late '83—Hart was flying back from a candidates' forum in upstate New York. He was sitting with Senator Patrick Moynihan. From one row behind, Dan Balz, from *The Washington Post,* kept poking his face between the airplane seats, asking Hart about the horse race. Balz was working the then-common wisdom that Hart was going nowhere in '84 (*everybody knew* that). "Gary," he said, "you've got no money, you've got no endorsements, you're a no-show in the polls—why don't you just give it up? . . ."

Well, it was the end of a long day, at the end of a long year, during which Hart had explained *a million times* that money, polls, and the nod from big pols was not what his campaign was about, and so . . . Hart went ballistic. He hiked one arm over the back of his seat and started pointing it in Balz's face. "Your reporting," he said, "is so shallow, it's . . . it's . . ." Hart had no words for this. His face was shaking. "You *always . . . miss . . . the point!*"

Of course, that wasn't exactly "cool and aloof." More like its evil twin, "icy and contemptuous."

Number two was "outsider," or "loner." This was a satisfying piece of code because it seemed to haul the reader from politics (where Hart would actually *admit* to insurgency) . . . straight into the dark and twisty corridors of psyche, which *everybody knew* was the locus of the weirdness. And "loner" had such a beautifully desperate air . . . it brought a whiff of the front page the day after some sicko shoots up a shopping mall with his Uzi: those dim and doleful stories wherein the sicko's neighbors say, "I dunno, I din' really know'm—he was quiet—kep' to hisself, pretty much. . . ." The one-column headline:

KILLER

WAS A

LONER

And then, too, there was "evidence": Hart had served two terms in the Senate, yet only one Senator (that well-known flake-o, Chris Dodd) backed him in the '84 campaign. This time, Hart was the clear front-runner and no Senator had signed on. Didn't that show they knew he was weird? Of course, it was also true Hart hadn't asked for endorsements. He never even used to ask those fellows to cosponsor a bill, or to help him with a vote. He thought they'd support his bill if they saw merit in it. Hell, Hart had to learn to ask for *voters'* votes—and money, well, forget it. The best he could manage, most of the time, was a sentence-with-no-subject that escaped his lips as a bark: "Needjurhelp!"

See, he didn't mean to ask for help *for him*. It was for the cause: *to change this country*. It could not be about him or his life. That would be . . . an awful presumption. That accounted, too, for the way he'd call the anchormen "Mr. Brokaw," or "Mr. Rather," on the *air* (so *stiff*, so *weird!*) . . . when they were "Tom" and "Dan" to every City Councilman or Police Chief in the country. But Hart didn't really know those news-bigs. He wouldn't presume. Never had that easy familiarity . . . not with anchormen, Senators, certainly not with the pink-jowled lunchers at Joe and Mo's ("political observers," to the readers of the smegma), who had no yuk-yuk stories about Hart, no pictures on their office walls of them-and-him in a grip-and-grin from last year's thousand-dollar-a-plate All-Star Sleazebag Salute to the Chemical Industry. No, not likely. There were no County Chairmen with scrapbooks full of his handwritten thank-you notes, and few state officials who owed their elections to him. Hart didn't want them to owe. He wanted them to think he was right. He was proud that way . . . and, withal, shy.

But "proud" and "shy" never made it as code. Somehow those words only meant what they said. They did not foster the notion of more explosive chemistry aboil within. That was the public purpose, after all, for this "analysis" marbling the Hart stories. Hart might be *dangerous*. . . who would protect the nation if the press fell asleep at the switch?

So sometimes, hints of menacing instability would haunt the Hart prose: what profile writers called a "streak of wildness." Howard Fineman strummed this chord with smooth concision, when he asked in his Who-Is-Gary-Hart paragraph:

"Is it Gary Hartpence or Gary Hart . . . Is it the devout child who pleased his mother in church or the escapee who the summer after high school took off for a week in Colorado, doing 105 at the wheel of a green Dodge—and who by that August had acquired corn-yellow hair from a bottle of bleach?"

(Jeez—Hart even changed his hair!)

It was the danger-code that went to the heart of the issue—the rattle of chains in Hart's psychic cellar. "A Candidate in Search of Himself," said the large type in *Newsweek*. "A driven figure . . . unfinished and unsettled. . . ." Why the hell should a voter let this guy get *near* the button?

This was the same killer doubt that Mondale managed to pin onto Hart in '84, with the red-telephone ad. It was a simple ad—quick, wickedly effective. The screen showed a red phone, ringing and blinking (in the Oval Office, one assumed) . . . while a voice-of-doom intoned off-camera:

"The most awesome, powerful responsibility in the world lies in the hand that picks up this phone . . .

(rinng, rinnnng)

"The idea of an unsure, unsteady, untested hand is something to really think about. This is the issue of our times . . .

(riiiinnnnngggg)

"Vote as if your life depends on it. Because it does. . . . Mondale. . . ."

God, it was beautiful! It played to the only thing voters liked about Mondale, who'd been around for so long. And it fit so well with the tap dance the press was doing on Gary's head . . . well, the combination pounded Hart right into the ground—at least in '84.

That's where the big trouble came from—'84, when Hart started to win. See, Hart snuck up on the press pack. They'd been writing he was nowhere, stinko, dead flesh in the sun . . . and then he finished second in Iowa. So they wrote him up as a "surprising challenger" . . . "better-than-expected," but still no threat—no way—it was Mondale and Glenn, just like they'd been writing. So then, the sonofabitch *won New Hampshire* . . . and their editors were on the phone—what the hell is going *on* out there?

It was embarrassing.

No, what it was, it was *fishy* . . . how could they *all* be wrong?

What the hell was this guy doing that they didn't see?

Who *is* this guy? . . .

They should go to Ottawa . . .

No—no time for that now.

There was Maine next week. (Hart won.)

And Vermont! (Hart won.)

And, Christ—then SUPER TUESDAY! How were they supposed to do profiles now?

Well, Chrissake! Pull the clips! We must have some goddam *clips* on the man!

And . . . there it was. *The Washington Post,* bless its bureaucratic workaday soul, had sent a man to Ottawa, months before: George Lardner—good man— and, thank God, Lardner had the poop. True, most of the story was that New Ideas drone, and Hart's Senate record, and other shit no one would read . . . but here, in the fifty-ninth graf . . . yeah, down here . . . was something:

Hart changed his name. Hmm!

And looka this—his office bio sheet listed him born in 1937, but the birth certificate said '36.

By this time, Hart's press pack had grown from a half-dozen to a hundred and fifty. They were hauling this gaggle around on two planes, and everyone had to ask Hart about the name thing . . . the age thing . . .

Hart said: It's no big deal—it's not what this campaign is about.

Then he went on TV and *they* had to ask about the age thing.

"It's no big deal—it's whatever the records say."

The name thing:

"It was not a secret—my family had talked about this for quite some time . . ."

But then someone called Hart's sister, Nancy, and she said: The name change was Gary's idea.

(What's this guy trying to hide?)

And someone else wrote that the age thing had to do with Hart's mother (who was wacky, anyway—everybody knew that—her and that church . . .), so everybody had to ask Hart about his mom: *C'mon,* what's the deal with your mother, *really*?

Hart reacted badly to this. He was racing around from airport to airport— two, three Super Tuesday states in a day, dead on his feet, voice about shot, and these people wanted to know, was he breast-fed?

Well, he wasn't going to talk about his mother—hell, no! Not even when his staff begged him. He wasn't going to talk anymore about his mother's church, or his name, or his signature, or any of it!

And that tore it with the press pack. What was *wrong* with this guy—didn't he believe in the public's *right to know*? Then, *every* story had at least a tip of the cap to name, age, momma . . . Hart's "identity problem," as it came to be codified. And although there were no new facts to report, these same desiccated Grape-Nuts—name, age, momma—were served up at breakfast tables across the nation. And Hart was officially a weirdo, a mystery man.

See, this solved the problem for the press: *that's* why they didn't know about Hart . . . because he was a man of many faces, a guy who did not know . . . no! . . . who was *hiding*—see?—his own identity . . . or, no! . . . a man who was . . . (drum roll) inventing his persona out of whole cloth! He was a fiction—a devilish clever bit of alchemy . . . illusion—see?

Who is Gary Hart . . . *anyway*?

The networks sang it in chorus the week before Super Tuesday. Hart still won six of the nine states (all the big ones), but the networks reported that Mondale "triumphed" by winning Georgia.

Meanwhile, Mondale came up with the red-telephone ad, and . . . well, the rest is history.

Hart still made it a fight—just what the pack wanted, after all—he fought on all the way to California (which he won) . . . but he could never shake the donkey's tail of doubt they'd pinned on him. Alas, that tail only grew.

Hart could not get through his head what the ethic of the pack was. He kept getting it confused with "freedom of the press," which he'd talked about for years . . . in the words of his idol, Thomas Jefferson, who insisted that a free press was the greatest bulwark of liberty that any society had yet devised. Hart believed it. And so, each name-age-momma episode could only increase his sense of injustice—no, *betrayal:* Is this the rotten harvest for which the saintly Jefferson toiled?

Well, he figured they'd drop it—they'd have to—after a while. It had to get boring, after a while . . . but he never could understand the investment the press had in Hart-as-weirdo . . . how much it explained, how he threatened them.

Later in the '84 campaign, when Hart was more accustomed to the herd of press, he tried to relax with them . . . maybe even have some fun. But a pack can handle only the most hammy humor. Any irony is lost in repetition—from the pool report to the press bus, to the full herd in the press plane, to the editors back at the office, who want to know: What the hell did he *mean* by that? . . . So Hart found, to his dismay, he couldn't relax. He couldn't say *anything* fun.

Here's how he found out: they were rafting, Hart and his son, John—with just a small pool of press to keep an eye on the candidate. And Hart was having a ball. The water, the sky, the rush of the raft—it was so elemental, so real, after weeks of endless talk, tactics, thinking his way through. Out there, on the river, there wasn't time to think—just react—and they hit some great white water, too. Hart felt alive that day, and pleased, as the guide told him they'd just skidded through type-four rapids. They should count themselves lucky they hadn't hit type five . . .

Oh, Hart said, I'd love that.

A reporter asked: You *would*?

And Hart arched his eyebrows, and said: "Oh, yeah. I love danger."

Well, that was all the press needed. The bells went off. Weird-alert! "Wait—lemme get this," they kept saying to each other back in the press plane. "Those are his words, right? 'I . . . love . . . danger.'"

Right.

There it was: the streak of wildness . . . the telephone ad confirmed . . . unsettled . . . unsteady . . . a loose cannon! Would this guy roll the dice with the lives of our children, the future of the planet?

What got lost were the eyebrows, the lilt in the voice, the hint of self-mocking smile . . . all absent by the time the quote hit the papers. That, and the fact Hart would never have said it . . . would *never* have tried to be confidential, even in jest . . . if the pool reporter, the one who asked, "You would?" . . . were not a woman, and a good-looking woman, at that: Patricia O'Brien, from the Knight-Ridder chain.

Not that this fact would have helped Hart with the pack—not one bit. Because another thing they knew, or thought they knew . . . oh, come *on*—*everybody knew* . . . this guy was getting laid.

—★—

What did they actually know?

Well, what they mostly knew was that *everybody said* they knew. They'd make jokes about it—at the supper table with their friends, you know—it was well known by people in the know . . . even though nobody wrote it.

That was half the problem, right there: no one *could* write it. Funny—isn't it?—how *everybody knew* for years, and yet no one had ever been able to write . . . anything. But anyway, this well-known "fact" dwelt enormously, malodor-ously, in the sealed and self-referential world of the pack—a spoiled fish in the bouillabaisse, a great steaming gob of a character flaw!—and no one could lift the lid!

It was maddening.

You'd have to be blind not to see it, really . . .

There was the way Hart was with women—good-looking women—so courtly, so charming, he almost purred to them (when they all knew, he was really cool and aloof). The women talked to each other about it. The playful eyebrows, the way he looked at them like they shared a secret . . . you'd have to get up awfully early to sneak *that shit* past a modern American woman . . . yes! And the female members of the pack were up extra-extra early.

And, of course, even wannabe-big-feet had the poop on Hart's separations from Lee . . . *two times* . . . and then they got back together, just in time for the next campaign!

And, then, too, all the Washington bigs knew Woodward—Bob Woodward, the *Post*'s investigative Ajax—and Hart had lived at Woodward's house during one of those separations. Except he didn't really live there . . . that's what Bob said, you know: Hart was just using his place as a mail drop—hadda be shacked up somewhere, right?—until Woodward got uncomfortable and asked Gary to leave. I mean . . . *come on*!

And—here's the kicker . . . Hart was *friends* with *Warren Beatty*! He'd go out to *visit . . . in Hollywood*! Do you think—come on, now—for even one minute . . . Warren Beatty is not getting laid?

Did you hear what happened with Hart and Pat O'Brien?

Yes, they'd heard . . .

Pat had left the business and was working for Michael Dukakis this time around, but there were still people in the Hart pack who knew about the time Pat had an interview in Hart's hotel room. It was '84, and Hart was in the whirlwind, and *everybody* wanted the candidate. It was late at night—and Hart came to the door in a bathrobe. A short one! And she *knew* he had nothing else on. A good-looking woman, Pat said, can *always* spot a man on the make. But she was so stunned, in this case, that she actually sat down and asked a question. And only when he answered, and she had a chance to gather her wits, did she say he was making her uncomfortable—with the bathrobe, and all—and she asked him to put on clothes. And Hart . . . he got *huffy,* like it was *her* dirty mind.

Well!

You could hear two or three of these stories for the price of a dinner. The staff, the Advance men, the local people who helped his campaign: they had stories about these . . . these . . . *women,* who would flounce up during Hart's speech, or just at the end of an event somewhere, and announce that Gary wanted them to come along on the plane . . . of course, no one could write *that.*

But couldn't you just die? . . .

It was *so obvious.* And so contemptuous . . . of *them*!

That's what really got to the pack.

It wasn't that they were friends of Lee Hart, who, after all, was the only one with standing in this case . . . when you got down to it. No one could suggest that Hart didn't do his job, or neglected to learn about the Middle East or something, because he was busy chasing skirt.

But for Chrissake, the man was *running for President*!

So what?

So, it said something about his *character*—didn't it?—his fidelity to his vows.

But what could *they* say about Gary and Lee's vows? Not a thing. Neither Gary nor Lee would discuss them.

Well, for God's sake, it showed something about his *judgment.* The man had to know he was living in a fishbowl.

But what could *they* show? That he came to the door in a bathrobe? That he called Warren Beatty a friend? That there were these . . . these . . . *tomatoes*! . . . on his plane?

No, they'd have to do better. It was awful . . . *knowing* . . . day after day, for months, with the stinking fish in the pot . . . and Hart climbing in the polls. . . . What it was, was weird.

They couldn't ask Hart! Well, they could ask. But that and a quarter would buy them coffee, so they could rev up and tell each other more stories. They could talk it over with their wise-guy friends—even Hart's own wise guys, the professional staff he'd assembled in Denver. Oh, the pros all knew the way the steam was blowing from this stockpot—sure . . . and they meant to keep their own index entries in the books, too. So they'd say: "Yeah, I asked about that . . . I didn't wanna get involved if he was gonna, you know . . . (Hey, don't use my name, huh?) . . ."

"Well, what'd he say?"

"Who?"

"*Gary!* What'd he *say,* when you asked?"

"He didn't say, I mean . . . you know, it wasn't him, personally, I talked to about it."

"Oh."

It was worse and worse—the steam on the stovetop—as April arrived, and Hart's announcement was imminent . . . and profile season was in full swing . . . and no one could spill the soup!

—★—

This particular odor actually went back to '72, the McGovern days, which was the first time Hart got famous in a hurry. The irony was, George McGovern was attracted to Hart for Gary's churchly, almost geeky goodness, his mannerly midwestern respect, his serious and stubborn application to the job at hand. (McGovern, son of a minister, was the man who'd built the South Dakota Democratic Party on three-by-five cards.) But by the time the press discovered Hart—descried his strategic genius, strangely enough, just after McGovern started winning—that was not the Gary Hart they introduced to the public.

No, their Gary bore almost no relation to the quiet, brainy Denver lawyer who prowled the campaign's ratty offices in a cheap suit and too-wide tie. Their Gary Hart wore jeans and cowboy boots, he was young, long-haired, flip, quirky . . . friend to movie stars, scourge of the old Party bosses . . . leader of the-young-and-the-restless (that bulge in the bell curve again), who, in those days, were so richly celebrated as the flower and the hope of a tired world. Their Gary was . . . in a word, sexy.

But that was okay. In fact, it was terrific: it fit with the story line, the ethic of the day. Remember, *Time* mag was doing Day-Glo covers, and "Make Love, Not War" still meant something—while there was a war. The political revolution that Hart was engineering followed on the bare heels of the sexual revolution—in fact, it seemed like one big mudpie. These McGovern kids were taking over the Party . . . in fringed jackets and miniskirts! The young were taking over the Earth . . . it was only Nixonites and like protofascists who had not the grace, or the God-given instinct, to bow toward this bright new light. And Hart? . . . Well, Gary was a Style Section darling, a political rock star. Even Teddy White, who by that time had seen too many campaigns, was stirred to note in his *Making of the President 1972,* young Gary Hart's "skin-fitting pants over slim cowboy thighs." (Yowlll!)

White also noted that Hart "drew the eye" of all the women in the campaign, though he was careful to add that Gary was too busy for romantic adventures. (Of course, White also called those women the "yearning maidens of the McGovern camp," so he can't have done much research there.) Alas, there were others of the older generation who were nowhere near so careful and kind—others who wanted Gary Hart's job. Even before McGovern started winning—surprise!—the old pros descended and counseled McGovern that he could no longer trust his affairs to Hart and those other kids. (*Sure, it's worked surprisingly well, but come on, now, George . . . get serious!*) Ted Van Dyk, an old Humphrey man, made a run, and later teamed up with his pal Frank Mankiewicz, an old Bobby Kennedy Press Secretary; and after McGovern won the nomination, they were joined in the dump-Hart effort by Larry O'Brien (ex-JFK, ex-LBJ) and his cronies from the Democratic mainstream. In each case, you could call it a political battle—or maybe a generational war—but it got personal in a hurry. Along the way, McGovern was informed that the office was a shambles! There was no control! No organization! (For God's sake, there weren't even meetings to attend!) And Hart—well, how could he restore order, when (they whispered) he'd been to bed with half the staff?

McGovern never did bite—not hard enough to dump Hart—but meanwhile, the Washington whispers were launched as extra ammo in the anti-Hart fusillade. Lee Hart had moved to Washington with Gary, but she was miserable and lonely (Gary was never home), and so, in the summer of '71, she took herself and the kids back to Denver . . . just when the first assault on Hart's job was kicking up the whispers and whines. By '72, when Hart's strategic success had made his job so much more appealing, the whispers got so public, so many, and so juicy, that Sally Quinn, the Style Section Queen (and a friend of Mankiewicz), descended to visit upon Hart . . . the profile.

It was a neat piece of work, an article Hart would rue for years. You could tell the interview was friendly—hell, here was Sally, urging, just for starters . . . show me your socks . . . no, *under* your boots.

Hart showed her his socks.

Then, there was Hart, explaining how he was with women—holding doors, lighting their cigarettes . . . and gosh, it was baffling, how they could call *that* . . . you know, macho! (You could almost hear him purr.)

From her first description of Hart's looks ("chiseled, movie-star profile, tousled styled hair, full lips, crinkly eyes") . . . "looks," Quinn adjudged, "with a hint of cruelty" . . . to the gambit with the socks (Hart "placed one long black-booted leg on the desk") . . . to the mention of a poster of Candice Bergen (bestowing upon Hart her "sultry smile") . . . it was a flirty fifty inches, from the start . . . but alas, just foreplay.

The climax had to wait for the last breathy column, where Hart was asked about his marriage . . . now that Lee was back in Denver, and Gary was alone. Quinn wrote:

"He will only say of his marriage, 'I have almost no personal life at all. I lead a completely political existence. If one party doesn't share the same interests you've got a problem. Let's just say I believe in reform marriage.' "

From the Monday morning when he saw the paper, Hart could not believe what she'd done to him . . . what he'd done to himself. He meant to be candid, charming, *at ease*. (At one point he was quoted: the best thing was "not just winning, but winning, and making it look easy.") But you don't learn ease on the job with Sally Quinn, no.

He was horrified at the hurt he'd done to Lee . . . and *himself*! It was so irresponsible . . . clumsy . . . *bush league*. He never would have said those things, if she hadn't been, you know, attractive . . . but even so . . . damn! Lee had gone and left him here . . . he barely saw his own kids. That part about no personal life—he meant it, but even so . . . why *did* he say it?

Well, he learned a lesson—the hard way. It didn't matter what he saw around him, the marriages on paper, the people in the campaign, on the press plane, in the field offices, all running away from hearth and homes, living for the day (and the night!) . . . you still couldn't *say* it! Well, he never would again. He'd never discuss his personal life—not with reporters—hell, no!

But then, too, never would that quote go away. It would come back with him, to Washington, when he took his seat in the Senate. It would surface in files in 1984. It was alive and swimming in the stinking bouillabaisse in '88—oh, very much alive!

And a strange, rotten bit of fish it seemed to this new pack, though they, too, had been young in '72. They were in schools, or coming out to first jobs. They, too, had long hair, and tight pants over slender legs . . . and if sex were money, they all would have been rich.

But here's what the wooers of this generation missed . . . Biden, Caddell, and all the trackers of this bulge in the bell curve: the salient fact about this boom generation had nothing to do with its love-and-drug-addled idealism, when it—when they—were the hope and heritors of the world.

By 1987, they still felt the world was theirs; the nation, the society (and everyone in it) ought, by all rights, to march to their tune. But the tune was changed, the times transformed. They'd done their own thing, they'd been the Me Generation, they'd sung "We Are the World" (and they *meant* it) . . . but the salient fact, at this point in their lives was . . . they were turning forty.

They were worried about their gums.

They were experts on soy formula.

They were working seriously on their (late, or second) marriages.

They were livid about saturated fats in the airline food. *What, no fiber?*

They did not drink, they did not smoke, drugs were a sniggering memory. They worked all the time, except when they were calling home.

And they certainly, God knows, did *not* mess around!

Sex! . . . It was tacky. It was dangerous. It was (sniff!) . . . *not serious.*

And being . . . (They Are the World) . . . *this* generation, no one else was going to get away with sex, either.

Or drugs.

Or ill health.

Or fouling *their* air with noxious smoke.

Or music so loud they couldn't hear their cellular phones!

Or driving without a seat belt, and a baby seat . . . like they had . . . so they could navigate the mortal dangers of the world, to get home, where there was some decent (i.e., French) springwater.

They had become the Thank-You-For-Not (smoking, eating, drinking, fornicating . . . or anything else I don't do) Generation. In their self-referential certainties, they were:

The ⊘ Generation.

Their mortality, their middle age, their growing and overweening fear must now become their world's fear.

And here was Hart—so dedicated (still!) to undermining the safe security of convention—even *their* conventions. Jesus, this guy just reeked of danger!

Here was Hart—(still!) unconvinced of their God-given bulge-driven *right* to decide what was right for him . . . or sane for the rest of the world. Well, if that wasn't arrogance!

Here was Hart (reform marriage, indeed!)—who *everybody knew* was (still!) getting laid . . .

Well, the sonofabitch was *prima facie* crazy!

—★—

So they all took their shots. In the trade, it's called "profile season," but it's actually akin to the first day of duck hunting. The candidate flies over on his way to announcement, and there's hot steel hurtling skyward from every marsh in the land. Every major paper in the United States, every big TV news outlet, radio guys, foreign press, news magazines, journals of opinion and polemic (even book writers!) . . . are bound (as guardians of the process) to opine on what this day, this week, this season means in the lives of candidate and country.

This is their chance to lean back and spend some time summing up *how this guy is* . . . in other words, what's wrong with him. And in '88, when *everybody knew* this whole election would boil down to Character . . . well, this was the wannabe-bigs' big chance!

Back in Denver, Sue Casey, the Scheduler, essayed at the meeting a radical suggestion: Why not let Gary talk to several at once? They all asked the *same questions* . . . and everyone around that table knew how Hart would get, if it went on for days, for weeks . . . on name-age-momma. "We could have him do, like, five in one swoop," Casey said with a smile of hope against hope. "And then, if they had special questions or something, after, you could put 'em in the car, five minutes, and . . ."

But Sweeney, the press guy, looked at her like she'd drooled on her shirt. Was she nuts? . . . Did she think *The Wall Street Journal* was gonna share with the *Chicago Tribune*? Get real! . . . Anyway, Sweeney already had talked to Hart, to explain that it wasn't personal. They weren't just ganging up on *him*. It was the system, after all. And Hart had sighed and said he'd do a certain amount—as much as he could. So the upshot was, Sweeney had just about *promised* these guys . . . not everyone, of course, just the top fifteen, maybe twenty. Well, call it two dozen.

So Hart was loaded up with interviews: at least one, usually more, every day. And in the product of this season, you could just about trace his jawline as it set, just about see his lips getting white. In the early profiles, you could tell he was all right—not that he liked the stories, much, no . . . they mostly took the line that *Hart* had improved. He was more *at peace with himself,* or *with his past* . . . the same kind of stories you see on the sports page when a star comes back from drug rehab. But that story line let the writer deal with current facts—Hart was doing everything right, his ideas were hot, he was winning everywhere—and still set the Grape-Nuts to rattling in the bowl.

It was later in the season, just before announcement, that matters got ugly. Hart had heard the questions too many times. "Come on, now," he'd say, at the first rattle of Grape-Nuts. He'd smile, like maybe he could jolly them past it. But, of course, he could not. Perhaps, he'd suggest, with patience too obvious, they were seeking mystery where there was none—or answers that didn't matter. "I don't think people are interested in that." Then he'd start lecturing the big-feet on what voters wanted to know. It wasn't name-age-momma, that was for sure. Hart himself had tried to put these matters to rest with an article, an autobiography, "One Man's Luck," *five thousand words* about Ottawa, his parents, church . . . and you know what? . . . No one wanted to print it! He finally placed the piece in *The Boston Globe,* but it was a struggle . . . because it just did not matter!

"*You* are the only ones who ask me about it." Hart didn't have to add: *you shallow-minded nincompoops!* Of course, the stories had him shifting in his chair, frosty, grim, beleaguered . . . *uncomfortable with himself.*

The apotheosis, the end of the line, came with E.J. Dionne. . . . Of course, it wasn't just one interview with E.J.—he was *The New York Times!* And Dionne did not mean to content himself with thirty inches off the front page on the day of announcement. He was planning a full-dress magazine piece, the cover of the Sunday *Times Magazine.* Sweeney thought E.J. was the one who might connect the dots—to *prove* Hart was not flaky. His ideas, his candidacy, his very being, had a long and intelligible history.

The white boys thought it was a splendid idea: E.J. was the smartest of the new generation, and if *The New York Times* said Gary wasn't weird, the whole pack might settle down. So Casey put E.J. on the schedule in Iowa, and on the schedule in New Hampshire, and in Denver . . . and wherever else he wanted. Meanwhile, the magazine's photographer got hold of Sweeney, to set up the shoot for the cover. The guy was a major-league New York portraitist, the kind who was looking to make that one magic moment—you know, by making the subject jump up and down to get loose, or by blowing a Harpo Marx horn at him, just to change the mood . . . whatever it took. This guy was an artist. Problem was, that one magic moment took time, so the photographer wanted Hart to pose for three hours.

Well, Sweeney wouldn't even ask Hart about that . . . the guy had to understand, this wasn't exactly, you know . . . Gary's *thing.* So Sweeney hondled and wheedled, and finally, the fellow said he'd settle for an hour.

So Sweeney went to ask Hart for a half-hour. "I know that's a long time," Kevin said. He was talking fast, trying to get a nod before Hart knew what hit him. "But it's a big cover, a big piece of paper. You know, it's for E.J.'s profile . . ." (Even Gary acknowledged that E.J.'s profile had to be good.)

"I'm not going to pose," Hart said.

"I know, I know," Sweeney said quickly, "but it's only going to be twenty minutes."

"I don't care. I'm not going to pose."

Sweeney was panicky. He tried to keep at his joke, keep it light. "I know, but it's only gonna be fifteen minutes . . ."

Hart was staring at him now, with that look. "I don't think you're listening," Hart said with precision. His voice did not rise a jot. "I'm not going to pose. I'm not going to pose. I'm not going to pose." Then he paused to see if that had sunk in. "I have got to run for President on my own terms. If I don't, I won't be a good President. I probably won't even be President."

There was silence. Sweeney had nothing to say. Hart tried to ease the sting: "Look. I'm not going to hide from the press—those people want to come in here, right now, take pictures of me and you talking . . . that's fine. Any event, in the meetings . . . that's fine.

"But I am not going to look at a camera and smile for more than thirty seconds. Because . . . I . . . feel . . . *cheap.*"

So that took care of the portrait, but not the profile, no. E.J. kept reporting, right through the announcement and beyond—his profile wouldn't appear till May. Meanwhile, he spent four hours with Hart in two separate interviews, nipping, yipping at the heels of his story, herding it toward the corral. Hart went through Ottawa with him, Bethany Nazarene College, and Yale, the Kennedy years, the McGovern campaign, the U.S. Senate, the run for the White House in '84 . . . he even talked about his kids, his marriage! And though it was hard for Hart to judge, he could tell that E.J. got it—mostly. The way he nodded, the questions that followed. . . . It seemed—at last—that Hart had made his life, *somehow,* transparent to a ranking big-foot. Still, there was something, something more . . . E.J. had to know.

So they met once again at a Formica table in a hotel cafeteria, in New Hampshire, early morning: a breakfast interview, and E.J. showed up with his baggage, fifteen years of Hart profiles in folders, which he stacked on the table, next to his paper place mat. E.J. was unsettled, uneasy that morning. He seemed to be yipping and dancing more than ever around his questions. He'd start to ask, then pause to brush a lock of hair off his brow, and knock his files of profiles into avalanche, and then try to gather himself, to ask, to try, or—well, whatever it was—again.

Finally, it was Hart who leaned across the table and stopped him: "E.J., what *is* it? What are you looking for?"

"Well, I don't know, I mean . . ." E.J. said, feinting at his forelock. "I mean, I wanted to know, from you . . ."

Hart fixed him with a parent's stare, a look of dwindling patience.

"Okay," E.J. said. "Why do *you* think . . . that *we* think . . . you're weird?"

— ★ —

Well, that was the end of Hart's profile season. He decreed, after that breakfast: no more. Sweeney was sputtering and fretting in the van—it was just the *system* . . . but Hart was clear: no more.

Of course, that didn't do much to relieve the sour steam in the stockpot. Hart was going to announce next week. Their profiles had to run this Sunday— next Sunday, max! And Hart wasn't doing interviews! Wasn't enough that the guy was weird: now he was hiding from them!

So Sweeney was out there spreading salve, trying to explain that Hart was tied up: focused on announcement, you know . . . which was true in its way, because Hart had got it into his head that he was going to announce like Van Buren, or Zach Taylor. He was going to have a few people up to his house, his cabin on a slope of the Rockies, and from his wooden front porch, he'd declare his intention to change this country.

They wanted roots? Well, let them see the real bedrock of his life, his old homesteader's cabin on the stagecoach road through the mountains to Denver. Let them stand with their cameras on the land Gary loved, on the old trail that he'd walk with his dogs, showing visitors where the stage used to run . . . where the Indians could overlook the road from those rocks . . . where the creek wound, rushing, down the slope, past his homestead. They wanted to see his life? Let them see something real . . . not the dime-store version they kept plugging into their stories.

"Gary, there's going to be hundreds of people. TV, radio, writers, photographers—everybody's got to come."

"Why do they all have to come?"

Well, they all had to come because they all had to come. That was the system, what announcement was about. The white boys wanted a nice, clean, faceless square in downtown Denver, with balloons and cheering crowds—you know, the regular stuff . . . but Gary insisted on something better.

"Well, it can't be the cabin. Where the hell would you put 'em?"

"They could set up their cameras right in front of the house."

"Yeah, but how about cars? Their trucks. *Satellite* trucks!"

Gary talked it over at home, and Lee wasn't happy . . . but it was Andrea who ruled it out. She was living at home; she didn't want that horde trampling over the place.

So Gary gave up on the house.

They settled on a park near Gary's house—Red Rocks Park—and Gary would have his mountain backdrop, they wouldn't have to build a crowd. They'd bus in the press, give them time to set up, then Gary would come, with the family . . . might not be bad! They could do a downtown rally after . . . but announcement, the tape that would run forever, would show the mountains, clean, strong, and bold . . . and set the theme of Hart's True Patriotism: "I am running for President . . . because I love my country."

Hart wrote his speech himself—eight minutes, no chaff. He spoke without notes, without a TelePrompTer. He thought if he could not say, without reading, why he was running—well, why should anybody listen? He said his campaign would likely make mistakes, but he would campaign on the issues that mattered. He would never talk down to the voters. He would never hold them cheap with appeals to passion. He would try to define the national interest, and rely on the voters' judgment to set this country on a better course. "Ideas have power," Hart said. "Ideas are what governing is all about."

Well, talk about weird!

The way the cameras got it, the picture was Gary Hart on a rock, and Lee and the kids on another, just below, with the mountains behind . . . that was fine . . . but there wasn't another human being in sight! In fact, most of the pictures were just Hart and cold stone in a forty-degree wind.

C'*monnnn*! Talk about a *loner*! *Chilly* . . . *aloof*! . . . There it was: right in the focus rings of their Nikons!

But by that time, it hardly mattered—or it mattered in a different way. Because that day, April 13, was the cover date of the *Newsweek* with Howard Fineman's profile, "A Candidate in Search of Himself." Let history record: smooth Howard it was, who tipped over the soup.

— ★ —

What he did, he got a wise guy, John McEvoy, who'd worked for Hart in '84 . . . and they're running through the weirdness . . . and Howard says: *Everybody knows* the guy is getting laid.

Howard says: It's so *obvious* . . .

Howard says: He's not even watching himself. Someone's gonna write it, and then there's hell to pay . . .

So McEvoy finally says: "Yuh, well, you know . . . he'll always be in jeopardy . . . if he can't keep his pants on."

Bingo! Howard writes him up . . . and there is hell to pay. McEvoy later insisted that line was off the record—and, anyway, pure speculation.

That's pretty much what Howard telegraphed, leading into the quote with one of the garbage source-codes:

". . . *many political observers* expect the rumors to emerge as a campaign issue. 'He's always in jeopardy of having the sex issue raised if he can't keep his pants on,' said John McEvoy," etc., etc. . . .

Hey, but what's the difference? The rumors were in print . . . and, therefore, fit matter for questions to Hart.

"*Senator, how do you respond to rumors about your womanizing?*"

In fact, that's all they were talking about in the plane on the grand announcement tour. Hart now had an official sex problem. The odor of bad fish filled the plane.

That didn't mean they could write any more than the rumor. Still, no one had anything, except a secondhand wise-guy quote. . . .

But then came Lois Romano, from the *Post,* the dread Style Section again. And she was after Hart: *Yes or no?* . . . She insisted: There are rumors.

Hart went ballistic again: "Come on, Lois, *who*?" he demanded. "Where do the rumors come from?"

So she told him they came from the Biden wise guys . . . then, too, the Dukakis camp.

Hart was seething. They were out to get him! (Just as he'd always suspected!) Of course they had to make *him* the issue: he was five miles ahead on every issue a President might actually have to face! But how the hell could he disprove rumors? He was running for President of the United States, and the only thing anyone wanted to know was whether he slept around.

Larry Barrett, the urbane chief of political big-feet for *Time* magazine, was next on the list for tête-à-tête. Barrett's come-on was calm, respectful. "Gary," he said, "I'm going to ask you once—and then we can get on with the campaign, okay? . . . Now, how 'bout these rumors?"

Hart made a fatal mistake. "All I know is what reporters tell me," he said. "If it's true that other campaigns are spreading the rumors, I think it's an issue."

Well, the back of the plane went crazy. Hart was accusing the other campaigns of starting rumors about his sex life! That was politics. That was fair game! At last, the lid was off, and they could all dip their ladles.

"He's gotta come back here and talk to us!" they demanded of Kevin Sweeney. "Kevin! He's gotta hold a press conference." Sweeney had no interest in a press conference on sex rumors. This was Hart's announcement tour. How about one goddam *day* where the message was *why the man was running for President*?

But that was not to be—not even for a day. Hart walked the aisle to the back of the plane and said with forlorn irony: "Anybody want to talk about ideas?"

No.

GARY: I'M NO WOMANIZER roared the headline on the front page of the *New York Post*. Inside, a story with quotes from the plane was flanked by a sidebar with *all* the rumors. . . . Here's how the paragraphs in the *Post* began:

"The whispers . . ."

"A lot of people thought . . ."

"Rumors that Hart strayed . . ."

"Tongues wagged after . . ."

The sidebar ended with this ominous graf:

"A number of newspaper reporters said around this time that they had received phone calls from women who claimed they had had affairs with Hart."

27

1961

DOLE WAS the one who met Kennedy—spring of '61, just after Bob got to D.C. JFK invited the freshmen in Congress to a dinner and reception. Phyllis was so excited—the White House! She set about making a new dress, in chintz with blooming roses, one of those wonderful sixties shapes with a high waist, straight skirt, a bow on the front. It was gorgeous! . . . But then Bob wouldn't say if they could go!

"Depends."

"Bob! On *what*?"

"Lotta things."

Bob had just been elected president of the House GOP freshmen. He didn't know if he was *supposed* to go to Democrat parties—even at the White House.

Phyllis didn't get an answer until that night: Bob showed up at their tiny house in Arlington, with a rented tux.

"Agh, we readyy?"

They drove to the White House in the Chrysler—then drove around trying to find the right gate. Marines in high-collar dress-blue tunics saluted them up the stairs, through the ceremonial entrance. In the Grand Foyer, the Marine Band, in white dinner jackets, serenaded the swirl of guests.

"I want to dance," Phyllis said. "I want to tell my grandchildren that I danced at the White House."

Bob and Phyllis stood with the other freshmen from Kansas—four of the six from their state were new. And when a sudden silence fell, and the Marine Band struck up "Hail to the Chief," the Doles and the others took one or two instinctive steps back, as the President and Mrs. Kennedy swept into the room.

There was no receiving line, no order, just everybody milling around in a sea of laughter, greeting, smiles. The Kennedys moved through the crowd with no apparent plan, yet they seemed to meet everybody. They were so gloriously at ease.

"Good evening, Mr. President," said one Kansas GOP freshman. "I'm Bob Ellsworth, from Kansas."

"Oh, yes," said Kennedy, like he'd been waiting all night to meet the Congressman from Lawrence. He turned to Jackie and said: "Dear, this is Vivian and Bob Ellsworth from Kansas." The Ellsworths were floored. The President knew Vivian's name! "Oh, yes!" said Jackie. "I'm so glad to meet you."

Then they were gone.

Bob's meeting was even briefer—a quick handshake in a hallway—the President had to leave early. (Turned out, that was a terrible night: the invasion of the Bay of Pigs.)

But Phyllis did have her dance in the White House. And Bob danced with his colleagues' wives, too. That night, the Marine Band played a song, "Mr. Wonderful," in honor of the new Commander in Chief. Rose Mary McVey, wife of Walter, the freshman Rep from Independence, said, "Oh, Bob, isn't it perfect?"

"Live it up while you can, Rose Mary," Dole advised. "We're parked in a ten-minute zone."

—★—

Glorious ease was not Bob's style. Another man might have taken a deep breath and told himself he'd arrived—a member of Congress at thirty-seven, president of his class in the Capitol. Not Dole. What he remembered from that election among the freshmen was that he'd *fought* to beat Clark MacGregor, from Minnesota—by *one vote*! MacGregor'd prob'ly never forget! . . . It was too easy for Dole to see the matter through MacGregor's eyes (or as he imagined MacGregor must see it): Who is this rube from Dust-burg, Kansas?

It was a heady climb for anyone coming to Congress at that moment, when Washington seemed to hold not only power, but promise of brilliance, glamor, and grace. There was money coursing through the government's pipes, and people who'd spend a private fortune on those with their hands on the spigot. There were lobbyists inviting them to parties, two or three *every night*—they really *ought* to go . . . and Washington hostesses—they loved these powerful young men. (Some ladies took liberties you'd seldom see in Kansas.) . . . All at once, there were reporters who wanted to know what these fellows thought—and cameras, TV cameras, and people holding doors for them, literally bowing them down the hallways of the Capitol.

Dole barely noticed this stuff.

Walter McVey, Rose Mary's husband, went off the deep end. He'd go to twenty parties in a week. He'd end up weary, pressed for time, not knowing

where or who he was, yelling at some poor elevator operator, "Let's go! Don't
you know who I am? I'm Congressman McVey!"

Walter was a smart man, a good lawyer, who served the southeast section
of the state. Dole liked him; but he couldn't understand why Walter couldn't
see himself. Dole was embarrassed when anyone held an elevator for him, or
put him on a plane ahead of other folks. Bob was embarrassed for Walter
McVey. . . . By the end of their first year, Walter had taken up with a secretary
in his office. Rose Mary went home and filed for divorce. And that was the
end of McVey. In another year, he lost his seat. People didn't like how he
behaved. He forgot himself.

— ★ —

Dole could not forget how he'd fought to get to Washington—*had* to fight!
He had a primary against Keith Sebelius, a popular attorney from Norton,
Kansas. Sebelius had run before, in '58, and come within an eyelash of knock-
ing off the incumbent, a giant in that district, Wint Smith.

Dole stayed loyal to Wint in '58—Wint had done him some favors, sent him
some law books (members of Congress got two copies of the Federal Statutes,
each year) . . . and Bob Dole was a loyal young man. Anyway, Wint told him
that '58 would be his last turn. Then, too, Bob figured if Sebelius got in, he'd
be there for years. So Dole, the four-term County Attorney, was the man who
delivered Russell County for Smith. . . . Wint held off Sebelius by a margin
of fifty-one votes.

And that's when it started for Bob. Two years before his 1960 race, he was
already meeting the powers in the big Sixth District, showing Wint's troops
that Bob Dole could lead. That meant Bob had to show he was as tough as
Wint ("the General" thought *Ike,* for Christ's sake, was namby-pamby on the
commies). . . . Meanwhile, Dole started driving . . . twenty-six counties, from
Salina west to the Colorado line, and all the way north to Nebraska—Dole hit
every town, every country store, every café and filling station.

He ran the campaign from the basement of his home. Friends from Russell
would crowd in, Friday nights, to drink Phyllis's coffee and get their assignments for the weekend. They weren't helping because they thought Bob was
going to win—no one from Russell ever won anything—it was just that Bob
was working so hard.

The problem wasn't only Sebelius (though Keith was problem enough—ex-
commandant of the American Legion, which meant he had friends in every
county post) . . . there was a third guy in the race, a State Senator named Phil
Doyle . . . Doyle, Dole, Philip, Phyllis—it was murder!

That's how Bob started with the juice—Dole (not Doyle) Pineapple. The
ladies from Russell would ride in the caravans, cutting up Dole-for-Congress
labels and pasting Bob's name on paper cups. When they hit the next town,
they'd set up a table on the courthouse square, or a Main Street sidewalk, and
fill the cups with pineapple juice from blue-and-yellow Dole cans. After a
while, they bought out the warehouse, they had to use Libby's juice. But that

was their little secret—they washed out the Dole cans and refilled them with Libby's.

Then Phyllis made sixteen red felt skirts for the Dolls for Dole—each with a blue elephant (trimmed with sequins), and on the elephant's trunk, lettering that read, "Dole for Congress" . . . but not just that, there was a banner across each skirt: ROLL WITH DOLE. That *oh* was the crucial vowel!

That's why it was perfect when Leo Meyer and Fay built that Conestoga wagon, a scale model you could take apart and put in the trunk of a car (Kenny had to beg or borrow a big car because the wagon only fit in a Lincoln or Cadillac)—that was the Roll-with-Dole wagon . . . and Fay's two girls each got skirts from Phyllis that said I'M FOR ROBIN'S DADDY! so they could ride the wagon, while the men, in red clip-on Roll-with-Dole ties, pulled it up Main Street or rode it on the back of Harlan Boxburger's flatbed, while Bob walked along, if it was a parade—Bob always walked in parades.

That's why he had his girl singers, whom Dole called the Bob-o-Links—though sometimes they were introduced as the Dolls for Dole Quartet—college girls who sang harmony (to the accompaniment of a ukulele) on Bob's theme song:

> *Everyone here*
> *Kindly step to the rear . . .*

Which let people know that *Bob Dole was coming*! That was the point: Bob was afraid that people wouldn't notice he was out there!

And that was certainly the point of Bob's appearance at Kansas Day, an annual GOP affair in the Jayhawk Hotel in downtown Topeka, where the faithful stood around sipping Cokes in the public rooms while the nabobs held court, with stronger drink and cigars, upstairs. All in all, a staid affair, mid-winter, gray, like the snow outside—until Bob Dole showed up, with his wagon Roll-with-Doleing through the lobby, and the Bob-o-Links in red Roll-with-Dole skirts hammering at their ukulele, and twenty men and women all dressed up to Roll with Dole, descending in ranks down the Jayhawk's grand staircase, singing:

> *Everyone here*
> *Kindly step to the rear*
> *And let a winner lead the way! . . .*

And then, there was a young man riding a Dole unicycle through the crowd; and a Russell farmer dressed in an elephant's head; and eight pallbearers toting an open coffin, in which sat Frankenstein's Monster, bearing a sign: YOU HAVE NOTHING TO FEAR WITH DOLE.

People noticed.

In fact, they talked about nothing else that day, save the young fellow from Russell (There he is! . . . "Bob Dohhlll! Goodta meetcha!") who had such a tough primary, against Sebelius—but, well . . . looked like he might have a shot!

To the other candidates at the Jayhawk, here was something to fear: Dole was a palpable energy force in that hotel. He was throwing himself at that crowd with such abandon, it was almost frantic. Bob Ellsworth saw Dole for the first time that day, and thought no other politician would have done that—maybe they couldn't have. Dole was turning himself inside out.

Of course, Sebelius wasn't standing still. As commandant, he had a list of American Legion members, and he was using it for mailings . . . almost drove Dole crazy, the unfairness: *Bob* was a Legion man! And Doran before him! Why shouldn't *Bob Dole* have the list, too? He complained to the Legion. He argued that the bylaws prohibited help to any candidate. He threatened a legal challenge. He whined and wailed about this in the newspapers, in speeches. By the end of the campaign, the issue did Dole more good than any list.

By the end, there would be other mailings, too. Kansas was teetotal country—home of Carry Nation. (Bob used to joke, the Women's Christian Temperance Union was the only union that ever endorsed him.) . . . So imagine the impact, when all those letters arrived, revealing that *Sebelius was a lush*!

Keith's own mother was a life member of the WCTU. She got a letter (with a Washington State postmark) that said her son was an alcoholic. She was in tears, and Keith was so enraged, he was close to crying, too. His mother had been a widow since Keith was six. He'd never do anything to disappoint her. Keith said to his wife, Bette: "If a guy wants an office this bad . . . well, it just isn't worth it." Of course, he assumed it was Dole's people doing the mailing.

Dole denied that.

Thing was, people knew Keith would take a drink—so it hurt him. No one could say how many votes it meant. All they could say was, in the end, some nine hundred votes separated Dole from Sebelius . . . and that sent Bob to Washington.

—★—

Anyway, Dole felt right away he had to make a splash! (Within two years his district would be combined with another—he'd have a Democrat incumbent as an opponent and *fifty-eight* counties to cover.) . . . So, before Bob and Phyllis settled into their rented house, off Lee Highway in suburban Virginia . . . before Phyllis had time to unpack all the linens and dishes she'd brought from Russell in the U-Haul (Bob flew ahead—didn't have time to drive) . . . and after Bob saw his first inauguration (it snowed the night before—Bob slept in the office and went in a shirt he bought at Drugfair) . . . after Bob set his office in the Cannon Building to cranking out mail, with the help of Wint Smith's old AA and a couple of gals from Russell . . . and as soon as he found his seat in the Ag Committee room and learned how to sprint from there to the floor . . . right away, he was on a plane again—back to Kansas.

In those days, the government paid for one or two trips home each year. Dole was back and forth every couple of weeks . . . and he sent out his newsletter every month (edited that himself), and handled his own press

. . . and he was on the phone to Kansas every day, working his mail every night. He signed every letter himself. Most he dictated himself. And then, in careful lefty print, he'd write on the bottom—just a few words—or he'd send along a picture and he'd write on that. He sent Aunt Mildred a picture of himself, smiling on the Capitol steps, and wrote: "Finally made it. Lots of Democrats here."

Too many Democrats: they controlled the House, the Senate, and the White House.

There were a couple of ways a GOP freshman could handle this. Bob Ellsworth worked on flood-control projects. Those bills would sail through, with the backing of the aged Democratic lions—Jamie Whitten from Mississippi, George Mahon from Texas. Ellsworth could just hang on for the ride, make sure his district got its share. Dole's district didn't care about flood control; ag was all, and Bob was fixated on the farm bill. But even on the Ag Committee, Dole wasn't interested in playing ball. He was interested in showing that JFK, LBJ, and (the Ag Secretary) Orville Freeman—all those Democrats and their bureaucrats—were going to be the death of American farming, of American farmers, their families, and all that was good and holy wherever God caused wheat to sprout.

JFK was the President of eastern monied interests—which *always* put the shaft to the heartland farmer.

The liberals in Washington were going to run this country *commie.*

Orville Freeman, for pity's sake, wanted to send our wheat to the *Russians*! (What's the point of fighting them and feeding them at the same time?)

Dole never missed a vote. He had the highest ratings from conservative "watchdog" groups—the antitax antidebt crusaders. He had one of the lowest ratios of support for the New Frontier. All this was in line with the views of western Kansas. But Bob, being Bob, was sure it wasn't enough.

In the summer of '61, he and Phyllis went home to touch base . . . and Bob announced that Phyllis and Robin would stay, for a year and a half—keep the home fires burning while Bob took care of business in Washington.

That fall, Bob flew back and took care of JFK's Agriculture Department. There were stories in the paper from Pecos, Texas, about a wheeler-dealer good-ol'-boy (friend of LBJ's, matter of fact) who'd made a shady fortune storing grain for the government. This fellow's name was Billie Sol Estes.

Billie Sol was a man who knew a good deal—and what he had with the feds was a good deal. Say, you had a grain elevator that was sitting empty . . . Estes would buy it—give you a good price—all in notes, understand, entirely on credit . . . after which, trains would start rumbling in with government surplus to fill the elevator. The government fees would pay off Billie Sol's notes, and everybody was happy—save for the fellows who used to store the grain, and a couple of spoilsport Ag Department guys who didn't think Estes should be storing every bushel the U.S. government bought. From '59 to '61, Estes stored fifty million bushels of grain and collected $8 million from the Ag Department . . . so taxpayers might have been unhappy, too—if they'd known.

They might never have known if Estes hadn't got himself in trouble with some bankers in Texas and Oklahoma who'd given him mortgages on 33,000 liquid-fertilizer tanks—when he owned, in total, only 1,800. (Billie Sol would just change the numbers on the tanks, depending on which bankers were coming by that day.)

At the same time, Estes was buying cotton allotments from farmers in the Old Confederacy and transferring these allotments to his lands in West Texas . . . which wasn't much good, as cotton land went, but price supports were so inflated that an allotment (in effect, a license to grow cotton) was like a license to print money. Anyway, there was an Ag Department man in Texas named Marshall, and he refused to approve these cotton transfers. Marshall ended up dead on his ranch: he'd been poisoned with carbon monoxide, beat over the head, and gut-shot five times (with his own bolt-action .22 rifle). Still, taxpayers might never have known. Henry Marshall's death was ruled a suicide. After that, Estes's cotton assignments went through.

But after that, the case was in the papers, too, and the smell of ink reached Bob Dole in Washington.

Bob's fellow freshmen thought he must be crazy: What did Dole know about Billie Sol Estes? Bob was messing with the White House—with LBJ's friends! Dole was going to get clobbered!

But Dole called in the Attorney General of Texas—got him into the office and started finding out about the case. ("Duck soup!") . . . A friend at the RNC put Bob in touch with Ag Department sources— holdovers from Ike's regime who'd blow the whistle. . . . There was one Ag guy, M. Battle Hales, who'd accused Estes of buying off the department. Hales was reassigned—his office was locked and he was denied access to his own files. His secretary was shipped off to a mental institution. That's when Dole brought the matter to the floor— and to the papers. He wanted the Ag Committee to hold hearings. He wanted Hales to testify. He wanted to know where Orville Freeman had squirreled away Hales's secretary. These were the sort of shenanigans by which the American farmer was bilked!

In the end, Bob Dole, freshman from Kansas, was the principal sponsor of the resolution that committed Congress to an investigation.

Bob Dole, freshman from Kansas, socked the Kennedy White House with its first taste of scandal.

Bob Dole, freshman from Kansas, made the case for the Republican Party, and the American farmer . . . in *The New York Times*.

"Agh, pretty *goood*! Front payyge!"

28

No Choice, Mike

KITTY WORRIED that she wouldn't measure up. It was so odd: Michael wouldn't have been in the race if Kitty hadn't wanted it so much. But the minute he got in, she was seized with dread: What if *she* hurt his chances? What if people looked at *her,* and found her wanting? What if her secret came out, and hurt Michael? She'd never forgive herself.

It was always that way with Kitty: she was so sure of Michael, her anchor, her rock . . . she was so sure *for* him. But her? She felt like a fraud.

That's how it was for twenty-five years, with the pills: after a while, she hated herself for taking them, for hiding them, for lying. . . . But if she did something—anything good—she was also robbed of the joy: it was the pills. Without them, she was sure, she never could have done it.

No one knew about the pills.

Except Michael—he knew, now—but Michael never saw it that way. "Look at her!" he'd say to the crowd, whenever she went with him to an event. "You tell me—wouldn't she make a *terrific* First Lady?" In his eyes, she was always . . . terrific. If she flew off the handle, snapped at someone who was only trying to help . . . if she fell into a mood where nothing was right, nothing worth doing . . . if she barged into a meeting in the State House, in a steaming rage that could not wait (it was just the mirror of her rage at herself) . . . well, that was just his Katharine. He adored her, his impetuous, tempestuous Jewish bride. In fact, her behavior fed him, his own idea of himself: it was left to him to be the steady one, the strong one, the stoic. *He* was fine, unperturbed—maybe, in the worst case, silent, down in his Mediterranean hunch—but *his* behavior was appropriate.

Which, again, let Kitty feed her own idea of herself: she was the one on the edge, the gambler, the high-wire artist, scraping through on charm, guile, and bursts of feverish energy—wringing the last drop of drama from her scenes. She was not hiding, no: she was a woman who would not be ignored. Intensely desirous of achievement she was, determined to have recognition—but certain, all the while, that someone would see through her act, straight to the fear at her core.

That was the fear rising now. They'd be looking at *her*. Surely, her secrets would be found out. She had her first major interview scheduled—the *Los Angeles Times,* Bob Drogin was coming to talk to her. Kitty was nuts with this thing, this interview. It seemed to others like unnatural dread.

Drogin was just getting his feet wet—his introductory story on Dukakis. Sure, he wanted to talk to Kitty, but he also wanted Michael's friend Paul Brountas, and the fund-raiser, Bob Farmer, and John Sasso . . . many other folks.

It's no big deal, they tried to tell Kitty. "I know Drogin," Patricia O'Brien, the campaign's new Press Secretary, said. "He's not the kind who's going to really, you know, *hammer* at you."

But Pat didn't know Kitty. . . . *No one knew.*

In the days before Drogin arrived, Kitty's face drew tight—everything about her got tight—and her eyes got darker, deeper in their sockets, like she wasn't sleeping well.

"Do you want me to sit in?" Pat asked Kitty.

Please.

So Pat sat in, and they set the thing up for Kitty's State House office, her own turf . . . and they held it (she's *awfully* busy) to twenty minutes—half an hour at most.

And Drogin came in, asked a few questions . . . it went fine. Kitty was stiff with fear, but Bob couldn't tell—it was the first time he'd met her. And he was an awfully nice guy.

It was only after the interview—Pat walked out to the hall with Drogin— that Bob brought up the thing he'd wanted to check out. There were rumors (you know, with the Hart thing in the air . . .) that Kitty'd had an affair . . . one of the troopers, one of Michael's State Police guards—Kitty and the trooper—it was all over town. Had Pat heard anything?

Nothing to that, Pat assured him. . . . She'd heard the talk, sure. She'd asked about it . . . and Pat was certain—it was nothing. Turned out, it was just a stupid rumor. Drogin nodded, and went on his way.

It was after that, Pat went back into the office: it was time to have a talk with Kitty. . . . Pat asked:

"Kitty, is there anything I should know—that I don't know? Something . . . anything . . . you want to tell me?"

Kitty stared up, bolt-still, like startled prey; she paused just a second
. . . and said:
"Yes."

— ★ —

Kitty Dickson started taking amphetamines—diet pills—at the age of nineteen. She thought she was fat, or thought she was going to be fat, or thought,
somehow, they were going to make her better. She'd seen the bottle in her
mother's dressing room, so she walked in one day and helped herself to a pill.
Next day, she was back to help herself to another. And soon she had her own
prescription.

They were easy to get in those days, '56, when doctors were happy to share
with their patients the pain-free miracles of modern chemistry. You wanted
to lose weight? Here was a pill. You wanted to sleep? Here was a pill. Felt down
in the mouth? Well, here . . .

And Kitty felt terrific. She was going to leave college—Penn State, she was
a sophomore—to marry her beau and start a new life. Turned out she barely
knew the boy, John Chaffetz . . . he just wanted her *so much.* She knew little
about herself, but she thought marriage would make her whole, somehow. It
would give her the sense of self that she craved. She thought, somehow, it
would make her better.

So she married the boy in a grand ceremony. (There was nothing her dad
wouldn't do for Kitty—she was the most wonderful girl.) And, amid great
flutter and attention—excitement was really her drug of choice—she set off for
her new world: an Air Force base in Texas, with her handsome new husband,
and a bottle of pills.

Alas, the excitement was over soon: there was another air base, and another—Florida, California . . . but it was always the same, she and John did
not really share a life. He had his work, his sports on TV . . . and she? Well,
after 1958, she had her son—a beautiful little boy named Johnny, whom she
adored—and she wanted another child, but she miscarried. And then, they
tried again, but again, she miscarried . . . and there was nothing much said
between husband and wife anymore in Kitty and John Chaffetz's house
. . . and at last, in 1960, they agreed, the marriage was over.

So by age twenty-four, she had a divorce, and a son, and a life to make on
her own. She moved back to Boston, and re-enrolled in college. She was
spiritually exhausted, physically worn down by stress—not much more than
a hundred pounds now . . . but still, she had the pills. How could she ever have
gotten through all *that* . . . without them?

And even after she'd met Michael, started dating, and fell so deeply in love
with that steady soul . . . even after she did finish college, and married again,
and had her own home, her own life in every sense of the word . . . even after
she did have more children, two lovely daughters (and another miscarriage,
and another pregnancy marred by German measles, that ended with the child's
death at birth) . . . even after she'd gone back to school, again, this time for

a master's in communications . . . even after she'd made a career for herself, first as an instructor in dance, then as an advocate for public parks and environmental beautification, an advocate for remembrance of the Holocaust, an advocate for the homeless in America, a rescuer of refugees overseas, the host of a television program, a leader of tours to the Middle East, the Orient . . . and for most of those years, all the while, First Lady of the Commonwealth of Massachusetts . . . even after she made a life, in short, that would have surfeited ten average women . . . she still had the pills. How could she have done all *that*, without them?

It was not till 1982, while Michael was in mid-course of his furious comeback campaign . . . in fact, by curious congruence, not until her husband had met his own loss (ouster from the job which was his definition of self), and faced his mistakes, faced himself, apologized, and come back stronger than ever . . . not until that moment when Michael bade fair to overcome his one great failure, did Kitty decide she had to face hers.

She told Michael about the pills. She told him she was going away, for help, to a clinic in Minnesota.

She told her children about her addiction, her lies, and she asked them to participate in the therapy.

She told her sister, and brother-in-law (in fact, it was Al Peters, Jinny's husband, a recovering alcoholic, who set her on the road to the clinic in Minnesota).

She told one friend, her old Penn State roommate, Ann Fogy, who lived in Missouri now and who'd cover for her, who'd tell anyone who asked that Kitty was visiting *her* to recover from "a bout of hepatitis."

But she told no one else.

And then, in mid-campaign, she got on a plane, took her last pill, and disappeared for more than a month.

(That's where the rumors of affairs got started: Where was Kitty? . . . Was there trouble in the marriage? . . . Must be trouble—she's never with him! . . . Well, of course—haven't you *heard*? . . . The trooper! . . . Kitty and the trooper! . . .)

Michael baldly lied for his bride. She didn't need anyone poking into her affairs. Nor did he: he was facing the most important election of his life in a couple of months. He didn't need weeks of ugly questions about his wife, her secrets, those pills . . . and how come he didn't know?

Michael himself couldn't understand—how could he not have known? He blamed himself—he should have seen. His wife! His bride! The light of his life! He'd always been there for her . . . tried to help . . . he'd paid attention. He'd scheduled time to pay attention! . . . How could he not have seen—for twenty years?

But when Kitty returned, that August, when she came back to him (she looked, well, just terrific!) without the pills—yes, she'd beaten those pills . . . she also had the answer for Michael: there was no way he could have known. She was taking pills before he ever met her . . . her behavior never changed . . . and pills are easy to hide. Hell, the way she'd sneaked those pills, Sherlock Holmes couldn't have found them!

And that was the answer she had ready for the day when she finally would, finally could . . . tell the world. She had to tell the truth, now, yes . . .

And sure enough, when she did tell all, that was the question everybody asked—how could he not have *known*?

Oh, she always knew what they were doing—trying to pin Michael for inattention, insensitivity . . . trying to beat up on Michael, for *her lie*.

But she wouldn't let them—not for an instant.

He couldn't have known . . .

I was using when he met me . . .

Pills are just too easy to hide . . .

She'd shut them down, in half a minute . . . with a smile.

But no one asked, or no one got a real answer (save for a shrug, and a flip "addicts lie") to the more interesting question:

Okay, it was her lie . . .

Okay, he couldn't have figured . . .

Okay, it started before, but . . . why, in a twenty-year "partnership," could she never let him see her failure, or her fear?

— ★ —

It was just the bare facts she told to Patricia O'Brien, but that was enough.

We've got a problem, Pat thought. She saw what they were doing to Hart, the way the whole pack was now Karacter Kops. She'd been on the job for less than two weeks . . . this was her first big—God, this had to be handled right!

"This is very big," she said quietly.

And Kitty looked better, right away: "It is?"

Pat said, of course . . . it had to come out. She wanted it to come out right, for Kitty's sake.

Kitty was a new woman, lighter, younger, excited again. She was so relieved . . . she'd told someone . . . who paid attention, who thought it was important.

She'd told Sasso, see, told him right away when Michael decided to get into the race. She'd gone to John and she told him about the pills, the treatment, her anguish . . .

And nothing happened.

"Lemme think about that," John said.

And nothing happened!

Of course, that was annoying to Kitty—confusing and hurtful . . .

Truth be told, Sasso had worked with Michael for more than five years now . . . and he wasn't going to get into Kitty-business. Not willingly, anyway. That was Michael's affair. Somewhere, Sasso had to draw the line . . . more and more, the line fell just this side of Kitty.

He wasn't confused about the politics, no: it had to come out, and they'd have to *put* it out. Sasso managed Geraldine Ferraro's campaign for the Vice

Presidency: he knew what a spouse's woes could do to a candidate. But this wasn't going to hurt Michael—not if they brought it out themselves. And Dukakis hadn't even announced yet. He could still barely say out loud that he wanted to be President. He needed an emotional crisis right now like a hole in the head.

So, when Pat O'Brien came marching to John with the stuff about Kitty, when Pat said it had to come out, had to be *handled right,* it had to be *planned,* this had to be *thought through* . . . Sasso said, with a shrug:

"I don't know if Mike'll go for it . . ."

That meant John didn't know when, or whether, he'd talk to Michael about it.

So Kitty brought it up with Michael . . . who didn't see why it had to come out. *His* health, sure, a clear issue. People had to know. But his wife's health? . . . Did anyone—did the public—have a right to poke into his bride's life? Where would this kind of thing stop?

—★—

So it ended up, again, at the kitchen table on Perry Street. The four of them gathered on a Sunday morning. Pat and Kitty were pushing to have the thing out . . . but Kitty wouldn't push hard—this was Michael's campaign . . .

And John's. But Sasso was quiet that day, sitting back—let the others thrash this out. He was adviser to Michael—that's all.

So it was Pat who carried the mail. She wanted this to be handled right, for Kitty . . . and for herself. Pat had just left the newspaper trade, and was prickly about her integrity. She was not going to get into a position where she had to cover up for anyone, on anything.

She'd been carrying the notes from her talk with Kitty about the drugs . . . she'd had the notes, for weeks, in her purse. And she'd told herself: *first reporter who asks . . . gets this story, gets it all.*

So she had to get the green light from Michael. Without it, she was going to lose her new job, or her fondest idea of herself.

"Governor," she said, "this could be terrible if it comes out any other way. It's a lot better for Kitty, if we do it now . . . it's the only way to keep control of the story, if we do it right . . . do a full press conference. Then it's *over* . . ."

Michael was already shaking his head. His wife's problems? No one had proved to *him* they had any bearing on the office he sought.

Pat tried to explain: it wasn't about the job, it was about the campaign, the pack on the plane. If this dribbled out uncontrolled, then BOOM, everything would go nuclear. "Governor, you don't know how bad this can be . . ."

But it was always a mistake to tell Michael he didn't know. She should have realized that, should have figured. . . . She was asking him to throw his wife—his bride!—to the pack. Not even asking—telling!

"Look," he said, in his laying-down-the-law voice. "If Kitty wants to share her . . . experience, that's fine. I think you know, I'm the kinda guy . . ."

He didn't have to finish that thought . . . Michael, the great allower. "But I wanna make sure no one thinks the campaign, this campaign, requires her to do it . . . because it doesn't."

You could just about hear his feet digging in, under the kitchen table. So Sasso said quietly, "Mike, you have to do it."

"Well," Michael said, "well . . . it's not gonna be a press conference."

At that point, they could almost see the ugly vision behind his eyes: Kitty being grilled by the pack on her woes. Twenty-five years he'd taken care of Kitty. She was high-strung, emotional . . . *they didn't understand.* . . . No one was going to put his wife through that.

". . . maybe the speech, at the drug event . . ."

Pat and John were already planning. There was a drug event for Kitty on the schedule. She could put her confession into the speech. No questions—not at that event, anyway.

Sasso had his eyes on Michael. Poor bastard didn't need this, didn't deserve . . . John said quietly, with sadness, like it was just the two of them: "No choice, Mike."

And Michael said to John: "I don't think she can do it."

Kitty said: "Michael! I can do it."

Michael turned to her, said nothing, just looked, with his dark, sad eyes . . . then got up. He went around the table, stopped behind Kitty, and, hand on her shoulder, slowly, delicately, lowered his face to hers—put his cheek next to her cheek. Just a touch—faces together, Michael's eyes were down. "Babe . . ."

It was almost too soft for anyone else to hear. "Babe . . . I just don't know if you can handle it."

And Kitty's throaty voice was as soft as his.

"I can, Michael . . . I know I can."

29

1964

GEORGE BUSH was still in Midland, in the big house on Sentinel, the last of George and Bar's homes in West Texas, when he first mentioned to a friend what he meant to do with his life.

It was George and C. Fred Chambers in the kitchen . . . the kids and wives were at the pool . . . no one else in the house that day. Bush said: "You ever had any sake?"

"No, let's try it," Chambers said. "Looks like a warm beer can to me."

"Well, that's how you drink it, I guess."

So they popped open this rice wine, and started feeling warm, pretty good . . . sitting at the kitchen table, talking oil, like they always did—Bush and Chambers were in deals together—when Bush said: "Fred, what do you wanna do? . . . I mean, for the rest of your life."

"Well, I'm here . . ." Fred said. "Oil bidness, I guess . . ."

Tell the truth, it caught him off guard. He never expected the question, not from Bush. He always figured George was like him—like everybody—just meant to hit the biggest field *ever* . . . pile it up . . . find the next one.

"You know what I think," Bush said. That wasn't a question. "I think I want to be in politics, serving, you know, public office."

Fred took that in, nodded: "Well, I think that's great," he said. "I thought of being a teacher or something, where you do something for people . . ."

But Fred could tell, as he said it, Bush wasn't just thinking about it. Bush had thought. Fred didn't ask him how, or when . . . it just seemed settled.

Bush'd do it, somehow. Fred didn't have to ask him why. He knew why. George had always felt that way about his dad.

—★—

Prescott Bush had the old-fashioned idea that a man who'd been blessed had a duty to serve. He'd always had public office somewhere in his mind. But what Pres saw was the service, the office. He did not take easily or quickly to the politics required to get there.

He first considered a run for Congress in '46, while Poppy was at Yale . . . but his partners at Brown Brothers Harriman took a dim view of the crowded House chamber. "Well, Pres," one of the Harrimans said, "if it were the Senate, we'd surely back you . . . but the House? We need you here more than the House needs you." And that was the end of that notion: there were no disputes among partners in the Brown Brothers' paneled boardroom.

So it wasn't till 1950 that he filed for office, and then for the Senate, and he ran nose to nose with a Democrat incumbent. But the Sunday before the vote, Drew Pearson predicted on his network radio show that Prescott Bush would lose the Connecticut Senate race . . . *because it had just been revealed that Bush was president of the Birth Control League.* Well, it didn't happen to be true, but more than half the voters in Connecticut were Catholics (state law actually prohibited the use of contraceptives), and Pres was denounced at every mass— it must have cost him ten thousand votes . . . anyway, just enough votes: he lost by eleven hundred, and his dream of service in the nation's best club was dashed. Two years later, he filed for the Senate again, but this time he narrowly lost the nomination to an upstate businessman named Bill Purtell, and Pres had to give up his dream: he'd run twice, he'd lost. He was finished.

But then—a Great and Godly Good stroke of fortune, or rather several, a Blessed Confluence: that same June, 1952, the senior Senator, Brien McMahon, died in office. Pres was handed the nomination . . . he had to campaign only two months in a special election . . . and, in the Eisenhower landslide, he beat young Congressman Abe Ribicoff by almost thirty thousand votes. At last, he would take up residence and the duties of a statesman in Washington. More- over, as he'd won a special election, to replace a Senator deceased, he could take up his duties the day after the vote: he did not have to wait for the new Congress (unlike Purtell, who had knocked Pres out of the *regular* election), and became, instantly, the *senior Senator* from Connecticut, a man of standing in the Capitol.

In fact, by Blessed Confluence, Prescott Bush found life in the capital almost unimaginably congenial. There was the fact that he'd backed the Eisenhower wing in the late Republican political wars, and so found friends in the White House—like Sherman Adams, the President's right-hand man. Then, too, Pres was one of the few golfers among GOP Senators—surely, the best golfer—and so he was often Ike's playing partner: that was most congenial. And then, too, Pres had been friends forever with Bob Taft—met him years ago, as sons of good family will, in Cincinnati (served on Yale's board with him, since '44)—

and as the GOP had taken back the Senate in Ike's landslide, well, Pres's friend Bob Taft was the Leader of the Senate. And it did not hurt that Taft's son, Bill, was a professor at Yale in those years, and so a constituent of Pres Bush, and when Bill Taft decided he'd like to be Ambassador to Ireland, it was Pres Bush who called his friend Sherm Adams, and pushed the nomination through the White House. And surely that was easier because Foster Dulles, at State, was a friend (lawyer to Brown Brothers Harriman, for quite a while) . . . as were the men at Treasury, and Commerce, of course—men of business whom Pres had known for years, and very congenial fellows all. And when there was friction between the Republican Senate and the Eisenhower administration (a good deal of friction—Ike was not really a pol, and notwithstanding his golf, not really a clubable man), it was Pres who hosted a dinner at the Burning Tree Country Club, to get all the fellows together—brought a wonderful quartet down from Yale to sing (Ike never forgot that, nor that Pres's son Johnny sang bass)—and things went along much better after that.

In all, it was a splendid time for a gentleman of business and grand personal qualities to serve in the Senate. And though he did not leave a long list of laws that bore his name, Pres was welcomed in the capital's councils of power, to have a look (perhaps a quiet word, here and there) on the most important and interesting matters in the Eisenhower years. He was such a sure-footed man, so impressive, so steady in his personal code . . . that people listened to Pres, though he was new in the Senate. He was a good ally—his word was his bond—and a good friend: they all noticed that. When Sherman Adams ran into such trouble with that Goldfine, and the vicuna coat . . . well, for a while, Pres and Dottie were the only ones who'd still have Adams to dinner. Pres took a leading role in the censure of Senator Joseph McCarthy—alas, that fellow did step over the line . . . but when McCarthy fell sick, in 1955, Pres was the last (maybe the only) member of the Senate to stop by the hospital and wish Joe well.

In general, Pres took to the job with grace, and assiduity. He traveled the world for a blue-ribbon commission for international trade. Later, as a member of the Armed Services Committee, he'd descend in a small plane onto the deck of some U.S. carrier, where he'd spend a few days with the officers, at sea. That was always most interesting. Meanwhile, each week, from the Senate studio, he'd make a TV broadcast for distribution in his state. (As a banker, in the thirties, Pres had helped launch CBS, and his friends there, Bill Paley and Frank Stanton, counseled him to do all the TV he could.) At the same time, he was a stickler for responding, personally, to every letter or telegram. Most weeks, he'd sign a thousand letters. He acknowledged every invitation, every contribution. His office worked six days a week, and Pres did, too. He spoke at a hundred public schools in the state, kept in touch with town officials, state officials, labor unions, the insurance companies of Hartford, the manufacturers of Bridgeport . . . he meant to show that they were his interest, that he was, as he put it, "a lift-up and bear-down sort of Senator." And though he had a bitter reelection campaign against the well-known Thomas Dodd, Pres made splendid use of TV—he was quite good with that camera now—and won by the largest plurality ever attained in Connecticut.

After that . . . and after 1960, when things did not quite work out for Dick Nixon . . . well, Pres wondered, as every Senator must, how he'd do, how he'd feel, at the other end of Pennsylvania Avenue. Yes, the thought occurred . . . he'd been around the White House quite a bit, what with the pleasant friendship he'd had with Ike. It did not seem oversized, or strange . . . and there was no clear standard-bearer for the Party, not from the mainstream, anyway. Yes, the thought occurred . . .

But things did not work out that way. Pres's own health was shaky, his doctors were quite firm about slowing him down. He would be sixty-seven when he'd have to run for reelection. And even Dottie, he knew—though she'd never say a word—was dreading the effort to come. Well, he had to take stock, and he did. He came to a firm decision: he would retire. He just could not drag Dottie through another campaign. Maybe if his health were better . . . maybe, if Kennedy hadn't beat Nixon by a hundred thousand votes in Connecticut . . . maybe, if Abe Ribicoff meant to stay, content, in the Governor's chair . . . maybe, if Pres had begun his own service as a younger man—well, surely . . . but no.

And so, with regret (with a stoic sorrow that would only grow, as his health improved), Senator Bush announced he was stepping down. He removed his name from consideration. That was the end of politics for him—an end, he was convinced, that came too soon. And that was 1962.

— ★ —

It was that spring, '62, when Houston's Party leaders came to Bush's house for lunch. Oh, they were in an awful bind.

The GOP was growing in Houston—in fact, it was on the rise all over Texas. (They'd even elected a Senator in '61, when LBJ had to give up his seat to assume the Vice Presidency. They got that runty professor, John Tower—a couple of Party leaders held him down on a table and shaved off his little Hitler mustache—and sent him out as a single-shot Republican against a field of about seventy Democrats . . . and he won!)

But the problem was *how* the Party was growing. The GOP had papered the state with its new slogan, "Conservatives Unite!" Of course, no one dreamed what that might mean. They *had* pried the right wing loose from the Democrats. The Party meetings were bigger than ever, but those new Republican voters—they were extreme, on the fringe, they were . . . well, they were *Birchers*!

These . . . these *nuts*! They were coming out of the woodwork! (Actually, they came out of a couple of fringy churches in the working-class suburb of Pasadena.) These people talked about blowing up the UN, about armed revolt against the income tax. They had their guns loaded at home, in case commies should appear that night. . . . Well, you can imagine how upsetting it was to *decent* Republicans—that is, to the lime-green pants crowd, who'd organized the GOP in Texas about the same time they'd founded their country clubs.

In fact, in the last Party convention, in Houston, right there in Harris County, it was everything decent folk could do just to hold on to the leadership. Jimmy Bertron was their candidate for County Chairman—such a fine young man!—the man who'd shaved John Tower and steered him to the Senate. But the Birchers poured in, they were packing the place! (Bob Crouch, one of the old-line faithful, had to head over to the black side of town, "to round up some Toms" . . . at least they'd vote right.)

Well, it was a bitter fight to the end. But when all the ballots were counted, Bertron held on—by sixteen votes! . . . Landslide Bertron!

The Party was saved!

But not for long. Now, in '62, Jimmy Bertron wanted to move to Florida. In fact, he was leaving, and leaving the chair . . . the Party was up for grabs again.

That's why they came to George Bush.

"George, you've got to help us! You've got to run for chairman!"

Well, wasn't it great, how it worked out?

— ★ —

Actually, Bush had his hands full—business, and all. Not that he was making a prophet of Fred Chambers, trying to pile it up . . . no, he was not that way. That was more his old partner's style—Hugh Liedtke—now, there was a man who gave new meaning to the verb "amass."

That's really why they'd split up—Hugh and George divvied up Zapata in 1958. See, Hugh was all for acquisition, corporate takeovers, buying production. He liked business. But George, he was more for the hunt, the future, the cutting edge, exploration. He liked the *oil game.* In effect, they split the company in half, and Hugh kept Zapata's land operations, and George took over Zapata Off-Shore, which was a subsidiary they'd created to drill for oil under the ocean bed. That was the future, according to Bush.

(Of course, he was dead wrong. Oh, offshore went fine—grew into a giant industry—that part was true. But the future, turned out, lay with the corporate takeover boys, and with Liedtke, who soon acquired South Penn Oil, and turned that into Pennzoil, and—well, it was just a pity that Uncle Herbie and his money men went with Poppy on that split.)

Anyway, it was the offshore business that carried Bush to Houston—and it wasn't any life of leisure. By 1962, Bush had four rigs to drill on the seabed; each cost several million dollars, and each had to keep working. He had more than two hundred people on his payroll, maybe ten times as many shareholders to consider. He had farm-outs of ocean-floor leases from the majors, he had contracts to drill, schedules to keep; he had business possibilities everywhere in the world there was oil under water. He had insurance, he had accountants, he had lawyers, bankers—he had debt. He had storms at sea that threatened his equipment . . . he had five kids who had to get educations . . . he had an ulcer.

So he looked at those Houston Republicans who came to lunch, at those desperate souls who wanted him for County Chairman, and he said: "Well, Jeez, sure! I mean, if you want . . ."

— ★ —

Well, after that, the pace of the Party picked up—everyone could feel it. The big difference was, the chairman *worked:* out every night, somewhere in the county, trying to find Republican election judges, or trying to find black precinct captains. No Republican chairman had ever been *seen* in the black precincts. They were thirty-to-one for the Democrats. But Bush wouldn't give up. He'd stand on some broken-down front porch, talking up the *two-party system,* how that was *good* and *right for the country* . . . until people inside either signed up or told him to get lost. Come Election Day, a lot of those captains would just take the money, stick it in their pockets . . . but George had them on the lists that he updated each week.

Most nights, he'd stop at headquarters, and the place seemed to swell with enthusiasm. Sometimes, Barbara would come, too—she'd stuff envelopes with the lady volunteers—but more often, it was only George. Aleene Smith, Party secretary, would have everything ready on his desk. George would read and sign the letters, sign the checks, write his memos, and clear the desk before he went home.

HQ was a dump on Audley Street, but Bush soon moved it to better quarters, a nice old house on Waugh Drive, near Allen Parkway. (Of course, people said he picked the place because it was on his way home from his office atop the Houston Club—but that's just how people are.) The house was perfect—volunteers had tables in the living room, the committee could meet on the side porch, or in the dining room. George put his office upstairs, in the front bedroom, and he fixed it up fine. He got the money from the first Neighbor to Neighbor Fund Drive—the kind of thing he used to do for the Midland Red Cross, a civic exercise. He got some local business friends to donate computer time, and he made lists of all the Republicans in the county. Then the precinct chairmen got the lists, just like they would for an election— but this time, for quarters and dollar bills. They raised more than ninety thousand dollars, probably double what the Party ever had. Then he used some of that money to support the campaign of Bill Elliot, who became the first City Councilman ever elected by the GOP—and that put more fire into the troops.

The troops were mostly women in those days, battle-hardened matrons who'd kept the flame when the whole county convention wouldn't fill a good-sized coffee shop, who'd fought like cheetahs for the last few years to keep the Bircher goofballs out of the office. Of course, the ladies loved George, adored him. He was so young, for one thing—just thirty-eight—and eager, enthusiastic . . . and so handsome, the way he'd stand up, tall and slender in front of the room, and talk about what the Party *meant,* with his high voice coming from up behind his nose, with that foreign eastern accent. Well, it was like Cary Grant, or David Niven, come to work at the office. And that was just the start: then they found out how kind he was, how interested in them, grateful for their work, eager to include them, to be their friend . . . he was so *decent*!

Too decent for politics.

They all agreed about that.

They had to protect him.

Poor George didn't even know who was a nut, and who was out to get him. He was so nice to those Birchers . . . really, sometimes, you wanted to shake him by the neck!

He couldn't see, the nuts *hated him*. They could *smell* Yale on him. Of course, it didn't help, the first time Jimmy Bertron introduced him to the executive committee: "Good friend of mine," Jimmy said. "George Bush . . . only thing wrong with him, he beats me at tennis."

Yuk. Yuk.

You could have heard a pin drop. Gene Crossman, one of the good ol' slimeball right-wingers, said: "Thass it, dammit. I'm not votin' for 'nother country-club asshole. Y'kin jus' fergit it."

But George had the idea they should all get along. He thought he could talk to the Birchers, make them *like* him . . . once they got to know him. They were probably good folks, underneath. He was always saying stuff like, "We all have the same *basic* goals . . ." He couldn't seem to get what was basic to the Birchers: being rid of *him* and everyone like him . . . like *Eisenhower, Rockefeller* . . . like all those rich, pointy-head, one-worlder, fellow-traveler, eastern-Harvard-Yale-country-club-Council-on-Foreign-Relations *commie dupes*!

No, George tried to talk to them, reason with them, involve them. He *wanted* them to come, participate, join the committees. He wanted to know them, to see their lives, to let them see his. He had them over to his house, for meetings, for breakfasts with him and Bar. He had *everybody* over to his house on Briar Drive. He wanted to share, see, him and Bar—they made everybody feel so *comfortable* there. It was a fine, big house in the Tanglewood section, but nothing austere about it: everything was comfy, the sofas, the chairs. You'd come in, sit down, and George would serve drinks, padding around with no shoes, in a sport shirt. The dog would come around—that dog who'd get crippled, psychosomatically paralyzed, any time George and Bar went away. That was always a joke with the Bushes. And the kids would be running around, in and out of doors that led from the family room to the backyard. They were all still in school—Doro was only three or four years old—but they were good kids, who'd always say hello to grown-ups. On the wall, there was the portrait of Robin, the little girl who died. You felt a part of it all, even when you just came for a meeting. Of course, that's how George wanted you to feel.

Wanted *everyone* to feel: sure, some of those folks had extreme ideas. But Bush was not one to judge a man on account of his *ideas* . . . no. So, first thing, he put out a half-page memo, telling *everybody:* no more name-calling. "We're all Republicans, and we're not going to divide ourselves, calling anyone 'crazies,' or 'nuts' . . ." He didn't want to *hear* the word "nut." (So what they did, they started calling everybody "Kernel" . . . Kernel Smith, or Kernel Crouch, or Kernel Nancy Palm, better known as Kernel Napalm . . . it was Bob Crouch who started it—had to have *some* word for "nut.")

Then—this was '63—Bush decided the Birchers had to have jobs, they had to be *involved,* he was going to give them *precincts!*

"George, you don't know these people," Sarah Gee, one of the stalwart ladies, tried to tell him. "They mean to kill you!"

"Aw, Sarah," he'd say. "There's some good in everybody. You just gotta find it."

The first was a gal named Randy Brown. George made them vote to give her a precinct. Sarah was livid. All the ladies were furious. Randy didn't even hide her contempt! What got into Bush? Couldn't he see? . . . He made them vote her in, and they were coming out of the dining room, after the vote, and he was coming downstairs from his office, at that moment. There he was, beaming like a kid, as he said, "Congratulations!" . . . Randy stared up at him, not a hint of a smile, and said: "George, you'll rue the day you made 'em put me on."

— ★ —

No, he couldn't see. Or didn't choose to. For one thing, he was too excited. There were too many good things happening. Good things for the Party. Good things for him. All those new friends! Nice things people said . . . they were talking to him about the U.S. Senate!

Sure, it'd be tough, but he had a shot . . . if he could unite the Party, draw some conservative Democrats . . . he'd unite them all around his person. They had to like *him* . . . he knew they would. Goldwater would unite the Party— just the kind of Republican the Texas GOP could get behind. Hell, just the man for Bush to get behind! He was so un-eastern, un-monied, un-moderate. Bush was big for Goldwater in '64—whole hog for Barry!—no one was going to out-conservative George Bush.

Tell the truth, Bush's program wasn't in conflict with Goldwater's . . . as Bush didn't have a program. Sure, he was conservative—a businessman who had to meet a payroll—but that's about as far as it went, on policy. One of the first times he ever made a speech—some little town just south of Houston— one good ol' boy stood up in the crowd and asked Bush for his position on the Liberty Amendments. Well, Bush didn't have a clue about the Liberty Amend- ments. (They were a series of Bircher Constitutional changes to get America out of the UN, repeal the income tax, abolish the Federal Reserve, a few other things like that.) Poor Bush was helpless. He turned to Barbara, the eastern matron, busy at her needlepoint on stage . . . no help there. So Bush said he hadn't had time, yet, to *study* those important amendments . . . but he certainly would.

Tell the truth, Bush wasn't much for programs, one way or the other. It wasn't that he wanted to do anything . . . except a good job. He wanted to *be* a Senator. . . . Just about the time he was thinking it over, about to announce his big move, there were stories in the paper—front page, it was awful!—about this little girl in the Houston public housing, sleeping on the floor, who'd got bitten by a rat! God, what a shame! . . . Bush didn't think about a program for housing, or maybe calling that Councilman he helped to elect—propose a rat eradication plan! No, he called home, that afternoon:

"Bar? . . . You think we could give that family our baby bed?"

And they did. That very evening, George came home, packed up that bed, and took it right over.

That's why Bush was gonna win the election: concern for the common man. Common values . . . common decency. That's what people had to know about him . . . that, and the fact—Bush could *see* it, everywhere—the Democrats were out of touch. They'd held on to Texas since the Civil War! They'd lost sight of the common folk . . . that was Bush's secret weapon. The Democrats were split, right down the middle. The incumbent Senator was an old-fashioned liberal, Ralph Yarborough—out of step with the new Texas, George Bush's Texas. The state was changing—Bush knew it, just as surely as Nixon beat Kennedy in Houston, last time—but old Yarborough hadn't got the wake-up call. He was still traveling the state in his white suit and big white hat, promising the world. . . . Bush *knew* he could take him. Jeez, even Lyndon couldn't stand Yarborough (Yarborough called Johnson "power mad"). And now that LBJ was Vice President—that had to hurt Yarborough, didn't it? Johnson would be running with Kennedy again—that was the good news for the Democrats. But people didn't vote straight ticket anymore . . . LBJ on the ballot might even *help* Bush . . . *everybody* knew how Lyndon hated Yarborough.

So Bush started talking it up—Senator!—just to friends, at the start. And there were more than a couple who suggested that maybe he ought to go easy, take it slow . . . maybe run for office once, you know, something local, or *Congress* . . . how 'bout Congress first? But Bush didn't want to hear that. He was going to announce, September '63. He'd do it with a splash! He knew where he belonged—in the U.S. Senate. Jeez, almost a year now, and his father *still* regretted leaving the Senate.

Oh, God—Dad! . . . Big Pres could be a problem!

Prescott Bush was not a Goldwater man. In fact, he was just the kind of fellow that the eastern wing was counting on to get behind *someone decent* . . . like Rockefeller, or Lodge—or Bill Scranton . . . someone to stop that *nut,* Goldwater. In fact, just a year or so after retirement, Pres would have liked nothing better than to keep his hand in, at least in Connecticut.

But George called, asked him flat-out: Don't do it! It was bad enough, they were talking in the churches of Pasadena about Bush's father, the Senator, a *member* of the Council on Foreign Relations! If he came out against Goldwater . . .

And so, Pres had to swallow it down, for his son. The torch had passed . . . to young George. It was his turn. Prescott Bush sat on his hands in '64. The whole campaign through, he could barely say a word. He confirmed and completed his sad political exile.

And in Texas, George Bush started campaigning in earnest. He'd have to have men in the field—area chairmen! It was time to make his move—so he called a meeting . . . and, as his first appointment, he turned to that slimeball Bircher, Gene Crossman, and appointed *him* to head up East Texas.

Well, that was too much for the ladies. One of the veterans, Linda Dyson, heard about Crossman, and she marched up the stairs of HQ, right to the front bedroom, George's office . . . where she flung open the door, and shouted in Bush's frozen face:

"George Bush! Y'know what your problem is? . . . You don't know the difference between a common man and a *common* common man."

— ★ —

But he knew how to make a man feel special—and that's what he did, all over the state. Bush had a four-man primary, and one of his opponents was Jack Cox, another young comer, a hot stump speaker who'd already run for Governor (and gave John Connally a run for his money).

Bush—well, he wasn't much on the stump. He'd get cranked up, dive into a twisty river of a sentence, no noun, a couple or three verbs in a row, and you wouldn't know where he was headed—sometimes for minutes at a stretch, while his hands sawed and pulled at the air, smacked on the podium, drew imaginary lines and boxes without name, without apparent reference to what he was talking about, which you couldn't exactly tie down, unless you caught a key word, now and then, like "Sukarno," or "taxes," or "lib-rull" (that one came up a lot), although you could tell it really hacked him off, the way his voice rose through the octaves—until he emerged on the other side of the Gulf of Mexico, red in the face, pleased as hell with himself, spluttering out the predicate, or maybe the direct object of that second-last verb, and a couple more random words that had occurred to him in the meantime, and you could see he cared, and it all went together in his mind, but it wasn't clear exactly how, or what it was he thought was so damned *important*.

Fortunately, there weren't many speeches required in the primary, which was a meet-the-folks affair in most Texas towns, where you could still get the registered Republicans into a single room. He did covered-dish dinners, cocktail parties, barbecues . . . and he was beautiful. He'd talk to everybody one-on-one, and they loved him. He was so eager to know about them! And he already had Party-official friends, after his year as chairman; and he knew all the oilmen, and a lot of fellows in business; and old neighbors, guys who'd drifted down from Yale . . . no one ever slipped off his screen. And after every dinner, every barbecue or picnic, Bush'd get back on his plane, and ask his area chairman: "Who're the ten people I wanna thank in Pecos?" And he'd do those ten notes before he was halfway home. Back in Houston, he'd do a few dozen more, banging them out on his own machine, with typos and x-outs and other endearing steno foibles, all explained in the top-right corner of the note, where he'd put: "Self-typed by GB."

Well, it worked like a charm. As did the Bush Bandwagon, a busful of friends dropped off in some neighborhood, working door-to-door from lists the volunteers had prepared . . . and not just in River Oaks or Tanglewood, but anywhere there were Republicans. They'd work in couples—safer that way— and Bar'd go with George's friend, a sweet-natured insurance man named Jack Steel. Jack was a bit older, and Bar already had her white hair, and everybody thought she must be Jack's wife—they used to laugh about that. They laughed about so many things: one man came to the door in his underpants; one woman hawked up a big gob, spat it into the flowerpot; once, the bus lost Bar and Jack, and they sat on a curb under a streetlight till ten o'clock . . . but she loved it. She became a campaigner. It wasn't politics with her—it was just for George. Her attitude was simple: it was anything he wanted to do.

Sometimes, they'd load up the bus and carry the whole show hundreds of miles across the state. They'd carry along a cowboy band, the Black Mountain Boys, who'd draw a crowd that Bush would ply with lemonade . . . and they'd dress up the gals in red, white, and blue, with white skimmer hats that said BUSH BELLES on the bands, and sashes with painted bluebonnets, that read BLUEBONNET BELLES FOR BUSH. Bar made purses for all the Bush Belles with a needlepoint elephant, and BUSH in big white letters. She must have made a hundred—the steady volunteers got handbags, too.

It was mostly volunteers in the big Houston office, an abandoned ballet school in an old loft on Main Street. The place was grungy, but the mirrors on the long walls made it look like there were hundreds of workers. And you couldn't beat the rent . . . or the maintenance: whenever anything broke down—plumbing, air conditioning . . . happened all the time—instructions were to call George's friend Bake. His daddy owned the building. Bake was a local lawyer—husband of a Bush Belle—James A. Baker III. Aleene Smith came over from the Party office, to keep the operation in line. (Anyway, she couldn't have stayed with the Party: when George resigned as County Chairman, the Birchers took over . . . Kernel Napalm at the helm . . . their first act was to throw out every scrap of paper that mentioned George, or Bush for Senate.)

Houston was the biggest operation in the state. (C. Fred Chambers worked from Houston: he was Finance Chairman. The Bush family worked from Houston, too: George W.—Junior—seventeen that year, poured his heart into that campaign, all summer.) But Bush also set up a statewide office in the capital, Austin. He wouldn't concede any bit of the state—not the Negro wards of Houston, or Dallas; not even the machine-Democrat Mexican shantytowns of the Rio Grande Valley—why shouldn't the GOP get Latin votes? Why couldn't Bush have friends there, too? . . . In Midland, heart of the oil patch, it seemed the whole town was out for Bush. Two weeks after his announcement, they scheduled a rally, strung a huge BUSH banner right across Wall Street; thirty oil wives and daughters dressed as Bush Belles; they rented the auditorium at San Jacinto Junior High—packed the place! A thousand people came . . . in Midland! George's local chairman, Martin Allday, an old friend, an oil and gas lawyer, did the introducing that night:

"Ladies and gentlemen . . . the only man I have personally known, who I thought should one day be President . . ."

But Bush was a long way from President—even Senator. There were 254 counties in Texas (in an area wider than New York to Chicago; longer than Chicago to Birmingham), and 200 of them never had a real Republican organization. Bush probably worked through half himself, and he had an amazing personal grasp of his affairs: by June '64, when he'd won a plurality in the primary, and beat Jack Cox head to head in a run-off (cleaned his clock: won better than sixty percent!); by the time Martin Allday left his law practice in Midland and moved to Austin to take over campaign management, Bush could run through the state, without any notes, county by county, knew the names of major supporters in each. Problem was, the list wasn't long enough. And by that time, Kennedy was dead, LBJ was President—he'd clobber Goldwater in Texas . . . and his name at the top of the ticket would pull thousands of extra Democrats to the polls, to give their favorite son his own full term in the White House.

Still, Bush was sure he could pull it off. He could feel things changing, everywhere he went. Bush for a Greater Texas! . . . Bush for a Greater America! . . . George Bush was the youth, the future: his brochures showed a bold young man charging into a crowd, his suitcoat slung over one shoulder . . . it was the style of "vigor," the style of a Kennedy. And he was sure he knew the people—he made *thousands* of new friends, he could *feel it* . . . they *liked* him! If he could just hang the lib-rull label on Yarborough . . . if he could just show the people that old phony was a *giveaway artist* . . . if he could just attack hard enough, long enough. . . . That was George's method, from the start. That's what state Party leaders had *told him to do:* attack, and keep attacking.

Alas, he was not that good on attack. It never seemed natural with him, no matter how many times he did it. The general election was all stump speeches, six to eight a day, with plane or bus trips in between. After weeks of this, Bush had a standard speech: Sukarno, the UN, foreign aid, taxes, the oil industry . . . but it never added up to a picture of Bush, or any kind of message—except Yarborough was too lib-rull. When he'd get onto Yarborough, Bush's voice would start to climb, his hands would leap up and slash the air—you couldn't tell where the hell he was going, except in a general drift to the right. And the farther right he drifted, the more frantic he became: Bush always screamed and sawed the air harder when he had to convince himself that he believed. . . .

Yarborough was *un-Texan!* . . . *left wing!* . . . *selling our state down the river!* . . . Bush opposed the new Civil Rights Act and lambasted Yarborough for voting to choke off a filibuster on it . . . Bush said America ought to get the hell out of the UN, if that organization seated the Red Chinese . . . Congress ought to cut off foreign aid if those foreign commie-leaning tinhorns didn't wanna play ball . . . the U.S. ought to arm the Cuban exiles . . . and get *tough* in Vietnam (including use of nuclear weapons—if that's what the military called for).

But the harder he screamed, the more he played into Yarborough's hands. LBJ was demolishing Goldwater by painting him as a right-wing extremist, a warmonger, a mad bomber . . . so Yarborough hopped on board: George Bush,

Yarborough said, was so extreme, so far out in right field . . . (What's that my opponent wants? *The H-bomb? . . . in Vitt-namm?*) . . . Why, no wonder that boy was . . . the darling of the *Birchers*!

The Birchers! George's friends couldn't believe it! You couldn't get those right-wing nuts to *say* the name Bush . . . without spitting. But how could you explain that to everyone in Pecos, or Waco, Brownsville, Texarkana? . . . How could you convince anybody, with George Bush out there, screaming himself hoarse?

Martin Allday, the new Campaign Manager, had a long talk with George one night, after hearing that stump speech. Maybe Bush should just, you know, try to be more like himself. . . . No, Bush said. He was doing what he had to. He had to attack, if he wanted to win . . . and he could win! He knew he was getting to Yarborough now, with those wild charges the Senator made. And Yarborough refused to debate him. "We got him on the run!" George said. He'd heard old Yarborough speak at a picnic—it was *scandalous*! The man just promised anything he could think of! That's why it was so important, Bush said. We need honest people in government. Honest people, together, can do good things for the country.

Bush wasn't shouting now, and he talked to Martin for a half-hour straight, about what the campaign meant to him. He talked about his father, how he'd served . . . how George felt that's why he was here: to serve . . . and about the notion of duty, courage . . . and what was *right*, what was *right in this country* . . . how it must be protected . . . that's why George had to serve.

And Martin, who loved Bush anyway, was moved: it made him feel *good, clean, excited* to be doing something like this. So he said to Bush:

"Why don't you say *that*? . . ."

"Nah."

That was private stuff.

And C. Fred Chambers heard Yarborough talking about his war record, so he said to Bush: "Why don't you mention your own service? Give people a feel for your life . . ."

"Nah . . . I'd just feel funny doing that."

He wasn't going to start thumping his chest, let *politics* change the way he was!

And George's brother, Johnny, heard him speak, and suggested a coach. Johnny was an actor—he knew the ropes—he knew a coach who could help. "Just so you can put your point across! . . ."

"Nah."

He wasn't gonna start acting now. He had Yarborough on the run!

He did get under the old man's skin: Yarborough wouldn't debate, so Bush and Allday invented the empty-chair debates. They'd rent a hall and advertise, and when the crowd got settled, they'd bring out Bush, and an empty chair. Then they'd play a tape of Yarborough speaking, and Bush would blast away at him—at his empty chair. Then they'd play another minute of the tape, and Bush would blast away again. It got ink in the papers—always a picture, too. Bush heard Yarborough was so pissed off, he threatened to sue.

But Yarborough never had to call in lawyers. He called in Lyndon, instead. In the home stretch, just as Bush felt he was making his move, pulling even, maybe pulling away (he couldn't be sure—he'd run out of money for polls) . . . LBJ flew back to Texas.

Sure, Lyndon hated Ralph Yarborough. Could not abide the man—said so a hundred times—but hell was gonna freeze over *twice* before he'd let Texas send *two* Republican Senators to Washington. He'd left the state alone for a minute, and for Chrissake got John Tower in *his seat*! This time, he'd keep ahold of the bacon: even if it was Yarborough bacon.

So Lyndon flew in, with the whole White House fanfare . . . and in front of, seemed like, half the cameras in the world, he categorically endorsed Yarborough, he *physically* endorsed Yarborough. Gave him a hug that nearly disappeared him.

Of course, the photo made the front of every paper. This was Lyndon come home! What the hell, this was the *President* . . . which still meant a good big deal in Texas.

Meant a good big deal to George Bush, too. When LBJ flew into Houston to endorse his opponent, Bush called Aleene at the ballet studio on Main Street . . . with instructions:

"I want everybody to go downstairs when the motorcade passes, and wave to the President."

"You gotta be kidding."

"No. Everybody downstairs."

It was a matter of respect—the personal code. He couldn't let politics change something like that.

— ★ —

Two nights before the end of the campaign, Yarborough went on TV for his last statewide address: there he was, painting Bush into the mad-bomber corner again. He asked his audience: "Doesn't he understand the terrible consequences of the atom bomb? The fallout . . . disease . . . cancer, leukemia?"

George had bought time for the following night. He was having a rubdown at the Houston Club, just before his last speech. Martin Allday stood by the white table, while the masseur worked on Bush's back.

"George? . . ."

"NgThe masseurnnnn?"

"You could really hit him in the teeth with that . . . you know, leukemia." Martin was thinking about Robin, the daughter who'd died.

"I know," Bush said. And then, softly: "I'm not gonna bring family . . . bring it up."

So he just went on with the UN . . . taxes . . . lib-rulls—the standard stump. Then he went to his last rally, at the Whitehall Hotel in Houston. You could see it on him like a light from above: George thought he could win. So did the crowd. They loved him like people loved the Kennedys. They were wild for him.

But the next day, LBJ swept the country, and swept Yarborough in behind him. The final count was fifty-six percent for Yarborough, forty-four for Bush. The Latin votes, Negro votes, which Bush had sought all over the state—they went straight-lever Democrat. The Birchers—their precincts went Goldwater, eight-to-two, but they took a walk on the Senate.

At the ballroom Bush had rented for his victory celebration, George W. Bush—Junior—sat with his back to the crowd, in tears. Aleene found him, sat herself down, said: "Can I cry with you?" And she did.

Martin Allday was crushed, couldn't forgive himself ("I just, by God, hurt in the stomach, for the next three weeks").

But George came to the podium late that night, and congratulated the Senator—who, he said, beat him fair and square. He'd looked around, Bush said, for someone to blame . . . and only found himself.

And the next day, George and Bar were in the office, to help clean up. Bar was a little weepy. But George, he'd spent the whole night calling people to thank them . . . and they were so *nice*!

What the hell? He'd got more votes than any Republican in the history of Texas. He said to friends:

"Don't worry. That's only the start."

30

1965

YOU HAD TO UNDERSTAND how Joe was about girls—so sentimental, sweet, even though he seemed such a ladies' man. Sure, he had all the dates he wanted: with that manly chin, the dazzle of teeth in the Biden smile, his bright blue eyes, his bushy hair brushed to the side—he was gorgeous. Then there was the way he carried himself on the Delaware campus: like the whole place was his backyard. You could spot him in a crowd of a thousand: tall, slender in his coat and tie, smoothly self-possessed, with an athlete's grace (though he'd stopped playing football after freshman year). Well, no mystery why there were dozens of girls—all of Val's friends, for instance—who'd drop anything if he looked their way.

But you really had to hear him talk about girls to understand—had to hear, first off, what he didn't say. Even with his buddies, the guys, locker-room pals, he never talked about what he did with girls, what they did with him, how he scored. Nobody'd even say that stuff *to* Joe—nobody who knew him. Joe had the Catholic-boys-school view: there were nice girls, and not-nice girls. Joe dated nice girls. If you asked about a girl he was dating, Joe was the kind who'd say: "You know . . . I could marry her. I really could."

But he was just trying out the picture in his head. He'd been saying that about his dates since high school—that's how long he'd been looking for the one. Meanwhile, he was nice to them all. Very gentlemanly, in a traditional way, was Joe Biden—and protective . . . just about drove Val nuts. When she enrolled at Delaware, big brother Joe was a junior BMOC . . . who insisted that he know every guy she went out with. He had to take care of her, and her friends—especially the homely ones: at dances, he'd make a point of talking to them.

That was the winter, her freshman year, Joe took Val skiing. They went to Snow Mountain. He put her skis on, and showed her how to snow-plow. Then he took her to the top of the mountain. "Joe, I can't do this!" Val protested. She'd never been on skis.

"Follow me," Joe said. "You're going down . . . you're a Biden."

That's how Joe carried himself.

Anyway, that's how he was on the slopes, on a date, in a car with the guys, in the campus halls as president of his class . . . there was nothing he couldn't do. Course work—that was another matter. A gentleman's C seemed good enough. It wasn't that Joe lacked the brains, or ambition. He probably had too much of both. It's just he didn't give a damn. He didn't want Harvard Medical School. Law school, probably, but it didn't much matter what law school. He didn't mean to practice—not for long. He was going into politics—Governor, or Senator. What the hell did Plato have to do with that?

He worked, instead, on the demanding curriculum of being Joe Biden. Everybody had to know him, like him, and trust him. He had to be the guy they could turn to, the one they could count on. He was a good friend, a good date, a good officer, a leader, a hell of a talker . . . a good brother, a good son . . . back and forth to Wilmington, to his family, his old friends, two or three times a week . . . still hanging out at the Charcoal Pit with the guys . . . they'd still spray each other with the first fire extinguisher they found in a building— just screwing around. . . . When was he supposed to study? Anyway, he got through—good enough—it wasn't hard.

Then, he went to Nassau—spring break, that same junior year, '64—and everything changed. Not all at once, no, but surely.

When he came back, he wanted the same things, had the same dreams—but all of a sudden he seemed to know how. It was like the dreams had become plans. Yes, he was going to law school—but he knew which school: Syracuse Law. He knew what he'd have to do to get there—and he'd do it, too. He saw the way. . . .

He saw her on the beach in Nassau. She was tall, almost five-eight, with long blond hair, green eyes, long lashes. She had a figure that . . . well, legs up to here and the rest defied gravity. She was a knockout—Neilia Hunter. She went to school at Syracuse—grew up around there, upstate New York. She said her folks ran a restaurant, but she might have come from money. She had that kind of confidence, poise. She wasn't flustered by Joe—not at all. He told her about himself, what he wanted, and she understood. She was smart. She was fun. She had a tan. She had class. She was the one. . . .

That was March; that spring, people saw the determination in Joe, a certain *gravitas*. He was busier, suddenly, on his own program. It wasn't that he hit the books so hard, or went to more classes. In fact, he cut all his Friday classes: he'd head out every Thursday—eighty miles an hour in his old Mercedes, north to Syracuse.

He showed up at her dorm, the weekend after they both came back. He was sitting in the lobby when Neilia told her friend Bobbie Greene, he was downstairs, the guy she'd met, *Joe* . . . go look! So Bobbie crept to the landing, and there he was, in a chair, with his long legs crossed. She checked him out: he had a tan now, too, a white shirt, that smile of white teeth, and those *eyes* . . . "God, he's incredible," Bobbie confirmed.

"You know what he said?" Neilia confided softly. "He told me he's going to be a Senator by the time he's thirty. And then, he's going to be President."

— ★ —

That May, he brought her to visit in Delaware, and they went to the beach. She could have taken the place by storm in a bikini, but she came with a simple one-piece suit. She didn't flaunt her looks. Some of Joe's friends were a bit disappointed when they met her—you know, they'd heard so much. . . . But she could put her hair up, glasses on—and pass for a librarian. If she combed her hair down, put on a dress, flashed her smile—she was dazzling.

In fact, she could look any way she wanted. And act any way, too. It just depended on making sure other people were comfortable. That was the same way she was about her brains: she didn't want to put people off. And there was ever a hint of the child in the way she spoke—a softness, which led people (especially men) to think they could put one over on her. But she saw everything. This was something beyond savvy: she had a sixth sense for how the other person felt. If there was a party, and someone was uneasy, it was radar: Neilia would be there, instantly.

That was the essence of Neilia's grace. It wasn't that she didn't have her own character—just the reverse: she knew who she was so surely that she didn't have to spend a minute proving that. She was a preppy by training, graduate of a fancy school called Penn Hall. But her parents never let her forget that they made their money in a diner: they were of the common clay. In fact, Robert and Louise Hunter still worked every day in the Auburn Diner, which was a hangout for kids—and Neilia was ever the princess there. Maybe that's where she learned her touch. . . . When she put on a party for the folks in Syracuse, everything had to be perfect . . . but when old George, the Armenian kitchen worker, blundered into the room, she brought him forward and introduced him, just as if he were a professor from Cornell.

That's what made her the one for Joe—that style, that grace, that giving, that . . . well, for once, he was lost for words. And when he got his first look at the Hunters' grand house on the lake, at Skaneateles, a huge place with a winding staircase, hidden dens, a sunroom that looked out on the long sweep of lawn down to the dock . . . now, that was class! And the way people gathered there—Neilia's friends, and her brothers' friends, the neighbors . . . it was just like the Bidens, only . . . well, more settled, older, refined. Joe was on his best behavior, sure enough, when he met the Hunters, though they couldn't have been nicer. Her mother was a down-to-earth woman, and she was the one who asked Joe what he meant to become.

"President," Joe answered.

For a moment, she just stared.

Joe added helpfully: "Of the United States."

By the end of one weekend, Mrs. Hunter had to concede: maybe the kid could make it. That boy could sure talk.

—★—

Senior year, he made the run to Syracuse almost every weekend. That's where he did his planning, in the car—he saw the moves in his head.

Joe did well on his LSATs—scored better than six hundred—so Syracuse offered him a partial scholarship. He'd got that piece locked into place.

Up there, law school, fall of '65 . . . then he'd ask Neilia to marry him . . .

They'd get married. Three years, *'68, he'll be out*—they'd head back to Delaware. That's where people knew him.

Neilia'll love the place . . .

That year, '68, the governorship would be up for election—but that'd be too soon . . . *he'd have to watch for his opening, make his move—it wouldn't be long* . . .

Governor Joseph R. Biden, Jr.

Senator Joseph R. Biden, Jr.

Joe Biden . . . for Delaware.

People'll say he's too young . . . but he'd use that . . . a fresh wind—he'd get the kids, hundreds of kids. *A young people's campaign* . . . they'd work *every street, every house* . . .

They'd hand out brochures. He saw the brochures. Him and Neilia. And the children . . .

They'd start a family—*a big family, big house*—he'd have to make some money before he ran . . . maybe real estate. *Have to get known, too*—in the city, everywhere upstate—his home county, New Castle: that's where the votes were.

There were only three counties in Delaware—a hundred thousand votes would win any race. And two-thirds of the votes were in the northernmost county, around Wilmington . . . Joe knew, *he could win it there.*

Not attacking, no . . . time for a change . . . *a new generation* . . . people said Kennedy was too young. But he'd show them. *A new generation, a new voice, time for a change.*

Joe Biden, For the Future . . .

Initially, political professionals dismissed the chances of the young challenger . . .

Joe could see the story in the papers, day after the vote. He could see the whole thing like it'd already happened. They'd wake up, and he'd be there, roaring by like a rocket!

They'd try to stop him . . .

Folks, I guess my opponent kind of took me for granted—took all of us for granted, but . . .

He could hear himself say it . . . six hours on the road . . . his victory speech . . .

When he got to Syracuse, he'd tell Neilia the new plan, exactly what he was going to say—when he was rolling, see, and they'd try to stop him, he'd say . . .

She'd always listen. But she'd also tell him the thing they had to take care of . . . today. She was organized in a way he wasn't, in the present. People used to tease her about being late. *Always* late—her friends used to lie to her, tell her to come an hour ahead of time . . . that way, she'd only be a bit late. But it was only because she was focused on this minute, this room, this person . . . now. Most people didn't see the organization. Her family knew: her mother, who could never find anything, would always call Neilia. "Mom," she'd say, "it's in the bottom drawer, in the back, under the red sweater . . ."

And Joe knew. That was his new confidence. It wasn't cocksureness—he'd always had that. This was quieter. He could do anything, everything he wanted, with Neilia. She'd take care of him. She'd take care of everyone else, too. He had the big piece of the puzzle locked in; now he could see the outlines of the others. He could live even more in the future, eyes to the horizon . . . because he knew Neilia saw the path at their feet.

When he graduated, he moved straight to Syracuse. He could have moved into the big house on the lake—plenty of room, no problem, he was welcome . . . but you had to understand how Joe was about this. They weren't married yet. It might not have looked right. He took a room in a boardinghouse—he'd live there for more than a year—while he ran back and forth to Neilia's.

— ★ —

That's what he did his first year of law school: back and forth to the Hunters' house . . . a little waterskiing in the afternoons . . . dinner dates at spaghetti joints with Neilia. Then, too, there was football or basketball with his new pals at school . . . and riding around in the Chevy that Joe, Sr., gave him for a present. Joe told his pals he always had a new car in high school—brand-new Chrysler 300—whenever he had a date or something . . . you know, his dad ran the dealership. He preened, too, about his driving—without question, Joe was the best driver *ever*. "You know I broke my record: four hours and seventeen minutes to Wilmington—six-hour trip."

That's the same way he was about sports: Biden was just . . . too good. Some guys thought he *must* have lettered at Delaware—they started hearing stories that Biden *broke every record* at Delaware . . . for God's sake, he was *Little All-American* . . . the only reason he'd fool with Syracuse intramurals was to get in shape for his *tryout with the Baltimore Colts*. . . . That's the way he carried himself: "If there was an Olympic event in football," Joe said, "I'd *be* in the Olympics."

In short, if Biden could have sucked as hard as he blew, Syracuse would have been a seaport.

But not with the guys who knew him best . . . and not about academics. Most of his friends figured if they didn't copy their notes for Biden (and make sure the notes got to Neilia so she'd read them) . . . there was no way in hell Joe was going to make it to the second year!

Joe himself blew hot and cold about his prospects. Most of the time, he was aw-shucks . . . Syracuse was going to cut a third of the class—it'd be a damn miracle if he didn't flunk. . . . But if anyone *else* suggested that Biden might not make the cut—well, Joe was ready to step outside and *settle* who was smarter. "I'll tell you something you guys may not know: I can learn more of this shit in *one day* . . . than you're gonna get if you study three weeks!"

Joe sure as hell wasn't going to be a grind. He didn't need to be one of the four or five top guys in the class—the ones who'd get the call from the big Wall Street firms. He didn't want to be a professor or a Supreme Court clerk. He was going back to Delaware; he just had to get through, pass the bar. And Syracuse *couldn't* be that tough . . . that's how Joe had it figured: They took him, didn't they?

They'd take a hundred twenty guys (it was almost always guys, in those days) and let about eighty-five come back for the final two years. It wasn't that the competition was so hot—some of those guys you wouldn't let fix a flat. But the cut was enough to put the wind up a lot of them. They worked like rats in a box! They'd get the assignments and skip lunch, run to the library.

Joe would never do that! . . . Problem was, he'd *never* run to the library— he'd stay in the students' lounge. The other problem was, the rats in the box saw that. Hell, you'd have to be blind *not* to see it: Biden didn't think he had to scramble, like them.

That's how he got into trouble, in fact—with that shithead Artie Cooper. It was in Legal Methods class, which was no big deal, just a course on how to cite a case, type up a brief . . . sort of trade-school stuff. Joe didn't pay it much mind. It was form, not content. He knew he could write. He'd hire someone to type the stuff up.

But in this course, they'd divide the students into groups, and then they'd grade one another's papers. The point was, the teachers wanted to see not only how you wrote a brief, but how you could rip one apart, too.

So Joe handed in his crappy brief—he didn't spend much time on it. He found a *Fordham Law Review* piece on the subject—"diversity jurisdiction"— and he took several cases from that. Thing was, when he took the facts of those cases from the law review, he took the journal's description of the facts. And then he copied the footnotes, too.

Anyway, Artie Cooper got Joe's paper for correction, and of course he saw where the whole thing came from—hell, Joe didn't try to hide it: he footnoted the law review piece at the end . . . but only once. So Cooper started acting like Joe was trying to pull a fast one—those weren't *his* citations, *his* research. . . . Well, Joe *was* trying to pull a fast one, but no faster than normal, no faster than the rest of the shit he had to pull to get through law school. But Cooper went mental! Artie didn't just rip up the research—he took Joe's paper to the teacher!

Well, the teaching assistant was a first-year guy, a local lawyer helping out, and he didn't know what to do with this, so he took it to the professor . . . and then the dean! All of a sudden, it was a federal case. *The dean* wanted Biden to write a letter—his version of what happened.

Of course, Biden was sick to death. Not to mention pissed off. What he would have liked to do was hammer Cooper into the ground like a tent stake. But that wouldn't help. Plus, then everybody would know. It would look awful. Nobody was gonna say that Joe Biden cheated. That just wasn't *him* . . . so what he had to do was write his letter, and show up at a faculty meeting to defend himself: he didn't mean to dissemble. He didn't know—*word as a Biden*. . . . He hadn't realized it *mattered,* where those citations came from, if he was only using the facts of the cases—he wasn't taking their conclusions! It was just a mistake!

Well, Joe was good on his feet. And he *had* them, in that room that day—he could feel it. They liked him . . . they believed him. But they couldn't just drop it—not after shithead Artie turned it into Murder One . . . so what they did was, they flunked him in that course, and let him take it again. Big deal.

He took it again, and did fine—got a B, which was a pretty good grade on Joe's transcript.

By the end of that first year, it was *Joe* who was just about mental. He must have read a million pages in the last three weeks. One test—for the whole damn year!—he had to get hot. Game day!

But he did it. By a hair's width. He ranked eightieth in the class, and they cut from eighty-eight down. . . . Well, what of it? He made the cut, like he said he would. . . . Hell, he had it figured from the start.

— ★ —

And that summer, he married Neilia. It was just like he'd imagined. No—it was better. It was a Saturday, August 27, 1966, and the day was glorious, with sunlight pouring down on three hundred guests at the country club, and sparkling on the water at the foot of the Hunters' lawn. They did the service at St. Mary's, Our Lady of the Lake—though Neilia was not Catholic, and didn't plan to convert.

It was just like her, how she thought about that: she did consider converting—her religious beliefs and Joe's were so alike—but then she thought she might somehow, someday, come to resent her conversion. And she didn't want anything like that to come between them. She didn't want to have anything to hold over Joe's head. She knew herself so well, see . . . just how she was.

And she knew what she wanted—to the smallest detail. Her bridesmaids' gowns were long and completely straight from the neck to the floor—chiffon—in a shade between deep pink and deep red. She could have had their shoes dyed the same shade, but no—she wanted them green, to pick up the ivy in their bouquets of three white roses. Her own dress was stunningly simple: white brocaded lace that took her shape to the waist, with a long straight skirt, no train. She wore a chapel veil, with a headpiece intertwined

with ivy, to match the greenery and shoes of her bridesmaids, and the matching
ivy to set off her own white roses in profusion. . . .

She was, as Joe would often tell her, the most beautiful woman he had ever
seen.

But he looked every bit her match that day, in his striped pants, gray
tailcoat, and pearly silver waistcoat. In fact, all the Bidens looked splendid:
Joe's sister, Val (every bit the princess of her own world), was Neilia's maid
of honor. And handsome brother Jimmy stood next to Joe, as best man. And
the father! Such a distinguished man!

There were some guests at the country club who thought the Bidens must
be quite a family in Delaware . . . to have such style—must be rich! Everything
about them looked so *perfect.* . . . Wasn't that part of their crowd landing in
a *seaplane*? Right there on the lake!

Neilia, of course, knew it was one of Joe's classmates who'd rented the
seaplane. She had no illusions of Biden wealth, Biden power. (On their second
date, she had to slip Joe a twenty under the table, so he could pay the tab at
the restaurant.) But she was very proud to become a Biden, and she understood, with her unerring instinct, exactly what it meant, how important it was
for everything to look *perfect.* . . . That's how she explained it to friends, later:
you just had to understand how Joe was.

31

Saturday Night

I
T WAS A MEASURE of his own mentality of siege that Hart didn't call the cops when he spotted the stakeout. Still, he couldn't quite believe it. It was so obvious, it was . . . comedic. There must have been five or six of these guys on the street and sidewalk across from his townhouse, and he saw they meant to look like neighbors—dressed in jogging suits, windbreakers, and such—but they kept checking with each other, at their car. Who the hell would be so *amateurish*?

He'd spotted the guy in the parka first—a *parka*—in May! He pointed him out to Donna Rice—it was Saturday night, they were walking to Hart's car, on their way to Bill Broadhurst's for dinner—and Hart told her, they were being watched. They turned right away and went back to the house. Gary meant to be calm. He was calm. It was just, suddenly . . . he was walking too fast for her.

Hart's front window, the kitchen window, gave a view of the street. He peeked out. Were they cops? Capitol Hill was a rough neighborhood, a lot of drugs . . . but they were watching *his house*. Were these guys from another campaign? What campaign desperadoes would *dare*? . . . No, they had to be press—were there cameras? Was there a van, or something, with a hidden camera?

Who were these guys?

What could he do?

Whom should he call?

He thought about the cops, but that would be a mess, and humiliating. What

would he say? *There're these GUYS, watching me, they're always WATCHING
. . . you have to make them STOP!*

Yeah, sure, okay, Senator, just calm down now.

Was he supposed to have his own muscle—guys in bulging suits, who'd take
care of snoopers? *Uh, nice car you got there, fellas. Shame if it should get
smashed up, parked out here on the street like this.*

What had his world come to? He was being stalked, at his own house.
Whoever these guys were, whomever they represented, Hart was sure of one
thing: he was their prey. The awful part was, he wasn't even shocked. He'd
felt hounded for weeks, ever since announcement—those *stories* . . .

Later—years later—he'd be asked: Wasn't he pissed off? Furious? But after
all that time (maybe because of it), Hart would not admit to anger.

He'd say he realized that night: it would never stop. He saw those guys on
his street and he knew: the whole campaign, he'd be prey. They'd never leave
him alone, with this *stuff* . . . his marriage, his debts, his name, his age
. . . he was facing another year and a half of fighting for his life—one damned
thing after another, he said—five years, or ten, if he won. And there wasn't
any way he could change that . . . change *them.*

He would say: he felt "just sad."

And worried.

But he was in his own home.

He hadn't robbed any banks.

He didn't shoo Donna Rice away, or shove her into a closet.

He didn't call anybody—save for Broadhurst. "There's somebody watching
this place," Hart said. "I don't *know* who. . . . I don't think we ought to leave.
Why don't you bring the dinner over here?"

Like anyone besieged, Hart's first thought was to shut the gates and stay in.
He'd be safer—he'd wait. Maybe they would go away.

— ★ —

The guys from Miami never had a doubt:

Big story!

Amazing!

Part of it was the way it happened—it was like fate. It started with the
rumors. Then Tom Fiedler, *The Miami Herald*'s political big-foot, wrote a
column *defending* Hart against the rumors, and some woman called to complain: *How can you defend him? He's having an affair with a friend of mine!*

Who's the friend?

No names were named.

Fiedler tried to blow off the caller, but she phoned again. She offered
pictures. She reported on calls from Hart to her friend. She said they went on
a *cruise*—Hart and this gorgeous blonde! She said her friend was flying from
Miami to D.C., *this weekend, to meet Hart!*

Well, you couldn't *not* sniff around.

And when the caller's dates checked out, and Hart headquarters said Gary had canceled Kentucky that weekend and was taking some time off in Washington, well . . .

"What flight?" Fiedler asked his source.

She said she'd call back, but she didn't.

So it was just a roll of the dice when the *Herald*'s top investigative hit man, Jim McGee—two hundred pounds, all swathed, for reasons unknown, in a parka—sprinted for a cab outside the newspaper office, whipped the driver to a lather for the airport, and made standby on Eastern's flight 996, the first nonstop from Miami to Washington that Friday night.

He saw three blondes—two pretty ones. He walked up the aisle of the plane to get a good look. He tried to watch them deplane. One of the blondes met a boyfriend. The other was met by a dark-haired woman . . . no Gary Hart, no campaign types.

What could McGee do? He got Hart's address—Sixth Street, SE—and went to take a look. At the end of Hart's block, and across the street, there was a park. McGee found a bench, sat down to watch the door, and an hour later, here came Hart . . . *with the second blonde from the plane*!

Holy shit! It's HER!

It was like God Himself had thrust this juicy pork chop into their mouths! . . . After that, it was a rush of phone calls, rent-a-cars, and fresh manpower (a photographer!) from Miami . . . *Chrissake, get up here!* . . . They had to tie this down!

It was Friday night when McGee spotted Hart and the blonde leaving Hart's house, late Friday night when McGee saw Hart and the blonde reenter the house. It was Saturday morning when the rest of the *Herald* troops boarded a plane in Miami, almost noon Saturday by the time they showed up on Sixth Street, with three more rent-a-cars. Someone, besides McGee, *had to see* Hart and the blonde! (Hey! Two sources! This was, you know, an *investigative team*!) . . . So they're sitting with the pork chop in their mouths, for *hours*—it's HUGE, there's juice on their chins—but none of the Miamis had seen Hart *all day*, and then it was Saturday night, which meant . . . shit! They were gonna miss the Sunday paper.

Finally, 8:50 P.M., darkness again, and McGee, in the alley, saw Hart and the woman walking from the back of the house. McGee made for the street, whispered to Fiedler, who trotted by in his jogging suit. Fiedler crossed the street to the park so Hart wouldn't spot him: Hart would know his face. Hart and the woman were headed for Hart's car. . . . But then, they turned and walked back to the house.

Fiedler thought Hart looked spooked.

This was big!

Of course it was . . . Hart was *in there*, in his *house*, with this, this . . . this *cutlet*! From MIAMI! . . . She was young, she was blond, she was . . .

Who was she?

They didn't know.

What was she doing in there?

They didn't know.

But, come *on*—what do you *think* they were doing in there?

Anyway, what did it matter?

This was legit—a *political* story—because the guy had spent the last few weeks *denying* . . . well, denying stories like this!

— ★ —

Broadhurst came over with Donna's friend, Lynn Armandt—and with barbecued chicken for dinner. But no one paid much attention to dinner. Hart was fidgety, stiff with worry and suppressed rage. What were those guys *after*?

He'd been set up! He was sure he was being set up. They'd been following him! . . . Or maybe, the girl. Maybe they followed the girls! Maybe one of these girls in *his own kitchen* . . . had set him up! At once, Hart was distant, removed, and angry. Everybody felt it. Broadhurst thought they should leave—him and the girls—they should just get out. Broadhurst always knew what the other fellow wanted—or needed.

In the aftermath, months later, some of Hart's people would blame Bill Broadhurst for the whole mess. They'd say he was the one who invited Lynn Armandt to Washington, he was the one who made that weekend happen. There were true believers who could excuse Gary for hanging around with two young women—but they'd never forgive him for *Broadhurst*! The guy was a *fixer*—wasn't he? . . . He was a political back-scratchin' lawyer who made it big when his pal Edwin Edwards got to be Governor of Louisiana. The true Hart wonks wanted to know: Why would Gary connect himself, politically, with that sort of backroom dealer?

But it wasn't all politics with Broadhurst.

32

Bill and Gary and Lynn and Donna

RAY STROTHER, Hart's old ad man, introduced Bill Broadhurst to Hart after the '84 campaign. Broadhurst did a couple of political events, at his Washington house, for Hart—and they hit it off.

Like so many people who attracted Hart, Broadhurst was a man of personal ease. If Bill was sitting with Washington politicos, he could chat urbanely about press and polls. With good ol' boys from Louisiana, Billy B. could drink hard and tell raunchy stories.

Perhaps his greatest talent was discernment. With Hart, Broadhurst discerned two things right away.

Number one, Hart needed time away from Senate business, and, later, campaign business. Anyone could see that—everyone on Hart's staff, for instance. But who had the money to finance a weekend getaway to Turnberry Isle? Who among the Hart wonks even knew Turnberry Isle existed? . . . Billy B. knew. He also knew fine food and wine. And he could pick up a check.

The great thing was, Broadhurst didn't ask for anything in return. He didn't insist on his status as a player, didn't try to insinuate himself into strategy sessions, issues, or political meetings. Broadhurst just wanted to be of help . . . to Gary. And the greatest thing, for Hart: he didn't have to sit through a chat-fest with Broadhurst.

That was number two. Broadhurst sensed that Hart valued space and silence. That's why Hart liked to travel with Billy Shore. They could sit through a flight across the country in silence. Broadhurst quickly learned to keep quiet around Hart. Broadhurst could sit for hours on a boat without saying a word—and without expecting Hart to say a word.

At HQ in Denver, no one knew much about Broadhurst. He was impressive, with that gray hair (though he was three years younger than Gary) and his southern manner. They knew he was a lawyer from Louisiana, he had connections, he had money. He could travel at his own expense, to make contacts for Gary. They knew he had to have a desk set aside for when he was in town. That's all they knew.

He was certainly generous. There were never dollars wasted in the office on Downing Street: it was wholly Spartan—used desks and chairs, no luxuries. Broadhurst hadn't been there three days before he gave one of the workers a hundred dollars for a coffee urn and another hundred for a microwave. People could eat and drink—Broadhurst was a hero!

Then he started working with the field staff. He was good about coming by to ask what he could do for them. He'd mention that he was going to Kentucky, staying at the Governor's mansion. He'd see who Gary could line up down there, where he should stand on local races. Broadhurst was on the road for Hart more and more, as the winter waned in '87.

The first sign of trouble came at a schedule meeting, in February, in the conference room. There were meetings every day in that room—that hole without windows. Broadhurst had never sat in before. This time, on the new block schedule, a weekend trip to Puerto Rico had suddenly been cut to one day. The second day of that weekend, suddenly, had no events. And Casey wasn't arguing—which was weird. Usually, she'd *obsess* about a day . . . Christ, a *whole day*? There were so many days lost to the law firm, so many for Iowa, or New Hampshire—never time enough. A day was precious!

But Sue was silent. And she knew more about the schedule than anyone. Still, someone asked: "Well, uh, what is *this*?"

It was Broadhurst who answered, quickly and firmly: "There's an extra day. Gary wants it, and it's on there."

That was a day Bill and Gary were going out on the boat.

The way Broadhurst saw it, that was just one small thing he could do for Hart—give him time for relaxation . . . away from it all. That was important in any campaign, Broadhurst said, and though this was his first Presidential campaign, he could see it was probably more important than ever at this level.

"You've got to have mental relaxation and talk about other things," he would say. "You need space and time."

He meant, Gary did.

— ★ —

It was on a boat, a charter boat, the last weekend in March, that Broadhurst met Lynn Armandt. That was just happenstance. What happened was, Gary and Bill were down in Florida for a weekend on this boat . . . and Gary ran into Donna Rice, invited her back to the boat for dinner, then for a cruise . . . and Donna called Lynn Armandt to go along. Donna didn't want to go with two men, alone. And Lynn was fun, she'd get along fine with new people. Lynn would know how to act—she was sharp, a woman of business.

She had a very hip and knowing manner—casual, like her clothes—Miami Beach funky (unlike Donna, who spent her working days in business suits). They were both twenty-nine years old. Donna had only known Lynn a few months—they were mostly just workout buddies at the Turnberry health club . . . but Lynn lived at Turnberry Isle, so she could come out to the boat on a minute's notice—that's why Donna called her.

Lynn Armandt wasn't exactly part of the actress-model-TV crowd in Miami; she was more a part of the Turnberry Isle crowd. She was one of the people (good-looking, or rich, for the most part) who were given free memberships and encouraged to hang around. Lynn had never fooled with college— what for? She had her own shop, the Too Hot Miami bikini boutique at Turnberry, which was a good place for business—a fast crowd and plenty of cash.

She was ever a young woman with her eye on the main chance . . . which, of course, Bill Broadhurst discerned. Right away, on the boat, he started talking to her about a business opportunity. His law office in Washington needed someone to coordinate its social functions. The woman who'd held the job had left the firm. Would that be something of interest to Lynn?

Yes, it would.

So, early on, Bill said he would invite Lynn to Washington to talk more about the job. It may have been that whiff of business on the Florida air that made Lynn so sanguine about the time spent with Bill and Donna and Gary. As she later told *People* mag (business again—big cash for her story), Lynn had doubts about this boat trip, at the start. But with a lunch of lobster salad, cold asparagus, white wine . . . and a detailed account of Gary Hart's latest novel, from the author, who was "a great storyteller" . . . Lynn relaxed. "So she made no objection when she found the boat was headed for Bimini. 'I felt very comfortable.' "

In fact, none among them felt any pain, by late afternoon, as they steamed into Bimini and pitched up in a bar called The Compleat Angler. They drank more, talked more, and took over the bandstand. It was Donna and Lynn singing "Twist and Shout," Broadhurst on drums, Hart's merry fingers on the castanets. It was on the dock that Hart had his picture taken with Donna Rice on his lap. (Come to think of it, that was Lynn's idea.)

It was Donna's camera, and Donna's picture—never intended for public . . . well, public anything! She never did let the negative out of her possession. It was always her picture, *her property*—which was partly what would gall her so when it made its very public debut on the front page of the *National Enquirer*. (The *Enquirer* had the nerve to claim copyright on the photo!)

By that time, Donna would know . . . it was a terrible mistake to lend the photos from that weekend to Lynn Armandt. (But Lynn was so insistent—said she *had* to show her boyfriend!) . . . And especially that one of Donna on

Gary's lap. (Donna *never* would have lent *that* if Gary had already announced his candidacy.) . . .

Of course, by that time, Donna would know . . . Lynn sold her out at every turn. She wasn't any kind of buddy at all.

In the end, Lynn was just a woman of business.

— ★ —

How could Donna not have known?

Well, she was quick to trust, chatty and voluble, confiding—why wouldn't she be? At twenty-nine, she had progressed through her brief adulthood from success to success—people always liked Donna. And admired her: she was a *magna cum laude* graduate of the University of South Carolina (serious about her grades, that meant), she was a cheerleader—*head cheerleader* (a serious responsibility)—she was a successful model, and an actress in commercials, industrial films, a few small parts on TV shows. She was always hunting opportunity—though, in those days, she was more and more convinced it was time to move on from the life she'd built in Miami. Her steady line of work was in pharmaceutical sales for Wyeth Labs, and she was serious about it, as was her wont—top salesperson in her district that year. Friday night, you'd likely find her home reading Wyeth reports or the journal of the AMA; she'd order in pizza, maybe watch some TV until she could fall asleep.

She was intelligent.

Worldly she was not.

Mention some name in the news, for instance, and Donna would get this sweet and serious look on her face like she knew she might know it . . . but . . . no connect.

Of politics she was blessedly unaware.

For instance: she was going out for some time with the rock singer Don Henley (she'd met him by chance, in Los Angeles, a couple of years before), and she was at Henley's place in Aspen for this party, New Year's Day, 1987. She was in the kitchen getting ready to serve some food she had helped cook, and she met . . . Gary Hart.

"Can I get you anything?" said Donna Rice . . . in complete and innocent ignorance of Gary Hart's career, his run for the Presidency in 1984, his fore-ordained front-runnerhood for 1988. This was her first hint that Gary Hart was on the planet . . . and tell the truth, even then, she did not take much notice.

Tell the truth, if a friend had not been shooting videotape of the party, all afternoon . . . if Gary Hart had not taken ax to firewood, entertaining with his imitation of Abe Lincoln the rail-splitter . . . if Hart, thereby, had not got himself prominently into the video record . . . if Henley's intimates had not sat around, after the party, and watched this video, and talked about "Gary, Gary, Gary," remarking that here was a political leader of the *nation* . . . Donna would never have remembered the name.

The face, of course, was something else. That's what happened, that Friday night in March, when Donna was at a cocktail affair at Turnberry Isle—it was a charity benefit, crowded and frantic . . . and that's why Donna and a dozen folks she knew walked out to get some air. They strolled along the docks toward a boat they knew (they knew the owner, actually) . . . unaware that it had been chartered for the weekend and was occupied, even then, by two older men, who turned out to be Bill Broadhurst . . . and Gary Hart—who invited the whole crowd on board for a drink. That's when Donna got a good look at Gary, and said: "Hey! I know you!"

And that's how they started talking.

But what did she know?

She didn't know, for instance, he was married (though Lee was also at that party, in Aspen, New Year's Day) . . . she didn't know where he lived . . . she didn't know what he'd done in his life. He was just a person . . . a nice person.

And so interested in her—at least it seemed so, when he asked her to dinner the next day . . . and then Sunday, on the yacht.

That was certainly the reason she accepted . . . and called her friend Lynn to come along. They both, these men, seemed so interesting. And she made another call—to her dad, who'd probably know:

"I met this man, Gary Hart—what is he? A Congressman? . . . A Senator? . . . What state?"

—★—

In a way, that only made it better—fresher. He was so sweet, funny and serious at the same time, and he wanted to know what *she* thought. He didn't hold forth like some distant, self-important politician. He didn't presume at all.

And she hadn't been with him long before she realized how much he wanted to get away from all the political talk, the pressure . . . in fact, he was tormented: here was a man who had to choose between devotion to his country and personal happiness. He was facing a run for the *Presidency,* when really, he—half of him . . . *didn't want to campaign at all*! . . . Donna understood, right away: here was a man facing the crisis of his life.

What stirred in her was not passion, but compassion.

At the same time, she knew that fate had put her with a man of exceptional vision, just as she was searching out a new path for her own life. *Here was the world of politics,* a new world to her. . . . Gary said the *best* thing about his life in politics—the one thing that *excited him the most*—was the freshness and idealism of the young.

He was charmed by her.

And she knew it was awfully quick, but . . . well, she was more than charmed—though she knew this was not reality, that boat was not reality, at all . . . but she was more and more interested—fascinated was her word . . . just after a day and a couple of evenings on that boat, and the morning after the cruise, coming back from Bimini . . . after which Gary and Bill went to the Miami airport. Lynn and Donna stayed behind, and talked about Gary.

Lynn was the one Donna would confide in, when Gary called, after that. He'd call from the road, and say he was thinking about her, remembering.

Sometimes, he was so sweet, she didn't know what to think—or where things stood. One week, Lynn might try to tell Donna this could turn into something *serious.* Next time she'd say, maybe Donna should just break this off. And Donna was in turmoil—trying to sort out what she really felt. That's why she had to think long and hard when he called and invited her to Washington—beginning of May. And in the end, that's why she went—why she decided at the last minute to go—she wouldn't know *what she wanted* until she could see him again.

33

Saturday
Night II

HART COULDN'T SIT STILL any longer. He had to find out what those guys were doing—at least let them know he was on to them, they could stop sneaking around his house. Maybe he could scare them off.

He walked outside, he was very alert. He'd try to bait them—he called it "trolling." He wanted to be certain they were after *him*. He got into his car, drove a couple of blocks, parked again, and started walking through his neighborhood. He'd walk a block, turn the corner, stop . . . listen. Sure enough, here would come the footsteps behind him. Hart doubled back toward Sixth Street, and made sure to pass their car. He gave it a good once-over, including the two guys inside. He let them see he was writing down their license number. Then he walked down the alley behind his house.

Jim McGee, investigative reporter, and Jim Savage, his editor, got out of the car and followed Hart down the alley. They turned a corner . . . there he was.

They introduced themselves. They were nervous. Hart was leaning against a brick wall, in his white sweatshirt, arms crossed in front of his chest . . . like he was waiting for an explanation.

McGee was saying, they wanted to know about the young woman who was staying in Hart's house.

"No one is staying in my house," Hart said, quite precisely.

Well, then, they wanted to know, what was his relationship with the woman?

"I am not involved in any relationship."

Then why did two reporters just *see* Hart and this *woman* going into his house?

"The obvious reason is that I'm being set up."

The *Herald* reported that Hart's voice was shaking. The stories described him as "nervous and evasive." But Hart was stiff with fury. Somewhere, there had to be a *line* behind which there was private life. Surely, the door of his own home ought to be a boundary. As Hart recalled, the *reporters* were shaky. When Tom Fiedler, in his jogging suit, joined the interview, Hart noted that Fiedler's voice quivered. He couldn't phrase his questions. He stuttered.

It went on for twenty minutes.

The *Herald* wanted to know the woman's name.

Hart wasn't going to reveal her name.

The *Herald* demanded to talk to the woman.

"I don't have to produce anyone."

What about the phone calls to the woman—what were they about?

"Nothing," Hart said. "It was casual, political . . ."

So what was his relationship with the woman?

"I have no personal relationship with the individual you are following."

Was he denying he met her on a yacht in Miami?

"I'm not denying anything," Hart snapped.

Did he have sex with her?

"The answer is no! . . . I'm not going to get into all that." Hart turned and started walking back toward his house. The *Herald*'s photographer started snapping pictures. "We don't need any of *that,*" Hart said, and he was gone.

The Miamis ran off to file their story. They still didn't know who the woman was, what she was to Hart, what had happened in the house. But they had Hart's denials . . . what the hell!

This was big!

They could still make the main edition for Sunday!

WASHINGTON—Gary Hart, the Democratic Presidential candidate who has dismissed allegations of womanizing, spent Friday night and most of Saturday in his Capitol Hill townhouse with a young woman who flew from Miami and met him. Hart denied any impropriety.

They would ram the story through in less than two hours.

While they were writing, Bill Broadhurst tracked them down by phone at a Quality Inn, twenty-some blocks away. Gary had called him. Broadhurst was outraged. He said he'd talk to these newsboys, straighten this thing out.

Broadhurst wanted to talk to Fiedler—but he couldn't. Fiedler was busy, writing. Broadhurst insisted to Jim Savage that the woman the *Herald* was after had slept with her friend, at his house, not Hart's. When Fiedler finally came to the phone, Broadhurst offered to host the *Herald* team at his house, give them his side of the story. "The girls" would be there. But Fiedler had to go. His deadline was *now* . . . he said he'd call Broadhurst back.

He did call back—when the story was headed for the presses in Miami. Six columns across the top of page one:

MIAMI WOMAN IS LINKED TO HART

Then Fiedler wanted to come meet the two women. Broadhurst said they were asleep. They weren't. But as Broadhurst pointed out: there was no point in showing the *Herald* guys anything anymore. Their story was filed.

Hart called Lee at the cabin, that night. He called his Campaign Manager, Bill Dixon, in Denver. Dixon called the other white boys into his apartment for a damage assessment. . . . Why the hell did Hart *talk* to those *Herald* assholes? Dixon would have to get to Washington right away! . . . Jesus! What was Gary *thinking*? . . . Did he think this wasn't going to hurt? . . . *Didn't he understand?*

No, Hart understood perfectly . . . that he was the *victim* of a *process that was out of control* . . .

He woke up the next day, worked on his economics speech, went out to get the *Times* (glad to see there was no one watching his house). He took the early calls from Denver—tried to answer questions for the white boys, to help them manage this problem. But the more they asked, the more he had the air of a man who was being picked on—picked to death.

In Denver, they thought he didn't understand. This was *front-page,* all over south Florida. The ABC Brinkley-fest gave it *big play—top of the news*! The wires were calling, the networks . . . the white boys told Gary he'd have to get out of his house, the press would be pounding on his door any minute.

"I am not going to leave my house."

Jesus! . . . This stubborn sonofabitch just didn't get it!

He got it.

By noon, he'd called his friend (and unofficial press counselor) Sidney Gruson. Gruson was a veteran *Times*-man, friend to Hart for fifteen years, who now had his job in the White House all picked out: Sidney Gruson, Special Assistant to the President. . . . Hart tracked him down in Vermont, at a golf camp. Gruson hadn't heard about the story. Hart told him. Gruson said it would go away.

"No it won't," Hart said.

"No, Gary," Gruson said. "It'll die."

"I don't think so . . ."

Gruson ceased to protest after Hart said: "I may have to withdraw."

34

Sunday

BY SUNDAY NOON, reporters and cameramen had gathered at the gate, fifty yards from the cabin. Their cars and trucks all but blocked the dirt road up Troublesome Gulch. Lee Hart was their quarry . . .

Or their prisoner: she couldn't go out . . . and let *those people* put her on TV? Never! . . . Certainly not now, the way she looked. She'd canceled her schedule a few days before because of a sinus infection. The left side of her face was puffed up. It hurt when she flew. So she stayed home, trying to take it easy. After the reporters arrived, she didn't want to go out. Then TV trucks showed, and the local stations had vans with masts and dishes on top for live shots; ABC nosed an air-conditioned semi up to her gate. Now there were twenty pairs of eyes and a half-dozen lenses trained on her windows. She'd have loved to tell those people what she thought of them. But how could she, with her face all swollen? "They'll think he beat me!"

Lee was skittish, her voice was taut. In the cabin, she'd insist she wasn't giving the reporters a thought. But every ten minutes she'd shout for someone to go out there. *They're coming over the gate! . . .* The phone was ringing. Lee was saying: "Thanks, Warren . . . I know . . . I know. All right, I will . . ." Warren Beatty was calling to check on Lee, to tell her, they'd get through this if they kept their heads up.

Ellen Strauss, the Harts' monied and imperious friend from New York, weighed in every hour or two.

"It's not true, Ellen," Lee would say to the phone. "You're wrong. You don't understand our relationship. . . . I believe him a hundred percent. No. It's *not* true! If he says it didn't happen, I believe him. He's never lied to me."

And when she wasn't staring out the window, sure she'd seen someone inside the gate . . . when she wasn't telling someone in the kitchen, she was sure, Gary didn't lie . . . when she wasn't on the phone telling someone else, she was fine, she was sure . . . then, unsure, she tried to remember his voice, the night before.

"I didn't do anything . . ."

She hadn't forced him to say more. She never made him explain. She just wouldn't do that.

"Gary . . ." She stopped him. Lee always remembered best what she said. "I believe in you. . . . Just tell me what happened, and we'll get through it."

"Babe, I didn't do anything wrong."

But he didn't tell her what happened. Not really.

She said, "It's okay. Don't worry . . ." And he might have said something more.

But she said: "No. Gary, just don't worry . . ."

Now she wished he'd call again.

—★—

The white boys thought someone had to get to Lee in a hurry. If she flew off the handle, the whole campaign would go tubular (that's white-boy for "down the tubes"). . . . By noon, Lee had called the campaign, to get someone up to the cabin, to manage the press. Within an hour, Joe Trippi was on his way. Trippi was a thoroughbred—young, smart, fast on his feet.

As he hopped out of his van to open the gate so he could drive up to the cabin, Trippi heard the Fox network man doing a stand-up, for *A Current Affair.*

"And here in Troublesome Gulch, Lee Hart is locked behind these gates. But staffers admit Lee and Gary Hart are talking on the phone."

Trippi wheeled on the guy: "Are you married?" Joe didn't wait for an answer.

"Of course they're talking on the phone."

Most of the reporters were half-apologetic. "Listen, it's not my idea to be here . . . but is there any chance? . . ."

Yeah, Joe thought, a fat chance. Trippi was full of his mission: he would protect Lee and Andrea Hart, he would cheer them, he would keep them from trouble, from woe. . . . He drove slowly up to the house. The low log cabin was built into the slope. The narrow side, facing the drive and the gate, held the kitchen and a side porch with a couple of old metal chairs. The living room with the fireplace, the TV, a couch, and Gary's armchair with the sheepskin to cushion his back, occupied the center of the cabin and most of its space. Off the main room, there was a small front bedroom where Andrea slept, and Gary and Lee's bedroom in back.

Andrea opened the front door, then retreated. The action was in the kitchen, to Joe's right. Linda Spangler, Lee's Scheduler, was there. Lee was sitting at the table. Lee's friend Trisha Cheroutas was across the table . . . they were giggling.

Lee was holding the phone away from her ear. Trisha was yelling at the phone, and at Gary Hart, in Washington:

"We should have cut your THING off, fifteen years ago!"

It was an old joke between Trisha and Gary—went back to 1970, when Gary goaded Trisha into a feminist rant at dinner one night.

"We should cut ALL their things off!"

When Lee hung up, she suddenly thought she'd better explain the joke to Trippi. He looked so stunned. (And so outnumbered! Look at him, with his poor left hand over his crotch.) It occurred to Lee, she really had to take care of Trippi. If he got the wrong idea, he could fall apart.

— ★ —

She thought: you had to see the humor . . . otherwise you're just prey to whatever people said, all the things they thought. . . . She stared out the window at the pack at the gate. They were all convinced she was going to divorce him. A woman wronged . . . a doormat! How could they understand? Twenty-eight years . . . how she tried, they *both* tried . . . why should she have to explain *to them*?

She'd had men in the house! Why didn't they ask about that? Friends of theirs stayed with her—lots of times. Gary knew. And nothing happened. That wasn't the point. Why didn't they ask *her* about *that*?

That's what she'd say to Gary. They'd laugh. She could hear how he'd laugh. *They never asked about her!* . . . And she knew. She knew there'd been women, yes. She'd tell him, she knew he wasn't a saint. But God knows, neither was she. She drove him crazy sometimes . . . she knew that. She wasn't easy. A doormat? A mouse? . . . For twenty-eight years?

The phone rang, and Lee jumped, but it was only Ellen Strauss again: "Lee, make him come to you. Don't go running after *him*!"

Lee said: "I'm not going to do that to him."

Ellen said it'd be good for Gary. Every woman in America would feel . . . *justice* . . . when he came crawling back.

Lee said: "You're wrong . . ." and she got off the phone.

She turned and said to the kitchen at large: "I'm not going to make him beg for forgiveness." And then: "She doesn't understand."

Who did?

Our top story: Did Presidential hopeful Gary Hart spend the night with a Miami . . .

She heard the TV from the living room. Andrea had the stupid thing on nonstop. It wouldn't shut up. Lee wouldn't even go into the living room . . . "Andrea! Turn that thing OFF."

"MOM! I want to SEE it!"

Lee turned to the window. "Joe! JOE! They're coming over the fence! Joe, you better go out . . ." Trisha and Linda came to the window to look.

"He's coming up to the house! . . . STOP HIM." Lee's voice was high.

Every time a new reporter arrived, the others, bored, would egg him on, to climb the fence, make someone come out. This had to stop. She was at the edge.

"MOM! Are they *kidding*? . . ." In the living room, the TV showed a picture of Donna Rice, the model, smiling come-on at the camera. Andrea said, more softly: "How could he be so *dumb!*" Lee thought there was no reason she should go in to look.

"JOE! DON'T LET HIM COME ANY CLOSER.

"DON'T LET HIM COME IN!"

The women watched Trippi out the kitchen door, down the stairs of the side porch. The phone rang—Lee jumped.

"Yeah, it's crazy here . . ." Now, her voice was low. She was trying to speak so no one could hear.

"Don't worry about it.

"No, we're fine.

"Love you . . ." Lee was almost whispering.

"No. We're all right. . . . Gary, we'll beat this thing."

—★—

At the campaign HQ, forty minutes away, in Denver, it was all-hands-on-deck. As staffers arrived at the office on Downing Street, Paul Tully, the Political Director, ran down the story—and the line of the day: "Stupid assholes never realized there was a back door! . . . Dumb Miami shits thought they had him!"

The Campaign Manager, Dixon, had flown on the red-eye from Denver to D.C. He was blasting away at the *Herald:* they were "hiding in the bushes! . . . peeking in windows! . . . They have taken a casual acquaintance and simple dinner with three friends and political supporters and attempted to make a story where there is none . . ."

The rest of the white boys were still firing calls into Washington, playing manage-the-damage, trying to find out from Hart, then from Broadhurst: What happened? Who the hell was this girl?

Hart sounded dejected. The anger was gone from his voice, but he clung to his victimhood. This was a sneak attack from the press, which he uncovered, and confronted . . . at his home! He insisted: Donna Rice, her friend Lynn, and Broadhurst, left Hart's house Friday night by the back door. Donna slept at Broadhurst's house.

Problem was, Hart had already talked himself off the high ground. There was his quote, *that very day,* in E.J.'s profile in the *Times* magazine: "Follow me around. I don't care. I'm serious. If anybody wants to put a tail on me, go ahead. They'd be very bored."

And it didn't make any difference that Gary hadn't meant, "Spy on me in my house," or that the Miami commandos hadn't read Hart's invitation to tail him before they set out to search-and-destroy. The way the timing worked out, it seemed clear: he was *daring* them. (Hey! Whadd'I tellya? Streak of Danger!) . . . In a conference call, Denver to D.C., Kevin Sweeney, the Press Secretary,

gingerly raised the option of saying: Look, it happened. I regret it, but let's
get on with the campaign.

Hart said, "Oh, that's just great! You know, Donna Rice has a right to
privacy. I'm not the only person involved here. I have a right to privacy and
she has the right to privacy. Besides, we didn't *do* anything."

Hal Haddon, defense lawyer, said to the white boys: "He's lying to us. He's
guilty. He fucked her."

None of the white boys said that to Gary.

Hart didn't tell them about his boat trip to Bimini.

Broadhurst said Donna Rice was too hysterical to come to the phone. He'd
had to give her three sleeping pills. . . . Great, Sweeney thought. He could see
the headline.

BLOND BIMBO DRUGGED BY HART CAMPAIGN!

What were they going to do with her? If she left Broadhurst's house, the
press would devour her. Sue Casey, the Scheduler, caught the next plane to
Washington, to babysit Donna Rice.

Judy Harrington, the Field Director, had three desk people working phones
all day. Even if the story on Gary held up, she figured the campaign had a
month: by that time, things could change. Meanwhile, she had to give the state
coordinators something to say.

"It was all a big mixup. It's not true. Someone tried to watch Gary's house,
but it's all wrong. It's just not true."

Most of the state coordinators tried to go along. "Damn papers! . . . They
wouldn't do this to anyone else." But a few just said, "Yeah, okay. Sure." She
could hear finality in their voices. She knew, just by calling (Sunday afternoon!)
she was sending a signal: *red alert!*

In the office, John Emerson, the Deputy Campaign Manager, had a meeting
for everybody, down to the volunteers. "Just remember," he said, "when we're
working in the White House for the President of the United States, the tough
calls, the toughest times, will be easier because of times like this . . ."

Most of that day, Emmo was closeted in his office, with Haddon, on the
phone to Washington, trying to build a record of the facts. People would walk
by and hear Haddon, the trial lawyer, grilling Gary—or someone:

"What time did you go to dinner?"

"What time did you get back?"

"Whose car did you come back in?"

"Was anybody with you?"

"Did anybody see you?"

That afternoon, Judy heard Emmo say to Tully: "I'm a team player. Hart
can trust me to the moon. But I'm not buying this shit." Tully didn't say a
thing.

Press calls were flooding Sweeney. Guys he knew, supposed to be big-feet,
were *frantic.* Guys like the *Post*'s Paul Taylor, or Paul West, from *The Balti-*

more Sun, were on the line for an hour. Sweeney knew there wouldn't be anything written about Hart except blonde-in-the-townhouse . . . *forever—* unless they knocked it down. But he didn't have anything to knock it down *with.* . . . Support would crumble, polls would go down . . . meanwhile, Taylor and West kept asking: Didn't this say something about Hart's judgment?

Every once in a while, Sweeney would say to Taylor, or West, "Paul, can you hold on a second? I have to pick up another call." Then he'd punch the hold button, put down the phone and scream, "Fuck!" . . . He'd stomp around the room for a minute, then come back on the phone and say, "Sorry about that. Just had to get this other call off the line."

After six o'clock, Judy went into Haddon's office. She sat on the floor. She didn't know how to ask.

"Hal? . . ." she said softly. ". . . How's this gonna go?"

Haddon just looked at her and shook his head.

Judy began to cry, quietly, in a heap on the floor.

Monday

MONDAY the Pinkerton guards showed up at the cabin. That put an end to reporters climbing the gate, but it only increased Lee's feeling of being jailed.

"I want to have a picnic," she said. "Being locked up is driving me crazy."

Lee and Linda Spangler made sandwiches. They all burst out of the cabin door, and made for the trees, forty yards away, with Andrea, Joe Trippi, and Linda walking in front of Lee, so no one could get her on TV.

The dogs went with them. Andrea worried about the dogs. People *killed* dogs: crazies went after the *dogs.* Andrea would freak out when she saw her big dog, Smoky, on TV. . . . Now the pack at the gate was filming the dogs again. They didn't care what they did! . . . That morning at school, reporters were staking out her classes!

"I've had it," Andrea said, and she stalked down toward the gate. "I'm gonna tell those bastards *exactly* what I think . . ." Trippi ran after her. "Andrea!" . . . But she got to the gate, and, face-to-face with the pack, she stopped. She looked at their grins . . . she was making their day! She turned away without a word.

Once they were in the trees, no one could get a shot of Lee, no one could see them at all. They slowed down, and walked a half-mile back on the land, to a boulder in a meadow . . . it was Lee's special place. Andrea went off with the dogs into the woods. Joe started tossing a football. They felt good to be out. They almost forgot.

"Why are they doing this to us?" Lee said, when they sat down. "They don't, you know . . . people don't understand what you give up . . . they don't know.

"They don't understand people like you, either." She was trying to pump up Joe now, to make sure he didn't feel he'd moved his life two thousand miles for nothing. Lee wanted him to know, she understood. "You picked up your wife and the baby—Joe, you've *got* to bring the baby out here. Tomorrow, will you bring her?"

Joe nodded. "I'll ask Katie."

"We talked about it," Lee said. "We knew the life we had was over. The minute he got into this. We knew it would never be the same . . . you know?"

Lee was looking at Joe intently. "Do you think I want to give him up? If I had a choice?" She shook her head. "But that's not right. I have to . . ."

She broke off to hand around sandwiches. Andrea was still off with the dogs. "It'd be easy," Lee said. "Just, you know, forget it . . ." She smiled at the thought.

"You know what happened when he called me?"

Trippi was chewing, shook his head. Linda was watching from the grass, below the boulder, never speaking, never taking her eyes off Lee.

"I told him, 'I'm behind you, hundred percent.'"

"He said, 'But, Babe, you know I don't want to be President.'"

She saw Trippi's face fall. If Hart didn't want to be President, what the hell was *Joe* there for?

Lee rushed on: "No! You don't understand! We decided to do it—*anyway.* See?"

Trippi nodded. He understood she was trying to buck him up.

But she was talking for herself, too. Gary was *called.* And that meant Lee had a duty. They hadn't drifted so far, after all, from Missionary class at Bethany. . . . Lee straightened up and looked at the clouds rolling over the ridge, the storm blowing in, with her chin up and a look of clear determination. S.T. Ludwig's daughter knew . . . if you walked away from your Duty on Earth, well, God help you.

Thunder echoed from behind the ridge. The storm was coming at them on a gale. Sandwich papers whipped away in the grass. There was no time to pack. "Come on," Lee said. "Up here!"

Lightning lit the sky as they ran up the ridge toward the back cabin. It was just a one-room affair, but with a fireplace—quite cozy—and they could wait out the storm there. They ran with fists full of paper and sandwiches, the basket, blanket, football. The rain started pelting down. The dogs came barking. The thunder was incredible. It made the air smack in their ears. Joe heard his head ringing, a high-pitched keening . . . it was Lee, laughing.

She'd got to the cabin, panting and wailing peals of laughter . . . she couldn't stop. She was flushed and wheezing. He thought she was going hysterical. "What is it? Lee?" He didn't want to sound worried. *"Lee? . . . What?"*

"They're at the gate!" she squeezed out with the last of her breath. She was thinking of the pack, dripping wet, in the lightning; they could have no idea there was shelter anywhere else on the land. "They're . . . *sure* . . . we're com-

ing . . ." She was wiping her eyes, but she couldn't stop laughing. It wasn't humor—it was coming out of her in a wail, like a steaming kettle. "So they're *standing . . . out . . . there . . . waiting!*"

—★—

Monday, *The Miami Herald* admitted (in the thirty-second paragraph) that no one was watching Hart's house in the wee hours of Saturday morning. And no one was watching Hart's back door from midnight on. In the critical hours during which the *Herald* alleged that Donna Rice and Hart were locked away in the townhouse, the five-man investigative team was actually Jim McGee, or McGee and a pal from the Washington bureau.

McGee saw Hart and "the woman" (he didn't know her name) return to Hart's townhouse between 11:00 and 11:30 P.M. *And then, he didn't see them come out!*

But if, as Hart said from the first, Donna Rice left his house shortly thereafter, *by the back door* . . . no one could prove him wrong.

Except, perhaps, Donna Rice.

—★—

Monday, Sue Casey shepherded Donna Rice back to Miami, and at a lawyer's office, Donna gave a press conference on her liaison with Hart.

"I don't know if he was attracted to me, but there was nothing between us," she said. "I'm more attracted to younger men."

She'd met Gary Hart at a party in Aspen, New Year's Day. She'd run into him, by chance, months later, in a crowd on a boat anchored near Miami. She and her friend, Lynn, went with Hart and Broadhurst on a boat trip to Bimini, to check on Broadhurst's boat there. And then she didn't see Hart again until . . . well, until this mess.

She told the small group of reporters, she didn't stay Friday night at Hart's house. Their association "was all very innocent. . . . If there was anything going on, we would have been cautious, but we had nothing to hide. Nobody did. We were all just pals. If there had been something fishy, we would have been sneaking around.

"That's why I'm so surprised about this whole thing. It's totally bizarre."

Of course, they asked if she'd had sexual relations with Hart.

"No."

Uhhnn, Ms. Rice, just to follow up on that, uh . . . no?

"No."

Well, did he ask?

"No."

So the only two people who knew what happened in Hart's Capitol Hill house—i.e., Gary Hart and Donna Rice—said nothing happened. Both said she left, Friday night, through the back door, which the *Herald* conceded it did not watch.

Donna answered all the questions. She was calm, friendly, ladylike, and absolutely clear. But the truest measure of her talent, her poise, was what she didn't say.

She didn't say that she hadn't slept since Saturday night, when Broadhurst told her it was *she* who'd been followed. Or that she hadn't known what it was about, what she'd done that was so horrible, but she could see in her mind, all night, for two nights, how Gary had *looked at her* . . . and all she'd wanted was to *tell him* it wasn't her, she hadn't meant to bring this trouble to his door—she didn't know *what had happened* . . . but they wouldn't let her talk to Gary—she *asked them all,* just let her talk to him. (He was the only one she trusted!) . . . For two days she hadn't seen *anyone she knew.* She'd barely talked to anyone, save to her parents, who were the ones to tell her, her picture was all over TV—that's how she found out her name had been released. Donna had pleaded with the Hart staff not to give out her name, but Dixon just wanted to know, was there anyone to "run interference" for her, and she hadn't even known what he meant till he said, "Don't you have a lawyer?" She'd never *had* to have a lawyer, so they put her with *their* lawyer—Tom McAliley—she'd never seen him before. They got to the airport in Miami and all she wanted to do was go home, but they wouldn't let her go home—there were reporters all over her home—so Casey made her go from the airport straight to McAliley's office, and they told her, she *couldn't go home* . . . till she did a press conference—her name was out there now . . . so, she did it.

They still wouldn't let her talk to Gary.

But she could show him—with this press conference, she was trying to *help him.* . . . That's what she couldn't tell the press—how much she wanted to help him. Couldn't *hint* . . . that's what the Hart folks had told her.

She was backed into a corner. She had to say something—*now.* She could have told how it really was for her—or she could say what they wanted her to say. So, she said . . . well, it was nothing.

And, of course, that day, she couldn't see ahead. But what could she possibly be after that, but . . . nothing?

What could she say, about herself, after that?

The only thing she ever would say in public (and this after more than a year): "I felt like a piece of chum tossed into shark-infested waters."

Even in private, to friends, she would never tell—not the way it was, for her. She'd get that serious and faraway look in her eyes, and say:

"I gave the press conference they told me to give."

She did let slip, once, she never heard from Gary Hart again.

—★—

Monday, they started coming out of the woodwork: strangers on the phone knew someone who'd slept with Hart . . . or they saw Hart and *someone,* not his wife . . . or they were sure this guy their friend had been seeing was *really* Hart—with a phony name . . . see?

They called newspapers, they called rival campaigns. They called the *Hart* campaign!

The flotsam that washed in at *The Washington Post* came with a picture—two pictures—and a detective's report. It was that report on Hart from last December . . . the one that said he went into this house on a Saturday night . . . *and he didn't come out* . . . not until Sunday, December 21, when those pictures were taken—there was the *woman* . . . there was the *number of the house* . . . this was *the goods*!

Or it looked that way. Tom Edsall was the reporter who got the detective's report. He bumped it up the ladder—Edsall said he thought this was something *the paper* had to decide. That meant Ben Bradlee, the maximum boss.

So Bradlee took a look at this stuff—Chrissake! He *knew* that gal! . . . Well, that was all the decision it required. *Ben* would check it out. The Big Hound was coming out of the kennel.

—★—

Monday, Hart traveled from Washington to New York—*made it* to New York, was how he'd say it. He had to drive to Baltimore (the press was staking out Washington National) . . . and slip onto a plane to La Guardia—which he left by a back door, to a waiting car, which bore him in blessed anonymity to Gruson's apartment in Manhattan. Hart canceled a funder in New Jersey that night to work on his speech for the ANPA, the association of newspaper publishers, who'd invited him to speak Tuesday, at the Waldorf.

Hart was scheduled to unveil there his grand economics speech—Strategic Investment—the last brick in his wall. His issue wonks, Dreyer and Steitz, had done their usual Pyramid-of-Cheops job. The speech attempted nothing less than a redirection of U.S. economic effort. It was true tectonic Hart-thought, the fruit of fifteen years' cutting through earth, and immense labor over the past six months. (Hart was still buffing the speech, by fax, Saturday morning, when the *Herald* SWAT team assumed he was in a sweaty tango with Donna Rice.)

But now, he wrote a new top for the speech—now there was only one issue.

"Last weekend, a newspaper published a misleading and false story that hurt my family . . ."

Now that the fight had come to him, it was not entirely unwelcome. He'd have hundreds of newspaper nabobs in one room—he'd stick it in their faces. His message was simple: *they would have to change.*

That same day, he told a reporter for *The Denver Post:* "Somebody's got to clean up your profession, my friend, or it's going to drive anyone that's got an ounce of integrity out."

That's why the professionals in Denver (and all the pros on TV—the Priests of the Process in the interview chairs) thought Hart was nuts, or too iron-headed to get it:

Did he mean someone had set him a trap?

Did he mean he didn't have sex with Donna Rice?

Did he mean the *Herald* shouldn't have been watching his house?

Or did he mean that even if *someone did* . . . and *he did* . . . and *they did* . . . no one should care?

That was closest to the truth. He meant all those things—they were all one to him. For Hart, this had become one filthy slurry of unfairness, of allegation, of invasion, of wanton and unworthy attack *on his person.* It was *so apparent* to him that *they were repulsive . . .* and the voters—well, Hart always thought the voters were like him.

He'd made the same case to his friend, his host, the *Times-*man, Sidney Gruson, a dozen times over the years. And Gruson always tried to tell Hart— there was *no way* he could make the press change. . . . The last time was at dinner in New York, an Italian joint, just a couple of months before—it was Hart, Gruson, Warren Beatty, and two or three fat-cat contributors. Gruson ran through the changes he'd seen in the ethic of the press since the days of JFK. "It's not the same this time . . . and there's nothing you can do about that." Hart raised his eyebrows with that look of his—wonder, naïve puzzlement.

"No matter what I do, they will not change?"

Gruson answered like he was talking to a child. "No, they won't change. They'll do the job they think they have to do." And Gruson would always remember, Warren Beatty turned to him and said, "Tell him. Tell him again and again and again."

Gruson did tell him, but he knew he wasn't getting through. Hart would do what Hart would do. Gruson liked him too much to make it a fight between them. In the end, Gruson would fall back upon a bit of Irish counsel he'd known since his own childhood in Dublin.

"Okay," he'd say. "Fuck 'em, all but six—you need pallbearers."

—★—

Monday night, Lee Hart was in her kitchen, making spaghetti. She was mincing garlic, with a phone to her ear—Warren Beatty, fourth time that day.

"I've got a great one," he was telling her. "You go out there and just tell 'em: 'You want a monk for President, you're not gonna have me for First Lady!' "

"That's great, Warren."

"You think so?"

"Yeah, that's great."

Everybody had great things for Lee to say. Everybody knew . . . she had to say *something.* Not that they meant to push, or dictate, but . . . the press was making hay with her silence.

HART'S WIFE WANTS DIVORCE, the *New York Post* announced. . . . "LIVID" LEE HITS CEILING & SKIPS CAMPAIGN TRAIL.

The phone rang again and Lee jumped for it . . . but it was just headquarters, calling for Trippi. "He can't come to the phone now. He's chopping onions." Lee's joke would show them, she was *all right.*

Trippi took the phone. "No," he said to it. "No. I don't think so, right now. Uh uh." He was trying to keep his voice light, as he stood in the kitchen. He didn't want Lee asking: What's wrong?

"We'll talk," Trippi said noncommittally. "Yeah. Tomorrow, fine."

Of course, what they wanted to know:

Was she ready?

When would she make a statement?

Was she going to meet Gary in New York?

Trippi didn't know that Lee already had told Gary: she'd meet him in New York, or anywhere. She'd make whatever statement would help.

But Gary had never trotted his family out for effect—he wasn't going to start now. He told Lee she didn't have to say *anything.* If they had to act like that . . . well, he'd lost.

He told her, he'd rather quit.

36

Tuesday

HART THOUGHT his fate still hung in the balance, Tuesday, in the ballroom of the Waldorf. He was still ahead of his nearest rival, three-to-one, in national polls. Only ten percent said the Donna Rice affair made it "less likely" they'd vote for Hart. Hart thought his future depended on how the story played—i.e., how soon it died.

And here were hundreds of publishers, editors (news *executives*) at tables stretching away from the stage as far as Hart could see. NBC was broadcasting live from the balcony (they cut away from the Iran-contra hearings). In the back of the hall, along the sides—in fact, onto every available foot of floor space—the working press was herded: reporters, columnists, photographers, video crews. . . . Waiters with steaming silver gravy boats were sweating through the crush: "*Steppahk, pleeese—comin' tru de food,*" they sang out in sonorous Caribbean accents. "*Steppahk, gentamen, pleeese—I like you to stay cleeen ahn fresh!*" The news nabobs seemed fascinated and horrified at the havoc their employees could create. (For God's sake, *reporters* were breathing down their *necks! At lunch!*) No one paid heed to the Daily News All-Star Jazz Band, or to the rabbi who blessed the swarm and adjured it to recall the founding fathers' dream of a republic "where the preciousness of personality was cherished."

On stage, it was Hart and Bob Dole . . . though Dole might as well have stayed in bed. ("You know, I have a feeling," Dole mused, as he got to the microphone, "I'm not going to make much news today . . .") As for Hart, he thought this must be the moment God made for his fight. In this room, among that crowd, he could *win . . .* if they would join him in denouncing the *Herald*'s stakeout.

"Last weekend," he said at the mike, "a newspaper published a misleading and false story that hurt my family and other innocent people and reflected badly on my own character. This story was written by reporters who, by their own admission, undertook a spotty surveillance; who reached inaccurate conclusions based on incomplete facts; and who, most outrageously, refused to interview the very people who could have given them the facts before filing their story, which we asked and urged them to do. It is now, nonetheless, being repeated by others as if it were true."

Hart's voice was strong in the vast ballroom. He was pale, composed, but his chin jutted out at the darkened crowd with obvious defiance. He was so sure he was bending over *backward* to accommodate this "process."

"Did I make a mistake by putting myself in circumstances that could be misconstrued? Of course I did. That goes without saying. Did I do anything immoral? I absolutely did not."

In the Q&A session after his speech (Hart laid on the full economics text), he acknowledged that voters had a right to ask what kind of man was running for the White House. He acknowledged that he'd put himself at risk.

"I will accept the responsibility for what I did, and I have done so, and will continue to, and will bear the consequences on that.

"But if someone's going to scrutinize me, I want them to scrutinize me. I want them to know all the facts. I guess what, among the other things, disturbed me the most here . . . first of all, I sought out the reporters; they didn't have to come find me. I knew I was being followed, and I went and confronted them, and we offered them all the facts in the story and they refused that until they filed their story to make their Sunday deadline. I leave it for you and the American people to decide who's at fault there."

After that, Dick Capen, the nabob for *The Miami Herald,* stood and made a speech. He was supposed to ask Hart a question, but he kept referring to Hart in the third person—as if he weren't there.

"The issue is not *The Miami Herald,*" Capen said. "It's Gary Hart's judgment. He's an announced candidate for President of the United States, and he's a man who knows full well that womanizing had been an issue in his past. We stand by the essential correctness of our story. It's possible that, at some point along the way, someone could have moved out of the alley door of his house.

"But the fact of the matter remains that our story reported on Donna Rice, who he met in Aspen, who he subsequently met in Dade County. He acknowledged that he telephoned her on a number of occasions. It is a fact that two married men whose spouses were out of town spent a considerable amount of time with these people.

"It is also true that our reporters saw him and Donna Rice leaving his townhouse on at least three separate occasions. And now, of course, it's been revealed by Miss Rice that she went with him on a cruise to the Bahamas. . . ."

From that point, it was apparent to Hart that the issue had shifted. The

Herald's six-column, front-page Sunday screamer had averred that Gary Hart and "the Miami woman" spent the night. Now Capen could only allege that Hart and Donna Rice were *seen leaving*—three times.

So, at that point, the test was changed: it was not whether Hart had slept with this woman last Friday . . . or at any time (to use Capen's phrase) as "an announced candidate for President." From that point, the issue had to become *anything* Hart had *ever* done with Donna Rice.

The old hounds at their tables took up the scent:
What about those phone calls?
What about that boat trip?
And Hart made a mortal mistake—he thought he could *answer*. Imagine!

— ★ —

Imagine, for a moment, that two people met in March, by happenstance—serendipity, it seemed—in a weekend out of time, a weekend that was a getaway . . . and they were charmed, freshened, made to feel more alive . . . not least by the un-normality of that meeting, but surely, mostly, by each other . . . and it was playful, exciting, with a hint of sex in the air—conquest, anyway, and the play of the eyes, the purr of voice, the happy racket of possibility in head and heart . . . but for their own reasons, for good or ill . . . for Donna Rice's ultraserious view of herself, suddenly and literally at sea with a man who, she found out (that day), was married . . . or for Gary Hart's own husbandhood, or his never-unfelt candidacy, his assurance to his white boys (*That* was not going to be a problem!), or his own metaphysically freighted sense of self . . . for whatever reasons of morality, respect, or fear . . . imagine . . . that what happened between these two people did not come to, did not have to do with, an act of sexual congress.

Just suppose this was, for Gary Hart, an argument he'd had with himself on three or four occasions, already, in the brief time he'd spent with Donna Rice . . . he knew, right away, and increasingly, how wrong this could be made to look, what someone might say about this . . . but he had, at the ready, like repellent for the bugs that would ruin his picnic, the assurance, the *certainty,* the chin-jutting *fact* . . . that they hadn't done anything wrong—you know, when you got down to it—all they'd done was have fun, and no one could tell him he wasn't supposed to have fun, and if they did, if they could, then he had lost, he was a goner! . . . So he could see in this woman's laugh in the sun on the bow of that boat the *necessity* . . . *the rightness* . . . of his independence. He'd said that from the start! And he knew—just imagine, he knew—he shouldn't make her like him so much, but it hadn't *got* to that point, past fun, not for him . . . and to tell him to stop was like telling him to stop being himself, and anyway . . . they hadn't done anything wrong!

So imagine . . . the second time they were together, he sensed, then he knew, with a terrible sinking thump in his gut, that it had all gone wrong—all his warnings to himself were true, or it seemed they were true: he'd been set up! And there were snoopers trying to say this was an *affair,* this woman had *spent the night* . . . but they were too cowardly to ask, they were sneaking around his house, trying to see . . . he went out to find them, and he *told* them: they had it wrong!

But he couldn't—wouldn't—explain.

Not how it was. How could he?

And they printed what they thought, anyway.

Six columns across the front page.

And they forced him, at the peril of his life's work, its purpose, to explain how he was with this person, who was just . . . fun . . . when all he wanted to say—he thought all he really should have to say—was he understood, probably better than they, what was the sin they imagined . . . and that was not his—no! And if the sin he *did* commit, of escape, of courting the rush in his veins, was so awful . . . well, couldn't they see they were driving him to it? They were stripping him away. They were trying to make him small, they were tearing down with their dirty little imaginings everything he had built. What right had they to know the conditions of his marriage, the state of his own heart? Now his wife was under siege, a prisoner in their house . . . he himself was running from a mob every time he tried to move . . . his staff in Denver questioned him like a criminal, his Campaign Manager had flown away in a rage (after he heard about the Bimini trip) . . . and Hart's ideas could not be heard in this—this din, this . . . was *unworthy.*

And they called *him* the sinner.

Imagine! . . . What a stubborn man . . . so convinced of himself, of his power to deny his rage, to show himself as he would be . . . what kind of a man would try, still, to answer . . .

"Did I do anything immoral? . . . I absolutely did not."

But matters had got beyond him, now. They changed the question.

—★—

On stage at the Waldorf, Hart said:

The phone calls were "no more than half a dozen or so. They, in a couple of cases, were returned phone calls that had been placed to me." Hart said they talked about Donna "marshalling support" from her friends in the "entertainment industry."

The boat trip to Bimini was Broadhurst's idea—he had a boat of his own under repair there . . . and "we were joined," Hart said, "by two or three friends of his and a crew of three, as I recall, in open daylight—there was no effort to conceal anything." The party was supposed to return that same day, but customs was closed. They stayed overnight, with the women ("the guests," Hart called them) sleeping on the charter boat, and the men ("my friend and I") moving over to sleep on Broadhurst's boat.

It was only weeks later, Hart figured out the answer he should have given: "None of your business."

That was the *only* answer . . . as it was for the *Herald*'s peepers in the alley. Afterward, he could have *kicked himself* for saying anything else. How could he have been so *stupid*?

Who's the girl?

Did she stay in your house?

"It's none of your damned business!"

But when the *Herald* asked him about the phone calls—What were they about?—Hart started a slide he could not stop. He answered:

"Nothing . . ."

He didn't think he could explain the truth.

The sad fact was: Gary Hart, master of the process . . . who was so sure he saw through "the system" . . . who'd spent the last six years trying to hold himself outside the bubble . . . ruined himself, trying to play the game.

Once he tried to color the truth, to tiptoe around it, by then he was lost. He wasn't right from the start—he wasn't bold, clear . . . or different. He looked like a squirming pol, lying to the press, and public.

Alas, that only came clear to him much later. That day, the snarl in his ears kept him from thinking. He was a hunted animal. His denials didn't settle the pack one whit. . . . The press found out while Hart spoke at the Waldorf: the boat on which he and Donna Rice had sailed . . . was named *Monkey Business.*

— ★ —

That sent the pack over the edge. It was feral. It was without thought. Hart was catching the dread and fatal affliction—he was ridiculous. Even callow wannabe-big-feet could smell blood on the forest floor. Someone was gonna . . . *take Hart down.* Why not them?

There was an ineluctible logic to the chase: Hart was on the run. They had to show him embattled, fighting the iron ring, or dodging the cameras. That just meant more cameras, more bodies straining in the scrum, more fights, more noise . . . more extraordinary video-rodeo to get the tape of Hart fleeing . . . which, of course, only made him more furtive, the hunted beast. Meanwhile, the print press had to have Hart *women.* If they didn't get one . . . some other reporter *would . . . today!*

There was terrible pressure.

Every incident of Hart-chase got hotter . . . blood pounding in the temples, bodies banging, elbows flying, pressure in the chest until it was hard to catch breath . . . and every *instant* increased the visceral certainty that something huge, historic, horrible . . . *was happening*! They had to *do something*! They had to have *at least a part* . . . if not, what were they doing? Who were they?

Before the nabobs' luncheon broke up, the pack had Sweeney, the Press Secretary, pinned in a side chamber of the ballroom.

". . . I know Mrs. Hart is interested in making a statement," Sweeney was saying. He was holding his own Pearl-corder in front of his chest, to make sure he could prove it when he was misquoted.

"I know she is interested in traveling with her husband. . . . No, she has an ear infection—I'm sorry, a sinus infection—that . . . no, she is very supportive of her husband. She has communicated that to him. She will make a statement, fairly soon."

KevinKEVINwhyzzinhetellwhathappenedintheHOUSE?RICE?WHATHAP-
PENEDFRIDAY?inlightofhisreputation! . . .

"He doesn't have to answer every detail about something he says is innocent
. . . he told the *Herald* the two women stayed at Mr. Broadhurst's."

Fiedler says he never mentioned Broadhurst! . . .

Tom Fiedler, the big-foot for the *Herald,* was, at that moment, ten yards
away, in his own press conference. He was rebutting Sweeney, rebutting Hart.
("Senator Hart is just not telling the truth. . . .") He was insisting the *Herald*
had no ax to grind, and never tried to characterize Hart's behavior—just
reported the facts. (Fiedler would get better play than Sweeney on the networks that night.)

Reporters ran with Fiedler's poop to Sweeney—instant reaction! There were
thirty or forty reporters shoving in on Sweeney now, and he felt for a chair
behind him, like an animal trainer, always facing the beasts. But he had no
whip! . . . Sweeney stood on the chair.

"It's fine to take a day or two off!" he was protesting.

Debby Orin from the *New York Post* was shouting: "Kevin! Why didn't
he—KEVIN! Why didn't he go see his WIFE?"

"Well, flying to Colorado when he has to then be on the East Coast is
illogical for someone who does not have a lot of time."

Paul Taylor from *The Washington Post* raised his voice: "He had time to
go to BIMINI!"

At that moment, Hart was leaving the Waldorf in a cops-and-robbers car
chase. Mike Stratton, a loyal and longtime friend, had flown in from Denver
to take over Advance. He was in charge of Hart's escape. The video rangers
had chase cars waiting. (No one knew where the sonofabitch was *staying*—
prob'ly shacked up somewhere! They *had to tail him*—see?)

Stratton got Hart in a car and peeled away from the hotel. The campaign's
crack Advance man, Dennis Walto, pulled a car out behind . . . and then he
stopped—*across two lanes.* The video chase crews went nuts! They slammed
on their brakes. They slammed on their horns. They started bouncing up over
the curbs to get past Walto!

He's gettin' away! . . .

Well, it *proved* the sonofabitch had something to hide.

In his car, Hart murmured: "Why do they have to chase me?" He couldn't
understand what they gained. He couldn't understand why they had to hunt
him down. It happened every time he tried to move now—like a bad movie,
speeding and dodging, sneaking back to Gruson's.

At one point, in the middle of a chase, Hart turned to Gruson with a look
that mingled irony and sadness. "I just want to have some fun," he said. "I've
never had any fun . . ."

Gruson replied: "Just wait until we get to the White House. I promise you
we'll have fun."

Hart just gave him that blank boy's stare. They were talking about different
sorts of fun.

That was the night they called out for pizza from Troublesome Gulch. Lee had phoned a few friends—a couple of whom stopped and picked up the pies. Andrea had over a couple of her friends. Linda Spangler was still at the cabin. Trisha Cheroutas was back in the kitchen. Trippi's wife, Katie, came out with their baby girl. It was ten for dinner—six cars on the drive.

When the pizza arrived, Trippi walked to the gate. He paused to chat with reporters. They gathered around him, then he asked them to wait, while he called over the Pinkerton man. "The guests are all gonna leave in an hour," he told the guard.

"Okay, Mr. Trippi!" This was the most important assignment the Pinkerton man had ever had.

"So when I turn out the lights, nobody in or out, okay?"

"Nobody, Mr. Trippi!"

"About an hour, that's it. We're goin' to bed."

"Okay, Mr. Trippi!"

Joe said goodbye to the reporters. Lee and Trisha, watching through the window, saw him pointing down the dirt road for one of them, obviously giving directions.

It was dark when the cars at the cabin loaded up, and their lights flicked on. Of course, Katie and the baby had to be getting home. And Joe was at the wheel of their van. No one saw Lee Hart, lying on the backseat, holding the baby on top of her as they jounced down the earthen drive.

As it turned out, Lee didn't need to hide. Most of the newsmen had abandoned the gate. Lee said to Joe: "What'd you tell them?"

"I told 'em there was a back entrance."

They were laughing as Joe hit the highway and turned toward town. Lee sat up in the backseat—free at last!

She would sleep at a friend's house in Denver that night, give a quick statement at the airport the next morning, then board a private jet to New Hampshire, to meet her man.

— ★ —

That was the night that Hart held a high-dollar funder in Manhattan—about two hundred souls. The white boys were fretting till the moment it began: What if they opened the doors and no one walked in?

They needn't have worried. This was New York, after all, and Hart was the talk of the town. They had maybe two cancellations. Everybody else showed up, with their checks. The campaign raised $300,000. The crowd fed Hart's certainty . . . and his victimhood.

"It doesn't matter," he said, "if the candidate is struck down in battle . . . or with a *knife in the back* . . ."

(Hart was now sure he'd been set up. The *Herald* stakeout was too convenient. There were people who could not afford to let him win.)

"Because the cause goes on! . . . And the crusade continues! . . . Anyone who wants to test my character is in for a surprise: I may bend, but I don't break. I can be bruised and I can be battered, but I *will come back* . . . because this fight must go on.

"These are hard days, but we will prevail for one single reason—the truth will prevail. . . .

"Fight on, and march on."

Sweeney was just about cheering, like the rest of the crowd, his eyes locked on his man at the microphone . . . when a woman walked up to him and murmured:

"Gary said I should talk to you. He told me they were coming after a lot of women he knew. He said I'm next."

— ★ —

It turned out Hart was wrong about that. That was the night Paul Taylor got the word from his editor at *The Washington Post:* the Big Hound was checking out a woman who looked like the real thing.

Taylor's marching orders: New Hampshire, tomorrow, with Hart. Stick close.

37

Wednesday

I T WASN'T even hard for Bradlee. He made one call, Wednesday morning. Not to the woman—Bradlee didn't want to ask her. He called a friend, a fellow who'd know. *He* could ask—get a quick answer.

A couple of answers, actually. That's all.

Was it an affair?

Was it recent?

Bradlee wasn't the kind to split ethical hairs. But if it was, you know, seven *years* ago . . . and now it was (in Bradlee-ese) "dormant" . . . well, the Big Hound would likely just gnaw that in private.

Bradlee didn't have any animus toward Hart—none that he could think of. Guy was kind of a friend!

Well, almost a friend . . . or a guy Ben knew. Ben's wife, Sally, had done a profile on him—hadn't she? . . . Come to think of it, she did sort of put the shaft to him. . . .

"But there was no *anti* in me," Bradlee would recall. "I just come to work with an empty bucket. And someone fills it up every day.

"That day, it happened to be Hart."

—★—

Wednesday morning, at the Denver airport, Lee Hart told a half-dozen se-lected reporters that she loved and trusted her husband. She didn't ask him about his weekend plans. She didn't ask him about his phone calls. "In all honesty, if it doesn't bother me, I don't think it ought to bother anyone else."

So she approved of Gary's weekend?

Lee said: "If I could have planned his weekend schedule, I think I would have scheduled it differently."

Then she boarded a Learjet and flew to New Hampshire.

She had an idea.

Gary was doing a World Affairs Council speech at Dartmouth. Then he was headed for a showdown press conference—a full Ferraro. Hart had decided he would answer questions until . . . until there were no more questions.

So Lee came up with the idea that Gary ought to *interrupt* the press conference . . . and he'd say: "Excuse me. My wife's upstairs. I just want to see her for a minute. Excuse me." He'd leave . . .

Then Lee would paint a *big shiner* on his eye—and Gary would go back to the press conference with this huge black eye, and say:

See? She loves me!

Then she'd come in and give him a big hug.

Trippi went so far as to call headquarters. "Look, this is gonna sound a little crazy. But this is what she wants, this is the idea . . ."

"Uh, Joe . . ." said the white boys on the squawk box in Denver, "that's a picture that's gonna be around for a long time."

"Yeah, but . . ."

"You know, for years . . ."

"Yeah, I know. Okay."

"Years and years . . ."

"Okay, forget it."

Anyway, schtick wasn't Hart's thing—and there wasn't time. When he heard Lee was in the campus hotel, Gary went up to the room before the press conference. He walked in with a half-sigh, without fuss, like a man getting home from a hard day at work.

—★—

Downstairs in the press conference room, they were fighting—for position and for dominance. This was their moment!

The room should have held eighty to a hundred, but the pack was two hundred strong . . . and, of course, there were tripods, cables, long lenses banging shoulders and skulls of the newsmen nearby, boom mikes poking crazily toward the front of the room, lights ablaze on spindly poles or burning hot white on the shoulders of the cameramen. It had to be a hundred degrees. Sunlight pouring down through the windows didn't help. People in smelly suits, sweating, waiting . . . like a New York summer subway, stuck in the tunnel . . . *C'MON! . . . Whatsa HOLDUP?*

When Hart walked in (alone—Lee stayed upstairs), the photographers surged. Stratton and Walto, at the head of the room, had to shove them back, leaning and straining. Stratton thought *they're gonna eat him*—he thought of Custer. . . . Hart felt the physical threat of the pack. He'd asked for no rostrum—nothing between him and them. But this was too close. Their bodies were too near—their faces were in his face.

He faced them, and he said:

"As I've made clear to everyone, I have nothing to hide. I've made a mistake. I've made a serious mistake, in fact. I regret those very much, not just for myself, but for all of those involved, the individuals who have been, I think, unfairly maligned. I think of my own family first of all. And for my supporters . . ."

Hart ticked off his charges against the *Herald* reporters: they lied about confronting him—he confronted them. They reported he "walked aimlessly" in his neighborhood—he was tracking them down. They missed his comings and goings, in broad daylight. He answered their questions for twenty or thirty minutes, that Saturday night—he didn't have to. He denied their charges— still, they rushed those charges into print. Later, Bill Broadhurst managed to track down the *Herald* team at a hotel, and he offered them a chance to talk, in his house, with his two houseguests present . . . but the *Herald* chose instead to file a quick Sunday story.

"Finally, let me say a word about my wife, Lee: she has been, if anything, under more stress because of these events of the last few days than I have. And she continues to astonish me with her strength and her courage. This is, needless to say, not a pleasant thing for anyone. Not for me. Not for our children. But particularly, not for her. She has said that we have been married for twenty-eight years. I hope we're married twenty-eight more—if that works out, and I think it will. Over that twenty-eight years, I have to tell you, of the people I have met in the world, friends that I have made, this is the most extraordinary human being I have ever had the pleasure of knowing—not simply as a wife, but as a human being. She is here today and will be with us on the campaign trail."

Then Hart turned his chin to the questions.

Doesn't this raise doubts about your judgment?

Yes, Hart said, but judgment was more than one weekend. Judgment, like character, had to take into account thousands of decisions over fifteen years of political leadership.

You complain about the reporters—but you wouldn't let them talk to the woman in your house.

Right, Hart said. And that was a judgment. There were three people in his house, none of whom had given him permission to involve them in a press imbroglio.

Everybody's heard the rumors about you. Haven't there been other times, with other women . . . just like this?

No, Hart said, though he'd had many women friends.

So why do so many believe the stories about you?

Goes with the territory. He and Lee had been open about their separations. But if he did mean to have an affair with this young woman—he'd written spy novels, he wasn't stupid—he wouldn't have done it like this.

Of course, they didn't believe *that* . . . they grilled him on the phone calls, the boat trip, the ins and outs of Saturday, the alley, the front door, the car, the garage . . .

Hart's answers were quick and sure. But they didn't take the steam out of the room. Hart was determined to do this—as long as it took. But it came clear, now, he would *never* answer: they didn't believe the answers, or they didn't want to. It wasn't about that Friday night, or even about Donna Rice. It was just him—anything they could get on him.

Why were you going to jetset parties?

Would you take a lie-detector test?

Didn't you say, "I love danger"?

("I don't love it that much," Hart said.)

His mind was working on every level—shocking clarity . . . like he saw himself from the ceiling, a figure surrounded, but firm against the mass focused on him . . . at the same time his lawyer-brain raced to the end of their questions while their mouths still labored on set-up and premise . . . at the same time, within, he worked his will on his eyes and voice—keep them steady!

He watched their faces. *They* were out of control. They were past reason. This *thing* . . . had ahold of them. The look in their eyes as they stared at him—it was *anger.*

It was *rage*!

What had he done to them?

Now it had got to *character*—i.e., anything they could get. Why? Why now? His eyes found Jack Germond, searched for David Broder—where was Witcover? Shogan? . . . He'd known those guys—they'd known *him*—fifteen years, since he started as a young volunteer for McGovern. Till now—a candidate for President of the United States. Fifteen years! Germond and Jules wrote a *book* with him in it. They never called him a liar before. They didn't see him as a "bad character" fifteen years ago, or ten, or five.

I'm either a bad character, or I'm not. . . . Are they ever going to ask themselves how they missed it—for fifteen years?

Hart thought it was like going back to a high school reunion . . . and suddenly your classmates *hate you*!

"Senator, in your remarks yesterday, you raised the issue of morality and you raised the issue of truthfulness. Let me ask you what you mean when you talk about morality. Let me be very specific. I have a series of questions about it. . . ."

This was Paul Taylor.

You had to understand how this moment was . . . for Paul. As he later would note in his book, Paul knew plenty. All rumors, alas, but Paul had heard stories. One time, he himself heard a story from a "trusted political source" about Hart having "a roll in the hay" with a woman in Texas!

But here was Hart talking about his high standards of conduct.

"The nakedness of his deceit," Paul wrote in his book, "put me in an uncharitable frame of mind."

He asked:

"When you said you did nothing immoral, did you mean that you had no sexual relationship with Donna Rice last weekend or any other time you were with her?"

Gary Hart: "That is correct."

Paul Taylor: "Do you believe that adultery is immoral?"

Gary Hart: "Yes."

Paul Taylor: "Have you ever committed adultery?"

There was a half-instant where Hart just stared—a blink. He'd been warned. Sweeney brought up the question, on the flight to New Hampshire. On the plane, Hart snapped angrily: "I don't have to answer that!" And Sweeney liked that anger—he let it go at that.

But now they were *asking* . . . Hart could hardly believe it. It was *absurd*! This had mushroomed from Friday night . . . to *ever*—in his *life*! Was that the new test of his candidacy?

"Ahh . . . I do not think that's a fair question."

There was no anger in his voice—he felt at sea. He looked at the pack, from face to face: guys he'd seen chasing anything that *smelled* female—women reporters, campaign staff, stewardesses, cocktail waitresses, volunteers—*interns . . . children! High school girls! HYPOCRITES!* . . . Hart's gaze was racing from face to face, looking for something . . .

The video boys zoomed for close-ups when they saw Hart's eyes go shifty. You could just about see the man sag. The air came out of him. Taylor was still after him.

"So that you believe adultery is immoral . . ."

"Yes I do," Hart said.

"Have you ever committed adultery?"

"I do not know. I'm not going into a theological definition of what constitutes adultery. In some people's minds, it's people being married and having relationships with other people, so . . ."

"Can I ask you whether you and your wife have an understanding about whether or not you can have sexual encounters with other . . ."

"My inclination is to say: No, you can't ask that question. But the answer is, no. We don't have that kind of understanding. We have an understanding of faithfulness, fidelity, and loyalty. That's our understanding."

Gary thought of Lee having to hear this. Why should he have to explain their marriage, their understandings? They'd told him, upstairs: *Lee has to be at your side.* "Nonsense!" he'd said. . . . Now Hart's chin came up. Lee shouldn't have to go through *any of this*! He called for more questions, the snap was back in his voice.

"Was it upon your invitation that Donna Rice went to Bimini?"

"She didn't force her way on the boat . . ."

— ★ —

It went on for forty-five minutes—and Hart stood his ground. He knew he hadn't won, but he'd taken their best, or their worst—everything they could throw at him, he thought.

More than half the pack loaded up to follow his motorcade north, to Littleton, New Hampshire. Hart had a town meeting scheduled. The motorcade was waiting, reporters milling around nearby, when all of a sudden, out of the garage squealed . . . Gary Hart, in a white Jeep. He'd commandeered it. He was at the wheel. And he roared away, left hand on the wheel, right hand holding Lee to him. She was sidling closer to him, as they disappeared.

The press went crazy. The cameramen were in a lather. They ran, shouting . . . *Let's go! Shit! Come on. He's goin'—move! MOVE!* . . . But an hour later, when they got to Littleton, Hart had arrived, the forum was started—no press.

There was a citizen Q&A. The people didn't ask about Donna Rice. They asked about nuclear arms, and trade, the oil import fee, and Gorbachev.

The press pack was outside the old wooden house, on the big lawn, badgering Sweeney.

Whaddabout when he saw Lee? . . .

Kevin! Kevin! Did they kiss?

Kevin! Did they kiss on the LIPS?

Did he kiss Lee on the LIPS?

Finally, the town meeting broke up. Gary and Lee came out. They had to get to their car, thirty yards away. But the pack assaulted them.

The still photographers were right in their faces, clicking off pictures. Thousands of pictures. They wouldn't let up. Motor drives, cyclops lenses, lights, and strobes. From everywhere, voices were screaming: *WhaddaboutDonnaRice?RICE!LEE!DonnaMRS.HARTonnarice?WHADDYATHINKAYER-HUSBAND?* . . . As Hart moved, the pack moved, backward, blindly, crushing whatever was in its path. There was a kid three or four years old who was getting trampled.

Hart was furious. He'd always hated those gang-bang photo-blitzkriegs . . . but now he was powerless. The pack was bigger than him. *Hey! Watch that kid! . . .* Who could Hart tell? Who could stop this thing? . . . The mikes were swinging over his head. Lee got clobbered with a Minicam. (Billy Shore, God bless him, slugged the guy.) . . . Then, right in front of his face, Hart saw a photographer he knew: Ira Wyman, from *Newsweek*. Ira had been shooting Hart for years—since '84, at least. He was a roly-poly guy, round face, always friendly—a bit of a pest, but he knew both Gary and Lee.

"Ira!" Hart said. Wyman was furiously making pictures, stumbling backward. Hart saw that little kid go down in the swarm and he called, "Ira! . . ." He reached out, and got Ira by the strap of one of his cameras. "*Ira! Help me! . . .*"

Wyman jerked backward, pulling the strap out of Hart's hand, and with his lens two feet from Hart's face, kept working his shutter.

— ★ —

Hart wouldn't stay in the same hotel with the press. Stratton quietly moved Gary out of Littleton, across the border to a town in Vermont. There was dinner—two tables—with the road crew, Lee, and Spangler and Trippi, who'd come with her from Denver.

Lee was lighthearted, telling stories from Troublesome Gulch—the stake-out, the picnic. Someone mentioned the stakeout of Andrea's classes at U of Denver. Gary said: "You're kidding. You didn't tell me that."

"Andrea was going to give 'em hell. You would have been proud."

Gary didn't look proud. You could see him sinking into himself. They were chasing his daughter! He ought to have been there with her. Where was she now? Why was she alone? . . . Why was he here?

Good question.

"Why did we do this event tonight? The press doesn't want to listen to anything I tell these people. The people don't want to ask anything the press is asking. But I can't get though to the people if the press isn't going to write what I say.

"If this doesn't let up, we can't do it . . ."

Hart kept trying to figure a way he could break out of this blood sport. Trippi and Casey talked about buying airtime. "Thirty minutes—go right over their heads. You'll never get it though the press, so the hell with 'em."

From the other table, someone pointed out: "The minute you're off the air, Dan Rather'll be on, and Jennings—everybody, you know . . . what he *didn't* say, what he *didn't* answer."

"We could do it straight," Trippi said. "We get a huge crowd. Build the biggest crowd we can do. Then you just tell 'em why you're running. Don't answer questions. Just right out to the people."

Hart liked the sound of that—*right out to the people.*

"Yeah," someone else said, "but it gets to the network news, they'll spin it any way they want."

"You just get back into the plane and go! What're they gonna use except the speech?"

"Yeah, but they'll say what they want, anyway."

Hart felt he had to think anew. He had to figure something . . . fundamental. He had to start it over, somehow. But a weariness was upon him. He couldn't find the clarity he required. His head was going too fast—or too slow. They tried to make a list of options, but there were too many—or too few. . . . He stood up. "Well, let's go home," Hart said.

He meant: Let's go back to the rooms. Didn't he?

—★—

Paul Taylor got the word straight from Bradlee that night. That woman in the photo, the detective's report . . .

Ben had gotten his call-back—only took one day. His pal said this was recent, this was real. This gal thought Hart loved her!

Bradlee told Taylor the woman was upset about Hart and Donna Rice. She was horrified that Hart had been followed to her house. She feared for her reputation, and her job. She wanted to keep her name out of the paper . . . and Ben, ever courtly, wanted that, too.

Of course, Taylor needn't tell Hart that.

That was the evening's work: Get Hart. Get a comment. Let him think the

Post was going to run the story, tomorrow, or whenever. Let him think whatever he wanted. That would, in Paul's phrase, "keep the squeeze on."

Squeeze for what?

Paul described his "exhilarating chase":

"My destination was the Eastgate Hotel in Littleton, where I expected to confront Hart with information that might sink his badly listing campaign. . . ."

Of course, when Taylor got to the hotel in Littleton, Hart was across the border in Vermont. But Paul didn't know that. He found Sweeney in a bar off the lobby, with three reporters—among them the *Post*'s Bill Peterson. Paul was delighted. He called Peterson out and whispered the poop on this *new woman—this was the moment!* And here was Peterson to *help Paul*—you know, to face Hart with this . . . ruin.

They could help each other, Paul and Bill, through the interview . . . and into history.

But Peterson didn't want to help. He thought it was sleazy.

So Taylor went back to Sweeney, asked him out to the lobby. They sat down, and Paul was exhaling in audible puffs.

"What?" Sweeney said, without slack in his voice. He was in no mood to sit through Taylor's moment. Paul had asked his smarmy questions at the press conference. Sweeney'd had about all the press contact he could stand. After his evening in the bar, he was sick up to his *throat* with reporters trying to *apologize* . . . "Well, *I* don't think it's a story, but, you know, *my editor* . . . " It was disgusting! They could see what this was doing to Hart, to his family and his campaign . . . they all wanted it known, it wasn't their doing. They were following orders. Bullshit!

"What? . . ."

Peterson came back to the lobby at that moment, and he said to Taylor: "We're not doing this."

Taylor snapped him a look: *We've been through this. . . .* But Peterson hung in there. "Paul, you don't have to do this. You *don't . . . have . . . to DO this.* "

Taylor lifted his arms up and shook his head. He shook his hands and shook his head. He said, "Bill, there's just a lot of pressure."

Then he told Sweeney:

"We have evidence of Gary with another woman. We have a detective's report that tells us that Gary was having an affair with another woman. We have corroboration from the woman. So, we have two of the three pieces. The only thing we need now is comment from Hart. I need to talk to him."

There was no way Sweeney was going to let Taylor near Hart. Not unless he had to—and that meant knowing what the *Post* had. Taylor opened up his laptop and started reading notes from his bosses in D.C.

He read it all—the suspicious husband, the detective's report, the pictures, the date. . . . It struck Sweeney—that was months before Hart declared his candidacy. The great *Washington Post* was peddling a private detective's report—from before the campaign . . . that was pathetic! . . . And then—that *date:* last December 20!

"God, I was with him," Sweeney said.

He remembered the day . . . Hart was so happy, just back from Russia—the meeting with Gorbachev! He picked up Kevin at his place, and they went out to Mutual Radio in Virginia. Hart had to do the answer to Reagan's weekly chat. Back in D.C., they went to a bookstore on the Hill, and then Hart dropped off Sweeney, and went home . . . Sweeney thought he went home. Taylor said the *Post* had pictures of Hart at the woman's home.

Sweeney took notes and told Taylor he'd get back to him. It was close to midnight—Hart might be asleep. Sweeney didn't know if he'd wake him.

Sweeney called Denver. The white boys were on the squawk box with Joe Trippi, Sue Casey, and Billy Shore in Vermont. They were working on the two-week schedule. Sweeney beeped in on Emerson's second line and told him to get the other guys out of the room. Sweeney had to talk to Emmo in private.

From Vermont, they could still hear Emerson, on his other phone. "Uh huh . . . uh huh . . . hnnnh . . . okay." Then Emerson came back on their line and said he had to talk to Billy Shore, in private.

It was Billy who called Hart—gave him the news, and said he'd better talk to Sweeney. Hart called Kevin within five minutes.

So Sweeney went through his notes—very deliberately: *Taylor said this . . . the detective's report said that. . . .* Sweeney was dry. He didn't want to sway Hart's reaction. This was Gary's call.

But Gary started to stumble around, explaining. "Well, I went out with, uh . . . when Lee and I were separated. And, uh, I saw her, um . . ." He was talking very slowly. Sweeney felt his heart sinking.

Then Hart stopped and said: "This isn't going to end, is it?"

Sweeney was surprised to hear the resentment in his own voice. "Well," he said, "you'd know better than I."

And that was it. Hart was alone.

Hart said: "Well, let's go home."

— ★ —

Stratton got the little plane Lee had flown to New Hampshire . . . got them in the air about dawn. No one was to know. They had to give Hart a head start, try to keep this mum till the Learjet got to Denver—till Gary and Lee could retreat behind their barbed wire.

No one had got much sleep. Stratton hadn't slept since the weekend. It was one of those mornings when the nerves are so close to the surface, your skin hurts; the light in the Lear's windows, from the early red sun, was like an assault. On the plane, there were only six: Stratton, Sue Casey, Billy Shore, Linda Spangler . . . Gary and Lee Hart, side by side, in the back seats. No one tried to talk above the whine of the engines. Gary was reading Tolstoy's *Resurrection*.

— ★ —

Sweeney and Trippi stayed behind to lead the press pack round the mulberry bush. They formed a motorcade outside the hotel. They loaded up the press. They set off for the first event on the schedule.

They got near the place for the first event, and the lead car started making turns, driving in circles—killing time. When they did stop, that was the end. The motorcade pulled up . . . *and no one was in Gary's car.*

What the hell?

Where's Hart?

Sweeney stood on a bench and announced: Hart was, at that moment, in the air, on his way to Denver. Campaign travel was suspended . . . as of now.

Of course, the press went ripshit! They'd been had!

Half of them were shouting at Sweeney. Half rushed for phones.

— ★ —

Paul Taylor didn't get caught in the morning's press ruse. He was on his way to Sweeney's hotel room shortly after 7:00 A.M. (What about *his interview*?) . . . when he ran into Trippi, who gave him the news: Hart was on his way to Denver, and the end of his campaign.

As Paul recalled in his book, he was *speechless*! . . . But Trippi filled in the blanks.

It was important that Taylor—the *Post*—get the message: Hart was *suspending his campaign.* Hal Haddon, Hart's old friend and counsel, would deliver the message, by phone, to Ben Bradlee. Taylor wrote that Haddon meant to offer a bribe, an *exclusive* on the end of the campaign . . . if the *Post* wouldn't run its story.

Not to worry! Paul's work was done.

"I gave him Bradlee's phone number," Paul wrote in his book, "but an exclusive was the furthest thing from my mind. I was too busy feeling relieved, then triumphant.

"The interview I never got had worked out fine. Just fine."

— ★ —

The *Post* wouldn't run its "other woman" story. That's what Bradlee told Haddon: "I don't see any reason why we should."

There never was an offer of any exclusive story on Hart.

This wasn't about a story.

As Bradlee explained it, he just heard Hart was going home—and out of public life.

"Suddenly, the chase is over," Ben recalled. "Ya got him! . . . The coon is up the tree!"

— ★ —

As the Learjet neared Denver, Hart didn't know whether it was over or not. He knew it couldn't go on—not like that. He'd go home. He'd stop campaigning for a while, and . . . maybe he hadn't thought past getting home.

At the last minute, they switched the flight plan. The press was all over Stapleton Airport, the big field in Denver. Hart's plane veered toward a little airport in Jefferson County.

But that little field was staked out, too. And NBC had a chopper to track Hart, like a perp who'd shot the clerk at a 7-Eleven. Three cars waited at the airport. Hart took the wheel of the lead car and he gunned it, through the mountains—eighty miles an hour—he was trying to lose the chopper . . . hopeless, of course. The noon news showed a helicopter shot of the cabin, and the dirt road—the ABC semi, and the satellite trucks, vans, rent-a-cars—a solid line, almost a mile, down to the blacktop. There were Minicam shots of the house, with the cameraman running, and the picture bouncing—like Vietnam. Reporters climbed the barbed wire; they were perched on boulders on the slope, over the house—vultures on the roof.

When Gary and Lee got inside, he nailed a blanket over the kitchen window to block the cameras. Then it was dark inside, and strangely quiet. John was at school—at least, he had been at school: Gary's old campaign friend, Paul Giorgio, had dived into a stakeout and pulled the Harts' son out of Worcester, Massachusetts. Andrea was no longer at the cabin. She'd fled her parents' home. She'd left town. She'd watched TV. If he'd been there, Gary could have warned her not to watch TV.

He thought—he had thought—he'd get home and, somehow, he'd go on with his life. But he was not going to have his life back.

The phrase occurred to him: *to the death.* He learned in the car . . . when he felt it rock with the impact of bodies, and a bare hand hit with a smack on his windshield, and there were people yelling and pounding on the car, with cameras in front, and he couldn't see to drive, and Lee was beside him, fragile he thought, as he gunned the engine, trying to *make them move . . .* and he *jumped* when a lens with a rubber sleeve hit—*THUNCK*—against his window and stuck there, filming him, shooting at him, and he couldn't see the human on the other side—but he learned . . . something new:

If he could have, he'd have jumped out and beaten them with his bare hands.

BOOK III

38

Pukin'
in the
Basket

JOE TRIED EVERYTHING to make it feel right—endless meetings with the gurus . . . all their messages, songs, and movies, which Joe tried on in rambling monologue, one after the other, like shoes in a store. Nothing fit. He could not see the moves. He could not find that overriding *reason* why he should be President, why he was *going* to be President, what he was going to be President *for*.

He tried to write university lectures—he'd do it better than Hart! People said Biden didn't have substance? Well, BANGO, he'd put out more goddam substance than they could swallow. ("Governance!" he'd grit out—his buzz-word that spring of '87. He'd say it with his chin out, jaw locked, so his teeth showed in front, like a *fightin'* word . . . "Gvrnnce!") But he had to scrap for every hour on those speeches (some of his gurus couldn't see the point), had to fight through every text (Pat Caddell thought the country was gone to hell, melted to a stinking ooze—dammit, he should have fired them all!), while he flew around the country, built a campaign staff in Washington and Wilmington, worked in the Senate, planned Beau's graduation . . .

And every weekend, he went back to Iowa. Lowell Junkins, the guy who lost for Governor last time, had signed on with Biden and was crying wolf—like the state would go Gephardt *tomorrow . . . today!* . . . if Joe didn't get his ass out there. Joe had new guys in Iowa—David Wilhelm was the chief, hell of a good guy . . . but it took time, and Joe didn't have time. Joe used to say, for every ten days the other guys spent in Iowa, Joe could spend one . . . but that was bravado, Biden bullshit, and he knew it. What's worse, he was pressing . . . and that was no good. Couple of weeks back, he was up in New Hampshire—nighttime, a living room, late already and it wasn't the last event—and some guy stood up and asked Joe about his education. Not his education *plan* . . . his own goddam education, like he wanted to make sure Biden went to college. Anyway, that's how Joe heard it . . . and he blew: he started yelling how he'd graduated with three degrees, went to law school on scholarship, clawed his way up from the bottom of his class—or some bullshit—he offered to compare IQs . . . all with the chin out, the hectoring voice, like . . . *I may be stupid, but I'm Einstein next to you! . . .* And Ruthie Berry and Jill, who were sitting, resting, in the next room, had to scurry in and steer Joe out of there. He coulda punched the guy out! Joe was always sensitive about his intellect . . . then, too, that was the day Joe found out he was *one percent* in the new Iowa poll—but, hell, the guy in New Hampshire didn't know that.

Then Joe gave the university lectures—the foreign policy speech, Harvard, the Kennedy School . . . and, of course, Joe and the boys had rewritten it, on planes, in cars, till the night before, and Joe tried to deliver the thing word-for-word . . . but the podium was low, the lights weren't right (Biden never could read aloud) . . . so it sounded like he was reading a speech he'd never seen. Then David Broder, Leader of the Pack, got hold of the text and *ripped* Biden in his column: What is *this*? *You call this a foreign policy?*

So the speech didn't quite work out . . . but that was no surprise: nothing was working out. The gurus were at each other's throats—and a couple had doubts about this *whole thing* . . . which, of course, got back to Joe. But that was no surprise, either: *Biden* had doubts. Just a week before announcement, he started to mutter aloud about "the timing" . . . "the feel." Then Joe mentioned to the new press guy, Larry Rasky, that he thought, well, maybe . . . he didn't want to run.

—★—

Then everything went nuclear: gurus in an uproar! Rasky had left his wife and home and a job he loved in Boston to live in a hotel and do this campaign for Biden. Debbie Katz, the new deputy to Ridley, had just left her job as John Kerry's AA. Vallely had fucked his own Governor and left Massachusetts to travel with Joe. For that matter, Marttila, too, was a Boston guru for Biden. They were all invested. Announcement, for Chrissake, was *next Tuesday!* So now Biden thinks maybe—*sorry, it was all a mistake*? . . . There was tremendous frothing on the phones, hourly bulletins from the plane, or from Wilmington . . . a cabal formed to coup Ridley (Joe would settle down if this campaign were *organized*), some people wanted to coup Caddell (he was making Joe *nuts*—everybody saw that), and, in general, the long knives came out. Which, of course, only made Joe shakier: *four days from announcement,* there's no speech because there's no message, the campaign's a zoo, and his merry men are amok in the forest, disemboweling each other.

So the Friday night before announcement, they all descended upon Wilmington, and Jill fed them dinner from a buffet on the side porch . . . and then, from an armchair in the grand living room, Joe made a little speech: he'd crossed the Rubicon . . . he was fine now, they shouldn't be alarmed . . . it was just the black Irish that came up in him every once in a while. He shrugged and smiled. He thanked them for their work, for bending their lives to his. He was gracious, all charm—and it almost ended there.

But then, from Joe's right, Rasky decided to get down and dirty: that speech was all very nice ("With all due respect, Senator . . ."), but if Joe didn't *feel* this, what the hell was he doing with his life—and *theirs*? And from the next chair, Billy Daley said his piece, and Vallely, and Marttila, right across from Joe's face, about how Joe had to make a goddam *commitment,* this wasn't a halfway kinda deal! . . . In fact, Marttila went weird altogether and turned the thing into group therapy, talking about how Joe had to *love* these people, LOVE THEM! He challenged Joe to tell each one, around the room, WHY HE LOVED THEM—GO AHEAD, RIGHT NOW! . . . and a few new people who didn't know Biden—never had a serious moment with the man—started looking at each other just to check if this was as nutso as it seemed . . . while a couple of the old guard—Kaufman, Gitenstein—took off after the gurus: they were outta line, this was *Joe's life* . . . the staff guys could see Joe getting pissed off in his chair, they'd *never* beat up on Biden like this. . . . And Ridley was bouncing off the walls: he had a $300,000 announcement, ninety hours away, five states, two hundred press, a plane, a special goddam *train* (he could see the headline: BIDEN CAN'T MAKE THE TRAINS RUN ON TIME . . .), and what are they gonna say now? Sure, uh, we said all this stuff, we raised all this money, but we *really thought it over this weekend,* see, and, uh, well . . . *come on!* It was time to stop this weirdness! . . . But it was out of the bottle now, it did not stop. It went around the room, twenty people had their say about Biden, how he had to stop screwing around with their lives—*his own life* . . . until Joe's jaw was working under his taut cheek, and his smile was showing just a ridge of bottom teeth. And Ted Kaufman jumped back in and said, of *course* Joe Biden was gonna run: it was just like Bill Russell, the great Celtics center—used to puke into a wastebasket before every game . . . "Hey! Relax! Joe's just pukin' in the basket!" . . . And Caddell meant to help, so when it got to him, he said, of *course* Joe's gonna run . . . Pat said: "I've been waiting to be President since I was twenty-two!" . . . Then everybody knew it was the Twilight Zone . . . with Caddell hallucinating to these people sprawled over the couches and the floor, cross-legged, in cutoffs, the new leadership of the Free World—whom Pat, without pause, without notice of their staggered stares, now lectured about "the best message . . . the best campaign . . . the best candidate . . ."

And Jill Biden, who was sitting on the arm of the best candidate's chair, her right arm draped across his shoulders, could feel Joe's spine going stiffer with every lecture. She could just about feel the heat rising off Joe's head, and she heard his breathing go shallow, like it did in a fight, and she knew he was going to blow them all off, shut those bastards up . . . for *good*! . . . And before he

could speak, she brought her left hand across and laid it on his arm and she
said, loud enough for most of them to hear:

"Joe . . . Joe . . . *don't* lose every friend you have in the world."

— ★ —

So they were running for President, Joe and his friends, and they'd have a big
announcement—the finest: Joe's taste in political theater ran with his taste in
houses. They'd rent the train station in Wilmington (that was the symbol, see,
for the way Joe took the train home, every night), and they'd run a special train
from Washington to Wilmington, with VIPs and plenty of press, and they'd
have drivers bring in the notables from Delaware, and stretch limousines to
deliver Joe and the family to the station, and every member of the family would
have his own body man—there were, in all, a hundred professional Advance,
led by the chief of Carter White House Advance, who had the thing timed to
the minute, with poster-sized charts of the schedule, a six-foot-long map of the
motorcade, a wall-sized plat of the station grounds . . . all of which were
unfurled that weekend in the living room of Joe's house, and explained, point
by point, to the Bidens, who sat in a row of chairs facing these grand schemata
and stared ahead with frozen grins of foreboding—the look of folks in the front
car of the roller coaster.

But that was only the start: then, *everyone* would board the special train,
which would carry them back to Washington, where Joe would repeat the
announcement in the rotunda of the Russell Senate Office Building, with more
press and more VIPs, after which the show would board a chartered airplane,
which would transport all supporting Senators, Congressmen, Governors,
notable pols, political press, distinguished Delawareans, Joe's brain trust, support staff, assorted hangers-on, and the Bidens, and the Bidens' friends . . .
onward to Des Moines, then Cedar Rapids . . . thence to Boston . . . and New
Hampshire . . . and, finally, to Atlanta, where the troupe would be met by
Jimmy Carter. The logistics were something like a space probe to Venus.

The payoff was, at every stop, Biden would give The Speech.

But there was no speech.

Pat was working on the speech, but when he flew in from California, what
he had was a forty-five-page exegesis of the nation's ills: the raveling of America's moral fabric, the cancer in the body politic . . . that kind of thing. So
Gitenstein and another able writer, Ron Klain, started whacking through the
kudzu, but Pat was there in valiant defense, and there was only one man to
fight with Pat.

But Joe was busy. That was the weekend of Beau's high school graduation:
that's the way Joe planned it, see . . . family first, the Biden way.

— ★ —

It was always Joe at the center of the family Biden—Joe and Neilia, from '68,
when they got back from law school: they were the ones who knew where they
were going. They could have stayed in Syracuse. Neilia would have liked that.

But she was willing to move for Joe. She became a Biden, and was devoted to Joe's dreams. They lived first in a farmhouse, off Marsh Road, north of Wilmington, but then Neilia got pregnant with Beau, so Joe did a deal with this guy who had a swim club. The pool had a tenant house—a cottage, really, but cute, stuck off in the woods—and Joe didn't have two bucks in his pocket, so he told the guy he and Neilia would live in the bungalow (free, of course) and watch the pool.

Actually, Neilia would watch the pool. Joe had to make his way in the world. He passed his bar exam as an intern at a blue-blood firm in Wilmington, but that didn't last . . . he switched over to a firm with connections to the state's Democratic pols. He wasn't much for slaving over a legal brief, but he was hell on wheels in front of a jury—Biden for the defense!

The next year, he started his own firm. He was the only young lawyer in Wilmington to set out on his own, certainly the only one to guarantee salaries for two *other* lawyers. His first move was to purchase an enormous Queen Anne desk—the finest—he knew it was his the moment he saw it. His partners thought he was nuts. He's living in a tenant house, he's got a law firm with three lawyers, no clients, and Joe drops a couple of thousand on this desk. It was huge! He put it in his office—he had to walk in sideways to sit down. Then he insisted on a blue leather couch, all tufted with blue leather buttons, for the front room—another fortune. Joe *had* to have it. "Look," he told his partners, "we're trying to act like an establishment law firm. People don't want to sit on *wicker chairs*." If he'd had the money, he would have paneled the whole place. "You know how important image is."

See, his major client was always Joe Biden. He had to spread himself around, get to know the players, make his name—in a hurry. Just months after he started his firm, in 1970, he was running for County Council. That would give him exposure for the big statewide race he'd always planned. And New Castle County was the power in the state. If he could win there, he could win it all. So, right away, he started with night meetings, too. Sometimes Neilia would drop off the baby with Mom-Mom, and go with Joe. He was better that way.

Sometimes, it seemed Joe was in such a hurry that he had to make you like him . . . now. But Neilia could slow him down; she made him easier, as she made him believe he could do it. Joe always knew what he wanted from people. But Neilia knew what *they* wanted.

One time, when her friend Bobbie called, Neilia said she couldn't stop to talk. "I've got to go over to Mrs. Baldicelli's—she's going to teach me to make spaghetti sauce."

"Spaghetti! Neilia, come on!" (Spaghetti was just about all Joe ate. Neilia would cook spaghetti ten, twelve days in a row, just to see how long it would take him to notice.) Bobbie said: "*You know* how to make sauce."

"I know," Neilia said. "But Mrs. Baldicelli really wants to teach me."

What she lent to Joe was the grace of effortlessness. Neilia never showed ambition. It was like she already had hers—whatever it was, a bungalow or a mansion. Of course, she knew Joe would go for the mansion—he did the wanting for two. But she understood what it was—the Biden way—the striving and the stretch required, for family, for friends, for the public. "You have to understand," she told a guest one day, when Joe was running late, running crazy, trying to do ten things . . . "Joe wants to be *so much* for people."

—★—

So came the day before announcement, Monday, June 8, and it got to be late in the day . . . and Pat was in his muscle-guy sweatshirt with the sleeves cut off, still stalking Joe's stately home, ready to go toe-to-toe on this speech, which was *very important.* And there were typists upstairs, waiting, and gurus present for consultations, and Joe's parents were over, just to help out, and Val, of course, and one of Jimmy's kids, and Joe's kids, in and out, and Tommy Lewis, Joe's old friend, who manned a stool in the kitchen, next to the three phones, because there were a hundred media calls and a million staff and volunteer calls and VIP arrangements—train passes and hotel rooms, Wilmington cops and state cops and Amtrak cops, the height of the podium (wrong, of course), money bigs with suggestions, food for the staff, people at the airport, people who called and said, "Is Joe there?"—and Val's kid, who wanted to know if Mom said it was okay to go to Billy's house, and friends who had to call (they were coming to the announcement, or they weren't coming—who gave a shit?) . . . somebody had to talk to them.

And Joe was going to have a nap, then do it with Pat—their duel, their dance—but Joe had just got ready to lie down upstairs when the TVs showed up: three satellite trucks in the driveway for three Philadelphia live-at-fives. So Joe went out on the lawn, from camera to camera, and, between takes, yelled back into the house, for Tommy: "SPIKE! How 'bout some Cokes for the fellas! It's hot!" So they were serving sodas to the TV crews while Joe should have been asleep—he didn't get upstairs for an hour . . . and then the phone rang and it was Tommy Bell and Charlie Roth and Larry Orr, *from Scranton* . . . they're in town! . . . They brought three gallons of spaghetti sauce . . . *from Preno's!*

"Joe's favorite!"

"Hey, uh, great . . ." Spike said to the phone.

"We're comin' out with the sauce!"

"Oh . . . yeah. Where you at?"

"Right here."

"What do you mean, 'right here'? "

"On the car phone. In your fuckin' driveway!"

So the guys from Scranton came in with the sauce. Spike put them on the side porch, and he still wanted Joe to sleep, but Joe came right down. "How're things in Scranton, boys?"

So they talked old times, but the boys were nervous, what with Joe going to be President . . . which made Joe extra-eager to set them at ease, so they had Cokes, talked more, and Ashley came out to say good night—it was her birthday, so they all wished her happy birthday—and Beau and Hunt came out, and Joe talked about the car he'd got for Beau, for graduation. It was family, then, like it always was, so they relaxed, they *really* talked old times . . . couple of hours. Caddell kept coming onto the porch, saying: "Excuse me, uh, Senator? . . ." Ten minutes later, he'd come back: "Senator, they're ready for you upstairs . . ." He came back four or five times.

The guys didn't like Caddell, and they were glad to see Joe wouldn't even look at him. "Yeah, okay," Joe would say, "I'll be right there . . ." They could tell he was pissed at Caddell. Joe was tired, anyway. He was getting to sleep at four, up again at six—that's what he said. But he was glad to see them—guys who knew him, from before all this—and it was dark when they left.

Only then did Joe get down to the speech, and the fight with Pat . . . but it was late, Joe was tired to his bones, his head ached—his head always hurt in those days, he was gulping Tylenol like candy, *never* took so many pills— and he still had to pack, get some sleep . . . tomorrow was *game day.* So they never quite fought it through. The speech just ballooned to hold both speeches: one line of apocalypse from Caddell, then a line of sanguine hope in the goodness and strength of the nation—that was Joe.

By the wee hours of announcement day, the speech was set to run an hour and a half—maybe twice too long, *three times* too long—but Joe didn't have time to make it short. As it was, the typing would go on all night, for the press copies, the podium typescript . . . and Joe figured he'd see it clearer in the morning—sure, he'd take another look in the morning—*game day* . . . after he got the family squared away. It was understood, always, without a word said, that Joe would take care, take charge of the family, at times like this, events like this. . . . If he could just get some *sleep* . . . but Jill was upstairs, and they talked till late . . . it was a big move coming, and Joe was revved up.

—★—

And then, the minute he was dressed, they were after him about the weather. It was a gray day, with low clouds scudding fast across the sky, and the early TV said showers, surely, and Joe had to decide—did he want it indoors?

"Outdoors," he said with a grin: he'd go with the luck of the Irish on this. (Biden weather—like Election Day '72, a brilliant day, crisp and shining, a day like a jewel. One hint of rain and Joe would have lost . . . but no, weather was nothing, with destiny fueling the wind.) So he said: "Don't even think about rain."

Then it started to rain.

So they went round and round—indoors, outdoors—and Joe had to make the call again: *Outdoors!* . . . And, sure enough, the rain stopped, and the wind was fresh. By that time, limos were in the driveway, Advance were in the foyer, along with Rasky, who was stooped with the weight of two hundred press, wet and waiting in the wind at the station . . . and Joe was going to get the family together, but Caddell called him, called them all, to gather downstairs: there was something they *had to hear.*

"Not now, Pat."

"No! Joe! You've *got to hear* this."

So the Bidens stood in announcement clothes, while Pat, as the majordomo, flicked on the stereo and cranked it up to TEN, till it felt like the speakers were slapping them in the face.

> *Do you hear the people sing*
> *Lost in the valley of the night?*

"LISTEN TO THIS NOW . . ." Pat yelled through the music. This was important . . . the finale to *Les Misérables* . . . and this was HOW THE CAMPAIGN HAD TO BE!

> *It is the music of a people*
> *Who are climbing to the light . . .*

"Yeah, that's great, Pat . . ."

Then, it was only minutes till three stretch limos rolled to a stop at the station and Joe leapt out of the last car, onto the sidewalk, about to call to Mom-Mom, to tell her where she had to go, and Jill and the kids . . . some family had to go straight to the stage, some inside to a holding room . . . Joe knew the drill, he'd take charge. He had his arms up to point, direct . . . but then he saw: the sidewalk was aboil with Advance—one to each Biden. They took Mom-Mom away, and Joe, Sr. . . . Jimmy, Frankie, Val, the kids, and Jill . . . and in a moment, Joe was alone, with the words frozen in his mouth . . . he just stared . . . alone . . . with the strangest, saddest look of resignation . . . until his arms dropped to his sides, and he felt a hand on his elbow. A voice said, "This way, Senator." And they led him off to announce that he meant to be President.

— ★ —

He'd run into town, Saturdays, join his friends at their pizza dive—Pala's ("The World's Worst Pizza")—and they'd be sitting there, talking trash, on their eighth pitcher of beer. Joe would have Cokes, but that didn't matter. He could bullshit just as surely, just as loud as they. The difference was, now that he was back—in '68—a lawyer, he wouldn't hang around: he'd only stay an hour, unless they were talking up some scheme.

Joe'd say: "C'mon, let's do it."

"What . . . now?"

"Yeah. C'mon. Let's *do* it."

Joe was going to make a fortune, see—he didn't have time to sit around.

One day he called his dentist-pal, Marty Londergan: "You gotta come down here. I got an idea and it's gonna make millions."

"Come down where?"

"Newark."

"What's the idea?"

"Day care."

"What? . . ." In '68, Marty didn't know what day care was.

"Listen. There's graduate students here. They're married. They work. They go to school. And there's no day care! They don't have any place to take the kids! I got the place all picked out. C'mon. Get down here."

"Joe, wait a minute."

"Come *on*! We'll get the girls in to run it. We can open 'em up all over the state. Marty, this is big."

"Did you talk to Neilia?"

"She'll love it."

In Newark, Joe dragged Marty to a big corner rowhouse, just off campus. "Look at the house!" Joe said. "It's perfect." In Joe's mind, it was already fixed up, filled with playing kids.

"I don't know, Joe . . ."

But you couldn't tell him no. He was on his way to the courthouse to find out who owned the building . . . a man who had a restaurant in Elkton, Maryland.

"C'mon, we're going to see him. . . . It'll *work*. Put on a suit. Come on, we're going back home. Put on a suit."

They drove back to Wilmington, and Marty dressed. Joe reappeared in his lawyer pinstripes. He had the briefcase. They drove to Elkton, straight to the restaurant. Joe asked for the owner, then introduced himself. "And this is Dr. Londergan . . ." Marty wasn't even out of dental school. Then Joe started to talk fast.

"See, here's how it works . . ." Joe was painting pictures in the air. Even Marty got excited. And when the flow would pause, or a sentence would finish, there'd be the grin, those beautiful Biden teeth. In no time, Joe got this leveraged deal sketched out. Of course, cash payments wouldn't start right away . . . but everybody would do well. What could go wrong?

"That's a pretty good deal, sounds like . . ." the owner finally said. "Why don't you have your lawyer draw up the papers, and my wife and I'll look 'em over . . ."

Joe opened his briefcase and started whipping out papers. Marty went bug-eyed.

"It just so happens," Joe said gravely, "that I have the whole business drawn up, here." He presented the owner with a multipage document. Joe had typed in the terms while Marty got dressed. Marty didn't know whether to laugh or leave for the men's room. The owner sat back in his chair like you could have knocked him over. He said: "Well . . ."

Joe said he'd leave the papers. He was already on to the next step. "Place needs to be fixed up," Joe said in the car. "Get some paint."

"But . . ."

"Place needs a coat of *paint,*" Joe said.

Marty went back to Newark with his paint and rollers. Joe was busy. He was thinking of the second branch. Marty worked in the house three days,

twelve hours a day, and he had the downstairs painted. He was ready to head
for the second floor when Joe walked in.

"Stop."

Marty looked down from the ladder. "What do you mean, stop?"

"Stop. Deal's off."

"Joe, what do you mean?"

"It's off. Fell through. I don't know. But listen. Get that paint in the car.
I got an idea . . ."

Thing was, the get-rich-quick schemes never did make him rich. Something
fell through, or Joe changed his mind. . . . If they worked, Joe had the money
spent six ways before it hit his hand. The sonofabitch could do a deal. Thing
was, he couldn't *not* do a deal.

Anyway, politics, houses . . . he never stopped moving up. One year after
he won for County Council, the state redistricted and took away half his term.
(They were going to make him run again, in '72—in a GOP district!) . . . Joe
told his friends, *forget* the goddam County Council! He was going for the *U.S.
Senate* . . . against Cale Boggs.

"Boggs! Shit, Joe! You haven't got a snowball's chance . . ."

"You just watch."

That was the same time he fixed up a couple of houses in Newark, sold them,
actually got some cash for a down payment on Northstar, his first real house
. . . a place for him and Neilia. It was actually out of his Council district—
major political headache—but he had to have it. It was beautiful, graceful—
perfect. That portico!

See, it was modeled on the White House.

39

Excessive
Consultitis

W HAT ate at Joe—the trouble in his soul—was he'd gotten exactly where he'd been going . . . for the last two decades, bearing down on this moment . . . but it didn't look like it had in his dreams. He said to the gurus: "I can't feel the tingle."

That announcement—he'd heard his call to the crusade, over and over in his head through the years . . . but it always sounded better, simpler, than the crap he delivered six times that June. He'd seen in his head how he'd build an organization—but it wasn't like this chickenshit outfit, no. He'd just got Iowa fixed, and New Hampshire fell completely to hell—had to send Ridley up to shitcan the state director and put in someone new. That first quarter, he raised more money than anyone else . . . but he needed more money, more and more. He had a solid two days of money-hunting now—the Hollywood Women's Political Action Caucus and a half-dozen other groups, all over California—when he should be preparing for the first debate.

Christ! That debate . . . how many times had Biden prelived The Debate—*his* debate? A thousand times? . . . There they'd be, Joe and his opponent, alone in the glare—High Noon, Main Street—and the other guy looked older, like Nixon . . . or Cale Boggs . . . and Joey would demolish him, seize the stage, with charm and wit. Joe knew *exactly* . . . how it was going to be.

But that didn't look anything like *this* debate, this turkey shoot set for July 1, seven Democrats lined up on stage in Houston for the Bill Buckley show—all answering the same questions, all struggling, squirming, to get off a good line, to say *something* . . . to somehow climb out of this unbecoming pack. Still, it was important, the nation's first look at the Democrats on TV. This could be the moment. He had to be ready. That's why he demanded two days, after California, strictly for debate-prep. He'd hole up in Chicago, get a decent suite, run some meetings, clear his head, get an idea . . . then fly into Houston the night before—he'd have a day to relax, to look and feel his best.

But he hadn't even got to California—still in the air—when the bells went off in Washington. Red alert! Lewis Powell had announced his retirement from the Supreme Court. The news was waiting when Biden landed: his nightmare was upon him. A Reagan nominee to the High Court, confirmation hearings in his committee . . . could take weeks, maybe months, maybe a floor fight to manage thereafter. Joe knew instantly: his plans for the year—hell, all his plans—were history, smoke! His campaign—well, his first thought was, he'd have to quit. How could he campaign? He couldn't quit the chairmanship, run away from his first fight—not if he ever meant to hold up his head again in Washington.

He got the office on the phone.

"I know who they want . . ." This was Gitenstein on the other end. He'd just talked to a right-winger friend in Ed Meese's Justice Department.

Joe knew, too . . . but he said nothing, as Mark said:

"Bork."

That was nightmare on nightmare. For the last few years, Lewis Powell had provided the swing vote that forestalled Ronald Reagan's "social agenda." Powell was the fifth vote for the right to abortion, the fifth vote for affirmative action. Gitenstein could tick off a half-dozen cases—each of them five-to-four on the Rehnquist court. If Bork got the seat, every one of those cases would turn . . . Bork had no respect for the decisions that made those policies law.

What was worse, Bork was unassailable on credentials, as a scholar, a thinker on the law. He was, in fact, the most revered conservative jurist in the country. Worse still, Biden had said as much, just after he got the Judiciary chair, in the fall of 1986. He'd told Larry Eichel, of *The Philadelphia Inquirer:* "Say the administration sends up Bork, and, after our investigation, he looks a lot like another Scalia. . . . I'd have to vote for him."

Now Rasky was on the phone. He wanted to know what they should say about the *Inquirer* quote.

"That was different," Biden protested. There was a plaintive note in his voice. All he was trying to say to Eichel was, he wasn't going to carry water for every liberal group in town.

"I'd have to vote for him," he'd told Eichel. ". . . And if the groups tear me apart, well, that's the medicine I'll have to take."

All he meant was, he was going to do it *his* way. All he meant was, he wasn't going to be their goddam Ted Kennedy! But he couldn't say that. Why the hell had he said anything?

What could he say now?

He wanted conference calls—legal scholars: Phil Kurland from University of Chicago (a good conservative, he'd have the poop on Bork), Larry Tribe

from Harvard, Walter Dellinger from Duke, Ken Bass, an old friend from
Wilmington. Joe would have to know what he was talking about. The press
was going to kill him. Anything he said was going to look like politics.

"Put the gurus on the phone," Joe said. There were three or four in the
office. They all wanted to talk. Biden cut them off, with one instruction:

"You guys just shut up. No statements."

"Joe! What are you going to say?"

Biden didn't answer. He was going to his hotel. He had to think. He didn't
want advice. "Don't worry," he said. "I know what I'm doing."

Which, they knew, was bullshit . . . but he'd hung up the phone.

— ★ —

The only thing he could do was try to steer them off Bork. Joe had to make
them see: they'd get a fight that could split the country. It wasn't just abortion
. . . but Jesus, that was bad enough. The women's groups would go berserk.
Biden couldn't afford that fight . . . he didn't have the kosher national Democratic pro-choice position—couldn't support public funding for abortions, for
instance. What he mostly did on the issue was duck. He was a Catholic. He
never wanted a vote on abortion.

What he wanted to know from Dellinger was all about the "advise" half of
"advise and consent." Joe had to know if the White House ever ran consultations with the Senate . . . *before* a nomination. He wanted examples, precedents. Dellinger had them. "I'm gonna call Howard Baker," Joe said. "I'm
gonna ask for a meeting."

Baker was the new White House Chief of Staff—came in after Reagan and
Regan got their asses in a sling with Iran-contra. Joe knew Howard Baker from
the Senate. They could talk. The question was: Would Baker talk to Reagan?
In fact, Howard Baker was under attack from the Reagan true believers the
minute he walked into the White House. They saw him as the evil "capitula-
tionist" who kept leading poor Ronnie into "deals" with Congress, "deals"
with the Russians . . . *deals with everybody*! . . . And they weren't going to let
it happen this time. Bork was their ticket to extend the "revolution" into
American law in perpetuity. They'd go to the wall for Bob Bork. And Howard
Baker, who had the Iran-contra hearings in progress, Ed Meese sinking in the
Wedtech scandal, arms talks with the Soviets, Kuwaiti tankers sporting U.S.
flags . . . not to mention Ronnie doing his thing and Nancy doing God knows
what . . . didn't have much stomach for a new fight.

But Joe didn't know that. He was in Chicago, trying to do debate-prep. He
had the issues staff flown out, and Ted Kaufman was there, and Gitenstein,
and Donilon. Caddell flew in from California. He had to make sure the
message stayed on track . . . but Joe didn't want Pat's message. Joe didn't want
Kennedy quotes, or Martin Luther King lines . . . it wasn't *working*. "That's
not how you lead a generation, by talking about it—you just do it."

So Pat and Joe got into it at the hotel. And Joe started laying down the law
about how *he* said things, in *his* words, how he had—what, Ted, how many?—

two thousand tapes in his attic, *every speech* he'd ever made, and people were going to be listening to *his* tapes . . . using *his* stuff, goddammit. . . . All the fear and frustration of the last few days poured out on Caddell.

There wasn't much Pat could do, except take it, and make a little face, like Joe had it all wrong . . .

But that was a bad move—the worst. Because that was the same face Joe always saw Pat make, in the back of the room, when Joe was doing a speech. . . . There were never press copies ready—not the way Joe worked on his speeches, until the last minute, until they were introducing him—but Pat would have a copy. And he'd stand at the back of the room and follow along until Joe changed something—said something his own way—and then Pat would start shaking his head, making that little prune-face, where all the reporters could see him . . . hell, *Joe* could see him . . . like Pat had fed this speech with a spoon to Biden, and now Joe was *fucking it up*!

"Pat, that's it . . ." Joe said in Chicago. "You know what? I don't want this crap. This is *your* story, not *my* story!

"I don't want you to come with me to Houston. I don't even want you there. I got one day to get ready . . . I'll fuckin' do it myself."

But Joe didn't have a day. That's when he got the call from Howard Baker. The meeting was on, ASAP—Meese and Baker would come to the Capitol, do a meeting with Dole, and Thurmond from the committee; then they'd meet with Byrd and Biden. When could Joe come? He'd have to charter a plane, hustle from the airport to the Capitol, maybe he could get home to sleep in Delaware. . . . Anyway, that was the end of debate-prep.

What he got instead was a Washington charade, a private meeting that half the nation's press seemed to know about. Meese and Baker showed up with a list of candidates—a nice list, with women, even a Democrat—very reasonable. And Joe went down the list with them, marking off the ones he thought would be trouble. Bork would be trouble. That's what he'd come to say. But this was like choosing sides after everybody knew what team they were on. The deal was down. There wasn't going to be any fight in the White House. Only Joe didn't know that. So he walked out and told the press that they'd had a fine meeting . . . he hoped the President would name a candidate with an open mind . . . someone who would not disrupt the balance on the court . . . he thought there was a chance.

It was only when he was back in the air, on his way to Houston for the big debate . . . the bells went off again in Washington. Reagan had moved expeditiously. Not only had he named Robert Bork, but he'd named the confirmation of Robert Bork as his number-one domestic priority. It seemed Reagan was convinced: the Bork fight would show he was back in the saddle, it would give the revolution focus again, haul it out of the swamp of Iran-contra.

Joe got the news in the airport again. That and the news the press was waiting. Every big-foot in the country had descended upon Houston and they wanted him . . . *now*. What was he going to say?

The answer was, not a goddam thing—not now. He had to have some *time*

. . . Christ! What the hell was wrong with this campaign? All those gurus, those smart guys, the head of the goddam *White House Advance*—and it's *Biden* who has to tell them he'd like to have a room . . . a few minutes to think!

So he blew up at the Advance, and Vallely, and Rasky. Cancel the goddam press! He went to his hotel. He had a debate tonight. The first debate, nationwide TV! *Game day!* He had to think!

But he never got a chance to think. There were conference calls all afternoon . . . and he had to write some kind of statement. And he had to get to the hall early—press conference in the lobby with two hundred banshee reporters.

Joe'd never had a press conference half that size. He'd never even *seen* a pack like that. He walked into the Houston convention center and thirty cameras swung around. The halogens pinned him. He stopped dead. He muttered through a frozen smile: "Holy *shit* . . ."

He only meant to say he had doubts about Bork . . . but he'd keep an open mind, give the guy a fair shake, a fair hearing. Actually, what he meant to say that night was nothing at all—or as little as he could.

But he couldn't really blow off the press conference, or delay it for a day . . . no more than he could hold off Bork . . . no more than he could hold back the debate . . . which went off that night, as scheduled. Biden seemed barely there. He never made a dent, couldn't seem to connect. Dukakis, Gephardt— they both made points. But Joe looked like he'd dropped in from outer space. The fact was, he'd chucked Pat's message one day before—and he didn't have a new one. He didn't have time to think up one line! On stage, his answers wandered, they went nowhere. His smile would jump up in the middle of a sentence, as if he'd thought of something funny but didn't mean to share it. Tom Shales, the TV critic, wrote the next day, for *The Washington Post:*

"Biden . . . appears to be overadvised and suffering from excessive consultitis. Worse, he comes across on TV as someone whose fuse is always lit.

"Unless we ditch television for the remainder of the campaign, Biden will never be President."

40

Leadership!

THE ONLY ONE who could have stopped it was the Bobster. When Baker and Meese came to the Capitol, the only "consultation" that could have derailed Bork was word from Bob Dole that he couldn't find the votes.

He could have warned them about a fight . . . but they wanted a fight, to show they could still do something after Iran-contra. That was half of Dole's dilemma—he didn't want Iran-contra buried. Dole could hardly believe that the truth about Bush-in-that-soup hadn't come out yet—*somehow,* between the Tower Commission and the Select Committee . . . well, maybe it would now. The Senate committee had Ollie North on the stand next week.

So Dole didn't need another hurricane to blow Ollie's testimony off the front page. . . . He didn't want a crisis that would rally the antiabortion nuts, the prayer-in-school nuts, the Uzi-under-the-bed nuts to the White House, to Reagan (and, by extension, Reagan-Bush).

But that was the other half of Dole's dilemma: with Bork as the darling of the Reagan right, Dole could not seem cool toward Judge Bork—nor even lukewarm. No! . . . Bob Dole would have to *lead the fight* for the White House.

That was the nub of Dole's appeal, his claim to the Gipper's mantle—and the Gipper's voters. "When Ronald Reagan wants something done," Dole would tell his crowds, "he doesn't call George . . . he calls Bob!"

"That's *leadership,*" Dole would say. "Leadership's when they give you the ball!"

Bob Dole would have to carry the ball for Bork.

When Ted Kennedy stood, within minutes of Bork's nomination, to *savage* the man ("Robert Bork's America is a land in which women would be forced into back-alley abortions, blacks would sit at segregated lunch counters, rogue police could break down citizens' doors . . ."), it was Dole who took the floor to defend him. Then he marched to his office to call Bork at the White House. "Well, you prob'ly heard, Ted Kennedy just attacked you—that's a good sign. Course, I stood up and said you were a Great American, so—here we go. . . . Well, keep your chin up!"

For reporters, Dole had nothing but smiles and confidence: people who attacked Judge Bork were playing footsie with *liberal interest groups.* "Judge Bork will be confirmed—I think, overwhelmingly, once people get a chance to look at his record." (In Dole's view, Bork *would* be a shoo-in—if Dole could set up the fight as the learned judge . . . against the gay-lesbian-affirmative-abortion-welfare-rights caucus.)

It was only in Dole's inner office, in his own car, or his own plane, that little comments started to leak, belying his cheerful Bork-boosting:

"Agh, first thing that guy oughta do is *shayyve* . . ."

And only true students of Dole-code understood the new line that crept into his stump speech:

"That's *leadership,*" Dole would say. "Leadership's when they give you the ball!

"Sometimes, you don't even *want* the ball . . ."

—★—

Thing was, Biden knew Dole could make it stick—poor Bob Bork, *victim of the liberals*!—unless Joe acted fast.

That Ted Kennedy speech, slamming Bork—that was hot rhetoric, good TV, great politics . . . for Kennedy. But Joe could think of three or four southern Democrats who'd *have* to be for Bork, if the contest came down to Bork v. Kennedy.

Biden knew he could lose even more votes if the interest groups didn't stop issuing threats. Hazel Dukes, New York State director of the NAACP, told reporters that Pat Moynihan *had* to vote against Bork—or she and her group would knock Moynihan out of office.

Hell, they were threatening *Biden:* even before Bork was named, Estelle Rogers, director of the Federation of Women Lawyers, warned that Biden had better "take time from his busy schedule to exercise the kind of leadership we expect from the Chairman of the Senate Judiciary Committee.

"If he can't," said Ms. Rogers, "he'd be wise to think carefully about resigning the chairmanship."

That was the fastest way to make enemies in the Senate. Biden always thought the liberal groups were a pain in the ass. Now they were going to lose the battle before it started.

One other thing Biden knew: Bob Dole would fight this out—right onto the floor. . . . Alas, Biden knew from experience.

In '86, he was running his first floor fight on a nomination, on a forty-four-year-old Indiana right-winger, Daniel Manion, whom Reagan had nominated for the Seventh Circuit Court of Appeals. Manion (a pal and protégé of Senator Dan Quayle) was a John Birch sympathizer—his legal briefs were barely in *English.* Law school professors and deans lined up against him. The American Bar Association wouldn't give him a clean endorsement. Then the Judiciary Committee voted the nomination out unfavorably.

Biden had all the ammo he needed. He walked onto the floor, jingling change in his pocket, like a gunfighter looking for an insult. *Game day! . . .* He had the votes. They *told* him he had the votes. In colloquy with Dole, across the aisle, Biden said, in effect: *Let's go! Let's roll the dice!*

Senators were absent. Biden offered to let them pair up—one pro-Manion, to one anti-Manion—they'd cancel each other out.

"Agghh! Now we're talkin' real turkey," Dole said.

Problem was, Biden wasn't really sure who was pro-Manion. And he thought Slade Gorton was anti-Manion—when, in fact, Gorton had sold his vote for control of a judgeship in his own state.

Anyway, Joe made them roll the dice . . . and he lost. He lost by two votes. Dole knew where his votes were, and Biden didn't. He fell on his face.

His liberal friends were livid, crying foul about the pairings . . . Dole was playing fast and loose!

They weren't any more livid than Biden. It was the civil rights groups that told him he had the votes in the first place. He *never* should have listened to them—should have taken care of business himself!

Biden knew, that day in 1986, he would never let the groups lead a fight for him again. . . . Just as he knew, the minute the Bork nomination hit, he had to get them off his back.

—★—

So he and the staff made a plan, a careful choreography of Biden's first day back in the Senate: Joe had to get control—establish the fairness of the process, and cool the rhetoric until the time was right.

Ten A.M., he'd meet with Bork, and assure him there'd be punctiliously fair committee hearings. Biden would maintain his two-step strategic position: he had "doubts" about Bork . . . but he would keep an open mind.

Next, he'd convene his panel of experts—Phil Kurland from Chicago, Walter Dellinger from Duke, Ken Bass (a former clerk to Justice Hugo Black), and Clark Clifford, the big-foot of Washington lawyers. Biden wanted their help to make his case for opposition, in one grand speech before the hearings in September.

Then, twelve-thirty, he'd meet with leaders of the civil rights groups. His agenda was short and direct: he wanted them to back off and let *him* make the move on Bork. If they wanted to help, they could sing from *his* prayer book. If not, they could just shut up.

But by the time he rolled into the leaders' meeting—almost an hour late—he was whistling with pent-up steam. There were nabobs from a half-dozen major liberal and minority lobbies: the Leadership Conference on Civil Rights, the Mexican-American Legal Defense Fund, the NAACP Legal Defense Fund, the Women's Legal Defense Fund, and People for the American Way. Biden started talking fast.

He meant to speak bluntly and confidentially, he said. He wanted them to know, they should stop whining about his devoting time to Bork. He would spend whatever time was required—even if it meant the end of his campaign.

Then he told them *he* would decide the strategy—it wasn't going to be a single-issue campaign. That was a shot across the women's bow, to let them know they could lose this fight (and lose him) if they made this a vote on abortion.

Well, that part worked fine. The feminist rep, Judy Lichtman, assured him she knew they couldn't fight Bork solely on abortion. Ralph Neas, from the Leadership Conference, said no one doubted Biden's commitment . . . they just wanted to discuss the timing of the hearings.

So Biden discussed timing. And he could have left it there. In fact, he meant to . . . but he wanted them to know *him*. He wanted them to feel the *connect,* before he left that room.

"Look, I'm gonna lead this fight—but you guys . . ."

And that was the critical mistake.

Within minutes, Biden was gone, he'd run off to a meeting with his Democratic committee colleagues.

But within hours, *The New York Times* was calling. Ken Noble, the reporter, wanted to know why Biden had said he'd keep an open mind—and then promised the civil rights groups that he'd "lead the fight against Bork."

Pete Smith, the committee's Press Secretary, got Biden on the phone—had to track him down in the gym. This was serious. "Uh, Senator, I think we have a problem . . ."

Biden didn't see why he should tell the *Times* anything.

Smith said they ought to draft a statement "to, uhnnn, bridge the two realities of those statements."

"Okay," Biden said.

So Smith issued a statement that Biden *was* planning to lead the fight—but hadn't meant to make that known until after he'd crafted a major set of speeches to set forth the case against Bork.

Well, that bridged the realities . . . but also left the impression that Biden had blithely lied to the world—and told the truth only when pressured by the liberal interest groups.

It also ended his two-step strategy.

He was committed.

BANGO!

Joe had bought himself a fight.

41

The River of Power

THEY WERE supposed to have another meeting on the porch of the big house in Wilmington, another session to figure out how to beat Bork. But Joe could not see the way, couldn't see a thing—he was too depressed.

"We fucked it up . . ." He must have said that five times. What he meant was, he'd fucked it up.

It wasn't that he'd messed up by coming down against Bork. He'd learned plenty about Bork in two weeks—and he didn't like what he'd heard. Anyway, politically, Joe had no choice: women, blacks, liberals of all stripes—they were going to the mattresses. One trip to Iowa, you'd have to be insensate to think any Democrat was going to be for Bork.

And it wasn't that he'd messed up by deciding he'd have to lead the fight. Hell, it was his committee! If he left it to Kennedy, with his rhetoric—the women in the alleys with their coat hangers—the fight was lost. That Teddy-firebrand stuff would lose every southerner, every Republican vote in the Senate. They wouldn't even have the votes to hold off cloture. They couldn't even *talk* Bork to death.

No, Joe had to do it, and do it without the interest groups. That's how he'd screwed up. He'd talked to the groups . . . and it leaked out that he'd make the fight. Like he promised *them*! Like he was their tool! Jesus!

"I made one big mistake," Biden said on the porch.

"Yeah, but Joe . . ." The guys were there to reassure him. But Biden was still talking:

"And it's probably fatal . . . the biggest mistake of my political career. You know, I didn't just screw up the campaign. It's my whole Senate career. It's over."

"Jesus, Joe!"

They'd never seen him like this, with the wind out so completely. He was curled into the white wicker, shrinking in his seat. He had his eyes turned away, toward the lawn, the fountain . . . it never worked. He would have fixed the goddam fountain, but he was going to move. He had that house. Beautiful deal! He shoulda bought the damn house . . . but no . . . he had to run. He wiggled out of the closing on the new house two weeks ago, just before Bork.

"Goddamnit!"

"Joe, wait a minute." This was Donilon, up from Washington, trying to put the thing on track. (Donilon *had* to get the thing on track. He'd cut himself loose from his law firm—as of July 1, the day they got Bork in their laps.) "Joe, you gotta remember, there's a tremendous up side . . ."

Donilon was always talking opportunity: national TV, for weeks, every day . . . *Joe Biden, Defender of the Constitution.* "Joe, just the name recognition . . ."

"Yeah," Joe would say. "But I gotta go toe-to-toe with Bork. I gotta show some substance."

Joe could not see his way to a win. For Christ's sake, there weren't fifty-one votes, today, for the simple proposition that Bork should even be *questioned* about his ideology, his politics, philosophy. Most of the Senate thought the Judiciary Committee should limit itself to one inquiry: Was Bork personally fit for the job by virtue of his education, experience, temperament?

Of course he was fit. Hell, they'd already voted him onto the U.S. Court of Appeals.

And Biden was already getting hammered for "playing politics" with the Supreme Court—and not just from Dole. Hell, Joe expected it from Dole. It was the press climbing all over Biden's back.

George Will led the charge, the day after the nomination:

"Six months ago, Biden, whose mood swings carry him from Hamlet to hysteria, was given chairmanship of the Judiciary Committee, an example of history handing a man sufficient rope with which to hang himself. Now Biden, the incredible shrinking presidential candidate, has somersaulted over his flamboyantly advertised principles. . . .

"Either Biden changed his tune because groups were jerking his leash or, worse, to prepare for an act of preemptive capitulation."

Then *The Washington Post* editorial page skewered him for his promise to the groups—before he'd even held hearings!

"As the Queen of Hearts said to Alice: 'sentence first—verdict afterwards.' . . ."

The next day, Mark Shields blew taps for Biden's Presidential hopes: "By seeming in the Bork nomination fight to be the prisoner or the patsy of liberal pressure groups, neither Biden nor anyone else will fill that bill of leadership for change."

The next weekend, in Cleveland, Joe was making a speech, and he mused aloud, he'd made a mistake, coming out against Bork.

Christ, then even Donilon got pissed off. From a phone booth, for hours, he tracked Biden's flight path—finally caught him in Iowa. "Senator, what the hell did you do out there?"

"Tom, you don't even know what I said. You had to hear the whole thing . . ."

"You were waffling."

"I was not waffling."

"Did you use the word 'mistake'?"

"Yeah. I gave an explanation of how . . ."

"You said 'mistake'! That's the lead tomorrow, I guarantee it."

Sure enough, the next day, Biden was not just a flip-flop . . . now he was waffling!

"Jesus! Everything I say ends up on the front of *The New York Times*!"

Biden had never been in this sort of shit-storm. There were two daily papers in Delaware, a couple of UHF towers in the cornfields outside Dover. Give him an hour, he could call every editor in the state. (And he would!) But how do you call every paper in the country?

No, he'd bought himself a fight. Not only would he have to win in the hearings . . . but to beat Bork he'd have to convince his fellow Senators that they could vote against a judge simply because he was too right-wing (not because he was unfit, or stupid, a bigot, a swindler—something easy) . . . he'd have to win over the editorial boards, the *Post,* the *Times, Wall Street Journal, Time, Newsweek* . . . he'd have to get control of the interest groups, bring them in line with his strategy . . . he'd have to find a message that could mobilize the voters—show them how a Justice Bork could affect their lives.

What he'd bought, in short, was another campaign . . . on top of his campaign. He could not fall on his face in one . . . and have any chance in the other. And this new campaign was not against Gephardt, Dukakis, Gore—any of those stiffs. He had to take on the Reagan majority, the forty-nine-state-landslide majority, and do it inside of two months.

What was it Will's column said? . . . No, it was the headline:

THE SENATOR IS OVERMATCHED

The horror was, it might be true.

— ★ —

See, you had to understand how Joe thought about Bork. This was what lay at the base of Joe's depression. This was why his son Beau was off to college next month at Penn. Hell, this was why Joe said that stupid quote to the *Inquirer* . . . *Send us a Bork,* he'd said.

Not because he knew about Bork. At that point, he didn't know squat
. . . except . . . Bork was big-time. He taught Constitutional law, for Chrissake,
at *Yale*!

You had to understand how that was, to Joe.

One time—this was years before, his sons were young, in grade school—Joe
was sitting around with his pals in Wilmington, a weekend, somebody's backyard.

Joe said: "Where's your kid going to college?"

One friend said: "Christ, Joe! He's eight years old!"

Another said: "Ahh, there's a lotta good schools now."

"Lemme tell you guys something," Joe said. And he wasn't just shooting
the shit. He had the clench in his jaw.

"There's a *river of power* that flows through this country . . ."

His buddies rolled their eyes, but Joe acted like he didn't see.

"Some people—most people—don't even know the river is there. But it's
there.

"Some people know about the river, but they can't get in . . . they only stand
at the edge.

"And some people, a few, get to swim in the river. All the time. They get
to swim their whole lives—anywhere they want to go—always in the river of
power.

"And that river," Joe said, "flows from the Ivy League."

Robert Bork came from the River of Power.

And now he was going to the Supreme Court.

Unless he was stopped by Joey Biden—Syracuse Law, '68.

42

Error-Free
Ball

THE IMPORTANT THING for Michael was: no mistakes. He didn't get in this thing to be embarrassed, and he didn't get in to give up his most precious attainment—control. He'd scowl at the schedule his mechanics brought up to the State House. What is this, leaving for New Jersey at four?

Fund-raiser there starts at six . . .

Michael's head would start shaking—no. "We said three days a week." He meant three days in the State House—state business. He did not mean three days, eaten away by interviews, meetings with the campaign staff, phone calls, fund-raisers. He meant three days as Governor Dukakis. The Governor did not leave his desk at 4:00 P.M. "Three days means three days, my friend."

Of course, he didn't mean friend, either.

— ★ —

No mistakes meant nothing could drop through the cracks. Certainly not state business . . . but more than that: the Governor could not be *accused* of letting anything drop. If the campaigns, the career, of Michael Dukakis were based on philotimy—the way the voters, and he, saw himself, the perception of his own correctness—then, certainly, this new, this largest campaign could not erode that view. Michael did things one way—correctly. And the correct way, to him, meant the way he'd always done things.

He always had a blizzard of bills before the legislature. So that year, he was working up a blizzard of bills. And not small bills: a thorough reform of condo conversion (Michael had introduced the bill to create the first condos, twenty-three years before—how could he drop the ball now?) . . . insurance reform (Michael made his name, in the sixties, with no-fault insurance—he wouldn't let the system crumble now!) . . . a multiyear attack on the state's solid-waste crisis . . . billions for reform and aid to higher education . . . a complex and expensive fix for the state's $9 billion pension gap.

There was a task force, supposed to come up with a bill for universal health care—the first such system in the country. (Six hundred thousand citizens of *his Commonwealth* had no basic health insurance—a disgrace!) But the problems were so intractable, politically explosive, that the task force only came up with two little demonstration projects. Dukakis announced that *he* would pull together a bill for universal health care. *He* would hold the meetings. *He* would forge a consensus. *He* would ride the bill through House and Senate. . . . Sasso almost choked at the news. This was just the thing to send Mike down in flames. And *time* . . . where would they get the *time*? . . . But Michael said it was the correct thing to do. End of discussion.

—★—

That was, after all, the point of brilliance that had brought Dukakis to this run for the White House. Government that worked (at least, his government) worked because everybody in it could count on Michael to do the correct thing—not most of the time, but every time. Dukakis would make policy on his understanding of the greatest good for the Commonwealth. And the policy he stated was the policy in fact—no deviation, no deals. No one had to check with the corner office for a secret political agenda. Good government was Michael's agenda.

Same with the campaign: the plan was the plan. There was a certain solid comfort, knowing always where the candidate stood. There was none of the pulse-thumping brilliance of the Biden nights. Then again, there was never the palm-sweaty fear, wondering what the candidate would say or do.

Michael would say what he planned to say. He would not add to a speech. (No, but he'd subtract: he had radar for the snappiest applause lines . . . he'd cross them out.)

Michael would do what he said he'd do, what he always did in a campaign. He would assemble the best machinery at hand, set it to puffing and pumping, then keep building it, steadily, prudently—always with an eye to *ekonomia*—until he was satisfied it could organize and control the territory he meant to cover.

Once (only once) he was asked about Hart's theory of concentric circles. Michael started shaking his head before the theory got to first circle. "You go out, you build a statewide or a nationwide organization as quick as possible," he said.

"I'm not a concentric-circle guy."

End of discussion.

But what an organization he built: experienced, professional, disciplined.

. . . Zealots, ideologues, true believers (first circle, indeed!) made Michael
uneasy. There was a job to do. Michael wanted smart, tough hands. These he
found mostly in Boston (to be precise, Sasso found them for him). Michael
liked to deal with people he knew, or, at least, people from worlds he knew.
Susan Estrich, the campaign's Deputy Manager, came from Lynn, Massachusetts, and was now a professor of law at Harvard. Jack Corrigan, Chief of
Operations, was a native of Somerville—Harvard College and Harvard Law—
who'd worked with Sasso since the 1980 Kennedy campaign. Chris Edley, chief
of the issues shop, was not only Harvard, but Swarthmore College before that.
Nick Mitropoulos, the body man, another son of Greek immigrants, was
associate director at Harvard's Kennedy School before Michael whisked him
off to the State House, after his comeback in '82.

To these, Michael now added a handful of the dispossessed Hart staff
. . . but none of the idea wonks, none of the believers. He got the most
professional, Paul Tully, as Political Director. He got Alice Travis, an experienced California organizer. He got Teresa Vilmain, the toughest young whip
in Iowa. . . . Actually, Sasso got them. By the time they sat down with Michael,
they'd already decided that here was a candidate who had the legs to go all
the way. Their (mandatory) interviews with Dukakis were mainly to foster his
sense of control—no mistakes!

And to this organization, Michael now added money—scads of money. This
was the province of his fund-raising superstar, Bob Farmer, another friend of
years, another Harvard Law graduate. (And no ideologue—Farmer started his
fund-raising for the Republican John Anderson.) Farmer promised Michael,
before the campaign, he could raise six and a half million dollars by the Iowa
caucus—enough to get Michael through to New Hampshire. By the time
Michael announced, and Farmer set up shop in Boston's Meridien Hotel, he
fondly forecast that Michael could beat Biden's impressive first quarter: one-
point-seven million dollars (in three months!). . . . But now Farmer was
shredding his own best predictions. Money arrived in a flood. Everybody who
was anybody in Massachusetts wanted to play. Greeks all over the country
wrote checks like this was a wedding. By the end of Michael's first quarter,
Farmer had raised four and a half million dollars.

Of course, it could have been more: but Michael would not take PAC
contributions, or more than a hundred dollars from state employees; he forbade Farmer to dun people who did business with the state; not one cent from
lobbyists; and anybody who wanted a job—send back his check! Michael had
to raise money *his* way . . . that is, correctly. Actually, Farmer had to raise
the money correctly. Michael only had to show up at the dinners. It was
Farmer's point of pride that Michael never had to sit down and talk with
money men . . . never even had to pick up the phone!

What a marvelous machine was Michael's campaign!

"We try," said the brilliant body man, Mitropoulos, with a puckish smile
(phyllo wouldn't melt in his mouth) . . . "to play error-free ball."

With Michael, it was more than try . . . more like compulsion. It wasn't just speeches (of course, he had to work over the speeches) . . . and not just his interview with every employee (the Dukakis campaign would spend five hundred dollars to fly the new receptionist for Washington to the State House, so Michael could tell her how to answer phones correctly) . . . Michael wanted to see, to edit, every press release. He wanted to see every questionnaire sent back to newspapers and interest groups. He wanted to see the thank-you notes.

Alas, that left little time to take care of business.

What business?

State business!

That was the summer, 1987, the Commonwealth of Massachusetts opened Route 25. It was a fine road, seven miles of clean new concrete to take an hour off the commute from the Boston suburbs to the Cape. Michael meant to go to the opening. He built the road.

Sasso said: "Mike, you're not Governor anymore. You're running for President."

Michael said he wanted to go.

"Mike! Who gives a shit whether Route 25 is open?"

Governor Dukakis opened Route 25.

— ★ —

He was on time. He was always on time, though he hauled along more staff, more press than anybody else. In fact, this day, for his lunchtime talk at the Colonial House restaurant in Boone, Iowa, Michael was early.

"Guys, what're we doin' here?" he demanded in the van. He had fifteen minutes till he was scheduled to appear in the restaurant's basement. What was he supposed to do—sit and *chat*?

No. He was out of the van, pumping down Main Street, like this was a power walk. Into the first shop:

"Hi! Mike Dukakis. Tell me who you are."

It was about a hundred degrees, a hundred and ten on the pavement. The asphalt was soft. Michael, in his dark blue suit, black shoes, red power tie, was breeze-in-the-Berkshires brisk. He was out of that shop, into the next one:

"Tell me who you are."

It was not a howdy—not like Boone was used to: five suits burst into a dark little tailor-shop-cleaners, and the one in front, with the red tie and the air of command, demands to know your name . . . in a hurry. The old guy behind the counter literally took a step back. Michael squinted through the darkness and winced a wintry smile with his mouth. "Thought we'd see how's business."

What is this . . . the IRS?

Half an hour later, in the coffee shop basement, Michael was lecturing voters on the IRS. Actually, what he said he was doing was listening ("I'm a guy who does a lotta listening these days, so . . ."), but what that really meant was questions. ("Any questions? Any comments?")

That meant Michael had answers.

To wit: the deficit's killing us—would Michael raise taxes?

"No one who's running for President will tell you—I *hope*—that they will never raise taxes. But the first thing is tax *compliance,* which is now running at eighty-one percent.

"Eighty-one percent!" Michael repeated this (arguable) fact with one palm turned up, in front of one narrow, half-shrugged shoulder, his head shaking, no, all the while, no, like he, *himself,* could hardly believe how management of *simple tax collection* had come to such a sorry pass. Then he started quizzing them, like children:

"What does the IRS stand for? . . . Can anybody tell me?

"Internal . . . Revenue . . . Service. I'd like very much to put the service back in the tax system. In my state, you get your refund back in nine days."

Michael was now nodding, both fists on his hips.

"Nine days."

Most of his answers ended up, somehow, in Massachusetts . . . with Michael nodding, head thrust forward, eyes almost closed, fists cocked bantam-bold on his hips, or one palm turned up in tacit insistence: *You tell me that doesn't make sense! Go ahead! Am I right or what?*

"You're looking at a guy who's a full-employment Democrat. Can I tell ya what that means? In my state, unemployment is running at . . . what? . . . Three-point-two percent.

"Three-point-two percent."

He even worked out a passable "my-state" patter on farming. (No, not fruit, or Belgian endive. He insisted: "I never said that!"—very upset was Michael at being mocked for "yuppie agriculture.") This was about new products from old crops.

"Look. What's the problem?" he'd start the quiz. "Overproduction! . . . So what do we do? Make a marriage! (Shrug) Make a match! . . . In my state, we've got a terrific new road, Route 25, to Cape Cod. It runs through the cranberry bogs. So, ya don't wanna use salt. Whadda we use? . . . A great new de-icer—costs a little more, but it's worth it. Can anybody tell me what it's made from? . . . Corn!"

It was always hard to tell what effect these certainties had on a crowd of Iowans. The little fella seemed smart, sure of himself—that much you couldn't miss. But it wasn't enough to make a crowd jump up and cheer. A nod of understanding, approval—that was about the most you'd see.

But you could also see that this was unsatisfactory to Michael. He seemed most intent on showing them, he was, on all points, correct.

And you could see, too, in the back of the room, a table manned by the local field staff, who would turn those nods of approval into names on the sign-up sheet . . . and you knew those names would get back to Des Moines, *today,* to be put into the computers (Michael's Iowa ops were computerized up the wazoo) . . . and those people in Boone would all get calls, and get names of their neighbors for them to call . . . and nothing would drop through the cracks . . . no mistakes!

No, Michael's machine was always working—as it was, forty-five minutes, to the minute, after Michael started speaking in the coffee shop basement, when his trip director, Jack Weeks (a boxer's build in a fancy suit and the light gray eyes of a wolf) held the door for the Governor, and Michael's black wing tips trudged upstairs . . . and even there, apart from him, Michael's machine was working, as Nick Mitropoulos, the body man, the eyes and ears, alerted him that Boston was also in a heat wave, and air conditioners were straining the supply of electric power, the state might have to go to alert, cut back supply in the grid ten percent, require reductions in demand from industry . . . Michael grabbed for the proffered phone:

"No!" he barked. "There's plenty of capacity. Yeah. Plenty. And I think you—you just go out there, say that . . . right. And we'll launch an immediate investigation. Monday. Yep. Tha-a-nk you . . ." He cracked down the phone.

And even in that minute he spoke, the machine was at work, as his state coordinator, Mark Gearan, discovered a wedding shower in the restaurant's back room, and Nick said: "Let's get 'im back there . . . and make sure we send her a note." So, in another minute, Michael burst in, like the IRS, upon a score of little white girls and white ladies, all dressed up in flowered things, while Nick—round and smiling, the pol's pol, like an old friend of the family— introduced him around, to the bride-to-be: "This is Christy . . . she'll be married Saturday . . . and the lovely hostess, Mrs. Irby . . ." Michael shook hands, posed for a picture, and he was gone, down the hall, while the side of Nick's mouth said to Gearan: "Make sure—a note."

Gearan said to the fresh scrawl on his clipboard: "Yessir."

And fifty minutes, to the minute, from his entry, Michael Dukakis settled his suit into the shotgun seat, reached for the shoulder belt, and with all certainties buckled in, rode away from a most satisfactory visit to Boone.

43

The
Age of
Dukakis

H E ALWAYS KNEW more than anyone else in that chamber. That
much you couldn't miss. The leg-
islature (especially the House) can be humbling—you need help to get anything through. But not for Dukakis. Year after year, through the 1960s,
Michael was convinced: things would be better if there were more people like
him in that State House.

And fewer ignorant hacks.

He had a million bills in the hopper—he was going to change this board to
a strong executive structure, or he was going to change that department into
a board . . . or he was going to reform this agency by requiring audits by the
state auditor, or he was going to reform the auditor's office by requiring audits
of the auditor—every year, a million tinkerings with the vents and valves
. . . all of which made perfect sense to him.

In fact, they were of such *obvious merit* that he would not brook opposition.
If you were against him, you must be drunk, or corrupt, or stupid. Half of his
remarks seemed to begin:

"Mr. Speaker, as I have explained before . . ."

Or: "As I tried to make clear to the Representative from . . ."

Or: "It should be obvious to everybody, by this time . . ."

One year, he'd lectured his colleagues so many times . . . when he got to
the speaker's well to explain yet another bill, he looked over the House, heaved
an audible sigh, and said: "Well. Here we go again."

Of course, he was disliked.

Well, it was mutual.

Actually, Michael's attitude was more like disdain. One time, he lectured a government class taught by his colleague Marty Linsky. Michael was asked if it was important to have a good relationship with the legislature. "No," Michael said. "That's not relevant." He wasn't there to make friends. And to throw a vote to a friend, well! . . . That would be a near-criminal breach of discipline and the public trust.

That's why he couldn't be ignored—that discipline: every issue, every bill, he probed for its government implications, and voted on the merits. When the three Reps from Brookline showed up together—Town Meeting, Kiwanis, or the Committee for Fair Housing—Linsky would insist on speaking first. It wasn't that Michael was such a hot speaker, but he was so sure of himself. If you came on after, even if you agreed, you'd only sound like a weak me-too. Even Beryl Cohen, elected two years *before* Dukakis—and no mean pol, a smart young comer (by '64 Beryl had moved up to the Senate seat from Brookline) . . . would keep an eye on Dukakis. You didn't want to end up on the other side.

That discipline, too, made Dukakis leader of the Democratic Study Group. This was a cabal of reformist legislators—not too many, maybe twenty votes on the best day . . . but they were young, serious, well educated, dedicated to the proposition that clean, activist government was the people's right, and their future. They'd meet, after sessions, at someone's home, or a restaurant . . . meetings would slide into dinner, drinks after that—but not for Michael. He was home for dinner, 6:00 P.M., and then he had meetings, or he had to do his radio show, or write his column for the Brookline paper, or he had legal work for Hill & Barlow . . . or Fran Meaney, his old law school pal, still the (unpaid) director of COD, would come by in his Volkswagen Beetle to drive Michael off to another corner of the state, to talk to clean-government Democrats. Michael and Fran had file cards on two thousand Democrats with whom Michael had discussed reform. No struggle was too remote, or too paltry.

Of course, people called them liberals—Michael and COD, Michael and his Study Group. But they certainly weren't liberal in their personal lives—straight arrows, to the core (and Michael the straightest of all). Nor were they wedded to the liberal Great Society. Michael was making his name, in fact, as a foe of the federally funded destruction of neighborhoods for urban renewal and expressways. Liberals were heading south, to march in Selma, or Montgomery. But Michael had no taste for the disorder, the unreason, of demonstrations.

Even at home, there were great liberal causes: for instance, the epic battle to desegregate Boston schools. Beryl Cohen (*there* was a liberal) was sponsor of the racial imbalance bill, to cut off state aid to any segregated school system. Beryl made his bill *the* litmus test for racial decency in Massachusetts. But he could never get Michael or the Democratic Study Group to help. In fact, Michael and friends seemed convinced that the irrational issue of race was impeding the crucial work of reform. When Martin Luther King led thousands

of Bostonians on a dramatic march to the Common in front of the State House,
Beryl marched. (Even a regular Democrat like Frank Bellotti showed up!) But
Michael was nowhere to be seen. High visions of racial justice were . . . well,
they were terrific . . . but when Michael said "power to the people," he meant
his people: the duly elected, responsible representatives of the Party, the
government—the clean, decent, educated few. That was his agenda. And as
the sixties drew to a close, the time had come for Michael to use his two
thousand file cards.

—★—

In fact, he'd already made one move: at the '66 state convention, Dukakis
almost grabbed off the nomination for Attorney General. That was the job he
had his eye on—second in clout only to the Governor, powerful enough to lure
into the race a former Governor (Foster Furculo), and the last Democratic
candidate for Governor (Frank Bellotti). Dukakis filed anyway. He was thirty-
two, with three years in the House. He urged Democrats to reject "the same
tired voices."

Fran Meaney managed the campaign. Carl Sapers, Michael's friend since
Harvard Law, had been counsel to a state crime commission, and fed Michael
a diet of scandal on Peter Volpe, the Governor's brother—which Dukakis
thereupon fed to the papers. Beryl Cohen, who was serving on a Senate
investigation, fed Michael a list of contracts allegedly influenced by contributions to Volpe, which put Michael back in the papers. Another friend, Hackie
Kassler, took care of fund-raisers—cocktail parties, ten dollars a pop. (But
before each party, the ladies of Brookline hosted turkey tetrazzini dinners,
each plate an extra fifteen bucks!)

Meanwhile, every weekend, most nights, Michael worked on the people who
mattered, the Party officials, the committeemen, who would pick delegates (or
would be delegates) to that convention. It was *obvious* to him: he simply had
to identify three to four thousand people and convince them—one by one, if
need be—that the Party had to do away with the clubhouse hacks and nomi-
nate active, progressive young people . . . like him!

And he was convincing. After all that free press, after a glowing nomination
speech by Beryl Cohen, after the Dukakis Girls (Kitty and some other Brookline matrons) made appearance in matching blue-and-green scarves, after
Michael's amateur troops charmed the convention by handing out fortune
cookies stuffed with slogans like "Happiness Is Dukakis for Attorney General!" . . . the first ballot left Bellotti some thirty votes short of nomination—
and Michael in second place.

Alas, that's as far as he got. Bellotti's floor lieutenants got the deal wrapped
up. The regulars were too strong in '66 . . . but Michael knew his time was
coming—and next time, 1970, he'd be ready.

—★—

And the Party would be ready for him. Reason and decency were on the
march! Kevin White, the polished and progressive Mayor of Boston, was

positioning himself for the 1970 Governor's race. (Michael was in close political contact with White.) . . . Beryl Cohen meant to run for Lieutenant Governor . . . and Michael Dukakis for AG—what a ticket!

They were all the shiniest of rising stars, who owed nothing to the clubhouse machine. Beryl and Michael talked about whether the state would accept two Young Turks from Brookline . . . but Michael said: Why not? They *were* the best, in tune with modern national Democrats, all in touch with each other, to better serve the people of Massachusetts. . . . This was Michael's dream come true.

And then, disaster struck.

Nixon won, in '68, and asked the Massachusetts Governor, John Volpe, to be Secretary of Transportation. Worse still, Nixon summoned Elliot Richardson, the state's Republican AG, to be Undersecretary of State. The Democrats in the legislature promptly nominated their favorite, an old-line Boston regular, the Speaker of the House, Robert H. Quinn, to fill Richardson's unexpired term as AG.

And there was Michael's problem: he couldn't stop Quinn, and he couldn't run against him: Michael was a Party-*builder.* He couldn't try to knock off a Democrat incumbent. Anyway, Michael wasn't strong enough to fight a bloody civil war.

So, he did what he had to: he voted *for* the old regular, Quinn . . . and then he walked over to the house of Beryl Cohen—his fellow reformer, and his friend since Brookline High. Michael knocked on the door, nine o'clock at night. When Cohen brought him in, Michael told him without preamble: Dukakis was now a candidate for Lieutenant Governor.

Beryl just gaped—he couldn't talk. His head was racing with the things they'd done together, the plans they'd made . . . twelve years! All he could finally pfumfer out was the horrible, obvious fact: "Michael, *I'm* running for Lieutenant Governor."

Dukakis just stared at the floor.

—★—

What else could Michael do? He'd gone too far, talked to too many people, rallied every reform group in the Commonwealth about the importance of the process, about *the kind of people*—serious people—who must come to the fore!

That was Michael's most characteristic phrase: "the kind of people." That's as personal as he got. Fran Meaney always tried to remind him: "You've got to ask for their help!" But it seemed to Michael, if they were informed of his credentials, apprised of his serious concern . . . it would be apparent that *he was exactly . . . the kind of guy.*

He showed them in so many ways. This was the time—amid the upheaval of the McCarthy campaign, Bobby Kennedy's race for the White House, his assassination, the inner-city riots, the Summer of Love, the intense anguish over Vietnam—that Michael Dukakis found his issues: highway planning and no-fault insurance.

Dukakis was the first legislator to help neighborhood groups save their homes from the highways. He was the first official to promote alternative plans and planners. And in '69, after Governor Volpe moved on to Washington, Michael lined up twenty members of the Democratic Study Group to demand from the new Governor, Frank Sargent . . . a *moratorium* . . . on highway construction in Boston.

Dukakis was also first to promote the new concept of no-fault insurance. Small cases would never go to court. A driver would collect from his own insurance—without regard to fault. This would streamline the courts, put money into the pockets of the aggrieved, and cut the cost of premiums in Massachusetts (at that time, the highest in the nation). This was not ideological, it was simply rational—in other words, vintage Dukakis.

Of course, no one thought he could do it. The lawyers, the insurance companies—they *loved* the old system. But they did not reckon with Dukakis, who went at this like a steam piston. The first year, he got his bill through the House, but was stopped in the Senate. After '68, when Quinn became AG and the House leadership was reshuffled, the new chairman of the Insurance Committee, Ned Dever, lined up against him. Michael's bill languished for another year while he worked on Dever. Finally, in 1970, Dever passed the bill to the floor, the House passed it again, but still, the Senate balked. So Michael went to work on the Senators: he'd sit them down and explain, in clipped, complete sentences, why his bill was the only reasonable and decent solution. He got Fran Meaney to organize a committee on the outside: Lawyers for No-Fault. The *Globe* piled on, editorializing for no-fault.

Dukakis went at his issue, in other words, just like he lined up his convention vote for Lieutenant Governor—with the same public-private mix of pressure and argument, the same meticulous organization, and dogged insistence on his own correctness. Eighteen hundred delegates, or twenty-six Senators—it was the same: Michael would hit them all.

If there was certainty to be had in this line of work, he would have it . . . at least he'd go to bed, on the last night, knowing there were no mistakes— no blank boxes on his checklist.

— ★ —

They stood no more than twenty feet apart, near the door of the convention hall in Amherst, Michael and Beryl Cohen. As candidates, they were barred from the convention floor, so all they could do was greet delegates at the door.

It was Saturday morning, June 13, 1970. The night before, the delegates had given the endorsement for Governor to the clubhouse favorite, Maurice Donahue, the Senate President. (Kevin White was rebuffed—but he'd fight on, in the primary.) Beryl was on top of his game, on top of the world. His candidate for Governor now held control of the floor. The Senators were Beryl's pals!

Then Donahue's man, Bob Kelly, came out to the gate, motioned to Beryl to step inside.

"I'm not supposed to be in there."

"It doesn't matter." Kelly sat Beryl down on the steps, then gave him the news: "You're not gonna win."

Beryl went berserk: "What the hell do you mean? . . . Donahue's gonna screw *me*? . . . How *could* he? . . . Why *would* he?"

Beryl asked: "Dukakis?"

Kelly shook his head. "Neither of you's gonna win."

Beryl jumped up, called to his guys—get the Senators outside the gates—right now! The vote was already starting. Delegations were mysteriously abstaining, taking dives . . . phone calls from Donahue's men must've frozen the chairmen.

Outside, Beryl saw Dukakis, just standing at the fence—poor little bastard had no idea.

"I just got told . . ." Beryl said. "Neither of us . . ."

Michael hardly blinked. Beryl thought he must not *get it*—Donahue was going to shaft them both!

Beryl couldn't stand still. He was going down the tubes! When the Senators got there, he gathered them under a tree. They had to help him! He was being screwed! They were all being screwed! Donahue wanted a deadlock so he could put in a ringer—his own man. They had to stop it . . . for Beryl. He was begging!

But how could they stop it? If you're working by deal . . . well, the deal can change.

And then, a funny thing happened on the floor. Dukakis's votes did not take a dive. They held him near the top through the first ballot—no one had a majority. Fran Meaney, Hackie Kassler, Allan Sidd, Carl Sapers, prowled the aisles for Dukakis. They wore red bandanas. They had hand signals, walkie-talkies. They had captains in the delegations. They had their plans, no matter what—they had assignments to rush the stage if the microphone suddenly went on the fritz and Donahue's men tried to mumble around, then raise someone's arm as the "victor."

A second ballot started. Up at the chair, delegates were coming forward: What was the deal? Was there a deal?

Donahue's men denied any deal.

Well, then, the delegates were voting Dukakis.

"The guy came to my house . . . twice!"

All of a sudden, it came clear, there wasn't going to be any deadlock, any deal—because Michael had not only beaten Beryl Cohen—he'd beaten Donahue, and anybody else who wanted his delegates. Michael had worked on those people for years . . . and no one could pick them off with a phone call—that era was over. This was another age—started that Saturday morning—the age of Michael Dukakis, who was, within minutes, the officially endorsed candidate for Lieutenant Governor of Massachusetts.

— ★ —

Well, it didn't quite work out in November. For one thing, Donahue and Kevin White spent the whole primary beating up one another. But even after White dispatched Donahue, there were problems.

The big problem was Frank Sargent.

Sure, he lucked into the Governor's chair (he was Lieutenant Governor when Volpe went off to work for Nixon) . . . but Sargent was no slouch. He, too, knew a new age was dawning, and sunrise was not going to find him acting like a Republican in a state where Humphrey beat Nixon, two-to-one. When Democrats in the House and Senate passed a bill to prohibit the President from sending citizens of Massachusetts to fight in "an undeclared war" . . . Sargent signed it. When National Guardsmen killed four students at Kent State, Sargent ordered the U.S. flag removed from atop the State House.

In fact, Sargent spent that whole year looking for ways to align himself with the state's Democratic "mainstream." Opposition to the war was not enough. He needed issues that hit closer to home.

And so, citizens of the Commonwealth were treated to a statewide TV address, in which the Governor revealed, he had rethought state policy, and was now announcing: a *moratorium* on highway construction in greater Boston.

In the summer, as the campaign heated up, Sargent asked for statewide airtime again, to announce that lobbyists for the lawyers and insurance companies were jamming the State House, trampling the interests of the citizens! Sargent would stand for it no more! He vowed to keep the Senate in session *till he got a no-fault bill.* . . . "I don't care if the session runs until hell freezes over!"

And the Senate passed no-fault.

There was great keening and rumbling from the insurance industry. This was the nation's first no-fault bill. Companies threatened to stop writing policies in Massachusetts. So Sargent went back on statewide TV—he signed the bill, on the air!

How could White and Dukakis match that?

They could not. In fact, White couldn't do anything in the last month of the campaign. A bleeding ulcer sent him to the hospital. Michael had to carry the ticket on his own.

And he did. Everybody saw how ably he ran, how he spoke on the issues. (And Michael only second man on the slate!) In fact, Dukakis wanted to debate: not against the Republicans' Lieutenant Governor nominee—he wanted Sargent.

Of course, Sargent ducked. He was cruising in the polls—and no one wanted to debate Dukakis: that was a pattern that would persist.

There were others:

Dukakis had to work with White's wise guys . . . but he didn't want their direction, their words in his mouth. He wanted his own people (who took their cues from him).

For the first time now, there was money—a different kind of money. (Though, still, there was turkey tetrazzini . . . in fact, Michael could cook a mean tetrazzini himself.) Michael had a friend doing money, Dick Geisser, a nonpolitician, a businessman who'd sold his company. Every night, Geisser would come to Michael's kitchen table with the checks, and read out the names.

"Nope," Michael would say.

"Nope, nope . . . send it back."

Michael wouldn't take more than five hundred dollars—though the law allowed one thousand. He didn't *like* contributions over a hundred. And no lobbyists—not a cent. And no one who did business with the state. No one who was *regulated* by the state.

His own guys—Carl Sapers, for one—told him he was crazy.

Geisser was the one who'd have to ask, "Why not?" . . . He was the guy who'd have to call up the donors, tell them why their money was no good. Michael would explain who this one was, and that one. It was a masterful tour of Massachusetts . . . by check.

That was the other pattern: Michael knew more than anyone else in that room. And the rest of the fellows—if they stayed, they fell into step. Everybody wanted good marks from Michael. You sure didn't want to argue: he'd give you a look—you weren't just wrong, you were on the wrong side!

In the end, the wrong side won. Michael's campaign ended a quarter-million votes short . . . but not without honor. Michael Dukakis had carried the Party standard, all by himself—and everybody could see . . .

Michael Dukakis should have been Lieutenant Governor.

That's what they said, afterward, in living rooms around the state. See, he never really stopped. After the election, he was out of the House, out of office—first time in ten years. He went back to Hill & Barlow (they made him a partner) . . . but, really, what he was doing was sewing up the state. The next time was his, to run his own race, his own way. He had earned it.

That's what they told him:

"Michael, you deserved it—you should be Lieutenant Governor."

Hell, more than a few said: Michael Dukakis should be Governor!

44

Their
Kinda
Guy

MAYBE THAT'S WHY it seemed so familiar—the living rooms, the coffee shops, the miles overland to the next little group. . . . Michael was convinced he'd done it all before. And that, in turn, fed his growing confidence in Iowa, his air of command, his self-possession. If it wasn't so efficient and purposeful, it could have been mistaken for ease.

Actually, it was more like relief. How could he have known, when he got into this, that it wasn't some mysterious sheet of sheer ice? He might have fallen on his face! People might have *ridiculed* . . . but they did not. Michael didn't even stumble. This wasn't any harder—wasn't any *different* . . . didn't feel different.

Sometimes, if he was alone, or with Kitty, or John, or the girls, he'd admit: it was almost unbelievable, how doable it was, how people looked at him as a *serious candidate* for the Presidency of the United States. That summer, *Newsweek* called him the Democratic front-runner . . . the man with the money and the horses . . . him! A child of parents who came to this country without one dollar, one word of English! It was . . . terrific.

Of course, that's not how it came out when he talked about his feelings . . . well, he didn't talk about his feelings. He might do a child-of-immigrants riff, but he'd rattle it off like one more credential, or some check mark on his to-do list:

Governmentthatworks . . .

Immigrantswhomadeit . . .

If a profile writer, or some other blip on his screen, asked what these months meant to him, they'd get a snappy answer that left no doubt: Michael was unswayed, unaltered . . . unmystified.

But, Governor, hasn't it changed, for you?

"When you first walk in, you don't know what to expect. Then you get your sea legs. You get your confidence. You have more information."

End of discussion. Michael's tone made it clear, he was past all that.

Sometimes, he'd say what a "terrific learning experience" Iowa had been. But when pressed for lessons learned, he'd say: "People here want very much the same things people everywhere want."

Of course, he meant people in Massachusetts.

By July, his wise guys were already after him to "broaden the message," to speak more "Presidentially," to be more "inspirational." Sasso's memo at the start of the month—the third-quarter plan, as John called it—gently suggested: "We have not hit that high note yet." Sasso urged him to reach for broader themes as he moved into the fall.

Of course, Michael took it from John—at least in concept. Sure, they could work more of that into the plan. . . . But if someone handed him a speech that strove for "that high note" . . . well, Michael went to work with his pencil, brought it back to "in my state."

They told him: People have to hear something more!

"It's a marathon, my friend . . . plenty of time for that . . ."

If they persisted, they found he had no more time for them.

"Nope. Nope . . . it's not me."

End of discussion.

The problem was, if he acknowledged that this was anything different . . . then, the next thing—they'd want him to be different. And he wasn't going to do that. Where would it stop?

"Nope. Steady as she goes, my friend . . .

"That's us . . . steady, strong."

He was most intent on proving that *he knew what he was doing.* And how could they argue? Ahead in New Hampshire . . . closing on Gephardt in Iowa . . . three million dollars *in the bank.* . . . Everything worked great!

Except when he *didn't* know:

He got to a café in Iowa, and ruled that the print press could follow him in—cameras out . . . nope, no cameras. (The iron ring still bothered Michael: the boom mikes, lights—how could people talk?)

Of course, the TVs went bullshit. They were doing stand-ups in front of the closed door: how Dukakis froze them out. . . . The Press Secretary, Patricia O'Brien, tried to soothe them: she knew campaigns, she understood . . . she'd talk to the Governor. . . . This was her credibility on the line, too!

So Michael came out, buckled up in the backseat, and Pat turned around from the front—she was on him.

"Governor, you can't do it that way."

"That's the way I do it."

"No, Governor, you can't do it. That is not the way you do it. Not in this."

"I don't want cameras . . . they change . . ."

"The cameras are why you're here!"

Now Michael glared at her in the front seat; he gave her the look. *"Will you listen to me?"*

"I'll listen to you when you start listening to me."

Of course, he knew she was right. That's what was galling. He was still staring at her with a look you'd give a misbehaving child . . . but he didn't have a leg to stand on.

"Well," he said. "Well. . . . Well! PUT ON YOUR SEAT BELT!"

—★—

The funny thing was, they got great press—respectful, serious—almost fond! This was partly because of the diddybops: they just assumed the race revolved around their man. But once the Duke's first-quarter fund-raising figures surfaced (*four* million?) . . . no one questioned again whether the guy was a player. He could play. . . . If anyone still made bold to ask *why* he thought he should be President, Michael had a neat and serviceable answer: opportunity for all, government that worked . . . he was more than airy ideas, he was the hands-on manager who *made it happen.* ("That's the *kinda leadership* I think we need in this country. I'm the *kinda guy* . . .")

Anyway, they seldom asked why. If they weren't speculating on the horse race, they were busy with Karacter . . . and it was apparent, Mike was their kinda guy.

Michael didn't screw around (but liked his wife), never took drugs (but blamed himself for not watching his wife), never got drunk (but would taste wine), never lost himself in fancy for a movie, a book, an idea of any kind . . . never overate, overslept, overworked, overpaid, overspent, overreached, overspoke . . . never lost control, in any way they could see.

And never changed.

Perfekt!

There was just enough for a nice, neat profile: a joke or two up front about how cheap he was (heh heh—that snow-blower is *twenty-five years old*—heh heh) . . . which played right into the "crisis of his life," the time he lost, in '78—because *he wouldn't raise taxes* fast enough . . . how sad he was, in loss, but how he got smarter (at Harvard!) and came back, better, harder, *brilliantly* . . . as Duke II.

Forty column inches—no loose ends.

There was a woman named Gail Sheehy on the prowl that summer—the Karacter Kops' drum majorette, she marched at the head of the parade. And after a long shiny-magazine inspection of Dukakis's life, she went (cautiously) gooey on her new squeeze:

". . . Or might we be ready for a hardheaded, thoroughly decent, pre-war model of a man, one who would wear very well indeed, never tell us a lie, give good value on the dollar, and keep Amtrak running on time?

"We have waited so long for a political leader to believe in with all our hearts . . ."

What higher praise could the Top Kop offer?

Even reporters, who actually tried to cover the man, could find no handle for dire speculation—secret failures, *frissons,* hints of danger . . . certainly not the Streak of Wildness.

Maureen Dowd, the most observant political writer on *The New York Times,* essayed The Profile that summer, and came out with:

The cheapness joke . . .

The passion for Kitty . . .

The crisis of his life, '78 . . .

And she wrapped up this life lesson as neatly as would Michael:

". . . When he recaptured the governorship in 1982, Mr. Dukakis had learned the art of politics. Duke II, as he is sometimes dubbed, does not scoff at patronage. He has created an awe-inspiring political machine. . . ."

God! She must have been talking to Sasso!

Actually, the big-feet were all talking to Sasso, though Patricia O'Brien was a splendid Press Secretary, and Sasso had ruled, by memorandum, that *all* comment—from *everyone*—had to funnel through Pat's shop. What he meant was, everyone but him.

John thought O'Brien hadn't quite made the leap from her previous life as a working reporter. She didn't quite *get* how the game was played. So every once in a while, he'd work a story, or a big-foot, himself. When it came time to announce Michael's extraordinary $4.5 million first quarter, John was rubbing his hands with relish. This was the kind of story that would put his man on the map!

Pat meant to announce the figure, on the day such figures were announced. But, no . . .

John meant to work this: Michael would be in Atlanta, ten days before the figures were announced. So Sasso would leak *partial* figures (not enough to step on the main story) to *The Atlanta Journal.* Then, just to cover his tracks (and take care of a friend, or two), he'd leak some numbers to *The New York Times* . . . so both papers would have partial stories. (Who could tell where they got the stuff?) Other papers and TV would pick up from that. *Then,* later, comes the main story. That way, John could get *a whole week* of play . . . with news organizations chasing each other to find out exactly how big was Michael's triumph. Gorgeous!

Pat said: "John, you can't choreograph reporters. They aren't puppets! It's going to cause a lot of ill will . . ."

John said: "You're right, Pat . . ."

But he did it anyway. Sasso knew which stories offered room for a few downfield moves and which he had to run straight up the middle. (The story of Michael's decision to run, back in March—no one got that early, not a whisper!) . . . Sasso was good with the press—that was part of his job—he was good at his job. And Pat didn't have to know everything. Who was she gonna complain to—Michael?

Michael didn't have to know everything, either. He'd long since come to rely on Sasso's friendships within the press, his handling of stories . . . to Michael it was a simple management problem, basic shop. Michael knew, John ran a good shop.

—★—

The proof was in the papers. In July, at last, Kitty made her announcement—she had taken speed for twenty-five years. This was a textbook piece of management.

Al Peters, husband of Kitty's sister, knew of a hospital in Norfolk, Massachusetts, that was dedicating a new wing for substance-abuse patients. The campaign got the hospital to dedicate it to Kitty.

Kitty's statement was a labor of weeks . . . three drafts, four drafts . . . they had to answer all questions—favorably, but firmly. They wanted to raise this once, then put it to bed. No second-day loose ends . . . and no lingering questions about Michael:

How could Mr. Hands-On not know about his wife's addiction for twenty years?

Why did he lie when she went for treatment, in '82 . . . that story about her hepatitis?

That was Sasso's worry—this could raise doubts about Michael. Tell the truth, John had no patience for this drug business. John didn't even want to deal with Kitty.

To Kitty, it seemed none of the men understood. It got to be very much a woman's affair: Patricia O'Brien and Susan Estrich worked with Kitty on her speech, and they worked in secrecy. If word got out, this would turn into a circus. The campaign had people calling doctors to make sure the medical facts checked out. Of course, they were only asking about "a friend." The doctors said there was no way five milligrams a day could constitute a physical addiction. But that was the word Kitty wanted to use: addiction. This was important to Kitty. This wasn't just a problem of press relations. This was her coming out.

That's why it was wonderful that Michael was there, when she told the world. Michael could have been on the road—Iowa, California—anywhere. Let Kitty do her thing. But Michael said no. He'd be with his bride. That's what made it so moving: he was next to her, at the hospital, as she started the story . . . and he started to cry. She paused to brush a tear from his cheek. And another . . .

"Michael didn't know," she said. "I was already taking the pills when I met him. Pills are easy to hide, and I hid them."

(She hid them in a shoe—she always hid the pills in her shoes.)

"But above all, I didn't tell my husband, because I knew, if I did, I would have to confront my dependency. I would have to stop. I was afraid I couldn't stop."

The small crowd applauded her warmly. And by the next day, the whole country was applauding Kitty.

And applauding Michael.

His ignorance for twenty years, his lie in '82—those issues disappeared overnight, replaced in the lore of the big-feet by his mastery of the story. The next day, E.J. Dionne quoted lunch-buddies:

"In its current mood, some politicians said, the nation may reward candidates who appear a bit vulnerable: confessional politics may also be smart politics."

In fact, he suggested, Dukakis helped himself by softening his icy image. E.J. quoted another anonymous source, saying Kitty made Michael "look like a warm, caring, loving and compassionate husband."

Of course, that referred to his tears . . . which appeared in only one paper, E.J.'s own *New York Times*. See, attendance at the hospital had to be controlled. No press circus—Kitty might crumble. So the campaign put the hospital event on the schedule—but without explanation. Only *after* she knew Kitty started her speech (this thing was timed to the minute—no mistakes!) did Patricia O'Brien make a round of calls alerting (only local) reporters that Kitty had something to say—did they want a half-hour with her that afternoon? . . . So, at the hospital that morning, there were just a couple of local TVs . . . and Maureen Dowd, from the *Times*—she did a great job. And the scene at the hospital made the story so much better.

Lucky she got there. She must have been talking to Sasso.

— ★ —

For Kitty, this was the start of a new world. She was scared . . . stressed out . . . and thrilled. She must have done fifteen one-on-ones that afternoon—same script, but still: one after another, after the other . . . it was brutal!

Susan Estrich or Patricia O'Brien would show in the next reporter, the next camera crew . . . for *hours* Kitty kept her place, in her living room, on one of the tatty old Danish-modern chairs (Michael would never spring for new furniture: What's wrong with our chairs?) . . . and Kitty was spectacular. She never lost her focus, or her charm, her vulnerability, her strength. The story never lost its freshness, or its intimacy. She just . . . well, she shined.

And she was calm, full of purpose.

It was strange, how collected she seemed, at the center of so much frenzied attention. But that's what gave her such focus. She knew she was doing something important—and it was right—because it was so important to her. This was not about Michael, or the state, or even the campaign. This was about *Kitty.* And in that line of reporters that stretched into the evening, there was interest, and more: there was connection, esteem, identity.

The local evening news had twenty minutes on Kitty.

The kitchen phone was ringing with requests for Kitty.

The campaign was working overtime on a new national schedule for Kitty.

When the last reporter had gone, Kitty walked back to the kitchen, exhausted, excited, satisfied. She popped open a bottle of wine—glasses for everyone. She knew she'd done a wonderful job.

But even she didn't know the chord she'd touched. She started to find out the next morning—6:00 A.M., she was off to Minnesota. She wanted to tell her story there, where she'd gotten treatment, where her triumph had begun. . . . She was flying commercial—back of the plane—and before they'd even taken off, a man, a stranger, came to her, down the aisle. He bent over the back of the chair in front of her, and almost whispered:

"You know, my wife had the same problem—nine years . . . and till yesterday, she thought she was the only one. God bless you . . ." Then *he* started to cry.

—★—

Kitty was always great when she had something to do, something important, whenever people were counting on her, paying attention to her. It's only when the music stopped—down time, delays—she'd get itchy . . . and then, watch out!

"I'm going to take a nap . . . I've *got* to get some rest, the way they have this *trip* . . . ucch, God! . . . *Andrew!* . . ."

That was her first body man, Andy Savitz, a Georgetown lawyer, a Rhodes scholar, and a wise-guy-in-training.

"*Andrew!* Is there some *reason* there's *no soda* in this room? . . . *Don't we have a list of everything to put in the room?* . . . Why don't we have a *list?* Would it be too much trouble to have a list? *I want to see the list!* . . . *Andrew!* When can we get the list? . . . Just a Perrier! How can I . . . really! . . . Ucch! *Dammit!* . . . *Is that too much to ask?*"

Savitz, of course, did not join that campaign to make lists of snacks.

But it drove her nuts if (it seemed to her) the staff didn't pay attention . . . or made her wait . . . or did sloppy work. Would they do that to Michael? They would not! He would not stand for it! Well, why should she?

She had a group of lady friends who'd rotate as traveling companions, paying their own way, to help with wardrobe, makeup, schedules, late-night conversation . . . anything she needed. But that was no substitute for staff she could rely on.

Why should she work without a full-time speechwriter? Wasn't she giving speeches?

Why was she flying commercial when Michael had his own plane? Didn't she do as much as Michael?

In fact, she did every bit as much as Michael—*had* to, with his time so short . . . his days, every week, in the State House. And Kitty was the campaign's way of saying: We Care About You. . . . She was the chief surrogate, the *emotional* surrogate for Michael. In fact, she could say, We Care . . . better than he!

And she knew it.

And now there was even more: she wasn't just Mrs. Governor, Mrs. Michael . . . she was Kitty. People knew about *her.* People wanted to hear *her.*

— ★ —

Near the end of July, there was a First Ladies' Forum, in Des Moines, a gathering of the Democratic spouses . . . all on one stage, like some horrid pageant—but this was about brains, commitment, passion, persona. Kitty meant to own the place.

This time the speech went through eight drafts . . . nine . . . and there was a speech coach, and the campaign's adman, Dan Payne. Kitty wanted to see tapes of herself speaking her speech—they rented a hall for practice at MIT, and Marilyn Chase, Kitty's Chief of Staff, got her husband and his professional crew to shoot the video.

Over and over and over . . . Kitty worked at this with a whip on her own back. This was about *her* . . . what kind of First Lady she would be. This was about her issues, her style . . . her substance.

And then, she flew to Iowa, to deliver her speech. The hall at Drake University was full—press everywhere, *a dozen tripods* on a platform in the hall! Kitty wore red. She looked spectacular.

And the way it worked out . . . it was too perfect!

Hattie Babbitt led off—education would be her priority: our children . . . Then Jill Biden—education . . . our children . . .

Then Kitty got up and laid into *her* issues: homelessness, refugees, Holocaust. She was . . . well, she was *different.* And it wasn't just different issues. She had *done things.* She had a record of concern, substance, and achievement.

She spoke about her *public identity.*

From the stage, she looked over the crowd with such a fierce and full elation . . . you could see what it meant to her. Same way you could see, afterward, when she said to Andy Savitz: "You should feel *really good. "* Of course, she meant that's how she felt.

They were driving to the airport. Kitty had to fly to Traverse City, Michigan, to meet Michael at the National Governors' Conference.

And . . . *at last* . . . there was a plane waiting for her—*her own jet!*—to fly her to her connection in Detroit.

Well, she was absolutely queenly in that plane . . . and absolutely alone. Savitz was *campaign* staff . . . and this was a trip in her role as the Governor's wife.

So she made her own connection to the commercial flight, in Detroit. And made it fine. She was so excited. She couldn't wait to tell Michael how her speech had gone! In fact, she was *wonderful* . . . until that little shuttle to Traverse City *sat there . . . sat there* . . . and *sat there . . .*

And Kitty blew:

"If this plane doesn't take off *right now . . . there is going to be TROUBLE, "* she told the pilot. In fact, she might as well have told everybody in the plane. "I have to meet my *husband . . . who is running for PRESIDENT . . . YOU MAY NOT KNOW WHO I AM, BUT YOU CAN TAKE IT FROM ME, THERE'S GOING TO BE TROUBLE . . ."*

She was right about that. The seat behind her was occupied by a reporter, who fed the incident straight to a columnist for the *Boston Herald.*

45

Shit
Happens

THE THING Jane saw from the stage was her kids. She got up to speak at the First Ladies' Forum, and she saw them in the front row—Matt, Christie, Katie—all staring down at their shoes. They were so nervous. Their mom! How was she ever gonna *do* this? . . .

Well, she'd had help. Bob Shrum put the speech together; and she had a coach, that man who helped Babbitt after they found out poor Bruce's head bobbed around like a dashboard doll's when he spoke. And Jane Gephardt did practice, marching around her bedroom, giving her speech to the pillows, to the mirror—that worried woman in the mirror!

How was she ever gonna do this?

It wasn't just the speech—the speech was fine. It wasn't any one thing. It was everything. At once. She had two houses already, one in Virginia, one in St. Louis, though Loreen took care of the one in St. Louis, and now they had two apartments in Des Moines—well, actually *West* Des Moines, which was more like East Jesus, a half-hour from anyplace . . . not to mention that Jane didn't know Des Moines, so a trip to anyplace started with directions, or a call to the staff, who didn't know Des Moines, so they'd drive her back and forth from the office to East Jesus on the main street of town, Grand Avenue, which was a Chinese water torture of stoplights, so that meant she was an hour from anyplace she had to go . . . usually someplace she had to go *now*. West Des Moines! It was one of those things that looked better on paper.

They were garden apartments (no gardens), one apartment for Loreen, another for Dick and Jane and the kids, except Dick wasn't often there, so

Betsy Bridge, the baby-sitter, would crash on the couch. And Frank, who was Don and Nancy Gephardt's son—he was going to work on the campaign that summer—took the other room at Loreen's . . . which meant that when his mother came—Nancy was going to travel with Jane—she would end up on Loreen's couch, or on the floor. And Carleen Overstreet, from Dick's Washington staff, who drove the van out with household chattel (except the dog, Rogue, who had to be dropped off at St. Louis), stayed a while at Loreen's, or Jane's. Tell the truth, if you came in at night, you didn't know whose body you'd have to step over.

It was like camping—without the woods. Without the privacy. And with lots more stuff. The staff had to rent beds, and mattresses, and dressers, and couches, and chairs, and TVs. Jane and the kids brought some of their own clothes when they flew out, each with a suitcase or two. And Loreen brought her own car, packed to the gills—pots and pans (they had to cook!) . . . and an ironing board. And then the van showed up with a solid load—kids do not live by clothes alone. And Jane had to go to a discount store for plates, forks and knives, pillows and sheets, and towels . . . and more sheets, when it came clear the couches were going to be beds, and more sheets, which she tacked up in lieu of curtains. And that didn't count the groceries . . . or the foodstuffs, as it turned out, since one of the campaign staff had a card to shop at a warehouse outlet, one of those deals for union men where you could buy food cheap but only in bulk—giant cans of this or that—or sometimes you could find regular-size, but you had to buy a dozen, or a case . . . so Jane would tote a twelve-pack of family-size Jif . . . along with a Brobdingnagian jar of jelly. All they needed was a truckload of Wonder Bread.

It was a great idea . . . move the family to Iowa for the summer. Dick said they'd be together. It'd be good for Matt, for the girls. It'd be greeaaat! And it always made the papers, every profile: *Gephardt is so serious about Iowa that he has moved his wife and children . . . and his seventy-nine-year-old mother.* . . . It was one of those things that looked better in the paper.

Like the schedule—the ninety-nine-county schedule. It was easy to say: "I've been to every county in this great state . . ." Except you'd be dead by the time you could say it. You'd take off in the van from some county courthouse and drive through a thousand square miles of corn before you got to the third county over, which was the next place you could yell *Fire!* . . . and more than two people would come. Of course, the staff in Des Moines (Gephardt had a big staff—that showed he was serious about Iowa) was only working from maps. What the hell . . . Monona County, Buena Vista County—same, uh . . . *quadrant* of the state! You put your thumb on one, you can touch the other with your pinky—look!

And Dick would do it. That was never at issue. In fact, that's what he'd talk about, when he got to Monona County: how this was his *second trip* to Monona County . . . that's how *serious* he was about Iowa. In fact, he'd tell them, he'd been to sixty-seven counties . . . and he was going to hit *all ninety-nine.* It was like the sign at McDonald's, where they change the number in front of the "billions." (Burgers must be good, right?) But sometimes, that seemed like all he did: he'd go around, and say how much he'd gone around.

Unless he had to go around some other state (forty-seven states in the past fourteen months!), or the place where they had to go around was just too dinky and distant, even for Dick . . . then Jane would have to go around. Jane and Nancy would pile the kids in the back of the van and drive—forever . . . while the kids whooped it up in the back and Jane tried to buy quiet with candy. Nancy drove. She was an Iowa girl, she knew the roads. They'd do a hundred miles to a coffee shop in some little town, and Jane would shell out another fortune in quarters for the game machines for the kids . . . while she talked to six people at one table about how they'd gone around. ("You know, we've been in seventy-one counties!") And then they'd pile back in the van—maybe make a pit stop, where Jane would buy more candy, pump herself a new tank of gas—and another county would rumble by, or two or three, till they got to another coffee shop, another video game, another tableful of Iowans.

Jane figured the staff didn't know what to do with all these willing Gephardts. She'd spend a half day on the way to . . . three people! She'd tell them that, when she got back—even if it was ten at night, she'd stop by the office. The young staffers were still there, of course. That's one of the things the Gephardt people talked about, when they worked—was how *long* the Gephardt people worked. Yessir, that midnight oil! . . . And they were always nice to her: "Jane, did you get to eat?" They'd offer some pizza they had ordered in.

No, she had to run. She was still a half-hour from East Jesus. The kids had to get to bed. She had . . . well, what did she have? If Dick got in that night, she could talk about her day: the drive to Ringgold County . . . she saw that nice Jim Whatsisname—Remle's friend, with the beard . . . and then Page County, and Cass, on the way back. And she stopped at the office.

Oh, what's goin' on?

"Nothing—same . . ." Jane would say. "They were all in front, eating pizza . . . d'you have any quarters?"

She'd given the kids all her quarters. Darn! She needed quarters for the washing machine in the hall.

—★—

Dick knew he was losing ground—to be precise, he wasn't gaining fast enough. And now, with Dukakis hitting his stride, and Biden's numbers finally inching up, and Simon starting to campaign full-time, Dick could feel it slipping. Just after Hart dropped out, the polls gave Gephardt twenty-four percent, called him the new front-runner. That was bullshit; but then, when the next poll knocked him down to eighteen, and then fifteen, everybody started asking: What's wrong with Gephardt?

That summer in Iowa, there were a thousand wise guys and wise-guys-in-training, doing business for seven Democratic candidates. And six-sevenths of these would be glad to explain *exactly* what was wrong with that blond-fascist-phony-protectionist-flip-flop Gephardt. Just buy them a beer! So all the writers in the Hotel Savery bar had these gorgeous wise-guy quotes, with which to *write* what was wrong with Gephardt . . . and they did. Then the editorial writers piled on: Gephardt was going to start a trade war with Japan! . . . And the next poll showed Dick's numbers down . . . again.

Whad I tellya? . . . Guy's a stiff!

Gephardt didn't need polls to tell him he hadn't got the system down. He'd go around the state, talking about how he'd gone around, and he'd see the same people. Nothing wrong with those people. He loved those people! But, uh, what about their friends? . . . What about those people he'd been calling in Cedar Rapids? Called them every two weeks—since last *year.* . . . Well, they still weren't quite, you know, *ready to commit.* (One of the kids in the office said he saw one at a Dukakis event.) What about the UAW? Chuck and Carol Gifford, they were like new cousins. (Just the other night, Dick was over, brought Jane and the kids, and the kids played around Chuck's garage, and Jane helped Carol straighten the kitchen, and Dick and Chuck had a *great* talk about the new patio Chuck built behind the house.) But what about their union members? How many were leaning to Biden?

Dick had a guy named Bill Fleming running Iowa—nice guy, clean, dedicated, well mannered, smooth with the press. He could talk just like a government report about his "concerns" . . . "impacting the agenda." But Dick didn't want to read memos on *modalities* . . . the Iowa staff couldn't even give him a hard count.

Gephardt knew this much about the system: what you needed was a list, thousands of names of actual people who actually said they would go to their caucuses and stand up for Gephardt. That's all that mattered. In the office, they called these people Number Ones. (That meant Dick was Number One with them.)

So every time Gephardt would get back to Iowa, he'd ask for the hard count. "How 'bout our Number Ones?"

"Uh, I think they were, uhm, gettin' 'em together today. Today and tomorrow . . . this week."

"I thought we were going to have them last week."

"We haven't got, uh, hard numbers yet, from the First District."

If Dick pressed the point, he could get the whole story about why they didn't have the numbers together, how Bill locked up Saturday night and Paula didn't have keys Sunday morning, and the phones were screwed up Sunday night, and the van broke down, and they had to send Glenn . . . but what was the point?

Mostly he'd get the briefer version, the standard slogan ever since Dick saw a bumper sticker out in his fifty-seventh Iowa county . . . and he couldn't stop cackling about it.

"Yeah," he'd say, and he'd laugh, every time: "Shit Happens."

He was trying to keep a good attitude. You start pressing, six months before the first votes, you're finished. People can smell fear. And he wasn't supposed to worry about mechanics—the hard count, the phone banks, the schedule, people who just hung around the office. That was Carrick's department, or Fleming's . . . they were the pros. Dick was just the candidate.

Anyway, he didn't know what more he could do. He was working flat-out just to hit the new counties, make the speeches, the visits, and the money calls, just to stick to the schedule, the plan. . . . Problem was, he didn't really have a plan—not since Hart got out.

The whole Gephardt plan was to sneak up on Hart, run as the Democrat who was *not* Gary Hart. (That's one reason Gephardt fastened onto the issue of trade—he knew he could use it to pick a fight with Hart.) If Dick could nick Hart in Iowa, he'd get ink. Even a strong second, and Dick would get the big Iowa bounce—the press has to have a contest. And if it went head-to-head, Dick and Hart . . . well, Dick was made to order for Super Tuesday. He was more conservative than Hart, more Reagan-Democrat, more tough-talk-on-the-Soviets . . . more mainstream, more border-state . . . more *electable.*

Fact was, Gephardt was always *not* someone. He was not an old ward-heeler Alderman (he was a Young Turk). He ran for Congress in the wash of Watergate as not an old politics-as-usual hack (he was a Fresh Face). He rose in Congress as not an old New Deal Liberal (he was a new-breed Hard-headed Democrat), and then he ran for President . . . but Hart screwed up *big-time* . . . so who was Dick going to be not?

—★—

That's why he started poking at Dukakis in the press, jabbing him on trade (the Duke's trade policy was like Reagan's—no policy at all) . . . needling Dukakis on the Massachusetts Miracle (it's no miracle when most of the money came from Pentagon contracts) . . . challenging Michael to say what he would do in the White House, say *something* beyond Good-Jobs-at-Good-Wages.

Anyway, those two spotted one another the minute the bell rang: Gephardt and Dukakis, both thinking their way through, two guys who'd go the distance, do whatever it took . . . and lose no sleep—the baddest German shepherds in the Alley of Process. And it did, frankly, bother Dick when Michael waltzed into the race (just a year before the first votes!) and claimed for himself the mantle of government-that-works . . . Mr. Know-It-All! Right! The guy couldn't find the men's room in the Capitol!

And it didn't improve Dick's mood that Dukakis immediately owned New Hampshire, where Dick had been trying to make friends for three years . . . or that Michael got away with mouthing some palaver about the importance of the family farm (and *The Des Moines Register* wrote it up like policy!) . . . or that Dukakis milked the developer-lawyer-banker-business fat cats of Massachusetts, and Greeks across the country, for more money in his first quarter than Dick would see in a year and a half.

That was the problem. You knew Dukakis would be in it till the end because he'd never run out of money. And you knew the diddybop Boston press (which provided New Hampshire with its "national" news) would cover Dukakis like the nominee—like no one else (and no place else) mattered. That's why Duke could go around saying, "I did a good job in Massachusetts—so make me President." Hey, get serious! . . . Massachusetts ain't Missouri . . . or Montana . . . or Moscow.

So Dick was going to hit him—first big debate, the TV debate from Houston—Dick was going to pound Michael's head. Foreign policy, trade policy, ag policy . . .

That was always the strategy from Gephardt's hired button men—go in there and kill. That was Dick's standard debate-prep: Shrum would feed him lines, egging him on to break the rules, jump in, interrupt, make the point— turn right to the guy and *take his head off.* . . . Meanwhile, Carrick would sit in a corner, mashing his fist into his palm, and grinning, like this was going to be fun. Carrick always figured you "won" if you gave the press "red meat." If you took someone's head off, you'd be in the lead in the next day's paper, you'd be the sound-bite on TV for a week! . . . And Reilly, the pollster, was blowing up the image of a smirking Dukakis like one of those balloons in Macy's parade. Reilly knew Dukakis, served as pollster to the last guy (the only guy) to beat him—Ed King, who threw Michael out of the Governor's chair in '78. So Reilly—dark, bearded, speaking dire truths in his savvy staccato—was Dick's font of Dukakis lore: "Y'think y'gonna kill him. Y'can't kill this little sonofabitch. He'll get up again—the comeback. That's his thing, the comeback. Y'gotta drive a stake through his heart."

See, Dick's hit men were convinced he couldn't pull the trigger. They had to . . . *make him kill.* And Dick, of course, he was trying to listen. He was trying to do the job, like they told him . . . same as the speech: look at the crowd, slow up, hit that next line, HIT IT. Same as the makeup: they thought he looked too blond, too boyish, too . . . nice. So, for Houston, they made him up in a death mask—couldn't smile if he tried. And they painted eyebrows on his head—guy's so fair, y'can't see his eyebrows! And they put him in the suit: not his own suit, but a suit of their devising . . . gray, with shoulder pads, made him look like Clark Kent coming out of the phone booth.

Problem was, the pads kept sliding around, down his arms, down his chest, till Dick felt he was growing tits, and it made him edgy in his chair, till he couldn't even, you know, cock his head, or make his dog face . . . you know, sit and listen . . . so how could he know when to break in and KILL . . . with new tits and eyebrows? So he never did deliver any lines on the Duke. And he knew he'd screwed it up, even before he got off stage and his guys started yelling: how were they s'posed to do their jobs when he couldn't even PULL OFF A SIMPLE GODDAM HIT? . . . Well, Dick felt awful. They wiped off his makeup while he hung his head in a chair in the holding room . . . damn! . . . damn! . . . *damn!*

"S'not too late," Carrick murmured. "All th'press's outside."

Dick looked up. Carrick started mashing his palm again.

"Mahcrophones . . ." Carrick said.

"Let's do it," Dick said.

"Camm'ras . . ."

"Come on, let's go!"

So Dick went out and stuck it to Dukakis in the pressroom, and that set off the rumble. Duke's wise guys started squealing: Knifed in the back! Sneak attack! Gephardt must be desperate! Never said a peep in the debate!

Gephardt's killers answered back in the press: Come on, come on . . . you wanna debate?

And that's how the great Duke–Dick Debate was born. And Duke's guys were crowing: Gephardt's supposed to be the front-runner . . . now he's making our guy the man to beat in Iowa!

Dick's guys were suddenly quiet in their suits. They were gonna get live TV in the Boston market (i.e., New Hampshire). . . . They were going to pin Dukakis, one-on-one, for an hour. . . . And they were damn sure going to cattle-prod Gephardt into a bloodthirsty serial-murder rage!

Well, it was all-around splendid.

— ★ —

So they started with "opposition research." That's what the hit men call it when they Hoover the ground behind another candidate, looking for a silver bullet they can promptly fire into the poor bastard's neck. In Dick's case, the big-nozzle vacuum was the CRS, the Congressional Research Service, an arm of the U.S. government created solely to serve members of the club—Congressmen, Senators—and their staffs. Campaign ammo wasn't *exactly* what the CRS was supposed to provide, but then again, none of the research requests—for example, "every published article in the last twelve years containing the words 'Dukakis' and 'tax' "—came *exactly* from Gephardt's staff. House staffers everywhere took a sudden interest in Michael Dukakis. (Hey, what are friends for?)

And it wasn't just "Dukakis" and "tax" . . . there was "Dukakis" and "trade" . . . and "defense" and "agriculture" and "economy" and "environment" and . . . and . . . and . . .

The upshot was, Dick got books: all kinds of crap. He didn't just learn what Dukakis said about the Harkin-Gephardt farm bill . . . or everything Dukakis said about farming in Iowa. He also had at hand what Michael said (July 1987) on a visit to North Carolina, about the current no-net-cost tobacco program of supply management.

And, Dick being Dick, he tried to learn the stuff. He carried those books around the country—or rather, Brad, the body man, carried them, guarded them like the magic sword. When, at last, Gephardt swooped back to Iowa (far too late, in the opinion of his killers) to prepare in earnest for the showdown, he was well informed:

"Massachusetts currently owes one billion dollars to the state retirement system."

He was lucid:

"Massachusetts mental health facilities ranked forty-first out of the fifty states in state support."

He was reasoned in his inquiries:

"Governor, you say the number of people on welfare in Massachusetts dropped significantly during your administration. What was that rate of decline?"

Of course, his killers were disappointed. This wasn't a town meeting on changes in Social Security—this was a fucking street fight! Why couldn't he get that?

They'd run him through practice, with one of the button men playing Dukakis, and they'd have to stop Dick in mid-disquisition:

"No, Dick, you've got to go right at him! Make the little fucker look at your chest. His eyes are only gonna come up to your chest. Try this: 'You say Miracle—it sounds like the Massachusetts Mirage!' "

"Okay, mirage. I understand."

In fact, he did understand, in a tactical sense—how he had to take the shine off Dukakis, how he had to make this a two-man race, how he had to become (in New Hampshire, at least) *not Dukakis*. What he didn't understand was why he had to be angry. They didn't have to be . . . enemies—did they?

He was the one who had to answer the Iowans: Why are you picking on Dukakis? Why did you start a fight among the Democrats?

Dick would answer, with an edgy smile: "Well, I think we can disagree . . . without being disagreeable, heh heh."

Problem was, he meant it. Dick was never disagreeable. He never made enemies—what was that for? Every campaign he'd ever run—there were people who were for him, and there were people who hadn't got to know him yet. Next time, maybe, they'd be for him . . . whenever he got a chance to sit down with them, and really, you know, listen.

The people who actually knew Gephardt—old staffers, like Don Foley, for instance—tried to tell the hit men: this slash-and-burn just wasn't Dick's style. So the killers made sure there was no one who knew Dick in debate-prep: they couldn't afford a mixed message.

"Kill'um . . ." Carrick would growl in the corner. "Kill'um good."

Reilly would pace, like the dark Prince of Mordor, launching his latest and most deadly attack against the Hobbit Castle. "Y'gotta break this guy. S'only way—fuck 'im up."

Of course, Shrummy was the genius, with his cigar, and a yellow pad to write out new lines, which he would read to Dick . . . then direct him on delivery. Shrum was deep into this—shirttail hanging out, arms waving—Maestro Koussevitzky with the baton.

And it worked—or it seemed to work. The night before the big debate, Gephardt came to look over the hall. With killers bouncing behind him, firing reminders, he strode onto the stage. There were two podiums, and a pot of ferns between them, a chair off to the side for the moderator. The hot lights were on.

Dick stood behind his podium. "THIS . . ." he barked, ". . . is the Harvard University RESEARCH REPORT . . ."

Opposition research had turned up a Harvard study on the Massachusetts economy. Dukakis, it concluded, hadn't hurt the state's recovery—but he hadn't helped much, either.

One of the killers called to Dick: "What if he says he wasn't try'n'a take the credit?"

"In front of TWO HUNDRED PEOPLE, at SAN ANTONIO, TEXAS, he SAID: 'They just wanna see if they can get a piece of the Massachusetts action!' "

Dick's face broke into a grin: "Isn't that a great quote?"

Don Foley asked quietly from the foot of the stage: "Dick, you want that typed out in brief?"

"No!" Gephardt snapped. "I wanna READ it, right here . . . and then I wanna HOLD IT UP." Dick had the sheaf of papers rolled in a fist, and was waving it next to his ear, like a club.

Under the white TV light—no makeup, white shirt—Gephardt glowed with menace. The light shone through his skin to the slash of his jaw, the fierce high cheekbones, the ridge of his forehead, with no softening hint of hair . . . like a visor of pale steel. He looked like a Visigoth arrived from the north to sack the city, the Avenging Teuton . . . as he stared over the empty hall.

"Where's our people?"

"Over here."

"Family in front?"

"Yeah."

"They'll come up after?"

Reilly said: "Yeah. Matt'll tower over him."

Dick's grin returned. "Yeah, he can stand eye-to-eye . . . with my daughter."

They brought Dick behind the other podium, so he could see the little step stool the Dukakis wise guys had built for their man. Reilly was in an ecstasy of Mordor-derision. "Remember how you'd sit on the telephone book—when you were *so little*? . . ."

"Well, I'm going home," Dick said, "stick pins in my Duke doll . . . *heh heh hackhackhack* . . ."

The killers fell in behind him. You could hear them trading lines through the hall, to the door, to the streets of Des Moines.

"Yeah. S'*more* pins . . ."

"Got some holes in it already!"

"Heh heh, you get done with it, bring it over . . ."

"Prob'ly can't figure out—OW—what's that *pain*? . . ."

"YOWWCH! Ooops! Sorry, Mike!"

"Yeah, sorry, Mike . . . *hackhackhack* . . . Shit Happens! *Hackhackhack-heeheehee.* "

—★—

"First, Mike, if you're the Democratic nominee, I'm going to work eighteen hours a day to help you get elected . . ." That was Gephardt's opening salvo.

What happened to the Killer Teuton?

Alas, shit happened . . . mostly to Dick. On the way to the showdown, he was already in the zombie-zone, trying to remember twenty lines at once, his opening, the way to turn . . . trying just to keep it together, when he got to the hall and ran into . . . Bonnie Campbell.

"Heyyy, great to see youuuu," he said. Bonnie was a friend. Her husband, Ed, former Iowa Party Chairman, was signed on with Gephardt, helping out with more or less constant advice. But now Bonnie was chair*person* of the Iowa Democrats . . . and in her official high-cheese capacity, she had words for Dick Gephardt that morning.

"You started this!" she said. Bonnie's chosen mission was Party unity. Dick Gephardt had picked a knife fight with a fellow Democrat, and brought his gore-stained blade back to *Iowa*!

"I don't see why you can't let us get through this without giving the Republicans all the ammunition . . ."

"Uh, really, Bonnie, I . . ."

"I don't appreciate it! Don't you come in here and leave *me* with blood and guts all over the streets!"

Well, the minute he got on stage, you could tell he'd lost it. Dick looked so clean, so young, so fair, so . . . *reasonable,* the way he stood, mannerly, looking down at the papers on his lectern—never turned on Dukakis, never *looked* at Dukakis, save with that Gephardt sympathy-of-listening, for God's sake, like he was trying to learn how Mike felt . . . so they could, you know, come to an understanding!

"There's a lot we agree on, Mike, and we're on the same team."

Gephardt did mention the Massachusetts Miracle (on the way to saying, "You've been an excellent Governor . . .") but he never called it a mirage. Never held up the report. Never read out any quotes. Never even *asked* Dukakis to defend his record in any regard. Instead, he led off with a cantaloupe of a question about the Harkin-Gephardt farm bill—could Mike support it? . . . It was just an invitation for Dukakis to do his sound-bite on the family farm.

Which Michael did. And along the way, he managed to stick it to Dick on his vote for the grain embargo of 1980 . . . and Dick's support of an import-oil tariff (that would cost the average farmer, Michael claimed, $400 a year) . . . then he fired off a nasty question on Dick's vote in 1981 for the Reagan tax cut. Did Gephardt think Michael would meet him halfway, in the Alley of Process, to shake hands? . . . Forget it!

Fifteen minutes into the thing, Michael was hectoring Gephardt:

"Well, I don't know how you can be proud of a tax bill that ran up the biggest deficit in history, and has about as much to do with destroying our international position in the world economy as anything I know . . ."

Michael delivered this tattoo with an eloquent shrug that told the world: *Anyone can see this—right? Am I right?*

"A hundred and six Democrats, Dick—a hundred and six of your colleagues—voted against that tax bill. And, look: I've been a legislator . . ."

Michael was nodding to himself now, as if we *all* knew the kinda crap *legislators* get away with.

"You're a [shrug] legislator . . ."

Fifteen minutes later, he was back on that theme (on the way to slamming Gephardt's votes for big-ticket weaponry). He was beating Dick black-and-blue with jabs:

"Well, that's the problem, Dick. You can't have it on-the-one-hand-on-the-other, in defense policy. That's part of the problem. You start with weapons systems, and then you stop. You move forward, and then you move back. I've been a legislator, and I've been a chief executive. The difference between being a legislator and a chief executive is that you can bounce around a little bit when you're a legislator. You have to make *decisions* when you're a chief executive . . ."

And through all this dismissive rat-a-tat-tat from Dukakis, Dick stared ahead, smiling, or busied himself at his lectern . . . and never once turned to Michael and asked: What damned decision have you *ever* made on a weapon?

And so, a half-hour after that, Gephardt was back in his holding room, staring at the floor again, while they swabbed him off with cold cream.

"Damn . . ."

46

There's
This Couple
in Bed...

I T WASN'T that Joe really had a plan. What he had was a speech, and he always felt better when he knew what he was going to say. "Biden is *speech-driven,*" his guys would explain. But that was just guru-talk for the fact that Joe often didn't know what he thought until he had to say it. Then, too, there was the sorry corollary: sometimes Biden spoke before he thought.

But not this time. He wanted a speech for the Senate floor, and he couldn't afford to screw around. He had to make his case to the World's Greatest Deliberative Body that Senators must look at Robert Bork's philosophy—hell, say it plain—Bork's politics . . . to decide whether he should sit on the Court.

"A really *serious* speech," Joe said, when he talked to the staff. Which was not to say he didn't take other speeches seriously . . . but they knew what he meant: no rhetoric, no poetry for the crowd. In fact, it wasn't a Biden speech at all. It was more like a law school paper—the kind he'd never done.

Joe could not resist a tiny flourish here and there: the second time he mentioned Justice John Rutledge, for instance, that jurist became, for Biden, "Old John." When he quoted a 1972 paper from his favorite conservative scholar, Philip Kurland, Joe stopped after the quote, as if he'd just heard it for the first time, and said: "Lemme repeat that . . . this is not repeated in the quote, but let me repeat that part of the quote." Then he hammered Kurland's point home again.

But the big point was, he had the quotes . . . and not just from Kurland, but from Senators (some still in the chamber) who had spoken in the Carswell and Haynesworth nomination fights, during Nixon's time . . . from debates on John J. Parker, a Hoover nominee in 1930 . . . quotes from Judge Learned Hand, Justice Felix Frankfurter . . . from the Senate speeches on Roger Taney, Andrew Jackson's choice for Chief Justice . . . and back to 1795—Old John— Justice Rutledge, a nominee of George Washington, whom the Senate rejected because it didn't like his views on the treaty with England.

Biden didn't have just the facts from the Senate and the nominees rejected (a list of which, lawyer-like, Biden inserted in the record) . . . no, he went back to Hamilton in the Federalist Papers, and beyond, to the draft language proposed at the Constitutional Convention in Philadelphia.

The fact was, the Senate's "advise and consent" was intended, from the start, to forestall the President from remaking the Court in his image. The Senate had, for most of its two hundred years, scrutinized the philosophy and politics of nominees—not just their competence, or honesty. And when a President picked a justice *for reasons of ideology,* it was the Senate's *duty* to examine that ideology.

Biden spoke for an hour straight, and at the end, no one could lay a glove on him. Mitch McConnell, GOP from Kentucky, actually *had* written on this subject at law school . . . but when he came at Biden, Joe hammered him with history.

And Dole, who had to carry the flag across the aisle, had a little speech ready, with a couple of zingers about "constituent groups" and "campaign promises." But he couldn't really knock down Biden's point . . . so he ended up just insisting that Bob Bork wasn't such a bad guy.

Biden said not a word about Bork (save to note his nomination, in the first sentence of his speech). He was arguing high principle. Tell the truth, he liked the view from high ground—Joe Biden, Defender of the Constitution! Anyway, if he could set the ground rules, he could take the fight to Bork. Through the millions of words that Bork had written or said, Joe Biden would paint a picture of the judge for the American people. That was how he could win the fight.

Problem was, he didn't know how he could paint the judge, or paint him into a corner, intelligibly. Joe had to make it connect.

And he would not know . . . till he had to make another speech.

— ★ —

The staff made him dozens of fat briefing books: antitrust, privacy, *stare decisis,* civil rights, First Amendment, Fourteenth Amendment . . . everything Bork had said on the subjects. Joe could almost recite chunks of Bork's 1963 *New Republic* article, where he blasted the Kennedy civil rights bill . . . Bork's 1968 *Fortune* piece, in which he defended the Supreme Court's *Griswold v. Connecticut* . . . Bork's 1971 article in the *Indiana Law Review,* wherein he changed his mind and attacked the *Griswold* decision.

That was the key, Biden was convinced: *Griswold v. Connecticut.* That was the 1965 case in which the Court threw out the old Connecticut law that banned the use of contraceptives (even by married couples under the advice of their physicians). A majority of the Court found that the Constitution guarantees a *right to privacy* . . . though those words do not appear in the document of the Constitution, the majority opinion called privacy "an un-enumerated right."

Robert Bork's problem was, he could not stomach the concept of "unenu-merated rights." In Bork's view, once a judge started stretching the Constitu-tion to cover some notion—however desirable—which did not appear in the document itself . . . where would it stop? Would some latter-day judge find a Constitutional right to recycling?

But *Griswold* was now important law: when the Court took the states out of the business of regulating abortions in *Roe v. Wade,* the majority upheld a woman's right to abortion *based on the unenumerated right of privacy.* If *Griswold* fell, *Roe* would surely be the next shoe to drop.

That's what Joe's adviser, Larry Tribe, meant when he said on the tele-phone, the day Bork was named:

"Bork's problem isn't just *Roe,* it's *Griswold.* "

That was the truth at the bottom of the polls (the Biden campaign took its own quickie poll in Iowa, when Bork was named, and later got national numbers from a poll commissioned by the AFSCME union). The country was deeply split on abortion, but an overwhelming majority thought the govern-ment should stay out of their private lives.

Hell, Joe didn't need a poll to tell him people thought they had a right to privacy. You stand up on a chair in Pala's Pizzeria and ask the guys *there:* Does the government have a right to make laws about what you can do in your bed . . . with your wife? Well, they'd knock over tables to punch your teeth out.

So now, when he worked through the case law with the experts, Joe kept bringing the sessions back to the ground floor:

"How're we gonna talk about *Griswold* . . . how do we tell people the story?"

Sometimes it was Tribe, from Harvard, or Kurland, from the University of Chicago. Joe went through the cases with them until he could render the law in the common tongue. Kurland and Tribe were an odd couple. Kurland was a conservative—roly-poly, he looked like Santa in a suit and tie . . . you could hear him breathe. Tribe was the liberal—svelte, tanned, worldly . . . likely to show up at Biden's house in an open-necked sport shirt, might catch a set of tennis between sessions. But they both hated Bork, so they kept coming to Wilmington. In August, when Joe took the family to Bethany Beach, Kurland or Tribe would show up. They were Biden's sounding boards . . . and his teachers.

In effect, Biden went to law school that summer, paced off the ground that he'd only hip-hopped at Syracuse. But this was the best law school in America. And Biden loved it. He had the kind of August he used to have before a football season—working on his moves, every day, all day.

"Tell me about the history of the Ninth Amendment. Why's it in there? . . ."

—★—

Campaigning was just a distraction now. He'd do it, if he had to—some event he couldn't miss. Biden had a new stump speech, mostly about foreign policy. It worked better than "my generation," but it still didn't give him the tingle.

One day that August, Bill Schneider, the columnist-pundit-pilgarlic-pollster-guru, showed up with a tape of a long, lovely TV ad for Neil Kinnock, the British Labour Party leader who was running against Margaret Thatcher. Kinnock had some beautiful stuff about what the Labour Party meant to working folk. To Joe, that was exactly why *he* was running: to give people a platform on which to build their futures. He grabbed that tape and took it home; he inhaled the thing. It was like when Barbra Streisand came on the radio—Kinnock was singing Joe's song!

—★—

He couldn't talk about Bork yet, couldn't do it piecemeal. He knew, when he laid out his case, it had to hit with a thump.

He had a speech scheduled that August at the ABA, the American Bar Association convention in San Francisco—another "serious" speech. He was going to give them a souped-up version of his Senate speech: advise and consent. That was scholarly ground he could stand on. But then he got to talking at his house one day—side porch again, another Bork meeting. The experts had left for the day, but Gitenstein was still there, and Donilon, and Vince D'Anna. Vince was from the Delaware staff, a "real guy," as Joe understood the term: smart as hell, sure, with tremendous political instinct, but not a Washington-head, not a suit, not a lawyer.

And that made all the difference.

Because Joe just started talking the stuff to Vince—like he would at Pala's—just shooting the shit about this privacy business . . .

"I mean, I'm serious! You know, you're in your bed, and a cop comes in, says, 'What do you think you're . . .' No! *Bork comes in!* I mean, can you see . . . wait! No! Here's the ad—here's the ad we oughta run, right? . . . There's this couple in bed, and the guy hears something, straightens up . . . it's dark, there's music, right? *DUM dum dum dum DUHHNN!* . . . And it's BORK! . . ."

They're giggling on the porch.

"That'd do it."

"Hell, yeah."

"Glad that sonofabitch wasn't around when I got married. Jesus!"

"Jail time!"

"Yeah, whole different ball game . . ."

"That's it, if he's the law . . ."

"Yeah, woulda been . . ."

"No, wait! I mean it. That's it! If he had been the law . . . that's how we show it."

"If Robert Bork had been on the Court . . ."

"If Robert Bork had been *Justice* Bork . . ."

"If . . . *Judge* Bork had been *Justice* Bork for the past twenty years, and he had *prevailed* . . . this would be a very different country."

"Thirty years . . . *Baker v. Carr.*"

"Forty years. If Judge Bork had been Justice Bork for the last forty years, we would have a very different—poorer . . ."

"No, let people decide that. We'll just tell them the cases—the things that wouldn't have happened."

"That's it. That's what we'll do for the ABA. We just lay it out: *These are the cases that Robert Bork would have reversed.* Let them imagine what it would be, without . . ."

"That's it."

"Let's do it . . ."

That was Joe, of course. He was revved up. He wanted to do it . . . now.

But it couldn't be now: it had to be careful, scholarly . . . *serious.*

He wouldn't get the speech for three or four days, but that same night—late that night—he could already hear it in his head. He could *see* it . . . the ABA, the Senate floor, the hearings . . . like stripes on the field to the end zone. He could see . . . *exactly* . . . how he was going to be.

"Ladies and Gentlemen, if Judge Bork . . ."

He was pacing in the night silence of his home.

". . . had been Justice Bork . . ."

47

A Platform upon Which to Stand

H<small>E ALMOST LOST THEM</small> at the ABA—a huge hotel ballroom, a thousand prosperous, comfortable suits, come to enjoy their week in San Francisco before returning to their life's labor, the protection of corporate America from a predatory government and citizenry. This was not an easy group to rally to the barricades. Then, too, Biden talked for an hour before he got to the point.

He'd left in a lot of "advise and consent," the whole nine *serious* yards. Joe's voice sounded reedy and dry as he backhoed the history. There were no applause lines. You could hear wool pants rustling on Naugahyde banquet chairs. A few folks stood up, all too visibly, and walked out of the hall . . . watched out the door by Joe's son Beau, who'd come to San Francisco, who was dying a slow death for Dad, in the back of the room, while Joe droned on . . . till Beau, toward the end, was staring at his shoes, murmuring, "Dad . . . finish."

But then Joe got to Bork, and the cases . . . not an attack—not obviously. He just laid out the facts at law, and Bork's opinions on the opinions.

First was *Griswold:* Bork not only called the decision "unprincipled," but he stated there was no difference—at law—between a husband and wife who wished to be relieved of regulation in their bedroom, and a utility company that wished to be free of smoke-pollution laws.

Then there was *Skinner v. Oklahoma,* where the Court struck down a state law permitting the sterilization of criminals. Bork called the majority opinion "intellectually empty."

There were cases where the Court struck down restrictive racial covenants, a case on poll taxes, the Voting Rights Act, affirmative action, a sixty-year-old decision allowing parents to send their kids to private schools, a case that overturned a state law forbidding the teaching of German . . . there was *Roe v. Wade* . . . there were two cases from the sixties, in which the Warren Court erected the doctrine of one man, one vote . . .

Bork had said of one man, one vote: "On no reputable theory of Constitutional adjudication was there an excuse for the doctrine. . . ."

By this point, the rustling in the hall had changed to silence, and then to whispered exclamations, as Biden hammered home seventeen cases. Most of these lawyers had had no *idea* . . . Bork was a flaming *radical*. Jesus! He meant to push down the pillars of *their temple*!

"We cannot be certain," Biden said, at the close—his voice rang through the ballroom—"that these are among the dozens of precedents that Judge Bork might vote to overturn. But we can be certain that if Judge Bork has meant what he's written for the past thirty years . . . that had he been *Justice Bork* during the past thirty years, and had his view prevailed . . . America would be a fundamentally different place than it is today. . . ."

When his voice died away, the suits jumped up and gave him a standing ovation. They came at Joe by the dozens, to shake his hand. The press in the hall badgered Rasky for a text—of course, Joe had screwed around with the text till way too late. Rasky snapped at the pack: "Why'n'cha learn to take notes?"

But it didn't matter. This was front-page, anyway—Biden Makes His Case.

Even Joe was amazed at the good press . . . they actually *got* it! And they wrote it! . . . Unbelievable.

Now he had to find a way to make the message clear in living rooms, and barrooms. Biden v. Bork . . . High Noon, Main Street . . . he had to get ready.

— ★ —

That's all he wanted to do—run through the moves, game it out:

"So then, if he comes back with Harlan, I'm gonna use that Harlan dissent. I'm gonna read the thing, right? That piece at the end—and then I'll say: 'Judge, do you agree with that?'

"So he can't, right? So I'm gonna read in the White House thing, saying he's in the tradition of Harlan . . ."

"What if he just says he changed his mind?"

"He can't change his mind on everything."

"What if he does?"

"I got his article. When's it from—'86?"

"Listen to this . . . listen to what he says . . ."

"Shit, this guy's completely out on the edge."

"Why don't you just use this?"

"Too legalistic—people gotta understand. Look, let's do it again—if I say . . ."

—★—

Of course, Biden wouldn't admit he was going to win—never. But you could see it sinking in.

He'd go down to Washington, Senators were coming to *him* . . . they'd read that stuff he sent over . . . you know, the civil rights cases—very disturbing . . . people aren't going to like that. The southerners were key—most of them won with black votes.

One offered advice: "Y'know this fella's *weeird* . . . Joe, y'jus' put a camm'ra off'ta *sahhhd* . . . y'show that *sahhd shot,* with the *beeard* . . ."

"Good idea," Joe'd say. He'd guarantee one thing: it wasn't going to be an Ollie North deal—the Senators on TV, creating an instant American hero—no way!

But, in truth, he didn't want to win with camera angles, Q-factors . . . or even personal stuff on Bork. He'd already told the committee: he'd get the FBI report—and that was it. Nobody else would even see it. He couldn't win by tearing down Bork, the man. Biden had to win on the cases . . . *Defender of the Constitution* . . . otherwise, it wasn't a win for him.

"Tom," he'd say to Donilon, "tell me again what's gonna happen."

"Look, Joe, these are the numbers . . ." Donilon would start again. He'd run through it a half-dozen times already. "Iowa is three-to-one against Bork . . ."

"Okay . . ." Joe would look down, concentrating on the words.

"Right now, your name recognition is ten percent—on its way to fifteen, twenty. That's up from three—and that's before the hearings. Your approval is up from one percent to five, maybe six—I don't know. But look: it's TV—not bites—it's hours of TV, day, after day, after day . . . you're the only candidate who's doing anything real. Your name recognition alone is gonna go to fifty, sixty, seventy percent. Some of those people are going to be for you—that's guaranteed, right? And since you're doing something they *approve* (it's three-to-one against this guy), your approvals go up *faster*—by a higher rate—than your name recognition. So that means you're gonna be at ten percent, and then you're gonna be at twenty percent, and then you're gonna win Iowa. Then, you're gonna win New Hampshire. Then, you're gonna be President."

Joe would nod at the floor . . . not agreeing, just nodding it into his head. Then, he'd look up at Donilon, and say:

"Go through that again."

—★—

In Iowa, he could feel it turning—he could see it: he's supposed to have thirty people at a coffee shop, a hundred show up. That packs the place, changes the feel . . . changed Joe's feel. But he still couldn't figure, exactly, *why?* . . . He couldn't feel the connect, the thump in his gut, the way he had to have it.

The Iowa guys were after him every week—how about next weekend? . . . How about a day and a half? . . . But Biden would get his chin out and insist he couldn't cut a day from Bork—not an hour. Even events he couldn't blow off—he'd be doing Bork in the plane.

That's how he was with the Iowa State Fair debate—it was a big deal, a Sunday, late August, Des Moines . . . if he missed it, he'd be explaining for months. And he still didn't know what he'd say: the staff had written a close for the debate, but it wasn't any good. Joe knew he had to redo it. But that weekend, he had Bork meetings at the beach house—Larry Tribe was flying in from Boston, with Marttila. There were a dozen guys driving up from Washington. And Caddell was flying in from his California exile, making his bid to come back . . . which meant, of course, he was coming back to take over.

They went at Bork all day. Joe ran through the moves, to Tribe, for hours, while the rest of the staff and gurus just hung around the deck and listened. All except Caddell, who was in there, pitching. Hell, he'd argue law with Tribe!

But you had to hand it. to Caddell—guy was a genius with a poll. The AFSCME pollsters had concluded that the best chance on Bork was to prove he was "insensitive to certain groups"—in other words, a bigot. But Pat knew Biden would never do that . . . and now that Pat had the cross-tabs from that poll, he picked them apart with ferocious precision—Biden wouldn't *have* to do that.

See, when people found out about Bork, they turned against him—fifty-one percent by the end of the polling . . . but why? That's where Caddell was a genius: he could find that single brick in the wall—pull it, the whole thing comes down in a heap.

"Lookit this: white southerners—that's the key, what every southern Senator has gotta watch. Look: *seventy-one percent* of white southerners are less inclined to support Bork when they find out he does not believe the Constitution guarantees a right to privacy.

"Who do moderate Republicans watch? Women under forty. . . . Privacy is the second most powerful argument against Bork for women under forty. For southern whites, it's *Number One* . . ."

That was the first day anybody heard Joe say, aloud, he might win this Bork thing. He just mentioned to Tribe, in passing, that if they could show this stuff, well . . . people wouldn't be for this guy.

For Caddell, Bork was *history:*

"Oh, we're gonna win *this.* I'm past that. That's done! I'm talking about taking back the *country.* This nomination is the end of the Reagan revolution. Don't you understand? This is the end of conservative intimidation! Over— *gone!* This is the end for them!"

The way Pat saw it—Chrissake, he'd been saying this since '84—if you push the right-wing social agenda hard enough, the whole Reagan coalition falls apart. There's no way all those Reagan Democrats want the Moral Majority fucking around with *their* lives. And Bork was just the maul to split the tree trunk—if Joe hit it hard.

That's why Biden was climbing in Iowa. They had the link now . . . lookit *this:*

Mike Donilon, Tom's brother, worked for Caddell, and he had a new poll from Iowa: Biden in double digits! Before the hearings!

Marttila said: "You're going to be the front-runner by October. . . . If you win Bork, you've got the nomination."

Joe wasn't so sure. He didn't know what moved the numbers in Iowa . . . didn't know what message they had that was working. Chrissake, he didn't know what he was going to say *tomorrow*.

That debate! Shit! He'd have to write on the plane.

—★—

But he got off the plane without a closing statement. David Wilhelm, his Iowa man, met him at the airport. "How you doin', boss?"

"Doin' great," Joe said, "but I don't have a close."

"Why'n'cha use the platform stuff? It's working great."

"Yeah, that's a good idea."

Joe asked Ruthie for paper the minute he got into the van. He knew that stuff from the Kinnock tape like a song in his head . . . he started writing it down, without hitch or pause:

Why is it that I am the first in my family ever to go to a university?

He'd done it four or five times: "You know, I saw a speech by the British Labour Party leader, Neil Kinnock, and he said something that I think is important . . ."

It worked great for Biden—without fail—because he felt it.

Why is my wife, Jill, the first of her family ever to go to college? Is it because our fathers and our mothers were not BRIGHT? . . .

He'd almost written it through by the time they got to the Savery Hotel—fifteen minutes for makeup. This debate would be on TV—PBS, all over the country . . . the big-foot press in Des Moines for the day. This could be big—this could be the moment. Joe kept running through the lines in his head, reading through the close, fiddling a word out, here and there, to make the words dance on the ear. He was acutely aware, he only had two minutes.

Is it because I was smarter than the rest? . . .

Those people who read and wrote poetry, who taught me how to sing verse? . . .

"Ruthie, gimme couple Tylenols, will you?"

Joe thought, surely, this was the message that could move Iowa. He could make them feel this . . . because this was him. He was thinking in the van, on the way to the fairgrounds: *this* is what he was—not some sixties campus radical with a broken heart from Vietnam . . . no. That was Pat, maybe . . . but Joe Biden was a middle-class kid who'd got a little help along the way—a chance, a platform to stand on . . . and *that's* what this country *had* to hold on to.

"You okay?" Jill asked him in the van.

"Yeah, good. I think I got it."

And when he did it that day, in the old debate hall, he had it—he took that crowd up, up . . . it was splendid!

"I started thinking, as I was coming over here . . . why is it that Joe Biden is the first in his family ever to go to a university? . . ."

Joe locked his eyes on the crowd, and he could feel it—like they bent an inch forward in their seats. He had them.

"Is it because they didn't *work hard*? . . .

"My ancestors, who worked in the *coal mines* of northeast Pennsylvania, and would come up, after *twelve hours* . . . and play *football* for four hours? . . ."

Joe's fist clenched as he leaned in toward the crowd, the cameras:

"No . . . it's *not* because they weren't as smart . . . it's *not* because they didn't work as hard . . . it's because they didn't have a *platform* upon which to stand. . . ."

The place was absolutely quiet—not a sound. Not one person even moved in a seat! . . . In fact, no one in the state of Iowa seemed to notice that Joe never mentioned . . . this was what *Kinnock* said.

It was only in Washington, in front of the TV, the gurus looked at each other. Someone had to tell Biden . . . he'd better credit this stuff, or he'd get his ass in trouble.

But, of course, no one could tell Joe at that moment. He was still locked on the crowd, had to feel *them* . . . feel it *hit*. . . . What Joe saw was that lady in front, watching him, with her face twisted up, tears streaming down her cheeks.

48

Six-Seven-One

IN THE BACK of the hall, Liz Kincaid felt so blue. She knew Dick had to do well that day . . . and Gephardt had a lousy debate. His closing speech was rambly, didn't seem to make any *difference.* . . . And Biden was spellbinding! She couldn't take her eyes off the man. She'd tell her husband, Kasey, that night: Biden had the closing of his *life*—all about his ancestors, in the *coal mines.* . . . She was almost in tears!

But that's the way she felt about the whole campaign that day. Liz had poured her heart into Gephardt's campaign. Liz and Kasey had been volunteers since last year. They used to joke with their friends: they were GBMQ— Gephardt Before Mario Quit. They were committed, yes, but more than that: they liked Gephardt, they cared for him.

They'd been with Hart in '84, but this time, they wanted a personal connection . . . and somehow, they sensed, Hart wasn't willing. That wasn't what it was about, for him. Anyway, this time, when he was so far ahead, his campaign didn't have that bravery, romance. . . . So they talked to Joe Biden, or rather, Biden talked to them. Liz thought he was Hart-in-reverse. He never talked about ideas. But he came at them so hard, so close, so quick . . . well, it made her back off. He was *so* come-on! (One time, she saw him kneel and kiss a woman's hand! I mean, come *on!*)

Dick didn't presume. Liz always said she had a peaceful feeling about him—she knew things would change for the better if he won—ever since she met him for the second time, and he walked up to her: "Liz! Great to see you!" (She told him later how impressed she was—he remembered her name—and

Dick just laughed. "I knew who you were for a long time.") But that was only the start: it was after that, the Kincaids used their vacations to work for Dick, and came to know how he was, how he listened . . . they knew, the Gephardts were people like them, who worried about *their* worries—paying the bills, schools for the kids . . . they knew Dick came from hardworking folks, that he meant to give people a chance, give kids in this country the same chance he'd had . . . and they saw how hard Dick tried, how he believed there was nothing people couldn't do, if they'd set their minds to it. In short, they came to love him . . . and that's what made it so awful.

Because it wasn't just his closing . . . it was signs—there *were* no Gephardt signs in the hall. And every other candidate had people at the fair, to hand out literature, or balloons . . . but where were Dick's people? It was like the lists she'd been waiting for, for *months*—lists of Democrats, people to call, work to hand out to volunteers. How could you know what to do without the lists? . . . She spotted people from the office, and asked, point-blank: What about signs, balloons? What about supporters to cheer for Dick? Where are our lists? . . . Everybody blamed somebody else.

That's why she talked to Jane—or talked to Jane the way she did. Jane was about to leave, probably asked just to be nice: "How's it going?"

Liz knew she wasn't supposed to bother the candidate . . . but she said: "You really want to know?"

"Yes!"

"We can't even get the lists!" And she was almost in tears again, as she loosed upon Jane her tale of woe.

Jane said: "I'll talk to Dick."

—★—

Just now, no one could talk to Dick—except Ed Campbell. When Ed talked, no one else talked. Ed, the former Party Chair, was not too tall, and bald . . . but not bald with a wimpy Mr. Whipple rim of hair around the bottom, no—*hairless.* And his head shone, bulging like a Schwarzenegger bicep . . . like his eyes bulged when he was pissed off—which he was.

He rode out with Dick after the debate, to tell Gephardt to get the *lead out* . . . or he was finished. Ed knew Iowa . . . and he told Dick: people were making their minds up—NOW. Babbitt was on the air with ads. Dukakis was pulling even with Dick (after that stupid goddam debate!), Biden was moving—why didn't Dick *do something*?

"I understand," Dick said.

But Ed was still talking. He wanted commercials on the air, NOW. "By Thanksgiving, it's *over! Understand?*"

Dick said he did understand, but his campaign professionals had decided to hold off on TV—save the money—till the end. . . .

Ed opined that Dick's professionals had their heads up their asses. Where the hell were his professionals at this debate? There were no Gephardt supporters. There were no Gephardt workers. There weren't even any damned *signs*!

Ed didn't have to tell Dick about signs. In St. Louis, Gephardt could call a race, within three percent, just by counting lawn signs.

"I know," he said. "I understand. You help me, I'm gonna fix it, just give me time."

"There IS NO TIME! . . . What's your hard count?"

Dick stared ahead, at the windshield: "Uh . . . I don't know."

— ★ —

Half of Dick's killers figured their Iowa chief, Fleming, must be a wily old fox: *never* tell the candidate where he stands—just cry the blues and beg for money. Oh, they knew the game! . . . The other half gave up asking for the hard count: it was easy enough to figure.

The rule of thumb was a hundred thousand voters would go to the Democratic caucus February 8. Thirty percent, thirty thousand souls, would make Dick a winner . . . right now, the polls had him at about fifteen percent . . . so maybe he had fifteen thousand—call it twelve, just to be safe. Of course, the true scientists-of-Iowa maintained that your hard count was always higher than your actual vote, because people lose interest, or their kid starts throwing up so they never get to their caucus, or they get a ride with their neighbor, who convinces them that *Simon's* the guy . . . or they tell your phone bank they're for Dick, just so their dinner won't get cold.

There was more-or-less continuous discussion of the *factors* . . . which was why it was so important to get the list . . . the people's names and numbers, so they could be tied down—*lock and load*! . . . That's why David Doak bestirred himself, at last, from his Georgetown office, to *field work*—he'd fly to Iowa and get the damn *count*. Doak had run field for Jimmy Carter in Iowa. No wool would shield the truth from his eyes . . . no.

But he couldn't get the count. What he got, by the time he returned to D.C., was a furrow in his forehead and a quaver to his voice, as he mused: "Maybe things have changed . . . I haven't done this for a long time . . . but I didn't see any, uh . . . *people.*"

He meant people for Dick.

Then Dick's fellow members of the House started coming back from Iowa. They'd popped out there to help, during the August recess. And one by one, they reported to him. "Well, I read about your army out there, Dick, but . . . Cedar Rapids, I hadda take a *cab*. There was no one at the office!"

That's when Liz Kincaid got the call: "Liz? Hi! This is Dick Gephardt."

"Sure, it is."

"No, it is!"

"Dick?"

"Yeah, I just thought I'd call, uh, see how it's going . . ."

That was about the same time Dick got the hard count.

Six-seven-one.

"Shit. Six thousand . . ."

"Six *hundred* . . . and seventy-one."

SIX HUNDRED! He couldn't believe it. He'd *baby-sat* for more Iowans than that. What was going ON? If he didn't score in Iowa . . . it was *over*! What was he doing wrong? How could he *be* so wrong? . . . And that office—that staff—all those salaries! . . . He was stewing when he got home that night, home to the woods of Virginia—God! His summer in Iowa was gone—squandered!

Dick said: "What are they doing with the *time*?"

Jane said: "They're eating pizza."

49

The
Secret
Weapon

Ⓘ T WAS Elizabeth who started to tell
the story that summer. She was doing
fund-raisers, two or three a week,
and at first her ambitions were modest. But then she raised fifty thousand in
one night in Dallas. . . . After that, she was tougher to please.

She set a goal—in an organized way, like she did everything—and made a
schedule with Dave Owen, Dole's top money man. Weekends, evenings, after
work at the Transportation Department, she would fly anywhere in the country. She was going to raise one million dollars for Bob.

Of course, you wouldn't hear much about that from Dole. The feedback
from Bob was secondhand—a comment to Owen from Jo-Anne Coe, the drill
sergeant in the Leader's office:

"Yeah, Senator was wondering what all that money for planes was about."

Like Dole thought they were wasting time—and his money. That's why
word came from Jo-Anne. Bob wouldn't say that sort of thing to your face.
So Elizabeth just worked harder, tried to get more money.

This came naturally to her. She was always telling people how Bob amazed
her—all he'd done, how much he knew, the way he held himself to such a
standard. She was sure people didn't understand him—thought he was mean,
for example, when she knew how he could hurt like a boy.

They couldn't see him—or her, for that matter. They wrote how she was
angling for Vice President, or President, herself . . . *the politics of Liddy Dole*
. . . there were none. She was the highest-ranking woman in the Reagan
administration, her name popped up in every piece of punditry about female
candidates for the GOP . . . but she had no instinct for electoral politics.

Owen knew—he went back with the Doles. Dave Owen was a former Kansas Lieutenant Governor, an Olathe boy who'd done well for himself in Kansas City. He'd been helping Bob Dole since Dole first ran statewide in '68. . . . Elizabeth he'd known since she married Bob, in 1975. He knew how she did things . . . by the numbers: every detail worked over till it shone, till it—till Mrs. Dole, herself, sparkled with intelligence and charm.

That was Elizabeth's one-two punch. She was not just Phi Beta Kappa at Duke. She was also May Queen. And it was the same skill that won her both honors, the same absolute insistence on preparedness—be it in Latin or lipstick. It was the same devotion that took her through Harvard Law, through a succession of government posts, to her current Cabinet rank—high pressure and power at the old boys' table. She'd won it her own way—no politics about it. With Mrs. Dole, it was always . . . personal perfection.

Everything she did was programed for control. She was a flawless administrator, never caught unprepared on her budget, or any report to Congress. She always had a grasp of where her projects stood because she scheduled followups—every week—with the persons in charge. If she had a luncheon speech for a Congressman in Michigan, she scheduled time to study his résumé, so she could mention his *sixty-four-percent* reelection victory and praise his *crucial work* on the Merchant Marine and Fisheries Committee. If she had a local TV interview, she was certain to learn in advance the anchorwoman's name . . . just as she was certain that her nail polish complemented her suit jacket . . . just as she was certain to raise her chin as she looked to the camera, to erase any unprepossessing thickness under the jaw.

So, that's how they did these funders—by the numbers. Owen would set up the events, then go with Elizabeth to every one. He'd speak first, give an overview of the campaign, the money raised, the hopeful polls . . . then wind up with how great it was to have their secret weapon—Elizabeth Hanford Dole—who was capable of being President herself!

She loved that. She'd step to the microphone, glowing, with a chuckle of dismay (Oh, that Dave! How he does go *on*!), and deliver her remarks about Bob.

"Bob is a man who's been TESTED . . . and Ah believe that Bob's colleagues, electing him to be their MAJORITY LEADER in the U.S. Senate, RECOGNIZED what Ah'd watched with AWE . . ." (That word always sounded like OWW!)

". . . And that is his ability to master the complexities of very TOUGH ISSUES, to use a keen, creative mind to WORK EFFECTIVELY with his colleagues in the Senate, to hammer out a solution to a TOUGH PROBLEM, even if it takes months to do it, or scores of meetings, and then to form that all-important COALITION . . ."

The lines were always the same. Solutions were "hammered out," and coalitions were "all-important." Once she got a line right, she could chuckle in the same place, smile to the front row with the same sudden pleasure, stress a key word with the same rise of voice . . . you could just about *see* the key words on an outline somewhere.

In fact, that's how it started—an outline that Owen wrote out on one yellow legal-pad sheet. . . . "You ask me," Owen said, "the bottom line is the war record. The punch line is that Bob Dole crawled out of a foxhole, grabbed his buddy under fire, and that's how he got shot. You know, that needs to be in your story."

". . . whose LEADERSHIP has been TESTED, tahm and tahm again, not only in the United States Senate, but also on the FRONT LAHNS, in World War II . . ."

Week by week, she worked on that speech, improving every night. She was a huge hit. Everybody loved Elizabeth. Owen did believe she was the secret weapon. All he had to do was tee it up—she never missed. There were weeks when she pulled in $200,000.

At the same time, of course, she was stretched to the limit. They got to California one night—they were going to stay over at Owen's condo—and Elizabeth had two funders, plus a meeting with some S&L fellow named Jim Montgomery. She thought it was going to be just a friendly visit with this man who'd signed on to help Bob Dole . . . but no: at the last minute, Owen told her she had to *put a move* on this guy. He was coming in cold . . . and they wanted him to be Finance Chairman for California.

Well, that was the last and lethal straw: Elizabeth was stressed already, trying to figure her *own* future. . . . She wanted to help Bob, of course, but she felt she couldn't resign from Transportation until her new airport regulations came on line—she'd tried *so hard* to sort out the crush at the busiest hubs—she was pushing the regs *as fast as she could,* she was working *as hard as she could,* but still they wouldn't be ready till fall, and if she left now, would it look like she was running away from the problem? She had a message at the condo to call Bob Crandall, the president of American Airlines . . . and now Owen wanted her to wing it with some *stranger*? . . . What was she supposed to say? She had no time to prepare! She didn't know *anything about this man*! She went into a bedroom—she started to cry. It wasn't fair! It wasn't possible!

But she did it. She pulled herself together and did the Bob Dole story—one-on-one. And before he knew what hit him, Montgomery was caught up—ready to fly cross-country for a meeting with the Senator, about to sign on as California chairman . . .

Which he did: Montgomery would raise another $1.1 million with a single event at L.A.'s Century Plaza.

You might say that made two million for Elizabeth and Owen.

You might . . . Dole did not. The word that filtered back to those two in California was a message from Jo-Anne, to Owen . . . about the condo:

"Senator says, if Elizabeth stays at the condo, you stay somewhere else."

—★—

She had a funder in Washington, at the J.W. Marriott, two blocks from the White House. Bob was in town, so he stopped in to see what the fuss was about. ("Lotta moneyy!")

When it came time for speeches, there was Bob, smoothing his tie, but, no:

the host, Dick Marriott, introduced Elizabeth, who stepped up and did the Bob Dole story.

"... not only in the United States Senate, but on the FRONT LAHNS, in World War II.... He was in a FOXHOLE in Italy ... they got him, BROKE HIS NECK with machine-gun fire ... BROKE HIS NECK, and he was PARALYZED ... he spent THIRTY-NINE MONTHS in the hospital ... he had EIGHT OPERATIONS ..."

It was likely the first time Dole ever had to hear a speech about ... his problem. He'd spent half a lifetime hiding its effects. For forty years, he'd labored, strained, so *no one* would have to keep that story in mind ... and here it was, laid out like a cheese platter for the delectation of this penthouse crowd.

They were cheering as Elizabeth introduced him, at last, and he made for the mike. He looked, for once, like he didn't know what to say.

"Well," he said, "at least you'll remember the introduction ..."

He'd remember, too. A hundred and fifty thousand dollars was raised that night, and not from a big crowd—maybe fifty people ... but they wrote checks and called on friends to write checks. Dole didn't need a dollar-count to see what'd happened. Those people felt they knew something about him. They were excited.

—★—

His injury wasn't the only thing—Dole never talked about himself at all. You'd hear five times a day what Dole said to Senator Moynihan on Social Security, what Dole said to Daniel Ortega about elections in Nicaragua ... but there was nothing about Dole: no intimacies about his home, his family, any book he'd read, any friends—nothing of the life that underlay the Leader.

Sometimes he'd proffer an illusion of that life with a joke about him and Elizabeth—that famous two-career couple. There was a picture in *People* magazine of Bob and Elizabeth making the bed. Dole said he got an angry letter from a man in California. " 'Senator, you're causing problems for men all over the country. Ever since that picture, I have to help my wife make the bed!'

"I wrote back: 'Brother, you don't know the half of it. The only reason Elizabeth was helping was 'cause they were taking pictures.' "

Like most Dole jokes, it was designed to deflect inquiry, not reward it. Anyway, Elizabeth was part of his high-gloss Washington power-persona ... which was the picture he'd polished for voters for the last twenty years.

In fact, you could just about see that persona take shape in the pictures—the press photos. In the sixties, they were almost all the same: Congressman Dole on the steps of the Capitol, leaning his perfect grin over the shoulders of some visiting Salina couple, or a Scout troop from Hutchinson ... thousands of western-Kansas-voter greet-and-grins that showed up in local papers with such frequency, uniformity ... folks in Russell said it was a darned shame no one would give Bob an office in Washington.

By the start of the seventies, when he'd won his seat in the Senate and was angling for the chairmanship of the Republican National Committee, the photos changed—they were indoor shots, power venues: the Senate floor, the White House . . . finally, Dole's splendid office at the RNC, with its huge wall map of the United States—Dole had visibly gone national. Now he looked serious, stylish, smoother. He didn't smile at the camera. He had those side-burns (modishly long). His suits fit better.

The other people in the pictures changed. From the early seventies (Lyn Nofziger, Bryce Harlow . . .) there were more and more capital smart guys and Big Guys. Cabinet Secretaries made appearance. Through the Ford years (Bill Timmons, Jim Baker, Bob Strauss . . .), the photo-buddies got bigger and smarter. By '76, when Dole ran for VP, men with earplugs showed up in the pictures . . . along with iron rings of microphones and cameras . . . foreign leaders . . . millionaires, movie stars, sports heroes.

The staff in the background changed. Through the seventies, guys behind Dole were mostly slab-shouldered Kansans—looked like they spent summers shoveling wheat, or at least they'd wrestled in school. . . . By the eighties, when Dole took over the Finance Committee, the corners of the photos showed pencil-necked Harvard grads—Columbia, at least—with piles of paper under their arms . . . tax-code geeks, trade-and-tariff experts, third-party-health-prepayment savants . . . with flashbulb glare on their glasses, all waiting for Dole to finish his press conference and head back to the hearing room.

(Dole always mentioned they were Harvard guys. "Oughta know something!" . . . He'd ask for their help on everything he touched for a month, then decide: "Well, nice guy . . . can't write." So he'd get a new favorite: "Aagh! Guy worked for Danforth! Must be good!" . . . They were all great if they came from worlds that seemed classy, unattainable to him. Once they worked for *Dole,* well . . .)

By 1987, when he set all his sights on the Other Thing, you couldn't see much Kansas in Dole. Dole always seemed to suspect, if people knew, if they could see, he was just a poor boy from Russell . . . they'd figure out he wasn't supposed to be here, at all.

But he saw what Elizabeth could do with his story. . . . And his smart guys said he *had* to talk about himself. Don Devine told him, like a broken record. In Washington, the whole campaign seemed tied up in production of a half-hour video on Dole's life, directed by a young media guru named Murphy. On the road, Dole's Communications Director, Mari Maseng, kept after him, every day, to let people into Bob Dole's life, make them see where he was "coming from."

Dole started gingerly, just a toe in the water: he'd tell his story about him and Pat Moynihan, saving the Social Security fund:

"I said, 'Pat! We've got to give this one more try!' . . ."

Then he'd add—just as part of the story:

"You know, some people don't have anything else except their Social Security. My mother was in that category!"

Pretty soon, in southern towns, or farm towns, Dole would mention:

"There's nothing complicated about Bob Dole! My father ran a cream and egg station . . . wore his overalls to work for forty-two years, and was proud of it!"

Dole didn't want to say too much—wear out his welcome—and he never meant to talk about the war. . . . But the crowds couldn't get enough—people came up to him after events, started talking about their fathers, how their families started out poor . . . or they had a kid disabled. It was like they found out they had a friend in court.

Dole started to work in: "So, I think I have been TESTED in life. . . . I think it proves, you can make it the HARD WAY."

And he found out something else: when he talked about the *hard way,* about people who caught some *tough breaks* in life, might not have the *advantages, rich parents, top schools*—then, voters started talking to him . . . about George Bush.

Dole didn't even have to bring up the name!

He'd wind up a speech:

"So I think the bottom line is, people are going to look at our records. I think I've got a strong record . . ." (He didn't have to add his tag line: *a record, not a résumé.*)

"I think people want to know whether we've *made a difference.* . . . I think I've made a difference!" (He'd leave it to them to judge whether Bush, in all his jobs, had made any discernible difference.)

And the next day, or the next stop, there'd be a few new lines:

"Times were tough. People had to be tougher. I was a County Attorney— people had real problems. Sometimes you had to take children away from their parents. . . . People can go bankrupt, lose their property. . . . I had to sign the checks for the welfare. I was going through the pile—there was my grand- parents' name . . ."

—★—

That's when the smart guys got nervous. What's going on? . . . Dole's out there, talking welfare!

Pretty soon, he started talking long-term medical care . . . child care! "People have real *problems* in this country!"

Don Devine, who thought of himself as the message cop, was going nuts. "Look, Senator," he'd say. "Voters want to keep their jobs. They want Amer- ica strong and at peace. Those are big issues. Child care is not in the same league."

Devine was Dole's designated right-winger. Republican conservatives didn't want to hear from *day care . . . the homeless!*

But these were issues to Dole. Real problems! . . . They were all coming up for a vote. Every one was some Senator's baby. The map in Dole's mind was still the Senate floor. That homeless bill—that was a *Byrd-Dole* bill. That meant a great deal to Dole: he was the only one who could cross the aisle, get it done with the Democratic Leader.

Alas, it might not ring the same bells with voters—not in GOP primaries. That's what Devine was trying to hammer home: "Senator, you were fine until you got to that bipartisan homeless bill . . . you've really got to stick to the outline. That's uh, not our issue."

Dole's best issue was "whatever."

He'd say: "Whether your issue's drugs, whether your issue's child care, Social Security—*whatever* . . ."

And then he'd make his point:

". . . I think you have to look at the record."

Or: ". . . I think I've made a difference."

Or: ". . . I can sit down with you and your group and talk about it without looking at notecards!"

And, certainly, he could talk about it without speech outlines . . . briefing books . . . or meetings. He'd call headquarters, on L Street, three times a day—everybody's in a *meeting*!

What are they meeting about?

"Strategy group, Senator."

"Agh! Whose strategy?"

Dole knew he had to have a *big* campaign. He wasn't going to end up like he did in 1980—no organization beneath him, nothing getting done anywhere, unless he happened to show up. Back in 1980, he had a grand theory on what he needed: the four M's—management, money, media, momentum . . .

"Well, maybe it was five M's," he'd say. "I forget the other. I didn't have any of 'em."

This time, he knew, he wasn't supposed to run his own shop. He was supposed to have experts—strategists, field men, finance wizards, media gurus, speechwriters. . . . God knows, he'd read enough big-foot punditry explaining "Dole's problem"—he wouldn't let himself be managed, organized.

That's why he rented a whole floor of an office building—Eighteenth and L streets, dearest downtown D.C.—just about enough space to manage General Dynamics. That's why he filled all those cubbyholes with smart guys. (He knew they were smart, the way he had to pay them—the Dole campaign was putting out tens of thousands of dollars every month, just for "consultants.")

And that's why he kept looking for a Big Guy . . . to run it! He was *ready to hand it over*! . . . But it had to be a *Big Guy*.

(It hadn't quite worked out with his Big-Guy-of-Choice, John Sears—not after that Christmas meeting, where Keene put the kibosh on the Sears deal. So Dole had installed his friend Bob Ellsworth as chairman. They called a press conference and rented half a hotel ballroom for the announcement—and Ellsworth did fine, explaining to the big-feet how Dole had changed, he was ready to be organized . . . despite a competing press conference conducted, ad hoc, by Keene and Devine, just outside the ballroom doors—mostly to leak how the deal with Sears had fallen apart. . . . So, Dole's continuing talks with Sears had to be semisecret, so as not to lose Keene and Devine—Dole had *Ellsworth* wooing Sears . . . but it wasn't much of a secret, what with Sears and Keene pissing on each other's legs, in the papers. . . . So Dole opened quieter negotiations with other Big Guys—Drew Lewis, Don Rumsfeld, Bill Brock—Cabinet-rank, one and all . . . but each had his own ideas and his own price, so Dole hadn't reeled in anyone yet . . . what the hell, a few months of negotiation wasn't unusual with Big Guys!)

It all went with Dole's Washington-Watergate-Town-Car-Brooks-Brothers persona. He would send a *big signal* on the capital tom-toms . . . show all the columnists, political observers, lunchers at Joe and Mo's, *everybody* who was *in-the-know:*

Dole was going big-time—he could pull in first-class talent!

Dole would have a manager of size, *gravitas*—his own Jim Baker!

Dole had mellowed—he was ready to do things right!

Hands off! . . . just the candidate! . . . *Presidential!* . . . Dole would *listen!*

Well, yeah, sure.

But that didn't mean a Big Guy—or any guy—was going to tell Bob what to *say.*

—★—

Why would they? Why should they? It was working! Dole could smell the wind out there. (Must feel kinda hot on Bush's neck!) . . . Dole was closing the gap all over the country. During the August Senate recess, Dole *was* everywhere in the country. He started in Ohio—Dayton, Columbus, Cleveland . . . then Red Bank, New Jersey, Manahawkin . . . Cheyenne and Casper, Spokane, Yakima, Vancouver, Portland, Denver, St. Louis, Mobile, Charlotte . . . back to New England—Vermont, New Hampshire, Maine, Massachusetts . . . back to Chicago, then Iowa—a dozen towns . . . Kentucky, Arkansas, New Orleans . . . then straight into Texas—Houston, Dallas, San Antonio . . . straight up Bush's wazoo!

That was just two weeks.

In one month, he hit and made news in seventy cities, twenty-nine states, D.C., and Puerto Rico. (Not to mention Nicaragua, Honduras, and Costa Rica.) He traveled light—one or two staff, no press on the borrowed corporate jet. There were no votes back in Washington—nothing to slow him down. Sun was out. Dole was making hay.

Hey! New polls showed Dole the most "electable" Republican (the one with support among Democrats and independents—still a majority in the nation). Dole had lower "negatives" than Bush. Dole had a slim lead in Iowa—in fact, across the Midwest. He'd cut Bush's lead in California by half, pulled ahead in Idaho, Colorado, maybe Washington State. North Carolina was solid for Elizabeth . . . and ¡caramba! Dole troops even hijacked the Partido Republicano in Puerto Rico! . . . Nationwide, *The New York Times* reported, Bush's ten-point lead was "shaky."

And it wasn't just cold numbers—Dole was hot! He'd hit a town, the press was waiting at the airport (and maybe the editorial board was waiting downtown). Dole knew the smell of ink—liked it! . . . In a dozen states he had a

committee of bigwig supporters to announce—his "leadership team." (Dole
liked a stage filled with pooh-bahs. In every state, he'd demand of his field staff:
"Are we organized?" That meant he wanted to see a list of names—big names,
like Senators, atop them all.) In another two-dozen towns, he'd be whisked
from the airport to a "presale meeting." That was for his committee-to-be, or
people who were going to put on fund-raisers. Back in D.C., he'd demand of
his money men: "What about St. Louis—z'at guy gonna make it? . . . New
York—that's supposed to be a million?" Dole still could not believe that
money wasn't a problem.

What he could believe, what he couldn't miss, were those events—those
crowds! It wasn't just the turnout, though that was startling (Gwinnett
County, Georgia, eleven hundred people—at four-thirty in the afternoon!)
. . . it was who they were. They weren't political types. They were working
people, farmers, small businessmen, homeowners, solid citizens . . . they told
him they'd never been to any meeting—not for President . . . school board,
maybe, years back. They told him they came because they saw him on TV, and
something he said . . . or they had an uneasy feeling, where the country was
headed—maybe Bush wasn't tough enough . . . or they had to let him know
how much they *admired* Elizabeth and him. . . . But they didn't really have
to tell him. He could see it, the way they wanted to believe. They were looking
for someone—it was *their* hope, on him. If it was him and Elizabeth, that was
something else. It was beyond hope, it was . . . adulation. The Doles would
speak, then hustle to the exits to shake hands as people left ("Agh! That's how
we Methodists do it—we get the *dorrs!*") . . . and the look in people's eyes when
Elizabeth had them . . . well, it was the look that movie stars see.

More and more, if they showed up together, Bob would want Elizabeth to
introduce him. He never gave her warning . . . drove her nuts. She'd just find
herself at the microphone—a bit breathless—"Whah, that *husband a-mine!*"
. . . But then she'd do the Bob Dole story, including the parts that he still
couldn't talk about . . . and by the time he said word one, that crowd was
locked on.

More and more, he gambled his political star-power on the lessons he took
from that story . . . a message Republicans hadn't heard for years:

There was a deficit—real money!

And debts come due—all Americans would have to pay.

Dole was the only Republican with the guts to point out this dirt under
Reagan's carpet . . . something a poor boy from Russell couldn't ignore.

But he'd also insist that he wasn't about to go Reagan one better and get
the money from the poor, the helpless . . .

People had real problems!

Government had to respond.

That was the other half of the message—apostasy in the Temple of the Gip!

"I think we also have to be sensitive to the needs of a lot of people out
there—some in this area—who may be white, some may be black, some may
be brown, some may be poor and old, or poor and young, or disabled. . . . What

we call vulnerable groups in America sometimes need a helping hand—sometimes, they can't find help. So what're you gonna do? I hope you'd agree, there's a responsibility for the federal government to step in."

The pinker and more prosperous the crowd, the more Dole insisted that "conservative" didn't have to mean "callous." He told a convention of Young Republicans in Seattle: "I'd like to see fifty wheelchairs in this audience. I'd like to see fifty black faces, fifty Hispanics, fifty Asian Americans. . . . The bottom line is how you treat others. We have a responsibility to open up the doors of this Party!"

The amazing fact was, the YRs started cheering.

Maybe Dole didn't have a vision. (He said that's why Sears wouldn't take over the campaign: "Agh, I guess I wouldn't go to the *mountaintop,* come back with a *vision,* you know . . .")

Dole didn't trust visions, or visionaries. Seen too many: they screwed up everything.

What he had was a stubborn recognition of facts. He'd long since seen through the hole in Reagan's silkscreen: Morning in America . . . the Shining City on the Hill . . .

Dole understood what the people understood: If we're all, for Christ's sake, Standing So Tall . . . why am I getting screwed? Dole knew what it was to make a mortgage, tuition for the kids . . . he knew voters saw the bankers getting richer, collecting interest on their debt—a hundred ways. The car loan, the mortgage, the credit card, the national debt . . . bleeding them all.

"We were in the *basement apartment* . . ." Dole would tell his crowds. "Had to *rent out* the top of the house. We didn't know where the next mortgage payment was coming from . . ."

Those were facts.

In Dole's hands that August, facts *were* message . . . and a link to the common millions that George Bush would never have.

Even schedule was message.

There was, first, the existence of a schedule, published in advance for the next six weeks. That was a *big* message on the capital tom-toms. Dole was being managed like the big boys. He wasn't going to sit in his plane with a map on his knees . . . and land anywhere he saw a crowd.

This was the first time anyone could recall that Dole checked off on weeks of a schedule, hit his marks—showed up where they told him to go—and never said a word about it. (At one point, he did call his Scheduler, a Russell, Kansan, Judy Harbaugh, who went back with him twenty-five years, but just to tell her: "This is the best week of campaigning I've ever had in my life.")

Then, too, there was the content of the schedule: nine states *in the South,* which Bush was claiming as his fire wall, his fortress. And then, straight into Texas—Dole didn't have to spell out that message. On one level, the contest between him and Bush came down to (as the Texans say) . . . who had the *cojones.*

Dole went into Houston, did a businessmen's breakfast, did both papers, one-on-one . . . then, an energy meeting with oilmen, twenty-five top guys. After that, an open lunch. They'd done some mailing and calling—figured seventy-five folks, at the Hyatt. They fed three hundred and five people.

Then he blew into Dallas, did both papers, all three channels' live-at-fives. He did a presale meeting with twenty-two couples who'd be holding a funder in November. And then the big one: the Dole campaign was planning a free reception for three hundred and fifty people at the Anatole Hotel. He drew fourteen hundred.

He spent the night in San Antonio. Van Archer, who was Reagan's guy in south Texas, had a breakfast for Dole the next day. Archer was a total right-winger. He was shocked: "In all the years I did these things for Reagan, I never had a crowd like this."

Dole was shocked, too: the acceptance of him, all that room to move . . . in the state Bush called home! Even *this* was not locked down for Bush! There was no state in the country where Dole could not compete.

"Agh! Let's *goooo!*" Dole was cooing that morning, with obvious goodwill toward the world. "Nnggh, car ready? . . ."

He had a big speech after breakfast—American Legion, the national convention. For the first time, Dole would follow George Bush on the same stage.

"Yuuoooh, yut-dut-dut-dut-dah . . ."

Dole was rasping out snatches of his march. The Legion! His crowd. Dole was winning Legion Halls when Truman was President.

"Bip-bip-bup-bah! Yut-dut-dut-dah!"

Mike Pettit, one of Dole's staff on that trip, would recall: it was like riding to the heavyweight fight—with Muhammad Ali in the car.

50

The
Badge
of the Big Gee

THAT MONTH, and stretching into September, George Bush spent twenty-five straight nights in his own bed, in his favorite bedroom, the big room with the windows looking out to sea off Walker's Point, at Kennebunkport, Maine. Twenty-five straight mornings, he woke as he liked—5:15, maybe a few minutes later—and after a while, he'd throw on a robe, hair still standing straight up on his head, he'd go past the utility room to the kitchen, grab a coffee. He had the coffee thing set for 5:30. Then, it was back to the king-size bed with coffee and papers, which he and Bar would read while propped up on pillows against the white headboard with its built-in shelves, and the dog, Millie, would hop up on the bed, too, and, after a while, the grandchildren (the Grands, as Bush called them) would tumble on with Ganny and Gampy while their parents (George and Bar's kids) sat in the armchairs for coffee and chat, as the fresh sun climbed above the trees and knocked the chill off the Maine morning, after which, Bush would stretch and throw on some sweats—6:30, maybe close to 7:00—to run.

Bush ran not by distance but by time, at a pace of nine or ten minutes a mile, with one Secret Service man running ahead, and one Secret Service man running behind, one big black car leading the way, and another, or two, big black cars purring behind, and more Secret Service struggling alongside, through the woods, over lawns, keeping up as best they could. Every so often, Bush would call out: "How long?" One of the Service men would call back: "Nine and a half minutes, Mr. Vice President!" Or, the next time Bush asked:

"Sixteen minutes, Mr. Vice President!" When they'd call out, "Twenty minutes, Mr. Vice President!" . . . Bang. Bush would stop and walk the rest of the way home.

After the run, it was shower, breakfast, out to the boat. Then a briefing. Then, maybe tennis—he'd be ready for some doubles. Or golf, if he could face it. (He just couldn't understand—what'd happened to his putting?) Maybe shower up again, for lunch. Then, perhaps, he'd head for the office, do some reading, take some calls. Unless Bar'd had the court for her doubles that morning; in that case, it was his turn—maybe him and son Marvin, or Jeb, or whichever son was available to make a side for the match, a good match, competitive . . . but likely to put the old man over the top, make him a winner. (Just before Labor Day, he ran a round-robin tournament for the Secret Service, to make match selection easier for the Ranking Committee.)

Late afternoon, it was back to the boat. Bush could be on that boat for hours, and never feel unease. He'd bring a friend, or a son, or a grandchild, but he wouldn't say much. He'd run in open, featureless water, trolling, trolling, trolling for bluefish. He'd tell about days when he'd bring home a half-dozen bluefish, but there was, on that score, a suspicious lack of confirmation. Anyway, fishing wasn't the point. Sometimes he'd hand over the wheel, busy himself with a screwdriver and a rag, fiddling, tightening, rubbing down that boat till it gleamed like a violin. And he'd be glowing, too. No one had a bigger, sleeker cigarette boat . . . except the Secret Service—took one off a drug dealer, and it was faster than the Veep's, which did sort of piss him off . . . but they had to run theirs wherever he wanted. The Service boat had a helmsman and two guys in frog suits, and then, a half-mile away, there were two Coast Guard cutters, and on the hill overlooking his bay, a chopper . . . not to mention the Secret Service man with a phone in the prow of Bush's boat. That's how he got away from it all.

He'd be back before sundown, for the cookout. Then, by 8:00 P.M., he'd be tired. "Let's see who's first into bed!" he'd tell the Grands. And that was the close of another big day.

— ★ —

It wasn't like he didn't get anything done. His two New England operatives, Andy Card and Ron Kaufman, bused in Republican officials from New Hampshire. John Sununu got the full treatment—the puffy Gov wasn't much for tennis, but there were rides on the boat, cookouts, lunches on the terrace. Of course, it didn't stop with Sununu . . . heavens, no! There were Republican members of the State Senate, and the world's largest State House of Reps (400 members—263 Republicans). They'd come up in gaggles and stay in hotels, and get, uh . . . Important Briefings, and invitations to cocktail things at the Point . . . the Vice President wanted to see *them.* And it did not stop with legislators. There were members of Party committees, Mayors, Police Chiefs, Town Selectmen, tree wardens, library trustees . . .

"This is ridiculous!" Bush would mutter. "I'm s'posed to be on vacation!"

Bush was always serious about "recreating," a verb that would occur to him, usually, in mid-protest ("Jeez, c'mon! I thought we were try'na recreate here!") and which he'd pronounce with stress on the "reck." He wasn't interested in his re-creation.

But that was the other interruption of his days and nights at Walker's Point: the white men of his campaign—the "G-6," they liked to call themselves— were always flying back and forth, scheduling meetings, bringing political pooh-bahs, setting up briefings, hauling experts from Washington, to re-create the Vice President as a thinker on education in the nineties, or on international economics, trade and tariff negotiation, or Third World development in the year 2000.

They'd set up director's chairs on the terrace, into one of which Bush would toss himself, with his long legs canted out over nearly four feet of stones, the laces of his Top-Siders jiggling while he tried to listen. He was always grateful for their effort . . . but he didn't say much. He'd sit next to the guy who was leading the talk, and he'd ask a question every once in a while—he'd ask the person who hadn't said anything. It was hard to tell if Bush wanted the answer, or just wanted that man to have a chance to talk. Bigger briefings were held in the living room, a grand and spacious chamber jutting out to sea, windows on three sides, pale green walls, chintz-covered couches and chairs in profusion, amid which the experts would set up easels, with charts that Bush would regard with polite attention, for maybe ten seconds apiece. Sometimes, his left wrist would cock and jiggle over his legal pad—and that was great psychic reward, when the Vice President would note an idea. Mostly his gaze moved from face to face—it was the people who interested him.

They'd show up overdressed, with black shoes and shirts that were meant to bear ties, and after a day, their noses would be burnt red, or their eyes would peer out from pale raccoon-masks, where their new sunglasses kept the skin Washington-white. They'd sit on the couches with their knees together, and they wouldn't interrupt. They'd scowl at their agendas, or their notes—pages of typed stuff that could take days to get through . . . plans on who would carry the ball on which portions of the discussion . . . the Top Ten matters they had to take up with the Veep. They'd be lucky if they got to Two.

See, it was over when Bush said it was over, and that was when he got to thinking what the Grands were doing out on the rocks past the pool, or whether the bluefish were biting, or that he hadn't stopped by his mother's house that day. He'd never embarrass them by cutting them off, or walking out—but it wasn't gonna go on all day, either.

He sure as hell wasn't going to memorize briefing books—fat tomes of policy-speak—no matter how many the pointy-heads compiled for him. Jim Pinkerton, the campaign's Director of Research, had fifteen guys up till five in the morning—for a *week*—before he showed up in Maine, bearing a briefing book as thick as his thigh. Pinkerton was a pale six-foot-nine tower supporting a brain strangely clarified by altitude. He looked like a guy who'd invent brilliant gizmos to defraud the phone company. But instead he was the chief pointy-head for the Bush campaign. Needless to say, Bush considered Pinkerton somewhat weird—and clearly, too brainy to be listened to. As for the briefing book, well, maybe he'd look at it.

See, a lot of guys had the wrong idea about Kennebunkport: they thought this was the place where Bush would sit in wave-washed stillness, to do some serious thinking . . . you know, *study*. They didn't understand Walker's Point at all.

Anyway, Pinkerton's book was designed for debate-prep: positions of all the Republicans on all contestable matters of state. Dole and Kemp, Haig, du Pont, Robertson—everything they'd said about everything. Pinkerton went so far as to analyze Paul *Laxalt's* Senate votes. In sum, this book held everything that Bush would need to joust with his opponents on the high-policy plateau. Therefore, it was useless:

Bush's white men did not want him to debate.

— ★ —

The question at hand was the first Republican TV debate, another special edition of William F. Buckley's *Firing Line*. The Bush campaign had been diddling Buckley for months with "scheduling problems." In the view of the white men, there was no acceptable schedule for the Veep to begin bleeding on stage. What if they could not stanch the flow?

Tell the truth, there were so many things Bush's white men did not want him to do, they were collegially, collectively content that he wasn't doing anything—except reck-reating. That's how the white men were, or how they wanted to be seen: collective, competent, controlling—in a collegial way, of course, so you couldn't really tell who said what, or who was culpable of knowing anything. No divisions among them, no individual opinions—just a blank white wall, the board of Bush, Inc. That was the first corporate decision, and the overriding ethic of the Gee-Six.

The name was the tip-off: it was a play on G-7, the Group of Seven—Prime Ministers and Presidents who'd meet, from time to time, for photos, and to decide what the dollar should be worth, what to do about oil, how the civilized world should fight terrorism, that kind of thing. It was the U.S., Japan, Germany, Britain, France, Italy, maybe Canada was in there . . . pretty much everybody who could make a decent car. The meetings, the group photos, were meant to convey to the world's unwashed that the Free World big boys, the guys with the twelve-inch GNPs bulging in their pants, were all agreed how the game should be played—stick to the rules, or do without friends.

That was the subtext of the Gee-Six in the world of Republican politics. These were supposed to be the big boys, titans all and each, allied on the bridge of the flagship, SS *Bush,* to steer the great white fleet through the roil of public waters, back to safe harbor in the White House.

". . . A formidable high command," said Germond and Witcover.

". . . An able leadership team," said the *Newsweek*s.

What it was, was a committee, playing defense.

Craig Fuller, of course, was a Gee-Six, and a natural at this. He must have been California state champ at fending. In the OVP, in the OEOB (that's how they talked at Bush, Inc.), Fuller fended off the public. He fended off the Veep's own campaign. He fended off the Veep's own friends. The press he fended with such efficacy, they couldn't get in the damn building! (Bush didn't have a Press Secretary after Iran-contra, when Marlin Fitzwater moved up to help the Gipper. No spokesman at all—went on for months. Of course, Bush didn't mean to say anything. Then again, he was kinda, you know, running for President. . . .) Anyway, Fuller was so busy fending off potential fender-benders, people who might tell Bush anything unplanned or unpleasant, that no one could get a call through to Fuller. He was "in a meeting," usually with his staff of fellow fenders, all working overtime, protecting the Veep, bumping memos back and forth, piling up pink message slips, having their secretaries check with Fuller's secretaries to make sure the paper flow didn't back up.

Actually, the OVP was set up as a wall of secretaries, and secretaries to secretaries, who were all young and presentable Republican women in suits, or dresses, and pearls, or fake pearls—one strand, not too large, like they never took them off after their graduation pictures—who were so awfully busy picking up the chiming phones and telling callers that their bosses were "in a meeting," which would be followed by "a three-o'clock," "a three-thirty," and "a four-o'clock" . . . that they barely had time to chime up the photo office to double-check the addresses to which smiling photos of George Bush and his newest friends should be sent (the photos were the major physical product of the OVP) . . . and if they had to be "away from their desks," you could *see* how they had to march double time in their no-wrinkle skirts, with their security badges swaying under their pearls, and hear the *clipclop-clipclop* of their high heels on the hard stone hallways (two or more sounded like arrhythmic flamenco), with the *crish-crish-crish* of their panty-hosed thighs rubbing desperate maraca beat . . . and you could understand why these well–made-up and well-spoken young women could get so hard-eyed, icy-voiced, if a caller (not to mention the occasional citizen who actually penetrated the echoing EOB and gummed up *everything* by *presenting* himself) suggested that their bosses had been in meetings, unable to call back, for months, and maybe the best thing would be a meeting—*for him* . . . well, you could imagine how disruptive it was to have to stop, to explain, that they did not "handle the calendar," and the woman who took care of that was "in a meeting" or "away from her desk," and the caller ought to send a letter . . . oh, the paper flow!

So, Fuller had the OVP organized effectively, but that did not take care of Fifteenth Street, or, in the parlance of Bush, Inc., GBFP—George Bush for President. That was three blocks away, two floors of a run-down office building (but not contiguous floors—six and eight, with locked doors on the stairways, so the Republican girls "away from their desks" spent a measurable fraction of their young lives waiting for two creaking elevators—no matter: if they won, they would all buy pearls and work in the White House) . . . this was the official locus of the Gee-Six. Two of them actually worked there.

Lee Atwater was the Campaign Manager, the Fuller and fender for this half of Bush, Inc., and as such, the man most responsible for the physical being and appearance of GBFP. That's why it looked rattier and more disorganized than it was. This was a matter of style with Lee, who was thirty-six and happy to have you think he was really just a frustrated blues musician, World Wrestling Federation fan, and encyclopedic B-movie buff who'd strayed into politics—uh, Republican politics—because he happened to grow up redneck in South Carolina, and happened to fall in with the Dixiecrat, Strom Thurmond, who happened to change over to the Republican Party when he felt the great wind of racial change on his own ancient and wattled neck, and anyway, what could a boy like Lee do when it was his lot in life to understand—almost without trying—the beady-eyed offa-mah-back aspirations of the newly suburban, newly Republican southern and western Sunbelt majority, which, according to Lee's own college master's thesis, was now the nominating wing of the Republican Party and the backbone of the GOP's electoral-college lock, which had elevated Ronald Reagan and which, with God in His Heaven, should control American politics for the foreseeable forthcoming eon? That's when Lee wasn't trying to show you he was really a deep and extra-rationally attuned Jedi-warrior disciple of the ancient Chinese philosopher and strategist, Sun Tzu, and also of the Renaissance Italian, Machiavelli, whose books, both and each, he carried with him, always, so he could pull them out and lend them for five minutes, or ten, if you were sitting in his office and he had to pick up the phone.

He would pick up the phone, which was another distinction of style at GBFP (where Fuller was reviled as a gutless paper-pusher), and growl into it: "Whuss happ'nin'?" . . . or sometimes, in the manner of a Vietnam platoon commander, watching through his infrareds for gooks in the night: "Whuss movin'? Anythin' movin'?" . . . unless it was (alas, so infrequently) George Bush on the line, in which case Lee would out with a bright "Yes, sir!"

You didn't have to read Sun Tzu to know how the bread was buttered, and you didn't have to know Lee's whole story (though you soon would) to know this was his Big Chance, his own shining shot at History . . . which was why all the bodies who were somebodies at GBFP had their offices on the same floor, in the same wing of Fifteenth Street, with their secretaries in full view of Lee's own pearl-necked Rhonda Culpepper. These somebodies included the aforementioned Pinkerton; the Deputy Manager, Rich Bond; the campaign's administrator, Ede Holiday; Field Director Janet Mullins; First Son and family spy, George W. Bush . . . but in the view of the White Men on the Bridge (I'm Gee-Six and you're not), the other *important* office was occupied by Bob Teeter.

Teeter was the pollster and strategist, purveyor of good and important reasons why GBFP was playing defense. Teeter was an old hand—Bush pollster in 1980, Ford pollster four years before, and before that, at age thirty-three, baptized by fire in Nixon's 1972 CREEP. He was not one to overestimate the interest of the American voter more than a year before the election. The only thing voters knew, Teeter's surveys showed, was who was big-league, the size of a President. Bush was big-league. Even if they couldn't vote for him, people could imagine him as President. Dole and Hart were the only other names voters knew—even so, they were only half big-league. Why should Bush elevate Dole by engaging in the campaign, joining him, contesting him (and Kemp, du Pont, et al.) on the same stage? Why should he subject himself to their leveling barbs? What if Bush opened his mouth, and out came a mistake?

Teeter was the mildest of men, and modest: twenty years in the big time, he never went Hollywood. He preferred his cabin in the Michigan woods. His office on the Wing of Power was without decoration—one ratty desk, no "seating group," no lamp other than fluorescents above, no shelves for his unruly hillocks of paper. With the air of a harried accountant, he'd work through polls and speeches, position papers, reams of memos. When he spoke, he'd do a half-hour of on-the-one-hand-on-the-other, unless some other Big Gee told him to cut to the bottom line. In other Fifteenth Street offices, they took to calling him Teets, which had the right air of milk-the-cow, hand-wringing caution. But when it came time to enunciate a Gee-Six position, or to carry some collegial poop to George Bush, even Atwater (whose idea of defense was to rip out the other guy's liver) was likely to agree: "Teets oughta do it."

See, it didn't have to do with how they saw Teeter, or how they (or Teeter) saw George Bush. The point (the whole point with the badge of the Big Gee) was how George Bush looked at *them*. Fuller and Atwater might have hands-on control, might be asked, in fact, to run the halves of Bush, Inc. But they were Washington creatures, men in their thirties . . . who worked for George Bush. Therefore, in Bush-life, the view from Kennebunkport, they were the lowest G-2 in Gee-Six. They were staff. Bush had run through a lot of staff. When they came for briefings, or brought pooh-bahs to Maine, Atwater and Fuller stayed in hotels. But Teeter antedated Bush in the big time—he'd worked for Nixon. He was not, in the Bush-mind, a total Washington creature, but a Michigander (i.e., from real America). Teeter had built his own business (Bong!—a big bell in the Bush campanile), so, at times, Teeter had stayed in the house on Walker's Point.

Teeter's complement in this higher G-2 was Roger Ailes, another professional op, a television guru, another antedater of Bush, builder of a business, a New Yorker who continued to work from New York. Ailes was a tough guy with a blunt, gray goatee, thick of appearance and slovenly: he looked like he was wearing someone else's suit—but one he'd borrowed years ago (now the guy didn't want it back). The point was, Ailes didn't care how he looked. If people didn't like his suit—fuck 'em, they were assholes! So Ailes, preemptively, acted like an asshole right back. That's one of the reasons Bush liked him: not that he was an asshole to Bush—but he didn't mind looking like an asshole *for* Bush.

Ailes was honest, and in his own way, modest. He didn't try to talk to Bush about U.S.–Soviet relations, or the War Powers Act . . . or anything outside his ken. In the highly compartmentalized acquaintance of the Veep (how else could one keep thirty thousand friends straight?), that showed up as something like sense. As a consequence, Ailes was invited to work his wiles upon Bush's image, his appearance, his speaking style . . . on which subjects Ailes was not shy. One hot day, Bush, at the podium, stripped off his suit coat to reveal his tie and a dress shirt with . . . *short sleeves*! The sweating and enraged Ailes met the Veep at the foot of the stage:

"Don't *ever* wear that shirt again! . . . You looked like a fucking CLERK!"

They got to be great friends. Ailes, too, stayed at the Walker's Point house . . . if there was room. But not if the First Friends showed up—Bob Mosbacher and Nick Brady. They were the last and the highest G-2 . . . *real* white men.

Mosbacher was Finance Chairman of GBFP, a friend to Bush for thirty years, a man whose life rang a half-dozen Bush-bells of respect: he came from money in a New York commuter suburb but eschewed daddy's business—stocks and bonds—for the oil fields of Texas. (Bong!) He made his own pile—vast oil and gas holdings—and devoted himself to raising money for the GOP, building the Party in Texas. (Bong!) He was Finance Chairman, nationwide, for Gerald Ford . . . a man of civic commitment—a chairman of Houston's M.D. Anderson Cancer Institute . . . a sportsman—U.S. sailing champ in Olympic-class yachts . . . a hale and handsome sixty-year-old with lively blue eyes and the charm of self-deprecation. (Bong, Bong, Bong!) In the argot of Andover men, Mosbacher was an all-rounder.

Nick Brady, Campaign Chairman, was a quieter figure, as became a private banker to the nation's most-monied. In fact, the Bush-bells of Brady's life rang harmony with those of Bush's father. Like Prescott Bush, Brady had climbed the rungs of his investment bank—in Brady's case, the firm was Dillon Read—while the principal, C. Douglas Dillon, lent service to the man in the White House. (Mr. Dillon was Secretary of the Treasury for Kennedy and Johnson.) Brady finally arrived at chairman of the board. Meanwhile, he served the nation's weal in his own way, for nine months as a Senator from New Jersey, appointed to fill an unexpired term, and then on blue-ribbon boards and commissions created by the Reagan White House. Brady was a diffident man to strangers, gray-granite-jawed, like a chunk of Manhattan schist. He went back with Bush only ten years or so—got to know him after Carter won and Bush had to step down as Director of Central Intelligence. But right away, Brady showed his acumen by offering Bush a partnership at Dillon Read. How did Brady know he wanted to lure Bush aboard when—in Brady's own words—he barely knew the man? The answer speaks to the method and worldview of white men:

Of course, he knew the family . . .

Then, too, he could just *see* Bush's "way of going" . . .

Bush was clearly "a very senior sort of person," Brady said. "It's like thoroughbred horses."

So, Nick and George were just neighing across the paddock fence. And Bush, with equal, instantaneous clarity, saw that Brady was, in Andoverese, "sound."

The interesting coincidence—well, not pure coincidence—was that Brady, so sound, so profoundly a conservator, was matched and met on his rung of the Gee-Six by Mosbacher, the go-go wildcatter entrepreneur . . . just as the clerkly and careful Teeter contrasted with the fiercely pugnacious Ailes . . . just as Fuller, in his Teflon pinstripes, contested with the flamboyant bluesman, Atwater.

You could call it balance . . . or uneasy stasis. In fact, it was more fluid than appearance would suggest—a constant rondo of alliance and agreement, depending sometimes on who had talked to whom, and when, or the fact that Atwater worked no more than fifty feet from Teeter, or someone's best friend couldn't get a call-back from Fuller, or the First Friends had just spent a weekend in the big house at Maine. . . . But it *was* difficult to win quick consensus. It *did* result in a campaign whose candidate spent twenty-five straight nights in his own bed, in a remote corner of the nation, four months before the first primaries. (It probably had been thirty years since a major contender for President took three or four weeks off—Ike, maybe.) . . . Anyway, whatever came up, you always had to think what your fellow Gees might say . . . and it was only prudent to consider what Bush (or some other Gee) might be talking about with that notable nonmember, Jim Baker (Gee-Squared). . . . In fact, there were so many ways that Gee-Six *meant* defense . . . the wonder was Bush ever left Kennebunkport.

— ★ —

But he did. About once a week, he'd motorcade down to Pease Air Force Base, climb aboard a waiting Stratoliner, and fly off to do something helpful. Last week it was New Orleans, where he spoke to a VFW convention. This week it would be San Antonio, to address the American Legion. Of course, the U.S. Air Force would have Bush back in his ocean-view bed that same night . . . anyway, this, too, was defense.

This was part of Atwater's southern fire-wall strategy, Lee's determination to erect an unassailable, insurmountable Super Tuesday bulwark, so that even if Bush lost Iowa . . . even if he fell on his face *big-time* and pissed away his lead (and Governor Sununu's help) in New Hampshire . . . even if Bob Dole got hot and swept the lesser early contests in Minnesota and South Dakota . . . even if Jack Kemp convinced the tax-cut-and-Star-Wars crowd that he was the Real and Rightful Reagan Heir . . . even if Pat Robertson's eye-in-the-middle-of-the-forehead charismatics crawled out by thousands from under church pews . . . *still, even so!* . . . on Super Tuesday, seventeen states would vote, most of whose citizens had never seen a candidate, and, as a consequence, they would vote in small numbers—small enough to match, or even overmatch, with a machinable bloc . . . just the kind of bloc vote that Lee could deliver, knowing, as he did know, every small-time white-shoe Republican op in the Old Confederacy, having worked with them on the Gipper's campaigns, having greased them now, assiduously, for nearly three years, as the head of the Bush PAC, and then the Bush campaign, having wheedled and threatened and bribed them aboard, every one, in every state . . . until the other campaigns must perish from lack of help, or lack of money, or, ultimately, votes . . . *one way or another,* George Bush was going to look like a winner on March 8.

This was defense by suffocation—you look to see where the other guy's breathing, then mash down the pillow of Bush, Inc.'s, superior resources. That's why these veterans groups (meeting in the South) were important enough to pull the Veep off his boat—you look at it like a white man (i.e., with cold-eyed literalness), you could see how the veterans might plump for Dole.

That was the same leak-plugging logic that led Bush to sign on a strange but Bush-devoted Christian, Doug Wead, as "adviser" and liaison to the born-again crowd. Wead was a preacher—Assembly of God—except he didn't have a church to pastor, never wore a clerical collar . . . seemed to have a second career as a motivational speaker for Amway. He looked like a standard Washington luncher, dyed his hair, showed up as man-in-the-know at politico-religious meetings, where he appeared to be well known. The convention of Christian Booksellers, for example: Wead was big—had a half-dozen books under his name. Now he was working on a book about Bush. *Man of Integrity* was Wead's new title. . . . Anyway, you'd see him at Fifteenth Street, or at the OVP, murmuring warnings about "the movement" and millions of Praise-the-Lord votes that Robertson would bring forth unless George Bush acted fast.

So, Bush made his moves. For one thing, he worked out a cover-the-bases statement on faith, which Wead and Bush, Inc., could retail when the occasion demanded. The problem, of course, was Bush wasn't born again. He was a born Episcopalian. So, Bush would say: "Well, if you mean by *born again,* 'Do you accept Jesus Christ as your personal Lord and Savior?' . . . then I'd answer, *Yes!* No hesitation. . . ." Meanwhile, he did not hesitate to issue a ringing endorsement of Jerry Falwell ("The nation is in crying need of your moral vision!") and to host Wead's friends, Jim and Tammy Faye Bakker, at the Residence. (This was before the Fall. Bush said he watched their television show.)

Atwater had elaborate theories to explain how these weren't just knee-jerk panderings but proactive stratagems on Sun Tzuian (or maybe Machiavellian) principles . . . how Bush would cut into the other guy's base, pick off maybe twenty-five percent, to keep rival campaigns from becoming real movements, forcing them to fight rearguard actions . . . Lee had theories on everything. He had a splendidly oriental filigree of justification for the way Bush pandered to the right wing—of course, that was Lee's idea in the first place.

It started in '85, shortly after Lee took over Bush's PAC, the Fund for America's Future. Bush agreed (after weeks of Lee's urging) to speak at a dinner tribute to William Loeb, the (blessedly, dead) publisher of the Manchester *Union Leader.* While he was still alive and spitting, Loeb had called Bush a "hypocrite" . . . "unfit to be the Republican nominee" . . . "up to his neck in Watergate," and accused Bush of taking illegal contributions from Nixon slush funds in his own '70 Senate race. (Of course, it could have been worse: Ike was "a *stinking* hypocrite . . . Dopey Dwight." And then, too, there was Ford—"Jerry the Jerk"—and "Kissinger the Kike.")

But Loeb (even dead) was big with the rabid right, so Bush showed up and praised his long career of vituperation. "Bill Loeb always spoke the truth as he saw it." Bush also appeared at the Conservative Political Action Conference (where a majority of the members—still—detested him for being Pres Bush's son) . . . and then, too, at a convention of the Conservative Party of New York (where he tried to make friends by questioning Mario Cuomo's patriotism). And those were just the public panderings: in private it was wackier.

In '86, the PAC arranged for Scott Stanley, editor of *Conservative Digest,* and Bill Kennedy, its publisher, to meet Bush in the West Wing of the White House. Just a chat—a search for common ground. ("Y'play tennis? . . .") And it went great! Kennedy and Stanley said to Bush: "What can we do for you?" Bush replied with gravity: "I would *love* to see the War Powers Act tested in court." They ate that up. He was making headway with these people! They were friends! (They'd already reprinted his Loeb speech in their March issue.) Then Kennedy suggested that KGB operatives were working out of Senator John Kerry's office. Bush turned momentarily and looked at Atwater (*You owe me for this* . . .) and then, with a polite smile, without argument, turned back to his guests.

Thing was, if you had a half-hour, Lee could explain why he (and Bush) had nothing to apologize for . . . how this was not *really* sucking up to the nuts, but the *appearance* of an effort to suck up to the nuts . . . an elaborate Sun Tzuian *feint*—see? . . . which would make the other candidates *think* . . . that *Bush thought* . . . that the right wing was still the muscle of the party . . . so they'd *all* run to the right, see? . . . when actually, secretly, Lee knew that the right wing was really just a quarter or a third of the Party—irrelevant!—and when they all, Kemp, Dole, du Pont, started scrapping over this fraction (a shard of which Bush would have grabbed off already), they would be fighting for a base that couldn't put them over the top, while Bush, having pandered and run, would move on toward the real Reagan center . . . see?

"That's one thing Ah kin do," Atwater would affirm happily. "Ah kin really make 'em chase the rabbit!"

Problem was—what Lee didn't calculate: that trail of timid, stinking rabbit spoor seemed to lead directly to the backside of his candidate, the much-defended VP.

51

A
Weanling
Woodlouse

IN FACT, *everybody knew*—for years, since 1980!—that Bush was kind of a weenie, a wuss, a wuh . . . wuh, wuh . . . well, that's when it started, in 1980, the first time Bush ran for President.

It wasn't that they didn't like him—the press, the lunch-buddies, the pink-jowled men-in-the-know at Duke Zeibert's—how could they not? Bush was so friendly, eager, engaging, so well bred . . . they called him "preppy," which was a word in vogue (there were books on how to become so). And though that struck Bush as inaccurate (in his mind, he was an *oilman,* a *wildcatter,* a West Texas *pioneer* . . .), he tried not to pick fights about it, as long as he was winning. In fact, it wasn't hostile while he was winning—Bush was the moderate against the troglodyte Reagan, the Great White Man Hope of the big-feet for a long and satisfying Republican bloodbath.

Then, Bush stopped winning and got out of the race. (Actually, Jim Baker pulled him out.)

Then, Bush accepted the VP slot and said he never disagreed with Reagan. No, *really*! . . . Bush was a troglodyte, too!

Well, Jeez, you know . . . didn't the guy *believe in anything*?

In fact, he did: he believed in George Bush . . . and winning—in turning this episode of his life into a win. Of course, when they did win, Reagan and Bush, things only got worse from the, uh, whi . . . whi . . . whillywha perspective.

At that point, not only was it standard Carter-era-Washington poop ("Political observers said . . .") that Bush had sold out his principles, his middle-of-the-road positions, his *essence* as the preppy son of the Council-on-

Foreign-Relations elite . . . but the new crowd, the Reagan wonks, never had forgiven him for contesting their hero. Bush (and worse still, his buddy Jim Baker, the new Chief of Staff at the Gipper's own elbow!) were worms in the apple of the Reagan revolution—for God's sake, *everybody knew,* they were *moderates*!

So it did not matter how many strident speeches Bush made in support of Reagan. (That only confirmed the suspicion that Bush was a wheedler, a weakling.) It did not matter how often or how ably Bush represented the President overseas. (So what? He's an errand boy, a whiffler!) It certainly did not redound to Bush's credit that he stood by Reagan while he caused a deep recession and enormous deficits (confirming Bush's judgment on "voodoo economics") . . . or as Reagan sent hundreds of Marines to their slaughter in Beirut, on a mission no one could explain (a mission opposed, untraceably, by Bush). By that time, Reagan had survived being shot, so no one could attach any blame to him. Anyway, heading into the '84 reelection, Reagan was supposed to stay on the big job of leading the Free World (i.e., chopping brush on his ranch) while Bush, the loyal deputy, flew around the nation to defend the administration.

That he did: a thousand chicken lunches and dinners were spiced by Bush-encomia on the Gipper, Bush-attacks on the Democrats, on the Congress, on the Sandinistas 'n' Soviets . . . and '84 was the worst—miserable! The problem was, every time Bush opened his mouth, some wise-ass reporter was sure to ask: *Why'd you say the opposite, in 1979?* Abortion, the ERA, taxes, arms talks . . . if Bush tried to deny the conflict, they had quotes, they had videotape! (That was *so* unfair.) Bush was waffling, he was a, uh . . . wiggler!

Of course, to Bush, this was all personal. He'd tried so hard to make friends! Why couldn't they see that? See him, like he really was? What got into these people? . . . He'd ask his Press Secretary, Peter Teeley—Teeley was an old pro, supposed to know reporters—but Teeley was too old a pro . . . kind of pissed off, in fact, that he still had to know reporters. He hated reporters! He wanted to be a real white man. . . . Teeley'd snarl: "Ahh, these stupid fuckers wouldn't know a story if it hit 'em in the mouth. No-counts! Second-stringers!"

Which wasn't much help to Bush, making friends.

He stayed away from the press when he could—cut back on interviews. Let 'em use the stuff from his speeches. Then he was elitist, afraid to take questions, a waxwork! . . . *Doonesbury* started working that stuff about Bush putting his manhood into a blind trust. (That sent Bush over the edge. Who was *that* guy? *Tru-dohhhh?* . . . *He's* the elitist—a Yalie! Junior knew him!—a spoiled sixties crypto-commie-intellectual snob!)

Well, it only got worse: the press pack was growing, had to file every day (Bush was out there making a spectacle of himself!) . . . and they couldn't use the stuff from the speeches—nothing *in* the speeches, except borrowed lines from the Gipper, America standing tall and all . . . and, the way Bush was, when the stuff wasn't *his,* he'd raise his voice to a scream on the borrowed lines, trying to show he *did believe* . . . his voice would leap an octave, and he'd whinny out these Rambo zingers, and wave his arms (someone must have told him that showed force) . . . speech coaches came and departed without effect, and the TVs would edit stuff just to show the mistakes, and the print press was worse: the *profiles . . . Jeezus!* They'd be asking about his watchband, his shirts and his shoes, trying to *prove* he was really still a preppy, expecting him to go through his, uh . . . *wardrobe* . . . when he tried to tell them, he was really sorta *Texan,* when you got down to it: he liked country music, he'd have a beer and popcorn—no! pork rinds! He *liked* pork rinds! And chili, and chicken-fried steak: we *love* all that stuff! . . . But they wouldn't believe it, wouldn't write his line-of-the-day. Instead they'd harp on some offhand remark, like *The Washington Post,* which had the gall to quote him on the *front page* when he said, just by the by, that, yeah, sure, as a last resort, you could probably raise taxes to cut the deficit.

And that was the day he was supposed to fly to California, to the *ranch,* for lunch! It was embarrassing . . . hauling in this planeload of banshees, screaming, *taxes, TAXES! What about the TAXES?* . . . At the Great Tax-Trimmer's *ranch.* Well, Bush denied that he'd ever *thought* about taxes . . . and Teeley—he was ripshit!—after the story persisted for a day, after the *Post* called the next day's speech an effort to bury Bush's tax gaffe, he called up the *Post* reporter in her hotel room, three o'clock in the morning, and threatened never to help her again, with *anything* . . . if she was *drowning!* And of course, that upset her: it was Dale Russakoff, on her second trip of her first campaign . . . so Bush had to go down the aisle of his plane, the next day, straight to Russakoff's seat, where he stopped, you know, just to chat . . . "Yeah, I heard y'play tennis! We'll have to get the Ranking Committee to check you out—maybe we can play!" And after that, he went back to the Power Cabin, but he didn't stop trying . . . no. An aide came down the aisle with a life-sized tennis racket made of chocolate (God knows where Bush had procured it), which was a Veeply gift for Russakoff. . . . You think it helped?

The *Post* editorial page essayed a comparison of the VP candidates, lauding Mondale for his "audacious and commendable" choice of a female. The paper called Ferraro "smart, strong and resourceful," conceding that her lack of foreign policy experience showed up in her speeches, from time to time . . . *but:*

"Something else shows when George Bush speaks—something that threatens to trash whatever esteem his impressive résumé and his private personal grace have earned him. Maybe it is just that he is a rotten campaigner (winning elections, after all, has never been his forte). But he seems to reveal himself, as all viewers of 'Dallas' will long since have noticed, as the Cliff Barnes of American politics—blustering, opportunistic, craven and hopelessly ineffective all at once. This impression has been so widely remarked in recent weeks by commentators of every political persuasion that it hardly needs elaboration. . . ."

(No, such poop was well known by everybody-in-the-know.)

That tore it with the *Post: Cliff Barnes!*

Russakoff never did get an interview—neither her nor the reporter from *Time,* another woman . . . so it got to be a "woman thing," which is how everything seemed to turn, after Ferraro was out there. Bush couldn't believe it! They'd compare *him*—after all he'd *done*—to a junior Democrat Congress-woman! It was ridiculous! Of course, he couldn't say that . . . couldn't go after Ferraro at all . . . wouldn't *be* that way about a woman, couldn't say, couldn't *breathe* his conviction that she, their darling, their symbol of liberality, was actually an *arriviste* . . . they'd think he was picking on her, as a woman, you know, or as an Italian from Queens (where he knew how gamey, grasping, the politics were—God! Look at Al D'Amato!) . . . so he had to just *take* it, while they *insulted* him with comparisons—and she came after him with knives: she started talking about *his* taxes—him and Bar!—how they only had to pay twelve percent that year . . . talk about *nerve!* When she and her sleazeball husband had piled up $4 million in New York, uh . . . well, you know that kind of business! Bar was furious. That's when she said, in the plane—she thought it was off the record—that she and George had *always* lived well, and didn't try to poor-mouth . . . "like that four-million-dollar—well, I can't say it, but it rhymes with rich." . . . Well, when that got into the papers, Bar was in tears (so mortified at hurting George) . . . and Bush threw the press off his plane altogether. They could ride in their own stinking plane—see how they liked it.

They didn't . . . and by the end of the campaign, Bush was well known as a worm, a weanling woodlouse, a weedy wort in the garden of politics, a wan, whimpering . . . well, it was war.

Of course, he won. That was the big thing—his team won reelection, big. Wasn't that the point?

Well, not altogether.

That's when Bush had to change his whole staff—in '85—because the campaign had been such a personal disaster. So he got Atwater . . . started courting the right wing . . . he did it because he wanted to win. But in January of '86, George Will wrote him up:

"The unpleasant sound Bush is emitting as he traipses from one conservative gathering to another is a thin, tinny 'arf'—the sound of a lapdog."

Later that year, when Iran-contra hit, Bush had to *prove* he was "out of the loop." And he did! He convinced the Tower Commission. . . . Of course, he had that wired, with his friend John Tower and his friend Brent Scowcroft as two of the three members . . . but everyone had to admit—right?—he won! He showed he was *unaware,* not a player—not culpable of knowing *anything*!

Of course, that had its price, too, as the lack of awareness was allied, in the tribal mind, with incapacity, imbecility, impotence. . . .

But he wasn't going to give anyone a chance to stick him with *that* . . . none of his opponents—oh, wouldn't they love to—if he sat on stage with them, got out there where they could all fire away. Hell, no! Why should he debate—let something happen? . . . If nothing happened, he was going to win!

See, at every stage of the game, George Bush did whatever he had to, to win.

And now, by the end of the summer of 1987, he was the clear front-runner for the Republican nomination, had a campaign command second to none, had more money, more operatives, more friends than any politician in the country . . . no wonder he could reck-reate for three weeks straight.

Still, the savants, pundits, pooh-bahs—even if they couldn't write it, wouldn't say it on TV yet—*everyone* who was in-the-know *knew* that Bush would never get there. . . . (God! *Look* at him, behind the fence of his mansion in Maine!) . . . Might as *well* say it:

The man was a wimp.

52

White
Men
at Play

THIS GROWING PROBLEM of perception had snuck up on the Veep: the
bubble imposes its own special
blindness, like one-way glass—you might see out, darkly, but you never can
see how it looks from the outside.

Not even by act of imagination, not for an instant, could George Bush put
himself outside the fence at Walker's Point . . . say, in a Chevrolet, the backseat
loaded with ketchup-smeared kids, stuck in crawling traffic on Ocean Avenue,
the two narrow lanes that led from the village of Kennebunkport, along the
coast, past the "cottages" (mansions, they'd call them, in the Chevy) that
looked out to sea, all built when building was grand and gracious, on the rise
of land to the left of the road, the landward side, across the street from the
ocean . . . except for . . . *one house* that owned the seaside rocks. It was a
compound, really—there was, in addition to the big house, a bungalow where
the VP's mother still summered, and a small guest house, The Wave, that was
once a wing of the mansion but had been rebuilt, after a great storm, as a
two-bedroom cottage separated from the main house by a narrow path.
. . . But what you saw from the road was one great house, dark and massive
on its private promontory of green and gray, that was so big, so distant, it
seemed to sail like a great ship on the ocean itself, and to conjure a world so
grandly *distinct* from the earthly present smell of french fries in the Chevy,
that it might be a picture in a shiny magazine, or a video-still from *Lifestyles*
. . . captured before the Secret Service man emerged from the gatehouse to hold
up a patient forestalling palm—no, not even *pictures* were ours to hold of this
embodiment of otherness, privilege, and ease.

That was the tourist's-eye view—more and more tourists drove by each year of his Vice Presidency, and the traffic was thick now, on summer weekends, in the year when his best shot at the White House approached. There were people in other "cottages" (and one or two at Walker's Point) who rued the day the road was "built through." . . . It used to be a dead end, so no one could pass on the way to anyplace else. But Bush wouldn't say such a thing. Very small-d democratic was the Veep about the little people—he never worried about the T-shirtification of the shops on the main street, or the crowds at Mabel's Lobster Claw. What the hell! If he meant to sup at Mabel's, someone would call and Mabel would clear out a whole side of the dining room—put half her tables together, fresh flowers for a centerpiece—and turn everyone else away. Of course, she wasn't supposed to tell the *reason* . . . but word would leak and tourists would line her porch three-deep, waiting for the motorcade. They couldn't eat—might as well see the show. So there'd be fifty people, or a hundred, waiting with their itchy kids when the motorcade showed up, with its long black cars, and the ambulance, lights flashing, and the earplugs, who'd jump out before the cars even purred to a stop . . . it was exciting. Sometimes, the crowd would break into applause! And Bush would wave and grin and thank them. It just showed him anew: all that sour press had nothing to do with the *people*—*they* liked him . . . and why not? In his mind, they were all on vacation, in Kennebunk, together. You know, no formality that *he* could see . . . just him and all those people from New Jersey—they were all at Mabel's together.

Bush could never understand all those reporters "who put me down on the couch."

Why was he always up in Maine? Wasn't it elitist? . . .

For God's sake, he'd been coming to this place every summer of his *life* (save for one, when he was bombing the Nips back to Tokyo). . . . He didn't pick it for status! He didn't pick it at all! Look, there was his *mother's* house, the anchor of the family . . . surely they could understand *that.* They wanted character?

Oh, he read the stories—though he said he didn't, or said he forgot them the minute he put them down. ("Bar's the one who'd remember that kind of thing.") . . . But he remembered, too. Some of the bad ones he could *recite.* And he remembered who wrote them. He always thought, in fact, it must be something about them—or them and him . . . a personal thing.

So he'd try to have them over to the house—drinks, or the boat . . . think it helped? Saul Friedman, the reporter for *Newsday,* known him for twenty-five years—Saul covered his first campaign in Houston!—Saul says, "Why'd you get a boat like *that*? What're you try'na *prove*? A sailboat is *your* kind of boat."

A *sailboat*!

Why couldn't these people see?

Just as he could not inhabit a french-fry-shocked Chevy, he could not *imagine* what it was like for reporters, to sit for fruitless days in a lousy hotel in a small town in Maine, killing time, trying to divine if something was ever going to happen in a campaign that didn't seem to be a campaign . . . not here, anyway—no matter how many white men flew in for conferences, briefings, and strategy set-tos, to which, of course, reporters were not invited.

The press could ask the pols who motored in for visits: "Whad'ja talk about with the Vice President?"

"Oh, you know . . . fishing." (That was the truth!)

Sometimes, reporters could catch one of the white men on his way to the airport, after a conference.

What went on?

Any actions, decisions?

Who said what?

Of course, the white men could never, uh, exactly remember, if anybody in particular said anything, you know, in particular . . . no, it was just nice to be up in Maine. (True enough, too.)

No wonder the stories said the Bush campaign had no positions. No wonder they implied that Bush was pandering and playing through the campaign. No wonder they started using the quotes from du Pont and Kemp—how Bush was ducking the debate, was not *man enough* to join a contest of issues, to put forth his agenda for the nation and its people. . . . The reporters came, they did their jobs, they asked around—and (in Al Haig's notable phrase), they didn't hear a *whimp*!

They looked at the distant house on the Point, and they saw:

White people at play.

They asked the candidate's main man, Atwater . . . and Lee talked about how great it was to get away from the noise and heat, to talk things over, all the white men together, in the sparkle of sun-on-water, the quiet cool of the night. Lee talked about how *classy* it was:

"What's *Bob Dole* gonna do?" said the gentle Campaign Manager. "Rent a trailer and invite all the New Hampshire Police Chiefs down to see him in his *Airstream*? . . ."

But Atwater (who was new at being a white man) missed the point—it wasn't class, or escape, not in the view from the big house.

Kennebunkport, all the "cottages," and Walker's Point in particular, had to do with America's *substitute* for class—that is, money and power. The stern gentlemen in their wing collars and boater hats who built these oceanfront mansions were not the idle rich of their day. They were men of big works and large affairs . . . they'd catch the *State o' Maine* sleeper Friday night from New York and, forty-eight hours later, they'd kiss their children goodbye again for the overnight trip back to Wall Street or midtown. Kennebunkport was their creation, for lives of the most rapacious striving.

Here is a fact about Walker's Point that should be borne in mind:

In the plan of the town, and through its early decades, this unique, irreplaceable spit of land was called Damon's Point, or more popularly, Damon's Park . . . because it was the townspeople's favorite retreat, a place (as the local historian wrote) of "wandering well-worn woodland paths; a small pond;

fragrant juniper and sun-warmed blueberries; and unsurpassed views in both directions along the shoreline of the Kennebunks. . . ."

That's before the Walkers bought it—so much for the public park.

Yes, proprieties were observed (white shorts and shirt on the court, please) . . . but the point, at the Point, was who played—and won. Yes, the Walker boys were expected at St. Ann's every Sunday—their mother was a very religious woman . . . imagine her dismay (though shock was unlikely) to find her sons, before church, in a circle by the driveway, laying down their bets on the first hymn—even or odd?

The W-word at the Point was Winning.

In the summer of 1987, while Bush reck-reated, David Broder wondered in print whether Bush was too much "an innocent" to survive the slaughter of a campaign. The Karacter Kops weighed in with profiles—mostly following the lead of the Chief Majorette: "*Is George Bush Too Nice to Be President?*" . . . They all stressed the privilege, the security of his youth, all the friends he made at school . . .

But what were friends for?

Remember the Andover newspaper poll: "The average student came to Andover with making contacts uppermost in his mind." Friends were the fellows who helped you play the game . . . and win. That was the real game—great doings, the lifelong King of the Mountain—the scramble onward and upward from Andover Hill to the boardroom, or the Cabinet table. . . .

Consider the transcontinental, transgenerational web of friendship, family, and power that supported one Bush-scramble, the creation and financing of Zapata Off-Shore Company:

George's main booster was still Uncle Herbie, whose company, G.H. Walker & Co., was underwriter for nearly all of Zapata Off-Shore's early public offerings of stocks and bonds. The law firm representing G.H. Walker & Co. was Winthrop, Stimson, the firm founded by Elihu Root in 1868. Henry Stimson (Andover's chairman and icon) was taken into the firm by Root in 1891. The actual lawyering on Zapata issues was done by Endicott P. "Cotty" Davison, a grandson of the legendary founder and headmaster of Groton, Endicott Peabody, and, with George Bush, a Bonesman at Yale in 1948. For Zapata Off-Shore's initial public offering, however, Bush wanted a Texas company to underwrite. Luckily, Robert Parish, who had been at Andover with Bush, was working at the Houston investment bank of Underwood, Neuhaus. (Parish and Milton Underwood took seats on the board of Zapata Off-Shore.) Parish called his friend Baine Kerr, who had experience in the oil and gas business, to do the Texas lawyering. Kerr was an associate at Baker & Botts, the prestigious Houston law firm founded by the grandfather of James A. Baker III. One of the early partners at Baker & Botts had been Robert S. Lovett, who became counsel to E.H. Harriman's Union Pacific and later served on the board of directors and as president of the railroad. Lovett was a self-educated man—his formal training ended after the third grade. But his own son, Robert A. Lovett, went on to the Hill School (with Herbie Walker and his brothers) and to Yale, where he was Skull and Bones. Lovett the younger, who commanded the first U.S. Naval Air Squadron, married Adele Brown, daughter of James Brown, a senior partner in Brown Brothers. Lovett also rose to partner at Brown Brothers and helped to arrange the merger of Brown Brothers with W.A. Harriman & Co., a company formed by E.H. Harriman's sons, Averell and Roland, and run for a time by George Bush's grandfather, G.H. Walker. Prescott Bush was a top partner in the firm for forty years. In fact, the Harrimans' top men, Pres Bush and Knight Wooley, had been Skull and Bones at Yale with four of the partners at Brown Brothers: Lovett, Ellery James, Laurence Tighe, and Charles Dickey. And just as Davison had been at Yale with Bush, so, too, Root, Stimson, the Harrimans, and all the Walkers were Yale alumni. And not only did they do business, but they were part of a line—from Root to Stimson to Lovett—that held sway in the U.S. departments of War and State, from the Spanish-American to the Vietnam War.

Tell the truth, the Walkers of Walker's Point were not so much interested in matters of public policy. More than most, they tended to strip the game to its essence—which was to put oneself and one's heirs firmly astride the fuel lines of the great economic engine. When Bush's Uncle Herbie shoved those new Zapata shares into the portfolios of his favored investors (with such blunt insistence that it actually caused some talk within the firm) . . . he did not have in mind the energy requirements and policies of the Republic. No, he was backing his favorite, Poppy. He was betting his horse to win.

Yes, there was security in the web—it could act as an extraordinary safety net: in the early years of Zapata Off-Shore, a hurricane in the Gulf of Mexico blew away one of Bush's three multimillion-dollar oil rigs . . . disappeared it, and with it, a third of Bush's business prospects. George was under great stress—though amid the Walkers and Bushes in Maine, nothing was ever really *said* about it. . . . Of course, Zapata was insured (through George's brother, Pressy) . . . but still, it was woeful news for the company, its investors and creditors. Sure enough, the officers of the Morgan Guaranty Bank were upset (most upset that they had not been told), so the bank president called his friend, Dr. Johnny Walker, in Kennebunkport. Johnny Walker told brother Herbie, who snapped: "What the hell are *they* calling for? I've got three or four guys who'll cover the whole thing!" . . . and Herbie called the president of Morgan Guaranty to tell him to get off of George Bush's back. . . . In fact, almost a week of sun-and-sea passed in Kennebunkport before Herbie or Johnny found cause to *mention* the matter to George.

Still, in the end, it was win or lose with the Walkers, and within the wider web of white men in which Bush came of age and became a star. Herbie was not cutting slack for his nephew—he was still betting to win. (He held on to Zapata Off-Shore to the end, till George Bush, himself, sold out in '65 to devote himself to politics. Even when the stock sank to two dollars and change, Herbie would insist: "Gonna be the *greatest* stock. Y'*gotta* go with management! . . .") The trick was to have enough muscle and will to stay in the game . . . and narrow the odds.

Herbie had the will. He was the second patriarch of the Point, which spoke volumes for his strength and standing within the web. In each generation, there was, after all, only one man to tend Walker's Point, and defend it, for the family and its heirs. . . . That was another easy misconception about this world of ferocious white men: in the end, there was nothing collegial about control, or winning. Only one man could have the big house.

And in his generation, George Bush was that man . . . that kind of winner. It was not Herbie's sons, Bert or Ray, who took the big house. And it was not for George Bush to take, in turn, the smaller bungalow where his parents, Pres and Dottie, had summered. The family was its own Ranking Committee . . . and Poppy was The One.

Maybe it was not entirely coincidence that it was at the Point, amid that family, that George Bush first said where *he* thought his life should lead. It was a summer evening in the sixties, the family was gathered, idly, with a TV on—pictures of a great hall, a national convention, a massed crowd cheering, and politicians on stage, waving and smiling . . . George Bush was lying on the floor of the living room, on his side, his head propped on an elbow, his eyes on the screen, as he said:

"I'm gonna be up there, sometime."

Maybe it was not entirely coincidence . . . when Herbie passed away, a decade later, and his widow, Mary, was going to sell the Point (a group of Arab investors meant to break up the parcel), Herbie's brothers brought matters to a head and prevailed upon Mary to sell the land and the big house (for a great deal less than it would fetch from the foreigners) to George Bush. It would not be easy for George. The house had been wrecked by a big storm. A wing was in ruins, the great parlor jutting out to sea was battered open to the weather . . . the place would need plenty of cash—more than George Bush had, at the time. But he was The One, family-ordained. . . . Maybe it was not entirely coincidence:

That was the year he first ran for President.

—★—

No one understood the web and George Bush's place in it—or appreciated it—like the First Son and chip off the block, George W. Bush. That's why he never offered the Veep advice.

It was *because* he knew his father: how Bush was about "team play" . . . about letting people do their jobs . . . about professional people who shouldn't have to look over their shoulders at every member of the family. That's why Junior tried to keep quiet—he put his head down, did his work.

But that work was in the campaign, every day. And George W. Bush had method—hard to see, sometimes, but . . . method, nonetheless. He'd have a rotating gaggle in his office all day, bullshitting, playing with the toys on his desk, giggling at the T-shirts and gimcracks tacked all over the walls, while Junior sat with his boots on the desk, a chew in his bottom lip, talkin' on the phone and spittin' in the basket . . . and listening. Sometimes people would get so easy in his office, they'd say what they thought.

That's how Junior knew—what they said and what they thought. He knew
. . . when they looked at his dad like a kid with his first bike—sure he was going
to crash and maim himself somehow. Like they were with the debate—oh,
Junior knew. It pissed him off. He knew *why* that stuff was in the papers, about
Bush ducking. . . .

That's why he brought up the stories.

They were playing golf—"electric polo," they called it. The way Bushes
played—and played through—the course was theirs to race. (*Whap!* Hit the
ball, gun the cart, jump out while the tires are still skidding grass—*Whap!*
. . . Two hours, start to finish! A truly athletic event!)

"*Shot!* . . ." Junior cried in approbation, and then, more quietly, into the
cart-wind: "These guys don't think you can do it . . . what we all know you
can do . . . this putt is *mine*—in the *CUP!* . . ."

That was about all—not much had to be said, *could* be said, within the web,
in Maine. . . . It was, actually, a couple of days later, in the air, aboard *Air
Force Two,* on the way to San Antonio, Bush told Fuller:

"When we land I want a statement saying I'll do the debate . . . October
28. I'll be there." Fuller was surprised: he hadn't heard any discussion about
that. But there was nothing in Bush's voice that invited discussion.

Bar said: "Oh, you'll have to call George . . ." (She meant George W.) "He'll
be so pleased."

Bush got up and motioned her into the forward cabin, told her there was
no need to rub Fuller's face in it. He didn't want the staff looking over their
shoulders at the family.

Junior got the news in the next day's *Post*—at least, one version of it:

". . . Bush announced his change of heart in San Antonio after discussing
it with aides on the way to a speaking engagement there, the aides said."

Anyway, the lead was true: George H.W. Bush was coming out to campaign.

53

Into
the Death-Star

YOU COULD SEE what happened in
San Antonio from the papers . . .
well, you could see what happened
to Dole.

It wasn't his speech. His speech went fine. He had those Legion fellows
laughing, cheering . . . he knew they were his.

But that part didn't make the papers—his speech. No, the stories were all
about Bush agreeing to debate . . . and then Bush's speech—that's what tripped
up Dole.

Bush used this line—just a throwaway, a passing dig—about the Congress
trying to micro-manage foreign policy instead of leaving it to the White House,
to the President . . . who, in Bush's view, was in charge of Standing Tall.

And Dole took the bait—he defended the Congress, or at least his Republicans, who were *backing* the President, *supporting* the White House!

Dole was extra-sensitive, as he was just then promoting his own five-point
peace plan for Central America, his own first adventure in Standing Tall.

Even so, he didn't make a big deal out of his defense. He answered one
question: it was probably four minutes out of his day. . . . It was just that those
four minutes were the next day's news:

BUSH, DOLE TRADE BARBS

Which was a clear violation of the "Be Nice" rule . . . but what was worse:
there was *no news* about Dole . . . nothing about his life, himself . . . what linked
him to that Legion crowd. He was off his message—and after that . . .

Well, it was hard to watch, after that . . . like watching a skydiver when his chute won't open.

Bush was safely back on his boat. Dole had to go on . . . but he wouldn't go on—not on his schedule. He was supposed to go to Austin—interview with a guy from *Texas Monthly,* a press conference with the statehouse press corps. That was the problem: Dole got it into his head they were going to ask him who he had in Austin—what pooh-bahs? And he had no bigwigs to announce. So he wouldn't go . . . and, worse:

He got out his maps in the plane, and announced: they were going to West Texas—Lubbock—*and then to Midland . . .* flying into the crack of the Empire's death-star—*Midland, Texas . . .* wrestling for Bush's own life. Set it up!

So at the next stop, the poor body man, Mike Glassner, sneaked to a pay phone and called in desperation back to headquarters—to Judy Harbaugh, the Scheduler, who was . . . not exactly sympathetic:

"I don't *care* who you call. Lubbock is *not on the schedule . . .* how should I know who to call?"

"Judy, come on, *please.* He says we're going to Lubbock. Don't you have a number? . . . Just the County Chairman!"

Of course, the County Chairman was a Bush guy, and anyway . . . they didn't call him till four o'clock on the afternoon before they showed up . . . so, the next day, Glassner's voice on the phone was smaller . . . calling from Lubbock. Dole was doing press, before the event, but Glassner had peeked into the hall:

"I can't tell him," Glassner said.

"You have to tell him! It's his own fault!"

"Judy, there's three *people . . .* the chairman and two old ladies! That's all!"

Of course, Dole was furious. That's why he demanded they *set it up for Midland*!

Glassner was on the phone, again:

"Judy, Senator says Jimmy Allison's wife will set it up. He says you know how to find Jimmy Allison . . ."

Judy's voice was ice:

"Tell the *Senator . . .* this is *not* the wife he remembers. . . . You might also mention: Jimmy Allison is dead."

Of course, Dole went anyway. It was disaster . . . but he had to do it. Alas, it was not just about Dole's life—not to Dole. It was about Bush's, too . . . that whole Texas business Bush liked to peddle—Dole couldn't believe it, couldn't see how anyone *would* believe it.

You could see how Dole looked at it . . . though he wasn't supposed to talk about Bush:

" 'Course, you could say *I* was from Texas," Dole told one crowd. "I was stationed at Camp Barkley, near Abilene, in the war. . . . I got to Texas before George Bush! . . ."

The crowd chuckled amiably. But it wasn't a joke. What had Bush *ever* done to claim Texas? . . . Sure, he ran there—and lost.

"I think what chairmen want is a qualified winner," Dole mentioned. ". . . Not a qualified loser."

Of course, that made the papers, too. Well, what of it? . . . He didn't say the guy's *name*! . . . Gaghhd! Come *on*! What had the guy ever *done*—that hadn't been *handed* to him? . . . Dole never could figure what they saw in George Bush.

54

1968

DOLE SAW HIM, of course, when Bush got to Congress, in '67 . . . people said the guy was a star. Nice guy, sure . . . far as that went. Not too far.

Dole had been in the House for six years! He figured he understood what Bush had going: he was the son of Prescott Bush. Well, Bob was the son of Doran Dole. That was a difference . . . so what?

Then, too, there was Bush's district—Houston—people talked about that. Made a difference.

Well, the difference Dole saw was, that district was made for Bush! Bob never had that kind of luxury. The minute he got to Washington, Dole was a marked man. His district, which was already huge, was going to be combined with Floyd Breeding's—a Democrat! Dole had to fight to survive!

But he toughed it out, he *worked* his way back.

Two years later, his race was even harder. Had to fight his way through the Goldwater disaster. Pulled it out by his fingernails, and five thousand votes— five or ten votes in every town, he had hit them all . . . in a district as big as New York State . . . driving all night toward the next lights on the prairie, with one big fear:

Flat tire.

What the hell would he do?

Of course, no one knew that . . . Dole wouldn't talk about that.

No one knew either what it took to get dressed—those mornings on the road. Bob could use a buttonhook for the shirt now, but the top button might take a half-hour—and still might not work. He'd tie his tie himself now, even if Phyllis was around—but he might tie it five times. Had to be just so.

Nobody knew how he had to do his letters. Thousands of letters—he dictated every one, every word. Then Judy Harbaugh would bring them in and hold them on the desk while Dole signed with his left hand . . . until he told her, one day: "I'll do it."

He lifted his right fist onto a corner of a letter, and held the paper himself. It was awkward. But he wouldn't let her help anymore. "There's so many things I can't do," he told her. "I've got to try something every day, just to see if I can."

He didn't expect anything to come easy.

He sure wasn't going to sit still in the House. He had a chance now, and he took it: Kansas's senior Senator, Frank Carlson, announced that he'd retire in 1968 . . . same day, Dole announced he was running for Senate.

He'd have a primary against a man who'd already run statewide and won— the former Governor, Bill Avery, a friend of Dole's (they'd served together in Congress) and a big name.

It would be tough.

Well, you had to be tough!

Actually, it could have been tougher: Dole might have had to face Garner Shriver, another Congressman who'd run a dozen times—never lost—in Sedgwick County, Wichita. Garner owned that part of the state.

But Garner dithered, then backed away. Nobody could figure . . . what did Dole say to Shriver to push him out of the race?

"No, he never talked to me," Shriver recalled. "Uh . . . you see, he had this war record. Well, I did, too . . . but I didn't have this, uh . . ."

Shriver cocked his arm at his side: ". . . that was, uh, very visible."

In the end, it wasn't even Bob's arm. Had more to do with stomach. Garner had watched Dole in Congress.

"I don't think I had the desire he had. . . . I just didn't have all that push."

—★—

People said Bob campaigned for that Senate seat like his life depended on it. Avery was well known (he'd won the governorship in '64 despite Goldwater's loss of Kansas by eighty thousand votes) . . . and Dole's name was new to most voters. Bob had to get around and make himself known—in a hurry!

He had a driver now, Bill Frazier, and they must have done a hundred thousand miles around Kansas. Frazier was a three-hundred-pounder, a trencherman, a smoker and drinker . . . but just the kind of guy Dole tended to rely on—big, ugly, and humble. He'd drop out of school every time Dole had a campaign. Probably never did finish school.

Anyway, it was always Dole and Frazier—they'd hit every wide place in the road. Dole only knew one way to campaign. He'd glad-hand his way up Main Street, on his way to a coffee-klatsch . . . if it was a big town, he'd start with coffee at some supporter's home, just to work up steam for the big event, at a rented hall. If it was a large hall, he might hook up with his quartet of girl singers, the Bob-o-Links . . . or his bevy of booster ladies, the Dolls for Dole—with their pineapple juice . . . or maybe he'd send brother Kenny ahead with the old "Roll with Dole" wagon. . . . Anyway, by the time Bob hit that hall, *he'd* be rolling—cracking jokes, telling stories, making up his speech on the spot . . . by the end, he'd be flying, barking out names, greetings, grabbing hands, chuckling for photos, moving through the crowd like a big steam engine. . . . Then he'd sink, in silence again, into the shotgun seat next to Frazier, and a hundred miles might go by before either one said a word.

Still, he talked to Frazier more than anyone—who else did he have to talk to? . . . Phyllis would come along for the big events, but they weren't her happiest evenings. You'd see her near Bob (not too near), with an edgy smile . . . unless she saw someone she knew—then she'd light up. But there weren't many she knew. (It always made her feel inadequate: she couldn't remember all the names, and a *microphone*—oh, God!—*petrified* her.) She'd never tried to be Bob's partner in politics. How could she start now? . . . She told him she didn't like that "Dolls for Dole" routine anymore—made her think of *Valley of the Dolls.* . . . Of course, Bob kept the gals. He wasn't much for advice.

Dole knew the Senate was the big league, so he hired a *consultant,* a guy named Roy Pfautch. Dole listened to him for about two weeks, then tuned him out. Never fired him, of course. He'd just stop listening . . . joke about the guy, behind his back.

Dole still talked to Huck Boyd; Huck was always there for Bob. But despite his national connections, Huck was a man of western Kansas—northwest Kansas, to be precise—and never had as much drag with the eastern Kansas nabobs, the old guard: Alf Landon, Oscar Stauffer, or Harry Darby, the Kansas City boss. That was Dole's problem. His district covered half the state, but the wrong half, the empty west. Nobody knew Dole in the cities—Wichita, Topeka . . . Kansas City! What could he do in Kansas City?

He'd have to put it together by himself—go around the old guard. Outflank 'em, outwork 'em. He scheduled big events in all three cities—fund-raisers, hundred dollars a plate—and he went major-league. He hired a famous singer—well, pretty famous—Marilyn Maye, to sing Bob's theme song, "Step to the Rear (and Let a Winner Lead the Way)." She had it in her contract, she had to be introduced as "Marvelous Marilyn May." Bob did that . . . but after Topeka, she announced she couldn't be bothered to go on. Bob had to hire a big band—in a hurry. He *lost* money on Kansas City.

The problem wasn't really Kansas City. That was Wyandotte County— mostly black, not a factor in a GOP primary. The problem was in neighboring Johnson County, the most Republican county in eastern Kansas . . . a political jungle—twenty-five separate municipalities, each with its Mayor and City Council, and all well-to-do suburbs, foreign turf to Dole. Those people spent more time in Chicago, or New York, than they ever did in Russell, Kansas.

Dole found a way: he found a guy—Dave Owen. Owen was a comer, running for State Senator. He had that county wired. By the time he'd put together his organization and held a big party at a hotel to show it off, nobody would even file against him. So Owen turned his organization over to Dole— whole hog. . . . Why?

"I don't know, I met him . . ." Owen said. "He had hero written all over him. He overcame his injuries. He never said a word about it. . . . I liked his style. There was something macho about him. He was kick-ass-and-take-names. Bob Dole stood for that."

So he did.

Dole's friend Bill Avery had lost the governorship, after one term, because he'd imposed a new income tax. The Democrats killed him, in '66, with that tax issue.

And so in the summer of 1968, when polls showed Dole flagging ("Gagh! What're we gonna *do*?") . . . he took a page from the Democrats' book:

Avery had the state studded with his trademark signs, verticals:

A
V
E
R
Y

. . . down the sides of a thousand telephone poles. So, every time Dole's workers found one of those poles, they tacked a horizontal sign on the bottom:

TAXES

By the day of the primary vote in August, it wasn't even close: Dole beat Avery two-to-one. Dole was going to the U.S. Senate.

55

1970

BUSH KNEW he was headed for the Senate. That's where he belonged, like his dad. He had no doubt. He could have held that House seat forever, like a birthright: that new district, Houston's Seventh, had been birthed for him. After one term (in fact, by the filing deadline—after thirteen months on the job), he was unopposed!

And he was a certified star: there were forty new Republicans elected to that Congress, in the rebound after the Goldwater debacle. Bush was chosen as president of the freshman class. For the first time in decades, a GOP freshman got a seat on Ways and Means. (Pres Bush had called on old friends for his son.) From the start, everybody knew about this bright, handsome young Republican . . . from *Houston*—a chink (at last!) in the solid South. George Bush was the Party's bold breeze of the future.

He was invited to address GOP luncheons, and breakfasts of bigwigs. He'd talk about the revival of the two-party system—change on the southern wind! What a hopeful vision! He wore that excitement like a suitcoat thrown over one shoulder, as he strode down the hallways with a greeting and a grin—he was having such a good time.

It wasn't legislating that ran his motor: he wasn't one of those annoying first-termers who think they've got to make floor speeches and pepper the House with bills. The only bills he pushed were aid for birth control (always an interest of Pres's—maybe unfinished business for the old man) and a short-lived proposal on Congressional ethics. (This pup published his tax returns!) . . . Most of his work he did in committee, as a quiet, respectful

student of the chairman, Wilbur Mills. (Mills loved him: after the kid filed that
birth-control bill, Mills always called him Rubbers.) . . . When the bells rang,
Bush would hustle to the floor, check in . . . but most days—just speeches, or
conference reports—he could leave with his new friend, the Mississippi Democrat, Sonny Montgomery, for a do-or-die dollar-a-game paddleball match in
the House gym.

It was the life, itself, that Bush found bracing: all the doing, new friends—he
was in such demand! There wasn't ten minutes to sit around: he had committee, he had a lunch, a meeting at Interior! . . . He'd grab his coat and bolt for
his office door, calling over his shoulder to Aleene Smith (she'd come with him
from Houston): "Allie! See what Mr. Holburn needs, will you—he's on the
phone!" . . . He'd *run* through the anteroom, with that lock of hair falling onto
his forehead, and the ladies of his office clucking, through their smiles: "Mr.
Bush! Tuck in your shirttail!"

(In Houston—it was Houston every other weekend, no matter the effort
required—the office ladies adored George Bush. Sometimes, if things got slow,
Bush would exit his inner office in a flying ballet leap—just to make *les gals*
giggle. Late one day, a little woman came by. She was a mousy sort, no
makeup, poor dress—probably a hard-luck case. She wanted to see Mr. Bush.
But the ladies had no time to tell him before he flew into the office in a twisting
tour jeté.. . . . Then he saw the woman. He froze . . . on the ball of one foot,
with his arms outstretched . . . and blushed crimson to the roots of his hair.)

No wonder they loved him—and talked about the way he was: how *a man
like that* could be so nice. He'd pick up the phone himself if it rang more than
twice, and he'd listen to some voter's tale of woe. ("No," he'd say to the phone.
"No, that doesn't sound right, at all. We'll look into it, right away. . . . No!
Thank *you* for calling!") Same with the mail: answers by return post. Aleene
would cram his battered briefcase every night—might be thirty or forty letters
typed up. He'd sign every one, add a couple of lines in his lefty scrawl. The
Capitol postman told Aleene that Bush got more mail than anyone else in the
Longworth Building. (That's because he sent more. One Houston lady wrote
him a letter. So, he wrote her back. So, she wrote to thank him for his response.
So, he wrote her back, thanking her for her thank-you note. Finally, she sent
him a letter that said: "You remind me of my aunt, Mrs. Ponder. She just won't
stay written to.")

This wasn't exactly politics with Bush—more like life. The day his moving
van arrived in Washington, it was a terrible snow: George sent Bar off to Sears,
through the storm, to buy sheets so the movers could stay the night—he
insisted! . . . Don Rhodes was a volunteer on his campaign in Houston. Rhodes
had a hearing problem, and people thought he was strange, maybe slow-witted.
(He wasn't.) Bush not only took him along for the Washington staff, he moved
Don into his house. . . . Visitors from his district (in fact, visitors from all over
Texas; Bush had run statewide before he ever had a district)—George might
have asked them to sleep over, too, if he'd had room. As it was, he had to hold
himself to fussing over them in the office, posing for pictures, leading tours of

the Capitol, making sure they got to see everything in Washington, and
. . . wasn't it great how it worked out? Bush inherited a couple of staff ladies
from the Texas Democrat who used to represent his part of Houston, so, of
course, they knew the crowd in LBJ's White House. They'd call up and get
special tours: not just the state rooms, but the Family Quarters (that picture
of George Hamilton on Lynda Bird's night table!)—well, you put that together
with a ride on Bush's *boat* (George just had to show them how the city looked
from the Potomac), and Bar's picnic, with the pâté, wine, and salad, and
. . . no wonder he was unopposed!

In fact, that was one reason he could make that vote—'68, the open-housing
bill—Bush knew he would face no opponent in November. Still, there'd be a
howl of protest. Sonny Montgomery told him, in the gym: "Your district ain't
gonna like this." Bush didn't need analysis from Sonny. For God's sake, some
of Bush's voters wouldn't ride in a car that a Negro had sat in—wouldn't play
the same *golf course*. . . . Bush agonized for weeks.

What stuck in his mind was Vietnam, his trip, those soldiers—black soldiers—in the jungle, in the uniform of their country . . . how could he let them
come back to a nation where they couldn't live where they chose? He could
not. He couldn't let politics change the way he was.

So he voted for the bill. He meant to take the heat.

But this wasn't heat. This was . . . ugly. First the calls—*les gals* had to hear
them:

"You tell Bush we don' need no Connecticut Nigra-lovers . . ."

"Are you half nigger-blood, too? . . ."

Then the letters—thousands of letters. Don Rhodes was up all night trying
to get out answers. But how could Bush answer?

"It's Communist says who I can sell my house to . . ."

"I know niggers are running the government . . ."

The threats menaced his staff and his family. One letter mentioned his
children by name. After a week, Bush looked like he'd aged ten years. His face
sagged. There was no excitement in his words or walk. He went back to
Houston, and . . . that was worse. The office felt like the Alamo. The ladies
tried to cheer him:

"They're just kooks," Sarah Gee said.

"They aren't thinking . . ."

"Everybody else is for you . . ."

Bush just sat at his desk, staring at the wall. Sarah saw the look of the
bereaved. She didn't even know why she said it—it just came out:

"Oh, George . . . I'm sorry."

Bob Mosbacher called, said the money men were up in arms. "You want
me to try to get 'em together, talk to them?"

Bush's voice was weary:

"No, I gotta do it myself."

So, he did: he got twenty-five big givers into a room. Bush had the air of
a man who'd been beat up. "I know we agree on so *much,*" he told them. He

didn't ask them to support his vote—just to keep in mind the other votes. It was almost pleading! "If you can't support me anymore . . . well, I hope I can still have your friendship."

He did feel he was beaten—not this time, no, it was too late to lose reelection . . . but what about next time? What about the Senate? All the great doings, the big plans ahead? . . . In fact, his loss went deeper than elections: it had to do with the choices he'd made for twenty years—in Texas—his feeling that he could speak for Texas. Was he wrong? . . . God! What if it was *all wrong*?

He wrote to a friend:

"I never dreamed the reaction would be so violent. Seething hatred—the epithets—the real chickenshit stuff in spades—to our [office] girls: 'You must be a nigger or a Chinaman'—and on and on—and the country club crowd disowning me and denouncing me. . . .

"Tonight [I was on] this plane and this older lady came up to me. She said, 'I'm a conservative Democrat from this district, but I'm proud, and will always vote for you now'—and her accent was Texan (not Connecticut) and suddenly somehow I felt that maybe it would all be OK—and I started to cry—with the poor lady embarrassed to death—I couldn't say a word to her."

He would always remember the moment when he knew . . . that night—a town meeting. The crowd booed him and muttered his name with a menacing hiss as he was introduced.

So he told them, he knew what they thought. He told them, he knew some people called him lib-rull. But it wasn't conservative or liberal—this vote. It was just . . . fairness. He told them about Vietnam—those soldiers—how could he let them come back? . . . How could you slam a door in a guy's face, just 'cause he's a Negro, or speaks with an accent? . . .

There was no more to say. He was going to sit down, in the silence. He turned to thank the moderator, and behind him he heard applause, a scattered few, and then, when he turned, more clapping, everybody was clapping . . . and then some stood, in front, and more behind. They were clapping—*for him*—because he did what he thought was right, and he'd said so. He didn't think they agreed—still—but they gave him a standing ovation.

God! He could have kissed them all!

— ★ —

That's how he knew, he was going to the Senate—not a doubt. This time, 1970, he would beat old Yarborough fair and square—he *knew* it—Texas was changing!

That's what Bush kept saying: Yarborough was out of touch! The state had passed him by. People didn't want that New Deal, promise-'em-the-moon kind of government, that kind of Senator—no. They wanted a modern conservative. They wanted George Bush!

This time, he'd have his ducks in a row. He'd been around, he had friends everywhere. This time, he'd have a professional Campaign Manager—Marvin Collins, great guy! He was signed on already. He'd have a big budget—two million, for starters. And a Bush-friend, John Tower, had taken over the

Republican Senatorial Campaign Committee—he'd send along whatever he could. And the President would help! President Nixon was on a roll: he was targeting races all over the country. Nixon said Texas was number one, and he asked Bush to run—personally! Even LBJ might help. Bush went to see him. The old man certainly wouldn't lift a finger to help Yarborough. Neither would John Connally. They all hated Ralph! . . . This time, Bush wouldn't have to scrape for issues—he'd had his eye on Yarborough for six years. He had the old snake-oil salesman locked in the cross hairs.

Bush had such big plans for 1970: ads all over the state, and not just in cities, but on every dustland radio station—Spanish, too! Bush didn't see why this race, his race, should not mark the *realignment* of Texas. Why shouldn't the GOP grab its share of the Mexicans? And Negroes—my God, he *ought* to get some Negro votes! (Election night, 1968, though he had no contest, he'd *grabbed* for the tally sheets: he wanted to see those colored precincts. Wouldn't you know it? Jeez! . . . After all that—two-thirds wouldn't even cross over for him—with *no Democrat against him!*) . . . But that wouldn't matter—that would be *gravy*—once he started hammering away at the old guard, the liberal, the tired voice of the past, Yarborough.

Then, the unthinkable happened: with a vicious, attacking campaign, a south Texas Democrat, a businessman (and former Rep) named Lloyd Bentsen . . . came out of *nowhere* (actually, he came out of Connally's hip pocket) . . . and took the senior Senator down. Yarborough lost his primary. George Bush lost his target.

Now it was Bush against Bentsen—and all of Bush's plans were air. George tried to tell folks it was fine—this would be *easier*—but even his friends couldn't see it. Bentsen was conservative—just like Bush, when you got down to it—and tough (he proved *that* against old Ralph). Bentsen could play the veteran card (he was a pilot in the war, too) and the business card (he'd made more of a pile than Bush). He had the same Congressional experience as Bush. He was just as nasty on Crime 'n' Commies, a practiced south Texas hand with the Mexicans, a Democrat Texans could live with. . . . So, here came Lyndon's pals from the Perdenales . . . and here came that greazy John Connally on the tube, making ads for Bentsen . . . here came all the courthouse Dems, the yellow-dog Dems, and the better-dead-than-red Dems. Bentsen brought them all back from the grave. Worse still, here came a ballot issue to allow sale of liquor by the drink. So thousands of rural Baptists would turn out against demon rum . . . and on the way, they'd likely vote the standard Democrat ticket.

And Bush? Well, he had the Republicans—but there still weren't many of those. (The electorate was at least four-to-one Democratic). . . . He had his friends in business, his constituents in Houston. . . . His manager, Marvin Collins, tried to cook a deal with the liberal Democrats (who hated Bentsen for what he'd done to Yarborough), and he nurtured a noisy group of Democrats for Bush. . . . Bush still had high hopes for the Negro vote. He'd gone to the *wall* for those people!

That was half the problem. Everybody knew about his open-housing vote—

Bentsen made sure of that. And about that time Bush had voted for the *Yeww Ennn!* Bentsen brought that up, too. . . . In fact, Bentsen ran close enough to the right-field wall, there was no way Bush could get outside of him. . . . Bush was the, uh, *lib-rull!*

Still, Bush was *sure* he could pull it out. People liked him! He had so many friends! He was working so hard! . . . Bush still thought he could cast the race as the Democratic past against the future. "We're on the threshold," he'd scream in every speech, "of a new de-*cade!*" (No one had the heart to tell him that Texans didn't accent that second syllable. He was working *so* hard—they didn't want to hurt him.) . . . If he could just show *he was* that future, that vigor, that youth. (With those kids rounded up by his Youth Coordinator, Rob Mosbacher, and Junior Bush, who'd cut away, when he could, from his National Guard flight training, the Bush campaign had the look of a Scout trip.) . . . If Bush could show, somehow, that Bentsen was just another page from the past . . .

But that was the other half of the problem: Bentsen didn't seem to have any past—not like Yarborough, not a past they could use. They dug up Bentsen's votes from Congress, but that was stuff from the *forties,* no one would give a damn. Oh, there was one guy came in with a tip—said it would *finish* Bentsen. Bush sent Aleene to the Ag Department in Washington. She sat there all day, writing down the information (with a couple of department lawyers at her elbow, clucking about how she might *embarrass* a former *Secretary*—most unfortunate!). . . . But when she brought the poop to Bush, he read the file and just shook his head: he wasn't going to be that way about politics. No, he could only be what he was.

That's how the problems started with Nixon. The President got it into his mind that George Bush *would not go for the kill.* . . . Nixon sent money—more than a hundred thousand dollars from one of his illegal slush funds . . . but Bush wouldn't use it to take Bentsen down. The White House offered to send Tricia Nixon, David Eisenhower . . . or surrogates who'd throw *red meat* to the press—bring in the tough guys. How about that Bob Dole? . . . Or Spiggy Agnew? . . .

Bush didn't want them . . . but when it got to Agnew, he could not say no: the Vice President of the United States! So Agnew came, and then Nixon himself. How could Bush say no to the President? . . . And in the last days of the campaign, both made blistering partisan speeches—wiped out any hope Bush had with Democrats.

On election night, family and friends gathered at the old Shamrock Hotel. Bush knew it would be tight—his last polls showed the race even. But he *knew* he could win—good things happen to good people. He had to believe. The family was in a suite—upstairs from the big ballroom, with the band, balloons, and streamers. George and Bar were on a couch: his arms around Doro and Marvin, Bar holding Neil and Jebbie. They turned on the TV, and . . . it was over. *Twelve minutes* into the broadcast—after two years of work (*seven* years, since he started for that seat)—Walter Cronkite said his computers called the race for Bentsen. Doro started crying. Marvin Bush started crying. George Bush hugged them, told them it would be all right. Neil and Jebbie cried in Bar's arms. The friends started crying. Aleene was sobbing. Sarah Gee started cursing the nuts. Nancy Crouch said she was through with politics. Marvin Collins felt like he'd been hit by a car. He went off to Junior Bush's apartment, and those two stayed teary till they were too blotto to care.

The one who didn't cry was George Bush. He went around the suite, telling everyone what a great job they'd done. Then he was on the phone. "Well," he'd say, "back to the drawing board." Downstairs, in the ballroom, he conceded, then stayed for an hour, answering anything the press had to ask. Then he was back on the phone . . . all night. At 5:00 A.M., he pulled out a list—hundreds of people he wanted to thank, and he started from the top. He'd be on the phone for sixteen hours straight. Bar couldn't sit there and watch—couldn't bear that, couldn't chip in, brightly, like she had in '64: "Well, there'll be another time." . . . No, 1970 was different. George Bush had run for the Senate twice, and lost—could there be another time? She went off with her girlfriends to the club: a tennis game, her doubles . . . but she was standing at the net and kept thinking of George, on his phone, trying to cheer people, telling them they'd done *so well* . . . and her eyes blurred with tears and she couldn't even see the ball . . . she felt the hand of a friend on her shoulder, and a voice:

"Oh, the hell with this, Bar. Let's go in and have a martini."

So they did. They may have had several.

56

1972

IT WAS DIFFERENT for Dole in the Senate. Harder, in some ways. Not that he'd complain. He'd made it past . . . well, he never would have thought of himself in company with Calhoun, Clay . . . Daniel Webster! Dole felt he'd climbed higher than he ever had any right to dream.

No wonder he didn't have—couldn't have—the same ease that made him popular in the House . . . holding court at the snack bar in the House cloakroom (must have eaten five thousand of those Nutty Buddy ice-cream cones), wise-cracking with Helen behind the counter, making jokes about the members who were sprawled (some asnore) on the couches . . . you wouldn't see that in the Senate. It was so formal, the gentleman's club.

Dole didn't say a word on the floor for months. He didn't open his mouth . . . until April 14 of his first year: that was the anniversary of the day he was shot, a quarter-century past—on that day, Dole made his maiden speech, a plea for housing for the handicapped.

But once he started, he was hard to shut up.

The issue with Dole was the Vietnam War. That was an issue for everyone, of course, but Dole took it personally. Like the Democrats were trying to stick *him* with that failure, that suffering, those body bags. *His* Party hadn't started that war!

Dole had always backed the White House on Vietnam, but in a quiet way (House Republicans didn't have any choice—they were quiet). But this was different: a different forum for Dole—everything he said made news; a different climate on the war—moratorium marches filling the Mall, and the jails. Most of all, a different White House.

Dole had such respect for Richard Nixon, it was near reverence. Nixon had come to Kansas to campaign for Dole in '66. Dole would never forget their talk—how Nixon said the GOP would make stunning gains in the House that fall. The Party was flat on its back after Goldwater . . . but *Nixon called it*—within two or three seats! Dole had never seen anyone who knew politics like Nixon: he had the whole country at instant command in his head.

But it was more than that. In Nixon, Dole saw a man who'd been knocked down by life. But he was too tough to stay down. He started in a dusty California farm town . . . times were bad: story was, the family made it through the week eating ketchup. That meant something to Dole . . . and to Nixon, who never forgot where he'd come from . . . who *could not forget* that he never grew up with the world on his side—like, for instance, a *Kennedy*. . . . Dole understood, very well.

He saw strength in Nixon, and nobility: Dole mentioned once that Nixon was the only one in Washington who stuck out his left hand to shake with Dole. *The only one.*

So, in the Senate, Bob Dole was The One for Nixon. Dole let nothing pass, no remark against the President, or his administration. They weren't going to get away with *that* while Bob Dole was on the Senate floor.

And he was on the floor, more and more. Dole thought he saw the lay of the land: no first-termer could make hay in committee, not in the Ag Committee, not the most junior member of the Senate's minority Party . . . but on the floor, it was wide open! Hell, half the time you could shoot off a cannon and not endanger one Republican life. . . . So Dole made the Senate floor his preserve, his patrol.

Democrats were his targets. Dole never ceased to remind them: it was *their* Party got us into Vietnam—another *Democrat war*! . . . Richard Nixon (with his "Vietnamization") was only trying to clean up *their mess*! . . . With his prairie voice rasping resentment and scorn, Dole called the antiwar Senators "a Who's Who of has-beens, would-bes, professional second-guessers, and apologists for the policies which led us into this tragic conflict in the first place."

Dole accused Ted Kennedy (his favorite target) of "the meanest and most offensive sort of political distortion." . . . Meanwhile, Dole accused Democrats of "parroting the propaganda of a *communist enemy.*"

Well . . . the Kansas GOP hadn't sent him to compete for Miss Congeniality.

In some ways, he was tougher on his GOP colleagues. He wouldn't just answer them on the floor—he'd argue in the *cloakroom*! Demand to know what got into them. He couldn't understand why they wouldn't stand up for the President—the *Commander in Chief.* Some of them were ducking and dodging on the war . . . some who called themselves *leaders* were just as bad as the Democrats!

Hugh Scott, who ran for Minority Leader (when Dirksen died, in '69)—

there was a perfect example. Scott was an old windbag from Philadelphia (he came to Congress before Dole even got his first bus ride from the Army) . . . he was one of those eastern Rockefeller gents who never failed to get under Dole's skin. Scott was kissing up to the other side, spreading balm, playing the game.

This was no game, to Dole.

When a Young Turk named Howard Baker—a Tennessean, just two years Bob's senior in the Senate—challenged Scott for the Leader's job (Baker promised a more active, partisan attack), Dole backed him. Bob was out front for Baker!

That made an enemy of Scott, who won.

When Scott (and some other statesmen of the GOP—Dole could name them all) would not stand up for the President and his High Court nominee, Clement Haynesworth, Dole saw his duty: *he* took the floor. He accused Haynesworth's opponents of toadying to the liberal lobby. When they mentioned their duty to advise and consent, when they cited the Constitution, Dole stood up to retort: "It talks about *rights* in the Constitution—not about special-interest groups."

Well, he got noticed. . . . He was making hay, wasn't he? . . . First year in the Senate, he got ink by the barrel. ("Agh, pretty good! Front payyge!")

But in the Senate, there was a thin line between notice and notoriety. When someone asked Bill Saxbe, Republican of Ohio, to react to the latest broadside from Dole, Saxbe shrugged it off:

"Aw, Dole's just a hatchet man. . . . He's so unpopular, he couldn't peddle beer on a troopship."

—★—

Dole was stung—stunned, more like it. Of course, he knew it all came from Scott. When Scott farted, Saxbe stunk, but . . . *hatchet man*? Is that what they thought?

He said to his old House colleague, Bob Ellsworth, "And these are my friends?"

Ellsworth had Dole's thorough respect. They'd come to Congress together, in 1961. After '66, when Ellsworth lost his bid for the Senate, he ended up working for Nixon as National Political Director—to Dole, an awesome credential. He used to say: "Ellsworth's smarter than the rest of us put together."

Now Ellsworth said to Dole: "Don't worry about them, Bob . . ."

Ellsworth thought Dole's problems came from being too hard-edged, too frantic. He only had to calm down.

"The shrubs are always attacking the roots of the oak," Ellsworth said. "They can't stand its being so tall and strong."

Well, Dole would stand his ground—tall and strong. He wasn't going to slink away to some corner, his tail between his legs, no. Sometimes you had to be tough!

The President understood! From time to time, in his second year, Dole would arrive at his office to find an envelope—from the White House! With a red tag—"Urgent!" Inside, there'd be a statement for Dole to read on the floor, a speech *for the President.* Dole would head for the chamber.

Then, too—more rarely—he was summoned to The Presence. The staff would buzz with the news all day. "Senator's going to the White House! . . . Dole's been invited by the President! . . ." This was heady business—though Dole tried not to show that.

One day, he did announce to his staff that next time, *he* would challenge Hugh Scott for the Leader's job.

"Senator, you can't do that."

"Why not? Jerry Ford did it in the House."

"But Senate's different—you gotta take some time, earn your way in."

"How do you do that?"

"Well, you know, Scott was already Party Chairman."

"Yeah . . . how do you go for Party Chairman?"

Turned out, you went by way of the White House—just the route Dole's duty had paved. There was talk that Rogers Morton would soon step out of the top Party job. Nixon's men wanted a kick-ass team for '72 . . . they needed someone who would *stand up for the President.*

John Mitchell told Dole in the first days of 1971: the job would be his—Chairman of the Republican National Committee.

Dole was moving fast, going national! (Who could tell what might happen now? Nixon might even get tired of dragging Agnew behind him!) . . . Dole told the good news to friends in Kansas, in Congress. . . . That's when Hugh Scott found out.

Scott protested to the White House, and within hours, other Senators weighed in, talking Dole down. (Publicly, Scott contended the job was too big for a sitting Senator—in private, he called Dole's selection a personal affront.)

H.R. Haldeman, the Chief of Staff, called Dole the next day, from San Clemente:

So sorry, Haldeman said. The President had changed his mind.

Dole was ashamed, enraged. How could they treat him like that? After his loyalty! . . . Did they expect him to go down without a fight? He found out that Nixon's palace guard was planning to install Tom Evans, from Delaware—an eastern money man! That night, Dole told his Big Guy friend Bryce Harlow: if that's how Nixon's men meant to treat him . . . well, he didn't think he'd even stay in the Senate. Harlow told him to forget that whine . . . then he brokered a deal: Dole would get the chairman's job, but the White House would name Evans cochairman at the same time.

Dole refused.

If they had to have Evans, *Dole* would make the appointment. . . . There could be only one chairman!

Till 3:00 A.M., Dole hung tough. ("They're not gonna do this to me!")

. . . In the end, he had to appoint two cochairs—Evans and Anne Armstrong, from Texas . . . but he won! Well—didn't he?

Bob Dole got the chairman's job.

He'd have a big press conference (biggest of his life!) to announce the glad news. . . . He was on the move!

What a shame, it left such a sour taste.

57

Phyllis

DOLE GOT the big office on the top floor on First Street—the one with the grand desk, that huge map behind . . . ("Heyy! Nice digs!") but his job was not to sit in the office.

He started crisscrossing the country, rallying for '72, raising money, trying to broaden the Party at its base. From the chairman's pulpit, Dole meant to open the Party to groups long-ignored: farmers, blue-collar ethnics . . . blacks, Mexicans, Asians . . . he never lost a chance to remind a crowd that his, *theirs,* was the Party of Lincoln, liberty, emancipation.

He never lost a chance at a crowd. Dole was determined to show his critics—show everyone—that he could carry his Senate load (he still never missed a roll call) and show up in every corner of the country to build the Party and its hopes for '72. Now, for the first time, a car came to fetch him, idling at the base of the Capitol steps as the Senate finished business for the afternoon . . . a jet was waiting at the airport . . . Advance men were waiting at another airport one or two thousand miles to the west. If Dole could pick up a time zone or two on his way to the dinner, the funder, the rally . . . he might have time for a press conference, too—or a stop, somewhere, refueling. . . . "Agh, better make it Kansas."

Kansans are always schizoid when one of their own grabs a glimmer of limelight: they're *so* pleased (can't believe, you know, a guy from *Kansas*) . . . that they're instantly on guard for some *slight* (that guy doesn't care about *Kansas* anymore!). . . . There's a window of about ten days before they decide: *That fellow's got too big for his britches! . . .* So Dole would stop in Kansas, two or three times a week—every time his plane poked west of Ohio, he'd order his pilot to gas up in K.C. or Wichita, Salina or Great Bend . . . while he scooted for a half-hour, hit a Kiwanis, or cut a ribbon for a new mall.

Of course, it was midnight, or after, when he'd land again in D.C. (that's the bad news with time zones—you end up paying them back). Dole would have the car drop him at his big house on Beechway, in Virginia—tell the driver what time to come back. Bob would head for the basement. If Phyllis was still up, she might bring him dinner on a tray. That's when she'd say anything she had to tell him. Then she'd go upstairs. . . . Bob would sleep on his bed, in his cellar.

Chet Dawson made a visit to Washington that year, and he came back to Russell shaking his head: "Bob came home at 2:00 A.M.," Chet told the boys in the drugstore. "I guess he didn't want to disturb Phyllis, so he just curled up downstairs. Four hours later, the limo showed up to take him away again. . . . What kind of life is that?"

That's what Phyllis wanted to know. Sometimes, she'd bring Bob's tray, with his food—all cut up, as he liked it—and she'd muster courage to announce: "We have to talk."

Bob would snap: "Whaddya want to talk about?"

She never had a good answer. There was no answer short or neat enough. It was just . . . they had to talk—didn't they? . . . What happened to their life? If they couldn't talk, well . . .

It wasn't that they fought. (Bob didn't have time.) Sometimes, she would have liked a fight . . . then she could *scream* . . . maybe he'd see how she felt—see her. But when? . . . She tried to think of ways she could be different, to fit in with his life. Maybe she should stay up, eat supper with him. But Robin had to eat. And had to get to bed—Robin had school. Phyllis could count—she went back and *figured out*—how many times they'd had dinner together, the three of them, that year, when Bob made chairman. Two times.

One day Robin told her: "Mom, all my friends' parents sleep together."

Phyllis put on a brave face: "Well . . . you don't know what happens when you're asleep—do you?"

She would ever remember the day she knew that life with Bob was never going to "straighten out"—was never going to be the life she'd thought of as a girl in New Hampshire, nor even the life she'd had in Russell, Kansas.

It was the mid-sixties, Robin was in grade school, maybe eleven years old, and she had a doctor's appointment. The doctor was a wise old head who'd dealt with hundreds of young girls. . . . So, just to keep Robin from worrying while he made his examination, the doctor asked—would she like to have her ears pierced? He offered to do the job, thirty-five dollars, including gold posts . . . of course, he'd take care of any complications, infections, whatever . . . Robin should ask her folks.

Well, Robin came out of that office, high as a kite—so excited! Could she get her ears pierced? . . . Mom? . . . Mom! Could she?

Phyllis didn't know what to say. (Where she grew up, the only young girls with pierced ears were gypsies . . . or, uh, worse!) "Well . . ." she said, "you'll have to ask your father."

That night, Robin left a note in the basement.

"Dear Dad: Can I please, please, please, *please* have my ears pierced? I talked to the doctor and he said it would cost $35 and that would cover any complications. Please, *please* . . . Love, Robin."

And she drew, at the bottom, two boxes: one marked YES, and the other NO. At age eleven, she'd left her father a speed-memo.

(His response was also characteristic. He drew a third box, checked it, and marked it MAYBE. He scrawled underneath: "I'll talk to you Tuesday." That was three or four days away—for a girl that age, an eternity. Of course, when they did talk, he was a pushover. Phyllis had to take Robin to the doctor, get it done.)

Anyway, Phyllis knew then. When she saw how surely Robin knew her dad, when she saw how her daughter accepted the facts—the way Bob was . . . then Phyllis had to accept, too: it would never be as she had dreamed it would be.

She rolled with it. Or she thought she did. She tried. She'd say what she had to, in the basement . . . then she'd leave him alone. If they got a social invitation, she'd tell him, but she wouldn't push. Sometimes, she'd go to the parties alone. When she got to feeling guilty about always being the guest, she'd invite everybody for dinner, then tell Bob: he was having a party . . . did he want to come?

They did get along—they *never fought.* That's why she felt like she'd been kicked . . . when Bob said, one night, in the basement:

"I want out."

—★—

He wasn't happy. They could see that—the ones who knew him, staff who'd been with Dole since Kansas: they always knew—from the comments that leaked as he worked through the day, jokes he muttered after calls from the CREEPs. (It was Dole who gave Washington that nickname for the CRP, Nixon's Committee to Reelect the President.)

The problem was, the CREEPs held all the cards (and the money—Nixon's reelection budget was ten times bigger than the RNC's) . . . they treated the Republican Committee like a poor cousin . . . or worse: like a trained dog they had leashed in the backyard, to be loosed whenever Mitchell, Haldeman, or Colson yelled, "*Sic 'em!*"

That wasn't how Dole saw the job. He'd learned a few things after three years in the Senate—he had more respect for his colleagues, and himself.

Sure, he'd attack George McGovern in speeches—try to paint him onto the left-wing fringe . . . or off the edge of the canvas! But Dole wouldn't let the Party newsletter use the cartoon (Chuck Colson sent it over) showing McGovern in the black pj's of the Viet Cong. He wouldn't send out the letter hinting that Hubert Humphrey had a problem with booze. He wouldn't use the collection of new, kindly comments from Ted Kennedy about George Wallace (Colson's headline: WHAT A DIFFERENCE A BULLET MAKES!).

Most of the envelopes with the red tags ("Urgent!") ended up in Dole's wastebasket now. Dole knew they didn't come from Nixon.

Problem was, he didn't know what Nixon wanted. The minute Dole demonstrated his independence, he was adjudged "unreliable" by the CREEPs and the White House crowd. By '72, Dole couldn't get in to see the President . . . couldn't ask what Nixon wanted . . . couldn't ask for Nixon's help. That frustration leaked from Dole, too—in the usual way:

"Agh, I called Haldeman, I said, 'Bob, I'm the National Chairman! I want to see the President!'

"He said, 'Fine. Tune in Channel Nine at ten o'clock. You can see him then.' "

In fact, so painful and public was Dole's estrangement from the power crowd . . . it probably saved his career. When burglars broke into the Watergate office of the Democratic National Committee, Dole couldn't even take the story seriously. He'd never believe those Big Guys in the White House were involved.

He did ask his Big Guy friend Bryce Harlow . . . who couldn't make much of the story, either. "It's got no legs," Harlow said. "It'll blow over . . ." Dole thought he might make a formal statement—say the Party had nothing to do with this fiasco.

But that might look like he was backing away . . .

"It'll fade in two or three days," Harlow said.

Dole raised the subject, once, at the White House. "I'm getting questions on the, uh, Watergate," he said. "Maybe we oughta make a statement, just to clear the air." But that suggestion lay on the table like a dead fish. Nixon didn't say a word.

So, Dole saw his duty: he hit the road, tucked his head . . . handled the questions in his own way:

"Agh, well, we got the burglar vote . . ."

Dutifully, Dole swiped at *The Washington Post:* the *Post* was in bed with McGovern! Doing the Democrats' dirty work! . . . More than dutifully, Dole flew around the nation, trumpeting Nixon's achievements: revenue-sharing for the states; draft reform, a volunteer Army; the diplomatic opening of China; the hundreds of thousands of boys he'd brought home—with honor—from Vietnam. Dole did believe that Nixon was solving the problems that mattered to Americans, that McGovern was out of step . . . that Nixon would win by a landslide . . . that Nixon could *reorder* the nation's politics—not just in the White House, but in Congress, in the states.

But the CREEPs only cared about the reelection—a landslide for the President. They didn't want to hear about down-ballot races. Dole couldn't even get a call through to Nixon's *staff* anymore. They treated the Party like an *enemy.* What could Dole do?

He kept flying. When the Senate went into recess, he stayed on the road for weeks. If they scheduled him a day to rest, an evening home, he'd remind them of some commitment he'd made, some emergency in a distant state. He didn't want to go home.

One night in D.C., he sat up late, in half-darkness, in his Senate office. Staff was gone—except for Judy Harbaugh and his RNC driver, waiting for Dole to call it quits. "I want to talk to you," Dole told Judy. "I'm going to need your help."

Judy tried not to gawk. Bob Dole never asked for help.

"Looks like I'm going to get a divorce."

She didn't know what to say. She knew—they all knew in that office—Dole didn't have much family life. They always figured that's the way he was cut out. The shock was that he meant to do anything about it.

— ★ —

It wasn't really what he meant to do. . . . After he said he wanted out, he didn't bring it up with Phyllis for weeks: they stuck to their routines. When Bob did try to talk to her again ("Well, we don't want lawyers gettin' their hands on everything—we prob'ly ought to talk") . . . it was too late.

"Here's the name of *my* lawyer," Phyllis said. "Talk to him."

Still, Bob didn't leave . . . he wouldn't go. He stayed at the house (as much as he stayed anywhere) all through the divorce. He didn't know where to go. It was Phyllis who finally called his RNC driver to come over and put Bob's belongings in the garage.

Bob told Judy Harbaugh: "I need you to find me a place to live."

She rented him a tiny place in the Sheraton Park hotel. She got him some linens, and kitchen stuff—plates, a couple of pans—so he could cook . . . if he could cook . . . what was he going to cook? For the first time in his life, Bob Dole was alone.

He hadn't felt like that since the Army, the hospitals. How could he end up like that again? . . . How could he not? He had no friends to call, no family in town. He couldn't even call his mother—Bina took that divorce hard. She took to the couch in the front room, in Russell. She blamed Bob . . . and herself. If she'd paid more attention to Phyllis—just a little more!—this wouldn't have happened. Never! She was so miserable, Doran couldn't even get her up for Christmas. Bina said: "There'll be no Christmas for me."

Phyllis's mom, Estelle, blamed her daughter. She thought Bob didn't really want to leave. She told Bob it would break her own heart if he went through with this, if he let Phyllis go. "Well," Bob replied softly, "if that's what she wants . . ."

The fact was, he had no idea how to work his will in a personal affair. Politics, sure—but not this . . . and not now. He was tired, stretched thin. He could not find the will.

He took sick, with a vicious infection that laid him out for days, while he thought what he might have said, or done—thought back through *years,* how it might have been different . . . but he could not make it different. He couldn't do any more now. He was in his bed . . . well, not his bed. It was that hotel, four walls . . . not much else.

— ★ —

He had his job, thank God, and he did it. As soon as he was out of bed, he was in the air again—another coast-to-coast swing. Bob Dole wasn't the kind to quit. Sometimes, you had to be tough! He flew a quarter-million miles in that election, for the Party, for the President.

That year, '72, Nixon piled up the biggest margin of any Republican in history. Of course, the President and his men were exultant . . . though Nixon did, sure enough, fail to mention any Party institutions in his victory speech.

Only Dole seemed to notice that.

Sure enough, Nixon's landslide did not raise the GOP to power in either house of Congress. In fact, liberal Democrats unseated Republican Senators from Maine, Colorado, Delaware, and Iowa.

Only Dole seemed to harp on that.

That was his reputation, by that time, in the White House: sour all the way—Bob Dole, crying wolf for the Party. One week after election, the capital's smart-guy community knew: Dole was on his way out—just a question of when.

Dole didn't need the tom-toms to tell him . . . it was almost time, anyway. He'd have his own reelection campaign in 1974. If he could bow out of the chairman's job with grace—say, mid-'73 . . . well, that would give everybody time.

Only Dole had grace in mind.

Two weeks after the election, Dole was summoned. It was his first visit to Camp David—his last for many years. Nixon had him flown up by chopper, with Attorney General Dick Kleindienst—who looked like a man on the way to his hanging. That's when Dole figured: maybe there was a noose for him, too.

Dole said, by way of small talk, "Agh, d'ya bring your *rope*?"

But, no . . . Nixon was awfully kind—talked about all the work Bob had done—helluva job! . . . The President had that big map from the office, all striped now with flight paths—that was a gift for Dole. And a jacket, emblazoned: "Camp David." Nixon couldn't have been friendlier—wanted to talk about *Bob's future*.

"Well, I have been working hard," Dole allowed. "I thought maybe I could stick around, have a little fun with the job, a few months . . ."

Nixon was nodding: yes, he'd figured Bob was ready to move on.

"No, well, I mean . . ."

No need to explain: Nixon understood! Well, who did Bob think should be his successor? . . . Of course, Dole caught the drift. He mentioned some Big Guys—Mel Laird might be good. . . .

That's when Nixon brought up the name George Bush. Nixon wanted to place Bush . . . but Bush didn't want to be number two anywhere. Maybe he could be number one at the RNC. Did Dole think Bush might take the job? . . . It was John Mitchell who suggested that Dole go to New York, sound out Bush—see if he'd be willing.

So, dutifully, Dole flew to New York, had his meeting with Bush, took his sounding, in the Waldorf. . . . Bush was cordial—nice guy, you know—he listened, smiled, didn't say yes, didn't rule it out.

Dutifully, Dole reported back to the White House.

It was only later, after Dole found himself and his daughter in the *last car* of Nixon's inaugural parade (well, just about the last car—maybe some cops behind them, or a sanitation crew) . . . after Dole learned from the papers that he'd been dumped as chairman (his demise unceremoniously leaked) . . . along with the news that he'd been dumped for George Bush . . . did Dole learn that Bush had talked to Nixon.

Bush had talked to Nixon before Dole ever flew to New York!

You'd think Bush might have said—somehow, let Dole know—it was all just a dog and pony show . . . he'd already taken Dole's job!

"Gaghhd! Guy just sat there! . . ."

Nice guy!

Well, didn't matter anymore—did it? Dole's job was gone. He was back in that hotel, alone, with those walls . . . his map, a Camp David jacket in the closet . . . and in his head, an unfading memory of Bush's blank, friendly smile.

58

1973

BAR TOLD HIM not to take that job. "Anything . . . but not that committee."

It was the first time she'd ever said something like that, but . . . the Republican National Committee? It was . . . just *politics,* just thumping the old tub! . . . Oh, she'd been to enough of those dinners to know the score. Bob Dole could run around the country, saying nasty things about the Democrats—fine . . . but that was a *lousy* job for George Bush! . . . George Bush was serving the country!

They'd been happy in New York, at the UN—in their grand apartment in the Waldorf (actually three apartments put together, on the forty-second floor of the Towers). After all those terrible things people wrote (she remembered well) when George got the job: how he was "just a politician," "ignorant of foreign affairs," who would "devalue the U.S. mission," whose appointment "demonstrated Nixon's contempt"—George had shown them, hadn't he?

He was a raging success . . . he'd done his homework, he knew the issues. He'd represented his country with honor. The staff at the mission loved him— as did the foreign diplomats, whom the Bushes entertained assiduously, with dinners in New York, picnics at his mother's place in Greenwich, nights at the ballpark to watch Uncle Herbie's Mets—George had made so many friends! . . . Actually, George and Bar had, since she got hold of a Blue Book, the list of diplomats and their wives—she memorized the names, made sure to talk to them all, at parties . . . then she'd take them over and introduce them to George—they made a wonderful team.

Bar would bring her needlepoint and sit through Security Council debates. She tried not to sit next to the wife of someone George would vote against—but if it happened, no matter: they could still be friends. After all, they were professionals. They had to take the line of their governments. Everybody understood that—understood there could be no deviation from that, no matter what one might think privately. In fact, there was no job (none in Bar's experience) where the power of mindset came in so handy. No one but Bar knew when George had argued for a different policy in Washington. (It happened seldom, as a matter of fact.) But George would *never* sow discord within his delegation, and he wouldn't allow any carping about the State Department, or Kissinger. No one but Bar would see Bush's heartache when he picked up the paper and found out Kissinger was secretly talking with the Red Chinese— pulled the rug out from under Taiwan . . . and from under George Bush, who was laboring to keep Taiwan in the UN. . . . No, Bush would simply take the *new line*—a two-China policy—no one would *ever* see him acting as if he did not believe it. . . . No one but Bar would ever know his humiliation and rage when the U.S. lost the vote on two Chinas, and the Third World delegates ("little wiener nations," Bush had called them) started laughing and whoop- ing, catcalling Uncle Sam, in the aisles. . . . No, he would gather the delegation and reassure them: they were a good team—no second-guessing and no looking back . . . "On to the next event!"

That was the loyalty he owed to his country—and his President. Richard Nixon had vouchsafed this job to Bush, after Bush lost his race for the Senate. No one would ever see Bush wavering from Richard Nixon. That's why the hard-eyed men in the White House thought of Bush for that RNC job. ("He takes our line beautifully," said a memo from Bob Haldeman.) And that's why Barbara Bush could hardly have been surprised when loyal George came back from Camp David and gave her the news she least wanted to hear. . . . Actually, he didn't have to tell her, straight out.

"Boy!" said George Bush. "You just can't say no to the President!"

> *Thank you for your note about the Watergate affair. I want to say I left the wonderful job at the United Nations to return to politics because I feel strongly that those of us who care must try to elevate politics.*
>
> *The connotations of Watergate are grubby and I don't like it. . . . There is a public distrust in government and to the degree that I can make some small contribution to correcting that, this new job in politics will be worthwhile.*
>
> *I appreciate your taking the time to write . . .*
>
> *Yours very truly,*
George Bush

He answered each letter personally, assuring Republicans that their Party had nothing to do with Watergate, promising the faithful that he'd spare no effort to trumpet the President's achievements, adjuring the Nixon-haters not to judge too soon or too harshly—to let the Constitutional process take its course. . . . What else could he do? He told his friends—the ones who counseled him to get off that sinking ship—that he wasn't just defending the President, he was defending the Party, and the Presidency.

> . . . *I fully share your concern about this sordid and grubby Watergate mess. . . .*
>
> *Watergate was the product of the actions of a few misguided, very irresponsible individuals who violated a high trust and who served neither the President nor their country well. . . .*
>
> *Keep in mind that the RNC and CRP are two separate entities. The whole Party shouldn't be blamed for the actions of a few zealots. . . .*
>
> > *Yours very truly,*
> > *George Bush*

But he was defending the President—no way around it. Richard Nixon had assured Bush, personally, that he had nothing to do with the break-in, the cover-up—any of that nonsense. . . . Bush had the President's *word*—man to man.

And how could he demonstrate his continued belief in the man who had become his friend, his patron . . . save by throwing himself into defense—personally? Bush knew no other way.

> *The President has said repeatedly he wasn't involved in the sordid Watergate affairs. I believe him. I am confident he will be fully exonerated once this matter is cleared up in the courts.*
>
> *I am also confident that people are basically fair. . . . The voters will not hold the Republicans responsible for what the Party was not involved in. . . .*
>
> > *Yours very truly,*
> > *George Bush*

If Bush was confident, he was more and more alone. Yale friends wrote, asking why he could not *do something* to rid the country of Nixon. Republican officials relayed forecasts of disaster in elections to come. Money for the Party disappeared. Bush had to fire half the staff at the committee. He handled each termination personally.

When GOP Congressmen edged toward impeachment, or Senators mused on Nixon's possible resignation . . . Bush's phone would ring. The White House was on the line—Chuck Colson, or one of his legion (Teeter, the Party pollster, called them "the after-dark crowd"). . . .

"*YOU GO OUT THERE AND TELL THOSE ASSHOLES . . .*"

You could hear Colson's snarl in Bush's earpiece, all the way across the office.

". . . THEY FUCK WITH US, WE'LL CRUSH 'EM . . . LIKE BUGS! ALL OF 'EM . . ."

And you'd see Bush's back go stiff, in his big chair, as he said with conscious quiet to the phone: "I'm not sure that would do any good . . . I'm not sure that's what the committee ought to be doing."

Then there'd be more of Colson, screaming . . . after which, Bush would set down the earpiece in its cradle, precisely, almost daintily, with thumb and index finger pincering its midpoint, only the tips of two fingers touching it. . . . "Well," he'd say, "that was pleasant."

> . . . *I have read every word of the transcripts, but I have not seen all the evidence, and thus, I am not going to join in suggesting that Richard Nixon authorized payment of hush money. Indeed, I am surprised that one who is concerned about government as you would not understand the point that all evidence should be seen and heard before definitive judgments are made by Members of Congress.*
>
> *Yours very truly,*
> *George Bush*

> . . . *I recognize that it is very hard to get the message of support out around the country, particularly when the press is having such a heyday with Watergate and the negative aspects.*
>
> *Yours very truly,*
> *George Bush*

> . . . *Last year for example, I traveled 97,000 miles, to 33 states, gave 101 speeches, 78 press conferences, was on national TV 11 times to speak for Nixon. . . .*
> *We really need you.*
>
> *Yours very truly,*
> *George Bush*

No, it could not be just letters, or phone calls. Bush flew around the nation with abandon, interposing his person between the Party and its date with a brick wall. The speeches and press statements were the same as the letters— same words—but Bush thought if people could *see him, hear him, in person* . . . see his hope for the nation, for its government, for his Party, its candidates, for *decency* . . . well, that would make a difference—wouldn't it?

That was what he had to give, that was the measure of loyalty—and the requirement of the code: personal commitment.

That's what made it worse, in the end . . . when he found out.

Nixon had lied to him, personally.

Bush never could shrug that off—couldn't chalk it up to politics . . . that wasn't politics to *him*. That was a personal breach.

Even a year later, Bush remarked to a friend, with uncharacteristic bluntness: "I wouldn't care if I never see Richard Nixon again."

Of course, by that time, Bush had less reason to be politic. In fact, he wasn't sure whether politics was his game, at all.

59

The
Cavalcade
of Stars

LOYALTY WOULD BE his watchword. He was still Vice President—part of the Reagan team. He'd said that so many times, even his white men understood: Bush—well, he probably *means* it. . . . Teeter, in fact, had good and important reasons why Bush had to run as Reagan's shadow: in the fall of 1987, it was the only way that made sense to the voters—it was his Veephood made Bush big-league.

But that didn't stop the white men from trying to hedge their bets—just a little. (Why not have your cake, too?) Especially when things got serious . . . like this Iowa event: the Iowa GOP would gather in September for the Presidential Cavalcade of Stars, a cattle show for Republican candidates . . . and a *straw poll.*

A straw poll meant *news stories.*

And that meant Bush had to win.

That's the problem with running big-league. You have to look big-league every time.

So the Iowa chairman of GBFP, George Wittgraf, a gentleman-lawyer from Cherokee, got a thunderstorm of calls from Fifteenth Street: tickets, buses, schedules, backdrops—everything had to be big-league! Several calls came from Rich Bond, who graced the Wing of Power as the Deputy Campaign Manager—deputy to Atwater . . . but saw himself, in the flowchart of his own mind, pendent on one thin line to the big box—George Bush. In fact, if you shot Bond up with truth serum, he might tell you: *it shoulda been him* (and not Lee) in that big corner office on Fifteenth Street.

It was Bond, after all, who'd run Iowa for Bush in 1980—Bond and Witt-graf—in that wonderful year when they'd won *every* straw poll, and then *whipped* the front-runner, Reagan, in the caucus . . . that put Bush on the map! . . . And after that campaign, it was Bond who moved into the gray granite pile, next to the White House, to serve as *political adviser* in the OVP. . . . It was Bond (and Wittgraf) who saw to the care and feeding of the old "Bush Brigade" in Iowa—meetings, mailings, reunions . . . *for eight years* . . . waiting for the next chance to trumpet George Bush for President.

This was the chance. This would be the first time Bush would work the same stage as his rivals. This was Bush's coming out. This was Bush returning to the scene of his (and Bond's) great triumph in 1980 . . . so Bond meant to cross all the T's on this Iowa Cavalcade.

He had his top deputy, Mary Matalin, watching the arrangements. Winning the straw poll meant having hundreds of people show up to vote . . . and that meant tickets—at twenty-five dollars a pop. So, the Bush campaign got people to buy tickets. Then they reserved buses to carry ticket holders to the hall in Ames. They sent a mailing to all known Bush supporters, statewide, explaining the importance of the vote. They followed up with phone banks—"Can you come on Saturday?" . . . Then, too, they had Bobby Holt, Junior's oilman friend from Midland, raise another forty or fifty thousand dollars for the Iowa GOP, so it could hand over *more* tickets for Republicans who'd be safe votes for Bush. . . . And that was before the blizzard of arrangements from the Schedulers (the VP had to speak first!), the Secret Service, the Chief of Advance, the Wocka, the White House Military Office . . .

And that was before the speech: that's where the white men wanted to have their cake and eat it. . . . See, the Gipper wasn't popular in Iowa—barely won there in '84. So this was Bush's *chance* to show he was his own man. He could illumine *his* issues—fill in the shadows of a Bush Presidency, open up a crucial crack of light between him and his Big Friend.

Well . . . couldn't he?

No.

Loyalty! Was that too complicated? . . . George Bush was not going to distance himself. Bush was not going to have *any issues* come between him and his friend. . . . Sure, he'd mention education—Reagan was for education, you know, as a concept . . . and ethics: Bush and the Gipper were *for* ethics in government!

But he wasn't going to mention ethics . . . and Ed Meese.

Ethics . . . and Mike Deaver. No.

What kind of team play would that be?

What kind of politics? . . . To Bush, it was simple: he was identified with Reagan. So, strengthening Reagan strengthened Bush. Anything to undercut Reagan would eat the ground out from under . . . George Bush! That's why he'd never show his cape in any of those White House bullfights—even when they begged him. The Don Regan thing! . . . The white men *all* told Bush, he had to say *something*—get out front!—to *show* he was easing Regan out, taking care of the problem: he was saving the President!

No!

In fact, Bush did help Regan out the door (had to fight off Nancy Reagan—let the Chief of Staff get away with his kneecaps!) . . . but Bush did his part invisibly. He'd never show that the Gipper couldn't clean his own house.

So, Bush got the speech he wanted: a loyalty speech. It wasn't much of a, uh, shocker, but . . . they did their best. The new speechwriter, Reid Detchon, gave it all he had: Bush meant to be a Boy Scout—how about a *tough* Boy Scout?

"For the last seven years, I've stood side by side with a GREAT President . . .

"And I'm damned proud of it!" . . .

That was the opener.

So the Bush Stratoliner swooped down upon Des Moines, and the choppers were waiting for an airlift to Marshalltown . . . where the limos and vans were idling in line for the scores of staff—everybody came—and the doctor, and the military aid . . . and the ambulance fell in with its strobes awhir, and the CAT squad rumbled in its armored Suburban . . . the whole big-league big top swept down Highway 30 into Ames, to a Holiday Inn, where the Service whisked the VP off to a holding room—security and comfort! The VP might want to rest . . . and thence to the campus of Iowa State, to the field house where the faithful had gathered . . . and everything went fine.

Except . . . Bond and Atwater split away and climbed to the top of the hall, last row of the balcony, where they could look down on the swarm below . . . it was like a convention floor: a press pen with two hundred reporters and crew—everybody came to a straw vote—and behind, the *thousands* . . . too many thousands! The place was teeming with Republicans! . . . Wait a minute! Were these Republicans? . . . They didn't *look* like Bushies—you know, with sport coats and flowered dresses. These wore *T-shirts,* and funny hats! And they were clapping, and whooping in rapture, like Christ was coming, and *the T-shirts said . . . Robertson.*

Atwater's head sank into his hands. "Oh, ohhh, oughhh," he was moaning. "Where's our people?"

"Well, they didn't all sit together," Bond said. "They . . ."

Atwater fixed Bond with a gaze of earnest menace.

"Ah'm gonna kill you."

Bond's eyes were fixed on the crowd. He said: "We're dead." (He meant, already.)

But . . . not so fast! The VP still had to speak!

So they brought Bush out from the holding room, and introduced him, and he stilled the applause, looked down at his speech . . .

"For the last seven years . . ."

Bush's eyes swept the hall—who *were* these people? Those *hats!* ROBERTSON . . . ROBERTSON . . . And the buttons: I WAS THERE WHEN ROBERTSON WON!

"I've stood side by side with a GREAT President. And I'm . . ."

God! They were, uh, Christians!

". . . very very proud!"

Of course, the Christians didn't know the difference . . . but a score of reporters circled the missing "damned" on their speech texts.

Couldn't pull the trigger on his own best line!

The wise guys were right!

Jesus! What a wimp!

—★—

What made Dole a star at the Calvacade—made this bit of guerrilla politics work—was that he had no speech. Well, that wasn't strictly true—there was a speech (*All typed up! Pretty gooood!*) . . . it's just that Dole never used it.

(By that fall, they'd stopped writing texts for him. They had to—he'd go through a writer a week. They'd hand him a speech and he'd drop one eyebrow, fix the writer with a glittering stare, and demand: "Aughh! Is this the best you can do?" The mortified writer would take it back, start over. . . . One time, he pushed a writer through four of those rewrites, till the day of the speech, whereupon Dole gave the squint-of-death to draft number five. "Gaggh! Is this the best you can do?" The frazzled writer practically screamed back: "YES!" . . . "O-*kayy!*" said Dole, rolling it neatly into his fist. "I'll read it now." . . . At any rate, by that September, they'd just tape him speaking off-the-cuff, then shred up his own words into new coleslaw. What the hell! He'd say what he wanted, anyway.)

One other key was the Kappa Sigma house, right there at Ames. Kappa Sig was Dole's fraternity. It was also the fraternity house of a couple of Dole's Iowa ops, and their friends on campus. . . . (In the end, the key may have been that Dole had young staff with friends at college.)

Anyway, the big Cavalcade in the field house was *televised* . . . but the candidates couldn't see—no TVs in the holding rooms. That's why Bush walked in cold.

But Dole had a guy watching TV at the Kappa Sig house . . . and that guy had an open phone line . . . to a phone in Glassner's ear, in the holding room, in the field house, where the Bobster was caged . . . and the upshot was:

Dole knew.

He knew how that crowd raised the roof when Robertson was introduced . . . and screamed and cheered two or three dozen times in the middle of the Reverend's speech. . . . Dole knew when Bush's speech fell dead, and the Veep just stalked off stage. . . . Dole knew how Kemp got nowhere with that crowd, bashing the Democrats, doing politics.

Dole knew enough not to talk politics—not traditional politics: he tossed away his own coleslaw . . . and he talked values—straight to that crowd.

He was glad to see them, he said.

He meant to *welcome them* to the Party, and the process.

Because their participation was a great sign for the GOP . . . and for the country, which was in need of moral leadership, the rudder of Christian values. . . . The stakes were high—as he well knew (leading the fight for Robert Bork, on the Court!) . . . but with *their help* . . . and *their prayers* . . .

Praise the Lord! He was like a visiting pastor!

The key to it all—the fact underneath—was that Dole knew more than the phone from the frat house told him. Dole knew why these people didn't look like Republicans, why they'd never shown up in any crowd before. Dole never needed a writer to tell him how to talk to the dispossessed.

These people were left-outs. (That's why they were watching Robertson's TV show!) . . . The message Bob Dole left with them, that Saturday, was simple: they mattered to him.

That was the day when Dole got the endorsement of Iowa's Senator Grassley ("Chuckeeee!") . . . and it was Grassley who introduced him, with the phrase that summed it up in one line.

"He's one of us!" Grassley said.

That line stuck with Dole. It was perfect for Iowa—for everyplace (and everyone) left out of Reagan's shower of gold. It linked Dole—in four words!— with the millions (these God-struck folk at Ames, for example) who felt that Washington was a place cut off from their town, from their lives, from the values they held dear.

Dole knew what it meant—the minute he heard Grassley twang it out! . . . He could *see* what it meant in that field house at Ames. . . . Bob Dole was One of Us. George Bush had to be one of *them*.

When the speaking was done, Dole did not leave, but stood at the door for an hour and a half, shaking hands.

By that time, Robertson had triumphed in the straw poll. Dole ran second, ninety-some votes ahead of George Bush.

By that time, the herd in the press pen was dispatching the news from portable computers . . . ROBERTSON SHOCKS GOP RIVALS. . . . Their stories were rolling into papers across the nation.

E.J. Dionne, in *The New York Times,* would note that some Christians expressed admiration for Robertson . . . and Dole.

But it was the *Post*'s story the Dole campaign would value (and Xerox) . . . if only for the subhead:

3RD-PLACE FINISH
EMBARRASSES BUSH

—★—

By that time, Bush was in the air, aboard *Air Force Two*—and a gloomy Power Cabin it was, that Saturday night, flying home from Ames. Bush didn't care about Robertson. Of course, he hated to lose—to a kook!—but Robertson probably bused in everybody in the state who liked him. Robertson was no threat.

Dole was another matter. That's what burned Bush: he finished behind Dole! . . . "He's one of us!" . . . Bullshit!

In the Bush-mind, Dole was a Beltway Bandito, an inside player, the kind you watch out for: Dole was *kick-boxing* . . . he'd do anything! Bush had known Bob Dole for twenty years—and never known him. Never could get comfortable—a personal thing. . . . Bush was pretty sure it wasn't anything on his side—not at the start. Seemed like something was making Dole tight inside, whenever he got around Bush. It came out in little things Dole'd say—always about other people. At the Bush dinner table, the subject of Dole would evoke the simplest and most damning judgment of the true White Man: not an attractive guy.

How could he lose to Dole?

How could he lose . . . like *that*? Third place! They were blown away! It sank in on Bush that all the planning, all the white men, all the staff, all the effort . . . was not getting through to *people*. He knew he had the team, the best in the business! What were they doing for the last two years? The PAC must have spent ten million dollars—all those people! Thirty staff in Iowa alone . . . and the Bush Brigade, his loyal cadre . . . from the first state he ever won! What went wrong? What the hell are they *doing* out there?

No . . . that wasn't fair. They were friends. Tried their hardest, Bush was sure. In fact, the first thing he'd ask, Monday morning—first call to the campaign office: "How's Wittgraf?"

"What do you mean, sir?"

"How's he feeling? What're people saying? People aren't making him the scapegoat, are they?"

Captain Bush wouldn't let his guys get down on themselves. They were a good team!

Even that night, in the Power Cabin, Bush spent his time trying to calm Atwater. Lee kept trying to take the blame, vowing they'd turn it around. "Ah wancha know, Mr. Vahz Pes'ent, Ah'ma take full sponsibility for this . . ."

The Veep told him there was nothing to worry about.

He would have told Bond, too, when Rich wandered up to the Power Cabin . . . but Bond was talking to Bar.

Actually, Barbara Bush was talking.

"So, Rich," she said with a smile into Bond's face. "When are you going back to Iowa to manage the Vice President's campaign?"

Bond jerked in place, for an instant, like a specimen pinned to a lab table. "Um . . . right away, Mrs. Bush!"

"Good!" said Bar. Her mouth was smiling, but her eyes had Bond's, as her head tilted back an inch or two.

". . . Because that's what George and I want."

60

The Big Guy

ELIZABETH DOLE harbored the fond and secret notion that when she quit her job to join her husband's campaign, she would, somehow, help Bob get *organized.* To Mrs. Dole, that did not mean lists of bigwigs pledging fealty. She had basic matters in mind: Whose job is it to run this project for us? Does this person know it is his job? Does he know when or how the job should be done?

Her every instinct was to administration . . . which, for Mrs. Dole, began with administration of self. If she were at Bob's side . . . well, things would surely be different. It was a matter of concern to her that Bob had not the faintest idea what he was going to say that afternoon. She was dismayed that Bob didn't even have *a set of notecards* for his basic speech. (No member of the Reagan Cabinet would be without!) She went so far as to bring this up with Bob's staff—as if this were something they had neglected.

Of course, not a word of this could be breathed aloud, because Elizabeth would not feed the canard that Bob Dole could not be organized. The Karacter Kops all repeated the fiction that Elizabeth had, somehow, *taught* her husband (suddenly, in his sixth decade) to "Be Nice." No one caught her working on her real agenda: "Be Neat."

Anyway, everybody was busy writing serious-minded feminist nosebleed on Mrs. Dole's "controversial" resignation. The idea was that we should *all* (harrrumph!) . . . *examine* the *assumptions* of a society where a (umph! umph!) *woman* . . . would give up her job in the *Cabinet of the United States* . . . to help her (hocchhh!) HUSBAND!

What about HER CAREER?

What all the earnest anguish ignored was that Bob was much more a part of her career than the next report on the next airliner to blow up in the sky over Pascagoula . . . that Elizabeth Dole would no more drop her career than would Bob Dole (or Barbara Bush) . . . that she *was* making a career decision . . . and anyone who did not know that being wife to the President of the United States is a better and more powerful job than being Secretary of Transportation was too dumb to work for government—though, alas, not too dumb to write for magazines.

The fact was, being Elizabeth Hanford Dole, she had no choice.

It wasn't just Bob's supporters *begging* her (the Secret Weapon!) to join them at the ramparts. Nor even his staff, who had taken to calling Bob and Elizabeth "The Dynamic Duo." No! It was *The Washington Post,* and *Washington Monthly,* and (the real Dynamic Duo) Evans and Novak . . . who were already beating tribal war drums, criticizing her for helping her husband *at all* . . . while (hoccchhh!) airliners were blowing up in the sky! For Elizabeth Dole, whose career was personal perfection, this was intolerable.

So . . . the real anguish was, she quit . . . and *then* she was hammered as a cop-out, a traitor to her gender, a feminist war criminal—no better than, than . . . than . . . a *WIFE*!

And the true upshot was, she joined her husband's campaign full-time and spent half her time in a new campaign to convince every audience that she was right to be campaigning. "What WE WOMEN have fought for," she said (and said), "is the RIGHT to make our own CHOICES!" Then, she'd take ten or fifteen minutes to explain that she didn't really leave her job because airplanes were blowing up in the sky—no! She'd met the challenges at Transportation. . . . "And as Ah left the Department [smile] . . . Ah felt Ah was putting aside ONE CAUSE, which Ah believed in very strongly, to take up ANOTHER. Ah wanted to be by mah husband's side—if not literally [chuckle], then at least figuratively!"

That was true, too: she seldom was with Bob. She was all over the country with her own plane and her own staff, working like a beast to be charming five times a day, in between which events, she'd try to memorize the résumés of another half-dozen City Councilmen while she shoveled M&M's, or Burger King fries, into her mouth and stood at attention in her hotel room, so her body man, Mark Romig, could zap her with his steam-gun, so her suit would be perfect, wrinkle-free, for her next event, her next interview, her next TV talk show, her next women's luncheon, where she'd explain again the CHALLENGE of participating in the PROCESS that selects the LEADER of the FREE WORLD . . . and . . .

She didn't feel too organized herself.

Which was okay with Bob, who had this organized just like he wanted—double the ink!

Besides, he was going to get a Big Guy . . .

This was *serious* now. He had a fish on the line—Bill Brock!

— ★ —

Even Dole's working staff—true, humble Dole-folk—were happy about this. (Well, there was a brief movement for Paul Laxalt as Big Guy. Laxalt wouldn't do *anything*. But if Laxalt was out of town, Bill Brock was the laziest man in Washington, so on the whole, everybody was pleased.)

As for Dole, he thought maybe Brock *could* help organize. (Elizabeth thought Brock was *so* organized! Elizabeth approved of Bill Brock entirely.) You know, Brock had been around! Brock was a grassroots specialist! Brock used to run that Youth for Nixon thing! Brock had run a *vicious* race to knock off Al Gore, Sr., and get to the Senate.

Didn't matter, really: whatever Brock *did* was gravy . . . because what Dole wanted was to show everybody that he *had* a Big Guy—and Brock was, number one and foremost, a *Big Guy*.

In fact, he'd been a Big Guy for so long that now there were *smart guys* . . . who were *Brock guys*! (As was his custom, Dole had hired some: his first campaign for President was managed, briefly, by Tom Bell—"Agh! Guy worked for Brock! Pretty *goood*!" Of course, Bell didn't last in that job, and Dole finished as an asterisk . . . but that did nothing to shrink Brock's Big-Guyhood.)

For twenty-five years, official Washington had linked Brock's name to titles of knowing power: *Congressman, Senator, Chairman, Secretary.* Brock had the bankable asset—he was well known, not least to Dole, with whom he'd served in House and Senate . . . where they'd voted together to *back Nixon,* and then *Ford* . . . after which, Brock moved on to *Chairman of the RNC,* in which post he worked to heal the Party, after Watergate . . . which healing was complete with the election of Reagan, whose ideology Brock did not favor, but from whom, nonetheless, Brock took jobs—first as *U.S. Trade Rep,* and then, *Secretary of Labor.* . . . This was another of Brock's apparent assets: he had held so many jobs and stood for so little, no one would be moved to quit if Bill Brock hired on—not even Devine or Keene, who measured themselves by their enemies, nor certainly Ellsworth, who got along with Brock, gentleman to gentleman.

In sum, Brock was perfect (i.e., no one would get mad at Dole). And Brock sent all the right signals.

"Kansan," said a headline in *The Washington Post,* "Has Expert Advice." The *Post* said Dole had cleared a giant hurdle to make himself Bush's most-feared opponent: "The selection of someone with Brock's stature is a clear signal that authority will be delegated in the 1988 Dole campaign."

Dole could not have thumped the tribal drums any better. Brock was worth all the waiting, all the talk . . . Brock was Big, Big, Big . . . Brock was, in Dole's backcourt eyes, better than Laxalt! Maybe better than Sears!

Brock was classy—heir to a candy fortune.

(Lotta moneyyy!)

Brock was southern—from Tennessee.

(Aghh! Super *Tues*-day!)

Brock was not only Cabinet *rank*—he was in the Cabinet *now* . . . which solved another ticklish problem.

Whenever she was questioned about her resignation, Elizabeth Dole would now rejoin: "Whah, *Bill BROCK* left the Cabinet just a few weeks after Ah did! For exactly the same reason—to be full-time in Bob's campaign. Ah'm sure he doesn't feel he's set aside *his* career! . . ."

— ★ —

So, Bill Brock *came aboard,* as Big Guys like to say . . . except Brock didn't hit the deck, just at that moment. He had important personal business, and some trips to make—he was awfully busy. So what he did, he sent a boarding *party,* a posse of guys in suits, to poke around L Street, asking questions of the Dole-folk, like: "How would you *describe* your work for Senator Dole's campaign?" . . . and similarly subtle queries, designed (as Big Guys say) to *evaluate the personnel.*

Of course, coming as they did, from the world of Big Guys, these posse men didn't have to ask much: it was obvious, the Dole campaign was . . . a walking disaster.

The *personnel*! . . . They were *so* humble—there wasn't one of them you'd want sitting behind you at a Cabinet meeting. And the *organization* . . . pathetic! These poor schlubs were all on one floor, together, everybody . . . you know, just . . . *working for Dole*!

Well, that was going to have to change.

For one thing, the campaign would have to bring in *first-class talent* (i.e., Brock guys) . . . and pay the freight: real talent never came cheap. And they'd have to rent another floor of the building, a couple of floors up, so no one could just burst in from the stairwells . . . there would be a decent reception desk, and a comely young woman, with pearls, to pick up the chiming phone and say:

"Senator Brock's office, please hold."

But, alas, that would take time. For the moment, it was all the posse could do to penetrate the mysteries.

My God! . . . They called a meeting with the bean counter, Kirk Clinkenbeard. Clink was a Dole-folk who'd left his father's CPA firm in Topeka (his dad was Dave Owen's first Campaign Treasurer) because of a problem with his vision. So . . . came the Brockies, asked their first question. Clink took off his glasses, held a piece of paper *one inch from his nose,* and announced there'd been $9.7 million raised. . . . Of course, the posse men started looking at each other like they'd landed in *Mork and Mindy.* C'mon, get *serious*! The campaign's finance director can't even see! This guy's got to go—*first* to go. . . . But what they didn't know:

Clink was the guy Dole called three times a day, to ask how much was in the till. Dole especially liked him because he had a disability.

Bill Lacy, who had run the whole campaign that brought Dole from amid

the pack to his current stance, toe-to-toe with Bush in the first five states
. . . he'd have to go. Guy didn't even have a strategic plan!

Mari Maseng, who juggled the press, ads, and speeches, who flew everywhere with Dole, telling him, "Senator, I think there's a positive way to say
this . . ." and still managed not to piss him off entirely . . . well, she'd have
to go, too. She could not supply a simple flowchart to show *who approved the
Senator's speeches*!

Kim Wells, the Kansas City lawyer who'd left his firm to work for subsis-
tence, to sleep in friends' houses for ten months, the man Dole relied on to fix
anything that looked broken . . . well, an obvious loser! (Couldn't even *find*
him on a flowchart!) The posse confronted him with a simple question: What
do you do in the campaign? Wells seemed to think that was funny! He said:
"Anything Dole wants."

It was Kim . . . (and Lacy and Maseng and Owen, and Judy Harbaugh, Scott
Morgan, Clinkenbeard—it was all the Dole-folk, after a while) . . . who started
with the Vulcan salute—that sign Spock used to give on *Star Trek:* one palm
raised, Injun-style, with the middle and ring fingers split to form a V. . . . "Live
long and prosper," they'd tell each other. That identified them as Vulcans—
true Dole-folk. The Brockies were the Klingons. The Dole-folk would pass
each other at L Street, and flash the V: "Live long and prosper! . . . Prepare
for Klingons!"

Of course, by the time it became *us* against *them,* the posse had identified
the problems . . . who were the people Dole called when he wanted something
done—they'd have to go. . . . Down the chart! Out of the loop! . . . Except Dole
still called them. Mostly, he'd call now to make sure they weren't mad at him.
(If they were, Dole wouldn't call. Elizabeth would call: "Whah, Bob was just
saying, just the other *day,* how *sorry* he was, the way that worked out . . .")

Dole was trying to be good—to hand the campaign over, to be organized,
like he promised—but he had doubts about the Klingons, too. He *knew* some
of them—"Gagghhh! Guy couldn't organize a two-car *fune*-ral! We gonna *hire*
him? . . ."

But he'd only say it in the plane, or his car. (Be Nice! . . . Hands off!) He
had to let them hire or fire whomever they wanted. Then, he found out they
wanted to can his Iowa chief—Tom Synhorst (just a farm kid—not Big enough
for the Klingons).

That was the one time Dole put his foot down. (Aughh! Only place in the
country he was *organized*!) . . . "Do what you want," he told Brock, on the
phone. "Don't touch Iowa."

61

What
Sasso
Loved

IF MICHAEL DUKAKIS could win
Iowa, it was over. That's how Sasso
had it figured. Michael sneaks into
a state where he's unknown . . . urban . . . an easterner . . . a Greek! . . . and
wins?

Then, surely, he wins New Hampshire, eight days later.

Then he sweeps into Super Tuesday as the only national Democrat, the clear
favorite in the rest of the nation. . . . Sasso had Super Tuesday all mapped out.
Michael wouldn't have to contest all twenty states—spread himself willy-
nilly—no. Massachusetts would vote that day. That's about eighty delegates
for Michael. Maryland, Washington State . . . Michael had solid chances at
wins. If he won one other big state—say Florida, where Kitty could help
. . . if he could, God grant, win Florida . . . and *Texas* . . . there's no way he'd
lose the nomination, if he didn't get hit by a bus.

But the first link was the weakest: Iowa.

Michael's polls there were holding steady—near the top. Michael's organization was the best. It would identify his voters and deliver them to their
caucuses. Sasso had seen to that.

But the race in Iowa was formless: Dukakis, Gephardt, Biden, maybe
Simon, Babbitt, or Jackson—someone was going to get hot and sweep the
thing.

Problem was, Michael wasn't going to get hot. Sasso had been leading him
gently to a higher pitch of speech. He had shown Michael, in a hundred small
ways, how "good jobs at good wages" was, at root, a *populist* message. What

could that mean . . . save that government had to take the side of working people, guarantee them a shot at the basics: a job, decent home, safe neighborhoods, good schools, a clean environment for their kids. . . . Michael was for all those things—but he came at them through the head, not the heart.

That's why Biden was a problem: he and Dukakis both appealed to middle-class voters. But Biden had the knack, an ear for their language . . . Biden talked straight to their hearts. And now, with weeks on the tube, every night, as chairman of the Bork hearings, he could build a record of "doing"—doing something that voters could see, *right now.*

Biden's numbers were rising. After Michael, Biden was the only Democrat with money. He could split Michael's middle-class base, all over the country. Biden could get hot.

Biden . . . could be *the* problem.

—★—

What Sasso couldn't understand was how Biden got away with all the bullshit. When John saw a tape of the Iowa State Fair debate, he couldn't *believe* it. Sasso knew the Kinnock ad—where the hell did Biden get off, using it word for word? It was like he was borrowing Kinnock's *life*! Did he think no one else in this country had seen it? That was bush-league. That was *bullshit.* . . . Why didn't anybody write that?

The Dukakis campaign had rented two floors of an old loft building in a grungy backwater of Boston . . . *ekonomia:* Michael must have got it cheap. John's corner room had a desk, a desk chair, a smallish glass table, two semi-clean ashtrays, and a few hard chairs covered with nappy polyester-tweed. But one side of the room was dominated by a black Sony video console, the only object in the room that gleamed.

Sasso got a tape of the Kinnock ad:

"Why am I the only Kinnock in a thousand generations . . ."

Then he slipped in the tape of Biden's close:

"Why am I the only Biden in a thousand generations . . ."

It was uncanny: it wasn't just the words—it was every gesture, every pause. And not one mention of the name Neil Kinnock!

He played the tapes for Tully, Corrigan, Edley . . . one after the other, his senior staff: they watched the Sony. John watched them. They couldn't believe it, either.

"Why didn't people write about this?"

"Maybe they didn't know . . . *must* not have known."

After that, for days—for a *week*—John showed the tapes to everyone who visited: politicians, wise guys, reporters . . . he watched them all. They were stunned. He didn't have to say a word. Surely, they'd talk about it. The reporters were bound to write it.

No one wrote a word.

He showed them to Tommy Oliphant, from the *Globe.* Oliphant sat there, staring, giggling! But then . . . not a word in print.

Was John crazy? . . . Was this not a story?

Then, on Labor Day weekend, Maureen Dowd called. She was doing a profile of Pat Caddell. But along the way, she brought it up: Wasn't it weird, Biden using stuff from a British Labour leader—who *lost* to Margaret Thatcher?

It was, John said, and weirder still, Biden didn't even credit Kinnock! ". . . Yeah, really. I've been playing the tapes! It's word for word—and no credit!"

Of course, Maureen wanted to see the tapes. John said he'd send a copy . . . as long as she didn't say where she got it.

And Tully said, why not cover their tracks? He was going to Des Moines to spend the weekend with Vilmain. Why not drop off a copy at the *Register*?

And Corrigan had a friend at NBC—hey, this shit is *made for TV* . . . so, a third copy went out.

And that was it.

The story was true . . . it deserved to be told.

So why, right away, did Sasso feel such gnawing unease?

And why did he never show the tapes to Dukakis?

— ★ —

Whenever John talked about Dukakis, about their history together, he always went back to 1978, and the first time he ever saw the Governor, in person.

Sasso was a New Jersey boy who'd come to school in Boston and stayed on to do politics. In '78, he was managing a statewide campaign for a fair-tax amendment to the state constitution. He signed up Governor Dukakis as a supporter—he signed up a lot of big pols. They were all supposed to come to Sasso's kickoff at South Station—he was sending a whistle-stop train across the state, just as the general election began . . . in fact, the kickoff was set for the Saturday after the primary.

But something unexpected happened in that primary—Dukakis lost! The voters threw him out! The state and its pols were still in shock that Saturday as Sasso loaded his train. John was standing on the platform . . . when he saw the little guy in a frowzy raincoat—Dukakis! He looked gray, beat-up, un-happy . . . it was only four days after the voters of the Commonwealth had kicked him in the teeth.

Sasso told the Governor how badly he felt. "I didn't think, uh, well . . . you didn't have to come."

Dukakis said: "It's an important issue."

End of discussion.

The picture John carried in his head, from that day on, was the small, hunched back of Dukakis's raincoat, as the Governor marched away.

Of course, there'd been a thousand pictures since—since Sasso signed on to manage Michael's comeback in '82 . . . since John gave Mike his new persona, elevated his plainness into something like public charm . . . since Michael and John took back the State House, together . . . since they planned, together, every day, and so many nights, at Michael's kitchen table . . . since they walked the halls of the State House, to Michael's every public event, with Sasso quietly running through the agenda for Michael, on that stage, that day . . . since they traveled together on Michael's first out-of-state forays, with John working dark reaches of the rooms, or the press pens, while Michael executed in the spotlight . . . since they thought through programs, and gave them names, and filed the bills, rode them through House and Senate . . . fought, together, to enact their shared vision, to install the best and cleanest officials, to confirm Michael's nominees, sustain his vetoes, enforce his budgets, fend off his enemies (and his friends) . . . to make Massachusetts work better, more rationally, decently, every day, for six years, together . . . John had a million mental pictures, sure.

But taken together—or even (here was the amazing thing) in particular—they did not belie that first vivid image of Governor Dukakis . . . marching down that gray station platform . . . head-down hard-cheese life-ain't-a-picnic *beat-up* . . . but in no way shaken in his belief, his *certainty*, that what was right was right: he knew, and would do, what was right.

John Sasso loved that.

The way the wise guys always talked about it—Sasso's friends, his poker buddies, the Thursday night savants who helped him dream up Mike-Dukakis-the-Persona . . . they all said: John was the *opposite* of Michael.

They loved the game, so they talked about how Sasso loved the game . . . and he did. They saw Michael's incapacities, so they talked about how John compensated for Michael . . . which he did. They'd said, for six years, since the comeback campaign, that Sasso was the politician, the man who loved people, the guy who made wheels turn for Dukakis so Dukakis never had to turn them himself—never had to foul his hands—never even had to know!

That was all true. But they never said why.

Why went beyond South Station, 1978 . . . beyond politics . . . to New Jersey, and Sasso's own hardworking father, who came to this country as a child (and became an electrical engineer) . . . and even beyond, to a village on the heel of Italy (just across the Adriatic from the rocky coast of Greece), a hard place, near Bari, where life held no shortcuts, where men named Sasso worked, cutting stone. Sasso means stone.

It went back to John's own stony notion of virtue: work, strength, discipline. . . . It went back to how Sasso saw himself—as a man who succeeded by hard labor, stubborn attention to detail, insistence on technical perfection.

See, Sasso did not consider himself Michael's opposite. Friends, admirers, talked about John's "gifts," his "ease," his "touch" . . . drinks and cigars in his office, late-night poker with the Speaker of the House . . . oh, that's Sasso, the *natural politician*. They missed the point: that was technical perfection.

Even Michael missed it: if John was yawning and mentioned to Michael that he'd been up late playing poker . . . Michael would shake his head in censure—how couldya live like that? He would never acknowledge the connection between the poker and the bills, or the budget . . . though he was happy enough to employ it.

Technical perfection was their compact—an unspoken Adriatic understanding. Hard work, they both understood. Discipline, of course. And fidelity, service . . . each in his own way.

Michael's was to march ahead, unyielding, eyes on the path in front of his feet. John's was to see all, even to the horizon, and to know the side routes darkened by Michael's blinkers.

But just as Michael made sure not to see if John darted down one of those side paths . . . so John made sure never to make him see.

And not just because it was important for Michael to maintain his view of himself, marching ahead on the straight and narrow. That view of Michael was just as important to John.

It was Michael's impossibly stubborn and straight march that gave Sasso license to practice his technical art, and still . . . remain a believer. With all that he knew about Michael, it was the unswerving, unseeing, maddeningly self-righteous trudge of the wing tips that John thought would, and *should,* put Dukakis in the White House.

He would never show Michael those tapes—not even as a matter of interest. That would be a lapse of technical perfection, a breach of the compact. Anyway, he knew what Michael would do—Dukakis would watch for a minute and conclude, satisfied, that emotional appeal was somehow flimflam. . . . He'd affirm, with a disgusted grunt, what he already held as a certainty: Biden had no discipline! . . . Michael would march on, surer still: he was worthy—Biden was not.

Of course, he'd forbid John to use the tapes to show any such thing. John would never suggest it! . . . Even so, just for showing them, Michael would give him the look, like John had tracked dirt onto the carpet. That's what John understood, and avoided. After so many years of believing, Sasso had to measure himself in Michael's blinkered gaze, too.

62

Destiny

I'S AN IMPROBABLE, exciting ride when a mechanism as complex, as ungainly, as a campaign (like a helicopter, you can't see *how* it'll work) suddenly begins to chudder, shudder, then roar . . . and takes off. The Biden campaign was like a miracle . . . once it started to fly.

Even Joe—a man of constant doubt, professional doubt (that was all part of gaming it out: seeing what could go wrong)—felt little but the wind under his wings, soaring into September, heading for the hearings . . . then Iowa, New Hampshire, the nomination, the White House. . . . He saw the moves, all the way down the field. He knew, at last, how he was going to be.

Which, in Biden's case, had to mean: he knew what he was going to say. He'd boiled it down to the nub of a message, in those months of work on Bork. He knew the crucial difference between himself and the judge—knew it so well he could say it in the commonest words, for every voter in the country.

This was the difference:

Judge Bork saw the Constitution (hence, the political life of the nation) as a finite set of concessions from the majority—the state—to individuals, who enjoyed the rights listed in the document. He saw the Constitution like a contract, a deed, a will . . . wherein each clause had fixed meaning, unchanged by time, unexpandable, except by amendment.

But Biden saw the Constitution as an enshrinement of natural rights that preexisted and informed American government. ("We hold these Truths to be self-evident," said the first document of the nation, "that all Men . . . are endowed *by their Creator* with certain *unalienable rights . . .*") To Biden, the noblest words of the Constitution—liberty, due process, equal protection of the laws—were guides to the aspiration of the American nation, and had to be interpreted anew in every age. The Constitution, in Biden's view, was a living document, intended from the first to change and grow with the country.

That made all the difference.

Because if Biden was right—right about the tenor of the country, the times, the voters and how they felt—then *that* would form the message he would carry into the campaign. If Biden was right (and he *knew* he was . . . not a doubt!), then the people did not want to *go back*—not even to the rosy Reaganaut fiction of an America that was right, and white, and neatly authoritarian in its prejudice, politics, and the polar absolutes of its worldview. If Biden was right, what the country wanted was a more perfect realization of its old ideals: Liberty, Justice, Compassion . . . and *that's* what he'd talked about—tried to talk about—for the last five years!

That's what he meant in Atlantic City, '82, when he told the Democratic Party that the country had not turned away from its ideals—only from old programs and policies that did not work. The special interests, Biden said, had become so wedded to their programs—old "solutions"—that they made busing the issue, instead of equality in education. They let food-stamp fraud become the issue, instead of food for the hungry.

That's what he meant when he told the interest groups—over and over— must have said it a *hundred times:* the solutions would not come from them, but from the people. The people wanted to move forward, to make the fight. The people were not scared of change, like their leaders were.

That's why the Kinnock stuff was so great—because that's what Americans wanted from their government: just a helping hand, to make the fight for a better life for their kids, just a platform to stand on . . . so they could reach higher.

When it came so clear to Joe, he could have *slapped* himself for ever saying anything else . . . listening to all his goddam experts! . . . when he should have just listened to the truth in himself. That was his life: he was just a middle-class kid who'd got a little help along the way . . . and that was all he had to show. But that's what connected him to the great body of voters in the country. That's all he needed! God-*dammit*! He never should have listened to anybody else.

It was strange how it worked out, like it always did, like it was, you know . . . all figured out. He'd cursed the day he ever took the chairmanship. Didn't want the job, didn't want the mess. . . . He'd cursed the day he got the Bork nomination—God, he thought his career was over! He'd never pull it off!

But what it was, was destiny. Someone up there had a plan for Joey Biden . . . he *needed* Bork, to get back, through all the bullshit, to the bottom, to the grit . . . to what Joe Biden believed.

And now he would say it, in the moment—the perfect moment—when the lights and the eyes of the nation were upon him, in the first day of hearings on the nomination of Robert Bork as Associate Justice of the Supreme Court. All three networks, and PBS, CNN, and C-Span . . . just about every TV screen in the *country* would flash Biden's opening statement . . . and then the cameras would linger, as Biden locked horns with Robert Bork, to discuss what each man thought must be *the nature and direction of the United States.* That was the moment. That would be the first speech—the first real speech—of the Biden campaign.

—★—

So the Bork campaign had become the Biden campaign, or vice versa. And the Biden campaign, which had seemed so muscle-bound as it herniated itself over speeches in Iowa coffee shops, suddenly straightened out with something big to push against—something that mattered. This Bork fight took everything a campaign had—a winning campaign. And the Biden campaign, suddenly, could win.

There was a message—all locked in now—not only for Joe, but for staff, and gurus, who could retail the thing to press and pols. For a few weeks, all the gurus were singing from the same page—they left off trying to kill each other.

And the staff—in mid-Bork, Ridley announced he was going to "unify the campaign," move *everybody* to Wilmington (that's the way Joe wanted it). So he gave the word: they'd close the D.C. office, and all Biden staff would pick up their lives a hundred miles north, in Delaware. It was a measure of just how gorgeous was the prospect of a win that the campaign didn't lose a soul.

Then, too—just as suddenly—there was a nationwide field operation. The biggest and best grassroots organization any candidate had in 1987 was the anti-Bork network run by the liberal interest groups—ACLU, NAACP, NOW, NARAL, and a cupful of lesser-known alphabet soup, all working together now on the Biden team.

There was the nationwide polling apparatus, led by Caddell, who did not stop at finding the magic brick for Joe. No, Pat put all his ferocious analysis into a memo, which he then personally took to the offices of undecided Senators (he could still open doors in Washington—they were flattered: Hey! Pat Caddell!) . . . where he explained why *their voters* were going to turn against Bork.

Suddenly, the press was all over Joe—BIDEN'S FIRST PRIMARY . . . SHOW-DOWN FOR THE SHOW HORSE—they wanted interviews, they wrote features . . . the editorial boards opened their doors. That was a moment, sure enough, when Biden, Donilon, and Rasky walked into the boardroom of *The New York Times*—two poor Irishmen and a Jew, walking into the Bastion of Established Opinion, the richest bottomland of the River of Power, with the original portrait of George Washington on the wall . . . to talk about the Constitution, and the Court. That was rich!

And Biden did fine. In fact, he did great—as he did, too, at *The Washington Post, The Boston Globe,* the *L.A. Times, U.S. News, Newsweek, Time* . . . hell, *Time* was fantastic! Dinner in the private dining room, top of the Time-Life skyscraper in New York, thirty River-of-Power types in gray suits and rep ties, down a table that would have bridged the Brandywine River in Wilmington. And Joe Biden, Syracuse, '68, took the place over, talked for five hours straight. After hour three, he had his jacket off, his ass perched on top of his chair back—so he could see them all—while he made sure these white men *understood* where *Joe Biden* was coming from, on every Constitutional issue of the day. About midnight, maybe after, they were shifting in their chairs, trying to say how *interesting* it had been . . . but Biden was just warming up.

"Hey! We haven't talked about foreign policy! Can I come back?"

The pieces were locking into place . . . he could *feel* it. He could see the thing—how it had to look, every detail: just a few days before the hearings, he decided that the dais for the committee had to come down. He had the same hearing room they'd used for Iran-contra . . . but he didn't want the Senators up on a platform, staring down at the witness—making a martyr, like Ollie North. Hell, no!

And there wasn't going to be any camera in the well between the committee and the witness, locked onto Bork's dewy eyes . . . no way. Cameras to the side, and in the back, where they could focus over Bork's head, onto the committee . . . and the backdrop. They'd have to get the backdrop right. And no staff whispering into Biden's ear. Keep it clean: Bork and Biden . . . toe-to-toe.

He had a run-through, with Larry Tribe playing Bork. They set it up in Joe's ballroom . . . chairs in an arc for the committee, Joe in the center, the witness table right across from him. Tribe was a terrific Bork. They set up video-cams so Joe could take a look, run through his moves, over and over. Joe brought in Jill, and Hunt, to see if they could follow every point.

It was planned as carefully, as ably, as a convention speech, a Labor Day rally. It was the biggest and best Democratic event since Ronald Reagan appeared on the scene. It was, well, it was so *right* . . . this was just the black Irish that came up in him, he understood . . . but it was so *perfect,* something had to happen.

63

What
Perfect
Was

H E KNEW what a perfect campaign was. In '72, Joe came from no-where—no one knew him, he was a *kid*. But something told Joe—like he *knew* it—J. Caleb Boggs, the beloved two-term Senator, twenty-five-year veteran of statewide office, a man with no enemies, a Republican with labor support . . . something told Joe he could beat Cale Boggs.

"Boggs! Joe, you're fuckin' crazy," pals told him.

"He's tired," Joe said.

Joe knew—hell, it was no secret—Boggs, already in his sixties, didn't really want a third term. It was Nixon who talked him into running. Still, when Boggs filed, no big-name Democrat wanted to run against him. So Joe could walk into the nomination. He'd run statewide, at age twenty-nine. Even if he lost, he'd make his name . . . but Joe didn't think he'd lose.

Neilia believed . . . she knew Joe could do it—they'd do it together, door-to-door, like they did the Council race. Mom-Mom would do the coffees—hundreds, before it was over. Brother Jimmy—he was twenty-four—he'd do finance. And sister Val, twenty-seven—she'd run the campaign, like she'd always run Joe's campaigns, since he ran for class president in high school.

That was about it, at the start: family, and a couple of friends who couldn't bet against Joe. Joe's pal from Syracuse, Roger Harrison, dropped his business career and came to help out—he did ads. Joe put the Biden rush on a lawyer in town, Roy Wentz, and he signed on. Wentz was tax counsel at du Pont, had a world of connections. But Joe's needs were basic: first thing Wentz did was buy up all of du Pont's secondhand office salvage—battered old steel desks and chairs. The campaign was working out of Mom-Mom's basement.

Joe knew he needed more than desks, more than volunteer kids from the Friends' School, where Val taught (she told them she'd flunk them if they didn't help). He'd seen this thing so many times in his head—he knew how it had to be.

For one thing, he needed experts. He had to know his stuff, better than anyone. He wouldn't even turn thirty (as the Constitution required for Senators) until two weeks *after* the vote. He was asking voters to make a hell of a leap. He had to show he could handle the job. So he'd spend all day talking with professors, days at a time with a guy named Dolan, a foreign relations specialist from the University of Delaware. Joe probably should have been knocking on doors, but he had to feel on top of his game.

The other thing he needed was money. Of course, Jimmy had the Biden brass balls. He'd knock on doors all over the country . . . but big givers didn't want to hear from the twenty-four-year-old brother of a twenty-nine-year-old hopeful, making his first run against Cale Boggs . . . Joe who?

So they raised money in dribs and drabs—crab feasts and backyard picnics. Then they'd spend days arguing how to use it. They must have drawn up five hundred budgets—still didn't have any money. A hundred dollars was a big deal. There was only one thousand-dollar contribution, and that had to be funneled secretly through the Democratic Senatorial Campaign Committee— it came from a partner at Cale Boggs's law firm.

Bobbie Greene, Neilia's college friend, was in Washington as a researcher for the Kennedy Library, and she introduced Joe to a few liberal thinkers and doers in the capital. They were the ones who saw what he could become. There was something about the kid, something fresh and clean, and sure about the way he handled himself. So he started getting money from national do-good groups, the Council for a Livable This, the Committee for Responsible That. And they put Joe with some campaign ops—a young guru from Boston named Marttila; a kid still at Harvard, but a hell of a pollster, named Caddell . . . see, they weren't going to give to a campaign that didn't have *professionals.*

But it was Joe who called the shots—Joe and Neilia. She was still the only one who could slow him down, or shut him up. He'd get all hot and bothered . . . something someone said . . . and Neilia'd tell him: "Joe, you don't say *anything* about that. That will pass. Don't make an enemy of him." Neilia now had their one-year-old, Amy, besides the boys. ("I'm not a keep-'em-barefoot-and-pregnant man," Joe had told the local paper. "But I'm all for keeping 'em pregnant until I have a little girl. The only good thing in the *world* is kids. . . .") Still, Neilia spoke at coffees, worked with the volunteers. She was out there, day after day.

Joe was the one who kept the campaign from sliding into liberal orthodoxy. He did raise his voice against the Vietnam War, but he never would make it the centerpiece of his campaign. He never went for busing, either—that didn't make sense to him, or to his friends, or to Mom-Mom's friends. Gun control—

why the hell would he bring *that* up? There were two farm counties downstate where everybody had guns . . . Joe meant to listen to those folks.

He was so sure he knew where the people stood. They were like him, he was like them. That's what he had to show—that he wasn't some millionaire from Brandywine Hundred, or a whiz kid from Harvard, come to straighten them out. No, he'd be *their* voice . . . he'd stand up for them. Even if it meant picking a fight. You know, Cale Boggs, sweet old man—"He really is a nice guy," Joe would say—but could you see him picking a fight? Standing up to Nixon? Forget it!

The people had been failed by their leaders, their government—that's what Joe said in his speech at the state convention. He didn't have to say they'd been failed by Boggs. When Joe's literature promised an activist Senator . . . he didn't have to say Boggs seldom sponsored a bill. When Joe talked about government letting corporations get away with no taxes, or government that hadn't got serious about pollution, or government that failed to manage the war, the budget, drugs, crime . . . he didn't have to say Boggs failed. If Joe could just get Boggs on stage, he wouldn't have to say anything about him: there they'd be, in the glare, Joe and old Cale, and Joe was twenty-nine, graceful, eager and strong, friendly, funny, smart, well dressed, well groomed, well versed . . . people would *see.*

Problem was, why would Boggs engage? Only twenty percent of the voters knew Biden's name. Joe was working animal days—door-to-door in the suburbs, the beaches at the shore. But, hell, it was summertime—what did people care? The good news was, when people knew Joe, eighty percent were for him.

That's when they started singing that song, that summer, at headquarters:

> *To know know knooow him . . .*
> *Is to love love luh-uhve him . . .*

That was Val and the kids—the volunteers. Val had hundreds now. It was a children's crusade. Of course, in '72, when the young were taking over the earth, that's how a lot of campaigns ran, but with Biden, it was like Beatlemania. Those kids adored him, and Val, and handsome Jimmy and Frankie. They'd do anything for the Bidens.

That's what made it destiny. That was the first year the eighteen-year-olds could vote . . . it was *important.* And after Labor Day, when school was back in, and the kids started talking to their friends, and their parents, it wasn't a campaign, it was a movement.

That's when everybody started to pay attention. Biden had these tabloids—sharp stuff, well designed, black-and-white: they told his story. And to save money, they never hit the mail. Every piece, to every house, was hand-delivered by those kids—*every door in the state,* all at once . . . a new piece, without fail, every weekend.

Then Joe was on the radio—all over the radio. They didn't have the money for Philadelphia TV, but Joe had a great radio voice—clear and calm, not too fast. He'd go to a shopping center and ask the people—man on the street—was it fair when millionaires paid no taxes? Well, Joe didn't think so, either. "I'm Joe Biden," he'd tell the folks at the mall. "Would you give me a chance?"

Then he started showing up in newspaper ads, on billboards . . . bus signs. The kid was everywhere! With that beautiful shining smile! . . . By the time Boggs woke up, it was late in the game—Joe was on a roll. You could see the sureness settling on him, like a blessing, the way he'd talk to folks—not about Washington mumbo-jumbo—about their lives, and his. They wanted to be with him. They were sure he could do it.

Boggs finally came out to meet him—just like Joe had dreamed: Joe and old Cale, toe-to-toe . . . it was perfect. At one point . . . and this was the key, this was the ball game, High Noon . . . they were face-to-face on stage, and some wise-ass asked a trick question about a treaty—the General Amnesty Treaty, or some such arcana. Joe happened to know what it was—he'd heard from Professor Dolan. But Boggs was confused. He stumbled around. Poor old guy looked terrible! So it came to Biden—and he *knew*—he could've *slammed* the guy . . . but, no. That was the key. Joe knew exactly how he had to be. If the beloved sixty-three-year-old did not know what the General Amnesty Treaty was . . . well, there was only one thing for a twenty-nine-year-old to say:

"Aw, I don't know that one either . . ."

That was the moment Joe knew he had him. It was destiny.

Boggs still had the papers—the *News* and *Journal* were owned by du Pont, and du Pont was the Republican Party. Boggs had a special insert planned . . . but then, the papers got hit by a strike. No one would see any Boggs insert.

Boggs still had the big name, most of the unions, the machinable vote . . . with cold rain forecast for Election Day—a low turnout—he could still pull it off. But then the wind blew fresh from the west, blew the rain out to sea, and Election Day came bright and clear, a *gorgeous* day . . . there would be no low turnout.

And the kids were everywhere at the polls, or driving voters with their parents' cars . . . they'd come too far now to let one vote slip. And Joe was out all day, and Neilia, and Mom-Mom, and Mom-Mom's friends. . . . Val had the state wired like a war zone.

And still, when the polls closed, no one could know. The Bidens gathered at a pasta joint. Joe, Sr., came in early, hauled himself up on a barstool and said, "Well, no one can say the kid didn't run a good race . . ." Even after dinner, they figured they'd better get to the hotel. Joe had insisted on the biggest ballroom in the state—the Hotel du Pont. What if it was empty? It'd look terrible if the family didn't show up soon.

But the Bidens were the last people in. Fire marshals closed the doors. It looked like the whole state was there, cheering . . . as the totals climbed, neck and neck, through the night . . . until it was clear, at last: Biden had won, with a margin of three thousand votes.

It was the next day, Joe and Neilia were in the car, when he looked at her—God, her smile that day!—and said: "Something's gonna happen . . .

"I don't know," he said. "But it's too perfect. Can't be like this. Something's gonna happen."

—★—

Even when they got the call about Kinnock, no one was worried . . . not about that. They had High Noon with Bork in four days.

Of course, the call was serious—the *Times*. Worse, it was Maureen Dowd. Rasky and Donilon knew the lineup: Dowd was the prima donna of the politics beat—whatever she wrote got play.

Still, it wasn't Mayday. The way Maureen was asking about Joe's close at the Iowa debate, it wasn't like she was chasing a scandal. It was a tweak—a one-day tweak. Donilon got on the phone: "Maureen, we're in the biggest Constitutional fight in fifty years, and you want to know whether Biden's great-grandfather was a coal miner?"

Alas, Joe had no coal-miner forebears . . . but he wasn't worried. There must have been a hundred reporters at the fairgrounds, and *not one* asked about the close. Most of them had heard him do the Kinnock stuff before—with credit. For Chrissake, the *Times* had covered the Kinnock stuff—with credit . . . when was that? Must have been a month ago! They had to get that story from their own paper—right? They had to see, he wasn't trying to fool anyone. . . .

Saturday, when the story hit, Ridley went to Union Station for the *Times*. He tore through it—every page—couldn't find a word. Great, he thought, they'd held it for Sunday. Gonna be page 42. . . . It wasn't till he closed the paper, he saw the piece . . . on the *front page*.

Joe was in Washington, with brother Jimmy, for the christening of Jimmy and Michele's new daughter, Caroline Nicole. That was an event Joe would never miss. Blood of my blood, as Mom-Mom always said.

Jill was in Iowa—she was campaigning alone all the time now—and when she called, she was sky-high: the people were so nice! (The ladies baked cookies, put them in her motel room!) They were glad to see her, they listened . . . they understood why Joe couldn't be there. They *wanted* him in Washington. *No one* was for Bork. . . . "That's great, honey," Joe said. He only talked about the christening, little Caroline, and Jimmy's party in the afternoon.

It was after the party, Jimmy and Michele flicked on the TV—CBS news with Connie Chung . . . there was Joe . . . and Kinnock. Shit, the story looked *awful* on TV. Ken Bode, on NBC, was worse. He ran the tape of Kinnock—then the same words from Joe . . . more Kinnock . . . then more Joe. It looked like Joe didn't just steal the words, it looked like he ripped off Kinnock's life!

Jimmy Biden had a nose for trouble, and for a brother's need. He was on the phone to Joe's house right away, and the next day, on his way to Wilmington.

—★—

It was Jimmy who got the call about Neilia, December 18, 1972. Joe and Val had gone to Washington, to interview staff. That month after the election was a whirlwind. There was a new life to make.

Joe had to people a new office in D.C., and one in Wilmington. He had to find a house in Washington—hey, he found a house! Hell of a deal!

The moving, of course, fell to Neilia. She had a ton of stuff to do, a list that never got shorter. She needed new beds—twins for the boys' room, a double for the guest room, a double for the master bed, a dresser . . . new rugs—green for the dining room, she knew exactly the shade, a deep oriental for the living room . . . and she'd have the two green chairs reupholstered, and the Williamsburg chair, and she had to find a mirror and a table for the hall . . . meanwhile, Christmas! Kids didn't care about moving . . . it was Christmas! So she got them all in the station wagon, Hunt in the front with her, Beau and baby Amy in the backseat, and drove off to shop. She was at a stop sign, just pulling out, when . . .

The truck smashed into her side of the car and drove it sideways a hundred and fifty feet, finally off the road, backward, into an embankment, where it crashed into three trees and came to a stop.

People ran from the road. *Ambulance!* . . .

The car was so bad, they didn't know who she was—until they saw the Biden brochures fluttering about the trees.

— ★ —

Jimmy took the call at the campaign office—a friend who worked with the state police. Neilia and the kids were in an accident—no information yet. They're on their way to the hospital.

Jimmy called Senator Byrd's office in Washington—was Joe there? No one knew where he was.

Then Jimmy heard it on the radio. *Jesus! Joe's going to find out* . . . so he called Washington again, with a message: "Come home . . . I'm on my way to the hospital."

Jimmy got the state police to pick up his parents, to get Frankie out of school. He called the family doctor to meet them at the hospital—at least he'd take care of the parents. He called the Hunters' doctor, in Syracuse, and told him to find Neilia's folks, and call Jimmy back, when he was at their side.

Fifteen minutes later, Jimmy got to the hospital. People were starting to gather outside the emergency room—public and press. Jimmy told the cops to keep them out.

The doctors came out to find him: "We lost Neilia and the baby."

The boys were still being worked on—broken hips, legs, arms. Beau was all cut up, and Hunter—concussion. Doctors weren't sure . . . brain damage possible. They'd have to transfer Hunt—another hospital, top pediatrics . . . they had to get Beau into traction . . . could Jimmy identify the bodies?

The family was all in the room when Joe burst in. One look, and Jimmy saw: Joe didn't know.

Jimmy told him.

For a split second, Jimmy saw in his brother's eyes that look—pleading.

. . . He just wanted Jimmy to tell him—no, it wasn't so. A mistake. A mix-up. It was . . . an instant—the only time he'd ever seen Joe helpless.

Then Joe asked to see his boys.

—★—

Then, the fucking ghouls started to show.

Oh, they're so sorry . . .

Oh, they can't believe it, it's so awful . . .

Someone who went to sewing class with Mom-Mom:

I understand . . .

What the fuck do you understand? What the fuck did any of them know?

Joe went with Hunt in the ambulance, for the transfer. "I'm gonna be right with you, son." Tests. X-rays. Skull fracture.

Then he was back, with Beau. Joe wasn't leaving.

The Hunters came down, right away. They couldn't accept. They had to see Neilia. Joe had to go with them. That was the worst. Jimmy went with Joe.

Jimmy stayed with Joe. It was raining. Hunt was back. They moved the boys to a private room. The boys' legs were going into spasms. Shots, IVs, traction. Joe wouldn't leave. He focused. The boys. This boy. His leg. Raise the bed. That lever. That cloth. Wet the cloth. . . . His boys were all that was left.

Joe watched over his boys.

The family closed ranks around Joe.

What the fuck did anyone else know?

64

Where
Do They
Stop?

HEY DIDN'T DO BADLY with the Kinnock story, considering. . . . By Sunday, one day after, Rasky had a good spin going—the *Post* did a rebuttal on the *Times,* pointing out that Biden had credited the Kinnock stuff in a half-dozen speeches, all over the country.

Meanwhile, the story showed up in Iowa. David Yepsen, the big-foot-in-a-small-pond for *The Des Moines Register,* had done the piece same day as Dowd . . . but Yepsen made sure to note: a tape (the "attack video," he dubbed it) of Biden and Kinnock had been provided *by a rival campaign.* So Rasky was pushing that, too: Who would be so dastardly as to attack Joe Biden, Defender of the Constitution . . . on the eve of the most important hearings of the century? . . . Was White House skullduggery behind this?

In fact, Joe had told Jimmy, he thought the White House was bound to come after him, once it dawned on the Reaganauts that their beloved judge might go down the tubes.

And Caddell was stomping around Joe's house—*sure* it was Shrum. Now that Doak and Shrum were working for Gephardt . . . *come on!* . . . Wasn't it just like that snake Shrum? He'd do *anything* to bleed Pat's candidate.

Everybody was at the house for the big rehearsal, day before the hearings. Tribe was playing Bork in the ballroom again. They had Scott Miller, from David Sawyer's firm, to work the videotapes . . . watched by the committee staff, the campaign staff, the Wilmington staff, the family . . . it looked like a wedding.

It was the finals of the U.S. Open that day, so between takes, everybody watched tennis. That day, a magazine had printed Gail Sheehy's latest opus, a machine-gun attack on Gary Hart . . . and everyone who'd ever known him. Hart had been out of the race for months—and she was still driving her heels into his skull. Joe couldn't believe it.

"Shit, I mean, she says he was *lousy at tennis . . . in high school!*"

But that wasn't Biden's life. People were *welcome* to look at Biden's life. And they would! Ridley told Joe that day: "By the end of this week, you're gonna be a household name in America."

Joe said: "That's what I'm afraid of." Just joking.

They joked a lot that day, until dark—people were leaving—when Rasky got the call from *The San Jose Mercury News.* He called the reporter back from Joe's kitchen phones.

The reporter asked:

What about these lines from the California speech? . . . Weren't those lifted? You know, *plagiarized*? They were straight from Bobby Kennedy!

— ★ —

They wanted character? They wanted to see what he was made of? . . . Biden would show them. He and the staff jerked around the opening-day schedule so the chairman's statement would come last—in the afternoon, when the networks were running live.

Meanwhile, let everybody else have his say. Alan Simpson, the Republican whip, started in on the process—how self-important we Senators are, as judges of the judges (when Simpson slips into his Will Rogers mode, he can aw-shucks the Senate for hours). "And, once in this room, unlike a defendant in a court of law, the nominee is not guaranteed any single right . . ."

After that, Biden broke in, and in the span of fifteen seconds, he dispensed with complaints about his fairness—one smile and a jaunty wave of his gavel . . . a gorgeous sound-bite:

"Judge Bork, I guarantee you that this little mallet is going to assure you *every single right* for you to make your views known . . . as long as it takes, on *any* ground you wish to make them. That's a guarantee [Biden smile]. So you do have rights in this room, and I will assure you they will be protected."

Joe Biden, Defender of the Constitution! (And, lo, even its wayward disciples.) That bite showed up on the news that night, along with Biden's noble prose about the God-given rights of mankind.

In the grand Senate Caucus Room, an echoing temple of marble pilasters and an acre of tables for the nation's press, eyebrows raised as Biden laid it on ever thicker: the terrific respect Bork's record inspired . . . the awesome Constitutional scholarship that Bork's writings bespoke . . . the difficulty which the citizenry (and certainly a plain ol' workin' lawyer like *Joe Biden*) might have, following the elegant reason of Bork's jurisprudence. . . .

It was cloying. But as Biden swung into his questions, he knew *exactly* . . . how he had to be. He was the eager student, trying to understand—you know, in the common words . . . why it was, that the venerated judge . . . ("I'm not trying to be picky here; I mean, clearly, I don't want to get into a debate with a *professor,* but . . .") *why* did Bork think it was okay to put cops in our bedrooms?

Why did Bork say a married couple had no more right to be free in their bed than a company had to be free of pollution laws?

"I mean," Joe said, through a bristle of Biden smile, "isn't that what you're saying?"

And Bork fell into the quicksand. He played professor to eager Joe.

"No, not entirely," he said. "But I'll straighten it out. I was objecting to the way Justice Douglas, in that opinion, Griswold against Connecticut, derived this right. It may be possible to derive an objection to an anticontraceptive statute in some other way—I don't know. But starting from the assumption—which is an assumption for the purposes of my argument, not a proven fact—starting from the assumption that there is nothing in the Constitution in any legitimate method of Constitutional reasoning about either subject, all I'm saying is that the judge has no way to prefer one to the other, and the matter should be left to the legislatures, who will then decide which competing ratification or freedom should be placed higher."

Biden nodded, concerned, through his smile. "Well, then, I think I do understand it . . ."

Yes, he did. Bork kept talking about originalist jurisprudence, neutral principles of Constitutional reasoning, the bankruptcy of the theory of penumbral emanations . . . while Biden talked about *cops in our bedrooms!*

The text of this exchange would take up a full page in the next day's *New York Times.* Biden just wanted to be sure, you know . . . he could understand, *exactly* . . .

Bork couldn't see any right of privacy—not in the reasoning of *that* case . . . right?

Some other case?

Well, no.

"Well, can you tell me . . ." Biden's voice was honey. "You've been a professor now for years and years . . . everybody's pointed out, and I've observed, you're one of the most *well read* and *scholarly* people to come before this committee . . . in all your [Biden smile] short life . . . have you come up with any other way to protect a married couple, under the Constitution, against an action by a government, telling them what they can or cannot do about birth control in their bedroom? Is there any Constitutional right . . . anywhere in the Constitution?

Bork: "I assume . . . I have never engaged in that exercise . . ."

BANGO!

In the boiler room that the gurus set up outside Joe's office, there were whoops of delight. "*That exercise! . . .*"

"That's it," they told Joe, when the hearings closed.

"You *got* him."

"God, that *answer*!"

But Biden was without elation.

That night, he didn't hang around. He went to dinner with Jimmy and Val. He was quiet, wary . . . every network news show had the same two stories at the top of the show: Bork's debacle . . . and Biden's copied speeches.

"What we didn't figure," Joe said at dinner, "was the stakes—the Court . . . and the White House."

Joe didn't talk about Bork that night, but about Jimmy's bankruptcy, Val's divorce, his own law school course where they flunked him, he didn't footnote . . .

It was sinking in on Joe. There were people he didn't even know who'd sooner destroy him than see him win. And the press didn't care. If they had to make Biden the issue, they would. What the fuck did they care about Biden?

"I don't see . . ." Joe said. "I mean, I don't see there's anywhere they stop . . ."

65

Just,
Why?

THE HOSPITAL was in a tough neighborhood, bad streets, and dark. If the boys could sleep, Joe and Jimmy would walk those streets, half the night. They'd tell the nurses they were going out for pizza . . . but they wouldn't eat.

They didn't even talk. The sound was their shoes on grit, or broken glass. . . . Joe was hoping someone would jump out from an alley, come at him. He would've killed the guy. He was looking for a fight. There was no place for his rage.

Sometimes he thought it would be easier . . . if he were the only one left . . . then he could kill himself. It was the boys, kept him alive.

He wasn't alone. Jimmy saw to that, and Mom-Mom, every day . . . and Val, who would move into his house, into Northstar. . . . But Joe *was* alone . . . or worse. He'd lost himself.

It wasn't even, *Why me?*

Just, *Why?*

Neilia never did anything . . . she took care of everyone. *His daughter!* She was the closest thing on this earth to perfect. They called her Caspy because she looked like Casper, the Friendly Ghost. His joke . . .

He used to say . . . he . . .

What did he matter? He didn't. That was obvious. All of it, all of them—all they'd done—*did not matter*. Gone.

People came up to him, talked about the Senate . . . his friends, told him he had to take his seat.

"That's what you are, Joe, you're a Senator."

What did they know about what he was? He didn't give a damn about the Senate. That wasn't what he was. What was he?

He functioned. He talked to them, told them thanks. Or he thought he did. He didn't know what he said. What'd it matter?

Mike Mansfield would call every day, talk to Jimmy. How's Joe? We gotta get him down here. We gotta get him occupied. We gotta get him back in the mainstream. Mansfield was great, like the other older Senators. Hubert Humphrey was a man of infinite compassion.

Jimmy told them not to come for the funeral.

Joe wanted no one but family at the funeral.

There was grumbling in Delaware—people had to pay respects.

Fuck *them*.

It rained the night of the memorial service, rained like hell, and people lined up. They felt they had to come. Bob Byrd was there, standing in the rain, waiting.

Joe would remember that, in the Senate. He was going to the Senate. At least, he'd try . . . try to be a father, and a Senator. He took his oath in the hospital, with the boys, and the cameras. People thought it was some kind of stunt.

Fuck *them*.

—★—

Second day of the Bork hearings, when they got the call about the law school stuff, Rasky didn't know anything about it. Donilon didn't know. They asked Jimmy.

"Oh, yeah, that . . ."

What the hell did Jimmy mean—oh, that?

"Joe was just talking about that, at dinner."

Jimmy told them the outline—one course, Joe flunked. Someone thought he was trying to cheat, but he wasn't. It was just a mistake.

That day, they asked Joe's old law school friend, Bob Osgood, a partner now in a New York firm, to fly up to Syracuse, get the records, bring them back. Osgood was back in five hours.

That was already too long. The press calls were coming in from everywhere. That was the scary thing. Everybody in the country was hunting up something on Joe.

The first to ask about law school was *Legal Times* . . . then CBS . . . then the papers. They were all talking to *someone* . . . or to each other. Biden was a *plagiarist*—from twenty years ago! . . . It was so *neat*! . . . The pack smelled blood again.

A guy from the *Journal* had a jones about Joe never taking a drink. He *must* have had a drink sometime. *The Wall Street Journal* was out to *prove*—Biden must've had a drink sometime.

The Philadelphia Inquirer was sniffing around Joe's civil rights claims.

. . . That, and the *Inquirer* meant to prove: Joe didn't *really* give the high school graduation speech.

There was an endless rolling meeting in Joe's conference room. Val and Jimmy, of course, and Donilon, Caddell, Marttila, Ridley, Rasky, Ted Kaufman, Vallely, Lowell Junkins from Iowa, Bill Daley from Chicago . . . they lurched from crisis to crisis.

Joe had to do the hearings. Bork was still at the witness table. The cameras were rolling. The nation was watching. Biden extended the lunch break so he could call the dean of Syracuse Law, make sure he gave the records to Osgood.

The hearings were perfect. The national polls were turning against Bork. On the committee, Dennis DeConcini probably would vote against the nomination. God only knew about Heflin, but Joe thought they might get Specter, a Republican. The votes were going to fall into place—unless it turned into Bork . . . against Biden, the cheater, the plagiarist. Then it would all be lost. In the afternoon, Joe met with the committee, privately: he offered to resign the chair. But no, they backed him, they knew him: he was doing fine.

Was he? He searched their eyes—they were for him. When he got back into the chair, Strom Thurmond came at him about the witness list . . . and the schedule—when were they going to vote? Strom wanted a date. . . . Donilon needed to talk to Joe in the back room: Who was the high school speech teacher? Spell the name? Is he alive? . . . Bork was speaking, but the cameras shifted briefly to Joe. He was bent toward old Strom, on his right, with his hand up, asking Thurmond to pause, while his left hand reached toward the glass on the table. He had to take a pill.

It was late, after the hearings, when Joe got to look at the law school stuff. In fact, he'd asked for the records before, back in May—but he'd stuck them in a drawer at home. Now he tore through the file in earnest. Jesus! Those marks! . . . God, there's his paper . . .

But that wasn't it . . . it had to be someplace—the letter from the dean, when he passed the bar. Here!

At his desk, Joe read out the letter, to Osgood, to the gurus and staff who were roaming the room. "Listen: . . . 'Mr. Biden is a gentleman of high moral character. His records reflect nothing whatsoever of a derogatory nature, and there is nothing to indicate the slightest question about his integrity, industry or ability. . . . Sincerely, Robert W. Miller, Dean.'

"Let's give this stuff out," Joe said.

"All of it?"

"Everything—just give it out. Questions, we'll do a press conference."

There was a boil of guru-foam all over the floor.

"Joe, wait, that's not how . . ."

"Senator, we ought to write out something . . ."

"After Bork, we . . ."

"Gotta give the press their pound of flesh . . ."

"You admit you plagiarized, but you know, you were young . . ."

At his desk, Joe fell silent. He watched their eyes. And he saw: they didn't believe him—*his guys* didn't believe him.

They wanted him to admit he cheated. They thought he cheated. They weren't looking at him when they talked. They looked at each other. Their eyes held fear, calculation.

"No—we go out there now, we're gonna get hammered on the news tonight, anyway . . ."

"Thing is, we get on top of this tomorrow . . ."

Tactics . . . and they didn't see this was his honor—why would they see? What the hell did they care?

Joe's eyes fell to the file—his letter, that he wrote the dean, when the deal went down.

November 30, 1965 . . .

It has been my aspiration, for as long as I can remember, to study the law, and now that there is a possibility that this desire will never be fulfilled I am heartsick, but this I could eventually overcome. However, the indelible stain which would mar my reputation would remain with me the rest of my life for being branded a cheat. This I could never overcome. I am aware that, in many instances, ignorance of the law is no excuse. Consequently, if you decide that this is such an instance and that I've broken the law, then any course of action on your part is justified. But please, I implore you, don't take my honor. If your decision is that I may not remain at Syracuse University College of Law, please allow me to resign, but don't label me a cheat.

Joe's eyes lifted to the office, the gurus. They were still talking.

". . . press conference, 9:00 A.M., before the hearing . . ."

"Yeah, we should rehearse it. Q and A . . ."

But they weren't really talking to him. The one who met his eyes was Jimmy . . . and they knew, they were alone.

— ★ —

Val moved into the house: when the boys came home from the hospital, she was there to take care. Jimmy stayed with Joe. Not to help—not obviously—that was the last thing Joe wanted. Jimmy was just there, four o'clock in the morning, when the last TV movie proved itself a dud. . . . If Joe wanted to talk, they talked. Otherwise, silence.

Joe had enough talk all day. The Senate was half bullshit, posture. Old men, full of wind. Talk, talk, talk. Politeness. Joe didn't know anymore how he was going to be—he didn't have the will to dream—but he sure as hell wasn't gonna be like them.

They showed him in a thousand ways they wanted to make him part of their club, but . . . what was their club for? That was half the problem: they were trying to be so nice. Teddy Kennedy sent a shrink up to Wilmington, for the boys . . . Kennedys knew about loss. Half the guys in the Senate invited Joe . . . to this dinner, that trip, their weekend place . . . but no, Joe would go home to his sons.

Oh . . . they understood.

They were so grave, solicitous. No one could talk about Joe without mention of the "terrible circumstance." The papers seemed to have a line of type that fell out of the machine every time they used Biden's name: ". . . whose life was touched by personal tragedy . . ."

Joe Biden (D-Del., T.B.P.T.).

Joe was so sick of it, he could puke. What did they know? He wanted to make them swallow their words. They'd start on him in committee, *commending* the young Senator from Delaware for his *fine work* on the bill . . . all the more *notable* because of the *"terrible circumstance"* . . . *T.B.P.T.* What they'd get from Biden was a snarl: "Thank you very much, but, uh, this befalls a lot of families, and we're, uh, talking about an issue here, so . . ."

So, fuck you. Shut up and deal.

They called him "brash," but he'd always been brash. You don't go after Cale Boggs and knock him off, at age twenty-nine, without being *brash*. But this was different . . . this had a bitter edge of contempt. Because Biden knew: they were *specks*, just like him . . . all their bullshit *did not matter*.

What he liked was saying the unvarnished truth, to make them squirm in their seats. When the Senators were dancing like Siamese virgins around the issue of a raise for themselves, it was Joe who stood up to say: "I don't know about the rest of you guys, but I'm worth a helluva lot more'n forty-two thousand."

When he stepped up to the podium for a speech to four thousand noisy muldoons of the Philadelphia Democratic City Committee, he got that crowd quiet in a hurry: "I've been in thirty-two states, and you're the worst damn audience anywhere," Biden said. He started to laugh. "I hope you can get out the vote like you talk, because you sure talk like hell . . . you're all a bunch of bums."

What he liked was the car phone on the long drive: Wilmington to Washington, and back, two hours, each way, every day. He'd call the boys three times each way. "Beau-y, what're you doin' now? . . ."

What he liked, was . . . well, there wasn't much.

66

That Is
the Process

I T WAS BETTER after the press conference—not that Joe knocked it out of
the park, but he had his say. He was,
by turns, humbly apologetic, then defiant. It reflected pretty well where he
stood.

He'd meant to be penitent. He had to bow to the press . . . which he did
in his opening statement:

"Ladies and gentlemen, I've been *dumb*. I did something very stupid,
twenty-three years ago . . ."

But then he asked for questions. And as much as he tried . . . as much as
he knew, in his head . . . well, he couldn't stop that hot juice rising in his craw.
They wanted him to say he was a *cheat*?

Fuck *them*.

What did they know about him? . . . Or care?

Someone had the gall to ask how he could represent himself as the leader
of the baby-boom generation, when he hadn't even, you know . . . *marched
against the war*?

Where the hell did they get off, questioning *his life*? He answered for fifteen
minutes straight, almost without a breath, with his voice rising, his chin jutting
out in sudden jerks, like his collar was tight.

". . . And look, I was twenty-nine when I ran for the Senate, folks. Other
people were marching, carrying banners. . . . I am not culturally one of those
guys who likes to—I don't fit very well, with—I'm not a joiner. I was, I was
out of synch with—by the time the war movement was at its peak, when I was

at Syracuse—I was married. I was in law school. I wore sport coats. I was not part of that. I'm serious! What you all don't seem to understand is—some of you, I think you understand, and I don't think . . . well, I won't characterize it—but, you know, there was a four-year period, folks, there's uh, uhh . . . light-years back, when I was on a college campus—those of you who go back with me, 1961–65—Vietnam was like Nicaragua is now. We all said, 'That's kind of stupid, but it's gonna end.' Well, you don't see many people marching on campuses. Go up to my son's campus in Philadelphia, or go down south, or go out west, it's nothing like the antiwar movement. That's about where Vietnam was in 1963, '64, and '65. So, I find, you all know better than: 'Well, where were YOU, Senator Biden, at the time?' You know, I think it's bizarre. I think it's *bizarre*! And THEN . . . when the movement *did* catch up, I was a twenty-three-year-old guy, married. And look: you're looking at a middle-class guy. I am who I am. I'm not big on flak jackets and tie-dye shirts, and, you know, that's not me. I'm serious! But that's the period. But I want to get this straight, man. Because I keep gettin' asked this all the time, and I'm not gonna get this many of you in a room again until I'm inaugurated, so . . ."

(At that point his staff burst into applause. But Joe wasn't done.)

". . . The second thing is, *when I got finished* . . . when I got finished—law school—I came back, I . . . the most important thing to me, in my life, is my family. And I got back, and I was gonna have a baby. Flat out. That's what was important to ME. And I was gonna take the bar exam—which was a bear—you know. I mean, I hated law school. I really did. But by the way, go out and ask *anybody* in Delaware whether you think I was not a *good lawyer,* and ask *any client* I represented whether they think they didn't get their *money's worth.* And ask anybody in Delaware that ever watched me *try a case,* and tell me that I wasn't a good trial lawyer. Go find anybody! I was a good lawyer. I am a good lawyer. And if you want to find out more about *that,* come down at ten o'clock, down at the hearing. So, you know, folks, I don't under-stand this. Now, how many other people twenty-nine years old *did* something about the war? I'm the guy who asked the Foreign Relations Committee—when Gerald Ford said he had a plan to end it—I remember, and some of you will remember, I looked at, at, uhm, Senator *Case* . . . so I asked: 'Why don't we ask to go see the President, and ask him what the plan IS?' . . . And they said, 'Well, no one ever does that.' And I said, 'Well why not?' And I remember, Jack Javits standing there, and saying, 'Well, it's not a bad idea. Let me call Henry.' And they called Henry Kissinger, and we all went down and, I think, if not the first time, but one of the few times in history that the entire Foreign Relations Committee went down and sat with the President and with the Secretary of State, and everybody played *pattycake.* Everybody went down and said, 'Yes, Mr. President.' 'No, Mr. President.' They were very polite. And I was young. I was thirty, I guess, then. And I'll never forget . . . you ask some of my colleagues, who were there. I said—and I remember being scared to death, saying it—I said: 'Begging the President's pardon, Mr. President. But if the President were the Senator from Delaware, I expect the President would expect me to ask the President this question . . .' I was a *fool*. I mean, I was so nervous, asking the question. But I said: 'Mr President . . . WHAT is the PLAN? . . . With all due respect, I've heard this all my career. . . . *What* . . . is the *plan*?' I did more in that meeting than a lot of people did that marched. So I don't take a backseat to the notion that, somehow, I did not go on the line. Other people marched. I ran for office. Got elected to the United States Senate at twenty-nine, and came down here and was one of those votes that helped stop the war. And I'm proud of it."

Well, damn right, he felt better!

Still, all the Friday headlines said:

BIDEN ADMITS PLAGIARISM

They didn't have room to deal with his life.

That's what Jill kept trying to tell him . . . he called her from Washington, night before the press conference, and she said, it wasn't about his life. It was politics. Life was something else.

Joe couldn't separate the two. But it did him good to hear it. She asked him, was there anything he wanted her to do?

"Just call me at five to nine. I just want to hear your voice, last thing before I go in there."

Now, when it was over, he only wanted to be home. What did these Washington bastards know about home?

Friday afternoon, Judge Bork was still the witness. Everybody wanted to wrap this thing up . . . but Biden wanted one more colloquy, and Thurmond wanted time, and Specter, DeConcini, Humphrey, Simpson . . . there was no way out—they'd have to come back Saturday.

Biden, Thurmond, with the staff and Bork's handlers, worked out the schedule: ten-thirty Saturday morning . . . then they'd finish, for sure. But ten minutes later, Biden interrupted to ask Judge Bork: "Would you mind if we started at twelve? That make a difference to you? . . ."

See, Joe had promised his son Hunter: Saturday morning—the *Archmere* game.

— ★ —

The royalty of Archmere doesn't sit in the grandstand at the fifty-yard line. Royals stand on the grassy rise that overlooks the field, as Father Diny used to do when he'd show up to halt practice. Justin Diny, retired headmaster, was there for the Christiana game, standing ramrod straight in a ratty civilian jacket and dark corduroy cap. The cold made the veins show through the skin over Diny's strong nose and brow.

It was a mortification to Joe that Father Diny had got involved in this mess. When *The Philadelphia Inquirer* meant to prove that Joe hadn't *really* been the graduation speaker, it was Diny who raked up his yearbooks, his memory. No, Diny had to say, Joey Biden was not the graduation speaker, but as president of the senior class (Father Diny had not let Biden run for student council president—too many demerits—Joe was crushed), Biden did welcome his classmates and their parents. Surely, that could count as a speech.

On the grass, above the field, three generations of Bidens clumped together in the chill. Mom-Mom was in front, with Jill next to her. Ashley played nearby. Brother Frankie was up in the spotters' booth, playing at assistant coach. Janine, his wife, was with the other Bidens, watching to see if Hunter, number 27, halfback/cornerback, would get into the game.

Joe was standing in a stiff little raincoat, talking to Father Diny. Joe started to tell about the letter he'd written the day before to the people at Archmere. He wanted them to know he hadn't forgotten all they'd taught him, the sense of honor, responsibility.

Father Diny interrupted to tell Joe a story about the World War II pilot with this slogan on his plane: *Non illegitimi carborundum.*

Biden looked at him quizzically . . . he didn't remember much Latin.

"Loosely translated," Father Diny continued, "it means: Don't let the bastards get you down."

Archmere was up by a couple of touchdowns at the half, a shutout, and the crowd was in a good mood as the band marched onto the field. Hunt still hadn't played, but he probably would if the score held. Joe moved through the crowd on the grassy rise.

"Hey, Joe!"

"You'll get 'em, Joe. Hang in there!"

His gait grew easier as he saw they didn't believe the stuff, as they told him, one after another, "This'll blow over . . . a couple of weeks, you'll laugh about it."

Joe said: "You're nice to say so . . . thanks . . . I hope so." But to the teachers, he meant to say more.

"No, listen," he told Coach Philibin. "You know, I wrote you a letter, a long one, to everybody here. Because I want you to know I didn't cheat . . . I mean, I didn't forget what you taught me . . ."

Vince Philibin was shaking his head—he didn't need to hear it. But Joe wouldn't stop: "No, you taught me a lot, the honor . . . I just want you to know . . ."

Joe moved on to his football coach, then his history teacher: "You did really teach me. Shoulda learned more, but really, you did. . . . Amazing, really, you know, the day after the bomb drops, I'm sitting there composing . . . I mean, what I wanted to do was let the people at Archmere know I didn't, uh, I wasn't like that . . ."

Tommy Lewis showed up in the second half. The plane was waiting, the Bork hearings were waiting. But Tommy knew enough not to push.

Hunt got into the game in the fourth quarter, at 24–0. Playing halfback, he got the ball on a sweep. Joe cut off talking in mid-sentence, jumped forward, his coat billowing behind him.

"Turn it up. Turn it! All RIGHHT!"

Hunt got eight yards. But Archmere had to kick. Later, at cornerback, Hunt was burned, and the Christiana receiver took it down near the goal line. "BIDEN. DIG IN, BIDEN!" Joey screamed as the boys bulked up in a goal-line defense. Christiana ran at the line and got nothing. They ran to Hunt's side and the linebackers knocked it down for a loss. They burrowed off tackle and got the spot at the one. Fourth down, fourth quarter, shutout at stake. Christiana snapped the ball, surged forward. Hunt piled into the line. Short! They came up short! Archmere took over on downs at the one!

"Good game," Joe said, as he caught up to Tommy at the car. "Hunt did okay. One good run. Finally got some playing time . . ." They were heading out the gates to Manor Road. Joe looked for the gash he made in the concrete pillar with the bumper of his new red Chevy roadster, twenty-seven years before.

"See?" he said. "Still there."

On the hill heading toward the highway, he said: "I used to live over there. When I first came back to town . . . beautiful place."

"And then, just a few blocks over that way," Tommy said.

"God, that was a great place."

They'd been driving these streets for almost thirty years. Back and forth to this same little airport for fifteen years, as a Senator. Ted Kaufman was waiting at the plane, like always. . . . Joe was almost jovial as he strapped himself into the four-seater.

"See," Joe said, as the engines started. "This is home . . . my staff just can't understand that. This is home. Whether I get to be President or not. Or after I'm President, I've got to live here. This is my place . . ."

Ted was nodding. He lived in Wilmington, too. He'd been with Biden fifteen years. Those two didn't really talk—it was more like Ted just helped out with Joe's monologue.

"You know . . ." This was Joe. "It wasn't easy coming back here, after all this. I mean, it was a lot harder than doing the hearings. The hearings were Washington. It was almost easy. I mean, everybody in Washington is so, uh, jaded already. They don't really . . ."

Ted said: "I think they almost liked you better for it . . ."

Joe said: "Yeah, I know . . . this all started in the first term. When I was always going home, instead of . . . you know. That's when people started saying that Biden . . ."

"I mean, here's this guy who goes home every night . . . *to his family* . . ." Ted's voice became a prissy whine. "Goody-two-shoes. Doesn't drink . . ."

"Yeah, that's what this Jeffrey Birnbaum from *The Wall Street Journal* can't believe. He's making an absolute inquisition now, about whether I ever took a drink. Ever. . . . I did once. My college roommate's wedding . . ." Joey trailed off and looked out the window at the land below.

"Now, is that going to be some big . . . I sound like I'm complaining . . . that's the thing. You can't sound like you're complaining, or you're being defensive. That's the thing, at the press conference, I wanted to tell them . . ."

And Joe was back into it. He ducked for his briefcase and pulled out the law school file once again. "Look, here's the footnote—see it? . . . See what I mean? It wasn't cheating." He was searching the eyes of his own friends to make sure they believed.

"But, you know, I deserve it. This is what I get for being lazy, for not doing my work till the last day, knowing I could get by . . ."

Joe sat back with a sigh. "So they write 'Biden admits plagiarism.' So . . . that's all right."

It wasn't all right.

"But I'll tell you," he said, with new toughness in his voice, as the plane dipped toward Washington. "My learning curve on this thing is moving."

A woman from the office was waiting with a car outside the private terminal. "How are you, Senator?"

"I'm all right," Joe said firmly. "All right. Really."

— ★ —

Joe was late for the hearings . . . didn't matter. This was just the loose ends. No one was watching, Saturday afternoon, with baseball and football on TV.

Biden had his closing planned, another stirring evocation of man's fundamental rights . . . but when he closed that afternoon, he talked instead straight to Bork. This was a different tone of voice than he'd had four days before. This was not for the cameras.

"You know, Judge . . . it is a lot harder on one's family than it is on the principal, when a member of the family is undergoing any test.

"You have been undergoing a test, but that is part of the process, as you well know, Judge. No judge, no nominee, is entitled to the spot. . . . It is not a presumption automatically made, any more than it is a presumption when one of us stands for election . . . that we should be elected."

In the chair at the center of the table, in the almost empty hearing room, Biden looked older than he had four days ago. There was almost a shrug in his voice.

"That," he told Bork, "is the process."

By that time, smooth Howard Fineman had phoned Biden's committee staff to ask about the comments Joe made in New Hampshire, a few months ago. *Newsweek* had a tape, from C-Span. . . . That stuff about his IQ, and his scholarships, how he graduated with three degrees, at the top of his class . . .

By that time, what could the staff say?

What could Joe say?

That he got pissed off? It was late? His head hurt? He only meant to shut the guy up?

No, he'd have to say: he lied.

That was the process.

— ★ —

Sunday, Joe was home, but there must have been a hundred press calls (he'd never worried about giving out his number). *Newsweek* wouldn't hit the stands till the next day, but half the world seemed to know about the piece (*Newsweek* fed the story to the wires, to assure the magazine got proper credit).

Thing about the calls—they didn't want explanations. There's a difference, Joe figured, when they know what they want to write. What they wanted was a comment—to show they'd called; a no-comment was just as good. He'd explain one thing, they'd bring up another. Jill couldn't stand it. She said: "There's no way to *answer* . . .".

For Joe, the calls were a blur—accusations, from voices he knew. People he *knew* . . . or thought he knew. The moment he would always remember—when the hopeless absurdity sank in—was one call: he was trying to explain that he *did* change in law school, he *did* buckle down, he *could* argue a case . . . yes, he *did* win the moot court competition . . . really! Honest!

And Val, bless her heart, came rushing to him on the phone with a frame she'd taken off the wall—his moot court certificate. He'd forgotten it was on the wall. She *ran* . . . with this stupid framed piece of fluff, like water for a man in the desert. She carried it in both hands, *running*!

What was awful was how happy they were . . . triumphant! His moot court certificate!

67

Biden's Waterloo?

HOW COULD he stop it? His campaign was hemorrhaging. Ridley was near emotional collapse. The gurus were clueless. Joe sent Val up to sniff the wind in New Hampshire, whence she fired back a telegram: THE PEOPLE ARE WITH YOU. VICTORY IS YOURS.

But that was just Val, being a Biden. They both knew that.

No less a savant that R.W. Apple, in *The New York Times,* was beating the tribal drums under the headline: BIDEN'S WATERLOO?

(And who was Apple's featured Washington wise guy, helping to drop the dime on Joe? "What's clearly revealed here is that his intellectual habits are lazy, undisciplined and sloppy," said Apple's "campaign expert," the pilgarlic-pollster-pundit-columnist-TV-guest-part-time-Biden-guru-who-gave-Joe-the-Kinnock-tape-in-the-first-place, William Schneider. "That's a major weakness, and it will seriously damage him.")

Worse, the papers were starting to speculate on whether Biden's woes would catapult Bork onto the Court. Joe couldn't let that happen. That would inflict his failure on the country, probably for twenty years.

But he couldn't give up the chair. That would be confirmation of everything they wrote about him.

That was the bottom line: he had to keep his life out of the Bork fight. Then, he would do whatever it took—however many years it took—to set the record straight on his own life.

Monday, Joe burrowed into the hearings like a kid hiding under the porch.

Bork was off the stand. Panels of judges and legal scholars were testifying for and against the nomination. No one could get to Biden while he sat in the chair . . . he didn't even get up to pee. He kept the committee in till eleven at night, while he stared ahead, mostly silent.

It really came down to three separate issues.

There was the Bork nomination . . . and the Biden campaign. He could not go out to save the campaign at the risk of the Bork nomination. He could not even take time now to defend himself, personally. If he screwed up on Bork, that would be the end of his reputation. That was the third issue—and the big one: his word as a Biden. That was the loss he could not overcome.

— ★ —

He took time, the next day, for one meeting: a session with his Congressional supporters. They'd stood up for him proudly, at announcement, a hundred days before. Now they only wanted to know: Any more shoes gonna drop?

And Joe, a hundred days ago the proudest of all on that grand stage, had to think before he answered. When he did talk, sadly, all he could say was: "I just, honest to God, don't know."

He'd been raking through his life in his head . . . anything else someone could use?

That speech . . . that line . . . was that his? Who wrote that?

Doak and Shrum—Pat was so sure they were bleeding him—what had he confided to those guys?

Or were his own people—guys with him now—leaving the ship?

Who could say, with blood in the water?

Word was spreading in the capital: Biden was about to call it quits. Joe had told the gurus to draft a withdrawal statement.

That day, there were two hundred press calls. Rasky had the twenty-foot conference table covered with messages. He and Donilon tried to call them all: of course, the big-feet first.

E.J. Dionne, from the *Times,* was ahead of the pack on Biden's withdrawal. He was on the phone every few hours. At some point, he asked Donilon: What was the story on Jimmy Biden's bankruptcy? The *Times* was thinking of doing a story. . . . But E.J. didn't press it: there was only one big story left on Biden—was there gonna be, you know . . . any announcement tomorrow?

At the close of the hearings, Joe walked into the conference room, found Rasky with his head down, like he was studying the grain of the table. "What'sa matter now?" Biden said.

"We're getting pressure from everywhere," Rasky said. "I just talked to E.J. . . . the great Paper of Record is trying to blackmail you out."

But Joe was spinning too fast—didn't have time to deal with cases. They'd deal with it all, that night, in Wilmington. He gathered gurus and staff—Donilon and Rasky, Gitenstein and Kaufman—but not Pat. Pat just wanted to attack the press: *straight to the people* over the heads of the press—take the road even Hart feared to tread. Biden wasn't going to do that. And Joe couldn't take a fight with Caddell now. So Pat stayed in D.C. (Ridley stayed behind as a fire wall between Caddell and Joe), and Biden took the rest home with him to Wilmington.

On the train, they clumped into an Amtrak coach, planning withdrawal. In Wilmington, the guys peeled off for dinner at a pasta joint. Biden would have dinner with family alone . . . they'd all meet at Joe's house to work out the final plan.

But when they got to Biden's, there was no more plan. Joe had talked it over with the family. It looked like he was back in the race.

— ★ —

Joe paced his living room, doing the moves: he was gonna *prove* why this charge was bullshit, and that charge was bullshit. The law school thing—he'd have the head of the Delaware Supreme Court open the case, a full investigation. The Kinnock stuff he already explained—he'd used that stuff before, always with credit. The Kennedy lines—Pat already said he stuck those lines into the speech, Joe didn't know. He'd said that at the press conference. The academic record—that was tough, but he'd explain . . . it wasn't three degrees, but he'd had two majors at Delaware. He did have a scholarship. He did improve in law school. If he could just get out to make the case to the people, he knew they'd be with him.

Yeah, but when could he make the case?

The campaign was dying.

Fund-raising . . . forget it.

Rasky and Donilon, the pros, couldn't see how Joe could do it. Not all at once. Something had to go. "You've had forty million dollars of negative TV dumped on you in the last week," Donilon said.

"You know," Joe said. "I've *never* been a quitter . . . never quit anything in my *life.*"

"That's right," Beau said.

Beau was the one who made the case for staying in. Beau and Hunt were furious, and hurt. They couldn't believe their father would even *think* of getting out. This wasn't about politics, or the public—this was about their dad's honor. "You've got nothing to get out *from,*" Beau said. "All the stuff they said—there's nothing real."

It was almost eerie how alike were father and son . . . and Beau made the argument with such feeling, such intensity . . . it looked like Joe might fight it out to the death.

"If you quit now, people will think that all that stuff about you is true. If you stay," Beau said, "keep the spotlight, you can make your case directly to the people—right over the heads of the press . . ."

Then Rasky got into it with Beau: What are you talking about—over the heads of the press? How? . . . Have you been talking to Pat?

No, Beau was not talking for Caddell. This was from Beau.

"If you quit," Beau said. "You'll be . . . like Hart!"

Caddell was on the phone now—not once, but every ten minutes. Pat had arguments for Joe, arguments for Jimmy to make to Joe, something he had to tell Beau—*right now.* . . . It was nuts. Caddell was stirring the pot to a froth from a hundred miles away.

Pat's next call, Rasky went to the kitchen—he'd try to calm Pat. . . . But no—how could Pat be calm?

"You guys," Caddell screamed, "have formed a *vigilante committee* to get *my candidate OUT OF THE RACE!*"

In the living room, Gitenstein was warning: this attack on Joe was going to contaminate the vote on Bork. "If we win on Bork, it's gonna be in spite of us. If we lose now, it's gonna be because of us. The only way you're going to shut the press up is . . . get out."

Ted Kaufman was the last to weigh in. After fifteen years with Biden, Wilmington to Washington every day, Ted wasn't talking about the press, the campaign, or the Bork fight—Ted thought of Joe. So it seemed like there was nothing more to argue, after Ted said . . . "Get out."

It wasn't that Joe didn't see the logic. He'd known since he got home, and started talking with the family: he'd have to get out. He had no way to fight. Christ, he knew that . . . with his head. But his heart—his family! his sons!—could not accept . . . "I quit."

He would not say it!

In the end, of course, it was all about family.

Jimmy, Frankie—they saw the logic. They were the ones who told Joe, flat out . . . it hurt, sure, hurt Joe, hurt the family . . . but that didn't change anything.

Jill wanted out. The calls to the house . . . so *nasty.* There was no explaining. Those people didn't want to hear the answers. They just kept . . . well, it was awful.

It was late that night, Rasky took Joe aside, into the library, told him more about the call from the *Times.* They were going after Jimmy; it wasn't just Joe anymore.

Soon after that, Joe called to Jill, and they started upstairs. Joe paused, turned on the staircase, and said quietly to Gitenstein: "Mark, you get to work on a statement."

— ★ —

The old Judiciary hearing room was packed an hour before Joe's appearance . . . the whole tribe assembled: government reporters who'd been sitting in the hearings, political reporters just back from Iowa, big-feet holding court at their seats. The back of the room filled, then the aisles. (David Broder would report that twenty-eight TV rigs were present.) The air was scarce. But it was social.

"Hey, what're you doin' here, slumming?"

"Hey, d'you have lunch?"

A reporter pressed against the side wall started paddling his arms and yelping. . . . Hah! Feeding frenzy—see?

The few who knew Biden were quiet. "I've covered him for eight years," said Nadine Cohodas, from *Congressional Quarterly.* She looked like she was going to weep.

Debby Orin, from the *New York Post,* was working the ones who knew—working hard: "There's something really wrong about this. I feel awful. I mean, don't you think it's wrong, there's something wrong?" She'd fix her sharp dark eyes on one, then the other: "Don't you think it's wrong? I mean, who did this to Joe? I've heard the White House on the law school thing, but, I mean, what about the other stuff, you know? Who? . . ."

(Gephardt, Gephardt, Gephardt . . . they answered. They all knew the poop on Doak and Shrum v. Caddell. If you weren't known to be in the know about Doak and Shrum . . . well, who were you? Anyway, Biden was dead meat. Next case.)

The door behind the podium swung open and Val emerged, with her husband, Jack, then brother Jimmy, then Jill and Joe. Biden stepped up to the podium, topped with a fungal bouquet of microphones.

"Hello, everybody. You know my wife, Jill. . . . Three and a half months ago . . ."

Jill was on his left, close, her right arm almost touching him. She stared straight ahead at the wall of cameras, the pack . . . but she met no one's eyes. She hated them. First time in her life . . . but it was true: this was hate. They were destroying what Joe worked for, twenty years. It was just another story for them. They were excited: the crowd at a hanging. She couldn't believe how Joe was—so controlled.

He kept it short and sweet: no ranting, no self-pity.

He'd made mistakes, he said. And now, with the glare on those mistakes, it was impossible to make people see Joe Biden. He had to choose between his campaign and his chance to influence the direction of the Court.

"Although it's awfully clear to me what choice I have to make, I have to tell you honestly, I do it with incredible reluctance—and it makes me angry. I'm angry with myself for having been put in the position, for having put myself in the position, of having to make this choice. And I am no less frustrated at the environment of Presidential politics that makes it so difficult to let the American people measure the whole Joe Biden, and not just misstatements that I have made.

"But, folks, be that as it may, I have concluded that I will stop being a candidate for President of the United States."

He thanked his supporters.

He thanked the press for being there.

Then he turned on his heel, and walked out.

— ★ —

It was a performance of grace and guts—everybody noticed. They commended him in "analysis" pieces that weekend. They said Biden did it to himself—at least he was sport enough to say so. It made everybody feel better.

Broder went so far as to write a column about the time he saw Joe stop in an airport and spend a half-hour with a man who had AIDS. See, Biden did have character.

It was okay to say so, once he bowed out so nicely—give the guy a break.

Like that story about Jimmy's bankruptcy: the *Times* never did follow up. Not a word. Probably thought they were being kind—pulling back, once Joe got out. They wouldn't see it otherwise . . . as the Bidens saw it . . . for instance, as blackmail.

Joe didn't have time for postmortems. He had the hearings, thank God. After his statement, he walked through the anteroom, straight to the hall and the Caucus Room. Jill and Mark Gitenstein walked alongside.

"I did the right thing," Biden said. He didn't even seem to be convincing himself. He was calm, quiet, clear. "I can concentrate now—do the hearings. At least, I can do a good job."

Mark was nodding. He was going to say . . .

"No!" Jill said. And it jolted them: her tone. Jill *never* cut in like that. Joe and Mark each thought she was talking just to him.

Jill said, with steel in her voice: "You have got to *win.*"

68

Missss-ter
Eagle Scout!

O F COURSE he wanted to win—wouldn't have tried if he didn't think he could. But when he started—when was it? four years ago? almost five!—Dick Gephardt didn't think he could lose.

Not that he thought himself inexorable victor—no, the odds were always against him. But if he just did *well,* if he ran a decent race . . . he'd have to end up better. A national figure, a force for the future!

It was strange, but the road to the White House was the path of least resistance. Dick made the turn in '83, after Senator Tom Eagleton tipped him off: Eagleton would not run again in '86. He was going to announce his retirement, and he wanted Dick to jump in the same day—say he meant to be the next Senator from Missouri.

Well, it was a hell of an invitation. Dick could emerge anointed, with Eagleton's blessing, Eagleton's money. (Lou Susman, the Senator's high-dollar man, was more eager than Tom! . . .) But it would have been bloody—a primary, statewide, against Harriett Woods, a go-getter liberal, a hard campaigner . . . a *woman.* It made Dick edgy: he'd have to talk about abortion. Gephardt had always voted with his district—pro-life—to outlaw abortion. But he didn't want to climb into bed with the antiabortion zealots in Missouri . . . they were crazy! Anyway, after that, he'd never be able to get *outta* bed. He could never run nationally as a pro-life Democrat (unless he meant to do without Democratic women).

So, Dick didn't jump. And when he balked at running statewide . . . well, the only choice was to go national. Jim Wright was already angling for Speaker (after Tip announced his retirement), and Dick could have made that a fight . . . but talk about *bloody*! He'd end up with enemies aplenty, even if he won. So he contented himself with Chairman of the Caucus—fourth in the leadership. That was his ticket to the top . . . and it wouldn't upset anybody.

Actually, the job was perfect: he could make of it what he chose—for instance, a straight shot to the evening news. Dick would be *invited* to speak for the Party, get out front to define the agenda. That would carry him all over the country . . . new friends, new connections . . . he was already running flat out for '88. At least, he was out there to offer himself, as he'd offered himself on St. Louis doorsteps. He'd see how it went, how people reacted . . . what did he have to lose? The filing deadline for his House seat would fall on March 29, 1988 . . . three weeks *after* Super Tuesday. The worst that could happen: he'd be back in the House—a stronger runner, after a practice lap.

But five years has a way of changing a man's mind. So much effort, by so many people . . . people counting on him. Other people's money, promises to keep . . . all the problems he'd talked about for years—as if he knew—now, he *knew*.

He'd voted, every year, for Meals on Wheels. Nice program: food for old people. Who's against it? . . . Dick was for old people—"senior citizens," he called them—always scored high on the rankings compiled by their lobbyists. But now, in Iowa—a campaign event, a photo op—he delivered a Meal on Wheels. And this old lady came to the door, on her walker . . . she was so *happy* he was there. She wanted to tell him what it meant . . . the food was fine—but what it meant was, a person came by, every day, to ask for her . . . a person who cared. She could live in her own house. She didn't have to sit in some warehouse for old bones. (She didn't call it a "senior citizens' home" or a "Title-Eight, Type-Two, Long-Term Health-Care Facility." It was that brick box across town, where people went in and never came out.)

He visited the GM plant in Fremont, California. It was shut down in 1982 because of low productivity, high worker-absentee rate, high defect rate . . . maybe the worst plant in the company (which was going some, in GM's case). And then GM switched it over to building the new Chevy Nova—a joint venture with Toyota—and replaced the plant's top brass. The new manager came from Japan: the son of Mr. Toyota himself. Well, the defect rate went down—among the lowest in the corporation . . . lower absentee rate, higher productivity. The high muck-a-mucks were eating with assembly-line workers in the same cafeteria, the workers were meeting in quality councils, showing up before shifts to do calisthenics . . . and they felt great about it!

That's just what he'd been talking about—attitude! You get people together and find out what they want . . . and then *do it*! You could turn it around! That's what the *country* had to do. That's what *he* could do . . . what he *had* to do!

It's like a drug, the feeling you could make a difference—a big, thumping, history-denting difference in the lives of all those people, those hundreds of thousands of hoping, hurting individuals who have stared at you in school auditoriums, coffee shops, and living rooms. The twelve hundred men and women from the J.I. Case plant, in Bettendorf, Iowa, whose jobs took off one day and landed in South Korea—he wanted to tell them, things would be better . . . he would *make* them better . . . he could *do it!*

But he had to win.

And that was different from not losing.

And the twist in his belly, that end of September 1987, was he was not winning. He wasn't even not-losing. When it mattered most, to *him* . . . he was sinking like a stone. But worse than that, he'd stand on a courthouse lawn (his seventy-ninth county!) and he'd wind up his speech . . .

"Give me your will . . .

"Give me your vision . . .

"Give me your commitment . . .

"Give me your belief . . .

"And, together, we can make America great, and strong again."

And maybe there'd be forty souls, forty pairs of eyes, maybe thirty seeing him for the first time . . . and he could not see in them any faith that he could make the difference. He could not even read belief . . . that he *wanted* to make things better.

What he saw was suspicion.

Even before Joe Biden withdrew, *everybody knew* . . . it was Gephardt who did him dirty.

— ★ —

It started in the sour soup of the pack, of course. Not that it showed up in stories . . . but still, everybody knew. Tell the truth, the pack was edgy—this Karacter Kop routine was screwing up their campaign, their own shining shot at History! Candidates toppling like trees in a clear-cut! Where would it stop? People were blaming *them!* . . . So, someone was gonna pay for Biden. That video started the whole sooty snowball—who sent it?

Gephardt, Gephardt, Gephardt . . .

The wise-guy community echoed back this delicious and well-known poop, the more avidly in Iowa (they might be in Council Bluffs, but hey!—they were in the know). And from that point, it was an epidemiological certainty that the "activist" population would be infected.

People stood up at events and asked Gephardt: Why'd you do it?

Gephardt said he didn't do it. As far as he knew, no one in his campaign did it.

As far as he knew! . . . Wasn't that wiggle room?

Even if they believed him—say, half those staring citizens on the courthouse lawn—they didn't believe for long. Their neighbor heard *for sure.* . . . Anyway, this thing spread like herpes B—no way you'd catch up with one man in a Ford van.

Dick was supposed to be bringing in the old Biden folks . . . forget it! Lowell

Junkins, the top of Biden's Iowa heap, the last Democratic candidate for Governor, was jobbing Gephardt every chance he got. And as he was the one man the big-feet consulted to find out where Biden-folk were likely to land . . . his chances were legion.

But the press didn't need persuading. They'd always had that Gephardt figured: the man would do *anything*! (He made his *mother* move to Iowa . . . what is she? Ninety?)

It was like his flip-flop on abortion . . . the guy got off the pro-life wagon just before going national—how convenient.

Then he discovered the trade deficit because he needed the unions.

Then he signed onto Harkin's farm bill because he'd need the farmers.

It all *fit*, see . . . not just Doak and Shrum plotting to ruin Biden because they hated Caddell. The whole Gephardt operation was a band of desperadoes! The newest was Joe Trippi . . . brilliant, yes, but his pockets were filled with grenades—*everybody knew that!* Trippi was going to do *message*—God only knew what Gephardt would say now, now that he'd tailored his whole image to Iowa . . . that whole Eagle Scout thing . . . and Iowa saw through it. (D'you see the poll? Guy's fallin' apart!)

Now there were rumors Gephardt meant to sack his Iowa operation (after Fleming put an *army* out there for him!). Was he getting rid of the guilty parties?

Everybody knew something was fishy in that Gephardt office. You never even saw those people out to dinner! . . . Teresa Vilmain, head of the Dukakis Iowa campaign, threw a party—it was for the Biden folks, but everybody came . . . everybody but the Gephardts. That's what people talked about, all night— and days thereafter. Not one Gephardt person! Teresa was nobody's fool—*she wouldn't invite them*! The Duke's people hadda know something . . . right?

Missss-ter Eagle Scout!

— ★ —

Dick was without tools to combat this disaster, unequipped by experience. His life's method was built on the certainty, the requirement, that people would look into his eyes and see he was decent, optimistic, patriotic, faithful to the Lord, considerate of his fellow man. . . . Seldom had he been mistrusted—never attacked.

He had no idea what to do.

His problem could not be solved by denial—they did not believe him. And his constant instinct in times of trouble—to work harder—was useless. He could not prove a negative by visiting three more Iowa counties, not even three a day. The intensity of his effort just made it worse. It made him laughable— the dread and fatal affliction.

His issues, his program, offered no protection: people did not believe that *he believed* in his issues . . . they were campaign-convenient, too clever by half. Reilly took polls in Iowa on the trade issue. Almost eighty percent of the sample agreed with Gephardt's position . . . but they wouldn't vote for him.

That's what was dawning on Gephardt: it was about *him* . . . the issues, the organization, were only important insofar as they showed *him*. . . . And not in the comfortable, unassuming way that had always worked before: Dick Gephardt, honest broker . . . that nice young man who helped the community association with its articles of incorporation . . . that knowledgeable young Congressman who cut through red tape at the VA . . . that patient legislator who sat through 165 conference committee meetings, just to buff the burrs off that Gramm-Rudman bill.

No, that was not enough.

"People in this country look at politicians like doctors—solve the problem . . ." That's the way Dick talked about his discovery. "They don't really know about the gall bladder . . . so they want to know something about the doctor."

This wasn't like his other campaigns. It was not just more doorsteps—this was something else. *He* would have to be something else. There were millions of people out there, going to pick their President. It didn't matter how hard Dick worked—he was not going to lock the baby blues on their faces and *listen* to them all. They weren't *going* to get in a room with Dick and figure out what they wanted to do. They wanted one guy, at the front of the room, to *tell* them what they were going to do—or, at least, what *he* meant to do.

Dick said, one day, in a plane over Iowa: "You know what's the amazing thing? The *people* elect the President . . ." He announced this with a grin of wonder—such a radical idea! "That makes all the difference. Isn't it un-be-*liev*-able? All those *millions of people* . . ."

Seeking one guy, of size, to fill the stage.

Problem was, he did not know how to be that man, or show himself to be that man . . . to bestride the stage, to impose his person. He could not impose himself upon his own campaign.

— ★ —

The most corrosive thing was, he could not know. When they came at him about the Biden mess, he didn't *think* his guys had done it. He'd never heard about it . . . but . . .

He asked Carrick, who said he was sure they hadn't done it . . . and Dick found himself listening in Bill's murmur for the thump of conviction.

So began the Great Chain of Doubt.

Because there was no conviction in Carrick's voice. He didn't *know* . . . surely, he ought to know . . . but Doak and Shrum did hate Caddell . . .

And Doak knew he hadn't done it . . . but Carrick . . . or Shrum! Shrum thought Biden was wifty anyway, and he would've known those Kennedy quotes *cold* . . . but Shrum was in Italy when those quotes came out, and . . . no, probably wasn't Shrum.

Of course, Shrum knew *he* hadn't . . . but Trippi—would he do it without telling? Could Joe do anything without talking about it?

Hell, Carrick could! Or that kid he hired for Deputy Press, that little killer,

Mark Johnson: ambition on his face *permanently,* like a birthmark! That kid could have done it . . .

Carrick could have told him to . . .

Dick could've told Carrick! . . .

"Mrs. Gephardt, did your husband put out the attack video?"

Jane got the question from a reporter in Idaho. She had to ask what he was talking about. She always *liked* Joe Biden—such a charmer! What was going *on*? She called the campaign, and Don Foley told her Dick was saying he had nothing to do with it. The line of the day: "We don't run that kind of campaign."

Well, that's exactly what Jane had said. Dick had *never* run that kind of campaign . . . but this was a new kind of campaign.

"Have Dick call me as soon as he can."

That night, Dick told her not to worry—they hadn't done it.

"Are you sure? . . ." Jane knew they were all "professionals," all the new people. Maybe this was part of the deal. "How do you know they didn't?"

Dick said he'd asked Carrick—and he had to back his guy! That was the *deal* with Carrick.

Jane said quietly: "You don't know anymore."

— ★ —

He'd make his move in Iowa: get rid of Fleming, bring back Steve Murphy, the almost-Campaign-Manager whom he'd dumped for Carrick. Murphy had licked his wounds and was looking for a role. And he was, in Dick's felicitous phrase, "a real ass-kicker." Murphy would take names.

It wouldn't look good—bound to get bad press: GEPHARDT CAMPAIGN IN DISARRAY. . . . And Dick never liked bearing bad news. But he had to! All his effort, money, hope . . . he sure as hell had to know what was going on! Dick had decided to make this campaign *his* campaign.

But it was like watching a kid learn to walk—one or two bold steps, then he'd fall over again.

He'd fly out that weekend—had a debate there, anyway—and he'd tell Fleming. (Well, actually, Carrick would tell Fleming—but Dick agreed!)

Murphy couldn't move to Des Moines for a week or so, but Dick was already talking to him, telling him the problems:

The schedule was stupid—they were plowing the same ground, over and over.

The field work was sloppy—people told Dick they'd tried to volunteer, no one ever called them back.

The speeches were always late—Dick didn't see them till the day he had to deliver the words.

"Well, all you gotta do is call 'em up and *tell* them," Murphy said. "Tell 'em what you want—*demand* it! You know? . . . *Get mad!*"

Dick said: "Okay, good . . . we'll do it." But he never called.

Meanwhile, till Murphy came, Trippi had to hold the fort—which was still besieged by suspicion. . . . The latest from HQ was, that Deputy Press kid, Mark Johnson, had been handing out clips on Biden's troubles—right in the middle of the feeding frenzy. Chrissake! The kid was Carrick's hire . . . but he had to be stopped.

So Trippi pulled an Al Haig ("As of now, I am in control here") and put out a memo—to *everyone*—forbidding any talk to the press without his explicit permission. In fact, he forbade talking to *the candidate* without his permission.

Then Don Foley went nuclear. He'd been Dick's Press Secretary for *ten years* . . . been working with Gephardt *since 1970,* since Don was a senior at St. Louis U and an eager lawyer-pol named Dick Gephardt had come by to organize Students for Symington. Foley was the one guy who knew Gephardt from back when. Foley was the one who told Gephardt *from the start:* this was *his* campaign . . . his values, his method . . . his person. (And Foley knew: that's why Carrick had to coup him. That's why Carrick "helped him out" with an assistant, Mark Johnson, the Pit Bull—the kid actually liked the nickname!— and why Carrick gave Johnson the word: Hey, if something should, you know, *happen* to Foley, well, the job is yours.)

So Foley went straight to Dick: This has got to stop! How could Foley do his job, help Dick . . . when Carrick and his killers were trying to cut off Don's nuts? This memo . . . after eighteen years, Don had to ask permission to talk to Dick Gephardt? It was ridiculous!

Dick agreed.

Don said: "Dick . . . it's got to the point, I'm thinking of leaving."

Dick said he'd hate to see that.

Well, then, now was the time, Don said, for Dick to put his foot down. Tell them what you want: Don Foley will be the spokesman, handle the press, travel with the candidate . . .

Dick said he really couldn't interfere.

So Foley was history . . . and just as the Kops were rooting up the forest floor, like hogs after a truffle, snouting out Dick's Karacter . . . there was no Foley to explain, to tell the old stories. . . . No, the campaign ended up with Mark Johnson prowling the press pens.

And he *had* been peddling hot clips on Biden . . . to CBS . . . where they fell into the hands of Lesley Stahl . . . who found out they'd come from . . . the GEPHARDT CAMPAIGN!

So she promptly went on the air with the first public confirmation that, indeed, the Gephardts were promoting dirt on Biden.

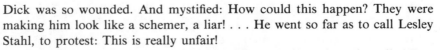

Dick was so wounded. And mystified: How could this happen? They were making him look like a schemer, a liar! . . . He went so far as to call Lesley Stahl, to protest: This is really unfair!

Mark Johnson went further (this could affect his future!) . . . he called Dan Rather. Of course, Johnson didn't get through. But he gave Dan's assistant an earful. He wanted a retraction!

Well, word must have got through . . . because Rather went on the air, the next night, and stuck it to Gephardt *again*.

So Carrick had to swing into action.

He gave the candidate a stern talking-to: "Dick! Y'don't pick a fight w'the goddam networks . . ."

And he called a meeting, a manage-the-damage. Dick had to come in for that.

They went round the table—who did what?—because they had to know where they stood. They ran through the answers to every charge—explanations for everything. Dick sat quietly through all that.

But when they got to the Lesley Stahl story, he picked up his briefing book . . . "This just shows . . ." he said.

He was standing now, in front of his chair.

". . . you can do *nothin'* wrong . . . and they'll *STILL* . . ."

Gephardt slammed down his briefing book.

": . . *FUCK . . . YOU . . . TO DEATH!*"

They were aghast. No one said a word. They'd never heard him talk like that. They looked at each other, then up at Dick.

He was smiling. He'd never heard himself talk that way, either.

He liked that. He'd got *mad*.

69

Matt

DICK WAS a first-year Alderman, a new partner at Thompson and Mitchell, a young lawyer-pol on the go, in May of '72, when Matt got the flu—they thought it was flu. Matt was eighteen months old, a blond, bright, and eager boy . . . until he got such terrible pains. He was miserable—he cried all the time, his belly hurt, he had diarrhea . . . and it didn't go away—two weeks of flu?

Then the doctor felt something in his abdomen, a hardness—probably a blocked bowel. He sent the Gephardts home with a laxative. Jane thought, later, she should have known . . . the change in Matt was so sudden, total. But how could a first-time mother know?

In time, X-rays showed a tumor off his prostate, squeezing the bladder and kidneys, pushed against his ureters. The pain came from his inability to urinate. The tumor was too big: surgeons could never cut it out without massive collateral damage. Worse still, the tumor was cancerous. Dick and Jane were told there was little chance for Matt.

What could they do? Hospitals . . . specialists . . .

And the answer, from the chief oncologist at Barnes Hospital, was . . . probably nothing.

Jane was devastated. She felt her life was ending—was ended. Matt had been her life, or its focus, for the last two years—she'd quit her job in advertising when she got pregnant, in 1970. She was a full-time mother, and she loved it . . . but now they told her her baby would be gone. She'd walk out from the the hospital, and see people on the street, hustling by: they didn't even look, they didn't know! "*Don't they know what's happening to me?*"

She could not accept . . . this was *not* happening to her, to her baby!
. . . And Dick could not accept. His whole life was testament to faith, and the
power of will. So Dick's answer was his most basic instinct: We'll fight, we'll
do . . . everything.

There was a young doctor named Ragab, an Egyptian, second man on
Matt's team. Abdul Ragab was the man who told Dick and Jane that there
was a treatment, developed in Texas—three drugs administered in combination chemotherapy, along with radiation . . . and it showed promise.

"It is possible . . ." Dr. Ragab spoke softly, with the soft consonants of his
native land. "Don't give up."

So Dick and Jane sat down with the chief of the team, Theresa Vietti, head
of pediatric oncology at Barnes, and they told her they wanted to do everything.

She said: "There are worse things than dying."

Dick stared at her across her desk. What the hell was she talking about? Did
she think they'd just let Matt slip away?

"The treatment could . . . could be worse."

Dick just blinked once, slowly, and looked her in the eye: "Do . . . whatever
. . . you have to."

— ★ —

Dick always said: "Once you're in the fight, then you're fighting, you're okay."
But this was not okay. They were throwing drugs into Matt as hard as they
could, bombarding his abdomen with radiation—they had to shrink the tumor,
or he'd be gone before the fight began.

If they could shrink the tumor, ultimately, they could operate—but how
soon? How well? And what would they find? No one could tell Dick and Jane
they would beat the cancer.

And Matt was shrinking, before their eyes, into a withdrawn and fretful
shadow of their son. Treatments were terrible. He came to fear the medicine,
machines . . . he'd grab for Dick's tie and hold on for all he was worth. He
lost his beautiful blond hair. He was so small, bald, weak . . . so frightened.

Sometimes, Dick and Jane—so allied in their activist, willful way in the
world—were frightened, too. And they had to wonder: were they right? Did
they have the right? . . . But they wondered to themselves. They were brave
for each other—for Matt. And, really, they could not look back: this was his
life!

And it was Jane's life—or that's how it felt. Dick still dwelt in the world,
day by day. He went to the office, he practiced law. He went to his aldermanic
meetings, he did politics. The amazing thing, said his friends from the time,
was they never saw the strain. Maybe it was harder to get him to laugh
. . . but they never saw him miss a step—he was so determined. Hell, there
were people, thought they knew Dick, who didn't know he had any troubles
at home. (They saw him just last week. He was talking about the billboard
ban!) Jane, they never saw—not that summer, not that year. She called it
"living in a vacuum." What it was: she lived in Matt's world. And that world

grew so small. With the treatments, he was hanging on the edge: his immune system was shot. He couldn't be out in crowds. You couldn't bring a stranger into the house. Jane would go out, and she'd find herself searching the people— as if she could *see* what germs she had to dodge.

Then Matt got pneumonia, and even that life stopped. The treatments stopped. The doctors said Matt couldn't hold on—he was going to die. He was in the hospital. Dick and Jane were in the hospital. Thompson and Mitchell gave Dick the time. Sometimes he'd sit in Matt's room all night. The hospital staff would bustle in and out, with drugs—antibiotics now—or to take blood, blood pressure, heart rate . . . seemed like a thousand stupid tests. They'd pound on Matt's back to try to loosen his lungs. Dick felt they were pounding on *him*. Matt had to fight! Dick wanted him to fight! How could he fight when he was so weak? They wouldn't even let him sleep, to get his strength! They were filling in boxes on their damned *clipboards*!

Dick moved his chair to the door of Matt's room. A nurse approached, middle of the night.

"You go in there," Dick Gephardt said, "and I'll deck you."

— ★ —

Jane was raised Catholic, and fairly religious. As a girl, in Nebraska, some-times she'd go to church without her folks. In college, she questioned . . . pulled away from the church. But now she found faith she never knew she had. She prayed for Matt, she prayed for strength, she prayed for the capacity to accept . . . but she couldn't accept. Downstairs in the house on Fairview, she had a prayer on the wall, over the washer:

O God, give us serenity to accept what cannot be changed, courage to change what should be changed, and wisdom to distinguish the one from the other.

Which was this?

Dick's faith was Loreen's. He knew this was God's will, but that would not stop his striving. When you accept God's will, when you give yourself into His hands, then He will help you work *your* will . . . that was Loreen's way. Praise the Lord . . . and pass the ammunition.

Matt's lungs cleared. The treatments resumed. But the doctors were juggling drugs. The surgeons thought they should go in to remove his bladder and bowel. The radiation specialists recommended starting with radiation. The chemotherapy doctors recommended chemotherapy first. Dick and Jane learned more medicine than they ever knew existed . . . and they learned: the doctors *did not know.* They *didn't have the answer*! Everybody said something different! That's when Dick and Jane started managing their own case.

Jane read everything she could get. The Gephardts traveled to specialists in Chicago and Philadelphia . . . they were on the phone twenty times to Texas. They looked into the Mexican Apricot Pit cure . . . the claims of miraculous recovery. There was one poor woman who called their house, several times, trying to get them to take Matt to Mexico—and take her along . . . she needed a cure, too. There wasn't anything that was too strange, no odds too wide, at least to check out. Loreen sent the three of them—Dick, Jane, and Matt—to a service in Pittsburgh by the Pentecostal faith healer, Kathryn Kuhlman.

And, meanwhile, day to day, week to week, there was the narrow, endless round in St. Louis: their house on Fairview (a couple of neighbors were permitted to visit), and Lou and Loreen's on Morganford (Dick's folks were on constant call, baby-sitting, cooking, yard work at Dick and Jane's). Brother Don and his wife, Nancy, came back to St. Louis that summer, for Don's doctorate at Washington U, so their home, too, fell within the straitened circle. But those were the only places, and people, in Jane and Matt's life . . . and, of course, the doctors, at Barnes Hospital. Back and forth to the hospital . . . Jane could do the route in her sleep. Once a week, twice a week, every day . . . back and forth. She'd take Matt for treatment in the morning, then they'd stop on the way home—White Castle belly-bombers . . . but Jane would eat in the car. She couldn't take Matt into a restaurant. . . . She'd get him home, try to put him to sleep—it was a blessing, when he could sleep . . . and she'd tiptoe back to his room, after he'd drifted off, and lay her hand on him, below his tummy, to feel . . . she couldn't *not* feel him:

Was it smaller?

She'd ask the doctors, over and over:

Was it shrinking? . . . At *all*? . . . *Was* it . . .

No.

—★—

Dick would rush home to be with Matt. Maybe he'd have to go out again, for an evening meeting . . . but, meanwhile, the time was precious—could be gone, like *that*! . . . Dick would strip off his suit coat and call, "Hey, Bugs!" (Dick had nicknames for everyone.) "Wanna ride?" . . . Then he'd pull Matt, in his little red wagon, everywhere he went.

The wagon was a near constant—or the stroller. There were times when Matt was too weak to get around any other way. If he felt stronger, if he could walk, and play, Dick would organize "orchestra." That was a game where everybody got an instrument—clappers, castanets, kazoo, bell, whistle . . . and they'd march around the house—Dick, Jane, Lou, Loreen . . . and tiny, bald Matt in the lead, as the grand maestro.

Sometimes Dick would go along to the hospital, to talk with the doctors. He could not understand why the surgeon said something different from the radiotherapist, the oncologists—they were different departments, sure, but they were supposed to work on Matt's case together . . . so he'd get them together. He'd talk to them all, he'd ask each in turn—what did they want to do? . . . And he'd listen to the positions—where's the bottom line? He'd tell each what the others said. . . . And in time, they had a treatment plan, Matt's team of doctors was a team. New drugs? Step up the radiation? They'd talk it out. The bridge was Dick Gephardt.

Of course, the expense was ferocious. Dick and Jane were hardly wealthy. Thompson and Mitchell had the compassion to hunt up a new medical plan, something to cover catastrophic care. They gave the assignment to Gephardt. And Dick worked it out: he read up on insurance, he talked to salesmen, to the hospital . . . he built the law firm a new health plan. Then he sold it, in-house, first to the senior partners, and then to the others—down to the last associate, they signed on—and Dick had his coverage (though the young associates were shocked to learn they'd signed away maternity coverage in the deal).

He was learning health care as he learned everything: you'd tell him something, and he had it forever . . . and not just Matt's case. What he learned was the *system.* He could talk about doctors, the equipment, treatments, insurance, the hospital, its costs. . . . Within a year, he was president of CURE, the organization of parents whose children had cancer. Within two years, he was appointed to the board of Barnes Hospital (and soon thereafter proved his worth in the system by casting the deciding vote on the Board of Aldermen to permit the hospital's expansion).

But that was just Dick's way of doing *everything* . . . what it all came back to, that autumn, was Matt.

The treatment ground on. It was months since the diagnosis, and Matt held on . . . though no one could say they were winning.

Till one day, Jane tiptoed up to his room, and felt his belly, and . . . *she couldn't feel it!* She felt and felt. *She could not feel it!*

Could that be?

Was that possible?

Even the *doctors* couldn't feel it. They took X-rays. . . . And the massive tumor was gone—shriveled to a tiny lump inside.

"Rare . . ." they said. "Must have been shrinking for some time . . . very strange . . ."

Jane said: "Well, if you believe in miracles . . ."

— ★ —

It was winter when they wheeled Matt in, and they cut out the tumor, the wizened lump—they got it all. The cancer had spread to his bladder, his prostate, so the surgeons had to remove them, along with part of his bowel.

"There may be problems," the doctors told Dick and Jane. Treatment would have to continue. If one cell was left, the cancer could come back . . .

"For how long?" Dick asked. "How long before you *know*?"

"Well, years . . ." What they meant was, forever.

But treatment for the first two years . . . and after that, if nothing happened . . . well, the chances were better.

"And after that?"

"Well, the first ten years . . ."

Ten years!

It seemed like a lifetime away, to Dick and Jane—another lifetime. *Any* years were a gift—they were bonus years!

Matt was in the hospital after the surgery. The healing was painful, the

damage immense. New tubes and bags . . . it would be difficult for him—
difficult, now, for Dick and Jane . . . but Matt was *there* . . . and he grew
stronger. At last, they brought him home.

Matt moved slowly through the rooms, looking at everything in its turn, as
if he had to check it against his inventory. . . . And then, he looked up at his
parents, at Lou and Loreen, standing by . . . and demanded:

"Orchestra!"

And he marched them around the house.

70

Happy
to Be Alive

DICK WAS IN Iowa, the following
weekend, when he got his re-
prieve. Michael Duffy, from *Time*
magazine, told him: *Time* had the story—it would come out Monday—it was
the Dukakis campaign that put the hit on Biden.

Thank you, Jesus!

Gephardt had a brutal schedule, crisscrossing the state—west to east, corner
to corner . . . followed by a few hours' sleep at his mother's apartment. Loreen
had decided to stay in Des Moines—the Lord had work for her. (It occurred
to her that the birthday of Lou, her late husband, was . . . *February Eighth*—
the night of the Iowa caucus! . . . "And did I tell you? The last four numbers
of my Social Security card? . . . *1988!*") And Dick had decided—one look at
his budget had decided *him*—there was no use spending money on a hotel
when Loreen had a perfectly good foldout couch.

Sixteen hours of work, six towns, five hundred miles . . . to a foldout couch?

"No, it's greeeaat!"

See, it didn't matter what he had to do. Didn't matter that his message cops
came to poke him after every speech. ("Dick, your first piece, up front, is that
you're gonna win . . . so your close has got to be, '*I want you on board, NOW!*'
. . . see? And it's, '*When . . . WHEN I'm elected, I will not forget . . .*' ")

Didn't matter that the Japanese Trade Ministry had an operative dogging
Gephardt's steps. For God's sake, they got her on his plane! . . . She was an
American, small and serious, who kept asking Dick to *explain* what was unfair
about Japan. ("Congressman, could we go into the beef situation?")

Didn't matter that the quarter was ending, and Gephardt had a hundred money calls to make. He had to pump up the total so the press wouldn't label him a pauper. ("Is Mr. Mitchelson there? This is Congressman Dick Gep-huh—? . . . He just hung up! He came right on, then he hung up! *Hackhack-hackheeheehee . . .*")

Dick was like a kid out of school for the summer. His whole body changed. He'd strip off his suit coat and toss himself into his airplane seat as if he'd lost twenty pounds overnight. Tail winds blew him into Muscatine forty-five min-utes ahead of schedule. ("Early! Can you be-*lieve* it?")

They gave him a room at the tiny airport, and he meant to work the phones. Brad hauled out the laptop computer and scrolled the lists. But there was a TV, and Dick flicked it on—C-Span, of course. He stared with his head cocked. The show was *Road to the White House,* and this edition had a tape of Dukakis working an event. It was unedited—the tape just rolled on, unblinking . . . a steady view of the Duke's shoulder and cheek as he handshook ("Hi, Mike Dukakis . . .") his way through a crowd. It was banal—and revealing. You could hear every lame mumbled pleasantry . . . every grunt.

"This is what killed Joe Biden," Dick said. "Video regurgitation. I mean, is this TV? Should this be on?"

He started laughing at Michael's halogen-lit mumbles.

"Would this be on . . . in any other country?"

Brad held the phone, uncradled.

Dick suggested: "South Carolina?"

"Uh . . ." Brad said, scrolling, "I got Minnesota."

Brad dialed. Dick made a few stabs, but people weren't in—6:00 P.M., not the best time. So Brad brought in a TV crew from St. Louis—they wanted an update on their hometown boy.

Had he changed?

"Nope," Dick said with a grin. "Not at all."

What surprised him?

"It's like being in prison . . . you never get to go where you want. You lose control. I expected us to have a plan, and we'd just go out and do our thing. But you're just out there . . . you lose control. You've *got* a plan—you plan for three years—doesn't mean a thing."

The TV woman from St. Louis asked if that made him unhappy.

Dick blinked once, slowly, and said to the lens:

"No . . . happy to be in this. Happy to be here. Happy to walk away. Happy to be alive."

Brad got the crew out. He was packing. They had a Democratic dinner in Muscatine . . . no use falling behind now.

But Dick got the phone.

He held up a hand . . . he'd dial.

"Hey, Bugs!" he said. "What's goin' on? . . ."

— ★ —

After the surgery, Matt underwent treatments for another three years. Sometimes they were awful, still . . . the doctors were always juggling the dosage of drugs. Sometimes it was scary, still . . . there were problems with the scar, sores, pains, side effects. . . . When would this ever settle down? Years from now . . . would there be years? That was the constant, overarching fear—so many times, with so many kids, the cancer came back, mostly in the lungs. But Matt's case was rare. This type of cancer usually showed up first behind an eye. Maybe his remission would be rare, too. How could the doctors know? . . . They could not. Dick and Jane could not. They could never be sure they were winning.

But they were winning. With every month of no news—not the worst news, anyway—Matt's chances improved. With every month, the treatments were less a dance with death, and more a part of life.

What changed was attitude. That's what Dick worked on, day by day. Dick said he wanted the most normal life for Matt, and for Dick that meant the most outward life. There were strangers at the house now—all kinds, Dick made sure of that. And trips for the family, and expeditions around the city. . . . Dick and Jane had to decide whether to have another child. Was it right for Matt? Was it right for them? Was it safe? . . . Dick said it would help take the focus off Matt. It would give *him* someone to look after. It would make everything more normal. Their daughter, Chrissie, was born in '73.

Dick pushed himself outward. He was leader of the Young Turks on the Board of Aldermen . . . and those fellows shook the whole city. They got the downtown—all of it—declared a "blighted area." (That gave the city the power to develop whatever it could dream up.) They changed the neighborhood renewals from tear-down-and-build to restore-and-renovate. They found millions in new money from the feds, and channeled every dollar through a new agency (which one of their own Turks went on to head).

They were only a handful—four or five votes out of a total of twenty-eight—so they needed the blacks, and at least acquiescence from the old guard. That was Dick's department: he was the bridge.

The leader of the old pols was one Albert "Red" Villa, a tavern owner from the South Side. Lots of politicians made pilgrimage to Red's bar—election night, for instance, they'd buy a few beers. But Dick was the only Young Turk who'd bring his wife—spend some time, sit down and talk.

The city's business nabobs formed a group, Civic Progress, that might have stopped progress altogether—but Dick would go out to the Bogey Club and talk to them, he was great with those folks. . . . Soon he had them convinced they *all* had to make the system work.

After Board meetings, the other Young Turks would sit down to lunch, plan the next week's mischief. They'd laugh about the old "Hoosiers" on the Board. (South to a certain line, those people had been in the city for years—they were Hoosierocracy; a bit farther out lived the Hoosieoisie; and way out, with the pickups and three-wheelers, were the Hoosietariat.) Those Friday lunches were a cackling self-congratulation for all they'd put over on the old farts . . . hah! Never knew what hit 'em!

But the real action went down the next day—Saturdays, 10:00 A.M., coffee and doughnuts in the Treasurer's offices. No one knew about it. City Hall was closed, and the guards would only let certain people in. No blacks. Few Aldermen. Nongovernment guys had to bring the doughnuts—the guy from Laclede Gas, the guy from Southwestern Bell . . . Midge Berra was the boss . . . Louie Buckowitz from the Tenth Ward, Sam Kennedy from the Eighteenth . . . and Dick was the only Young Turk who could come.

In '73, the Young Turks ganged up against the Mayor, Cervantes. They backed the City Comptroller, John Poelker, a straight arrow, a white knight . . . it was a risk, they rolled the dice—and they won. They made John Poelker the Mayor. They'd knocked off the boss . . . and Gephardt had run the campaign.

A year after that, they were talking up Gephardt for Mayor. Hell, he had backing all over town, he had ideas, he had energy. And he wanted to get something done—*now*.

Some of Dick's old friends—his cousin, Joe Kochanski, for instance—used to tell him: Don't rush in. The Mayor's job was a dead end, a citywide headache, a mess . . . and for what? . . . Wait a few years, something better would come along.

Dick would nod, and go right on. If something better came along, that was fine. The one thing he wasn't going to do was wait. He was going to do something—*now*. What Joe didn't understand—what none of them seemed to understand—it could all be gone, tomorrow . . . like *that*!

The point was, Dick could do something *now*. Things were changing in the city, in the country. After all of Nixon's troubles—Agnew, Colson, Haldeman, Ehrlichman, CREEPs, Plumbers, and all the rest—the voters wanted something new . . . fresh faces, untainted, people they could trust. (There was a man named Carter, saying the same in Iowa.)

The point was, after Watergate, Gephardt knew his time had come.

The point was, after Matt, Dick's time was always . . . *now*.

71

1974

AFTER WATERGATE, it was a wonderful time to be a reform-minded Democrat. The clean would inherit the earth! . . . And there was no one cleaner than Michael Dukakis—or readier to seize the day.

He had started again on his trips around the state. The earnest evenings in the living rooms, the drives through the darkness . . . they were just part of life now. For the first time, Michael had staff—young men pounding the highways, building the card files for reform.

He created Dukakis's Raiders, modeled after Nader's Raiders in Washington. Michael's young issue wonks would investigate state agencies, like the Outdoor Advertising Board, or the Massachusetts Port Authority, to make sure the Commonwealth was being served cleanly, rationally . . . and, of course, it didn't hurt if Michael's name cropped up, from time to time, in the newspapers.

Or his face on TV. . . . He met a man named Greg Harney, a producer for public TV, who had helped to create *The Advocates,* a weekly PBS issues forum about disputes in the news. The show was set up like a courtroom, with an audience, and a panel of experts "testifying" from the liberal and conservative sides. In 1972, Harney was hunting a new moderator to introduce the topic and the experts, to keep the discussion on track . . . and he recruited Dukakis.

Well, it was a political godsend—weekly, prime-time identification with the issues that mattered most. There was Michael, earnest, intense (power of brain—like a young Rod Serling) . . . keeping company with Senators, Secretaries of the Cabinet, professors, and political thinkers . . . and *he never had to take a position.* He was somehow above positions—the embodiment of fair-minded reason.

Just as he was, when Watergate took over the *Globe*'s front page, a well-known public-interest Raider . . . the personification of good government.

Just as he was, heading into 1974, the best-organized Democrat in the state of Massachusetts.

Dukakis was organized before he knew what he was organizing for. When Michael hosted his first meetings on Perry Street, back in 1972, he still had in mind to run again for Attorney General. He was sure the incumbent, Quinn, was going to make the jump to the Governor's campaign. But Quinn refused to tip his hand. He'd announce his plans when he was good and ready . . . very confident was Quinn—he had the boys on Beacon Hill lined up behind him. So Fran Meaney devised a plan to *force* Quinn to make the jump.

Michael would start making noise—about the *Governor's* race! Quinn would *have* to jump in, lest Michael get a head start. Then Michael could drop down and gracefully accede to run for AG . . . very clever.

Except Quinn wouldn't jump. Michael's out there, talking Governor . . . his toe, and then, his *whole foot* in the water . . . and still Quinn wouldn't jump!

But a funny thing happened—other people jumped. Reformers, do-goods—they wanted to help. (They even sent money.) They loved it!

And nobody laughed. The *Globe* called Dukakis a serious candidate. The neighborhood groups, who loved him for fighting the roads . . . the East Boston people, who hated the Port Authority . . . the consumer types who recalled Dukakis's no-fault bill . . . and, of course, antimachine insurgents all over the state—they all said it was time they had an alternative.

Michael Dukakis should be *Governor*!

And that's what everybody thought, in those meetings in his living room—especially the guy at the front of the room.

— ★ —

MIKE DUKAKIS SHOULD BE GOVERNOR. . . . That was actually the slogan—a bit peremptory, perhaps . . . but Michael thought no one could disagree. Actually, it was meant to be part of a larger ad campaign—tied in with his issues:

The Port Authority should work for the people . . . Mike Dukakis Should Be Governor . . .

People should have decent housing . . . Mike Dukakis Should Be Governor.

Like that . . . but it ended up, there was no money for the ads. Michael's campaign never had that kind of money. (Smart money was all with Quinn, who finally did declare for Governor, after Michael.) Michael couldn't even vet the checks overnight, to send back the dirty ones. His Campaign Manager, Joe Grandmaison, insisted: if those donations didn't get to the bank *today,* Michael's own checks would bounce all over the state.

Grandmaison was Michael's first professional Campaign Manager. He'd made his name, in 1972, as McGovern's (and Gary Hart's) man in New Hampshire. Of course, Michael wasn't for McGovern. (He was a Muskie man!) . . . But he signed up Grandmaison in '73, and reluctantly agreed to a salary of twenty thousand a year.

That's about all Michael spent. Through a bitter two-year primary campaign, Dukakis's media expenses were only twenty-four thousand—statewide. And through all but a month of that long march, Quinn was ahead in the polls, confident he'd take Michael to the cleaners in the September primary. Quinn had the big pols, a big name, money . . . and the logic of one immutable fact: he was an Irishman.

But he was also the perfect foil for a Michael Dukakis morality play: old-guard Irish, slap-on-the-back, job-for-a-friend . . . politics as ever it was in Massachusetts. Quinn could feel no new wind.

Michael was stumping the state, promising to rid the State House of the "cancer" of patronage. He released five years of his tax returns, which proclaimed his frugal cleanliness. He promised an administration so rational, so efficient, that state voters could finally escape the cycle of deficits, followed by tax hikes, followed by deficits. . . .

No new taxes!

How could Quinn answer that?

Well, for months, he didn't even try. Even after the race drew even—near Labor Day—Quinn refused to debate Dukakis. Quinn thought if he could hold the Irish . . . and Italians (his wife was Italian) . . . well, how could he lose?

But Dukakis was winning the Italians from the shore towns, promising to stop the Port Authority from eating away at their neighborhoods.

How could Quinn answer that? His old buddy, Ed King, was the head of the Port Authority.

Then Dukakis went at Quinn's record as AG, implying there was something shady about the way he administered federal law enforcement grants.

And at last (just as new polls showed Dukakis ahead for the first time), Quinn went nuclear. One week before the primary, he put ads on TV, accusing Dukakis of favoring abortion. And then he dropped leaflets in Boston, accusing Dukakis of backing busing. (Hey, he voted for the Racial Imbalance Law!)

What he did was play into Michael's hands.

Michael got *free* TV time to denounce Quinn's last-minute smears . . . dirty tricks! (Nixon, though departed, was still on the mind.)

"This," Michael intoned, "is *the kinda hack politics* that has been hurting the state for forty years."

No one could do righteous indignation like Dukakis.

Quinn withdrew the ads, but it was too late. He had allowed the campaign to become a referendum on political morality. He had revealed himself as exemplar of the politics that Michael was born to displace.

The Sunday before the vote, President Ford pardoned Richard Nixon. Voters in Massachusetts were disgusted—an obvious deal!

Monday, the *Globe* withheld comment on most candidates, but singled out

Dukakis as worthy of support. (Michael was not like a candidate, by that time. He was nothing less than the new wind itself.)

Tuesday, Dukakis beat Quinn in a landslide, by more than a hundred thousand votes.

— ★ —

After that, he could have just shut up and won. The *Globe*'s first poll of the general election showed Michael ahead by eighteen percent.

And the Democratic Party was uniting as never before. By grace of God, Michael was blessed with a Lieutenant Governor nominee who was Irish—an O'Neill! . . . In fact, Tommy O'Neill was the eldest son of Tip O'Neill, Majority Leader of the U.S. House and the best-loved star in the old-guard cosmos. That meant Tip and Tommy would whip up the hoary machine, even as Michael cried reform.

You couldn't dream it up any better.

Withal, even for the liberal Frank Sargent, this was a lousy year to be an incumbent Republican. It wasn't just Watergate—or the pardon!—though that was bad enough. . . . Before he vacated the White House, Richard Nixon had punished Massachusetts (the only state to vote for McGovern) by closing *five* military bases. The end of the war in Vietnam stripped the state of megamillions in defense contracts. The Arab oil embargo had stuck the voters in gas lines, raised heating bills by fifty percent, caused a horrific recession that drove unemployment toward ten percent.

People were hurting, and they were pissed off.

But, of course, Michael wouldn't shut up.

He thought he knew—he was *sure* he knew—the cause of the inflation, unemployment, the terrible business climate: it was not Arab oil, not Nixon, not the plunging dollar—no. It was . . . inefficiency in the State House!

"It is," Michael told the Greater Boston Chamber of Commerce, "the utter failure of state government to manage itself effectively and responsibly."

Of course, he was trying to stick it to Sargent, but really . . . what was the point?

The point was, Sargent was not Michael Dukakis.

Michael promised that he—being him—could wring *$100 million* out of state budgets and thereby make good his vow, "No new taxes."

Sargent said that was preposterous. What was Michael going to cut? (Here was Sargent, the Republican, talking compassion for the hard-pressed poor. And Michael running like a Yankee Republican.) Dukakis insisted, he wouldn't have to cut anything (he wasn't going to lose the liberals—they thought he was one of them). No! Better management! Efficiency! *Ekonomia!* A hundred million was less than three percent of the budget. No one could tell Michael he wasn't smart enough to find three percent.

In the last month, it came clear to all the knowing men of the State House that the next Governor was going to have to find a lot more than a hundred million—just to tread water. With a recession, people out of work, welfare and

social service expenses were shooting through the roof. Tax collections were
falling. The state was bleeding red ink.

Sargent couldn't admit that. He'd have to concede that he'd failed to manage. And Michael *would not* admit it: he'd have to go back on his boast that
he could manage away the problem. No new taxes!

The *Globe* asked him, point blank:

No taxes? Are you serious?

Serious was Michael's middle name.

Lead-pipe guarantee?

Absolutely. He'd close the deficit in the first six months!

Michael could smell triumph now. He was galloping toward it—on his high
horse. In a letter to the Governor, he offered to meet Sargent personally to
work out details for the final debates. ". . . But not at the State House, and
not on the public's time."

When Sargent misreported a $40,000 loan from his wife to his campaign,
Michael said that reminded him of Watergate. (At the same time, he was
denouncing Sargent for running a "scurrilous" campaign.)

Michael was so sure he bestrode the highest, purest moral axis . . . well
Sargent was *prima facie* sleazy—just for contesting the election! And so sure
was Michael that reason and decency were on the march, he actually agreed
to take a $10,000 loan—personally—to fund the last week of his campaign.

When Grandmaison got to Michael's room in the 57 Hotel, on election
night, that was the first question Michael asked:

"Did you pay back the loan?"

"Yeah."

Then, Michael asked:

"How'm I doing?"

"You won."

Then, Michael Dukakis grabbed Tommy O'Neill in a hug, and in each
other's arms, they jumped up and down on the bed.

72

Betrayed

THE AWFUL THING about it was—Michael was so happy! He'd *just about* got to the point where he knew this Presidential campaign was doable . . . as he meant to do it. He'd *just about* got to deciding . . . he liked it. It *was* different—the excitement, the way people looked at him, the way he felt, talking to them—it was . . . just terrific.

Michael was even prepared to concede (this was the true measure of his comfort) there were parts he didn't understand. The way to communicate what he meant to do, the *kinda guy he was*—he hadn't got there yet, didn't have the lines. But he would! . . . Or, at least, he'd try. What he'd lost was the fear of the strangeness and size—this wasn't going to swallow him whole.

He didn't have to give up his life!

Not all of it . . . some things. (He'd lost his cucumbers . . . very upset about his cucumbers. He should've *known,* the way his Katharine was, she'd *never* water them!) But not the big things—he could govern. He could stay on top of state business—three days a week! And here was the delicious secret:

He'd come back to the State House, and he saw—like a grown man who goes to see the house where he grew up . . . it was so small! One day that September, he said to his finance chief, Frank Keefe: "You know, my friend, this is a big, wonderful country we live in. You oughta go out and see it."

A big, wonderful *world.* . . . He had a splendid chat with a man named Lenihan—Deputy Prime Minister of the Republic of Ireland. Lenihan actually came to see *him.* Michael had actually *been to Dublin.* They had plenty to discuss! It was most cordial! Most agreeable. . . . This foreign policy stuff—this was not from Mars. He could do this!

And then . . . *then*! Came to visit *Oscar Arias*.

The President of Costa Rica . . . winner of the Nobel Peace Prize . . . came to Michael's office, and they talked—very well, indeed. They agreed that Reagan's contra war was bankrupt, immoral, *illegal*. . . . Michael and Oscar Arias agreed on the Arias Peace Plan!

And the best part—in the middle, Kitty called. His bride! . . . Jean Hines, Michael's secretary, put Kitty right through.

"I'm sitting here with President Arias . . ."

She could hear the pride and pleasure in Michael's voice.

"Katharine? What do you want me to tell President Arias?"

"Oh, God, Michael! I don't know! Tell him we all have great hopes for his peace plan . . ."

Michael turned from the phone, and relayed this message in perfectly precise Spanish.

Why wouldn't he be happy?

He was taking the measure of a new world, and it fit him!

He was taking the measure of this huge new campaign . . . and he was of size.

—★—

How did he know? The way he always knew: his *organization* was covering the ground. Michael was, first, an organizer. That was the root talent that had hauled him into the State House. And now . . .

His organization dwarfed his opponents'. Hart was gone. Biden was gone. Jesse Jackson had no pros on the ground. The rest were lightning-seekers: they had to hope for a big win, then try to catch fire. Fire was not Michael's style.

"Nope . . . it's a marathon, my friend."

The difference, of course, was money . . . and Michael was having another sterling quarter—another *$4 million quarter*! In fact, at the end of September, he was scheduled for a million-dollar evening in Boston. One event: one million dollars.

It was a dinner—with musical entertainment: the plan was for Michael to come on stage . . . and play his trumpet! Michael hadn't touched a trumpet for years, but such was his comfort now, he agreed. And, being Michael, he went to work—he practiced.

Friends would call the house, talk to Kitty:

How's Michael?

"Oh, God. Don't ask! He's upstairs, playing his trumpet."

In the State House, they asked him: "How's the trumpet going?"

"The lip?" Michael would answer, with a shrug. "The million-dollar lip?" Of course, by the big day, he was ready. He would play trumpet, correctly.

That was the day . . . Sasso came to the State House, four o'clock. He told Michael: he was the one who sent out the tapes about Biden.

Michael just stared, fiercely . . . then he sagged in his chair. He shook his head slowly. His voice came from far away.

"*Why?*" he said. "John . . . *why?*"

— ★ —

Michael told no one. He had his million-dollar dinner. Steady as she goes . . . he went into his hunch. He went to his funder. He played the trumpet, correctly. A group of schoolkids sang a song, on stage. Michael was supposed to watch. He watched.

"Michael! Smile! . . ."

That was Kitty, next to him.

"Smile!" she whispered. "They'll think you're not enjoying it."

Michael winced a sick little smile.

"Mi-chael!"

He muttered darkly: "Come on, babe."

She knew the tone: get-off-my-back. There were people around . . . they'd talk at home.

How could John not tell him?

Michael had told the press, the day before: that tape had nothing to do with him—*nothing*! If *anybody* in his campaign was involved, he'd be furious! He wouldn't stand for it!

How could John let him go out there—in ignorance?

How could John betray him?

The funder seemed to last forever. Then they had a driver. Michael sat silent. Kitty worried. Something was terribly wrong. (On the way to the dinner, Michael had forgotten his trumpet—so unlike him!) In the backseat, she lit a cigarette. Michael didn't say a word.

"Okay," she said, after he closed the door on Perry Street. "What's wrong?"

"Sit down."

"Michael!"

"You better sit down. . . . I found out today it was John who made those tapes."

"Oh, God."

Michael was standing slumped in the middle of the floor. She went to him, hugged him. But he did not give himself to her touch. He was beyond comfort.

She heard him on the kitchen phone: he called Paul Brountas. Paul was one of Michael's oldest friends, a Greek, a law school pal, now a corporate *consigliere,* a successful man. Michael had made him chairman of the campaign . . . but Paul didn't have to do much. As chairman, he'd been mostly what he ever was—Michael's friend.

Now, Michael told him, he needed Paul's help. They talked about John. Paul thought John should go. Paul had never trusted Michael giving himself over to John . . . it was an old story. Michael said they'd have to see what happened.

But what could happen?

Michael would have to make an announcement.

Tomorrow.

Early.

He would have to announce . . . he had not known what was going on in his own campaign. How could he have known? John was the one he trusted. The one . . .

He would have to announce, admit . . . well, he had to talk to John. He dialed John's number at home. Maybe John would not have to go . . . a leave of absence . . . an exile . . . a penance. . . . Michael had to think. He didn't want to act from emotion, but there was so much hurt.

— ★ —

That's not what John heard on the phone. He heard Michael's voice, and he knew: Mike was going to be . . . correct.

Michael's pain, his need, was for family. John had erred. Therefore, John had betrayed. From that moment, John was not family.

And Sasso did not defend himself. He should not have to explain: what he did, he did for Mike. Anyone else, any member of the staff, John would have gone to bat for him—gone to the wall! . . . But he would not say a word for himself, though he knew, if he did not sway Michael . . . he was gone. His dream for himself was gone.

He shouldn't have to argue with Michael.

For God's sake, where was Mike's loyalty?

Gone: in a contest between human loyalty and Michael's idea of his own correctness . . . there was no choice. It did not matter how Michael needed John, or what John needed. Compared to Michael's idea of himself, astride the moral axis, human need—even his own—was *nothing*.

That's what stung Sasso into prideful silence, what he heard in Michael's voice: nothing.

73

Dr. Dukakis

W HEN Governor-elect Dukakis took the T to the State House, after the '74 election, the first news to land in his lap—Boom!—the deficit was not one hundred million, nor even the whispered one hundred fifty. . . . Try *three hundred and twenty-one million dollars.*

Michael didn't bat an eye. He knew he'd have a problem to manage. Now he'd have a bigger problem. That was the only difference he saw. Did he doubt he could manage this problem away? . . . Not for an instant. Was he unhappy? . . . Not exactly. The pols and reporters who talked to the young Governor-elect strove to describe his air: they used words like "optimism" . . . "eagerness."

In fact, this was joy.

He was born to solve problems. Dr. Dukakis had trained himself for forty years to cure the ills. The problems were his reason for being. So the problems were bigger—*huge*—aha! Just as he'd suspected, as he'd *said* . . .

He was correct!

He set out to make a government unlike anything the citizens of the Commonwealth had ever seen. "The best government," he promised, "this state has ever had."

This would be a government of principle, not patronage. That was the first order of business: a radical patronage-ectomy, a *professional* personnel operation. No one would have a job because he was friend to Dukakis. In fact, no one of any political persuasion or prominence could get a job of any description for a friend.

Of course, he wasn't asking others to swallow anything he wouldn't. When anybody from his own campaign asked about a job in the State House, Michael would give them that dirt-on-the-carpet look, and scold: "You know that's not possible." . . . Why? Because they were friends!

And Michael didn't stop with jobs—all favors *had to cease*! The Governor had at his privy command the power to dispense low-number license plates. This was a harmless, much-coveted sign of standing, something like the Order of the British Empire, or a Lenin Medal for Valiant Factory Production. Best of all, it cost the Commonwealth . . . nothing.

"Nope. No special plates. That's not the way we're gonna do business."

"But Michael, *somehow* you gotta thank your friends."

So Michael told Kitty to schedule a dinner—not too big, maybe twenty-five people.

"Good. I'll hire a caterer."

"The way they charge?"

"Michael, *I* can't do it!"

So . . . the Governor-elect made turkey tetrazzini for twenty-five.

Then he cleaned up.

Then, thanking was over.

—★—

The first thing he thought of was to cut the Governor's payroll in half—who needed staff? (No, actually, the first thing he thought of was to give back ten thousand of his salary—who needed more than thirty thousand a year? . . . But Kitty talked him out of that.) Next, he got rid of the limo, and the state cop who drove it—what's wrong with the T? . . . The cops, of course, still had to protect him. Now they *all* had to ride on the T.

Next, he had to find a cabinet. That was serious. That was principle! No, that was a matter of *multiple* principles. . . . In fact, so complicated was the web of Dukakisian imperatives that Michael put Fran Meaney in charge of the talent search. Only Fran, his longstanding partner in reform, could find the correct people.

First, they had to be clean.

And bright—that went without saying.

And not from Michael's campaign—no one would say he gave jobs to his friends.

And *generalists*—they should not have friends among the issue groups they'd regulate. (In practice, that meant most would know nothing about their subjects. Not everyone found it as easy as Michael to keep from having friends.)

Then, at his first press conference, someone asked the Governor-elect how many of his ten cabinet secretaries would be women.

On stage, next to him, Kitty said: "Four!"

Michael said that sounded correct.

So, four women became a principle.

And minorities—that was a principle, too.

"That's great," said Fred Salvucci, the transportation sage. "Now all's we need is an Italian woman whose mother was Hispanic and whose father was Chinese and spoke Swahili."

"Cute," said Michael. "Very cute, Frederick."

Somehow, Salvucci slipped through the web and got appointed Transportation Secretary . . . though he knew the field, had helped Michael's campaign, and could even be described as a friend. (Then again, he was correct, and clean, and had been virtuously ignored for years while he and Michael inveighed against the roads.)

In Michael's pure vision, the cabinet would actually run the state—the Secretaries and the Governor would make the hard choices—without interference of politics . . . not even the politics of the Governor's office.

That's why Dukakis could cut his own staff . . . why he could hire another rookie, David Liederman, as his Chief Secretary: because the *cabinet* would act as his counselors. They were all going to be on the same team, weren't they? They'd meet together, pull together . . . cure the ills, make Massachusetts work—wouldn't they?

Of course they would! They'd work in concert, they'd reason and discuss . . . at least until some reporter started writing something into a notebook . . . after that, the Secretaries mostly ceased to reason—what they did was make speeches.

See, that was a principle, too: not only would the cabinet run the state, give the Governor its candid counsel . . . it would do so in meetings open to the press and public. Michael thought it important for citizens to see clean government. They ought to come and watch!

So they did, until one cabinet meeting wherein the Secretaries of the Commonwealth were interrupted in their reasoning by demonstrators who stood up to shout: "No welfare cutbacks! No welfare cutbacks!" And Michael wasn't going to stand for that crap! He called an emergency recess, and told Liederman:

"Deal with them."

Of course, by that time, his mood was different. He and his bright generalist counselors had been reasoning together, reforming, cleaning, cutting—administering the physic of honest government for more than three months . . . to an anguished crescendo of protest from welfare-rights groups, mental health groups, the elderly, the disabled, the medically afflicted, veterans, and a half-dozen other interests—not to mention a threatened strike by fifty thousand state employees, a rumble of disaffection from the leaders and their myrmidons in Senate and House, and a rataplan of angst from the state's newspapers . . .

And the deficit was climbing toward $500 million.

—★—

They begged him! From the minute he got into office, the sachems of the State House—the Senate President, the Speaker, the chairmen—all urged the Governor to bite the bullet: send down a tax plan! *Now* . . . while the next election was still more than three years away, while the deficit could still be labeled as Sargent's red ink . . . while they could still make the case that there'd been no way to know the size of the mess until Michael got in to set matters aright.

It was mostly true . . . and it was the only way to shield the new administration (and the legislators) from blame: delay would help no one—least of all, Dukakis.

But he didn't want to hear it. What kinda talk was that? He wasn't going back on a commitment! That's not the kinda guy he was! No, he was going to manage the problem. *Ekonomia!*

So he didn't stop with his own car—he took away the state cars from cabinet secretaries and commissioners. Of course, people weren't happy. But it must have saved . . . well, *thousands.* And he wouldn't buy stationery. No! He had his staff use *existing* stationery, crossing out Frank Sargent's name. There was no telling how much he could save.

He set out to abolish all jobs in the Fraudulent Claims Bureau of the Insurance Department. His own no-fault law had made those people superfluous. Problem was, those people were friends of the Speaker and Majority Leader, so Dukakis's bill got abolished in the House. Same with his bill to kill the Governor's Council: he got hammered on the vote.

That didn't mean he'd listen to the sachems. Why should he? . . . A reporter asked Dukakis if he might have to take his scalpel to the state's human services programs. Dukakis replied: "It might be a meat cleaver." That's when the public protests found their symbol.

One problem was, Michael didn't know diddly about the budget. Another problem was, he didn't want to know.

His own top man, Chief Secretary David Liederman, was dedicated to clean government. He was smart, independent, a thoroughgoing public servant— even by Michael's standards. Liederman had served with Michael in the House, but in contrast to Michael's fascination with pure government, David's interest lay in specific state services—housing, community development, children's programs. In other words, he had to know where the money came from, and where it went. Now he told Dukakis: "Michael, you're not gonna squeeze it out. You can squeeze ten million, twenty . . . maybe fifty. You can play with fifty million. But not two hundred. *Not three hundred.*"

"Steady as she goes!"

Michael announced he would not release the (contractually required) cost-of-living raises for state workers. (That's when the unions passed their strike vote). He ruled out the (legally required) cost-of-living raise for welfare. Michael froze the accounts by which services were purchased for the mentally retarded, the disabled, all the state's poorest and most helpless. He held up thousands of welfare checks to ram temporary month-to-month "budgets" through the legislature. He announced that human services would have to take twenty million in immediate cuts . . . and next year ('76 looked even worse than '75), he would cut welfare alone by $300 million.

He insisted he wasn't cutting people's only income . . . no! "In human services, for example," he said, "we may cut back on some consulting contracts. We may stop publishing brochures and bulletins at the rate they've been rolling off the presses."

Three hundred million in brochures?

"All of us," said Michael, "are going to have to make sacrifices."

But even his longtime supporters (all those liberals who thought he was one of them) pointed out with obvious justice that Michael's choice—his instinctive choice—was to balance the budget by cutting benefits and services to the poorest people, to save the middle- and upper-income brackets from the burden of further taxes.

That was another part of the problem: Michael didn't know anyone who couldn't find a job. No one on welfare. Like Panos before him, he couldn't understand why these people shouldn't *work*! Thirty-five-year-old people! Men! Taking money from the state? What got *into* them? . . . Where was their *discipline*?

That's what he wanted in his Commonwealth: discipline . . . for the public weal. He'd hector his cabinet in their (now private) meetings:

"You guys don't wanna do it! We can do it! It's not a lotta money—we can get it!"

See, it wasn't just his public commitment—no new taxes. It was his private compact: no one could tell Dukakis he wasn't smart enough.

"You guys just don't wanna do it! . . . I don't wanna hear that!"

So, after a while, he did not.

No one wanted to get in his face. Not even when they were poking around in the Welfare Department—cleaning, literally—and came across *shoe boxes* full of unpaid bills . . . they went back years! Tens of millions of dollars in back bills!

Don't tell Michael!

Nor even when his finance guys, Jack Buckley and his deputy, Tex McClain, got the latest revenue estimates, and thereby arrived at a new figure for the deficit—the amount of money coming in, compared to the totals going out.

They called Liederman.

"David, you better get down here."

There they were, Jack and Tex, with their faces hanging halfway to the floor.

Liederman said: "What's the number?"

"Six hundred and twenty million."

In the end, he had to raise taxes. But by the time he did, he could never raise enough to close the gap for the current year. So he had to borrow almost five hundred million, and then raise taxes—more than a hundred million a year—to pay back the bonds at nine percent.

That still didn't take care of the next year. So Michael would have to raise taxes again.

The legislators *begged* him (well, actually they begged Liederman) to roll all the taxes into one revenue bill. Don't make them vote for two hikes in one year!

Michael would hear of no such thing. They were separate issues!

So, one week after he signed his first tax hike, he asked the legislators—rather, he told them—to raise $687 million in new annual taxes. That was the steepest tax bill in the history of the state.

He would still cut thousands of people from the welfare rolls, diminish benefits and services for everybody else, stiff sixty thousand state employees on cost-of-living raises, and lay off at least a thousand workers more.

That's when it came clear the legislature might not be in a mood to hand him two-thirds of a billion dollars. Six months into his term, he had become the enemy of the poor *and* the middle class. He had become the target for every cartoonist in the state. (Michael-with-his-meat-ax was too good to pass up.) And he had managed to alienate a solid majority (of Democrats!) in the legislature. Maybe they'd give him his budget—maybe not.

Of course, Michael was furious.

Was he, or was he not, *Governor*?

What it was, of course, he felt betrayed.

74

Wilting from the Heat

ASSO GAVE Michael his resignation, the next morning, at the State House. Michael didn't look well. He hadn't slept much. But he was brisk, managing the problem.

Nope . . . no resignation.

Michael had his press conference already scheduled. He would announce: John would take a forced two-week leave, an exile. Michael, of course, would take full responsibility.

The politics were tricky, they both knew that. This would draw exhaustive and negative attention while people were forming their first opinions of Michael. Iowans were famous for the gentle orderliness of their politics. And now Michael's campaign would admit to hitting Joe Biden, just as he was to lead the Democratic *jihad* against Bork.

But Michael wasn't talking politics. "I don't have to tell you," he said, in his chief-executive tone, "that's not the kinda campaign I wanna run."

No, he didn't have to tell John.

Any other time, Sasso might have told *him:* "Mike . . . is this room bugged? Is anybody listening? . . . Mike! This is just us!"

Any other time, John surely would have told him: what he did, he did for Mike—this was no betrayal—John did nothing for himself. John had no way to know his tweak on Biden would start an avalanche. The tapes were the truth. He'd added nothing, taken away nothing. And he never lied about them afterward. (Tully denied the story in the press. Just yesterday, Paul had denied it again—at a contributors' luncheon. Tully would have to go.) Of course, John didn't step up and volunteer that he was the source of those tapes. And he waited way too long to tell Michael. But he *never lied*.

It was important to Sasso that Mike realize that. But there was no way to tell Michael that morning, with Michael in his hunch. *Monos mou* . . . he didn't want to talk.

Michael called Paul Brountas to tell him the decision: John would be spared . . . after an exile. Brountas wasn't happy, Michael knew. But Michael didn't want to talk.

See, to fire John, to cut him off . . . that would be the *old* Dukakis. Michael meant to show he had learned . . . as he'd said in '82, he could listen now, he could bend . . . he was flexible, more humane. In other words, this was about Michael's own idea of himself.

"John offered to resign," Dukakis said at his press conference. "I considered it seriously, but rejected it. I did so, even though what he did was a very, very serious error in judgment, a very serious mistake."

Dukakis apologized to Biden.

He took full responsibility.

He took questions, and dismissed them, one by one.

Then he walked off stage . . . and the heat began.

— ★ —

Kitty soon joined Michael at the State House. She'd already gotten calls at home—Michael should know. Brountas was reporting calls stacked up at his law firm. People thought John had to go. Was Michael condoning this attack on Biden?

Michael took the calls from Senators, Joe's colleagues . . . Teddy Kennedy, John Kerry, Michael's old law school pal and fellow Greek, Paul Sarbanes. Congressmen were calling, Democratic Committeemen . . . Biden had friends!

And they all said, John had to go, *now*. This couldn't wait for another news cycle. Mike had to realize. The networks would kill him!

"I don't understand why John did it," Michael kept saying. "I think you know, this is not the kinda campaign I run . . ."

They told him it didn't matter what they knew, or what kinda guy he was—it was what people saw. And Michael had to act—now.

Of course, it was terrible for Michael. That's why Kitty said, more than once, how *outrageous* it was, what John had done . . . how he'd put Michael into this . . . *position*!

And at some point, near noon, Michael stopped answering into the telephone, "I think you know . . ."

Now he just said, "I know . . ."

— ★ —

No one could remember, at the campaign loft on Chauncy Street, when it came clear . . . this was not over: it didn't matter what Michael had said. He was still taking heat, and he was wilting.

Maybe it was a phone call from the State House (there were scores that day—staff swapping rumors).

Maybe it was the questions still aswirl in the press pack. The diddybops were camped in the hallways, waiting for Sasso . . . trading the story up to spine-tingling scandal: Sasso did the tape—Michael hadda know! . . . Michael must've known—Kitty hadda know! . . . Tully knew—Vilmain in Iowa hadda know. . . . Who knew? Farmer? Corrigan? Edley? Estrich? Patricia O'Brien? . . . What did they know . . . and when did they know it?

Or maybe it was John, who was sure: this wasn't over . . . no, not the way Michael was treating this—as a moral question. Once it got to that, there was only one place Michael could come down.

Sasso was closeted in a hideaway office, upstairs, with his wise guys and a few staff. John was going to do his own press conference that afternoon—three o'clock. They had to get this thing square, to bed, in time for the TV news. If they couldn't kill the questions, this would slop into another day's news, and another, then another. They could bleed to death like Biden.

But all the talk was strange, strained. They talked about Tully! Did Tully have to go? How should Tully go? . . . As if no one thought that Michael would—that he could—let John go. They were Sasso's people, after all—not Michael's. Michael was a weight they bore.

It was afternoon when it sank in . . . still, no one could quite believe . . . Michael *couldn't* . . . he had to *think* . . . God, they had to stop him!

Dan Payne, the ad man, called the Governor at the State House. Michael took the call, but that was it. He didn't want to talk.

"Look," Payne said, "can't this wait, hold on, like, *one day*? You're under a lot of stress. John is . . . I mean . . ."

"No—you should be here," Michael told him. "The calls are coming in, it's unbelievable. Everybody says . . ."

Payne tried to break in, to say what Sasso would not say: "You guys haven't even really *talked* . . ."

"There's no time," Michael snapped. "Gotta do this." He took a call on another phone and, for some reason, handed Payne off to Kitty.

Jack Corrigan, Sasso's right hand, told the Governor he was making a mistake. Corrigan was a man of few words—mutters, actually—not the kind to make speeches. But that day, he got in Michael's face, and told him: "Governor, you have *no idea* how hard this campaign is going to be . . . you're going to need John."

But Michael acted like it was Corrigan who needed John: "Look, I know how close you two are . . . but it's gotta be done."

Susan Estrich made her first call ever, directly to Dukakis. She'd always dealt through John. But she felt she had to tell Michael that John would stay. She *knew* John would stay. If they could only talk—they had to talk. . . . But she knew, John would not call.

No, John would not call. So Michael called John, at Chauncy Street. Michael's voice was clipped.

"You're gonna have to go. You're gonna have to do it, make the announcement . . ."

And, after an instant's silence . . . at last, John tried:

"Do you want to talk about this for a few minutes? . . . Later this afternoon? . . . You wanna talk, tonight?"

"No," Michael said. "You gotta do it, at your three-o'clock."

John didn't say more. Was he worth twenty-four hours? Apparently not. Was he worth one face-to-face discussion?

Michael would not look John in the face for the next three months.

At his press conference, Sasso announced he had resigned.

75

Old
Friends

I N THAT FIRST TERM, as the Governor took his meat-ax to the budget, there was no use coming at Michael with threats to resign. Abandonment seemed to hold no terror for him. Isolation in his correctness only made that correctness more splendid—and more dogged. People used to say he couldn't hear criticism, but that wasn't true. He heard, he understood the words (he wasn't stupid!) . . . that's why he acted ever more sure that he was right.

And not just right . . . but sure, all the while, that he'd be *proven* right, and soon! Reason and decency (*he*) would prevail. And not just sure . . . but eager, optimistic, every day, as he marched the wing tips into the corner office, shrugged off his boxy suitcoat, rolled his shirtsleeves a couple of times, and sat down to *govern*. . . . This was the life!

Sure, the press and pols might be fixated on welfare cuts, taxes . . . but Michael took great satisfaction from his reform of the Public Utility Commission, the Outdoor Advertising Board, the Insurance Commissioner's Office, the Banking Commissioner's Office. Michael could talk for hours about resuscitating the state's decaying mill towns. (He'd found a sharp young planner in Lowell, Frank Keefe, and he was working on some Urban Heritage Parks that were, well, just terrific!) . . . Salvucci and the neighborhood do-goods had managed to oust that idiot, Eddie King, who ran the port and the airport, and Michael was pressing ahead with a *full reform and reorganization* of the Port Authority! . . . These were great doings, to Dukakis—the stuff of his dreams.

So what if demonstrators were shouting obloquy from the curb on Perry

Street? He was elected to *govern*—not to give away the store. In the end, the static only sharpened Michael's sense of all he had to bear, to be right. His children were upset and confused. Kitty thought the attacks were an outrage. And her mother (who called Michael "the Saint") told him he was *too good* for this job! She could hardly believe how well he bore such wickedness and idiocy.

So what if his erstwhile liberal supporters were conniving and combining to oppose him—somehow—in the next election? Their desertion only showed he'd been *correct* in his mistrust of them. (And Kitty, for one, knew that most of them—oh, she could name names at the dinner table!—were in the pockets of the interest groups.) Anyway, Michael was sure, in the end, they would have to see, he was right. Anyone who knew would have to admit, he was right.

In the old days, from time to time, some friend (a Brookline veteran or an old compadre from the reform wars) might find a chance to talk with Michael—some evening, some Sunday—make him think twice, or at least make him listen. . . . But Michael had so little time now. He was so wrapped up—and so excited—in the corner office.

And the old friends . . . well, it was strange, how it happened.

The toughest for Michael was Allan Sidd, the Treasurer of Brookline, a friend since Michael's first campaigns. Allan loved politics, understood politicians, and relished the game—as much as he loved food, drink, and smoke. Allan died of a heart attack—he was only fifty-three—just two years into Michael's term.

By that time, Carl Sapers and his brother, Bill, had split with Michael—they'd been allies since Town Meeting days, since "Vote Group Two!" . . . but after Michael started running statewide, they'd had it with his attitude. He didn't seem to know who his friends were. (He wouldn't help Carl in a race for Brookline Board of Selectmen!) Anyway, the Saperses were gone.

Maybe Michael's oldest friend in politics was Sumner Kaplan, the Prometheus of reform, Dukakis's first political model, the first Brookline Democrat to break into office, the man whose House seat Michael had stepped into. In 1977, Kaplan wanted to become a judge—Brookline District Court. But Governor Dukakis wouldn't appoint him. Why? Because everybody knew how close Michael was to Sumner Kaplan! Michael had to be correct! . . . So, Sumner Kaplan was no longer talking to Michael.

Then, too, Fran Meaney, Michael's closest political ally—his partner in COD, his companion on countless drives through the dark in service of reform, his manager in '66 and '70, and his chairman in '74, the campaign that put him into the corner office . . . Fran Meaney's law firm got a bond counsel contract with the state!

Lord help us!

It did not matter to Michael that Fran had not got the contract by his influence (or by any other means—he hadn't been involved) . . . it did not matter to Michael that the State Treasurer (a man named Crane) was not part of the Dukakis administration, but an independent elected officeholder who ran his own shop, picked his own counsel . . . it did not matter to Michael that Fran's firm—Mintz, Levin—was in every way competent and eligible for this contract. It certainly did not matter that Fran had worked with Michael Dukakis for fifteen years, without taint of compensation, or any accusation of self-interest . . .

No.

People might think that Michael was, in some way, not correct! So Michael wanted Fran to force his firm to give up the contract.

No way.

Fran announced: "I am not a satellite to Michael Dukakis." Then, he resigned all volunteer jobs that Michael had loaded upon him.

Michael said: "If that's the way he wants it, so be it." Then, he went back to work.

The important thing was, Michael was correct . . . the more (and more) splendid in his isolation.

76

Apology
Weekend

EVERYONE COULD SEE, that week-end in Iowa, what this meant to Dukakis, what it took. He marched around the state—twenty-four stops in three days—apologizing, taking the blame . . . *insisting* on the blame.

"We've had six wonderful months in Iowa," he'd tell each little crowd in each little town. "Something unfortunate happened this week, as you know. Maybe there are bumps in the road to the Presidency. I guess there are. But I apologize for . . . what happened."

This was grim work, and Michael's mien matched the chore at hand. He looked gray and weary. His eyes were sunken in a protective wince. In front of the crowds he'd stand up straight, but between stops, or back and forth to the van, his eyes sought the ground, his shoulders would hunch toward his ears. He'd called Andrea, his daughter who was working in the Des Moines office, to ride with him that weekend. He kept her at his side every minute, for three days.

He was hauling a Greyhound full of diddybops and national press, and between stops, he made time for everyone who wanted a shot at him. Not that they'd get a different answer to The Question (Did he know about the tape? How could he *not* know?) . . . but he meant to tell every reporter who would listen:

"I'm a guy who's been involved in public life for twenty-five years. I'm the kinda guy who's always believed very strongly that the only way to campaign and the only way to be a political leader, is to campaign positively . . ."

Then he'd get out at the next backyard, the next high school, or coffee shop, and apologize again, try to tell another forty or fifty voters the kinda guy he was.

From the first, it was apparent that most Iowans didn't quite get what was so *awful.* How could they understand Michael astride his moral axis? They thought this was just a campaign.

— ★ —

No one was going to rob Dukakis of his opportunity to disown this, this . . . this . . . *behavior.*

Michael was riding in a plushy van, owned by his volunteer driver, Steve Lynch, who'd dolled up the truck, named it *Van Force One,* when he drove for Gary Hart, his first love in politics. For each ride, Michael would climb into the back, to an armchair on a swivel, just behind the shotgun seat. Patricia O'Brien would put a new reporter on the bench, facing Dukakis. And Michael would have at apology again. Or, to be precise, Michael worked at disassociation.

To Germond and Witcover, he called John's act "incomprehensible."

To the *Globe:* he "never imagined."

For the *Boston Herald:* he "couldn't conceive" of John's being involved.

To *The Washington Post:* it was "inconceivable."

If the reporter in his van didn't have the good sense to ask, Michael would bring up his "incomprehension" himself.

With *Newsweek* as witness, he stared off (unseeing in his misery, so *Newsweek* supposed) at the fields of brown autumn cornstalks, and sighed aloud (twice): "Why did he do it?"

No member of the pack could remain insensible to Michael's blamelessness, his victimhood, or his loss (he and John were "like brothers," Michael said).

Many of the interviews in the van harkened back to Michael's defeat in 1978. That was the accepted "crisis of his life" . . . when he learned loss . . . and learned apology. Michael was perfectly willing to run through the lessons. He'd start nodding before the question was through, and recall the history:

"I hadn't failed at very much politically to that point. I worked *so* hard in those first two years. Late 1977, early '78, things had turned. The best year, economically, in the state since World War II. . . . I really didn't understand a lot about campaigning. And the polls had me forty points up . . ."

Then, the shrug—incomprehension, loss remembered, the "public death"— it was neat. . . . Thirty column inches—no loose ends.

But when some woolly writer suggested that wasn't the same kind of loss . . . when it was suggested to Michael, instead, that the analogue occurred before '78—when he dismissed Fran Meaney from his life, Michael snapped:

"It's not the time to talk about *that!*"

There was silence for a mile or two, before Michael swiveled toward the windows, and returned to the accepted text:

"I just don't understand why John did it."

The writer suggested it wasn't so hard to understand. The Campaign Manager spends twenty hours a day thinking how to get Michael past the other guys . . . how to bring Michael up, bring the other guys down. . . . "It's not a personal thing against the other guys. They're just the targets."

And Michael's face went dark, as he wheeled in his little captain's chair and his fist came crashing down on the arm:

"NOT in this campaign. They are NOT TARGETS!"

Well, that shut everybody up.

And with that smashing fist came the answer to the only hard question: Why couldn't Sasso tell his "brother" Mike?

— ★ —

The public contrition was over in a week. Michael stopped apologizing. The big-feet had spent themselves of features and analysis . . . they stopped asking Dukakis if he knew about the tapes. Michael stopped saying how sad he was.

It was Kitty, as usual, who summed up the emotional truth. "I think that we have a sense of sadness, and that's appropriate, under the circumstances," she said while on damage patrol in New Hampshire. "But my husband's competency and his integrity are what matter. We will go on with another Campaign Manager, and things will go on as before."

So Michael appointed his new Campaign Manager, Susan Estrich. She came from within Sasso's executive cadre. She would provide continuity, calm his organization. Michael didn't know her well, wasn't sure if he could rely on her judgment. But that suited him. He and Brountas had discussed this: Michael had relied too much on John Sasso.

Now Michael would take charge. He called every member of the staff who might have dealings with the press, to tell them:

"I don't want any disparaging of any opponents. I don't want any leaking. I absolutely won't tolerate it. I don't like it, and I'm telling you, we're not going to have it. Republicans, Democrats, I don't care. I'm talking about everything. Not just the little stuff on the edges. I'm talking about everything. I don't want any of it . . . you got it?"

They got it . . . and lest they did not, there was a lawyer, a Hill & Barlow man named Dan Taylor, acting for Brountas, scouting around the loft on Chauncy Street, building files for an internal purge, asking disingenuous questions like: "Tell me . . . is it *usual* to make tapes of things and hand them to reporters?"

Susan Estrich soon canceled that investigation. She'd inherited an organization that was already shaky in its shoes. She needed more pointing fingers like she needed a skin rash. The *Boston Herald* was still poking around Corrigan's involvement in the tapes episode. Susan managed to stonewall that question—Corrigan stayed.

The *Globe* still had a "spotlight team" grunting up a mega-turd on the Biden tapes. Patricia O'Brien favored that team with a long, anguished interview about how she should have known there was bad fish in the soup. Patricia was soon gone.

As for Sasso, Michael said a dozen times that he would have no role in the campaign, now or in the future. Yet the first time Estrich brought up a question of political strategy, Michael asked:

"What does John think?"

What he wanted, of course, was a campaign that took full advantage of Sasso's wisdom, and his wiles. . . . Just don't tell Michael.

He would not see John, no.

That's what he assured Joe Biden, when he called him, to explain: he'd had no knowledge of this whole affair. He'd been shocked, stunned, when he found out it was Sasso. And he'd *acted* . . . to cut that kinda thing out.

Biden, of course, didn't believe him. Biden would have known. Hell, yes—if it was his campaign! No one could convince Biden that Michael was not involved—or that Dukakis and his minions hadn't *deliberately* hit him, just at the start of the hearings on Bork . . . just when he couldn't hit back.

That's what galled Joe—the *worst:* they hit him just when he was saving the country from Bork! . . . Biden didn't want to talk to Dukakis. He didn't want a lot of holy explanations. He had only one point to make to the Governor:

"Don't you assholes understand? This shit is important!"

77

It's
Hard
to Smile

THE WIN ON Bork turned out to be—
as Caddell had insisted—the swish of
the guillotine on Reagan's "revolu-
tion." Biden carried his committee with an extra vote to spare—didn't know
about that till the last day, when Heflin came off the fence.

Armed with a nine–five negative recommendation, Biden took the Bork
nomination to the Senate floor in early October. Outgunned, outnumbered, the
judge's supporters tried to make the confirmation process the issue. But Biden
would not give them the satisfaction.

"Forty million people *watched* him," Joe insisted. "He spoke. I, time and
again, raised the gavel and said, 'Are you certain, Judge, you've had enough
time to respond to questions?'

"When it was all over, I said to Judge Bork: 'Now, Judge Bork, do you think
you got a fair hearing?'

"He said, 'Yes.'

" 'Anything else you want to say, Judge Bork?'

" 'No.' . . ."

The fact was, Biden ran a long and serious hearing, the best discussion (and
a high enactment) of the Constitution in the TV age: he could not let them
take that away. And he would not let them repaint the battle as a liberal media
attack on Bork. Biden made his case, and the people who watched turned away
from the judge. The Senate vote reflected the shift among voters.

In the end, the Senate voted fifty-eight to forty-two against Bork. Joe had
his win. But he did not have his vindication. Nor, to tell the truth, much
satisfaction.

"Some wins are more enjoyable than others," he said that afternoon. "This is one of the wins that's less enjoyable. . . . Because we're talking about a man who had to sit home and watch this."

Biden knew how that felt.

Sometimes, at night, he'd get home, talk to the kids and Jill, and then after dinner, he'd flip on the TV. The other night, the kids had the VCR cued up with a video. Biden hit PLAY . . . and there he was, smiling, with David Frost. They'd taped his interview for Frost's series in the summer, months before . . . and there he was *telling Frost about the Kinnock speech* . . . how he saw that tape from Britain, how Kinnock moved him—because they were talking about the same kind of life! . . . God, he'd explained the thing perfectly—for *national TV* . . . but it never made TV. Biden had dropped out before the show aired.

Sometimes he'd tune in C-Span, PBS . . . and his mind would race ahead: he knew *exactly* what he'd say . . . what Gore, Gephardt, Dukakis would say next—then how he'd break in and . . . leave those sonsabitches *in the dust!* . . . God, he could see it. The other night, the live debate, Dukakis started in with that *pablum*—good jobs, good wages. Jesus! . . . But Joe only watched a minute. Jill came in.

"We're not gonna watch that, are we?"

"Well, I just thought I'd . . ."

"Well . . . I'm going downstairs." And she walked out.

— ★ —

The hard thing for Jill was, she'd thought it was finished. Standing at that press conference, she'd thought—well, at least it's over. But she hadn't counted on this feeling, the emptiness: the death of a dream she didn't know she'd had.

Joe had his life. The Senate went on, and the hearings. He started looking forward to a chance to travel, to dig into foreign policy. And she was teaching. But it was different. They were going through the motions, like they were underwater. Life was so slow. There was no weekend schedule—jump on the plane to Iowa . . . funny, she loved Iowa. He could've won there. They would have *won* . . . after the hearings, when everybody was paying attention, everybody would've known Joe, what he did on Bork . . . he was brilliant.

God, of all the things they could've thrown at Joe . . . his character, his *honesty*—that's why she *married* him! . . . She would have liked to get people by the neck and *tell* them. But there was no way. What was she going to do—scream it out in the Pathmark? She was the one who was out every day: the Pathmark, the drugstore, or Janssen's, the little market. People were trying to be nice. They'd tell her: "I wish Joe hadn't got out . . ." And Jill would have to smile, say it was all right. Or they'd say: "There'll be another time . . ." And Jill would try to keep her voice light, when she said, "Yup. Sure will."

They all wanted to defend him, but there was no way. The boys wanted to hit back. Beau had been out to Arizona for the Young Democrats, and Hunter had been at the meetings in the house. They were all a part of . . . of what?

They weren't doing anything.

There was no Delaware schedule, either. It was like they just closed down. Days would go by, no one would say a word. Funny—it was Jill who had to talk.

They'd talk in the bubble bath, in the big bathroom upstairs—it was huge, with old blue-gray scrollwork decorating the walls of cream tile, a cream-colored rug on the floor. This was their system: Joe would come home, maybe ten, he'd eat at the counter in the kitchen, see the kids. The kids would want to talk to Joe down there. But then he'd go up to the bathroom—their place. Jill would lie in the deep bath, Joe would pull up the vanity stool.

"It's hard to smile."

"I know," Joe would say. "Things'll get better."

It was great the way he had his eyes fixed ahead: things he was going to do, things they could do. Sometimes, she could look ahead. That was better. "There's a lot for you," she'd say. "You can keep going on the child care . . ."

"Yeah, I talked to Kennedy . . ."

"It's important, people really need . . ."

"Yeah, there's a lot . . ."

Seldom would they talk about what was, or had been. It was sad. It was hard to understand, and accept.

"I didn't know . . ." Jill said one night. "Do you have to be just ruthless?"

"I don't know."

"They are."

He didn't have to ask who. They were Kitty and Michael Dukakis.

"I don't know," he'd say. "Maybe you do."

— ★ —

It felt like drowning. That was the first thought. Joe had to strain, to fight to fill his chest with air. He was down—might as well admit that. It wasn't just the losing, it was the helplessness, the shame.

How could it blow up in his face like that? The answer was the depressing thing: he could not make it, and be like he was. If he wanted to have his dream, he'd have to be like someone else—some other way altogether.

He couldn't accept that. Probably couldn't do it . . . but anyway, what good would that make the dream?

He heard Jill say to a friend: "It's just about power. Joe was naïve."

Was that it? Yeah, he was naïve. He knew why they hit him. Sasso made no bones about that: Biden was getting the blue-collar vote. Biden's numbers were on the *move*. (Joe took grim satisfaction in that.) . . . But he never figured they would use the Constitutional fight of . . . of the *century* to come after him. No, he never figured.

Still, that didn't explain, didn't excuse . . . the helplessness. There were things he couldn't have known. No one can know, till they're in it. He didn't know what they meant when they said his whole life would tumble out in the glare. He didn't know what the press would do—wouldn't do . . . he never understood how *lazy* . . . that no one would go back and really do his record, make the picture whole. He didn't understand how much they mistrusted *him*, ever since he'd come to the Senate—since that first term, when he pissed people off. He thought he was past that . . . but you never get past. He didn't understand how the gurus would be no help, how they'd make him look hapless to the press. He didn't understand how the big-feet hated Caddell, or what they meant when they wrote about Biden's "oratory"—he didn't understand the code. God, how a guy like Johnny Apple—with a brain like that—could write that Biden was an *empty vessel* that Caddell poured a candidacy into . . . Joe still didn't understand how Apple could write that.

He knew they'd come after him, somehow—or he should have known. But when they came, he had no way to fight. How could he have been so *wrong* about the way it would be? This was the weight Joe had to push off his chest. How could he have been wrong—about his destiny?

If he lost his idea of that . . . what was left? If he gave up what he was going toward . . . where was he? Everything had to happen for a reason. That's what destiny meant, to Joe. Why did this have to happen?

He could not accept that it did not matter—that he did not matter. That would put him back—a speck . . . he *could not* go back to that despair. God, he hadn't felt that way for ten years—twelve!—since Jill . . . not since Jill came, and put his life back together.

78

Jill

I T WAS a couple of years after Neilia died before Joe even got himself back. Not that he was a basket case. Thirty-two years old, a Senator, rising star in the Party . . . that was fine. The boys were healthy and strong, off to school, doing well. Val was living at Northstar, with Joe. Mom-Mom was around every day, and Uncles Jimmy and Frankie. Those boys had more familial care than . . . well, they never lacked.

Parents? Joe was the parent. Period. No confusion: not Val, not Jimmy, or Mom-Mom. Joe didn't want anybody else raising his kids, thanks. He was there every night, every weekend. They had stories at bedtime, games of catch on the lawn, outings, trips, places to go: out to the Charcoal Pit for burgers, steak sandwiches . . . "Beau-y, Hunt! C'mon! Let's go!" . . . drag-racing the eighteen-year-olds down the Concord Pike in Joe's green Corvette—"Let's see what this kid has under his hood." The boys never saw the air out of Joe's lungs. Not once. He would not allow that.

That's partly why it took so long. He could not let down, could not turn away. What took years to win was absence of mind—when he wasn't working, or focused on the boys—to wake, stretch, look outside, and think: It's a nice day.

Not: A nice day—we would have been doing this, if . . .

Not: A nice day—can I dream up something for the boys to do outside? . . .

Not: A nice day—I oughta get home early, give Val a chance to get out . . .

"It's a nice day."

That was the elusive prize. How do you work at feeling normal?

How could he spend a day without thought for the hole in his life, when everything was set up to compensate for that hole? The commute back and forth to Washington . . . the car phone in that huge Cadillac that Jimmy insisted on . . . weekends home . . . Aunt Val at home . . . that home!

He started looking for a house. Too many memories at Northstar.

He tried to go out, tentatively . . . it was hard. In Washington, he felt . . . well, he had to get home. In Delaware, it was almost too close. Everybody knew, or thought they knew. Not to mention, all those eager . . . well, Mrs. Johnson thought her daughter would make a *perfect match* for a Senator . . .

He saw Jill's picture in the airport—one of those photos selected by committee, this one mounted by the Department of Parks. She was blond, young, smiling . . . she was gorgeous. Brother Frankie knew someone who knew her—Jill Jacobs. Frankie got the number for Joe.

When he called, he wanted Jill to go out that night. She had other plans. "Well, can you break them?" Joe said he had to leave town the next day.

So, she broke her date. God knows why. She didn't know much about him. She knew the name, of course, and about his wife. She'd voted for him in '72 (thank heavens). In fact, she was at the Hotel du Pont that election night—but that wasn't for Joe. That was a date: Jill's interest was in dinner.

Funny thing was, by the time Joe called, she'd almost resolved to quit dating. She'd married young, it didn't last, and after that, when she went back to college, well . . . she was a senior, but twenty-four years old. She was out in the world, student teaching, and the guys at school were only boys. Anyway, most guys were awful. In 1975, if they bought you dinner, they figured they bought . . . you know, the whole thing.

That was the first way Joe was special. For a start, he showed up in a suit. She hadn't gone out with a guy in a suit for—probably since high school. And then, when he brought her home that night, he took her to the door and . . . shook her hand.

She told her mom on the phone: "My God, I think I finally met a gentleman."

That, and the other part: he didn't quit. He wasn't one of those guys who said, "I'll call you . . . maybe we'll get together next weekend." No, he was on the phone, the next day, and the next. He wanted to talk to her.

They didn't talk about the past—his or hers. With Joe, it was now . . . or better yet, times to come. He always had something he wanted to do, something they could do together. Second date, he drove her out to a street called Montchan Drive, pulled up at a huge old house.

"This is the place I'm gonna buy," Joe said. "C'mon! You gotta see it!" Of course, it was midnight, pitch-dark, and Joe couldn't find a light that worked, the place was surrounded by mud, and . . . Jill sat in the car. But Joe was so excited.

Then he called and told her he didn't think they should date anyone else . . . after two dates! Then he wanted to bring the boys. Then he wanted to take her out with the family, the brothers, Val, his folks . . . that's where Jill held back. She didn't want to get involved with the family, to feel she was under inspection. Only later she figured out: Joe didn't want an inspection. It wasn't any special trip for her to meet the family. The family was how "we Bidens" lived.

By that time, of course, Joe's head was racing. He was starting to see how it could be . . . in the new house, with Jill, the boys. The boys loved her. Half the time, she was over there for dinner, in the kitchen, easy in the life. . . . And the boys wanted to be married. That's how "we Bidens" thought about it. Beau or Hunt would say to his dad: "Are we gonna get married again?"

And Joe was so attentive. Every day he called her. Every night. If he got home at ten, he'd run over to her apartment, just to say hello. And he was so interesting—though, God knows, she didn't care much about politics. Joe didn't mind. He got enough of that in Washington.

No, he'd take care of the politics, and Jill . . . well, he could see her taking care of them, the way she was with the boys—with everybody. She could talk with anyone. Not that she believed everyone. No, she believed what she believed. She had backbone. She was private—Joe liked that, her cool way of hiding the girl inside, and old hurts . . . he could see that. She had that way of looking at you, to make sure you meant what she thought was so funny . . . and then that quick shy smile, half-doubting—she could sniff out bullshit. She'd tell him, too—especially when it was his bullshit—she'd tell him straight. Very soft of manner was Jill, but smart: she knew who she liked.

She could do it . . . he could *see* it . . . and when that started, well, he could see things falling into place. If he could put that back together, if he knew they'd have their home, their family . . . then he could reach outward again. It wasn't just the schedule—he could travel, he could speak. It was more like the center was in place . . . so he could lift his eyes. That's how Joe talked about it—his words:

"What Jill did . . . she was the one who let me dream again."

79

One of
the Great Sins

LEE HAD ALWAYS SAID, she wanted
their life back . . . but this was not
their life. There was a hole at the
center: What was Gary going to do? That's what so much of their life had been
about. The simplest things, and the biggest—like where they lived—had always fallen into place around Gary's plans. Even day-to-day doings—the
schedule, a calendar . . . Lee might go a week now and never write a thing on
her calendar. If she did, it didn't make any difference—she never looked at the
darned thing anymore.

It was drastic, overnight; the future was a blank sheet. And not just her
personal future, next week. They'd always shared a larger *public* future, for
their kids, for the country. On that Gary and Lee had stood, unalterably,
together. They'd given up so much for that—but now she was conscious of how
much that had given them.

Public purpose . . . it was never really for *her*. Over and over, Lee had tried
to explain: she wanted Gary to be President—not for her, *personally*—but just
because he'd be great. *She* never wanted to be in the White House. But people
couldn't seem to credit her with that. If they didn't think she was a doormat
. . . well, she must be so greedily ambitious that she'd let Gary trample her
as long as he hauled her into the White House.

She'd tried to explain . . . but what was the point now? Her friend Sally
Henkel told her she ought to write something, or go on TV—Oprah!—to show
she was not a conniver or a victim. But to Lee that seemed like looking back.
She always said (and not just her—Gary always said) you only look back to

learn, to make yourself better. Otherwise, it's just morbid—too debilitating. You have to get on with your life, unless you want to curl up in a ball and die. She had to see this as a *new challenge*. She had to *look ahead*—which was hard enough, with all the . . . information.

It wasn't that she asked. People called *her*! . . . Just a few weeks after Gary got out, a friend of Lee's (such a good friend) called to make sure she knew the whole dismal poop on the *Post*'s "other woman." This friend not only had the woman's name, just for starters, but what she was like, what she looked like, what she felt about Gary, even what she'd said when the *Post* grilled her. (This friend was sure: a *team* of three *Post* reporters had gone at this woman for six hours!)

And it wasn't till months later, Lee found out that most of this information was wrong. She should have known: Lee had *seen* one of those reporters in New Hampshire—while he was supposedly grilling the "other woman" in D.C. But how could Lee know what to believe?

Another friend called to say Gary's car was seen outside this other woman's house, for *months*—from January to the campaign's end, in May . . . while Lee knew, John had driven his dad's car back to Colorado in December of '86. . . . Of course, when Lee tracked down a charge and confronted somebody with the facts, they'd start backpedaling: that wasn't what they really said . . . or they must have meant '86 . . . or they must have meant a different car. . . . What was the point?

She didn't even ask Gary about a lot of this stuff—he didn't want to talk about it. And some things just weren't worth bringing up. They were unimportant, compared to the big things in life. And with Gary, you just didn't keep going *over* things. "You get it out of your system," he'd say, "because at some point it's got to stop."

Lee believed you shouldn't put a person on the spot. This wasn't just for Gary's sake—it was her way with her children and friends, too. "You don't want to push people into positions where they have to lie," she'd say, "or just stop talking. There are times when you can be put into a position where you have to lie—just to protect yourself. That's the way to teach people to lie."

It wasn't that they didn't talk. There was time now to talk about personal things, things they'd just let slide for the last ten years. With Gary it was never easy. But at some point you had to talk. And she told him, this was the *stupidest* thing he'd ever done. But she knew, even as she said it . . . she didn't have to. That's why she had to laugh about those stories—*Cosmopolitan,* or some magazine like that, made such a big deal about things she wouldn't even ask! Well, after nearly thirty years, there's so much you don't have to ask.

And Sally Quinn—the feminists—were pathetic! You work hard at a marriage for twenty-eight years, and then when somebody makes a mistake, you throw it over? . . . And in this case, when you really got down to the facts, it wasn't such a horrible mistake. Just stupid.

She never would understand how he could be so *stupid*. "But," she said, "those things happen."

She said she never shed one tear.

—★—

People would call—they were so blue without the campaign—and Gary would end up consoling *them:* life would go on, there would be other challenges, other ways to carry on the mission.

Him? . . . He was fine. He'd remind them: he got out of the race on Friday and was at the law firm, 9:00 A.M., Monday morning.

Which was true, but it didn't say anything about him . . . except he wasn't going to sit home. If anyone tried to ask about his work for the firm, he'd roll his eyes to show: he wasn't really a part of *that*—he was just a rainmaker, a money-raker, supposed to put the firm into the middle of deals. It seemed so empty to him.

He had to do it.

He had engaged himself to do it, for one thing . . . and the partners had tried to be good to him. And he had two kids in college, and never took the time before to make money. And his option on the land around the cabin—137 acres, his one personal place in the world—would come due in July '87, two months after he quit the race. (And the campaign contributor who was going to loan Gary money to buy the land suddenly withdrew the offer. Life changes when you're a loser.)

Hart had to make money in a hurry. (In the end, he had to ask Warren Beatty . . . who gladly lent him the money.)

So this wasn't therapy, or Hart settling into a new life. There were demands, as ever. Gary put his face to the phone. . . . But that wasn't what his life was about.

He'd defined himself for so long by his public purpose, there was no way to do without it. You couldn't fly around for six years in a race to change the country before its future be squandered or scarred . . . and then, after a ten-minute concession speech, walk away with a shrug, a smile. He could not.

He was religious, in his way—and one of the great sins was to fail to make use of your talents and abilities. He never meant to suggest he was *selected by God*—nothing like that—terrible presumption. But he had something to offer . . . that had carried him for *fourteen years,* if you went back to the Senate campaigns.

There had to be a way.

A friend would call and Hart would bring up an idea: someone had suggested he might write semi-regularly for *The New York Times,* op-ed—you know, opinion, foreign policy, defense . . .

"Sounds great."

"You think so?" Hart would say. "May come to nothing . . ." He'd mention the L.A. Times Syndicate—a column . . . or he thought he might give his remaining economics speech at a college. He'd been talking with a professor who thought it might be good to do a series of lectures.

There were always possibilities. Next week, they were still possibilities. Nothing happened. But he had another idea: PBS might want to do a series of interviews—if he could get Gorbachev . . .

The fact was, he didn't want to commit to anything real and large enough to hold him. He wouldn't take a step in any direction if that would pull down the pillars of his life . . . not when there was a *chance* he could build anew.

He wouldn't bring it up. People called him! . . . Had he seen that poll about the press? (*Two-to-one,* people thought the press went overboard on Hart.) Had he seen that southern-states poll from Atlanta? (When Hart's name was added, he was still the Democratic front-runner.)

"Really!" Hart would say. (Like he hadn't talked about that poll thirty times.) He'd tell them about the letters—hundreds of letters, came to his house, to the law firm . . . hundreds he couldn't even get to yet that came to the campaign address.

People were writing to tell him he never should have quit—the cause and the country required him. There were letters that offered theories on who'd set Gary up; letters from lifelong Republicans who said they'd vote for Hart; there were senior citizens who sent five dollars from their pensions—all they could afford. There was a hundred dollars from one couple who'd just birthed a baby girl. They had this money to buy a new crib, but they decided it was more important to do something for their baby's country.

Of course, there were letters on the other side. But they were few, or from obvious sickos, or people who didn't . . . well, Gary said they weren't worth mentioning.

> *Dear Mr. heart sorry your bLue. Evrybody thinks your sLezzy. But I don't!*
>
>> *sincereLy,*
>> *Rand Olson*
>
>> *P.S.*
>> *Your a nice Guy.*
>> *here is my*
>> *picther*

Hart never mentioned, anymore, anyone who wanted him gone for good. If he heard any bad news about his standing, it didn't register. Or it only *proved* to him that the politics-as-usual hacks were afraid of him, ganging up. That's how the real Hart people knew. Friends or staff who'd gone through the wars with Gary could tell: Jesus, he was *serious*! . . . He was getting ready to be a majority of one again.

The Hart people would call one another, like consulting physicians. Billy Shore would dial Sue Casey and say: "I saw him today." He didn't have to say who.

"Yeah," she'd say, like she wasn't sure she wanted to hear.

"He's doing it again."

"Like, how bad is he doing it?"

"Well," Shore would say, "he asked me three times, 'Do you really think any of the others really *get* it?' . . ."

Occasionally, one of the physicians would hump up Hippocratically and try to talk to Gary. Casey was still in Denver. She'd call his law office, get him out to lunch.

"Look," she'd say. "There's life, and there's running for President. And there's just things you've got to resolve in life first."

"There you go again," Hart would say. "Pass the bread."

"No, really! What do you want? What's really going to make you happy?"

"It's good bread . . ."

Sometimes, Casey would resort to bitter memory-dose: "Think what you're going to put people through! Your family. Yourself! All these stories . . . it's gonna be, like, *slap me again*! . . . Have you *forgotten*? . . . What it's going to be like?"

Hart would insist, his family was ready. "The kids—you don't understand."

Casey did understand. Andrea had given her an earful—she was furious at Sue for opposing a new campaign. It was *betrayal,* like Sue was siding with the assholes! . . . *How come you're not part of the family anymore?*

But even Casey couldn't understand what happened in Gary Hart when he looked into his daughter's eyes and saw doubt . . . *about him.* If he'd done nothing wrong, why did he quit the race? Why didn't he get back in? The truth will *always* prevail—he was the one who'd taught her that!

If he believed what he'd always said, he had no choice!

Ideas *had* to make a difference in life.

How could he duck the battle now?

The worst was when she wouldn't talk. Hart would be up late, reading in his chair in the main room of the cabin. Andrea would walk in and, with one glance, fill the room with the question.

"Andrea . . ." he'd say. "If people as smart as Billy and Sue don't think it's possible, you have to think . . ."

But she'd just keep going to her room. He already knew what she thought.

In some ways, John was harder. He'd never wanted this before—to be a part of a campaign. But now he wanted it *so much.* It was like bitter fate was trying to insure that Gary and his son always passed each other, going opposite ways.

"Dad, you gotta do it!"

"John, you cannot imagine what it'd be like."

"I don't care."

"I don't mean just for me. I mean, for your mother . . . for you, and Andrea."

"We can take it. The family's strong."

They were strong, Gary thought. And he would not sacrifice that. He wasn't confused about the arguments that Casey made—she was right, of course. Billy was right. If Hart raised his head out of the ditch, there'd be a thousand people trying to kick it. They'd hit him with everything they could grab.

He knew that. But how much would he pay for the respect of his son?

That's why he asked John to meet him in Ireland. Hart had business in Europe that August—John could meet him for a week, before returning to school. They both loved Ireland. Gary would get the time with his son. John would have the chance to make his case.

— ★ —

That's when it happened, when Gary and John were in Ireland: Bill Dixon, the former Campaign Manager, told *The Washington Post* that Gary would reenter the race within a few weeks, to run a low-budget guerrilla campaign . . . because supporters and family were urging him back. "His wife and children want him in."

Then all hell broke loose. Everybody had to get Hart, but Hart was in Ireland—where, precisely, no one would say. Irish Radio finally tracked him down, but Hart went cute—wouldn't confirm or deny. "I'm not going to get into a debate here in Ireland." (In fact, the resumption of the hunt caught Hart flat-footed; he wasn't even sure what Dixon had said.)

There were hundreds of press calls to the white boys, who were back in D.C. now, or in their home states, in new jobs, new lives. . . . If some Hart people tried to knock down the story, all they could say was, they'd heard nothing. Then, they were presumed to be *out of the loop.* Dixon must have the inside track! He hadda be talking to Hart, right?

Lee Hart was besieged anew, and she was furious . . . at Gary! He had to be talking to Dixon, right? Bill wouldn't just *say* such a thing—how *she* wanted Gary back in the race? . . . She and Gary hadn't even talked about it! But she couldn't say that . . . what was she supposed to say?

It was a national fever.

The papers were already moving on to the tactics of reentry. Dixon said Hart would have to apologize, of course, for the conduct that drove him out of the race . . . he'd use the free debates to make up for his lack of ads . . . and put together a bare-bones national staff—three people instead of three hundred . . . he'd pick his states, to maximize his impact, and . . .

Whadda story! The sonofabitch was gonna rise from the dead! . . . Now the papers were digging out that Gallup Poll, where they left Hart's name in the mix: the guy was *still* ahead of Jackson, two-to-one, and everybody else at least *four-to-one.*

Did he think he could turn those numbers into votes? . . .
Did he think they'd let him get away with that? . . .
Did he think all the stories went away in four months? . . .
What got into the guy? Why would he do this to himself? . . .
Why? Why? . . . Why?

On the first day, the *Post* offered a piece of speculation that was just chewy enough for perfect political cud: Hart was still in debt—$1.4 million, from his '84 campaign. If he got back in, his '88 contributions would qualify for matching funds from the federal treasury: that would be a million dollars, right there.

Aha! . . . The official and well-known secret reason!

After that, it did not matter that Billy Shore got hold of Hart and retailed, at last, a Hart denial. (In fact, Shore offered a Hart *quote:* "Oh, no, no, no.")

It did not matter that Hart could not (without a legal fight) apply any '88 funds to clear off his '84 debt.

It certainly did not matter that Hart was *apparently* not running for anything; was running away, in fact, from the fond attentions of the press in the green and voteless countryside of the Republic of Ireland.

Nobody believed *that* pose!

Hart was gonna have to come back and *say something*. Hart was gonna have to *answer questions*—answer *to them*. It was just a matter of when, a matter of how. . . . *Nightline* was calling—how 'bout it?

—★—

Hart did *Nightline* on September 8—but not without a struggle. He insisted, for one thing, that ABC break its format and put him in the studio with Ted Koppel. He had to be face-to-face, on equal footing with the host. He had to avoid that frog-on-a-lab-table look that guests get when they cannot see Koppel but only the needle of a camera lens poked at their brains.

The show went on for more than an hour, but as Koppel conceded in his opening tease, there were only two questions everyone wanted to ask: Was Gary Hart running for President? . . . And if so (or even if not—what the hell!) . . . did he have an affair with Donna Rice?

Koppel asked the second question twenty minutes into the show. Hart nodded, squared himself on his seat, and fiddled with the ring finger of his right hand.

"Mr. Koppel," Hart said (even now he could not presume to "Ted"), "I was asked a question last spring, which I refused to answer—and your clips showed that. The articles to which you've referred have commented not only on Miss Rice, but, I must say, an outrageous number of people with whom I have been linked—a large number of whom I have never met, let alone been involved with. It has also been suggested that I don't tell the truth because I would not reveal all about my personal life. And I've tried to figure out the best way to answer these questions—not only for my sake but for other elected officials' sake, in the future, other candidates for national office. And so, it seems to me, I have no choice but to answer the question that was asked me last spring, and I will do that. If the question is, in the twenty-nine years of my marriage, including two public separations, have I been absolutely and totally faithful to my wife, I regret to say, the answer is no. But I also am never going to answer any specific questions about any individual. . . . It isn't anyone else's business."

At last, Hart's line was drawn. And despite a half-hour of intelligent follow-up (Tom Shales, the TV critic, remarked that Koppel looked like a *splendid* candidate), Hart held to that line.

He dodged the question about the *Post*'s "other woman." (It wasn't just the *Post*'s threat that drove him from the race. It was the fact that any—*every*— other paper would now hound him with other women.)

Hart explained (sort of) the *National Enquirer* photo of him holding Donna

Rice on his lap. (". . . this attractive lady, whom I had only recently been introduced to, uh . . . dropped into my lap, I was embarrassed, I chose not to, ah . . . dump her off, and the picture was taken. I shouldn't have been in that situation.")

He even responded with patience to the theory (propounded by the Chief Majorette) that Gary Hart didn't really want to be President. His unstable chemistry made him *act out* in a tacit plea to the Karacter Kops: *Stop me, oh, stop me PLEASE . . . before I win.*

No, Hart said. He wanted to be President.

So, how 'bout it, Koppel asked, at last: Are you back in the race?

"Mr. Koppel, I am not a candidate for President, and I'm not making any plans to become one. . . . I am frankly in a kind of a perplexing situation. We have been talking about sin here, this evening, I guess—that's what it gets down to, not crime, sin . . ."

"And bad judgment," Koppel offered.

"And bad judgment. Uh . . . but the Bible that says that being unfaithful is a sin also says we're all sinners, and that only those who are without sin can cast the first stone. And it says, further, that one of the greatest sins is to waste God-given talent. I've been given some talents, and what I've realized in the last three months is that I can't waste those talents. And I've got to figure out a way to contribute. . . .

"I'm not going to create a campaign organization. I'm not going to raise money. I'm not going to hire a pollster or a media expert. But I am going to give speeches, and I am going to try to have an impact."

It was perplexing, indeed.

Hart didn't reveal any definite scenario for his future, save that he would not go back to hiding in Troublesome Gulch. . . . He did reveal the reason, obliquely. He asked Koppel for a clean shot at the last thirty seconds of the broadcast.

"Mr. Koppel," he said, full face to the camera, "I appreciate the chance to be on this program. I just want to say . . . to one very special young woman, and young man—how sorry I am for letting them down . . . for many others like them.

"Have courage.

"We are not defeated. And we will not be.

"*I will find some way—I promise you—to continue on.*"

Of course, it was instantly well known to those in-the-know: Hart was talking to his own kids. On national TV.

C'monn . . . talk about weird!

— ★ —

The big-feet lost interest in Hart's new speaking tour, after the first speech. The news was that Hart had crawled out of his hole. After that, it was a yawn. They never did write much about what he said—New Ideas, and such. The problem was, you couldn't count on members of the public to ask the right questions, to make him squirm about Donna Rice—they didn't even try!

Even Hart was surprised by the questions. Maybe people at the campuses, the community halls, were just too nice to ask whom he'd slept with. Or maybe he'd been right *from the start*—they didn't care! They asked about the candidates who were running. They asked about Gorbachev, arms control, Iran-contra . . . they asked about the deficit, taxes, education.

The halls were packed, most of the time. Sometimes, they had to move Hart's speech to a larger room, or the gym. There were a couple of stops where *nobody* showed—Gary was crestfallen, of course. But he found out (would not rest *until* he found out) that the posters never got printed, or the organizers never put them up . . . there was always a reason.

Billy Shore would travel with him, and in most cities, there was some old supporter who'd pick them up at the airport, who'd put together a bunch of people to attend the speech. These weren't organized like campaign events, but someone was always calling Billy—anything they could do?

Well, maybe check the podium.

Then, two days later, they'd call back: "Can we do a reception? Will he stay for a dinner?"

The point was, it felt like a campaign . . . but better—none of the pressure. There were reporters at the speeches—but local reporters, who'd write about the warm reception he got. People waited a half-hour sometimes, just to shake Hart's hand, or tell him he never should have quit. Hart didn't have to watch what he said, or temper his positions. If he wanted to blast away at the teachers' unions . . . well, give 'em hell! And the crowds—he played to those crowds like he never would as a candidate. They gave him back a warmth that was . . . it was like life again.

Invariably, he'd get back to Denver with some eyebrow-raising fact-on-the-ground:

"They say we can do it in Ohio."

"They say we could put it together in upstate New York."

"They say it's still there in North Carolina."

"Gary . . ." the attending physicians would warn. "They'll beat your brains out. They'll burn you alive! Blow torches!"

"I've got asbestos feet now . . ." And he had a theory. (With Hart, there was always a theory.) If the press turned up the heat too high, reaction would kick in—the backlash would fuel his campaign.

"Gary, you can't be serious . . ."

More and more, as October waned, Hart would say: "Why not?"

He was the one who was out there, with the people—they were begging him: just say the word!

—★—

He had the scene in his mind, like a piece of a novel—it would be sensational. He had a speech scheduled at Boston University . . . he'd do it there.

Boston was a great town for him. A few weeks before—Boston College, a speech about Bork—Hart drew a mob at the basketball arena, a line around the block . . . must have been four thousand people (though the *Globe* nincompoops called it "over a thousand") . . . and that was charging five bucks to get in . . . up against a *hockey game*! . . . Boston was spectacular.

Anyway, for BU, he wasn't going to tell anyone. Except John. He called John in Worcester and read him the statement—Why Hart Must Speak Out. Actually, he'd written it while he and John were in Ireland together. John was so excited . . . his dad was coming out to fight! He had prevailed!

Gary would read the statement at the end of his speech . . . to the hushed hall . . . which would break into *cheers.* It really couldn't be better. The BU student activities group had a rule, no press—which meant they'd be fighting to get in. (The BU group was going to refund the tickets if the press came in.)

The place would be full—Hart knew exactly how he'd construct the speech, idea by idea, the need for reform, the need to speak out, the *emptiness* of the current campaign . . . which was *why* . . . it was so *simple,* so *apparent* to him . . . he would reveal:

The next day, they were going—Gary and John, together—to New Hampshire, to the statehouse in Concord. Gary would deliver a check for a thousand dollars . . . and file for the primary. Gary Hart would be *back in the race*!

Let the people decide!

It would be *simply explosive.*

When Gary got to Boston, to the hotel, there was John . . . in a *suit.* John was so excited, he went out and *bought a suit.* . . . Gary said to Billy Shore:

"Give me ten minutes. I've got to go to the room." He had to take John upstairs—to tell him.

"John . . . I can't do it."

Hart saw his son's face fall. "John, I've told you, this is going to be hard. Everybody's got to be together, in the family . . ."

Gary could see he wasn't getting through. But he didn't want to say more. He couldn't say . . .

"Your mother may not, uh . . . this may not be the right time."

He didn't want to say what had *happened*—the extraordinary fact: he was on his way to Boston, to his destiny, the new campaign . . . when, for the first time in their lives together, Lee Hart told him:

"No."

She wouldn't have it. She wasn't ready. No one had asked about *her* life. They hadn't really talked. She needed time, she needed . . . what? She didn't know. But she was not going through it again. Not like this.

"No! Gary, I will not."

So Gary had to explain to John, and he didn't want to seem like he was blaming Lee. It was so . . . it wasn't her fault. She shouldn't have to feel forced . . . but John was so set on this, he might . . . suddenly, it wasn't simple at all.

"This may not be the right time . . . your mother looks at this differently than you do. It may be harder for her. John, you have to un—John!"

John had turned and was heading for the balcony of the room. Gary started after him, but the phone was ringing. He went around the bed and picked it up.

"We gotta go . . ." Billy's voice.

"Take your time. I've got John here, we have to talk. Even if we're late. Just give me a few minutes."

Hart cradled the phone and straightened himself. He walked to the balcony door. "John . . ."

But John was gone. Gary's heart went to his throat . . . and stayed. Jesus! Did he jump? No . . . God, where was John? Hart had to go to that speech . . . he had to give that empty speech . . . with the question screaming in his head: Where was John?

Was he, at that moment, driving Gary's car on some dark road, a hundred miles an hour? . . . In rage? In tears? . . . Headed where?

Where was John?

80

I Am a Man

To Vice President George Bush, it was simple. He'd do whatever it took, to win—he had no doubt about that . . . his family had none. Strange he should have to prove it.

But that's what they told him. He had to go down to Florida—the state convention in Orlando—and show those delegates he wanted their support. It was another straw poll. Bush had to win. (After his debacle at the Ames Cavalcade, he *really* had to win.) There were 220 press credentials issued, 2,400 delegates, and an expectation among the big-feet that Bush had to win fifty percent—or he'd look like dead meat in the papers again.

(The "new" Press Secretary, the old Veep-friend Pete Teeley, tried to peddle the line that they'd be happy with any win—one vote better than their nearest opponent . . . but Atwater already told *The Miami Herald* he wanted a clear majority. So much for Teeley's spin control.)

By the day of the convention, Bush, Inc., had the place wired: delegate lists, field staff, floor captains, coordinators, walkie-talkies, minions running in and out. (The guy at the door wasn't supposed to let anybody back onto the floor once they'd left the hall. But he sold out for a picture with the Veep, so Bush, Inc., had people shuttling all day.) . . . This time, the Bush campaign would not rely on organization alone. They wheeled in the juice. Jeb Bush lived in-state—he was big in the Party. And they brought in Junior, with Atwater and the rest of the brass. And then the Big Gulp: they flew in the Veep a day before the vote and worked him like a pump, till they couldn't find any more hands for him to shake.

He did four meetings with leaders from all over Florida: four speeches, each

to about a hundred people. That night he did a rally—another 750 souls. Then
he stood grinning and chatting, for hours, so every single leader could have
his picture-with-the-Veep. The day of the vote, GBFP set up three hotel rooms:
one for Jebbie, one for Junior, and one for Congressman Clay Shaw. Then, in
groups of ten or fifteen, they ran the uncommitted delegates through. Jebbie,
Junior, or Shaw would get to talking about the importance of this vote, and
Florida, to George Bush, who was just saying, on the plane yesterday . . . and
then there'd come a knock at the door, and Bush, Sr., would walk in, sit down
on a bed . . . and just flat visit. Knocked those delegates for a loop, every time.
(He came in—just regular, you know. Asked for their votes . . . personally!)
After he closed the deal—ten or fifteen minutes—he'd get up, walk down the
hall, and "surprise" another group of uncommitteds. They moved 130 votes
through those rooms that morning. Then Bush went downstairs and gave his
convention address.

As he stepped off the stage, the crowd was chanting "*Bush, Bush, Bush, Bush
. . .*" and the Veep wore a weary grin as the wall of suits wedged him
back to his holding room . . . where Atwater stepped forward, and said: "Ah
gotta talk to you, Mr. Vahz Pres'ent . . . uh, Ah gotta explain somethin'."

"Yeah, what?" Bush almost snapped the question.

"Well, our numbers show we kin git up to fifty-five percent *plus* . . . but,
uh, our *count* only shows us up to fifty-two. It's, uhhh . . . *conceivable* we could
be closer to fifty . . ."

Bush lifted his nose like he smelt bullshit. *Now* they were telling him he
could fall under fifty percent? . . . Matter of fact, it was starting to smell like
. . . Iowa.

Lee was very busy explaining:

There were 2,400 votes, but so far they couldn't physically *find* 300 of the
delegates. "We just don' know where they *are,* sir . . ."

Junior broke in:

"Why the hell *don't* we know where they are?"

"Okay, Lee. What do you want?" That was from the Veep. The side talk
stopped. Atwater said:

"Uh, Ah'd like you to work the undecided who, uh . . ."

"How long?"

"Half-hour?"

"Well, let's go."

Of course he'd do it. He hadn't come down there to lose—or to look like
he'd lost. They ran a hundred more delegates in, and he pumped their hands
and told them how great it was to know them. And as they were ushered out,
Junior grabbed them at the door. "*Listen,*" he'd say, and they'd stop in their
tracks, to hear that same Bush-voice from that same Bush-face, only
younger—and right in *their* face.

"*Listen,* there's only *one candidate* in this race who came down here,
personally, to ask for your vote. And that's George Bush. I hope you'll remember that."

Yes, they'd remember. They'd give him his fifty percent, and more. That was after Bush made it back to the airport and onto his Stratoliner, up to the Power Cabin, into the Power Chair, where stewards hied with a Power Martini . . . after Bush left the matter in the hands of Atwater, with a Veeply warning, uttered in the holding room, in the hearing of a dozen campaign ops and Secret Service men. Bush fixed Atwater with a stare, none too friendly:

"Lee, I hope no one's coverin' their beehives on me here."

— ★ —

Beehives?

Bush was always playing net with himself. He was so sensitive to the currents around him, so desirous that he not offend, so quick of mind and sense, it was almost reflex: he'd doublethink his own mouth.

"Listen, sonofabitch: you lie to me again on this, I'll kill you . . ."

(No. God! There's a dozen people in the room, strangers, voters!)

"Listen, Lee, you better not be coverin' your ass on this one . . ."

(No! No threats. We're all on the same team!)

"Lee, I hope no one's coverin' their ass on this one . . ."

(No! "Ass"—bad word! "Behinds?")

"Lee, I hope no one's coverin' their beehives . . ."

It was the brilliance of George Bush that it all happened in a second. It was the price of being Poppy that it made him sound like a prep school weenie . . . or, as the press would have it, a wimp.

The reporters kept lists of these things: that time he said the Russians were "tough as horseradish" . . . that time in Denver, after a speech, when they tried to ask about taxes and Bush didn't want to say anything, so all that came out was: "Zippedeedoodah! It's off to the races!"

There was the time he was trying to recap his experience as Vice President, at Reagan's side, through good times and bad. . . . *We've had successes, we've had setbacks* . . . but then, he thought, he couldn't accuse the President of *failures*. . . . It happened somewhere between "successes" and "setbacks," so all that issued from the Bush-mouth was: "We've had sex . . ."

Oh God, oh God, oh God!

But all this was as nothing, as . . . air—wind! no! a fart in the wind! . . . compared to the stinking granddaddy, the one that stuck to George Bush like dog, uh, droppings on his shoes.

It wasn't a big deal at the time—1986, and Bush just back from a mission to China. The Veep was pretty relaxed, in fact, and that was the start of the problem. He was kicking back in the Power Cabin, over a beer and the public popcorn, with a reporter from *The Wall Street Journal,* and he remarked upon the reception he'd received in Peking. So friendly! They loved him! . . . And Bush wanted people to understand the depth of his *personal knowledge* of China, and how far we'd come, which was a ratification of sound Republican foreign policy and *just the kind of thing* that people didn't understand about *him*—his ease, his steady certainty in foreign affairs, which was built upon *experience* of the sort he'd obtained a decade before, *in China,* when things were *tough,* when you couldn't even talk *weather,* or, you know, *tennis,* with any decent Maoist, because the poor fellow would wind up with electrodes hooked to his balls, and you'd be thrown out of the country, of course. That's the way it *was* . . . which people didn't *remember* . . . which was why Bush wanted to *point out,* was *going to say,* if the official who'd greeted him so warmly in Peking last week had talked to him like that *when Bush was envoy to China,* well, that fellow would've been in knee-deep shit. So he said: If the guy had been that nice ten years ago, he woulda . . .

(But then Bush thought it might seem undiplomatic, and if the Chinese . . . well, they might not get the, uh, metaphor.)

". . . been in . . ."

(Well, it was true! Jeez! The Chinese ought to recognize it, too!)

". . . *deep* . . ."

(Shit? No! God! His mother's friends read the *Journal!*)

". . . *doo-doo.*"

Oh, God! . . .

Of course, by October 1987, it was too late for explanation: no one even used the full quote. But there were, in the year of his announcement for President, scores of references to the D-words in newspapers across the nation.

And doo-doo was never deeper than the week of his announcement.

— ★ —

Announcement, of course, meant Profile Season . . . and that's when it happened. Came out, in fact, on October 11, the eve of his announcement. Bush was in Houston for the Big Day. He had the whole magazine read before breakfast. Well, he didn't read it through . . . how could he? What was the point, after that cover?

They'd called him a *wimp* . . . on the *cover* of *Newsweek* . . . on the day of his announcement! It made his stomach turn, just to look at it. Jesus! . . . Those *shits!*

Margaret!

That was the other heartache: Margaret Warner wrote the story. He liked her! The whole family liked her—such a lady! *Had her up to the house*—she was a friend! . . . And then, she fucked him. Coast to coast, in every checkout line of every supermarket from Maine to California.

GEORGE BUSH: FIGHTING THE "WIMP FACTOR"

There was a picture of him, at the wheel of his boat, body bundled into a jacket, face set against the wind . . . like he was battling the cold, clammy whoosh of wimpdom that threatened to blow him away.

The picture wouldn't have been bad, by itself.

But there was the word—wide as his fist—*WIMP* . . . on the cover!

Bush wanted to hit them . . . we'll see who's a *wimp*—or, no! Get *them* out on the boat. (Tom Pettit, NBC, got *him* out in the boat, opened her up

. . . *wham*! Pettit went down on his ass—broke his *tailbone*! That oughta, uh, drive the point home, heh heh.) Show those sonsabitches, in their building in New York—what the hell did they know about this country, about who gets along in this country when you dump them out in the middle of Texas and they got to get along with people who work in the sun and dust and mud, see how *those* sonsabitches get along in the *Navy* when it's sink or swim . . . those . . . those . . .

Ailes was right. They were assholes!

Bar was right. They'd never understand him.

Junior was—oh, God, the kids: this would hit them hard. Doro's probably in tears . . . he ought to go to her room, right now, tell her . . . no! He had to be on TV—now, this morning, all day! Had to do his announcement—five cities, speeches, interviews—and look like nothing was wrong! . . . While they asked him, every stop—what did he think about the Wimp Cover?

What the hell could he think?

— ★ —

He did not, could not, understand that kind of journalism—he called it "impact journalism." (Like Lawrence Taylor was an "impact player" in football: he'd "impact" the other guy insensate.) He could not understand, could not accept, Margaret Warner's explanation that it *wasn't her*—she never used that word! (No, the editors in New York stuck it in her story, then used it for the cover line.) Bush wanted to know: Who was it? . . . He could not accept that it was no one in particular—that no one person was out to get him—nothing personal!

It was personal to Bush. He couldn't understand why they'd do it to him on the *day of his announcement.* . . . What did he know about Profile Season? . . . He couldn't even understand what they *meant*! Did that word mean coward? (He didn't see any air medals on *their* chests.) . . . Did they think he was a weakling? (Let's play two sets, see whose ass is dragging!) . . . God! They didn't mean he was a, uh, *homo*—did they?

They talked about how he had no positions—except Reagan's positions. . . . Well, how the hell else was he supposed to do his job? Did they want him to deny he was Vice President?

He could not *figure* how they got to that word—from *his life*!

But the editors of *Newsweek* weren't looking at his life. This was a political judgment . . . about Bush's *political identity*.

Who defines political identity?

Why . . . *political observers*!

Who all knew Bush was a wimp.

In other words, wise guys, smart guys, and big guys . . . who'd talked, *just the other day* . . . with people who were *very plugged-in* to the campaign . . . who heard from people who talked *all the time* with the Gee-Six . . . who all knew (these guys aren't stupid, you know) . . . what lunch-buddies always knew, which was: this campaign had a problem—which was the candidate! Just *look at the numbers*!

Bush was still ahead in the polls nationwide, but people couldn't give a reason why they were for him.

His support was soft, could bleed in a hurry.

Dole had gained five points in a month.

People didn't see Bush as a leader.

(C'mon! Whadd-I-tellya? . . .)

The *Newsweek*s had to stay ahead of the curve! So they commissioned their own numbers. Here was the key question:

"Some people say that George Bush's loyal service to Republican Presidents over the years has hurt his political image and made him look like a wimp. Is this criticism a serious problem for Bush's candidacy or not?"

Well, fifty-one percent said it sure was!

Of course, if you picked it apart, it wasn't fifty-one percent saying Bush was a wimp. It was *Newsweek* said . . . that "some people" said . . . that Bush's "political image" . . . "made him look like a wimp."

The only question asked: Is a wimp problem a *serious* problem?

It was a wonder that forty-three percent said no.

Anyway, this only went to prove what everybody knew. And now everyone could ask about his "wimp image." It wasn't just *some people said* anymore . . . *Newsweek* said!

And it was amazing, when you thought about it, how the *facts* bore out the magazine's prescience. . . . This guy couldn't even project a decent image at his own announcement!

— ★ —

For one thing, he didn't look happy. People talked about it—how the whole event seemed a bit somber. . . . Of course, no one in his hometown crowd brought up the *Newsweek* story. These were friends, after all.

There were hundreds of friends . . . but not sufficient hundreds to fill more than half the Imperial Ballroom of the Houston Hyatt, nor certainly to overflow the overblown *haute plastique* atrium-lobby that stretched aloft 300-some feet in a vertiginous striation of balconies.

What happened was, Bush, Inc., got big eyes and took over the whole hotel—gave the Secret Service men a nightmare job, with all those balconies overlooking their goose . . . had to commandeer every elevator. They filled three overhangs with high school bands, blaring brass . . . the bar in the well of the atrium was closed and given over to supposed Bush-revelry . . . tens of thousands of balloons were roped into nets, thirty stories above . . . they built a big stage at one end, big camera platforms at the other, hung banners supposed to look homemade (looked like they were all from one home) . . . there was a press-filing room sufficient for a Super Bowl, and a satellite truck so that any little station, anywhere in the country, could get free pictures of the big do.

And into this overscale they marched a slump-shouldered George Bush. Actually, in the ballroom, they marched in the Houston Astros blowhard announcer, Milo Hamilton, who introduced "our celebrities." (. . . "Would

you *welcome* . . . and with *resounding applause* . . . the RIGHT FIELDER
FOR THE ASTROS—*KEVIN BASS!*") . . . Then Milo gave way to Bob
Mosbacher . . . who introduced Congresswoman Lynn Martin . . . who introduced Governor John Sununu . . . who introduced former Senator John Tower.
. . . And somewhere in the middle, Junior got introduced, to introduce the
family . . . and then John Tower took his spot at center stage again to say the
name people had come to hear: George Bush!

By then, the crowd was clapped out.

Bush said he knew he'd have to come home, to Texas, to say the most
important words of his life:

"I am here today to announce my candidacy for President of the United
States. I mean to run hard, to fight hard, to stand on the issues—and I mean
to win!"

They gave him a big cheer, and he launched into his speech.

"We don't need radical new directions—we need strong, steady, experienced
leadership."

Small applause.

"We don't need to remake society—we just need to remember who we
are . . ."

No applause at all.

It was actually a nice speech to read—Bush had the cleverest White House
writer, Peggy Noonan, on the case. But it took too long to deliver . . . at least
for this hard-eyed crowd, which spent its time looking around for someone
important. Minicam men switched off their lights and started roaming, looking
for a more interesting shot. There was so much noise, it was hard to hear Bush,
or pay attention, as he read out the most amazing part.

It was about his experience: all his jobs—they showed up in most of his
speeches. But this time, instead of naming the jobs, Bush said:

"I am a man who . . ." (Navy flier.)

"I am a man who . . ." (Texas businessman, Congressman, RNC Chairman . . .)

Seven times: "I am a man."

It was sad to watch him drumming it home. Sad to note that this was the
big windup, the final argument for his candidacy . . . the litany that ended with
Bush at the side of a great President, where he realized . . .

". . . What it all comes down to, after all the shouting and the cheers, is the
man at that desk. And who should sit at that desk. . . .

"I am that man."

That was it. Bush started shaking hands, saying hi to all those friends. The
Secret Service had him pinned at one corner of the stage with a ropeline
. . . so, for friends who couldn't get to the front, Bush would just point and
make a goofy face of welcome. There was a Chinese couple who worked up
to the rope. "Ah! The Asian contingent!" Bush cried. He grabbed for a hand,
but the woman reached her arms around his shoulders. Bush was going to kiss
her cheek, but then doublethought (God! Awfully *public*!), so he pulled back

a twitch and . . . (Oh, what the hell!) went for her . . . but the woman had been bobbing and weaving her cheek into position while Bush played net with his kiss, so her head pulled away just at the moment—Bush ended up slurping her neck.

He had to go.

He had to get to the lobby! To do it all again . . . with those long camera angles—the balconies, the bands . . . or maybe he was supposed to do just part of the speech again, or maybe make another speech . . . hard to tell.

Because by the time Mickey Gilley's band stopped playing and Milo Hamilton yammered on again, and they brought George and Bar out on stage again as the high school bands played "The Yellow Rose of Texas," while the elevators . . .

Well, that was the problem. The Hyatt had those elevators, all shiny lights and glass, that rode up and down *outside* the balconies, so the rubes could gawk up the atrium . . . and these four *magnificent* elevators were supposed to rise behind George Bush—just to the top of camera frame, where they'd all stop at a single floor, each with a letter in lights, in the outside glass, to spell:

B   U   S   H

Except they got it screwed up, so it said:

B

U   S   H

So they dicked around with the elevators until the B finally landed, bobbing like Groucho's duck, next to the U . . . and it must have thrown off the schedule, because Bush was saying:

"I am going to *be* . . . the next President of the United States . . . and let me just say, before the balloons come down . . ."

But balloons already were coming down, the dead ones that lost their air, picking up thirty stories of speed—trash from the sky, little rubber turds, falling on the heads of Bush's old friends, who were all looking up like turkeys in the rain . . . and the place got very noisy, and what Bush wanted to say . . . was lost.

81

It All
Began in
Russell!

WHEN BOB came home a couple of nights before his announcement, November 9, brother Kenny Dole had to pick him up at the airport. Kenny and his wife, Anita, went to Great Bend. They had to wait—two planes . . . Bob and Elizabeth flew separate planes. But it wasn't any more than two or three hours for Kenny—no more than usual. He didn't mind, though he groused about it the usual way. He always got the call when Bob needed fetching . . . a voice on the phone from Washington: "Senator says pick him up in Hays, nine o'clock tomorrow night." That's all. No questions. No please or thank you. If Kenny knew the voice, maybe he'd say something.

"Is he bringin' his sandals?"

"Uh, excuse me?"

"I thought Jesus Christ always wore sandals."

Kenny used to say he was going to start the BOB Club. "B-O-B stands for Brother of Bigshot." But he was used to it. He probably would have been offended if they hadn't called him, now that Bob was going to be President.

Kenny wouldn't say that, of course. In Russell, it's best not to talk about your dreams. But you could see the idea had got to him, like a flu making the rounds. Everybody had a touch of it, whether they'd admit it or not.

Russ Townsley, the newspaper chief, had been whipping up folks for months, trying to get all the businesses in town involved in Bob's announcement, not to mention the Chamber, the Legion, Kiwanis. . . . It got to be quite some pressure—like Russell had to pass this test for Bob, and for the country.

The whole nation would be watching, Russ said. But as the big Monday drew close, it was easier, the fever took hold: the kids in the high school choir and band were practicing . . . their parents ordered signs for their storefronts, and bunting from Topeka . . . Bob's ex-wife Phyllis sent handsome handmade wooden buttons: DOLE '88 (Bob's Aunt Gladys Friesen sold them in Russell) . . . in Kenny and Anita's office on Main Street, you could buy tiny stone fence posts like the pioneers once carved in Kansas, except these said DOLE FOR PRESIDENT and sold for forty dollars a pair . . . Dean Banker got a sign for the front of his department store: BOB DOLE SUITED UP HERE FIRST . . . the men of the Russell Volunteer Fire Department polished the pumper they'd named *The Doran Dole* . . . the *Russell Record* printed every hopeful poll that came over the wire, and readied two special sections with pictures of Bob, his family, his house, his school, his campaigns . . . national reporters came to town in ones and twos, collecting "color," which could be anything down-home, folksy, or Kansan—anything at all about the town—so it got to be like everyone in Russell *had done something,* just by living there, and knowing Bob (though many were hazy on Bob; it *had* been almost thirty years). . . . It came clear to everyone that something big *was happening,* that it started with Russell, and people in the Chamber thought they ought to consider what would happen, you know, if it got to be like Plains, Georgia, or Abilene, with its museum for Ike . . . so it wasn't really politics—more like a *civic* thing, but emotional, because of the Bob Dole story . . . which was the centerpiece of this festival, like a passion play the town was putting on, about Bob (and the apostles, who were the family, the exiled Phyllis, and Bub Dawson from the drugstore).

That Saturday night, when Bob got home, Kenny made sure to drive him up Main Street, so Bob could see the banners (IT ALL BEGAN IN RUSSELL!), the new mural, the storefronts, the grandstands, platforms . . . then it was straight to Bina's old house. It was late, Bob and Elizabeth had to rest. Kenny would be back early the next day, to take Bob to the graveyard.

Sister Gloria had gone out to clean off Bina and Doran's headstones, and make sure there were fresh flowers. Doran had died in 1975, Bina eight years later. Gloria's own cancer was under control from chemotherapy, but she had only one kidney, and her blood pressure was just *shooting* up. The problem was the family reunion that Sunday before announcement. Gloria had made a ham boat with twenty pounds of ham and pork—it was thirty pounds by the time she added twenty eggs and the rest of the trimmings. She'd made a loaf of cheese potatoes in the big electric roaster, and a load of candied sweet potatoes—from scratch, like Bina used to do. And two loaves of buttered French bread, a plate of pumpkin bread, a big black cherry salad, a cranberry-apple salad, fresh applesauce, a plate of cookies, a banana cream pie, and chocolate, cherry, and apple pies, a hundred-and-some cinnamon and pecan rolls, and homemade ice cream, with the corn starch, like they always had.

Then Kenny called and said he'd invited that cousin from the power company—he was a cousin, wasn't he? Anyway, the fellow said he'd be delighted, and now he was bringing sixty more "cousins" . . . so Kenny was yelling for help, and Gloria swung into a higher frenzy of cooking.

Gloria had a houseful, too, with her kids, their spouses and babies, all come back to town. And Aunt Gladys, Doran's sister, had all her beds filled . . . and *then* Bob asked her to take in Mrs. Kelikian. (She put her off on Faith and Harold Dumler, who weren't even family, but there was no choice—and Faith would do a lovely job.) Then Robin wasn't comfortable in Bina's house, where nothing had changed—nothing had been moved—since Bina died. There were all the fussy matching drapes, with valences, and the carpets, and Doran's favorite chair. But there was no more scent of honeysuckle, rose, wax, or baking bread . . . no life. Robin thought it was creepy, like sleeping in a shrine. So she came to Gloria's and asked if she could stay. Gloria didn't have a spare inch, but she took Robin in, put her with her own girls.

After the graveyard, Bob and Elizabeth went to the Methodist Church, where three rows in front were roped off for them. Aunt Gladys was hoping for a word with Bob, after the service, but his back was turned—he was being interviewed. After that, it was Dawson Drug, which was packed with press and photographers, and then to the 4-H for the family reunion. There were more than two hundred people there, and it almost broke Gloria's heart. Bob was working the whole time. He didn't get to eat anything. They had red-checkered tablecloths . . . and they were paper. There were six Republican women in the kitchen . . . they didn't know what to do with the food. The fourth cousins ate like they wouldn't get another meal all year. Bob was busy shaking hands. He took more than an hour, working his way through the crowd, and then he was gone. Kenny had to take him to the hospital and the nursing home.

Elizabeth came over to Gloria's. She was hungry again. Gloria fixed her some chicken noodle butterball. When Elizabeth finished, she said, "That shore was good!" And Gloria said, "Cherry pie?"

"Whah, yes!" (Gloria never could figure why that woman didn't weigh three hundred pounds.)

That's when Gloria got to ask how Bob was—she asked Elizabeth . . . who said Bob was just *saying,* the other day, how pleased he was to be coming home to Russell. Elizabeth was sure the welcome had touched Bob's heart.

Gloria was going to doll up and go to Bob's party at the VFW that night— they were going to show Bob's new video. But when the time came, Gloria didn't feel well. . . . Aunt Gladys got everybody in her house together—she had ten in tow—got them out to the VFW. But by nine, when she arrived, she couldn't get in the door.

People were backed up from the door of the hall. It was dark inside. Everyone was watching the video. It was spectacular—all about Bob's child-hood, and Russell, Bina and Doran . . . Bob went off to war, and came back, just broken bones and heart . . . he picked himself up, and never forgot . . . and by the end of the film, when he's running for President, standing in a cornfield, making a speech, with the cornstalks eight feet tall around him, and that wonderful music welling up under his words—when he talked of opportunity, freedom, our future . . . you were guaranteed to end up crying if you knew Bob, or his folks, or the town—or even if you didn't, you felt like you did. Even the reporters stopped talking (there were hundreds staying over that night—some had to sleep in Hays). The people from Washington—staff and smart guys—you could almost see it dawn on them: this stuff they'd been *saying,* Dole and the heartland, small-town, hardworking . . . it was *real,* here it *was,* the Veterans of Foreign Wars, Post Number 6240, Russell, Kansas . . . they were *in it*! And as the lights came up, everybody was talking at once—wasn't that *great*? Did you see that picture of Bob, so *skinny*? . . . And people who knew him, even slightly, felt they were *part of something,* something great *was happening*—no one left the hall . . . except Bob and Elizabeth (who had to go, so Kenny took them) and Gladys—she got in the back door, saw all those strangers, and just went home.

—★—

"Good morning, ladies and gentlemen," said Dave Owen—first at the microphone on Main Street, early that Monday. "Good morning, and welcome to Russell, Kansas!" There was a cheer from the big crowd, shivering in shadow. The sun still hadn't peeked over Banker's Mercantile, to the left of the stage. The wind was blowing straight down Main Street, the temperature was in the twenties, the air was frozen clear.

Up on stage, behind Dave Owen, stood Chuckie Grassley from Iowa, Bill Brock, Bob Ellsworth, and every Republican official from Kansas. To the right of the stage stood the Russell High School Bronco Pops Choir, which warmed up with its choral rendition of "Twist and Shout." Then the emcee, Russ Townsley, got the mike and boomed out:

"Boy! On a morning like this, does *anybody* have any doubt they're in Kansas?"

Behind Russ, Doran Dole's old grain elevator was the first building to catch the sun. From the top of the tanks, a banner announced: RUSSELL, KANSAS. HOME OF BOB DOLE. Townsley was in a transport of local pride. "I say, '*Hey, America!*'" he yelled. "'*You take a good look at who we are!*'"

Russ introduced Larry Ehrlich, Chairman of the Russell County GOP, who said: "We *know* he's going to make it . . ." Then Bob's old friend and opponent, the gentlemanly former Governor, Bill Avery, stepped up to talk about three icons of Kansas Republicanism: Huck Boyd, Alf Landon, and Dwight Eisenhower. The Russell High School Bronco Marching Band followed up with a fight song, and the kids in the bleachers were waving little flags, as the sunshine, at last, lit them in sharp glare. Cheerleaders cued them:

"Go Bob go!
"Go Bob go!
"Eatem up! Eatem up!
"Go Bob go!"

When the band swung into "Yankee Doodle Dandy," the Bobster emerged from Dawson Drug, stage right, and climbed onto the platform. He was wearing a gray topcoat and red power tie, and was bouncing to the music like Bob Crosby of the Bobcats. Elizabeth was splendid in purple. Robin matched entirely, in rose.

Russ Townsley read out the telegram received in Russell, in May of 1945. "The Secretary of War wants me to express our deep regret . . ." Then, Bub Dawson was on stage: "If I can take you back forty-two years . . ." Bub talked about the collection for Bob. "There was a cigar box on the counter," Bub said, "with Bob Dole's name on it."

Then . . . *Bub produced the cigar box*—the relic of the passion play!

But this time, the box contained *one hundred and thirty-five thousand dollars* . . . from Russell, Kansas . . . for Bob's campaign.

The band played "God Bless America," an up-tempo rendition—fast, in fact—it was still cold as hell. Nancy Kassebaum, Dole's Senate colleague from Kansas (and daughter of the icon Alf Landon), had the honor of introducing Bob. "In a real sense . . ." she noted (no flies on Nancy!), ". . . Russell is what this campaign is about."

And when she said the name, kids screamed "Dole! Dole! Dole! Eeeeeeeeeeeeee!" and the band let loose with "Step to the Rear (and Let a Winner Lead the Way)" . . . and there was the Bobster, in front now, with a smile of fierce elation, bouncing to the music, swinging his arm—bringing on the action!

Lord, what a story! An American Everyman drama for our age! And not done yet—no! Bob had a speech to make . . . but first, his part in the drama:

There was a woman who'd traveled with him to Russell, Sophie Vavlety, a strange Park Avenue New Yorker who was in love with Bob Dole, and everything he touched. She gave her fur coat to the Mayor's wife at the airport. She gave Kenny a lambswool Italian scarf, and Anita a silk kimono. She gave two dresses to Doris Henderson, the owner of Russell's Country Squire Motel. Sophie was an emblem of Bob Dole's new world, which he'd brought back to Russell. Now Bob called the Mayor to the stage and presented, from Sophie Vavlety:

A $10,000 check for the poor of Russell, Kansas.

Well . . .

Bob still had to speak . . . but what was left to say?

What were *words* about opportunity, compared to this allegory-in-life of righteous GOP redemption? . . . What were prosy visions for the nation's next four years, compared to the miraculous *fact* of Dole's life—his *future*—sun-sharp and solid as the bricks on Main Street?

82

No Future
at All

IT DAWNED ON Dole only slowly that he'd have to fight for his life—when Watergate burst open like a bad cantaloupe, when everything around him turned foul, all at once.

It wasn't that Watergate snuck up on him. He didn't try to wish it away, or deny its import . . . not anymore. Once he'd left the Party chair, there was no Republican more vocal, more candid about the scandal. Dole saw the cover-up killing Nixon's Presidency, and he knew Republicans would suffer, at the polls. Still, it was a stomach-turning shock to him—an affront—when they came at *him,* in Kansas!

It started with Norbert Dreiling, "Mr. Democrat," from Hays. Dole showed up in Kansas, around the turn of the year, 1974, for the first quiet *ta-rappa-tap-tap* of his reelection soft-shoe . . . and Norb was already slamming him with the portentous question:

What did Dole know, and when did he know it?

Either Dole was *culpable of knowing* (and was, therefore, like his President, an unindicted coconspirator) . . . or Dole (the National Chairman!) was *unaware, out of the loop* (therefore, impotent, imbecilic) . . . which would Bob have us believe?

Dole was so enraged by this line of inquiry that he threatened to *sue* . . . at which point Norb, a lawyer by trade and a brawler by temperament, replied in every Kansas paper: "Let him file his damn suit! Then he can answer the question under oath!"

Only the mildest stuff made it into the papers. As usual, in Kansas, the real poison spread by word of mouth. People would take Dole aside, after events—these were supporters!—and quietly, half-ashamed, ask if it was true, what they heard:

"Bob, they say the burglars kept their tools at your apartment!"

Sure, that one was easy to knock down—Dole wasn't renting at the Watergate until the year after the burglary. But how could he tell that to the thousands who *didn't* ask? . . . As usual, Dole feared the things people would not say.

For instance, the divorce: no one brought it up with Dole. But *everybody knew,* of course, how Bob dumped that gal, Phyllis—you know, when he went fancy-pants, with Nixon . . . just as they knew that Phyllis was *his nurse* . . . nursed him back *from the dead* . . . now he didn't need her anymore, he . . . well, people knew how *that* went, with men. (Prob'ly got some chippy in that *Watergate—everybody* knew about *that* place!)

There was no way Dole could silence the whispers.

No more than he could shut down the standard Kansas whine: Bob Dole had been National Chairman—must not *care about Kansas* anymore. (Maybe that Dole's gettin' too big for his britches!)

He couldn't stop the cover-up from ruining his patron-President . . . any more than he could stop Jerry Ford from issuing his pardon. (Someone asked Dole, after the pardon, whether he'd get campaign help from Ford. "I think Ford's given me 'bout all the help I can stand," Dole said.)

There was no way he could stop the Democratic Senatorial Campaign Committee from naming Kansas—him!—as a "vulnerable target" . . . sending money to fuel his opponent—his *respected* opponent, the Topeka physician and two-term Congressman, Bill Roy . . . any more than Dole could forestall Dr. Roy from stumping the state (to increasing approbation) for "integrity in government" and an "independent Senator for Kansas."

What could Dole do?

Well, he could use his new national connections to raise hundreds of thousands of dollars . . . which he could spend for *professional help*—high-tech consultants! He hired a Campaign-Manager-guru named Herb Williams ("Agh! Pretty *good*—guy worked for *Dann*-forth!") . . . Dole got a fast-talking pollster, Tully Plesser; a top-notch adman, Jack Connors, from Boston. . . . Dole had airplanes to fly him around the state—or *choppers*! . . . He would spare no effort, or expense.

Which made it all the more depressing, through that long summer of '74, as Dole's high-tech campaign ground to a bitter standstill in Kansas. The consultants couldn't get along with the Kansans. Herb Williams proved he could handle a flowchart, rent offices, hire staff; he could denounce everyone else's ideas as bullshit, rend the air with a blue streak of oaths, work everyone around him to a frazzle, and spend a fortune—for nothing—or at least without benefit to Dole. (And Dole, of course, couldn't fire him—never fired anybody!) The highly creative admen in Boston had yet to produce a single ad. (They did design a handsome tabloid—printed tens of thousands—but they spelled

Wichita *Witchita,* so those landed in the trash.) And Dr. Bill Roy (who began as an unknown in four-fifths of the state) drew even in the polls, and then pulled ahead, by five points, ten . . . by *thirteen points* (in Dole's own pricey polls!).

Dole knew, by that time, he was in a fight for his life. But he seemed like a boxer who'd been punched woozy in the ring. He wasn't quite sure how he'd got there . . . or what the hell to do to get out . . . he didn't seem to have any plan, any will, to pull out of his swoon tomorrow, next week . . . at any point in the future!

Dole couldn't convince himself that he had any future at all.

— ★ —

George Bush thought he deserved some consideration, some future. God knows, he'd paid his dues. Everywhere he went, there were people who thought he was mixed up in that mess—people couldn't keep all the names straight—Haldeman, Colson . . . Ehrlichman, Dean, Stans, Butterfield . . . Bush! . . . But that was over, thank God.

Ford was President now. Ford was a friend.

Gerald Ford had to pick a Vice President.

This wasn't something Bush dreamed up. He was encouraged to consider the job. People who were close to the President—very close—told him . . . no guarantees, but everyone agreed it made sense. George Bush had friends in a hundred nations, from his days at the UN . . . friends all over the country from his term at the RNC—State Committeemen, County Chairmen . . . friends in Congress, strength in Texas—he could help Ford all across the South . . . he was a seasoned pol, but just a month or two out of his forties—Bush was the future of the Party. He'd make a hell of a Veep!

In fact, this wasn't the first time Bush had been considered. Back in '68 his name had come up, when Nixon got the nomination in Miami. Bush's friend, Dick Moore, brought the name up at a meeting . . . but Bush was only a first-term Rep; Nixon thought he needed seasoning.

In '73, when Agnew copped a plea in a Baltimore courtroom, Dick Moore was once again at Nixon's side. . . . What about George Bush? Hell of a guy! Hell of a résumé! . . . Nixon thought Bush wasn't tough enough. Nice fellow—Nixon always liked his dad—but George was, maybe, too nice (not "one of us" to Nixon and his crowd), an Ivy Leaguer, through and through. Nixon was so surprised to hear that Bush was captain of the Yale ball team! . . . Really? *Bush?*

Anyway, Nixon took Jerry Ford . . . but things worked out for Bush. *Now* . . . his time had come. Good things happen to good people. Loyalty and patience could not fail to bring rewards.

Not that Bush was going to lie back, let nature run its course . . . no. He did what he could:

From the chairmanship of the RNC, it was an easy matter to poll the National Committee (just for the President's information, understand).

Behold! The favorite, nationwide, of Republican Committeemen and women was . . . George Bush!

Then he arranged for a poll of Republican members of Congress. Who would they choose for Veep?

George Bush!

From the Oval Office, it had to look like a groundswell: all those people, letters, telegrams—Republicans, all over the country, talking up Bush! . . . Actually, Bush had a friend, a Committeeman from Omaha, Dick Herman, who moved into Washington's Statler Hilton, whence he ran a telephone boiler room, beating the tom-toms for Bush.

At last, in Kennebunkport, Bush got the call: White House on the line! The President had made his decision. . . . The new Vice President of the United States would be . . . Nelson Rockefeller.

Bush was hurt, then angry. What did a guy have to do? He'd stood up—taken heat, put his own good name on the line—through the worst shit-storm his Party ever faced.

What did it get him?

Ford said they'd have to get together soon "to discuss the future."

Goddammit, there'd better be some discussion—because George Bush was through with the RNC.

—★—

Well, Ford couldn't have been nicer, more solicitous—after the fact, of course. He said there were two *top-notch* diplomatic posts (Ambassador was still the title Bush used in Washington)—Paris or London . . . Bush could have his pick.

Bush had another idea—China.

China?

It wasn't even an embassy! Just a "listening post." Anyway, China policy was mapped and made by one man—Henry Kissinger. The Liaison Office in Peking had nothing to do. It was there simply to be there. "You'll be bored beyond belief," Kissinger said.

No, Bush was sure it would be *a wonderful adventure* (he and Bar had decided). China was exotic. China was important!

China was . . . his choice.

See, you had to look at it as Bush did—that is, through the woeful misadventures of four years.

Here was a young up-and-comer who'd given up his safe House seat to run for the Senate. The President had asked him—and Bush so much wanted into the big game . . . but he caught that bad break with Bentsen . . . and that dream was dashed.

So he went to the UN—but not before he made sure he'd have a seat at the table, Cabinet rank, and the President's ear. "No problem!" the President's men assured him. . . . But in New York, he found he wasn't in the game at all. Nixon and Kissinger were the whole team.

So, loyally, he took the RNC job—making sure he'd keep his seat at the Cabinet table, and *this time* (for sure!) he'd be a player on the President's team . . . But by that time, the captain was about to be drummed out of the league, and the badge of team membership was a public shame.

The loss of the Vice Presidency was just the last straw.

So, China was important . . . enough. China was intriguing . . . enough. China, best of all, was seven thousand miles away.

When he got established in Peking, he wrote to a friend: the warnings were true—there wasn't any work. "So I'm trying to do this job, and meanwhile figure out what I'm going to do with my life."

Bush felt he'd played the game—as hard as he could.

Maybe it wasn't the game for him.

83

A Fight
for His Life

THIS WASN'T any game to Dole. This was the only part of his life that meant anything, that was left to him. But everything ended up looking wrong—he couldn't make people see. . . .

The buzz in Congress that year, '74, was inflation: Whip Inflation Now! . . . That was the first time Dole put forth his instinctive notion that Congress (that he) could cut the budget fairly. But every finger of government, every program, would pay the price—say, five percent . . . just tighten up the belt! On the floor of the Senate, Dole proved his *bona fides* when he offered an amendment to cut five percent from the agriculture appropriation. "I offer this amendment," he said, "because every Senator's got to take the hit."

By the time Dole got back to Kansas, Bill Roy had the state half convinced that Dole was *taking money from the farmers*—stealing the sneakers off their children's feet! Why would Bob Dole vote against his farmers?

Well, to serve his President, and Party . . . just as he opted for President and Party when he took the RNC chair . . . and forgot about Kansas, spent his time all over the country, making "hatchet-man speeches for Nixon." . . . Bob was a caustic fellow, anyway, and partisan, with those nasty jokes— not a caring man, like Bill Roy, who was a *doctor,* a healer (delivered five thousand babies!) bringing *life* . . . and then, in concern for the public weal, decided that he must study law, as well . . . which he did, at night, *with his wife* (who also became a lawyer) . . . Dr. Bill Roy was a man of concern, credentials, family, faith . . .

Bill Roy was about to bury Bob Dole.

At the start of September, Lieutenant Governor Dave Owen (he'd decided not to run for another term) became the working chairman of the Dole reelection campaign. In D.C., Dole's top Senate staffers quit the federal payroll to volunteer in Kansas. They found a campaign in ruins:

There were no ads, no money to run ads. (Dole had raised half a million dollars, but Herb Williams spent it. Dave Owen would find eighty thousand dollars in unpaid bills in Williams's credenza.) There were true Dole-folk all over the state, but they'd almost given up. The campaign was flirting with the fatal affliction: it was ridiculous. Williams and his high-tech campaigners had managed to contract for billboards . . . but no one had come up with art or copy—Dole was renting empty billboards.

Somehow, they had to get rid of Williams . . . but the campaign could not take another bad-news story. Somehow, they had to make some good news— some ads! . . . but where was the money?

Owen and friends called some guys together at the Petroleum Club—twenty or thirty good fellows—and walked out that same day with $130,000.

Then Owen called the ad agency in Boston and threatened to start making ads himself. He did, in fact, hire a local announcer to sit on a stool, with a smoke in his hand, and stare straight into the camera while he took the hide off Bill Roy. (That was an old format used by Governor Bob Docking—it was ugly, but it'd worked before.) Jack Connors called from Boston, to protest: just hold on forty-eight hours! . . . Sure enough, on day two, Owen got tapes, air express.

The ads showed a standard campaign poster of Bob Dole, and off-camera, a narrator said:

"Bill Roy says Bob Dole is against the Kansas farmer." (FWAP . . . a big glob of slimy mud hit the poster, and slid down Dole's face.)

"Roy says Bob Dole voted to cut school lunches." (FWAP . . . another glob of mud.)

"Roy says Bob Dole voted against cuts in the federal budget." (FWAP . . .)

Then the announcer rebutted all the charges, and said Dole was *for* budget-cutting, school lunches, and the Kansas farmer. . . . Meanwhile, the film was reversed, the mud started flying off the poster, leaving a handsome and smiling Bob Dole.

"All of which makes Bob Dole look pretty good," the narrator said. *". . . And makes Bill Roy look like just another mudslinger."*

The ads caused an uproar. Kansans had never seen their politics played out so graphically. Half the voters thought these were Bill Roy's ads—they were furious: How could he fling that slime at Dole? The other half understood they were Dole ads—they were mad at *Dole* for throwing mud at his own face! . . . Voters called the TV stations, wrote letters to the papers, they denounced dirty campaigning and candidates who sullied the airwaves—and Kansas!

Dole thought he had to pull the ads. (Of course, he wouldn't say that. He had Huck Boyd call Dave Owen to suggest that *Owen* ought to pull the ads.)

But how could anyone pull the ads? Dole would look like a waffler! He'd look ridiculous!

Owen and the boys thought up the play:

First, Dole quietly reserved for Herb Williams a soft landing pad with the RNC in Washington. Next, Williams held a press conference—in Kansas— and quit Dole's campaign . . . because *Dole would not permit him* to run any more mudslinger ads.

Eureka! The ads came off the air, and Dole got rid of his Campaign Manager, six weeks before the vote. . . . But instead of two killer stories—DOLE CAMPAIGN IN DISARRAY—Dole got one plump creampuff: Bob was too nice, too honorable, for dirty politics.

In the end, it was Bill Roy who couldn't pull the trigger. The Democrats had prepared ads on Watergate—Dole as Dick Nixon's political twin and alter ego . . . but the state chairman didn't want to take the low road. So Roy held back the ads—despite warnings from Norb Dreiling, who knew Dole well. "You let Bob Dole get his head off the mat," Norb said, "and you'll never hold him down."

Then, too, the Roy campaign decided not to answer the antiabortion nuts. They were after Roy as an obstetrician who had performed abortions when the health of his patients required them. In fact, Roy had hated abortion since his residency in Detroit, when he watched a teenage girl die in his emergency room because a back-alley abortionist had perforated her uterus. But the Roy campaign decided not to "dignify" the issue. Abortion was a matter of medical ethics—and Roy was, first and foremost, a doctor. He'd jumped from medicine to Congress, in 1970, in a three-month campaign—politics was not his life.

He would find out, it was Bob Dole's life.

The great confrontation was the half-hour Agriculture Debate at the Kansas State Fair, in Hutchinson. Dole insisted on the Lincoln–Douglas format—no moderator, no panel, just the two candidates, toe-to-toe, in a tent, and on statewide TV. Both candidates tried to pack the arena. The Dole crowd, Russell folks, were *convinced* that Roy's people were nothing but thugs (who'd been *paid* ten dollars apiece to show up!). Those Roy people were cheering when their man asked Dole:

"Why did you support legislation to do away with the Department of Agriculture, when it's so important to the farmers of Kansas? . . ."

Dole didn't know what legislation Roy was talking about. (His staff had put together a fat briefing book—last minute, of course, dictated from phone booths—Bob never looked at it.) Dole hemmed and hawed: he couldn't answer, and that threw him off track.

Near the front of the crowd, Bina Dole kept her eyes on her son, and as he began to press, she saw his brow grow dark. She knew that look—he was enraged. Bina stopped whispering with the other Russell ladies, her own mouth drew into a tight line—she was rigid with worry, her hands worked in her lap. Bill Roy was pressing his advantage, painting Dole as a thoughtless political slasher . . . *Look who you are . . . compared to me—a doctor!*

How could Bill Roy know . . . that's what Bob Dole always wanted to be? How could Roy understand what had been stolen from Dole . . . as Roy seemed now to be stealing the rest of Bob's life?

With one minute left, Dole strode to the podium. "Why do you do abortions?" Dole said. "And why do you favor abortion on demand?"

There was an instant's hush in the tent . . . the crowd began to boo. This was so ugly . . . hundreds of people—not just Roy's crowd—were hooting Dole back to his chair.

Roy stammered out words, but nothing like an answer. He knew he had less than thirty seconds. The statewide broadcast ended with his senseless mumble into the microphone, the angry hoots of the crowd, and Bob Dole stalking off stage.

The folks from Russell planned to stay for dinner, but Bob didn't come. He had a plane waiting to take him to Parsons—just a three-seater. Dole asked Bill Wohlford: "Whyn'cha come on to Parsons?"

Wohlford was one of Dole's Washington staffers who'd quit his job to help in Kansas—one of those big, humble Dole loyalists who didn't expect much talk from the Senator. Wohlford hardly knew what to say in the plane— though he saw: Dole was down. For the first time that Wohlford knew, Dole seemed to want reassurance. It was dark in the plane—just dim nightlights, the glow from gauges . . . Dole was slumped in a sling-seat.

"We can do it," Wohlford said, heartily. "We just got a lot of work, but we got a lot of people now . . . we just have to turn it loose!"

He meant, to win.

"Yeah," Dole said. ". . . I'm just not sure it's worth it."

In the end, there was no time to wonder—no way to change *anything*. The campaign tumbled to its close with a relentless ferocity that everyone tried to disown. No one could deny, though—the Dole campaign did "turn it loose."

Dave Owen found an account of Dole's war service in a vets' magazine; he had the story reprinted on hundreds of thousands of fliers, under the headline GUTS! . . . then dispatched crews in motor homes to hand them out—for days at a time, one Main Street after another. It was the first time the Bob Dole story had been told in anything other than whispers.

In the end, there was also a mailing to Legion vets, which alleged (in another headline): THE ONLY MILITARY TERM BILL ROY KNOWS IS AWOL. Then there was a little asterisk. You had to go to the next page to find a box that explained: Bill Roy was absent from the House of Representatives for two votes on military matters. (They'd happened to fall on Fridays—Roy was back in Kansas.)

In the end, there were stops at local high schools, where Dole would tell the kids, at the close: "Go home and ask your parents if they know how many abortions Bill Roy has performed."

In the end, the mudslinger ads went back on TV—no one seemed to think they were shocking anymore. . . . By that time, there were newspaper ads, too, showing a skull and crossbones: one bone was labeled "Abortion," the other

"Euthanasia." Underneath, it said: "Vote Dole." By that time, the last week (especially that Sunday of the last weekend), there were thousands of fliers found on windshields. Those showed photographs of dead babies in garbage cans: "Vote Dole."

Dole said this stuff didn't come from him. He was trying to stop it. This kind of thing didn't help him!

But it did.

In the end, a switch of two votes per precinct would have made the difference. And one of the most Democratic precincts was around the Catholic church in Kansas City—Bill Roy lost there. His own Catholic precinct, in Topeka, he used to win two-to-one while running for Congress. He broke even in that one.

In the end, Bob Dole was returned to the Senate. On election night, his supporters gathered in jubilation at that Ramada, in Topeka. They could hardly *believe* it: they'd turned it around. They'd pulled it out! Dole could not believe it either. (He kept saying that night, "Well, 'fraid we didn't quite make it . . .") Dole would not come downstairs to speak till after two o'clock the next morning. Dave Owen said they had it won. The reporters downstairs said Dole had it won. The network TV said Dole had won. But Dole called 105 County Clerks before he would claim it.

Even then, there was no jubilation for Dole. Even while the crowd whooped and chanted his name, Dole had a stubborn grip on the facts. He was a winner, he'd escaped. He was going back to the Senate. But he wasn't going to go through this again. He could not. Something had to change.

— ★ —

How do you change a life that has lasted fifty years? With difficulty, and mostly at the margins. But Dole was lucky. There was a woman in Washington, Elizabeth Hanford, whom he'd called from the road almost every night of that bitter campaign . . . sometimes two in the morning—didn't matter—he always felt better when he heard her.

That election night, he was even later: he wouldn't call till he knew he'd won. He told her he wanted to celebrate with her, back in Washington. He was crestfallen when she said she wouldn't be there . . . she was scheduled to depart for three weeks in Japan.

Of course, that's one of the reasons he liked her: she'd never be the type to sit home, waiting for him to finish his meetings. She never stayed home—unless she was sleeping, or working there. She was just as serious about work as he was. (Maybe more: she'd fret about next week's work, or next month's—as he never would.) She was a rising star in the capital, a member of the Federal Trade Commission. She was good-looking, soft-spoken, raised with the graces of the well-to-do in Salisbury, North Carolina (Lotta moneyy!) . . . she was smart, well schooled (after Duke, aghh! *Harvard!*) . . . she demanded perfection from herself (they had that standard in common) . . . she was a woman who achieved, who *shined,* in his Washington world. . . . In fact, she seemed so polished, accomplished, he almost missed his chance.

He'd met her in '72, just months after his own divorce. Elizabeth was working as assistant to Virginia Knauer, the White House adviser on consumer affairs. Knauer wanted a consumer plank in the GOP platform, so she asked for a meeting with the chairman, Bob Dole. Elizabeth said, years later, that the minute Bob walked in, she thought: "My! What an attractive man!" Bob said, years later, that after the meeting, he wrote her name on his blotter. But what happened at the time was . . . nothing.

In fact, he saw her again at the opening of Nixon's campaign headquarters in Washington . . . and at the convention in Miami . . . in fact, it was months before he called, and they talked pleasantly for forty minutes, about nothing in particular, a conversation that led to weeks of more . . . nothing.

After which, he called again, and they had another long talk—yes, they certainly did see eye-to-eye on many subjects! . . . But at the end of that call, all he could muster was that it might be nice to get together.

"Whah, yes!" said Elizabeth. She waited for him to name a place, a date . . . something.

But the poor man could not. There was thirteen years' difference in their ages: she was only thirty-seven—would she be interested? He was, after all, a man divorced, not a raging success in affairs of the heart . . . and she was the Belle of the Capital Ball!

So she was . . . but she was also, at that point, almost convinced that she had outpaced all suitors. There were men who thought she must be a tigress (and came on doubly strong to show their stripes); and plenty who thought she was great—if she'd only drop that government stuff; and men who never would get close enough to find out anything (it was the capital, after all, and she *outranked* them!)—to put it simply, she scared most men to death.

Bob was shy (he finally did choke out an invitation to dinner at the Watergate Terrace) . . . but not afraid. He was a man not unused to strong women (Elizabeth seemed a fragile flower next to Bina Dole). He was not worried about outranking her, out-politicking her, out-thinking, or out-talking her . . . those were stripes he'd proved elsewhere. His concerns were more innocent (and winning): mostly he wanted to prove he could be a nice date.

But he was! She was interested in what he *really* did . . . he didn't have to make small talk, make up hobbies, keep telling jokes. She understood his world, understood his talent in it. And still . . .

What he discovered, little by little (this was, perhaps, the hook that fetched him into the boat) . . . she was a woman of surprising innocence. There was her faith in the system: she believed government—public service—could make lives better. There was her faith in the Lord, which she talked about with unaffected certainty that one did not often hear in Washington. There was her startling *un*certainty about herself, wherein, slowly, one discovered the fuel for both her compulsive work and her faith in a Higher Power. . . . When she got back from Japan, she found a gift of champagne and a dozen long-stemmed red roses. Bob Dole had a life to remake—he did not want to be alone.

That was almost the turn of the year—1975, the year they would marry. Bob never did propose. They just started talking about their future, together. In fact, Bob said he'd known for more than a year . . . before that election night. He said he was waiting, just to make sure he had a job.

Of course, once he had a job, he had work to do. So they waited some more, until the Senate was out, that December . . . which gave Elizabeth time to select a chapel (the Washington Cathedral) and to find a gorgeous white dress, a veil of lace, and the organist, and to ask the Senate Chaplain, Edward Elson, to preside. Elizabeth memorized and rehearsed her vows, Bob figured he could wing it. . . . It was a Saturday, nearly evening, and the small guest list, mostly family, heard Dr. Elson's welcome to the happy occasion, this solemn sanctification, this fulfillment of God's plan, and His command . . .

Dr. Elson paused, perhaps for breath. He hadn't yet turned to Bob and Elizabeth—much less, asked them anything. But Bob wasn't waiting anymore. His prairie voice echoed in the Bethlehem Chapel:

"I *dooo*!"

84

1975

BY THAT TIME, Dole was making speeches about opening up the Republican Party, repairing what he called its "antipeople image." It wasn't enough, he said, to rail against welfare cheats. Everybody knew what the GOP was *against*. Republicans had to demonstrate they could also take care of the needy, that the Party was not against *helping people*.

What had got into Dole?

The shamans of the Washington tribe were confused: just when they had him neatly pigeonholed, the hatchet man went mooshy. (Was this some kinda trick? . . .)

Then he started in on *food stamps*!

Dole was a member of the Senate Select Committee on Nutrition (most members were Ag guys) . . . and he found out that people who needed food stamps had to *apply for eligibility*. They had to prove they were so poor, the government ought to sell them stamps worth, say, one hundred fifty dollars, for the princely discount of one hundred dollars. It took weeks, of course, to prove eligibility.

So in '75, Dole advanced an amendment: if people were hungry, sell them stamps *now*—let them *self-certify*. (If the paperwork didn't square, next month . . . well, time enough to deal with it then.) At the root of this proposal was a radical idea: *feed the hungry*—you could trust people, even though they were poor!

Well, conservatives sent up a howl. They were promoting a bill by Senator

James Buckley to knock thousands (or tens of thousands) *off* food stamps
. . . now Dole wanted to make the system work?

But Dole didn't stop there. With the Chairman of the Select Committee, he
authored a complete overhaul of the program, a reform: for the first time, there
would be an income limit for people who got food stamps (that was the bone
for the conservatives) . . . but at the same time, the government would just give
the stamps away. Dole was acquainting his fellow Republicans with another
radical truth: people who were hungry might not *have* a hundred dollars for
stamps.

Well, that sent up great clouds of ash from the op-ed volcano. It wasn't just
Dole's radical ideas. It was his coauthor (to be precise, his coconspirator), the
chairman of the committee, the Senator from South Dakota, and the right
wing's favorite *piñata,* George McGovern. This reform was called the *Dole-
McGovern bill.*

C'monnnn! . . . What was Dole try'na *pull*?

The wise-guy community was profoundly split on what everybody-who-
knew was supposed to know:

Some knew for a fact that Dole was playing clever hardball to win a bigger
market for the Kansas farmer. (It was true, Dole saw this as a spur to markets
. . . but the Kansas wheat farmer didn't give a damn about food stamps.)

Some others descried a plan—*a plot*—to position Dole on issues of national
substance, in furtherance of his overweening long-term ambition for higher
office. (It was true, Dole meant to build a record of substance . . . but if he
were picking issues out of a hat—why not postal rates?)

The Washington Post essayed the bold notion that Dole was actually trying
to help people. A series of editorials commended Dole for his farsighted stand.
(Of course, those truly in-the-know knew it had to be more than that—Dole
was, you know . . . trying to Be Nice!)

Dole, himself, told anyone who asked: there was nothing miraculous here.
Bill Roy almost beat him because voters didn't think he cared about *anyone*
. . . wasn't true!

Well, how could the lunch-buddies accept that?

Everybody knew Bob Dole was . . . a hatchet man.

(They'd all heard what he said to Senator Buckley. They held hearings on
Buckley's hard-line food-stamp bill. Dole asked—in open session!—"Agh,
d'you put in a *burial allowance . . . f'the ones who starve?*")

But Dole kept making speeches, affirming that people who were hungry
should *get food*! . . . In Washington, someone spotted him at a prayer breakfast.
That was probably Elizabeth, got him to come . . .

Aha! . . . Elizabeth!

All at once, the official-secret story emerged. Elizabeth Hanford Dole (who
was *so* nice!) was working on Bob.

All at once, everybody knew the *same story*—most satisfyingly well
known—how Elizabeth sat Bob down (at home—yeah, in the kitchen, with the
little lady!) . . . and made him watch tapes of himself . . . and showed him how
to Be Nice! . . . She was *making* him *Nice*! . . . She was his *Nice coach*!

Well, Bob didn't go out of his way to correct that. Seemed to him, if there had to be credit, Elizabeth ought to get it. He probably *was* nicer, liked himself better—once he got past reelection . . . once the new Congress moved the capital past the Nixon bitterness . . . once he got to flyin' around the country . . . come home, there's Elizabeth—he *loved* coming home.

Matter of fact, he was in love . . . why wouldn't he be mellow?

For God's sake, he's getting good ink from the *Post*!

— ★ —

Barbara Bush was in love with China. It was her first trip overseas . . . such a wonderful adventure! There was the compound in Peking—a small building for the office, a larger house behind: first floor given over to reception rooms and a spacious dining room; family quarters above—quite cozy. . . . There was a house staff of six (so *interesting*, with their Chinese ways, and strange Maoist stringencies) . . . and a tennis court (with a Chinese pro), where she and George could team up for mixed doubles. . . . There was a new community of foreign diplomats to woo and watch: receptions, reciprocal dinners, national days (such a grand and festive barbecue she and George mounted for July Fourth— the Chinese had never seen anything like it). . . . There were visitors, occasional trips; wonderful food (their head cook, Mr. Sun, was an artist); lots of letters to the kids, who stayed at school in the states. There was an early-model VCR, with tapes of *M*A*S*H* from a friend at the network. There were daily lessons in Chinese (Bar picked up more than George) and three thousand years of history to learn. There were her bike rides through Peking, to ancient tombs, into strange corners of the city—with friends, or alone, or, best of all, with George.

That was the great thing. Bar had moved into too many different houses (this one in Peking was her twenty-fifth) to fall in love with another pile of brick; staff she'd had, and would have more; new friends—there were always new friends. But in Peking, for the first time since Odessa, Texas (maybe the first time in her married life), she had George Bush to herself. He had no work in the evenings—often none in the afternoons. There were no long cables to write back to Washington, describing his contacts with the Chinese government. Save when Kissinger came to town (twice in their year-long sojourn), there were no serious contacts with the government . . . unless you counted the tennis pro.

So Bar and George did everything together. They'd pedal off, side by side, in the afternoons, on their way to the Ming tombs, or the Forbidden City, with George waving and smiling to the Chinese on the streets. . . . *"Ni-how!"* he'd call, through a gap-mouthed grin. That was Chinese for "How are ya?" . . . except with Bush, sometimes it came out like an indeterminate rodeo whoop. Anyway, if anyone really answered, they'd soon exhaust Bush's stock of Chinese words. But still, they had to come away with a sense of his freshness, his eagerness to know them. What he brought to the historic reopening of U.S. relations with one billion Chinese was the same gift that carried him through every job—his person.

And no one enjoyed that person more than Bar. She was never happier. "I think it's great," she told one friend, "to have a new life every ten years or so." She called China "a whole new leaf in both our lives . . ."

But it was not altogether a new leaf for George—or, he hadn't quite finished turning the old one. In November '75, he got a cable from Kissinger: THE PRESIDENT ASKS THAT YOU CONSENT TO HIS NOMINATING YOU AS THE NEW DIRECTOR OF THE CENTRAL INTELLIGENCE AGENCY.

Bar said: "I remember Camp David . . ."

What she meant was, she remembered that day, at Camp David, when George accepted the worst job of his life—the RNC. What she meant was, the CIA was under the same sort of cloud as the Nixon campaign of '72. Senator Church's Select Committee on Intelligence was turning up evidence of illegal operations, assassination plots, domestic spying. *(What did they know? When did they know it?)* . . . She just wanted George to stop and think: Did he want to walk into another swamp?

But she had no illusions; George would never refuse the President. Anyway, she could see how he felt: this was a *big job* . . . worldwide . . . critical to the country, critical to the man in the Oval Office. He wouldn't have to fight for the President's ear—would he? . . . He cabled back to make sure.

No, he'd have full access, control of his own shop, his own staff. (Bush started calling himself Head Spook.)

And, within days, he found out that this—that he—was part of a major shake-up: a new Defense Secretary, Don Rumsfeld; a new National Security Adviser, Brent Scowcroft; a new Commerce Secretary, Elliot Richardson . . . and most intriguing—a new opening for the national ticket, in 1976 . . . Nelson Rockefeller had bowed out as Ford's running mate.

Who could tell what would happen now?

There was a whole new team taking the field . . . and, at last, Bush would be in the great game!

He cabled his acceptance. He flew back to Washington.

Only weeks later did he learn that some Senators (and not just Democrats) didn't want Bush in the game. Only then did he hear the theory (it had occurred to him, as a matter of fact) that they'd brought him back just to smear him in another swamp of misfeasance . . . to give him a job from which he'd *never* recover—not politically, not in the public mind . . . that they'd brought him back to *bury him forever*. Worse still, as the price of his confirmation, they wanted him to remove his name from consideration as Ford's running mate.

How *dare* they? It was like taking away his right to *vote*! It was . . . unconstitutional! Had to be!

Well, maybe. But the decision was out of his hands. Before the Senate Armed Services Committee confirmed Bush's nomination, Gerald Ford wrote a letter, assuring the committee:

". . . There should be continuity in the CIA leadership. Therefore, if Ambassador Bush is confirmed by the Senate as Director of Central Intelligence, I will not consider him as my Vice Presidential running mate in 1976."

85

1976

WHEN DOLE got the call from Gerald Ford, at the GOP Convention in Kansas City, he was so excited, he blurted out: "Mr. President, I can't believe it!" Then, with his next breath, he accepted the Vice Presidential nomination.

A lot of people couldn't believe it. Elizabeth was stunned. The family went into a tizzy. Kenny told a reporter in the Muehlbach Hotel: "I'm looking for my cleanest dirty shirt." ABC had a crew on a chartered plane, already bound for Howard Baker's hometown—they had to U-turn in midair and head for Russell, Kansas. Nelson Rockefeller, the retiring Veep, had only hours to put together his speech of nomination.

"The man of whom I speak," Rockefeller said that night, in the Kemper Arena, "can take the heat! He can not only take it, believe me, he can really 'Dole' it out!"

With that rhetorical flourish, Ford's Advance men appeared with blue-and-white Ford-Dole signs, still smelling of ink . . . but Dole's name set off a floor demonstration that lasted, alas, less than ten minutes. UPI was already on the phone to Bill Roy, who had the bad grace to bring up dead babies in garbage cans. "It may be," Roy predicted, "what some people will call a dirty campaign."

Newsweek called Ford's selection "impulsive," and called Dole the "cut-and-shoot junior Senator from Kansas."

The New York Times got hold of Phyllis (at that point, Mrs. Lon Buzick, wife of a cattleman and prominent Republican in Sylvan Grove, Kansas), who thought Bob would make a bored Vice President—too aggressive. But with Ford thirty-three points behind, Phyllis said, Bob might save the day. "Bob Dole," she said, "will just tear into Jimmy Carter. He is just as smart, and just as tough, and just as hard . . . he can campaign forever if he has to—even with the arm."

That's what Ford and Co. had in mind. The President would stay in the White House, conducting himself Presidentially. (Polls showed Ford lost support when he went out to campaign.) What Ford wanted was a running mate who would bleed Carter with a thousand cuts, make news, get the ink, take the heat . . . meanwhile, shore up the GOP in the heartland (where farmers still resented Ford's cutoff of grain sales to the Soviet Union).

Dick Cheney, Ford's Chief of Staff, told Dole: "You're in charge from the Mississippi west."

Bob Teeter, the President's pollster, told Dole they'd have to win (or win back) 130,000 votes each day.

Ford said: "You're going to be the tough guy."

It wasn't supposed to be a "nice" job . . . or easy. The point was, Dole had a chance! Point was, they gave him the ball! Bob was so pumped up, he was racing around his hotel, grabbing hands, spreading cheer. He had one phone to his ear and another uncradled, on the hotel bed—someone else waiting. He was *thanking* people. (Never did *that* before! . . .) He was so excited he invited Ford to begin the campaign in the *real* heartland—Russell, Kansas—the next day! Tomorrow!

That was the first time Dole brought the national show to Russell, and it hit with such a jolt . . . the town would never be the same. *The President of the United States* was coming, twenty-some hours from now. The Air Force took over the nearest decent airport, seventy miles east, in Salina. The Secret Service choppered into Russell to pick out a site—the courthouse lawn. The Chief of Police called in reinforcements from a hundred miles; he placed them, with rifles, on the courthouse roof, the Legion roof, the buildings across the street; state cops poured in to help with traffic. Paramedics and ambulances arrived from nearby towns, the hospital went to alert: they had to have the President's blood type in stock. The telephone company strung hundreds of new lines. Ev Dumler, head of the Chamber of Commerce, borrowed three sections of bleachers, and trucks to carry them in; he tracked down a P.A., took all the chairs from the Armory, and from the 4-H, too; dismantled and hauled in the stage from the fairgrounds, along with stock tanks for icing down thousands of sodas (the President wanted an old-fashioned barbecue). Scores of Republican ladies brought their grills from home to cook twenty thousand hotdogs (a bakery in Hutchinson put on a special shift for buns). The VFW color guard was scrambled to attention, the high school band crashed into rehearsals of "Hail to the Chief," the Dream Theatre gave its marquee to the message WELCOME PRESIDENT FORD AND BOB, the radio station went live remote from the courthouse, the *Russell Daily News* swelled with extra pages of Dole-pictures, Dole-bio, Dole-record, and Dole-remembrance, all topped

with the two-inch headline: BOMBSHELL HITS RUSSELL. . . . Of course, no one
got any sleep.

Who wanted to sleep?

Mae Dumler, Ev's wife, said: "Well, I got so excited, I didn't know what
to do. So, I just made a pie."

Bina Dole got so excited when the President was going to come *into her
house* . . . she lost it, on her front step. She couldn't find her key. Fifteen men
in suits were standing, waiting, while Bina scrabbled around in her purse, until
Jerry Ford said, "Bina, let me have a look." Then Bina about dropped dead.
The *President's hand* was *in her purse*! (Elizabeth, at last, found the spare key
behind a drainpipe.)

That day, as Bob stood on stage to speak, the President, Bina, Elizabeth,
and Robin sat behind him. The sun was shining on the people, massed so tight,
they hid the courthouse lawn. There were ten thousand souls in Russell that
day. At the edge of the crowd, at the curb, on Main Street, the farmers leaned
against their pickups—Doran's friends. . . . Doran Dole died the December
before (Bob and Elizabeth cut short their honeymoon). Bob got the Vice
Presidential nomination on August 19—that would have been his father's
seventy-sixth birthday. What would Doran say if he could see his town, and
his son, now?

"I am proof . . ." Dole told the crowd, "that you can be from a small town,
without a lot of material advantages . . . and still succeed . . . if I have
succeeded.

"If I have had any success, it is because of the people here. . . . I can recall
the time when I needed help . . . and the people of Russell helped . . ."

Then he stopped speaking. He looked down. His left hand came up to his
forehead, hiding his eyes. He was crying.

The silence was awful. It went on for a minute—felt like forever. Elizabeth
wanted to go to him. No one knew what to do. Bob was sobbing, and could
not stop.

Then President Ford rose from his chair behind Bob, and he started to
applaud. And ten thousand people stood in front of him, clapping, cheering,
until Bob looked up again and said, in a croak that was nearly whisper . . .

"That was a long time ago . . . and I thank you for it."

— ★ —

Jerry Ford flew straight from Russell to a week or two of golf in Vail, Colorado. Dole hit the road . . . and did not stop. He'd never seen a national
campaign from the inside—now he was supposed to build one, on the fly.

Dole had Dave Owen doing money—Owen took an office in Washington,
(Eighteenth and L streets), slapped a couple of million Ford-for-President
dollars into the Riggs Bank on the corner. That same day, Owen rented a
Northwest Orient 727 for the next ten weeks . . . so there wasn't extra money
to throw around.

In fact, it was a wicked combination—a plane, and not much money. For one thing, to pay costs, they had to rent half the plane to the press, who'd badger Dole constantly . . . and since they had the plane all the time, there was no point paying extra money to stay anywhere. So mostly, they'd fly Dole out and back—same day. To be precise, they'd load him up at National Airport for a godawful 6:oo A.M. hop to some breakfast, and do three or four stops across the country, picking up hours, heading west . . . by evening, they'd be in the Southwest or the Rockies, or on the West Coast . . . after which, they'd fly Dole back across the country all night. It did save money, and time. It just about killed Dole.

The demands were horrendous. Dole was supposed to hit every major media market . . . but concentrate on the farm states . . . but make news every day . . . and hit Carter, always, hit him, and hit him. Ford was in the Rose Garden. Dole had the press to himself. He did all the speaking. He needed things to say, and he had no issues staff, no speechwriters (save for his own humble Senate folk).

They were piling on staff as fast as they could: press Advance and Larry Speakes from the White House; Lyn Nofziger, Charlie Black, and Paul Russo from the Reagan team. Dole tended to rely on his Kansans—Owen, Bill Taggart, Kim Wells . . . but he didn't listen to anyone, really, save to the White House, where Teeter's polls and Jim Baker's instincts determined the program (more farm stops, more and more . . .). On the plane, there was a continuous turf war, constant bickering about who was giving Dole the best advice. The last thing Dole would do was sort out that cockfight. True to form, Dole's staff did whatever it wanted—except for the ones he trusted, who did whatever he asked.

He was supposed to hit Carter . . . but hit him with what? So the Washington smart guys started a briefing book, which would travel on the plane, for the Senator's study. Within weeks, there were special briefing books, depending on the issue—all color-coded, so the *master* briefing book referred to appendices: "See Blue Book" . . . "See Red Book" . . . "See Green Book," and so on. It was weeks before Dole said: "Doesn't anyone on this plane know I'm color-blind?" So they stuck big labels on the books: "THIS IS THE RED BOOK" . . . "THIS IS THE GREEN BOOK." Dole never opened the damned things, anyway.

In fact, he was mild about Carter—by his standards. (*Time* mag called him a disappointing "tabby cat.") Before his nomination, Dole said Carter looked like "southern-fried McGovern." But the White House Big Guys got nervous (southerners might be offended), so they warned Dole off that. Then Dole started telling his crowds: "I *used to* call him southern-fried McGovern . . . but I have a lot of respect for Senator McGovern . . ."

(That was true—and mutual: one of the first calls to Dole-for-Veep came from George McGovern, suggesting a few ways Bob might get under Jimmy Carter's skin.)

In his own view, Dole was "sticking to the issues." Carter was committed to the Humphrey-Hawkins bill for full employment. So Dole would suggest, at every stop, that a Carter White House would have two hotlines—one to the USSR, the other to the AFL-CIO. Carter could not make clear the arithmetic of his "tax reform." He had to clarify, then reclarify. Dole snapped: "Carter's got three positions on everything. That's why he wants three debates."

Actually, there would be four debates: for the first time, the nation would see the Vice Presidential nominees square off. (Dave Owen tried everything to scuttle that plan—to the point of making Ford's Big Guys watch a tape of Dole at the Kansas State Fair. But the Veep debate was scheduled, nevertheless.) Dole was supposed to take one day a week to study his briefing books and practice answers . . . but whoever made the plan for Dole to sit still in mid-campaign could not have known the man. Elizabeth (who was on leave from the FTC) rode along with Bob for days, tried to engage him in pepper drills . . . but even with his new wife, Bob was not much for games. As the fateful date neared, Dole's thin staff devoted itself to preparation: they had to find a quiet, secluded space for practice (finally begged a room at Nelson Rockefeller's Washington estate) . . . they set up a studio to duplicate the stage Dole would find in Houston . . . they hired a video crew . . . they had Senators Domenici and Stevens help with new briefing books . . . they got Dave Gergen, one of Ford's top aides, to bring up questions and to play Mondale . . . it took weeks to get the thing set up perfectly, for practice. Then Dole wouldn't come. He sat in his office, making phone calls. Finally, on the last day, he came to the house, stood behind the podium, looked at himself on the monitor . . . and walked out.

It wasn't till he got to Houston, the day of the debate, that Dole would sit still to run through questions . . . but by then he was so offhand (or trying to look offhand), he'd just toss off wisecracks.

"I think tonight may be sort of a fun evening," Dole said, in his introduction to the national TV audience. He said he'd been friends with Walter Mondale, in the Senate, for years . . . "and we'll be friends when this election is over—and he'll still be in the Senate."

Dole seemed determined to keep this light. (Mondale, on the other hand, seemed just determined.) . . . But it's tough to be light with the nation's networks, a thousand of the nation's press, and tens of millions of the nation's voters judging every word.

How many thought it was funny when Dole said George Meany (head of the AFL-CIO) "was probably Senator Mondale's makeup man"?

How many thought it was funny—or fair comment—when Mondale linked Dole to Nixon and Watergate? . . . Or when Walter Mears, of the AP, asked Dole about his criticism of Gerald Ford, when Ford pardoned Nixon?

Dole didn't think it was fair, or funny. You could just about see his spine go stiff, his brow grow dark, as the anger took hold. He said he didn't think Watergate was an issue . . .

". . . any more than the war in Vietnam would be . . . or World War II, or World War I, or the Korean War—*all Democrat wars* . . . all in this century."

Mondale's mouth fell open a notch, and hung there—he couldn't believe Dole had slipped into partisanship about . . . a world war!

But Dole didn't slip—he stalked in . . . and he didn't stop:

"I figured up, the other day: if we added up the killed and wounded in Democrat wars, in this century, it would be about 1.6 million Americans . . . enough to fill the city of Detroit!"

After that, Mondale let him have it:

"I think that Senator Dole has richly earned his reputation as a hatchet man tonight . . ."

Of course, Dole thought that was *so* unfair. He said, after the debate: "I thought I was very friendly. I called him 'Fritz' a couple of times. He called me 'hatchet man.' "

In fact, Dole was sure he'd won the debate—scored his points, made his jibes stick. It was a shock to him when the flood tide of editorial condemnation crested. ("Democrat wars" was common political discourse in Russell—like "Republican depressions.") . . . Dole tried to *explain:* he didn't really mean the Democrats *caused* all those deaths, those wars—he just wanted to let Mondale know, if he made Watergate a Republican millstone . . . well, there were weights to drag the Democrats down, too. He even hinted that if *anyone* had the right to talk about the suffering of war, it was *him,* Bob Dole! . . . You want to make something of that?

Of course, that only made it worse.

Why couldn't Dole just . . . back off?

All the hatchet-man Grape-Nuts that reporters had stored now came rattling into "analysis" pieces—character will out, after all! Pat Caddell, Carter's pollster, filled the breakfast bowls when he told the big-feet that Mondale was a plus for the Democratic ticket . . . but Dole was dragging the President down! This poop got to be so well known by those in-the-know, that Dole became the subject of the Carter campaign's only negative ad. (With four of the last six Vice Presidents moving up to the top job, who would *you* like to see a heartbeat away?)

Dole just kept flying. What else could he do?

In the last weeks, he hit four or five states a day—mostly through the Midwest and South . . . where he'd rasp out his message that the name of his candidate wasn't Nixon-Ford, it was Jerry Ford! . . . Carter could talk about trust, but Jerry Ford had earned it!

Dole was getting sick, his voice was almost gone. Elizabeth would call the Schedulers to tell them Bob *had* to rest—they were killing him. Then Bob would call and add a stop to the day after next . . . they were so close, just a little more push . . . they could make it—Carter could still go sour! . . . Carter's margins were melting away in Texas, Illinois, Ohio, Florida, Oklahoma—Dole got the tracking polls every day. Jerry Ford was, at last, loosed from the White House, and he thumped and stumped around the country, showing the grandeur of his office (thousands came out, just to see *Air Force One*) and the Everyman values to which he still clung (every Ford rally featured the Michigan fight song). There was a half-hour TV show in all the major markets, with Ford answering questions from that penetrating interviewer, Joe Garagiola . . . and lots of negative ads, feeding the public doubts about Carter.

And in the last week, the final Gallup Poll showed . . . Ford and Dole edging into the lead! . . . It wasn't really a lead—just one point—easily within the margin of error. But that statistical nuance was beside the point. They had come from *thirty-three points behind*! . . . On the last weekend, Ford called to say: "You're doing a great job. I know you must be exhausted—but keep it up. We're going to make it, Bob!" . . . They had climbed back to even—against all odds. And they were moving—Dole could feel it:

"I smell VICTORYYYY! . . ."

—★—

They lost by two percent . . . by fifty-seven electoral votes . . . by the barest handful of votes in Ohio and Hawaii. Those two states would have turned it around: if 9,244 votes had changed (one one-hundredth of one percent of the votes cast nationally, or one vote in every ten thousand), it would have thrown those two states to Ford and Dole . . . and completed the miracle comeback.

Dole had so many ways to measure how close they came—and how far they'd come: the farm vote held solid for Ford . . . Dole won all of his assigned states—the West, the heartland (save for Missouri—he was *sure* the Democrats stole that in the cities!) . . . Dole did not want to give up—they could demand recounts in the tightest states. . . . But Ford ruled that out, day after the vote.

By that time, Dole was in bed—fevered and weak. He only got up to host his party. He was giving a party for reporters who'd traveled with him. . . . That's when Barbara Walters asked the question—like a knife in his ribs:

Didn't Dole think, Ms. Walters asked, *he was the one who lost the White House for poor Jerry Ford*?

That sent Dole back to his bed. How could she *say* that?

He did his job! . . . Did it well!

He showed he could play in the big leagues—the biggest!

He showed himself, anyway.

It was a couple of days later, when Dole got back to the office, Taggart asked: "Well, think you'll run for national office again?"

"Not for four years," Dole said.

Actually, he started just weeks after the vote—Dole did a speech in South Dakota, then a stop in Illinois, and then . . . he was flyin' around. He made sure to bring up the VP race himself.

"Well," he'd say, "they told me to go for the jugular—so I did. . . . It was mine."

He knew he would run again—in four years, eight, or . . . as long as it took. Next time, he wouldn't do dirty work for anyone else. It would be his campaign . . . so he knew, it would start in Russell.

86

Vision Music

ON MAIN STREET, as Dole was about to begin his announcement speech, a man in the crowd keeled over from the cold. Dole stopped, bent, stared down at the pavement with a look of concern . . . murmured something about a doctor . . . but he was live on the morning shows, so after a few minutes he had to go on.

In fact, there were eight people who collapsed that Monday morning, from cold, or excitement, or by happenstance. Frostbite? Heart attack? . . . No one knew. The hospital wouldn't distract attention from the show, so no information was released on the patients or their conditions.

The point was, Bob looked wonderful up there. And no one could miss how real was this frozen street scene, compared to Bush's high-gloss Hyatt . . . and the cameras here had a beautiful shot from the riser in the center of Main Street—but they blocked the view for local folks, who had to come around the riser to the foot of the stage so they could see, and so Bob could see their signs . . . and that meant people in the near folding seats, like Bob's sisters, Gloria and Norma Jean, had signs in front of them . . . and when the signs blocked the cameras, the techies had to shift in a hurry . . . so Anita, Kenny's wife, got clonked in the head with a camera, or a tripod leg, as Bob got toward the end of his speech, as he improvised that terrific close . . . where he's sitting in the sun on his Capitol balcony, *thinking:* Could he be, should he be, President?

"And I thought to myself, 'I could make a difference.'

"And I thought, 'I will make a difference!' . . . 'I *can* make a difference!' . . . 'I *have* made a difference!' . . ."

That was the bottom line with Dole, and probably why he looked so happy as he ended his speech and the music kicked up again, and he grinned out over the crowd, swinging his fist, bouncing to the beat . . . and then he climbed down to the street, to the people in the front row, people in wheelchairs.

(Advance had wanted to move those folks—make an aisle in front of the stage, but Kenny warned them: "You're makin' a big mistake. Bob Dole. . . . That's what it's all about.")

Kenny had to scoot to a storefront, where station KAKE had a makeshift studio—a panel discussion on Bob Dole, featuring Kenny, Bub Dawson, and Bob's old coach, George Baxter. The three men were wired with earplugs to hear the anchor-humans in Wichita.

"Kenny, what is it that's so special about your brother?"

Kenny started to answer . . . but he had his head cocked at an angle, like he couldn't figure how to speak to this voice in his ear. The cameraman was silently, frantically, motioning at Kenny to sit up straight . . . sit *still* . . . stop *mumbling*!

Kenny said, after it was over, "Might as well had a corncob in my butt as that plug in my ear."

Gloria, Norma Jean, Gladys, and the rest crowded into Dawson Drug, waiting for Bob. Gloria was fretful. There'd been such a rush to get out of her house, she hadn't time to pack a bag for Bob—no goodies! And when Bob got off stage in the rush, everyone was pushing, she couldn't even grab his arm to tell him. . . . And, then, Bob never came back to the drugstore.

In the end, Gloria had to go to one of the cool, crisp strangers with the microphones in their sleeves to ask if she could go into the alley where they'd parked Bob's car. "I'm his sister," she said. "I just want to hug him." The stranger's sunglasses looked her up and down.

"I always hug him . . ."

They finally let her into the alley, and she caught Bob getting into the car. She just had time for a quick hug. "Got any goodies?" Bob said.

"No, Bob. I . . . there wasn't time."

"Oh-kayy. Gotta gooo . . ." He was into the car. He had to get to Iowa, to make his speech again.

Gloria couldn't go to Iowa. That was not for her. The press would go, Bill Brock, the Big Guys. . . . Gloria stayed in Russell.

She was exhausted. Bob's announcement just about finished the family. When she got back to her house, she got her makeup off, got out of her dress, collapsed into a chair, and it looked like she didn't have the strength to draw breath. The grandkids had the house jazzed up with bunting and posters—but in the middle of it all, Gloria only looked grayer. She was barefoot, in her robe. She had that sick blood-pressure feeling, her kidney was giving her trouble.

Kenny came over, and Aunt Mildred Nye. They were sitting at the table, Mildred was scanning the paper for more Kenny Dole quotes. "Here it is!" she cried. "The *'sacks of concrete'* . . . why, Kenny, you're nothin' but a bullshitter!"

Kenny was spluttering. "When are you leavin'? We've got things to do here! Don't you have a long way back? . . ."

In her armchair, Gloria was musing: she really could do a White House cookbook, all the recipes, if Bob, well . . . she was the one who *knew* how he liked everything—like she told that reporter, the liver and onions, told him just how to make it . . . it wasn't hers anymore. Bob wasn't theirs anymore. That's what she told the reporter. "He belongs to all of you now."

But Bob looked happy. Didn't he?

Oh, yes, Bob had Dave Owen call Anita, and Dave said Bob was pleased. "That's good," Gloria said.

In Russell, in the exhaustion, there was no way to tell . . . but, yes, Bob was happy. He was, well, he was so pumped up, they got to Great Bend, to the airport—big plane, *Presidential Airways!*—and they loaded up the press, the Big Guys, and finally the Bobster, who came up the front stairs and ducked his head into the cabin, where he heard the music, the theme from *Star Wars,* with the trumpets and those echo-spacey laser-whooshes . . . Gaaggh! It was fantastic!

"Heyy! We got *vision!*" Dole said. "We even got vision *mu-sic!*"

What Else?

BY THAT FALL, it was painfully clear, Dukakis had no vision for Iowa—or anywhere else. He'd lost the thread, the excitement that used to lend his prosy words their urgency. He'd been saying the same thing too long.

He'd still talk about his Massachusetts Miracle, but his sentences would start: "I don't have to tell you, I hope . . ." He'd still talk up new uses for farm crops, but—this was so *obvious,* it was hard to believe he should still have to say it:

"We've got more productive capacity than we know what to do with! [Shrug] . . . I think we ought to be *getting on* with this, folks."

Yes, he did. It seemed to him like a lifetime, he'd been saying this stuff . . . and nothing was happening! And he had not a clue as to how he could *make* something happen. These Iowans were kind, polite, serious, deserving . . . he never ceased to tell them how grateful he was for their attention, their reception of him—terrific . . . but he had no idea what they liked, or disliked, or why.

He thought they still mistrusted him.

He thought they looked at him funny.

Of course, no one said anything.

But he did look like a foreigner. He talked fast. He had an accent. Or they thought he had an accent. Or he thought they thought he . . . well, you know. He thought they didn't like him. What it was . . . *he* didn't like him—because he didn't know what he was doing out there!

What was it for? Why did he get into this thing? Because Sasso and Kitty told him he should. Sasso was gone. Kitty, he never saw—not from one end of the week to the other. She was taut with stress and wear. He wasn't doing any good for her, not like this, not in this—he was . . . well, he didn't like what he had to do, the way this thing crowded and stole from his life . . . work a day in the State House, and then, four-thirty, five o'clock, not home—no trolley, no dinner, no Kitty, no—straight to New Hampshire, or to the airport, a jet, a flight to some funder . . . a wise guy waiting at the airport, with a car, in which he'd pick at Michael about Presidential Vision, or National Per-spective—"Governor, these people don't wanna *hear* Massachusetts, ya know? . . ."

Well, actually, he didn't know—he didn't know what they wanted. They talked about vision, message, national outlook . . . he'd say: *Give me the lines.* They'd write him long, eager memos, how he had to develop a Presidential voice. He'd say, *Gimme the speech—I'll take a look. . . .* That's all he wanted— to see what they meant—something he could read. What the hell was Media Strategy? *Gimme the scripts. I'll tell you what I think.*

He could tell in a minute if it fit him.

Most of it didn't.

Most of it was *junk.*

"Nope . . . nope. It's not me," he'd say. "What else?"

That meant he wanted to see some more lines.

"Guys, c'mon! What're we doin' here? I don't talk like that. That's not me."

Bang . . . bang . . . back in the briefcase: he could knock down a new speech and three ad scripts in a quarter of an hour on his jet. He'd put them away with neat X's drawn through whole pages. Then he'd take out his State House papers, spread them on the table in front of his seat, and bury himself in something real—the new draft of his health-care bill—lest someone else essay a pep talk, tell him, again, he had to engage.

He shouldn't have to *tell them* he was engaged *seven days a week* . . . doing the plan, back and forth across the country, like a yo-yo . . . ninety-nine Iowa counties, for God's sake! He hadn't had a day off, home with his bride, to walk in Brookline, cook a soup, write a letter to Kara at school . . . he hadn't taken a day off in what—six *weeks?* It was ridiculous! No wonder he was . . . well, Michael wasn't the kinda guy to wear down—no, steady, strong . . . or lonely—nope, he wasn't the kinda guy who even knew what that meant—that wasn't him, no, no, sadness, no . . . that wasn't . . .

"Look, Governor, I'm Mediterranean, so I can say this . . ."

This was Mike Del Giudice, a New Yorker, a graduate of Cuomo's Capitol, a friend of Sasso's, a big help with Wall Street money, and the latest to take a shot at Mike in a backseat on a ride to another event.

"Governor, whatever we have in our emotions is all over our goddam face . . . and you've got to get over this thing with John. Because you're hurting yourself, and you're hurting the campaign. A lot of people are investing a lot of time, and money, and energy, and everybody's going down the tubes to-gether . . .

"So, if you want this thing, do it. If you don't want it, get out. It's as simple as that. You can't just drag on. John's behind you."

Michael didn't argue, or shake his head.

"It hurts," he said. "John was, well, I don't have to tell you . . . it hurts like hell."

— ★ —

The campaign staff did everything to set the engine puffing down the track again—or at least make it look that way.

On the day that Sasso resigned, Susan Estrich and Farmer's enforcer, a woman named Kristin Demong, arranged to hold back the checks from the night before, September 29, the million-dollar funder. That way they could announce that the Duke's megamoney wasn't disturbed by the shame of the tapes—no. Steady as she goes! October was another million-dollar month!

That ingenuous Hill & Barlow lawyer, Dan Taylor, proved his acumen even after his internal snooping was called off. He found a flaw in the federal campaign law that limited spending in Iowa. He discovered that a simple fund-raising tag (two seconds on the end of a TV ad) would allow the campaign to charge the ad to fund-raising expense—not to the Iowa campaign. Through that tiny loophole, the Dukakis campaign now drove a truck.

They went on the air with a bio ad—the kinda guy Michael was. They followed with a beautiful spot wherein a tarnished, dented silver bowl was hammered and buffed back to glowing grace while an announcer ticked off the facts of the Massachusetts economic revival. The minute the ads went up, Michael's numbers started climbing—he was back in the hunt—and with the loophole, which only Dukakis had the money to use, he could have put on a lot more ads.

Problem was, he didn't like any ads. He must have x'd-out twenty-five scripts. . . . Meanwhile, the Iowa troops complained bitterly about the new ads—it was a shame to have those ads on the air—they didn't say anything! . . . It was Michael, of course, who didn't want to say anything.

Well, that wasn't strictly true. It was just . . . whatever they gave him didn't seem to be the kinda thing he ought to say. It was all so . . . political, sour, so negative! Michael was still trying to prove what a *positive* guy he was. He didn't want to talk about problems. He didn't want to talk about Reagan and Bush. He surely would not say one word about the other Democrats!

What did that leave?

Good-jobs-at-good-wages . . . the thinnest gruel.

Estrich was aware of this problem—issues, message, communication . . . these were her specialties. Plus, she was smart as hell. Even Dukakis once remarked she was the kinda gal who probably got better grades in law school than he did! . . . Of course, that was on the way to saying, she didn't know practical politics like he did. Nope . . . he'd just have to show her—she'd just have to learn . . . *he knew what he was doing*!

So he showed her, in a thousand ways . . . he hadn't brought her in there to tell him how campaigns were run.

"I've been doing this for twenty-five years!"

Actually, he seldom brought her into his presence—or into his thoughts—in any way. When he came back to Boston, he'd head for the State House—state business! . . . He didn't want to be interrupted with calls from the campaign, speeches to read, strategy, message . . . no! "We said three days, my friend."

Thursdays, he'd host a handful of campaign staff (which he was careful to balance with a half-dozen government types) to go through his schedule. He'd sit them down at his State House conference table—that's where he was at his worst. His every action at the head of that table was intended to show them he was—still, in *real life*—the Governor of the Commonwealth. He'd snap down the agenda, dismissing any discussion—they were taking time from things that mattered. Then, too, the campaign ops, and all political concerns, had to wait while he took any call that came in about state roads, the pension bill, a sludge program, the Governor's Anti-Crime Council. . . . There were people from the campaign who wouldn't even go to the State House. "Why should I?" said the pollster, Tubby Harrison. "I'm just a prop."

And Estrich, who would stay on, after that meeting, for her private sit-down with the Governor—a half-hour, her only scheduled session with Dukakis, week to week—found herself an unwilling prop in a private drama: his determination to prove he could do without John Sasso, his demonstration of his own correctness, all the more splendid in its, in his, isolation.

She'd bring up some way to broaden the message—a good idea! Dukakis was the only man among the front-runners who could stand outside the Washington miasma . . . he could make that distance an advantage—people mistrusted the old federal runaround. What they wanted, what he could show, was *know-how*! Basic American know-how, like they'd shown in Massachusetts! . . . It was *perfect*—hands-on government that worked, but with a theme, a set of words, that dovetailed with voters' preconceptions. She'd have the thing—a *communications strategy*—all set out in memo-prose by her Director of Communications, Leslie Dach.

"I'll take a look," Dukakis would say. "What else? Anything else?"

And that would be the last she'd hear. Dukakis hated Dach, and everything Dach touched. What was this—try'na make him *bash Washington*? "That's not the kinda thinking we want in this campaign."

This made Estrich very nervous—and more determined to show Dukakis he could repose some trust in her. She had worked in politics plenty long enough to handle this job. By age thirty-five, she had habited the top echelons of three Presidential campaigns—which was precisely two more than Dukakis had seen.

She had known for months: this campaign was never going to get anywhere if it didn't find something to say. She could confirm now what she'd always suspected: that communication of some vision was the weakest of Sasso's skills; he did *anything else* first. "This campaign's got everything . . ." she announced at one of her first meetings, ". . . except a fucking message!" She'd chide the surviving wise guys (they were all guys): "I don't understand how you ran this thing for six months without a fucking thing to say!"

Of course, they knew she was right. But what she didn't get—yet—was what it took to move Dukakis . . . the way Sasso kept him swaddled in reports of progress, good news, feedback from the field . . . the constant weaving of the web of confidence that would keep Dukakis out of his hunch, let him move at his trudge-of-the-wing-tips pace toward some new idea that would, in time, come to seem like his own.

That wasn't Susan's style. She wanted Michael to *face his problem.* She took it as a challenge—a personal commitment. The easiest, the cheapest, way would be to let Michael trudge on—to confine her mission to making sure there was someone to meet him at the airport, money in the bank, field staff in the districts—she could have done it well, and saved herself a lot of woe. But she owed him better than that.

So, she pushed harder—and she could push! She could also smoke up a black cloud, swear like a tugboat captain, talk loud and insistently, make her points with vicious humor—all in service of her fierce determination, and all . . . alas, like nails on the blackboard to Dukakis, who didn't like nerves, or pressure from his staff. No. "Calm, steady—that's us."

Well, in fact, that wasn't us . . . not at that point. That's part of what was eating Dukakis. He just wanted to know what he had to do next week, and the week after that, next month, next quarter, first month of next year! Like Sasso used to do in his quarterly memo . . . he just wanted to see the plan!

Well, Estrich got that. She set Corrigan to producing a plan—a full battle map, with a strategy for the delegate hunt, a timetable, a budget. . . . But, of course, the start of the plan was to put on a move in Iowa. Get tough! Go after the thing! Knock the other bastards out of the box, in a hurry . . . and then, start work on the general election.

Michael wouldn't hear of that. This was a marathon. He'd told them that! No one, for *twenty-five years,* had got very far by pushing him—telling him he had to win this, or do that, or he'd be lost! No. Steady, strong . . . we're going to win because we're raising more money . . . we're employing more staff . . . we're organizing, one vote at a time. He didn't need these kids to tell him how to build a campaign, for God's sake!

At last—more in desperation than eagerness to share Michael's spare attentions—Susan asked Dukakis: Who did he *like* to listen to? . . . Who did he *want* to help with the message?

Dukakis mentioned Tom Kiley, a noted Boston guru, a pollster, partner to John Marttila. He came from a world that Dukakis knew. And Dukakis knew that Sasso—before he left—was trying to get Kiley into the campaign. (In fact, Kiley turned down the Campaign Manager's job before Michael and Brountas settled on Estrich.)

So Susan went to work on Kiley. She did her job. She called him, invited him, inveigled him, cajoled him . . . Kiley was reluctant. But she landed him—brought him on as the *new message guru.*

Great doings!

Kiley came to a couple of meetings, sat with Dukakis, rode along while Michael worked, then retired to his office, and wrote . . . The Memo. Kiley was clear and calm—and smart: he knew Dukakis's history, he had ideas about the field, the voters, the mood of the nation. . . . All of this, he poured into The Memo.

It was a call for National Purpose, a renewal of Real Leadership . . . a plan for Michael to establish—by his issues, his speeches, his ads, his every action—*his own voice*. A Presidential Voice! He had to stop running for National Governor . . . and engage!

Kiley gave The Memo to Susan, who gave it to Michael. They scheduled a talk. They came to the State House—Kiley and Estrich—sat down with Michael. . . . Had he read it? Well? What did he think?

"Okay," said Michael, "try to be more Presidential. What else?"

88

Bambi

THING ABOUT IOWA—no one could call it. The old rules seemed not to apply. The Gephardt campaign poured everything it had into the J-J, the Jefferson-Jackson Day Dinner. For Democrats, that was always the focus of the fall. Jimmy Carter won the straw poll at the J-J in '75, and that put him *on the map:* he showed he could organize the state, he had the troops—after that, there was no stopping the man.

And after that, of course, no Democrat would ever again ignore the J-J. Mid-November, every fourth year, they'd pack the hall, they'd hire on buses, they'd scheme and bribe for extra tickets, they'd dress their people like *Let's Make a Deal*—whatever it took to "win" the J-J. . . . And that year, the Gephardts went berserk. This was gonna show, the new team in Iowa could kick ass! This was gonna put the lie to their declining polls. This was gonna get them back in the network roundups, make the big-feet *take notice.*

They were running out of dollars all over the country, and they poured *thousands* into extra tickets—they bought the floor. Joyce Aboussie rounded up a herd of St. Louisans and flew with them to Des Moines aboard a chartered jet. (That was the mildest of Joyce's endeavors—what she wanted was a team of Budweiser Clydesdales to circle the hall, parading Dick's name.) Carrick brought back Barry Wyatt, the Advance whiz who'd yanked Dick's announcement into line, to move Dick in and out of the hall and whip the floor demonstration to a proper frenzy. There was a SWAT team of kids to decorate—they sprinted into the hall when the doors opened, climbed into the rafters, stood on each other's backs to get their signs well up on the walls.

(Dick would note no dearth of signs here—there were Gephardt stickers in the bathrooms!) Of course, they had Shrummy on the speech—first team—and Doak actually *came*! That's how big it was. Doak was strolling the floor, next to *Carrick* . . . walking together, talking and laughing—proud owners at Grand Opening—smoking big cigars.

But by that time, alas, the cream was off the milk—skimmed by cruel circumstance, and a bit of heads-up politics.

The circumstance: Judge Ginsburg, Reagan's post-Bork nominee for the Supreme Court, was discovered to have smoked a bit of dope while at Harvard. By the time Gephardt got to the hall, all the Kops wanted to know was: Had he ever smoked marijuana? (Gephardt answered as he always answered character-queries: he looked them in the eye, and said, "No." At which point, someone yelled the best—unanswered—question of the night: "Well . . . why not?")

The politics: the Simon campaign convinced the state Party to *cancel the straw poll* . . . there would be no vote, no clear winner in the papers the next day. So when the Gephardt faithful leapt up at their man's introduction, when they made the whole place ache with noise, when they conga-danced in the aisles and poked their pole signs heavenward, when they stood on their chairs and bayed their man's name at the roof, when they stomped on the floor till it seemed the balcony must come down, when they exceeded their time limit for "crowd response" by a factor of three, when, in short, they *took over the goddam J-J* . . . well, there was no one to notice.

Anyway, no one who could be trusted to notice. E.J. Dionne, in the next day's *Times,* made no mention of Dick's demonstration . . . though Dick did get his own subhead in the story:

Hit a Brick Wall

> Mr. Gephardt, who has spent more time here than any other Democrat, and has built a substantial following, was seeking to reverse the perception that his campaign, as one prominent Iowa Democrat put it, "has hit a brick wall."

And E.J. noted, higher in the story:

> One candidate who likes the way things are going just fine is Mr. Simon, of Illinois. . . . Mr. Simon seems especially strong among precisely the sorts of Democratic activists who attend the caucus.

Simon! . . . Gephardt couldn't understand it. Paul Simon was a nice man—a friend of Dick's, matter of fact: they had served together in the House, sometimes took the same plane home to their districts (Simon's home was southern Illinois, closer to St. Louis than Chicago).

Back in '80, Dick even put Paul's name up for Chairman of the House

Budget Committee . . . of course, Simon got slaughtered. Dick could have told him. But Paul said he *had* it. Jesus—just 'cause people told him they were for him! At least Dick could count votes! Paul might have a good idea, a lot of good ideas . . . and was sincere, sure, good-hearted, independent . . . but that was different from getting things done. Paul was off in left field (playing deep!) . . . you'd see a vote: 364 to one . . . that one was Simon.

President Simon?

But sure enough, after Dick had shrugged off all the bad press and installed his new kick-ass Iowa squad . . . after he'd finally got the Biden monkey off his back . . . and schemed and spent to take over the J-J . . . after he was ready to make those polls *jump up and say Hi!* . . . Who got the bump? Whose numbers shot up?

Paul Simon.

There he was—a Senator now, but same guy, exactly—saying the same airy nonsense, in the same honey-graham baritone: *"Weee wanta guvvverment that caaares!"* . . . In fact, that's what he wanted you to see: that he hadn't changed a lick. He had the same pendulous ears, same folds in his face, same glasses, same stentorian Our-Friend-the-Government promises he had in 1956! . . . And the same bow ties.

That was his trademark, see . . . and it was beautiful, Dick had to admit: all his supporters with lapel pins in the shape of bow ties . . . *instant identification,* like the pictures of cows and chickens they use for the different parties in India. In other words, you didn't have to know nothin' . . . that's why Dick admired it so.

"It's a *visual,* see . . ." That's how Dick explained it, because that's how his killers explained it to him. He'd ask:

Why is Simon going up?

Why is Dukakis going up?

(While Gephardt's falling below ten percent—the second tier!)

Carrick and his button men would tell him those other guys were on TV with ads. It gave people a *visual* to hold on to . . . and Dick's ads were still a month away.

So Dick was trying to think visually—think ahead to his ads. (It's always the next hope in campaigns—the next thing, surely, will fix all the ills.) He had a legal pad on his knee while his small plane bounced over Iowa. He was sitting between the new members of his road crew: Debra Johns, who did press on the plane, and Ethel Klein, who did . . . well, no one knew what Ethel did, but she was smart and she talked to Dick.

Dick drew a box on his pad—big and neat, like Dick always drew—and on the left, he wrote "RAG" . . . him. In the middle, he wrote "Duke," and on the right, "Simon." Then he wrote words for each. Under "RAG," he wrote: "Midwestern, Honest, Young, Cleancut . . ." Under "Duke": "Leader, Massachusetts Miracle, Eyebrows . . ." And under "Simon": "Honesty, Caring, Bow Tie, Glasses . . ." Then he sat and stared at the page, till he said:

"See, after what happened to Hart, and Biden, and now Dukakis, people are fed up. Simon's the symbol, antipolitics—the bow tie, the glasses, you add that voice: 'I-I-I-I . . . C-A-A-A-R-E.' . . . It doesn't matter what Paul Simon says—everywhere he goes, he carries that *visual* in front of him.

"See, people look at Dick Gephardt, they don't have a connection. . . . 'Young,' okay, 'Honest' . . . but then, they think, 'Protectionist.' They're confused. They don't know. See, what the image has to be is Energetic, Leadership, Doer, Fighter—that's the visual we need."

Ethel finally broke in: "Yeah, but that visual is not passive, like the bow tie, or the eyebrows. If you want that image, you've got to *be* energetic, fighting all the time. You can do it—I've seen you enough to know you can do it—but you've got to *BE* it."

(*That's* why Ethel was on the plane. As Brad Harris, the body man, catered to Dick's body, so Ms. Klein ministered to the head.)

Dick said: "Right. I understand . . . *be* it."

But he was still trying to think of something like a bow tie. Had to have it! . . . That, and he had to hit Simon—*hard*—at the next debate, the big one December 1, a network show, prime time, NBC! Brokaw! . . . Democrats *and* Republicans. Everybody would watch. Dick had to go in and *kill*. . . . That's the other thing Carrick and the fellas had told him.

—★—

Here is the official button-man analysis, from Joe Trippi (ex-Mondale, ex-Hart), Gephardt's message-doctor, heading into the NBC debate:

"It's simple. . . . Dick would never hit Simon. Why go after Paul? Paul is just out there, caring. You hit Paul, you look like a monster. Paul is Bambi, skipping through the woods, eating leaves. No one wants to kill Bambi.

"But then we get out from under the Biden tape—it's Duke, after all, and he looks like shit . . . so Dick figures: 'Jeez, all *right*! Finally, we're gonna *do* something!'

"And next time he turns around, here's Bambi, running by in the woods, eating leaves, and Bambi is getting big!

"Still, you don't kill Bambi, right? Dick says to Carrick: 'That's not gonna last, is it?'

"And Carrick says, 'No. Can't last. Don't worry.'

"And there goes Bambi, munching leaves.

"So we're into November, and Dick is slipping. The Biden thing left a sour taste. People in Iowa are looking for someone, anyone, without the smell of blood:

"Gephardt, somehow, he was involved, right?

"Duke, he had to *fire* his guys.

"Jackson, he's black—can't win.

"Babbitt is a wonk.

"Gore won't even come to the state.

"Who's left?

"Ah, Bambi!"

"Bambi is getting bigger. Dick says: 'When's this gonna stop?'

"Carrick tells him: It's gotta stop. Don't worry.'

"Dick says: 'The guy's got thirty percent! I got ten, going south.'

"Now, everybody admits: Simon is rolling. He's gonna win Iowa big.

"So who's gonna kill him?

"Babbitt? He's the Son of Bambi. Babbitt is gonna kill no one.

"Jackson is all peace and love. Gotta be. He's a scary black man.

"Duke doesn't wanna kill Bambi. Duke thinks: 'If Bambi wins Iowa and I win New Hampshire, then it's just me and Bambi. . . . I'm it!'

"Gore? He's not gonna touch him. If Bambi wins Iowa, Duke wins New Hampshire, then these two *martians* have to come south, to Gore. One talks about making better 'cahs,' and the other one says: 'I want to spend a lot of money on poor people.' Let 'em come!

"Meanwhile, Gephardt, the one guy who might get to white, middle-class people in the South, will be dead meat.

"So, in the NBC debate, Gephardt takes out a .357 Magnum, and blows Bambi's head off."

— ★ —

That simple. That's why the killers were leaning on Dick so hard to go in and *kill.* . . . They were sinking so fast, they were panicky. There must have been twenty debates that year, but they were nothing compared to this NBC thing . . . that's what they wanted Dick to know. This was *it!*

That's why they tried so many lines, wrote them on cards for him to memorize:

"You know, Paul, I've heard you promise more aid to education, more grants for higher ed, a guaranteed jobs program, long-term health care for seniors . . . so, there's plenty of beef. What I want to know is—where's the dough?"

(That's how they were going to hit Simon, see: Paul had no idea how to pay for Our-Friend-the-Government.)

Then, the staff speechwriter, Paul Begala, wrote out on a briefing sheet: "*Simonomics* is just the flip side of *Reaganomics.* "

Then, in a mock debate, Trippi blurted out: "*Reaganomics with a bow tie!*" . . . They all had a giggle about that.

But they should have known: you couldn't toss four different lines at Gephardt—he was *listening.* The Washington staff used to call him Memorex. (Lately, it was RoboCandidate.)

This time, the practice was harder, because Carrick and the boys brought in hotshot lawyers to play the other candidates. Their instructions: beat the shit out of Dick—make him hit back, make him kill. . . . Of course, that, too, sent the message to Dick that this was the *big one:* suddenly, he was looking at $2,000-an-hour worth of Washington smart guys.

But the thing was, he *knew* this was it. For God's sake, it was *December* . . . the caucus was nine weeks away . . . it was network! All those *millions of people*! And he wanted to do something . . . *so badly*—he was pushing himself harder than they were!

So they were running mock debates, beating up Dick, and their smart-guy-Gore said something about Dick's vote for Reagan's tax cut. Dick just wheeled on the guy, started yelling:

"Where were *you*? I led the FIGHT for the Democratic alternative! Where were *YOU,* Al? You were on the BACK BENCHES!"

The button men were silent, staring. Dick had hit back! But it sounded screechy—like the interviews with pro wrestlers. It wasn't . . . Presidential.

So Shrum broke in again. Now he was trying to back Dick off: "Uh, Congressman? I hate to say this, 'cause, you know, I always . . . but that seemed, uh, a little harsh. Maybe we could try something like Dukakis does, where you say, 'You don't understand . . .' or 'Those are not the facts . . .' "

Dick cocked his head, said he understood . . . but behind his eyes, that just turned the screws tighter. Why were they now telling him *not* to kill? They didn't think he could do it? They were giving up on him! . . . Or they were wrong? They changed their minds? . . . They didn't *know*!

And from that point, Gephardt knew, he was alone. He'd always wanted their help. He'd always been good at asking for help. But this was the big one—and he was out there . . . naked. They wanted him to kill, but be himself, but show some balls, but Presidential . . . and there were no answers. He was going to have to get it from himself, and he didn't know anymore where it was . . . with all of them working on him, to rev him up, back him down—calm, it had to be calm, they said . . . but as he left the room, there was Carrick, pounding his fist into his palm.

—★—

Ethel Klein, who always talked like a shrink, called it a "generalized web of anxiety." And it only tightened on the big night. First, there was Ethel, driving him through D.C. to the Kennedy Center. God knows why they wanted her to bring him. Maybe they thought she'd calm him down. But how could she? She didn't even know how to get to the place! She was a New Yorker . . . she wasn't the body man, couldn't answer his questions: Where do we go when we come in? Where do we sit while the Republicans are on? . . . She knew what he wanted: some piece of certainty—just logistics!—but she was helpless, her hands white on the wheel.

Then they got to the holding room, and there were Doak and Shrum. That was another signal. Shrum hated debates, never came. He was like a playwright who can't stand opening night—his beautiful lines get all screwed up, and people hate it . . . but Carrick insisted. Shrum was trying to make jokes—that's what Carrick told him: Lighten it up! But Shrum was a mess, and nobody laughed . . . so pretty soon Shrummy didn't have any jokes. He paced the room, chafing his neck with his Italian scarf, fiddling with the fringe on the end, like a hungry Jew waiting for Yom Kippur to end. "Dick," he said, "you're just gonna have to get me through this."

Doak was calmer—outwardly. He slipped into country-lawyer mode, like he used to when he had a big murder case, as a Public Defender in rural Missouri. Doak always tried to keep it simple—one truth for the jury to hang on to. Tonight, his one message for Dick was: Don't ask a question if you don't know the answer. And just to drive that home, fill the air, he told a story—one of his old murder trials. Doak had his client *off,* the case was going *great,* but the cop was on the stand . . . and Doak asked a question when he didn't know the answer: How did the cop know what happened in the house? So the cop went into forensics, how he pieced it together . . . how this elderly lady, in her own home, was hit in the head, but then she ran through the house, and the guy hit her again, and she fought, and he hit her again where there was blood on the wall, and again, he bludgeoned her, where they found part of her scalp, and again, and he hit her, and hit her, until . . . heh heh . . . the jury saw that old lady's brains and blood all over the walls . . . heh heh—that case went down the drain.

Dick was staring at Doak, like this was a bad dream: her brains *on the wall?* . . . It was time to go. All the candidates had to meet backstage for their pictures, smile for the cameras. . . . Jesse Jackson took the occasion to rally the Democrats. He wanted them to remember: *Party unity.* They didn't want to give the Republicans ammunition. . . . Of course, Jesse couldn't know, but he was only turning the screws on Gephardt—like *Bonnie Campbell,* before the Duke-Dick debate! . . . Well, Gephardt wouldn't pussy out this time.

So they got on stage, and it happened: Gephardt looked edgy, white under his makeup, bloodless, angry, wooden. He screwed up his first answer (though it was one they'd rehearsed forty times). In the audience, Shrum was looking through his fingers, like you do at a horror movie when you can't bear to watch . . . as Simon said something . . . and Dick turned slowly . . . and he *hit him:*

"Paul, you're not a pay-as-you-go-Democrat . . . you're a promise-as-you-go Democrat."

There was a moment's hush in the hall—the attack had come out of *nowhere* . . . and Simon, with his lips parted, just stared at Dick in quizzical paralysis— he looked stunned, almost sad . . . oh, God! . . . Bambi caught in the headlights.

But Dick couldn't stop: he hit him again—Simonomics is the flip side . . . Reaganomics with a bow tie . . .

And no one knew how to stop the thing—least of all, Simon . . . or Dick. So he hit Paul again: "Where's the dough? . . ."

It was just like Doak's hoary ax-murder, where the killer couldn't stop. And even the knowing Washington crowd was sending up a low, rustling murmur of incredulous revulsion . . .

Until, mercifully, Gephardt was out of lines.

— ★ —

In the holding room, while the Republicans were on stage, no one had the guts to bring it up with Dick. They talked about Gore (Dick had called him a back-bencher).

"Well, he deserved it," the killers said. They were trying to sound hearty. Dick was staring ahead, looking at no one.

He had to bring up Simon himself:

"I hated that," he said.

The killers had nothing to say. Ethel tried, but she was so panicky, she was squeaking. She wanted Dick to explain to *her* why it was all right: "I don't know, I really felt, I mean, God, you know, you have to give people some access, some way to like you, and . . ."

Dick turned on her—screaming at her face:

"SOMEBODY HAD TO DO IT! . . . HE HAD TO TAKE THE HIT, AND *SOMEBODY . . . HAD TO DO IT.*"

—★—

That night the killers sent Dick home, went out and got drunk. What else could they do? It was over.

Some unemployed pollsters had a people-meter operation rigged up in Iowa during the debate. The Iowans had dials with which to register their likes and dislikes. When Dick blew Bambi's head off, the Iowans were so unhappy they dialed Gephardt's graph off the bottom of the charts. When they walked out, Dick was at *zero*—not one person said they'd vote for him.

Shrummy took to his bed, convinced he'd ruined the campaign—too many lines. The gloom filtered down through the Washington office. RoboCandidate had gone haywire—green slime was oozing out.

And that was just Washington. The road show went to Iowa, 6:00 A.M. the following day. Dick looked terrible. The rest looked worse. They landed in Des Moines, and there was . . . Ken Bode, NBC, full crew. Bode was full of beans and news of the people-meter disaster: *Well, how does it feel to be the most hated man in Iowa?*

That's all Dick got, all day, as he slogged east across the state:

How do you explain your campaign falling apart?

Looking back, how did you lose your lead?

Would you say attacking Paul Simon was your last chance?

No, he would not say . . . but what could he say? He got to his last event, late . . . and it was Waterloo.

Waterloo, Iowa, was supposed to be his stronghold, a blue-collar town that had lost its jobs, UAW country. Gephardt had a big rally scheduled. Dick got to a holding room in the basement of a church: he had ten or fifteen calls, people to sign on. The local field man dialed, and Dick came on: "We need your help. . . . You're the kind of people who make things happen here . . ."

Not one signed on—he lost them all.

He walked down the hall to his rally, and there was no one—well, twenty or thirty old folks, just the faithful. The UAW was supposed to bring in busloads . . . no bus. No show. He started his speech, the stump speech, same speech . . . but it was not the same.

He started telling stories in the middle, talking about the people he'd met. And they weren't polished stories, for effect. He was just talking. Like he meant to tell them what it meant to him, all those months—now that he'd got to the bottom. "You know, I took a meal to this lady—she was ninety-four years old, she came to the door on her *walker* . . ."

In the back of the room, the regional field man, Don Miller, whispered to the road show crew: "We're in trouble . . ."

"Did you tell Dick?"

Miller shook his head. It was the moment when the guys in suits stop telling the candidate the truth.

Ethel Klein told Miller: "You have to do something. You have to make him feel good, tonight. You get somebody to call this guy!" Then she went to a phone and tracked down Carrick. Half a dozen calls. "You've *got* to call him," Ethel said. "You have got to call this guy, *tonight.*"

Dick was still telling stories:

"This man said, 'How'm I gonna send my daughter to college?' And I *saw the daughter* . . ." Dick stopped, looked away, like he could see the girl, still . . .

It was late. They needed sleep. But Dick needed this more. He had to draw these people to him—not to his candidacy, to him.

At the end, he did his pitch for precinct captains . . . but he did not leave. He thanked every one of them for coming . . . went around the room, shook hands with everyone. Still, he stayed.

Then a farmer, Carroll Hayes, a thick guy with sideburns, in a jacket and cap, said to Dick, to everyone: "You don't just need precinct captains. I'm a captain. Been with you a long time. You need money, too." He put his ankle up on his knee, took out a checkbook, and wrote Dick a hundred dollars, right there.

Dick said quietly, he'd never forget that.

Then Hal Lennox walked up with a check. He was an IBEW man, and there were only a couple of dozen IBEW men with jobs in Waterloo. Hal wasn't one of them. He hadn't worked for a while. But he handed Dick a check for twenty dollars.

It was almost midnight when they finally left—night-silence in Waterloo, and a sudden, soft snow. Ethel said to Dick at the car: "That was wonderful . . ." She got his eyes, like Loreen used to do, and she told him: "You were so . . . great."

In the hotel that night, Carrick called. He talked about the ads. This month, they'd be on. The ads were gonna be killers.

Then the Iowa Field Director, Jim Cunningham, called: "Dick, there ain't no quit in any of us. Only thing means a damn here is my Number Ones, and we're up this month, thirteen hundred . . ."

Dick was played out. His voice was small. But he took the calls. . . . At last, he called Jane. He always finished with a call to Jane.

She could hear it in an instant. She always knew. The words were the same, but there was no air in him.

"Bug-man, you're the best," she told him.

Over and over: "You're the best . . . you'll make it. You just have to believe you can do it. That's what I learned from you, Bug-man. You can't go by the polls. Believe in you! You're the best . . ."

89

God
Is Doing It

DICK WOULD get downstairs early in the mornings. He'd have the paper read, front to back, by 7:00 A.M. On March 9, 1976, he never got past the front page:

REP. LEONOR SULLIVAN TO RETIRE . . .

Dick had just committed to his Young Turk friends to run for Mayor. Well, actually, they'd talked to him about it . . . and Dick agreed.

But by 6:45 that morning, Loreen was on the phone—just to make sure: "Dick, did you see the paper?"

By 7:00 A.M., Dick was on the phone with cousin Joe Kochanski. (Joe never liked that Mayor idea . . .)

"D'you see? . . ."

"I'll pick you up in ten minutes."

Before the morning rush hour, they were out of St. Louis, on their way to Jefferson City, to file Dick as a candidate for the Congress of the United States.

In fact, they spent the whole morning in Jeff City while Dick worked the Capitol . . . introducing himself, passing out cards, telling everybody he saw that he was running. He had to make as much noise as he could—scare as many people out of the race as he could.

That's what they talked about on the way home: old Leonor had an heir apparent, a State Senator and IBEW union official named Don Gralike. Gralike would have Sullivan's troops, the unions, Democratic clubs, committeemen, and captains—all the machinable vote. If Dick had to split the rest with a crowd of eager hopefuls, well . . . he might as well save his filing fee.

"We gotta show something on the ground, right now . . ."

"Yeah, we gotta get a printer—brochures, lawn signs . . ."

"Somebody's gonna have to write some positions."

"Have to get something down on paper."

"Who's gonna run it?"

"We can get Carol Higgins . . ."

"Vicki can help . . ."

Vicki was Dick's secretary at the law firm, wonderful woman . . .

But what kind of noise could they make with a campaign of Vicki and one typewriter?

That night, Dick went to the Morganford Avenue storefront of his own club, the Fourteenth Ward Democratic Organization. There was a meeting in progress, and the captains cheered as he walked in.

"Hey, Congressman!"

"Count on me, Dick . . ."

But that was the only ward club he could count on.

That night, he called Don Foley, the young political op—Dick had met him while Foley was still in college. By that time, Foley was in Chicago, working for Governor Walker, of Illinois.

"Did you hear about Leonor? She's gonna retire."

Foley said: "What're you gonna do?"

"I already did," Dick said. And he asked: Would Don come back and run this thing?

That night, too, he gathered the family—Cousin Joe, Lou, Loreen, Jane, even little Matt, in the house on Fairview . . . and he told them they had to commit. Unless they all helped, he couldn't do it . . . but if they all worked, if they believed . . .

"Oh, I know you'll do wonderfully."

That was Loreen. She was committed, but much more than that: she'd been thinking all day how perfect it was, the way Mrs. Sullivan said she'd step aside, *just at the moment* . . . how Lowell Jackson, her old boss at International Shoe, had told her, when Dick was *sixteen years old,* "That boy is going to be President" . . . how every year, Loreen would think she could not be prouder of Dick—how could she be?—and then, every year, her hopes were exceeded . . . and now, the path cleared, *just at the moment* . . .

Loreen said: "God is doing it."

And Dick agreed.

—★—

He had five months till the primary—no time to wonder who was going to do this or that. He'd just start doing it . . . if someone came to help, that'd be great.

Gralike was the heavy favorite with the unions—but Dick went straight to the unions: that was his first instinctive Gephardt move. He asked for their support. He knew he wouldn't get it . . . but he wanted them to know him. He wanted them to know, here was a guy who'd play ball.

"Well, if I win the primary, do you think you could support me?"

Sure, Dick—no problem! (What did they have to lose? Gralike was a shoo-in!)

Meanwhile, Gephardt went right around them. He was out the next day, and the day after that, and after that . . . door to door: "Hi, I'm Dick Gephardt, and I'm running for Congress. Everything okay in the neighborhood?"

He'd do it all day . . . he'd spend two minutes at a door, or an hour, depending on what they wanted to say . . . how the city didn't do nuthin' about that tree that's got a limb right over the house . . . or the way the trucks make the house shake when they hit that hole at the end of the block . . . or the way the colored act in the city, it's no wonder nobody goes downtown. . . . Gephardt nodded, listened. He never argued, never fogged over. His blue eyes were clear, locked on their faces.

Issues, position papers, he farmed out. He'd read them over when they came in—but quick, like he'd scan an associate's legal brief . . . just to see if it would pass muster. (One woman to whom he'd assigned a paper was so rattled by his unconcern that she started screaming at him in the Bevo Mill—a public restaurant! She shouted that he had no *business* in Congress. Dick asked someone else to do the paper.)

The contacts with community groups, the neighborhood stuff, he left to a fellow Alderman, Jim Komorek. Komorek was another Young Turk, an advertising man. He helped with the signs, too. Dick was fanatic about signs.

The money, the books, the thickets of post-Watergate election law—Joe Kochanski took care of that. (Joe had the files and forms stacked all over the office of his heating and air-conditioning business.) They didn't have much money . . . didn't matter.

"How many doors did we hit today?"

That's all Dick wanted to know.

There wasn't a day off. There wasn't an hour off. If he had thirty minutes between appointments—well, he might get one side of a block. They had the blocks numbered, and they'd hit them one by one . . . every house . . . hundreds every day. Dick would call in from someone's kitchen—did Jane get all of thirteen and fourteen? . . .Well, he'd go over there tonight, when he finished.

Gephardt tried to make it look like he was everywhere at once—out on the fringe of the countryside, Tuesday; Wednesday, up the tight streets of South St. Louis. . . . Gralike mailed into all of those houses. But Dick showed up on their porches.

By summertime, the Gephardts were a drill team. They'd pull up at the foot of some street, in Kochanski's heating-supply panel truck, and Dick would work one side, Jane the other—or Jane and Loreen together. If someone insisted on talking to Dick, Jane would stand on the lawn, waving her arms. Dick would trot across the street, or down the block, in 105-degree heat. But he'd never sweat.

By that time, they had a schedule of neighborhood picnics, church fairs, block parties . . . they'd roll up in Joe's truck, tank of helium in the back

. . . every kid got a Gephardt balloon, a leaflet for every voter—bang, bang, bye-bye, back in the truck . . . next block.

By that time, too, Gralike had to debate . . . and that's where it showed—before one word was spoken. Gralike was an old-fashioned pol, a dark and serious-looking man . . . and there was Dick, across the stage: young, blond, eager . . . with his beautiful family in the front row . . . well, it did your heart good. You could *see* that young Gephardt was honest, decent, smart . . . and he *cared so much.*

But Gralike was not going to roll over, play dead. He'd been lining this up for a long time. He had his union households, and his home neighborhoods were studded with lawn signs. . . . God, this guy was the *king* of lawn signs!

That's what got to Dick, in the summertime . . . those signs, *everywhere:* he'd work a sixteen-hour day and then have to drive home in the dark, past GRALIKE . . . GRALIKE . . . GRALIKE . . .

One night, Dick sagged through the door and dropped himself onto a chair in the kitchen: "I don't know," he said to Jane. "I just . . . I think we can't do it. I think we're gonna lose it."

Jane said, "Well, we are going to lose it, if you don't think we can. That's what you always say. . . . But we're *not going* to lose it. We'll just have to work harder."

—★—

Dick had his first downtown fund-raiser—hundred dollars a plate! (Night before, he had a ten-dollar beer party, in the district, so people wouldn't think he'd gone country club.) After that, he cut his first ad.

It was a beautiful shoot, in the backyard of the house on Fairview: Dick, Jane, Matt, and Chrissie . . . a picnic table on the lawn in the sunshine. "Hi, I'm Dick Gephardt . . ."

Dick ran through the script two or three times—perfectly. Dick could just *do* that sort of thing. But Chrissie was small—just three—she started yammering, and hammering a spoon on the table.

The TV guys (friends of Komorek's) wanted to get rid of that take, do it again—maybe get rid of her . . . but Dick said no, it would be fine that way. Leave it in. . . . It was a move of instinctive genius.

After all, it was 1976, when Jimmy Carter was thirty points ahead and *cruising* on the promise, "I'll never lie to you." People wanted candidates they could trust . . . Christian values . . . family values. Imperial, impervious, impersonal government was the *problem.* That was the first thing Dick was *not* . . . part of the old guard, part of the problem.

No . . . much better to be personal. Jimmy Carter was personal. (He'd called Dick's *home* . . . Carter *called,* he talked to Jane!) Much better to be genuine. Jimmy Carter was genuine. And Dick Gephardt thought Carter ran a campaign of genuine genius.

So, by the end of July, everybody in the district seemed to know that Gephardt was the fellow with those beautiful young kids. (That little girl! She didn't like that camera, one bit! . . . Well, they knew how that was . . .)

Of course, Gralike had ads, too. But he didn't have those lovely kids—no kids at all, to judge from his ads—or sunshine, or grass . . . just men in suits, shaking hands . . . and—woe unto Gralike—*photo-gray glasses* . . . that turned dark in the bright light . . . dark glasses in the middle of a dark face . . . a union man, hmm?

In the end, it wasn't even that close: Gephardt beat Gralike fifty-five percent to thirty-seven—by sixteen thousand votes. (The next day, Dick was on the phone to the unions . . . to tell them how *glad* he was they were on the same team now. See, he didn't want them to feel bad—have a hard time coming to him.)

He would have a Republican opponent in November: Joseph L. Badaracco, a well-known man, former president of the Board of Aldermen . . . but another old-style pol. Dick made him look like part of the problem.

The race with Badaracco was even more lopsided: Dick won by fifty thousand votes . . . and two months later, he was on his way to Washington, where he was invited to the White House, and he found himself (he could hardly be-*lieve* it), shaking the new genius-President's hand.

90

Roll Up
the Net

WHEN THEY set out to run for the White House, Dick and Jane went to see the Carters. Plenty of Democrats made public pilgrimage to Plains, but Gephardt didn't go for a photo op. He wanted to sit down and talk . . . actually, he wanted to listen.

When you got down to it, he meant to run Jimmy Carter's campaign— twelve years later, different issues, new wrinkles, but still, he meant to hike the trail that Carter blazed. He would come out of nowhere, win Iowa . . . get the bump . . . and then the hot light would hit. Dick had to be ready. He had to know how to run in the South, how to make his campaign truly national; had to know what the press would do, how to get the money while his name was hot, how to tie down the pols who meant to ride with a winner . . . how to build momentum until his nomination, like Carter's, could not be stopped.

So he sought Carter's advice, and he followed it. He started early. He made sure his contact with Iowans was not only broad, but deep—and deeply personal. Though his money was tight, he staffed not only Iowa and New Hampshire, but offices in several southern states. He picked his campaign team, and he backed it—even in the worst times, he never second-guessed. He worked small towns, and corn boils, church picnics, county fairs . . . he did everything, in short, that Jimmy Carter did . . . did it just as hard, and much longer . . . and with two months before the Iowa caucus, he could see . . . it hadn't worked worth a damn.

Why wasn't it working?

Dick had asked himself a million times, answered himself maybe fifty different ways . . . and tried to fix every problem he discerned. Meanwhile, things got worse.

After the NBC debate, the *Register*'s December poll showed him fallen . . . to six percent.

After five years of effort, after 110 days campaigning across Iowa, after thousands of hours in the air, and tens of thousands of rent-a-car miles, after tens of thousands of staff hours, tens of thousands of phone-bank calls, after more than a million dollars, after personal visits to ninety-four counties, after rallies, meetings, breakfasts, lunches, dinners, picnics, fairs, ice-cream socials, cocktail parties, meet-and-greets, coffee shops, motel meeting rooms, main street strolls, senior citizens' homes, factory floors, auction barns, grain elevators, farmyard tours, debates, press conferences, interviews, photo ops, satellite stand-ups, speeches, notes, phone calls, visits-at-home, candy-for-the-hostess, and flowers-to-the-hospital . . . after thousands of deliberate personal acts of will and wile, by Dick and every Gephardt, all in blandishment of one sparsely peopled midwestern state, he had won and held . . . six percent.

It could not be true.

He was better than that!

There must be a mistake!

But if there was not?

And if his hardy six percent read this poll and felt, as he did, the chill of disaster on the back of the neck—how many would stay with him? How many could he count on?

Dick got another piece of advice from Jimmy Carter—a warning, really.

"You will reach a point," Carter told him, "where you can only be sure of two votes—yours and your wife's . . .

"That's when you've got to still go on."

— ★ —

Gephardt got a day home after the latest poll hit the streets. It was a good time to be out of Iowa. Matt picked him up at the airport. He had actually cleaned Dick's Pontiac—took it to the *car wash*. . . . That was the first sign.

Dick had promised to help Matt set up the Christmas tree. Jane backed off, to let those two be together. Matt was full of questions—but only certain questions.

"How're *you* doing, Dad?"

"Where have you been lately?"

"Are you tired?"

"How do you *feel*?"

That's when it sunk in on Dick: his kids were worried about him. Matt never brought up the polls . . . but, of course, Dick knew that Matt read everything.

At dinner, the girls were the same way: never mentioned the polls, but . . .

"Are you okay, Dad? . . . Really okay?"

— ★ —

Was he? What was okay? Yes, he was tired . . . after years of pumping up a balloon that always seemed to have a hole in it somewhere. He was worn down . . . but he didn't want to lose. Not like this. In ignominy.

Could he really expect to win?

And if he could not win, then . . . what was it for?

Somehow, he had to get back to the why . . . and why *now*?

Back in '81, '82, when Reagan was new and strong, the President had set the agenda, and swept all opposition before him. The feeling Dick remembered was helplessness . . . being shoved to the margins. He would have meetings with his Democratic colleagues, they'd plan, they'd propose, they'd put together packages . . . and then Reagan would call those phones in the cloakroom . . . and their votes were gone. Their plans were air.

Now Reagan was out of steam, not even treading water. But you still couldn't get the people together to *do something*. Not with a veto in the White House. Not with the members running scared. Their districts might not like it if they stuck their necks out. They had to take care of this group, or that. . . . And there was no one to get them together.

Dick liked the House, he loved those guys (by now, he'd signed on eighty of them to back his campaign) . . . but, Jesus, what a mess! Planned chaos! . . . Four hundred thirty-five members, running half-crazy with their separate agendas. And *nobody had the power* . . . to do *anything*.

That's what shoved Dick out to Iowa. Someone had to supply the will to *do something*. He didn't have all the answers. But the point was, he'd *do something*. And if that didn't work, he'd do something else. That was the why—to get something done. And that was what he had to offer, that will.

But this was the awful calculus of the polls:

How could he swallow that will now, that ambition, that drug of denting history? How could he go back to the House now, with his tail between his legs?

Powerless? . . . His life had never seen that sort of futility.

He could not do it.

He would not go back!

He would return to Iowa, and make a move . . . or it was over. Not just this campaign—all the campaigns. He was not going back to the House.

He told Jane: this was it. They'd fight it out on this line . . . win or lose—then it was over. All of it. They'd talked about the money for college (Matt was a junior, applying next year) . . . maybe they'd have to sell this house, or the house in St. Louis, maybe both . . . well, maybe it was time to make money— Dick could practice law.

He talked about where they'd live, what they could do. He talked about spending time with Matt, and the girls. Time was precious—they wouldn't be home for long . . . God, he'd missed the time! They wouldn't have to run from this campaign to St. Louis—another campaign to save his House seat. They could take a trip!

Jane didn't say much. She wasn't one to count her chickens . . . she was just relieved to hear Dick working up all the good things . . . so much happier. She'd missed that.

Back in Iowa, they had no idea what had happened to Dick at home. How could they know he'd rolled up his safety net, and was swinging free over the floor? He never said a word.

Ethel Klein was on the phone the next morning, back to Steve Murphy in Des Moines, as Dick came out of his first event. She said into the phone: "Dick just gave me a big thumbs-up. He's got this huge grin. Is there some really great news? . . . Or has he completely flipped?"

The Washington HQ was going to hell . . . rumors that everybody was fired. There was bickering among the killers, great struggle and teeth-gnashing over the ads. The campaign was flat out of money. They were going to have to close up the South . . . those people would have to make their way to Iowa—limping into the last fort . . . with Apaches already at the gates.

But Dick was beautiful: funny, tireless, full of good juice . . . he made his speeches, and then at every stop, he did a second event for his people, his captains—pep talks—as he poured his will into them. "What I want to do tonight, is to get *you* to *believe*. I'm looking you in the eye now. . . . My mother always said, when you talk to someone, you look them right in the eye. I want your commitment! I want your belief! Because if I can get you to believe . . . then we are going to win this thing, and we are going to change this country. . . . WE HAVE THE POWER!"

And all of a sudden, he had them standing, yelling:

GEP-HARDT . . .
GEP-HARDT . . .
GEP-HARDT . . .

No one could figure it out. They only knew that for the next month, by force of pure conviction, Dick Gephardt carried that campaign on his back.

91

Gorby Juice

BUSH COULDN'T UNDERSTAND—
why wasn't it working? This was
the state where he'd made it hap-
pen, where he'd felt Big Mo settle on him like the hand of God. He'd worked
his heart out in this state—two *years,* against all odds. And he showed he could
win!

That was Iowa, 1980. Not so long ago . . . same people with him now
. . . and he was the same guy, same kind of winner, maybe better. Hell—sure
he was better!

So why wasn't it *working*?

—★—

He had liked those odds, starting out . . . back in '77, '78. His name recognition
stood at zero-point-three percent. One in 333 voters knew Bush's name. His
three staff kids (Jim Baker hadn't even come aboard—he was running, unsuccessfully, for Attorney General of Texas) would, in time, call themselves the
Asterisk Club: Bush was an asterisk in every poll.

The campaign . . . well, they called it "George Bush's two thousand closest
friends." That was the major asset: Bush had the Christmas card list, his
politician friends from the RNC days, his business friends—quite generous
with money—and his school friends. That turned into money, too. Bush had
been chairman of Campaign for Yale, an ambitious reendowment of Old Blue,
which, by degrees, became Campaign for Bush.

And he had one other asset: Jimmy Carter. It was Carter who gave Bush
his reason for running—not to mention the time. Bush went to Carter, close

of the '76 campaign, and offered to stay on at the CIA. He offered his service—
let Carter send a message of bipartisanship . . . Bush would finish the job he
had started a year before: restoring the CIA to its proper standing—*above
politics.* . . . Carter could have sent a strong signal with that move, but he never
really considered it—didn't understand.

Bush was more and more convinced: Carter couldn't see the big picture.
Carter was going to be a disaster. Bush had briefed him during the campaign.
Once Carter became the nominee, he was entitled to the precious awareness—
so Director Bush tried to bring him up to speed: the latest from the listening
posts, the poop on the new satellites . . .

"What's the angle on that gimbal? . . ."

"Excuse me?"

"What's the angle on that camera gimbal on the new satellite? What's the
maximum angle? . . ."

"Uh . . . we'll check on that."

Who the hell cared what's the angle on the GIMBAL? . . . The point was:
What can we see? . . . What about forty-five Russian divisions on the *Chinese
border?* . . . Can we see if they're *moving?*

To Bush, Carter would ever be a small-time, liberal Governor from Georgia
. . . who didn't have a clue to how the world really worked, who was going
to . . . *screw* . . . *everything* . . . *up.*

So even as Bush drove Bar's Volvo back to Houston . . . as she settled them
into another new house . . . as George got on a bank board, started talking
up his business career . . . he started turning over the big question:

Could he knock Carter off? . . . Could he get there?

Bush was pretty well convinced that by 1980, voters wouldn't be in the mood
to sit through another four years of outsiders, men who didn't know the levers,
who ran against Washington. No more Carter—he'd bet on that . . . and maybe
no Ronald Reagan. Everyone said Reagan had the 1980 nomination sewed up,
after his near miss against Ford, in '76 . . . Bush didn't believe it. Reagan was
old hat—and old: Bush would *relish* running that man's aged ass into the
ground.

He talked it over with Jim Baker . . . Bake thought they might do it like
Carter—work the grassroots in Iowa, establish themselves with a respectable
second place as the sensible alternative to Reagan, then burst through (somewhere) with a winner's grin, into the glare.

Candidates in a half-dozen states were already asking Bush to speak—help
them out in '78. . . . In an office next to his own in the Citizen's National Bank,
Bush set up a PAC to handle the requests, the schedule, the money. That much
was fine—he could stop with that . . . or go whole hog.

But could he get there? (Zero-point-three percent!)

He could make a career in business. The bank board, Eli Lilly's board,
Purolator, Inc. . . . that came easy to him.

Bar was so much happier since he'd left a job he couldn't talk about—not
even to her. She'd felt so left out.

The new house was fine. Houston was homey. He'd drive himself to the bank in the morning, then Don Rhodes would pick him up in his truck, if Bush had a meeting, or a date somewhere.

Wasn't it great how it worked out?

They were in Rhodesy's pickup, spring of '78, on their way to the Ramada Club—Bush had a lunch date.

"Don, I've really gotta decide if I want to run for President."

Rhodes was driving—didn't even turn his head.

"Run," he said. "Y'don't have anything better to do."

— ★ —

The '88 campaign ought to be easier—more comfortable, surely . . . with his Stratoliner sweeping down now upon Des Moines. There was an Air Force Reserve base at the back of the airport, aswarm with men on duty, trucks scooting across the tarmac, snack bar flippin' burgers one a minute . . . every bit of brass in the Iowa Reserve on alert—seeing to the landing of *Air Force Two*.

Here it came: gorgeous stainless steel in the sunshine . . . elegant, serifed, black capital letters on the side: THE UNITED STATES OF AMERICA. Right away, traveling press tumbled out the back door, and a half-dozen young Advance shepherded them to a ropeline. There was a plywood stage and a microphone in front of the ropeline, and behind, some kids—looked like one busload—with hand-painted signs: LET GEORGE DO IT and IOWA   BUSH. Another two or three Advance (maybe the same ones, they looked alike in their pod-people suits) were herding dignitaries to the base of the front stairs, to form a line to greet the Vice President.

Still, something was missing: What was it?

Public.

Nobody had come to see George Bush. Maybe the Air Force base was off limits. The question was: Could Bush tell?

He was waving from the door of the plane, atop the flight-stairs, and . . . from up there, it looked glorious: hundreds of people in sharp winter sunshine—people being *held back* by a ropeline, kids cheering . . . he bounded down the steps. Now, sure as hell, he couldn't tell if anyone was there because he was surrounded—people smiling, grabbing for his hand. Advance wanted to lead him to the platform mike, and after they showed him, he strode over like it was his idea. He was giving jerky waves to this side and that. He waved to reporters. He waved to his own staff. He made a face—delighted to be here! He was all delight today.

Bush had something to say. Mikhail Gorbachev had just come to Washington with the INF agreement in his pocket. The Gipper signed the deal—killed off one class of missiles in Europe—the first major treaty with the Russians in ten years!

Everybody knew, peace was big in Iowa.

Bush was for peace—*for* the treaty.

Gorby was the hottest thing in Washington since . . . speakerphones. And

Bush had a *sit-down with Gorbachev*. They had breakfast! (And whom did Bush take to breakfast-with-Gorby? Cooper Evans! A grain dealer, a friend . . . an Iowan!) Best of all—*then* . . . when Gorby took his famous walk, got out of his car on Connecticut Avenue, and *waved to Americans* . . . who was with him? . . . George Bush!

So Bush had juice today. He had INF juice. He had peace juice. He had Iowa juice. He had . . .*Gorby juice.* It was like some made-up concatenation of best-selling buzzwords—like one of those have-it-all headlines in the super-market tabs:

JACKIE O'S SEX-BUDGET-UFO DIET!

This could turn Iowa around!

"As you know," Bush was saying, "we've just come from Washington, where we've just signed the *I-N-F* treaty . . ." Bush laid into those letters. He looked like he'd hammered out the treaty himself. He decried critics on the left, who blamed the Gipper for hanging tough against the Russians. He decried critics on the right, who were raising doubts about the new treaty.

Dole had not come out for the treaty. Big mistake. Bush was trying to drive this treaty through Dole's heart like a wooden stake.

"And I think it's good. I think it's good for America. I think it's good for my ten grandchildren."

He spread his hands to indicate he'd take a question.

A voice behind the rope called out: "How good is it for you in Iowa?"

Bush's eyes lit up. A lob! . . . He swung into Iowa juice—how he'd taken heat for having Cooper Evans in that breakfast with Gorby.

". . . An Iowan, a grain expert, presenting the views of American agriculture. So let the political opportunists take some shots. I think it was very good. And I kinda resent it, that because somebody's from Iowa, and happens to be a friend of mine, that he should be excluded." Bush was shaking his head: as long as he was in charge, his Iowa friends would *always* breakfast with Gorby.

There was a question on whether Bush expected more summits, more arms control. This was from the national press, which never got to ask Bush anything—except at these local press-avails. Bush took the chance to spread more Gorby juice.

"Well, clearly, he's a man who's in control. You may know, I was with him when he jumped out of the car . . ." This was rich! His voice fell to confidentiality—but then, it was nearly inaudible, so he had to belt it out.

"You know, we're riding in this big Russian limousine they have, and he says to me: 'How do you like my *bunker*?' . . ."

Bunker! Bush was enchanted with the word. But curiously, it was the only line of Gorby-talk that Bush would share in Iowa. That, and one other word:

"Stop!" . . . Gorby had barked that to the KGB man in the front seat.

"And I was with him, and I sensed, uh . . ." Bush was trying to get the story out—it emerged in jagged bursts. ". . . The adrenaline pumping . . . 'Stop!' . . . And we stopped. And he got out of the car. So, he controls the agenda. And I saw that. Yeah. You."

"Last question!" one of the pod-people shouted, as Bush pointed to a local. The guy was dressed in a blazer, with a rep tie. He had his own microphone, and his cameraman swung around to point the lens at him. This was footage! This was:

Action News caught up with the Vice President at the airport . . .

"Vice President, you've said you feel your advice to the President should remain secret . . ."

Bush's lips drew into a thin, crooked line. He hiked his back straight and stiff, flashing his power tie.

". . . As a candidate," Action News was saying, "would you now ask the President to let you reveal, now, what you told him about Iran-contra?"

Bush's head was already shaking. This was a Dole line. Like Bush was going to ask permission to dive into that shithole again.

"No . . . no." He'd beaten this answer around so many times, it was an omelette in his head. ". . . So, the point is, mistakes were made . . . but, uh, you give me the credit for half of all the good things, and I'll take all the blame, but, ah, I'm not going to start now to tell you . . ."

Tell who? . . . The camera hadn't moved. It was still focused on the Action News guy. The point to this was not the answer but the cutaway shot: the picture of the newsman asking the question, then scowling and nodding while the Big Gulp provided the audio.

"So, yes, mistakes were made. The President said that. But you move on."

And he was moving. "Thank you. Thank you all very much." Like it'd been great to be there . . . and he steered off across the tarmac, toward his choppers, while the pod-people screamed: *Traveling press! Over here! Traveling! Traveling ONLY!*

On the riser, the Iowa press was filming Bush's back as he greeted one of his Air Force crew like he hadn't seen him in years . . . then he looked up, waved an instant of spasmodic friendliness to a steward in the door of his plane . . . then craned his body around to wave to the press, like he'd forgotten to say goodbye . . . and lunged to greet the Army men standing at the choppers . . . and he was gone—disappeared into the helicopter.

Damn!

He'd flown in here with Gorby juice . . . but it was clear, what was on TV tonight . . . was Action News made him say, *again:*

"Mistakes were made."

—★—

The great thing about that 1980 campaign was how personal it was. Bush didn't have to work with strangers. Of course, with Bush, no one stayed a stranger for long . . . but for most of those two years, you could meet the whole staff in one weekend hop from Houston to Iowa, and on to New Hampshire.

As for those few select, the Bushies of '78–'79, they were spoiled by all the time spent with him, his endless personal attention. They'd travel with him— Bush and one body man, maybe a local who'd pick them up at the airport. Or, if they weren't along for the ride, there'd be calls from him, every day . . . a personal note if he got ten minutes . . . an invite to burgers and bloodies in the backyard, if he happened to catch a Sunday home in Houston.

There were few days home. In his first year of campaigning, he traveled 180,000 miles, mostly flying coach. After that, the pace picked up. The normal road crew was Bush and David Bates, a twenty-seven-year-old Houston lawyer and body man—child of Bush-friends, childhood friend to Bush-son Jeb—and possessor of a hypereager sunniness that made him seem like a young copy of Ambassador Bush. Bates would show up, early A.M., at the new Bush house on Indian Trail. Don Rhodes would come by with the truck—they'd throw their bags into the bed. By nine in the morning, they'd be in the air to some midday event—Fred Jones for Congress, say—and after Bush told the crowd what a splendid friend was Fred Jones, he'd do a little press conference, if any reporters could be cajoled to hang around. Then came the heavy lifting— private meetings: Party leaders, activists, money men . . . one-on-one, twenty minutes apiece, for as many hours as it took.

"How's Janey? The kids? . . . Jeez! College already!" (Bush had the names from his travels for the RNC.)

"Listen . . . I really think I've got a good shot at this thing—think I can *win,* and, uh, if you could help, I'd really love to have you on the team."

Some wanted to know how Bush thought he could win . . . and he was ready for that:

"I think I can make a more *active* campaign than Reagan" (i.e., that guy is *ancient*). . . . "I can show I have more experience than Reagan." (Guy doesn't know where the Treasury Department *is,* for God's sake!)

Then they'd ask: Who would he have for State Chairman? Bush was always ready to discuss local politics. He could reel off the names of his supporters in the state without notes, without pause—like some people always know how much money's in their wallet.

Sometimes, a meeting would wind up with the pooh-bah telling Bush: "George, you know I wish you the best . . . but I'd like to give it some thought." Some would say, "Well, George, I know you're going to do well, but I'm committed . . ." (to Dole, John Anderson, Howard Baker, or, usually, Reagan).

Bush always understood if they were committed to somebody else. But if they said they were with him, and didn't come through, they were off the list. That was a breach of the code. The ones that really got to him were the friends who didn't sign up. What did friendship mean, if they weren't going to help?

Whatever they said, Bush would follow up with a note. That's how he spent his time on his afternoon flights: handwritten notes to the one-on-ones. "Really enjoyed the chance to catch up . . . sitting down with you . . . just want to reiterate that I'd really like to have you along." So, if they ever fell off the Reagan boat . . . or when Dole, Baker, or Connally foundered . . . well, those pooh-bahs had a *relationship* with George Bush. Meanwhile, word got around that Bush was working hard, making friends.

That he was: there were also notes to Fred Jones ("Great to see you again . . ."), to the chairman of the Fred Jones event ("Thanks for having me . . ."), to the guy who herded the local press toward Bush, to the drivers, the cooks, the waiter who brought an extra glass of water. . . . Those would be carried back and typed in Houston. Meanwhile, Bush was on his way to a dinner of the World Affairs Council in Indianapolis, or the Rotary in Keene, New Hampshire, or the Chamber of Commerce in . . . well, he did the Chamber everywhere.

Actually, the schedule was more of a bitch than it had to be, because Bush would never say no to a friend. Bates learned to say no by reflex, right away. Margaret Tutwiler, the Scheduler in Houston, tried to train Bush, for months, to say: "Margaret's the one who handles my schedule." They couldn't let a friend even *talk* to Bush . . . because Bush would start fretting about ol' Fitzy in San Francisco, or Binky in Cleveland ("Well, God . . . Binky—shit, he's been so *good* to me—maybe we could blow off that Chicago lunch!") . . . and he'd fly halfway across the country and back to show up under a tent in Binky's backyard.

The fact was, he didn't mind: the endless miles, the eight-event days—he liked the athletic feel of the race. If they made their motel at midnight, with just hours to collapse till the next event . . . it was Bush who'd show up with coffee for the troops at 6:00 A.M. If they made their last plane at 9:30 P.M., with nothing but another airport, another long car ride, another motel ahead . . . it was Bush who'd buoy them with his boyish routine: "Tray tables down!" he'd bark, like he used to run the flight-check in his TBM Avenger. "Note paper out! . . . List! . . . Pen! . . . Commence!" If they ended, by chance, at a decent hotel, Bush would stroll the suite, noting aloud each luxury appurtenance. He'd end up at the door to his room, where, with a hint of a bow, he'd announce: "Batesy, I hope this is adequate to your needs."

In Iowa alone, there were ninety-nine counties, and he was organized in every one. He worked *every* Kiwanis, Moose Lodge, Legion Hall, VFW . . . he worked chicken barbeques, ladies' auctions, cattle barns, farmyards . . . he toured packing houses. He held ("Jeez, warm little critters, aren't they?") *piglets*!

And he made speeches, hundreds—actually, the same speech hundreds of times, a conservative speech about American strength . . . in the world: how Carter let U.S. interests slip away by his moralistic fixation on human rights . . . in the economy: how the nation's vitality was sapped by inflation and overblown government spending . . . in energy: how energy companies had to be unshackled to explore and exploit . . . in intelligence: how a Bush Presidency would beef up the CIA and back it against its critics. (He started by playing down his connection to the Agency, but then he heard the applause when his devotion slipped out one day—after that, there was no speech without mention of the CIA.)

And that led him to his own life—or at least to his résumé. Here, too, Bush was conservative—he didn't give much away. The point of the litany was that he'd *had* all those jobs, *been* all those things ("A President We Won't Have to Train!") . . . not the effect of those jobs on him. The lessons he did adduce were conventional, or conventionally expressed: the CIA taught him *how the world really was* . . . China showed the *blessings of freedom we take for granted.* . . .

Despite the drill of repetition, despite visits to a speech coach (four hours at a stretch with a woman in New York—thousand bucks an hour!), Bush never became a great speaker. He could not really haul his listeners into his life. He did stop pointing with every phrase . . . but now he'd mash the air with spasmic karate chops, or grab fistfuls of air and hold them to his breast to show how much he *meant* those words, or these, which his voice, arising, was *about* to strain forth into that mike. . . .

But at the scale that Iowa offered—forty, fifty folks in a room—what they could see, or, precisely, feel, was his endless energy, the intensity of his want . . . wanting to know them.

"I *know* about the cycle of seasons—the snow, the green, the upturned fields . . . your sense of family. These things will make me a better President. I just *know* it."

What they could feel—especially when they met him, one-on-one (Bush always tried to stay, to meet them)—was his rising confidence in his organization, in himself . . . it was working! He could sense the momentum, the shift . . . he could feel his time, feel the world, come to him! He couldn't tell them how yet—the reporters, the pols, the Washington-wise who came out to Iowa—he just knew it was working.

And in that final winter, when Rich Bond and the boys brought the phones to fever, and all those County Chairmen got their captains out, and the buses lined up to bring the Bush Brigades to the big straw votes . . . they clawed past Ronald Reagan as if he were standing still—Bush won every straw poll! . . . Well, then, everyone could see. This guy had more than a hope. This was a guy to watch! (And such a nice guy—you know, they met him, they rode with him in that Oldsmobile, Bush made them so comfortable!) . . . This guy *was* special! This guy was a *winner*. This could be The One.

That's when Jim Baker and Teeter told him he had to *define himself.* He had to start giving people a clearer idea of what Bush believed in . . . what President Bush would do.

"I don't know," Bush said. "I don't get the feeling people want that."

They argued . . . but Bush just wouldn't believe it. *Personal quality* was his "thing." He thought people would *see* it . . . once they took a look at him.

The fact was, he hadn't a clue how to define himself. Some people saw him as moderate . . . some, conservative—that was fine! He didn't want to rope himself into . . . *positions.*

Why should he?

The fact was, he wanted to *be* President. He didn't want to be President to *do* this or that. He'd do . . . what was *sound.*

When people would ask—reporters, usually—*why* did he want to be President, he'd talk about Big Pres: "My father inculcated the idea of service."

True enough. But one could serve by raising money for United Way. Why President?

One time, a reporter kept asking. Bush said: "Well, you know . . . doesn't everybody grow up wanting to be President?"

Maybe where he grew up.

Anyway, Bush beat Reagan by two percentage points in Iowa, 1980 . . . he got the bounce. He got Big Mo. He never did define himself. So it was in New Hampshire, 1980, that Reagan started painting the picture *for* Bush—a portrait Bush could not live down.

—★—

By December 1987, Bush's claim to the Presidency rested on an even longer litany of being. Not only had he *been* all those good things: airman, oilman, Congressman, etc. . . . Now he had *been Vice President*—seven years!

This was his time. He *knew* he could do the job. . . . He just had to *show* that.

That's why he'd had his people angling with the Reaganauts to *let Bush be Gorbachev's host* . . . let him spend the time, show up with Gorby, day after day, everywhere, on TV.

But, no . . . the President's men couldn't see it. Reagan could not *favor* Bush—not like that. The President had to be *impartial* in the campaign. (Not to mention Mrs. Reagan: *Oh, no! It's Ronnie's summit!*)

Seven years of loyalty . . . and Bush got breakfast.

Alas, it would be left to him to make people see George Bush—to define himself—and still he had no clue. He wasn't—couldn't be—"not Reagan." What kind of loyalty would that show? In fact, he couldn't *do anything* on his own—to make people *feel* his confidence, his sureness . . . at least his want.

How could they feel him at all?

That winter, Bush was scheduled to stop at a country store; actually, he wasn't *scheduled*. Rich Bond had been back in Iowa for months now—kept demanding that Bush get out of the bubble, *mix it up with the people*! So Bush's stop did not appear in the bible. He was going to *happen by*—like Gorby telling the KGB: *Stop!* . . . then Bush would jump out, walk into this store, and *talk* . . . with *people*!

Nick Brady was in the armored car that day, applying the balm of First-Friendship to Bush's Iowa woe. ("He just couldn't get unwound," Brady said.) And he watched Bush get up for this happen-by . . . with pleasure: he *liked* meeting people . . . we *love* this stuff! They got to the store, the limo swept onto gravel . . . and stopped. The Secret Service hopped out . . . and stopped. The staff vans, the pool-press vans, the rest-of-the-press bus, the cop cars, the ambulance . . . stopped.

Then, Bush sat. The Service wouldn't let him out of the car.

A minute, two minutes . . .

What was the holdup?

People from the store came out and stood in the cold parking lot. They were smiling and bending to wave at the Vice President through his shaded glass.

Three minutes, four minutes . . . Bush sat in the car.

"What the hell are they waiting for?" That was Brady. The gray-granite schist was rumbling. You can't put people *out* like that! (Look at them, standing with their arms clenched, in the cold! They were waving no more.)

The Service men were in confab on their wrist radios.

Five minutes . . .

Bush didn't want to tell the Service how to run its job. ("You might as well be protecting yourself then.") But he was catching the dread and fatal affliction. He was ridiculous.

"Well, I'm getting out," he said. And he did—but what the hell could he say after that . . . Hi?

So much for mixing with the people.

On this weekend—his Man of Peace trip—Bush did his speech at a Moose Lodge, took questions at Grinnell High School, did a motel funder for the Johnson County GOP, stayed overnight in Iowa City for a morning address to the Foreign Relations Council, spoke to GOP activists in Keokuk, got a lovely crowd in Keosauqua . . . and he didn't meet a soul.

By nightfall of the second day, he was back at the air base—it was after the TV news deadline, so there was no stage, no questions, no kids with signs. Just a couple of cameras stabbing light toward his plane, and the shadowy ant colony of trucks and reservists on the dark tarmac. Anyone—any voter, that is—who'd come to see him was stopped a quarter-mile from *Air Force Two.*

Did Bush know?

He stood atop his flight-stairs to wave . . . he must have known. He was so far away . . . a tiny man, lit in the doorway of his big plane . . . waving with slow exaggeration, his whole arm—like he was cleaning a plate-glass window.

He turned to enter the plane. He was tired, he could stand a drink. He'd have *Meet the Press* tomorrow to praise the treaty, and the rest of the day off, before another week of travail.

That was the week—when he got back to Washington—he learned Bob Dole would endorse the treaty . . . in the White House press room, *on stage with Ronald Reagan.* The Gee-Six howled protests at the President's staff . . . to no avail. Howard Baker, Chief of Staff, said Bob Dole had to *vote* on the treaty. Bob Dole would *lead the fight* for Ronald Reagan.

That was the week the White House and the Iran-contra Committee agreed to declassify and publish a note from 1986—a memo from Admiral Poindexter that was rescued from the White House computers: the memo named George Bush as a "solid" supporter of the arms deal with Iran. (The memo was published in a joint statement by the Committee Chairmen, and the ranking Republican, Senator Rudman—who was chairman of the Dole campaign in New Hampshire.)

That was the week new polls showed Dole had climbed sixteen points ahead of Bush in Iowa. "Bush got no immediate benefit," said Paul Taylor's front-page story, "from his high-visibility meeting with Soviet leader Mikhail Gorbachev . . ." Nationwide, over the last two months, Dole had cut Bush's lead in half.

The only break for Bush was that this woeful sequence played out in shadow. Bush atotter was not the lead story—barely made the papers. . . . That week, there was only one story.

92

Like
Old Times

I T WAS LIKE old times in New Hampshire, when there were just a few around Gary, the first circle: Sue Casey, Ned and Sally Helms, Dan Calegari. They were there in '82–'83, and here they were, on the morning of December 15, 1987—like family . . . like a family coming together again. And Lee was with Gary, and John was coming. (John was supposed to meet them at the Helmses'—where was John?) Only Andrea was missing. She had to stay behind for exams at the University of Denver. (But she was so proud of her father—and excited. She was going to be his Campaign Manager!) And Billy Shore stayed in Washington. But he was busy, like old times, working the phones for Hart.

And it didn't matter that Billy couldn't see the path ahead. Or that Sue Casey argued, almost to the last minute ("Gary, they'll kill you, it's gonna be *miserable!*"), until they all met at Ned and Sally's house in Concord. Or that Ned Helms had signed on months before to help Al Gore in New Hampshire . . . or that Calegari came by just as a friend—he was Gephardt's northeast regional director—he arrived in a rent-a-car from the Gephardt campaign.

Didn't matter. They were together . . . and once again, with a shared secret: only they knew what was going to happen that morning, on the granite steps of the statehouse. Even they didn't know how it would go. Sue Casey had called a few friends and a few of the big-feet the night before, just to warn them—naturally, word leaked out . . . and that morning, they heard on the radio, from the wires:

Sources say Gary Hart is on his way to the statehouse . . .

Casey wished she'd had time to make a bigger round of calls, to make sure there were press, not to mention citizens—a crowd! If only fifteen or twenty showed up, Hart would look awfully lonely—he could end up looking ridiculous! Sue was seized with spasms of panic—Hart alone on the gray steps, shouting into the wind. . . . There were a couple of friends supposed to check out the scene and report back to Ned and Sally's before Gary and the rest piled into the van. But the friends never showed. No scouts. No report. "Gary," Sue warned him, "I only had a chance to call, like, eight people. I don't know who's gonna be there."

But that was like old times, too—the oldest times. Hart seemed serene. He didn't know how it would go. He *couldn't* know . . . but he had that certainty within himself. It was like all those times in his life when he did what he thought was right, pushed open that door, and . . . there it was, just as he'd imagined—the opportunity, the path only he had seen.

He used to say, in tough times, in '72—even '82: "The Lord will provide." People thought he was joking. But he wasn't.

The fun was in watching.

Just as Hart watched now, as his friends at Ned and Sally's house went outside, one after the other, to try to start the van in the cold gray wind. . . . The van wouldn't start. And it was all they had to drive.

Sue Casey looked at Dan Calegari.

"Casey, no!" he said. It was Gephardt's car.

"Danny, it's the only way."

"I'm not even supposed to be here!"

"You can let us off, like, a couple of blocks away."

"Ohh, shit."

So the Harts and their shrunken first circle packed into Dick Gephardt's rent-a-car and drove through the first flakes of a snowstorm toward the state-house.

— ★ —

In the end, Lee decided she would not be the one to say no. She would not be the focus of the doubt, years later. (*You know, it might have worked, if it hadn't been for Lee.*) No! She would not do that to Gary. She would not do that to herself.

He didn't pressure her to help . . . just like he told his friends, the supporters who'd moved on to other campaigns, other lives—he didn't expect them to drop anything . . . that would be a presumption. He told Lee: "You don't have to do *anything*. You could stay home. You don't have to go anywhere."

Well, that was ridiculous. She told him: "Are you kidding? If you go out there, I'm coming along."

Sure, she was apprehensive—what if people laughed, or said ugly things? But she would not let that apprehension get hold of her. She told herself, you can deal with anxieties. You don't have to let them destroy you—Gary always said that.

In the car, Gary was asking how many people might be there . . . and Lee was surprised to hear apprehension coming from *him*. Casey said, too tersely: "Maybe you're all alone. I don't know." She added: "You're on the steps, you're gonna have your back to the statehouse. People that do come, supporter types, we're gonna have them behind you."

"Behind me?" Hart said. "I want to talk to them."

"Gare—read my lips. They're behind you. You walk up to the podium. You give your speech."

Casey was snapping answers . . . because she didn't really know. She'd asked for a podium. She had no idea what the hell was out there. . . . Then she realized she wasn't the only one snapping with nerves. Gary just wanted some friendly faces to talk to. She said, more gently:

"You're gonna talk to the cameras. It'll be okay."

God, please, let there be cameras.

They stopped a couple of blocks away, got out of the car . . . and they knew. They couldn't see the steps yet, but they could *feel* it—the crowd. And a gaggle of cameras, lights on in the gray air, still photographers, pencil-press writing mile-a-minute in notebooks—and no one's said a word yet! And everybody pumped up from the cold and the wait, and the . . . *history happening.* They cheered the moment Hart came into view. They waved leftover Hart placards and raggedy homemade signs—Magic Marker on dull brown cardboard from a cut-up box! STILL THE BEST . . . WELCOME BACK, GARY! Lord, wasn't that *beautiful?* . . . People he'd never seen! And they weren't just behind him on the steps—they were all around, and all around the press, cheering . . . steam from their hot breath rose in the glow of TV lights—no one could miss the feeling. It was electric. Hart was dressed in a blue pin-stripe suit. No coat, no hat, no gloves. He wasn't cold. There was the podium. There was a microphone! There was *John* in the crowd, eyes shining as he watched his father. . . . Hart stepped up and let the cheering subside; he would wait just one extra beat, so his voice—high and clear with the cold air tightening his throat— would cut into expectant hush, a shock through the winter air. He knew exactly how he'd begin.

Sometimes, the best thing to do is what you feel you must do . . .

But he waited, yet another moment, to let silence generate that extra ache . . . while he looked over the crowd—he would remember this . . . while he found Sue Casey's eyes so he could flick his brows up, with the joke—he knew she knew—his eyes flashed with light from the cameras and asked without words:

Pretty miserable, hmmm?

—★—

". . . Getting back in this race is about the toughest thing that I have ever done. And believe me, it is not done lightly. My family, Lee, John, and Andrea, understand clearly the difficulties that lie ahead. And they are totally behind this step, because we believe in ourselves, and we believe in the American people.

"We are together on this decision, because we love this country, and because we are not quitters.

"There is no shame in losing, only in quitting. If you believe in yourself, and if you believe in what you're doing, then we believe—I believe—you don't give up.

"We want to let the people decide. We believe in the American people, because you are fair and you have been good to us. You've been generous with your friendship, your support, and your kindness. We trust the fairness of the American people, and we are prepared to let you decide.

"This will not be like any campaign you've ever seen, because I am going directly to the people. I don't have a national headquarters or staff. I don't have any money. I don't have pollsters or consultants or media advisers or political endorsements.

"But I have something even better. I have the power of ideas and I can govern this country.

"Let the people decide!

"I'm back in the race."

— ★ —

Hart gave his thousand-dollar check to the Secretary of State. He signed his filing papers. Then he was going to walk Main Street, Concord—direct to the people! Just as he'd said.

He, Lee, and John walked away from the statehouse, down Main Street, and the press surged upon them—they had to get this! What would people say to Hart? What would they say to Lee? . . .

They didn't get to say anything.

GARYGARYLEEwhaddyaMRS.HART!thinkaDONNARIy'gonnaWINthink yaWINPOSTgonnaprintaLEEstorygottaRICEGaryMONEYLEEEEHEYYY!

The noise from the press got louder, closer, the more Hart showed he was trying to look past them . . . he was looking for *the people.*

He couldn't see a thing.

The cameras were solid around Gary and Lee. Reporters in the back were pushing in, thrusting tape recorders forward, into the air over the shoulders of reporters in front of them. They thought Gary must be talking to voters. Hart couldn't get to a voter.

He stopped. He spread his hands, long enough so the picture would be boring. He said, very quietly:

"Look—just a three-foot path, please." He caught the eye of one cameraman, and with one hand, made a motion to one side—just a bit to the side. "You have your job to do," he said, "and I have mine."

It went on like that for a block and a half . . . and Hart didn't even get testy. He stopped to plead for room, three times . . . and then he was laughing. It was just silly. They had to get away.

"Where we going?" he said.

Casey looked at him and smiled. She'd spent maybe ten minutes, total, on a schedule for the rest of the campaign. She figured they could go down to Nashua, to a shopping mall.

"Where's the car?"

What car? . . . Calegari brought his rent-a-car to the end of Main Street, all the while, protesting: "I gotta get to work!" They got in his car, and decided on lunch.

"Let's stop somewhere."

"Is everybody hungry?"

"What do you want?"

"Let's go. Come *on!*"

Reporters were running for their cars while the Harts acted out America's noontime drama—Heyy! How 'bout lunch on the way to the mall?

"What about pizza?"

"Let's sit down somewhere."

"Come *onnn!*"

"Danny, make a few turns and we'll lose 'em." This was Casey, who was not ready for a chase scene. The snow was falling steadily. All they needed was a high-speed pile-up:

THREE DEAD AFTER HART ANNOUNCEMENT

Great.

"Danny, just lose 'em and find someplace for lunch."

"We don't have any gas."

"Jesus, Danny!"

They doubled back through the narrow streets to the bottom of Main Street, near the Ramada, and turned into the first gas station. They were still packed in the idling car, at the pumps, waiting for the full-service guy. Calegari craned around to look into the station . . . and there it was. In the window, a hand-lettered sign—white paper, black felt-tip marker:

GIVE 'EM HELL GARY HART

That's what good Advance would have done—would have found the place, told the guys at the station to be nice, even if they were Republicans . . . then made sure the candidate had to get gas . . . so he'd see. He'd feel good.

But Hart didn't have Advance. This was magic.

Gary was instantly out of the car, into the station office, talking to the guys. From outside, you could see him throwing his head back, laughing—that bark of delight. Guy was saying, his wife was *never* gonna believe this! . . . He was *always* for Gary, *always!* . . . "Who gives a shit about that stuff they wrote up on you? You show 'em!"

Hart's face was a study in pleasure, and excitement . . . his *posture* was different—chest out, head back, like he wanted to see all he could of this *scene* . . . in which it was *shown,* unalterably: he was right! People didn't care about things the press harped on. He was right, from the start! *It did not matter!*

After that, of course, Hart was insufferable. "Pretty horrible, huh?" . . . "Kinda miserable, Casey?" Then he'd crack up at his big joke. He was too cute for words.

They stopped for lunch near the Amaskate Bridge—little place, mostly takeout, five booths—Pappy's Pizza. They got in the door, and here came Pappy in his wheelchair.

"Can we get lunch? . . . Do you have a phone?"

"Come on back—use my phone," Pappy said.

"I've got a credit card," Casey told him.

"No, just pick it up—use it!" Pappy said. "And food's on me! . . . Greatest thing that's happened to my place! Greatest thing that's happened to this country!"

They looked at Gary, ready for his laugh. His eyes held the joke—they all knew. But, tell the truth, he wasn't sure anymore whether to laugh . . . or heed that tightness in his chest that only happened . . . when things got *very serious*.

93

Serious
About the
Business

THE *Globe* said this was good for Dukakis. (To the diddybops, everything was either good or bad for Dukakis.)

Hart would raise the stakes in New Hampshire. He'd won there, in '84, and started his amazing surge that almost unhorsed poor Walter Mondale. The *Globe* pundits thought Hart still had strength in New Hampshire. If Dukakis could hold on and beat him there . . . well, that would make Michael's neighborly triumph mean a great deal more.

Hart, after all, was somebody.

Beating somebody, like Hart, was better than beating nobody—dwarves like Simon, or Gephardt, Babbitt, Jackson . . . or Gore. Who's gonna notice?

Just to make sure, the paper cited a quickie poll, which confirmed the fondest hopes of The Hub:

Duke . . . 39.

Hart . . . 19.

Gorgeous!

And then, to make doubly sure, the day after Hart came back, the *Globe* attached to his name the following epithets:

"Unbelievable."

"Weird."

"Crazy."

"Out of his mind."

Those were in the news columns, mostly on the front page.

The inside pages were chockablock with wise-guy quotes, like this pearl of analysis from the ever-reliable William Schneider: "An act of pure narcissism, a show of contempt for the party. I think it's contemptible."

And, lest the reader miss the drift, a *Globe* editorial harrumphed: "The element of the bizarre in Hart's reappearance hurts Republicans, Democrats and anyone else who takes seriously the business of electing Presidents."

Ah! There was the nub of the matter, and the reason the *Globe* was in such comfy Hart-bashing company . . . why even the gentlemanly David Broder (such an admirer of Hart's speeches only months before) felt constrained to weigh in with a column of condemnation—the headline: WHEN AMBITION OVERRIDES ALL OTHER CRITERIA . . . why the influential *Des Moines Register* ran a front-page cartoon with Hart as a seventh dwarf, Sleazy, pushing the other six over the side of a cliff.

They were all—the *Globe,* Schneider, Broder, the *Register,* the other purveyors and publishers of triple-E big-foot punditry—*serious about the business . . . their business.* They were brothers of the cloth, the Priesthood of the Process (from which Hart was excommunicant).

And this, ultimately, would be very good for Dukakis. Because he, like they, had devoted his life to the proposition that government and politics could be made cleaner, more rational, more able . . . by constant prosaic attention to the process: that *this* was the worthiest calling for a man, what they (and he) did every day—O watchdogs on the stoops of Government Halls—*this* (and this alone—not bold ideas, nor shining dreams, nor grand ambition) . . . this would make *all the difference* for the Citizens of Our Republic.

Serious was Michael's middle name.

"The New Hampshire primary," the beetle-browed Dukakis scolded Hart that same day, "is more than a *symbolic exercise.*"

— ★ —

But even the brethren of the cloth could not know how good this was for Dukakis. It was a new campaign, a new life—at least, a spark of life.

Yes, it gave him someone to beat . . . but better still: someone he *could* beat. Michael had ten million dollars in the bank. Hart had fifty thousand and his personal credit card. Hart had no staff. Michael had 263 paid professionals in thirty-nine offices in fourteen states. If Dukakis's native instinct to order, his fifty-four years as master mechanic, his quarter-century as the premier organizer of Massachusetts politics, told him anything . . . it was this delicious truth, which he proffered as a vow to the press:

"I'm gonna beat him."

He must have said it twelve times: "Gary Hart's perfectly welcome to run, but . . . I'm gonna *beat* him in New Hampshire."

It was the first time in months—since Apology Weekend—that Dukakis said anything so bellicose . . . the first time since the Biden tape, he'd admit: he meant to thump some other Democrat.

Michael had worked out his own answer to all the urgent horse-race questions, the cinch of the campaign's anxiety belt: What would he do if he finished out of the money in Iowa? What if his lead in New Hampshire slipped? What if it was *true:* no short, dark Greek could run for office south of Maryland? . . . "Well," Michael would say with a small smile, "if it doesn't work out, I've gotta great job. I'm an hour from the Cape. My bride and I will be on Nantucket for the Strawberry Festival in May. . . ." (Estrich hit the roof when she heard that. She was working eighteen-hour days, three thousand miles from her husband. Everyone on Chauncy Street was sacrificing a family, a career, a decent salary, at least their leisure . . . fuck Michael and his flowers in May! . . . "Don't *ever,* " she said, "let anybody hear you say that." Of course, he went right on saying it.

But not after Hart came back.

With Hart in the race, Michael Dukakis could be *obviously* cleaner, more moral, more rational, more disciplined: here was a foil for the Dukakis morality play. "This guy," said Michael, "has gotta be stopped."

He'd never thought much of Hart. Dukakis looked at Hart's telegenic allure as some kind of sleazy trick. Hart was flashy. Hart was cheap and easy . . . *politics*! And then . . . *then:* to give himself, and his campaign, and his *family,* over to *whim* . . . to a girl who—well, Michael didn't talk about this kinda thing, and if he did, it would probably be in Greek, with a coupla guys, but . . . *well*! That lack of *discipline* . . . *fidelity* . . . *basic human decency*! . . . Hart was, in every way, an affront to Michael's uxorious eye.

Michael got the news Hart was back in a handwritten note passed to him in a meeting, in Burlington, Vermont, at the Northeast Governors Conference. And he left the room! . . . Michael left an *important government meeting,* wherein his fellow chief executives were discussing the future of federal super-conductivity contracts . . . and he scooted . . . to make a call about *politics*!

That day, Estrich and Corrigan were meeting him in Vermont to fly to Texas (he hadn't allowed them to schedule a meeting in Boston—not in the State House, no!) . . . and that was the day, at last, he signed off on his plan of campaign. In fact, he accepted the thing whole, with barely a glance, all the spending, all the millions—all except the part about sweeping the field in Iowa. ("Look. It was never part of the program that I hadda win Iowa.") No . . . for Michael, this campaign would begin in New Hampshire—the campaign of philotimy—against Gary Hart.

In fact, it had begun. Michael took questions all that day—and the next, and the next—about (ta dummm!) the Karacter Issue. The reporters were working on weekend thumb-suckers: whether it was right for the pack to turn up the heat again under the stinking bouillabaisse. They were diffident questions: Michael was, in a way, a victim of this same cookery . . . what with his sadness, and Sasso, and . . . well, anyway, this was the kind of "other-campaign reaction" that most candidates would dismiss. But no, Michael couldn't have been nicer—or more supportive.

"I think we're gonna be held to the *highest standard* . . . and we should be. People have a right to know the kinda guy . . ."

Michael had no message problem if this campaign was about the kinda guy. He had no trouble rousing himself to combat, once candidate Hart was quoted on "the Massachusetts Miracle" . . . or in contemptuous derision of Michael's "solution" for the budget deficit (better tax collection!). . . . Michael had no trouble at all.

And Estrich had less trouble, once she set the staff to scouting out *every* Hart comment about Dukakis . . . or Massachusetts . . . or any other Hart quote that would make Michael see red. She made sure each clipping found its way under Michael's nose—so he'd have a chance to react . . . which he did.

It got so, even the diddybops noticed: "Why've you got him attacking Hart?"

Estrich said: "At least he's attacking someone."

Someone who was *someone:* by that weekend, new national polls had Hart in the lead, with thirty percent of Democrats—compared to twenty-two for Jackson, fourteen for Dukakis. In Iowa, Hart had thirty percent—nearly twice the total for any other Democrat.

94

Out
of the
Monkey Suit

IT DIDN'T MATTER to Gephardt who was in the lead. He wasn't. A month and a half to the caucus, and the message wasn't getting through. Six percent! He was better—he *knew*. He could feel it in the room, or the barn (he was doing farm rallies—he loved them) . . . but it was too late to work forty folks at a time.

Somehow, he had to make people listen anew—a lot of people, in a hurry. But with everybody chasing Hart, Dick couldn't get on the network news to save his life. And the papers—well, he only *wished* they'd ignore him. They were vicious!

"Could we—just *once!*—get *one* decent story from the *Post-Dispatch* . . . so we could raise a little money?" Dick would fume at the tearsheets from St. Louis: "They don't understand! They're killing the campaign!"

And the *Post-Dispatch* was benign compared to the *Register*. Iowa's biggest paper had a bad jones for Gephardt. It wasn't the poll, though that was a monthly knife in his heart. The editorial page slammed him regularly. (Hey, they might be in Iowa, but they were just as tough as *The New York Times!*) And the paper's political big-foot, David Yepsen, was the man who had let Dick twist in the wind . . . for *weeks* . . . when he knew, of course, it wasn't the Gephardts who had handed him the Biden tape. In fact, the *Register* had written Gephardt off. In that newsroom, *everybody knew* . . . Iowans had heard his message—plenty of it—and rejected it.

Of course, Dick couldn't accept that. People didn't know him! He hadn't yet got to them. Somehow, he had to get it across that he was *for them* . . . the ads! It would *have* to be the ads.

— ★ —

There would be four ads. They were going to be great. (Dick believed in Shrum—Bob was a genius!) One would be a bio, introducing Dick. Then, one for farmers, one about seniors, and one about trade. Some of Dick's fellow Reps were urging him off that trade horse—people were tired of that—and the newspapers were *hammering* Dick for being "protectionist . . . against free trade." But Dick was not getting off any horse. Not any more. . . . There were friends in Iowa who told him he could forget about seniors. Simon had the seniors all wrapped up. But Dick had Claude Pepper, the eighty-eight-year-old Representative from Florida—he was going to be in the ads. Pepper was Chairman of the Committee on the Aging, a hero to seniors and their organizations. In fact, Pepper was even in the bio ad, talking about Dick's concern for health, which he developed, Pepper said, "in his young son's struggle with cansuh . . ." Jane didn't like that reference at all. Loreen would go nuts. They'd always kept Matt's health private. What would Matt think? Jane couldn't even bring herself to tell him. She argued with Dick . . . but the line about Matt stayed in. The ads were the next hope. Everything had to go into those ads.

But the ads got held up—the killers were split. Now that they had to boil down the message, dream up a slogan to tie the ads together, no one could agree on a *verb*. Murphy, Klein, Trippi—who were trying to get Iowans to like Dick Gephardt—said they had to hammer the word "change." People wanted a change. Carrick, and the killers back in D.C., said it had to be "fight." That's what this came down to—were they gonna fight? . . . Murphy said "fight" wasn't Gephardt: Dick would always split the difference. . . . Someone from the staff tossed in "stand." Maybe they could all agree: *"Stand up* for Gephardt . . ." But that wasn't really *it* (and Babbitt was already "standing up") . . . no. Carrick, Doak, and Shrum insisted it had to be "fight" . . . but "Fight for Gephardt"? Iowans didn't *like* to fight.

So Dick had his yellow pad on his knee again, this time in the middle of sweating passengers and squalling babies at an O'Hare Airport gate, waiting for a flight to Des Moines. He was flying commercial—coach, at that. He'd left the road crew in Iowa: money was tight.

"I gotta get it down to five words," Dick explained. "That's what it's gotta . . ." He was drawing a neat square on his legal pad, as if he somehow had to fit the words into that box. "Something people can hold on to . . . five words."

They had to be about him, but couldn't be exactly him . . . or not just him. That was the strangest part. Dick said he knew now: voters wanted someone larger than life . . . Olympian. So it couldn't be that red-haired lawyer from St. Louis who got home from work and fell asleep on the floor of his family room with his mouth open in front of the TV. . . . No, they told you to be yourself, but they didn't want you to be like yourself. They wanted you to be like a President! They wanted you to be something *huge* for them.

"I'll tell you the weird part—is when you *stop*. . . . I was in Louisiana. Little town . . ." He named the town. "I don't think they'd had a Presidential candidate since, uh . . . Millard Fillmore.

"So, I get there, and there's cops and motorcycles, and a limousine the size of Ohio. There's the Mayor, and *marching bands* . . . and they treat me like the King of Spain.

"I do my speech, I get back in the limo, get to the airport . . . and two hours later, I'm back in O'Hare . . . hauling my suitcase off the plane . . . carry it half a mile . . . I gotta wait in line for a lousy *hot dog* . . .

"All of a sudden, I'm back, I'm a . . . a, uh . . ." He was hunting a word. "I'm a, uh . . . a *shit-bum!*"

But he wasn't going to finish as a bum. No . . . he stared down at his pad, as if it must hold the answer. But there were no words in the box.

— ★ —

"It's Your Fight, Too!" came from David Doak—and Gephardt loved it. Didn't that just say it all? You know, not only was he out there *for them* . . . but now, they had to stand up *for him* . . . *and for themselves!* . . . Beautiful!

Murphy still tried to fight against "fight," but it was time to shoot the ads, and no other word worked. ("What do you *want?*" Shrum protested. " 'It's your tussle, too'?")

Anyway, the strangest thing happened. As soon as they started hammering down the ads—refining the scripts, sending drafts back and forth—Gephardt started using the lines. . . . "They work *hard* all day to make a good product. . . . If we don't stand up for our workers, then who *are* we? . . . *It's your fight, too!*"

And right away, he could see it in the crowds, the way they *locked on* . . . *finally,* he was talking their language! And his speeches, his rallies, started giving off heat. Voices called to him, from the crowds:

"Give 'em hell, Dick!"

Dick would stop in his speech and call back: "I'm like ol' Harry Truman—I just tell 'em the truth . . . and they *think* it's hell."

His van crunched to a halt in the snow on a farm lane, and he hopped up on a wagon in the barn—mid-December, cold like a meat car on a coast-to-coast train . . . cold air through the walls, cold floor, cold gray light filtering in through forty feet of loft above . . . great dull cold-steel mantis-machines, stored for the winter, looming over Gephardt like monster sculptural tribute to debt and difficulty, futile fertility—thousands of tons of Iowa corn that no one could sell.

Dick was dressed in a ballcap and a bulky (borrowed) blue jacket that advertised a seed company. He shouted through the steam of his breath:

"Costs about two dollars eighty cents to make a-bushel-a corn!" (Dick was talking full St. Louis now. . . . He pronounced it "cahrn.") You get about a *dollar and a half* for it . . . *that's* the program now! A few months back, it was a *dollar!*"

"That's right . . . tell 'em, Dick!"

"Why shouldn't farmers *vote* on the program? . . . Let's pass Harkin-Gephardt and let the farmers *VOTE* on what the program is! . . . You want a fair *PRICE* for your cahrn! . . ."

"Yeaahhhh!"

"Give 'em hell, Dick!"

They were slapping their big gloves together, stomping their feet.

At the back of the barn, Ethel Klein was clapping, too, squealing to be heard over the cheers: "He's never done this before! It's all *him*! It's all *him*!"

And Gephardt was so pumped up, he was *screaming*:

"Lemme tell you something! I'm a Democrat that cares about the American worker and the American farmer . . . AND I'M NOT GONNA LEAVE 'EM BEHIND! . . ."

Fight was the word—he'd show them a fight!

They loaded him in the van, and Ethel got his eyes: "I am so *proud* of you . . ."

But Dick didn't need that. His voice raspy from strain, he demanded of Brad: "What's next?" He could hardly sit still.

Problem was, there was Brad, and Ethel, Debra Johns, sometimes Trippi, or Murphy—Dick, and a driver, of course—and they still only needed one van. There wasn't enough press for two. The big-feet weren't going to screw around with a candidate at six percent. . . . So there wasn't any way to tell the world: Gephardt was fighting back.

—★—

Every morning, at Loreen's apartment, or a motel in some corner of the state, Dick would rip through the *Register* . . . in vain. They just wouldn't *get* it! At a press conference that December, David Yepsen asked Gephardt (rather, told him): "You sound horrible. You look tired. Do you really think you're getting any votes here?"

Then came Chickengate. It wasn't much of a story. God knows who fed it to the *Register*. It was about some vote in Congress—a procedural vote on a poultry bill—and Dick had voted no (couldn't even remember what the vote *was;* it was chickenshit). But the *Register* was going to prove with this vote that Gephardt was really *against the farmers*.

Well, the story never caught on . . . no one could understand it. But it did wonders for Dick. Because, finally, he realized: *they didn't like him.* He wasn't going to make a friend of Yepsen. He wasn't going to get a good story from the *Register*. It wasn't that he hadn't got to them yet, hadn't worked hard enough to get to know them. They didn't *want* to be got to—didn't *want* to know him.

Can you beat that!

It occurred to Gephardt that the message wasn't getting through because they didn't want it to get through! . . . It made him angry.

And that anger fed back into the ads, into the final scripts, and the shoot. They filmed about ten days before Christmas, and Dick poured his outrage and resolve into those ads. It wasn't just the words, it was him and the camera—he could just *do* that: show that camera exactly what he meant. And what he meant to show was a steely indignation . . . at the *unfairness.*

Of course, the words were about unfairness to the workers, the farmers, the seniors . . . to voters.

But the anger was his.

— ★ —

"You got any Contac or anything?" he croaked in the dark, aboard his puddle-jumper, heading east—his last stop in Iowa before Christmas. "I think I'm gettin' a cold. . . . At least it's the end. Be home tomorrow night."

They had him scheduled the next day in New Hampshire—one last effort before decency required that he look like he was relaxing. One of the Iowa crew asked what he was going to do in New Hampshire. Gephardt shrugged.

"I don't know . . . walk around."

He shook his head. Now that he was saying what he meant to say, it just didn't make any sense to be doing . . . well, half of what they asked him to do.

Brad said: "Did you talk to Jane yet about that *USA Today?*"

Gephardt slumped five degrees in his seat. "Not yet."

USA Today wanted to shoot a family picture at his home—the day after Christmas. Dick hadn't had the guts to tell Jane.

Brad said: "So you'll talk to her?"

"Yeah . . ."

Brad started laughing. "When?"

"Okay, I will . . ."

"Yeah, and, uh, we want a media hit in New Hampshire tomorrow . . . so they want you to shop."

The look on Gephardt's face was as close to disgust as he could manage. "What am I gonna shop for?" he said. "A seed hat?"

"I think they want you to shop, uh, for Jane . . ."

Gephardt wasn't paying attention. He liked that seed-company jacket—first time he'd been warm in a week. "It was lined, inside, like a sweatshirt. I wanna wear it . . . I got to get out of this monkey suit. You know, when I go home tomorrow, I'm not gonna wear a suit. Blue jeans . . . I HATE suits. When I was in Congress, I *never* wore my jacket. Got into a meeting, and right away, just threw it in a corner."

Gephardt was talking about Congress in past tense.

"You know, I saw it on TV, the other night. Got in late, and I turned on the TV, and they had the House . . . I saw it, like a *citizen.* The budget resolution. I mean, for *hours* . . ." (He started waving his arms in a parody of an earnest solon.) "Mister SPEAKER! . . . *Heh heh hackhackhack.*"

The new Gephardt was molting before their eyes. And the road crew didn't know what to make of it. He was good, loose, but . . . maybe the guy *was* getting sick.

"So, uh, Dick . . ."

Gephardt announced he was giving up ties!

"I HATE ties. Always worried to death I'm gonna get something on it."

Brad pointed out it was his tie, not Dick's.

"Well, I'm giving it back."

"It's up to you, boss," Brad said. He looked worried, prim, in his own gray suit.

"That's what I'll do," Gephardt said. "I'll shop for a tie for you. *You're* the suit. Brad is the suit! *Hackhackhack* . . ."

Brad said: "I always feel I have to be dressed . . . to meet the President."

There were three beats of silence in the plane. Brad was *serious.*

President Dick said: "Yeah, but the President's wearin' a *seed jacket hackhackhackheeheee* . . . I'm gonna, too. I'm gonna do it. This is it . . ."

Brad said: "Uh, so you'll shop?"

"Yeah, okay . . . I'll shop."

Which he did, the next day, at the Mall of New Hampshire. He did exactly what they told him: walked into a store, straight to the sweater (the Advance man had it all picked out), held it up while he smiled for the camera, took it to the register, and bought it for Jane.

Which was great, except the Advance man forgot to check—the sweater was made in China . . . which didn't really bother Dick . . . but it made for a snide little wire story (Mr. America First!) . . . which *The Des Moines Register* ran the next day.

95

Who
Would Have
Thought?

IT WAS SO MUCH NICER to be with Michael, once he'd settled his stomach, once he'd started to try again. It was like something loosed in him. Even the air in the plane felt . . . well, it wasn't light—it was somehow more solid. It was sensible, purposeful . . . but an enjoyment: like the feeling you might have after one of Michael's meals. This was his favorite meal:

"Soup, salad . . . and a hearty piece of bread."

Michael had taken a day off. He felt so much better after he got a day off, after he got with his staff and *demanded* one day in fourteen, just to stay home, take a walk, cook . . . he cooked a soup, his chowder. The way he did it was, he'd cook enough so he could eat, then he'd put up leftovers in the freezer. Clam chowder, Bermuda fish chowder . . . he could freeze four containers after a *feast* of turkey soup—after he used the turkey. "I make turkey tetrazzini," he said.

And he'd demanded more time with Kitty. "I told Nick, what we gotta do is give her a separate schedule. But we could kinda connect in the evenings, and then, during the day, go our separate ways." Michael shrugged his mystification: Why should he have to tell his staff simple stuff like that?

How was Kitty?

"Just . . . terrific. We're having so much fun together."

Maybe everyone in the family did feel better when Michael felt better . . . or maybe he was the sort of husband and father who makes everyone put on a sweater when he's cold. Anyway, he was certain, they were flourishing.

"Two weeks ago, Kara put together *seven hundred people* at Brown . . ." (her university, in Providence, Rhode Island). "Here was my baby, looking around, moving like a seasoned Advance man. I was so proud of her. Kara might have a future in politics yet. She's got the talent. John, almost certainly. Andrea, no."

Andrea, his twenty-two-year-old, who'd been working in the Des Moines office since June, since her graduation from Princeton, was sitting across the airplane table. It wasn't clear if she'd heard this judgment upon her . . . though she wouldn't have disagreed. She'd always been the nonpolitical one who suffered for her father through the public slights, attacks in the press . . . he'd been campaigning ever since she was alive. Anyway, she hadn't spoken till he brought up her name. The day was wet and raw, on the ground—above, in that prop plane, bucking the stratus clouds, it was wild. Andrea looked pale, and tight around her dark eyes—Kitty's eyes.

"Dad, it's the Maytag *repairman.*" (Now, it was clear, she'd been waiting to correct the errors in his new stump speech.) "You always say the Maytag salesman. It's supposed to be the Maytag repairman."

Michael's head immediately bent to her. Eyes down, his face softened to an uncharacteristic expression—absolute attention. "And I say salesman?"

"Yeah," she said. "And precinct *captains.*"

"What do I say?" His eyes looked up at hers submissively from his half-bowed head, like a communicant at the altar.

"You always say *chairmen.* But it's *captains*—women, too. You should say captains."

"Okay."

He'd fought off fifteen drafts of that new speech for two months, but clearly: he'd try his best to say the lines exactly as suggested by his nonpolitical daughter.

—★—

The new speech was meant to be inspirational, Kennedyesque—that was the new vision. "Twenty-eight years ago, another son of Massachusetts . . ." Michael called this reheated soup "The *Next* Frontier."

Underneath, it was his same cautious program—good-jobs-at-good-wages . . . to be achieved by means of "a strong, vibrant public-private partnership." These words meant something to Dukakis, but to his listeners they remained opaque.

The difference the crowd could sense was Dukakis's own confidence, and his obvious attempt to show them how he *felt.* He had two new TV ads (from a new adman, Ken Swope, a friend of Kiley's) that showed his *outrage* at the U.S.-backed contra war in Nicaragua and, at home, the plight of the homeless. They were striking ads, grainy black-and-white photos of destruction and deprivation, backed by creepy music and Michael's voice, squibs from his speeches: it was time to stop the killing—start the war on poverty and injustice. . . . But the best by-product of the ads was, Dukakis had to take on the Reagan ethic in his speech. He had to perform his anger.

It wasn't easy.

"Folks, I don't *comprehend* what's been going on in this country for the last seven years . . ."

That was as close as he'd come to taking on the Gipper by name. But, clearly, Michael was reaching for the common tongue.

". . . They gave it a name—supply-side economics. It was *wacko* economics!"

This key word he pronounced with such precision, it sounded like the syllables had never before escaped his lips. He called to mind that boy in Brookline who practiced new words in front of the mirror.

"*Whack—oh* . . ."

Well, it was a start.

The confidence, of course, had its root in organization. The Dukakis campaign was growing—Michael was going to field-organize his way to the White House. But at the same time, the way Dukakis worked, part of his old staff spent its days ferrying new staff all over the state . . . so the Governor could interview each new hire.

Today, in Council Bluffs, it was a kid named David Behar—a New Yorker who'd recently spent time in California and landed somehow in the middle of the nation to apply for a dweeb job organizing for Dukakis. Michael bearded the boy in a small room that fairly vibrated with poor Behar's anxiety.

Dukakis asked a couple of quick questions, didn't wait for answers. "Didja? Whadja do out there? Oh, yeah. Whadja thinka that?"

Behar hadn't yet got to the point where he could form a coherent sentence. But Dukakis didn't have much time. He cut him off:

"Look, David, three things I say to everybody who comes aboard on this campaign. One, is your personal standards. Your personal conduct and ethics and standing—very important to us. Very important. People are looking very closely at us. And at you. And that goes for everything. Your own morality, conduct, ethics . . . I don't have to tell you more than that.

"Second, I'm not kidding when I talk about a positive campaign. I mean it. We're running for the Presidency. We're not running against anybody. I don't want it. It doesn't help us. It doesn't achieve anything. That goes for Hart, too."

Behar tried to speak. Michael didn't stop.

"If he wants to run, he's welcome to it."

"But it's . . ."

"Look. The way to beat Gary Hart is to beat Gary Hart. So, in the meantime . . ."

"But . . . I just want to give back to people what they're giving me . . . which is . . . it's just ridiculous!"

Michael held up a palm. "I know. But hold it back. I don't do it. I don't want it."

"Yes, sir."

"And third is memo. There've been more campaigns sunk by people who feel they've gotta write a memo . . . so when you put anything on paper, just assume it's gonna be on the front page the next day. If it can't be—don't write it. Okay?"

Behar was nodding, eyes down.

"Good to have ya aboard." Michael stuck out a hand, and departed.

— ★ —

Why wouldn't he be pleased? Just a few days until Christmas, and then the home stretch . . . at last! If Michael could finish well in Iowa—above Hart, clearly—it would give his people in New Hampshire all the confidence they required. No one had an outfit like Michael's. Not Paul Simon, his closest rival . . . and Gephardt, Babbitt, Jackson—they were too far behind. Michael had taken their measure.

In fact—this was the swelling secret in his breast—Michael had decided he could *win* Iowa. He didn't have to attack, flail around, making promises, mouthing themes . . . no! The *basic economic message* . . . was going to win Iowa. He'd been correct, all along!

Of course, he wouldn't say that aloud—the winning part—that was for family. Back on his plane, bouncing toward Waterloo, there was a writer who'd wormed his way aboard. He was asking questions. Michael grudgingly conceded, things were going well, he was more comfortable, sure. But that didn't mean anything had changed—he'd been doing this kinda thing for twenty-five years!

"Long campaigns are nothing new for me. I was holding meetings—forty people in my living room, 1972—two years before that election. It's a building process. You've got to keep moving ahead—slowly, surely—not getting distracted by anything . . ."

Then, Michael addressed himself with solid equanimity to a club sandwich.

Actually, it was two chunky quarters, half of a club sandwich—which was all Michael removed from an enormous tray of club sandwiches that rose volcanically on the table between him and his daughter. With the oversized, purposeful hands of a surgeon, Michael lifted Saran Wrap from one half of the tray, and extracted his meal. Then, he stopped. Andrea was not eating. Over the sandwich mountain, Michael fixed her with a father's look—Pan's look, from the head of the table. But he didn't scold. Andrea was fighting the blustery bump of the clouds.

"I talked to your mother . . ."

Andrea just looked sick.

"You weren't along, of course, for our honeymoon . . ." Michael smiled at his joke. ". . . but, you know, I've got to go to Puerto Rico. I think we've got a good chance to get the delegates there. So I was talking to the Governor. Lovely guy, Rafael Hernández . . ." Michael pronounced the name with precision and relish.

"So he said, whenever I come, he'd love to have us stay at the residence there, *La Fortaleza* . . . fabulous place . . ." Michael's hands rose and sketched a great cliff, as his words described the old Spanish fortress above. "So I called your mother . . .

"I said: 'Twenty-four years ago, I took you to stay in the Hotel Atlantico . . .' "

(It was kind of a fleabag.)

". . . 'Now, how would you like to go back and stay in the palace, *La Fortaleza*?' . . ."

Michael had the air of a kid who shows his girlfriend how he can lift the back of a car.

"She said she thought she could use that."

His smile was broad now, as he sat back.

"Who would've ever thought?"

96

1978

Y CHRISTMAS 1977, all the papers thought Dukakis was a safe bet for a second term. He still had enemies aplenty on Beacon Hill, and in the banks, insurance companies, high-tech companies, business groups and welfare groups, state employees and . . . sometimes, even his friends didn't like Michael. But even enemies thought they'd have him, lecturing from the corner office, for another term. Moreover, *Michael* thought he was a sure thing. People were bound to see all the good he'd done, all the hacks he'd chased, the mess he'd hosed away from the State House. Sure, he'd ruffled feathers. But anyone who knew anything would have to see—he was right.

That year, two hundred thousand more people had jobs than in '75. Unemployment was down to six percent. There were four hundred new businesses—some in the old mill towns that were dying when Dukakis took over. The flow of red ink was stanched. The Commonwealth had a budget surplus. State aid to local schools was up, two to three hundred percent. All this, Michael Dukakis could claim—and rightly—he had done.

Anyway, he didn't have a popular opponent. There were two Democrats against him. Barbara Ackermann was a liberal Mayor of Cambridge who'd never run statewide. She went after Dukakis just to show him he couldn't beat up on the poor—and get off scot-free. The other opponent, Eddie King, was a former Boston College football star (then a Baltimore Colt) who was running because he was pissed off at Michael and the neighborhood do-goods who did him out of his cushy job at the Port Authority. Eddie hadn't ever run for anything. Nice fella, in a glad-hand way—not much of a speaker, not a thinker. Dukakis viewed him with unalloyed contempt.

Then came the snowstorm: February '78. Snow fell for three days. High tide and screaming winds flooded the Massachusetts coast. People were stranded. Everything shut down. The power failed. Jimmy Carter declared Massachusetts a federal disaster zone . . . and, through it all, Michael Dukakis managed the problem. People who were with him during those three days said he was never so great—so even-tempered, happy, masterful. He shut the roads, he mustered the National Guard. He just about lived on TV, three days and nights, in a turtleneck, under a crewneck sweater . . . he was calming, resourceful, good-humored . . . informing the citizens of the latest snow news, the actions of government, the availability of help. He pulled his state through. He managed the problem.

After that, he was up fifty points in the polls.

Then Dukakis set out to manage his reelection. He eschewed a professional Campaign Manager (they cost a fortune!) and gave his friend Dick Geisser that title. Geisser had never run a campaign—but that was all right . . . Michael would take care of this. There were people in his administration who might have helped (some with political smarts did manage to sneak into jobs). But Michael *prohibited* that. "You guys run the government," he said. "Let me worry about the campaign."

But why should he worry? . . . He interviewed consultants—two sharp young guys, Dan Payne and John Marttila, showed him flowcharts, talked about in-house polling, computer-targeting, direct mail. (What did he need with that?) . . . Michael decided on his own ad budget—zero. (What'd he spend last time—twenty-five thousand? This time, he was Governor! Why should he toss money around?)

And who was there to *make* him worry? . . . Allan Sidd was gone, the brothers Sapers, Fran Meaney . . . who was talking to Michael? His erstwhile liberal allies were thumping the tub for Ackermann—they were still pissed off at Michael for cutting back on welfare. (He refused another three-percent hike for the poor that year—then he announced his surplus.) The sachems of the State House were in cabal against him, stoking up the hoary machine to help a man who'd play ball, Eddie King.

Meanwhile, King was running a smart campaign. He didn't know politics. But he knew he didn't know politics. He had a sharp young pollster, a killer named Ed Reilly . . . and when Reilly told King the five hot-button issues, King listened. They were:

A cut in taxes—now.

The death penalty.

An end to state funding for abortion.

Mandatory sentences for drug pushers.

A return to the twenty-one-year-old drinking age.

Whatever he was asked, King would give one of those answers—the one closest to the topic, usually . . . it really didn't matter to Eddie.

Michael couldn't believe King would get anywhere with that sorta know-nothing irrationality. King was *craven*! People hadda see through that kinda crap! . . . Still, by the summer, Dukakis said he sensed anger from the voters. It puzzled him.

It wasn't that he didn't work. He drove all over the state, thousands of miles, all day, all night, doggedly retailing his record. He'd campaign at the beaches till his neck and nose were burnt from sun, his hands swollen and scratched from women's rings, Band-Aids all over, feet hammered and throbbing from the sand in his wing tips . . . and maybe he saw a thousand people that day. Meanwhile, on the tube, King was talking up his tax cut to four hundred thousand viewers. By August, Michael figured out, *he* should be on the tube . . . but he was out of money (he never raised much), and he wouldn't *talk* about going into debt.

He was still ahead. King was a moron. People had to see that . . . and no one was telling Michael any different.

There was one debate—statewide TV—Michael could have turned it around. Ackermann hammered at Dukakis from the left; King did his five points (whatever they asked), hammering from the right, but Michael . . .

What the hell was wrong with Michael?

He looked dead! . . . He wouldn't answer back!

He kept trying to *correct* their errors—like a robot! He never spoke up for himself . . . much less, threw anything back at them. His staff, his friends, Kitty—no one could figure it out. . . .

It happened, actually, before the debate, before the red lights on the cameras flashed on. They were on stage, doing microphone checks, and one of the reporters who was going to ask questions, a TV guy named Tony Pepper, just to be a wise ass, instead of saying, "Testing, one, two, three" . . . he said: "*My name is Mike Dukakis, and I promised no new* . . ."

He didn't have to say "taxes."

Michael looked like someone had punched him. He went into his hunch and he never came out till the lights shut down, the cameras were off . . . and the election was lost.

In fact, it would have been kinder if he'd known it was lost. But he still couldn't see . . . even to primary day, and primary night, when the vote started coming in. Michael still would not believe. . . . "Michael Dukakis Should Be Governor." They'd had *four years* to see the Governor he was!

He held that hope through the night—the 57 Hotel. . . . He thought maybe Pittsfield, out west, would turn out huge. He'd killed himself for Pittsfield! He'd saved that town from the dead!

He lost Pittsfield.

He lost to King by eighty thousand votes. Ackermann took sixty thousand—all from Dukakis. But he couldn't blame her. He wouldn't blame anyone—but himself. He told Geisser: "I lost this. You didn't. I blew it. . . . I blew it."

People told him: "You'll be back."

He said: "Don't be ridiculous."

That night, he told Kitty: "I'm a has-been."

Next morning, he was back in his office, 9:00 A.M. He gathered his people and told them: they were going back to work, for the next four months, to give the citizens of the Commonwealth the best government they'd ever had, to turn the government over to the next administration with the best transition the state had ever seen.

And three days thereafter, on a raw, gray, Saturday morning, he went out campaigning for a fair-tax amendment to the state constitution. South Station . . . a whistle-stop train . . . he met the organizer, a bright young man, John Sasso. They posed for a picture, both of them in rumpled raincoats, neither smiling . . . like a couple of G-men.

That was the only picture Sasso ever had on his office wall.

97

Sasso

H E HADN'T seen Michael for three months. Mike had not found occasion to have Sasso in the same room with himself. Or to call. . . . Estrich would ask Nick Mitropoulos: "Did you get him to call John?" Nick would purse his mouth, shake his head. "I'll get him to do it this week."

Estrich stopped calling John. God knows, she could have used his help. She wouldn't have been in that campaign if not for John—she'd signed on (without salary) to work with her friends, Tully, Corrigan . . . and Sasso. But how could she call—if Michael would not?

Of course, John would not call. Sometimes, he wanted to know, wanted to talk, so badly, it was physical—this had been his life for seven years. But he would not call. If they wanted to do without him, so be it.

Then, he got the invitation: New Year's Day, at Perry Street. John and Francine, and their kids, Robert and Maggie, would join the Dukakises for brunch—a family affair. John tried not to be excited. He was excited.

Well, it couldn't have been nicer. Michael and Kitty served a lovely meal, in the dining room—you could see what effort had gone into it . . . and there was so much warmth, with all the kids, the way Michael and Kitty were teasing Kara, who'd come home so late she'd just woken up—for *brunch* . . . the way Michael was with the Sasso kids—he insisted little Maggie have an egg in bread, a Greek good-luck tradition, for New Year's . . . Kara and John Dukakis ran to the attic to rummage through Michael's things (visiting pols get great gifts), and they brought down an Indian feather headdress for Robbie Sasso, who was seven, in heaven . . . it was *so* nice.

And Francine Sasso was so grateful, for the kids, who'd seen their father on TV like a criminal, over and over, Sasso, Sasso, Sasso . . . and they knew Daddy didn't work anymore for the Governor—but they weren't sure why . . . why did the Governor turn on Daddy? So wrong! . . . And it was *so* wrong, for three months, in the Sasso house, with John so sad, Francine on eggshells—sometimes, in the dark, at night, awake, she'd think, she'd dream, it was all just like it was before. That's all she wanted, to be back . . . like it was before.

So they were, that day. Michael asked Francine about her job at the AG's office, and John told Mike about the new job he'd lined up at Hill, Holiday, the big ad agency. . . . Michael talked about the State House, the way the legislative sachems buried his health-care bill. And Michael and Kitty talked about the campaign: how long it seemed, out in Iowa, the cold, the endless events, the people, the press . . . the fights with the staff on Chauncy Street. The way the staff badgered Michael to say such-and-such about trade, to go after Simon, to talk about PACs.

They wanted him to say this, or that . . . why? What was it for?

Sometimes, he didn't know what he was doing any of it for.

And John fell right into it . . . he talked to Michael, earnestly, about how they started, with one simple idea—opportunity for all—how that fit, with the American dream, Mike's own life, the kinda guy he was . . .

"Remember, Mike, those numbers we looked at, a while back, the things people actually wanted, how . . . *modest* it was? What they really thought was the dream? A little chance, a job, a home, a little better shot for their kids? . . . Remember?"

And there was Michael. He was getting it, from John, again. "Yeah . . . yeah . . ." he said, nodding, eyes almost closed. "Yeah . . ."

"That's why you got into this race . . ."

"Yeah . . ."

"That's what we tried to do . . . that's what it's about, Mike!"

Francine did not attend the words. But she was so glad—John was talking to Mike again. Absently, she noticed her hands were twisting together. She'd been fighting this habit for months—her fingers fretting, twisting over one another till they hurt. She kept her hands under the table. She didn't understand why her hands wouldn't keep still.

She didn't understand, in the car, why she felt so bad, so . . . depressed. John didn't say anything. The kids had a great time. It was such a wonderful day, a wonderful reunion—wasn't it?

"Ahh, I don't know," John said. John could not have told her what it was—not then. It was only later . . . he felt the hole in the middle—the way everything was perfect, all together (they acted like it was all together), except John and Mike—they weren't doing anything together. It was only later, John felt so . . . *stupid,* so *used* . . . for falling in again, playing his role, acting the part, in some private play of Michael's.

What did Mike want—for John to tell him he'd been right?

98

A Cornered Marmot

DICK GEPHARDT flew to Iowa the day after New Year's—five weeks to give it one more hard shot. His ads were on the air—they started the day after Christmas, and reaction was good. He didn't know how good. (His vacation was four days' skiing with the family, and Jane had docked his phone privileges—he only managed a few stealthy calls from the phone at the top of the chair lift.)

But as soon as he was back in the state, he could feel the ads. The trade ad hit the hardest. Voters came up to Gephardt and quoted the ad back to him—as if, maybe, he didn't know and they had to *tell him* about this ad . . . unbelievable! It said just what he'd been *talking about*!

So Gephardt started using the ad, almost word for word, in his speech:

"We make a car here called the Chrysler K-car . . . costs about ten thousand dollars in the United States. Competes against the Hyundai. That costs about seven thousand dollars. So that's the competition, and I accept that. . . . But if we took a Chrysler K-car and tried to sell it in Korea, they put on nine different taxes and tariffs . . . and when they're done, that K-car that cost ten thousand dollars here would cost *forty-eight thousand* in South Korea. . . .

"So, when I'm President I want to have a meeting with the South Koreans . . . and I'll say two things: first, we'll keep our military commitments, because that's the kind of people we are. We give our word, we keep it. But, second, I'm gonna ask them to take off the taxes and tariffs that *we* don't have on *their* products. And if they *don't,* they're gonna leave that table wondering . . . how many Hyundais are they gonna sell here, for forty-eight thousand dollars a copy!

"They can bring the Mitsubishis, and the Toyotas, and the Mercedes-Benzes, and the Volvos, and the record players, and computers—all of it—I don't mind it. But, *by golly* . . . if they can bring their products here and sell them with *ease,* I want us to be able to take our products there—and sell them with *EQUAL EEEASE*! . . ."

That's what Dick was talking—*equalese!* . . . And now, every time he gave them equalese, the crowd would halt him with cheers.

In a state hit hard by a slump in exports, where so many workers had lost their paychecks, lost their plants, as manufacturing moved overseas, the issue was a good one . . . but, God knows, he'd been drumming Iowa with the Gephardt Amendment for *years,* and it got him . . . six percent.

True, these words were better, as he wasn't talking about his arcane bill, or the unfathomable billions in the national balance of trade. He was talking about two cars (that they knew) and one (unknown) set of menacing Asians . . . and that lent focus, a target for ire. . . . But why would this new *example* turn the tide when, for years, they'd watched their own factories shut down and their neighbors or kin put out of work? Were they confused before about what Gephardt meant?

No, but now he'd become something palpable in their lives. He was on that screen, whence the great world came to them . . . not once, but several times a night: he was a presence, a force, of size, he was . . . bigger than Geraldo!

And just as angry.

And more serious, more important . . . almost (dare one say?) noble . . . because, in the end, he was not on TV for money, or ratings, syndication, selling soap, no . . .

It's Your Fight, Too!

He was . . . for them.

And as TV validated Gephardt—made him larger than life, the size of celebrity (which is like in degree unto personage, or President)—so, then, his appearance in their town, their school, their neighbor's home, or their own freezing barn, validated that enormous presence on TV. It was not just slick hoopla cooked up in Hollywood—or Washington. He was *there* . . . and he said the *same thing* . . . and they heard him, and cheered him, and they were, thereafter, linked to that huge figure on TV.

And the last shining strand of this gossamer pulled straight back through the heart of the web . . . because their cheers (so loud, so many new people!) validated Gephardt in his instinct, his effort, to *be* that man on TV.

And when that happened (it was only a matter of days—Gephardt could just *do* that kind of thing) . . . he *was* huge. He was coming like a freight train.

— ★ —

And he knew it. He called his killers in Washington and told them: "This thing is gonna *happen.* We can *win.*"

That's when Shrum came out to listen to the new stump speech. If something was happening out there, he had to know. The next speech, the next ad, had to build from these new facts on the ground.

So they drove Shrummy out to a one-street town—just a car dealership and a Catholic church, way up north, by the Minnesota line, where the windchill could crack the skin on your face. It was Sunday, they had to wait for people to come from church. And the farmers stood in Sunday-best, in a shed with a concrete floor, while Dick climbed onto a wagon in front, with his own new shiny green seed jacket on, a tractor behind him . . . and he was belting it out:

"*Why shouldn't farmers VOTE on the program?* . . .

"*Why should BIG GRAIN COMPANIES TELL YOU THE PROGRAM?*"

Shrummy tried to listen, but he had nothing on except a nice little corduroy jacket and a fine, white Italian scarf, and he was gingerly dancing on the concrete, where the cold ate through the soles of his Italian shoes, and . . . well, he just couldn't concentrate, with his *feet,* you know . . . while he hugged himself for warmth and hopped on the cement, and he said: "No *wonder* these people are unhappy. S'not economic problems! It's fucking *cold here* . . . there's not one decent piece of architecture, and no decent *restaurants!*"

That was about the time the pack decided it was Shrum who'd created this monster new Gephardt—laid him down on a marble slab and poured in that angry populist juice. . . . *Everybody knew* Shrummy was a genius.

—★—

Had to be *someone,* see . . . because the pack had written Gephardt off—the guy was a stiff! (Of course, they hadn't watched him lately—who's gonna watch a guy at six percent?) Then they'd gone home for Christmas, his ads went up . . . and the first poll they saw when they drag-assed back to freezing Des Moines—the guy was even with Dukakis! (Their darling!)

It was a *trick*—had to be . . . a stratagem . . . which they'd have to ferret out.

Must be the ads—who did the ads?—Doak and Shrum! Those two sly desperadoes must have body-snatched ol' Eagle-Scout-conference-committee-split-the-difference Dick . . . and trotted him out for '88 as a fire-breathing class warrior!

So the big-feet went straight to the source—Doak and Shrum—and what could the boys say? . . . That the Hyundai ad was Trippi's idea? That Gephardt had been saying this same stuff for two years? That, so far, they'd gurued the man to the point where his kids thought he was going to lose, he had promised his wife he'd hang up his spikes, he was facing total political extinction . . . he was fighting like a cornered marmot?

No. Their man was on the move! This was their own shining shot—they'd be in all the books. Not to mention, this was their livelihood. (They'd grown to love those year-end ceremonies where they wrote each other million-dollar checks.)

So they talked about the ads—modestly, becomingly—and they made sure to mention, Dick had input.

And some of the press followed up on that tip, and rode along with Gephardt (he was so happy his herd was growing) . . . and asked:

Who told him to talk so tough?
What happened to Gephardt, the consummate insider?
Wasn't this kind of a transparent ploy? . . .
But Gephardt was no fun. He'd look them in the eye, and say, "No."
He had the gall to insist: he meant what he said!
Of course, they didn't believe that crap for one minute.

— ★ —

He went to dinner with the editors of the *Register*. The maximum boss, Jim Gannon, was host at his house, and he had his editorial chief, Jim Flansberg, and the publisher, a fellow named Charles C. Edwards . . . and their wives all came . . . Gephardt brought Murphy. Gannon had the thing catered—drinks and dessert in the living room.

It was a wonderful talk, a wonderful night. They liked him! Gephardt was *sure.* He'd been in politics twenty years. Surely, he could tell who liked him. Afterward, Dick called Carrick: "I think we really got to them. They caught on . . . even the editors, I think . . . they really listened!"

Yes, they did. The next editorial in the *Register* was entitled: HITTING THE WRONG NOTE.

"Actually, if you listen closely, Gephardt is not as protectionist as his stump rhetoric would indicate, but that's not reassuring. It smacks of demagoguery, which may be his real problem."

That was the same day Gephardt picked up *The Wall Street Journal,* and read: "The farm crisis is over."

Gephardt leapt out of his airplane seat, waving the paper. "Look at this! This is the *problem!* Where do they *get* this stuff?" (Well, the *Journal* had an expert to quote: one James P. Gannon, editor of the *Register.*)

The next day, Gephardt gave a blistering speech—a new phase of the campaign, he called it. He said he meant to refocus the issues: American jobs, the family farm, our children's educations, Social Security, Medicare—they were all in jeopardy . . . and why?

Because the multinational corporations, the grain companies, the oil companies, the bankers, the Wall Street traders . . . all of Reagan's favored friends, were making money hand over fist by selling off America's economic base! And what's worse, the gray-suited savants of the boardrooms—and *editorial boardrooms*—insisted that American workers, farmers, old people, poor people . . . must cut back *their* standard of living . . . to compete!

Dick called this cabal "the Establishment." (That was Shrummy's word.) . . . Of course, the forty-year-old big-feet-in-bud went nuts; they hadn't heard that stupid word since they'd failed to drive ROTC off campus!

Who'd this guy think he was?

Where was *he* in the sixties?

At that point, the well-known poop on Gephardt leaked off the editorial page and onto the front page:

GEPHARDT'S NEW TACTIC—ANGER

It was so *obvious*! . . . Gephardt's rage was just a creation of Doak, Shrum, Carrick, et al. . . . Just as the Eagle Scout, door-to-door Dick was their creation before. . . . In fact—*everybody knew*—Gephardt had been their creation *since the start of the campaign*!

That was the problem: the knowledge of this knowing claque reached back all the way . . . to last February! . . . Shrummy was try'na make this guy sound like Ted Kennedy!

How could they know . . . what "Establishment" actually meant to Dick was "big shots."

The way the big shots have it rigged, the little guy doesn't have a chance!

Dick didn't sound like a Kennedy.

He sounded like Lou Gephardt.

99

Hollywooood!

W HAT DOLE'S PACK couldn't credit: Bob was not mean. The press was always watching, with dread and fascination, for Mount Bobster to blow—never happened. There were a few puffs of smoke, around the turn of the year, when Bill Brock, Campaign Chairman, decided (five weeks before the voting began) that the time was right for his winter Caribbean vacation.

And there was a brief belch of ash when Dole actually *found out* what the Klingons were paying themselves: Skip Watts, for example, who used to be the volunteer chairman in Vermont, but now, in the Brock administration, was the Political Director, at, uh . . . $11,000 *a month*—not to mention the cost of the Washington condo the campaign was renting for him and the weekly airline tix back and forth to Vermont, along with incidentals, like, you know, Skip's dry cleaning. . . . Well, Dole did note that Watts couldn't organize *Vermont.* But he only said that in his car . . . and he never tried to do anything about it. What could he do? . . . He asked Bill Brock for a list of Klingon salaries, but Brock said real talent never came cheap—and he added: "I'm running the campaign." Dole couldn't pick a fight with his Big Guy . . . which would only *prove* Dole could not be *organized* . . . so, he dummied up.

Anyway, Watts was a feeder of mere middling appetite at the trough of Dole consultants. Dole's old pollster, Tully Plesser, was adjudged to be not Big Guy enough, so Dole for President hired on Dick Wirthlin—about fifty grand a month (but, to be fair to Wirthlin, that was only supplement to his ongoing deal with the Republican National Committee, good for 800,000 simoleons per annum). . . . Murphy and Castellanos, the media ops who produced the splendid $30,000 video of the Bob Dole story, clearly were not Big enough . . . so DFP engaged a new guru by the name of Don Ringe, who came *aboard* for the satisfyingly Big Guy sum of $40,000 a month—which was just a retainer, ads would be extra . . . which was no threat, as Dole observed: Ringe did not produce any ads.

But Dole only said that in the car.

He really had handed it over. . . . Of course, the press pack didn't believe *that* for a minute. *Everybody knew,* Dole was just trying to act Presidential.

The pack could not accept his excitement, all the good feeling he brought to his events—had to be a tactic, right? They were sure Dole was hiding his Karacter (everybody knew he was a bitter hatchet man) . . . so, uh, he was trying to *act* upbeat . . . right?

Well, it was a hell of an act! He looked, for all the world, like a man who thought he was going to be President. People were telling him, he was going to be President. They were asking him questions they would ask a President.

In New Hampshire, one afternoon that January, Dole cut away from his press herd to do a sit-down with the editors and bosses of *The Portsmouth Herald*. It was a conference-table affair, most cordial.

One of the news pooh-bahs said he'd seen Elizabeth on a recent stop. "She was terrific, really good. Made everybody feel real comfortable."

Dole's comment was entirely candid: "She's a very disciplined person."

Dole said he'd be in New Hampshire often, with Congress adjourned. "You know, I've seen six or seven Presidents, and they're never happier than when Congress is out." Right away, the room eased with knowing male chuckles. Dole said: "One of 'em told me, it's like being *born again* when Congress leaves town."

Dole was going to take these guys for a quick tour through the cloakroom, the insider world of verbal nudge and wink. Within ten minutes, he was in *deep* cloakroom, telling a story—him and the President, arguing the INF. "So I told the President, I said, 'You know, you got Cranston and all these liberals for your treaty now—but what happens when you want more for conventional weapons? They're going to vote no, and then we're really in the soup! You know, you got Jim Wright already talking about a *peace windfall!*' " One Dole eyebrow descended in eloquent disapproval. "There isn't going to be any *windfall*. Conventional arms cost more than nuclear."

Robert J. Dole, Commander in Chief, was not going to let Speaker Wright *touch* the Pentagon—that much was clear.

It was also clear, these spellbound editors thought they were sitting with a winner. The general manager, Azio Ferrini, asked Dole: "How do you feel about just the enormity of the responsibility?"

Dole leaned back in his chair: "Well, you gotta use your Cabinet more. You gotta find some good people, gotta know everything . . ."

When it was over, Dole stayed behind for a minute or two, to say goodbye. When he got to the car, he was almost skipping. He said to Mari Maseng: "I don't know if he's going to endorse me, but he's *for* me! He's *FOR* me—says I'm going to win!'"

The driver, a local, said: "Then he'll probably endorse you."

Dole was still talking: ". . . Says Bush is soft! Says what we got is an *appointee* against a professional politician!" Dole's eyebrows were dancing. "I said, 'Well, I never put it exactly like that, but . . .'

"Well. Let's goooo!"

— ★ —

Dole was trying not to get too excited. He said that was one thing he learned from Ronald Reagan (maybe the only thing): the Gip never seemed to get too up, or too down—he was always just a little optimistic. Dole thought that was a good way to be.

Good way, maybe, for someone else.

Dole might as well resolve to be Sudanese.

The fact was, Dole couldn't act, at all—couldn't act like he didn't care (when he did), couldn't act like he might just have a chance (when he was winning), or act like criticism rolled off his back (when, clearly, it was aimed *at his throat*) . . . Dole couldn't act like he was having a fine time, playing the game—no matter how often Mari, at his elbow, hissed: "Senator, smile!"

This was no game. For one thing, he couldn't afford to lose. "You know, I'm not running again," he said, on one midnight flight back from Iowa. "Sometimes you have to lose, and it makes you stronger. You can come back. But I'm not running again. This is my time."

It was even more than that:

For the first time, he felt he *ought* to win. Who was going to row the country out of this sea of red ink? The Democrats? (Steering the wrong way!) . . . George Bush? (Who'd do the paddling for him?) . . . Dole saw only one man tough enough. For the first time, in his mind, he was The One.

And the most delicious fact in his grip: he could do it!

Not just the election—though his standing was on the rise everywhere ("I was in Texas and Alabama and Mississippi yesterday, and it's *happening!*")—he could change the direction of the country, thereafter.

It didn't even look that hard to him. He knew the job . . . and he knew what people could take. Sometimes, when voters asked about the deficit crisis—What had to be cut?—Dole would break off his answer with a shrug: "Come *on!*" he'd say. "This is America! Nobody's gonna hurt that bad."

To Dole, it boiled down to a matter of will, and the glorious fact was, that's what he brought to the job. He'd read enough history to know how they talked about the times calling forth a single man. . . . No one from Russell, Kansas, would talk aloud in terms that grand, but . . . Gagghh! Kinda looked like it was working out!

He had to stop at another newspaper—*Foster's Daily Democrat*—he went to toodle the editorial board . . . meanwhile, the crew from *Tanner '88* would be waiting at the door. They were shooting a cable TV series about a fictional

Presidential campaign, starring the mild and charming Michael Murphy as the mild and charming candidate—a fictive Democrat—Jack Tanner. Dole was supposed to help out with a cameo.

While Murphy waited for Dole's meeting to end, he talked about how easy it was to work with real candidates. He thought that running for President must be a lot like acting. (The one who surprised him, he said, was Gary Hart. "He just—the elevator doors opened and there he was, with just one guy, frail, alone. . . . You know, suddenly, I *believed* he had to push that girl off his lap.")

When Dole came downstairs, he barely broke stride, just paused on the sidewalk with Tanner. The cameras rolled.

"Hi. Jack Tanner."

"How ya *runnin'*?"

"Good, good . . ."

"You're closin' the gap!" Dole said.

"Well, not like you! I'm envious," said Tanner.

Dole dropped an eyebrow, flashed a hint of smile, and said: "We're workin' on it!"

Dole was flawless. "O-kayy . . . good luck!"

Of course, he wasn't acting. He was being Bob Dole . . . as he was, just out of camera frame, at the door of his car, when he uttered into the winter air this prairie haiku:

"Agh! Hollywooood! . . . Let's go! . . . The big moneyyy!"

—★—

Dole had no fear of cameras—nor of the herd: he knew how to make news, and he was surely the only candidate to admit he would listen to the press. (When voters asked how Dole would avoid the fog that suffused the White House in Iran-contra, Dole's first remedy was press conferences. "They'll tell you if you're missing something.")

So, of course, he was offended when the press kept asking about his money— his income, taxes, net worth. He knew the stuff came from Bush. (It came, precisely, from the Bushies in Iowa, who were panicky now, trying to prove Bob Dole was *not* "One of Us.") That made sense—Bush was losing. Bush had nothing to say for himself, so he was trying to knock down the Bob Dole story. Okay . . . but Dole could not believe *the press* was going to help! They were trying to make Dole admit . . . he was rich!

Well, it was gonna be a cold day in hell—Dole had just got so he could talk about being poor!

And what did it matter, anyway, if Bob Dole, at age sixty-four, had a million dollars, or a couple of million? The point was *not* where people ended up—it was where they started.

If he had a few dollars now, well, uh, well . . . *he worked for it.* He made it the *hard way*! He, he . . .

He married it.

But he wasn't going to say *that*.

In fact, he wasn't going to talk about that money.

In 1974, when he had to make his first disclosure, Dole's fortune was $30,000, in a cash account, in a bank in Russell. . . . That changed the next year, when he married Elizabeth Hanford. But that didn't mean Bob *did* anything with that money . . . or even knew much about it. In fact, Elizabeth didn't know much. When she asked Dave Owen, Bob's money man, if he'd help with her finances, she brought a shopping bag to the office. She was in a meeting when Owen picked it up: he was on his way out of town, and he took it with him, on and off airplanes for a few days. When he got a chance to poke through the bag, he was horrified to find *bonds,* bank statements, old receipts, *savings certificates,* check stubs, *insurance policies,* credit card reminders, *stock certificates* . . . everything jumbled in a heap that was worth . . . well, to put it simply, Elizabeth had two million in a shopping bag. She wanted Dave to take care of it.

So, he did. Elizabeth signed over a power of attorney, and Owen became her personal investment adviser . . . until 1985, when the Doles (by that time, Senator and Secretary, the capital's pet power couple) set up Elizabeth's blind trust. The trustee was to be Mark McConaghy, Dole's old staffer on the Finance Committee who now worked for Price Waterhouse. Of course, McConaghy was a policy wonk, not a businessman, so he brought in Dave Owen as investment adviser.

Anyway, Dole never seemed to notice that he lived like a millionaire: cars waiting, airplanes, staff. It seemed to him an extension of his Senate stature. He wasn't rich—he just had work to do! As for *money* . . . well, Dole didn't think about the money. *He* had nothing to do with that money!

Alas, he did, of course.

He didn't just have his apartment anymore, and his parents' old house in Russell: he had a condo in a Florida white men's preserve. Well, legally, Elizabeth had the condo—but that nicety didn't stop *The New York Times* from turning its "candidate profile" into a heavy-breathing investigation of how the Doles did the condo deal. (In the end, the *Times* couldn't pin down anything improper.)

Dole couldn't content himself anymore with writing the occasional shy and secret thousand-dollar check to some charity, or some down-and-outer, like he used to whenever he felt the urge, to help people (usually disabled people) get back on their feet. Now he had the Dole Foundation, which was another million-dollar affair, with its own intricate and legalistic exigencies.

Dole could not issue anymore a one-page Senate disclosure, listing his salary and maybe some speaking fees. . . . Now he was earning another forty thousand a year from his *Face-Off* radio shows with Ted Kennedy; he had investments— and possible conflicts of interest with industries affected by legislation in the Senate; and then, too, there was income from Elizabeth's trust, part of which had to be reported jointly, and . . .

Alas, inconvenient as it was, Dole was rich.

And what was *worse:* after Bush started *pointing out* that Dole was rich, the newspaper in Hutchinson, Kansas (Dole's old nemesis—"the Prairie Pravda," he called it), suddenly found itself in possession of a stack of information about investments made and contributions passed along by Dole's friend, Dave Owen. (Jeez—wonder where *that* stuff could have come from!)

So *The Hutchinson News* launched its own investigation, to suggest that Owen was making *a dirty fortune* . . . wielding *Dole's political influence* . . . to steer *federal contracts* . . . to *friends* who would *contribute* . . . both to Owen's favored *political campaigns*—and to the engorgement of the *Elizabeth Hanford Dole Trust.*

Phew!

Well, it was complicated—all of Owen's business was too complicated by half . . . and by the time the *Times* went to work again, reporting the stuff reported by *The Hutchinson News,* it didn't just look intricate—it looked *awful.*

It looked—it *smelled*—to the pack on Dole's plane like . . . bad fish!

So, in New Hampshire, Dole conducted a bang-up event in a packed pancake house: Elizabeth introduced him with the Bob Dole story, then Bob came on with a charming appeal to *open up the Party* . . . to let the government respond to people's *real problems* . . . and to *preserve the opportunity,* which was America's hallmark and her gift to the planet . . . and, amid a standing ovation, Bob made for the door, where the press was waiting.

Senator! What's your net worth, jointly, with Elizabeth?

"Beats me."

WhatchurestimateSenatoryoumustknowabouthowmuchYOURNETWORTH?

Dole stopped and faced his accusers. "I'm the candidate," he said. "My net worth is very little. But I don't have any idea."

Are you a millionaire?

"Me? I doubt it. I own an apartment and a car, and I don't know how much money is in the bank, but . . . I guess very little."

Don't the voters deserve to know?

"They'll find out. They know. I publish it every year, so it's no secret."

Will you release your income tax returns?

"I don't know. I'm not going to let *him* set the timetable. . . ."

(He didn't have to say he was talking about Bush. It was Bush who demanded that Dole release his tax returns.)

"This has got nothing to do with my background! . . ." In the shadowed entryway of the restaurant, Dole's face was getting darker. This was what he got for taking questions.

". . . I can't understand why the press would swallow this in the first place! Obviously, this is a diversionary tactic. And some of the press bought it. They like to poke around! Every year, I put my disclosure in the *Record*—everything, including joint . . . which makes me look rich. My little holdings, I think, will be made available, but that's not the point. The point is, where did we start in this life? I know where I started, and I know where

I got—where I am. Just because I've been somewhat successful is, I think, sort of the American dream! . . .

"Nobody gave it to me. I didn't have rich and powerful parents! . . . I don't really have much. . . . I've given about half a million to charity over the last several years. I'd like to see the Bushes match that."

There was a question about how voters might regard this pissing match between Bush and Dole.

"We didn't start it! We want to talk about the issues and leadership. Others don't want us to talk about that. I'm not going to stop talking about that—I'm a strong leader, that I've got more done, that I've got a *record*—if I stop all that because someone doesn't like it, then I don't have a campaign. And I think it's working! When you say, 'Vote for Bob Dole, because he's One of Us,' that hits a tender spot—I can't help it. I am what I am. And I was what I was when I was growing up. And a lot of people out there identify with that."

Dole walked out into the sunshine. He'd stated his case.

Of course, on the news that night, there was no sunshine—and none of Dole's pancake-house speech—just a dark hallway, a scowling hatchet man, bragging about his half-million to charity:

"I'd like to see the *Bushes* match that!"

— ★ —

It went on for days, everywhere Dole stopped: less than a month now until the voting began, and the only questions Dole heard were about his money.

The Bush campaign was challenging Dole to release *five years* of his tax returns. So the pack asked Dole: Would he release five years of tax returns? The Bushies were distributing hot poop from *The Hutchinson News.* Reporters asked Dole about the poop from the *News.*

Sometimes, Dole's answers were plaintive ("You know, we're running for *President of the United States*—and someone's going to win! Let's be serious!") . . . and sometimes, blustery ("Gaghh! You swallowed that story from Bush?") . . . but nothing seemed to satisfy. To Dole, it was apparent: they thought he was going to *win* . . . they were trying to *take it away* . . . they were coming *at his throat* . . . and the knife in their hands was Dave Owen.

Always, always, there were more complicated questions about Owen and his real estate deals, his banks, corporations, partnerships, loans from the Dole trust, sales of property to the Dole trust. . . . *Senator, were you aware that the Dole trust had purchased the office building in Overland Park, which is listed as the address of the E.D.P. and Eagle partnerships, through which Dave Owen participated, with your former aide John Palmer, in supplying food service to the Army at Fort Leonard Wood?*

Dole's Senate Press Secretary, Walt Riker, tried to calm the waters ten times a day, pointing out that Dole knew nothing about the deals for the trust: "You know, that's why they call it a blind trust."

From Kansas, Dave Owen issued blanket denials of wrongdoing—specific denials wherever he could get a hearing. He got the Kansas City *Star* to knock down one charge—that he'd formed shell corporations just to make contributions to campaigns—but that's because he knew the reporters in Kansas City. What about the other hundred and fifty newspapers, all trying to penetrate his business?

Owen talked to the editor in Hutchinson—knew him from years back, in Topeka—but the fellow said he couldn't interfere with a news investigation. Owen called Kim Wells because Kim's father was on the board of the company that owned the paper; but Kim, of course, couldn't get the stories squelched. Owen called to assure Dole's Big Guys that there was nothing to these stories, but the Big Guys were busy assuring the national big-feet (just on background, understand) that Owen never did much for Dole's campaign, he was just a hanger-on, despite his title of Finance Chairman (just the kind of guy they were trying to *clean out* of the campaign; they'd warned Dole about him, but, uh . . . don't use my name, huh?) and somehow they couldn't find time to call Owen back. Owen was supposed to meet Dole in Miami and travel with him back to the Midwest, but what with trying to answer the charges (*The Washington Post* wanted full explanation—*now!*), Owen was pinned down, so he sent word to Dole, in Springfield, Missouri, that there was nothing to this brouhaha—nothing wrong—but when Dave called the plane, he only got the body man, Glassner, who neglected to mention where Dole was going to stay that night, so Owen never did talk to Dole. He did talk once to Mari, who said Dole wasn't in a good mood . . . but after that, Mari didn't return Dave's calls. So Owen called Kim Wells again, and Kim said he'd talk to Dole . . . but somehow Owen never heard from Wells.

Somehow (maybe when the Minicams staked out his office) . . . Owen got the feeling he was being nudged off the back of the sleigh. . . . *Bill Brock* bestirred himself to call and suggest: "Dave, I think we've got a *problem.* I think this is just unfortunate, but, ahmm . . . maybe you need to cease doing anything for the campaign."

At that point, Owen *had* to talk to Dole . . . but he could never get through. True to form, Elizabeth called instead. But Elizabeth just asked about Dave's family, and told him this would all work out—the cool Christian sympathy of the hospital hallway.

That's when Owen got the message: he stopped trying to call Dole . . . and he scheduled a press conference to announce he was leaving the campaign.

Dole was busy, arranging for the Office of Government Ethics to give *him* a clean bill of health—Elizabeth, too—and preemptively announce that. ("There is no indication," said the deputy director, "that the Doles did anything improper.") Of course, the Ethics office couldn't say the same for Owen—not without a proper investigation!—wouldn't say a thing for Owen.

Nor would Dole.

On the afternoon of Owen's *auto-da-fé,* Dole did conduct a quick interview with Angelia Herrin of the *Wichita Eagle-Beacon.* Angelia told Dole of Owen's announcement—he was stepping down from the campaign until these questions were resolved.

"WHAT?" Dole barked. "No! *No!* . . . I want it resolved. I want it *final.* His role has *ended!*"

There was silence in the car. They were riding through northern Iowa, in the half-light of a scarlet sunset. Angelia asked, gingerly:

"How do you feel?"

Dole stared at the angry red horizon . . . then he wheeled from the window. "How would *you* feel?"

He'd *asked* Elizabeth, the minute she got into that deal with Owen. "What're we paying *him* for?" Owen was making a *career* out of the Doles! Doing deals! Guy's become a millionaire! Dole never wanted that. . . . And too cute: you look in that trust, it's not IBM stock—you pick up a rock, you see *worms* underneath.

"How would anyone feel? *Nobody* has the right . . ."

When they got to Dole's next stop, there were thirty more reporters who wanted to know: Would Owen's departure put an end to Dole's problem?

"I don't *have* any problem," Dole snapped.

"Maybe Dave Owen's got a problem. I don't."

— ★ —

Dole was correct about that.

From that day, Dave Owen would face three and a half years of investigation from the Office of Ethics, the Securities and Exchange Commission, the FBI (in service of a U.S. Attorney in Missouri), a committee of the U.S. House of Representatives, the Federal Election Commission, the Kansas Public Disclosure Commission, and the Kansas Attorney General. Owen's legal fees would eat up several hundred thousand dollars, his business opportunities would shrivel, he'd be shunned by former friends, his daughters would be scorned, his wife wouldn't know if *she* should believe him, she would have to take a job as a secretary, Owen would spend his time playing golf—so he wouldn't stay in bed all day. He owned a gun, and he surprised himself by thinking of suicide. . . . In the end, he would plead guilty to one Class C misdemeanor in the state election law—the moral equivalent of parking in front of a hydrant.

In the end, he would never hear another word from Bob Dole.

Dole was correct about *his* situation, too.

From the day that Bob Dole cut off Dave Owen, Dole would no longer have a problem. He handed out *twenty years* of tax returns . . . and nobody cared. The story of his money all but disappeared. In fact, from the moment Dave Owen was kicked off the sleigh, Dole was immediately and richly applauded. The big-feet, the smart guys, and everyone they talked to, approved.

Finally!

Finally, they said, Dole had learned to act . . . like a President.

100

President
Dick

ALL OF GEPHARDT'S killers flew out to Des Moines before the big *Register* debate, January 15. They were primed and ready for a good twitchy wrangle on the message, the strategy, the electoral imperatives in the last Democratic face-off before the caucus.

Of course, Dick had been through thirty debates . . . but this was the big one for Iowa—three weeks before the vote. This could be the ball game. Not to mention, it was national TV, and the country would be watching for its first look at Hart-risen. . . . How should they handle Hart? What if Hart came at Dick?

They gathered in the party room at Loreen's apartment building. They had most of two days blocked out on Dick's schedule. They wanted to mount a mock debate; they'd videotape, critique the tapes. They wanted to rehearse his answers. The other candidates knew Gephardt was surging: there were bound to be attacks on his trade bill, his farm bill . . . his campaign, his *character*! . . . They had to have a game plan!

But Dick already had a game plan. They might have been thinking about the message, but Gephardt had been doing it—eight times a day. He was on that weird white tractor beam that brushed away everything in his path. He was saying what he meant to say, more clearly than he ever had. What did he need them for?

"Okay, what about the deficit figure?" Doak began. (The trade deficit had diminished—bad news for Gephardt's campaign.) "What're we gonna say?"

But before Shrummy or another maestro could start, Dick said: "Look, it's not numbers. It's people. It's American jobs. It's American workers and their families . . . that's all I haveta say."

"Uh, okay . . . well, what're we gonna say if Duke says your ag bill will raise food prices?"

Dick said, calmly: "Mike . . . you know how much you pay for a boxa Wheaties? Buck and a half? Two bucks? . . . You know how much goes to the farmer for that wheat? A penny and a half? Two cents? Four cents? . . . If that price goes up two cents, you think that's gonna hurt the American public? But that two cents makes all the difference to the family farmers of America. Why shouldn't their labor earn them a living?"

They ran through three or four more questions—just the toughest, the ones they'd been stewing over in Washington. And every time, Dick would answer—boom—it was over. After twenty minutes, Shrum said: "I move that we end debate-prep . . . unless Dick's got any questions . . ."

They looked to Gephardt.

"Yeah," he said, and his eyes fell upon Trippi. "Joe—find out: How much is the wheat in a boxa Wheaties?"

— ★ —

Trippi was exultant. "Tonight," he announced, before the debate, "you're going to see a President of the United States."

President Dick!

"He's unbelievable. We didn't even prep. He's absolutely calm, absolutely certain. It's scary . . . he's Mr. President!"

Trippi had a highly developed theory on what a President was—though, alas, he'd never been able to make one. He started working Iowa for Kennedy in '80 . . . but Kennedy couldn't knock off Jimmy Carter. In '84, Trippi was in Iowa as the deputy maestro for Walter Mondale, who swept the state . . . though, again, Mondale fell short in the end.

That's why Gephardt had his eye on Joe—Trippi knew Iowa . . . Gephardt had to have Iowa. He started calling Trippi back in '86—August '86, the day Joe's daughter was born. Trippi was a half-hour out of the delivery room when the phone rang:

"Joe? This is Dick Gephardt . . . I just heard about the blessed event, and, uh, I just want you to know, I think it's great!"

Christmas that year, Gephardt tracked down Trippi at his in-laws. Dick was trying to decide whether to dump Murphy in favor of Carrick. Trippi told him: "Dick, you may have a problem . . . I just want you to know, Murphy has told twenty people that he has your personal assurance . . ."

Within days, Gephardt had dumped Murphy. That's when Trippi thought Dick might be a President.

"See," Trippi said, "he might have *had* to make that decision. That's what I mean, being ready to be President . . . it's too important for personal loyalties.

"That kind of decision—like cutting off a Pat Caddell . . . Joe Biden will not have a problem making that kind of decision anymore.

"That's what we demand in a President."

But Trippi did not go to work for Gephardt—not right away. He went to Denver, to work for Gary Hart.

"That was a man," Trippi said, "who was ready to be President. He showed straight determination . . . even after the bomb hit. That day when he had the press conference in New Hampshire—a hundred fifty *banshees* in that room, just trying . . . to take . . . him . . . *down*.

"It wasn't once he was asked about adultery. They must've asked eight different ways. Joe Biden would've fallen apart. Anybody would have. But Hart stood there like a *rock*. He would not leave until there wasn't anything left to ask. He took every bit of shit they could throw, and he handled it. He did . . . whatever it took.

"That's a President."

So why wasn't Trippi busy prepping Hart for the big *Register* debate?

"No, that's what I mean," Trippi said. "There's this horrible logic to the process. The next day, when Hart decided to go home, when he decided he couldn't put his family through it, or the women who were gonna be named, or whoever . . . when he put anything else before this . . . then he wasn't ready to be President."

101

Time's Up!

H ART DIDN'T DO debate prep. He
didn't have briefing books. (Who'd
write them?) He had no Washing-
ton smart guys to act out parts in a practice. He had no opposition research—
he didn't want any. It wasn't the polls—he was still on top of the national polls.
(His was the only name voters recognized among the Democrats.) Even Hart
didn't quite believe those polls. It was just . . . he was so sure he was miles
ahead of those poor saps:

Gephardt—he's for American workers and farmers. *Who's against them?*
Or Simon—"We caaarrrre!" *Who cares? What are you going to DO?*

That's why this debate, January 15, was Hart's great chance: he knew what
he wanted to do. He was preparing his own fiscal '90 federal budget—a
blueprint for taxes and spending, so people could *see* what he would do. Hart
had printed a campaign booklet, his sole piece of literature—ninety-four pages,
cheap paper, solid type. (Hart was fond of saying, as he waved this chunky
volume at his crowds: "My brochure is not three or four glossy folds, like other
people's; it's printed in one color, black-and-white; there are no pictures of my
family here, or of our dog, MacArthur.")

This debate would offer his one chance to wave those positions at all the
voters of Iowa . . . and the *nation:* this was coast-to-coast TV, all the big-feet
were in Des Moines for the night; the networks had bought out whole floors
of hotels, there were satellite trucks from thirty cities—the plaza in front of
the Civic Center was *hidden* by satellite trucks, side-by-side, nose-to-tail, like
buffalo on the prairie, before the white hunter showed up with his gun.

Free media, the Priests of the Process called it.

For Hart, it was manna.

— ★ —

He wasn't even supposed to be in Iowa . . . probably wouldn't have competed, without this debate to lure him. The Iowa caucus rewarded organization— Hart had none. What's more, this wasn't like a primary—the flick of a finger in some booth, behind a curtain, in privacy, anonymity. . . . No, each caucus voter had to show up (and stay for hours) on a Monday night . . . to publicly name his candidate of choice . . . and then *defend his vote to his neighbors.*

Hart's was a candidacy that presented a voter with problems. And while there were thousands of Iowa voters (and maybe millions in the nation) who could resolve, or ignore, those problems for themselves . . . it was quite another matter to have to explain. Could you tell your neighbors (say, your wife's friends from church) that you really didn't give a damn if Gary cheated on Lee?

Hart was aware of this problem. He could read a poll as well as any pol, and "negatives" of forty-some percent were not negligible. Somehow, he had to make a vote for Hart *simpler.* He had to put the questions to rest. He had to give his supporters something to say, something clear, direct, of overriding moment. It would help, of course, if they could talk about his issues. But no one was writing about Hart's issues. They wrote about *Hart*—psycho-investigations.

Richard Cohen, the columnist for *The Washington Post,* wrote about Hart's apology for his "mistake" with Donna Rice . . . the very *word* revealed Hart's character, or lack. "By characterizing the Donna Rice episode as a 'mistake,' Hart shows that we have learned more about him than he has about himself. He persists in his Presidential race as if behavioral patterns were slips of the tongue or blunders made at the end of a long and tiring day. They are nothing of the sort. What he calls 'a mistake' is representative of who Gary Hart is. His real mistake is not realizing that."

Ellen Goodman, the columnist for *The Boston Globe,* examined the "talisman" and "key" to Hart's campaign—Lee Hart. "Why does she do it? Why does she shake hands every day with people who are often uncomfortable in her presence, people who shared her public humiliation, who see mental images of Donna Rice on her husband's lap when she comes into a New Hampshire hall? What makes Lee run?"

The Leader of the Pack, David Broder, weighed in with a stunning reexamination of Hart's campaign debt. "The problem is," Broder wrote, "that as long as voters have known Hart, and for years before that, he has exhibited a pattern of 'walking away.' He left behind in Kansas the family's name and church affiliation. He left divinity school for law school. He left his marriage twice and twice returned. He left the Senate to seek the Presidency. And he left the Presidential campaign, only to return to it again."

Broder noted with a sniff that Hart talked "constantly" about issues. "But he answers only rarely and reluctantly the questions that go to his consistency and his character.

"He leaves it to the voters to judge whether all that is past—or whether he is, once again, just walking away from himself."

When Hart came to Iowa, he didn't know about Broder's psycho-insight. The column hadn't appeared. But, clearly, copies were available to subscriber papers. Hart had a crucial meeting with editors and reporters for *The Des Moines Register*—he had to put to rest as many questions as he could . . . and one woman at the table kept asking:

"Aren't you just walking away?"

Hart didn't know what she was talking about.

Well, uh . . . your marriage—for one thing?

Wait a minute! Gary and Lee had problems, but they stuck it out—twenty-nine years! Ronald Reagan walked away. That's called divorce.

Yeah, well . . . Hart could not deny that he walked away from his campaign, in May.

And Hart, without awareness of Broder's epiphany, had not the information—or the bad grace—to suggest that he didn't "walk away." Broder's newspaper hounded him away!

Hart did discuss what the *Register* called his "personal failings." Broder's certainties notwithstanding, Hart invited all the character questions they could muster. He called himself an adulterer (and said he wouldn't be the first in the White House). He said that in May, "I let myself down, I let my family down, I let my supporters down." He admitted that he hadn't been able to pay all his '84 debts (but pleaded for fairness—at least acknowledgment that his problem was not unique).

At that point, Lee Hart joined the rumble in Gary's defense—reminded the *Register* pooh-bahs that Gary had run McGovern's campaign and two Senate campaigns without one dollar of debt; she talked about all the work Gary did to whittle that '84 debt from four million to one; she talked about the nights he'd spent away from home, to raise money, how the family hated that, but they understood, duty came first . . . how everyone in the family understood, now, that they'd let themselves in for a cudgeling—but that *did not matter,* compared to the nation's future; she told them about the letter from the parents who were going to buy a crib, but sent the money to Gary instead . . . then, Lee started to cry. And Gary was thinking, as Lee spoke—how could they say he always "walked away" . . . when the easiest thing in the world would have been, simply, to walk away? But *he could not*—he thought of his kids, their faith . . . and Gary started to cry.

The next day, of course, there was a front-page picture of Hart in tears . . . as he talked about "his failings" . . . and it went *so perfectly* with the Broder column. . . . In sum, Hart had answered questions for an hour and a half, and it didn't make anything simpler.

—★—

There was a rule for this debate—no more than six cars in the motorcade that brought each candidate to the hall. That was five cars more than Hart required. He got the biggest dressing room. (Rooms were awarded in order of standing in the Iowa Poll.) But Hart had no use for the extra space. Lee and Sue Casey sat in the dressing room. Hart and Billy Shore made for the stage.

Hart brought a copy of his campaign booklet. He had it rolled into a cylinder, which he carried in his right hand like a sceptre of office. At last, his rivals would have to face him *on the issues* . . . they would have to discuss the *future of the nation, and the planet* . . . while the voters watched. And Hart, at last, would have a chance to show why he was still ahead where it mattered, though his campaign was without money, media, pollsters, staff . . .

It was strange without staff—inconvenient, tiring . . . but it was easier to stay clear, on the things that mattered. Big ideas did not come from staff.

That was Hart's strategy, as far as it went—big ideas. He knew the other candidates would try to nickel-and-dime him with detail. It was Hart's job to show that niggling would not suffice. "That's not the issue," he would say. "There are broader questions that have to be addressed . . ." Hart would have to haul the discussion up to the level where a President must operate. He would steer the talk to foreign affairs—that was his strong suit, a weakness for the rest. He knew he would have to be forceful. But he was ready, confident . . . cocky, more like it.

Backstage, the candidates held last-minute huddles. Billy Shore whispered to Hart: every one of those staffers had worked for Gary. They were all his people! . . . Hart nodded, lips pursed. He'd insisted they must move on . . . now he felt they'd abandoned him.

Well, he would show, the issues were his, still. . . . He took his seat on stage, between Dukakis and Jackson.

First question, from the editor of the *Register,* Jim Gannon:

Last week, in his interview, Hart said he wouldn't be the first adulterer in the White House. . . . Did that mean voters should just ignore questions of character and trust?

Before Gannon finished, Hart's head was twitching—probably meant to be a nod. He looked grim as he tried to respond. "I've made mistakes. I probably should have said in that interview that I'm a sinner. My religion tells me, all of us are sinners. I think the question is whether our sins prohibit us, or prevent us, from providing strong leadership. . . .

"I think there's another level of morality at stake here, and that's the morality of an administration which is really bankrupt in terms of its commitment to public ethics. . . .

"I would never lie to the Congress or the American people. . . . I would never shred documents. I would never sell arms to terrorists. And I would never condone anyone in my administration who breached the highest standard of the sacred trust of the public duty."

As Hart concluded, there was only a scatter of applause from the crowd. Hart settled back into his seat, trying to look unconcerned, trying not to stick out. . . . And that was the problem. After Gannon finished with him, Hart didn't look oversized, at all.

—★—

The awful part was, Hart knew what he had to do. And he knew—probably better than anyone there—what a President had to do. He had the same ideas and proposals that had attracted such praise eight months before . . . in fact, now they were better refined, they fit together like a Lego set. He'd been thinking hard, for eight months.

What he hadn't been doing was debating every week, or twice a week, like the rest of those fellows. Once Hart got himself together after Gannon's question, he had still to get up to speed on the picky stuff. It'd been a long time since he'd formed his two sentences on rural telephone policy or Medicaid extension for catastrophic care.

So he'd take a second or two to think about his answers, then he'd say his piece—he did nicely—and then he was supposed to say: *But the broader issue that has to be addressed is . . .*

Meanwhile, the yellow light would flash on, which meant he had ten seconds. It happened three times in a row. . . . Hart would settle back again. *. . . Well, I missed that question.*

Second and third time, he started to remind himself *he wasn't doing what he had to do!* . . . He started pressing himself to be faster, more forceful . . . he couldn't take time to consider an answer. Then he couldn't clean the question with a couple of sentences. He had to add another . . . and then—time's up! . . . Dukakis and Simon had to ask him questions, and they both pinned him with detail on health-care costs—same stupid question! What about America's place in the world? Her promise to a new generation of citizens? . . . Hart's cheeks were showing an unhealthy flush—he looked too pink, hot, as he edged forward on his chair, and his hand jerked up a couple of times, like he wanted to break into the discussion . . . but he couldn't—he just . . . didn't have the moves.

By the end, Hart's mien was grim . . . as Jesse Jackson reached over and touched Gary's arm, whispered to him—consolation . . . everybody could see.

And when everybody stood for pictures, then walked off the stage, Hart was shaking his head, looking down. He didn't want anyone to tell him he'd done fine—he knew he hadn't done *anything*. . . . Lee was in the holding room, and she was saying—No! It really went fine! . . . But Shore and Casey were silent, trying to keep disappointment from their faces—little smiles.

Hey, it's just . . . no big deal.

—★—

Of course, it was a big deal, as the spin doctors insisted, in the pressroom gang-bangs after the debate. Hart didn't have any spinners. He went to dinner.

"Big loser's Hart . . ." breathed Simon's Iowa Campaign Manager.

"He didn't do anything," said one of Gephardt's road crew.

"Six guys tied and one guy lost," said Dave Nagle, an Iowa Rep who cast himself as neutral. "The candidate of New Ideas might have shared just one of them tonight."

That comment took prominent place in *The Washington Post* analysis, next day, under the headline:

HART FAILS TO DOMINATE IOWA DEBATE

Hart, meanwhile, had moved on to Kansas—Ottawa, to be precise—where he once again returned to his roots, and made a speech to a Chamber of Commerce dinner, to reveal for the first time his federal budget.

This was a document that would reorder the entire federal government: it covered every subject—defense, space and technology, agriculture, energy, natural resources and environment, infrastructure, housing, education, health, welfare reform. . . . Hart would propose major new investments ($67 billion over five years) in research and development, new technologies, education, retraining, and social services. He would cut several defense programs (which he named) to save $45 billion, rebase Medicare payments to hospitals (to save another $28 billion); he would retain the thirty-three percent income-tax bracket for the highest earners (which would bring in $57 billion); he would tax capital gains at death (which would bring another $22 billion); he would tax Social Security payments for families with incomes over thirty-two thousand dollars a year (which would yield another $21 billion); and he would institute or increase taxes on major polluters, on imported oil, on cigarettes and liquor (which would yield another $150 billion, over five years) . . . and with those new sources of revenue, Hart's budget projected a deficit of $41.5 billion, instead of the $150 billion predicted by the feds for fiscal '93 (which would actually turn out to be more than $300 billion), which meant a savings on federal interest payments of at least $66 billion, all of which would be available for investment in the economy.

Hart, in other words, proposed a plan for the nation. But it didn't get much coverage. Hey, the big-feet had *been* to Ottawa with Hart—last year! Why go back?

Anyway, after that debate, everybody knew: Hart didn't have New Ideas—not really. Hart had nothing to say.

Thermonuclear

HE'D SAID all he had to say on that subject—answered the questions *a million times* . . . Jeezus! What did they want?

They wanted an answer on Iran-contra: What did Bush know . . . and when did he know it?

For more than a year, ever since late '86, Bush had been holding the line:
I did what I did . . .
I told the President what I told the President . . .
And honor forbids me to say more.

Bush had said that so many times, he was frustrated. He thought he had answered *every conceivable nuance.* Of course, he never actually said anything.

But once he'd made his point . . . well, anyone who insisted on bringing it up was just *rehashing* . . . try'na make him *look bad.* They were, you know, acting like bullies. And the old school code treats a bully with . . . contempt.

That's why he couldn't believe—wouldn't hear it!—when his white men warned that Dan Rather was going to jump him. . . . "No," said the Veep. "Dan's a friend." (He'd known Rather since Texas—Dan was just a local newsman, Bush was in the oil bidness . . . Jeez, it'd been more than twenty years!)

But Fuller got tipped off that CBS News was trying to make the scandal *stick* to Bush. Teeter got tipped off. Teeley called a friend to confirm. Ailes said he knew *exactly* what those shitheads were planning. Atwater said he could *feel* they were up to no good. . . . *Everybody knew*—or said they knew—except Bush, who insisted to Fuller, in New Hampshire:

"Dan's been over to the house . . ." (They played tennis!)

On the plane back to Washington, Fuller was trying to write out answers to questions Rather might ask.

"This is much too tough," Bush said. "Why are you so uptight about this? Are the others worried?"

"Yes, sir, they are."

"Well, you see, I'm okay with this."

It was in the car at Andrews Air Force Base—Ailes had come out to meet them—Fuller said: "Look, if he really just trashes you on Iran-contra, why don't you tell him, 'How would you like to be judged, your whole career, on the seven minutes you walked off the set?' . . ."

Fuller was referring to the semi-famous incident in which Rather went ballistic because a tennis match delayed his newscast, and while he was on a phone, bitching to the powers-that-be, the tennis match ended, CBS had no anchor on the set, everybody panicked, and the network went to black. It was an incident much retailed by the pink-jowled lunchers—in other words, inside baseball.

But Ailes loved the line. He went *crazy*—repeated it about six times. Fuller knew, from that moment, it would be Ailes's idea . . . but Bush insisted: "It isn't going to be that way. Dan's a friend."

And that's why Bush played such a rabid net game, on the *CBS Evening News,* the night of January 25, after he *sat there,* and watched that . . . that . . . *crap* Rather put on the air, before the interview: it was *all* Iran-contra, it was *all* rehash, it was . . .

How could Rather understand he wasn't just conducting a tough interview? . . . He was proving George Bush wrong in front of his *friends,* he was violating Bush's *trust*! . . . It was *betrayal*!

The short answer was, Rather had no clue.

"Mr. Vice President, we want to talk about the record on this because . . ."

"Let's talk about the whole record . . ."

"The framework here is that . . ."

"That's what I want to talk about, Dan."

"One-third of the Republicans in this poll, one-third of the Republicans and one-fourth of the people who say that, you know, they rather like you, believe you're hiding something."

"I am hiding something."

"Here's a chance to get it out."

"You know what I'm hiding? What I told the President—that's the only thing. And I've answered every question put before me. Now, if you have a question . . ."

"I do have one."

"Please."

"I have one."

"Please, go ahead."

"You have said that if you had known, you said, if you had known this was an arms-for-hostages swap . . ."

"Yes."

"That you would have opposed it."

"Exactly."

"You also said that you did not know . . ."

"May I answer that?"

"That wasn't a question, it was a statement."

"It was a statement, and I'll answer it."

"Let me ask the question, if I may, first."

"The President created this program, as testified or stated publicly, he did not think it was arms for hostages."

"That's the President, Mr. Vice President."

"And that's me. Because I went along with it because—you know why, Dan?—because . . ."

"That wasn't a question, Mr. Vice President."

"I saw Mr. Buckley, heard about Mr. Buckley, being tortured to death— later admitted as a CIA chief—so if I erred, I erred on the side of trying to get those hostages out of there and the whole story has been told to the Congress."

"Mr. Vice President, you set the rules for this talk here. I didn't mean to step on your line there, but you insisted that this be live and you know that we have a limited amount of time . . ."

"That's why I want to get my share in here on something other than what you want to talk about. . . ."

The fact was, Bush wouldn't listen to a question . . . much less answer anything. Meanwhile, million-dollar minutes were bleeding away, the producers were yelling into Rather's ear to *wrap it up! CUT . . . DAN! WRAP IT UP!* . . . And Rather was still trying to get his first clear answer.

"I don't want to be argumentative, Mr. Vice President, bu . . ."

"You do. Dan, this is not a great night, because I want to talk about why I want to be President, why those forty-one percent of the people are supporting me, and . . ."

"And, Mr. Vice President, these questions are . . ."

"I don't think it's fair to judge a whole career, it's not fair to judge my whole career by a rehash on Iran. How would you like it if I judged your career by those seven minutes when you walked off the set in New York? Would you like that?"

—★—

Turned out, Rather didn't much like it. Nor was Bush, at that moment, his most sanguine self. After nine minutes of Bush stonewalling, taunting . . . after Rather finally cut him off and went to commercial . . . after CBS switchboards lit up with calls of protest (how could Dan treat the VP that way?) . . . Bush was still so fired up in his Capitol office that he ripped out his earpiece and announced, with a sneer:

"Well, I had my say . . . *Dan.*"

Ailes tried to tell him: his mike was still live. Bush didn't care.

"He makes Lesley Stahl look like a *pussy,*" Bush said. The CBS crew tried to get Bush to take off his microphone. But Bush was like a warrior with his foot on his enemy's neck, whooping to the heavens.

". . . But it's going to *help me.* Because that bastard didn't lay a *glove* on me.

". . . And you can tell your God damn *network* that if they want to talk to *me,* they can raise their hands at a press conference! No more 'Mr. Insider' stuff."

The next day, Pete Teeley tried to tell the press pack: Bush meant Lesley Stahl was, you know . . . a pussy*cat.* Bush apologized for his language, insisted he never would have taken the Lord's name in vain if he'd known people could *hear* him. (As if the commandment read: Thou Shalt Check Thy Mike.)

But the interesting thing was how everybody around Bush, Inc., *loved it* . . . the Killer Veep!

Atwater was spinning a cloud of sparkling dust about "defining events"— one or two such moments would make a President—and the Bush-Rather face-off was, in Lee's terms, "the defining event." Teeley said the "debate" would put an end to all "the wimp bullshit." Bush had gone toe-to-toe with the toughest! Rich Bond insisted Rather had tried to "bully George Bush"— that would help Bush in Iowa. George Wittgraf, Iowa chairman, showed himself an attentive Atwater acolyte when he talked about the dust-up as the . . . "shaping event."

Bush was *so* pleased: couldn't believe all the nice things people said, all the calls of congratulation, the way people cheered at his events. Publicly, he went into Audie Murphy mode—he conceded it was "tension city" in the studio, joked about deserving "combat pay." But he also said Rather was just doing his job. (You see, he wasn't wrong, after all—Dan *was* a friend.) . . . Everybody came out fine, as far as Bush could see: his press pack was *delighted,* writing "defining event" analyses, thumb-suckers on the Age of TV Politics, delicious Karacter studies on the virile New Bush, or even-more-delicious behind-the-scenes blow-by-blow on how Ailes had *planned* the whole showdown . . . you know, who sandbagged whom?

Wasn't it great how it worked out?

It was left to Bob Dole to point out: Bush never answered anything.

And how would Bush deal with Mikhail Gorbachev . . . if he got so riled up by Dan Rather?

— ★ —

That was the problem: Bush couldn't run a nice, clean campaign against Dan Rather without Dole spoiling everything—pointing out *he* was still in the race . . . still *ahead,* where it mattered, in Iowa, where polls showed a jagged post-Rather blip for Bush . . . for about four days . . . after which Bush's numbers settled back to nowheresville.

It was *so* frustrating.

And there was Dole, sailing around the state, talking farm, talking Midwest-neighbor, talking "One of Us" . . . the man had the nerve to stick to that poor-boy-from-Kansas routine (when Bush-for-President had gone to such lengths to *prove* that Dole was rich) . . . he had the gall to announce he was organized in every Iowa *precinct* (when everybody knew Dole could not organize) . . . he had the *cheek* to conduct himself like a statesman, a man with a mission—like a winner!

This was not the Bob Dole the Bushies were counting on. They never bargained for efficient good humor.

These were the worries of George Wittgraf, Bush's Iowa chairman, as he made his familiar drive, three hours east and south from his hometown, Cherokee, to the capital, Des Moines.

Wittgraf had been working Iowa for George Bush for nine years—almost a quarter of his time on the planet . . . and now Bush was stuck (forever, it seemed) in second place . . . and all of Wittgraf's efforts were headed for the thirsty drainpipe of history (he wasn't going to make a *footnote* for Germond and Witcover) . . . unless, somehow . . .

He had to get under Bob Dole's skin—show him up! Show him to the voters of Iowa as the volcanically nasty, shifty-eyed, razor-tongued, dark-hearted, mean-minded, bile-besotted *snarler* . . . that Wittgraf (and all good Bushies) knew him to be.

And Bush, Inc., had one week to pull it off.

Actually, Wittgraf started typing the minute he got to the office, at the start of that last week before the caucus:

"Iowa Republicans must weigh Bob Dole's record of cronyism and his history of mean-spiritedness carefully, before they decide whom to support as our Party's nominee for President. . . ."

The heading at the top of Wittgraf's page said "Press Release," but in Wittgraf's lawyerly mind, it was a summation to the jury—his last chance to make the case. The defendant (Dole) . . .

". . . showed his mean-spirited nature in 1976, when he nearly single-handedly brought the Republican national ticket down to defeat.

". . . fails to mention that he and his wife are now millionaires, and had an income of $2.19 million from 1982 through 1986."

Wittgraf also could not neglect to mention that the Doles lived in "Washington's posh Watergate apartment complex" . . . that they took vacations (regularly!) at a Florida condominium (purchased with the help of Dole's agribusiness buddies) . . . that Elizabeth's blind trust was *under federal investigation. . . .*

The next day, Wittgraf sent this screed to the *Register* . . . and waited for the explosion.

— ★ —

Dole was at a school in Latimer, Iowa, when Bush's love note caught up with him. Mari Maseng, Dole's former Communications Director (now Press Secretary—the Klingons demoted her) backed the Senator into a broom closet.

"Senator, I think this is the kind of thing that—granted, you know, it's upsetting, but . . . you know, the kind of thing where a lot of anger is probably not what we . . . you, you probably want, you know, a 'more-in-sorrow-than-in-anger' kind of thing, that . . ."

Dole just nodded, listening, looking down at the closet floor, with the air of a man who was waiting. Was she finished?

"Senator . . . more in sorrow . . ."

What she meant was: *Oh, God,* please—five days to the caucus, *please*—don't go nuclear now! *Be Ni-i-ice.*

Dole stepped out of the closet, and into the waiting iron ring. What he said was . . . sorrowful—this kind of thing made him feel sorrow . . . because it was *pathetic*—a pathetic, *desperation tactic . . . by George Bush.*

After that, Dole was warmed up.

Someone asked: Was Dole sure that Bush was behind that release?

"Either George Bush is responsible for this kind of campaign . . . or he's totally out of control," Dole said.

"Maybe he *isn't* in charge. . . .

"Maybe he's not *in the loop*! . . .

"I want George Bush to hold this in his little hand and say, 'I stand by every word.' "

Of course, Bush meant to do no such thing. When his pack pinned him, in Clinton, Iowa, the Veep said of the press release:

"I don't endorse it. But I don't reject it."

Oh, yes, he said, he'd authorized it—he was in charge!

But, no, he couldn't comment on specifics—he hadn't read it.

— ★ —

That's what sent Dole over the edge—*thermonuclear.* Both men were in Washington the next day for a Senate vote on aid to the contras: on the floor, Dole would carry the ball for the Gip and his favorite guerrillas; Bush would preside, up front, in the chair.

But no sooner had the VP got to the dais, than Dole was making for the front of the chamber . . . he was heading for Bush! He was carrying the press release!

It happened so fast, Bush was frozen . . . he looked at Dole, then away, as if the doings on the floor might require the attention of the Presiding Officer.

Dole was waving the press release and yammering at Bush. Bush said something back, but that only seemed to set Dole off again.

"I asked him, 'Did George Bush authorize this?' . . ." Dole reported in the press gallery, within the hour.

". . . Because I couldn't believe that he had authorized this . . . very personal attack on me, and on my wife, Elizabeth, and I think we—as I told the Vice President—*we're running for President!* This is a very important office! And I said, 'Did you authorize this release?'

"He said, 'Yes.' "

"I said, 'Did you read it?'

"He said, 'No.'

"And I said, 'Do you know what it contains? Do you know what it *says,* about me, and *Elizabeth*?'

"I couldn't believe it!"

What Dole could not believe was that Bush would try his game of yin-yang Washington knowing . . . on this! Bush knew all about the press release . . . without being culpable of knowing anything.

That's why Dole poked the paper onto the desk, under Bush's nose ("Well, *read it*!") . . . then stalked away.

Bush wouldn't pick it up.

Bush could not *believe* that Dole had made a public *spectacle* of this, let it get under his *skin*—a bit of rough and tumble—tipped him over the edge! . . . Did he expect Bush to cut and run from a guy like Wittgraf? Been with him for years! . . . It had to be phony somehow—Dole was *acting*—waving that paper ("My *wife*!"). Dole was acting . . . like a bully! Came right *at* Bush—in his *face*. That face! . . . Bush said later, Dole's face went strange—like something took over. Dole was *out of control*!

103

Into the Bubble

I N THE LAST WEEK, the Democrats were neck and neck . . . and neck, like thoroughbreds pounding for the finish. The latest Iowa poll had it:

Gephardt: 19

Dukakis: 18

Simon: 17

That's when Simon went after Gephardt—radio ads, accusing Dick of flip-flops. "Some candidates now profess to be friends of the working men and women, when their votes helped create the problems we face."

In the bar of the Savery Hotel, Simon's wise guys were whining because their man wouldn't go nuclear—put the ads on TV. But radio did the job: Gephardt got a steady drizzle of questions on his votes.

The '81 tax-cut vote was the favorite. Why did Gephardt vote for Reaganomics?

Well, the short answer was, Dick voted with his district—to be precise, his district-to-be. Redistricting, after the 1980 census, was going to pack a new swatch of Jefferson County suburb into his district—he was nervous, he did the popular thing. Sure, he could kick himself now. He should have known, he should have *seen* what it would mean if he went national. (*When* he went national was more like it . . . that's what was frustrating—he should have known himself.)

But that was a long time ago . . . anyway, not the kind of answer he could give. So he had this patter worked out—we were headed for recession, we needed a tax cut, he led the fight for the Democratic tax cut . . . but the votes weren't there, so he voted for Reagan's cut, which was better than none. . . . And then, for the next five years, he pushed for tax reform, which closed up a lot of those tax breaks Reagan engineered for the rich.

It was all true, in its way . . . but it took about two solid minutes to say, even with no wasted words—and was difficult for a voter to get as he passed by the tube on the way to the fridge. So Dick didn't like to have to say it . . . but he said it.

Some guy in the crowd would stand up, after Dick's speech, and ask: he heard on the radio . . .

Dick would do the patter.

Then he'd start back to the car and some visiting reporter from Chicago would stick a tape in his face, and ask:

Now, what about the '81 tax vote?

What the hell did she want him to say? He saw her, at the event, hunched over her tape in the back of the room, transcribing his answer the first time. Did she think he'd change his answer for her?

No, he'd blink, once, slowly, and start:

"I led the fight for the Democratic alternative . . ."

"Yes, yes," she said, after the patter. "But the *deeper* question, the deep issue, is that you're being expedient . . ." She tried to make her voice rise at the end, so it sounded like a question.

But Gephardt knew it wasn't a question. The net result was, he spent less time with the press. He had two vans-ful trailing him now, and rent-a-car paratroops dropping in for an hour or two. He was the front-runner: they all wanted a chat.

Well, let them get in line.

He had to husband himself as a campaign resource. Eight events a day were draining enough. At every stop, he had to bring up that hot resolve they expected from the TV. Dick would ask, as the Advance man's hand reached for the door of his van: "Where's my *Wall Street Journal?*" Someone would hand him a fresh copy of the *Journal* editorial, the one that claimed the trade deficit was "just a fact of life." And Dick, in his shiny-green parka, would take that clip on stage—and wave it.

"I wish the people who wrote the editorials would come with me out of their office, out of New *York,* and sit with the *workers* at the J.I. *Case* plant in Bettendorf, Iowa. *Twelve hundred jobs* in that plant six months ago—today none.

"Talk to people thirty and forty and fifty years old, who lost their life insurance, lost their health insurance, lost their pension. Have no idea how they're gonna support their families . . . standing in welfare lines and unemployment lines . . . tell them it's JUST A FACT OF LIFE that their jobs left Bettendorf, and they're now in South Korea. Or go to the Farm-All plant in the same town. *Three thousand* jobs. And tell those people the same thing. People making twelve and thirteen dollars an hour. Or go to the Caterpillar plant, which is half closed down—in six months *WILL* be closed down—*two THOUsand* more jobs in the same town. *SIX* to *seven THOUsand jobs* in one town . . . *HERE in Iowa.* And the jobs are *GONE,* in the last six months . . . tell *THEM* it's just a *FACT OF LIFE* . . .

"Well I don't *LIKE* their facts of life. I wanta *CHANGE* the facts of life. And if you'll stand with me on February 8th, we'll confound the critics, we'll surprise the Establishment, and we will turn this country in a new direction. *IT'S YOUR FIGHT, TOO!*"

They'd be screaming and stomping when he finished, men pumping his hand, hammering his shoulders, women in union jackets busting through to kiss him, and tell him he's going to win.

The crowds were bigger now, and hotter, pumped for his arrival by Bruce Springsteen ("Born in the U.S.A.") thudding and wailing though the P.A. Barry Wyatt, the Guru of Advance, had moved into Iowa for the final push, and he was training a feral pack of twenty-year-old triggermen. ("Goddammit, is that the best goddam sound system you could find? . . . You call that a fuckin' *backdrop?*") Those kids would fan out through the state, living off the country-side, begging or stealing what they needed, leaving a trail of abandoned rent-a-cars and shell-shocked locals—but Dick's events were beautiful TV. . . . Then they'd come back to Des Moines, through the big new office, with their premature suits and premature swaggers, boasting of their all-night ride on this corn combine, or the way they talked that car dealer out of his thirty-foot flag. ("put it up behind the stage—Dick looked like fuckin' Patton!")

And it wasn't just the new Advance pack that swelled the office—the staff had tripled in a month, as everyone from the southern offices and most of the people from D.C. sped to Iowa, where the action was. In the new downtown storefront, they'd scream to one another over the tacky walls of their carrels. ("JIM! This six-eighteen from Burlington First, is that today or last week? IS THAT LAST WEEK? NO . . . *SIX-EIGHTEEN!*") There were scores of women on scores of phones—updating hard counts every day and every night. Joyce Aboussie had moved in from St. Louis and was whooping and whipping a cadre of Missourians into making noise everywhere Dick went. Murphy had a closed office in the back, from which he'd emerge, screaming imprecations, at irregular intervals. There were press and camera crews, come to talk to Murphy or record this frenetic scene, and they moved more or less at will through the chaos.

And the net result was, Dick didn't come to the office. He couldn't wander in, to ask how it was going, or talk to Murphy, or do an interview. It was a public event when he appeared. He'd have to make remarks. He'd have to show some fire to match the heat in that storefront.

No, if someone had to talk to Dick—members of the House, money men, Washington smart guys—the Schedulers would tuck them in, in Waterloo, or Iowa City . . . they could join up there, maybe have ten or fifteen minutes with Dick on the trip to Quad Cities. . . . Most of these VIPs felt constrained to bring Dick some warning or complaint. Sandy Levin, a House member from

Michigan, set up a constant mewling whine about Dick's us-versus-them rhetoric. Levin assured his fellow mewlers in Washington: this was not Dick Gephardt . . . he knew Dick . . . he'd talk to Dick . . . to let him know, he could, uh, make *enemies*. . . . Jack Guthman, Dick's old pal from Northwestern, now a hot-shot zoning lawyer in Chicago, was trying to position Dick in Illinois—and he had to warn him, his business friends didn't like what they were hearing. Jack was afraid Dick was losing perspective, pouring everything into Iowa, losing track of the rest of the country.

Dick, of course, would cock his head and keep the baby blues on their faces, and say at the end, they were right, he understood. But the fact was, he *was* pouring everything into Iowa . . . and he didn't mean to stop. The fact was, he wasn't worried about enemies, back in Congress. He wasn't going back.

But he wouldn't say that. So, the net result was . . . he didn't talk much to his old pals. What was the point? . . . Loreen was upset about the ads, the way they brought up Matt's illness, the way they repeated that falsehood about Lou Gephardt losing his farm, but Dick didn't talk to her about that. What was the point? . . . Even Jane was cut off from his new world, off in a smaller, grimmer bubble of her own, as she plied ladies' luncheons and coffee-shop patrons in other parts of the state. Jane didn't understand—what was the point of running her around, her and Nancy, or her and Liz Kincaid, driving hundreds of miles through the snow to another cheap motel with its clattering heater and nubby polyester bedspread? She and Dick would talk at night from their two motel rooms, but all he could say was, they'd do the best they could. The Schedulers had to know what they were doing—or he had to assume they did.

Only the road crew and the killers knew what was happening in Dick's narrowed world. They were the only ones he really heard.

"I gotta hand it to the guy," Reilly said at lunch one day, with Ethel Klein. "He's really stickin' with us. You know, all these people are coming at him, complaining, but he's just not paying attention. I gotta say, the guy is backin' us—the guy is amazing! Those are his old friends!"

"Yeah," Ethel said, quietly. "But pretty soon, we'll be his old friends."

Finally, the Secret Service arrived to seal off Dick's world from everyone who did not have a badge. And then it was easier. The motorcade was longer, but the cars ran better. There was less for the boys in the bubble to think about . . . rides, planes, motels—all arranged. There was less dissonance in Dick's ear . . . less information altogether. He had to call meetings to ask his crew—what was happening out there? . . . Were they doing okay? . . . Were they winning?

He thought they were winning. He could feel that much, at events.

But he couldn't know.

In the last week, the *Register* endorsed Paul Simon. That had to stop Simon's slide. Dick thought Simon's support was holding—he could see Simon people at his own events.

What about the Duke?

Dick was worried . . . he wanted Dukakis to run second. If it ended Gephardt, Dukakis—first, second . . . that would kill off Simon. Dick could go to New Hampshire as the clear alternative—he could be *not* Dukakis. But he couldn't see Duke's people on the ground . . . where were they?

He kept asking Reilly, Ethel, Trippi, Murphy: "What's he *doing*? Where's the Duke?"

104

Ucch, God...
Their Life
Was Over

THE STAFF screwed up, booked them into a single room at the Savery. Kitty hadn't been sleeping. Michael, of course, slept correctly. He only needed five hours a night. But Kitty couldn't sleep. It would happen before every primary.

She was awake at 3:30 A.M.—no place to go. There was no second room. She didn't want to sit in the bathroom. She couldn't wander the halls. She was *Kitty Dukakis.* She was in prison, tossing and turning.

She was supposed to talk, that evening—some event—but the snow was too bad. Kara, her youngest, had to fill in. Kitty wondered how Kara did. She must have done all right. She had the political moves. Kara had to get back to school next week. That would be hard for her. Andrea hated politics. Anyone who wasn't for her father was an insult. Kitty wondered what this campaign was doing to the girls. Would they ever be the same? Probably not. This was too long. Oh, God! . . . She had to do the *Today* show the next day! . . . Kitty thought about the snow—in Boston, did it snow? Would the neighbors clean the walk? If they were home, Michael would be out with his old snowblower. That thing ought to go to the Smithsonian! . . . Maybe it *would* go to the Smithsonian! Would they ever be back in Brookline, Michael blowing snow? . . . Oh, God, if they won, they would *never* . . . Who did the snow? Secret Service? . . . *Ucch, God . . . their life was over.*

She was tossing. Michael stirred. Concern, annoyance, and sleep were in his voice. "*What,*" he said, "is the problem?"

"I just can't sleep anymore."

He grunted. "What is it, babe?"

"I'm afraid you're going to win . . . I mean, I don't want you to lose . . ." She could hear him stirring. "But I'm not sure I want you to win."

Michael sighed. "This," he said, "must be part of your ethnic heritage."

— ★ —

Michael didn't have any second thoughts. No, this was not the time . . . he was getting out of Iowa. Like a veteran runner, he could smell the tape—that close! He could feel this thing turning. He could win! He was better every day—the crowds could feel the striving. All of a sudden, it wasn't like being in a meeting with Michael . . . he was trying to reach them.

And they fed his certainty. He dug in his heels against his staff—against all comers. He wasn't going to hit the other guys in this race. Not on PACs, not on anything. He wasn't gonna start that kinda politics now. Hart's bubble had burst. Hart was going to finish nowhere. . . . Simon had crested. Michael was convinced his organization would grab off the voters who'd been "leaning" to Simon. . . . Gephardt was a phony. Michael said everyone would see Gephardt was a phony. Michael would not have to say one word.

Everyone would see he was *right*. . . . Three days before the caucus, his phone banks rang up thirteen hundred Number Ones—a record! In sixteen hours the following day, they pulled *twenty-three hundred Number Ones*. . . . That was the day, even his wise guys had to admit . . . he *might* be right . . . Michael had a chance.

That was the day, he started in the west of the state, Council Bluffs . . . with Richard Gere. There were seven hundred people in a mall at 9:00 A.M. Young girls were screaming—sounded like a jet engine. The music on the P.A. made the tiles of the mall rattle. And Gere was eloquent—Gere was *perfect*!

He said he heard about Dukakis when Michael refused to send the Massachusetts National Guard to Central America. "I thought, 'Now *there's* a ballsy move' . . .

"I have a confession to make. From the time I was twenty-two to the time I was thirty-six, I didn't vote. But Mike and I met . . ."

Gere looked at Michael with something like apology on his face. ". . . in December, in L.A. It was about eleven o'clock."

"Three A.M., East Coast time," said Dukakis.

"I was tired," Gere said. "Michael had been campaigning all day. He had a bad cold. But we sat down and we talked. And this man talked to me from the heart . . . person to person. And I really felt good about him in my heart."

The girls screamed for Gere, and for the man of his heart, Dukakis.

That was the day Michael finished in Des Moines with a neighborhood walk, a canvass, door-to-door. On the press bus, the trip director, Jack Weeks, promised "old-fashioned local politics."

Sure.

There were 150 people waiting outside—plus thirty camera crews. People stampeded Michael's bus. Advance men were trying to hold them back with ropes. (Michael still insisted, no Secret Service. He said he didn't want a buffer between him and the voters. All it meant was, the campaign supplied its own muscle.)

Dukakis was engulfed by the iron ring—cameras, boom mikes over his head, in his face. His Advance guys were shouting: "*Move toward the house. GOV-ERNOR . . . TO THE HOUSE. THE HOUSE!* . . ." Michael couldn't see the house. He couldn't see anything.

But he knew, that day, he could win.

The next morning, at the Savery, there was a breakfast for his precinct captains. The ballroom looked like a piece of a national convention. The crowd was studded with waving signs, cameras, and blinding lights. The Boston TVs were doing stand-ups while the crowd was yelling . . . and on the stage, for once, Michael dropped his speech and started to talk.

He talked about his first trip to Iowa, a year before, his first visit to a farm, in Osceola—the Barretts. And on the same trip, his discovery of Gus and Tom's Pizza and Steakhouse—his Greeks. . . . He talked about the people he'd met since, the farmers who had to take city jobs, and meat-packers who had to take cuts in pay. . . .

He talked about a woman in Sioux City who had a seven-year-old son, and no health insurance. Her son had had pneumonia, thirteen times. "I asked her, 'What do you do when he gets sick?' She said, 'I hope and pray, and when he gets really bad, I take him to St. Luke's. But, Governor, now I have a bill at St. Luke's—this long! . . . I'm embarrassed to go there.' "

At last, Michael was trying to say what health insurance *meant.* He didn't talk about his pending bill in Massachusetts, or statistics on the national problem. This campaign had done something for him, after all.

"One more thing I want to say. . . . This is a very close race. I know it. And you know it. And in a race like this, five people in a precinct can make the difference between a good result and a great result. . . . And it's up to you.

"Let me tell you something, folks. Those other campaigns, they're worried about you. They *know* . . . how good you are."

His captains stopped him with cheers.

". . . One more thing: I'd like to introduce someone who has been the love of my life, and my partner, for twenty-five years. In fact, Kitty and I will celebrate our twenty-fifth wedding anniversary on June 20th . . ."

Another round of cheers.

". . . which just *happens* . . . to be the end of the primary season. . . . And wouldn't it be a *terrific* twenty-fifth anniversary present . . . if I could take her away to our favorite place . . ." (That is, schnorring off Tiky and Viv, in Fort Lauderdale.)

". . . and I could lean across the table, and say . . ."

Michael paused while his eyebrows danced.

". . . 'Baby . . . you're gonna be the next First Lady of America!' "

The ballroom erupted. People were screaming and hopping around. And why not? After a year in Iowa—the day before the caucus—Michael had started to tell them, honestly . . . *why* he was running.

Kitty came on stage. He put his arm around her. They looked so happy there, while the people cheered. . . . Kitty turned in his embrace, and she looked out on the crowd with a glorious smile. . . .

At the side of the ballroom, the Advance men noted: that was wrong—she should have her arm around *him,* that puts *him* a half-step forward . . .

"What's she doin' in fronta him?"

"He's gonna have to quit with that arm."

Someone was going to have to tell Michael.

105

Juice

THE NETWORKS were wired into Des Moines with millions in equipment, hundreds of people from each . . . Dan Rather prowled the Savery with his new CBS consultant, Tom Donilon . . . cables as thick as anchor chain snaked up the fire stairs in all the big hotels . . . but no network wanted to bore the nation with a nightful of the Iowa caucus, so the killers kept an eye on *Happy Days,* waiting for a trail of numbers across the bottom of the screen.

It was maddeningly slow.

In the Gephardt family suite, Reilly couldn't wait—he was on the phone with friends from the networks. Trippi had a cigar, unlit. His wife, Katie, watched their tiny daughter, who was toddling on the tan shag carpet. There were two bedrooms and a center parlor in the suite at the beautiful Best Western. In the center room, there was a bar with trays of food, untouched. A long couch (nubby polyester to match the shag) faced three TVs—one for each network—and that's where the killers gathered. Doak and Shrum were in and out (poor Shrummy was a ball of nerves), Murphy was fretting and pacing, Paul Begala, the speechwriter, watched the TVs.

"Here it is—HERE!" They'd call out when the numbers rolled—twenty percent of precincts, then thirty-three . . . Dole was way ahead in the GOP (and, God! Robertson second—Bush wiped out!) . . . but the Democrats were not clear-cut. Dick was holding over thirty percent, a wavering three- or four-point lead over Simon; Dukakis was third with twenty-two percent. On the walkie-talkie, a staffer at Democratic Central said hard numbers put

Gephardt at thirty-three percent . . . but still, no call from the network gods of election.

Just before eight, CBS came out—called it for Gephardt. There were whoops . . . but the other networks held off. Did they know something? . . . Trippi's cigar remained unlit. Murphy was frozen: if they declared victory and then, somehow, lost their lead, they could turn a near tie into disaster. Reilly dove for a bedroom, punched at the phone—"When're you guys gonna *call it? Come on! . . ."*

The family filtered in. Not Dick, of course, he was doing TV . . . but Jane and the girls went into one bedroom, and Matt took the other, watched TV in the dark. Nancy Gephardt and her son, Frank, stayed in the center room, with Loreen, her friends the Halls from Third Baptist Church, and her brother, Dick's Uncle Bob, and his wife, Kay. They hung back at the bar, tried to see the TVs . . . but without Dick, this wasn't their room, and the TVs somehow belonged to the killers, who turned their backs, and traded rat-a-tat spin.

"Okay, spin doctors," Trippi was saying, "I think we oughta say this makes it a three-man top tier . . . kill Gore in the South—it'll be too late for him."

"We gotta say this weakens the Duke . . ."

"Wait . . ."

There was silence. ABC had called it for Dick . . . and there he was, on the screen, with Peter Jennings asking if he could pull it off in other states . . . "the politics of grievance—what makes you think it will work, anywhere else?"

"Well, Peter . . ."

Loreen Gephardt meant to see her boy, and even his face on the screen emboldened her to take the couch, so she settled in with Mrs. Hall, and the killers had to part, so she could see.

Jennings was boring in on the flip-flops.

"Well, Peter . . . I've been in public life fifteen years now, and I'd rather change and be right, than be rigid and wrong . . ."

Loreen was in pink fuzzy cashmere, and she snuggled against Mrs. Hall. Her hand absently reached for Mrs. Hall's jacket and she fingered the wool, as if she had to touch something, to know . . . it was real, all her hopes, all the effort—God did have a plan. Loreen tugged gently on Mrs. Hall's jacket. She turned her shoulders so she could look straight into her friend's eyes, as she whispered: "He *looks* like a President."

Uncle Bob Cassell had a bag he was fingering, and now he pulled out his portrait of Dick, just like the ones he used to paint when Dick was twelve years old . . . but now Dick had the Capitol dome and an American flag floating behind him, against an azure sky.

"Oh, Bob, it's a wonderful picture," Loreen said.

"Gee, that's great!" said Jane. She was distracted, trying to be nice. "I've gotta find a place to put it . . . in the White House!" It sounded strange. She'd never thought of *living* in the White House.

There was a *Newsweek* reporter in the suite, who had to come over now to get the poop on the picture. Loreen introduced her brother: "You know, people always said Dick looks a lot like Bob." And Bob drew himself up, beaming, to look like a President, too.

Debra Johns kept other reporters at bay, in the hall: "Debra! Where'd he eat *dinner*? . . . Debra! *What'd he have for dinner?*"

And now, Dick's voice was in the hallway, too. He was taping out there— *Good Morning America.* A few friends from the suite went out to watch. But Loreen stayed behind—she had the Lord's work to do.

"Bob, it's such a lovely picture, I think you should present it to him on stage."

Bob was diffident. The picture wasn't quite finished. "I really can't make it a big deal . . . I'll just give it to him upstairs, in the room."

No, Loreen insisted, and she bent to pull the bag back over the portrait.

"Well . . ." Bob was accustomed to his sister's will. "I'm just going to sort of present it, then. That's all."

And, finally, their Dick was in the room, and he was pumped up, he was huge . . . and pink under his makeup. But he had the victory speech to do—an important speech, the same one he would give in New Hampshire the following day—and he had to freshen up. He brushed by into the bedroom—not even a hug for Jane. She and the kids were milling at a mirror, last-minute makeup and hair. No time for talk. Nancy was firing stage directions at Frank and Loreen and the Halls. Brad, the body man, was standing at the door of the bedroom, yelling, *"Now, let's talk about what we're gonna do here! . . ."*

There was no time to be a family. They had to learn how to look like a family.

— ★ —

Downstairs in the beautiful Starlite Ballroom, the crowd was whoop-it-up happy, and a bar band lashed the air with electric guitars. It was a long, low room—and packed. The Des Moines staff couldn't recognize half the country folk who'd poured in. They must have driven for hours. In the end, it was the farmers who put Dick over the top—he won sixty of Iowa's ninety-nine counties.

Against the long back wall, there were platforms studded with tripods, cameras trained on the podium like a firing squad, and mounds of gear in heaps at the feet of surly crews. It was hot, it was late. They were supposed to go live in Kansas City . . . and Cincinnati . . . Atlanta, Houston, Chicago, Boston . . . and St. Louis! Every two-bit station with a satellite truck had its anchor-wanker there, and a big chunk of the budget tied up in (ta *dummm*) . . . *Decision '88!* But they weren't asking these Iowans about their decision. They weren't going to get on the air with some stupid *voter* . . . no. They needed juice.

And, at last, here it came, in the person of Dick Gephardt, and his wife, and children, his mother, her friends and family . . . who busted into the hall along a little cattle run that Advance roped off, and straight onto stage, in front of twenty-two American flags . . . and the halogens snapped on, and the crowd sent up a fevered yowl that drowned the bar band's "Theme from *Rocky.*"

Jane hit her mark on stage—behind Dick, and to his right. The kids were on the other side, in a rising diagonal row—Katie, Chrissie, and tall Matt closest to the crowd. Loreen stood directly behind Dick, with a view of his pink Presidential neck, and the rest of the family off on the flanks, with Congressman Tony Coelho (always a nose for a winner, Tony had). And it was quiet— Dick was talking.

". . . We will fight the Establishment! . . . We will pry open foreign markets! . . . It's time to tell the forces of greed: ENOUGH is ENOUGH! . . .

"In our America, land is a place to raise cahrn and soybeans, wheat, and most importantly, a place to raise our kids AGAIN . . . we will save the family farm in America, because . . ."

The crowd was onto this song now, and they joined in as chorus: "NUFF is E*NUFF!*"

Loreen was jolted back to the here and now by the noise of the crowd, and she woke with a pleasant shiver of joy from a reverie on her boy's neck, and she looked over the crowd, into the lights, with a smile of blessing and vindication, at the faces in front, staring up at her boy, who was pink as her fuzzy cashmere, and wailing:

". . . they've done nothing but paid their taxes, fought our WARS, raised our KIDS . . . we don't need to give them a FAVOR . . . WE OWE THEM . . ."

And the crowd yelled:
"*NUFF izza NUFF!*"

Dick was yelling, too: "We will WIN in New Hampshire . . . We will WIN in NOVEMBER . . ."
Gep-HARDT
Gep-HARDT . . .

"And when we WIN, we're gonna TAKE BACK THE WHITE HOUSE and GIVE IT BACK to th'*MERICAN PEOPLE* AGAIN . . ."
Gep-HARDT-Gep-HARDT-Gep-HARDT-Gep-HARDT-Gep . . .

"I thank you for your help on this cold and snowy night, and I ask for your help . . . to change America and give it back its soul."

With that, the band issued a few bars of Neil Diamond's "Coming to America," and the crowd noise swelled higher in a rhythmic scream . . . *Gep-HARDT-Gep-HARDT* . . . as Dick gathered himself, and roared out the only line outside his text, the simple thought closest to his heart:
"*WE'RE GONNA WIN THIS THING!*"

And the band sped the song into full cry, as the crowd screamed *GepHARDTGepHARDTGEP-HARDT* . . . except with two or three thousand people screaming off the beat, only the strongest consonants came through, so the noise was just a frantic bark:
GARP-GARP-GARPT-GARPT-GARPT-GARPT . . .

And there was no script anymore, so Dick turned and hugged his mother, and he missed Jane, but he found his kids, and he bent way down for Katie and hugged her hard and quick, and then Chrissie, hard and quick, and then Dick stood and looked straight into Matt's eyes, and threw open his arms and advanced on Matt, who grasped him tentatively, and was going to step back, but Dick grabbed him harder, and Matt forgot the crowd and disappeared into his father's embrace, and Dick laid his head on Matt's shoulder, and they held like that, neither one would let go. And when they did, they were both fighting tears, but Dick was being pulled to the podium—some business . . .

It was Bob, who took the sack off the portrait, and Dick's eyes popped open a few millimeters at the shock of azure . . . and . . . Hey! That's him! He gave Bob a big thumbs-up . . . and he started to wander the stage again—Tony Coelho, a hug, Nancy Gephardt, Frank . . . and the band was thumping hell-for-leather, but the crowd couldn't keep barking like that, and the halogens were clicking off, as Dick listed from hug to hug . . . and it could have been over—Dick had his back turned—but Loreen understood, maybe better than her son, just what this was about.

She took the painting and strode to the podium, she faced it away from her, and with her fingers grasping the sides of the frame, she mounted upon the podium the Portrait of Dick Regnant. She disappeared behind this icon . . . even Dick alive in his hugs disappeared . . . and the halogens clicked back to full glare, and the crowd looked up at Dick, and the Dome, and the Flag . . .

GARPT-GEHPT-GARPT-GEHPT-GARPT-GARP . . .

106

We Won
the Bronze

DUKAKIS HAD his own "victory" party—it looked fine on TV. He announced to his crowd:

"Tonight . . . we won the bronze!"

Like there were three guys standing on a victory platform.

That was a brilliant piece of spin, the brainstorm of Estrich's husband, Marty Kaplan. (In fact, Kaplan's coup saved Michael's bacon. Once the Duke's people started mounting this "bronze" conceit, the triple-E pundits fell into line. Though Dukakis was soundly beaten by Gephardt and Simon, John Chancellor told NBC's millions of voters: "Well, third place, so far from home, is no disgrace.")

Anyway, the problem was, Dukakis liked this "bronze" business so much— he *believed* it. At least, he said he did. Didn't matter that Michael worked a year to eke out twenty percent of the vote. No one could tell Michael he was going to have to do (or say) anything more.

Estrich was in Des Moines for the caucus, and she explained, as calmly as she could: "If we survive tonight, we survive by the skin of our teeth. You're never going to make it if you don't get out there and throw some punches."

But it wasn't just Susan—and it wasn't all calm.

Bob Farmer, king of the money men, came to Des Moines to have it out with Michael. Farmer was killing himself. His finance committeemen were killing themselves. They had raised more than $10 million! . . . Could he go back and promise that Dukakis would *never again* settle for third place? . . . *Well, could he?*

Paul Brountas, mild-mannered friend, went ballistic in Des Moines. Since Sasso left, Brountas saw himself as Michael's friend . . . and strategist. That didn't mean Michael listened. But it meant Paul saw his duty, and did it. . . . Why couldn't Michael see? *This was an unacceptable performance!* . . . Brountas had watched his friend Ed Muskie slide down the tubes, with a flush and a gurgle, in '72—that campaign fell to pieces in a matter of days! . . . Michael had to get into the game! *Michael had to stop being so damned stubborn!*

They beat up Dukakis all day, all night.

He didn't give an inch. "You guys . . . we did *fine.* We're on track. Let's not get down on ourselves. I *told* you . . ."

Actually, what he'd told them was that the "basic economic message"— good-jobs-at-good-wages—could win. But he forgot that now. . . . He had the bronze!

After midnight, after the speech, after his live shots with the networks, and a few for the diddybop TVs, Michael was back in his suite at the Savery. He had to sleep. He'd be up before six to do the A.M. shows, then fly to New Hampshire.

In the adjoining hospitality suite, there were a couple of slack-jawed staff and a stray writer, come to cadge a beer. They were picking at dry broccoli on the food trays, when . . . in walked Dukakis.

He couldn't sleep. Or maybe Kitty was beating him up, too. He asked how they thought it came out. No one answered.

They were gawking at Dukakis in an undershirt—hairy arms sticking out from floppy short sleeves, his thin neck protruding from the white V-neck, which sloped halfway down his slight shoulders. Even his physical self was pure economy.

Then, they talked all at once, tried to buck him up, with borrowed wise-guy patter:

No problem!

Third place was the best thing that could have happened!

Now the campaign would move to his turf, New Hampshire, with two kamikazes splitting the vote against him—instead of one strong Gephardt. If Simon had finished third, he couldn't go on. Now Gephardt would have to fight a rearguard action against Simon . . .

Michael said: "You really think so?" He was nodding with his eyes half-closed, as if he'd already thought that out, but the eagerness in his voice gave him away.

They could see, in an instant, poor Michael was making this up as he went—just like everybody else. He really didn't know whether he was still breathing . . . didn't have a clue.

They warmed to the task of cheering him up, told him he was in *perfect* position . . .

Michael nodded. He ought to sleep. But he stayed, asking more questions— actually, it was the same question: Was he okay?

They told him he'd done a great job, come from nowhere in this state, on issues he knew nothing about less than a year before. "I had a lot of help," Michael said, with his tone of automatic denial. And that was his cue. He rose to go. "It's a marathon," he said. "We're just at the start—long way to go." He meant the words to sound determined, but what they heard was sadness. They watched his little back through the door. There was hardly any body to him, just a spare, hairy machine to house that *schtarker* of a brain.

107

President Bobster

DOLE WAS STILL ON TV. . . . For hours, he marched the Hotel Fort Des Moines—second floor, tenth floor, third floor, ballroom, up and down the stairways with the TV cables— from Jennings and Brinkley on ABC, to Dan Rather on CBS, to Bernie Shaw on CNN, back to CBS for *Nightwatch* . . . putting out the message: "Well"— smile—"I think the voters saw sharp differences between me and the Vice President. I think voters want someone who can make the tough choices . . ." Dole was drubbing George Bush, thirty-seven percent to nineteen, and he was working the global village like a Kansas Main Street, hitting every storefront, every hand . . . and meanwhile—as they fiddled with a new plug for his ear, or the halogen lights on the interview chair, or the cables that would link him to Peter, David, or Dan—the Bobster kept dribbling: "No, I can't hear Dan . . . got my Dan Rather sweater on . . . that's all I could get—couldn't get an interview . . . yeah! . . . Yeah, Dan! . . . Aaghh, well, you really know how to finish 'em off hegh-hegh-hegh . . . o-kayyy—we ready?"

The rooms were small, stacked with equipment and tense with technicians who had to get it right, first time, every time—live TV. And then the Dole entourage—Elizabeth and her body man; Kenny and Anita Dole from Russell ("Told'ya I'd win," Kenny said); Bill Brock and one besuited flunky; Tom Synhorst, Dole's triumphant Iowa chief; Mari Maseng ("Smile, Senator"); Kim Wells (Dole might need something written); and Mike Glassner, with his leather folder—would fill the place to bursting, the hindmost peering in from the hallway. But Dole was never crowded. They'd sit him in a chair; the mess of machinery and mankind would bump and stumble into array around the walls, into corners—out of camera frame, of course . . . the holy-white circle of light fell only on the Bobster. In one of his first interviews—CNN, Bernie Shaw—Dole tried to move the halo, broaden it, share it: "Bernie, before I forget, there's somebody on my left here who's been a tremendous help in this campaign . . ." But the lens would not move—Elizabeth wasn't lit correctly, or something, so she was left, standing, chin up, smiling her most brilliant smile at no one. Bernie just asked Bob another question, and Elizabeth said she had an awful headache.

The strange thing was, it was the same away from the cameras—in the hall, on the stairway. No one got too close to Dole. No one touched him. (Save for one time, when Dole began to fiddle one-handed with his tie. "Z'at straight, Mari?" She hopped up. "Yes, Senator." But he could tell the knot wasn't perfect. "Why'nch you go ahead, Mike." So Glassner came, half-leaping on tiptoe, over equipment, to kneel before the Bobster and straighten the red power tie.) . . . No one spoke unless spoken to—or invited by his eyes—and then they mostly scrambled to offer some information. "Senator," Synhorst ventured, "did you hear what Bush said?"

"Yeah. He said he didn't know what, aghh, mis-*stakes* he made to get this result." Dole's eyebrows dipped, he lifted a little shrug. All the courtiers broke up laughing. He said to Synhorst: "You talk to Wittgraf?" Synhorst's brow furrowed—was he supposed to? But Dole was rasping his prairie cackle. "Hegh-hegh-hegh, send him a bo-kayyy."

There was no discussion of what to say to the cameras, to the voters—or how. (Dole would say whatever he thought best.) There was no political talk (save with anchormen)—what this meant to Iowa, to New Hampshire, to the country, to Dole for President . . . nor certainly any personal talk—what this meant to Dole, to Bob and Elizabeth, or to all of them, together. In the end, they were not together. In the end, it was Bob, alone. And despite the jokes he dropped behind him, the trail of breadcrumbs . . . in the end, that trail led back to an opaque curtain of reserve—Bob alone. You could just about see the curtain fall, when he got to another network room, and he had to wait, and his darting gaze found no work to do. Then his eyes would roll up to where ceiling met wall, where there was no one smiling at him, no one to greet . . . and he could think: this thing *was happening*!

Things were happening *for* him—different things—he was *making* them happen. That's what he meant when one TV man suggested that Iowans had responded to Dole as a neighbor. "Well, I was out here as a neighbor in 1980, too—no one noticed." They weren't going to take this away by discussing the *factors* . . . no.

"It's still up to Bob Dole to deliver the message, to attract the votes." That's what Dole said.

"It's up to Bob Dole . . ."

The way people looked at him now, the way they cheered him, the hope in their eyes when they listened to him . . . the way he stood, without a doubt, to meet that—that's what was different, that was the excitement. It was no dream, no pipe dream, it was a *plan,* a work of will: *that's what he meant* at his announcement, when he tried to tell that freezing crowd how he'd sat in the sun, on the balcony of his office, and he'd looked out at the Mall, the White House, the monuments—and he *had to think:* Could he do it? Could he meet that? Could he, by the same will that had kept him alive when he was *nothing, garbage,* could he meet hope of that size now, make that kind of difference? Was that in him? . . . And he'd answered: *Yes! He could make that difference—he* . . .

"Senator? . . ."

They moved him to the ballroom floor. NBC had rented a corner of the big room where Dole's faithful had gathered. And they'd built a platform between their space and the Dole-crowd, so Brokaw could interview the Senator with the Iowa folk going nuts behind Dole—for effect, you know, good TV. And you could see, when Dole arrived at the head of his train (longer now: they were joined by Bob's nephew, Jeff Nelson, and his wife and daughter—they lived in Des Moines), it was going to work like a charm. . . . Dole went straight to the platform and stood, and the techies fired up the lights on the Bobster, and the crowd caught a look at him—and even before Elizabeth struggled up, in her tight skirt, to stand next to him, the crowd was yelling: "Go *GET'EM BOB*! . . . DOLE! DOLE! DOLE! . . ." And the Bobster was crooning: "Howwe*DOOOnn*? . . . How'*DOOOOnnn*?" . . . with his thumb poking the air, fist pumping—he was bouncing on the balls of his feet. And then . . . NBC was not ready. They were okay in Des Moines, but they didn't have the network, or Brokaw was busy, or it was time for local commercials—something . . . they told Dole it would be a few minutes, so he climbed down, and Elizabeth after . . . and then, everybody was standing around.

Jeff Nelson offered to get Cokes . . . and the rest just stood, all but silent in a semicircle around Bob Dole. He was still half-bouncing, looking around, all dressed up and nowhere to go—everybody else staring at him, with pleasant party faces, searching themselves for something to say to him.

At last, Jeff's daughter, Kristen, said to the circle at large:

"You should have seen Dad's precinct! Where's Dad? Show him Dad's precinct."

And everybody perked up: they were going to engage the Bobster. They, too, had a piece of this night-of-nights to show him. So Jeff was summoned, and he went into a paroxysm of patting—his jacket, his shirt, his pants—trying to find the slip of paper where he'd written the numbers from his precinct caucus. All eyes bounced from Jeff, to the Bobster, back to Jeff, and all his pockets . . . until he *found the numbers*!

By that time, Dole was half-turned, back toward his ballroom crowd, the platform, the camera, the bright lights—he had the print press to do after this, then tape for the overnights, the morning shows—*Let's gooo!* . . . Jeff was holding the numbers in midcircle, midair—but no one would touch the Bobster, or say, "Hey, Bob! Here's the damn numbers! Turn around!" . . . Jeff held his little paper up for four or five seconds—it was getting embarrassing—while everybody stared at the back of the Bobster's head, shining in the halogen corona of the platform lights behind him . . . and, then, too, at six-foot-two, they were staring *up* at Dole, and the lights shining down from NBC glistened in their eyes . . . till Mari finally plucked the paper offering, tapped the Senator, and handed him the numbers. They stared up. There was an instant, it was clear, where the Bobster did not know what the hell they had stuck in his hand . . . there was the heart-stopping chance he would conclude this was trash— some mistake—and wad it up, and that would have made everything so awkward. But someone said, "It's Jeff's!" and the Bobster understood, this was a gift of a sort, and . . . he popped his eyebrows up in a show of interest and pleasure. The scary thing was the look on *their* faces—Jeff, Karen, and Kristen Nelson, Mari Maseng, Bill Brock, Kenny, Anita, Elizabeth Dole—the up-turned smiles that *erupted,* with the holy-white network light in their eyes . . . it was a look from Renaissance paintings, Adorations, when the faithful gaze upon the Body, the figure at the center, with the golden light around His head—a look of awe, love, and fear.

— ★ —

It was rock 'n' roll on the Dole plane, after three or four hours' sleep, flying east—big plane, a Bahamas Air 727, and not a spare seat from the cockpit to the narrow tail. Anyway, no one stayed in a seat. In mid-takeoff, the Dole staff was perched, smiling, on the arms of the chairs. One Advance man gave Mari a high-five as he passed in the aisle. Chuckie Grassley, Bill Brock, and the pollster, Dick Wirthlin, were dispatched to the back of the plane to spin. Wirthlin was saying:

"The political world has been changed. The mountain moved."

The press was crowded around these Big Guys, standing in the aisle and on the seats. Boom mikes raked the ceiling of the cabin. The pack mushed and trampled the neat breakfasts in neat plasti-packs. One of the stewardesses of Bahamas Air said, "I've done a political charter, but it was . . . more, uh . . . contained."

Wirthlin was saying to the *L.A. Times:* "Absolutely, if there is no Robert-son, there would've been only one headline—DOLE BEATS BUSH. As it is, there's two headlines—both of them bad for Bush."

In the front, Brock was rocking on his heels and toes in the aisle next to Dole's chair. He said something to Dole and then threw his whole torso back, laughing. Everybody was back and forth, from the press section to the staff in front. They were yukking it up about George Bush, quoted from New Hampshire—it was on the wire: "Iowa is Iowa," he'd said, "and New Hamp-shire is New Hampshire." Yuhhhh! That was rich! Next, they'll teach him how to spell O-hio!

On the tarmac in New Hampshire it was a mob scene. Now the camera jockeys had aluminum ladders, so they wouldn't have to shoot through a swarm of shoulders and heads. Between the plane and a long motorcade, Dole was surrounded by the iron ring of cameras and tapes—ten to twelve bodies deep. Advance men tried to keep the herd from crushing the Bobster flat. Dole *was* President that morning. He was on his way to the statehouse to address a joint session of the New Hampshire legislature. The topic of the speech was *national security.* It was a Presidential speech.

Meanwhile, the staff was handing out Xeroxes of a letter from Ronald Reagan. It was dated February 5, 1988—four days before—and it said:

> *Dear Bob:*
>
> *I want to express my personal gratitude to you for your support of my request for assistance to the Nicaraguan Democratic Resistance. I particularly appreciate your sponsorship of the resolution to approve my request, and your leadership in achieving a successful vote in the Senate. . . .*
>
> *Sincerely,*
> *Ronald Reagan*

It was the sort of roto-pen "courtesy letter" that Presidents send out routinely. If it showed anything, it showed that Dole's friend Howard Baker was still in control, as Chief of Staff. But it looked like more—looked like Reagan was hedging his bets . . . or, at the very least, like Dole was welcome to ride shotgun on the Gipper's old mule train . . . as it rolled in a cloud of golden dust toward greater *national security.*

Who could ask for a warier shotgun man?

The speech text handed out on his four press buses, pitching and rocking toward the statehouse in Concord, was true troglodyte target-practice: Bob Dole trusted *Russk*—uh, you know, *Soviets* . . . 'bout as far as he could *throw 'em.* And let no one forget it! Especially not the right-wing, white-flight, tax-flight droolers who had overrun the southern tier of New Hampshire ("Live Free or Move!") . . . and now voted in overwhelming numbers in the Republican primary.

Here he came, through the grand white doors of the old House chamber, with his beautiful wife . . . both of them *glowed.* (Where'd he get that *tan?*) The legislators on the aisles leapt up—and took a step back. Everybody was standing . . . and cheering. The Doles sat down, but the cheers went on, for two minutes more.

At last, a minister at the rostrum intoned:

"O God of all . . . winners and runners-up . . ."

The business at hand, you know—a blessing for the political show that arrived with Bob Dole. When Dole stood to speak, the assembled legislators gave him another standing ovation. Doug Scamman, Speaker of the House, had arranged this for Dole—this session. Couldn't *be* better timing—couldn't be better anything.

Poor Gephardt was, at that moment, yelling his speech in a shopping mall. Dukakis had to rent a theater. Jack Kemp, God bless him, was freezing his buns at a spare press conference on the steps of that very statehouse. But Bob Dole was warm, bathed in white light, anointed with the cheers of the suits in joint session . . . to whom he said, before his discourse on strategy vis-à-vis the Soviets . . .

"Thank you . . .

"It's good to be here.

"Good to be awake.

"Good to feel good."

And then, President Bobster went to text—he actually *read out* a speech— had to get it right. He knew Gorbachev was listening.

— ★ —

He had a meeting, after his speech, in the Speaker's office—a ten-minute sit-down with the Big Guys: Where do we stand?

All his New Hampshire Bigs said, "It's winnable." Dole asked Wirthlin. And Wirthlin, without benefit of any new numbers since the previous night, sketched a scenario of a Dole win. They would overtake Bush that weekend. They would win New Hampshire February 16, the following Tuesday. "And then," Wirthlin said, "it's a roll."

He was looking at Dole to see if Dole was pleased.

Dole looked back without expression, and in the voice designed to cut through wind, he said: "Wait a minute. Back up a minute. What if we don't win?"

Everyone was silent. Everybody figured, *Win! Win! We're winning!* But Dole had enough Russell, Kansas, left in him to wonder. . . . He'd been saying for months that he couldn't feel things building in New Hampshire. He got a big boost a few months back when Senator Warren Rudman signed on, and Rudman's people took over the Dole operation. (Actually, they *were* the Dole operation. There was nothing before.) Then Dole started hearing that Rudman's "organization" was a paper tiger. (Rudman himself said organization didn't count in New Hampshire.) In mid-January, a poll showed Dole almost in *third place* (even with Jack Kemp!) . . . and Dole about hit the roof. Wirthlin told him not to worry: that would all change, once he won Iowa. Bob would be on a roll! . . .

"If we don't win?" Dole said in the statehouse. "What happens?"

Wirthlin bestirred himself anew, and said: "Well, it's less rosy, but, uh . . . we can do it. You come out of here, you go down south, our numbers show . . ." He ended up again with a Dole win—at the wire.

So Dole nodded, then fell silent. They could see him turning it over in his head: Maybe this thing was on the downhill . . . these guys were pros—maybe they're right! Maybe he was just ultra-sensitive because he did so badly in New Hampshire last time, still didn't trust the people's smiles. Maybe he oughta just . . . accept—people prob'ly weren't any different here than they were in Iowa, or Kansas . . . pretty much the same!

So it was President Bobster, still, who boarded his motorcade for a date at

Chubb Insurance, out in the woods, miles from any town. It was a tanned, handsome, and confident candidate who marched through the snow, into the low brick building, straight to the cafeteria where a crowd of employees waited. The cafeteria (in fact, the whole excessive exurban brick fort) bespoke the easy money of the Reagan recovery. It was a long room, hung with corporate philodendrons, kept alive on a service contract with the Corporate Philodendron Company. Fake butcher-block tables made things homey. There were Chubb employees at the tables . . . clapping, kind of.

In streamed Dole's entourage, and Dole's herd, smiling and bouncy. They were riding with a winner, making the big turn. They were showing a new state what they'd seen *for months,* in Iowa . . . yes, they still had a bit of Iowa about them: it was that frank, friendly, mannerly air that went so well with Dole's midwest verities—like mashed potatoes with fried chicken.

There was a thick woman in a brown pants suit leaning on one of the faux-maple tables near the aisle. One of the Dole-herd, a particularly friendly and polite writer, proffered her a grin, and said:

"How you doin', ma'am?"

This flower of New Hampshire looked him full in the face, and said: "We don't need people like you around here."

108

White Men at War

TUESDAY MORNING, after the Iowa caucus, Bush was already in New Hampshire. (No use lingering at the site of a massacre—Bush left Iowa before the vote began.) He and the white men were walled away in the newest, most futilely fancy motel in New Hampshire, the Clarion, near Nashua, a box of white cement rising eight stories tall in the middle of a deserted snow-covered bog, a half-mile distant from the nearest road, miles away from anything else. It was the hotel embodiment of the oversized and isolated Bush campaign . . . more perfect as symbol, still, because inside, amid the pink marble and olde-Englishy prints, there was . . . *red alert*!

Bush was up before first light. Tell the truth, he hadn't slept much. He was out at a factory gate, shaking hands in the numbing cold . . . cold to make the pain creep from the feet up, from the hands in, from the back of the neck . . . who cared? Bush was newly, nervily aware: he could lose! (*That* was pain.) He could lose New Hampshire, then Minnesota and South Dakota . . . he could lose every state until South Carolina—or Super Tuesday! . . . and that would be the end: the South would crumble. He would lose everything.

The white men were abustle in the hotel hallway. They looked bad, ill-rested, unshaven, no ties . . . there was, on the Hall of Power, a bad smell of stress and failure. "Ah knew it," Atwater was claiming. "Ah kin feel the wind! Ah *tol'* him it was a hunnert percent he was gonna lose, and Ah said it was fifty-fifty he was gonna run *thirrrd*!" . . . What did it matter what Lee knew? They didn't just run third—Dole beat them two-to-one! Bush did not win a single county in Iowa.

Teeter looked like an actuary whose years of patient calculation had just revealed the median death age . . . was *his* age. Overnight polls in New Hampshire showed Dole cutting Bush's lead to eight or nine points—*before* the news from Iowa. God only knew what the swing would be after that humiliation. The problem was, voters couldn't see any *political* difference between Bush and Dole. And Dole was trouncing them with his man-of-the-people work boots. Half the Bush vote came from people who just thought Bush was going to win. Well, Iowa would take care of *that*—Dole looked plenty big-league now. . . . Somehow, they had to show those voters that Bush and Dole were not the same—they'd make different leaders. "We gotta show, they're different guys!" But that meant showing who George Bush was, and they hadn't been able to pull that off for two years. How could they start now?

Ailes looked even worse than usual—he had pneumonia. He was fevered, full of antibiotics. But he said he could tape an "Ask George Bush"—a half-hour, statewide TV . . . fill the audience with Bushies who'd lob softball questions and let the man stand up and talk. That's what Ailes did for Nixon in '68, when they had to *show* the New Nixon! . . . Goddammit, it was time to *show George Bush*! . . . Not Bush's plane, Bush's cars, Bush's staff—that's all people ever saw! . . . "We gotta get rid of this VP shit!"

"Goddam, Ah'm with ya!" Lee said.

This was another thing Atwater said he *always* knew . . . all that motorcade shit's jussa pain inna ass! . . . He *tol'* 'em, said Lee, back in, uh, September: *We gotta git close to the GROUN' in this thing.* . . . Tol' that asshole Fuller that Sununu was complainin' 'bout the motorcades, uh, blockin' the traffic, an', uh, *pissin' people off*!

That's what Lee *always* said, *always*. People couldn't *feel* the man! Didn't know him! . . . *That's why they were losing!*

Then George Bush came back to the hotel, called a meeting. He didn't want to hear more talk about losing. He didn't want to hear about Iowa, what happened, or who did it. That was over—gone. "There's no sense looking back. It's nobody's fault. We either go on, win in New Hampshire—or I go back to Kennebunk, and go fishing."

Captain Bush, the one-minute manager.

Of course, that didn't amount to a plan.

But Governor Sununu was with Bush . . . he said they didn't *need* a plan—not a new one: they were going to *win*.

That's how Sununu was. First thing he wanted to show you: he was in control. Second thing: he was smarter than you.

Of course, it was Sununu's organization they were doubting—what Sununu called the best organization in the history of New Hampshire. And it was Sununu's plan: for the last year in New Hampshire, George Bush had gone where Sununu took him . . . what Sununu called his "see-me-touch-me-feel-me" campaign. The Governor was proudest of last New Year's Eve in Concord, where people come out, with their children in tow, to stroll Main Street . . . before they go get loaded at their parties. Sununu's boys took over a clothing store and set George and Barbara Bush in there with borrowed furniture—instant living room. They had three thousand people lined up in the cold, waiting for hot chocolate and a handshake with the Veep.

Sununu was sure: that would not be forgotten. Nor would that big picnic at Congressman Judd Gregg's, the Fourth of July parade in Bristol, the community fair on the green in New London. . . . "You've invested a lot of time and effort," Sununu said. "The only thing we've got to do is show George Bush is the same guy they met and wanted to support before. Just get him out on the street!"

Okay, the street . . . when?

Now—today! Every day!

The bible called for Bush to leave for Washington—lunch with Reagan. Then a day in New Orleans at the Southern Republican Leadership Conference . . .

Scrap it.

Scrap the bible?

They *had* to have their lunch with Reagan. (Maybe get TV in there!) . . . Reagan's approval stood at eighty percent with New Hampshire Republicans. This wasn't Iowa—they loved the Gipper!

So, okay, lunch—get him down there, picture with Reagan—then back for see-me-touch-me . . .

And "Ask George Bush" . . .

Yeah . . . Ask Bush.

And we gotta hit Dole.

We gotta show they're not the same.

The Straddle Ad!

That was an Ailes script—an attack on Dole that said the Bobster always tried to fudge where he stood. The ad suggested Dole was going to raise taxes . . . no matter what he said.

Bush didn't want the ad—too tough. He'd rejected the script: *no Straddle Ad.*

You got to say *something* about the sonofabitch!

He can't pull off that "I'm One of You" stuff in New Hampshire.

But *you* gotta say something . . .

That was the problem—Bush had to say something—about Dole, about himself, about the country . . . *something*! People had to hear, had to feel, that Bush believed he was the man for this job, that he wanted it enough to come out of the bubble.

Let's get out there!

Where?

Everywhere. Anyplace there's more than five people.

And no motorcade bullshit!

Just stop.

Service isn't gonna like it.

Fuck the Service!

So that was the new plan. After seven years of careful building, after twenty million dollars spent, after all the briefings, coaching, debate books, the cautious positioning, luxuriant staffing, the hundreds of speeches, the thousands of events, hundreds of thousands of miles, after *seven years of detail* . . . it came down to one state, where Bush would hit the streets, and do . . . everything—at once.

So he did. He went out and hit the high school in Hopkinton, an insurance office in Keene . . . and in the middle, he *stopped* . . . at a mall, then a grocery store, where he saw people across the street, behind a rope . . . he *ran* to shake their hands.

And he said . . . well—Dole was in the state with a tough speech on the Soviets, so Bush had to show *he* was tough on Soviets—he was supposed to talk about himself, after all . . .

"I don't know whether your history teaches you," said Bush to the high school students at Hopkinton, "back into the early days of the Korean War and that kind of thing . . . but there was an old tough guy named Yakov Malik at the United Nations . . . and I was the UN Ambassador then—uh, I started dealing with the Soviets about then, 1971, 1972 . . ."

Somehow, the story about Yakov Malik never did come out.

Dole was promising to solve the deficit with a freeze of federal spending—so Bush said *he* could freeze federal spending: "A flexible freeze . . . that would give uh, *flexibility,* but would keep that overall level, so . . ."

But that wasn't about him, at all.

He tried to sum up why *he* was the man New Hampshire voters would turn to . . .

"I'm one of you."

What?

"The reason is . . ." Bush said, "because I am. I was born in Massachusetts, grew up in Connecticut, live across the way—uh, have a house across the way—in Maine . . . and I understand New Hampshire."

Three Greyhound busloads of press could not *believe* it: the poor desperate bastard was lifting Dole's slogan! *Wimp-o-rama!* . . . Bush did not *get it*—thought it was about geography!

They were yelling at him from risers and ropelines:

WHADDABOUT TEXAS?

"I'm one of them, too."

Y'BORN IN MASSACHUSETTS!

Bush shrugged. "Can't vote in Massachusetts. Born there. I'm one of them, too."

This was a game Bush could not win. He tried to explain:

"It was s'posed to be funny. . . . Maybe nobody got it."

Next stop, it was worse:

WHYD'YA SAY YOU'RE FROM TEXAS?

"Look," Bush said. "I'll *drop* the slogan."

Testy, testy!

Well, goddam right! "They nitpick every word I say!" . . . While he was

out there, trying *so hard* to keep a life's work from sliding down the tubes
. . . trying to spread himself everywhere around that state till he almost pulled
himself apart . . . trying to show he was coming back . . . trying to show the
fighter he was . . . but *loyal* . . . but *determined* . . . but *friendly* . . . trying,
in one week, to be for them everything he thought they wanted—to do *everything*!

Almost everything . . .

No. Everything.

While Bush was trying to be one of them, Ailes was on the phone to his wife,
in New York. Ailes's fever was a hundred and two. He had a towel over his
head to trap the steam from a vaporizer. He was gray. His voice was a nasty
croak. But he'd have to be dead—at least unconscious—before he'd stop trying
to hit Dole.

"You go in, tonight," he said. "Make the Straddle Ad."

Norma Ailes was a TV producer.

"Do we have authorization?"

"They don't air it, I'll eat it. We're gonna need it." He dictated the ad: "Dole
straddled on the INF . . . straddled on the oil import fee. Bush led the fight
for INF. He's against an oil import fee. . . . Then we say, 'Bush won't raise
taxes, period.' Put the period on there. 'Dole won't promise—you know what
that means.' . . ."

Norma Ailes wanted to know: "What do we use for visuals?"

"Use what you find."

It didn't have to be pretty.

"Just go make it."

The tape arrived by messenger, Wednesday, before noon.

— ★ —

Wednesday, before noon, Peggy Noonan was in her car, on the way home to
her house in the woods of Virginia. Peggy had left the daily grind at the White
House. She meant to stay home, write her book, raise her little boy. That's why
she was hustling now—home to her son. She'd left her mother with the boy.

She had the radio on—news from New Hampshire . . . and she heard Bush's
voice, tinny in the speakers:

"I'm one of you . . ."

Oh, God, that was *awful*! The poor man had nothing to *say*!

She liked Bush. She didn't know him well, but he'd asked her to do a couple
of speeches . . . the first time, he only had an hour or two before the Steedham
thing. Steedham was the sailor whom the TWA hijackers killed and threw off
the plane, onto the tarmac in Beirut. His body was coming home, to an Air
Force base—just after 6:00 P.M.—it would be live on every news show in the
country. Bush was going to represent the White House. He worried for Steedham's parents: they'd have to stand there, watching their son's body come off
the plane, with the newsies poking telephotos at their faces. He had to say
something of comfort . . . so he called Peggy.

That was her reputation in the White House. She was the designated "sensitive"—ever since she did that speech for Reagan after the *Challenger* blew up. As for Bush's reputation . . . well, Noonan couldn't understand why he was so much demeaned, why the Reaganauts didn't trust him. He was a Goldwater man! . . . And such a sweetie: so interested in *her* . . . charming—handsome! She was struck by his maleness, the way he threw his legs out from the edge of his chair—big legs—an athlete. . . . Why did people think he was a wimp?

"*I'm one of you* . . ."

God, he *sounded* like a wimp!

She got home and asked her mother, in the kitchen: "Mom, could you take care of the baby for a week if I'm away?"

Then she called Fuller's office.

Fuller was "in a meeting."

"Well, tell Craig if he wants me, I'll be there."

An hour later, word came back: Fuller's assistant, Diane Terpeluk, said that Craig said . . . 2:00 P.M.

"Really? What are we doing?"

"They're all getting on *Air Force Two,* going to New Hampshire."

She saw Bush on the plane for a moment, when she walked into the Staff Cabin. "Oh," he said, "come to pick us up off the mat, huh?"

That was the calmest thing anybody said. The purposeful quiet of *Air Force Two* was gone. Atwater couldn't even say hello. He was scratching his head, like he did when he was nervous. "Ah kin see this slippin' away! Ah got bones for this! Ah got skin that kin feel *everything* . . ." Teeter was edgy, earnest. He wanted a sit-down right away. "Look, we gotta show who this guy is—they're not the same, Dole and him. Different lives. Be totally different leaders."

Peggy set to work on a new stump speech.

That night, she sat down at dinner in the Clarion with Teeter and the VP. They sat in the restaurant—in the main room, with regular people. That threw the place into a tizzy. The Secret Service was around Bush like angry bees. No waiter would approach.

She showed Bush the new speech. He read it with his head back.

"Oh," he said. "The me-me-me stuff."

Peggy said, "You know, it's the *person* we're electing here. It's who you are . . . that's the difference."

Bush said the difference was: "I know the other guys—they shouldn't be President."

He said: "Well . . . would you like a drink?" His voice held a boy's eagerness.

Teeter broke in, right away: "No, I think I'll just have a Coke."

Bush turned to Peggy. She was on a diet, wasn't supposed to have anything. She was going to say no . . . but she could see he'd be crushed.

"How about you, Peggy?"

"Well, I'd *like* to . . ."

"Good!" said Bush. "Then I'll have one, too."

He got a martini, and he drank that sucker down.

"Well," he said. "Would you like another?"

Even Teeter caught the drift now—he got a drink. Peggy got another glass of wine. Bush got another martini. But he stopped at two.

And the next day, Thursday, Bush went out into the cold again. This time, it wasn't just chat at a grocery store: he showed up in a parka and a ballcap. He drove an eighteen-wheeler (with two Secret Service agents hanging off the side mirrors) around the lot at Cuzzin Richie's Truck Stop. He parked his backside on a greasy vinyl seat and had him some breakfast. He pulled out his wallet and paid for his own. Then he moved on to a lumberyard, drove a forklift . . .

This time, he said a budget freeze was a "cop-out"—in fact, the worst kind . . . a *Congressional* cop-out! Bush's voice held something new: conviction . . . and contempt.

"Congress isn't the *real* world," he said. "They don't *decide*. It's all one long Continuing Resolution. They pass the bills that make the constituencies happy: pig farmers get Baby Pig Development Grants. Districts that wish they had a river get a bridge! . . .

"Bob Dole, my opponent, says the answer here is a freeze. . . . A freeze will freeze in all those studies of pigs and mating habits of butterflies!"

It was the first time Bush had taken Dole on, by name.

And he did something else for the first time, too:

He got to an old people's home, late in the day—too late for network news—and he started to talk . . . about his mother.

"You know, she calls me. She says, 'I don't like the things they're saying about you, George.' " His hand grasped air to his heart. "So . . . it's a mother, to her little boy, still."

And that led him to . . . himself—not his jobs, all the things he'd been—but the way he felt about himself:

"I have a tendency—I confess to it—to avoid going on and on with great eloquent statements of belief. Some are better at that than I am."

He was speaking softly to the small crowd.

"I don't always articulate . . . but I do feel. And I care too much to leave now. Our work isn't done. So I'm working my heart out up here . . . and I'm asking for your help."

On the press bus, in gathering darkness, they were playing tapes, over and over, trying to catch the soft words, and buzzing about the "new Bush."

That evening, for the first time, tracking polls showed Dole even with Bush in New Hampshire . . . and Bush still bleeding everywhere.

— ★ —

That was the evening Bush saw the Straddle Ad. He winced. "God. That's awful."

It wasn't pretty: every time Dole showed up on the screen, there were two Dole-faces—two-faced—pointed toward one another with the word "Straddled" across the screen.

The INF . . . the oil import fee . . . then taxes.

On taxes, the screen said "Straddle"—present tense—which faded out, to: "Taxes—He can't say no."

The voice-over said: "Bob Dole straddles, and he just won't promise not to raise taxes. And you know what that means."

Mosbacher stood behind Bush in the Clarion. "Well, it's true," he said.

"Is it?" Bush said. "Are you sure?"

Sununu had the backup research from Pinkerton: full memo—Dole's votes, back to the Kennedy tax cut of '63. . . . They were covered.

Fuller said it seemed awfully negative.

Teeter said, no-no-negative-no.

Ailes did not defend the ad. He'd made the goddam thing on his own hook—that was statement enough.

Atwater didn't weigh in, either . . . but that night, George W. Bush called his father. . . . Junior had been briefed by Atwater.

"Dad, have you looked at the ad?"

"Yeah. They seem to think it's too negative. I do, too."

"Are you sure all the others agree?"

"I think so."

"Well," Junior said carefully, "I'm not sure all the others agree. . . . I just wanted to make sure you had, uh, full input."

That kept the question alive. Friday brought it roaring back onto the table. Friday was the worst. For one thing, it snowed like hell. No one could get around on the roads. Bush had a breakfast speech at the Clarion—a hot speech, a zinger on Dole . . . and no one came. No press, anyway.

When the white men got back to the Hall of Power, they found out Haig was pulling out . . . and endorsing Bob Dole, at another hotel, in front of musta been three hundred reporters.

The problem wasn't *Haig backs Dole*—Al Haig was two percent in the polls, and that was probably rounded off from something less. The problem was, with the snow, Haig-and-Dole was the only fresh video of the day—CNN ran that SOB *a hundred times*! . . . The clip had Haig calling it quits . . . Haig saying Dole was a man "who'd been there—and made a difference" . . . Bush was a man "who'd just been there—period." . . . Then, there was Dole, striding up to the podium to grasp Haig's hand, the two of them grinning and muttering jokes that only the other one could hear.

Bush himself, cooped up in the Clarion, must have seen the thing six times . . . before Atwater switched off the TV—or switched it over to the VCR. Lee had something to show the Veep—a tape of Dole's current ad, the one with a picture of Bush that fuzzed and faded in symbolic futility until it disappeared.

"It's just like ours," Lee said, "or, uh . . . worse."

Atwater was always, sometimes edgily, aware that he did not come from George Bush's world. But Lee thought he knew Bush: he'd watched the man for fifteen years—since 1973, when Atwater was a rising star in the Young Republicans and Bush was RNC chairman. (In fact, it was '73 when Atwater said to Bush, there was this sweet little intern in Strom Thurmond's office. Lee was going to bring her by that night, to a fund-raiser. If Bush could mention, somehow, he just *could not get along* without Lee . . . maybe she'd be impressed. Bush played his part, but he could see the young woman couldn't care less about the Chairman of the GOP. So he called Atwater over: "Listen. Why don't you take her out on my boat? Maybe get another couple of friends . . . call Don Rhodes, tell him I said to use the boat." That was Lee's first date with his wife, Sally.)

What Lee always talked about was the Bush-code of conduct . . . it drove him nuts. Bush had to be talked into doing what was good for him. Sometimes, he still wouldn't do it. There were small things—like yesterday, someone asked about Noriega. *Perfect* chance for Bush to tee off on a drug-dirty dictator. . . . But the Reagan White House was trying to cut a deal with Noriega. Bush wouldn't say a word. . . . Then there were big things—like this ad. Lee was sure Bush had to run the Straddle Ad . . . or *something,* to take Dole down. But Lee knew he had to deal with the code. "George Bush," Atwater would sometimes say, "is everything I'm not."

"Sir . . . he's hittin' *you!*" Lee said.

Sununu volunteered that the people of New Hampshire would not be confused if Bush hit back. They understood "comparative" ads. Sununu was always singing up the voters of New Hampshire—sagacious souls who'd elected him three times.

"Mr. Vahz Pres'ent," Lee said gravely. "You may, uh . . . this may, uhm, lose me mah *job*—but Ah think we're *behind* . . ."

Bush turned toward Teeter.

They *were* behind—for the first time—but it was tight. And Teeter did not want the ad. Teeter's every instinct was to moderate Bush—rub every rough corner off until he rolled like a marble to the deep center of the bell curve. "Overnight, it's within the margin of error," Teeter said. "On the other hand, if you look at . . ."

This wasn't the time for on-the-one-hand-on-the-other.

"Mr. Vahz Pres'ent, Ah think we gotta, uh, hit 'em."

Bush knew it was up to him—nothing collegial about it, in the end. But he could not sit there anymore, talking about it—he had to get moving . . . *do something.* He'd go outside . . . see how daughter Doro and her husband were doing, down the hall—maybe take a walk . . . find some voters! He was out of his chair, hunting a coat . . . he was out the door.

But not before he heard, or overheard, more talk about the ad, from the white men—and Barbara Bush, who said:

"I don't think ours is that bad."

109

Believe Me,
Bob

DOLE DIDN'T THINK Bush could take the pressure. He'd known the guy for twenty years. Never worked with him (that's how Dole got to know most guys)—but he'd seen Bush, for hours at a time, when the Veep presided in the Senate . . . seen him in a hundred meetings—politics, White House briefings. Bush never said anything in the meetings. He'd stare at his own tie, the arm of his chair, or whoever was talking—if it was the President, Bush always agreed. . . . *Hey! Hiiiii! Hey!* He'd be kissing up to people afterward, talking tennis. *Y'play Jimmy yesterday? . . .*

Nice guy—far as that went.

Tennis, terrific. Prob'ly great on a golf course.

Politics, that was another sort of sport.

— ★ —

Dole had seen to Bush's bottom, he thought—in New Hampshire, eight years ago, 1980 . . . when Bob Dole was nowhere and Bush was riding in the curl of the great wave. In those days, the Iowa bounce *was* a bounce—front page of the papers, cover of the newsmagazines, lead story on the six o'clock report. . . . Bush was everywhere after he won Iowa—shot up twenty-five percent in the polls. Bush versus Reagan—that was *the* story. "There is a widespread perception," *The Washington Post* reported, "that Reagan is fading fast."

That's why Reagan arranged to debate Bush, one-on-one—the *Nashua Telegraph* would sponsor the event. It was recognition that the race had boiled down to two men—why not make the face-off fact? Just two guys on stage at the local high school, Saturday night, three days before the vote.

It was high electoral theater.

And the last straw for Dole.

How could they freeze him out? How could they act like Bob Dole didn't exist? Dole, Howard Baker, Phil Crane, John Anderson . . . were they non-candidates?

Dole peppered the papers with angry quotes about Bush—the "Rockefeller candidate" . . . who was "hired help for the big banks" . . . "a member of the Trilateral Commission!" (Bill Loeb, publisher of the *Union Leader,* was happy to retail the slurs.) . . . Dole-lawyers filed complaints with the Federal Election Commission to stop the *Nashua Telegraph* debate. The newspaper had to pull out as sponsor. But Ronald Reagan picked up the costs.

At that point, Dole began calling the other campaigns, working out an ambush. They would *all* show up at the high school—force a showdown, right there on TV—let Bush *try* to keep them out . . . while the whole state watched.

The beauty part was, Reagan's people were in on it! John Sears, Reagan's number-one man, helped script the drama. Dole sent his young Advance kid, Mari Maseng, to find a holding room for the four excluded candidates, and someplace they could talk to the press. By phone from his Manchester hotel, Dole worked the details with relish. How long was that hallway to the stage? Where would Bush be sitting?

On the night of the debate, there were fifteen hundred people in the high school gym. Jon Breen, the *Telegraph* editor, moderator of the debate, was shuttling between the Reagan and Bush gangs, trying to work out what to do about Dole, Anderson, Crane, Baker . . . four candidates had invaded! Would George Bush accept their participation?

Bush refused even to *talk* to those guys—this was his shot at Reagan! Rules are rules!

They sent New Hampshire's Senator, Gordon Humphrey, to reason with Bush: "George, give 'em a chance. It'll be good for the Party!"

"Don't lecture me about the GOP," Bush snapped. "I've worked a lot harder than you have to build the Republican Party."

In the gym, the crowd was yelling—the debate was forty minutes late. Finally, Bush came on stage, smiling and waving. Reagan appeared, to cheers from his faithful. . . . But then the *other* four guys filed in, behind the desks, like spectres from a Dickens tale. The moderator, Breen, announced that he meant to stick to the rules—this would be a two-man debate.

Governor Reagan started a speech—how everybody ought to be included. Breen instructed the technicians to turn off Reagan's mike. That's when Reagan started yelling—he was beautiful! A line from an old movie: "I paid for this microphone, Mr. Green!"

The crowd cheered—even Bush supporters cheered. The other four guys on stage started clapping, waving to the crowd. Breen was trying to get them off stage. The crowd was yelling. Reagan gracefully stood, and shook all the other fellows' hands as they left. But Bush froze, like a kid who'd rather take his ball and go home. He sat there steaming, couldn't say a word. . . . He looked like a perfect weenie.

Well, Bush got his debate with Reagan—but no one remembered anything they said. What they remembered was that gorgeous Reagan moment ("I paid for this microphone!") . . . and maybe a couple of lines from the press conference Dole arranged in a schoolroom.

Howard Baker said of George Bush: "If he is the front-runner, he wears the crown most unbecomingly."

Dole, as usual, was more direct: "As far as George Bush is concerned, he'd better find himself another Party."

Bush was so rattled he left the state—went to Houston for two days, to "rest" before the New Hampshire vote. Meanwhile, in those two days, Reagan bounced past Bush in the polls. Bush lost New Hampshire . . . and Big Mo. Ultimately, he lost any chance to unhorse Ronald Reagan.

Worse still, he left behind an image of George Bush as a wimp *extraordinaire*—a stickler for form who choked when it counted. It was a portrait that would haunt him for a decade, a gift from the Gipper (who would never forget how Bush *just sat there*) . . . and from Bob Dole, who wanted Bush to know that the damage would not be confined to that night—nor even to that campaign.

"George!" Dole rasped as he left that stage in Nashua. "There'll be another time."

— ★ —

This was his time, Dole said—'88 was Bob Dole's year. For three days after the Iowa caucus, Dole ate into Bush's lead in New Hampshire. Dole made up eighteen points—and he was still climbing. Wirthlin reported on the tracking polls every morning.

"You're up . . ."

"It's moving . . ."

"Undecideds are breaking for us . . ."

One week before, Dole would have been happy to finish in the same *bracket* with Bush—to cut the Veep's lead to ten points. But now he could smell . . . victoryyyy!

Dole would ask new reporters on his bus: "D'ja see Bush out there?" They thought it was a Dole joke. But Dole wanted to know—was Bush just gonna *sit there*?

Tell the truth, Dole couldn't make sense of what the *Dole campaign* was doing: he'd spend all day, snaking around the state in huge motorcades—convoys, more like it—forty ragtag vehicles (Greyhounds, rent-a-cars, Winnebagos, a big snowplow that said "Dole" on the front) and two hundred people . . . descending on some little town library . . . or a school! ("Gaghh! What're we doin' with fourth-graders?") . . . But Senator Rudman and his smart guys insisted: that's how it was *done* in New Hampshire.

Dole could have done without ninety percent of his own crowd—hell, he'd get along with one car and a kid to drive. But everybody wanted to be with Dole. Rudman was his corner man, Wirthlin was a constant, Brock—well, Bill Brock was the Big Guy. Dole's D.C. offices were empty (Senator might need help in New Hampshire!) . . . Washington lawyers, lobbyists, experts from the Finance Committee—they all had to talk to the Senator about New Hampshire! There were paratroop pooh-bahs dropping in from other states—they needed to "touch base with Bob." There were reporters—a hundred, at least, that Dole had to carry along—and the networks wanted Dole to wear their microphones, or maybe they could ride a crew in his car, for a day-in-the-life: you know, minute by minute, on the way to the White House.

They wanted face time.

Face-to-face with Dole.

Dole wasn't sure how this airborne, mechanized assault brigade looked to voters. He wasn't sure anymore what he was trying to show to voters. "One of Us" didn't quite fit here. The family farm was not an issue. "People with real problems" could perish unaided, as far as the State of New Hampshire was concerned. These people were conservative—a funny kind of conservative: talk about a couple of trillion dollars for Star Wars—people cheered. Bush could spend a million flying himself and fifty staff into the state for a dinner— nobody made a peep. People liked that go-go, write-a-check, paint-it-gold style . . . as long as *they* didn't pay any taxes.

Dole thought *he* might have a problem with taxes. Jack Kemp had spent the last year—for a while, he put ads on TV—painting both Dole and Bush as closet tax men. So Dole was going to cut his own tax ad. First night after Iowa—a GOP dinner in Nashua—Dole was going to tuck a line into his speech, how he'd veto any new tax bill from the Democrats. Kim Wells wrote the line—went so far as to *type it* on a half-sheet of paper. Rudman's guys got the film crew into the dinner . . . they were all set up. But this being the Dole campaign, they didn't have a TelePrompTer—and, of course, no one could make Dole rehearse. So when Dole tried to unload the line, he had to pull out the paper, and he scowled at the sentence (couldn't read a thing without his glasses) . . . he stumbled in the middle and it sounded like something someone told him to say. The upshot was, the tax stuff looked lousy. So they made an ad with different film—Dole talking Gorbachev, U.S. strength, and peace.

Maybe they'd have another chance—Dole already said, a million times, he'd veto any bill that raised the income tax *rates*. . . . Anyway, Wirthlin said the tax issue wasn't cutting with voters. And Kemp was not the problem—just Bush: What was he doing?

Not much.

Four days before the vote, Dole's smart guys checked around and announced, to the delight of all, that Bush wasn't doing *anything*! He had no new ads scheduled—hadn't bought any *airtime* for the weekend—save for one half-hour roadblock, all channels, for one of Ailes's specials, "Ask George Bush."

That was Friday—that wonderful snow day—and Dole with the only news on TV. (Al *Hayyyg*—great American! . . .)

Late afternoon, in his hotel room, Dole was closeted with Wirthlin and Rudman, who were telling Bob things were going . . . great. ("Bob, I know New Hampshire and, believe me, Bob . . .")

Dole's new ad ran before the local TV news: it was Dole talking off the cuff about national security. "So we haveta be strong! . . . Not for war—Bob Dole doesn't want war. Bob Dole wants *peace!*" The camera went to freeze-frame on Dole's face.

"I love it!" Wirthlin said.

Dole was squinting at the screen. "I don't get it," he said.

Walt Riker poked his head in. "Agh! C'mon *innn*," Dole said. "What's cookin'?"

"Senator, you're ahead! These're from CBS—I just got 'em . . ." He read off the numbers:

Dole 32 . . . Bush 29.

"They gonna use 'em?"

"Think so."

"Pretty *goood!*"

It was better than good. It sent Rudman into orbit: Believe me, Bob, the people of New Hampshire, Bob—remember, I told you, Bob?—Bob? . . . Meanwhile, Riker was conducting, channel to channel, a Dole TV rondo. After seven years as Press Secretary, Riker was a cable-ready maestro: he hit four networks, three Boston news shows, PBS, New Hampshire's Channel Nine, Headline News *twice* . . . and Dole was never off the screen for more than a minute. Dole, Haig-and-Dole, Haig, Dole, Haig-and-Dole Dole Dole. . . . Wirthlin had his black book out, he was on the phone to *Time* and *Newsweek.* Strictly off the record, understand: he was promoting Dole for the cover. "You guys're gonna want it. Dole's going to win this thing!"

Dole couldn't pay attention, as he wanted, to the TV (Gagghh! Haig was live with Dan Rather—*killing* Bush—should've made an ad with Haig!) . . . or the phone calls ("No, *this* week is the cover!") . . . or the "Bob-Bob-Bob." . . . He had to think—this thing was *moving fast.* He lifted his eyebrows, murmured to Riker, who told the others, "Senator's gotta get a little rest."

Dole couldn't feel it—that rush of certainty, when it all comes together— and he thought there had to be *something* more. There had to be some way to lock people on, something to say, something about him . . . something he had to do. It couldn't happen like this—sitting in a hotel and Bush's numbers melting away. *Didn't* happen like this—how could it? . . . Unless Bush was going to sit on his hands—play dead all week. Why would he?

What was he *doing*?

110

Doing
Damage

GEORGE BUSH was having a snowball fight with the press in a parking lot outside the Clarion. He spotted a guy trying to unstick his car—he ran over, offered to help. (The man refused.) Bush ran the other way to shake another voter's hand, pat his dog. Everywhere Bush ran, the Service ran. Sununu puffed behind. The press tried to run along, but the Service kept them away . . . and there really wasn't anything to ask.

Bush had the air of a kid trapped inside on a rainy day. He walked through the snow, with Doro and her husband, Bill LeBlond, to some horrid housing project—condos, or townhouses—the nearest evidence of civilization (or at least Reagan-era lending policies). Bush was hunting voters, but the condo-stalag was new and unpeopled. So, with son-in-law Bill, who was a budding builder in Maine, he earnestly talked construction.

Bush wondered what Dole and the others were doing in the snow. He was pretty sure Dole wasn't taking the afternoon to walk with *his* daughter. Dole always struck Bush as a lonely man—didn't have the same, well . . . blessings as the Bush clan. Or values: "family" and "values" were words in near equation to Bush. He couldn't figure how it was for Dole. . . . That *look* he'd seen on Dole's face when Dole came at him, in the Senate, waving that Wittgraf press release . . . "My wife!" . . . Dole was upset, sure—but it wasn't like he wanted explanation. Didn't want to talk—you do that in private . . . decent guys do. Bush called it "that stunt Dole pulled"—like it was bad taste . . . *bad form!* . . . Dole was acting like a bully.

Friday night, Bush went over a new speech with Peggy Noonan. The speech attacked Dole . . . the language made Bush edgy, so he fiddled with it, made it ungainly—but he made it something he could say.

"I don't want to say he's a bad guy," he told Peggy. Bush's voice held no protest—more like explanation—he was searching: not a *bad* man . . . just not the *right* man.

That night, Junior called again about the ad:

"Yeah, I was watching TV," Bush said. "A lot of the others are more negative. I mean, if you put it in context . . ."

Saturday morning, before Bush left for the north of the state, Atwater and Ailes were in urgent conference in the hotel hallway. (Ailes had come out from under editing "Ask George Bush.") . . . "Look," Ailes said. "I can tell him he needs this ad. But me supporting it, just sounds like I made the damn thing . . ."

"Goddam, Ah 'gree with you!" Atwater said. "We gotta, uh, kick 'em in the *nuts!*"

They went together into the VP suite. This time Teeter said they were behind—maybe *five points* . . .

"Shit," Bush said to the floor. "I thought . . ."

"There's been slippage," Teeter said. "There's enough undecideds to go either way, but if you look at . . ."

"Mr. Vahz Pres'ent, you may not wanna hear this from me, but Ah can't go out of this room without . . ."

"Look," Sununu said, "if it's a problem of being negative . . ."

Bush was slumped in a chair. The problem was how it was going to *look.* "The press is gonna say we're desperate. Have we checked those facts?"

Ailes was going to wade in again: the ad was no more than a statement that . . .

But . . . that's when they got the word. Actually, Ailes never caught the word—from Bush.

Bush was saying, ". . . this is your business, not mine . . ."

As Ailes would recall: "Atwater just ran out of that room like a scalded goddam dog."

Ailes and Sununu caught up with Lee in the hallway.

"Can we get it on?"

Traffic departments at the TV stations were closed for the weekend. By Monday, of course, it would be too late.

"I got a friend at one station in Boston," Ailes said. "Twenty years I know the guy . . ."

"Lemme see," Sununu said, "what I can do with Channel Nine." That was the only station in New Hampshire. Sununu wore his accustomed smirk of control. "I think I may be able to help."

In fact, Sununu knew he could get the ad on Channel Nine. One month before, the station had asked for an interview with the Vice President. Sununu brought Bush down from Maine on a Sunday. They taped the interview, and another segment for that night's news. Then they hung around for another hour while the Veep posed for pictures with every staffer at the station. He posed with their children. In Washington, he wrote personal notes for every photo.

Now, *that* . . . was see-me-touch-me-feel-me.

The Straddle Ad would go on the air that same afternoon.

— ★ —

On the long ride over the mountains to Wolfeboro, Peggy Noonan sat next to Bush in the limo. Teeter faced Bush on a jump seat. Bush was silent. Peggy read the papers—the stories about Haig backing Dole. She got to a quote, something Haig said to Dole (someone overheard them on stage, after all) . . . "Well," Haig had said, "I did as much damage as I could."

"Mr. Vice President," Peggy said. "Have you seen this?"

Bush looked at the quote. Then he looked at Teeter, at Peggy, then he stared out the window.

"That's *sick,*" he said.

Doing *damage* . . . to his life, his reputation. Didn't that just show?

Lee Atwater was, at that moment, buying eighteen-hundred points of air-time for the Straddle Ad. That meant hundreds of thousands of dollars. More important, it meant the average New Hampshireman with a TV would see Bob Dole made a two-faced liar eighteen times over the next sixty hours.

That was different . . . that was just a comparative ad.

Anyway, after the smoke cleared, Sununu said the ad wasn't really crucial— just one more positive statement of Bush's tax principles. Sununu said that often. Sununu was a guy who showed judgment, Bush thought. The Veep mentioned, amid the family, that Sununu would make a good Chief of Staff. Meanwhile, Sununu was increasingly in evidence at Bush, Inc. By the spring, he would become a Campaign Cochairman, a de facto seventh on the Gee-Six.

By that time, Bush, too, would decide that New Hampshire turned, in the end, because of all the friends he'd made. All those contacts Sununu talked about. See-me-feely . . . whatever that was. Bush said: "We didn't win because of that ad."

That was the only fight he ever had with Ailes. It got pretty hot: "Let's don't rewrite *history,*" Ailes said.

"I didn't win because of that ad."

Ailes had to drop it. "Well," he said, "let's just say it didn't hurt."

111

Sandbagged

THAT WEEKEND, Dole felt it slipping away. Before he ever saw the Straddle Ad . . . before network numbers showed his curve topping out and Bush on the way up again . . . even with Wirthlin still telling him, "You're going to win—three or four points, at least . . . maybe big—ten or better."

"No, I'm not," Dole said. "I'm going to lose by five or six."

What Dole felt was the heat slipping from his own events. What disappeared was that feeling of history pushing with him. He could still go out and say (as he did) that momentum was his: five days ago, Bush had led in New Hampshire by twenty points—now Bush's lead was *nothing* . . . but the reason for that momentum was back in Iowa—there was nothing new bringing voters to Dole.

What Dole saw on TV were pictures of Bush—Bush touring with Ted Williams, Bush throwing snowballs, Bush at McDonald's . . . on a forklift . . . driving a plow. The guy was showing he wasn't going to curl up and die. There was news tape of busloads of college volunteers for Bush, arriving in state, met by Atwater. Each kid got a map and a kit and an area to cover. They were organized—twenty colleges! (Dole was lucky to have people who'd been to college.) The Bush operation put out tens of thousands of fliers and made twenty thousand calls, reminding voters to watch "Ask George Bush." It was an obvious phony, a "town meeting" of Ailes-town . . . but by the time the Bushies had thumped the tub so hard, the TV ran snips of the thing like it was news!

Dole did his events—schools, old-age homes, town halls—remembering to say, at almost every stop, that Bob Dole was not going to raise taxes. He'd look for revenue—anyone facing a deficit had to look everywhere he could—but Dole would not raise the rates in the new income-tax law. The crowds applauded—good crowds—hundreds of people in a little town! But, as Dole muttered in the car, he was "dipping the ocean with a spoon." At that moment, Bush might be reaching a hundred thousand viewers with the message that Dole could not wait to get at their wallets.

By that weekend, even Rudman's people were bitching: their plan had been ignored—they were sold out! Where was Dole's tax ad? Rudman himself came at Dole to complain about Brock. "Even a half-baked Senate campaign can turn an ad around in two days!" Dole just said: "What can I do now?" . . . In fact, he *had* an attack ad on Bush—the Footprints Ad: boots crunching through snow while a narrator ran through Bush's résumé . . . the last shot showing the snow—undisturbed. (Bush never left any footprints, despite all those Important Jobs.) The ad was ready before the week began, but Rudman said it was too negative. (They were winning! Bob had to Be Nice!) . . . Now it was too late. Dole hadn't bought airtime.

There was one chance to send a message, statewide: a televised debate at St. Anselm College. Dole spent most of ninety minutes trying to Be Nice . . . and angling for a chance to answer Bush on taxes. But all of a sudden, from Dole's other side, Pete du Pont pulled out a copy of the standard New Hampshire no-tax pledge—and poked it at Dole.

"Sign it," du Pont said.

Dole wasn't going to sign anything—couldn't hold it down to sign it, couldn't read it without his glasses! (If Dole were the kind to sign whatever they handed him, he could have saved himself a huge headache on the INF treaty—he could have signed on, like Bush, before he'd even seen the thing.)

But now he was squinting at this paper, on stage, on TV—with du Pont and everyone else staring at him . . . what was he supposed to do? This kind of stunt was fine for du Pont. But if Dole got to be President, he was going to have to close a gap of $200 billion a year.

Dole let the paper drop from his gaze. "Give it to George," he said. "I'd have to read it first."

Good line. Got a laugh. And Dole lost his chance to make his point on taxes.

Dole would replay that scene in his head for years afterward. Sometimes he'd lie awake at night, thinking what he could have said. Maybe he should have signed the damn thing.

It was certainly bad politics to refuse—his supporters said it killed his chances in New Hampshire. They said it was the only time in '88 that anyone lost on a matter of public policy.

—★—

He did lose, decisively. By Tuesday, it wasn't close, though Dole kept hoping it wasn't true—maybe the feeling in his belly was wrong, things had changed, or . . . maybe his Big Guys were right! There were Wirthlin's numbers in the paper, again: Dole was going to win!

By Tuesday, it came clear with a sickening lurch that the big mistake was saying—ever—Dole was going to win. If Dole could have set his goal for the week to cutting into Bush's lead, he might have looked terrific. But it wasn't Dole who said—aloud—he was going to win. That's what he had Big Guys for. That's what people told Dole to do: find some guys and turn the campaign over. Well, he did that! . . . What'd it get him?

They'd sat there all weekend and done *nothing* . . . while Bush killed him! Seemed like every ten minutes on TV: Bob Dole was gonna raise your taxes! Bob Dole wouldn't back Reagan on the INF! Bob Dole would raise the price of *heating oil* . . . for God's sake, in the middle of winter! Bush might as well have said that Dole liked to bury children in ice! . . . Bush and Ailes . . . *killed him* . . . while Dole and his Big Guys sat in their hotel.

Dole did his events that Tuesday morning—enough to get on TV . . . then it was lunch, and back to the hotel for a meeting with the savants. Bill Brock was there, along with the Political Director he'd hired (another twelve grand a month), Bernie Windon. There were a couple of true Dole-folk who shrank into the woodwork, as they did whenever high Klingons were present. Rudman's smart guys were in and out, with news from local polling places. Wirthlin was there, of course, as was Dole's old pollster, Tully Plesser—both calling friends at the networks for news of the exit polls. David Keene, Dole's right-winger consultant, flew up from D.C. He was drafting a statement ("We've come a long way . . . proud of our volunteers . . .") for Dole to use if the news was true—if he had fallen short.

Keene detested Brock and disrespected Windon—not just as ideological sellouts, but incompetents, wastrels, and failures. Rudman's people were furious at Wirthlin, contemptuous of the Dole command that pissed away this chance in New Hampshire. The true and humble Dole-folk reviled all Klingons and regarded the New Hampshire ops with secret but satisfying sneers of comeuppance—those were the know-it-alls who tried to tell *Bob Dole* what to do! . . . That evening, CNN reported "a high official in the Dole campaign said this election was kicked away by people who didn't know what they were doing." The source might have been any man in that room. (The sad fact— Riker breathed the word amid the faithful: the "high official" was Dole.)

Dole was sitting on the luggage bench at the foot of his bed while this gaggle of helpers discussed his prospects. That meant he had his back to half of them. That was okay. They tell you, you've got to hand the campaign over . . . till you lose—then it's your fault.

He thought it was his fault—he could have signed that paper from du Pont. He could have insisted they make the ad about taxes. He could have ordered them to run the ad about Bush. They tell you, people don't like that kind of ad—maybe they don't. But they watch it. Bush knew that—his people did. Dole thought it would have been different if he'd had an Atwater, someone to carry the attack. Dole couldn't get Brock to *answer* Atwater—Brock thought it was beneath him. Dole said, "I'll do it myself." Then everybody's wringing their hands: *Oh, no! Senator's got to Be Nice!* He was nice. No one answered Atwater.

But nobody's got to be nice when they're kickin' you in the face! A *President's* got to be tough. People didn't know Dole was tough. People knew what they saw on TV—they thought Bob Dole was a liar. *Bush made him a liar.* All the while, they told Bob Dole he was winning—so he sat on his hands and took it.

"Look," Keene was saying, "we get through Super Tuesday if we target right, we got four million for media, if you target that, we get back to the Midwest with a spending edge, and then . . ."

Brock said: "We've got eight hundred thousand."

Dole looked up, his eyes on the wall opposite. He didn't speak. He looked like he'd frozen.

"Eight hundred thousand for Super Tuesday?" Keene was humphing—he wanted it clear whose doing this was. "Well, if I were *you,* I'd start cannibalizing everything I could get my hands on. We gotta have at least . . ."

Brock said, "Eight hundred thousand for the campaign."

"Total?"

"There's four million budget!"

"Things have changed."

Dole knew things changed last fall, when he handed it over . . . changed at L Street—had to rent another floor of that building, glass walls. You walked in, there were glass walls, two or three layers, you could look through, past the valets and flunkies, to Bill Brock. Cars waiting downstairs—limos, drivers, guys standing around . . . staff, consultants. Clink said it cost a hundred thousand a day just to keep the doors open. Hands off! . . . Dole was hands off—and they spent his money.

He turned it over and they cut his throat!

He would *never* do that again.

When would he ever have the chance again?

It was over. The Big Guys were talking about the South, Super Tuesday, Illinois. But Dole knew it was over. The way Bush was organized down South, Dole's only chance was to win New Hampshire, to win everything on the way to Super Tuesday. Dole didn't speak again in that meeting. Didn't talk to Brock that afternoon.

That night, George Bush won New Hampshire by nine points. Dole spent the night trying to be gracious: he hit his marks, he made his statement, he thanked his volunteers and supporters, he vowed to go on. He smiled ruefully and told the cameras: he'd made up a lot of ground in a week—he never expected things to be easy.

At the end of the night, the very end . . . he was on live remote with NBC . . . and who was next to Brokaw—beaming like the cohost of the big election special? George Bush! . . . But Dole didn't know that. He had no monitor . . . no one warned him. He was sandbagged.

Brokaw said to Bush: Any message for Dole?

"Naw, just wish him well," Bush said. "And meet him in the South."

Then, Brokaw and Bush, both smiling, turned toward the monitors—to see Dole . . . but he couldn't see them. He was sitting in a hotel room, looking at a camera lens. The talk in his earpiece sounded like the chatter before any interview:

Senator, can we get a mike check? . . .

Senator, can you hear Tom? . . .

And then Brokaw's voice:

Senator? Any message for the Vice President?

It was Dole's face on the air—but he didn't know that. . . . The camera caught the dark flash in Dole's eyes, as he said:

"Yeah. Stop lying about my record."

Dole said later, he deserved one chance to tell the truth.

Elizabeth said later, Bob was *so* tired . . . he was not himself.

Of course, the wise-guy community said right away, Dole was a hatchet man. New Hampshire proved, the voters *saw,* Dole could never learn to Be Nice.

— ★ —

What did it prove? What did any of it prove? All the work, all the people who helped him—little people who never took a dime, didn't want anything— they're the ones who got shafted for trying, against the odds. Dole thought he should have known. He blamed himself. There were a hundred things he could have done, could have *tried.* God knows, he tried, but . . .

He couldn't sleep—couldn't sleep at all, lay there all night, tried to lie still . . . until he couldn't try anymore and it was five o'clock and there was no reason to lie in bed. That's when Dole came down to the lobby of the hotel and sat—no one around, he just sat. Pen in his hand. Careful suit. Perfect shirt, tie. And no one around. What would he have said, anyway? He was sorry? . . . He *was* sorry. He didn't say that often . . . but that's what it was, this time.

This was his time. And now, it was over.

He'd lost it, lost the feeling—and the hope. It was always going to be tough in the South, even if he'd won New Hampshire. Bush had been making friends in the South for . . . well, ten years, probably more. People would say to Dole: "Well, we like you, Bob. But this is George's time . . ."

When was Bob Dole's time?

This was his time. And they took it away! . . . He'd lost before. He wasn't going to whine. But this time was different. This time, he couldn't sleep at all, couldn't stop his head: things that could have been different . . . all the things he'd done . . . probably wrong—half the things, anyway.

But the worst part wasn't things he'd done. It was the pictures of Bush— that's what he couldn't stop—*pictures of Bush!* In his head! Bush throwing snowballs, driving trucks, forklifts . . . unwrapping his Big Mac. Dole never wanted to see that in his head. And he never wanted to say—even in his head . . .

It would not leave him alone . . . five in the morning! Had to come down to the lobby . . . but he couldn't get away from it. For the first time in his career—first time in thirty years, anyway—Bob Dole said to himself:

"Maybe I could have done that . . . if I was whole."

112

What
Joe Biden
Knew

BY THE TIME Biden got to the motel, his headache was picking up steam. He probably should eat— had to eat! Christ—he did the forty-five-minute speech at the University of Rochester, then stood and answered questions for four and a half *hours*.

What happened was, he did the INF speech—a new era dawning with the Soviets on arms control. But the first question was about plagiarism. So Biden answered for twenty-five minutes straight . . . after that, his motor was racing.

Bob Cunningham, from the Delaware staff, was traveling with Joe on this run—first time Biden had got moving since the Bork, Ginsburg, and Kennedy nominations; first time he'd hit the campuses since his own campaign fell to shreds. After an hour and a half of questions, Cunningham gave the signal— held up his watch, so Joe could see. Biden nodded, but he just kept talking. So after another hour, Cunningham cut off the audience mikes. That just made Biden come down, off stage, so the kids wouldn't have to shout their questions. After four hours, Cunningham went to the lobby, got his coat, Biden's coat, the briefcase . . . then walked back into the hall and stood next to Joe, with coats and all . . . but Biden just threw an arm around him and kept on for forty minutes more.

"Hey!" Joe said, on the way to the motel. "You think we can still get a pizza?"

But this was Rochester, near the airport, one A.M. Nothing was open. Biden went to his room, sat down on the bed and . . . WHAM.

It hit in his head like a brick. He must have blacked out. He didn't know how long. It was like that time in New Hampshire—but worse. He couldn't move. *His legs wouldn't move . . .*

He had to move. He had to prove he could move. He forced himself off the bed, to be sure his legs would do . . . he stared at his hands, and they moved. He couldn't think . . .

It couldn't be a heart attack. He wouldn't be standing, thinking, talking . . . he talked out loud in the empty room. His voice. It sounded right, his voice. But his *head!*

God, there was never pain like this. Not in Joe's life. What the hell was *happening, GOD?* He felt sick, dizzy . . . the *pain.* . . . He tried to throw up. He had nothing to throw up. It couldn't be food. He'd had no food.

He had to lie down. He'd be better, sure, if he just got down and kept still. He gingerly laid himself flat, on the bed, in his clothes.

He did not move all night, save to the sink, the toilet, to try to throw up. He thought if he could just stick it out through the night, get to the plane . . . if he could just get *home.*

— ★ —

Tommy Lewis met the plane in Philadelphia. Cunningham came off.

"Hey. Where's Joe?"

Cunningham had the briefcase. Joe asked him to carry his case. That's how he knew it was bad. He'd been with Joe since they'd served together on the County Council . . . Joe *never* wanted people toting for him. He'd rather lose an arm.

"He's coming. He's sick."

"Bad?"

"He had his face in the bag the whole way."

Then Joe came. He was gray. He looked like death. He said he'd be all right. Just get him home.

Tommy got him home, but it took a half-hour to get him out of the car, and up to his room. Tommy half-carried him up the stairs. He got Joe onto the bed. Tommy had to take Biden's shoes off for him.

Joe thought if he closed his eyes, he could will the pain away, control it. But he could not.

Jimmy Biden called. Tommy gave him the news.

"D'you call a doctor?"

"Joe said just let him rest. He's got a plane again, two-thirty . . ."

"Bullshit. Get a doctor."

Tommy called Joe's local doctor, the same guy who'd diagnosed Joe's pain as a degenerated spinal disk, a couple of weeks before. Tommy was trying to figure out how to call Jill at her school without scaring her to death.

But Jimmy called Jill: no more screwing around. Hospital for Joe—right now.

— ★ —

Jimmy was in Washington, he was the one who fixed it up at Walter Reed—the Army Medical Center, on the Beltway around the capital. He went to the boss. That's how Jimmy worked. "Will you take my brother?"

"Of course, Mr. Biden."

They were going to fly Joe down in a chopper, but it was snowing like hell that day, February II. Anyway, Joe was too fragile to fly. The doctors at St. Francis in Wilmington had found blood in his spinal fluid—they were pretty sure that Biden had an aneurism in the brain. If it blew—change of pressure, a jolt in the air—it was curtains.

So they'd have to ride him down in an ambulance, through the storm. Police from Delaware would ride escort. The family piled into cars. Beau would ride up front with the cops. Jill would ride in the ambulance with Joe.

She stood by the back door of the truck while they lifted him in on a stretcher. "You know," she said, bending over him, "you really screwed up Valentine's Day."

Maryland cops were supposed to meet them, but they never showed. Deep into Maryland, the Delaware cop turned to Beau: "Where we goin'?" Beau had a windbreaker on, and a ballcap—must have looked like a federal SWAT guy. So he had to explain, he was Biden's son . . . he had no clue where they were going.

So they stopped by the side of the road, tried to radio. Five minutes, ten minutes, by the side of the road, until Jill started hammering on the back wall of the ambulance: "Get going! I don't care what you don't know . . . get this goddam thing *going.*"

— ★ —

Dawn came at Walter Reed, while the family hung in the hallway outside Intensive Care.

An aneurism is a weak spot in the wall of an artery. Like a thin spot in an innertube, it balloons with the pressure. To be sure of what they had, doctors had to take an angiogram, which was a delicate procedure in itself. They fiddled a catheter into an artery in Biden's neck, whereupon they loosed a dye that would show up on a scan, to outline the arteries climbing Biden's brain.

Dr. Eugene George was the surgeon in charge. A top man . . . but Jimmy Biden was working the phone. He wanted to know the top five guys in the world. Who were they? Where? Would they come? Jimmy didn't know a lot about surgeons. He guessed they had egos like everybody else. But he looked Dr. George in the face, and said: "Doctor, I hope you don't take this the wrong way . . ." (He really didn't give a shit how he took it.) "I want a second opinion."

"Good. That's fine," George said. Jimmy liked that.

He narrowed it down to four, apart from George: one guy in Switzerland, one in Toronto, one in Texas, and Virginia. Joel Boyarsky, a big fund-raiser in the campaign, now a family friend, had a team ready to come from New York—the surgeon who did the work on James Brady after he was shot with

Reagan. Jimmy was going to hire a jet for the doctor in Texas. He could be in D.C. by late afternoon.

Too late, said Dr. George. He gathered the family in the hallway that morning. He showed them the scan. There was the balloon in Joe's head. Doctors were sure it had bled—that was the pain. If it blew now, it would kill him: not the blood loss, but the jolt from the blood on the brain—there's no protection for the brain—it's like a riot hose that blows the tissue away.

There weren't many options. There wasn't any talk of waiting. They'd wheel Joe in, by 3:00 P.M. Mom-Mom tried to play nurse, asking questions, but Jimmy and Val jumped on her. George was trying to tell them the chances, complications: if he lived, yes, there might be impairment . . . left side of the brain . . . he could be paralyzed . . . he could lose his speech. Mom-Mom turned away then, couldn't listen. Joe, Sr., thought of his dad, died of a stroke. Dr. George was telling Jimmy that the Virginia surgeon was in town. He'd assist, if that was all right with Jim. . . . Then there was silence in the hallway for an instant—until there was a nod from Jill. It had to come from Jill. Then, everything started whirring again.

—★—

They gave Joe a paper to sign.

"What does this mean?"

"It means you understand the risks."

"The . . . what kind of chance do I have?"

"Pretty good chance."

"Fifty-fifty?"

"Just about fifty-fifty. That doesn't count morbidity."

Joe didn't even know the word. But he understood "just about" . . . they were going to cut open his skull; he was less than fifty-fifty. He didn't want to know about the other stuff, the loss of speech, of movement, of sense—morbidity. He signed.

A priest came in to give him last rites.

Joe asked to see the Bidens—one at a time . . . Jill, Val, Jimmy, the boys. It wasn't like the movies—there wasn't big stuff he had to fix. He didn't have to tell them he loved them, after all, or adjure them to take care of each other. They knew that stuff. . . . But he wanted them to know what he'd found out fifteen years before: they would go on.

When the boys came in, he told them he knew—whether or not he lived, he knew—they would be great men. Not a doubt in his mind.

"And I guarantee you," Joe said, "that any . . . every single time you have a problem, when you got a tough decision to make, you look: I'll be there with you. Every time."

—★—

In the VIP wing, where they moved the family, the Bidens settled in; it was like an Irish wake . . . except there was no body. That was downstairs.

Ted Kaufman was the only guy from the staff. He was like family. Anyway, Ted was the kind who'd always see the silver lining. During the campaign, Ted was the designated optimist.

"Okay, Ted," Valerie said. "Tell me something good about *this.*"

Ted tried, fumbled around, and they laughed at him.

It was like the campaign, with everyone there, and disaster a cloud outside the room. Someone said: "We gotta stop meeting like this."

Ted and Jimmy went out and got pizza. The Bidens told old stories.

"God, remember when he jumped off that cliff?"

"Oh, God . . ."

"Then he got pissed off at *me!*"

"You let him."

"I dared him. He's screamin' at me: 'I coulda broken my leg!' "

"He could've broken his head."

"That's good, Mom."

"Oh . . ."

"Aw, don't start now . . ."

They'd told these stories so many times, but there was a tricky edge to the punch lines now . . . they weren't funny unless they all lived to tell. There were too many things they thought of that caught on their tongues.

Mom-Mom whispered to Val—no one else—"Oh, God, if he lost his speech . . ."

Michele, Jimmy's wife, had an uncle—he was up in a cabin, with his wife and one other guy. They had to haul him off that mountain: aneurism. Michele told Jimmy—no one else—her uncle was a vegetable.

Jill was thinking the whole time: thank God he wasn't campaigning . . . New Hampshire. He never would've stopped. Up in the snow. They never would've got him down here. Not in time. He would have died. Joe would have been dead . . . already.

My God, what's happening down there?

Nobody wanted to ask out loud.

Dr. George said four hours, four and a half . . . that meant 7:00 P.M., it ought to be over.

"Time is it now?"

"Ten of ten."

"Jesus, Mary, and Joseph."

Biden would be on that table for nine hours.

—★—

It was midnight when George finally told them: it went well, in a technical sense. Of course, they couldn't know the result until Joe woke up—that would be hours more. But George, for all his careful Army-doctor words, had the look of a trapeze man who'd just done the triple—backward, no net.

"The timing, I think, was appropriate," he said. What he meant was, they weren't a minute too soon. In fact, the moment they cut into Biden's head—

maybe it was the disturbance of the surgery, maybe just a godly coincidence—the aneurism burst like a gusher.

Dr. George called it "friable matter." He meant blood and tissue, everywhere. "There was quite a bit of friable . . ."

Biden was lucky. His artery burst outward, toward the wall of his skull. As far as George knew, the brain tissue had not been disturbed. Dr. George got a clip on the wall of the artery, through all the mess. That much was fixed. As to the rest . . . time would tell.

It was dawn again before Biden was lucid enough to know he'd been lucky. Jill came into Intensive Care, told him he was going to be fine. But Biden had to prove to himself he was there—all there.

He worked his fingers and toes under the sheet. Brought a hand up to touch his nose. Blinked his eyes. Saw the clock. Told himself the time, and figured the duration of his unconsciousness. He estimated the square footage of the ceiling by multiplying the tiles. He could think. He could move. He could talk. Thank God.

Thank God . . . he would've been dead . . . in New Hampshire, he would have been dead.

That was the luck that descended like blessed peace on Biden in his hospital bed. It wasn't just the fact of survival, no. There was a plan for Joey Biden, after all. There was a reason . . . there was destiny.

Ted Kaufman was the first man from the staff to see Joe that morning. Joe's head was a swollen swaddle of bandage. Tubes ran in and out of him everywhere. His voice was small, but he said to Ted:

"I'm gonna be all right."

"I'm sure of that," Ted said. "It's a much better story if you live. It's gonna increase the legend."

Biden managed a smile. But this wasn't a joke.

"No, now I know," he said, "why the campaign ended like it did."

113

Dangerous
Magic

IT'S ALWAYS DANGEROUS when you start to believe in magic . . . the hand of God propelling you by the small of your back, smiting your enemies a shot to the chops. The pros warn against it. But when it's the pros who are God's Own Agents . . . well, then, look out—there's no one to warn you.

When Dick Gephardt escaped New Hampshire with second place, he knew it had to be God's work—because Dick hadn't had a good week, on his own. It started well enough—he came steaming in from Des Moines Tuesday morning (*eight planes* full of press, crew, and hangers-on). He was ready to ride the famous Iowa bump, close the gap on Dukakis, and raise hell about the Establishment . . . but the Establishment, turned out, had gotten tired of taxes and poor people in Boston and moved, en masse—to southern New Hampshire.

By Wednesday, the press herd had digested the Iowa results and moved on to the serious business of destroying the new front-runner, Congressman Gephardt. There was the flip-flop analysis, the insider-outsider analysis, the Doak-and-Shrum-as-Mephisto analysis, and one heady new entry: Gephardt-as-candidate-of-regional-discontent.

Thursday, Simon went nuclear, put ads on TV just *ripping* Gephardt—by name—for his tax votes, his weapons votes, his everything-Simon-could-think-of votes. Turned out, Bambi knew how to hold a grudge, and now he was dripping foam from the mouth!

Friday, Dick actually saw a Simon ad, and it put him into a rage. That night, at a candidates' forum, Dick was the only Democrat who did not get a standing ovation. He was flat, angry, stiff. After his speech, he held an ugly press conference, tried to slash at Simon, but all he could manage was: "He ought to take off that bow tie, because he's just another politician."

That night, Dick woke Jane with a call. She could hear—his first four words—he'd sunk to the bottom again. "He lied to me. . . . Paul promised me he wouldn't do that."

She tried to buck him up, but the good words didn't get through. Dick asked about the kids, but she knew he didn't hear the answers.

"You're really down, aren't you?"

"Yeah, I guess I am. I oughta get some sleep."

But she knew this would be one of those nights when he'd wake with a start, at three or four . . . and never get to sleep again.

So Dick spent the weekend fighting off Bambi, fighting with the press, making money calls to fat cats who were, uh . . . out of town, in a meeting, or indisposed . . . and by the day of the primary, Tuesday, eight days after his apotheosis in Des Moines, Dick had ceased to wonder what had happened to his Iowa bump and was wondering instead if it'd be him, or Simon, who would squeak through in second place, and leave New Hampshire alive.

That Tuesday, when there was no more schedule, and darkness fell, and the killers gathered in another motel—this time a Howard Johnson's, no food, no couch, no Loreen, and not a suite, just a row of rooms along a dim hallway— no one could tell Dick he would survive the night. They told him it was too close to call . . . and sent him out again, to stand in the snow and dark, outside polling places—who could tell? Maybe he'd change a few votes. Then, they were so frantic, they sent Jane to other polls—"Now! Y'gotta get out there *now!*" . . . She had to tell them to wait *five minutes*! Could she go to a bathroom? Could she get some gloves?

That evening, when the polls closed, Dick came back, and the killers tried to leave him alone with Jane—private time, they called it. But Dick just sat on the bed, flipping channels—why didn't anyone have any damn *news*? She tried to talk about the day, but he didn't want to talk. ("Fine . . . no, it was fine.") So she shut up, and hunched back against the pillows with a sick, empty feeling inside. What would this do to him? Would he always regret? How would he get past this sadness? He kept flipping channels, and no one was telling him . . . *anything*. She could see from his back how alone he was. So she walked down the hall, and she brought the killers back to him.

They came in like angels of death. Even Carrick was accepting blame that night, for getting so panicky during the week—that had thrown Dick off his game. Doak and Shrum had spent most of the week fighting with Trippi over who was the genius behind the magic-bullet Hyundai ad. Ethel Klein was in her last night—the white boys had driven her off the plane when it looked like they were headed for the White House. So all they could offer Dick now was a chance to polish his third-place speech, a "fight-on-to-change-this-country" speech . . . and after Dick had worked that over, at his narrow motel desk . . . after the TVs had started scrolling some numbers . . . and a couple of the dim rooms filled with suits and smoke and spin . . . after Reilly had read his tea leaves, and punched up his friends at the networks, and as he was pouring into Dick's ear the news, but only the good news, or the maybe-at-least-okay news, while Dick studied the carpet in the drab HoJo hall . . . then Tony Coelho burst out of Dick's room, calling into the hallway, as he came:

"CBS just projected you got SECOND!"

And Dick lifted his eyes from the rug and looked up at the cheap ceiling tiles, two feet above his head, as if they were Uncle Bob's azure heavens, and he grabbed Coelho with a hand behind Tony's neck and pulled him closer, till their foreheads were touching and Dick saw Coelho's eyes as one, and he said, grinning, giggling: "This thing just might *happen!*"

And everyone was so *relieved* . . . they didn't notice—not that night—that Dick's cry of triumph had shrunk in eight days from a roar to a gurgle. No one thought to comment on the strange and dangerous air of *deliverance* in that hallway. . . . Not to mention (no one did that night), they hadn't closed the gap on Dukakis all week.

—★—

To be precise, when they rolled into South Dakota the next day, they were, by Reilly's reading, sixteen points *behind* Dukakis . . . in a farm state . . . in the Midwest. It looked like another grim week. As a matter of fact, the week couldn't have started worse: Dick hit the ground, and the first guy he saw was . . . Paul Simon.

"God*dam* that man! . . ." he muttered. "Won't he die?"

(Actually, Simon was dead, but his Illinois pol friends didn't believe in Death with Dignity. Hey! They wanted to go to the convention!)

So Dick began to ply South Dakota . . . and for two days he toiled, but he could not close the gap fast enough. He had the endorsement of the state's reigning politician, Senator Tom Daschle . . . and that endorsement he publicized on TV. He had the Harkin-Gephardt farm bill . . . and his midwestern roots . . . and his victory in neighboring Iowa . . . and all those positives he publicized. But he was still eleven points behind. And he could not go into Super Tuesday, trailing a string of second-place finishes, limping, impoverished. He had to do *something*.

So he scraped together an extra ten thousand dollars and . . . he went negative.

That's when the dangerous magic happened.

The killers had the ad ready Thursday night—they read Dick the script. They had to have a decision within hours, to buy the airtime Friday for weekend spots—give the sludge a chance to cook.

The ad was quick and cheap. A narrator's voice carried the freight:

Gephardt was for a tough trade bill . . . Dukakis was against.

Gephardt was for the Harkin-Gephardt farm bill . . . Dukakis—well, who could tell?

Dukakis was the man who told Iowa farmers to diversify: ". . . flowers, blueberries, Belgian endive . . .

"Those are some of the reasons why South Dakotans are for Gephardt—not Dukakis."

Then, the Gephardt slogan appeared . . . followed by the narrator's voice, again, as if he had to make sure he got that right:

"Belgian endive?"

In Carrick's gentle phrase, the ad was "a fuckin' killer." It went up Friday night, and Dukakis started bleeding support. By Sunday, the gap had closed to six points, and by the last tracking poll, Monday, they were even.

One ad . . . a lousy ten thousand bucks!

Dick had struck the rock . . . and lo, it gave water.

114

Lobster
Salad

I T WASN'T that the Dukakis campaign was asleep at the switch. All the wise guys on Chauncy Street realized they had a fight on their hands . . . everybody but Michael.

He was still striding the boards, speaking the lines of his private play . . . relishing the stirring climax of Act Two, when he'd won New Hampshire and stood on stage while his bride, Katharine, draped a gold medal around his neck.

What an orgy of diddybop photos!

What a luscious piece of marathon spin!

"I always wanted," the *Globe* had him whispering to Kitty, "to win a gold medal."

"That's not true!" Kitty corrected. "What he said was: 'I love you, babe.'"

Well, the point was, the happy warrior marched off with a tremendous victory. He'd worked New Hampshire every week for a year, opened offices in every town with more than two gas stations . . . he suffused that state in TV ads, TV interviews, a tidal wave of Duke-news from the Boston papers . . . he paid enough staff to call 200,000 households, augmented his paid staff with hundreds of volunteers, who drove north from Boston to bring out the vote . . . he had his two closest rivals at each other's throats with broken bottles, and most of the nation, withal, ignoring the Democrats to see if Bush would bleed to death . . . and the Dukakis juggernaut won the state with . . . what? Thirty-six percent?

That is, with sixteen percent less than the polls gave him, six months before.

Fantastic.

Of course, that showed Michael he was right. He was running the kinda campaign people liked. They were moving now. Things were happening! They were . . . right on track.

So when Kiley suggested, day after day, that they try to move the speech off good-jobs-at-good-wages, show the nation the passion for justice, the can-do spirit, the bedrock of conviction that underlay the campaign of Michael Dukakis . . . well, Dukakis took the new lines out of the speech.

When Estrich suggested, again, that they hit Gephardt with the flip-flops . . . when she showed Michael a computer list of business PACs that contributed to Gephardt's campaign, or a subset of that list—PACs that gave to Gephardt *and* to George Bush—Michael gave her that dirt-on-the-carpet look, and snapped: "I don't wanna hear it!" (Of course, the list didn't go to waste. It showed up in *The Boston Globe*. . . . That was fine. Don't tell Michael!)

They planned TV ads on Gephardt's PAC contributions and the flip-flops. Michael wouldn't authorize production. (He didn't want *attack tapes* lying around the office—no!) He asked someone—his Advance man, or a local pol—and they didn't like the idea, either. That was one of Michael's favorite moves. He'd ask anyone he saw about a line in a speech, an ad, a debate-prep zinger . . . he'd ask until he found someone who didn't like it. Then he'd report back to Chauncy Street that the *local* people didn't like that stuff.

In desperation, Estrich flew out to meet Dukakis on the road, to show him their polls on the PAC issue. It made a difference to people! If they could show Democrats that Dick Gephardt was taking that money (Mercantile Bancorporation, Inc., Political Action Committee—$5,000; Monsanto Citizenship Fund—$5,000), voters would finally see a difference between the campaigns! . . . Michael immediately asked his driver, a kid in his dad's Chevrolet: What did *he* think? Should a responsible candidate, should a *Michael Dukakis,* engage in that kinda, that sorta, that negative branda . . . *politics*?

"Yeah!" said the kid. "You know, that's one of the things that really bothers me! They're taking that money! . . ."

Michael gave Estrich a dirty look, like she'd set the kid up.

Mostly, he heard what he wanted to hear. Michael was enough of a lawyer for that. Anyway, the campaign had moved beyond the states where he had to *know* people, where they might tell him something unpleasant. Now it was mostly airport to airport, with local pols on the tarmac, telling him he was doing . . . well, fine . . . things were looking great!

So they were. Babbitt had dropped out. Simon was crippled. Hart was still out there with his daughter, and a single car, nosing around the South—why, Michael couldn't figure. But Michael wasn't going to stoop to attack now . . . when people seemed to be catching on to the kinda guy he was.

That was the problem. Michael saw his fortunes rising, and concluded: people were taking a good look now . . . and they liked him!

"We're starting to connect out there," he told friends back in Boston. "It's something . . . well, you oughta see it, it's just . . . terrific."

—★—

The problem was, Michael wasn't going to hit anyone. That's not the kinda guy he was. But there was a time . . .

In 1979, when Ed King supplanted Michael in the State House, Michael thought he was finished. If Ed King did a *half-decent* job, he'd be good for two terms. Michael was washed up. Paul Brountas convinced him he had to keep a little office for politics—if nothing else, just to thank the people who wrote in to tell Dukakis how sorry they were.

"Just keep their names on file!"

So he rented an office, one room, and staffed it with one young supporter, Andy Sutcliffe, who sent the thank-yous, kept the file cards, and took the calls . . . some of them calls from Dukakis people who were still in the State House, who were terribly upset by the King administration.

King was a Bozo!

King was hiring hacks!

King was disassembling all their reforms!

So Sutcliffe had hot poop on the King administration. And this poop promptly found its way into the papers. King was doing a hell of a job of ruining his reputation—on his own. (During National Clown Week, he posed for a picture with a clown nose—then *everyone* called him a Bozo.) But Michael's office-in-exile did what it could to help out.

The best was the lobster salad.

Ed King liked lobster salad for lunch. Of course, his bodyguards (King liked bodyguards) had to have lunch, too. So when Sutcliffe got word that Eddie King wanted the state to pay his take-out lunch bill . . . *twelve hundred dollars of lobster salad in one month* . . . well, it wasn't long till the *Globe* ran a front-page exposé, along with a handsome picture of a lobster . . . and Ed King had a new reputation as a *wastrel* Bozo.

Michael could not have been more pleased. He knew, of course, about the leaks to the *Globe*. He and Sutcliffe plotted them. The public deserved to know! A wanton arrogance! . . . The story deserved to be told! It was true!

Just as true as the tapes that Sasso put out.

But that was different. No one found out how the *Globe* got the lobster salad.

Anyway, Michael had lost to this guy!

—★—

In his Georgetown office, the day of the South Dakota vote, February 23, David Doak got the word from his TV friends: Gephardt was blowing Dukakis away.

"How big?" Doak breathed into the phone.

A small chuckle followed. He traded some numbers from previous calls . . . when he hung up, he was smiling broadly. But . . . back to business: he was explaining how the magic happened.

"No, our one advantage was, we could turn on a *dime* . . .

"Bob and I went through four or five ideas, Wednesday and Thursday . . .

"Flew it out there . . . got it up Friday night . . ."

Doak waited patiently while the writers wrote that down.

No, he said, Dick wasn't any problem on this. Dick understands now. Dick is on track . . . took some doing.

"You know, he kept waiting for someone to pin the fuckin' merit badge on him . . .

"He's done everything right—much better than anybody expected—and the shit is only getting tougher."

But Reilly's numbers showed them ahead by a hair in Texas, closing in Florida, tied for the lead in Georgia . . . of course, Missouri would be a lock for Dick. With the magic in South Dakota, they'd even have some money— close to a million for Super Tuesday . . .

"You wanna see something?"

Doak led the way to the mailroom, opened the door. The bright fluorescents banished the early-evening darkness, shone on Doak's hair as he looked to the floor. There, gleaming white, purple, and orange . . . were seventy-five Federal Express packs filled with ad tapes . . . lined up in stacks, as neat as bullets in a cartridge clip.

For an instant, as he looked up, the lights flashed in Doak's eyes. The next day, those packs would blanket every market in seven states. Doak chuckled again, more in satisfaction than mirth.

"You're lookin' at it," he said.

He didn't have to explain what *it* was . . . it was the next hope.

How could he have known, that same night (faster than FedEx could travel), Michael Dukakis would hear the vote from South Dakota (forty-four percent for Gephardt, thirty-one for Dukakis) . . . and know he'd made a mistake. Of course, he wouldn't say that . . . but he'd have very much the same *it* in mind when he'd tell Nick Mitropoulos they could go with the ads on Gephardt.

"I'm not gonna let it happen again," Michael would say. "Anywhere."

115

The
Plane
from Hell

REPORTERS were calling it the Plane from Hell—even while Dole was still winning. South Dakota, Minnesota were good states for him—wide-open, clean-living, midwestern places where Bob Dole could be "One of Us." Bush meant to duck both states. Dole couldn't lose.

Still, Dole's charter—a dingy 727 from Presidential Airways—was filled with the smell of death. Too much room, for one thing: on some hops, there were eight or nine reporters rattling around the back, where there was space for fifty. Up front, it was emptier: just Dole and Glassner and sometimes a field guy; no one to talk politics, no one writing anything for Dole; there wasn't a *typewriter,* much less a computer, a fax, even a phone. Mari was still aboard, supposed to deal with the press, but she was so sick with pneumonia, it was all she could do to haul herself along. Dole was sick, too, but not like Mari—mostly sick at heart. He'd sit up front, staring, silent: he didn't understand his schedule, why he was doing these events. He had no idea what he was supposed to be saying. There was no plan, no sign of activity at L Street. What were they doing? He'd call headquarters from the airports—couldn't even find any Klingons! They must have split when the money ran out.

That's why he called Dave Keene to come along—actually, he had Judy Harbaugh call Keene:

"Senator wants you to meet him at the airport, 7:00 A.M."

Keene had grown increasingly sour since Brock and the Big Guys froze him out. "I don't think a meeting's going to do much good."

"No, he wants you. He wants you to go along on the plane."

So Keene climbed aboard the Plane from Hell, and Dole at least had someone to complain to. "Senator, don't get too down," Keene told him. "Things can happen with Bush, too. I know Bush: he can get down if he has setbacks. He might have trouble, handling . . ."

Dole snapped at Keene: "I can handle . . . *losing*. You tell me I'm gonna lose sixty-forty, I can handle it. Don't say I can't handle it! . . . But I've got a right to *know* what's going on. Don't tell me I'm gonna win sixty-forty when I'm not."

Dole said no one was telling him *anything*! "They give me the schedule, but they won't tell me *why* we're doing anything . . . look at this!" He showed Keene the schedule for Tuesday—Dole was supposed to sit in Missouri on the night he was winning Minnesota, South Dakota.

Keene couldn't figure that, either: "We need good news."

"That's what I thought, too. . . ." Then Dole asked: "What does Devine think?"

"He's in Minnesota."

"You think he'd come with us?"

"He would if you asked."

"You get him."

So then it was Keene and Devine—just like old times! Keene was spouting lines for Dole mile-a-minute ("Why don't you start asking, 'Where's Bush?' Haven't seen him anywhere! How can he write off the heartland of this country?") . . . And Devine was hunched over his computer (he had a *laptop*!), trying to figure out where Dole might win delegates—maybe delegates enough to . . . make this a fight! They couldn't fight Bush all across the South, but they could pick off Missouri, Oklahoma . . . North Carolina, surely—a district or two in Florida? . . . They were actually nosing toward a *plan* . . . and Dole started to perk up. He kept hovering over Devine:

"What about the delegates? Aghhhh . . . you got 'em?"

"Yeah, I got 'em," Devine said. "But I'm not telling you because you'll hold me to the numbers."

"Nooo," Dole said. "I won't do that."

Keene said: "Yes, you will!"

And they started to laugh. It was the first time in a week anyone had heard laughter on that plane.

"Just tell me," Dole said. "Can we still do it?"

Devine said: "You can do it."

Auughhh! It was like someone breathed air back into the Bobster. He seemed physically bigger! His tan came back! . . . He got right on the phone to L Street—get Brock on the line! *We need computers for the plane, and phones!* . . . Where's Judy? . . . *We're stayin' in Minnesota, Tuesday night!*

At L Street, this was terrible news: Dole was on the warpath! He was *ruining everything*! Judy Harbaugh couldn't keep the schedule tied down long enough to send Advance out ahead of Dole. She ended up advancing in cities where

Dole never showed. Then the ancient and freckled Dixiecrat, Strom Thurmond, endorsed Dole in South Carolina—where Dole wasn't even planning to fight—so for the next week, the only place Dole wanted to go was South Carolina.

Brock called Judy: "Is he sticking to the schedule? Don't change it!"

"I can't get anything put together! He's messing with everything!"

Brock called Dole and chewed him out. *Who's running this campaign, anyway?*

And that about sent Dole over the edge: *Why aren't we staying in South Dakota, or Minnesota . . . on a VICTORY NIGHT?* Dole said he couldn't understand it, Keene couldn't understand it, Devine couldn't understand it!

Keene and Devine sent Mari home—she was too sick to do any good. Dole had someone call Riker: "Senator says, meet him in Duluth tomorrow morning!" . . . They called back the young ad guys who'd done that great Dole video—Murphy and Castellanos—hired them on an emergency basis, and they cut two dozen ads in ten days, more than the Dole campaign had managed to produce the previous year. . . . On the phone from the road, Dole reeled in an endorsement from Jeane Kirkpatrick. She was the soul of the Reagan revolution. She knew Dole *and* Bush—and she was coming out for Dole! So he called Judy Harbaugh again, ordered her to schedule him back to Washington for a big press conference. . . . Meanwhile, he spent his victory night in Minneapolis.

What he did, in effect, was cut his own campaign out of the loop—made up a new one from the plane . . . and not a bad one! At least, it felt like a campaign.

That's when Keene got a call from his buddy, the columnist, the big-right-foot, Bob Novak. He was going with a piece, the next day, quoting a "high official in the Dole campaign" who said the Plane from Hell had been "hijacked" by Keene and Devine.

Well, that was trouble . . .

That could only be one source . . .

That could only mean . . . the Big Guy . . . was pissed!

—★—

Bill Brock met the plane, the night after the Minnesota and South Dakota wins. They were in Orlando. The next morning, Keene was eating breakfast in a coffee shop—Dole was speaking in the back room—when a newsmagazine photographer asked Keene:

"Mind if I get a picture of you and your Campaign Chairman?"

Keene said: "It's all right with me if it's okay with him."

The photographer said: "He's on his way over."

Bill Brock sat down in the booth, and as the photographer was taking his picture, Brock raised a finger into Keene's face and announced:

"I'm cutting the string. You're finished! You're off the campaign!"

Keene started to pfumfer through his breakfast. (He had egg on his face!)

. . . Don Devine wandered over, and Brock wheeled on him: "You, too! You're fired! You're off the payroll! And you're off the plane in Jacksonville. You can find your own way home. And you can *pay* your own way home!"

Devine said: "I don't know if I'll *get* off . . ."

Brock said: "You'll get off, or we'll throw you off!"

When Dole finished his speech, and was headed to the cars, Keene sidled up: "Uh, are you aware that Don and I have just been fired?"

Dole just stared . . . then he said to Keene: "I'll talk to Brock. Don't worry."

But still, Dole could not pick a fight with his Big Guy. Anyway, there was no time to talk—they were on their way to Universal Studios. Dole had a photo-op! Movie stars! . . . Then they were back on the Plane from Hell—just a short hop into Jacksonville, and when they landed, here came Brock, down the aisle:

"Get their stuff off the plane! Throw it off! They're off the plane!"

Keene scurried up the aisle toward Dole. "How do you want me to handle this?"

"Aghh . . . gingerly, I hope."

"You gotta be kidding."

So Keene gingerly told every word, every seamy bit of background, to every paper in the nation with circulation of a hundred thousand or better: if Brock and his pricey flunkies hadn't steered Dole's campaign into such desperate deep water, Keene never would have *been* on that plane! . . . Meanwhile, the Big Guy could not content himself this time with Klingons peddling his response—no, he bestirred himself *personally* to apprise the big-feet (just on background, understand): if Dole and his humble helpers hadn't reduced the campaign to such a mess *before Bill Brock got there* . . . well, things would *never* have come to this pass. It all made delicious cud for Super Tuesday chewing, as everybody-in-the-know analyzed Dole's desperation (the only thing upon which all sides agreed) . . . an impression reinforced by Wirephotos of Dole, at Universal Studios, grinning (hegh-hegh-hegh) . . . next to Franken-stein's Monster.

116

Back
to the Bible

Office of the Vice President, Washington
Schedule of the Vice President
for
Asheville, North Carolina
March 5, 1988

EVENTS: Visit to Asheville Flea Market

DRESS: Men: Casual
Women: Casual

CONTACTS: Vice President's Advance Office
John G. Keller, Jr.   202-456-7935
Trip Coordinator
Tracy J. Spahr   202-456-7935

ADVANCE: Nancy Pilon   LEAD
Tom Johnston   USSS
Mike Williams   WHCA

WEATHER: Mid 50's/Chance of Showers

Contact Sheet
for
Asheville, North Carolina
March 5, 1988

HOTEL: Holiday Inn West
275 Smoky Parkway Hwy
Asheville, NC 28806
705-667-4501

NAME	AFFILIATION	ROOM	TELEPHONE
Nancy Pilon	Lead	200	704-665-1703/38
Gregg Hall	Site		
Ray Joiner	Press		
Staff Office		202	665-1703/38
FAX			665-1907
Press Line			665-2014

USSS: Tom Johnston Lead   684-5652
       Marshall   TSD   684-4850
       Command Post   684-4467

WHCA: Mike Williams Lead   684-5575

ASHEVILLE REGIONAL AIRPORT   684-6873
    VP Holding Room   684-5472
    Air Force II (Line 1)   684-5048
    Air Force II (Line 2) Ramp Phone   684-5373

ASHEVILLE FLEA MARKET   253-1691
    VP Holding Room   251-1114
    Senior Staff Holding Room   251-1115
    Staff Holding Room   251-1116

CELLULAR SERVICE: To reach one of the following numbers
              dial: 1-704-777-7626 then:
    VP Chief of Staff Motorcade Car   301-520-4020
    VP Chief of Staff T-8000   301-520-5891
    VP Chief of Staff T-8000 (McBride)   301-520-3942
    VP Mil Aide T-8000 (Menarchik)   301-520-3941
    USSS Supervisor T-8000 (Johnston)   301-288-4029
    WHCA Lead T-8000 (Williams)   301-520-3018

SPECIAL INSTRUCTIONS FOR TRIP-SITE CELLULAR USERS:
    Your cellular phone has been activated for use in the local cellular network. The local network is a nonwire-line system. Before using your cellular phone please insure that the internal program is set on scan b. A telephone credit card IS NOT required to complete long distance calls.

SPECIAL INSTRUCTIONS:
    To reach the White House dial: 1-202-395-2000
    To dial Long Distance dial: 1 + AREA CODE + NUMBER
    To reach Greensboro, N.C., S.O.: 1-919-852-4549
    To reach Greensboro, N.C., R.P. dial: 1-919-854-5609
    To reach Greensboro N.C., C.P. dial: 1-919-852-0012

Schedule of the Vice President
for
Asheville, North Carolina
March 5, 1988

9:15 A.M.   THE VICE PRESIDENT arrives Asheville Regional
               Airport, Asheville, North Carolina.

               Met by:
                   Mr. and Mrs. Jim Bailey (Diana)
                   GBFP Buncombe County Chairman

                   Mr. and Mrs. Wes Potter (Dottie)
                   Shana Fagan (granddaughter, 14 years old)

                   Mr. John Veach (Jack)
                   GBFP Supporter

                   Dr. Reuben Holden (Ben)
                   GBFP Supporter

                   Mrs. Katheryn Kenny (Cockie)
                   Buncombe County Co-Chair
                   Women for Bush

                   Mrs. Ruth Brandon
                   Buncombe County Co-Chair
                   Women for Bush

9:20 A.M.   THE VICE PRESIDENT boards Motorcade and
               departs Asheville Regional Airport en route Ashe-
               ville Flea Market.

- -

Motorcade Assignments
          Lead   N. Pilon
          Spare   Dr. Savage
          LIMO   THE VICE PRESIDENT
                         Follow up
          Control   C. Fuller
                         J. Keller
                         D. Menarchik

Support	S. Hart
	D. Valdez
	T. McBride
Staff Van	All Remaining Staff
Guest Van	
Press Bus	B. Zanca

- -

(Drive Time: 25 Minutes)

- -

Guest and Staff Instructions

Upon arrival at the Flea Market,
Guests and Staff will be escorted to
Viewing Area.

Please board Motorcade no later 10:00 A.M.
for transport to Airport.

- -

EVENT: **Visit to Flea Market**

OPEN PRESS

9:45 A.M.   THE VICE PRESIDENT arrives Asheville Flea
Market and proceeds through Flea Market.

10:00 A.M.   THE VICE PRESIDENT concludes participation
in Flea Market and proceeds to Motorcade.

10:05 A.M.   THE VICE PRESIDENT boards Motorcade and
departs Asheville Flea Market en route to Asheville
Regional Airport, Asheville, North Carolina.

NOTE: UNSCHEDULED CAMPAIGN ACTIVITY EN ROUTE =
10 MINUTES

— ★ —

George Bush walked through a flea market in North Carolina. Actually, he
got out of his car and walked about fifty yards, shaking hands and chatting.
Someone—maybe a reporter who worked his way through the Service cordon—asked him about Panama. Noriega was acting up again: canceled the
elections and beat up the winners. Bush said something—his mouth moved,
anyway—which sent the rest of the press running, asking: *"Whadd'e say?*
Whadd'e say?" After a minute, one reporter announced:
  "Panama. Democracy will prevail."

There were glum nods. It was shorthand. The reporters had heard the Veep's nonanswer on Panama. Bush had nonanswers on everything. One of the reporters said, "I don't think I'd drive three minutes to see this." In fact, she had driven and flown a hundred thousand miles.

One woman, a flea-marketeer, brought a jar of honey for Bush to autograph. One man got his dog, Cocoa, patted. ("What's the dog's name?" press wanted to know.) And then it was over. . . . The limo drove straight into the middle of the flea market, the Secret Service made a Gardol shield on one side, and the pod-people started shouting: "All right! Let's get the bus! Bus! BUS! PRESS THIS WAY!"

They were mostly back on the bus when there was a sudden bustle, and someone muttered, "Ah, shit!" Bush had grabbed the microphone in his limousine and was standing on a rocker panel, in an open door. George Bush was going to *talk*!

His high, nasal voice filled the flea market. "I just want to thank you very much for that . . ." The press was running back, six-legged, whipping out tripods and boom mikes.

"I just want to thank you very much for that warm North Carolina welcome. Thank you very much for that warm North Carolina welcome. . . . And if I may be permitted, I need your vote on March 8th. . . .

"And if I get it, if I do, you'll . . . you can say you went shopping with the next President of the United States!"

The limo was rolling—Bush was inside.

"Ah, shit!" The press went running again—back to the bus. The press was restive. It'd been weeks since Bush said anything.

It was three days till Super Tuesday. South Carolina would vote today. Bush had that wrapped up in ribbons—Atwater's home state. He would win South Carolina—big. And that would be the headline, into Super Tuesday.

If nothing else happened, he was going to win. He was going to win everywhere on Super Tuesday. He was going to win it all.

— ★ —

George Bush had come out of the bubble for that one needy week in New Hampshire. When he won there, he dove back inside with purposeful finality, and he would never have to come out again. His Super Tuesday style made his Iowa campaign look homey and personal. Through fifteen states in twenty days, he met people he knew, or people who were picked to meet him—anybody else, he'd barely stop to shake hands. He said nothing for ten minutes at a stretch at three dozen airports, and nothing for five minutes a pop in a hundred local TV "interviews" in three dozen media markets. Meanwhile, he spent $3 million buying airtime everywhere there was a vote: there were ad images of Bush-with-Reagan, Bush-with-soldiers, Bush-with-grandchildren, Bush-with-ocean, Bush-with-farmland, Bush-with-flags.

He wasn't negative.

He didn't need to be.

Super Tuesday was invented by southern Democrats as a grand and futile prophylaxis against a liberal nominee . . . but the way it worked out (what a Good Godly stroke!) . . . Super Tuesday was made for George Bush.

As it turned out, New Hampshire and South Carolina would restore (just in time!) Bush, Inc.'s, most successful rationale—inevitability.

As it turned out, that rationale was strongest when the campaign schedule threw together, on one day, so many contests, so widely dispersed, that no one could make (for more than a couple of hours) a concerted appeal to any set of voters in any one place.

As it turned out, Bush, Inc., was the only campaign with the reach and resources to play everywhere across the South. Super Tuesday was so vast and vacant of content, it rewarded pure movement and muscle—or at least the money to buy muscle . . . everywhere at once.

As it turned out, Bush's strongest opponents were beset in these same three weeks by dire self-inflicted woes: Bob Dole's smart guys and Big Guys had eaten through the fortune he'd raised and were now busy eating one another in an orgy of press leaks and attempted coups. Pat Robertson was visited by revelations (of nuclear missiles in Cuba, and the exact location of U.S. hostages in Beirut) . . . which the Reverend announced with some fanfare but, alas, could not begin to prove.

Bush alluded with mild derision to his rivals' troubles—"unstable" was a word that popped out—but he didn't have to name names. To him, their incapacities were evident, and the real and final rationale for his candidacy:

They shouldn't be President.

To him, the noiseless, newsless operation of his white men and their hirelings, all across the South, was the confirmation of his bedrock faith:

This was *his* time—he was ready for this game, like no one else.

As it turned out, Bush, Inc., was blessed in these weeks with a candidate who was closer, each day, to the full flush of confidence . . . uniquely able, by virtue of his resources and the inability of rivals, to project across one-third of the country, without static—almost without argument—a clear and faithful view of his own beliefs, the issues that informed his candidacy, the outlines of his possible Presidency . . . his hope for the nation, which he meant to serve . . .

Oh, the vision thing.

As it turned out, there was none.

At every stop, in every state, he shot for the safest common ground. Speeches . . . well, he didn't make many. Mostly he'd blow into a room and assure the crowd, with a grin:

"Don't worry. I'm not gonna drop the full load on you . . ."

Often, he'd bring up the word "change." (Teeter's numbers showed that voters wanted "change"—a *good word,* Teeter said.) But change, for Bush, turned out to be just a change of watch at the helm of the great ship. The point was to . . . *be* . . . the next President of the United States.

He'd like to "*be* . . . the Education President." But he wouldn't want the federal goverment interfering in local schools (i.e., the only schools we have).

He'd like to "*be* . . . the Follow-on President for Arms Control." He was the *first U.S. official to meet Gorbachev* (at a funeral). But he would not affirm any fundamental difference between Gorbachev and his predecessors . . . nor envision a shift in U.S. policy toward the Soviets . . . a reevaluation of containment . . . no.

He'd like to have a *line-item veto* . . . the better to battle Congress over federal spending. But that would require a Constitutional amendment, which would take years (if it ever happened). Meantime, his plan to balance the budget . . . was no plan.

He did repeat his vow not to fool around with taxes.

In fact, from the Super Tuesday evidence—local interviews (his only interviews)—Bush was not going to fool around with anything. From the evidence, he did not see anything to do.

Sure, there were U.S. factories closing . . . the Reagan flood of guilt-free debt left a few million have-nots high and dry. "There's some people still hurting," Bush allowed. "Some jobs gone. But, generally speaking, a very successful President." (Bush also referred to the Great Depression as "the thirties, when we had some economic difficulties.")

One of the local anchormen asked: "What will distinguish a George Bush Presidency from . . . from anything? What will be your place in history, if you have your choice?"

Bush said: "It's hard to say at this juncture. But, I hope, peace." Then, there was a pause, before Bush mentioned, for a second time, he'd like to be the Education President.

Mostly, he answered horse-race questions:

Was he going to win South Carolina?

"I will win South Carolina . . ."

Would a win in South Carolina echo into Super Tuesday?

"It will have an effect . . ."

Thank you, Mr. Vice President.

Curiously, the vacuity of George-Bush-winning was not discussed as character . . . nor even Karacter. Maybe the Kops had spent themselves in the war of wimpdom. At any rate, the Karacter query on Bush *was* the Wimp Factor . . . and no man is a wimp to the political press corps whilst he win.

So the dive of George Bush back into the bubble was discussed in the press as tactic—on which ground it was hard to fault. In these three weeks, Bush was appealing to Republicans across the South. He knew who they were—how they came to be Republicans.

They were Democrats all, when he first moved among them, in the forties . . . when the Democrats brought to the South the schools, hospitals, the electric lines that it so desperately needed. And he lived among them through the fifties, while the region caught up in development and wealth . . . and into the sixties, when the Democratic Party identified itself with the struggle for civil rights. . . . For four decades, Bush had watched these people as they moved in from the countryside—or the cities moved out to meet them—where they now had roads, schools, hospitals, country clubs . . . and homes in suburbs, attained and established, they insisted, by their labor . . . and the last goddam thing they wanted was the government to come in and get in their way . . . to take more taxes, for example . . . or, worse still, to erode, to *take away,* any measure of the security and comfort they had attained . . . those schools, houses, neighborhoods, jobs . . . in any effort to bring along the have-nots— blacks, for instance, or the poor in those rotting cities, the workers in rust-belt factories . . . bailouts, affirmative action, Congressional mandates, federal court orders . . . no!

These were the got-mines that Joe Biden used to talk about:

"Got mine . . . go get yours!"

These were people who thought they wanted government to do . . . well, not much . . . save to stand tall for America, God bless her.

"I'll never apologize for her," Bush vowed, in Super Tuesday speeches.

As it turned out, George Bush was perfect for Super Tuesday.

— ★ —

"I wouldn't mind if I could get the paper to recognize how mindless it is . . ."

This was David Hoffman, *The Washington Post*'s lead reporter on the Bush campaign. He was in Greensboro, North Carolina—the Four Seasons Mall. Bush was receiving a merit badge from the Boy Scouts at the Greensboro Scout-o-Rama—six months of Advance, six minutes of event: "The Boy Scouts," Bush said, "represent American values."

Hoffman was a man near the end of his rope. He was, among the big-feet, the most thorough and ambitious reporter. He had files that went back years, on everything Bush said. He had them organized for instant access to the history of Bush-thought—or at least Bush-speak—on any subject of moment: arms control, Soviet relations, civil rights, education, the environment . . . Hoffman was ready.

"The Boy Scouts," George Bush affirmed, "represent the best of America!"

Hoffman was stuffing his mouth with a two-dollar cookie. He'd just got off the pay phone outside of Scribbles 'n' Giggles. "I can't get this shit in the paper."

Behind him, Marie Cocco of *Newsday* was on the phone with her editors. "He hasn't talked to the traveling press in eight days," she said. "The other day, we jumped him about something in his speech, and it was right behind a diesel. He acted like he couldn't hear—just like Reagan."

Bush was already finished with the Scout-o-Rama. He'd been whisked away for three local TV "interviews" at a hotel. The big-feet and big-feet-to-be were not invited. It was just the VP and a single blow-dry in matching armchairs— very intimate—they could really get to know one another . . . you know, for four minutes and thirty seconds.

("You really must be running around!" said Action News, Channel Five. "Oohhhh," said George Bush. "Exhausting!")

Meanwhile, the fleet of Greyhounds had deposited the national press in a cold gray wind in the middle of a rock quarry. There were craters in the ground and mountains of gray gravel and stone. No one could figure why they were standing for a half-hour in this chill moonscape.

David Hoffman was furious. He'd had a standing request to interview George Bush for a year and a half—since October 1986. Once he got so close as to have a talk with Bush about why he should get to talk to Bush. Then he called Craig Fuller forty times. Then he had to write a letter. But by that time, Iran-contra had transpired and Bush had gone to ground—Bush talked to no one. Then, the Wimp Factor surfaced—Bush talked to no one. The only interview Hoffman ever saw was a wet kiss from David Frost, the celebrated English brownnose. Hoffman said the white men had prepared Bush for *days* . . . "like it was some kind of goddam summit meeting." Bush never did the Marvin Kalb interview, like all the other candidates.

"He's never done a substantive interview on *anything*," Hoffman said.

George Bush was arriving, in a whoosh of thirty vehicles . . . straight into the rock quarry, where the pod-people set up a ropeline. Secret Service held the limo door for Bush, and Hoffman was at the rope, screaming:

"WHY ARE YOU HERE? . . . WHY ARE YOU HERE?"

Bush just waved and grinned, climbed into the cab of a front-end loader. Off to the side, all the plant brass were gathered, and local Bush supporters— women in fur coats. There was a man on the ladder, next to Bush, who knew how to run the machine. He pointed to a lever. Bush pulled the lever.

"WHY ARE YOU HERE?"

Beep-Beep-Beep . . . the loader drowned out all other sound with its elec- tronic warning, as the front scoop lifted a ton of rock, preloaded for the Deputy Commander in Chief.

A dump truck rumbled into camera frame.

The man on the ladder pointed to another lever.

"Great," said one reporter. "Now he can finally drop the full load."

The next reporter kept his eyes on Bush: "Does he remind you of a three- year-old?"

"My three-year-old has more maturity and sophistication." There were some hoots behind the rope. "And vision," someone said. The one with the three-year-old said: "Helen Keller has more vision."

Bush pushed the lever. Rock tumbled into the dump truck.

The cameras were rolling. They could mock all they wanted. Bush was getting *his* work done—and they were helping.

Bush Advance and the mobile white men were having a good yuk about Hoffman's question: "Why the hell do you *think* we're here?"

Meanwhile, Bush was ending his inspection of a rock separator. He came to the ropeline for a minute of spasmodic friendliness. Someone got his atten- tion for a question—what was he doing in this quarry?

Bush shrugged. "There's a lot of show-biz in politics. There are a lot of things about campaigning that I don't like. One of the things I *do* like is meeting the people who hold a job, and do the work, building *the strongest economy this country's ever had."*

The limo came purring through the moonscape behind him. Bush disappeared into the backseat. He was having a chuckle, too. These reporters didn't understand the value of the bubble. The limo was backing to turn around when he grabbed the microphone inside.

"See you, guys!" he called to the quarrymen. One of his arms was flapping out the side of the limo. "See you, guys! Thanks for the visit! Thanks, guys! Appreciate the visit!"

117

The White Lightning Curve

IT WAS JUST Hart and Lee sometimes, or Hart and Andrea (Lee's sinuses were hurting again) . . . and one or two friends who'd help. Sue Casey had tried to run the whole campaign from Denver, but she burned out—there were days now you couldn't find Casey anywhere. When he could, Billy Shore would travel with Gary. Or Mike Stratton would go along. There was a new guy who showed up for some trips, a Californian named Bernie Schneider—Hart called him Bernie the Attorney. Four Advance kids were half-killing themselves, hip-hopping the South, trying to set up something ahead of Hart.

But that was it: his campaign, his crusade, had shrunk to this hardy, hopeless few. You could seat them all at one table for dinner—which he did, almost every night, along with anyone else who took an interest—people who wanted to be delegates, the kid who drove him to his speech at the local campus, the poli-sci professor who introduced him in the lecture hall, a guy from the local radio who'd never met a Senator.

They were strange and fascinating dinners—a dozen people, or fifteen, at a table thrown together by a flustered restaurateur . . . with Gary in the center, recalling the doings of the day, theorizing, answering questions, telling stories, feeding the gathering from his faith and experience, that inexhaustible store.

He'd start with a drink, one of his white lightning specials—Stolichnaya vodka on the rocks—and that would loosen the tongue. Someone might mention the Secret Service . . . which would remind Hart of a story—had they ever heard about the time the Service and the California Highway Patrol closed the San Diego Freeway for him?

"It was *4:30* . . . on a *Friday* . . . in *May. Everybody* was trying to get out of town. I was coming in—Friday before the primary . . . and the Highway Patrol had the freeway blocked for *ten miles*—all the entrances. . . ."

Hart's eyebrows danced with droll horror.

"And we're going TWENTY-SEVEN MILES AN HOUR! . . . I see guys out on the ramps, shaking their *fists* at me as we go by—at FUNERAL SPEED! . . . I'm literally beating on the shoulders of the shift commander, yelling: *'GET GOING!'* . . .

"So, we get in. The Secret Service guy is hanging his head—like this. I said: 'NEVER . . . do that again. NEVER . . . DO THAT! You just lost me a quarter-million votes. Do you understand? NEVER!' "

Then Hart would lean back and laugh, softly. No one ever mentioned how the Service had now departed Hart's side—they left after he finished under four percent in Iowa and New Hampshire.

Over dinner, or after, there might be another Stoly . . . and Hart's remarks would grow sharper, more topical and telling. He talked about Dukakis, piling up delegates, step by cautious step. Dukakis never got more than thirty-five or forty percent *anywhere*—he had a ceiling, he couldn't win—why didn't anybody write that? It reminded Hart of Mondale, in '84, plodding on with that same stupid inevitability . . . reminded him of Barbara Tuchman's book *The March of Folly,* in which the Great Powers lurched to war—"like this . . ."

And Hart's hand darted toward the edge of the table, then disappeared below.

". . . like watching someone go over a cliff."

The other night, in debate, after Hart brought up an idea, said he hadn't heard it from the other candidates, Dukakis swiveled in his chair, and with an edge of contempt in his voice, reminded Hart (and the audience): "You'd have heard it . . . if you'd been *around* for the last six months . . ."

That was when Jesse Jackson reached over, patted Hart's hand, and whispered: "I don't like that guy . . . he's *mean.* "

It was a good word, Hart thought. *Mean* was the word they used in Ireland for small, ignoble . . . they used it for cheap, or stingy, narrow . . . a *mean* understanding was not much understanding.

That was one reason Hart couldn't get out of the race—why his gut wouldn't let him get out. All the others (save for Jesse) were playing traditional *old-line politics*—pleasing the interests. Every day, Hart would comfort his crowds (and himself) about the polls, or his own dismal results in the first primaries: the rest of the field, he'd say, was contesting only for the mantle of old Mondale-style politics . . . then the winner would have to face Gary and his New Ideas. Sooner or later, Hart would not be ignored—or ignorable—if he could just stick it out. And he would, he vowed. He knew he was right—right about Mondale, right about Dukakis. *He's for good jobs at good wages. . . . I'm waiting for the candidate who's for bad jobs at low wages.*

That always got a laugh on the stump. Hart's crowds laughed at all the right places, they cheered the right lines, they were impressed, informed, swayed

. . . but he could see this *thing* behind their smiles: they were listening, they liked what they heard—but the doubt and derision, that *thing* was tugging at them, pulling them away from him. That's why he told his Advance kids: no podiums. Hart could not afford to put anything between himself and the voters. He had to get so close, they *could not pull away*. . . . "The closer I can stay—*physically closer*—somehow, I need that. It's very curious. . . ." Still, he couldn't get the people to articulate their doubt about him, so he could *answer*, he could make them see him again—he'd make the *press* see . . . if there were press.

The CBS crew had stopped trailing Hart after he finished as an asterisk in Minnesota and South Dakota. Now, before Super Tuesday, the whole traveling corps consisted of Judy Penniman from ABC. But she had to scramble at every stop to get a crew from the local affiliate, if she wanted any chance of getting a story on the air. Most days, there was no chance. Hart had become a nonstory, or at best, a *feature,* an "On the Road" piece: it was Gary Hart and his daughter, campaigning through the South . . . or some guy who'd built a four-story castle out of tin cans in his backyard. Hart was a curiosity.

And that's what got to him, late at night—say, with the third Stolichnaya, on the backside of the White Lightning Curve. You could hear the sadness creep into his voice, it got smaller . . . you could just about see the lights go out, behind his eyes. He was wracking his brain for some way to beat the dread and fatal affliction . . . but there was no answer. He had to stop thinking, sometime. The Stoly helped, it sent him to sleep. "I'm hacking a path through the wilderness," he'd say, "with no map and no compass. Sometimes, true north is hard to find."

—★—

He was better off in daylight, in better command. He was never at a loss with an audience—he was of size, and absolutely sure. He was at his best on a campus—he'd ask for a blackboard on stage . . . then he'd strip off his beat-up brown herringbone sport coat, and with his issues book in his left hand, a piece of chalk swooping like a baton in his right, he would begin to inform the room.

Four days before Super Tuesday, he took as his text the job of President. He asked the audience: What is it?

"Make the budget," someone offered from the seats. Hart turned to the blackboard and wrote: *Head of Government.*

"He has to meet Gorbachev . . ."

Hart's chalk baton pointed in approval, and he turned to write: *Head of State.* "What else?" he demanded. "One more!"

People called out answers tentatively . . . Hart's eyes peered through the stage lights to locate the voice that had said "Defense."

"Who said that? Defense—who was that? What's your name?"

Students were embarrassed to name themselves in front of a crowd. The answer—Sandra McDowell—echoed back timidly. So while he wrote on the blackboard, *Commander in Chief,* Hart boomed out:

"VICE PRESIDENT McDOWELL SAYS DEFENSE! AND SHE'S RIGHT!"

Then they were laughing, and he had them . . . as that answer led to military reform, a concept he'd helped to invent, a subject he'd worked on since 1978. It was a topic much misunderstood . . . but not with Hart at the blackboard.

"Now, I want to ask another. Which of you brilliant people can tell me: What wins wars? . . . What is the one essential element of combat that's going to make the difference between victory and defeat? . . .

". . . SECRETARY OF DEFENSE GOLDSTEIN SAYS *PEOPLE*! Exactly right! . . . Now, most of the generals and Defense Department bureaucrats would have said weapons. The whole defense debate in this country has been about weapons and spending—do we buy more, or do we buy less? But think about it . . ." And he was on another dive back to Hart-fact, bearing down for a moment into the battle deployment of NATO forces, the folly of naval power based on thirteen gigantic aircraft carriers. . . .

He'd turned out to be a hell of a teacher, or a preacher, after all. There was in his "chalk talk," as he came to call it, the kind of detail that demystified the job, and that detail built back to the fundamental question—what the nation would require from its President.

"The economy of a country is like a house. . . . What Reagan did—he put a coat of paint on, no scraping, nothing repaired—put a coat of paint on, put glass in the windows, and the house looked a lot better, for a while."

Hart drew a house on his blackboard—too near the top of the board, and out of kilter. He drew like a child.

"But what he did that was worse—he did not repair the foundation! Now, what are the pillars of our national house's foundation? They are: manufacturing—we've lost three million jobs!" (Hart now started to fill in the board with fat foundation pilings.)

". . . Agriculture and energy, that's another. . . . Infrastructure—now what is that? That's our roads and harbors, and public works, our sewer systems, transit systems, and bridges—there's bridges falling down in this country in every state of the union! That's how to put our people back to work! . . .

"Now let's look: what would happen with the HART BUDGET . . ."

By this time, Hart's voice had risen to a messianic contralto. He'd wave his budget and slap the air with his black-and-white brochure, and in those moments, he was riveting—and convincing: there *was* a better way . . . *this could be done*! This was the optimism that wins elections. This was an effort to *empower* . . . and it was without effect.

Because the underlying premise—the required leap of faith—was that *they and he* would do it . . . and they'd all seen on TV, of course, that Hart couldn't really do *anything* . . . he was a flake, and a fuck-up. He was out there alone. What kind of candidacy was that?

—★—

Three nights before Super Tuesday, there was a J-J dinner in Raleigh, North Carolina, in a cinderblock shed about the size of a football field. It was an unprepossessing place to make a speech. Hundreds of people stood in long, noisy lines for chicken, iced tea, and shiny, gelatinous pecan pie. Wizened salads in soldierly ranks had sat out on tables since the afternoon.

Now, at 8:00 P.M., here was Al Gore, screaming about Working Men and Women. Gore discovered Working Men and Women after Dick Gephardt won Iowa. Actually, what Gore discovered was that phrase, which was rebounding off the concrete floor and cinderblock walls once every ninety seconds or so, whenever Al finished up another of his daddy's ol' country stories.

Vying with Gore's grits-and-gravy scream was the din of people howdying, talking at the tables, the scraping of a thousand folding chairs on concrete. Hart was busily writing at the head table, head down.

". . . changing and growing and learning, ladies and gentlemen!" Gore was wrapping up. He had two more events that would land him in Tampa that night. "One trillion dollars a year! . . . We can do it, ladies and gentlemen! I want you to dream with me!"

Al got half a standing ovation, and he started working the front of the room, tending generally out the door and south, to Florida. But he was busy about it—he couldn't seem to get gone. He kept acting surprised and tickled to see the next person who wanted his hand. *Why, gosh! It's good to see you!*

Meanwhile, Hart was introduced, and he got a quarter of a standing O. Only half the folks were clapping at all. The rest were talking.

"It is with a note of sadness," Hart began, "that we must acknowledge that our Party has won only one national election since 1964. . . . Will we win this time?"

The believers, people who were listening, readied their tribal affirmative cheer.

"The answer is *no,*" Hart said. "We will not win this election . . . with slogans and platitudes."

The noise in the place dropped a notch, probably from shock: Hey! They hadn't come to hear any downers!

"We will inherit the Republican legacy of debt and deficit . . . we are going to have to pay taxes on luxuries. We are going to have to put a ten-dollar-a-barrel tax on imported oil, to avoid losing lives unnecessarily in the Persian Gulf . . .

"We must reform our military to a true national security force that can fight, if called upon, in a Third World arena . . .

". . . and that is why, at the University of North Carolina, I proposed a voluntary national service, so young people, and all people, can give something back to this country."

They started to applaud him. Not all, to be sure. But it shut some more people up. There were actually hundreds of people trying to listen. Hart was telling them that he knew it was harder to vote for him now. . . . "But I stay on because I love this country. And I believe that the Democratic Party represents the best hope for our nation."

With his chin out and his voice high and clear, he quoted Winston Churchill: "Never give up. Never give up. Never . . . never . . . *never* give up . . ."

The applause started again, and this time it didn't stop, but built unaccountably—now people were standing. From the podium, Hart stared out over the hall, startled and pleased. Then he saw that the people standing were faced not toward him, but toward the corner, where the former Governor, Terry Sanford, had entered.

Hart stood waiting while Sanford climbed to the head table and acknowledged the applause. Sanford raised his arms above his head, and the cheering swelled. Then he reached down and grabbed the right arm of Al Gore. (He was still there!) He raised Gore's arm up with his.

On the other side of Gore, Hart reached down and grabbed for Al's left hand, so the three could stand with arms raised in tableau. But Gore yanked his left arm down and pulled his hand away. Hart flushed red, smiled shyly, and turned away.

—★—

Two nights before Super Tuesday, from his hotel room, Hart returned a call from Roy Romer, his home-state Governor in Colorado. Romer told him he was going to endorse Dukakis—within twelve hours, 7:00 A.M., Monday . . . *the day before Super Tuesday.*

Hart's face fell. He was stricken. He said nothing at first. Then, stiffly, " 'Preciate the call, Roy."

One day before Super Tuesday—his home state! It was a personal embarrassment. The Colorado primary was almost a month away! Why now? Because Hart was still in the race? . . . Romer said Dukakis wanted it now.

Mike Stratton was already on the phone to Romer's Chief of Staff, just to let him know: Hart still had a lot of friends in Colorado—they kick Hart now, they could break a toe. Subtlety was not Stratton's long suit. Hart turned to Bernie the Attorney: "What do you think?"

"It's unfair," Bernie said. "It's unnecessary. It's bullshit. What purpose does it serve?"

There was no purpose, Hart thought. It was just . . . mean. He ought to stay in—just for one more debate, just to turn to Dukakis and ask him: "What are you going to *do,* Mike? What are you going to do about soldiers who can't read their manuals? Call a conference in Davenport? Start an enterprise zone? What are you going to do about the countries you've only read about, where the bulk of the world is living, where the battles are going to be fought? What are you going to do about Gorbachev? . . ."

But what for? Just to give back meanness for meanness? That was not Hart. . . . Mean was the cautious median, the safe zone between the poles of the old ideas—the average, the well-worn path, the same old down-the-middle that Hart had fought, since the start, since RFK . . . twenty years!

And now they said Hart was hurting the Party?

Stratton was dialing again, stabbing the phone with his thick fighter's fingers, making the keypad clack . . . the sound of toes breaking. He got the Chief of Staff to Tim Wirth, Hart's successor in the Senate. "Well, I thought Tim ought to have some warning . . ." (Translation: *Wake up! You let Romer get on board with Dukakis, and Wirth will be hanging out there all alone!*) Stratton was making sure this would be a long night for the Governor.

It was going to be a long night for Hart, too. . . . It would be different if there were some way to turn it around. Hart couldn't see the steps. . . . He'd thought of a major speech, but not if TV wouldn't cover. He could ask to go on *Nightline,* but why should they do it? He could concentrate on one state—say, Connecticut, where he won 121 out of 122 townships last time . . . but no, he knew, people voted nationally. That's why Al Gore's southern strategy was wrong: they were all in the same media tangle. Hart could try to find a major figure, someone to say: "Come on! Give the guy a chance!" But who? Safire came as close as he could—really stuck his neck out . . . nothing happened. Iacocca? Cronkite? . . . Hart made his head hurt, trying to think of the way.

They looked at him now, and they just saw his . . . *unelectability.* Bernie the Attorney called it "the Tinkerbell problem." They didn't believe Hart could fly. And if they didn't believe . . . well, then, Hart could not fly.

Hart couldn't allow himself even that thin cushion of metaphor. The papers printed the candidates' schedules—but not his. He couldn't get on TV anymore—even in the wrap-ups. "Someone in New York has decided," Hart said. "I just don't matter anymore."

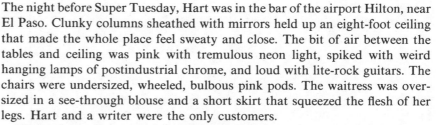

The night before Super Tuesday, Hart was in the bar of the airport Hilton, near El Paso. Clunky columns sheathed with mirrors held up an eight-foot ceiling that made the whole place feel sweaty and close. The bit of air between the tables and ceiling was pink with tremulous neon light, spiked with weird hanging lamps of postindustrial chrome, and loud with lite-rock guitars. The chairs were undersized, wheeled, bulbous pink pods. The waitress was oversized in a see-through blouse and a short skirt that squeezed the flesh of her legs. Hart and a writer were the only customers.

He drank tequila, up, with lime and salt. He was near the peak of the White Lightning Curve, ready to talk about awful truths.

This was the truth:

He would have to get out. His dream was over. He would not be President. He never wanted to say it, to let go of that . . . he'd given his life to that. "But I don't want another round of editorials and op-ed pieces, day after Super Tuesday, saying I'm obsessed, I'm ridiculous, I'm pathetic. . . ."

Could they hurt him anymore?

Yes, they hurt. And in the end, they could kill his ideas.

Between his two '88 campaigns, he'd shopped a book proposal around—no takers. . . . Then a woman from the New York Times Syndicate called to talk to Hart about a column. She was sure it would be a big winner. He sketched out thirty-six columns . . . but then he heard nothing. She finally called to say, all reactions were negative. There was no place for Hart's column. . . . Finally, there was an agent in New Jersey who worked hard to put him on the lecture circuit. . . . "And when I finally did go out to speak, no less a publication than the *L.A. Times* editorialized: 'Sit down, Gary. You have nothing to say. You have no place in public life in this country.'

"They can take my platform away, altogether. . . .

"I'm in a struggle to the death over who I am. And I feel my opponent is the press, who cannot allow me to define myself—they have a stake in this. They're all on record, and they can't bear to see me reemerge as a serious person in this country, because they went so far out and said such terrible things. They can't allow me to succeed."

The writer asked about Hart's own argument: that he was the only reform candidate, that sooner or later, when it narrowed down, they would have to pay attention.

"You don't understand," Hart said. "I'm making these things up as I go along. I got up in front of the cameras after I got one percent in Iowa, and I had no idea what I was going to say. Out came this notion that I was the only reform candidate—happened to be true. It's the muse. The muse was with me that night.

"But . . . I don't know how it can happen.

"Do you know, Mike Stratton came out here to tell me that all my friends want me to get out now? That's the message. . . ." Hart was staring at the rime on his tequila glass.

Said his companion: "What's the point of being the stubbornest man in the world if you have to start listening to your friends?"

"Really?" he said. "The stubbornest?" He looked more cheerful. "Well . . . I'm going upstairs." His eyebrows leapt once, with the joke. "Big day, tomorrow."

—★—

It would be a big day . . . but not for him. In twenty races, Hart would gather, total, three percent. His best state would be Texas, with five percent—but no wins in any district, no delegates anywhere. And three days thereafter, at a calm press conference in Denver, Hart would get out . . . and let go his life . . . with no commotion, an absence of noise—with the sad and final quiet of a man in deep water who ceases to kick.

118

The
Alamo

DICK KNEW it wasn't going to work—even while the polls were still good . . . in fact, they were on the rise after his win in South Dakota, and the numbers said he had a chance everywhere . . . at least in Texas, Florida, Georgia, Oklahoma, Arkansas, even Louisiana. It was Gephardt and Dukakis, with Gore trailing badly . . . and Jackson was solid, though the polls would miss many of his voters. The killers were no twitchier than usual. Money was an awful strain, a constant disappointment: those southern bigs who said they'd be there if Dick won Iowa . . . well, where were they? . . . But neither was that different than usual. The press was actually better: the big-feet and pundits had Gephardt in the mix—somewhere along the line, he stopped having to prove he was a serious candidate (*everybody knew* Gephardt would be a major player on Super Tuesday! *Newsweek* made him the "smart-money favorite") . . . and camera crews were waiting at the airports.

Still, he knew, it was somehow wrong—the feeling. That was the first to go: the feeling, inside . . . that he could make a big, thumping difference. Happened the very first day.

He left South Dakota and went to Waco, Texas—the district of his House buddy, Marvin Leath. And Marvin, God bless him, had a crowd that would have filled a ballpark! It was great . . . they came for Marvin—didn't know a thing about Dick . . . but a hell of a crowd, and Dick felt fine.

But then he got back on his little jet, and the next stop was Florida . . . so he flew, and flew . . . and he flew, and . . . *four hours* in the air! And it dawned on Gephardt, the way it never did with schedules and maps: he had *twelve days* till Super Tuesday . . . and *twenty states* would vote that day!

And he was *four hours* in the air, to get to his second event . . .

And the next day, he'd do four stops in Florida, and he would be on the plane *seven hours* . . .

It dawned on Gephardt, he could spend twelve days on Florida alone . . . and not even scratch the place! It dawned on Gephardt: he could not cover the ground. He could show up in this media market, or that media market, make a *hell* of a speech. . . . But what about the *other* seventy-five markets?

And that was the first pillar of his life to slide out from under him—maybe the most unsettling, because it had to do with *him* . . . and when that history-denting difference went out of his own days and nights, when that strength left him . . . well, what he felt was helpless.

—★—

After that, it was like one of those crash scenes, where you *see* the kid on his bicycle . . . it's all in slow-motion . . . but so is your foot on its way to the brake . . . and the wheel when you yank it . . . and the car tipping over . . . and the tree, the ditch . . .

You can *see* the whole damn thing going wrong—and there is . . . *nothing you can do!*

He wasn't stupid. He knew he'd have to win it on TV.

But this wasn't like Super Tuesday four years before, when Gary Hart, winner of the Iowa bump, was also winner of New Hampshire . . . he was cleaning Fritz Mondale's clock . . . that was *the story.* Hart had network news every night. (And that meant he had a dozen volunteers in D.C., just ripping open envelopes to get to the checks.) . . . But with Gephardt's pitiful Iowa bump, he couldn't get more than ten seconds on the news—usually a ten-second clip in a roundup, meant to show how this whole campaign sucked wind.

So the only chance was his own paid TV—the magic bullets! But that took money . . . which he didn't have. This wasn't a matter of an extra ten thousand. He'd wheedled and begged almost a million for Super Tuesday, but that just spread him around seven states so thin . . . you might see a Gephardt ad once a night. His killers had decided they couldn't afford the bio ad. They had to cut the Hyundai magic to thirty seconds . . . which basically left just a smile and a threat. They taped an endorsement from Marvin Leath, which they ran all over Texas (even though nine-tenths of Texas had no idea who the hell Leath was). They taped an endorsement from Claude Pepper, but they only had the money to run it in South Florida (where Michael Dukakis's marriage to a Jewess had already sewn up the senior sunbirds in their condos).

What could Dick do? . . . Spend twelve hours a day in a motel in Atlanta, working the phones for money? Not likely. His schedule averaged out between one and two thousand miles a day. Anyway, it didn't seem to matter who he called, how often—or what was said. The commitments only lasted until he hung up. So he scheduled another fund-raiser in St. Louis, and another in Springfield, Missouri . . . raised another quarter-million . . . but that just burned one day out of twelve in the one state he shouldn't have had to visit at all.

That was the day he said, on the plane, with a bitter tone that startled his crew: "If they'd *told* me I'd have to raise ten million . . . I wouldn't have *run!*"

There was a new edge of darkness to his humor, like when he visited Texarkana and did the expected photo op, standing with one foot in Texas, one in Arkansas, and said, through too thin a smile, to Trippi: "Is this our idea of covering two states?"

There was an unwonted snappishness to his answers on his tax votes, abortion, the MX missile . . . he'd get the flip-flop questions everywhere he went now . . . that's how he knew Gore's ads were on the air.

It seemed like Gore had a new persona every month: first was Herald-of-the-High-Tech-Future . . . that bombed. Then he tried the hawkish Voice-of-the-Sunbelt . . . apparently didn't play in the polls. Anyway, by Super Tuesday, Al was Defender-of-the-Working-Man! And that meant Gore was head-to-head with Gephardt for the same votes. So Al *borrowed* his way to a two-million-dollar budget . . . and used the bulk of that to dump on Gephardt's head.

And Gore was only the thunder to Dukakis's lightning bolts. The Duke's people made a killer ad. They hired an acrobat, gave him a strawberry-red wig, and put him in a suit. And then they filmed him, physically flipping and flopping all over a studio . . . while a narrator read out a half-dozen back-and-forth Gephardt votes. Gorgeous! . . . So the Duke had *another* three million dollars to spend, dumping on Gephardt's head.

What did Dick have? . . . Well, in the end, he scraped up $80,000 to run some pitiful ten-second kamikaze ads on Dukakis. Forget about answering the charges against Dick Gephardt! All he could say was, the Duke's campaign was the one that smeared Joe Biden . . . and a Dukakis op was accused of trying to infiltrate Paul Simon's campaign . . . and now Dukakis was trying to smear Dick Gephardt . . . so don't believe him. It was ugly . . . and futile.

No one who hadn't lived through Iowa would understand what those charges meant . . . and in ten seconds? Forget it! . . . Anyway, the ad would only run once a night.

When Reilly saw it, he knew Dukakis would *never* forget, or forgive . . . *no one* was allowed to suggest that Michael Dukakis had somehow strayed from his moral axis. Reilly called the plane and got Trippi—Joe had to talk to Dick. If Gephardt *ever* thought of Vice President, on a ticket with the Duke . . . that ad could never run.

So, Trippi asked, gently as he could—no one likes to be the first to mention the V-word. It was dark in the plane, unaccountably cold, and Joe was mumbling around the subject. He said the ad was rough . . . something had to be done, but . . . there were some, uhhh . . .

Dick broke in: "You have a better idea?"

Joe shook his head.

"Then, don't you think we ought to run it?"

Trippi gathered himself. "Uh . . . Reilly knows Dukakis, and I know Dukakis. I mean, Dick . . . he'll *hate* you. There's a good chance he'll hate you *personally,* and that means . . . you just won't have . . ."

Gephardt cut him off. "That's okay. He's not gonna be my Vice President, either."

So it was go . . . but this was no magic bullet—not with $80,000 . . . more like a BB, against cannon.

— ★ —

In Texas, the weekend before Super Tuesday, Dick got an hour of downtime, another motel . . . he flipped on the TV, got the news. But the news came between newscasts: one hour of TV, *five* ads from Gore and Dukakis, five shots to his belly.

The Duke's acrobat ad . . .

Gore's charge that Dick tried to cut Social Security (a lie) . . .

A Duke ad slamming Dick for accepting money from PACs . . .

Over and over, and over, in Texas . . . where Gephardt's oil import fee ought to take off . . . where his farm bill could make a difference . . . but who knew anything about his bills? He'd come into Texas with a lead! *Still* could make a run of it in Texas! He knew he could! . . . But how was he going to hold any votes with five ads against him in one hour!

— ★ —

He could not . . . and that's how he knew: nothing he tried was going to work . . . not against five million dollars on his head.

So he did what he was supposed to, he did his schedule, he did his best: he went to his next event, and his next, till the end, his last event, the day before the vote, and it was . . . the Alamo.

There was a huge plaza in front of the old fort, and a grand monument in the center of the plaza, where flags whipped in a gray wind. Dick's Advance had him standing with the doors of the fort as backdrop—that way, the crowd would only have to fill the pavement between the fort and the monument.

It wasn't a bad crowd—hell, close to a thousand people! A crowd that big in Iowa, or New Hampshire, puts the smell of a *win* in the air. But those little states were gone. And this crowd . . . he just couldn't feel the heat coming back from them.

He said the words—same words!

We will take back this country's economic DESTINY! . . .

And he could see, he could feel, they didn't know what the words meant. They weren't against him. They just didn't know anything about him . . . all the years he'd been speaking these words, these people had not heard a thing! . . . And there was no way now he could echo up to size, the size of that *figure* in the ads—what ads?

He had to try! He had to believe . . . for them! It *could* not work if he did not believe. He *knew* . . .

We're gonna WIN in Texas . . .
We're gonna WIN across the SOUTH . . .
We're gonna WIN BACK THE WHITE HOUSE!

But he could not believe . . . any more than he could take the words and plant them by will, by his own force, behind the eyes of those staring Texans . . . any more than he could fill, with his own breath, his own battered voice, what looked like a thousand miles of empty, gray, Texas sky.

— ★ —

And he was not surprised when he got the word from Reilly, then Carrick in Washington, that the bottom was dropping out . . . everywhere. The last states—Texas, Arkansas, Oklahoma—states where he had a chance, till the end . . . well, this was the end. His numbers were melting like butter in a pan.

And even then, they meant to fly him on that lousy plane (no bathroom—no one would trust himself to have a beer) . . . across four hours of the country . . . *again* . . . to Miami, to another motel, middle of the night. . . . Florida was only on the schedule for a fund-raiser in West Palm Beach. But the funder was canceled now. . . . All he had was breakfast at a senior citizens' center—seven in the morning on three hours' sleep, in a state that was lost . . . yet the pros scheduled Dick to eat Raisin Bran and chat with his elderly tablemates while an old man in plaid pants and dyed orange hair entertained with his rendition of "New York, New York."

And even then, on Super Tuesday, the day of his demise, Dick did it.

119

Tough
Night

IT WAS THREE DAYS before Super
Tuesday when Elizabeth Dole saw
where things were headed. She
knew how unhappy Bob was, of course . . . how New Hampshire hurt . . . how
people talked about him. Even in her own state, North Carolina, some women
would mention *to Elizabeth's face* that "their neighbors" wouldn't vote for
Bob, on account of him being so mean . . . well, it just made her more
determined. She had to show, they were all wrong! . . . Somehow, she had to
win North Carolina for Bob!

She had to put herself on the line. Her speechwriter, Stan Wellborn, told
her: "You have to tell these people, *you* want *your husband* in there! You have
to tell them, they should want *you* in the White House!" . . . It was risky. If
she lost, it would be rejection for her, too. But she prayed for courage, and she
did it:

"Let's put a North Carolinian in the White House!"

Every stop, every two-bit town, eight events a day:

"Ah say it's *tahme* for a *North Carolinian* in the White House! . . . What
do you say?"

Well, they whooped her name to the skies. If she could just hit enough
towns, enough crowds, enough hands, enough hearts . . .

The Saturday before the vote, she was hip-hopping in a twin-engine plane
(Bob wouldn't let her fly in single-engine jobs), with two pilots (Bob wouldn't
let her fly with one pilot), and her staff and her cavalcade of stars—Al Haig
was along, and Dick Rutan, who was such a celebrity at that moment, for

flying his own plane around the world without stopping for gas. . . . It was Rutan who saw, or maybe smelled, trouble: a fan in the roof of the plane that was supposed to cool a coil, it quit, or melted, and something in the ceiling got hot during takeoff—the pilots had the engines at full throttle when Rutan jumped off his seat, yelling for the brakes . . . and they barely made a stop at the end of the runway . . . Rutan kicked out the door—the plane was filled with smoke—another minute, they would have been goners.

Mercy!

Then they were trapped at that flea-circus airport while they tried to find a plane with two engines, and two pilots, for rent, that weekend day, for Elizabeth . . . who had to *win North Carolina* . . . and who had two more events that day—two more crowds.

It took hours. They had to call all over the state. . . . But the unfair part was the view, for hours . . . at the end of the runway . . . that gorgeous, gleaming, stainless steel 707, lettered on the side *The United States of America* . . . silent and still, its four jets protected by custom engine-caps, which was standard procedure for the backup *Air Force Two,* which was always in position, at the ready, in case any hitch should befall the VP's number-one plane.

— ★ —

That weekend, new Bush ads went on TV in North Carolina: "Bob Dole says that President Reagan calls him to get things done. But under Bob Dole's leadership, we lost the Bork nomination, and in sixteen of the thirty-four votes Reagan lost in the Senate, Dole couldn't deliver even half of the Republicans. . . . So, when President Reagan wanted a Vice President he could count on, he didn't call Bob Dole. He called George Bush."

Elizabeth and her mother and her mother's friends organized the Prayer Network. The night before Super Tuesday, they would all pray, from six o'clock to six-fifteen.

Monday, in a van rolling toward Winston-Salem, a staff member said: "Mrs. Dole, it's six o'clock."

Elizabeth said: "I wonder if we could just be quiet for a few minutes now . . ." They drove up the road in absolute silence, while Mrs. Dole prayed.

— ★ —

Super Tuesday, they moved Dole out of the South (no sense lingering) to the next battleground, to Illinois, where he holed up in a Hyatt near O'Hare Airport. There was a ballroom, a small crowd, a black-tie band to play "Chicago, Chicago" . . . arranged for his one required appearance.

The walls were festooned with blue and yellow balloons and victory signs . . . but Dole hadn't won a damn thing. There were a few close states— Oklahoma was tight, Missouri was too close to call—but the only color on the TV maps was Bush-red. Dole was getting blown out from Texas to Florida and all the way to Maryland, right up the East Coast.

In the ballroom, a rumor was swirling among the press that Dole was going to call it quits—right there—tonight! Guy's getting *killed*! . . . But on stage, Lee Daniels, Dole's chairman, the Republican Leader in the State House of Reps, was vowing to stop the tide in Illinois on March 15. "A hundred and seventy-two thousand phone calls! Every supporter gets a card! Every county is organized! We're going to turn this thing around!"

The crowd was obliging, yelling: "We want Dole! We want Dole!"

And there was the Bobster, thumbs up, while the strobes lit his smile . . . and he said to the crowd:

"Well, I'm available."

It was clear in an instant, Dole had no intention of quitting. Nor did he mean to satisfy expectations with a snarl of any sort. He seemed oddly at peace.

When the crowd got quiet, he thanked his southern supporters. "Sometimes, in politics, we forget to say thank you. And that's all some people ever ask . . ."

Dole's tone was reflective, gentle. He talked about what Illinois meant to him. "A lot of great people . . . one was a doctor, Hampar Kelikian. . . . And I remember, almost forty years to the day, walking out of Wesley Hospital, on the road to recovery. . . . That's what I'm going to be, next week, in Illinois—on the road to recovery!"

It could have ended there, but Dole wanted to talk. He started on the polls, how they *showed* he was electable . . . he beat every Democrat—better than Bush! He challenged Bush to debate—one-on-one, to have it out—not in a mean or negative way . . . but just to show who was who, who was the strong one.

"I'm proud to be a candidate," he said. "I'm proud to be a Republican. I'm pleased to be in Illinois. I do want to make one final—not a plea, but a statement. I think you've got to be strong in this business. It's not a piece of cake . . ."

He got a big cheer when he came down the steps to the floor. He wanted to shake hands, he was trying to thank these people . . . but the cameras closed in, and Dole was pinned against the stage, with his thumb up, a frozen grin. "That's good, that's good," Mari murmured.

A radio man stuck a microphone in Dole's face and said, "Tough night . . ."

Hegh-hegh-hegh . . . Dole was grinning.

Another mike—a question about Bush's clean sweep.

"I feel good," Dole said. "It's not over yet." Then he cut himself off. He had to get away from the mikes. On stage, there were a couple of codgers from the Tenth Mountain Division . . . so Dole climbed up again, stood with them for photographs.

When he came down to work toward the door, the crowd got him. In the crush, a teenager came at him head first, or skull first. The kid had "Dole '88" shaved into the stubble on his scalp, along with a silhouette of Illinois. The crowd shoved them together: Dole's face leapt in an involuntary flicker of horror as he inspected this artwork from a distance of six inches. . . . A woman with a voice like a club and makeup like Naugahyde was yelling at Dole—

offering lingerie, nylons, shoes for Elizabeth. "Agh, gimme a discount?" Dole said. "YOU GOT IT, HONEY!" the woman roared. "ANYTHING YOU WANT!" Dole's eyes were twitching for a route of escape. Mike Glassner and Mari were trying to push to the door, trying to shepherd Dole, but they wouldn't touch him. A lovely young woman had a hold of his left hand, and she was pressing up to him, whispering something. Dole's eyes faced the floor as he listened. He winced. She was saying, she was going to be a doctor, she understood all that he went through, those thirty-nine months . . . she *knew his pain!* She still had his hand, and he started to shake it, up and down, hoping she'd let go after that. . . . Mari was pushing, but with her hands three inches from his back, his shoulder, while her voice was at his ear, murmuring, "Senator, we have to go, Senator . . ." Glassner pulled the door; he stood away and held it, both arms stretched out, to keep five and a half feet of crowd at bay. A couple of microphones darted at Dole, bidding him pause: *Senator whaddabout the vote tonight? Isn't it all over? . . .* But Dole brushed by, muttering: "Gotta gooo. S'posed to be upstairs."

"G'LUCK, BOB!" a man yelled as Dole hit the door. Dole wheeled, halfway out, tried to wave . . . "Keep *workin'*!" he barked.

He caught a glimpse of the pretty med student as the door was closing. Dole's voice echoed in the hallway as he disappeared:

"Agghh! Might *need* a doctor . . ."

—★—

Elizabeth didn't make it to Chicago till after ten o'clock. She had to stay in North Carolina, for her victory party . . . but there was no victory. North Carolina was lost to her, to Bob, by six percentage points.

When she got to the Oak Brook Hyatt, she swept through the lobby. She stopped for no one. She looked at no one . . . straight into the elevator, where she stared ahead, at the door. A couple of reporters ducked on for the ride . . . and they tried, gently:

"Mrs. Dole?"

But she didn't even turn.

"To the suite," her body man, Mark Romig, said to the Advance man. To the reporters, he said Mrs. Dole was tired.

In the elevator light, she looked pale, not well—like a woman they'd never seen. Her face was a different shape . . . no one had ever seen it unaffected by her will to please.

When she was gone, the reporters rode down to report to the pack at large. She looked, they said, like she was going to a hanging.

Someone said: "How would *you* like to be in that room with him?"

There were grim chuckles . . . like everyone knew how Bob would be.

120

That
Slow-Motion
Horror

FUNNY, how it worked out, how most of Dick's killers couldn't be there—in St. Louis, that dismal Super Tuesday. Carrick was sick with the flu—and Reilly, Doak . . . well, what could they do in St. Louis? They'd already done what they could: by noon, they'd had their conference call with Dick, told him he was going to lose . . . everywhere.

Dick was calm. He wanted them to know: "You guys did a great job. I'll always appreciate it."

Jane was in bed with fevered flu in Virginia, the kids were with her . . . so when Dick took cover at a hotel in St. Louis . . . there was no one around.

The road crew came with him from Florida, and Shrum was on the plane in those days . . . but they all told each other Dick must be awfully tired. They left him to "rest" in his suite.

Dick Moe flew in, Jack Guthman from Chicago, Don and Nancy Gephardt from New York; Joyce Aboussie showed up with her St. Louis crowd; Uncle Bob came to the hotel with his wife, Kay . . . but no one had the heart to barge in on Dick. They mostly stayed downstairs, in the bar. If they were talking in the hall, and happened to pass his door, they whispered past the Secret Service man.

The suite was plush, tan and taupe, and empty, dim in the afternoon light. There was Dick, and the TV, and no one . . . except Loreen.

"Come sit down," she told him. She patted the couch. They sat, touching, holding hands, fingers locked—his right hand, her left . . . they talked a bit, but mostly sat silent, while the afternoon light gave way to darkness. Dick didn't want the lights on, no . . . thanks. Loreen watched her son in the lurid splashes of TV light while Dick stared at the screen, waiting for the news he hoped would never come.

It came, of course, over and over, in that slow-motion horror . . . for *hours*—maps flashing, check marks studding the screen next to the other guys' names . . . sadness, resentment, the cry in his throat of woulda-been . . . and then, he was numb. He had hoped, to the very end, for *something*—not a state, perhaps, but a few local districts . . . a few delegates. But, no. Everything was lost. Florida, Texas—Dukakis picked the two biggest plums. Gore swept the border states. Jackson won the cotton South. The anchors had a hard time picking the "winner" . . . in time, they gave up.

"But the big surprise, Peter, on the Democratic side, is the disastrous showing by Congressman Richard Gephardt . . ."

"If we'd had the money . . ." Dick said, in the suite.

But Loreen was beyond the comfort of earthly explanation. "If it was supposed to be," she said, "it would have been."

Dick nodded . . . but he could not accept—not that night.

"This is the best for us," Loreen said. She made Dick look straight at her eyes. "There is a reason . . . even if we don't know the reason. The Lord is doing it."

Dick said he agreed.

— ★ —

It was late when Gephardt appeared on TV, from the ballroom of his St. Louis hotel. (Why rush? Maybe people would go to bed . . .)

But Carrick was still watching, in D.C., and he saw Dick embrace every person on stage. There was a long hug for his brother, Don. Then, Loreen: they stood near the podium, hands on one another's shoulders, eyes locked. They stayed like that for what seemed like a minute. (Loreen was telling Dick: she was never more proud of him than she was that night.)

On the screen, Dick turned, and the hometown crowd sent up a cheer: *Gep-HARDT Gep-HARDT* . . . Dick laughed aloud, into the mike. "You bet!" He posed there with a double thumbs-up. When they were quiet, he began:

"Well, I never told you it was gonna be easy . . ."

Carrick was proud of Dick's grace. He thought *he* couldn't have done it. Not that way. Not that well.

Then, there were interviews with the networks. It was the first time Carrick could remember anyone congratulating his opponents for their victories.

Carrick felt sick at heart. It occurred to him, again—the thought he'd been living with, all day, since that conference call: we have not really served this man . . . not as he deserved.

— ★ —

The next day, they all flew to be with Dick. Gephardt was still on his schedule, moving on to South Carolina—another disaster in the making. . . . Carrick and Reilly rented a plane, a small King Air. Murphy, Doak, and Tony Coelho came along, as did the money man, Terry McAuliffe, his deputy, Boyd Lewis, and the field director, Donna Brazile. They called ahead to let Dick know: they'd meet at a supporter's home, outside Columbia, South Carolina. Debra Johns told the traveling press that Dick had a private dinner that night. The last thing they needed was a deathwatch story. Carrick and the killers snuck through the airport. No one could know Gephardt's future was on the line.

It was a long night, full of talk—argument, as always, but the heat was gone . . . no point fighting for the biggest stateroom aboard the *Titanic*. And they all felt another change: there was the campaign . . . and there was Gephardt's life. In the last days, those had ceased to be the same.

Carrick ran the show: he started with McAuliffe, to run down the money. Dick was a half-million in debt . . . maybe a million, once all the bills came in. If Dick chose to fight on in Michigan (Illinois was too expensive, too soon—hopeless) . . . well, that would be another half-million. Dick would have to grind it out, retail . . . smart money was gone. Dick would have to get his face in the phone, and beg.

Coelho just wanted Dick back in the House. He'd told Carrick, that morning, maybe it was time for Dick to quit. . . . But now it came clear: if Dick blew up in Michigan, he'd have so much debt he'd *have* to come back to Congress. No way to raise the money otherwise. . . . So, Coelho said maybe Dick ought to go on.

Shrum said there was no disgrace in getting out. Shrummy could write the speech! A beautiful exit. Shrummy was sure: there would be no lingering negatives on Dick.

Reilly was sure there would be. His numbers showed the flip-flop tag had stuck like tar—get out now, and history would conclude that Dick's own record drove him from the race. Gephardt had traveled forty-eight states, asking people to stand up and *fight*. . . . How could he quit now, first time he got a bloody nose?

Donna Brazile said the field staff could do Michigan—they'd own the place! Precinct by precinct, just like Iowa . . . and they'd do it all in two weeks.

Murphy said: "You're not gonna win Michigan."

Doak had the quaver back in his voice: "Look, it's been a crazy fuckin' year . . . who knows? I think you could win! If Duke finishes third in Illinois, how's he gonna get the delegates? It's a brokered convention! . . . Let's mix it up, let it happen!"

Trippi said maybe it was time to let Dick unite the Party. Get out now, endorse Dukakis . . . go to the Hill, get those guys behind Duke . . . back to Iowa, urge those delegates to unite behind Dukakis. The goal was a Democratic President: if Dick got out, he could *un-broker* the convention, unite the Party . . . and Dukakis would know, it was Dick who made him king.

Reilly said he knew Dukakis, they didn't. If they thought for a minute that little shit would be *grateful* . . . well, forget it.

It was Debra Johns, who'd been so quiet, who finally turned to Dick: "What do you think, Dick? Everybody's talking . . . what do *you* want to do?"

They all turned, and Dick dropped his RCA-dog look. He didn't even pause: "I've been doing this two and a half years now. I'm not getting out until they cut my head off and hand it to me."

There was silence. Everybody staring . . . Dick was so fierce. They hadn't realized, the want had always come from him.

So, Michigan became the next hope.

People started getting up. Shrum said he never really thought Dick should quit. Trippi said he just thought the idea had to be considered. "Yeah," Coelho said, "and dismissed out of hand . . .

"So . . ." Coelho turned to Dick. "So, if you don't win Michigan, we're gonna file for Congress?"

Dick hadn't moved. His eyes were locked on a corner of the room. He wasn't seeing them.

He was thinking back . . . how he started, after '82, because he had to—someone had to—get control . . .

And he was thinking ahead—how would he get the money? Money for Michigan . . . money for the debt . . . money for college.

March 29th was his filing deadline.

Michigan would vote March 26th.

He was going back to the House. He had no more control . . .

"Yeah," he told Tony, absently.

No one in that room knew he'd charged up a hundred thousand dollars on his personal Amex Gold Card. No one knew.

"God," Dick said, as he stood. "Who's gonna tell Jane?"

The
Secret
Plan

DOLE FOUND OUT they'd taken a million dollars from his Senate re-election fund—that could have been his *retirement* money!—and spent it on ads all over the South . . . states they never had a prayer of winning. They threw it away! (Gyagghh! They ran the Footprints-in-the-Snow Ad in *Florida*—people never *seen* snow . . . not to mention, Bush was forty points ahead there.)

The Big Guys promised Dole they'd pay it back. Then the smart-guy lawyers figured out—a week too late—the campaign laws wouldn't let them pay it back. That money was history.

That's when Dole pulled his ads off the air in Illinois.

Then the press found out, and the Friday papers (four days before the Illinois vote) were filled with speculation:

Dole was going to call it quits (sources said . . . observers said).

Dole denied he was quitting.

Of course, they didn't believe *that* crap for a minute!

And Dole did not, could not, tell them about the TV time he was trying to buy—the Saturday special, the half-hour statewide.

That was the whole point: he wanted to spring that, make it a big deal—couldn't give Bush time to get ready! That was Dole's secret plan.

Then, too, the Dole campaign still had to tie down a few, uh . . . loose ends.

—★—

Dole had in mind a TV show . . . but *live* TV—he would *make something happen.* He picked a little town, Galesburg, near the Iowa border, 185 miles

west and south of Chicago, the site of Knox College, host to a Lincoln–
Douglas debate in 1858—that's where Dole would challenge George Bush to
meet him, one-on-one. Bush was going to be in Galesburg Saturday night for
the Lincoln Day Dinner . . . so Dole would show up in Galesburg, too . . .
crowd the VP, get in his face, make him *react,* on the spot . . . *just like Nashua,
in 1980*—while the whole state watched, live, on TV.

So they flew in the video wizards, Murphy and Castellanos, to Chicago—
that was Friday. Brock had a limo waiting at the airport to whisk them into
the bunker at the Hyatt. The smart guys were already calling all over the state,
trying to buy a half-hour time block. Hot-shot Washington communications
lawyers were threatening million-dollar lawsuits if the Illinois stations
wouldn't sell the time. Dole-folk were on the phones to Galesburg, trying to
map a battle plan: *We could crash the Bush event—just buy a ticket! Y'know,
we'd challenge him right there: C'mon, you wimp! . . .* Dole's Illinois chairman,
Lee Daniels, came in with some of his Chicago mob—guys with pinky rings
and broken teeth. Daniels was throwing a fit over the stories that Dole would
quit. Henry Hyde, the smarmy Rep from the Sixth District, was going to
endorse Dole—now *that* was in jeopardy. Daniels demanded that Brock call
Hyde. One of Daniels's mob, a guy named Paulie—who had not only the ring
and the teeth, but shades and a shoulder holster—was informing the Dole-folk:
"We're gettin' *focked*! In Du Page County. You got that? Focked *over*!"
. . . Then the phone rang in the staff room. It was the Bobster, from his suite:
What about his TV show?

"Impossible," Murphy said.

They only had twenty-eight hours! They hadn't even bought the time. They
couldn't hire a crew until they got the time. Dole wanted *remote TV*—no
studio, they'd need a camera truck. He wanted *live TV* in a small town 185
miles away—that's *satellite time.* Where would they get the trucks? St. Louis?
Would the stations in Illinois *take* a live feed? . . . Why not tape? Why not
Chicago? Guys . . . *Guys! . . . What* was the show?

Wasn't ten minutes later, an Advance man strode in, told Murphy: "Room
320, five minutes." When Murphy got there, the phone rang.

"Whah, *hah,* Mike!"

Mrs. Dole was just thinking how *great* that Bob Dole video was, how it
touched her hort . . . and . . . by the way: Bob *really wanted* his show from
Galesburg.

"Well . . . there's problems . . ."

"Let's *trah* to do it."

"Uhnn . . ." Murphy said.

Mrs. Dole was relentlessly, sugar-sweetly implacable. "Mike, it's awfully
important to him."

"Uhnn . . . alrighty . . ." he said. "We'll do our best."

After that, she called again—for Castellanos: same message.

Then her staff called: the speechwriter, Aram Bakshian, *had* a half-hour
speech, *already written*—wasn't that *great*? (Actually, it wasn't great. It was
just a half-hour speech. Aram had in mind that Dole would *read* this thing,

staring, full-face, into the camera. Murphy started calling it the People of Earth speech. ATTENTION, PEOPLE OF EARTH!)

Another Advance man grabbed Murphy: "Come with me." He pulled him down the hall to the staff suite. Bernie Windon said to a phone: "Here he is, Senator . . ." He handed Murphy the phone.

"Agghh! What'sa *prob*lem?"

"Well," Murphy said, "there's four problems. Number one, we need a satellite truck, and there's NCAA basketball all over the country Friday night, so all the trucks are out on the road. Number two, we'll need a camera truck with switching—right now we're looking in Milwaukee for one. Number three, we're going to need a lighting truck so it doesn't look like a home movie. I think we can get one. Number four, if we get the time, we're not sure the station'll take a live feed, and we'd have to get satellite time, and all that."

As usual, Dole was surprisingly hip:

"Aghh, have you tried Conus?"

"I'm sure we have," Murphy said.

"Well, check with Walt Riker in Washington. He's working on this, too."

"Okay, I will, Senator."

Dole wanted Murphy to know he was not unaware. . . . "I think we've got to do this live. Not in a sterile situation," he said. His voice was soft, almost pleading. "We wanna get Bush in there. If he walks in, you can't tell him, no, it's already taped. It's got to be interesting—big event for the press—build it up . . ."

Murphy said: "Well, Senator, we're trying to put it together."

"I know it's not easy," Dole said, "not an easy situation. We're twenty-five points down. It's gonna be hard to win. But we gotta try."

Murphy said nothing—he didn't know what to say.

Dole's voice was even softer, a bit husky—he said: "If we can't do it right . . . if I'm just going down the tubes, we could save the money—not do it . . ."

There was silence. He was breaking Murphy's heart. "Senator, I'll find a truck if I have to steal one. We'll do everything we can."

"O-*kayy!*" The Bobster's voice was back. "Don't wanna *keep* you. *Get to it!*"

—★—

Friday afternoon, they bought the time, 6:30 P.M., Saturday, on WGN, Chicago's Channel Nine, and on smaller stations downstate. They bought the satellite time for the feed through the heavens, they found a satellite truck, a lighting semi, and a case-portable control room—no truck, alas, for the switching equipment, so they'd have to hand-carry twenty-five metal trunks and thirty smaller cases and build a control room on the spot. They had to bring in thirty guys from Chicago for the crew—along with four cameras, wireless microphones, a TelePrompTer, makeup. . . . The satellite truck was a big C-system rig—the pro kind—but there was a glitch in the equipment, so they had to scramble and all they could find was a smaller KU-band truck, in Little

Rock, Arkansas. That crew would have to drive all night. WGN couldn't take a KU transmission, so they scrambled and lined up a KU earth-receiving station in Chicago, which would take down the feed from the Dole extravaganza and pipe it, underground, to WGN, which would air it, live, and feed it back to the satellite for the other local stations, and to cable nationwide. There were scores of people and a couple of million dollars in equipment heading for Galesburg, which was overwhelmed already by Bush. The Knox College pooh-bahs agreed to give Dole the historic room with the Lincoln chair, but they were finicky: *Please, don't move the table . . . and don't park on the grass.* They had no *clue* about the army of TV Vandals bearing down on them in eighteen-wheel trucks.

In Chicago, Mrs. Dole called all the smart guys again, and brought them into one suite to announce: this had to be *organahzed.* She didn't want fifty people telling Bob what to do. Murphy and Castellanos wanted Bakshian's speech boiled down to seven minutes. Then, Mrs. Dole would talk. Then, they'd cue WGN to run the video of the Bob Dole story. Then, the Bobster would come on live again, to close. (Then again, all this planning would be scrapped in an instant if Bush could be lured near their cameras.) Wellborn went to work on Mrs. Dole's remarks. Bakshian was set to cutting his text. Murphy and Castellanos were finishing a last-minute Dole ad about the *Chicago Tribune*'s endorsement—by now it was 1:00 A.M.—and then they found out the truck from Little Rock had broken down en route. So at 2:00 A.M., they tracked down a Conus truck in Minneapolis, but that was a fourteen-hour drive and there was a snowstorm—that crew would have to start now. At 3:00 A.M., the Dole-folk chartered a plane to Galesburg, arrived at the college before dawn, and set to trashing the precious Lincoln room. They built their control panels behind the room where Dole would speak and started taping cables everywhere—across the ceiling, down the walls, up Abe's desk leg. Dole Press Advance arrived in time to mention there would be a hundred national press—where were they gonna watch?—so they ran cables down the hall, to monitors in the gym, and then, too, they had to run cables to line-feeds, because the networks were coming with their own trucks. There was only one phone line to the gym, so the phone company had to chopper in a hundred phones. One piece of the portable control room went flooey, so by midmorning the video wizards had a new box on its way from Chicago. An ABC crew was filming the set-up when they broke a piece of the Lincoln Chandelier. Mari Maseng and Kim Wells arrived for a meeting with Wellborn and Bakshian, to polish the speeches—but there was no speech for the Bobster: Aram still had his thirty-page tome. They got him a room at the Galesburg Howard Johnson's, but Aram turned out to be a real stonecutter: *click . . . click . . .* they could hear him pecking deliberately at his typewriter—*click . . .* at midafternoon! The truck from Minneapolis arrived. The technical trunks and gee-gaw boxes were piling up in the college hallways, and the Dole-folk took over the Dean's Office. At 3:00 P.M., the control-room boys fired up the power, and . . . they got a test pattern in Chicago! . . . *Hurrah! We're on the air!*

Auughh! Four-thirty, two hours before airtime, there was still no speech for

the Bobster! Kim and Mari were locked up with Bakshian, *all* typing, trying
to get pieces of the text hammered down. Dole still hadn't seen word one.
. . . Five-thirty: still nothing to show the Senator. The video wizards let the
lights burn for three hours straight—better safe than sorry—and tested what
they could on their rig. Dole didn't like his makeup. He was having it redone.
He was asking if there was any sign of Bush—Dole hadn't given up his dream
that somehow he would dare Bush into that Lincoln room and expose him in
the hot white light as a loser, a choke when the going got rough. Kim and Mari
and Aram were writing transitions for Dole's speech in longhand—handwritten bridges that Dole was supposed to puzzle out. Brock was in there, trying
to gather the pages in order—this stuff had to get to Dole! It was twenty-one
minutes to airtime when the power failed in the control room—so they grabbed
an extra cable, strung it around the circuit box (to hell with fuses!) and got
the power back six minutes later. No one could tell whether anything was
damaged. Nobody told Dole about the power failure—no sense promoting a
panic. Dole got his speech eight minutes before his broadcast. He showed up
in the Lincoln room, two minutes to air.

"Aghh, we ready? Hear me o-kayy?"

And they rolled.

— ★ —

Ladies and gentlemen, good evening, and welcome . . .

The intro went fine: half the Lincoln room held a small crowd to clap for
Dole, and those folks did their part; the Bobster came in right on cue, started
talking. There were three cameras in front of him, a wall behind, with a door
over his left shoulder—the fourth camera was hidden back there. Behind that
wall, the control room was crowded with eight monitors, instrument panels,
a jungle of wire.

Six and a half minutes into the show . . . Dole was talking about drugs: "So,
we've got a problem! . . ." *Pow!*—all eight monitors went to black. The Bobster
was still talking—they'd just flashed him the five-minute card—the holy-white
light was upon him . . . but the control room went dark—no power—and there
was nothing on the *screen.* Behind the wall, there was an instant of silence,
then a frantic scraping of the wizards' chairs being shoved back, amid a
whispery hiss of oaths. In opaque darkness, they tore at the floor to get to
cables. Chicago was on the phone with Castellanos: "You just went bad—what
happened? You're a freeze-frame. You got nothing! What happened? Dead air!
Dead air! . . ."

Alex was yelling into the phone, "Fire the tape!"

"Dead air! . . ."

"Go with tape! *Fuckin'firethetapeTAPE!NOW!*"

A minute fifty-five into the disaster, the Dole video rolled in Chicago. No
one knew if they could get the power fixed in Galesburg. If so, how much time
would they have left? They'd have to switch out of the video on the fly. How
long would Dole have to speak? What would he say? What would he have time
to say?

In the Lincoln room, Bob had finished his speech. Elizabeth was talking, introducing the video—she *thought* she was introducing the video. Then the Doles walked back to the control room, and Brock said to Murphy: "Tell him. You have to tell him. Tell him."

Murphy said: "We lost power in the middle."

Dole looked stricken: "Where'd you lose me?"

"You were in the drug thing."

"You didn't get any Elizabeth?"

"None."

Dole sagged. "What'll we do now?"

"Well, we're gonna try to get this fixed and go to a live close after the video. If we can't get it fixed, we'll let the video run out, and that'll be the end."

Dole nodded.

The power came up about five minutes later. But they had no feed from WGN—they didn't know what was on the air at that moment. Castellanos had to dope out a transition point, kill the tape, and go to Dole. The technicians in Chicago were holding a phone up to a speaker in their studio so Castellanos could hear the sound track. They'd have to cut it off at the cornfield . . .

"Okay, Senator. Stand by."

Castellanos was counting down. Two or three people fired orders at Dole:

"Twenty seconds . . ."

"Two-and-a-half-minute close, okay?"

"No, wait Senator . . ."

"TEN seconds . . ."

"Maybe three minutes."

"SIX, FIVE . . ."

"Just watch the time cards."

The audience started clapping. The video wizards threw the switch to feed from Galesburg again. There was Dole, scowling in the Lincoln chair. He started talking. He watched the time cards. He talked about education—that was two sentences in his script. He talked for two minutes straight. His eyes darted from the cameras to the cards. He segued into child care, day care . . . whatever . . . animal rights.

Then it was over.

His chance.

—★—

They were going to do it again, for tape, for a few local stations that would broadcast tomorrow—might as well get it right once. Bob still had in mind to get over to the big Bush dinner, crash the place, *make something happen* . . . but Elizabeth insisted: they did it all again. The tape went without a hitch—save for one tiny moment, when Bob said the Lincoln–Douglas debate was in 1958. So everyone stayed fifteen minutes longer while Dole recorded that sentence, over and over, so the video boys could dub in 1858. The Lincoln room was now an oven. Bob and Elizabeth waited in a hallway. Bob sat on a corner of a desk, with his coat on, slumped amid the dislocated furniture and stacks of video detritus. Elizabeth came and sat on the side of the desk, and leaned her head against his left shoulder. With their legs hanging down, they looked like a couple of kids on a dock—sad kids at summer's end. Mari snapped a photo—she knew Mrs. Dole would love that picture. Dole kept telling people to call the Lincoln Day Dinner—see if they could still catch Bush, see if they could hold the crowd . . . maybe Bob could get up and talk, at least say hello. But the organizers were all Bushies. They wouldn't lift a finger to help.

Worse still, they passed the word to Bush—Dole was on his way! So by the time the Doles packed into three freezing cars and drove to the dinner . . . they were just in time to be pinned, helpless, ordered to a stop by police, while they witnessed the departure of Bush's fifty-vehicle motorcade—cop cars, blue lights, the lead limo, the Bush-limo, VIP cars, staff vans, press buses—the incumbent magnificence arrayed against Dole.

Bush had gone, and the crowd was on its way out. Dole jumped out of his car as if he meant to stop them, but it was like trying to stop a river with your body—you're lucky just to stand your ground. The press was set up outside in respectful ranks for Bush's departure, and now they came, six-legged, snapping their tripods shut as they ran after Dole. Mari had her head in her hands, moaning: "This is disaster. I can't believe we're doing this . . ."

But she thought Dole was too exhausted and stressed out to see how helpless he looked. He was trying to grab hands, say hello, fight his way into the hall. People were streaming out, bumping into him, trying to get past him. When he finally burst into the hall, there were only a few waiters and a couple of hundred people. He might as well have just sat down. It was . . . gone.

—★—

When they got all the Dole-folk onto the plane—Dole had his big plane, the one the press now called the Sky Pig—the staff drifted toward the back. They left a lot of room for Dole. No one had any idea what to say to him. . . . Everyone knew—thought they knew—how Dole would be.

Murphy would have liked to crawl under the seats . . . especially when Bob Dole came down the aisle and dropped into the seat next to him.

"Aghh, howsa *goinn'*?"

Murphy loosed a flood of apology. He felt so awful, things were so fucked up, he couldn't even tell the Senator, at that moment, what had really *happened*—he'd tried to look into it, just to know—maybe sabotage. "But I, uh . . . technically, we just don't know what the line filter—if it was the line filter, it would . . ."

And in the middle of this heartfelt technoblather, Dole dropped one eyebrow as he glanced for an instant into Murphy's eyes, and said:

"Agh, really liked that video. Good music!"

And above the whine of the Sky Pig's engines, Dole's prairie voice scraped the air, as he began to hum . . . *Hnnghhh gnngh hnnnnnggh* . . . the music from the beautiful cornfield scene:

Dut dut duunnnnghhh dghn-dughhhnnnnnn!

Even true Dole-folk turned to stare in shock and fascination.
Illinois was lost.
Yut dut dut dunggghhhh . . .
The Other Thing was gone.
Yut tuughh tugh tunggghhhhhh.

122

Jesseee!

JANE WAS with Dick for the day of the Michigan vote. In fact, that day the schedule moved them on to Milwaukee . . . the Wisconsin vote, April 5, was the next hope—though not for Gephardt.

They were in a cinderblock holding room at the Mecca, Milwaukee's big basketball arena. All the candidates would show up for a Democratic dinner. Murphy and Carrick worked pay phones in the hallway for the first news from Michigan. The holding room was horrible. Some public works genius had the thing painted smile-face yellow . . . *cheerful* cinderblock . . . and wake-the-dead fluorescent light, two hard plastic chairs, and one window that looked not onto the world, but the gray arena floor, two stories below.

"Got numbers," Murphy said. He shut the door softly.

Dick tried to sound hearty. "Count on Murphy to bring in real numbers."

Murphy handed him a scrap of paper. "That's with thirteen percent of precincts."

Dick read them out.

Dukakis . . . 42

Jackson . . . 36

Gephardt . . . 22

He held his eyes on the paper just one beat too long. He turned to Dick Moe, with feigned interest: "That's just about what the poll said, isn't it?"

"That's about it."

Dick turned away, toward the window. He leaned against the wall, his eyes staring down on the gray hall below. It was set up with bare rectangular tables in ghostly ranks across the floor, like a graveyard.

Carrick broke the silence. "S'that where our dinner is?"

Nervous laughter.

"No," someone said, "that's for the Supreme Soviet . . ."

"The Presidium . . ."

Jane was at Dick's side, instantly. She didn't talk, just stood at the window, with her arm touching his. The cement gray light from that vast hall cut across one of Dick's cheekbones like a dark scar—came right through his skin, so pale . . . he looked so fragile.

Moe was talking quietly to the side of Gephardt's face: "You might want to think if you want to say anything to the press. They're getting numbers, too. They'll ambush you here, outside the door."

Gephardt nodded. He didn't talk. He had one more event to do, before the dinner. One last time: "Give me your belief! . . ."

In a minute, he squared himself in front of the door. A Secret Service man pulled it open, and the halogen fireflies blinded Gephardt as he tried to move out to the hall.

Congressman! Yer running third in Michigan! . . . Congressman! Any comment on the vote in Mi—Dick, would a LOSS mean . . .

He couldn't even see who was screaming at him. He tried not to squint, tried to keep his eyes on the back of the Service man, who was shoving the fireflies back. They jiggled crazily ahead of him.

"Have to see what happens . . ." Dick said to the air. "Haveta see what happens . . ."

Areyagonnaquit? WHYD'YATHINKYOULOST? . . . Wouldn'alossbe CONGRESSMAN! Wouldn't you say a loss in MichiDICK! WHYD'YATHINKYA LOST?

—★—

He'd campaigned bravely through Michigan, in cold rain and snow, in arctic wind outside shuttered auto plants, in predawn darkness at factory gates . . . and in sadness.

In the end, the UAW took a dive on Dick. He'd come to them after Super Tuesday, with the smell of loss upon him. "Well, uh, you know, Congressman, we've decided we really can't, uh, endorse a *specific* candidate at this point in the process . . ." Then Douglas Fraser, past president of the UAW, showed up in a Dukakis ad, applauding Michael's brave new tough talk on trade.

The networks started pulling their crews off Dick's bus—they had their own tracking polls. The reporters couldn't bear to tell him straight. But they'd mention, offhand one day, how it just occurred to them—they didn't have a single photograph of them and Dick, together, you know . . . would he mind posing, just for a minute? . . . Dick would oblige, smiling big, like they'd come to be best friends . . . on the way to the White House.

The press that was left asked him every day, every hour: What percentage

would he have to win in Michigan? Didn't he *have* to win? Wouldn't he quit
if he didn't win? *When* was he gonna quit?

"I think we'll do well . . ." he'd say.

"I think we'll do very well . . ."

Then he'd get off his bus, and tell the crowd at the next Democratic club:

Give me your vision!

Give me your belief!

. . . and March 26th will be the day of the MICHIGAN MIRACLE!

But Dick was past March 26th, past miracles:

"You know, I told Jane last night, I'm looking forward to everything we're
gonna do. We get that back now . . . we never would have had a normal life.
It's absolutely impossible. I couldn't take my kids to the movies, the store, buy
them a pair of gloves . . .

"We'd have nothing.

"You know, Matt's going to be gone in another year. He really needs me
now. I called him, the other night, he said, 'Dad, how you doing?' I said, 'Well,
we're at seventeen points in the polls—he's got thirty-five.' He says, 'You can
do it, Dad!' . . .

"I want to spend a *lot* of time with him now. He needs me now." Dick raised
a finger, like he did in a speech when he wanted to pound home one point:
"He's gonna know, before he leaves . . . I'm there."

Then the chipmunks leapt on his cheeks: *Hackhackhackheeee . . .* "I'm not
in the vacuum tube!

"I'm the luckiest guy in the world."

— ★ —

They had a hotel room to wait an hour or two, before the dinner. It seemed
like a long time. Dick flicked on the TV. There was Gore, Defender of the
Working Man.

"We oughta sell him our ads."

"Deficit reduction. We'll sell 'em our ads."

Jane said: "What time do we have to go down there?"

"Eight, maybe eight-thirty . . . it keeps getting later." All the candidates
were speaking, in turn, at the dinner. A dozen of Dick's Advance pack, the
kids, had straggled into Wisconsin. They knew, by now, they didn't have to
come . . . they hadn't been paid for a month. But they came. They were all
at the Mecca. They kept phoning word to his hotel—minute-by-minute updates, like it was the Democratic convention.

Jane said: "Do we have to work the tables?"

There was laughter.

"Why not?" she said. "I'll get withdrawal symptoms." She was giggling,
pawing the air, grabbing for make-believe hands.

"Somebody get her a Valium."

"I hope it's a nice day tomorrow . . ." That was Dick. He meant in Virginia.
He wanted to sleep late, and wake in sunshine.

The screen was flashing numbers.

Dukakis . . . 38

Jackson . . . 34

Gephardt . . . 21

Simon . . . 4

Gore . . . 3

Someone said, to break the silence: *"Simon's* beating Gore."

"Good."

"Jackson's cleaning up in Detroit. He could win this . . ."

"I hope it's a nice day tomorrow. . . . When do we get rid of the Service?"

"Monday."

"Do you have to tell them in writing? Or can you just walk out to the trailer and say, 'Guys . . .' " Jane jerked her thumb in the air.

Dick was laughing. He stood up. "That's it, guys! . . . We're goin' t'the five-and-dime!"

— ★ —

Outside the grisly holding room, in the Mecca, the killers were conferring with the Service. "When does he go in?"

"They said eight," the Service man said.

"No," Murphy said. "Forget the tables. He doesn't need to sit and listen to those assholes speak. Get him on, get him out. He doesn't have to talk to anyone tonight."

But he did have to talk. Barry Wyatt, wizard of Advance, came into the holding room, and his pack, a dozen kids, all talked their way in behind him. Now, sadly, sweetly, they were trying to say goodbye to Dick. "Thank you for the opportunity," said a young man named Mark Stump. "I learned from you. So you are in me now."

Dick went around the quiet room, shaking hands with each. He knew every name. Then he stood with his back to a wall and held up a hand. He started to tell them they had to go on . . . this was about more than him . . . more than what they'd done for him.

Dick's voice was steady and brave. He wanted them to see this as a start—the only way this made sense—as a cause . . . this loss, his loss, did not matter.

Then, a noise . . . Dick stopped. The door opened . . . and it was filled with Jesse Jackson.

Jesse was huge that night: he was blowing Duke away in Michigan—a late surge from the central cities, a flood tide—it wasn't even close. And Jackson, always a presence, was on this night enlarged, engorged by triumph. In the doorway, his big face seemed to give off light. His suit was so dark blue, it looked black. He had a red tie, a red pocket handkerchief, and a thousand-watt smile.

"Jesseee!" Dick came across the room, South St. Louis polite . . . he held his hand out in front of him.

But Jackson spread his arms. And he gathered Dick in a bear hug that *disappeared* him. All they could see was the reddish top of Gephardt's head.

Jesse Jackson knew loss. He knew what was going on in that room. And there was, in his embrace, not just his triumph of that night, but his understanding of Dick's effort, the *years* . . . the hope, the exhaustion, the loss.

He would not let go.

Gephardt's head wiggled briefly. Then it settled against Jackson's suit.

Jesse would not let go.

And just for a short while, half a minute, perhaps . . . the only time that night . . . on the breast of the only man in that room who could really understand, Dick Gephardt wept.

123

The
Priesthood
Is Obeyed

MICHAEL HAD a problem. He'd lost to Jesse Jackson. He'd lost big— two-to-one. He had allowed momentum to slip into the hands of a black man who'd never held elective office, who owed nothing to the elders of the Party, and who, the Priests of the Process were convinced, had no chance as the nominee.

Accordingly, the Priesthood discovered:

Dukakis was uninspired.

Dukakis was arrogant and distant.

Dukakis had nothing to say.

That's because he lost. In fact, Michael had lost two in a row—big, visible whiffs:

First, he steamed into Illinois, fresh from his Super Tuesday triumphs, and got *big* crowds—Chicago loves a rally. Back on Chauncy Street, the plan was for Dukakis to duck Illinois. Paul Simon was a native son, fighting for his political life. Jesse Jackson lived in Chicago, and he'd have a lock on a quarter of the vote. But in his own breast, Dukakis was the nominee-to-be. He wasn't gonna *duck*! (What kinda respect for the process would that show?) Anyway, what about those crowds? They loved him! . . . He insisted: "Something's happening out there. We're really connecting. . . ." So he went all out, spent $400,000, and got . . . nowhere. Simon won, Jackson got second. Delegates for Dukakis—zero.

By the next week, in Michigan, Michael was acting like the *inevitable* nominee. Actually, he wasn't in Michigan. He was in his State House, or flying coast-to-coast, collecting more money, posing for pictures with the big pols endorsing him. He meant to put the lie to this brokered-convention pipe dream . . . and demonstrate that responsible Democrats, the duly elected representatives of the Party, wanted to unite behind a *serious* candidate (the kinda guy he was). So one morning he was in New Jersey—had a nice picture taken with Bill Bradley . . . and that night, California—another $200,000 dinner . . . maybe in the middle, he'd stop in Michigan—refueling. One day he flew in to receive the endorsement of Michigan's Senator Don Riegle . . . in return for which, Michael endorsed Riegle's trade bill (Son of Gephardt). . . . So Dukakis was a flip-flop and a panderer, too. . . . Anyway, Jackson stomped him big-time, and Michael had a problem.

STUNNED PARTY LEADERS QUESTION DUKAKIS' ABILITY TO COMPETE, said the headline on the front of *The Washington Post*. The next day, it was: DUKAKIS TOLD TO SHARPEN MESSAGE. The story was filled with suggestions from politicians and consultants. Dukakis faced a must-win in Wisconsin on April 5 . . . or Armageddon in New York, on April 19. He had to provide "a compelling rationale for his candidacy." He had to "draw the distinctions" between himself and Jackson. Estrich had a stack of message slips from people who wanted to tell her more of the same.

Everybody knew Dukakis had a problem . . . except Dukakis. He didn't have any problem. Illinois, he ran against two favorite sons. He started late—no time to organize. . . . Michigan was crazy—the Party ran the caucuses, not the government—Jesse's people musta voted five times apiece! It was a fluke! . . . So when Estrich showed up with a two-page memo—changes in the campaign plan for Wisconsin (new speech, new ads, new schedule)—Michael said no. They were correct! They were on track! Steady as she goes!

"No, that's not what I mean," said Estrich. "You're right. You don't have to change . . . but when you lose, you get a lot of advice. I'm getting a lot of advice."

Michael was nodding. "Yeah . . . yeah." He'd had his fill of advice, too.

"But when you get that much advice, you have to look like you're taking some advice . . ."

"Yeah . . ."

". . . and it's got to look like you're willing to listen . . ."

At last, she rang the right bell. He looked over the memo again.

"Okay," he said. "What else?"

So Michael got a new speech (wherein he actually criticized Reagan for undermining American workers!) . . . new ads (pictures of farms at auctions, chained factory gates, little girls hunting food in garbage cans) . . . a tough schedule, day after day in Wisconsin (factories, union halls, ethnic clubs) . . . and no more hunting for endorsements.

It was (and would be) the only time in her tenure when Susan went to him with a plan from Chauncy Street . . . and he read it, got it, and did it—he even drank a beer with some guys in Milwaukee!

It was great fun. And it worked.

Dukakis beat Jackson in Wisconsin by twenty percent. Of course, that was the same spread the polls showed the week before. Dukakis always thought he was going to win.

But the press noted his changes with satisfaction. The Priesthood was obeyed, the process well served, and Michael had his must-win, on the way to New York.

Except he wouldn't go to New York. He blew off his schedule, went back to the State House.

His health insurance bill was up for a vote.

— ★ —

That's what this campaign was about—this campaign, the Oval Office, that job . . . it was all about *governing*. . . . *That's what Mike Dukakis could do.*

He could still govern, and campaign—he could do it all!—as long as the campaigning didn't change the kinda guy he was. . . . So he worked on his health bill, he got it through the House . . . and *then* he went to New York—where, after all, it was *apparent* . . . he was on a roll!

He had a rally in Astoria, Queens . . . his Greeks. They came out by *thousands.* There were so many people *on the street*—the Crystal Palace could not hold them!—they were hammering his car, rocking it crazily. . . . Inside, people rushed the stage for pictures with him, for his autograph. The New York cops had to shove them back. They were waving flags, Greek and American. Men were yelling his name:

"BRA-VO DU-KA-KIS . . . BRA-VO . . . BRA-VO DU-KA-KIS."

And for them, Michael departed from his speech, to tell them about his father, Panos, who was so proud of his heritage . . . so in love with this great new land. . . . Michael only wished that Panos could be there, at this moment, at the Crystal Palace, to see what the times had wrought, for his son . . .

And for all Greeks in America . . . for this was the same hall, where Michael had stood, the summer before, when his mother, Euterpe, speaking in Greek, told another cheering, keening crowd that Michael Dukakis was not just her son . . . but from that point, he was a son to them all.

And so Michael talked to this crowd about their sons and daughters, who were like children of his own now . . . and his hope for them, that they would see him, see this, feel this great moment, in this hall . . . and think about a life of public service—the highest calling, the finest honor, in this great land!

And he could see some of those children staring up at him. He saw mothers weeping, next to them. And with the image of Panos alive behind his eyes, and before them, the future of his people . . . and not just his people, but all the children of all the peoples who came to this nation . . . he knew, at that moment, what he was called to do: *he* was their bridge, their hope . . . he would not disappoint them.

Michael told them, correctly, in Greek . . . the words with which the Athenian commander, Miltiades, rallied his outnumbered forces against the Persians, in 490 B.C.:

"*Tha nikisoume! . . .*"

"We shall win! . . ." And the place exploded in a roar of righteous pride.

"*BRA-VO . . . BRA-VO . . . BRA-VO DU-KA-KIS . . .*"

How could he live through that and fail to marvel? How could he not be borne almost off the ground by that hot rush of . . . well, it was *love,* what he felt from that crowd. How could he conclude anything but . . . he *was* their hope, their elect? Him! . . . And he was on his way—from triumph to triumph, ahead in New York! He was on his way to another win, his biggest, the win of his life . . . and beyond—to the nomination for President of the United States. Dukakis . . . *President.* On his way to the White House! It was *happening . . . to him.*

124

1982

H E KNEW that feeling of blessed elation—even the same sense of wonder, that it should happen to *him,*
a *miracle* in politics. He knew what that was—from '82. It's said that most
politicians rerun forever their first successful campaigns. But Michael's model
was his comeback—the campaign that said the most about him.

It was all about him—from the start, when Ed King took his job away.
Michael never blamed anybody but himself. Even when he thought his career
was over, even in the first months of sad disorientation, he never allowed
himself the luxury of alibi. The problem was him. Something was wrong with
him.

That's what made it so devastating. It was not about policy, or competence,
or performance. He knew he'd run the state well. Massachusetts was booming.
He left the state with a surplus. He'd cleaned up, straightened up, speeded up,
every bit of government he touched. People had to see that!

But they did not see that . . . or they didn't care. Or they weren't willing
to see him . . . or maybe they *did* see him.

What *was* it about him? . . . For the first time in his life, Michael had to
take inventory of himself—the one thing he'd never spent a minute worrying
about. He was the steady one, the smart one, the strong one. He'd spent from
a bottomless reserve of ability and will on everything outside—Kitty, the kids,
the town, the state, his citizens. . . . He had no way of working on himself,
even seeing himself. He had not the habit of mind, the language, the history
. . . no ground from which to start.

He asked friends: "Was I really that bad? That lousy?"

Of course, they told him no.

Well, then, what *happened*?

Son John would find him in the afternoon, just staring, sitting in the kitchen, dark, sad eyes fixed on nothing. No one had ever seen Michael Dukakis without something to do. No one had ever seen him at a loss. It was like the power went off, and the house on Perry Street was at a standstill. Then he saw how people tiptoed around him, and he felt worse. He was a drag on them! He was a dead weight. He was finished! . . . That was the cinch of the circle: Michael was depressed. But Michael was a man who was never depressed—not for one day in his forty-five years. He never took more than one aspirin! . . . Now he didn't understand what had happened to him, what was wrong with him . . . he felt awful. He felt bad for feeling bad. He'd let them all down. He'd let himself down. And he could not understand, now, why he couldn't pick himself up.

— ★ —

He had that one-room office, but he wasn't going to sit there. What would he do? He couldn't go back to practicing law. His life was about the public weal. So he took a job at Harvard's Kennedy School—he would teach the managers of state and local governments . . . and meanwhile search for his answers.

There was opposition to his appointment—professors didn't want the school to look like a dumping ground for failed politicians. But Michael soon showed his seriousness. He went at teaching as he went at everything—full speed, with dogged attention to the unglamorous mechanical chores: faculty meetings, curriculum, committees . . . he pulled his weight. He'd ride his bike to his crowded cubbyhole office . . . a far cry from his elegant corner suite in the State House—but Michael never mentioned that. He'd roll up his sleeves, he had students to serve! And these weren't kids, fresh out of college. Most had finished law school, some were working officials. The method of instruction was case studies—problems confronted by governments in states and localities around the U.S. Michael would work through the problems, along with his class. That part was easy—too easy.

Michael was so ferociously smart, so sure his answers were *correct,* that he barely paid lip service to the notion of class discussion. Students who presented a different solution would see Michael's head start shaking—nope, nope . . . even when he tried to say something nice: "Well, you've almost got it. You're *close* . . . " At the end of his first summer session, his faculty ranking from students was third from the bottom (the two who ranked lower were not asked back).

But Michael was learning. By his second year, the tone in his classes had changed. There was no single right answer, and Michael didn't have to prove he knew what he was doing. In fact, he'd decided what he had to prove was . . . he knew how to listen.

He started asking questions—even when he *thought* he knew. He started questioning his own assumptions—*everything* he thought he knew. For a

while, he was like a kid with a new word: you couldn't *stop* him asking
everyone's opinion. In his classes, he started to preach the value of "broadening participation," asking legislators, community leaders, labor leaders, businessmen, to help hammer out policy, which would then have the force of
"consensus."

In fact, he was already building consensus, off hours, on Perry Street. He'd
host roundtable discussions on topics of personal fascination: welfare reform,
economic development, affordable housing . . . this was Michael's idea of fun.
He wanted to bring himself up to speed on ideas from other states. He wanted
to know what was happening in the King administration, the Carter administration. He'd sit down three or four experts, in his kitchen, and he'd quiz them:

"Where's the youth employment policy going? . . ."

"What are you finding out about what we need to do? . . ."

"Do you know what we did in Lowell, with the Labor Department?"

He didn't want soliloquies, didn't want to know what they thought. He
wanted to know what they *knew*—data, facts, statistics, studies. They didn't
have to break it down into bites for him. They could talk high-policy govern-
ment-speak, and in a minute he'd start nodding. "Yeah . . . yeah." He got that.
He'd move on. The excitement was his urgency, and the speed of his comprehension. But he also wanted these experts, gurus of the policy groups, to *see
him listening.*

He was rebuilding his base from the ground up. He wanted the liberals and
good-government groups, the ones who abandoned him in '78, to *know* he was
different. They had to see *him*—and see, he had learned.

— ★ —

What had he learned? Well, that it wasn't enough to be right . . . unless he
got the politics right. Without the politics—that grooming and stroking he'd
always disdained—he might be *absolutely* right . . . and have no office from
which to govern. What's more, politics would not make him less correct—only
more effective.

He had learned to value effect. When he won the Governor's chair in '74,
he thought it was a new age in the State House, and the Commonwealth. But
now Ed King was taking apart his reforms, piece by piece. (They were bad for
business, Eddie said. King was a business *booster*!) And Michael saw that by
a failure of politics, of his own persona, the Age of Dukakis was without effect.

He saw that he had failed. That was the defining fact in his new awareness.
He had tried as hard as he could, worked *so* hard—and nevertheless. . . . If
Michael got back to that big corner office, he would not show the same
impatience toward people who ended up, somehow, with the short end of life's
stick. He wouldn't assume a want of will, or discipline . . . not anymore.

Two years after his loss, Michael dusted off his file cards and sent a Christmas mailing—first notice to the Commonwealth that Dukakis was on his way
back. It was an odd document, Christmas greetings coupled with Dukakis's
first public broadside against the man who'd taken his job.

"We worked hard to bring integrity and competence to state government,"

Michael wrote. "But during the past two years, you and I have seen that progress slowed, stymied and reversed by the present state administration. . . ." To restore confidence, competence, and integrity, "and with your continued support and encouragement, I intend to be a candidate for Governor in 1982."

In addition, there were messages from the Dukakis children—this from twenty-two-year-old John:

". . . My father made some unpopular decisions, and there was a lot of anger directed at him—and sometimes at us. If I felt it, I know he and Mother must have felt it a hundred times more. So I've thought about that—the price you pay.

"But we've all grown through those experiences, and learning to understand them and deal with them brought us all very close together. I'm really proud of my father. I'm proud of both my parents. And I'm glad the campaign is on."

The mailing sparked an extraordinary reaction—not just political support, not just money (though it drew an amazing number of checks) . . . but the personal appeal for expiation was met with an equally personal response. It was remorse for what the voters of the Commonwealth had done to Michael Dukakis.

—★—

After the mailing, he moved fast: he had to get the politics right.

This time, there would be no campaign-on-the-cheap. Dukakis wanted money and plenty of it. So he signed on a strange new friend—a fellow who actually *loved* to raise money—Bob Farmer.

This time, Michael wouldn't manage his own campaign. He signed on a pro—a young man who'd formed that splendid consensus around the fair-tax amendment to the state constitution—John Sasso.

This time, he would not ignore the liberal interest groups, the neighborhood associations, big labor—even business groups. . . . He went to their meetings, and told them, he *had to have their help*. Dukakis had made errors in his first term—he admitted that, night after night. But he wanted them to know, he had learned, he had changed, he meant to listen . . . and with their help, he would start the march of progress anew.

It was like statewide group therapy, wherein Michael presented himself to be yelled at, lectured, reminded of his failings. But he took it, and every room he left held a core of supporters—some new . . . but many who had turned away from him before. There were so many people who told him, they really never meant for him to *lose* . . . it was just . . . well, by '78, they were so pissed off, they couldn't even bring themselves to vote!

"I know," Michael told them. They needn't feel bad: "That was my fault. I blew it. I made a lotta mistakes."

The state's newspapers worked out their own guilt: King had slipped by them, King had put one over. So they hammered him at every turn, never failing to mention his bodyguards, his limousines, his lobster salad . . . his bumbles in the State House, his shady appointments, his rich business pals. . . . Sure, Michael helped out with that. But not as much as King helped: everything he touched turned to dust.

King had promised to cut taxes—"Taxachusetts is dead!"—but he couldn't convince the legislature. His tax cut was stillborn.

King had promised to cut violent crime, but crime had risen by thirty percent. The Boston papers were a daily freak show.

In December '80, King turned a labor tiff on the T into a full-blown crisis that ended with a strike and shutdown of all transit—at the peak of the Christmas shopping season.

Then, in July 1981, King's Secretary of Transportation, Barry Locke, was arrested and indicted on bribery charges . . . he'd become the highest-ranking state official ever to land in jail.

You couldn't write a better play for Michael Dukakis . . . it had a story line, surprise, suspense, a moral . . . and then a clever friend of Sasso's, Dan Payne, gave it a name:

The Rematch.

—★—

In the spring, before the primary, there was one televised debate. And this was Michael's chance to exorcise the greatest failure of 1978.

This time, in the microphone checks, it was Michael who departed from the standard *"Testing, one, two, three . . ."* Dukakis growled into his mike:

"Under Ed King, violent crime has increased thirty percent in Massachusetts . . ."

And that was mild compared to Michael's tone once the show began. Here's one of his "questions" to King:

"Your Secretary of Transportation, Barry Locke, was convicted and jailed for stealing public funds. Your Commissioner of Insurance was a front man for the industry and had to resign after one week. Three other officials in your administration were forced to resign because they lied or were unfit for public office. The Ward Commission documented that corruption is costing each taxpayer in Massachusetts three thousand dollars, per capita, that goes directly into the pockets of corrupt public officials, and never gets spent on public services. That adds up to six billion dollars—and you say that 'Taxachusetts is dead'? With your record of bad judgment and bad appointments, what can you say to us tonight to convince us you've changed, and that we can expect anything better over the next four years?"

By the end of the question, King was white under his makeup, with his head shaking denial, confusion, and rage. All he could mumble, by way of answer, was: "I'd urge everyone listening to disregard your totally absurd, without foundation, statements . . ."

Who could disregard the spectacle of Dukakis ripping the man to shreds, under spotlights, in front of the whole state? Michael never stopped—never gave King a chance to breathe. He attacked without rest, without remorse. He had to beat Ed King—*take him down* . . . and he did. After that debate, statewide polls showed Dukakis ahead of King by more than forty percent.

— ★ —

Then John Sasso got in trouble with a tape . . . this was an audiotape, a parody of a King radio ad. The ad had King's wife telling how Ed took care of her through her battle with polio. The parody (made by a supporter of Dukakis at a radio station in the town of Ware) changed Mrs. King's words to an anatomy of Big Ed's sex life. It was just a joke, a private joke . . . or so Sasso thought, when he shared it with a friend from the *Globe*.

But word of the joke spread, and the King campaign (with the *Herald*'s help) played it for all it was worth. SEX TAPE SCANDAL, the front page screamed. King's minions described in loving detail how Big Ed jumped out of his chair when he heard. He was gonna punch Dukakis's *lights out* . . . they hadda *restrain* him! (Actually, King and his campaign had known about the tape for weeks before the story blew.) For days, there was hardly anything else in the papers. Radio call-in shows were nonstop outrage about that slimy Dukakis . . . *makin' fun of a polio victim*!

Michael called from Western Massachusetts when the story hit. "What the hell is going *on* back there?"

Sasso offered to resign—for the good of the campaign—but Michael wouldn't hear of it. "Are you *crazy*? . . . C'mon! We've got a lotta work to do!" Michael had to *beat Ed King*—he wasn't going to get distracted by some nonsense with tapes.

And he was right about the work. King was climbing. With Tape-gate, Michael was losing the moral high ground—which was his entire platform. On the issues, voters mostly agreed with King—at least in spirit (who's for taxes, crime, welfare?). Michael lost votes every time the race strayed from competence, management, cleanliness. By midsummer, King's pollster, Ed Reilly, put the gap at only eight percent. Michael knew he could lose . . . unless he took King down.

That summer, a man named Stanley Barczak, a minor official of the Revenue Department, got arrested for taking a bribe. Barczak tried to save himself—he sang. A grand jury started looking into charges that any tax delinquency could be "settled" by payment of cash to the right parties at the Revenue Department. One of those under suspicion was a schoolfriend of King's, John J. Coady, the Governor's Deputy Commissioner of Revenue. In late July, King learned that his old pal was a target of the investigation. Nine days later, Coady was found dead, hanging by the neck in the attic of his home.

The papers ran stories revealing that Barczak had been hired by Coady.

They revealed that Barczak had served time for tax fraud, in '53.

They found out Barczak was carrying King bumper stickers at the time of his arrest.

They found out Barczak had visited King, in the State House.

They examined King and Coady's friendship.

They found out King had been told that Coady was a target. Was it King who let his pal know the grand jury was after him?

It was altogether a riveting scandal . . . altogether a godsend for Dukakis. But it wasn't an act of God. Most of those juicy news stories had come from sources in the office of the Attorney General—and the AG was Frank Bellotti, Dukakis's old ally.

Coady was barely cold when Dukakis attacked with a new TV ad:

"Corruption and cronyism in the State House! . . .

"How much does the Ed King Corruption Tax cost you?"

—★—

Dukakis beat Ed King by 83,000 votes, almost seven percent. Of all the campaigns in the state's living memory, The Rematch was the most brutal and fascinating. There was no one in the state who did not know King and Dukakis—and no one was neutral. Turnout was up thirty-six percent.

On the primary night of his resurrection, September 14, 1982, Michael was humble and touched by wonder. "You've given me," he told his supporters, "something that one rarely gets in American politics—a second chance. . . . And I'm very grateful."

He would go on to beat his Republican opponent two-to-one in November . . . and then, without pause (and with Sasso at his side), on to the triumphal politics of his second term. That's when the papers started to write about Duke II . . . this new, more flexible, more humane politician.

In time, of course, they ceased to compare Dukakis with King, or even Duke II with Duke I . . . the scars of his loss and The Rematch healed. Memory faded. But even years later, Michael hugged around himself the lessons he'd educed.

"I'm a guy who does a lotta listening, these days, so . . ."

"I think we need the kinda leadership that builds strong consensus, real partnerships . . ."

"I want to be the kinda President who can work with the Congress. There's some terrific people in the Congress! . . ."

So, surely, he must have taken, too, the scrappy political lessons of his comeback—the way he'd fought, kicked, and clawed . . . to make his miracle happen.

"No!" Michael would snap. "Get your facts straight!"

That wasn't how he saw it, at all.

The story line he favored came from the ancient Greeks—the story of Aristides the Just.

In the version Dukakis told, Aristides was a wise and upright ruler in Athens—fifth century B.C.—who was so honest he would not do favors for anyone. So, of course, he made enemies. His integrity got to be grating—they threw him out, *exiled* him. . . . Until, six years later, Athens was in a total mess, corrupt and floundering, and the people went to Aristides, and they *begged him* to come back. *"Aristides, we've got to have you!"*

They had thought anew, see . . .

They had seen the kinda guy he was . . .

And after that . . . they loved him!

125

The
Big
Enchilada

IT DIDN'T LOOK LIKE a triumphal march—more like a walk through a minefield. New York was the ugliest primary, a roiling suspend of particulate fears and hatreds that could not be dissolved, or even altered, by a week of rallies. Blacks and Jews hated each other (and Jews felt bad about that), the blacks hated Mayor Koch (who thought he spoke for the Jews), the Latins resented Koreans, Koreans feared the blacks, the Irish and Italians thought the city had long since gone to Junkie-Mugger-AIDS-and-Homeless Hell, the Williamsburg Bridge was falling down, and the Japanese were buying midtown. . . . Three candidates landed in this bubbling mess, and responded, each in his own way:

Jesse Jackson spoke brilliantly for peace, love, and hope for every minority group—except the Jews. (He even marched for the ailing bridge.)

Al Gore tried to be Jew for a Week. Gore attacked the PLO. Then he attacked his fellow Senators for "wavering" on Israel. Gore signed up the obstreperous Mayor, who promptly attacked Jesse Jackson. Gore attacked Jackson, and then he attacked Dukakis (for *not* attacking Jackson). Gore attacked everyone but Yitzhak Shamir.

And Michael Dukakis hunched his shoulders and insisted that everything was *fine.* . . . Divisive? He didn't notice anything, uh, divisive . . . he was a *positive* kinda guy . . . steady as she goes!

It wasn't easy. For one thing, the press was on him like an enraged beast. It wasn't just the New York stations, New York papers, diddybops, and big-feet-to-be. Every network, station, paper, wire in the world seemed to have

someone in New York: financial-beat writers came uptown for this spectacle
. . . UN correspondents from Jugoslavia, Indonesia . . . not to mention all the
camera agencies, free-lance video-ops . . . and Super-8 documentary auteurs
who emerged, blinking, from basements in Brooklyn. Wherever Michael
stopped, the press would engulf him—then reengulf itself . . . until there was
a mindless, sightless mob backed up into some city street that was immediately
awail with car horns and curses, while the people in front shoved cassette
recorders closer and closer to Michael's mouth, and the people in back bruised
his head with boom mikes, and the New York cops (Michael still refused
Secret Service—he didn't want a *fuss*) tried to keep the mob from crushing him
and meanwhile hissed at Michael: "Move, Governor! Keep movin'!"

Michael kept moving.

He went upstate, and the herd followed. Michael had to rent his first big
plane, an aged commercial airliner that smelled inside like the stuff men spray
in their gym shoes. The six-legged men became ten-legged men as they brought
along their aluminum ladders, which they'd snap open, slap down on the
pavement, and ascend, to espy Michael's head in the crush. Rochester, Buffalo,
Syracuse . . . big crowds, big cheers . . . Michael did good-jobs-at-good-wages.
No one even suggested that he try to say anything more. Why should he? He
was winning. Gore was nowhere—he'd pandered his last. Jackson was a
threat—but too unsettling. Michael was the acceptable vote, the comfortable
choice. He was the Jackson-stopper. He would be . . . the Last White Man
standing.

All he had to do was keep moving. No mistakes!

He had a meeting with the *Daily News* editorial board, where they tried to
knock him off his pins with foreign policy: NATO, the Soviets, first use of
nuclear weapons. . . . But he had answers! He answered like the briefing book
said, about the use of nuclear weapons to stop the Soviets if they were overrun-
ning Europe. He knew that stuff, he'd read all that!

He made a speech to the Conference of Presidents of Major Jewish Organizations, and he *knew* they wanted him to rule out a homeland for the Palestini-
ans, declare that Jerusalem was now and evermore a Jewish city. But he would
not! He was the nominee-to-be! That was all right for Gore . . . but Michael
had to think about *governing*!

He had to sit through a debate in the Felt Forum, with Gore snapping at
his shins like a nasty Pekingese. Al had the nerve to bring up Michael's
problem with prison furloughs—murderers who left the pen on furlough and
never came back. Gore claimed two of them had murdered again. Michael had
been back and forth with that crap for *months* with a newspaper up in Lawrence, Massachusetts. . . . Finally, the legislature changed the furlough law,
and he went along . . . ancient history. "Al, the difference between you and
me," Dukakis snapped in the New York debate, "is that I have to run a
criminal justice system. You never have."

End of discussion. Michael pulled out his old executive-versus-legislator war
club . . . and Gore shut up, for the moment. Michael said no more.

Why would he? He was winning. He was going to win New York. He was going to be the nominee for President of the United States!

So, he went back to his State House.

— ★ —

It should have been one of the great days of his life. His health-care bill—*universal health insurance,* for every citizen in Massachusetts—had finally passed both houses. Michael was about to sign the bill. He called a press conference.

"This is the culmination of months of work—*years* of work, by a great people, in the state and across the country . . ."

Michael looked over the crowd of press in room 157, his room, his homey little conference chamber, with its pale blue walls and the portraits of his predecessors in the best job in the world, the Governorship of the Commonwealth. . . . He smiled to his right, to his partners in progress, who had crowded in near the door.

". . . And it was one of the best examples of teamwork I've ever seen in this building—couldn't possibly have been done without the leadership of the Senate President and the Speaker, Chairman McGovern, Chairman Voke, and countless, countless others in the legislature, of a broad, very strong coalition among the health-care community, among working people, business people, who care very deeply about our fellow citizens . . .

"Any questions about that? . . ."

The press had no questions about that. They wanted to know about Michael's statement to the New York *Daily News* that he would nuke the Russkies if they overran Europe. "Governor . . . did you advocate a first strike against the Soviet Union?"

"No. No."

"So they got the story wrong?"

Annoyance concentrated Michael's features in the middle of his face. For God's sake, he'd used the words out of his briefing book! They'd told him that was the policy, for years!

"The policy I advocated, and the policy that governs the United States for many, many years, is the policy of the NATO alliance." Michael looked to another corner of the room.

"So what did you say to them?"

Michael went silent on the platform. There were four or five seconds of silence in the room.

"To whom?"

"To the *Daily News* editorial board! . . . Whaddidya *say*? . . . Because they reported this morning that you advocated a first strike against the Soviet Union."

"I did not!" Dukakis responded. "Look at the transcripts of what I said, and what I advocated—the policy of no-early-first-use!" (No one was going to challenge Michael's answers to this quiz.) "A very, very different thing, which

has been the policy of our government and the policy of the NATO alliance
for many, many years."

"Yeah, but under . . ."

"But . . ."

". . . what circumstances . . ." This reporter did not want the answer to the
quiz. He wanted to know when Michael thought he would or should use
nuclear weapons.

". . . *fortunately* . . ."

". . . under what . . ."

". . . the *challenge* of the next President, I expect, will be not that . . ."
Michael was in segue to another of his sound-bites. ". . . but also a series of
negotiations to limit the conventional forces in Europe, on the ground . . ."

Michael turned to his left, seeking safe haven. But there was no haven
. . . no questions on health insurance.

"The *Daily News* also says this morning that you would advocate letting
American hostages die, rather than making concessions to terrorists. Is that
true?"

"What I've said repeatedly . . ."

"Would that include letting American hostages die?"

". . . never, ever make concessions to terrorists . . . what we did in Iran-
contra . . ."

"*So the* Daily News *is correct when they say that you would allow American
hostages to die?*"

"*Senator Gore has responded to your statement in the* Daily News *today,
saying that, uh, you are unwise and irresponsible in both those statements* . . ."

"*Governor, if Soviet troops did overwhelm Western conventional forces, on the
ground in Europe* . . ."

"*Sir, did the* Daily News *misquote you? Because they said you advocated
using* . . ."

On the platform, Michael looked like a man who'd suddenly remembered
his dentist appointment. He stopped pointing to this one and that one, and took
the question from the loudest voice.

One reporter had the temerity to ask him what any government could do
about good-jobs-at-good-wages.

Another question actually began: "Governor, now that you've equivocated
on the issue of a Palestinian homeland . . ."

Fifteen minutes in, the Governor rediscovered his watch. Thereafter, he
checked it every minute or so.

Finally, a reporter asked: Wasn't it racist for white voters to vote for a white
candidate just because he's white?

Dukakis snapped: "Of course." Then he marched out of his own press
conference.

How could he have known, he would never have another press conference in
that room—in any room—that was uncolored by the leap of faith he was

making in New York? When Michael Dukakis finally said to himself, and to the world, he was going to win, he was going to be the nominee, he meant to be President of the United States . . . well, that didn't mean *he* was different—did it?

He didn't think so.

But everything was different.

He went back to New York for the big Salute to Israel Parade. Jesse Jackson wouldn't march—that was the news of the day. But the news to Michael was the day itself, a splendid spring morning of fresh sunshine and a breeze that held promise of warmth, of restoration, growing things. It seemed to Michael, he'd spent the last six months in the perpetual twilight of airplanes and cars, the dead fluorescence of meeting rooms, or wincing into wake-the-dead television lights. But here he was in God's good sunshine, marching the wing tips down the center line of Fifth Avenue, with thirty feet of glorious open space on either side, between him and the crowds—cheering *him: "Mike! Go get 'em, Mike! . . ."* He waved. They *loved* him. All he had to do was keep marching, straight down the center line: *"WE LIKE MIKE! . . ."* Sometimes they screamed for a smile and a wave from *"KITTY" . . . "KITTEEEEE!" . . .* which made him happier still. Because there were times, in the last six months, he worried—*had* to worry: Had he done the right thing? Could she take it? Those nights in Iowa she couldn't sleep . . . so serious in New Hampshire . . . the way she felt that Florida rested on her shoulders—his bride! The way she suffered—sinuses that hurt every time she flew. He told her! See a doctor! What d'ya do when you have a problem? How long since you've seen an ear-nose-and-throat man? *"KITTEEEE!" . . .* His Katharine! She didn't have quite the same steady stamina as, ahh, her *husband . . .* no. But they came through, together, to this day, to this wonderful . . . street and straight line, just as far as he could see, open all the way, for *him*! This win . . . for *him,* for *them*! . . . A miracle! A wonder. *"MIKE! . . . MIKE! . . . MIKE!"* He turned to Kitty, and she looked beautiful, waving to the crowds. "Remember when I first brought you to this town, twenty-six years ago?" She turned her smile to him in the sunshine. Good as new. . . . How could he have known, his bride would never be the same?

Michael always thought, somehow, if they could just get this thing locked up, get past this . . . *crazy* time—*somehow* . . . well, things would settle down. Not all the way—he knew . . . but somehow, back to his life. He had to hold on to his life. That's why he wouldn't take the Secret Service. He didn't want to take that last step (he thought it must be the last) into the bubble, where he would just . . . *his life* would disappear. He told Estrich he was going home—the night of the primary: he was going to win New York, he was going home. End of discussion. Susan wouldn't fight anymore. She'd lost too many—spent her last on Wisconsin. Well, they won that, and his prize was . . . home. He thought, maybe, he could plant . . . well, a little early, but he could start, turn the soil. . . . If they could just get by *this*—how could he lose? He wasn't afraid of the White House. The job was governing. They'd be together. He'd be home for dinner, six o'clock. You live over the shop! . . . And if not—well, thank God, he could go back to a job, a life, that he loved. If he could just keep marching. This was . . . terrific. . . . How could he have known, he would never have his life back?

He went to a shelter for AIDS patients—Bailey House. He finally made the Advance team pick a small pool of reporters. He didn't want to crash in with a halogen circus—he wanted to show concern. This wasn't easy for Michael. He didn't approve of homosexual—well, any of that kinda strange (he could only imagine!), that kinda . . . but he went. He talked to the patients, they asked him questions. But it never turned into a conversation. Michael was uneasy. There was a patient named Petrillis (a *Greek*?) who asked Michael if he'd invite AIDS patients to the White House. Michael shrugged. "I *might* . . . I've been inviting everyone else." So when the pool report got to the bus, everybody wanted to know: What the hell did *that* mean? What it meant was: there was work, and there was home. What did *they* mean, "to the White House"—to his *home*? . . . But how could he explain that to a hundred and fifty reporters? For that matter, how could they ask, in a mob on the street? They could only shout their questions into the knot of tape machines around his head. So they screamed: *WHAT ABOUT AIDS? . . . WHAT ABOUT AIDS? . . .* Michael didn't know why they were screaming at him. What had he done wrong? Just an offhand remark! He'd gone to show his concern—tried to be correct! . . . How could he have known, there would be no more offhand remarks?

The day before the primary, he was flying upstate. Overnight, the U.S. Navy had shot up an Iranian oil platform—retaliation for mines sown in the Persian Gulf. The press wanted to know: What did Dukakis think of the action in the Gulf? Michael was careful. He said he'd have to study the reports. He was seeking full information. . . . Then he walked down the aisle of his big new plane, to the bathroom in the rear—one thing about these events: if you're the star, you never get a minute to pee. So he was trying to edge into the can, and the Reuters guy asked him again: "How 'bout the Gulf?" Dukakis just wanted to get by—for God's sake, he had to pee! "Well, it, ahh, seemed like a measured response." So, of course, next stop, the Reuters guy filed . . . and everybody else went bullshit! Their desks wanted to know: "Why no Duke-react? Reuters has Duke-react!" . . . So on the plane, they were screaming: *WHADDABOUT IRAN?* And in front, Michael's wise guys were bawling him out: "Don't *do* that! Don't go back there."

"I was going to the bathroom!"

They told him not to go to the bathroom.

He could not understand—he would not—that life, as he knew it, was over. He wasn't gonna lose . . . anything. No! He was winning! He was right! He was doing everything right! He could feel it turning—that was good, wasn't it? This was what he'd been working for—this moment!—when he knew . . . and everybody conceded, he was going to be the nominee. The chosen. Him!

On the last night, he went to Brooklyn—a gym in a beat-up school. Charles Schumer, the Congressman, made Michael come. For what? For basketball! Anyway, that's what they promised the press bus—film of Michael, playing ball. So they got to the gym, and the place was a madhouse. There wasn't any basketball game. A few huge guys, on the court, shooting, and the bleachers full of Puerto Ricans—God knows what Schumer promised *them* . . . and in the middle of the gym floor, politicians, the school principal, a hundred and fifty pissed-off reporters and cameramen, and sound men, auteurs. . . . Marie Cocco, *Newsday,* was screaming at Jack Weeks, the Trip Director, near mid-court. "You assholes said a basketball game! There isn't any fucking basketball game!" Weeks just shrugged. What the hell could he do . . . what could anyone do, with this? They put Michael into an orange T-shirt with a big number 8 on the front, and on the back the words: "Street Corner Stuff." Michael got onto the floor—set shots. Fifteen feet, twenty feet—a miss, another miss. Then he hit. He was such a cocky little bastard, he clapped his hands for the ball. *Hey! C'mon! I hit my shot. Gimme the ball!* . . . Schumer was screaming at the crowd through a cheap P.A. *"On the last night before the New York primary, we have the next President of the United States. He's come to Midwood to do us proud . . . "* All of a sudden, the three huge guys on the court had ahold of Michael, and had lifted him up like a beachball, in front of the basket, with the ball in his two hands like a kid would hold it, in his stupid T-shirt, his wing tips kicking little spasmic kicks with the effort . . . WHAM . . . he stuffed the ball. Greek Thunder! So everybody with a camera was enraged because Schumer was screaming they'd missed it, so up Michael went again, with the "Street Corner Stuff," and the wing tips wiggling . . . and he almost missed. They were filming. He looked . . . well, not to put too fine a point on it: he looked ridiculous, undersized, out of place.

How could he have known how he looked? He never worried about that. They were happy, right? He did his basketball thing—right? It's over? Good. Let's go.

And they were happy—the wise guys, the press. It was over, this mess of New York . . . their man was *winning.* They were going on to Pennsylvania, Ohio, all the way to California—L.A., the pool at the Century Plaza! And beyond, to the convention . . . the White House! Jesus! . . . They all felt the turn. In the press bus, Jack Weeks barked at the driver, in Southie patois: "Awright, Fred. Fastasyacan! Everybody get yer seats! *Wahp speed.* " So the diddybops were yelling at Weeks: "What's a Wahp? Whadd'yahave against Wops?" Weeks was yelling back at them: "What's the headline? What's the HEADLINE? Duke slam-dunks New Yawk? . . ." And from the back of the bus, catcalls: *"WHADDABOUT IRAN, JACK?"* . . . *"WHADDABOUT AIDS?"*. . . Phil Lintz, from the *Chicago Tribune,* had an electronic keyboard he was hauling home, a gift for his kid. So now he started picking out the tune the Puerto Ricans sang . . . a catchy Latin thing:

> "Mike Du-ka-kee . . .
> "El Presidente . . .
> "Mike Du-ka-kee . . .
> "El Presidente . . ."

The bus was pitching and rolling—sixty miles an hour on the humps and ruts of a Brooklyn street, while they sang . . .

"*Mike Du-ka-kee* . . ." Stomping the floor, banging the windows. "*Presidente* . . ."

And in his quiet car, Michael turned against his belt in the front seat and arched his eyebrows: "So, gentlemen," he said. "A year later, wiser . . . but still standing. Taking nourishment. And it's nice to be escorted by New York's finest." That was for the cop at the wheel. Michael was expansive, inclusive . . . he'd made it through.

He wasn't counting chickens—but he could read a poll. He was beating George Bush—ten points. . . . "Not too bad for a guy from Massachusetts whom thirty percent of the people don't know." Michael said everybody assumed the GOP had some kind of lock—a built-in advantage. He couldn't see it. "The country is coming offa that." He was out there! He saw the way people *responded* to him—especially now, when it was coming down to Bush . . . and him.

Who would have thought?

All the rest had fallen away—Hart, Biden, Gephardt . . . Gore, too, after this . . . just Jackson and him. He would go on and beat Jesse in Pennsylvania, Ohio, West Virginia . . . that would be different—him and Jesse. It was always the other guys who helped Michael to define himself. Not that he hauled them down.

"Nick, you remember that black guy in the little restaurant? You know, before the Wall Street rally? . . ." They'd used a small Greek restaurant as a holding room. A black lawyer there said to Michael: *Thank you for running a real Presidential campaign.* . . . "Ya know what he meant, don't you?" Mitropoulos knew. Michael was the one who wouldn't hit Jesse. That was a great satisfaction.

God, he loved New York . . . he loved his life . . . he loved . . .

"Kitty has been *wonderful.* Down here, she's been using Yiddish—I couldn't believe! . . . Nick, what was it she pulled out the other day? 'Why does a duck have webbed feet?' . . . in Yiddish? I couldn't believe it! There was a terrific story in the *Globe* today, her with these old Jewish people, using Yiddish . . . and they're sitting back there, whispering, 'I didn't know she was Jewish!' "

Michael threw his head back and laughed.

Someone suggested there were times Kitty wasn't sure she *wanted* Michael to win. "Not anymore," he said. Now she was more determined than *he* was.

"This is serious now," Michael said. "This ain't beanbag, as Dooley said. Kitty is a hundred percent. The whole family. . . . This is for all the marbles. *This* . . ." Michael said, so vehemently he forgot his accent, ". . . *is the Big Enchilada.*"

—★—

The night of the vote, Michael and Kitty stayed in New York. Kitty *insisted* they stay in New York. The campaign rented a ballroom at the Omni Hotel—

terrible room, hot, smelly, packed with money and *machers* of all description who thought they had a right to be there . . . very important people, and too many. That was the idea. TV doesn't show the size of a room. The one thing you don't want is empty spots—looks like you can't draw a crowd. So the wise guys made sure there'd be a fight for space, and air—the heat of a mob.

Then, at 10:35—perfect for live shots at the top of the late news—Michael and Kitty appeared on a balcony that ran around the mezzanine. The cops had closed that level. Michael and Kitty emerged in regal isolation. From the right rear corner, they walked the length of the room while the crowd cheered and five thousand eyes tracked their progress. From that sweaty floor, they looked . . . well, splendid, distant . . . perfect. They stopped in mid-progress, to smile, and wave—the kind of thing Presidents do. Then, invisibly, they descended, and reappeared from the back of the stage . . . to the front, where they stood, each with an arm around the other (perfect—someone taught them how), each with one open palm raised, smiling and waving, while the band struck up "New York, New York," to a frantic percussion of motor drives, and the mob on the floor yelled *"Let's go Mike!"* . . . and for the first time, he looked the part.

"Thank you, thank you, thank you very much," his mouth was saying. But no one could hear. The band stopped. The crowd was yelling: *"Beat Bush! Beat Bush! Beat Bush!"*

Michael finally bent toward his microphone:

"My friends, we won the bronze in Iowa. In New Hampshire, we won a gold. . . . And tonight . . . tonight, in New York, we won the Oscar!"

The crowd stopped him with cheers again, while Michael hugged his cousin, Olympia—fresh from her *Moonstruck* triumph. It was, as Michael liked to say, "the year of the Dukaki."

". . . And all it took . . . was a strong message . . . a lot of hard work . . . and a lot of charisma!"

And as he said the word "charisma," he started to laugh. Michael Dukakis was laughing, in front of a microphone. And the crowd started yelling again— no way he was going to talk. *"Beat Bush! . . . Beat Bush!"*

So Michael stood back, grinning, put his arm around Kitty. She looked wonderful, joyous. Her smile was huge. She put her hand up behind him, lightly fondled his back. The crowd was still screaming, *"Beat Bush! . . . Beat Bush! . . . Beat Bush!"* and stomping the floor, clapping in rhythm. Kitty's head nodded time. But Michael didn't mark the beat. His face was a small smile. He was looking at his bride.

How could he have known, just a few days later, he'd get home to Brookline, to Perry Street, his prize . . . and find his bride on their bed, drunk, passed out—poisoned insensate by vodka. He would not be able to rouse her. He'd have to call for help. And he would stand over the bed, eyes half-closed, speaking to no one:

"Kitty, Kitty, why? . . . Why do you do this?"

Mercury in Retrograde

GEORGE BUSH did not know why he couldn't feel it. He'd won . . . he'd wiped the field clean! He'd won every state in Super Tuesday—a *shutout* . . . and never had to break a sweat in Illinois. . . . Wisconsin—no contest—Dole just hung in for one more week, to make a speech, have his say . . . Bush could understand that. He understood too well. "Dole must be tired," he said. "It's hard to snap back . . . feels like a death in the family."

It was hard for Bush to snap back . . . or snap *to* the fact that he'd won. This course he'd been running for ten years was at an end—he was the nominee. Let go that baton! Take a bow!

Friends told him, Super Tuesday night: Hey! It's over—done deal!

"I just don't see that," Bush said. "I don't feel that. I don't want to feel that. If I felt that, I'd do something wrong, or I'd react in a bad way . . . not working hard, or whatever it is."

So he went on to Illinois and vowed that no one would work harder. He acted like he was holding on for dear life—in a way, he was. And he wouldn't give up on Wisconsin—didn't want to hear that it really didn't matter.

It was like a muscle that he couldn't unclench. He won and he won and he won . . . and, at last, he flew back to Washington. They were on the ground at Andrews Air Force Base, and Bush wandered back from the Power Cabin— he came to wish the staff Happy Easter. They wished him congratulations on his victory.

"Somehow," Bush said, "I don't have that . . . exhilaration."

— ★ —

For one thing, there wasn't much to do. Back in Washington, Dole hosted a
"reception" for Bush: he invited all the Republican Senators to affirm fealty.
It was a nice gesture—Dole, trying to go that extra mile . . . but Bush seemed
oddly disengaged. Either all that heat he'd directed at the figure of Bob Dole,
now standing next to him in that Capitol office, was somehow out of scale—or
this was . . . this piece of theater: everybody smiling, acting like all those words,
those months, those years, did not matter anymore. It robbed purpose from
the past—made it empty, like this present.

Bush meant to thank his family for their efforts, the way they'd all bent their
lives . . . but they were so spread out, all over the country, the best he could
do was a conference call. That wasn't really what he had in mind—staring at
a box on his desktop while they all tried to talk through the White House
switchboard. It didn't have the feeling of getting them together, like in Maine.
He just didn't feel it, that sense of completion he craved.

Bush was ever a man of missions: a mission isn't over till all planes are on
deck, debriefing's done, the forms are filed. . . . Pat Robertson hadn't given
up. Word came from the Reverend's campaign that he wasn't trying to beat
Bush—just keep his troops in shape, win some votes, restore some lustre lost.

Tough noogies.

Bush sent word back: Get on board—ship is pulling out! It wasn't said
exactly that way. It was more like: if you want to *be* mainstream . . . then
act mainstream. The Reverend got the message, no one got hurt.

And that was the last plane on deck—Bush had no more opponents. He had
the delegates to make him the nominee. The white men scheduled a rally—in
Washington, a full tribal salute. They called it the Over-the-Top Rally . . . it
was going to be big.

Of course, it wasn't really for Washington—real Washington was twenty-to-
one for Jesse Jackson. This was for official Washington, a town where Bushies,
suddenly, were legion. (You could get almost a thousand young folk at the
Fifteenth Street warren of GBFP . . . and a few hundred more from the OEOB
. . . and you could pack a rally *full* with staff from the offices of consultants
and smart guys—the car-phone-in-the-Beemer crowd was so eager to help
now—their people would all be in from Virginia, you know, on a work day.)
. . . So they'd get all these folks to wave signs and scream for Bush—cheer him
on toward the Oval Office. And then . . . *then!* . . . from the Oval itself, they
would march in the Big Brush-Chopper—the *Gip!*—who would finally be free
to drop his pose of disinterest, end his official, statesmanlike neutrality . . . and
at last . . . for the good of the Party, and in tribute to the loyalty of seven years
. . . put his shoulder to the wheel for the *one man* he trusted to stand beside
him . . . *at last!* . . . Ronald Reagan would endorse George Bush.

So GBFP and the OVP set to work on a Reagan speech about their man
. . . beautiful stuff about Bush at the President's elbow, a force for calm, for

strength, for decency, for true conservatism! . . . They had pages of praise, all typed up, sent in to the White House writers.

And they held the rally: first week in April, weather just right, crowd big enough—noisy, too—and Bush made a speech, said they were going to *win in November* . . . and he looked like a winner, or deserved to, with all those delegates in his column, the nomination locked up, the Party united, everybody behind him . . . almost.

Bush finished speaking, the crowd finished cheering and . . . no Gip.

Where's the President?

No President.

No explanation.

Mercury in retrograde?

—★—

Luckily, it didn't make news—the Reagan nonappearance at the big Bush rally. The stuff about Mercury, Uranus, and all . . . that was front-page. Don Regan's book was seeping into the papers, newsmagazines, and TV—TV loved that book! Nancy and the astrologer—*too delicious!* . . . Bush started getting questions on astrology: *What did he know and when did he know it* . . . about Sagittarius rising.

Then, too, there was Attorney General Meese, whose top staff resigned, and he couldn't hire replacements. No one wanted to play in the slush with Ed. It was only a matter of time before they'd have to throw Meese off the sleigh, to the wolves. (Actually, Meese was sliding off, on his own lubricious conflicts of interest.) Now Reagan had to act deaf every time he left the White House. Bush couldn't show up anywhere without being asked if Meese should be fired. *What was he gonna do about Meese?*

Meanwhile, there was a steady drip, drip, drip . . . from Panama and General Noriega. The Reagan White House wanted Noriega out . . . then it turned out that U.S. intelligence (the CIA, for example, under Director George Bush) had been paying Noriega as a stoolie for years. The Reaganauts contended Noriega was a drug kingpin (Bush insisted, he only just found out) . . . then it turned out the Drug Enforcement boys had been awarding Noriega citations of merit! The Reagan Justice Department indicted Noriega in a South Florida court . . . then the Reagan State Department sent legations to tell him: the indictments would be dropped only if he'd take his dirty money, and go.

Noriega wouldn't leave Panama.

Meese wouldn't leave the Justice Department.

Don Regan was on every talk show in the country.

Dukakis was hopping from state to state, beating Jesse Jackson every Tuesday and beating up on Bush with "White House astrology" . . . "the sleaze factor" . . . "deals with drug-running Panamanian dictators." Late April, a *Time* magazine poll had Bush eleven points behind Dukakis in a head-to-head race. Early May, Gallup had Bush thirteen down.

Which, of course, made the white men *very nervous.* Teeter's private numbers were worse—not just the head-to-head—*Bush had problems:* a majority of Americans thought he hadn't told the truth about Iran-contra. (That was the only Bush-news in the papers—new dribble on Iranamok—unless they were running that picture of Bush chatting with Manuel Noriega.) Forty percent had a negative opinion of Bush as a leader. (That was worse than Jesse Jackson.) And women! God! They hated Bush! "Big gender gap," Teeter said. "Lot of bad numbers." That was strong talk from Teeter. His solution, of course, was to moderate Bush, or decorate him with an appliqué of "good words" that might push the button with women—"day care," "college tuition credits." . . . Teeter took over the issues groups—which meant they were packed with quiet, solid professor-types from Michigan State, Purdue, or other places that rang no Bush-bells. The Veep didn't want new programs. Bush thought the issues groups were weak.

Which made Atwater *very nervous.* Lee could *feel:* he was losing control. All this bad news was leaking into the papers, stuff about the campaign clueless, and he *knew* how the VP *hated leaks*! . . . Lee was sure his enemies were floating *bad balloons* . . . so the campaign would look chaotic . . . so they'd bring in *Jimmy Baker* . . . and Lee would *lose his job*! . . . He'd be on the phone before seven, calling staff—*"D'ja read th'Post?"* . . . (No, they hadn't read the *Post*! It was six-thirty in the morning!) . . . *"Well lookit page five, call-me-back!"* . . . Lee thought he was going to have to quit—this was gonna set back his career! He'd *have* to get something like Chairman of the RNC—just to save face. But he wouldn't dare bring that up with the Veep. So he'd wander across the Wing of Power and mention the RNC in Junior's office.

Junior wanted Baker in—now! The Vice was in trouble! What the hell are friends for? . . . Get Baker in to run the campaign, let him convince George Bush to *save himself* . . . act like a candidate! Move his whole office out of the White House and into campaign HQ—get him out of asshole-Fuller's clutches, that'd solve half the problems right there! Teeley, the Press Secretary, was in Junior's office every day, complaining how Fuller cut him out of the loop. Teeley wanted to be Gee-Six . . . and Fuller wouldn't even take his damn calls! Teeley was going to quit. What the hell was he Press Secretary for . . . if no one but *reporters* would talk to him? Junior said to Teeley: "Talk to Baker. We gotta get him over here."

Baker didn't want to come. He had a straight deal with Bush—he would come for the general election . . . meanwhile, he *liked* being Secretary of the Treasury. Baker didn't want to be the top political op in town—he'd been that. Now . . . he was a statesman! He had his own shop—gorgeous office!—he roamed the world, doing *big* deals: James A. Baker III, Savior of the Free World Monetary System! . . . So Baker called in Hugh Sidey—the white man's tom-tom, a columnist for *Time* mag—and fed him the line that the best thing Baker could do for Bush . . . was to stay where he was! . . . James A. III had to coax breath, life itself, into the world economy. James A. III had to keep a healthful finger on the pulse of M-1, M-2. . . . James A. III would control the *climate* in which Bush hip-hopped the nation, repainting rosy the *whole perception* of the Reagan years, saving the heritage that was Bush's to claim . . . saving, in sum, the Reagan administration.

But it looked like even Baker could not save the Gip. The curtains had parted—the Wizard of Oz was finished. Everything he tried, to show renewed force, control, blew apart in a cloud of sawdust and swamp gas. Inauspicious planetary transit! Nancy wouldn't let Ronnie out of the house to endorse George Bush. . . . What did it matter? . . . Reagan's polls were at an all-time low, along with his political charm. Reagan was part of Bush's problem.

Which gave the white men an idea: *Hey!* . . . How 'bout if we get Bush to *separate from Reagan*? . . . He could be *his own man*! . . . Say something about Meese?

"No!"

Noriega?

"No!" said George Bush. "I'm not gonna start that now!"

— ★ —

What *would* he do? . . . Well, he'd *keep going*! . . . He wasn't going to sit around, fretting. But he was dropping in the polls! Dukakis was beating Jackson every week! One thing Bush hated—second to leaks—was panic. It made him *nervous* to see the white men in such a state. Plus, he knew they'd decide in the end, the problem was somehow . . . him.

So he went on to states where there were primaries—even though he had no opponent—and showed up where the reporters were, collected some endorsements, got his face on the news. He set off to Ohio, Indiana . . . then, Stratoliner to California. Anywhere the Democrats went, Bush was sure to follow.

But it wasn't so easy to get on the news, without a horse race that week. Endorsements? . . . Every Republican had already endorsed him—who else could they be for?

How about movie stars? Or *sports*! We love that stuff!

Well, Muhammad Ali would come out for Bush—but only if his pal, a guy named Salzman, could get a job with Ed Meese. . . . In Ohio, Bush picked up the endorsement of the legendary football coach Woody Hayes. It had to be noted, however, that Woody died the year before . . . but he did say he liked Bush—you know, before he croaked—really!

Bush was soon reduced to his standard photo op—heavy equipment. Since the eighteen-wheeler and forklift saved the bacon in New Hampshire, Bush, Inc., had not let a week go by without perching the Veep on some steel behemoth. His press pack had a name for this:

"What's he doing in Indiana?"

"Same—you know, Tonka Toys."

(Actually, in Indiana, it was a military vehicle to replace the Jeep. The head of the plant ushered Bush to a brand-new unit, carefully tested and cleaned. . . . Feel free! Hop right in! . . . Only hitch was, Bush had been limoed for so many years, he plopped into the passenger seat. There was a pause of skin-itching awkwardness while he waited for someone to drive him.)

The real problem—the fact at the root of all this unease—was, Bush couldn't make news because Bush had nothing to say. Without an opponent—*me* instead of *him*—the Bush campaign was about . . . nothing. Bush took some swipes at the Democrats, but Dukakis hadn't finished his work, and Bush could not appear to play favorites. So he made his attacks against "Jacsis," which, in his mind, was an amalgam of Jackson and Dukakis . . . nobody else knew what he was talking about.

And every time he stopped talking—if he couldn't disappear into a car, or a plane—someone would ask about Meese, or Noriega. . . . What was he going to say?

"I'm not gonna get into the Meese thing."

Did he pay Noriega, while he was the head of the CIA?

"I can't confirm or deny . . ."

If they pressed him—which they did, every day—he lied.

Well, it wasn't exactly a lie in his mind—just another schizoid unease that came from being candidate and Vice President.

Vice President Bush supported the administration's efforts in Panama. Candidate Bush saw the drip, drip from Noriega washing his campaign down the toilet. So George Bush was on a secure phone, every day, trying to get the White House to pull the plug on negotiations with Noriega. He'd try to get the National Security Adviser, Colin Powell, to tell him: What the hell were they negotiating *about*? Why should they offer Noriega *anything*? Why was it *public*? . . . It wasn't just that Bush hated leaks. Most of all, he loved secrets.

Secrets, and power, and loyalty, and government—they all went together in the Bush-mind. So this was his secret: he knew Noriega was dirty . . . he thought the Panama policy was nuts. But he wouldn't tell the *public*! He'd rather lie.

Meese—Bush said it wasn't his place to ask the Attorney General to step down. In fact, that's exactly what he had done, two weeks before, when he had a talk with Meese and asked him pointedly: Didn't he realize the damage he was doing to the President, by hanging on? Meese said he didn't see why he should resign—he hadn't done anything wrong. He said he'd think about leaving after the Special Prosecutor issued his report.

Vice President Bush wouldn't reveal *that*—no way! . . . And as usual, when he was lying, Bush felt the need to *prove he believed* . . . in terms ever stronger . . . to the point of an aggrieved shriek. When word leaked that Bush advisers considered Ed Meese a drag on their campaign—and that Bush, privately, thought so, too—Bush was at such pains to knock down the story, he said:

"I deny that I have ever given my opinion to anybody on anything."

Thank you, Mr. Vice President.

Bush thought if he could just hold on, the bad news would go away. That was his text, in sermons to the white men—when they'd *beg* him to take just one shot at Meese, or *something,* to signal he had an opinion of his own. No, Bush said. This was a time for discipline, faith! He wasn't going to cut and run. Reagan would be back in the polls—the pendulum would swing back.

In the end, Bush had faith in his yin-yang knowing, in the Washington way:

no one would ever prove he knew anything. He could outlast the capital's attention span.

And he was right. The Special Prosecutor finally issued his report. Meese declared victory (hell, he hadn't been *indicted* . . .) and resigned. That was the end of Bush's Meese problem.

Noriega hung on in Panama—a bit embarrassing to the America-standing-tall crowd. But Bush solved *his* problem. In mid-May, in California, he told a crowd at the Los Angeles Police Academy that he would not "bargain with drug dealers . . . whether they're on U.S. or foreign soil." He didn't mention Noriega by name—certainly did not mention Reagan—but Fuller filled in the blanks in a "background briefing."

BUSH SPLITS WITH REAGAN . . . was the lead story in the *Post* the next day. There was rejoicing among the white men (save for Teeley, who resented Fuller briefing the press). Yale friends and Andover friends, Houston friends and Maine friends poured calls of congratulation into the OVP. "Let Bush be Bush!" There was a two-day blizzard of stories about Bush and James A. Baker III waging a "battle royal" within the White House to quash any deal with Noriega. . . . And then it was over.

The only attempt at explaining Bush's change of heart was the mention of the latest poll (Gallup had Bush sixteen back). Lost in the back pages were accounts of his meetings with Noriega—stretching back to 1976—and clear indication that he'd known about Noriega's drug connections, at least since 1985. After a week, that story disappeared, too. No one ever pinned Bush about his standards for truth in the public discourse.

"I've said what I had to say," Bush said.

So he had, in a tactical sense. If the issue ever came up again, it was discussed as another "Bush loyalty thing." There were so many fish to fry: new polls (worse and worse for Bush), Reagan Democrats shifting to Michael Dukakis . . . Teeley quit—turmoil among the white men . . . Reagan wanted to ship new warplanes to Kuwait . . . Reagan was going to visit Moscow and Gorby . . . Reagan announced the end of negotiations with Noriega.

There was, too, the interesting issue of Reagan's loyalty to Bush.

— ★ —

The Gipper did finally endorse him . . . at the annual President's Dinner—a knowing crowd, black tie, fifteen hundred dollars a plate—but 9:00 P.M. . . . after the news. The Bush campaign had promised the President would "preview" his endorsement that afternoon, for the cameras at the White House . . . but for some reason, Reagan never showed.

So there was a goodly press contingent that night at the Washington Convention Center—a huge place, a perfect Reagan event. There were gigantic mockups of federal buildings. There was a lovely, gauzy twenty-minute film of "Great Moments" in the Reagan years, all set to music and splashed with sunshine, like the Gipper's "Morning in America" ads.

Just like old times! . . . And the Gip was in form, reminiscing about Jimmy

Carter's interest rates with fond and practiced contempt. Then he got to the end of his speech—the last paragraph, matter of fact. Ronald Reagan said to the crowd:

"If I may, I'd like to take a moment to say just a word about my future plans. In doing so, I'll break a silence I've maintained for some time with regard to the Presidential candidates. I intend to campaign, as hard as I can. My candidate is a former member of Congress, Ambassador to China, Ambassador to the United Nations, Director of the CIA, and National Chairman of the Republican Party. I'm going to work as hard as I can to make Vice President Bush the next President of the United States."

There was a round of applause as Reagan said the name . . . though, alas, he mispronounced it. ("Bush," he said, like it rhymed with "slush.") Then the crowd stilled for the big windup.

But there was none. Reagan turned back to the mike, and said: "Now it's on to New Orleans, and on to the White House."

That was it? . . . After eight years?

It turned out, in the agonizing aftermath (the white men were crestfallen, Bar was furious, *The New York Times* front page announced: BUSH CAMP LONGS FOR SIGNS OF MORE SUPPORT BY REAGAN) . . . that the White House writers *had* used some of the splendid Bush-staff prose, but Nancy wouldn't *hear* of it. ("No! It's *Ronnie's* dinner!") . . . So the President had to write, in his own block print, what *he* thought about his Veep—which wasn't much.

And the heartbreaking thing was, he'd called in George Bush . . . and showed him! . . . Bush could see it wasn't much. But he also saw his Big Friend laboring, at his legal pad . . . what could he say?

"I think that's great, Mr. President."

127

Science at Kennebunkport

THE NEGATIVES came from Jim Pinkerton, in research. Atwater gave him a file card and told him:

"You git me the stuff to beat this little bastard. Ah wancha put it on this card."

The card was three inches by five.

"Use both sides," Atwater said.

Pinkerton came up with seven entries: Dukakis's national defense positions, his record on taxes and spending, the pollution of Boston Harbor, his opposition to the death penalty and to mandatory sentences for drug offenders. . . . The longest entry on the card was Dukakis's policy on prison furloughs—including one case in which a murderer named Horton got a furlough from a Massachusetts pen and attacked a couple in Maryland, raping the woman, stabbing her fiancé.

Pinkerton found out about the case from the question Al Gore asked Dukakis at the New York debate. Pinkerton called up Andy Card, his best Massachusetts source—did he know about this? Card did, indeed. He pointed Pinkerton to the *Lawrence Eagle-Tribune,* which had won a Pulitzer Prize for its investigation of prison furloughs. What shocked Pinkerton was not the incident, but that Dukakis refused afterward to change the policy. Massachusetts was, at that time, the only state allowing furloughs for murderers who had no chance of parole.

"I don't get it," Pinkerton said. "When they find out this thing is all screwed up . . . why wouldn't he change it?"

"You don't know Dukakis," Card said. "You can't tell him anything." Card had served in the Massachusetts legislature. He told Pinkerton how they'd passed a bill to require recitation of the Pledge of Allegiance, ". . . so this guy vetoes the Pledge of Allegiance!"

Pinkerton tucked that onto the file card, too.

— ★ —

To Atwater, this did not require a lot of thought: Bush, Inc., had a candidate who was fifteen points behind—and falling. George Bush had "negative ratings" of forty percent with the voters. Dukakis's "negatives" were only twenty percent. There were two choices: they could work on building a more positive Bush-image . . . or they could stick so much shit on Dukakis's head that his "negatives" would shoot through the roof.

They'd tried for three years to show what a sterling fellow was George Bush.

To Atwater, there was only one choice now.

— ★ —

The day before the white men went up to Kennebunkport for the big Memorial Day sit-down with the Veep, they gathered in a shopping center in Paramus, New Jersey, for a focus group with the sort of voters that Bush, Inc., would have to turn around.

They were suburbanites, forty thousand a year, or better . . . they used to be Democrats . . . but they voted for Reagan . . . now they were for Dukakis. Why?

Well, he seemed able, middle-of-the-road, nonthreatening. Seemed like a good man, a successful Governor, and smart.

The Bush white men watched from behind a one-way mirror. There was a moderator—one of Teeter's ops from Michigan—at a table with the voters.

The moderator told the story of Willie Horton and the prison furloughs. Then he said Dukakis was against the death penalty. Then he said Dukakis was against prayer in the schools. Then he said Dukakis vetoed the bill to require kids to say the Pledge . . .

Within ninety minutes, half the voters had switched to Bush.

— ★ —

As the family liked to tell it, George Bush was the calmest hand on deck. Friends were calling from all over the country, wringing their hands and moaning: Why couldn't he *do something*? The Gee-Six were in a lather . . . panicky about Dukakis's lead.

Junior knew that, of course, with his office on the Wing of Power. Hell, he was among them enough to worry, too. He knew all the bad news: the polls, the "internals," the "gender gap," the "negatives." He knew the schedule for the next two months held nothing to help Bush get back on the evening news. Dukakis looked like the centrist statesman in his week-to-week wins over Jesse Jackson. He would hold the spotlight through July, as the Democrats convened in Atlanta. George Bush couldn't even throw his own body around the country to get onto *local* TV. . . . GBFP had spent the legal limit; the travel budget was a hundred thousand *overspent* . . . no one wanted to tell the Veep.

Junior talked to his father, just before Memorial Day. He kept it casual—the normal stuff: Laura's fine . . . the kids . . .

Only at the end, Junior asked: "How are you, Dad? . . . Are you okay with this thing? You think it's all right?"

"Yeah," said George Bush. He sounded surprised by the question. "People don't know who this guy is . . ."

He meant Dukakis. There was no doubt in Bush's mind what the issue would be in this campaign. And also no doubt: Dukakis had no idea about life in the bubble.

That would make all the difference.

"I mean, who is this guy? . . . You've got to remember, Dukakis has never been here before."

— ★ —

As Atwater liked to tell it, the focus groups proved they had the silver bullet. Hell, they had enough ammo to perforate Dukakis. And Lee was just the man to make Bush pull the trigger. Lee brought videotapes of the focus groups to Maine. If Bush could only *see* those voters . . . when they found out how liberal Dukakis was . . . well, he'd have to agree! He'd have to go negative.

Atwater meant to get the whole Gee-Six, present Bush with a blank white wall of consensus: he *had* to attack. Lee had to make sure of Mosbacher. He was the only Gee-Six who had not seen the focus groups. "Ah'm tellin' you, this is *it,*" Lee said. "These people were, uh, *stunned* when they started hearin' this shit . . ."

Teeter had the numbers: by his count, Bush was seventeen points down— worse with women. Voters didn't know much about either candidate . . . but they knew what they liked. Bush was behind on the critical "internals," like "leadership" and "able to get things done." Worse, still, most voters described themselves as "conservative," or "somewhat conservative." And when asked which candidate was more "conservative," the majority answered . . . Dukakis!

Lee went to work on Teeter to convince him: Bush had to attack, *now.* They had to drive up the negatives on Dukakis—*now*—or risk falling so far behind that Bush would never catch up. Like Jerry Ford against Carter, they could run a *perfect* campaign, and still fall one or two points short. "You gotta tell George Bush," Atwater said. (Lee knew, if Teeter would play ball, Brady would fall into line.) "Ah'll tell 'im th' same thing," Lee said. "But don't you come in there an' fuck me, now!"

Ailes maintained he didn't need the numbers, focus groups, or any high-tech bullshit to prove to *him* what Bush had to do: he had to paint Dukakis as an out-to-lunch-in-left-field *liberal* . . . from the *most liberal corner* (Brookline) . . . of the *most liberal state* . . . who'd never been anywhere, or done anything, that taught him *a single goddam thing* about the rest of the country. Ailes and

Atwater were in agreement on tactics: hit Dukakis, early and often. Atwater thought it was crucial for the race. Ailes thought it was crucial for Bush.

Ailes had devined a fact about the Veep—it came clear while Ailes interviewed Bush for a bio ad. They were talking about World War II, about the bombing run over Chichi Jima. Bush recounted how he saw flames shoot along the wing of his plane, and smoke fill his cockpit.

"Why didn't you bail out?" Ailes asked.

Bush didn't pause, didn't think, didn't blink. "I hadn't completed my mission," he said.

That's when Ailes knew: if you gave Bush that sense of mission . . . the only way you'd stop him, after that, was to kill him.

So Ailes was working on the Veep. "Two things voters have to know about you," Ailes said. "You can take a punch, and you can throw a punch. . . . You're gonna have to make the hit."

By the time they all arrived in Maine, the Gee-Six were collegially, collectively agreed: they would make the case for attack—*right now.* They would come at Bush from every angle, and convince him—or wear him down. Teeter would do the numbers. Atwater would show the ammo—he'd *make* Bush watch those tapes. Ailes would sketch out the language, the ads. Mosbacher would assure Bush that Party surrogates would sing the song. Fuller (Fuller was in!) would make sure the White House hummed along.

All together, they would make George Bush go after Dukakis. It was their only hope! They had to do *something*! . . . They gathered at dinner—the night before their first sit-down with Bush at Walker's Point—and rehearsed their roles. They would not back down! They would all insist! They'd fight all week if they had to.

— ★ —

They didn't have to fight. From his terrace, Bush gazed out at the rocks and sea and said, mildly: "Well, you guys are the experts . . ."

Sure, he'd watch the focus-group tapes.

He didn't mind going after Dukakis.

He didn't need surrogates—he'd do the attack himself.

It was over in five minutes.

True, they sat around most of that day . . . but there was nothing more to decide. On the schedule, there were five more days of meetings in Maine . . . but that would be just blather with the issues groups. The real issues were settled over one cup of coffee.

Atwater was on a plane for D.C. the next day. Lee was triumphant . . . but mystified. He never even had to speak!

What none of the white men could quite concede was that the issue was settled before coffee was served . . . before any Gee-Sixes got to the big house, to tell George Bush what he had to do.

Bush knew what he had to do.

Bush would do what he had to, to win.

If that meant *mano a mano* with Dukakis—so much the better. There, at last, was a message that meant something to Bush:

That guy shouldn't be President!

— ★ —

It all went back to the view from that big house. (Maybe it was not entirely coincidence that the course was set at Walker's Point.) All the research, the focus groups, were just detail, to Bush—had nothing to do with the decision. *One look* told Bush all he had to know.

In the view from the Point, Dukakis was *obviously* a little outsider (Who *was* he? Where'd he ever *been*?) . . . who did not know the world, as it was to George Bush.

Dukakis was another one-worlder, blame-America-first, UN, World Court, human-rights *liberal* . . . who was going to *give away the store*!

Dukakis was another put-on-a-sweater, turn-down-the-thermostat, fifty-five-mile-an-hour, five-thousand-pages-of-Energy-Department-regs *Governor* . . . who'd try to thin the mixture in the great economic engine.

Dukakis was another brainy tax-and-tinker-technocrat *Democrat* . . . who was going to . . . *screw* . . . *everything* . . . *up*!

Dukakis was . . . *Jimmy Carter.*

That solved a lot of problems for George Bush.

Bush could vow (in fact, he did, while he hosted the press that weekend) that he'd labor to define himself . . . he'd show the country what he believed in . . . he'd work like the devil on that vision thing. . . . But he wouldn't have to. The Bush campaign would not be—could not be—about nothing . . . as long as it was about Dukakis. *He* shouldn't be President!

From the moment Dukakis appeared in the bombsight, there would be no lack of mission. Bush would protect the heritage!

If the W-word at the Point was Winning . . . if there was only one man to tend the big house . . . if there was, in every *good* family, one in each generation who must be steward . . . then there must be one to take his turn at the helm of the great ship, and steer it on, unharmed, to the shores of well-being. Bush lived his life to be that man.

There was a line that crept into his speeches, after that weekend. It never got famous, like the catchy bluster of "Read my lips!" . . . but people in the crowds would look up when he said it . . . there was such an (unusual) air of conviction in Bush's voice. . . . It came at the end of his praise for Ronald Reagan, how people felt differently about the U.S.A. now . . . how different was the economy, the business climate, the tax code . . . Bush would praise all these supposed achievements, and then say:

"And I'm not going to let them take it away."

There was the mission! (It wasn't just "me-me-me," after all.) There was the message of the campaign, in one line. And that line made perfect sense to Bush—once "them" became Michael Dukakis.

After that, Bush would do . . . whatever it took.

—★—

By the time that started to show, the white men had told everybody—everybody who was in-the-know—how they got together (collegially) up in Maine, on Memorial Day, and set the course . . . they convinced George Bush.

For the book writers and other keepers of the index entries of History, there were long, loving analyses of the focus groups, the people-meters, the attitude sampling, the ad testing . . . the science behind the lightning bolts that leapt from trembling white fingers. There were accounts of the fateful dinner, where the Gee-Six hammered out the crucial consensus, *the attack on Dukakis* . . . which they carried, thence, to Walker's Point.

It was all that loving, knowing science that let the newsmagazine savants declare this . . . (ta dumm!) . . . The Year of the Handler.

It was the handlers describing their dinner.

Of course, Bush had to eat, too . . . but there wasn't the same level of science: just a motorcade to Mabel's Lobster Claw . . . cheers on the porch . . . Mabel made her usual fuss . . . got everybody seated, got the Service squared away, and came over to shoot the shit with Bush.

"George, do you know how to potty-train a Greek boy?" She didn't wait for an answer. "Do ka-ka!"

Bush threw his head back and laughed at the ceiling. Then he motioned her close, and asked her, in a near whisper: "What's fourteen inches long, and hangs in front of an asshole?"

Mabel gave him a dirty look. He must have heard that one from her own cook!

"Oh, George, I heard that! . . . Dukakis's tie!"

128

Monos Mou

MICHAEL WAS DOING just enough. He was beating Jesse Jackson every week, every primary: Pennsylvania, Ohio, Indiana, West Virginia . . . no mistakes! Dukakis meant to sweep every race, to the last checkered flag, in California, June 7. He meant to win enough delegates to be absolute master of his convention. He wouldn't need help from any other candidate. He wouldn't need anybody . . . no deals! So he had to keep beating Jackson.

Michael liked to win, and this was the easiest winning he'd ever done. Every Wednesday, front pages all over the country confirmed to him everything he'd done right. Every week, new polls showed him edging higher in a head-to-head contest with that hapless Bush. Every month, new Farmer-funders pushed Michael's bank balance higher—twenty-two million . . . twenty-five million . . . until, at last, he'd raised the legal limit, *twenty-seven million dollars* (lucre like no Democrat ever had) . . . after which, Farmer began to raise "soft money" for the Party. On the road, six or seven times a day, another group of greeting pols would tell Michael how excited they were about his chances, their chances, in November . . . what a marvelous machine was the Dukakis campaign. What a marvelous candidate—three days a week!

Actually, it was more like two, or two and a half. The closer Michael got to the nomination, the harder he clung to his *real life*. (The day after he won New York, when Michael *knew* his miracle would happen, Al Gore wanted to meet, to make peace. Michael couldn't spare the time. He had to fly at 7:00 A.M. back to Boston, his corner office . . . where his crucial meeting dwelt for a half-hour upon spring shrubbery planting at the State House.) Whenever the issues staff wanted the Governor for a briefing on foreign policy or defense, Michael would insist: that was campaign time. Sure, he'd sit for a briefing (well, he'd sit for twenty minutes, then pick up a newspaper)—but they'd have to cancel Indiana. . . . But they *couldn't* cancel Indiana—because Robin Toner, in *The New York Times,* was already questioning where the hell Dukakis was spending his days (God forbid she find out, Michael hadn't sat for a foreign-policy briefing in the last month and a half) . . . Farmer and Kristin Demong needed Michael three nights, for *another million dollars* (Fine! But that was campaign time) . . . and the Washington office could not explain to the Party powers why their nominee had not deigned to come to the capital *once* in the last two months. (Said the dean of smart guys, Robert Strauss: "Doesn't he wanta call me?") . . . And, of course, that didn't count things like strategy sessions, message, advertising, or communications in general, which Dukakis would never discuss for more than four minutes, anyway.

Why should he? He was winning every week!

There were folks who suggested to Michael (well, actually, they suggested to Estrich, or to Brountas, or to Kiley, or they'd call John Sasso in exile— Michael had no time for suggestions) that he might want to change his, uh . . . *priorities* . . . now that he bade fair to become the leader of, you know, the *Free World*—maybe he could scale back his work on the state sludge-dumping program, maybe leave off interviewing District Court judges, let someone else chair the next few meetings of the Governor's Statewide Anti-Crime Council.

Out of the question!

In Michael's view, the campaign was going fine! His problems were in the State House. What did all those campaign wise guys know about his revenue estimates for fiscal '89? . . . He was going to have a heck of a time closing that budget gap! . . . Serious problems with the Senate President, Mr. Bulger . . . a thorny dispute on aid to parochial schools. When Estrich had the temerity to suggest one extra day to meet with important pols in Washington ("Governor, those guys can kill us in the press!"), Michael reminded her about that *extra weekend* he'd given her when she got so panicky about Wisconsin.

To Michael, this was just the standard whine about his schedule. The wise guys told him he had to win Iowa, or else! They cried alarums when he lost South Dakota . . . when he lost Michigan to Jackson . . . when he wouldn't ratchet up his schedule for New York. But he never listened! Strong, steady Michael had won it *his way* . . . he'd been correct!

For God's sake, he'd won Nebraska! . . . "Do you know," he asked a table-ful of wise guys, in Boston, "how long it's been since a *Democrat won Nebraska?* . . ." (To their shame, none of the wise guys pointed out that Dukakis had not run against a Republican.)

West Virginia—he won every county! Michael told his cabinet: "They *love* me in West Virginia!" (His Chief of Staff, John DeVillars, did *suggest* that the opposing candidate was black, and could have got lynched in West Virginia.)

Anyway, the point was, they could *try* to tell him that people were watching him, now, in California . . . now that he was the nominee, he had to start filling in the blanks . . . say *something* to begin the fall campaign with a bang . . . but Michael simply shrugged them off. Steady as she goes! The basic economic message (good-jobs-at-good-wages) would win California—and everywhere else.

They could tell him he had to expand his circle—reach out to the leaders of the Party, broaden his base . . . in fact, Estrich did put Dick Moe (the senior Mondale hand, late of the Gephardt campaign) on the plane with Michael for California . . . and Congressman Tony Coelho came along (what a nose for a win!) . . . but that didn't mean Michael *talked* to them. In fact, as his entourage grew, Dukakis talked less and less to anyone. He'd sit in the front of his big plane (a different plane—this one had a bathroom in front, for him) . . . and he'd do his State House paperwork . . . or he'd read a newspaper . . . one night, he balanced his checkbook.

He just had to keep marching. . . . One week into June, California and New Jersey would vote, and Michael would have his delegates.

He just had to let people see the kinda guy he was.

He just had to keep hold of his life.

Then, the foundation of his life crumbled.

In Los Angeles, Kitty took her morning walk, her left foot started to drag. She couldn't get it to move properly. Her head was throbbing. She had hot flashes, chills. . . . She'd felt the symptoms before. She tried to ignore them— like the drinking: it was just the stress. It would pass. It wasn't a problem. . . . Still, she couldn't ignore this . . . God! Multiple sclerosis! . . . A brain tumor! . . . She wasn't sure she wanted to know. But she was scared now. She went to a doctor, had a scan. Two disks were pressed against her spinal cord. When the L.A. neurologist sent the tests to Michael's old friend, Nick Zervas, head of neurosurgery at Mass General, Zervas ordered Kitty home.

She made it back on Wednesday, six days before the California vote. When Zervas scheduled surgery (he said there was risk of paralysis), Michael got the word in San Francisco. He called Jackson and canceled their evening debate. He made it back to Boston by midnight. Motorcycle cops led his car down the Storrow Drive. Michael slept on a cot by his bride . . . 6:00 A.M., they wheeled Kitty to the operating theater. Kitty's sister, Jinny, sat with Michael in the hospital room. Michael spread his State House papers on a table and looked like he was working.

"God," Jinny said, "this came at the worst time . . . just before California."

Michael looked up. "It doesn't matter," he said. "Without her, I don't want to do anything."

—★—

Nick Zervas called Michael with updates every hour or so. They were taking bone from Kitty's hip, they were cutting open her neck, they were replacing her disks with the extra bone . . . it looked okay, Nick said. After each call,

Michael would go back to work. Kitty was on that table more than four hours.

He should have known. He blamed himself. He *told* her to see a doctor! He should have *made* her slow down. . . . Staff from the State House came to Michael for instructions on the press. There was a crowd downstairs. The hospital switchboard was overwhelmed, calls from Washington, flowers arriving . . . Michael didn't want to hear about that. . . . Finally, Zervas came back, said it looked fine. "As soon as she can wiggle her fingers and toes, we'll be all set." Zervas had scans and X-rays to show . . . Michael might want to talk to the press. "No," Michael said. "You talk. It's not my place." He just wanted to see his bride.

In Intensive Care, she asked for a raspberry Popsicle. Michael was beaming. The nurses went *running* to the dieticians, who went *running* to find her Popsicle. "I feel like a Mack truck hit me," Kitty said. Zervas asked: Could she wiggle her toes? Kitty wiggled. Her eyes were shining. Michael thought she looked like a queen. "I need an ice cream and a massage," she said. "Well, we can do the former—I *think* . . ." said Michael. He looked twenty years younger. His voice had snap. "The other [his eyebrows danced] . . . that'll have to wait." The dieticians were still in a lather for Kitty's raspberry Popsicle. Jinny told them: "You know, she'd take grape."

They just couldn't do enough at the hospital. They were wonderful. Kitty had a big room with a view of the Charles River. Michael had to leave for a fund-raiser. But the staff was around, the Secret Service. Kitty got her friends on the phone, collect, from Intensive Care. (If they were on their phones, operators broke in and told them to get off the line—Kitty Dukakis wanted to talk to them!) Flowers came in and out by the stretcher-load. Kitty's room looked like a Mafia funeral. Jesse Jackson sent a ficus tree as tall as Michael. Thousands of letters, cards, telegrams. Press and citizens crowded the lobbies. Patients from other floors hobbled by, just to get a glimpse of Kitty. Kitty's dad flew back from California. He rushed in and saw his daughter, amid the flowers . . . she looked wonderful! "How're you feeling," Harry said. Kitty said: "Turn on the television, Dad. They've been talking about me all day."

"You know, Kitty," said Harry, who'd lived his life on stage—no mean showman was Harry Dickson—"you have a real talent for making a career out of catastrophe."

Jinny found it so strange what was happening to her sister. Not just now, in the hospital—but through the whole campaign. The spotlight, attention, tension—Jinny could *see* her changing. Kitty was so . . . queenly, more and more, every day . . . like their mother! That attitude . . . a-lady-does-not-go-out-without-gloves *bearing* . . . Jinny never thought she'd see it from Kitty! Kitty was always the softie, the emotional *case:* she'd burst into tears at the *thought* of unhappiness—for anyone. She still had that impulse to help. That weekend, she was supposed to speak at the high school graduation of the Vietnamese refugee whom she'd rescued from a camp in Thailand. He was graduating with a full four-year scholarship to Brandeis. Kitty was so proud. She couldn't look at a picture of him without crying. . . . In her hospital room, she read to Jinny the speech she'd planned for the graduation . . . and they both cried. That's how it always was, with them. . . . But the way Kitty arranged now, to have a staff person do the speech for her . . . the way she told him *exactly* how she wanted it done, *exactly* what she wanted in the press, what she didn't want— the way her staff buzzed around, told her how her last speech was so great, the way they talked about her interviews, TV shows, messages from leaders all over the country, scheduling sessions, a new Press Secretary—the way her sister *handled* it, that was . . . a new Kitty.

Jinny didn't know the half.

A few days into her recovery at Mass General, Kitty summoned Susan Estrich to the hospital. She wanted to talk about her staff. So Estrich schlepped across the river, to present herself.

Kitty said: "I want you to get rid of Andy and Marilyn."

Estrich gawked. Andy Savitz had become Kitty's spokesman. Marilyn Chase was her Chief of Staff—since the start! They'd both *killed themselves* for Kitty. Marilyn was one of the highest-ranking blacks in the campaign. Estrich wasn't going to blow her off. Savitz thought he and Kitty had a relationship! (She called him by a Yiddishe nickname, Andilla). Estrich said Andy would be crushed!

"Well, they're just not up to it," Kitty said. "Get rid of them."

"Look—do *you* want to have this conversation with them?"

"No," Kitty said. "I don't feel like it. I don't want to see them anymore. You just do it. I'm in a different league now."

— ★ —

Michael was in another league. He knew that—in his head. It was just . . . he wasn't any different, was he? He didn't want to be. Estrich took as her new personal mission the effort to move Michael's head past the last primaries, beyond New Jersey and California, to his contest for the *nation* . . . with George Bush. In daily phone calls, she'd tell the staff on the plane with Dukakis: "You gotta get him to talk about *after* June 7 . . ."

Michael was ready for that.

"In a few days . . ." he mused from a podium in California, "I'll be planting tomatoes in my front yard."

No. No! NO! . . . Not what she had in mind.

The grungy loft on Chauncy Street had become the focus for intense aspiration—and not just from within. There were hundreds of calls coming in each day from officials, Party leaders, gurus, consultants, Washington smart guys. They had ideas, people to propose, concepts for the campaign against Bush, warnings from their home states, gossip, lines for Michael to use. Dukakis was their hope! And such a shining shot—their best chance for the White House in . . . well, since Reagan started dying his hair. And they *all* said Dukakis had to take the attack to Bush, sharpen up his message, inoculate himself on crime and taxes . . . and defense! Foreign policy! . . . He had to form a team of admen . . . start his consultations with the Party's best and biggest . . . he had to get busy! Michael had to *focus*—start listening! Start planning! High concept! Put an A-team with Michael on that plane! Come *on*! . . . *Who's talking to Mike?*

Well, poor Dick Moe didn't have much success.

Kiley had just about given up. Losing every day wears a man down. Kiley was ready to go back to polling.

Nick Mitropoulos had Stockholm Syndrome—he sounded more and more like Dukakis.

Brountas was supposed to take care of the VP—and Michael wouldn't even sit down *with Paul,* to talk about that!

Susan asked Michael: Who do you *want* to talk to? . . . What about Bob Shrum? . . . Bob Squier? . . . Tom Donilon?

Michael didn't want hired guns from Washington.

What about a senior Party pro like Bob Beckel?

"Ahh, John Sasso is worth three of Beckel."

Sasso!

Actually, it wasn't Susan who brought up John's name—but everyone else did, ticklishly, secretly. They all had the idea that Susan would go batshit if John came back. Actually, Susan made it clear she'd never stand in John's *way* . . . but that was a different matter. Mitropoulos, Kiley, Corrigan, Kitty—even Brountas—whispered John's name.

But the fact was, Michael liked it *monos mou.* He'd shown—hadn't he?—he could do without Sasso . . . not to mention the legions from D.C. He would admit: "Maybe we need some help with communications . . ." Sure. (Maybe they could get Kirk O'Donnell, a Boston man, a Kevin White, Tip O'Neill hand—a guy from Michael's world.) But that didn't mean Michael would hand *himself* over. Or make himself over. Change the kinda guy he was?

His checklist was clear. First, he had to win, to settle this matter with Jackson. People said he had to talk to Jesse . . . of course he'd talk to Jesse—once he'd beaten him.

Then, the VP selection—Paul was working on that. His Campaign Chairman! What more could Michael do?

Then, the convention. So he got Susan's memo on the convention . . . all her ideas, for speakers, themes, strategy . . . he read the memo, and he said: "Okay. Fine. Sounds good. Anybody you want me to call? Anything I should do?"

What was so complicated? The only thing he wanted from Estrich was a name for a Transition Director—someone to start working now on the first hundred days—Michael had to *govern.*

Sure, Bush would come after him—just as his opponents had tried to knock him off for the last year!

But he'd won!

That last night, he won Montana, and he won New Mexico, and he won New Jersey, and he won California—*a sweep.* Jackson never got close. Michael got his delegates. What else did he need?

He made a speech on his last night—another mobbed ballroom:

". . . What quicksand for our opponents if they waste this opportunity on mudslinging and name-calling! Because the American people are not interested in what Mr. Bush thinks of me, or what I think of him. They want to know which one of us has the strength and the ability, and the values, to lead our country . . ."

Just a warning.

That day, the exit polls showed Dukakis ahead of Bush by thirteen percent. In California (where both men campaigned), the split was *seventeen* percent.

The front of the *Los Angeles Times* proclaimed:

DUKAKIS GAINS VICTORY WITHOUT SPLIT IN PARTY

Yes, that was a great satisfaction.

The New York Times was even closer to Michael's fond philotimy:

WITH DISCIPLINE, NOT DAZZLE, DUKAKIS OUTLASTS HIS RIVALS

And a couple of days later, he was bent to his tomatoes, in his front yard, in Brookline . . . black mulch in his garden—his dream, his prize . . . with his bride at home, resting more comfortably every day, on the mend, soon to be . . . good as new!

I'll
Take Care
of This Guy

A COUPLE OF DAYS later, John Sasso arrived, to have a talk with Michael. "Mike, I want to come back. I can help. Do it *now,* while you're on top . . ."

"Ahh, I don't know," Michael said. "It'll be a bad story. The papers'll kill me . . ."

"The papers are calling *me,* Mike . . . you know? I'm tired of ducking so you won't be hurt. If you can't bring me back, I'm gonna come out. I gotta start doing something for myself now. I've gotta stop acting invisible. I'm gonna talk to some people, start moving around. I'm gonna do some interviews."

"Whaddya *talkin'* about?" Michael said. "You know everybody loves you— you *know* they think highly . . ."

John thought: So what's *your* problem? . . . This was not the first time John had asked Dukakis. He'd started in March, trying to get Mike to take him back.

Now he said: "Mike. It's time. I wanna come back. They're gonna try to kill you. You're gonna need help . . . I can start to think through a plan . . ."

Dukakis was shaking his head, looking down. "I said you were out . . . what would I say?"

"You say John has suffered enough. It's almost a year, Mike. It's enough. . . . You say you want to put your best team on the field . . . this is too important!"

"Look," Dukakis said. "I'm gonna beat this guy. This may be a *blowout.*" Dukakis looked up at Sasso: "You start thinking about the first hundred days. I'll take care of this guy."

The Mission

O<small>N</small> J<small>UNE</small> 9, 1988, George Bush strode on stage at the huge convention center in Houston—a concrete mega-box, brand-new—filled, for the first time, with the faithful of the local GOP. There were Bush-buttons on a thousand lapels, Bush-stickers on plastic straw hats, thousands of blue-and-white Bush-signs dancing in clenched fists over the heads of the delegates and alternates and hangers-on who filled the floor. It was the 1988 Republican State Convention—a crowd made to order for the VP, and for the special message he'd brought, that day.

"Our campaign may have seemed quiet these past six or seven weeks . . . but today, it's a new ball game! . . . Spring training is OVER! . . . The season has begun, and there's no reason to wait till the World Series to . . . START SWINGING!"

Bush was shouting. He shouted through his whole speech, like he was mad at someone. Maybe he was.

"First, on TAXES . . . Michael Dukakis has been a proponent of HIGHER TAXES . . . He imposed the BIGGEST TAX INCREASE in Massachusetts HISTORY . . . despite a campaign pledge not to."

It didn't take the crowd long to catch on. They started whooping in derision at Dukakis and his taxes, urging Bush on with pep-rally screams. Ladies in flowered dresses were yelling *Wooooooweeee!*

"Just two days ago, Governor Dukakis said this, in California: 'No serious candidate for President would rule out raising taxes.' . . . Well . . . I'VE RULED OUT TAXES. AND YOU *BET* I'M SERIOUS!"

Wooooooweeee! Gittem George!

"On foreign policy, my opponent . . . says he would rely heavily on multi-lateral organizations, such as the *Yeww Ennn* . . .

"A PRESIDENT can't subordinate his decision-making to a multilateral body—he can't sacrifice ONE OUNCE OF OUR SOVEREIGNTY . . . WE ARE THE UNITED STATES OF AMERICA!"

Yowoooooowheeeeeeee!

They were stomping the floor as they screamed—stopping Bush with cheers. He looked up from his speech, and stared back at the crowd with a gap-mouthed grin that showed his top teeth.

"Governor Dukakis—his foreign-policy views born in HARVARD YARD'S BOUTIQUE—WOULD CUT THE MUSCLE OF OUR DE-FENSE . . .

"Michael Dukakis on *crime* is standard old-style SIXTIES LIBERALISM . . . he has steadfastly OPPOSED THE DEATH PENALTY . . . he supported the ONLY state program in the WHOLE COUNTRY—THE ONLY ONE!—that gives unsupervised WEEKEND FURLOUGHS to *FIRST-DEGREE MURDERERS*! . . ."

By the time Bush had finished with Dukakis that day, the crowd in Houston was yelling *Bush! Bush! Bush! Bush!BUSH!BUSH!BUSH!*

They sang to him, for his birthday, three days thence . . . while Barbara Bush joined her husband on stage, pointing out friends so he could make goofy faces of delight.

He did feel goofy. He'd done three time zones in the last twenty-four hours—still had to stay up to do *Nightline* (three times, he'd call Ted Koppel "Dan") . . . and he'd be up early the next day—flight to Denver. . . . The Houston speech had been late—they had to fax it to his plane . . . barely got a chance to read the thing before he found himself on stage, shouting it out.

But he heard that crowd.

GITTEM GEORGE! YOWOOOOOOOOEEEEE BUSH!BUSH!BUSH! BUSH!

The next morning, in Denver, in the car from the airport, he would say for the first time, to his son Neil: "You know, I feel . . . I can sort of see the target. I think we're gonna win this thing."

EPILOGUE

I N HOUSTON, on Election Day, November 8, 1988, George Bush was not happy. I could see that even from the ropeline, twenty yards away. Security was suddenly brittle and beyond talk—a new layer of earplug people recognized no one, only badges and pins, and there was no way to feel anything from Bush in their midst. The White Men were all around him, vibrating with unease and ill tidings. In the final week, Bush had skittered every which way in the tracking polls, flopping and darting and standing tall again, like a beast of the veldt in fight-or-flight . . . all the while flinging *Air Force Two* about the country, to Michigan, California, Missouri—wherever Teeter said the tall grass held menace. Twelve days before the election, Bush was twelve points up in New Jersey . . . five days out, he was four points behind. So twice, Bush flew halfway across the nation— back to New Jersey. He took $500,000 out of Texas, and threw it at New Jersey. He had to ask the *Gipper* to descend upon New Jersey. In the end, he'd win New Jersey by fourteen points. But how could he know?

And it was the same everywhere—Ohio, Michigan, Illinois, California . . . how could he know about California? In the final push, just a few days before the vote, Bush was riding a bus cavalcade down the farm valleys of California. Six or seven stops a day—open-air rallies. A half-dozen B-level show-biz stars would stand behind him to whip up the crowds while Bush screamed out disconnected vows and threats. Star Wars and Line-Item Veto and Pledge of Allegiance and *yes* (O God, yes!) to Prayer in Our Schools and No New Taxes and No Coddlin' Criminals and No Cuttin' Missiles and no,

No, NO! It got so he made no sense at all, and it didn't seem to matter; after every hoarse hyenic gale of code words, Chuck Norris or Phyllis Diller or Mike Love or some other wizened talk-show goat would start to clap, and local schoolgirls in itty-bitty skirts would jump and pump their pom-poms, shrieking *Eeeee Eee Eee Eeeeeeeeeee* . . . and sure enough, the crowd would answer with its best for the national blood-roar. I came to think it was cynical, a Devil's pact between the goats and the sheep, all acting like this made sense, in a plot to promote the Big Hyena . . . until I talked to Bush on his bus. I was *going* to talk to Bush, but he was tied up on a bench seat with Mike Love, the old Beach Boy, who looked about seventy-something, thin beyond Slim-Fast, etched about the eyes and mouth with tiny, pale, X-acto age lines; everything was pale about him, like a sci-fi visitor from the Planet of a Dying Sun, come to steal the Earth-Grass . . . but no, quite of this world was Mike Love, as he talked nonstop at George Bush's ear about massage—Mike was big on massage—and when Bush said he liked a rubdown, too (common ground!) . . . well, Mike had a world of advice, and he was just in the part about the method that was really good, the way he liked it, see, which he recommended to the Veep at length—"You get two girls, y'know, one side and the other and, uh, two girls at once, y'know, workin' on you, yuh oughta, uh, s'cool, really, y'know?"—and Bush was staring at the bus floor, nodding, polite, like he wanted to pay special attention to the *placement* of the girls, and I thought this was part of the Devil-deal, Bush pretending this made any sense . . . until Bush looked up, and I happened to see in his eyes—he didn't expect me there, and before he knew it, I saw through the watery blue to the bottom— and there was . . . no one home. There was no Devil-deal, the sheep were just sheep, the goats knew no better, and Bush made no sense because he had no sense left in him. The Outgoing Message was still spinning, but the tape had snapped a couple of states back. That amplified whinny he loosed at events was just the last torn and random snatches flapping around with the reel—*ReadmyLIPS! ReadmyLIPS! ReadmyLIPS!* After that, the rallies didn't seem cynical—just the response of a system that was intact, an answer that made explicable a total lack of sense, reassuring, like the *Eeee Eeee Eeeeeeeeee,* which sounded now like a signal that the national phone was off the hook and we should expect no communication until November 8, when we'd slap the booger back in its cradle and, at last, have done with the noise.

And it only got worse after that, more frantic, exhausting, and senseless for Bush, with the White Men so teetery, pointing his plane everywhere Dukakis seemed likely to make trouble, and Dukakis flying his Sky Pig charter back and forth across the country *day and night*—without even *sleep,* for God's sake, shaving five times a day and yelling "We're On Your Side!" in ten different states, trying to goose up those polls, which was goosing Bush . . . same thing, in the end, a perfect identity . . . and now that Dukakis had finally wakened and was screaming random slogans into the wind, people said he'd really improved, you know, and some brave pundits who needed a niche made bold to suggest that *Dukakis was not dead,* which was just a hot poker

grazing Bush's privates—he'd killed the little sonofabitch a *thousand times*—
and a single shaky poll was guaranteed to send *AFII* rumbling down another
runway, while in the Power Cabin, Atwater muttered oracular apocalypse
("California is the *death-star* for Dukakis") and Ailes emitted bilious fulmina-
tions on the enemies of Right and Good, like the press, which Ailes saw
"carrying the little Duke-corpse around, doing mouth-to-mouth, trying to
keep it alive."

Blood-roar . . . the nation seemed to demand it, or at least to expect it, in
the closing days. How else to explain those gatherings of thousands where the
candidate screamed and people screamed back, no one said anything, and the
papers wrote it up as the campaign "picking up steam" . . . blood-roar homage
to our political lineage, to vengeful northern conquerors and their forest-gods
(Normans, surely—French cuisine for state dinners, with five forks gleaming
beside each plate, but give us the heads of our enemies on pikes). Bush knew
it, too. He always said he understood the values of the American people—
better than Dukakis—and people laughed: *D'he learn 'em from his chauffeur
on the way to Greenwich Country Day?* But Bush was right—he did know
better. A hundred times, his White Men, or his family, old school friends, or
someone else who mistook breeding for behavior, tried to steer Bush off the
Pledge of Allegiance, or Willie Horton, Crime 'n' Commies, Furloughs, Flags,
and Read My Lips! It was ugly, brainless; Bush had worn it out . . . but Bush
kept at it. He understood what the forest-gods demanded, what the people
wanted in a chief: his enemies felled and bleeding, drawn limb from limb and
thrown to earth for the people to dance, in blood-roar. America defiles its
losers.

And Bush knew he had to keep it up to the end—not just blood-roar, but
the full measure, till the cup was dry, till he, too, was brainless. The system
demanded totality. That's why this system of picking the chief retained its
defenders, who'd concede right away that it was long—horrible, in fact; it
cheapened the issues, or ignored them; it dumbed down the dialogue to noise;
it was spendthrift, exhausting, hurtful, and it savaged its protagonists . . . that's
why the savants would get those dreamy looks at the end of the talk shows,
and say it wasn't such a bad way to pick a President—a stress test that was
a match for the job. In the end, we have only one nonnegotiable demand for
a President, the man we hire to watch the world at our backs: that is totality.
We may differ on our seven-point plans for child care, the six-hundred-ship
Navy, one-man-one-vote for Namibia. But every adult in the country knows
instinctively: that job in the White House is brutal, and the bastard who gets
it works for *us*. We will not allow anything to be put ahead of it—not friends,
family, nor certainly rosy self-regard . . . nor ease, restoration of self—forget
it! Gary Hart admitted adultery and asked us to forgive his sin. But unforgiv-
able was his assumption that he was supposed to have any life "outside."
Whatever he did with that lovely girl, he put his enjoyment ahead of our good
opinion, and he was erased from consideration. He would not concede that his
life was our chattel.

Dukakis couldn't figure it either. Poor Michael and his brainy young patriots on Chauncy Street used to tell each other every day that Bush would never get away with this crap. This furlough crap, this flag crap—Bush was *craven*. People would *see*. . . . Of course, people saw and concluded, rightly, that here was a guy who'd do what it took. Bush met the nonnegotiable criterion—they voted him in. Their only other choice was a guy who showed in a hundred ways, he didn't know what it took, he knew only what he wouldn't do, and he was not gonna lose hold of his life! *No!* Dukakis was the King of No . . . and no was just another way of saying he wouldn't see this as bigger than himself. He would not concede, his life was meat. People put all kinds of words on this failure; the wise guys pointed to defining moments. The favorite was the national gasp in the second debate, when Bernie Shaw tried to draw Michael forth by asking about the rape of his bride; Michael turned his sober, hooded eyes to the camera and answered with statistics on capital punishment. Thereafter, a million words recapitulated Dukakis's fatal lack of passion, and a couple hundred thousand decried the vulgarity of the question. But passion was never nonnegotiable (Bush would win no ribbon in that bake-off), and the question always struck me as kindly: an invitation for Michael to give us a purchase upon his life. He refused.

And this was no momentary choke. Dukakis could never *get* that he had to (as Arsenio says) *give it up!* You could have seen the campaign's disastrous end months before that debate—soon after Dukakis returned to Brookline, seventeen points ahead in the polls, with his primary triumphs like a neat stack of bills in his briefcase. Kitty was recuperating from her neck operation, still confined to Perry Street. So her new press honcho, her new body woman, and her new Advance staff brought the world to her. So it happened one morning, 6:30 A.M., Michael padded down his steps and ran into the crew, camera, lights, cables, field producer, coffee-in-a-paper-cup and doughnut-wrapper-on-the-floor of *The CBS Morning News* . . . in his living room. So much for lack of passion. Michael Dukakis, in his little striped pj's, stood at the foot of his stairs, bellowing, "KATHARINE! WHY ARE YOU DOING THIS TO ME?"

Give it up! (Woof-woof-woof-woof!) . . . Only one man could. He would become President . . . which goes a long way toward answering the final, most persistent and troubling question: Why . . . when at last we mop up the quadrennial bloodbath and shove one of these fellows toward the White House, why . . . when no matter who he is, he rides a national flood of goodwill, bears the public's hope for a fresh start and better times, why . . . when he surfaces, smiling, under the Great Eagle Seal to become the embodiment and emblem of our age, why, *invariably* . . . does this poor bastard seem so *out to lunch*?

Because he is stunned with blood-roar; witless; spent . . . which explained, also, the sour, furrowed face on George Bush, November 8, 1988, his great day. He just wanted it to be over.

—★—

But it seemed like the day that would not die. There was the smile for TV at the polling place—had to get that tape on the air; then a drop-by at the phone banks, where Bush made a couple of ritual calls; then the schedule went blank, but it really was a white heat of White Men calling network friends for exit polls, then badgering Bush for satellite chats with anchoroids in Markets That Might Make a Difference. If it had been up to the White Men, Bush would never have got to Houston; they planned to fly his raggedy beehive to five or six contested states *on Election Day* . . . until Barbara Bush emerged from the forward cabin of *AFII* and announced, "Well, *we're* going to Houston." She meant her and the Veep, of course—which meant the White Men could do what they wanted, but they'd have no bloody shirt to wave. It was Jeb Bush, second son and heritor of the Walker steel, who put the kibosh on the satellite chats: "Let the old man have his peace!"

Alas, there would be no peace while the polls were open, or even after—not till the network Gods of Election had painted their maps Bush-blood-red across the South and West, proving Bush had held on to the Gipper's old homestead and would soon take over the big house. Bush went to dinner with family and pals at the home of his old neighbors on Indian Trail, the Nebletts. The way Charles and Sally Neblett planned it, this was to be the real celebration with real friends, the Hugh Liedtkes and the Bill Liedtkes, the Chamberses, the Kerrs, the Fitches, the Pressie Bushes, the Jonathan Bushes, and, to leaven the mix, Jim Baker, and then, too, Nick Brady, and for politeness's sake, Teeter, and Fuller, and Atwater, and, of course, the body man, McBride, who could eat in the kitchen with the Veeply traveling doctor, who couldn't drink on the job anyway . . . and the friends were properly ebullient and ready to kick it out in glee for George, once they'd gone through the buffet in the dining room and drifted with their plates into the living room, where the Nebletts had arrayed four TVs . . . but Bush was slumped in a chair where no one could come between him and the screens, and what with all those White Men still twitchy on the job, it just never took off. Some state would start flashing red, and a friend would shout, *Hurray! Kentucky!* But Baker would snap, like a teacher who heard giggling at the back of the class, "That's our *base,*" and then he'd march upstairs to make another Important Phone Call, which let people know what they saw downstairs didn't really matter a good goddamn. . . . Before 8:00 P.M., ABC's computers bumped Bush to 240 electoral votes—just thirty shy! But Teeter said, "Yeah, and ABC called six states wrong last time." So no one got to yell. . . . Even after one network called it, then another, there was, still, that sonofabitch Dan Rather—just wouldn't call it—hoping for a miracle, Atwater said. . . . And even at 8:17, when CBS finally lit Missouri and put Bush over the top, Bush just mumbled, "Nuhh, premature," and bent his face toward the screens like the maps might change if he blinked. So, finally, just on his own say-so, the Nebletts' son cranked up the stereo with "Chariots of Fire," and in the living room, Dr. Neblett asked Bush, "Would you come with me?" And Bush hemmed and hawed, but he couldn't be impolite, so he let himself be led to the garden room, where everyone was gathered, and they showed him the cake, with the candles and the frosting that read: "Congratulations Mr. President!" But Bush still didn't want to *admit it,* so he mumbled around, and said, "I really think I could do a good job, if I win—but if I don't win, I still have my friends, and . . ."

And he had to go, back to the hotel to get ready for the real Big Victory Thing, which would employ the brand-new convention center, dolled up for the night with a grand scale model of the White House, and confetti cannons, towers for balloon drops, and two stages, and huge banners that said *AMERICA WINS,* and there'd be bands and singers of famous name, and hundreds of fat-cat contributors who called themselves The Eagles, and The 100 Club, who'd have gold tickets for admittance to their own rooms (with open bars and potted palm trees) that Bush would have to stop by, after he stood on stage for the nation and read a speech that Peggy Noonan wrote (that's how Big this deal was), with a buffalo herd of satellite trucks and all the big-feet on duty to describe the dawn of a national era, and the networks, of course, with correspondents and crews and producers and even *news execs,* who had come in person to make *damn sure* they and their outfits were *in on the ground floor* of the Age of Bush—heavy power-tripping in heavy power suits—all amid massive security, for this was a night that would bring out the nuts, like Christmas spurs suicides, peak of the curve, and the Service could read an exit poll, so they had, seemed like, a thousand earplugs, to the point where Advance could pretty much pick and choose who was going to get to the front of the room, where Bush might have to see them, and surely who'd get to the ropeline, where Bush might have to talk to them or hear them talk, which was a good thing because they worried for days about this one guy, Judge Lindsay, who wasn't a nut but an old Bush friend and the current dean of the Harris County GOP, who was hosting a party for *thousands* of visiting Young Republicans, who learned their manners in frat houses and who would surely be shitfaced and creating a scene—what Bush Advance was pleased to call "a real goat fuck"—but Advance knew, if Lindsay got to the ropeline and asked the President-elect to stop by, well, Bush would *never* say no to a friend, so then they'd have the Free World's Leader-to-be in a YR goat fuck, and the fretting went so far as suggestions that someone could, you know, "take Lindsay out," or "maybe just put him away for a while."

They needn't have worried. By the time a tiny, distant, slope-shouldered Bush got on stage and gummed Noonan's chewy prose down to fast food, and stopped by The Eagles and the 100 fat-cats (about four minutes apiece amid the potted palms), it was clear he wanted to go nowhere but home. He saw old friends, but he couldn't even say thank you, they couldn't get near him, what with all the earplugs—who were suddenly *strangers* (where was his own detail?)—and people calling him Mr. President, like that would please him, when all at once, he really wanted to be George. And he didn't know yet, but they were screwing around with his hotel, too, which was as close as he had in Houston to home, assigning new guards to close off his hallway all the way from the ice machine, moving "safe people" into rooms all around, even above and below his old rooms, where they even changed the seal on the door (how's a guy to sleep with a new seal on his door?)—tired as he was, he wasn't going to sleep well . . . but at least it was over. He made for his motorcade, then fidgeted behind his bulletproof glass while they loaded all the cars, and he really didn't seem to relax till they moved, past the buffalo herd and off the convention center grounds, onto his hometown streets, heading for the Houstonian. . . . They took a route through the center of town and swept past the Hyatt, where Lloyd Bentsen's disappointed Democrats were streaming out— that was the first time Bush seemed to inhabit his own skin. On the corner, three lady Democrats took the opportunity to salute Bush's limo, each with her middle finger upraised.

"Isn't that nice?" Bush said mildly to his plate glass. "They're already saying, 'We're Number One.' "

—★—

By that time, the networks were frantically filling between ads already sold, trying to breathe life into their telecasts by turning a couple of tight Senate races into a national crisis and flashing around the studio and stratosphere to stiff-shouldered correspondents who were encouraged to fritter a few minutes apiece, discoursing upon news they'd squeezed out, fast as they could, a couple of hours before.

"So . . ." said a desperate Dan Rather. "Did he have any coattails? How big a mandate does he get? All of those things are still very much up for grabs. Ed Bradley! In your conversations with voters today—keeping in mind that that was your assignment, to go out and *talk to actual voters,* uh, what was their reaction to the tone of the campaign—do they agree with the press and a lot of the pundits that it was particularly nasty?"

"No question, Dan," said the candid Bradley. "As you know, we've all talked to, uh, a number of people, and a lot of people expressed the opinion, uh, recently, that this has been a very negative campaign, and that was, uh, carried out, borne out, by the numbers we're seeing from our exit-poll survey. Most people thought that both of the candidates spent more time attacking the other man than they did explaining their own positions, uh—but they blame George Bush more for that negative tone. In fact, if we take a look at the numbers . . ."

That was the truth that everybody-in-the-know was known to know, that this campaign had turned so (unphh, unphh!) *ugly*—so *personal* (How could it get that way, a mystified press wanted to know)—that it really, well, it wasn't *about anything,* like, you know, running the government, and so . . . *everybody knew,* there would be no mandate, no national consensus, no societal satisfaction, no, no . . . *no honeymoon for Bush!* Not after he'd helped them defile their own bit of history—no! . . . Said the Wednesday morning *Boston Herald:* "The honeymoon is over before it even begins." Said the well-known TV-guest-in-the-know on well-known knowledge, William Schneider: "*I* would argue, the honeymoon is *over* . . ."

Everybody knew, but Bush. By the time he appeared that morning, after church, for his first press conference in the Age of Bush, he was convinced: all rancor (all politics, in fact) was behind him . . . "and the American people are wonderful when it comes to understanding when a campaign ends and the work of business begins."

So, though he was gray as his suit, and more wrinkled, Bush turned to the work of business. He announced that he meant to become the President of all. He said he never ridiculed liberals. He commended Dukakis and Bentsen as distinguished patriots who "have given a major portion of their own lives to public service. I have the greatest respect for that commitment. I know that each one is going to serve the public interest as they see it, with the same energy and conviction that they demonstrated so well in this campaign." Bush worked in some praise of Bob Dole—said he'd "done a wonderful job. I think we can work harmoniously together." Bush promised to use the phone, unceasingly, to maximize his personal contacts. He promised frequent press conferences. Two or three times, he commended the press for "a magnificent job" in the campaign and thanked its representatives gathered before him that morning— in fact, Bush would not cease to praise and to thank everyone, that day, or for months thereafter. At least a dozen of those reporters in Houston would find in their mail one of Bush's stiff, cream-colored cards with the embossed seal, and an intimately charming note of *personal* thanks . . . as would, of course, Bush's friend and OVP honcho in Houston, Jack Steel; and Bush's hosts for election night, Charles and Sally Neblett . . . and the Reverend Tom Bagby, who presided at St. Martin's Church that morning-after and gave Bush a Bible to guide him. The note to Bagby was dated that same day, and mailed from Washington, D.C. "Tears came to my eyes," Bush wrote, "when you mentioned all five kids by name at today's service. Thanks for being there, thanks for my Bible, and thanks for your love and friendship." Of course, Tom was an old friend. And Bush was determined not to lose a friend—not now, when he felt on the brink. There was a note Bush wrote earlier that year, when it came clear he was facing the prospect of life in the White House. Apropos of no occasion in particular, he wrote to Bob Boilard, a fishing guide and Bush fishing-buddy, in Biddeford, Maine: ". . . *Bob, I'm going to win, but I'll promise you one thing—it won't affect our fishing together. Life is about friends and values. You are my Friend. Keep your fingers crossed. Love to Maddie. George B.*" As Bush said in his press conference, "Reach out and touch someone!"

And by the time that press conference ended, the Bush honeymoon had begun. One of the reporters said at the door, "D'you notice how many questions he took?" His happy pal nodded, "Yeah! He gave short answers, but at least we got a chance!" In the next month or two, those happy scribes would discover Bush knew their names, he'd call on them in press conferences, he'd joke with them (on camera! even better!), they'd get invited for *cocktails* with the President-elect . . . and, not entirely by coincidence, they would discover his thousands of friendships, his endearing affection for country music, for baseball, and popcorn, and horseshoes, and grandkids, burgers-and-bloodies,

Chinese food at the mall in Virginia, speedboats, fishing boasts, tennis rankings, goofy smiles . . . God, Bush was *so nice*! Bush, in short, would have a
honeymoon and a half—a gorgeous romance with the myth-makers of the
capital that would last till inauguration (when George and Bar got *out of their
car* to walk on Pennsylvania Avenue!) and beyond, through the first weeks of
his administration (when Bush greeted tourists at the White House gates!), and
would not fade, even as the cherry blossoms burst forth, which blooms Bush
was wont to point out to guests from the windows of the White House's *third
story,* the floor of "private residence," where guests had never been brought
before—fourth- and *fifth-term Senators* had never seen those rooms—but he
so much wanted to share . . . and he knew how they'd love to have their
pictures taken while they sat on the Lincoln Bed, so he'd snap them himself,
with his Polaroid, and then sign the pics—*the man knew how to make friends!*
And after all, that's how he planned to confront the enormity of the job: the
same way he got it—Bush would *make* his honeymoon, he'd *earn* it—making
friends, one by one, if need be, or now by the thousands, or the millions, with
each halogen-lit gesture. There wasn't any feeling but good feeling, when
George Bush wanted to be friends. You could see it all over the guy! . . . As
you could that morning-after, at the close of his first public appearance, as he
was ushered into a holding room, and he executed his first written act as
President-elect.
    "We really gotta get moving," Jack Steel was warning.
    God! It was true! November already!
    George Bush tore a strip of paper off the bottom of a letter, and with his
pen in his left hand, leaned his forearms flush against a wall, and wrote:
    "We count our special blessings.
    "We are grateful for our friends.
    "We give thanks to God."
    "Don't lose that!" Bar commanded Steely. "That's our only copy."
    True enough, but soon to be replicated, for *so many thousands* . . . the first
written order of the Age of Bush: the message for the annual Christmas Card.

—★—

That day, Michael Dukakis had a press conference in Boston. He looked
weary, punch-rumpled, hard-cheese-beat-up—but in no way shaken. Michael
knew what he had to do. "I spent the morning," he announced, "in my State
House office, getting reacclimated and going back to work on my job as
Governor of the Commonwealth. . . ." In fact, he'd marched into his office
before 9:00 A.M.—"Good morning. Good morning, good morning," he said
briskly, then put his coffee cup on his desk, stripped off his jacket, and sat down
on his hard-backed chair—to *govern.* This was the life! . . . In the autumn of
the campaign, when he was sure the detested press could not overhear, he'd
murmur to one or two Boston friends, "At least I've got something I love to
go back to." Here was Michael's real life renewed.
    In the last twenty-four hours, since he'd flown, for the last time, all night

again, across the country again, and landed in Boston, there were friends who tried to cheer him, or comfort him, who told him he'd done "a terrific job," done "great things," made them "proud." Michael would shake his head, look away, mumble, "No, no. I blew it." He'd take the blame. He insisted on the blame. In Michael's view, he'd made one critical error—he let George Bush and a hateful herd of press depict him as a weak-kneed, possibly unstable, pastel-patriotic, ineffectual technocratic tinkerer who had no business on the national stage . . . *while he refused to hit back.*

That was all true, in a mechanical way . . . but this was more than technical analysis to Michael. If loss was visited upon him because *he would not stoop* to that sorta, that branda *cheap politics* . . . then Dukakis did not have to change his view of himself, at all. If Michael had simply *failed to show the kinda guy he was* . . . the campaign was about exactly what he said it was—he was correct all along!

And if—here was the crucial cam on this pumping engine—Michael had redressed these failings at the end of his campaign (alas, a tad too late) . . . if he had, in those last two or three weeks, hit back at Bush, shown the public the kinda guy Mike Dukakis was, made his case for the kinda values, the kinda ideals, the kinda *positive public service* that his Party and his career and his life had been about . . . well, it was true, then, he'd been surging (he just ran out of time!), he'd been climbing in the polls (once they really got a look at him, they loved him!), he'd been making . . . on the grandest stage, before the eyes of the world . . . *a comeback!*

That was the object of all the pumping, his fondest, most familiar conceit—the comeback: he amazed them, the way he got off the canvas, like he always did, he would amaze them, he would . . . but that was a secret, still. That was his delicious secret—Kitty had only just started to mention it, the possibility . . . that his greatest comeback was *just beginning,* here and now . . . no, that was not the kind of thing the Duke would talk about, nor even admit to himself, that bud of an idea, that glimmer of light, that small ironic smile that played for an instant on Michael's mien as he took his first question, November 9, 1988 . . .

Governor, what are your plans for 1992—are you running?

There were scattered groans from the press, but not at the head of the room; Michael ruled out nothing. "At this point, my job is here. I'm going to be the very best Governor of this Commonwealth that I can be. I have lots to do. . . . What happens in the future remains to be seen."

—★—

Oh, but he would *make* them see. Michael was the most optimistic of men. Now he believed (as he had in every comeback) that in his own Commonwealth, from his own corner office, he would make them see what they'd *missed*—and what injustice had been done to Michael Dukakis. How? . . . He would govern! He would institute those splendid programs he proposed for the nation in the last month of the campaign. He would lead the way on health care, *of course.* And on economic development—that went without saying. But now he had ideas on education, too—and tuition finance. He would shelter the destitute; he would make home ownership possible for people of modest means. In his beloved State House, he would resume the mastery he'd missed in his campaign. He would make of his Commonwealth a model for what might have been . . . or what might be still. How much greater now was his experience in the nation's states, and his appreciation of his home. The *opportunities* he saw were . . . just terrific. And here was the joy, the stomach-soothing peace: he could *do it* in his home, his own orbit, that perfect ellipse—all he had to do was what he loved. He knew there were problems— the numbers from Revenue were deplorable. He'd have woes with his budget, sure. But solving the problems was his reason for being. Dr. Dukakis was keeping office hours again!

So, briskly, he took ten more questions and dismissed them. There'd be no looking forward to '92. There'd be no looking back (no farther than those last three weeks, "the surge," that "terrific comeback"). Michael's gaze was blinkered to all but his home and his State House. (He thought he'd take maybe one weekend off, and then, you know, dig in.)

After that press conference, Michael went home to Perry Street—he took John Sasso along—and on his driveway, behind the police barricades, Michael signed the paper releasing himself from the care and protection of the Secret Service. "You've been terrific," he told the agents. "Good luck." And that was that. Michael and John sat at the kitchen table. They talked—not too deeply. They never had recaptured entirely the brotherly candor they enjoyed before Sasso's exile. So no one at the table acknowledged that the "terrific comeback" was a fabrication—wish fulfillment for the wise guys and a press corps that needed a story.

It was John who'd made the comeback, after Michael panicked in September. Michael's fear-of-bad-story was overwhelmed by a *great new fear*—a poll showed he might *lose Massachusetts,* his real life!—and he called Sasso back from exile. If Dukakis looked better in those last few weeks, it was because that huge and overweening fear—he could lose *everything,* he could look *ridiculous*—made him stop trying to prove he was right. He started begging for help! At last!

But what was the point of rehashing? After an hour at the kitchen table, Michael walked John out to the curb. They parted, as they'd ever parted— neither would say they shared no more business between them.

"Call me," Michael said.

"You be in the office?"

"Yeah, call."

"Okay." . . . And then they saw, both at once . . . it was what they didn't see. The barricades were gone. And the agents. And the cop cars, the van, the *people*—that block had been wall-to-wall demonstrations; Jesse Jackson made a *speech* there; crowds spilled off the sidewalks; there were TV trucks with satellite masts; newsmen doing stand-ups, with lights blazing down and microphones at their mouths—the photographers, the tourist cars . . . all gone. Less than twenty-four hours after the polls closed, there was not one person on Perry Street, not a neighbor, nor a mailman, not a sound, save for . . . birds.

"Nobody," Michael said.

"Yeah." And Sasso bestowed that smile that was a gift.

Michael said, "It's just like it was . . ." and he paused, just an instant, to figure, ". . . twenty months ago." Then he turned and, with a light step, walked up the driveway toward his half-a-house.

The next morning, with no limo attending, Michael happily set out on foot for the trolley. Kitty Dukakis saw him off, then went to the liquor cabinet in the dining room, measured out four ounces of booze, drank it down, and went back to bed, to pass out.

— ★ —

Kitty's campaign had been a splendid procession . . . the last few months, since that night in July, that stage in Atlanta, after Michael finished the speech of his life and she ran into his arms, embraced him, and the nation could read his lips—"I love you." She was in glory. And this was not reflected light from Michael. She was no pale moon. The radiance was hers, and triumph—every day.

Every day, she would wake in nervy excitement for what she had to do. Her schedule was packed. Her speeches were packed. She'd talk about Michael, but she'd talk about herself, too—about her issues, her drugs, her growing up, her growing sense of self. She was Kitty Dukakis—that's all she had to say! She could get anyone in the country on the phone: "This is Kitty Dukakis . . ." She could raise money for causes, bring powerful people together, have ten reporters waiting at her next stop, or ten organizers. She didn't even have to make the call, she had staff. She stated, several times, she had the biggest and most professional campaign staff that any spouse ever assembled, which was likely true: they were the best in the business, and devoted to her; she just had to *mention* something she might want, and it was *done*—a room was waiting, a meal, a masseuse, a hairdresser . . . a plane. Her plane!

Kitty wrote a whole book of remembrance. But her plane was enough—it told the story. It was a Gulfstream jet—taupe carpets and leather, TV, stereo, everything built in so cunningly, like a pricey yacht—a twelve-seater, with two pilots, and a stewardess, Marlene Dunneman, who was lovely, impeccable. She was an artist with food, lavish in her attentions, sweet, correct in all things. Marlene (*Marleyna,* she pronounced it) was German, a fact not lost on Katharine Dukakis, former member of the U.S. Holocaust Memorial Council. Of course, she was wonderful with Marlene. Why not? "Marlene?" she'd call. "What's for breakfast?" In answer, Marlene would arrive with the golden flatware, large linen napkins, Scottish smoked salmon, capers, lemon, chopped egg, onion, assorted rolls, toast and bagels, fresh pastries, cinnamon buns and muffins, butter, preserves, cream cheese, and plates already garnished with strawberries cut into the shape of crowns or kiwi sliced so thin you could see the china through the translucent green fruit.

Kitty called her plane Sky Heaven, which drew the contrast she wanted, to Michael's Sky Pig. She hated to fly with Michael, not just because of the unlovely Aero Swine, but because of its cargo—a-hundred-and-some press and staff, and hangers-on, and Secret Servicemen, and such hubbub and awful food, and waiting to load and unload, and the schedule, she had no control—and once they finally got somewhere, what was she supposed to do? Sit and stare at Michael, with an idiot's adoring smile, while he gave his speech? . . . She would not. She was better than that. She could speak for herself, she could do for herself—better than Michael. She'd proved that. I once told her, she had built for herself "the better bubble." She loved that—never failed to mention it as a secret between us. But it was no secret. As Michael's lead blew away in the Bush-wind, there were scores of reporters and hundreds of voters who told Kitty, *she* was the one who should run. She was so warm, so giving, so caring, so dynamic, passionate, sympathetic . . . and Michael was a *stiff.* Kitty would defend Michael, she'd say he found it hard to show his feelings, except to her: he was better, with her—which was true . . . and an interesting response. Because, day by day, she fought his staff's schemes to bring her along with him. She wouldn't give up Sky Heaven. She'd tell reporters from Michael's plane, "You ought to fly with us!" And when they would . . . when perhaps, they'd settled into a leather seat, with their first sundowner cocktail . . . and Paul Costello, Kitty's Press Secretary, had hooked his CD player into the Gulf-stream's stereo and fired up "Les Miz" (one of Kitty's passions), or Tracy Chapman (so hip—and from Boston), or even the country-western twangers that Kitty's Service detail favored . . . and Marlene had served some savory broiled mushroom caps, to go along with drinks, to tide everyone over till dinner . . . then Kitty, mischievous with vodka, queenly in her chair, all eyes upon her, would solicit comment: "We're taking a survey: Who would *you* rather fly with?"

And it might have gone on like that—triumph and control within her realm—had it not been for the crisis in Michael's fortunes after that disastrous second debate. How could he *answer like that* when they were talking about *her rape*? She jumped him, in the car, afterward. She was steamed—why wasn't he *ready* for something like that? But she couldn't harp, he was so contrite, so upset. She tried not to beat on him, but Kitty wasn't good at holding things in. The next morning, with Michael still in such a terrible funk, sitting on the bed in their suite, Sasso and Mitropoulos standing beside him, trying to console him, pick him up, while Michael stared at the carpet, muttering, "I blew it, I blew it" . . . Kitty wanted to scream. But she couldn't scream at Michael. She had to figure what *she* would say—everyone was going to ask *her* about it, no one was figuring out what *she* could say . . . surely not Nick or John, who had eyes only for Michael, and least of all Michael, who was *hanging his head:* "I blew it, completely." So she burst into the bedroom and demanded: What about her? Why wasn't anybody working on what she was supposed to say? What was she going to say? . . . Until John Sasso turned on her with a look he seldom employed, and all but screamed at her to *just keep quiet!*

After that, she traveled more with Michael. She'd introduce him, she was his passion passport—living evidence that the man was not just a brain in a jar. She'd tell the crowds that this was the man who won her hand twenty-five years before, this was the man who won her heart with his loving attentions to her son, this was the man who was *by her bedside* when they *lost their first child* . . . "my passionate partner for twenty-five years, Michael Dukakis." It was a performance that never lost its riveting horror. It was so raw, spoke so bluntly of need—the crowds went nuts for her. Then Michael would step up. Each with one arm around the other, they'd wave a couple of times, wave to the left, wave to the right . . . when things got quiet, he'd begin: "I always said, if Kitty were the candidate we'd be twenty points ahead." Heh heh.

She knew, they were not going to be twenty points ahead. She knew, they were not even going to catch up. Those were the weeks—the proud weeks of Michael's "surge"—when Kitty's staff started stocking her suite with a bottle of Stoly. They were going to lose. Kitty knew. But she also knew she couldn't face that knowing, couldn't dwell on that fact—and get up the next day, to do it again. The Stoly helped. She'd have one drink, or two. She never lost it on the road. She did spectacularly well. She was a star.

— ★ —

It never occurred to her what *she* would lose—until it was over. There was suddenly nothing, back in that house with the Formica table and the Danish-modern chairs, and the phone wasn't ringing, there was no schedule, no cars waiting, no Secret Service, no local cops to thank, no newsmen to dodge, no interviews, no TV shows, no friends trying to find her, no one to greet, grace, praise, or bawl out, nothing she had to tell Michael, no menu, no manifest, no guest list to finalize, no posing for pictures, no Greeks sending food, no day-care center, no high school, no campus, no women's refuge, no hospital, no homeless shelter, no soup kitchen, no seniors' center she had to visit, no issue she had to learn, no speech to work over, no speechwriter, no body woman, no Chief of Staff, no Press Secretary, no Advance, no airport, no plane, no pilots, no Marlene, no makeup artist, no hairdresser, nothing to buy or pack, no itinerary—she wasn't going anywhere today, this week, or next, or next. She'd get up and there was nowhere she had to go.

There were her issues. She thought she might go back to her work at the Harvard Open Space program—but she didn't: it was too small, too hard, to make the kind of difference she craved. She signed up with an agent for speeches, and a literary agent—she was going to write a book. She got a splendid advance, $175,000. But she wondered, did she have anything to say for herself? For Kitty? . . . Mrs. Candidate Dukakis was gone. She didn't want to be Mrs. Governor. She was *Kitty Dukakis*—what did that mean now?

Her friend Sandy Bakalar came by and asked, "All right, Katharine, what's our next project?"

Kitty said: AIDS. She wanted to establish a Boston support center and food bank for AIDS patients—like the one she'd visited in San Francisco.

"Good!" Sandy said. Then she got her friend's eyes. "Katharine. You are incredible."

But Kitty didn't feel incredible. She got together one meeting on AIDS, but it was mostly people from the campaign; it felt like they were trying to hang on to old times. Then, too, things didn't get *done*. She'd pick up the phone to call her big-money supporters: "Tell him it's Kitty Dukakis . . ." It was strange how many were out of town, tied up with business, or working on something else. Everything seemed strange—she had to drive herself around, she had to *think* how to pull into a station and fill her tank. It was so slow, so . . . well, she blamed herself for feeling things were so hard. Just because she had to go to a beauty salon: *it shouldn't make any difference*—but it did. She couldn't put a dime in a meter without thinking: How long had it been since she had to fish out a dime to park?

More and more, things just seemed too hard. When Michael would leave, she'd cancel any dates she had, and get drunk. Looking back, Kitty would mark those weeks after the election as the time she became a "binge drinker." But those words don't convey her purposeful efficiency. For her, binge had nothing to do with spree. She didn't sit around with a glass, on the phone, or in front of the TV. She'd pour out the booze, down it, and pass out. When she woke, she'd do it again. She'd stop before Michael got home—to get herself together—he shouldn't know.

Of course, he knew. He tried to help. He reasoned, he explained away. He blamed the stress, exhaustion, sadness. He blamed himself. His campaign had brought her to this. She'd counted on him, and he blew it. He bore the sadness, too. The loss was with him every day. He worked, thank God. She should come to the State House. She had her office at the State House, down the hall from his. But Kitty didn't want to show up at the State House. She didn't want the dirty looks from people who blamed her—she got him into this. She didn't want to hear the ugly things people said about Michael.

Michael was finding no ease in his State House. The money was drying up. They'd rip open the tax envelopes—no checks—refund, refund, refund. Massachusetts wasn't alone—California, New York, same story, big shortfalls. But that was meagre consolation. Michael's budget was out of line, getting worse. Who could tell how many millions he'd have to find?

He fumed aloud: Why wasn't he told?

He blamed himself—he should have known.

The last budget, six months before, he'd balanced only by his own clout and guile—with a pencil, literally, writing in the margins, nickel-and-diming the local aid grants, writing in new numbers for each city and town, line-item vetoes at night in his office, hours before he had to leave for Atlanta, his convention, where the whole country would hail his Massachusetts Miracle.

He was brilliant on that budget—everybody said so. (And that was when Michael declared to the nation: *This election is about competence!*) . . . Maybe too brilliant—a bit too quick. Those were the days when no one wanted to get in his way. He was the favorite son, the hope of the Party.

Now, he'd spent that hope. This budget would be different. The mood was ugly. They said he should have started cutting earlier, to avoid the crisis—but no, his *campaign* came first.

Well, he'd dragged them all down.

What a loser.

On Boston talk-radio, they started calling him Pee Wee.

Michael would have to ask for new taxes. But things were so vicious. The legislature would vote to rip up all the triumphs of his past two terms—money for day care, retraining for workers, in-home care for the elderly. They'd take a knife (might be a meat-ax) to his government-that-worked . . . just to cut him up! The bold new plans he brought home from his campaign were *dead*—not just because of their cost, but because they came from him. People said they'd paid enough for his ambitions. There was talk about *repealing* his universal health-care law—before it ever took effect.

Michael was heartsick. And weary—though he'd never confess it. (He insisted, he was fine!) . . . But what happened to these people? Where was their faith? Things would turn around—steady as she goes! He would show he was right.

In December, Michael took his bride to their special place, Tyke and Viv's, in Fort Lauderdale. It wasn't much of a break, just four or five days. It was cold, and Michael was not in high spirits. But when he came back to Boston, after Christmas, he knew what he had to do.

He announced: he would not seek reelection. He was renouncing the job he loved, the Governorship of Massachusetts, to rid the Commonwealth of its greatest distraction: him.

Then he asked for new taxes. As a lame duck. And they tore him to shreds.

That was the same month Kitty called a couple of close friends to tell them: "I'm an alcoholic." They couldn't believe it, they tried to argue. But she insisted. "No! I have to face it." There was an odd excitement in her voice—vindication. There *was* something wrong, there was a *name* for what she felt. "I'm Kitty. I'm an alcoholic." That was the first step toward a new life, or a step she required, when the old life was gone.

— ★ —

Gary Hart was free to have his life outside the bubble—then he had to live with it. Andrea took an apartment in Denver, and John moved out to Boulder—he was in school there. Still, Gary and Lee were in close quarters in their mountain cabin. They were building a new kitchen and an addition on the back. But by '89, they started planning to supplant the house of their old dreams with a new structure—a great log thing set into the hill.

Lee would superintend the building. Gary was on the road, restlessly, under the aegis of his law firm; he traveled Europe and Asia, putting people of ideas and influence together with people of business. He was making more money than the people he once wouldn't *talk to* (they were *fat-cats*). But it wasn't money that drove him—hopscotching, say, Eastern Europe for a week, lighting in Moscow for the next four days, flying through London, New York, to Denver . . . then heading back to the airport, with fresh shirts, after a day and a half. The spur was inside him.

He was probing with that diamond bit for something—anything—that was interesting. He wasn't going to shrivel, sitting months at a time in an office in Denver—or anywhere else. What was interesting was the wider world he'd once planned to remake. Overseas, people weren't hung up on his past—those parts of it that made his countrymen so teen-giggly. In Europe and Asia, people could not understand what had happened to him in American politics (no more could he). They judged his ideas, they treated him as a statesman. The business part he made up as fortune and wile dictated. He created a job for himself where none existed—by the same kind of self-creation that fueled a hundred streak-of-danger profiles, written by Kops who could never reason to the truth that a shot of supercharged self-envisioning was the necessary first act-of-campaign for any poor boy who would be President.

The Soviets were wonderful, warm to him—and such a source of excitement. *They* were changing the world—by imagination. Gorbachev was drawing forth the greatest minds, to think anew. Hart began to nurture the germ of a book—an anatomy of that great new revolution. With his contacts among the Soviet elite, with his background in U.S.-Soviet relations, with his lifelong love for the Russia of Tolstoy and Dostoyevski . . . perhaps Gary Hart was the man to make the Soviets' spiritual upheaval come alive on the page. At least, to make it clear. Hart was sure the Soviets would help. Maybe *Mikhail Gorbachev* would help! It was that important: if the world were to change, America would also have to think anew. And even in those first months of Bush's term, Hart could see—it was so *apparent* to him—Bush was stuck in the old rules. Gorbachev was trying to pull walls down in Eastern Europe, *right now*—and Bush wouldn't help. Bush hadn't budged on arms control—on *anything*. He kept waiting for some stupid *committee* to "review the policy." Bush couldn't feel the rock shifting below the soil. . . . Hart thought, maybe *he* could make the people see—and they would lead their leaders. Hart thought—he hardly dared say—this book might lead *him* back into his own country's policy debate. That was the part of his dream that lingered: he wanted to put forth his ideas—let them rise or fall by their own power. He still believed, had to believe, ideas had power. Over drinks or dinner, he'd sometimes ask friends: "Do *you* see any way . . . I could come back?"

Not for public office—nor even national politics—he'd given up that hope, perforce. . . . It was in July '88, at the Democratic convention, that they shot him up with poison enough to kill that dream—even in his stubborn soul. The world was celebrating how cleverly Dr. Dukakis had staved off infection by Jesse Jackson's genius. God knows why Gary showed up. . . . Why wouldn't he show up, when he'd given his adulthood to that Party, trying to make the country better? He showed up because that was his life. . . . But even before he got to Atlanta, he heard dark rumors he was not to be seen—not by the populace, surely. The Party powers scheduled speech slots for former candidates—except for Gary Hart. Then the wires hooted to the world that Gary Hart had been issued a *press pass*! (He'd agreed to write a column for a Denver paper.) So a thousand desperate mediapersons all had one piss-and-giggle feature to file—and Hart was assaulted as he tried to drop off his column.

How's it feel to be on the other side?

"I'm not on the other side."

Then what're you doing here?

Y'ask people questions 'n' y'write it down?

Have ya got a little PRESS sign to put in your hat?

Hey, Gary! Hey! Gary! Hey! Y'gonna write f'The Miami Herald?

When he walked onto the floor of the Omni, to visit the Colorado delegation, young men in the employ of Party Chairman Paul Kirk blocked off the aisles—so no one could get to Hart, no delegates, no camera crews. It got a bit rough—Kirk's goons had to use a little goon-force—but the nation was spared reminder that Gary Hart was a Democrat. After one day, Hart got the message: "I've become a nonperson." They couldn't make him leave. They didn't have to. By the second day, he was on his way back to the airport, and home. He never should have come. His kids told him, he never should have come. But he hadn't known how it would be. . . . "I'm an undigestible—what is it? In Dickens? I'm an undigested piece of gristle," he said. "That's not what I want to be in life."

After that he knew enough to stay out of the line of fire. But well into the Age of Bush, you'd see his name in boldface, in leering People-column squibs—this, for instance, from *The Washington Post:*

"Yes, that friendly couple sitting in the lounge of the Jefferson Hotel Monday evening did look familiar. It was none other than the man who once wanted to be President, Gary Hart, and he was having drinks with an attractive dark-haired young woman. They came and left separately and Hart paid for his vodka and her scotch with his American Express Card. The Jefferson always has been one of those dark intimate spots where meetings take place . . ."

Occasionally, some thinker of the press would solicit a quote, or more rarely, a column, about an actual issue—say, the disintegration of Soviet empire, or the twenty-first-century needs of the Pentagon. More rarely still, some large-bore thinker would note that every Democrat well known to be knowledgeable was using issues brought forth by Gary Hart: the death of the New Deal, the concern (as Democrats) for economic expansion, tough talk for unions and interest groups, worker retraining, reinvestment in infrastructure, military reform, postcontainment foreign policy. . . . New Ideas became Big Buzz-words.

Mostly, they'd call Hart when the capital was seized by a Karacter convulsion. The Bush administration went into spasm in the starting gate when John

Tower, the Secretary of Defense nominee, was depicted as a weasely foul-breathed little sot near whom no decent woman was safe. Hart got hundreds of press calls and invitations to discourse on TV. What were they think-ing? . . . *And speaking of peccadillos, we're joined now in our Denver studio by former Senator Gary Hart* . . . Fat chance! What Hart found out was, it did not matter if he said anything or not. Wannabe-big-feet (a new crop rising) had a responsibility to *analyze the similarities* between the Donna Rice Scandal and the current, lamentable Tower Affair. Then, as the Tower story dragged on (alas, with nothing new and juicy), there were analyses of the *differences* between Tower and Hart. (Hart, for instance, had a well-known death wish.)

Once, on the phone, Hart asked what I thought about the "business with Tower." I answered with my newest, hottest, wise-guy whispers about two Senators, *two votes,* that *Bush could turn around—just a phone call* . . . but he wouldn't play hardball!

There was silence on the phone, until Hart said, in a tone reserved for worms: "You gave me a Washington answer." Of course, it came clear in-stantly: Hart saw the Tower mess as the government's, the nation's, bitter harvest . . . *poisoned* . . . by the same blight that ruined him. Hart thought the sickness stemmed from a dangerous fallacy—Americans think they can know (have a right to know!) everything about their leaders. But that certainty of knowledge is not available. People can't be tied down, reduced to facts. More dangerous still, politicians try to toe the line. Hart quoted, from his friend Warren Beatty: "When forced to show all, people become all show."

Months later—the Tower imbroglio was history, though the postmortems and press-apologia were still extant—I saw Hart and noted that the wheel was turning. Maybe the country would scare itself and think twice about Karacter. Maybe Hart would come out a winner.

Hart smiled and looked down. Too late for him. "I'm a failure."

But everybody was out there, still using his stuff—couldn't he see any victory there?

"With Mondale and Dukakis as the nominees of my Party? No . . . I wasted my time. I should never have gone into politics."

— ★ —

It was after the Tower fight, little hints started to leak from the Bobster . . . maybe life in the Senate wasn't all the life he cared to live. While the fight was on, he was fine—mile-a-minute quotes, jokes, ideas: he tried to get Tower onto the Senate floor to answer his accusers; he brought Tower to a weird press conference wherein Tower took the pledge—he wouldn't touch a drink whilst he serve in the Pentagon; in the end, when the Democrats had the votes, Dole tried another tack—put Tower in the Pentagon for *six months*—a trial sub-scription! Dole offered everything but free storm windows.

Of course, he lost.

Only three Democrats voted aye—and that left Tower three votes short. Tower was finished. (He died in a plane crash, two years later.)

George Bush got a sharp demonstration of what those White House tours were worth: a picture on the Lincoln Bed—plus a quarter, you know. Bush had pals. Votes were something else. (Of course, it never occurred to Bush that this showed the limits of friendship. Bush just concluded, Tower didn't have enough friends.)

Meanwhile, the lunch-buddies concluded that Bob Dole was back—he *proved* he would carry the ball for Bush. *Flat-out* for the White House!

Yes, Dole would carry the ball. But that wasn't what the fight showed *him*. "The bottom line in this place," he said, "is how many votes do you have." The answer was, only forty-four Republicans—Bush got *his* win in '88, but the GOP *lost* two seats in the Senate . . . and Dole saw no prospect that Bush would spend one minute, lose one friend, or one percent in a poll, to change the lineup. What Dole saw were *years* ahead where he'd have to sweat and scrape for fifty-one votes to declare National Peach Week!

He wasn't going to give up—Dole didn't know how to give up. That came clear in New Orleans, at the Republican convention. Dole was in a foul mood all week, complaining about being held up for inspection, like a beef carcass at sale, while Bush made up his mind about his Vice President. People kept asking Dole: What had he heard? What could he do to make himself more attractive to Bush? Dole wasn't going to do a thing! He never campaigned for the job, never asked to be considered . . . *never wanted anything from George Bush*! That's what he said—especially after Dan Quayle was named. (What had that guy ever done?) . . . None of it mattered to Dole. That's what he said. He and Elizabeth left town, as soon as they could. Then we got to tour their suite. It was glorious—best hotel in New Orleans—four rooms, all connected, a *piano* in Elizabeth's wing. But what I noticed were the wires, thick cables, running past the piano, into Bob's room, ten extra phone lines: if Bob got the VP nod from Bush . . . he wanted to be ready.

For forty years, Dole had worked flat-out to make a difference. That's what his first campaign was about, in 1950. That's what all the moving up was about. That's what the Other Thing was *for*—bottom line: he had to make a differ-ence, or what was his life about?

What was it about now? The climbing, planning, scrambling, all the up-and-up-and-up—was over. The Other Thing was gone. Dole's majority in the Senate was gone. No way to control the agenda. Forty-four votes, plus Bush, was not the same as forty-four, plus Reagan. Dole would lead the fight for the White House program. But what program? Darman came to the Capitol talking up a five-year budget deal—but Bush wouldn't pull the trigger. Maybe next year, or next, or next. Why wait? Without a deal on the deficit, no one would start anything new—how could they? No money. Democrats would pass the programs—no way for Dole to shape the bills. If the GOP lost another seat or two in '90, Dole wouldn't even have *influence*. He'd just be in the business of obstruction. Of course, Bush would veto all the spending bills. And Dole would have to work—flat-out—just to enforce paralysis.

Dole got to see Camp David again—first time in sixteen years, since Nixon flew him out there to give him his jacket, and the rope. This time, Dole said, he only got invited 'cause Elizabeth was Secretary of Labor. Bob was a Cabinet spouse. He left before the weekend was through. When he got back to the Capitol, some eager reporter asked breathlessly: *"Senator! How was Camp David? Was it beautiful?"*

"Woulda been," Dole said, and strode on, toward his office.

Of course, there was '92. Reporters asked, did he think he'd ever run for President again?

"Aghh, wait a minute. Haven't even said I'll run for reelection."

What?

"Might not."

Dole was thinking . . . he could get on some boards. Make a little money. Bob Strauss heard whispers, and called to say there was always a place in his Big Guy law firm. Warren Rudman talked to Dole about *both* of them leaving—they could start a firm and (Believe me, Bob!) write their own ticket! . . . For that matter, the Cabinet table ceased to hold its former fascination for Elizabeth. She had to think of some life beyond her old life. Maybe she could run for Governor in North Carolina—or take on Terry Sanford for Senate, in 1992. (Bob could be a Senate spouse.)

When he went back to Kansas, the old Dole-watchers in the press asked him, point-blank: "Senator, you serious y'might not run?"

"Aghh, don't *knoww!*" Dole would answer. "Gotta look at it, one of these days."

At first, no one made much of it—he'd said the same in 1980, the last time he lost for President. . . . But then they saw the Democrats lining up, for '92. (Dan Glickman, Rep from Wichita, stood at the head of the line.) . . . Then they heard Dole had talked to Kim Wells, about running on the GOP side.

Dole told one group of reporters, "Have to look it over, look at my options. I wanta make certain I'm in good health." Dole was sixty-six. Wasn't gonna live forever. Sister Gloria's cancer had come back, and brother Kenny had to sit with an oxygen tank, fighting emphysema. How long did Bob have?

Word started to ricochet around the Big Guy circuit in Washington. The staff was on the phones, all day, whispering: *It's serious.*

Serious? Gaggh! It was *horrible*—Dole was locked away in his inner office . . . with *carpet samples!*

The Bobster was going to redecorate his apartment.

— ★ —

Every once in a while, Biden would catch Bush on TV, greeting a foreign visitor, talking at some ceremony . . . and just for an instant, Joe would get that sinking anxiety for the guy, like when you see a comedian and no one's laughing—"Oh, God, he's gonna screw this up."

And then Joe would wait for the other shoe to drop: the thought that *he ought to be the guy up there* . . . but that seldom happened anymore.

It wasn't that Biden's politics, or his vision for the country, had changed—

they were the same, maybe more important to him now. What changed some-how was the notion that *Joe Biden* was the *one guy* who could step into the breach. Maybe it was less ego . . . though Joe felt he was paying more attention to himself now. Maybe he was just paying less attention to what people expected of him.

He really didn't know why he'd changed—what to call it—but he knew when it happened, or when he felt it . . .

It was May '88. Biden was still in the hospital after his second operation. Doctors often find a "mirror aneurism" on the other side of the skull, and that's what they found in Joe—along with a vicious blood clot that almost croaked him, actually required a third operation, set him back in his schedule, and gave everybody the shakes again. Anyway . . . Joe was finally recuperating, after months of concentrating strictly on the basics—eat, sleep, get some strength. He was lying on his hospital bed, staring up idly at the TV, and he saw: Bush and Reagan on stage, in black tie, in front of a huge model White House, with a fancy crowd and cameras, lights shining in the Gipper's old eyes as he gave Bush his endorsement, or whatever—a big White House do. . . . And Joe was on his way back, gaining strength, he knew, and he clenched his teeth, lifted his jaw, and thought, "I oughta be up there."

Then he thought, he didn't want to be up there.

And then he was seized by fear—*why* didn't he want to be up there? Had he lost his motor? Shit! What would he be worth, if that drive was gone? . . . But it wasn't gone—he'd just lost the panic that kept it near his throat: the feeling that it all had to happen now, today, this instant!

This was not the time in his life that he saw himself up there.

And then he knew, he was all right. He didn't just relax about his present, his future, but about his past. He understood why he had not been able to save his campaign. It wasn't like before, his first morning in that hospital, when he had Destiny to explain everything. This was more personal, human-scale. He just never had seen himself living that life, being that President. Even at the end, when he thought he was going to beat Bork, and he saw how he had to campaign . . . still, he never saw himself in the White House.

It was the only time in his life he'd tried something like that, something big, when he hadn't been able to picture how he would be. He ran because people told him he should—their expectations . . . he'd tried to do it by the numbers, so much money, so many consultants, positions, speeches, state directors . . . but he couldn't picture himself there, so he never could take control of how people saw him. He never had seen the *why now,* and why *it had to be him.* So how could he make others see? He would never do that—never do anything big again—without that certainty of obligation.

And that's what he told people, after he was well, when they came to him in the Age of Bush and told him he had to run next time. He said he was exactly where he belonged, for this time in his life; he was doing exactly what he should. He was doing good work in the Senate. He was taking care of his wife and his children, enjoying them, and enjoying them having him.

It was strange—a man like Biden, he'd had his face rubbed in mortality so hard, you'd think he would hear, for evermore, his earthly clock ticking . . . but no. He thought, there would be time. If there came a time when he should run for the White House, he'd know . . . but more than that. And this was at the bottom. This was what gave him his blessed absence of fever. There would be time, in his life, to establish in everyone's mind, that he was of good character. If he lived long enough, that, too, would come. People would know, he never cheated in law school.

—★—

Dick and Jane Gephardt went to work on their lovely house in the woods of Virginia. They hadn't touched the place for two years, and Jane's list, just the basic stuff, was as long as her arm: new paint everywhere, lighting fixtures, new appliances—*everything* had to be done, at once . . . so they could sell. After the campaign, the family finances left no choice. Matt was a senior already, and Chrissie was only two years behind him. Matt wanted to go to Duke, where tuition, room, board, and such would run at least $20,000 a year. Dick and Jane would buy a smaller, cheaper house in a new tract, farther out in Virginia, in a town called Herndon.

And then, too, they had to sell their lovely house on Fairview, in South St. Louis, where Loreen had lived, where she'd tended to the flowers and the graceful shrubs for a decade past. She had to move to their new home-in-the-district, which was a condo near the expressway leading out to Jefferson County—new construction again, a heck of a deal . . . though even Loreen, who was the Queen of Good Attitude, did concede that it would be *more wonderful still* after there was grass or plants around the buildings and after she got to know somebody, and had neighbors again, someone to talk to.

Still, being Gephardts, they swung into this program whole hog, sold the Virginia house in one day, and moved everything to the new house—except half the furniture wouldn't fit, so they stacked that in the basement. But they were in, and Dick had only twenty minutes extra on the trip to the Capitol—two hours and change in his Ford, round-trip, if he worked late and missed the traffic. Jane had maybe a half-hour each way—well, forty-five minutes in the morning, with the traffic—to take Katie back to her old school, before Jane could take herself to her job. Matt was already driving, so he could drive himself and Chrissie back and forth, a half-hour each way, to their high school, which he certainly didn't want to leave, as he was president of the student body—Matt had become quite a pol in Dick's campaign, a development which Jane viewed with wry ambivalence, but Dick said it was great. Dick and Jane decided, at length, that the strain of moving was *the best thing* that could happen . . . because they were so busy now, it kept their minds off their disappointment (Dick had never lost an election) and the upheaval, *God was doing it* . . . because the campaign takes your life away, and when you come back, nothing feels the same, and it would be too weird to hang on and act like nothing had happened. "You have to do something," was the way Jane put it, "to start over and make it different."

It was weird for Dick, in the House, but he had no choice. He had to raise money (he was still working off his debt), and it wasn't that he didn't like the job—it was fine, day to day. I went along with him once, while he raced from his dark, cramped, two-room office suite to the floor of the House, to his car and to Baltimore, for a speech on the greenhouse effect; then back to D.C., Capitol Hill, to the Ways and Means Committee, where Rostenkowski was trying to ram through a vote on the S&L bailout, but it wasn't yet time for the vote; so Dick walked out to give a talk to some Texas Democrats who were meeting in Washington (who knows why); then back to Ways and Means for the vote (finally); and back to the office for a couple of meetings; then down to a demonstration of the new Cray supercomputer; then back to the office to dress (black tie!) and off to meet Jane for dinner in a ballroom full of Democratic fat-cats. "I'm like a butterfly," Dick explained. "I light here, light there. It's great, each part of it, but you can't tell what happened."

I asked him, how about reading, or study? Dick was supposed to be writing a book. And learning Japanese.

"Nah. Just running."

And thinking. His home-state Democrats wanted Dick for Governor; his favorability ratio stood at seventy-two to eight—there was no one Dick couldn't beat, Missouri could be a Democratic state! Dick's Capitol Hill staff wanted him to move up to the Senate—he could beat Kit Bond in '92, and *still* run for President in '96. Steve Murphy said opportunity lay in the House. The long knives were out for the Speaker, Jim Wright (payback for Tower, lunch-buddies said), and Murphy thought Wright was a goner. New jobs for everyone! . . . So the killers came back for a meeting—they set aside two days—and Carrick (who'd moved to L.A. to become a TV exec) sat at the head of the table, like old times. And they went around the table, like old times, and everybody had his say, until someone asked Dick, who said he didn't like the Senate, didn't want to be a Senator . . . didn't want to be Governor (sure as hell didn't want to tell Jane she had to move again, to Jeff City, Missouri) . . . if things happened in the House, fine. . . . "Now," Dick said, "let's get back to '92. How much would we have to raise by the end of this year?" They could have done the meeting by phone in one hour. Gephardt just wanted to be President.

Within weeks, all his plans were smoke. Not only was Speaker Wright a goner, but Dick's pal, Tony Coelho, third in the leadership, got blowtorched in the papers, too. No one had a better nose for trouble than Tony: he didn't wait for his clothes to catch fire—he left the Congress . . . and Gephardt was Majority Leader.

It had to be God who was doing it. That's what Loreen said when she toured Dick's new nine-room suite in the Capitol, with the vaulted ceilings painted with state seals, and the hideaway lounge with the wine rack and wet bar, and the small black TVs next to the chairs (so the Leader could keep abreast of doings on the floor). It wasn't just the luxury, nor even the *opportunity* (Gephardt was second-in-command to Tom Foley, who was already *sixty years old*). No . . . this was the job of Dick's dreams! It was his role now to call the members together, and ask: *Okay, guys, what do you want to do about this? Okay, good—let's do it!*

And Dick thought, what with his new skills from the Presidential campaign, he could craft for House Democrats a unified message—for the first time, they would be not just a ragged crowd-noise of ills, bills, and interests. They would sing in chorus to make one point about *where they stood,* what they *stood for* . . . and how they stacked up against George Bush.

So after Dick settled into the job—in just a few months—he started meeting every morning with his message hit-team, about twenty members who were interested and showed some talent. They worked out the spin and the lines for the day, and they all used them. . . . And it worked to perfection. By the time Bush conceded his paralysis and called a Budget Summit to work out some mega-deal on the deficit . . . Dick was chairing the Summit and calling the tune for the Message Chorus. Democrats stuck it to Bush for months, had every-body in the *country* saying Bush was for a capital-gains cut because it would *benefit the rich*—Bush was *for the rich* . . . the Democrats were for "tax fairness," and "a break for the middle class."

It was gorgeous!

And they finally did pummel Bush to submission. They made him admit he'd have to raise taxes, have to take the heat *with them.* . . . They cornered him, finally, in the Oval Office, where Bush stared glumly at his desk drawer and said, okay . . . he had Darman write out a statement: *It is clear there is a need for taxes* . . . which, of course, was no good because the sentence mentioned no human beings (*mistakes were made*) . . . so they sat there till Bush inserted the words "to me."

It is clear to me . . .

And that took half a year.

By that time, Gephardt was talking to the killers again—what if he *did* go in '92? Actually, the killers talked. But Dick agreed!

"If he didn't want to *do* anything," Dick kept saying about George Bush, "why'd he run?"

— ★ —

The most eloquent sign was his putting came back. Any weekend golfer knows, you hit the long drives with your legs and back, full swing of the arms, turn of the torso—big body action, muscle and mechanics . . . but a dinky four-foot putt puts the mirror to your troubled soul. And Bush . . . well, not to be harsh, but . . . Bush stunk up every green for *eight years* as Vice President. He had the yips.

When he got the nomination wrapped up, he got one of those long semi-legal putters and went out to play . . . that was the first hint. He got back to the big house on the Point and broke in on his sons, who were planning a golf match—"Don't count me out!" . . . After he won the election, he'd stand behind that big putter, and he could see every inch of the path that ball would travel, the hole looked twice as big and . . . bingo! In the cup! That's when he announced to the family, and the world:

"Mr. Smooth . . . is back!"

And through the first couple of months of his administration, you'd barely find anyone to argue. Bush looked so happy in the job—like he knew exactly what he'd find, and he'd just been waiting to sit in that chair, to show the right way to do things . . . it was instantly well known that this was a transition unlike other transitions. A real insider, said the triple-E pundits—a sure-fingered masseur of Congress and the agencies. A confident and sharing man, said admiring reporters in his press conferences—he took questions about *anything*! You could see him thinking up the answers, *himself*! He didn't have to wait for six months of staff work, he picked up the phone and called Gorby—to chat. This was a man who knew the ropes in the rigging of the great Ship of State.

Of course, that's exactly what Bush meant to show. He laughed off the idea that the job was oversized. Not that he meant to brag—anything but! He'd say something humble, like, the Gipper left the shop in great shape, or the fine people in the government were wonderful about cooperating, or he was lucky enough to have had some experience . . . Mr. Smooth! He looked like he had come to believe his old campaign slogan: "Ready on Day One to Be a Great President."

But there are different ways to become President—not all of them easy to pin down. Bush won the vote, November '88, and became President, politically. He took the oath at the Capitol, January '89, and became President, Constitutionally. But it would take time, he knew, before his Presidency, the look and sound of him in that office, could settle into the public mind as fact, when the words "President Bush" would sound easy together, like "Washington" and "D.C."—that date could not be predicted. Nor could the date of dread and dreams when the nation's fortunes would seem to be at stake, and the people would turn to their President—*to him*—and expect him to act, and to win. Nothing about that moment could be predicted, except . . . that would mark the last becoming—at that moment, for good or ill, the Presidency would descend upon him.

And that was the moment for which Bush waited. When friends gushed to him about approval polls (over sixty percent!), the splendid press he was getting, his graceful (so effortless!) personal success, Bush would say the polls could be fickle. The press would surely turn. As for him, he'd say, he hadn't yet "been tested by fire."

—★—

He was right about the polls—they started sliding. In his third month, the Senate killed off his Cabinet nominee, John Tower, the first time in thirty years such a slap was dealt to a new President. Hundreds of top-level jobs in the government were still vacant, or filled with Reagan holdovers who were doing the country the service of keeping those paychecks warm. Bush had no major bills before the Congress. He had yet to answer Gorbachev's call for accelerated arms control. The foreign policies of the U.S. were said to be on hold for mysterious "reviews" by unnamed officials and experts . . . and, sure enough, Bush was being hammered in print.

"A Presidency 'On the Edge of a Cliff' " was the lead essay in *The Washington Post*'s Sunday Outlook section. In it, no less than David Gergen declared the administration atotter. Bush was a "Mexican Jumping Bean," traveling too much, giving speeches about nothing; he was neglecting the "vision thing" and frittering time on details; he'd stuck with Tower so long he'd created a political bloodbath; he was clueless without his campaign White Men, dependent on the low-brow John Sununu; Bush was "being nibbled and nicked to death," he was too often "surprised," "reactive," "chained to his in-box"—this went on for fifty solid inches . . . and, of course, Gergen was not alone. *Everybody knew* poor Bush was out to lunch. And not just OTL, but egregiously, obtusely, willfully lackadaisical—close to *negligent* (Bush didn't *want* to do anything, well-known people-in-the-know insisted) . . . because everybody had just finished writing (last month) how Bush-the-insider knew everything about being President . . . so how could they turn now and report he was having a hard time?

That was the first time I caught a glimpse of Bush the President. I was in a White House hallway, waiting to go upstairs to see Barbara Bush, when . . . came flying out of a doorway, George Bush, twenty feet away and closing. He had a pack of suits behind him, Secret Service guys and policy guys, the military guy, and who-knows-what guys—twelve, at least, fanned out in his wake, in a ragged V, like Canada geese, pumping their arms to keep up and wearing purposeful scowls, all . . . except for Bush. I murmured to Bar's aide, at my side, "There's the boss!" Bush whipped his head around with a vague smile—trying to locate the source so he could make a goofy face at whoever it was, give that personal gift that had brought him to these great halls—but he had the loose-eyed and inward look of an athlete in the final quarter, deep in the game, everything pumping in him with an internal roar that would dim all outside . . . except, of course, he was George Bush, so the game *was* every person outside—each one, individually, owed a measure of his energy and a tick off his clock, which he was trying to give (*Who was that?*) while he's still the lead goose, couldn't miss a step, because the others would march up his back, and the next meeting (and the next, and the next) couldn't start till he got there, and anyway, he's the *boss,* supposed to be out front . . . all the time.

It seemed to me, Bush wasn't lackadaisical *for one instant,* and all the stray facts that were retailed at lunch tables fell into a pattern of another shape.

President Bush stuck to the bitter end with John Tower, not because he courted (or didn't know enough to avoid) the political showdown . . . but because Captain Poppy stood by his ungainly chum, Ovie, when the rest of the Andover squad would have shooed Ovie off the field.

President Bush had two daily go-rounds with his Chief of Staff, John Sununu, morning and evening, while Sununu ticked off items from his notebook and Bush knocked them down, one by one (trying to do, with each, whatever seemed sound) . . . not because Sununu, Rasputin-of-the-Rocky-North, had a chokehold on the President or his agenda . . . but because George Bush was the Harris County Chairman who *always* stopped by the office at night, to read the memos, sign the mail, and clear his desk before he went home to Bar and the kids.

This President charged about the country giving airy, friendly speeches about nothing-in-particular, not because Sununu was fearful of competition from bright speechwriters, or because this White House was without the political edge of the G-6 . . . but because George Bush ("Watch the *action!*") had risen for forty years in business, politics, and government, *always* on the move, always by the coin of his person—he was practicing the *essence* of his politics, precisely by jumping on a plane and *showing up.*

President Bush picked up the phone to chat with Gorbachev (and Thatcher, Kohl, Mitterrand, Andreotti, Takeshita, Mulroney, Salinas, Aquino, Mubarak, King Hussein, King Hassan, King Fahd, and forty or fifty lesser-known heads of state . . .) because the Commander in Chief and Leader of the Free World was going to save the planet from conflict . . . the same way George Bush saved the county GOP from warfare with the Birchers—by interposing his person: they were all going to like him, he *knew* they would, they were going to be friends.

The horrifying fact was, he didn't know any other way. He was using everything he ever knew—and some things he wished to God he knew better . . . but all he had to go on, all he could bring to the job, was his own life before he hit the bubble. And God knows, he was spending it—pouring it out, to do this job. Mr. Smooth was working his withered old buns off.

— ★ —

And heaven help the fellow with whom George Bush did not want to be friends—especially if that fellow happened to run some small troublemaking nation, one of those "little wiener countries." The personal coin, like any other, had two sides.

Manuel Noriega, the Panamanian strongman, was once an informant to DCI Bush. In the eighties, Bush knew him as one of the Reaganoids' unsavory anticommie pals. By '86, when Noriega's goons started killing off his opponents, the General became an embarrassment—even to the Gip. Worse still, though the Reaganoids blustered—the Justice Department *indicted* the General, in a U.S. court in Florida—Manuel Noriega refused to leave power!

Worse still, Noriega had shown his most cheeky recalcitrance in the middle of George Bush's campaign.

Noriega may not have known, but his life was dogfood. He made his great mistake December 15, 1989, eleven months into George Bush's term. An off-duty U.S. Marine was shot by Noriega's troops at a roadblock in Panama. At that same roadblock, a Navy lieutenant and his wife were arrested, the man was beaten up, the woman was threatened with sexual assault . . . and that was the end. George Bush was once a young Navy lieutenant, with a young wife . . .

The next day, a Sunday, George Bush broke away from his Christmas Party and went upstairs to the White House residence to hear the Pentagon's plans for invasion. Bush had on his bright red socks, one of which said "Merry," and one of which said "Christmas."

Twenty-four thousand U.S. troops would destroy Panama's force of sixteen thousand (only three-thousand Panamanians were considered "combat-ready"). The U.S. would take over the country, depose its government, swear in the new guy, and prop him up while he cleaned up the mess. As for Noriega, they meant to snatch him, and bring him to Miami for trial, like a street criminal.

"Okay," Bush said. "Let's go."

Two years later, there would be millions of words expended about the "emergence" of the Warrior Bush in the Persian Gulf. There would be foreign-affairs dissertations about the way he made *himself* the linchpin of a worldwide alliance against Iraq. There would be high-level semiotic *analysis* of the steps by which Bush *personalized* the war—turned it into a crusade against one man, Saddam Hussein, whom Bush used (so the savants said) as the focus for public enmity, to build support for a war about oil.

Two years later, even Washington people well known to be in-the-know were amazed (and not a little horrified) to discover the miracle of combat-ardor in this friendly, well-bred President Bush.

But George Bush found the leitmotiv of his administration on Christmas Eve, 1989. He needed no calculation to personalize his combat—or the conduct of alliance. What it took was a lifetime's training—and he had nothing else to throw at a crisis.

—★—

U.S. troops shot up Panama in a hurry. They controlled all the strong points and the city streets. They held the water and electric plants, the canal, the bridges and airports. The invasion went better than any God-fearing man would have dared to hope. It was over in one night. By the time the U.S. news crews got there, Panamanians were celebrating in the streets.

But no Noriega.

The second day, the news crews showed looting. And no Noriega.

The third day, weeping Panamanian widows, wounded Americans! Snipers, still firing! . . . And no Noriega.

George Bush had sent twenty-four thousand young Americans in harm's way—twenty-three servicemen were dead. Bush had gone on TV and said the purpose of this extravaganza was . . . to get Noriega.

And he had no Noriega.

The fifth day was Sunday, Christmas Eve . . . the President and family had gathered at Camp David . . . and George Bush was wound so tight that his back seized up—he was hunched, walking like a hundred-and-eight-year-old man. *Where was that sonofabitch Noriega?* Was he headed for the hills like Augusto Sandino? Was George Bush going to spend months—*years?*—greeting body bags at Dover AFB?

It got so bad with Bush's back, he couldn't even play *sports* with his sons. He didn't sideline easy when a game was on the line, but . . . Mr. Smooth couldn't even stand up.

So it came to pass, that Christmas Eve, Bush was standing on the white-tiled balcony of the squash court. (The game at hand was wally-ball—a volleyball, rocketing around a closed court—fast, and rough.) And all Bush could do was watch his sons, George W., Jeb, Neil, and Marvin, dividing into teams, with a couple of Marines, contesting for the wally-ball *championship* of the Camp, and the clan. It was a tight match—hard fought, long, and near its brutal climax . . . when the phone on the balcony rang.

George Bush talked on the phone for a minute . . . and then he was back at the rail of the balcony. Suddenly six-foot-two again, looming on his clean white perch over the white court, George Bush held up one hand to still the game below.

"Noriega," he said, "has given up to the Papal Nuncio in Panama."

And with that, the entire male line of the Bush clan let the ball bounce to standstill on the gleaming white floor, and . . . looking up at the white balcony, applauded their father, who had become President.

— ★ —

In 1991, after the Persian Gulf, when Bush was over eighty percent in the polls, Dick Gephardt was deciding not to run for President. He couldn't pull the trigger—couldn't leave the House, not after he'd stood for a full term as Leader. Reporters and wise guys came after Dick, demanding an answer: *Why don't you run?* Gephardt shot back: "Why don't *you* run? You talk about it like it's goin' across the street for lunch!" He was uncharacteristically snappish. He made the smart move, but it didn't feel quite right. What he'd lost was a matter of attitude: Do it now! That, and a certain faith. "It's just kind of an accident who you get. The system doesn't work too well."

— ★ —

I saw Joe Biden early in '92. People were trying to get him to run, too. Joe didn't even nibble. He was doing what he wanted. We were in his house— scaffolding everywhere outside, workmen in masks and hardhats appearing in the windows like moon-people. The gutters gave out, see, and the drainpipes, fabulous copper, were set into the walls between courses of brick . . . anyway, it was a lot of work. But these days, Joe just sat and let his insurance pay contractors to do what they could do. Biden said he was content with the house, couldn't think of moving with the market so rotten . . . except, maybe— he'd been thinking this out—maybe he and Jill could get a place in Washington . . . get involved with the life of the capital, outside of work. Might be important—you know, for people-in-the-know to get to know him better.

— ★ —

Dole went out to Topeka for Kansas Day, January 29 . . . and the press jumped him. It'd been more than a year he'd been playing footsie about reelection. He had a press conference. *"So . . . you running?"* Dole made his one-word announcement: "Yes." He'd been hanging back because his doctors told him he had prostate cancer. But he'd had his operation, and they got it—every bit. He also announced he'd be campaigning in each of the 105 Kansas counties— and maybe a bit around the country, too. Who could tell? Might hit a hot streak, things could happen . . . might pick up a couple of seats, get up around forty-six, forty-seven votes, he could do some things—might not be bad. A few nights later, he went on Larry King, promoting early detection for prostate problems. A caller asked if Dole would run for President again. Said the Bobster: "Never say never."

— ★ —

Dukakis was not a man to give up easily. But the comeback never took root in the poisoned last two years of his term, and he finally had to concede, the Massachusetts Miracle was dead—the state was in a slump. In '92, Michael took a job lecturing at Florida Atlantic University, which put him and his bride near their special place—Tyke and Viv's in Fort Lauderdale. Kitty was training to become a substance-abuse counselor. She'd fought through ups and downs, a couple of them horribly public . . . but she fought on. She said now, she never would have survived if they'd won the White House, if she'd had to live her life on display. Michael thought about speaking out, during the new campaign, to defend Bill Clinton. Somehow, the Clinton people never spotted just the right opportunity for him. . . . Occasionally, there'd be a story about them—Michael and Kitty—or you'd see them on TV, side by side in beach chairs . . . he looked a bit grayer, she looked fragile. She didn't say much in the interviews. Michael always said, they were fine.

— ★ —

Hart's book came out the end of '91—it traced the ideas that propelled Mikhail Gorbachev to greatness. But alas, the same week the book came out, the Moscow coup marked the beginning of the end for Gorby. *The New York Times* did not see fit to review Hart's book, but poked fun in a bottom-of-the-page editorial. *The Washington Post* ran a box on the front of the Style section, with the headline: GARY HART'S SECOND MISTAKE. Of course, Hart got hun-

dreds of calls when the press (led by the tabloid *Star*) started snouting out Bill
Clinton's Karacter. But he ducked the questions.

— ★ —

They were still having parades for Desert Storm, in the summer of '91, when
the White Men and the pundits started pecking on Bush to *get out there*—start
thumping the tub for four more years! He had to get a campaign team in place,
get down to business in the states—polls were slipping with the economy—he
had to define himself, make some speeches . . . that kind of thing. He delayed.
He didn't want to turn to it. Didn't want to turn himself over. Shouldn't have
to. Of course, he had to.

When he did, of course, it wasn't enough. People said the new team wasn't
good enough—faceless white people. Atwater was dead, alas; Ailes wouldn't
play this time; no Jimmy Baker, he was busy at State; Fuller was out of the
loop, successful as the head of a consulting firm (like his predecessor, Dan
Murphy, and his successor, John Sununu: they were all well known to know
the President) . . . people thought the President's speeches didn't pack any
punch, so they sacked the speechwriters and gave Bush new words to prove
he cared about the recession . . . for a while, with Pat Buchanan raising
cain, and the polls in a terrible swoon, Bush was riding *Air Force One* everywhere across the South, yelling at rallies—vows and threats . . . but people
said that wasn't Presidential, so he stayed in the White House again. He didn't
look well. For God's sake, he puked on his pal, Miyazawa. The White
House doctor diagnosed hypertension. He said Bush never got a chance to
unwind.

The odd thing was, you didn't hear a word anymore about that friendly,
eager, granddad-goofy George Bush . . . who was *so nice*. There were no more
stories about his horseshoes, his speedboat, his wave-washed rocks (a storm
made a wreck of the big house in Maine) . . . no sneaking out to the movies,
Peking duck at the mall, no . . . tours of the third floor, pictures on the Lincoln
Bed, tourist-greetings at the White House gates, no . . . nor phone calls to his
thousands of friends, to keep him in touch with the world. What world? This
poor bastard was so cut off, he didn't know from supermarket scanners! Or
so the papers said. Marlin Fitzwater had to screw a statement out of Bush, that
he did know scanners. A White House communiqué affirmed, the President
had seen a supermarket.

In the spring of '92, I checked with Bob Boilard in Maine. Bush did call.
"Let's go fishing!" So they did. Boilard raced out there, and Bush came out
in his boat, with the Secret Servicemen and Brent Scowcroft—Bush always had
Scowcroft along now, like a Pocket New World Order Doll. There were chase
boats, and the chopper, boats from the press cutting four-foot wakes, tourists
making noise like fireboats—*There he is! Eeeeeeeeeeeee! Eee Eee Eeeeee!* The
nearest sentient fish had to be three miles away. After twenty minutes, Bush
had to go. It's tough to have friends when you're the President . . . and they're
trying to take it away.

You do things you have to do. Nothing personal. He'd look better once he had an opponent in the crosshairs.

Bush did give one interview before he dived back inside the bubble. He told the celebrated David Frost that he would do anything—whatever it took—to win again. It caused a lot of comment. It did sound kind of hard-edged. People wondered . . . why would he say a thing like that?

About the Author

RICHARD BEN CRAMER was a newspaperman for ten years with *The Baltimore Sun* and *The Philadelphia Inquirer.* His reporting from the Middle East won the Pulitzer Prize in 1979. Since 1984, his magazine articles have appeared in *Rolling Stone* and *Esquire,* where he serves as a contributing editor. He lives with his wife and daughter on a bank of the Choptank River, on Maryland's Eastern Shore.

About the Type

This book was set in Times Roman, designed by Stanley Morison
specifically for *The Times* of London. The typeface was introduced in the newspaper in 1932. Times Roman had its greatest
success in the United States as a book and commercial
typeface, rather than one used in newspapers.